Principles of Economics

Second Edition

Principles of Economics

Second Edition

Dirk Mateer
University of Arizona

Lee Coppock
University of Virginia

W·W·NORTON
NEW YORK · LONDON

W. W. Norton & Company has been independent since its founding in 1923, when William Warder Norton and Mary D. Herter Norton first published lectures delivered at the People's Institute, the adult education division of New York City's Cooper Union. The firm soon expanded its program beyond the Institute, publishing books by celebrated academics from America and abroad. By midcentury, the two major pillars of Norton's publishing program—trade books and college texts—were firmly established. In the 1950s, the Norton family transferred control of the company to its employees, and today—with a staff of four hundred and a comparable number of trade, college, and professional titles published each year—W. W. Norton & Company stands as the largest and oldest publishing house owned wholly by its employees.

Editor: Eric Svendsen

Developmental Editor: Steven Rigolosi

Manuscript Editor: Janet Greenblatt

Project Editor: Melissa Atkin

Media Editor: Miryam Chandler

Associate Media Editor: Victoria Reuter

Editorial Assistant: Lindsey Osteen

Media Editorial Assistant: Sam Glass

Marketing Manager, Economics: Janise Turso

Production Manager: Eric Pier-Hocking

Photo Editor: Nelson Colón

Photo Researcher: Dena Digilio Betz

Permissions Associate: Elizabeth Trammell

Text Design: Lisa Buckley

Art Director: Rubina Yeh

Cover Design and "Snapshot" Infographics: Kiss Me I'm Polish

Composition: Jouve

Manufacturing: Courier Kendallville

Library of Congress Cataloging-in-Publication Data

Names: Mateer, G. Dirk, author. | Coppock, Lee, author.
Title: Principles of economics / Dirk Mateer, University of Arizona, Lee Coppock, University of Virginia.
Description: Second edition. | New York: W.W. Norton & Company, [2017] |
  Includes index.
Identifiers: LCCN 2016027501 | **ISBN 9780393264579 (hardcover)**
Subjects: LCSH: Economics.
Classification: LCC HB171.5 .M435 2017 | DDC 330–dc23 LC record available at
  https://lccn.loc.gov/2016027501

This edition: ISBN 978-0-393-26457-9 (hardcover)
W. W. Norton & Company, Inc., 500 Fifth Avenue, New York, NY 10110-0017

W. W. Norton & Company Ltd., 15 Carlisle Street, London W1D 3BS
wwnorton.com

1 2 3 4 5 6 7 8 9 0

In memory of our editor, Jack Repcheck, whose zest for life was contagious. Thanks for believing in us and challenging us to share our passion for economic education with others.

D.M and L.C.

BRIEF CONTENTS

CONTENTS

PART I   Introduction

1 Five Foundations of Economics   4

2 Model Building and Gains from Trade   26

PART II The Role of Markets

4 Elasticity   110

7 Market Inefficiencies: Externalities and Public Goods   214

PART III The Theory of the Firm

8 Business Costs and Production   244

9 Firms in a Competitive Market   274

PART IV Labor Markets and Earnings

14 The Demand and Supply of Resources   430

15 Income, Inequality, and Poverty   466

PART V Special Topics in Microeconomics

16 Consumer Choice 504

PART VI Macroeconomic Basics

19 Introduction to Macroeconomics and Gross Domestic Product   596

PART VII The Long and Short of Macroeconomics

24 Economic Growth and the Wealth of Nations   756

PART VIII Fiscal Policy

PART IX Monetary Policy

PART X International Economics

32 International Trade

33 International Finance   1058

PREFACE

We are teachers of principles of economics. That is what we do. We each teach principles of microeconomics and macroeconomics to over a thousand students a semester, every single semester, at the University of Arizona and the University of Virginia. To date, we have taught over 40,000 students.

We decided to write our own text for one big reason. We simply were not satisfied with the available texts and felt strongly that we could write an innovative book to which dedicated instructors like us would respond. It's not that the already available texts were bad or inaccurate; it's that they lacked an understanding of what we, as teachers, have learned through fielding the thousands of questions that our students have asked us over the years. We do not advise policymakers, but we do advise students, and we know how their minds work.

For instance, there really was no text that showed an understanding for where students consistently trip up (for example, cost curves) and therefore provided an additional example or better yet, a worked exercise. There really was no text that was careful to reinforce new terminology and difficult sticking points with explanations in everyday language. There really was no text that leveraged the fact that today's students are key participants in the twenty-first-century economy and that used examples and cases from markets in which they interact all the time (such as the markets for cell phones, social networking sites, computing devices, and online book sellers).

What our years in the classroom have brought home to us is the importance of meeting students where they are. This means knowing their cultural touchstones and trying to tell the story of economics with those touchstones in mind. In our text we meet students where they are through resonance and reinforcement. In fact, these two words are our mantra—we strive to make each topic resonate and then make it stick through reinforcement.

Whenever possible, we use student-centered examples that resonate with students. For instance, many of our examples refer to jobs that students often hold and businesses that often employ them. If the examples resonate, students are much more likely to dig into the material wholeheartedly and internalize key concepts.

When we teach, we try to create a rhythm of reinforcement in our lectures that begins with the presentation of new material, followed by a concrete example and then a reinforcing device, and then closes with a "make it stick" moment. We do this over and over again. We have tried to bring that rhythm to the book. We believe strongly that this commitment to reinforcement works. To give an example, in our chapter "Oligopoly and Strategic Behavior," while presenting the crucial-yet-difficult subject of game theory, we work through the concept of the prisoner's dilemma at least six different ways.

No educator is happy with the challenge we all face to motivate our students to read the assigned text. No matter how effective our lectures are, if our students are not reinforcing those lectures by reading the assigned text chapters, they are only partially absorbing the key takeaways that properly trained citizens need to thrive in today's world. A second key motivation for us to undertake this ambitious project was the desire to create a text that students would read, week in and week out, for the entire course. By following our commitment to resonance and reinforcement, we are confident that we have written a text that's a good read for today's students. So good, in fact, that we believe students will read entire chapters and actually enjoy them. Many users of the first edition have indicated that this is the case.

What do we all want? We want our students to leave our courses having internalized fundamentals that they will remember for life. The fundamentals (such as understanding incentives, opportunity cost, and thinking at the margin) will help them to make better choices in the workplace, in their personal investments, in their long-term planning, in their voting, and in all their critical choices. The bottom line is that they will live more fulfilled and satisfying lives if we succeed. The purpose of this text is to help all of us succeed in this quest.

What does this classroom-inspired, student-centered text look like?

A Simple Narrative

First and foremost, we keep the narrative simple. We always bear in mind all those office-hour conversations with students where we searched for some way to make sense of this foreign language—for them—that is economics. It is incredibly satisfying when you find the right expression, explanation, or example that creates the "Oh, now I get it . . ." moment with your student. We have filled the narrative with those successful "now I get it" passages.

Real-World, Relatable Examples and Cases that Resonate

Nothing makes this material stick for students like good examples and cases that they relate to, and we have peppered our book with them. They are part of the narrative, set off with an **Economics in the Real World** heading. We further feature **Economics in the Media** boxed examples that use scenes from movies and TV shows that illustrate economic concepts. One of us has written the book (literally!) on economics in the movies, and we have used these clips year after year to make economics stick with students.

🛒 ECONOMICS IN THE REAL WORLD

Internet Piracy

The digitization of media, along with the speed with which it can be transferred across the Internet, has made the protection of *intellectual property rights* (that is, the protection of patents, copyrights, and trademarks) very difficult to enforce. Many countries either do not have strict copyright standards or fail to enforce them. The result is a black market filled with bootlegged copies of movies, music, and other media.

Because digital "file sharing" is so common these days, you might not fully understand the harm that occurs. Piracy is an illegal form of free-riding. Every song and every movie that is transferred takes away royalties that would have gone to the original artist or the studio. After all, producing content is expensive, and violations of cop[...] ing a fair return on [...] content don't often se[...] the copyright encryption i[...] in question or bought it legally o[...] ent. One reason copyright exist[...] are fully specified and enforced acro[...] tors receive compensation for thei[...] violated, revenues to private busine[...] and movies produced will decrease[...] and society will suffer. (For other be[...]

Think about the relationship be[...] each side needs the other. In that se[...] watch is not a true public good, b[...] make the good excludable but no[...] always have an incentive to violat[...] insist on ever more complicated er[...] ests, and for the betterment of soci[...] to enforce copyright law to prevent[...]

Incentives

▶️ ECONOMICS IN THE MEDIA

Direct Finance

The Big Short

The Big Short (2016) is based on the book with the same title by Michael Lewis. The movie is essentially a documentary that doesn't feel like a documentary as the actors carefully explain the details of the financial collapse that led to the Great Recession in 2007.

The movie introduces Mark Baum (played by Steve Carrell) and Michael Burry (played by Christian Bale), who were among the few people who recognized the dangers in the economy's rampant reliance on overvalued mortgage-backed securities.

In the movie, Baum and Burry travel to Florida to interview real borrowers. They knock on home doors and visit local businesses. These interviews help them see what almost nobody at the big banks sees: that the borrowers will not have the income to repay their loans when their low introductory interest rates increase. When these borrowers stop paying, their securitized mortgages being sold to investors will become worthless. When Baum realizes that he can make a lot of money by betting that these losses will happen (a process called "shorting" the mortgages), he recognizes that the economy will take a nosedive when other financial insiders finally reach the same conclusion. In the meantime, he determines, the very biggest invest-

In the movie *The Big Short*, we get a look at the complicated world of finance.

ment banks (including Goldman Sachs and Lehman Brothers) are in over their heads, have no idea about the dangers that are brewing, and do not realize how dangerous subprime loans are to the economy.

At the end of the day, *The Big Short* helps you understand secondary markets, securitization, and mortgage-backed securities. In addition, it provides a good look at some of the perverse incentives and dangers that lurk inside the real-world loanable funds market.

Applying Economic Decision-Making Through Problem-Solving

Most instructors in this course want students to learn to think like economists and to apply economic principles to their decision-making. This text shares this goal. To get students thinking about economics, we first open each chapter with a popular **misconception**. Students come to our classes with a number of strongly held misconceptions about economics and the economy, so we begin each chapter recognizing that fact and then establishing what we will do to clarify that subject area. Then, in each chapter, several **Practice What You Know** features allow students to self-check their comprehension while also laying the foundation for the step-by-step problem solving required for the end-of-chapter **Study Problems**. And throughout the text, key equations are used, and the **five core foundations of economics** (incentives, trade-offs, opportunity cost, marginal thinking, and trade creates value) are reinforced with a special icon to ensure that students are constantly connecting the dots.

Incentives
Trade-offs
Opportunity cost
Marginal thinking
Trade creates value

PRACTICE WHAT YOU KNOW

Income Elasticity

Question: A college student eats ramen noodles twice a week and earns $300 a week working part-time. After graduating, the student earns $1,000 a week and eats
s once every other week , or 0.5 time a
the student's income elasticity?

Yummy, or all you can afford?

income elasticity of demand using the midpoint method is

$$E_I = \frac{(Q_2 - Q_1) \div [(Q_1 + Q_2) \div 2]}{(I_2 - I_1) \div [(I_1 + I_2) \div 2]}$$

the values from the question yields

$$E_I = \frac{(0.5 - 2.0) \div [(2.0 + 0.5) \div 2]}{(\$1000 - \$300) \div [(\$300 + \$1000) \div 2]}$$

yields

$$E_I = \frac{-1.5 \div 1.25}{\$700 \div \$650}$$

= −1.1.

elasticity of demand is positive for normal goods and negative for
s. Therefore, the negative coefficient indicates that ramen noodles
or good over this person's range of income—in this example,
)0 and $1,000 per week. This result should confirm your intuition.
ostgraduation income enables the student to substitute away from
es and toward other meals that provide more nourishment and

PRACTICE WHAT YOU KNOW

The Japanese government estimated total damages of $309 billion from the 2011 earthquake and tsunami.

Changes in Resources: Natural Disasters

In 2011, a major earthquake and tsunami in Japan destroyed significant physical capital, including roads, homes, factories, and bridges.

Question: How would you use an aggregate production function to illustrate the way a major destruction of capital affects a macroeconomy in the short run?

Answer:

This is an unusual situation in which the level of capital in a nation actually falls. Because capital (K) is on the horizontal axis of the production function, the decline in capital moves Japan back along its production function. This means less GDP for Japan (Y falls) until the nation can get its capital rebuilt.

Question: With no further changes, what happens to real GDP in the long run?

Answer: With no further changes, real GDP returns to the steady-state output level in the long run. At the new level of capital after the earthquake (K_2), the marginal product of additional capital is relatively high, so there is a greater return to building new capital. But in the long run, because there was no shift in the production function, the level of capital returns to the steady-state level (K_1), which means that output also returns to its steady-state level (Y_1).

Big-Picture Pedagogy

For beginning students, economics can be a subject with many new concepts and seemingly many details to memorize. To help keep students focused on the big ideas of each chapter while continuing to emphasize critical thinking, we use several unique features. First we introduce students to the objectives in each chapter in the form of **Big Questions** that students will explore rather than memorize. Then we come back to the Big Questions in the conclusion to the chapter with **Answering the Big Questions.**

BIG QUESTIONS

* What is monopolistic competition?
* What are the differences between monopolistic competition, com[
  and monopoly?
* Why is advertising prevalent in monopolistic competition?

ANSWERING THE BIG QUESTIONS

What is monopolistic competition?

* Monopolistic competition is a market structure characterized by free entry and many firms selling differentiated products.
* Differentiation of products takes three forms: differentiation by style or type, location, and quality.

What are the differences between monopolistic competition, competitive markets, and monopoly?

* Monopolistic competitors, like monopolists, are price makers that have downward-sloping demand curves. Whenever the demand curve is downward sloping, the firm is able to mark up the price above marginal cost. The results are excess capacity and an inefficient level of output.
* In the long run, barriers to entry enable a monopoly to earn an economic profit. This is not the case for monopolistic competition or competitive markets.

Why is advertising prevalent in monopolistic competition?

* Advertising performs useful functions under monopolistic competition: it conveys information about the price of the goods offered for sale, the location of products, and new products. It also signals differences in quality. However, advertising also encourages brand loyalty, which makes it harder for other businesses to successfully enter the market. Advertising can be manipulative and misleading.

Another notable reinforcement device is the **Snapshot** that appears in most chapters. We have used the innovation of modern infographics to create a memorable story that reinforces a particularly important topic. By combining pictures, text, and data in these unique features, we encourage students to think about and understand different components of a concept working together.

Solved Problems Pedagogy

Last but certainly not least, we conclude each chapter with a selection of fully solved problems that appear in the end-of-chapter material. These problems show students how to approach material they will see in homework, quizzes, and tests.

SOLVED PROBLEMS

5a. The equilibrium price is $4, and the equilibrium quantity is 60 quarts. The next step is to graph the curves, as shown here.

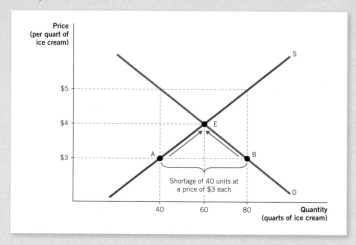

b. A shortage of 40 quarts of ice cream exists at $3 (quantity demanded is 80 and the quantity supplied is 40); therefore, there is excess demand. Ice cream sellers will raise their price as long as excess demand exists—that is, as long as the price is below $4. It is not until $4 that the equilibrium point is reached and the shortage is resolved.

8.a. The first step is to set $Q_D = Q_S$. Doing so gives us $90 - 2P = P$. Solving for price, we find that $90 = 3P$, or $P = 30$. Once we know that $P = 30$, we can plug this value back into either of the original equations, $Q_D = 90 - 2P$ or $Q_S = P$. Beginning with Q_D, we get $90 - 2(30) = 90 - 60 = 30$, or we can plug it into $Q_S = P$, so $Q_S = 30$. Because we get a quantity of 30 for both Q_D and Q_S, we know that the price of $30 is correct.

b. In this part, we plug $20 into Q_D. Doing so yields $90 - 2(20) = 50$. Now we plug $20 into Q_S. Doing so yields 20.

c. Because $Q_D = 50$ and $Q_S = 20$, there is a shortage of 30 quarts.

d. Whenever there is a shortage of a good, the price will rise in order to find the equilibrium point.

9a. The reduction in consumer income led to a negative, or leftward, shift in the demand curve for gasoline. Because this is the only change, the equilibrium price of gasoline fell. In fact, by the end of 2008, the price of gasoline had fallen to under $2 per gallon in the United States.

b. The significant drop in the cost of production led to a large increase, or rightward, shift in the supply of gasoline. This increase in supply led to a decrease in price. In fact, by early 2015, the average price of a gallon of regular gasoline in the United States fell to under $2 per gallon.

Looking at parts (a) and (b) together, you can see that very different causes led to steep drops in the price of gasoline. In 2008 the cause was a decline in demand; in 2014 it was an increase in supply.

10. Because alcohol and Solo cups are complements, the key here is to recall that a change in the price of a complementary good shifts the demand curve for the related good. Lower alcohol prices will cause consumers to purchase more alcohol and therefore demand more Solo cups. In other words, the entire demand curve for Solo cups shifts to the right.

Principles of Microeconomics— Hallmarks and Updates to the Second Edition

When we wrote the first edition of *Principles of Microeconomics*, we decided to follow the traditional structure found in most texts. Though every chapter is critical, we believe that supply and demand, elasticity, and production costs are the *most* fundamental, since so many other insights and takeaways build on them. We tried triply hard to reinforce these chapters with extra examples and opportunities for self-assessment.

Feedback from the first edition led us to move the chapter on market efficiency earlier so that instructors can discuss consumer and producer surplus when they teach price controls. We also added a chapter on international trade (from *Principles of Macroeconomics*) after we heard that many of our *Principles of Microeconomics* instructors emphasize that content.

We have made other important updates based on reviewer feedback. Content updates include a thoroughly revised chapter on income, inequality, and poverty, in particular adding discussions of GINI coefficients and the Lorenz curve. Our coverage of game theory in Chapter 13 now includes sequential games, backward induction, and decision trees. Of course, we have updated our examples, adding features showing how students see inequality in the *Hunger Games* movies, how Uber is changing the New York City taxi market, and how Thomas Piketty's *Capital in the Twenty-First Century* has influenced notions of economic inequality—to name just a few. Lastly, we have added new study problems at the end of every chapter.

One hallmark of this textbook that is not found anywhere else in the Principles markets remains. This text includes a separate chapter on price discrimination. We have done this because the digital economy has made price discrimination much more common than it ever was before, so what was once a fun but somewhat marginal topic is no longer marginal. What's more students really relate to it because they are subject to it in many of the markets in which they participate—for example, college sporting events.

We also place a stand-alone consumer theory chapter toward the end of the volume, but that does not mean that we consider it an optional chapter. We have learned that there is tremendous variation among instructors for when to present this material in the course, and we wanted to allow for maximum flexibility.

Principles of Macroeconomics— Hallmarks and Updates to the Second Edition

Principles of Macroeconomics follows the traditional structure found in most texts, but it contains several chapters on new topics that reflect the latest thinking and priorities in macroeconomics. First, at the end of the unit on macroeconomics basics, we have an entire chapter on financial markets, including coverage of securitization and mortgage-backed securities. The economic crisis of 2008-2009 made everyone aware of the importance of financial markets for the worldwide economy, and students want to know more about this fascinating project.

Economic growth is presented before the short run, and we have two chapters devoted to the topic. The first focuses on the facts of economic growth. It discusses in largely qualitative terms how nations like South Korea and Singapore can be so wealthy, and nations like North Korea and Liberia can be so impoverished. The second chapter presents the Solow growth model in very simple terms. We've included this chapter to highlight the importance of growth and modeling. That said, it is optional and can be skipped by those instructors who have had time for only one chapter on growth.

Coverage of the short run includes a fully developed chapter on the aggregate demand—aggregate supply model, and a second chapter that uses this key model to analyze—essentially side by side—the Great Depression and the Great Recession. We feel this is a very effective way of presenting several of the key debates within economics.

Finally, we have written a unique chapter on the federal budget, which has allowed us to discuss at length the controversial topic of entitlements and the foreign ownership of U.S. national debt.

Feedback from the first edition has driven important revisions for this new edition. In particular, we have added a new appendix on the Aggregate Expenditures model to chapter 14. We have also expanded our discussion of the origins of the great recession in this chapter, added new sections on "GDP and Happiness" in chapter 6 and the equation of exchange in chapter 8, and made major changes to Chapter 13 on the Aggregate Demand —Aggregate Supply model. Of course, we have updated the examples in the book, including new features on using the movie *The Big Short*, and how GDP is calculated in Europe. We have also added additional study problems at the end of each chapter.

Supplements and Media

 ## Smartwork5

Smartwork5 for *Principles of Economics* is an online learning environment that helps instructors meet the teaching goal of connecting concepts and showing applications. Richly varied questions and intuitive functionality give users the flexibility to create the type of learning best for their students. Try a demo of the following features at digital.wwnorton.com/prineco2.

Easy to launch, easy to use
Simple course setup and intuitive student registration minimize administrative headaches at the beginning of the semester. Instructors can use prebuilt activities or customize their own assignments and questions to suit their needs.

Integration with campus LMS platforms
Smartwork5 integrates with campus learning management systems. Student grades flow automatically to the instructor's LMS course. Single sign-on between the LMS and Norton digital products simplifies student access—and this means fewer password/log-in woes.

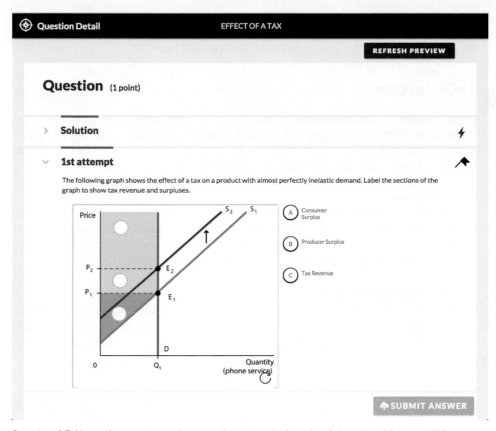

Smartwork5 Norton's easy to use homework system designed to integrate with your LMS.

Trusted economics tools and content

Smartwork5 teaches students not just how to solve problems but how to problem-solve, connecting concepts to learned skills through varied applications. Smartwork5 includes assignments based on real-world economic scenarios, "Office Hour" Video Tutorials presented in the learning moment, analytical and interactive graphing questions, and application problems. Rich answer-specific feedback builds students' confidence and economic skills. Questions are book specific, matching the terminology and conventions that students see in their textbook. They are developed in collaboration with instructors actively teaching with the Mateer and Coppock textbook.

Rich performance reports

Intuitive performance reports for both individual students and entire classes help instructors gauge student comprehension and adjust their teaching accordingly.

An intuitive easy-to-use graphing tool

The Smartwork5 graphing interface consistently employs the same coloration and notation as the in-text art to underscore continuity and reduce confusion. The interface is easy to understand, and it functions on computers as well as tablet devices. Students are invited to manipulate precreated graphs or draw their own graphs from scratch.

Answer-specific feedback and hints

Smartwork5 teaches students to problem-solve, not just solve a single problem. Many online homework systems only offer solution explanations after the student has answered a question. Smartwork5, in contrast, provides explanations throughout the problem-solving process, giving answer-specific feedback and hints for common misconceptions.

 ## InQuizitive

Award-winning InQuizitive is Norton's gamelike, adaptive quizzing and practice system. Developed with book-specific questions and content, this system lets students compete with themselves as they prepare their material for class. Demo InQuizitive at digital.wwnorton.com/prineco2.

Play with a purpose
Gaming elements built into InQuizitive engage students and motivate them to keep working. Students wager points on every question based on their confidence level, gain additional points for hot streaks and bonus questions, and can improve their grade by continuing to work in InQuizitive.

Active learning, helpful feedback
InQuizitive includes a variety of question types beyond basic multiple choice. Image-click, numeric entry, and various graph interpretation questions build economic skills and better prepare students for lecture, quizzes, and exams. Rich answer-specific feedback helps students understand their mistakes.

Easy to use
Instructors can set up InQuizitive for their students in less than 5 minutes. Students can access InQuizitive on tablet devices as well as on computers,

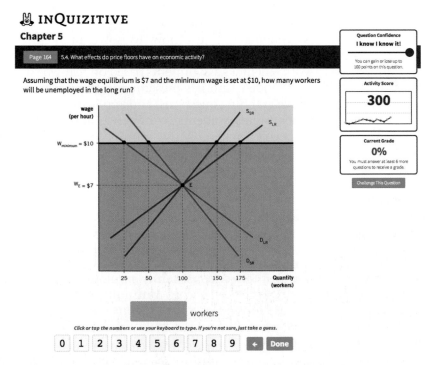

InQuisitive Norton's game-like adaptive quizzing and practice system.

making it easy to study on the go. InQuizitive integrates with campus learning management systems; when integration is enabled, grades flow automatically to campus LMS gradebooks.

Formative assessment works

The efficacy of formative assessment is backed by education and psychology research (see inquizitive.wwnorton.com). Furthermore, performance-specific feedback, varied question types, and gaming elements built into InQuizitive have been shown to increase student engagement and retention of material.

Norton Coursepack

Bring tutorial videos, assessment, and other online teaching resources directly into your new or existing online course with the Norton Coursepack. It's easily customizable and available for all major learning management systems, including Blackboard, Desire2Learn, Moodle, and Canvas.

The Norton Coursepack for *Principles of Economics* includes:

* Concept Check quizzes
* Homework quizzes
* Office Hours video tutorials
* Interactive Scratch Paper modules
* Flashcards
* Links to the digital landing page for the e-book, InQuizitive, and Smartwork
* Test bank

The Ultimate Guide to Teaching Economics— Now with teaching tips for online courses

The Ultimate Guide to Teaching Economics is much more than an instructor's manual, it is two handbooks for becoming a better teacher. The Ultimate Guide—the most innovative instructor's manual ever created for Principles of Economics—includes 1,000+ teaching tips from the classrooms of the authors and other innovative instructors, to help instructors, both new and experienced, incorporate best teaching practices and find inspiring ideas for enlivening their lectures.

The tips in *The Ultimate Guide to Teaching Microeconomics* and *The Ultimate Guide to Teaching Macroeconomics* include:

* New—A Taking It Online appendix in each chapter that shows how the Ultimate Guide's class-tested teaching ideas can be adapted to online teaching environments
* New—Writing to Learn tips that give instructors short (one-page or less) paper prompts with ideas for potential student responses
* Think-pair-share activities to promote small-group discussion and active learning
* "Recipes" for in-class activities and demonstrations that include descriptions of the activity, required materials, estimated length of time, estimated difficulty, recommended class size, and instructions. Ready-to-use worksheets are also available for select activities.

✳ Descriptions of movie clips, TV shows, commercials, and other videos that can be used in class to illustrate economic concepts
✳ Clicker questions
✳ Ideas for music examples that can be used as lecture starters
✳ Suggestions for additional real-world examples to engage students

In addition to the teaching tips, each chapter begins with an introduction by Dirk Mateer, highlighting important concepts to teach in the chapter and pointing out his favorite tips. Each chapter ends with solutions to the unsolved end-of-chapter problems in the textbook.

Interactive Instructor's Guide

The Interactive Instructor's Guide (IIG) brings all the great content from *The Ultimate Guide to Teaching Economics* into a searchable online database that can be searched and filtered by a number of criteria, such as topic, chapter, key word, media format, and resource type. Instructors can even save their favorite assets to a list so they don't need to hunt for them each time they revisit the IIG.

To make it quick and easy for instructors to incorporate the tips from *The Ultimate Guide to Teaching Economics,* the IIG will include:

✳ Links for music and video tips when an online video is freely available
✳ Links to news articles for real-world examples when an article is available
✳ Downloadable versions of student worksheets for activities and demonstrations
✳ Downloadable PowerPoint slides for clicker questions
✳ Additional teaching resources not found in the Ultimate Guide

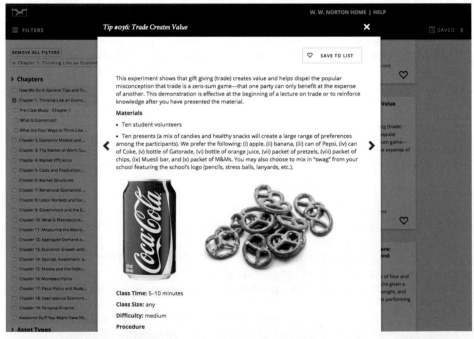

Interactive Instructor's Guide This searchable database of premium resources makes lecture development easy.

Office Hours Video Tutorials

This collection of more than 50 videos brings the office-hour experience online. Each video explains a fundamental concept and was conceived by and filmed with authors Dirk Mateer and Lee Coppock.

Perfect for online courses, each Office Hours video tutorial is succinct (90 seconds to 2 minutes in length) and mimics the office-hour experience. The videos focus on topics that are typically difficult to explain just in writing (or over email), such as shifting supply and demand curves.

The Office Hours videos have been incorporated throughout the Smart-Work online homework system as video feedback for questions, integrated into the e-book, included in the Norton Coursepack, and included in the Norton Coursepack.

Test Bank

Each chapter of the test bank for the second edition has been fully updated and expanded based on reviewer feedback. Each chapter includes between 100 and 150 questions and incorporates graphs and images where appropriate, The test bank has been developed using the Norton Assessment Guidelines. Hundreds of new questions have been developed for the second edition that focus on graphing, scenario-based questions, and calculations. Each question in the test bank is classified according to Bloom's taxonomy of knowledge types (remembering, understanding and applying, analyzing and evaluating, and creating). Questions are further classified by section and difficulty, making it easy to construct tests and quizzes that are meaningful and diagnostic.

Presentation Tools

Norton offers a variety of presentation tools so that new instructors and veteran instructors alike can find the resources that are best suited for their teaching style.

Enhanced Lecture Powerpoint Slides

These comprehensive, lecture-ready slides are perfect for new instructors and instructors who have limited time to prepare for lecture. The slides include elements such as images from the book, stepped-out versions of in-text graphs, additional examples not included in the chapter, and clicker questions.

Student Note-Taking Slides

This resource is a trimmed-down version of the lecture slides with instructor notes removed for instructors who prefer slides that are more visual and with limited bullets. These are great for posting to the LMS for students to download for note-taking during lecture.

Art Slides and Art JPEGs

For instructors who simply want to incorporate in-text art into their existing slides, all art from the book (tables, graphs, photos, and Snapshot infographics) is available in both PowerPoint and .jpeg formats. Stepped-out versions of in-text graphs and Snapshot infographics are also provided and optimized for screen projection.

dirkmateer.com

Visit dirkmateer.com to find a library of hundreds of recommended movie and TV clips and links to online video sources to use in class.

leecoppock.com

This blog serves as a one-stop-shop for all the "econ news you can use." Here you will find timely economic data, graphics, and teaching materials you will need to keep your course fresh and topical.

ACKNOWLEDGMENTS

We would like to thank the literally hundreds of fellow instructors who have helped us refine both our vision and the actual words on the page for two editions of this text. Without your help, we would never have gotten to the finish line. We hope that the result is the economics teacher's text that we set out to write.

Our class testers:

Jennifer Bailly, California State University, Long Beach
Mihajlo Balic, Harrisburg Community College
Erol Balkan, Hamilton College
Susan Bell, Seminole State College
Scott Benson, Idaho State University
Joe DaBoll-Lavoie, Nazareth College
Michael Dowell, California State University, Sacramento
Abdelaziz Farah, State University of New York, Orange
J. Brian O'Roark, Robert Morris University
Shelby Frost, Georgia State University
Karl Geisler, University of Nevada, Reno
Nancy Griffin, Tyler Junior College
Lauren Heller, Berry College
John Hilston, Brevard Community College
Kim Holder, University of West Georgia
Todd Knoop, Cornell College
Katharine W. Kontak, Bowling Green State University

Daniel Kuester, Kansas State University
Herman Li, University of Nevada, Las Vegas
Gary Lyn, University of Massachusetts, Lowell
Kyle Mangum, Georgia State University
Shah Mehrabi, Montgomery College
Sean Mulholland, Stonehill College
Vincent Odock, State University of New York, Orange
Michael Price, Georgia State University
Matthew Rousu, Susquehanna University
Tom Scales, Southside Virginia Community College
Tom Scheiding, University of Wisconsin, Stout
Clair Smith, St. John Fisher College
Tesa Stegner, Idaho State University
James Tierney, State University of New York, Plattsburgh
Nora Underwood, University of Central Florida
Michael Urbancic, University of Oregon
Marlon Williams, Lock Haven University

Our reviewers and advisors from focus groups:

Mark Abajian, California State University, San Marcos
Teshome Abebe, Eastern Illinois University
Charity-Joy Acchiardo, University of Arizona
Rebecca Achee Thornton, University of Houston
Mehdi Afiat, College of Southern Nevada
Carlos Aguilar, El Paso Community College
Seemi Ahmad, State University of New York, Dutchess
Abdullah Al-Bahrani, Northern Kentucky University
Frank Albritton, Seminole State College
Rashid Al-Hmoud, Texas Tech University
Farhad Ameen, Westchester Community College
Giuliana Andreopoulos, William Paterson University
Tom Andrews, West Chester University
Becca Arnold, San Diego Mesa College
Giant Aryani, Collin College
Lisa Augustyniak, Lake Michigan College
Dennis Avola, Bentley University
Roberto Ayala, California State University, Fullerton
Philip Baca, New Mexico Military Institute
Ron Baker, Millersville University
Saad Bakir, Alabama State University

Mihajlo Balic, Harrisburg Area Community College
Kuntal Banerjee, Florida Atlantic University
Ryan Baranowski, Coe College
Ruth Barney, Edison Community College
David Barrus, Brigham Young University, Idaho
Jude Bayham, Washington State University
Mary Beal-Hodges, University of North Florida
Michael Bech, University of Southern Denmark
Stacie Beck, University of Delaware
Christian Beer, University of North Carolina, Wilmington
Jodi Beggs, Northeastern University
Richard Beil, Auburn University
Ari Belasen, Southern Illinois University
Doris Bennett, Jacksonville State University
Karen Bernhardt-Walther, The Ohio State University
Joel Beutel, Delta College
Prasun Bhattacharjee, East Tennessee State University
Richard Bilas, College of Charleston
Kelly Blanchard, Purdue University
Inácio Bo, Boston College
Michael Bognanno, Temple University

Antonio Bojanic, California State University, Sacramento
David Boldt, University of West Georgia
Michael Bonnal, University of Tennesse, Chattanooga
Heather Bono, University of West Georgia
Andrea Borchard, Hillsborough Community College
Feler Bose, Alma College
Inoussa Boubacar, University of Wisconsin, Stout
Donald Boudreaux, George Mason University
Austin Boyle, Penn State
Jared Boyd, Henry Ford Community College
Elissa Braunstein, Colorado State University
Elizabeth Breitbach, University of Southern California
Kristie Briggs, Creighton University
Stacey Brook, University of Iowa
Bruce Brown, California State Polytechnic University, Pomona
John Brown, Clark University
Vera Brusentsev, Swarthmore College
Laura Maria Bucila, Texas Christian University
Bryan Buckley, Northeastern State University
Richard Burkhauser, Cornell University
W. Jennings Byrd, Troy University
Joseph Calhoun, Florida State University
Charles Callahan, State University of New York, Brockport
Douglas Campbell, University of Memphis
Giorgio Canarella, University of Nevada, Las Vegas
Laura Carolevschi, Winona State University
Nancy Carter, Kilgore College
Amber Casolari, Riverside Community College
Nevin Cavusoglu, James Madison University
Valbona Cela, TriCounty Technical College
Semih Cekin, Texas Tech University
Rebecca Chambers, University of Delaware
Jason Chang, California Polytechnic State University, Pomona
June Charles, North Lake College
Sanjukta Chaudhuri, University of Wisconsin, Eau Claire
Parama Chaudhury, University College of London
Chuiping Chen, American River College
Shuo Chen, State University of New York, Geneseo
Monica Cherry, State University of New York, Buffalo
Larry Chisesi, University of San Diego
David L. Cleeton, Illinois State University
Marcelo Clerici-Arias, Stanford University
Steve Cobb, University of North Texas
John Colletti, North Central College
Kristen Collett-Schmitt, University of Notre Dame
Rhonda Collier, Portland Community College
Michael Coon, Hood College
Gary Cooper, University of Minnesota
William Cooper, University of Kentucky
Carlos Cortinhas, University of Exeter
Chad D. Cotti, University of Wisconsin, Oshkosh
Richard Cox, Arizona State University
Erik Craft, University of Richmond
Antoinette Criss, University of South Florida
Zachary Cronin, Hillsborough Community College
Glynice Crow, Wallace State Community College
Patrick Crowley, Texas A&M University, Corpus Christi
Damian Damianov, University of Texas, Pan American

Morassa Danai, California State University, Fullerton
Ribhi Daoud, Sinclair Community College
Patrick Dolenc, University of Massachusetts, Amherst
John Donahue, Estrella Mountain Community College
Oswaldo Donoso, Lone Star College, North Harris
Kacey Douglas, Mississippi State University
Whitney Douglas-Buser, Young Harris College
Chelsea Dowell, Upper Iowa University
William Dupor, The Ohio State University
Harold W. Elder, University of Alabama
Diantha Ellis, Abraham Baldwin Agricultural College
Harry Ellis, University of North Texas
Amani Elobeid, Iowa State University
Tisha Emerson, Baylor University
Lucas Englehardt, Kent State University
Michael Enz, Framingham State University
Erwin Erhardt, University of Cincinnati
Mary Ervin, El Paso Community College
Molly Espey, Clemson University
Jose Esteban, Palomar Community College
Sarah Estelle, Hope College
Patricia Euzent, University of Central Florida
Brent Evans, Mississippi State University
Carolyn Fabian Stumph, Indiana University–Purdue University, Fort Wayne
Leila Farivar, The Ohio State University
Ben Fitch-Fleischmann, University of Oregon
Oscar Flores, Minnesota State University, Moorhead
Michael Forney, Austin Community College
Irene Foster, George Washington University
Roger Frantz, San Diego State University
Gnel Gabrielyan, Washington State University
Craig Gallet, California State University, Sacramento
Susan Garrigan-Piela, Hudson Valley Community College
Wayne Geerling, Pennsylvania State University
Karl Geisler, New Mexico State University
Elisabetta Gentile, University of Houston
Erin George, Hood College
Menelik Geremew, Texas Tech University
Linda Ghent, Easter Illinois University
Dipak Ghosh, Emporia State University
Edgar Ghossoub, University of Texas at San Antonio
J. Robert Gillette, University of Kentucky
Gregory Gilpin, Montana State University
Joana Girante, Arizona State University
Lisa Gloege, Grand Rapids Community College
Robert Godby, University of Wyoming
John Goddeeris, Michigan State University
Rajeev Goel, Illinois State University
Bill Goffe, State University of New York, Oswego
Michael Gootzeit, University of Memphis
Paul Graf, Indiana University, Bloomington
Alan Green, Stetson University
Barbara Grey, Brown Foundation
Natalia Grey, Southeastern Missouri State University
Jeremy Groves, Northern Illinois University
Gail Hayne Hafer, St. Louis Community College
Dan Hamermesh, University of Texas at Austin
Mehdi Haririan, Bloomsburg University
Oskar Harmon, University of Connecticut

David Harrington, The Ohio State University
David Harris, Benedictine College
Darcy Hartman, The Ohio State University
John Hayfron, Western Washington University
Beth Naynes, East Tennessee State University
Jill Hayter, East Tennessee State University
Densie Hazlett, Whitman College
Douglas Heiwig, Ivy Tech Community College
Marc Hellman, Oregon State University
Amy Henderson, St. Mary's College Maryland
Jessica Hennessey, Furman State
Wayne Hickenbottom, University of Texas at Austin
Mike Hilmer, San Diego State University
Ashley Hodgson, St. Olaf College
Adam Hoffer, University of Wisconsin, La Crosse
Jan Höffler, University of Göttingen
Lora Holcombe, Florida State University
Charles Holt, University of Virginia
James Hornsten, Northwestern University
Nancy Howe, Hudson Valley Community College
Gail M. Hoyt, University of Kentucky
Yu-Mong Hsiao, Campbell University
Alice Hsiaw, College of the Holy Cross
Yu Hsing, Southeastern Louisiana University
Amanda Hughey, University of Delaware
Brad R. Humphreys, West Virginia University
Greg W. Hunter, California State Polytechnic University, Pomona
Miren Ivankovic, Anderson University
Meredith Jackson, Snead State Community College
Sarah Jenyk, Youngstown State University
Kristen Johnson, Metropolitan State University of Denver
Paul Johnson, University of Alaska, Anchorage
David Kalist, Shippensburg University of Pennsylvania
Mustafa Karakaplan, Oregon State University
Nicholas Karatjas, Indian University of Pennsylvania
Reza Karim, Des Moines Area Community College
Hossein Kazemi, Stonehill College
Janis Kea, West Valley College
Michael Kelley, Oakwood University
Carrie B. Kerekes, Florida Gulf Coast University
Frank Kim, University of San Diego
Sandra Kinel, Monroe Community College
Linda Kinney, Shepherd University
Vivian Kirby, Kennesaw State University
Ara Khanjian, Ventura College
Colin Knapp, University of Florida
Mary Knudson, University of Iowa
Brian Koralewski, Suffolk County Community College, Ammerman
Dmitri Krichevskiy, Elizabethtown College
Lone Grønbæk Kronbak, University of Southern Denmark
Daniel Kuester, Kentucky State University
Jean Kujawa, Lourdes University
Sylvia Kuo, Brown University
MAJ James Lacovara, United States Military Academy at West Point
Becky Lafrancois, Colorado School of Mines
Ermelinda Laho, LaGuardia Community College
David Lang, California State University, Sacramento

Carsten Lange, California State Polytechnic University, Pomona
Tony Laramie, Merrimack College
Paul Larson, University of Delaware
Teresa Laughlin, Palomar College
Jason Lee, University of California, Merced
Logan Lee, University of Oregon
Jenny Lehman, Wharton County Junior College
Mike Leonard, Kwantlen Polytechnic
Amy Leung, Cosumnes River College
Eric Levy, Florida Atlantic University
Herman Li, University of Nevada, Las Vegas
Ishuan Li, Minnesota State University, Mankato
Jaclyn Lindo, University of Hawaii, Manoa
Charles Link, University of Delaware
Delores Linton, Tarrant County College
Arthur Liu, East Carolina University
Weiwei Liu, Saginaw Valley State University
Xuepeng Liu, Kennesaw State University
Monika Lopez-Anuarbe, Connecticut College
Heriberto Lozano, Mississippi State University
Brian Lynch, Lake Land College
Lynn MacDonald, St. Cloud State University
Zachary Machunda, Minnesota State University, Moorhead
Bruce Madariaga, Montgomery College
Brinda Mahalingam, University of California, Riverside
Chowdhury Mahmoud, Concordia University
Mark Maier, Glendale Community College
Lucy Malakar, Lorain County Community College
Len Malczynski, University of New Mexico
Margaret Malixi, California State University, Bakersfield
Nimantha Manamperi, St. Cloud University
Amber Mann, Corretta Scott King High School
Sonia Mansoor, Westminster College
Daniel Marburger, Arkansas State University
Emily Marshall, Dickinson College
Jim McAndrew, Luzerne County Community College
Michael McAvoy, State University of New York, Oneonta
Kate McClain, University of Georgia
Myra McCrickard, Bellarmine University
Cara McDaniel, Arizona State University
Scott McGann, Grossmont College
Christopher McIntosh, University of Minnesota, Duluth
Craig McLaren, University of California, Riverside
Shah Mehrabi, Montgomery College
Mark Melichar, Tennessee Technical University
Diego Mendez-Carbajo, Illinois Wesleyan University
Evelina Mengova, California State University, Fullerton
William G. Mertens, University of Colorado, Boulder
Charles Meyrick, Housatonic Community College
Frannie Miller, Texas A&M University
Laurie Miller, University of Nebraska, Lincoln
Ida Mirzaie, The Ohio State University
Kaustav Misra, Saginaw Valley State University
Kara Mitchell, Belmont University
Michael A. Mogavero, University of Notre Dame
Mehdi Mohaghegh, Norwich University
Moon Moon Haque, University of Memphis
Sheena Murray, University of Colorado, Boulder
Yolunda Nabors, Tennessee Technical University

Max Nagiel, Daytona State University
Mijid Naranchimeg, Central Connecticut State University
Mike Nelson, Oregon State University
Gibson Nene, University of Minnesota, Duluth
Boris Nikolaev, University of South Florida
Jasminka, Ninkovic, Emory University
Caroline Noblet, University of Maine
Daniel Norgard, Normandale Community College
Stephen Norman, University of Washington, Tacoma
Grace O, Georgia State University
Ichiro Obara, University of California, Los Angeles
Fola Odebunmi, Cypress College
Vincent Odock, State University of New York, Orange
Lee Ohanian, University of California, Los Angeles
Paul Okello, Tarrant County College
Gregory Okoro, Georgia Perimeter College, Clarkston Campus
Ifeakandu Okoye, Florida A&M University
Neal Olitsky, University of Massachusetts, Dartmouth
Martha Olney, University of California, Berkeley
EeCheng Ong, National University of Singapore
Stephen Onyeiwu, Allegheny College
Sandra Orozco-Aleman, Mississippi State University
Lynda Marie Ortega, Saint Phillip's College
Stephanie Owings, Fort Lewis College
Caroline Padgett, Francis Marion University
Jennifer Pakula, Saddleback College
Kerry Pannell, DePauw University
Pete Parcells, Whitman College
Darshak Patel, University of Kentucky
R. Scott Pearson, Charleston Southern University
Jodi Pelkowski, Wichita State University
Faye Peng, University of Wisconsin, Richland
Erica Perdue, Virginia Polytechnic Institute and State University
Andrew Perumal, University of Massachusetts, Boston
Brian Peterson, Central College
Dorothy Peterson, Washington University
Michael Petrowsky, Austin Community College
Rinaldo Pietrantonio, West Virginia University
Van T.H. Pham, Salem State University
Inna Pomorina, Bath Spa University
Steve Price, Butte College
Irina Pritchett, North Carolina State University
Guangjun Qu, Birmingham—Southern College
Gabriela Quevado, Hillsborough Community College
Sarah Quintanar, University of Arkansas at Little Rock
Aleksander Radisich, Glendale Community College
Tobi Ragan, San Jose State University
Mona Ray, Morehouse College
Ranajoy Ray-Chaudhuri, The Ohio State University
Mitchell Redlo, Monroe Community College
Ann Rhoads, Delaware State University
Jennifer Rhoads, St. Catharine University
Samual Riewe, Sonoma State University
Matthew Rolnick, City College of New York
Leanne Roncolato, American University
Debasis Rooj, Northern Illinois University
Brian Rosario, American River College
Ildiko Roth, North Idaho College

Matthew Rousu, Susquehanna University
Jason Rudbeck, University of Georgia
Nicholas G. Rupp, East Carolina University
Anne-Marie Ryan-Guest, Normandale Community College
Martin Sabo, Community College of Denver
Hilary Sackett, Westfield State University
Shrawantee Saha, College of St. Benedict
Ravi Samitamana, Daytona State College
Rolando Sanchez, Northwest Vista College
Jeff Sarbaum, University of North Carolina, Greensboro
Naveen Sarna, Northern Virginia Community College
Supriya Sarnikar, Westfield State University
Noriaki Sasaki, McHenry County College
Thomas Scheiding, Cardinal Stritch Community Collge
Douglas Schneiderheinze, Lewis & Clark Community College
Jessica Schuring, Central College
Robert Schwab, University of Maryland
James Self, Indiana University, Bloomington
Sean Severe, Drake University
Sheikh Shahnawaz, California State University, Chico
Gina Shamshak, Goucher College
Neil Sheflin, Rutgers University
Brandon Sheridan, North Central College
Dorothy R. Siden, Salem State College
Cheri Sides, Lane College
Joe Silverman, Mira Costa College
Scott Simkins, North Carolina A&T State University
Robert Simonson, Minnesota State University, Mankato
Brian Sloboda, University of Phoenix
Gordon Smith, Anderson University
John Solow, University of Iowa
Robert Sonora, Fort Lewis Collge
Todd Sorensen, University of California, Riverside
Maria Sorokina, West Virginia University
Christian Spielman, University College London
Denise Stanley, California State University, Fullerton
Leticia Starkov, Elgin Community College
Kalina Staub, University of North Carolina, Chapel Hill
Rebecca Stein, University of Pennsylvania
Joe Stenard, Hudson Valley Community College
Heather Stephens, California State University, Long Beach
Liliana Stern, Auburn University
Joshua Stillwagon, University of New Hampshire
Burak Sungu, Miami University
Paul Suozzo, Centralia College
David Switzer, St. Cloud Sate University
Vera Tabakova, East Carolina University
Ariuna Taivan, University of Minnesota, Duluth
Yuan Emily Tang, University of California, San Diego
Anna Terzyan, Loyola Marymount University
David Thomas, Ball State University
Henry Thompson, Auburn University
James Tierney, Pennsylvania State University
Aleksander Tomic, Macon State College
Suzanne Toney, Savannah State University
Mehmet Tosun, University of Nevada, Reno
Steve Trost, Virginia Polytechnic Institute and State University

Mark Trueman, Macomb College
Nora Underwood, University of Central Florida
Gergory B. Upton, Jr., Louisiana State University
Mike Urbancic, University of Oregon
Jesus Valencia, Slippery Rock University
Robert Van Horn, University of Rhode Island
Adel Varghese, Texas A&M University
Marieta Velikova, Belmont University
Tatsuma Wada, Wayne State University
Jaime Wagner, University of Nebraska, Lincoln
Will Walsh, Samford University
Yongqing Wang, University of Wisconsin, Waukesha
Thomas White, Assumption College
Johnathan Wight, University of Richmond
Eric WIllbrandt, Auburn University
Nick Williams, University of Cincinnati

Douglas Wills, University of Washington, Tacoma
Ann Wimmer, Iowa Lakes Community College
Kafu Wong, University of Hong Kong
Kelvin Wong, University of Minnesota
Ken Woodward, Saddleback College
Jadrian Wooten, Washington State University
Ranita Wyatt, Paso-Hernando State College
Anne York, Meredith College
Han Yu, Southern Connecticut State University
Kristen Zaborski, State College of Florida
Arindra Zainal, Oregon State University
Erik Zemljic, Kent State University
Tianwei Zhang, University of Georgia
Ying Zhen, Wesleyan College
Dmytro Zhosan, Glendale Community College
Kent Zirlott, University of Alabama

All of the individuals listed above helped us to improve the text and ancillaries, for the first and second editions but a smaller group of them offered us extraordinary insight and support. They went above and beyond, and we would like them to know just how much we appreciate it. In particular, we want to recognize Alicia Baik (University of Virginia), Jodi Beggs (Northeastern University), Dave Brown (Penn State University), Jennings Byrd (Troy University), Douglas Campbell (University of Memphis), Shelby Frost (Georgia State University), Wayne Geerling (Penn State University), Paul Graf (Indiana University), Oskar Harmon (University of Connecticut), Jill Hayter (East Tennessee State University), John Hilston (Brevard Community College), Kim Holder (University of West Georgia), Todd Knoop (Cornell College), Katie Kontak (Bowling Green State University), Brendan LaCerda (University of Virginia), Paul Larson (University of Delaware), Lucy Malakar (Lorain County Community College), Ida Mirzaie (Ohio State University), Charles Newton (Houston Community College), Boris Nikolaev (University of South Florida), J. Brian O'Roark (Robert Morris University), Andrew Perumal (University of Massachusetts, Boston), Irina Pritchett (North Carolina State University), Matt Rousu (Susquehanna College), Tom Scheiding (Cardinal Stritch University), Brandon Sheridan (North Central College), Clair Smith (Saint John Fisher College), James Tierney (Penn State University), Nora Underwood (University of Central Florida), Joseph Whitman (University of Florida), Erik Zemljic (Kent State University), and Zhou Zhang (University of Virginia).

We would also like to thank our partners at W. W. Norton & Company, on both the first and the second edition who have been as committed to this text as we've been. They have been a pleasure to work with and we hope that we get to work together for many years. We like to call them Team Econ: Melissa Atkin, Hannah Bachman, Jack Borrebach, Miryam Chandler, Cassie del Pilar, Sam Glass, John Kresse, Pete Lesser, Sasha Levitt, Lindsey Osteen, Eric Pier-Hocking, Jack Repcheck, Victoria Reuter, Spencer Richardson-Jones, Carson Russell, Nicole Sawa, Eric Svendsen, Janise Turso, and Stefani Wallace. Our development editors, Becky Kohn and Steve Riglosi were a big help, as were our copy editors, Alice Vigliani and Janet Greenblatt. The visual appeal of the book is the result of our photo researchers, Dena Digilio Betz and Nelson Colón, and the design teams at W.W. Norton and Kiss Me I'm Polish: Tiani Kennedy, Rubina Yeh, Agnieszka Gasparska, Andrew Janik, and Annie Song. Finally, we would like to thank Kailyn Amos for the help she provided generating photo ideas in this edition. Thanks to all.

ABOUT THE AUTHORS

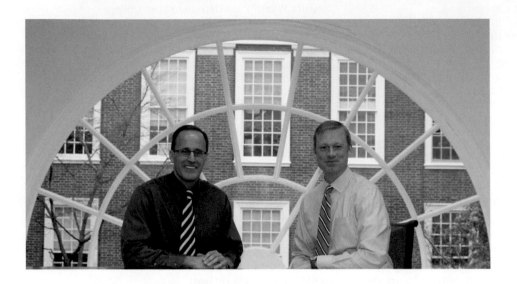

Dirk Mateer is the Gerald J. Swanson Chair in Economic Education at the University of Arizona. His research has appeared in the *Journal of Economic Education* as well as other journals and focuses on media-enriched learning. He is the author of *Economics in the Movies* (2005) and is an award-winning instructor. He has been featured in the "Great Teachers in Economics" series and he was also the inaugural winner of the Economic Communicator Contest sponsored by the Association of Private Enterprise Education. While he was at Penn State, he received the George W. Atherton Award, the university's highest teaching award, and was voted the best overall teacher in the Smeal College of Business by the readers of *Critique Magazine*. Now at Arizona, he received the best large class lecture award in the Eller College of Management.

Lee Coppock is Associate Professor in the Economics Department at the University of Virginia. He has been teaching principles of economics for over twenty years, specializing in principles of macroeconomics. Before moving to UVA, he spent 9 years at Hillsdale College, where he learned how to reach college students. At UVA, Lee teaches two large sections (500+) of macro principles each spring. He has received teaching awards at both Hillsdale College and UVA. Lee lives in Charlottesville with his wife Krista and their four children: Bethany, Lee III, Kara, and Jackson.

Principles of Economics

Second Edition

INTRODUCTION

Five Foundations of Economics

Economics is the dismal science.

Perhaps you have heard of the "dismal science"? This derogatory description of economics was first used by historian and essay-

MIS CONCEPTION

ist Thomas Carlyle in the nineteenth century. He called economics the dismal science after economist Thomas Mal-thus predicted that population growth combined with the planet's limited resources would ultimately lead to widespread starvation.

Malthus was a respected thinker, but he was unduly pessimistic. The world population was 1 billion in 1800, and it is over 7 billion today. One of the things that Malthus did not take into account was increases in technology and productivity. Today, the efficiency of agricultural production enables more than 7 billion people to live on this planet. Far from being the dismal science, economics in the twenty-first century is a vital social science that helps world leaders improve their citizens' lives.

This textbook provides the tools you need to make your own assessments about the economy. What other discipline helps you discover how the world works, how to be an informed citizen, and how to live your life to the fullest? Economics can improve your understanding of the stock market and help you make better decisions. If you are concerned about Social Security, this textbook explains how it works. If you are interested in learning more about the economics of health care and some of the challenges it faces, the answers are here.

In this chapter, you will learn about five foundations of economics—incentives, trade-offs, opportunity cost, marginal thinking, and the principle that trade creates value. You will find that many of the more complex problems presented later in the text are based on these

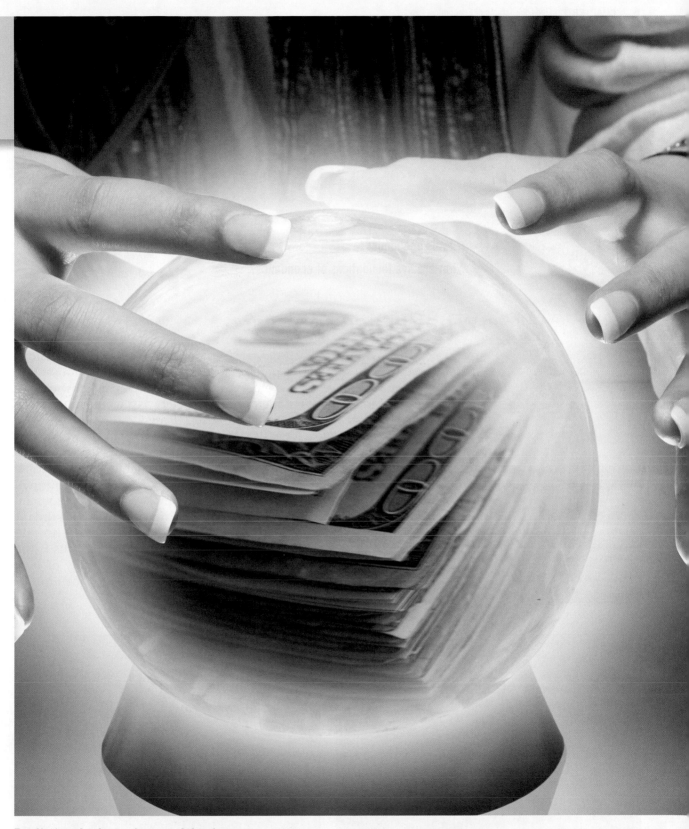

Predicting the future is a tough business.

foundations, either singly or in combination. Think of this chapter as a road map that provides a broad overview of your first journey into economics. Let's get started!

BIG QUESTIONS

✳ **What is economics?**
✳ **What are five foundations of economics?**

What Is Economics?

Economists study how decisions are made. Examples of economic decisions include whether you should buy or lease a car, sublet your apartment, or buy that Gibson guitar you've been eyeing. And just as individuals must choose what to buy within the limits of their income, society as a whole must determine what to produce from its limited set of resources.

Of course, life would be a lot easier if we could have whatever we wanted whenever we wanted it. Unfortunately, life does not work that way. Our wants and needs are nearly unlimited, but the resources available to satisfy these wants and needs are always limited. The term used to describe the limited nature of society's resources is **scarcity**. Even the most abundant resources, like the water we drink and the air we breathe, are not always abundant enough everywhere to meet the wants and needs of every person. So how do individuals and societies make decisions about scarce resources? This is the basic question economists seek to answer. **Economics** is the study of how individuals and societies allocate their limited resources to satisfy their nearly unlimited wants.

Scarcity refers to the limited nature of society's resources, given society's unlimited wants and needs.

Economics is the study of how individuals and societies allocate their limited resources to satisfy their nearly unlimited wants.

Water is scarce . . .

. . . and so are diamonds!

Microeconomics and Macroeconomics

The study of economics is divided into two subfields: microeconomics and macroeconomics. **Microeconomics** is the study of the individual units that make up the economy, such as households and businesses. **Macroeconomics** is the study of the overall aspects and workings of an economy, such as inflation (an overall increase in prices), growth, employment, interest rates, and the productivity of the economy as a whole. To understand the difference, consider a worker who gets laid off and becomes unemployed. Is this an issue that would be addressed in microeconomics or macroeconomics? The question seems to fit parts of both definitions. The worker is an individual, which is micro, but employment is one of the broad areas of concern for the economy as a whole, which is macro. However, because only one worker is laid off, this is a micro issue. If many workers were laid off and the result was a higher unemployment rate across the entire economy, the issue would be broad enough to be studied by macroeconomists. However, macroeconomics is more than just an aggregation of microeconomics. Macroeconomists examine, among other things, government policies regarding the federal budget and money supply, the reasons for inflation and unemployment, economic growth, international trade, and government borrowing—topics that are too complex to be understood using only microeconomic analysis.

Microeconomics is the study of the individual units that make up the economy.

Macroeconomics is the study of the overall aspects and workings of an economy.

What Are Five Foundations of Economics?

The study of economics can be complicated, but we can make it very accessible by breaking it down into a set of component parts. The five foundations presented here are key components of economics. They are a bit like the natural laws of physics or chemistry. Almost every economic subject can be analyzed through the prism of one of these foundations. By mastering the five foundations, you will be on your way to succeeding in this course and thinking like an economist.

The five foundations of economics are:

- Incentives
- Trade-offs
- Opportunity cost
- Marginal thinking
- The principle that trade creates value

Each of these five foundations reappears throughout the book and enables you to solve complex problems. Every time you encounter one of the five concepts, you will see an icon of a house in the margin. As you become more adept at economic analysis, you will often use two or more of these foundational ideas to understand the economic world around you.

Incentives
Trade-offs
Opportunity cost
Marginal thinking
Trade creates value

Incentives

When you are faced with making a decision, you usually make the choice that you think will most improve your situation. In making your decision,

Incentives

PRACTICE WHAT YOU KNOW

This mosaic of the flag illustrates the difference between micro and macro. The small-sized pictures represent microeconomics and the roles that individual decisions play in the overall health of the economy, which is the composite we see when we look at the entire picture.

Microeconomics and Macroeconomics: The Big Picture

Identify whether each of the following statements identifies a microeconomic issue or a macroeconomic issue.

The national savings rate is less than 2% of income.

Answer: The national savings rate is a statistic based on the average amount each household saves as a percentage of income. As such, it is a broad measure of savings that describes a macroeconomic issue.

Jim was laid off from his job and is currently unemployed.

Answer: Jim's personal financial circumstances constitute a microeconomic issue.

Apple decides to open 100 new stores.

Answer: Even though Apple is a very large corporation and 100 new stores will create many new jobs, Apple's decision is a microeconomic issue because it is best understood as part of an individual firm's competitive strategy.

The government passes a jobs bill designed to stabilize the economy during a recession (an economic downturn).

Answer: You might be tempted to ask how many jobs are created, but that information is not relevant to answering this question. The key part of the statement refers to "stabiliz[ing] the economy during a recession," which is an example of the government taking an active role in managing the overall workings of the economy. Therefore, it is a macroeconomic issue.

Incentives are factors that motivate a person to act or exert effort.

you respond to **incentives**—factors that motivate you to act or exert effort. For example, your choice to study for an exam you have tomorrow instead of spending the evening with your friends is based on your belief that doing well on the exam will provide a greater benefit. You have an incentive to study because you know that an A in the course will raise your grade-point average and make you a more attractive candidate on the job market when you are finished with school. We can further divide incentives into two paired categories: positive and negative and direct and indirect.

Positive and Negative Incentives

Positive incentives encourage action by offering rewards or payments. For example, end-of-year bonuses motivate employees to work hard throughout the year, higher oil prices cause suppliers to extract more oil, and tax rebates encourage citizens to spend more money. *Negative incentives* discourage action by providing undesirable consequences or punishments. For instance, the fear of receiving a speeding ticket keeps motorists from driving too fast, higher oil prices might spur some consumers to use less oil, and the dread of a trip to the dentist motivates people to brush their teeth regularly. In each case, we see that incentives spur individuals to action.

Conventional wisdom tells us that "learning is its own reward," but try telling that to most students. Teachers are aware that incentives, both positive and negative, create additional interest among their students to learn the course material. Positive incentives include bonus points, gold stars, public praise, and extra credit. Many students respond to these encouragements by studying more. However, positive incentives are not enough. Suppose that your instructor never gave any grade lower than an A. Your incentive to participate actively in the course, do assignments, or earn bonus points would be small. For positive incentives to work, they generally need to be coupled with negative incentives. This is why instructors require students to complete assignments, take exams, and write papers. Students know that if they do not complete these requirements, they will get a lower grade, perhaps even fail the class.

Direct and Indirect Incentives

Incentives can also be direct or indirect. For instance, if one gas station lowers its prices, it most likely will get business from customers who would not usually stop there. This is a *direct incentive*. Lower gasoline prices also work as an *indirect incentive*, because lower prices might encourage consumers to use more gas.

Direct incentives are easy to recognize. "Cut my grass and I'll pay you $30" is an example of a direct incentive. Indirect incentives are more difficult to recognize. But learning to recognize them is one of the keys to mastering economics. For instance, consider the indirect incentives at work in welfare programs. Almost everyone agrees that societies should provide a safety net for those without employment or whose income isn't enough to meet their basic needs. In other words, a society has a direct incentive to alleviate suffering caused by poverty. But how does a society provide this safety net without taking away the incentive to work? If the amount of welfare a person receives is higher than the amount that person can hope to make from a job, the welfare recipient might decide to stay on welfare rather than go to work. The indirect incentive to stay on welfare creates an *unintended consequence*: people who were supposed to use

Public assistance: a hand in time of need or an incentive not to work?

government assistance as a safety net until they can find a job use it instead as a permanent source of income.

Policymakers have the tough task of deciding how to balance such conflicting incentives. To decrease the likelihood that a person will stay on welfare, policymakers could cut benefits. But this decision might leave some people without enough to live on. For this reason, many government programs specify limits on the amount of time people can receive benefits. Ideally, this limit allows the welfare programs to continue meeting people's basic needs while creating incentives that encourage recipients to search for a job and acquire skills that will help them get a job. We'll learn more about welfare issues in Chapter 15.

ECONOMICS IN THE REAL WORLD

How Incentives Create Unintended Consequences

Let's look at an example of how incentives operate in the real world and how they can lead to consequences no one envisioned. Two Australian researchers noted a large spike in births on July 1, 2004, shown in Figure 1.1. The sudden spike was not an accident. Australia, like many other developed countries, has seen the birthrate fall below the replacement level, which is the birthrate necessary to keep the population from declining. In response to falling birthrates, the Australian government decided to give parents a "baby bonus" of $3,000 for all babies born on or after July 1, 2004. (One Australian dollar equals roughly one U.S. dollar.)

The policy was designed to provide a direct incentive for couples to have children and, in part, to compensate them for lost pay and the costs of car-

FIGURE 1.1

Australian Births by Week in 2004

The plunge and spike in births are evidence of an unintended consequence.

Source: See, Joshua S. Gans and Andrew Leigh, "Born on the First of July: An (un)natural experiment in birth timing," *Journal of Public Economics* 93 (2009): 246–63.

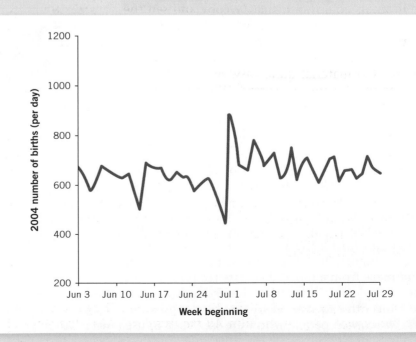

ing for a newborn. However, this direct incentive had an indirect incentive attached to it, too: the couples found a way to delay the birth of their children until after July 1, perhaps jeopardizing the health of both the infants and the mothers. The delayed births were clearly an unintended consequence. Despite reassurances from the government that would-be parents would not put financial gain over their newborn's welfare, over 1,000 births were switched from late June to early July through a combination of additional bed rest and pushing scheduled caesarean sections back a few days. This behavior is testament to the power of incentives.

On a much smaller scale, the same dynamic exists in the United States around January 1 each year. Whether a child is born in January or in December, parents can claim a tax credit for that child for the entire year. Thus, parents have an incentive to ask for labor to be induced or for a caesarean section to be performed late in December so they can have their child before January 1 and thereby take the tax credit. Ironically, hospitals and newspapers often celebrate the arrival of the first baby of the new year even though his or her parents might actually be financially worse off because of the infant's January 1 birthday. ✳

Incentives and Innovation

Incentives also play a vital role in innovation, the engine of economic growth. An excellent example is Steve Jobs. He and the company he founded, Apple, held over 300 patents at the time of his death in 2011.

In the United States, the patent system and copyright laws guarantee inventors a specific period of time in which they have the exclusive right to sell their work. This system encourages innovation by creating a powerful financial reward for creativity. Without patents and copyright laws, inventors would bear all the costs, and almost none of the rewards, for their efforts. Why would firms invest in research and development or artists create new music if others could immediately copy and sell their work? To reward the perspiration and inspiration required for innovation, society allows patents and copyrights to create the right incentives for economic growth.

In recent years, new forms of technology have made the illegal sharing of copyrighted material quite easy. As a result, illegal downloads of books, music, and movies are widespread. When writers, musicians, actors, and studios cannot effectively protect what they have created, they earn less. So illegal downloads reduce the incentive to produce new content. Will the next John Lennon or Jay-Z work so hard? Will the next Suzanne Collins (author of *The Hunger Games*) or J. K. Rowling (author of the Harry Potter books) hone their writing craft so diligently if there is so much less financial reward for success? Is the "I want it for free" culture causing the truly gifted to be less committed to their craft, thus depriving society of excellence? Maintaining the right rewards, or incentives, for hard work and innovation is essential for making sure that inventors and other creative people are compensated for their creativity and vision.

Incentives Are Everywhere

There are many sides to incentives. However, financial gain almost always plays a prominent role. In the film *All the President's Men*, the story of the Watergate scandal that led to the unraveling of the Nixon administration in the early 1970s, a secret source called "Deep Throat" tells Bob Woodward,

Incentives

Ferris Bueller's Day Off

Many people believe that the study of economics is boring. In *Ferris Bueller's Day Off* (1986), Ben Stein (who was an economics major at Columbia University) plays a high school economics teacher who sedates his class with a monotone voice while referring to many abstract economic theories and uttering the unforgettable "Anyone, anyone?" while trying to engage his students. The scene is iconic because it is a boring economics lecture that inspires Ferris and his friends to skip school, which leads to their wild adventures. In fact, the movie is really about incentives and trade-offs.

Was this your first impression of economics?

an investigative reporter at the *Washington Post*, to "follow the money." Woodward responds, "What do you mean? Where?" Deep Throat responds, "Just . . . follow the money." That is exactly what Woodward did. He eventually pieced everything together and followed the money trail all the way to President Nixon.

Understanding the incentives that caused the participants in the Watergate scandal to do what they did led Bob Woodward to the truth. Economists use the same process to explain how people make decisions, how firms operate, and how the economy functions. In fact, understanding incentives, from positive to negative and direct to indirect, is the key to understanding economics. If you remember only one concept from this course, it should be that incentives matter!

Trade-offs

Trade-offs

In a world of scarcity, each and every decision incurs a cost. Even time is a scarce resource; after all, there are only 24 hours in a day. So deciding to read one of the *Hunger Games* books now means that you won't be able to read one of the Harry Potter books until later. More generally, doing one thing often means that you will not have the time, resources, or energy to do something else. Similarly, paying for a college education can require spending tens of thousands of dollars that might be used elsewhere instead.

Understanding the trade-offs that exist in life can completely change how you view the world. Let's look at Psy's song "Gangnam Style." The video for this song has been viewed over 2 billion times on YouTube, making it the most watched video of all time. Imagine what could have been accomplished if people had used that time differently. *The Economist* magazine considered this question and came up with a list of the trade-offs. "Gangnam Style" is 4 minutes and 12 seconds long, which means that more than 140 million hours have been spent watching the video. In the same amount of time, six Burj Khalifas (the world's tallest building, located in Dubai, United Arab Emirates) or four Great Egyptian Pyramids could have been built or the entire contents of Wikipedia entered! 140 million hours also would have been enough time to build three aircraft carriers, an example that brings us to the trade-offs involved in fighting a war. Dwight Eisenhower was aware of trade-offs in 1953 when he stated:

> The cost of one modern heavy-duty bomber is this: a modern brick school in more than 30 cities. It is two electric power plants each serving a town of 60,000 people. It is two fine, fully equipped hospitals. It is some 50 miles of concrete highways. We pay for a single fighter with a half million bushels of wheat. We pay for a single destroyer with new homes that could have housed more than 8,000 people.

What might have been achieved in the time it has taken to watch this video 2.5 billion times?

Ultimately, thinking about trade-offs means that we will make more informed decisions about how to utilize our scarce resources.

Opportunity Cost

The existence of trade-offs requires making hard decisions. Choosing one thing means giving up something else. Suppose that you receive two invitations—the first to spend the day hiking and the second to go to a concert—and both events occur at the same time. No matter which event you choose, you have to sacrifice the other option. In this example, you can think of the cost of going to the concert as the lost opportunity to go on the hike. Likewise, the cost of going hiking is the lost opportunity to go to the concert. No matter what choice you make, there is an opportunity cost, or next-best alternative, that must be sacrificed. **Opportunity cost** is the highest-valued alternative that must be sacrificed to get something else.

Every time we make a choice, we experience an opportunity cost. The key to making the best possible decision is to minimize your opportunity cost by selecting the option that gives you the largest benefit. If you prefer going to a concert, you should go to the concert. What you give up (the hike) has less value to you than the concert, so it has a lower opportunity cost.

The hiking/concert choice is a simple and clear example of opportunity cost. Usually, it takes deliberate effort to see the world through the opportunity cost prism. But it is a worthwhile practice because it will help you make better decisions. For example, imagine you are a small business owner. Your financial officer informs you that you have had a successful year and made a sizable profit. So everything is good, right? Not so fast. An economist will tell you to ask yourself, "Could I have made *more* profit doing something else?" Good economic thinkers ask this question all the time. "Could I be using my

Opportunity cost

Opportunity cost is the highest-valued alternative that must be sacrificed to get something else.

Do you have the moves like Jagger?

time, talents, or energy on another activity that would be even more profitable for me?"

Profits on an official income statement are only part of the story, because they only measure how well a business does relative to the bottom line. Accountants cannot measure what *might* have been better. For example, suppose that you had decided not to open a new store. A few months later, a rival opened a very successful store in the same location you had considered. Your profits were good for the year, but if you had opened the new store, your profits could have been even better. So when economists talk about opportunity cost, they are assessing whether the alternatives are better than what you are currently doing, which considers a larger set of possible outcomes.

Mick Jagger thought about opportunity cost. Before joining the Rolling Stones, he had been attending the London School of Economics. For Mick, the opportunity cost of becoming a musician was forgoing a degree in economics. Given the success of the Rolling Stones, it is hard to fault his decision!

PRACTICE WHAT YOU KNOW

The Opportunity Cost of Attending College

Question: What is the opportunity cost of attending college?

Answer: When people think about the cost of attending college, they usually think of tuition, room and board, course materials, and travel-related expenses. While those expenses are indeed a part of going to college, they are not its full cost. The opportunity cost is the next-best alternative that is sacrificed. This opportunity cost— or what you potentially could have done if you were not in college—includes the lost income you could have earned working a full-time job. If you consider the cost of attending college plus the forgone income lost while in college, you can see that college is a very expensive proposition. Setting aside the question of how much more you might have to pay for room and board at college rather than elsewhere, consider the cost of tuition, which can be $40,000 or more at many of the nation's

Spending thousands on college expenses? You could be working instead!

most expensive colleges. Add that out-of-pocket expense to the forgone income from a full-time job that might pay $40,000 a year, and your four years in college can easily cost over a quarter of a million dollars.

ECONOMICS IN THE REAL WORLD

Breaking the Curse of the Bambino: How Opportunity Cost Causes a Drop in Hospital Visits When the Red Sox Play

If you are injured or severely ill, you head straight to the emergency room, right? Not so fast! A 2005 study published in the *Annals of Emergency Medicine* found that visits to the ER in the Boston area fell by as much as 15% when the Red Sox were playing games in the 2004 playoffs. Part of the decline is attributable to more people sitting inside at home—presumably watching the ballgame—instead of engaging in activities that might get them hurt. But the study determined that simply staying at home did not explain the entire decline in emergency room visits. It turns out that a surprising number of people are willing to put off seeking medical attention for a few hours. Apparently, for some people the opportunity cost of seeking medical attention is high enough to postpone care until after the Red Sox game. ✳

Emergency room beds are empty. Are the Sox playing?

Marginal Thinking

Marginal thinking

The process of systematically evaluating a course of action is called economic thinking. **Economic thinking** involves a purposeful evaluation of the available opportunities to make the best decision possible. In this context, economic thinkers use a process called *marginal analysis* to break down decisions into smaller parts. Often, the choice is not between doing and not doing something, but between doing more or less of something. For instance, if you take on a part-time job while in school, you probably wrestle with the question of how many hours to work. If you work a little more, you can earn additional income. If you work a little less, you have more time to study. Working more has a tangible benefit (more money) and a tangible cost (lower grades). All of this should sound familiar from our earlier discussion about trade-offs. The work-study trade-off affects how much money you have and what kind of grades you earn.

Economic thinking requires a purposeful evaluation of the available opportunities to make the best decision possible.

An economist would say that your decision—weighing how much money you want against the grades you want—is a decision at the *margin*. What exactly does the word "margin" mean as used in economics? In economics, **marginal thinking** requires decision-makers to evaluate whether the benefit of one more unit of something is greater than its cost. Understanding how to analyze decisions at the margin is essential to thinking like a good economist.

Marginal thinking requires decision-makers to evaluate whether the benefit of one more unit of something is greater than its cost.

For example, have you ever wondered why people vacuum, dust, scrub the bathrooms, clean out their garages, and wash their windows, but leave the dust bunnies under the refrigerator? The answer lies in thinking at the margin. Moving the refrigerator out from the wall to clean requires a significant effort for a small benefit. Guests who enter the kitchen can't see under the refrigerator. So most of us ignore the dust bunnies and just clean the visible areas of our homes. In other words, when economists say that you should think at the margin, what they really mean is that you should weigh the costs and benefits of your actions and choose to do the things with the greatest payoff. For most of us, that means being willing to live with dust bunnies.

The *marginal cost* of cleaning under the refrigerator (or on top of the cabinets or even behind the sofa cushions) is too high, and the added value of making the effort, or the *marginal benefit*, is too low to justify the additional cleaning.

ECONOMICS IN THE REAL WORLD

Why Buying and Selling Your Textbooks Benefits You at the Margin

New textbooks are expensive. The typical textbook-purchasing pattern works as follows: you buy a textbook at the start of the term, often at full price, and sell it back at the end of the term for half the price you paid. Ouch. Nobody likes to make a bad investment, and textbooks decline in resale value the moment that students buy them. Even noneconomists know not to buy high and sell low—but that is the textbook cycle for most students.

One solution would be to avoid buying textbooks in the first place. But that decision is neither good nor practical. To understand why, let's use marginal analysis to break the decision into two separate components: the decision to buy and the decision to resell.

Let's start with the decision to buy. A rational buyer will purchase a textbook only if the expected value of the information included in the book is greater than the cost. For instance, say the book contains mandatory assignments or information that is useful for your major and you decide that it is worth $200 to you. If you are able to purchase the book for $100, the gain from buying the textbook would be $100. But what if the book is supplemental reading and you think it is worth only $50? If you value the book at $50 and it costs $100, purchasing the book would entail a $50 loss. If students buy only the books from which they receive gains, every textbook bought will increase someone's well-being.

A similar logic applies to the resale of textbooks. At the end of the course, once you have learned the information inside the book, the value of hanging on to the book is low. You might think it is worth $20 to keep the textbook for future reference, but if you can sell it for $50, the difference represents a gain of $30. In this case, you would decide to sell.

We have seen that buying and selling are two separate decisions made at the margin. If you combine these two decisions and argue that the purchase price ($100) and resale price ($50) are related, as most students typically think they are, you will arrive at a faulty conclusion that you have made a poor decision. That is simply not true.

Textbooks may not be cheap, but they create value twice—once when bought and

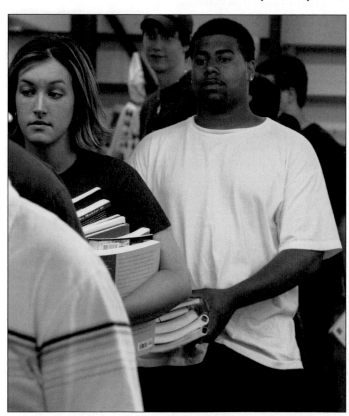

Why do students buy and sell textbooks?

again when sold. This is a win-win outcome. Because we assume that decision-makers will not make choices that leave them worse off, the only way to explain why students buy textbooks and sell them again later is because the students benefit at the margin on both sides of the transaction. ✳

Trade

Imagine trying to find food in a world without grocery stores. The task of getting what you need to eat each day would require visiting many separate locations. Traditionally, this need to bring buyers and sellers together was met by weekly markets, or bazaars, in central locations like town squares. **Markets** bring buyers and sellers together to exchange goods and services. As commerce spread throughout the ancient world, trade routes developed. Markets grew from infrequent gatherings, where exchange involved trading goods and services for other goods and services, into more sophisticated systems that use cash, credit, and other financial instruments. Today, when we think of markets, we often think of eBay or Craigslist. For instance, if you want to find a rare DVD of season 1 of *Entourage*, an excellent place to look is eBay, which allows users to search for just about any product, bid on it, and then have it sent directly to their home.

Trade creates value

Markets bring buyers and sellers together to exchange goods and services.

The Circular Flow

The **circular flow** shows how resources and final goods and services flow through the economy. There are two groups in the circular flow, *households* and *firms*, which want to trade with each other. Households are the people we usually think of as consumers. *Firms* are businesses. Households want the goods and services produced by the firms, and firms want the resources owned by the households in order to make goods and provide services. The circular flow shows how households get the things firms produce and how firms acquire the resources to produce those things. Both of these trades happen in a market.

The circular flow contains two markets. The first market is the *product market*. In this market, households are the buyers and firms are the sellers. This is the type of market you're probably most familiar with. When you go to the gas station or the mall, you are acting as a buyer. The store is the seller.

The second market is the *resource market*, and here the roles are reversed. In this market, the household acts as the seller and the firm is the buyer. The market for labor is a resource market. When you go on the job market, you are basically selling yourself. Firms are looking for employees to help them produce goods and services. They are buying labor.

Figure 1.2 shows the circular flow. The households and firms are the actors. They interact in the two different markets. The arrows show the flow of goods, services, and resources through the economy. This basic view of how things work is actually incredibly accurate. However, we can add one more thing to make the picture of economic activity more complete. At this point we are assuming that the households and the firms trade goods for resources. In other words, they barter. **Barter** involves individuals trading a good they already have or providing a service in exchange for something

The **circular flow** shows how resources and final goods and services flow through the economy.

Barter involves individuals trading a good they already have or providing a service in exchange for something they want.

FIGURE 1.2

The Circular Flow

(a) Circular Flow Model: Goods and services move counterclockwise from one part of the economy to another. Firms produce goods and services and send them to the product market. Households buy these goods and services in the product market, but households provide the inputs necessary to make goods and services. Households sell these inputs in the resource market, where firms buy them and turn them into goods and services.

(b) Circular Flow Model with Money: Instead of bartering for goods and services, people use money to make the transactions much easier. Money acts as a medium of exchange, enabling the economy to avoid the double-coincidence-of-wants problem.

(a) Circular Flow Model   (b) Circular Flow Model with Money

A double coincidence of wants occurs when each party in an exchange transaction has what the other party desires.

they want. The problem is that barter requires a **double coincidence of wants**, in which each party in an exchange transaction has what the other party desires.

A double coincidence of wants is pretty unusual. Consider how you would get what you want in a barter economy. Let's say you are hungry. To get something to eat, you get a job at a Subway restaurant. At the end of the day you get paid. You eagerly choose a foot-long meatball sub as payment for your day's work. Satisfied, you walk home, where you find that your landlord is demanding payment for the rent you owe him. You agree to pay him with a six-inch turkey sub every other day for the next month. Fortunately, the landlord likes Subway sandwiches. In this situation, there is a double coincidence of wants. Unfortunately for you, when you get upstairs there is a message from the cable company. It needs to be paid as well. You call the company and offer food from Subway, but the company doesn't want food. Instead, it wants to be paid with gasoline because its service trucks don't run on sandwiches. To pay your cable bill, you need to find someone who will trade sandwiches for gasoline so you can trade gasoline for cable TV.

You probably see where this is going, and you probably already understand what is missing in our simple model: money. We'll discuss money in a later chapter, but for now it is clear that having some common commodity that buyers and sellers both want will increase the efficiency of the market. Thus, we see societies develop some form of money. Adding money to our model, as we do in Figure 1.2(b), makes it look more like reality. Money flows in the opposite direction of the goods, services, and resources, illustrating that money is being used as a medium of exchange. Now we have two flows, one of goods and services, and one of money, moving in a circle. Hence, the term "circular flow."

Trade Creates Value

Trade is the voluntary exchange of goods and services between two or more parties. Voluntary trade among rational individuals creates value for everyone involved. Imagine you are on your way home from class and you want to pick up a gallon of milk. You know that milk will be more expensive at a convenience store than at the grocery store 5 miles away, but you are in a hurry to study for your economics exam and are willing to pay up to $5 for the convenience of getting the milk quickly. At the store, you find that the price is $4 and you happily purchase the milk. This ability to buy for less than the price you are willing to pay provides a positive incentive to make the purchase. But what about the seller? If the store owner paid $3 to buy the milk from a supplier, and you are willing to pay the $4 price that he has set in order to make a profit, the store owner has an incentive to sell. This simple voluntary transaction has made both of you better off.

By fostering the exchange of goods, trade helps to create additional growth through specialization. **Comparative advantage** refers to the situation in which an individual, business, or country can produce at a lower opportunity cost than a competitor can. Comparative advantage harnesses the power of specialization, a topic we discuss in more detail in Chapter 2. As a result, it is possible to be a physician, teacher, or plumber and not worry about how to do everything yourself. The physician becomes proficient at dispensing medical advice, the teacher at helping students, and the plumber at fixing leaks. The physician and the teacher call the plumber when they need work on their plumbing. The teacher and the plumber see the doctor when they are sick. The physician and the plumber send their children to school to learn from the teacher. Likewise, Mick Jagger made a decision to specialize in music instead of pursuing a career in economics. This decision makes sense because he was better at music than he was at economics.

The same process is at work among businesses. For instance, Starbucks specializes in making coffee, Honda in making automobiles. You would not want to get your morning cup of joe at Honda any more than you would want to buy a car from Starbucks!

On a broader scale, specialization and trading of services exist at the international level as well. Some countries have highly developed workforces capable of managing and solving complex processes. Other countries have large pools of relatively unskilled labor. As a result, businesses that need skilled labor gravitate to countries where they can easily find the workers they need. Likewise, firms with production processes that rely on unskilled labor look for employees in less developed countries, where workers are paid less. By harnessing the power of increased specialization, global companies and economies create value through increased production and growth.

Trade is the voluntary exchange of goods and services between two or more parties.

Comparative advantage refers to the situation where an individual, business, or country can produce at a lower opportunity cost than a competitor can.

However, globalized trade is not without controversy. When goods and jobs are free to move across borders, not everyone benefits equally, nor should we expect this outcome. Consider the case of a U.S. worker who loses her job when her position is outsourced to a call center in India. The jobless worker now has to find new employment—a process that requires significant time and energy. In contrast, the new position in the call center in India provides a job and an income that improve the life of another worker. Also, the U.S. firm enjoys the advantage of being able to hire lower-cost labor elsewhere. The firm's lower costs often translate into lower prices for domestic consumers. None of those advantages make the outsourcing of jobs any less painful for affected workers, but outsourcing is an important component of economic growth in the long run.

Conclusion

Is economics the dismal science?

Now that you have begun your exploration of economics, you know that economics is not dismal. Economists ask, and answer, big questions about life.

Our economy depends on specialization.

This is what makes the study of economics so fascinating. Understanding how an entire economy functions may seem like a daunting task, but it is not nearly as difficult as it sounds. If you remember learning to drive a car, the process is similar. When you are first learning to drive, everything seems difficult and unfamiliar. But once you learn and practice a few key principles, you can become a good driver quite quickly. With experience, you can drive any car on the road. Learning economics is similar; once you have learned the fundamentals of economics, you can use them to analyze almost any problem. In the next chapter, we use the ideas developed in this chapter to explore trade in greater depth.

Five Foundations of Economics

In this book, we study five foundations of economics—incentives, trade-offs, opportunity cost, marginal thinking, and the principle that trade creates value. Once you have mastered these five concepts, even complex economic processes can be reduced to smaller, more easily understood parts. If you keep these foundations in mind, you'll find that understanding economics is rewarding and fun.

OPPORTUNITY COST

INCENTIVES

In making a decision, you respond to incentives—factors that motivate you to act or to exert effort. Incentives also play a vital role in innovation, the engine of economic growth.

TRADE-OFFS

TRADE CREATES VALUE

MARGINAL THINKING

Marginal thinking is the hallmark of economic analysis. It requires forward thinking that compares the extra benefits of each activity with the extra costs.

REVIEW QUESTIONS

- Which of the five foundations explains what you give up when you choose to buy a new pair of shoes instead of attending a concert?

- What are four types of incentives discussed in the chapter? Why do incentives sometimes create unintended consequences?

Midcareer Earnings by Selected Majors

A recent study surveyed full-time employees across the United States who possessed a bachelor's degree but no advanced degree. Twenty popular fields are listed in the graph below along with the salaries they command. Note that economics ranks quite high on the scale!

Not all majors are created equal. However, the majors that produce more income initially do not necessarily keep their advantage a decade or two later. That means that today's newly minted economics majors, with a median starting salary of $50,100, will likely surpass those who majored in physics or computer science in earnings by the time they reach midcareer. The same holds true for political science majors, who have a lower starting salary than business majors but eventually surpass them. In the long run, pay growth matters to income level as much as, if not more than, starting salary. In terms of salary, any decision about what to major in that looks only at starting pay is misleading. How much money you make over your entire career is what matters!

Will you make more by majoring in economics or finance? Check out these median (what the typical person earns) salaries!

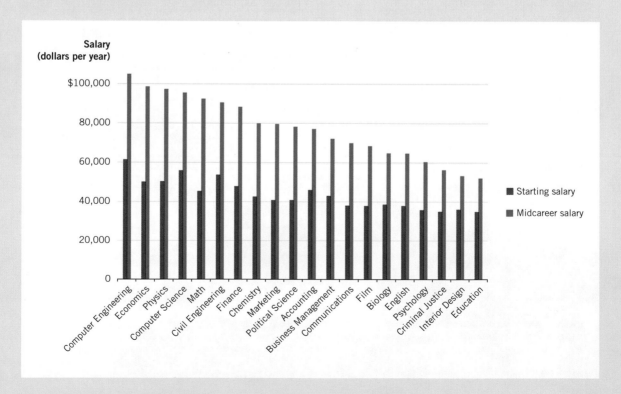

ANSWERING THE BIG QUESTIONS

What is economics?

* Economics is the study of how people allocate their limited resources to satisfy their nearly unlimited wants. Because of the limited nature of society's resources, even the most abundant resources are not always plentiful enough everywhere to meet the wants and needs of every person. So how do individuals and societies make decisions about how to use the scarce resources at their disposal? This is the basic question economists seek to answer.

What are five foundations of economics?

Five foundations of economics are incentives, trade-offs, opportunity cost, marginal thinking, and the principle that trade creates value.

* Incentives are important because they help explain how rational decisions are made.
* Trade-offs exist when a decision-maker has to choose a course of action.
* Each time we make a choice, we experience an opportunity cost, or a lost chance to do something else.
* Marginal thinking requires a decision-maker to weigh the extra benefits against the extra costs.
* Trade creates value because participants in markets are able to specialize in the production of goods and services that they have a comparative advantage in making.

CONCEPTS YOU SHOULD KNOW

barter (p. 17)
circular flow (p. 17)
comparative advantage (p. 19)
double coincidence of wants
  (p. 18)

economics (p. 6)
economic thinking (p. 15)
incentives (p. 8)
macroeconomics (p. 7)
marginal thinking (p. 15)

markets (p. 17)
microeconomics (p. 7)
opportunity cost (p. 13)
scarcity (p. 6)
trade (p. 19)

QUESTIONS FOR REVIEW

1. How would you respond if your instructor gave daily quizzes on the course readings? Are these quizzes a positive incentive or a negative incentive?

2. Explain why many seniors often earn lower grades in their last semester before graduation. **Hint:** This is an incentive problem.

3. What is the opportunity cost of reading this textbook?

4. Evaluate the following statement: "Trade is like football: one team wins and the other loses."

STUDY PROBLEMS (✳ *solved at the end of the section*)

✳ 1. What role do incentives play in each of the following situations? Are there any unintended consequences?
   a. You learn that you can resell a ticket to next week's homecoming game for twice what you paid.
   b. A state government announces a "sales tax holiday" for back-to-school shopping during one week each August.

2. Compare your standard of living with that of your parents when they were the age you are now. Ask them or somebody you know around their age to recall where they were living and what they owned. How has the well-being of the typical person changed over the last 25 years? Explain your answer.

3. By referencing events in the news or something from your personal experiences, describe one example of each of the five foundations of economics discussed in this chapter.

✳ 4. Suppose that Colombia is good at growing coffee but not very good at making computer software and that Canada is good at making computer software but not very good at growing coffee. If Colombia decided only to grow coffee and Canada only to make computer software, would both countries be better off or

worse off? Explain. Can you think of a similar example from your life?

5. After some consideration, you decide to hire someone to help you move from one apartment to another. Wouldn't it be cheaper to move yourself? Do you think the choice to hire someone is a rational choice? Explain your response.

✳ 6. Would you wait in line three weeks to be the first customer at Best Buy on Black Friday (the day after Thanksgiving, the "official start" of the holiday shopping season)? Two women from California did just that, taking turns holding their positions in line around the clock for over 500 hours. They waited in order to get a doorbuster deal on a new 50-inch television for $199 (the normal retail price of the model is $399). Discuss why they might be willing to wait in line three weeks in terms of incentives. Do you think their choice makes sense? Answer this question by considering the marginal benefit that they receive versus the marginal cost they must pay.

7. *Whiplash* (2014) is about an aspiring college-age drummer who wants to become the best drummer in the world. He is willing to

sacrifice personal relationships, practices tens of thousands of hours, and suffers mental and physical abuse from his teacher in order to achieve his goal and earn the recognition he craves. Watch the full movie trailer on IMDB.com or go to www.youtube.com /watch?v=MsWlktW0kj4 and watch the break-up scene with his girlfriend. What trade-offs are you making in your life right now to achieve your goals?

✴ 8. We have talked about how trade creates value. Use the information in each example below

to compute the total value created in each exchange:

a. Patrick bought an orange pen from Jill for $2.00. Patrick would have been willing to pay $2.50 for the pen, and Jill would have been willing to sell the pen for $1.25.

b. Hillary found a car on Craigslist for which she would have been willing to pay up to $10,000. The car's owner, Jason, needed to sell the car right away and would have accepted $6,000. The price they agreed on was $7,500.

SOLVED PROBLEMS

1.a. Because your tickets are worth more than you paid for them, you have a direct positive incentive to resell them.

b. The "sales tax holiday" is a direct positive incentive to buy more clothes during the back-to-school period. An unintended consequence of this policy is that fewer purchases are likely to be made both before and after the tax holiday.

4. If Colombia decided to specialize in the production of coffee, it could trade coffee to Canada in exchange for computer software. This process illustrates gains from specialization and trade. Both countries have a comparative advantage in producing one particular good. Colombia has ideal coffee-growing conditions, and Canada has a workforce that is more adept at writing software. Since both countries specialize in what they do best, they are able to produce more value than they could produce by trying to make both products on their own.

6. The women have a direct positive incentive to wait in line. They will save $200 when they buy the TV. There are many trade-offs that they face: missed sleep, time they could have spent with family members and friends, and the time they could be working instead of waiting in line, to name just a few.

It is hard to see the women's choice as rational when examining it using marginal analysis. They will save $200, but they will spend hundreds of hours in line. There is a high opportunity cost here and the hourly rate that they are using to value their time is very low. Saving $200 but spending 500 hours to save that money makes their time worth 40 cents an hour. They could work an extra job at minimum wage for 40 hours and earn enough money to purchase the TV at full price and still have over 400 hours free to do something else. In short, they don't seem to be aware of the opportunity cost of their time.

8.a. In this example, Patrick is better off by $0.50 because he was willing to pay $2.50 but paid just $2.00. Jill is better off by $0.75 because she would have accepted $1.25 but Patrick paid her $2.00. So the total value created is the additional value to Patrick ($0.50) plus the additional value to Jill ($0.75), which sums to $1.25.

b. The value added for Jason is $1,500, which is the difference between the minimum price he would have accepted ($6,000) and the price he received ($7,500). The value added for Hillary is $2,500, which is the difference between the maximum price she would have paid ($10,000) and the price she actually paid ($7,500). In total, $1,500 + $2,500 = $4,000 in new value was created through the exchange.

Model Building and Gains from Trade

Trade always results in winners and losers.

When most people think of trade, they think of it as a zero-sum game—that is, a game in which one side wins what the other side loses. Think

about international trade, for example. Many people believe that rich countries exploit the natural resources of poor countries and even steal their most talented workers. In this view, the rich countries are winners and the poor countries are losers. Other people think of trade as the simple redistribution of goods. If you're in the cafeteria and trade your apple for a friend's cup of chocolate pudding, how can this trade possibly create value?

In this chapter, we will see that trade is not an imbalanced equation of winners and losers. First, we will consider how economists use the scientific method to help explain the world we live in. These foundations will serve as the tools we need to explore the more nuanced reasons why trade creates value.

Elementary school children trade lunch items to get something better.

BIG QUESTIONS

* How do economists study the economy?
* What is a production possibilities frontier?
* What are the benefits of specialization and trade?
* What is the trade-off between having more now and having more later?

How Do Economists Study the Economy?

Economics is a social science that uses the scientific method to develop *economic models*. To create these models, economists make many assumptions to simplify reality. These models help economists understand the key relationships that drive economic decisions.

The Scientific Method in Economics

On the television show *MythBusters*, Jamie Hyneman and Adam Savage put popular myths to the test. In Savage's words, "We replicate the circumstances, then duplicate the results." The entire show is dedicated to scientific testing of the myths. At the end of each episode, the myth is confirmed, decreed plausible, or busted. For instance, in a memorable episode, Hyneman and Savage explored the reasons behind the *Hindenburg* disaster. The *Hindenburg* was a German passenger airship, or zeppelin, that caught fire and became engulfed in flames as it attempted to dock in New Jersey on May 6, 1937. Thirty-six people died.

Some people have claimed that the fire was sparked by the painted fabric in which the zeppelin was wrapped. Others have suggested that the hydrogen used to give the airship lift was the primary cause of the disaster. To test the hypothesis (proposed explanation) that the paint used on the fabric was to blame, Hyneman and Savage

The scientific method was used to discover why the *Hindenburg* caught fire.

built two small-scale models. The first model was filled with hydrogen and had a nonflammable skin. The second model used a replica of the original fabric for the skin but did not contain any hydrogen. Hyneman and Savage then compared their models' burn times with original footage of the disaster.

After examining the results, they "busted" the myth that the paint was to blame. Why? The model containing the hydrogen burned twice as fast as the one with just the painted fabric skin. It seems reasonable to conclude that hydrogen caused the disaster, not paint.

Economists work in much the same way as Hyneman and Savage: they use the scientific method to answer questions about observable phenomena and to explain how the world works. The scientific method consists of four steps:

- First, researchers observe a phenomenon that interests them.
- Next, based on these observations, researchers develop a *hypothesis*, which is a proposed explanation for the phenomenon.
- Then they construct a model to test the hypothesis.
- Finally, they design experiments to test how well the model (which is based on the hypothesis) works. After collecting data from the experiments, they can verify, revise, or refute the hypothesis.

The economist's laboratory is the world around us, and it ranges from the economy as a whole to the decisions made by firms and individuals. As a result, economists cannot always design experiments to test their hypotheses. Often, they must gather historical data or wait for real-world events to take place—for example, the Great Recession (economic downturn) of 2007–2009—to better understand the economy.

Positive and Normative Analysis

As scientists, economists strive to approach their subject with objectivity. This means that they rigorously avoid letting personal beliefs and values influence the outcome of their analysis. To be as objective as possible, economists deploy positive analysis. A **positive statement** can be tested and validated. Each positive statement can be thought of as a description of "what is." For instance, the statement "The unemployment rate is 7%" is a positive statement because it can be tested by gathering data.

In contrast, a **normative statement** cannot be tested or validated; it is about "what ought to be." For instance, the statement "An unemployed worker should receive financial assistance to help make ends meet" is a matter of opinion. One can reasonably argue that financial assistance to the unemployed is beneficial for society as a whole because it helps eliminate poverty. However, many argue that financial assistance to the unemployed provides the wrong incentives. If the financial assistance provides enough to meet basic needs, workers may end up spending more time unemployed than they otherwise would. Neither opinion is right or wrong; they are differing viewpoints based on values, beliefs, and opinions.

Economists are concerned with positive analysis. In contrast, normative statements are the realm of policymakers, voters, and philosophers. For example, if the unemployment rate rises, economists try to understand the conditions that created the situation. Economics does not attempt to determine

A positive statement can be tested and validated; it describes "what is."

A normative statement is an opinion that cannot be tested or validated; it describes "what ought to be."

Incentives

who should receive unemployment assistance, which involves normative analysis. Maintaining a positive (as opposed to normative) framework is crucial for economic analysis because it allows decision-makers to observe the facts objectively.

Economic Models

Thinking like an economist means learning how to analyze complex issues and problems. Many economic topics, such as international trade, Social Security, job loss, and inflation, are complicated. To analyze these phenomena and to determine the effect of various government policy options related to them, economists use economic models, which are simplified versions of reality. Models help us analyze the components of the economy.

The Wright brothers' wind tunnel

A good model should be simple, flexible, and useful for making accurate predictions. Let's consider one of the most famous models in history, designed by Wilbur and Orville Wright. Before the Wright brothers made their famous first flight in 1903, they built a small wind tunnel out of a 6-foot-long wooden box. Inside the box they placed a device to measure aerodynamics, and at one end they attached a small fan to supply the wind. The brothers then tested over 200 different wing configurations to determine the lifting properties of each design. Using the data they collected, the Wright brothers were able to determine the best type of wing to use on their aircraft.

Similarly, economic models provide frameworks that help us to predict the effects of changes in prices, production processes, and government policies on real-life behavior.

Ceteris Paribus

Ceteris paribus means "other things being equal" or "all else equal" and is used to build economic models. It allows economists to examine a change in one variable while holding everything else constant.

Using a controlled setting that held many other variables constant enabled the Wright brothers to experiment with different wing designs. By altering only a single element—for example, the angle of the wing—they could test whether the change in design was advantageous. The process of examining a change in one variable while holding everything else constant involves a concept known as ***ceteris paribus***, from the Latin meaning "other things being equal" or "all else equal."

The *ceteris paribus* assumption is central to model building. If the Wright brothers had changed many design elements simultaneously and found that a new version of the wing worked better, they would have had no way of knowing which change was responsible for the improved performance. For this reason, engineers generally modify only one design element at a time and test only that one element before testing additional elements.

Like the Wright brothers, economists start with a simplified version of reality. Economists build models, change one variable at a time, and ask whether the change in the variable had a positive or negative impact on performance. Perhaps the best-known economic model is supply and demand, which we study in Chapter 3.

Endogenous versus Exogenous Factors

Models must account for factors that we can control and factors that we can't. Factors that we know about and can control are **endogenous factors**. The Wright brothers' wind tunnel was critical to their success because it allowed them to control for as many endogenous factors as possible. For example, the wind tunnel enabled the Wright brothers to see how well each wing design—an important part of the model—performed under controlled conditions.

Endogenous factors are the variables that can be controlled for in a model.

Factors beyond our control—outside the model—are **exogenous factors**. Once the Wright brothers had determined the best wing design, they built the full-scale airplane that took flight at Kitty Hawk, North Carolina. At that point the plane, known as the "Flyer," was no longer in a controlled environment. It was subject to the gusting wind and other exogenous factors that made the first flight so challenging.

Exogenous factors are the variables that cannot be controlled for in a model.

Building an economic model is very similar to the process Wilbur and Orville used. We need to be mindful of three factors: (1) what we include in the model, (2) the assumptions we make when choosing what to include in the model, and (3) the outside conditions that can affect the model's performance. In the case of the first airplane, the design was an endogenous factor because it was within the Wright brothers' control. In contrast, the weather (wind, air pressure, and other atmospheric conditions) was an exogenous factor because the Wright brothers could not control it. Because the world is a complex place, an airplane model that flies perfectly in a wind tunnel may not fly reliably when it is exposed to the elements. Therefore, if we add more exogenous variables, or factors we cannot control—for example, wind and rain—to test our model's performance, the test becomes more realistic.

The Danger of Faulty Assumptions

When we build a model, we need to make choices about which variables to include. Ideally, we would like to include all the important variables inside the model and exclude all the variables that should be ignored. However, no matter what we include, using a model that contains faulty assumptions can lead to spectacular failures. An excellent example is the financial crisis and Great Recession that began in December 2007.

In the years leading up to the crisis, banks sold and repackaged mortgage-backed investments under the faulty assumption that real estate prices will always rise. This assumption seemed perfectly reasonable in a world where real estate prices were rising annually. Unfortunately, the assumption turned out to be false. From 2006 to 2008, real estate prices fell. Because of one faulty assumption, the entire financial market teetered on the edge of collapse.

In the late 1990s and early 2000s, some investors believed that real estate prices could only rise.

PRACTICE WHAT YOU KNOW

Positive versus Normative Statements

Question: Which of the following statements are positive and which ones are normative?

1. Winters in Arkansas are too cold.
2. Everyone should work at a bank to learn the true value of money.
3. The current exchange rate is 0.7 British pound per U.S. dollar.
4. On average, people save 15% on insurance when they switch to Geico.
5. Everyone ought to have a life insurance policy.
6. University of Virginia graduates earn more than Duke University graduates.
7. Harvard University is the top educational institution in the country.
8. The average January temperature in Fargo, North Dakota, is 56°F.

You should eat five servings of fruit or vegetables each day. Is this statement positive or normative?

Answers

1. The phrase "too cold" is a matter of opinion. This is a normative statement.
2. While working at a bank might give someone an appreciation for the value of money, the word "should" indicates an opinion. This is a normative statement.
3. This is a positive statement. You can look up the current exchange rate and verify if this statement is true or false.
4. Geico made this claim in one of its commercials. It is a positive statement because it is a testable claim. If you had the data from Geico, you could determine if the statement were correct or not.
5. This sounds like a true statement, or at least a very sensible one. However, the word "ought" makes it an opinion. This is a normative statement.
6. You can look up the data and see which university's graduates earn more. This is a positive statement.
7. Some national rankings indicate that this statement is true, but others do not. Because different rankings are based on different assumptions, it is not possible to identify a definitive "top" school. This is a normative statement.
8. This is a positive statement, but the statement is wrong. North Dakota is much colder than that in January. The statement can be verified (in this case, proved wrong) by climate data.

What Is a Production Possibilities Frontier?

Now it's time to learn our first economic model. However, before you go on, you might want to review the appendix on graphing at the end of this chapter. Graphs are a key tool in economics because they display the relationship between two variables. Your ability to read a graph and understand the model it represents is crucial to learning economics.

In Chapter 1, we learned that economics is about the trade-offs individuals and societies face every day. For instance, you may frequently have to decide between spending more time studying or hanging out with your friends. The more time you study, the less time you have for your friends. Similarly, a society has to determine how to allocate its resources. The decision to build new roads will mean that there is less money available for new schools, and vice versa.

A **production possibilities frontier (PPF)** is a model that illustrates the combinations of outputs that a society can produce if all of its resources are being used efficiently. An outcome is considered *efficient* when resources are fully utilized and potential output is maximized. To preserve *ceteris paribus*, we assume that the technology available for production and the quantity of resources remain fixed, or constant. These assumptions allow us to model trade-offs more clearly.

Let's begin by imagining a society that produces only two goods—pizza and chicken wings. This may not seem like a very realistic assumption, since a real economy produces millions of different goods and services, but this approach helps us understand trade-offs by keeping the analysis simple.

Figure 2.1 shows the production possibilities frontier for our simplified two-product society. Remember that the number of people and the total resources in this two-product society are fixed. If the economy uses all of its resources to produce pizza, it can produce 100 pizzas and 0 wings. If it uses all of its resources to produce wings, it can make 300 wings and 0 pizzas. These outcomes are represented by points A and B, respectively, on the production possibilities frontier. It is unlikely that the society will choose either of these extreme outcomes because it is human nature to enjoy variety.

If our theoretical society decides to spend some of its resources producing pizzas and some of its resources making wings, its economy will end up with a combination of pizza and wings that is somewhere along the PPF between points A and B. At point C, for example, the society would deploy its resources to produce 70 pizzas and 90 wings. At point D, the combination would be 50 pizzas and 150 wings. Each point along the production possibilities frontier represents a possible set of outcomes that the society can choose if it uses all of its resources efficiently.

Notice that some combinations of pizza and wings cannot be produced because not enough resources are available. Our theoretical society would enjoy point E, but given the available resources, it cannot produce that output level. Points beyond the production possibilities frontier are desirable but not feasible with the available resources and technology.

At any combination of wings and pizzas along the production possibilities frontier, the society is using all of its resources in the most efficient way possible. But what about point F and any other points located in the shaded

Trade-offs

A **production possibilities frontier (PPF)** is a model that illustrates the combinations of outputs that a society can produce if all of its resources are being used efficiently.

FIGURE 2.1

The Production Possibilities Frontier for Pizza and Chicken Wings

The production possibilities frontier (PPF) shows the trade-off between producing pizza and producing wings. Any combination of pizza and wings is possible along, or inside, the line. Combinations of pizza and wings beyond the production possibilities frontier—for example, at point E—are not possible with the current set of resources. Point F and any other points located in the shaded region are inefficient.

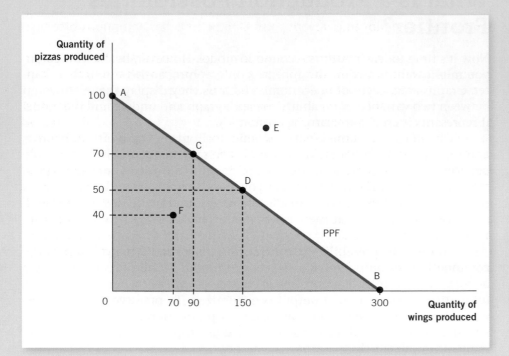

region? These points represent outcomes inside the production possibilities frontier, and they indicate an inefficient use of the society's resources. Consider, for example, the labor resource. If employees spend many hours at work surfing the Web instead of doing their jobs, the output of pizza and wings will drop and the outcome will no longer be efficient. As long as workers use all of their time efficiently, they will produce an efficient amount of pizza and wings, and output will lie somewhere on the PPF.

Whenever society is producing on the production possibilities frontier, the only way to get more of one good is to accept less of another. Because an economy operating at a point on the frontier will be efficient, economists do not favor one point over another. But a society may favor one point over another because it prefers that combination of goods. For example, in our theoretical two-good society, if wings suddenly become more popular, the movement from point C to point D will represent a desirable trade-off. The society will produce 20 fewer pizzas (decreasing from 70 to 50) but 60 additional wings (increasing from 90 to 150).

Trade-offs

Opportunity cost

The Production Possibilities Frontier and Opportunity Cost

Because our two-good society produces only pizza and wings, the trade-offs that occur along the production possibilities frontier represent the opportunity cost of producing one good instead of the other. As we saw in Chapter 1, an opportunity cost is the highest-valued alternative given up to pursue another course of action. As Figure 2.1 shows, when society moves from point C to point D, it gives up 20 pizzas; this is the opportunity cost of producing more wings. The movement from point D to point C has an opportunity cost of 60 wings.

Until now, we have assumed a constant trade-off between the number of pizzas and the number of wings produced. However, not all resources in our theoretical society are perfectly adaptable for use in making pizza and wings. Some workers are good at making pizza, and others are not so good. When the society tries to make as many pizzas as possible, it will be using both types of workers. That is, to get more pizzas, the society will have to use workers who are increasingly less skilled at making them. For this reason, pizza production will not expand at a constant rate. You can see this effect in the new production possibilities frontier in Figure 2.2; it is bowed outward rather than a straight line.

Because resources are not perfectly adaptable, production does not expand at a constant rate. For example, to produce 20 extra pizzas, the society can move from point D (30 pizzas) to point C (50 pizzas). But moving from point D (280 wings) to point C (250 wings) means giving up 30 wings. So moving from point D to point C has an opportunity cost of 30 wings.

FIGURE 2.2

The Law of Increasing Opportunity Cost

To make more pizzas, the society will have to use workers who are increasingly less skilled at making them. As a result, as we move up along the PPF, the opportunity cost of producing an extra 20 pizzas rises from 30 wings between points D and C to 80 wings between points B and A.

Opportunity
cost

The **law of increasing opportunity cost** states that the opportunity cost of producing a good rises as a society produces more of it.

Now suppose that the society decides it wants even more pizzas and moves from point C (50 pizzas) to point B (70 pizzas). Now the opportunity cost of 20 more pizzas is 50 wings, because wing production declines from 250 to 200. If the society decides that 70 pizzas are not enough, it can expand pizza production from point B (70 pizzas) to point A (90 pizzas). Now the society gives up 80 wings. Notice that as we move up along the PPF from point D to point A, the opportunity cost of producing an extra 20 pizzas rises from 30 wings to 80 wings. This higher opportunity cost reflects the increased trade-off necessary to produce more pizzas.

A bowed-out production possibilities frontier reflects the increasing opportunity cost of production. Figure 2.2 illustrates the **law of increasing opportunity cost**, which states that the opportunity cost of producing a good rises as a society produces more of it. Changes in relative cost mean that a society faces a significant trade-off if it tries to produce an extremely large amount of a single good.

The Production Possibilities Frontier and Economic Growth

So far, we have modeled the production possibilities frontier based on the resources available to society at a particular moment in time. However, most societies hope to create economic growth. *Economic growth* is the process that enables a society to produce more output in the future.

We can use the production possibilities frontier to explore economic growth. For example, we can ask what would happen to the PPF if our two-good society develops a new technology that increases efficiency. Suppose that a new pizza assembly line improves the pizza production process and that the new assembly line does not require the use of more resources—it simply redeploys the resources that already exist. This development would allow the society to make more pizza with the same number of workers. Or it would allow the same amount of pizza to be made with fewer workers than previously. Either way, the society has expanded its resource base. Figure 2.3 shows this change as a shift in the PPF.

With the new technology, it becomes possible to produce 120 pizzas using the same number of workers and in the same amount of time that it previously took to produce 100 pizzas. Although the ability to produce wings has not changed, the new pizza-making technology expands the production possibilities frontier outward from PPF₁ to PPF₂. It is now possible for the society to move from point A to point B, where it can produce more of both goods (80 pizzas and 220 wings). Why can the society produce more of both? Because the improvement in pizza-making technology—the assembly line—allows a redeployment of the labor force that also increases the production of wings. Improvements in technology make point B possible.

The production possibilities frontier will also expand if the population grows. A larger population means more workers to make pizza and wings. Figure 2.4 illustrates what happens when the society adds workers to help produce pizza and wings. With more workers, the society can produce more pizzas and wings than before. The PPF curve shifts from PPF₁ to PPF₂, expanding up along the *y* axis and out along the *x* axis. Like improvements in technology, additional resources expand the frontier and allow the society to

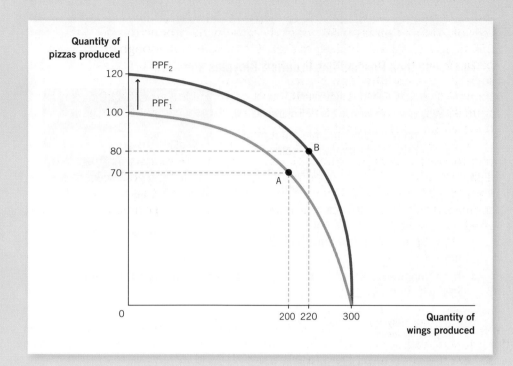

FIGURE 2.3

A Shift in the Production Possibilities Frontier

A new pizza assembly line that improves the productive capacity of pizza makers shifts the PPF upward from PPF_1 to PPF_2. More pizzas can be produced. Comparing points A and B, you can see that the enhanced pizza-making capacity also makes it possible to produce more wings at the same time.

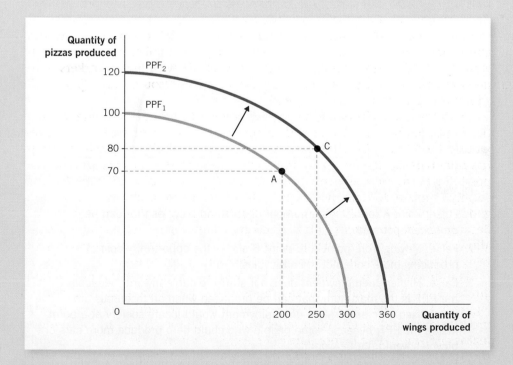

FIGURE 2.4

More Resources and the Production Possibilities Frontier

When more resources (such as additional workers) are available for the production of either pizza or wings, the entire PPF shifts upward and outward. This shift makes point C, along PPF_2, possible.

PRACTICE WHAT YOU KNOW

The Production Possibilities Frontier: Bicycles and Cars

Question: Are the following statements true or false? Base your answers on the PPF shown below.

There is a trade-off between making bicycles and making cars.

1. Point A represents a possible amount of cars and bicycles that can be sold.

2. The movement along the curve from point A to point B shows the opportunity cost of producing more bicycles.

3. If society experiences a substantial increase in unemployment, the PPF shifts inward.

4. If an improved process for manufacturing cars is introduced, the entire PPF will shift outward.

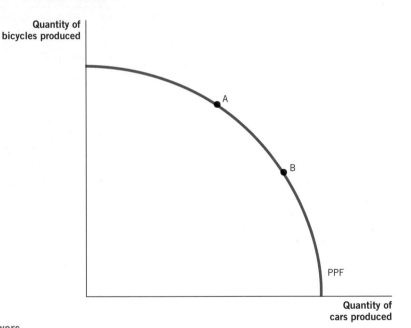

Answers

1. False. Point A represents a number of cars and bicycles that can be *produced*, not sold.

2. False. Moving from point A to point B shows the opportunity cost of producing more cars, not more bicycles.

3. False. Higher unemployment does not shift the curve inward, because the PPF is the maximum that can be produced when all resources are being used efficiently. More unemployment would locate society at a point inside the PPF, because some people who could help produce more cars or bicycles would not be working.

4. False. The PPF will shift outward along the car axis, but it will not shift upward along the bicycle axis.

reach a point—in this case, point C—that was not possible before. The extra workers have pushed the entire frontier out—not just one end of it, as the pizza assembly line did.

What Are the Benefits of Specialization and Trade?

We have seen that improving technology and adding resources make an economy more efficient. A third way to create gains for society is through specialization and trade. **Specialization** is the limiting of one's work to a particular area. Determining what to specialize in is an important part of the process. Every worker, business, or country is relatively good at producing certain products or services. Suppose that you decide to learn about information technology. You earn a certificate or degree and find an employer who hires you for your specialized skills. Your information technology skills determine your salary. You can then use your salary to purchase other goods and services that you desire and that you are not so skilled at making yourself.

In the next section, we explore why specializing and exchanging your skilled expertise with others makes gains from trade possible.

Specialization is the limiting of one's work to a particular area.

Gains from Trade

Let's return to our two-good economy. Now we'll make the further assumption that this economy has only two people. One person is better at making pizzas, and the other is better at making wings. In this case, the potential gains from trade are clear. Each person will specialize in what he or she is better at producing and then will trade to acquire some of the good produced by the other person.

Figure 2.5 shows the production potential of the two people in our economy, Debra Winger and Mike Piazza. From the table at the top of the figure, we see that if Debra Winger devotes all of her work time to making pizzas, she can produce 60 pizzas. If she does not spend any time on pizzas, she can make 120 wings. In contrast, Mike Piazza can spend all his time on pizzas and produce 24 pizzas or all his time on wings and produce 72 wings.

The graphs illustrate the amount of pizza and wings that each person produces daily. Wing production is plotted on the x axis, pizza production on the y axis. Each production possibilities frontier is drawn from the data in the table at the top of the figure.

Debra and Mike each face a constant trade-off between producing pizza and producing wings. Debra produces 60 pizzas for every 120 wings; this means her trade-off between producing pizza and producing wings is fixed at 60:120, or 1:2. Mike produces 24 pizzas for every 72 wings. His trade-off between producing pizza and producing wings is fixed at 24:72, or 1:3. Because Debra and Mike can choose to produce at any point along their production possibilities frontiers, let's assume that they each want to produce an equal number of pizzas and wings. In this case, Debra produces 40 pizzas and 40 wings, while Mike produces 18 pizzas and 18 wings. Since Debra is more productive in general, she produces more of each food. Debra has an

Trade creates value

FIGURE 2.5

The Production Possibilities Frontier with No Trade

(a) If Debra cannot trade with Mike, she chooses to produce 40 pizzas and 40 wings, because she likes both foods equally.

(b) If Mike cannot trade with Debra, he chooses to produce 18 pizzas and 18 wings, because he likes both foods equally.

	Daily production	
Person	Pizzas	Wings
Debra Winger	60	120
Mike Piazza	24	72

(a) Debra Winger

(b) Mike Piazza

TABLE 2.1

The Gains from Trade

Person	Good	Without trade		With specialization and trade		Gains from trade
		Production	Consumption	Production	Consumption	
Debra	Pizza	40	40	60	41 (keeps)	+ 1
	Wings	40	40	0	47 (from Mike)	+ 7
Mike	Pizza	18	18	0	19 (from Debra)	+ 1
	Wings	18	18	72	25 (keeps)	+ 7

absolute advantage, meaning she can produce more than Mike can produce with the same quantity of resources.

At first glance, it would appear that Debra should continue to work alone. But consider what happens if Debra and Mike each specialize and then trade. Table 2.1 compares production with and without specialization and trade. Without trade, Debra and Mike have a combined production of 58 units of pizza and 58 units of wings (Debra's 40 + Mike's 18). But when Debra specializes and produces only pizza, her production is 60 units. In this case, her individual pizza output is greater than the combined output of 58 pizzas (Debra's 40 + Mike's 18). Similarly, if Mike specializes in wings, he is able to make 72 units. His individual wing output is greater than their combined output of 58 wings (Debra's 40 + Mike's 18). Specialization has resulted in the production of 2 additional pizzas and 14 additional wings.

Specialization leads to greater output. But Debra and Mike would like to eat both pizza and wings. So if they specialize and then trade with each other, they will benefit. If Debra gives Mike 19 pizzas in exchange for 47 wings, they are each better off by 1 pizza and 7 wings. This result is evident in the final column of Table 2.1 and in Figure 2.6.

In Figure 2.6a, we see that at point A, Debra produces 60 pizzas and 0 wings. If she does not specialize, she produces 40 pizzas and 40 wings, represented at point B. If she specializes and then trades with Mike, she can have 41 pizzas and 47 wings, shown at point C. Her value gained from trade is 1 pizza and 7 wings. In Figure 2.6b, we see a similar benefit for Mike. If he produces only wings, he will have 72 wings, shown at point A. If he does not specialize, he produces 18 pizzas and 18 wings (point B). If he specializes and trades with Debra, he can have 19 pizzas and 25 wings, shown at point C. His value gained from trade is 1 pizza and 7 wings. In spite of Debra's absolute advantage in making both pizza and wings, she is still better off trading with Mike. This amazing result occurs because of specialization. When Debra and Mike spend their time on what they do best, they are able to produce more collectively and then divide the gain.

Comparative Advantage

We have seen that specialization enables workers to enjoy gains from trade. The concept of opportunity cost provides us with a second way of validating the principle that trade creates value. Recall that opportunity cost is the

Absolute advantage refers to the ability of one producer to make more than another producer with the same quantity of resources.

Trade creates value

FIGURE 2.6

The Production Possibilities Frontier with Trade

(a) If Debra produces only pizza, she will have 60 pizzas, shown at point A. If she does not specialize, she will produce 40 pizzas and 40 wings (point B). If she specializes and trades with Mike, she will have 41 pizzas and 47 wings (point C).

(b) If Mike produces only wings, he will have 72 wings (point A). If he does not specialize, he will produce 18 pizzas and 18 wings (point B). If he specializes and trades with Debra, he can have 19 pizzas and 25 wings (point C).

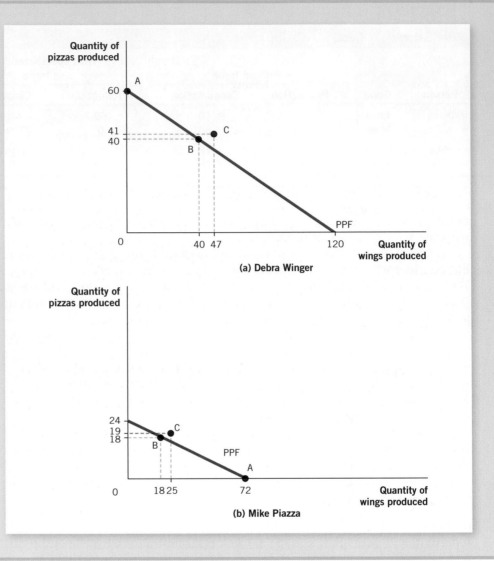

highest-valued alternative that is sacrificed to pursue something else. Looking at Table 2.2, you can see that in order to produce 1 more pizza, Debra must give up producing 2 wings. We can say that the opportunity cost of 1 pizza is 2 wings. We can also reverse the observation and say that the opportunity cost of one wing is $\frac{1}{2}$ pizza. In Mike's case, each pizza he produces means giving up the production of 3 wings. In other words, the opportunity cost for him to produce 1 pizza is 3 wings. In reverse, we can say that when he produces 1 wing, he gives up $\frac{1}{3}$ pizza.

Recall from Chapter 1 that comparative advantage is the ability to make a good at a lower opportunity cost than another producer. Looking at Table 2.2, you can see that Debra has a lower opportunity cost of producing pizza than Mike does—she gives up 2 wings for each pizza she produces, while he gives up 3 wings for each pizza he produces. In other words, Debra has a

Opportunity cost

TABLE 2.2

The Opportunity Cost of Pizza and Wings

	Opportunity cost	
Person	1 Pizza	1 Wing
Debra Winger	2 wings	$\frac{1}{2}$ pizza
Mike Piazza	3 wings	$\frac{1}{3}$ pizza

comparative advantage in producing pizzas. However, Debra does not have a comparative advantage in producing wings. For Debra to produce 1 wing, she would have to give up production of $\frac{1}{2}$ pizza. Mike, in contrast, gives up $\frac{1}{3}$ pizza each time he produces 1 wing. So Debra's opportunity cost for producing wings is higher than Mike's. Because Mike is the low-opportunity-cost producer of wings, he has a comparative advantage in producing them. Recall that Debra has an absolute advantage in the production of both pizzas and wings; she is better at making both. However, from this example we see that she cannot have a comparative advantage in making both goods.

Applying the concept of opportunity cost helps us see why specialization enables people to produce more. Debra's opportunity cost of producing pizzas (she gives up 2 wings for every pizza) is less than Mike's opportunity cost of producing pizzas (he gives up 3 wings for every pizza). Therefore, Debra should specialize in producing pizzas. If you want to double-check this result, consider who should produce wings. Debra's opportunity cost of producing wings (she gives up $\frac{1}{2}$ pizza for every wing she makes) is more than Mike's opportunity cost of producing wings (he gives up $\frac{1}{3}$ pizza for every wing he makes). Therefore, Mike should specialize in producing wings. When Debra produces only pizzas and Mike produces only wings, their combined output is 60 pizzas and 72 wings.

Finding the Right Price to Facilitate Trade

We have seen that Debra and Mike will do better if they specialize and then trade. But how many wings should it cost to buy a pizza? How many pizzas for a wing? In other words, what trading price will benefit both parties? To answer this question, we need to return to opportunity cost. For context, think of the process you likely went through when trading lunch food with friends in grade school. Perhaps you wanted a friend's apple and he wanted a few of your Oreos. If you agreed to trade three Oreos for the apple, the exchange benefited both parties because you valued your three cookies less than your friend's apple and your friend valued your three cookies more than his apple.

In our example, Debra and Mike will benefit from exchanging a good at a price that is lower than the opportunity cost of producing it. Recall that Debra's opportunity cost is 1 pizza per 2 wings. We can express this opportunity cost as a ratio of 1:2. This means that any exchange with a value lower

Opportunity
cost

TABLE 2.3

Gaining from Trade		
Person	**Opportunity cost**	**Ratio**
Debra Winger	1 pizza equals 2 wings	1:2 = 0.50
Terms of trade	19 pizzas for 47 wings	19:47 = 0.40
Mike Piazza	1 pizza equals 3 wings	1:3 = 0.33

than 1:2 (0.50) will be beneficial to her because she ends up with more pizza and wings than she had without trade. Mike's opportunity cost is 1 pizza per 3 wings, or a ratio of 1:3 (0.33). For trade to be mutually beneficial, the amount exchanged must fall between Debra's opportunity cost of 1:2 and Mike's opportunity cost of 1:3. Outside of that range, either Debra or Mike will be better off without trade, because the trade will not be attractive to both parties. In the example shown in Table 2.3, Debra trades 19 pizzas for 47 wings. The ratio of 19:47 (0.40) falls between Debra's and Mike's opportunity costs and is therefore advantageous to both of them.

Trade creates value

As long as the terms of trade fall between the trading partners' opportunity costs, the trade benefits both sides. But if Mike insists on a trading ratio of 1 wing for 1 pizza, which would be a good deal for him, Debra will refuse to trade because she will be better off producing both goods on her own. Likewise, if Debra insists on receiving 4 wings for every pizza she gives to Mike, he will refuse to trade with her because he will be better off producing both goods on his own.

ECONOMICS IN THE REAL WORLD

Why LeBron James Has Someone Else Help Him Move

LeBron James is a giant of a man—6'8" and 260 pounds. Given his size and strength, you might think that LeBron would move his household himself. But despite the fact that he could likely do the work of two ordinary movers, he kept playing basketball and hired movers. Let's examine the situation to see if this was a wise decision.

LeBron has an absolute advantage in both playing basketball and moving furniture. But as we have seen, an absolute advantage doesn't mean that LeBron should do both tasks himself. When he signed with a new team, he could have asked for a few days to pack up and move, but each day spent moving would have been a day he was unable to work with his new team. When you are paid millions of dollars to play a game, the time spent moving is time lost practicing or playing basketball, which incurs a substantial opportunity cost. The movers, with a much lower opportunity cost of their time, have a comparative advantage in moving—so LeBron made a smart decision to hire them! ✳

Opportunity cost

PRACTICE WHAT YOU KNOW

Opportunity Cost

Question: Imagine that you are planning to visit your family in Chicago. You can take a train or a plane. The plane ticket costs $300, and traveling by air takes 2 hours each way. The train ticket costs $200, and traveling by rail takes 12 hours each way. Which form of transportation should you choose?

Answer: The key to answering the question is learning to value time. The simplest way to do this is to calculate the cost savings of taking the train and compare that with the value of the time you would save if you took the plane.

Will you travel by plane or by train?

Cost savings with train	Round-trip time saved with plane
$300 − $200 = $100	24 hours − 4 hours = 20 hours
(plane) − (train)	(train) − (plane)

A person who takes the train can save $100, but it will cost 20 hours to do so. At an hourly rate, the savings would be $100/20 hours = $5 per hour. If you value your time at exactly $5 an hour, you will be indifferent between plane and train travel (that is, you will be equally satisfied with both options). If your time is worth more than $5 an hour, you should take the plane. If your time is worth less than $5 an hour, you should take the train.

It is important to note that this approach to calculating opportunity cost gives us a more realistic answer than simply observing ticket prices. The train has a lower ticket price, but very few people ride the train instead of flying because the opportunity cost of their time is worth more to them than the difference in the ticket prices. Opportunity cost explains why most business travelers fly—it saves valuable time. Good economists learn to examine the full opportunity cost of their decisions, which must include both the financials and the cost of time.

We have examined this question by holding everything else constant (that is, applying the principle of *ceteris paribus*). In other words, at no point did we discuss possible side issues such as the fear of flying, sleeping arrangements on the train, or anything else that might be relevant to someone making the decision.

Opportunity cost

Opportunity Cost

Saving Private Ryan

In most war movies, the calculus of victory is quite apparent. One side wins if it loses fewer airplanes, tanks, or soldiers during the course of the conflict or attains a strategic objective worth the cost. These casualties of war are the trade-off that is necessary to achieve victory. The movie *Saving Private Ryan* (1998) is different because in its plot the calculus of war does not add up: the mission is to save a single man. Private Ryan is one of four brothers who are all fighting on D-Day (June 6, 1944)—the day the Allies landed in Normandy, France, to liberate Europe from Nazi occupation. In a twist of fate, all three of Ryan's brothers are killed. As a result, the general in charge believes that the family has sacrificed enough and sends orders to find Private Ryan and return him home.

The catch is that to save Private Ryan, the army needs to send a small group of soldiers to find him. A patrol led by Captain Miller loses many good men in the process, and those who remain begin to doubt the mission. Captain Miller says to the sergeant, "This Ryan better be worth it. He better go home and

Saving one life means sacrificing another.

cure a disease, or invent a longer-lasting light bulb." Captain Miller hopes that saving Private Ryan will be worth the sacrifices they are making. That is how he rationalizes the decision to try to save him.

The opportunity cost of saving Private Ryan ends up being the lives that the patrol loses—lives that otherwise could have been pursuing a strategic military objective. In that sense, the entire film is about opportunity cost.

What Is the Trade-off between Having More Now and Having More Later?

The **short run** is the period in which we make decisions that reflect our immediate or short-term wants, needs, or limitations. In the short run, consumers can partially adjust their behavior.

The **long run** is the period in which we make decisions that reflect our needs, wants, and limitations over a long time horizon. In the long run, consumers have time to fully adjust to market conditions.

So far, we have examined short-run trade-offs. In looking at our wings–pizza trade-off, we were essentially living in the moment. But both individuals and society as a whole must weigh the benefits available today (the short run) with those available tomorrow (the long run). In the **short run**, we make decisions that reflect our immediate or short-term wants, needs, or limitations. In the short run, consumers can partially adjust their behavior. In the **long run**, we make decisions that reflect our wants, needs, and limitations over a much longer time horizon. In the long run, consumers have time to fully adjust to market conditions.

Many of life's important decisions are about the long run. We must decide where to live, whether and whom to marry, whether and where to go to college, and what type of career to pursue. Getting these decisions right is far more important than simply deciding how many wings and pizzas to produce. For instance, the decision to save money requires giving up something you want to buy today for the benefit of having more money available in the future. Similarly, if you decide to go to a party tonight, you benefit today, while staying home to study creates a larger benefit at exam time. We are constantly making decisions that reflect this tension between today and tomorrow—eating a large piece of cake or a healthy snack, taking a nap or exercising at the gym, buying a jet ski or purchasing stocks in the stock market. Each of these decisions is a trade-off between the present and the future.

Trade-offs

Consumer Goods, Capital Goods, and Investment

We have seen that the trade-off between the present and the future is evident in the tension between what we consume now and what we plan to consume later. Any good that is produced for present consumption is a **consumer good**. These goods help to satisfy our needs or wants now. Food, entertainment, and clothing are all examples of consumer goods. **Capital goods** help in the production of other valuable goods and services in the future. Capital goods are everywhere. Roads, factories, trucks, and computers are all capital goods.

Education is a form of capital. The time you spend earning a college degree makes you more attractive to future employers. When you decide to go to college instead of working, you are investing in your *human capital*. **Investment** is the process of using resources to create or buy new capital.

Because we live in a world with scarce resources, every investment in capital goods has an opportunity cost of forgone consumer goods. For example, if you decide to buy a new laptop, you cannot use the money to travel over

Consumer goods are produced for present consumption.

Capital goods help produce other valuable goods and services in the future.

Investment is the process of using resources to create or buy new capital.

Study now . . .

. . . enjoy life later.

spring break. Similarly, a firm that decides to invest in a new factory to expand future production is unable to use that money to hire more workers now.

The decision between whether to consume or to invest has a significant impact on economic growth in the future, or long run. What happens when society chooses to produce many more consumer goods than capital goods? Figure 2.7a shows the result. When relatively few resources are invested in

---

FIGURE 2.7

Investing in Capital Goods and Promoting Growth

(a) When a society chooses point A in the short run, very few capital goods are created. Because capital goods are needed to enhance future growth, the long-run PPF$_2$ expands, but only slightly.

(b) When a society chooses point B in the short run, many capital goods are created, and the long-run PPF$_2$ expands significantly.

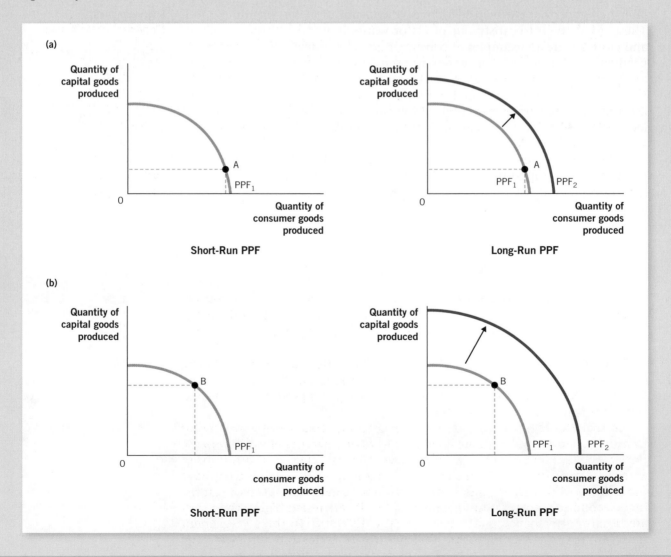

The Trade-off between the Short Run and the Long Run

A Knight's Tale

Before the late Heath Ledger starred in *Brokeback Mountain* or played the Joker in *The Dark Knight*, he played an entrepreneurial peasant in *A Knight's Tale* (2001).

In the movie, three peasants unexpectedly win a jousting tournament and earn 15 silver coins. Then they face a choice about what to do next. Two of the three want to return to England and live the high life for a while, but the third (played by Ledger) suggests that they take 13 of the coins and reinvest them in training for the next tournament. He offers to put in all 5 of his coins and asks the other two peasants for 4 coins each. His partners are skeptical about the plan because Ledger's character is good with the sword but not very good with the lance. For them to win additional tournaments, they will have to invest considerable resources in training and preparation.

The movie illustrates the trade-off between enjoying consumer goods in the short run and investing in capital goods in the long run. The peasants' choice

Learning to joust is a long-term skill.

to forgo spending their winnings to enjoy themselves now in order to prepare for the next tournament is not easy. None of the three has ever had any money. Five silver coins represent an opportunity, at least for a few days, to live the good life. However, the plan will elevate the three out of poverty in the long term if they can learn to compete at the highest level. Therefore, investing the 13 coins is like choosing point B in Figure 2.7b. Investing now will allow their production possibilities frontier to grow over time, affording each of them a better life in the long run.

producing capital goods in the short run, very little new capital is created. Because new capital is a necessary ingredient for economic growth in the future, the long-run production possibilities curve expands only a small amount.

What happens when society chooses to plan for the future by producing more capital goods than consumer goods in the short run? Figure 2.7b shows the result. With investment in new capital, the long-run production possibilities curve expands outward much more.

All societies face the trade-off between spending today and investing for tomorrow. China and India are good examples of emerging global economic powers that are investing in the future. Over the last 20 years, the citizens of these countries have invested significantly more in capital goods than have the citizens of wealthier nations in North America and Europe. Not surprisingly, economic growth rates in China and India are much higher than they are in more developed countries. Part of the difference in these investment rates can be explained by the fact that the United States and Europe already have large capital stocks per capita (per person) and therefore have less to gain

PRACTICE WHAT YOU KNOW

No pain, no gain.

Marginal
thinking

Trade-Offs

Question: Your friend is fond of saying he will study later. He eventually does study, but he often doesn't get quite the grades he had hoped for because he doesn't study enough. Every time this happens, he says, "It's only one exam." What advice would you give him about trade-offs?

Answer: Your friend doesn't understand long-run trade-offs. You could start by reminding him that each decision has a consequence at the margin and also later in life. The marginal cost of not studying enough is a lower exam grade. To some extent, your friend's reasoning is correct. How well he does on one exam over four years of college is almost irrelevant. The problem is that many poor exam scores have a cumulative effect over the semesters. If your friend graduates with a 2.5 GPA instead of a 3.5 GPA because he did not study enough, his employment prospects will be significantly diminished.

Trade-offs

from operating at point B in Figure 2.7b than developing countries do. China clearly prefers point B at this stage of its economic development, but point B is not necessarily better than point A. Developing nations, such as China, are sacrificing the present for a better future, while many developed countries, such as the United States, take a more balanced approach to weighing current needs against future growth. For Chinese workers, this trade-off typically means longer work hours and higher savings rates than their U.S. counterparts can claim, despite far lower average salaries for the Chinese workers. In contrast, U.S. workers have much more leisure time and more disposable (spendable) income, a combination that leads to much higher rates of consumption in the United States.

Conclusion

Trade
creates
value

Does trade create winners and losers? After reading this chapter, you know the answer: trade creates value. We have dispelled the misconception that every trade results in a winner and a loser. The simple, yet powerful, idea that trade creates value has far-reaching consequences for how we should organize our society.

We have also developed our first model, the production possibilities frontier. This model illustrates the benefits of trade and also enables us to describe ways to grow the economy. Trade and growth rest on a more fundamental idea—specialization. When producers specialize, they focus their efforts on those goods and services for which they have the lowest opportunity cost and trade with others who are good at making something else. To have something valuable to trade, each producer, in effect, must find its comparative advantage. As a result, trade creates value and contributes to an improved standard of living in society.

In the next chapter, we examine the supply and demand model to illustrate how markets work. While the model is different, the fundamental result we learned here—that trade creates value—still holds.

Failing to Account for Exogenous Factors When Making Predictions

Predictions are often based on past experiences and current observations. Often the least accurate predictions fail to take into account how much technological change influences the economy. Here we repeat a few wildly inaccurate predictions as a cautionary reminder that technology doesn't remain constant.

PREDICTION: "There is no reason anyone would want a computer in their home." Said in 1977 by Ken Olson, founder of Digital Equipment Corp. (DEC), a maker of mainframe computers.

FAIL: Over 80% of all American households have a computer today.

PREDICTION: "There will never be a bigger plane built." Said in 1933 by a Boeing engineer referring to the 247, a twin-engine plane that holds 10 people.

FAIL: Today, the Airbus A380 can hold more than 800 people.

PREDICTION: "The world potential market for copying machines is five thousand at most." Said in 1959 by executives of IBM to the people who founded Xerox.

FAIL: Today, a combination printer, fax machine, and copier costs less than $100. There are tens of millions of copiers in use throughout the United States.

These predictions may seem funny to us today, but note the common feature: they did not account for how new technology would affect consumer demand and behavior. Nor did these predictions anticipate how improvements in technology through time make future versions of new products substantially better. The lesson: Don't count on the status quo. Adapt with the times to take advantage of opportunities.

Source: Listverse.com, "Top 30 Failed Technology Predictions."

ANSWERING THE BIG QUESTIONS

How do economists study the economy?

* Economists design hypotheses (proposed explanations) and then test them by collecting real data. The economist's laboratory is the world around us.

* A good model should be simple, flexible, and useful for making accurate predictions. A model is both more realistic and harder to understand when it involves many variables. To keep models simple, economists often use the concept of *ceteris paribus*, or "all else equal." Maintaining a positive (as opposed to normative) framework is crucial for economic analysis because it allows decision-makers to observe the facts objectively.

What is a production possibilities frontier?

* A production possibilities frontier (PPF) is a model that illustrates the combinations of outputs that a society can produce if all of its resources are being used efficiently. An outcome is considered efficient when resources are fully utilized and potential output is maximized. Economists use the PPF to illustrate trade-offs and to explain opportunity costs and the role of additional resources and technology in creating economic growth.

What are the benefits of specialization and trade?

* Society is better off if individuals and firms specialize and trade on the basis of the principle of comparative advantage.

* Parties that are better at producing goods and services than all their potential trading partners (and thus hold an absolute advantage) still benefit from trade. Trade allows them to specialize and trade what they produce for other goods and services that they are relatively less skilled at making.

* As long as the terms of trade fall between the opportunity costs of both trading partners, the trade benefits both sides.

What is the trade-off between having more now and having more later?

* All societies face a crucial trade-off between consumption in the short run and economic growth in the long run. Investments in capital goods today help to spur economic growth in the future. However, because capital goods are not consumed in the short run, society must be willing to sacrifice how well it lives today in order to have more later.

CONCEPTS YOU SHOULD KNOW

absolute advantage (p. 41)
capital goods (p. 47)
ceteris paribus (p. 30)
consumer goods (p. 47)
endogenous factors (p. 31)
exogenous factors (p. 31)

investment (p. 47)
law of increasing opportunity
cost (p. 36)
long run (p. 46)
normative statement (p. 29)
positive statement (p. 29)

production possibilities frontier
(PPF) (p. 33)
short run (p. 46)
specialization (p. 39)

QUESTIONS FOR REVIEW

1. What is a positive economic statement? What is a normative economic statement? Provide an example of each (other than those given in the chapter).

2. Is it important to build completely realistic economic models? Explain your response.

3. Draw a production possibilities frontier curve. Illustrate the set of points that is feasible, the set of points that is efficient, the set of points that is inefficient, and the set of points that is not feasible.

4. Why does the production possibilities frontier bow out? Give an example of two goods for which this would be the case.

5. Does having an absolute advantage mean that you should undertake to produce everything on your own? Why or why not?

6. What criteria would you use to determine which of two workers has a comparative advantage in performing a task?

7. Why does comparative advantage matter more than absolute advantage for trade?

8. What factors are most important for economic growth?

STUDY PROBLEMS (*solved at the end of the section*)

✳ 1. Michael and Angelo live in a small town in Italy. They work as artists. Michael is the more productive artist. He can produce 10 small sculptures each day but only 5 paintings. Angelo can produce 6 sculptures each day but only 2 paintings.

	Output per day	
	Sculptures	Paintings
Michael	10	5
Angelo	6	2

a. What is the opportunity cost of a painting for each artist?
b. Based on your answer in part (a), who has a comparative advantage in producing paintings?

c. If the two men decide to specialize, who should produce the sculptures and who should produce the paintings?

✳ 2. The following table shows scores that a student can earn on two upcoming exams according to the amount of time devoted to study:

Hours spent studying for economics	Economics score	Hours spent studying for history	History score
10	100	0	40
8	96	2	60
6	88	4	76
4	76	6	88
2	60	8	96
0	40	10	100

a. Plot the production possibilities frontier.

b. Does the production possibilities frontier exhibit the law of increasing relative cost?

c. If the student wishes to move from a grade of 60 to a grade of 88 in economics, what is the opportunity cost?

3. Think about comparative advantage when answering this question: Should your professor, who has highly specialized training in economics, take time out of his or her teaching schedule to mow the lawn? Defend your answer.

✳ 4. Are the following statements positive or normative?

a. My dog weighs 75 pounds.

b. Dogs are required by law to have rabies shots.

c. You should take your dog to the veterinarian once a year for a checkup.

d. Chihuahuas are cuter than bulldogs.

e. Leash laws for dogs are a good idea because they reduce injuries.

5. How does your decision to invest in a college degree add to your human capital? Use a projected production possibilities frontier for 10 years from now to compare your life with and without the college degree.

✳ 6. Suppose that an amazing new fertilizer doubles the production of potatoes. How would this invention affect the production possibilities frontier for an economy that produces only potatoes and carrots? Would it now be possible to produce more potatoes *and* more carrots or only more potatoes?

7. Suppose that a politician tells you about a plan to create two expensive but necessary programs to build more production facilities for solar power and wind power. At the same time, the politician is unwilling to cut any other programs. Use the production possibilities frontier graph below to explain if the politician's proposal is possible.

✳ 8. Two friends, Rachel and Joey, enjoy baking bread and making apple pie. Rachel takes 2 hours to bake a loaf of bread and 1 hour to make a pie. Joey takes 4 hours to bake a loaf of bread and 4 hours to make a pie.

a. What are Joey's and Rachel's opportunity costs of baking bread?

b. Who has the absolute advantage in making bread?

c. Who has a comparative advantage in making bread?

d. If Joey and Rachel both decide to specialize to increase their joint production, what should Joey produce? What should Rachel produce?

e. The price of a loaf of bread can be expressed in terms of an apple pie. If Joey and Rachel are specializing in production and decide to trade with each other, what range of ratios of bread and apple pie would allow both parties to benefit from trade?

9. Where would you plot unemployment on a production possibilities frontier? Where would you plot full employment on a production possibilities frontier? Now suppose that in a time of crisis everyone pitches in and works much harder than usual. What happens to the production possibilities frontier?

10. Read the poem "The Road Not Taken," by Robert Frost. What line(s) in the poem capture the opportunity cost of decision-making?

✱ 11. Suppose that you must decide between attending a Taylor Swift concert or a Maroon 5 concert. The concerts are at the same time on the same evening, so you cannot see both. You love Taylor Swift and would pay as much as $200 to see her perform. Tickets to her concert are $135. You are not as big a Maroon 5 fan, but a friend has just offered you a free ticket to the concert. If you decide to take the free ticket to see Maroon 5, what is your opportunity cost?

SOLVED PROBLEMS

1.a. Michael's opportunity cost is 2 sculptures for each painting he produces. How do we know this? If he devotes all of his time to sculptures, he can produce 10. If he devotes all of his time to paintings, he can produce 5. The ratio 10:5 is the same as 2:1. Michael is therefore twice as fast at producing sculptures as he is at producing paintings. Angelo's opportunity cost is 3 sculptures for each painting he produces. If he devotes all of his time to sculptures, he can produce 6. If he devotes all of his time to paintings, he can produce 2. The ratio 6:2 is the same as 3:1.

b. For this question, we need to compare Michael's and Angelo's relative strengths. Michael produces 2 sculptures for every painting, and Angelo produces 3 sculptures for every painting. Because Michael is only twice as good at producing sculptures, his opportunity cost of producing each painting is 2 sculptures instead of 3. Therefore, Michael is the low-opportunity-cost producer of paintings.

c. If they specialize, Michael should paint and Angelo should sculpt. You might be tempted to argue that Michael should just work alone, but if Angelo does the sculptures, Michael can concentrate on the paintings. This is what comparative advantage is all about.

2.a.

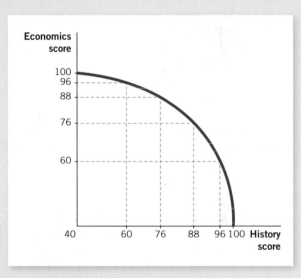

b. Yes, because it is not a straight line.

c. The opportunity cost is that the student's grade falls from 96 to 76 in history.

4.a. Positive
b. Positive
c. Normative
d. Normative
e. Normative

6. A new fertilizer that doubles potato production will shift the entire PPF out along the potato axis but not along the carrot axis.

Nevertheless, the added ability to produce more potatoes means that less acreage will have to be planted in potatoes and more land can be used to produce carrots. This makes it possible to produce more potatoes and carrots at many points along the production possibilities frontier. Figure 2.3 has a nice illustration if you are unsure how this process works.

8.a. Rachel gives up 2 pies for every loaf she makes. Joey gives up 1 pie for every loaf he makes.

 b. Rachel

 c. Joey

 d. Joey should make the bread and Rachel the pies.

 e. Rachel makes 2 pies per loaf and Joey makes 1 pie per loaf. So any trade between 2:1 and 1:1 would benefit them both.

11. Despite what you might think, the opportunity cost is *not* $200. You would be giving up $200 in enjoyment if you go to the Maroon 5 concert, but you would also have to pay $135 to see Taylor Swift, whereas the Maroon 5 ticket is free. The difference between the satisfaction you would have experienced at the Taylor Swift concert ($200) and the amount you must pay for the ticket ($135) is the marginal benefit you would receive from her concert. That amount is $200 − $135 = $65. You are not as big a Maroon 5 fan, but the ticket is free. As long as you think the Maroon 5 concert is worth more than $65, you will get a larger marginal benefit from seeing Maroon 5 perform than from seeing Taylor Swift perform. Therefore, the opportunity cost of using the free ticket is $65.

Graphs in Economics

Many students try to understand economics without taking the time to learn how to read and interpret graphs. This approach is shortsighted. You can "think" your way to the correct answer in a few cases, but the models we build and illustrate with graphs are designed to help analyze the tough questions, where your intuition can lead you astray.

Economics is fundamentally a quantitative science. That is, economists often solve problems by finding a numerical answer. For instance, economists determine the unemployment rate, the inflation rate, the growth rate of the economy, prices, costs, and much more. Economists also like to compare present-day numbers with numbers from the immediate past and historical data. Throughout your study of economics, you will find that many data-driven topics—for example, financial trends, transactions, the stock market, and other business-related variables—naturally lend themselves to graphic display. You will also find that many theoretical concepts are easier to understand when depicted visually in graphs and charts.

Economists also find that graphing can be a powerful tool when attempting to find relationships between different sets of observations. For example, the production possibilities frontier model presented in this chapter involves the relationship between the production of pizza and the production of chicken wings. The graphical presentations make this relationship, the trade-off between pizza and wings, much more vivid.

In this appendix, we begin with simple graphs involving a single variable. We then move to graphs that consist of two variables.

Graphs That Consist of One Variable

There are two common ways to display data with one variable: bar graphs and pie charts. A **variable** is a quantity that can take on more than one value. Let's look at the market share of the largest carbonated-beverage companies. Figure 2A.1 shows the data in a bar graph. On the vertical (y) axis is the market share held by each firm. On the horizontal (x) axis are the three largest firms (Coca-Cola, PepsiCo, and Dr. Pepper Snapple) and a separate category for the remaining firms, called "Others." Coca-Cola Co. has the largest market share at 42%, followed by PepsiCo Inc. at 30% and Dr. Pepper Snapple at 16%. The height of each firm's bar represents its market-share percentage. The combined market share of the other firms in the market is 12%.

A **variable** is a quantity that can take on more than one value.

FIGURE 2A.1

Bar Graphs
Each firm's market share in the beverage industry is represented by the height of the bar.

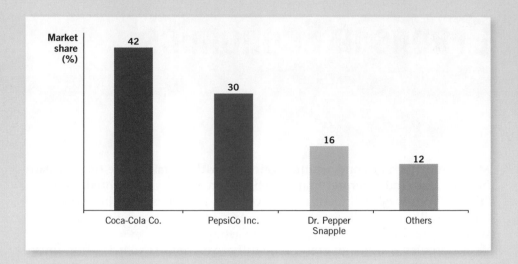

FIGURE 2A.2

Pie Chart
Each firm's market share in the beverage industry is represented by the size of the pie slice.

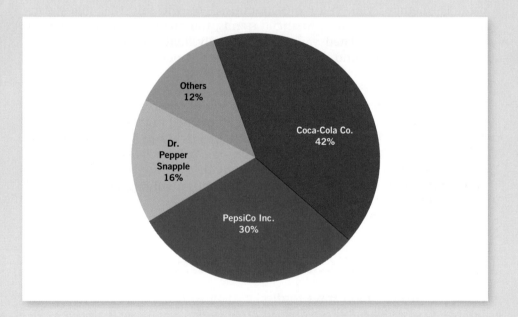

Figure 2A.2 illustrates the same data from the beverage industry on a pie chart. Now the market share is expressed as the size of the pie slice for each firm.

The information in a bar graph and a pie chart is the same, so does it matter which visualization you use? Bar graphs are particularly good for comparing sizes or quantities, while pie charts are generally better for illustrating proportions (parts of a whole).

FIGURE 2A.3

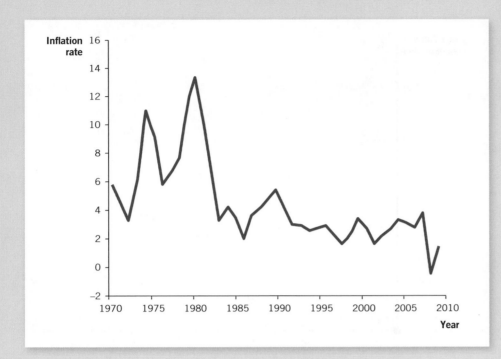

Time-Series Graph
In a time-series graph, you immediately get a sense of when the inflation rate was highest and lowest, the trend through time, and the amount of volatility in the data.

Time-Series Graphs

A time-series graph displays information about a single variable across time. For instance, if you want to show how the inflation rate has varied over a certain period of time, you could list the annual inflation rates in a lengthy table or you could illustrate each point as part of a time series in a graph. Graphing the points makes it possible to quickly determine when inflation was highest and lowest without having to scan through the entire table. Figure 2A.3 illustrates this point.

Graphs That Consist of Two Variables

Sometimes, understanding graphs requires you to visualize relationships between two economic variables. Each variable is plotted on a coordinate system, or two-dimensional grid. The coordinate system allows us to map a series of ordered pairs that show how the two variables relate to each other. For instance, suppose that we examine the relationship between the amount of lemonade sold and the air temperature, as shown in Figure 2A.4.

The air temperature is graphed on the *x* axis (horizontal) and cups of lemonade sold on the *y* axis (vertical). Within each ordered pair (*x*, *y*), the first value, *x*, represents the value along the *x* axis and the second value, *y*, represents the value along the *y* axis. For example, at point A, the value of *x*, or the temperature, is 0 and the value of *y*, or the amount of lemonade sold, is

FIGURE 2A.4

Plotting Points in a Coordinate System

Within each ordered pair (x, y), the first value, x, represents the value along the x axis, and the second value, y, represents the value along the y axis. The combination of all the (x, y) pairs is known as a scatterplot.

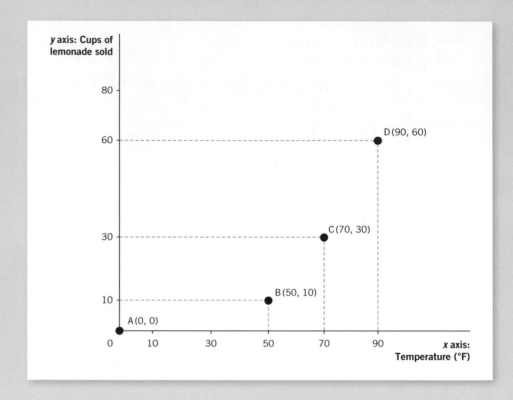

also 0. No one would want to buy lemonade when the temperature is that low. At point B, the value of x, the air temperature, is 50°F, and the value of y, the number of cups of lemonade sold, is 10. By the time we reach point C, the temperature is 70°F and the amount of lemonade sold is 30 cups. Finally, at point D, the temperature has reached 90°F, and 60 cups of lemonade are sold.

The graph you see in Figure 2A.4 is known as a **scatterplot**; it shows the individual (x, y) points in a coordinate system. Note that in this example, the amount of lemonade sold rises as the temperature increases. When the two variables move together in the same direction, we say that there is a **positive correlation** between them (see Figure 2A.5a). Conversely, if we graph the relationship between hot chocolate sales and temperature, we find that they move in opposite directions; as the temperature rises, hot chocolate consumption goes down (see Figure 2A.5b). This data set reveals a **negative correlation**, which occurs when two variables, such as cups of hot chocolate sold and temperature, move in opposite directions. Economists are ultimately interested in using models and graphs to make predictions and test theories, and the coordinate system makes both positive and negative correlations easy to observe.

Figure 2A.5 illustrates the difference between a positive correlation and a negative correlation. Figure 2A.5a shows the same information as Figure 2A.4. When the temperature increases, the quantity of lemonade sold increases as well. However, in Figure 2A.5b we have a very different set of ordered pairs. As the temperature increases, the quantity of hot chocolate sold falls. We can

A **scatterplot** is a graph that shows individual (x, y) points.

Positive correlation occurs when two variables move in the same direction.

Negative correlation occurs when two variables move in opposite directions.

FIGURE 2A.5

Positive and Negative Correlations

(a) This graph displays the positive relationship, or correlation, between lemonade sales and higher temperatures.

(b) This graph displays the negative relationship, or correlation, between hot chocolate sales and higher temperatures.

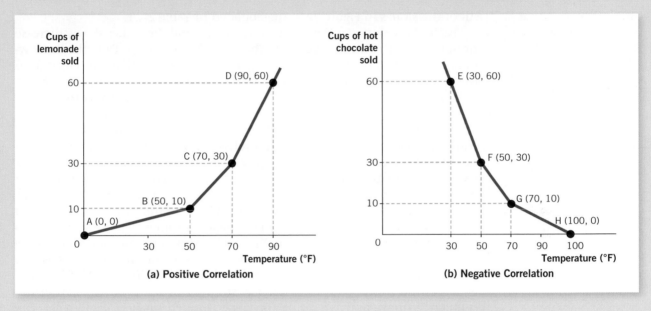

(a) Positive Correlation

(b) Negative Correlation

see this relationship by starting with point E, where the temperature is 32°F and hot chocolate sales are 60 cups. At point F, the temperature rises to 50°F, but hot chocolate sales fall to 30 cups. At point G, the temperature is 70°F and hot chocolate sales are down to 10 cups. The purple line connecting points E–H illustrates the negative correlation between hot chocolate sales and temperature, because the line is downward sloping. This relationship contrasts with the positive correlation in Figure 2A.5a, where lemonade sales rise from point A to point D and the line is upward sloping. But what exactly is slope?

The Slope of a Curve

A key element in any graph is the **slope**, or the rise along the *y* axis (vertical) divided by the run along the *x* axis (horizontal). The *rise* is the amount that the vertical distance changes. The *run* is the amount that the horizontal distance changes.

$$\text{slope} = \frac{\text{change in } y}{\text{change in } x}$$

A slope can have a positive, negative, or zero value. A slope of zero—a straight horizontal line—indicates that there is no change in *y* for a given change in *x*. The slope can be positive, as it is in Figure 2A.5a, or negative, as it is in Figure 2A.5b. Figure 2A.6 highlights the changes in *x* and *y* between

Slope refers to the change in the rise along the *y* axis (vertical) divided by the change in the run along the *x* axis (horizontal).

the points on Figure 2A.5. (The change in a variable is often notated with a Greek delta symbol, Δ, which is read "change in.")

In Figure 2A.6a, the slope from point B to point C is

$$\text{Slope} = \frac{\text{change in } y}{\text{change in } x} = \frac{(30 - 10) \text{ or } 20}{(70 - 50) \text{ or } 20} = 1$$

All of the slopes in Figure 2A.6 are tabulated in Table 2A.1.

Each of the slopes in Figure 2A.6a is positive, and the values slowly increase from 0.2 to 1.5 as you move along the curve from point A to point D. However, in Figure 2A.6b, the slopes are negative as you move along the curve from point E to point H. An upward, or positive, slope indicates a positive correlation, while a downward, or negative, slope indicates a negative correlation.

Notice that in both panels of Figure 2A.6, the slope changes values from point to point. Because of this changing slope, we say that the relationships are *nonlinear*. (In contrast, the relationship is *linear* when slope does not change along the line.) The slope tells us something about how responsive consumers are to changes in temperature. Consider the movement from point A to point B in Figure 2A.6a. The change in *y* is 10, while the change in *x* is 50, and the slope (10/50) is 0.2. Because zero indicates no change and 0.2 is close to zero, we can say that lemonade customers are not very responsive as the temperature rises from 0°F to 50°F. However, they are much more responsive from point C to point D, when the temperature rises from 70°F to 90°F. At point D, lemonade consumption—the change in *y*—rises from 30 to 60 cups, and the slope is now 1.5. The strength of the positive relationship is much stronger, and as a result, the curve is much steeper, or more vertical. This part of the curve contrasts with the movement from point A to point B, where the curve is flatter, or more horizontal.

We can apply the same analysis to Figure 2A.6b. Consider the movement from point E to point F. The change in *y* is −30, the change in *x* is 18, and the slope is −1.7. This value represents a strong negative relationship, so we would say that hot chocolate customers were quite responsive; as the temperature rose from 32°F to 50°F, they cut their consumption of hot chocolate by 30 cups. However, hot chocolate customers are not very responsive from point G to point H, where the temperature rises from 70°F to 100°F. In this case, consumption falls from 10 cups to 0 cups and the slope is −0.3. The strength of the negative relationship is much weaker (closer to zero), and as a result, the line is much flatter, or more horizontal. This part of the curve contrasts with the movement from point E to point F, where the curve is steeper, or more vertical.

TABLE 2A.1

Positive and Negative Slopes

(a)		(b)	
Points	Slope	Points	Slope
A to B	0.2	E to F	−1.7
B to C	1.0	F to G	−1.0
C to D	1.5	G to H	−0.3

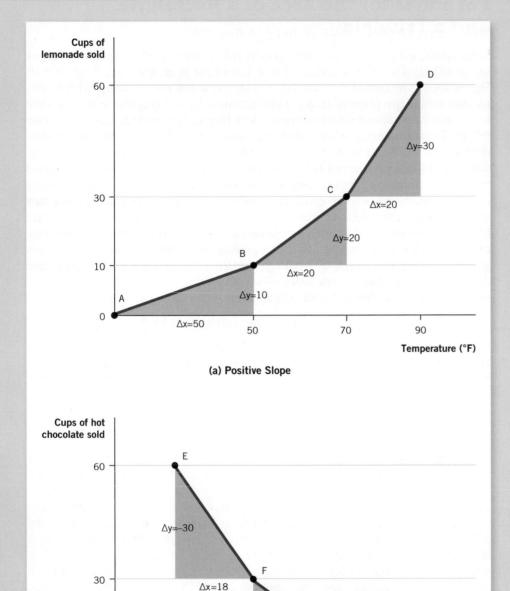

(a) Positive Slope

(b) Negative Slope

Positive and Negative Slopes

Notice that in both panels the slope changes value from point to point. Because of this changing slope value, we say that the relationships are non-linear. In (a), the slopes are positive as you move along the curve from point A to point D. In (b), the slopes are negative as you move along the curve from point E to point H. An upward, or positive, slope indicates a positive correlation, while a negative, or downward, slope indicates a negative correlation.

Formulas for the Area of a Rectangle and a Triangle

Sometimes, economists interpret graphs by examining the area of different sections below a curve. Consider the demand for Bruegger's bagels shown in Figure 2A.7. The demand curve (labeled D) has a downward slope, which tells us that when the price of bagels falls, consumers will buy more bagels. (We will learn more about demand curves in Chapter 3.) But this curve also can tell us about the revenue the seller receives—one of the most important considerations for the firm. In this case, let's assume that the price of each bagel is $0.60 and Bruegger's sells 4,000 bagels each week. We can illustrate the total amount of Bruegger's revenue by shading the area bounded by the number of sales and the price—the green rectangle in the figure. In addition, we can identify the surplus benefit consumers receive from purchasing bagels; the blue triangle shows this amount. Because many buyers are willing to pay more than $0.60 per bagel, we can visualize the "surplus" that consumers get from Bruegger's Bagels by highlighting the blue triangular area under the demand curve and above the price of $0.60.

To calculate the area of a rectangle, we use the formula

$$\text{Area of a rectangle} = \text{height} \times \text{base}$$

In Figure 2A.7, the green rectangle is the amount of revenue that Bruegger's Bagels receives when it charges $0.60 per bagel. The total revenue is $0.60 × 4,000, or $2,400.

To calculate the area of a triangle, we use the formula

$$\text{Area of a triangle} = \tfrac{1}{2} \times \text{height} \times \text{base}$$

FIGURE 2A.7

Working with Rectangles and Triangles

We can determine the area of the green rectangle by multiplying the height by the base. This gives us $0.60 × 4,000, or $2,400 for the total revenue earned by Bruegger's Bagels. We can determine the area of a triangle by using the formula $\frac{1}{2}$ × height × base. This gives us $\frac{1}{2}$ × $0.60 × 4,000, or $1,200 for the area of consumer surplus.

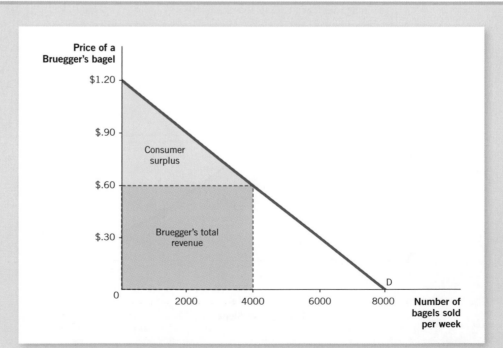

In Figure 2A.7, the blue triangle represents the amount of surplus consumers get from buying bagels. The amount of consumer surplus is $\frac{1}{2} \times \$0.60 \times 4,000$. Note that the value of the height, \$0.60, comes from reading the y axis: \$1.20 at the top of the triangle − \$0.60 at the bottom of the triangle = \$0.60.

Cautions in Interpreting Numerical Graphs

In Chapter 2, we utilized *ceteris paribus*, which entails holding everything else around us constant (unchanged) while analyzing a specific relationship. Suppose that you omitted an important part of the relationship. What effect would this omission have on your ability to use graphs as an illustrative tool? Consider the relationship between sales of lemonade and sales of bottles of suntan lotion. The graph of the two variables would look something like Figure 2A.8.

Looking at Figure 2A.8, you would not necessarily know that it is misleading. However, when you stop to think about the relationship, you quickly recognize that the graph is deceptive. Because the slope is positive, the graph indicates a positive correlation between the number of bottles of suntan lotion sold and the amount of lemonade sold. At first glance this relationship seems reasonable, because we associate suntan lotion and lemonade with summer activities. But the association does not imply **causality**, which occurs when one variable influences the other. Using more suntan lotion does not cause

Causality occurs when one variable influences another.

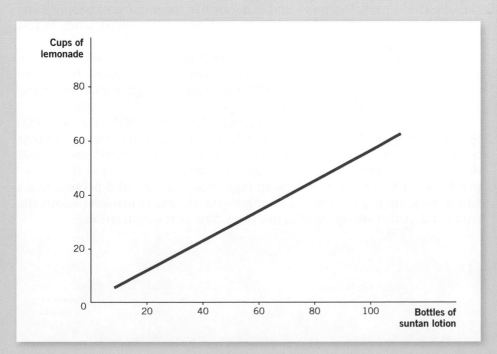

FIGURE 2A.8

Graph with an Omitted Variable
What looks like a strongly positive correlation is misleading. What underlying variable is causing lemonade and suntan lotion sales to rise? The demand for both lemonade and suntan lotion rises because the temperature rises.

FIGURE 2A.9

Reverse Causation and an Omitted Variable

As you look at this graph, you should quickly realize that important information is missing. AIDS deaths are associated with having more doctors in the area. But the doctors are there to help and treat people, not harm them. Suggesting that more doctors in an area causes more deaths from AIDS would be a mistake—an example of reverse causation.

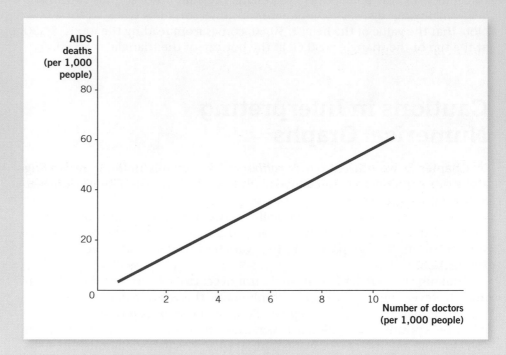

people to drink more lemonade. It just so happens that when it is hot outside, more suntan lotion is used and more lemonade is consumed. In this case, the causal factor is heat! The graph makes it look like the number of people using suntan lotion affects the amount of lemonade being consumed, when in fact the two variables are not directly related.

Another possible mistake is **reverse causation**, which occurs when causation is incorrectly assigned among associated events. Suppose that in an effort to fight the AIDS epidemic in Africa, a research organization notes the correlation shown in Figure 2A.9.

After looking at the data, it is clear that as the number of doctors per 1,000 people goes up, so do death rates from AIDS. The research organization puts out a press release claiming that doctors are responsible for increasing AIDS deaths, and the media hypes the discovery. But hold on! Maybe there happen to be more doctors in areas with high incidences of AIDS because that's where they are most needed. Coming to the correct conclusion about the data requires that we do more than simply look at the correlation.

Reverse causation occurs when causation is incorrectly assigned among associated events.

CONCEPTS YOU SHOULD KNOW

causality (p. 65)   reverse causation (p. 66)   variable (p. 57)
negative correlation (p. 60)   scatterplot (p. 60)
positive correlation (p. 60)   slope (p. 61)

STUDY PROBLEMS (✳ *solved at the end of the section*)

1. The following table shows the price and the quantity demanded of apples (per week).

Price per Apple	Quantity Demanded
$0.25	10
$0.50	7
$0.75	4
$1.00	2
$1.25	1
$1.50	0

a. Plot the data provided in the table into a graph.
b. Is the relationship between the price of apples and the quantity demanded negative or positive?

✳ 2. In the following graph, calculate the value of the slope if the price rises from $20 to $40.

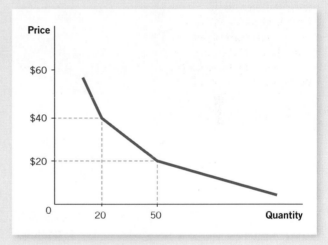

3. Explain the logical error in the following sentence: "As ice cream sales increase, the number of people who drown increases sharply. Therefore, ice cream causes drowning."

SOLVED PROBLEM

2. The slope is calculated by using the formula:

$$\text{Slope} = \frac{\text{change in } y}{\text{change in } x} = \frac{\$40 - \$20}{20 - 50} = \frac{\$20}{-30} = -0.6667$$

The Role of
MARKETS

The Market at Work
Supply and Demand

Sellers determine the price of the good.

What do Starbucks, Nordstrom, and Microsoft have in common? If you guessed that they all have headquarters in Seattle, that's true. But even

more interesting is that each company supplies a product much in demand by consumers. Starbucks supplies coffee from coast to coast and seems to be everywhere someone wants a cup of coffee. Nordstrom, a giant retailer with hundreds of department stores, supplies fashion apparel to meet a broad spectrum of individual demand, from the basics to designer collections. Microsoft supplies software for customers all over the world. Demand for Microsoft products has made large fortunes for founder Bill Gates and other investors in the company.

Notice the two recurring words in the previous paragraph: "supply" and "demand." Economists consistently use these words when describing how an economy functions. Many people think that the seller determines the price of the good. Often our first instinct is to wonder about the price of something rather than how much someone will pay to get it. This one-sided impression of the market undermines our ability to fully appreciate how prices are determined. To correct this misconception, this chapter describes how markets work and the nature of competition. To shed light on the process, we introduce the formal model of demand and supply. We begin by looking at demand and supply separately. Then we combine them to see how they interact to establish the market price and determine how much is produced.

Black Friday rush at Target means more demand.

BIG QUESTIONS

* **What are the fundamentals of markets?**
* **What determines demand?**
* **What determines supply?**
* **How do supply and demand interact to create equilibrium?**

What Are the Fundamentals of Markets?

In a **market economy**, resources are allocated among households and firms with little or no government interference.

The **invisible hand** is a phrase coined by Adam Smith to refer to the unobservable market forces that guide resources to their highest-valued use.

Markets bring trading partners together to create order out of chaos. Companies supply goods and services, and customers want to obtain the goods and services that companies supply. In a **market economy**, resources are allocated among households and firms with little or no government interference. Adam Smith, the founder of modern economics, described the dynamic best: "It is not from the benevolence of the butcher, the brewer, or the baker, that we expect our dinner, but from their regard to their own interest." In other words, producers earn a living by selling the products that consumers want. Consumers are also motivated by self-interest; they must decide how to use their money to select the goods that they need or want the most. This process, which Adam Smith called the **invisible hand**, guides resources to their highest-valued use.

The exchange of goods and services in a market economy happens through prices that are established in markets. Those prices change according to the level of demand for a product and how much is supplied. For instance, hotel rates near Disney World are reduced in the fall when demand is low, and they peak in March when spring break occurs. If spring break takes you to a ski resort instead, you will find lots of company and high prices. But if you are looking for an outdoor adventure during the summer, ski resorts have plenty of lodging available at great rates.

Similarly, many parents know how hard it is to find a reasonably priced

Peak season is expensive . . .

hotel room in a college town on graduation weekend. Likewise, a pipeline break or unsettled political conditions in the Middle East can disrupt the supply of oil and cause the price of gasoline to spike overnight. When higher gas prices continue over a period of time, consumers respond by changing their driving habits or buying more fuel-efficient cars.

Why does all of this happen? Supply and demand tell the story. We begin our exploration of supply and demand by looking at where they interact—in markets. A firm's degree of control over the market price is the distinguishing feature between *competitive markets* and *imperfect markets*.

. . . but off-season is a bargain.

Competitive Markets

Buyers and sellers of a specific good or service come together to form a market. Formally, a *market* is a collection of buyers and sellers of a particular product or service. The buyers create the demand for the product, while the sellers produce the supply. The interaction of the buyers and sellers in a market establishes the price and the quantity produced of a particular good or the amount of a service offered.

Markets exist whenever goods and services are exchanged. Some markets are online, and others operate in traditional "brick and mortar" stores. Pike Place Market in Seattle is a collection of markets spread across 9 acres. For over a hundred years, it has brought together buyers and sellers of fresh, organic, and specialty foods. Because there is a large number of buyers and sellers for each type of product, we say that the markets at Pike Place are competitive. A **competitive market** is one in which there are so many buyers and sellers that each has only a small impact on the market price and output. In fact, the impact is so small that it is negligible.

At Pike Place Market, like other local markets, the goods sold by each vendor are similar. Because each buyer and seller is just one small part of the whole market, no single buyer or seller has any influence over the market price. These two characteristics—similar goods and many participants—create a highly competitive market in which

A **competitive market** exists when there are so many buyers and sellers that each has only a small (negligible) impact on the market price and output.

One of many vendors at Pike Place Market.

the price and quantity sold of a good are determined by the market rather than by any one person or business.

To understand how competition works, let's look at sales of salmon at Pike Place Market. On any given day, dozens of vendors sell salmon at this market. If a single vendor is absent or runs out of salmon, the quantity supplied that day will not change significantly—the remaining sellers will have no trouble filling the void. The same is true for those buying salmon. Customers will have no trouble finding salmon at the remaining vendors. Whether a particular salmon buyer decides to show up on a given day makes little difference when hundreds of buyers visit the market each day. No single buyer or seller has any appreciable influence on the price of salmon. As a result, the market for salmon at Pike Place Market is a competitive one.

Imperfect Markets

An **imperfect market** is one in which either the buyer or the seller can influence the market price.

Market power is a firm's ability to influence the price of a good or service by exercising control over its demand, supply, or both.

A **monopoly** exists when a single company supplies the entire market for a particular good or service.

Markets are not always competitive. An **imperfect market** is a market in which either the buyer or the seller can influence the market price. For example, the Empire State Building affords an iconic view of Manhattan. Not surprisingly, the cost of taking the elevator to the top of the building is not cheap. But many customers buy the tickets anyway because they have decided that the view is worth the price. The managers of the Empire State Building can set a high price for tickets because there is no other place in New York City with such a great view. From this example, we see that when sellers produce goods and services that are different from their competitors', they gain some control, or leverage, over the price that they charge. The more unusual the product being sold, the more control the seller has over the price. When a seller has some control over the price, we say that the market is imperfect. Specialized products, such as popular video games, front-row concert tickets, or dinner reservations at a trendy restaurant, give the seller substantial pricing power. **Market power** is a firm's ability to influence the price of a good or service by exercising control over its demand, supply, or both.

In between the highly competitive environment at the Pike Place Market and markets characterized by a lack of competition, such as the Empire State Building with its iconic view, there are many other types of markets. Some, like the market for fast-food restaurants, are highly competitive but sell products that are not identical. Other businesses—for example, Comcast Cable—function like monopolies. A **monopoly** exists when a single company supplies the entire market for a particular good or service. We'll talk a lot more about different market structures, such as monopoly, in later chapters. But even in imperfect markets, the forces of supply and demand significantly influence producer and consumer behavior. For the time being, we'll keep our analysis focused on supply and demand in competitive markets.

The Empire State Building has one of the best views in New York City.

PRACTICE WHAT YOU KNOW

Markets and the Nature of Competition

Question: Which of the following are competitive markets? How will each firm price its products, and how much market power does each firm have?

1. Gas stations at a busy interstate exit
2. A furniture store in an isolated small town
3. A fresh produce stand at a farmers' market

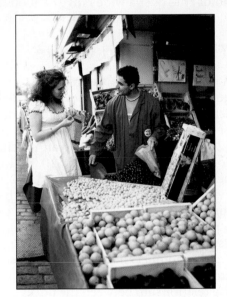

Is this a competitive market?

Answers

1. Because each gas station sells the same product and competes for the same customers, they often charge the same price. This is a competitive market. However, gas stations also differentiate themselves by offering conveniences such as fast food, clean restrooms, ATM machines, and so forth. The result is that individual stations have some market power.

2. Residents would have to travel a significant distance to find another furniture store. This situation allows the small-town store to charge more than other furniture stores. The furniture store has some monopoly power. This is not a competitive market.

3. Because consumers can buy fresh produce in season from many stands at a farmers' market, individual vendors have very little market pricing power. They must charge the same price as other vendors in order to attract customers. This is a competitive market.

What Determines Demand?

Demand exists when an individual or group wants something badly enough to pay or trade for it. How much an individual or group actually buys depends on the price of the good or service. In economics, the amount of a good or service that buyers are willing and able to purchase at the current price is known as the **quantity demanded**.

When the price of a good increases, consumers often respond by purchasing less of the good or buying something else. For instance, many consumers who would buy salmon at $5 per pound would likely buy something else if

The **quantity demanded** is the amount of a good or service that buyers are willing and able to purchase at the current price.

The **law of demand** states that, all other things being equal, quantity demanded falls when the price rises, and rises when the price falls.

the price of salmon rose to $20 per pound. Therefore, as price goes up, quantity demanded goes down. Similarly, as price goes down, quantity demanded goes up. This negative (opposite) relationship between the price and the quantity demanded is the law of demand. The **law of demand** states that, all other things being equal, the quantity demanded falls when the price rises, and the quantity demanded rises when the price falls. The law of demand holds true over a wide range of goods and settings.

The Demand Curve

A **demand schedule** is a table that shows the relationship between the price of a good and the quantity demanded.

A table that shows the relationship between the price of a good and the quantity demanded is known as a **demand schedule**. Table 3.1 shows Ryan Seacrest's hypothetical demand schedule for salmon. When the price is $20.00 or more per pound, Ryan will not purchase any salmon. However, below $20.00, the amount that Ryan purchases is negatively related to the price. For instance, at a price of $10.00, Ryan's quantity demanded is 4 pounds per month. If the price rises to $12.50 per pound, he demands 3 pounds. Every time the price increases, Ryan buys less salmon. In contrast, every time the price falls, he buys more. If the price falls to zero, Ryan would demand 8 pounds. That is, even if the salmon is free, there is a limit to his demand because he would grow tired of eating the same thing.

A **demand curve** is a graph of the relationship between the prices in the demand schedule and the quantity demanded at those prices.

The numbers in Ryan's demand schedule from Table 3.1 are plotted on a graph in Figure 3.1, known as a demand curve. A **demand curve** is a graph of the relationship between the prices in the demand schedule and the quantity demanded at those prices. For simplicity, the demand "curve" is often drawn as a straight line. Economists always place the independent variable, which is the price, on the y (vertical) axis and the dependent variable, which is the quantity demanded, on the x (horizontal) axis. (If you need a refresher on these terms, review Appendix 2A.) The relationship between the price and the quantity demanded produces a downward-sloping curve. In Figure 3.1, we

TABLE 3.1

Ryan Seacrest's Demand Schedule for Salmon

Price of salmon (per pound)	Pounds of salmon demanded (per month)
$20.00	0
$17.50	1
$15.00	2
$12.50	3
$10.00	4
$ 7.50	5
$ 5.00	6
$ 2.50	7
$ 0.00	8

FIGURE 3.1

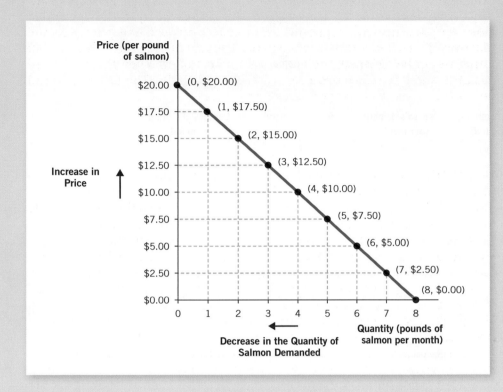

Ryan Seacrest's Demand Curve for Salmon

Ryan's demand curve for salmon plots the data from Table 3.1. When the price of salmon is $10.00 per pound, he buys 4 pounds. If the price rises to $12.50 per pound, Ryan reduces the quantity that he buys to 3 pounds. The figure illustrates the law of demand by showing a negative relationship between price and the quantity demanded.

see that as the price rises from $0.00 to $20.00 along the *y* axis, the quantity demanded decreases from 8 pounds to 0 pounds along the *x* axis.

Market Demand

So far, we have studied individual demand, but a market is composed of many different buyers. In this section, we examine the collective demand of all of the buyers in a given market.

The **market demand** is the sum of all the individual quantities demanded by each buyer in a market at each price. During a typical day at Pike Place Market, over 100 individuals buy salmon. However, to make our analysis simpler, let's assume that our market consists of only two buyers, Melissa Rivers and Ryan Seacrest, each of whom enjoys eating salmon. Figure 3.2 shows individual demand schedules for the two people in this market, a combined market demand schedule, and the corresponding graphs. At a price of $10 per pound, Melissa buys 2 pounds a month, while Ryan buys 4 pounds. To determine the market demand curve, we add Melissa's 2 pounds to Ryan's 4 pounds for a total of 6 pounds. As you can see in the table within Figure 3.2, by adding Melissa's demand and Ryan's demand, we arrive at the total (that is, combined) market demand. Any demand curve shows the law of demand with movements along (up or down) the curve that reflect a price change's effect on the quantity demanded of the good or service. Only a change in price can cause a movement along a demand curve.

Market demand is the sum of all the individual quantities demanded by each buyer in the market at each price.

FIGURE 3.2

Calculating Market Demand

To calculate the market demand for salmon, we add Melissa's quantity demanded and Ryan's quantity demanded.

Price of salmon (per pound)	Melissa's demand (per month)	Ryan's demand (per month)	Combined market demand
$20.00	0	0	0
$17.50	0	1	1
$15.00	1	2	3
$12.50	1	3	4
$10.00	2	4	6
$ 7.50	2	5	7
$ 5.00	3	6	9
$ 2.50	3	7	10
$ 0.00	4	8	12

Shifts of the Demand Curve

We have examined the relationship between price and quantity demanded. This relationship, described by the law of demand, shows us that when price changes, consumers respond by altering the amount they purchase. But in addition to price, many other variables influence how much of a good or service is purchased. For instance, news about the possible risks or benefits associated with the consumption of a good or service can change overall demand.

Suppose that the government issues a nationwide safety warning that cautions against eating cantaloupe because of a recent discovery of *Listeria* bacteria in some melons. The government warning would cause consumers to buy fewer cantaloupes at any given price, and overall demand would decline. Looking at Figure 3.3, we see that an overall decline in demand will cause the entire demand curve to shift to the left of the original curve, from

D_1 to D_2. Note that though the price remains at $5 per cantaloupe, demand has moved from 6 melons to 3. Figure 3.3 also shows what does *not* cause a shift of the demand curve: the price. The orange arrow alongside D_1 indicates that the quantity demanded will rise or fall in response to a price change. *A price change causes a movement along a given demand curve, but it cannot cause a shift of the demand curve.*

A decrease in overall demand shifts the demand curve to the left. What happens when a variable causes overall demand to increase? Suppose that the news media have just announced the results of a medical study indicating that cantaloupe contains a natural substance that lowers cholesterol. Because of the newly discovered health benefits of cantaloupe, overall demand for it will increase. This increase in demand shifts the demand curve to the right, from D_1 to D_3, as Figure 3.3 shows.

In our cantaloupe example, we saw that demand shifted because of changes in consumers' tastes and preferences. However, many different variables can shift demand. These include changes in buyers' income, the price of

If a new medical study indicates that eating more cantaloupe lowers cholesterol, would this finding cause a shift in demand, or a movement along the demand curve?

FIGURE 3.3

A Shift of the Demand Curve

When the price changes, the quantity demanded changes along the existing demand curve, as indicated by the orange arrow. A shift of the demand curve, indicated by the black arrows, occurs when something other than price changes.

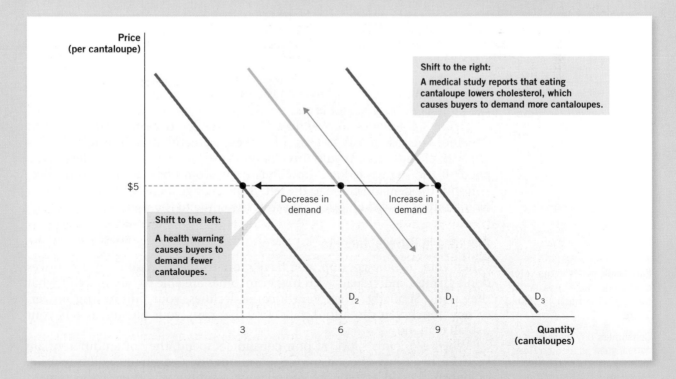

FIGURE 3.4

Factors That Shift the Demand Curve

The demand curve shifts to the left when a factor decreases demand. The demand curve shifts to the right when a factor increases demand. (*Note*: A change in price does not cause a shift. Price changes cause movements along the demand curve.)

**Factors That Shift Demand to the Left
(Decrease Demand)**

- Income falls (demand for a normal good).

- Income rises (demand for an inferior good).

- The price of a substitute good falls.

- The price of a complementary good rises.

- The good falls out of style.

- There is a belief that the future price of the good will decline.

- The number of buyers in the market falls.

- Excise or sales taxes increase.

**Factors That Shift Demand to the Right
(Increase Demand)**

- Income rises (demand for a normal good).

- Income falls (demand for an inferior good).

- The price of a substitute good rises.

- The price of a complementary good falls.

- The good is currently in style.

- There is a belief that the future price of the good will rise.

- The number of buyers in the market increases.

- Excise or sales taxes decrease.

related goods, changes in buyers' tastes and preferences, price expectations, the number of buyers, and taxes.

Figure 3.4 provides an overview of the variables, or factors, that can shift demand. The easiest way to keep all of these elements straight is to ask yourself a simple question: Would this change cause me to buy more or less of the good? If the change reduces how much you would buy at any given price, you shift the demand curve to the left. If the change increases how much you would buy at any given price, you shift the curve to the right.

Changes in Buyers' Income

Purchasing power is the value of your income expressed in terms of how much you can afford.

Consumers buy more of a **normal good** as income rises, holding all other factors constant.

When your income goes up, you have more to spend. Assuming that prices don't change, individuals with higher incomes are able to buy more of what they want. Similarly, when your income declines, your **purchasing power**, or how much you can afford, falls. In either case, your income affects your overall demand.

When economists look at how consumers spend, they often differentiate between two types of goods: normal and inferior. Consumers will buy more of a **normal good** as their income goes up (assuming all other factors remain constant). An example of a normal good is a meal at a restaurant. When income goes up, the demand for restaurant meals increases and the demand curve shifts to the right. Similarly, if income falls, the demand for restaurant meals goes down and the demand curve shifts to the left.

While consumers with an increased income may purchase more of some things, the additional purchasing power will mean that they purchase fewer inferior goods. An **inferior good** is purchased out of necessity rather than choice. Examples include rooms in boarding houses, as opposed to one's own apartment or house, and hamburger and ramen noodles, as opposed to filet mignon. As income goes up, consumers buy less of an inferior good because they can afford something better. Within a specific product market, you can often find examples of inferior and normal goods in the form of different brands.

> An **inferior good** is purchased out of necessity rather than choice.

The Price of Related Goods

Another factor that can shift the demand curve is the price of related goods. Certain goods directly influence the demand for other goods. **Complements** are two goods that are used together. **Substitutes** are two goods that are used in place of each other.

Consider this pair of complements: color ink cartridges and photo paper. You need to print a photo in color. What happens when the price of one of the complements—say, color ink cartridges—rises? As you would expect, the quantity demanded of ink cartridges goes down. But demand for its complement, photo paper, also goes down because people are not likely to use one without the other.

Substitute goods work the opposite way. When the price of a substitute good increases, the quantity demanded declines, and the demand for the alternative good increases. For example, if the price of the PlayStation 4 goes up and the price of Microsoft's Xbox remains unchanged, the demand for Xbox will increase while the quantity demanded of the PS4 will decline.

> **Complements** are two goods that are used together. When the price of a complementary good rises, the demand for the related good goes down.
>
> **Substitutes** are two goods that are used in place of each other. When the price of a substitute good rises, the quantity demanded of that good falls and the demand for the related good goes up.

Changes in Tastes and Preferences

Fashion goes in and out of style quickly. Walk into Nordstrom or another clothing retailer, and you will see that fashion changes from season to season and year to year. For instance, what do you think of madras shorts? They were popular 20 years ago and may be popular again today, but it is safe to assume that in a few years they will once again go out of style. While something is popular, demand increases. As soon as it falls out of favor, you can expect demand for it to decrease. Tastes and preferences can change quickly, and this fluctuation alters the demand for a particular good.

Though changes in fashion trends are usually purely subjective, other changes in preferences are the result of new information about the goods and services that we buy. Recall our example of shifting demand for cantaloupe as the result of either the *Listeria* infection or new positive medical findings. This is one example

Are these boots Sn-UGG-ly or just plain UGG-ly? It depends on consumers' tastes in fashion at the time.

ECONOMICS IN THE MEDIA

Shifting the Demand Curve

The Hudsucker Proxy

This 1994 film chronicles the introduction of the hula hoop, a toy that set off one of the greatest fads in U.S. history. According to Wham-O, the manufacturer of the hoop, when the toy was first introduced in the late 1950s over 25 million were sold in four months.

One scene from the movie clearly illustrates the difference between movements along the demand curve and a shift of the entire demand curve.

The Hudsucker Corporation has decided to sell the hula hoop for $1.79. We see a toy store owner leaning next to the front door waiting for customers to enter. But business is slow. The movie cuts to the president of the company, played by Tim Robbins, sitting behind a big desk waiting to hear about sales of the new toy. It is not doing well. So the store lowers the price, first to $1.59, then to $1.49, and so on, until finally the hula hoop is "free with any purchase." But even this generous offer is not enough to attract consumers, so the toy store owner throws the unwanted hula hoops into the alley behind the store.

One of the unwanted toys rolls across the street and around the block before landing at the foot of a boy who is skipping school. He picks up the hula hoop and tries it out. He is a natural. When school lets out, a throng of students round the corner and

How did the hula hoop craze start?

see him playing with the hula hoop. Suddenly, everyone wants a hula hoop and there is a run on the toy store. Now preferences have changed, and the overall demand has increased. The hula hoop craze is born. In economic terms, we say that the increased demand has shifted the entire demand curve to the right. The toy store responds by ordering new hula hoops and raising the price to $3.99—the new market price after the increase, or shift, in demand.

This example reminds us that changes in price cannot shift the demand curve. Shifts in demand can happen only when an outside event influences human behavior.

of how information can influence consumers' preferences. Contamination would cause a decrease in demand because people would no longer want to eat cantaloupe. In contrast, if people learn that eating cantaloupe lowers cholesterol, their demand for the melon will go up.

Price Expectations

Have you ever waited to purchase a sweater because warm weather was right around the corner and you expected the price to come down? Conversely, have you ever purchased an airline ticket well in advance because you figured that the price would rise as the flight filled up? In both cases, expectations about the future influenced your current demand. If we expect a price to be higher tomorrow, we are likely to buy more today to beat the price increase. The result is an increase in current demand. Likewise, if you expect a price to decline soon, you might delay your purchases to try to get a lower price in the

PRACTICE WHAT YOU KNOW

Shift of the Curve or Movement along the Curve?

Cheap pizza or . . .   . . . cheap drinks?

Question: Suppose that a local pizza place likes to run a late-night special. The owners have contacted you for some advice. One of the owners tells you, "We want to increase the demand for our pizza." He proposes two marketing ideas to accomplish this goal:

1. Reduce the price of large pizzas.
2. Reduce the price of a complementary good—for example, offer two half-priced bottles or cans of soda with every large pizza ordered.

Which strategy will you recommend?

Answer: First, consider why late-night specials exist in the first place. Because most people prefer to eat dinner early in the evening, the pizzeria has to encourage late-night patrons to buy pizzas by stimulating demand. "Specials" are used during periods of low demand, when regular prices would leave the establishment largely empty.

Next, look at what the question asks. The owners want to know which option would "increase demand" more. The question is very specific; the owners are looking for something that will increase (or shift) demand.

Price (dollars per pizza)

A reduction in the price of pizza causes a movement along the demand curve.

D₁

Quantity (pizza)

(CONTINUED)

(CONTINUED)

Consider the first option, a reduction in the price of pizzas. Let's look at this option graphically (see graph on previous page). A reduction in the price of a large pizza causes a movement along the demand curve, or a change in the quantity demanded.

Now consider the second option, a reduction in the price of a complementary good. Let's look at this option graphically (see graph below). A reduction in the price of a complementary good (for example, soda) causes the entire demand curve to shift. This is the correct answer, because the question asks which marketing idea would increase (or shift) demand more.

Recall that a reduction in the price of a complementary good shifts the demand curve to the right. The other answer, cutting the price of pizzas, will cause an increase in the quantity demanded, or a movement along the existing demand curve.

If you move along a curve instead of shifting it, you will analyze the problem incorrectly.

future. An expectation of a lower price in the future will therefore decrease current demand.

The Number of Buyers

Recall that the market demand curve is the sum of all individual demand curves. Therefore, another way for market demand to increase is for more individual buyers to enter the market. The United States adds 3 million people each year to its population through immigration and births. All those new people have needs and wants, just as the existing population of 325 million does. Collectively, the new people add about 1% to the overall size of many existing markets on an annual basis.

The number of buyers also varies by age. Consider two markets—one for baby products (such as diapers, high chairs, and strollers) and the other for health care (including medicine, cancer treatments, hip replacement surgery, and nursing facilities). In countries with aging populations—for example, in Italy, where the birthrate has plummeted over several generations—the demand for baby products will decline and the demand for health care will expand. In other words, demographic changes in society are another source of shifts in demand. In many markets, ranging from movie theater attendance to home ownership, population trends play an important role in determining whether the market is expanding or contracting.

Taxes

Changes in excise taxes (which are taxes on a single product or service) and sales taxes (which are general taxes on most goods and services) affect demand as well. Higher taxes lower demand because consumers must now pay the higher tax in addition to the price they pay for the good. Lower taxes reduce the overall cost to consumers and therefore increase demand.

What Determines Supply?

Even though we have learned a great deal about demand, our understanding of markets is incomplete without also analyzing supply. Let's start by focusing on the behavior of producers interested in selling fresh salmon at Pike Place Market.

We have seen that with demand, price and output are *negatively related*. That is, they move in opposite directions. With supply, however, the price level and quantity supplied are *positively related*. That is, they move in the same direction. For instance, few producers would sell salmon if the market price were $2.50 per pound, but many would sell it at a price of $20.00 per pound. (At $20.00, producers earn more profit than they do at a price of $2.50.) The **quantity supplied** is the amount of a good or service that producers are willing and able to sell at the current price. Higher prices cause the quantity supplied to increase. Conversely, lower prices cause the quantity supplied to decrease.

When price increases, producers often respond by offering more for sale. As price goes down, quantity supplied also goes down. This direct relationship between price and quantity supplied is the law of supply. The **law of supply** states that, all other things being equal, the quantity supplied increases when the price rises, and the quantity supplied falls when the price falls. This law holds true over a wide range of goods and settings.

The Supply Curve

A **supply schedule** is a table that shows the relationship between the price of a good and the quantity supplied. The supply schedule for salmon in Table 3.2 shows how many pounds of salmon Sol Amon, owner of Pure Food Fish, would sell each month at different prices. (Pure Food Fish is a fish stand that sells all kinds of freshly caught seafood.) When the market price is $20.00 per pound, Sol is willing to sell 800 pounds. At $12.50, Sol's quantity offered is 500 pounds. If the price falls to $10.00, he offers 400 pounds. Every time the price falls, Sol offers less salmon. This means he is constantly adjusting the amount he offers. As the price of salmon falls, so does Sol's profit from selling it. Because Sol's livelihood depends on selling seafood, he has to find a way to compensate for the lost income. So he might offer more cod instead.

Sol and the other seafood vendors must respond to price changes by adjusting what they offer for sale in the market. This is why Sol offers more salmon when the price rises and less salmon when the price declines.

When we plot the supply schedule in Table 3.2, we get the supply curve shown in Figure 3.5. A **supply curve** is a graph of the relationship between the prices in the supply schedule and the quantity supplied at those prices. As

The **quantity supplied** is the amount of a good or service that producers are willing and able to sell at the current price.

The **law of supply** states that, all other things being equal, the quantity supplied of a good rises when the price of the good rises, and falls when the price of the good falls.

A **supply schedule** is a table that shows the relationship between the price of a good and the quantity supplied.

A **supply curve** is a graph of the relationship between the prices in the supply schedule and the quantity supplied at those prices.

TABLE 3.2

Pure Food Fish's Supply Schedule for Salmon

Price of salmon (per pound)	Pounds of salmon supplied (per month)
$20.00	800
$17.50	700
$15.00	600
$12.50	500
$10.00	400
$ 7.50	300
$ 5.00	200
$ 2.50	100
$ 0.00	0

you can see in Figure 3.5, this relationship produces an upward-sloping curve. Sellers are more willing to supply the market when prices are high, because this higher price generates more profits for the business. The upward-sloping curve means that the slope of the supply curve is positive, which illustrates a direct (positive) relationship between the price and the quantity offered for

FIGURE 3.5

Pure Food Fish's Supply Curve for Salmon

Pure Food Fish's supply curve for salmon plots the data from Table 3.2. When the price of salmon is $10.00 per pound, Pure Food Fish supplies 400 pounds. If the price rises to $12.50 per pound, Pure Food Fish increases its quantity supplied to 500 pounds. The figure illustrates the law of supply by showing a positive relationship between price and the quantity supplied.

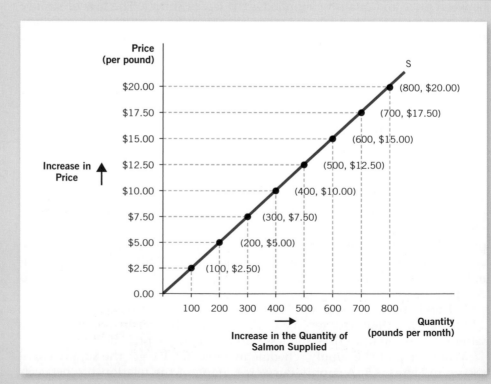

sale. For instance, when the price of salmon increases from $10.00 per pound to $12.50 per pound, Pure Food Fish will increase the quantity it supplies to the market from 400 pounds to 500 pounds.

Market Supply

Sol Amon is not the only vendor selling fish at the Pike Place Market. The **market supply** is the sum of the quantities supplied by each seller in the market at each price. However, to make our analysis simpler, let's assume that our market consists of just two sellers, City Fish and Pure Food Fish, each of which sells salmon. Figure 3.6 shows supply schedules for those two fish sellers and the combined, total-market supply schedule and the corresponding graphs.

Market supply is the sum of the quantities supplied by each seller in the market at each price.

FIGURE 3.6

Calculating Market Supply

Market supply is calculated by adding together the quantity supplied by individual vendors. The total quantity supplied, shown in the last column of the table, is illustrated in the market supply graph below.

Price of salmon (per pound)	City Fish's supply (per month)	Pure Food Fish's supply (per month)	Combined Market supply (pounds of salmon)
$20.00	200	800	1000
$17.50	175	700	875
$15.00	150	600	750
$12.50	125	500	625
$10.00	100	400	500
$ 7.50	75	300	375
$ 5.00	50	200	250
$ 2.50	25	100	125
$ 0.00	0	0	0

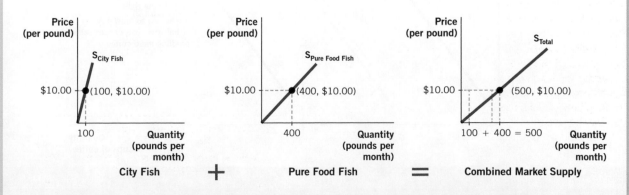

Looking at the supply schedule (the table within the figure), you can see that at a price of $10.00 per pound, City Fish supplies 100 pounds of salmon, while Pure Food Fish supplies 400 pounds. To determine the total market supply, we add City Fish's 100 pounds to Pure Food Fish's 400 pounds for a total market supply of 500 pounds.

The first Starbucks opened in 1971 in Pike Place Market.

Shifts of the Supply Curve

When a variable other than the price changes, the entire supply curve shifts. For instance, suppose that beverage scientists at Starbucks discover a new way to brew a richer coffee at half the cost. The new process would increase the company's profits because its costs of supplying a cup of coffee would go down. The increased profits as a result of lower costs motivate Starbucks to sell more coffee and open new stores. Therefore, overall supply increases. Looking at Figure 3.7, we see that the supply curve shifts to the

FIGURE 3.7

A Shift of the Supply Curve

When the price changes, the quantity supplied changes along the existing supply curve, illustrated here by the orange arrow. A shift in supply occurs when something other than price changes, illustrated by the black arrows.

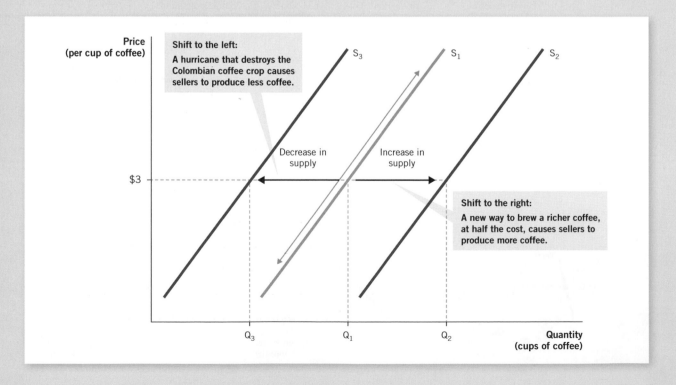

right of the original curve, from S_1 to S_2. Note that the retail price of coffee ($3 per cup) has not changed. When we shift the curve, we assume that price is constant and that something else has changed.

We have just seen that an increase in supply shifts the supply curve to the right. But what happens when a variable causes supply to decrease? Suppose that a hurricane devastates the coffee crop in Colombia and reduces the world coffee supply by 10% for that year. There is no way to make up for the destroyed coffee crop, and for the rest of the year at least, the quantity of coffee supplied will be less than the previous year. This decrease in supply shifts the supply curve in Figure 3.7 to the left, from S_1 to S_3.

Many variables can shift supply, but Figure 3.7 also reminds us of what does *not* cause a shift in supply: the price. Recall that price is the variable that causes the supply curve to slope upward. The orange arrow alongside S_1 indicates that the quantity supplied will rise or fall in response to a price change. *A price change causes a movement along the supply curve, not a shift in the curve.*

Factors that shift the supply curve include the cost of inputs, changes in technology or the production process, taxes and subsidies, the number of firms in the industry, and price expectations. Figure 3.8 provides an overview of these variables that shift the supply curve. The easiest way to keep them

FIGURE 3.8

Factors That Shift the Supply Curve

The supply curve shifts to the left when a factor decreases supply. The supply curve shifts to the right when a factor increases supply. (*Note*: A change in price does not cause a shift. Price changes cause movements along the supply curve.)

Factors That Shift Supply to the Left (Decrease Supply)

- The cost of an input rises.
- Business taxes increase or subsidies decrease.
- The number of sellers decreases.
- The price of the product is anticipated to rise in the future.

Factors That Shift Supply to the Right (Increase Supply)

- The cost of an input falls.
- Business taxes decrease or subsidies increase.
- The number of sellers increases.
- The price of the product is expected to fall in the future.
- The business deploys more efficient technology.

straight is to ask yourself a simple question: Would the change cause a business to produce more of the good or less of the good? If the change would reduce the amount of a good or service a business is willing and able to supply at every given price, the supply curve shifts to the left. If the change would increase the amount of a good or service a business is willing and able to supply at every given price, the supply curve shifts to the right.

The Cost of Inputs

Inputs are resources used in the production process.

Inputs are resources used in the production process. Inputs may include workers, equipment, raw materials, buildings, and capital goods. Each of these resources is critical to the production process. When the cost of inputs change, so does the seller's profit. If the cost of inputs declines, profits improve. Improved profits make the firm more willing to supply the good. So, for example, if Starbucks is able to purchase coffee beans at a significantly reduced price, it will want to supply more coffee. Conversely, higher input costs reduce profits. For instance, at Starbucks, the salaries of Starbucks store employees (or baristas, as they are commonly called) are a large part of the production cost. An increase in the minimum wage would require Starbucks to pay its workers more. This higher minimum wage would raise the cost of making coffee and make Starbucks less willing to supply the same amount of coffee at the same price.

Baristas' wages make up a large share of the cost of selling coffee.

Changes in Technology or the Production Process

Technology encompasses knowledge that producers use to make their products. An improvement in technology enables a producer to increase output with the same resources or to produce a given level of output with fewer resources. For example, if a new espresso machine works twice as fast as the old machine, Starbucks could serve its customers more quickly, reduce long lines, and increase its sales. As a result, Starbucks would be willing to produce and sell more espressos at each price in its established menu. In other words, if the producers of a good discover a new and improved technology or a better production process, there will be an increase in supply. That is, the supply curve for the good will shift to the right.

Taxes and Subsidies

Taxes placed on suppliers are an added cost of doing business. For example, if property taxes are increased, the cost of doing business goes up. A firm may attempt to pass along the tax to consumers through higher prices, but higher prices will discourage sales. So, in some cases, the firm will simply have to accept the taxes as an added cost of doing business. Either way, a tax makes the firm less profitable. Lower profits make the firm less willing to supply the product; thus, the supply curve shifts to the left and the overall supply declines.

The reverse is true for a **subsidy**, which is a payment made by the government to encourage the consumption or production of a good or service. Consider a hypothetical example where the government wants to promote flu shots for high-risk groups like the young and the elderly. One approach would be to offer large subsidies to clinics and hospitals, thus offsetting those firms' costs of immunizing the targeted groups. The supply curve of immunizations greatly shifts to the right under the subsidy, so the price falls. As a result, vaccination rates increase over what they would be in a market without the subsidy.

A **subsidy** is a payment made by the government to encourage the consumption or production of a good or service.

The Number of Firms in the Industry

We saw that an increase in total buyers (population) shifts the demand curve to the right. A similar dynamic happens with an increase in the number of sellers in an industry. Each additional firm that enters the market increases the available supply of a good. In graphic form, the supply curve shifts to the right to reflect the increased production. By the same reasoning, if the number of firms in the industry decreases, the supply curve shifts to the left.

Changes in the number of firms in a market are a regular part of business. For example, if a new pizza joint opens up nearby, more pizzas can be produced and supply expands. Conversely, if a pizzeria closes, the number of pizzas produced falls and supply contracts.

Price Expectations

A seller who expects a higher price for a product in the future may wish to delay sales until a time when the product will bring a higher price. For instance, florists know that the demand for roses spikes on Valentine's Day and Mother's Day. Because of higher demand, they can charge higher prices. To be able to sell more flowers during the times of peak demand, many florists work longer hours and hire temporary employees. These actions allow them to make more deliveries, increasing their ability to supply flowers while the price is high.

Likewise, the expectation of lower prices in the future will cause sellers to offer more while prices are still relatively high. This effect is particularly noticeable in the electronics sector, where newer—and much better—products are constantly being developed and released. Sellers know that their current offerings will soon be replaced by something better and that consumer demand for the existing technology will then plummet. This means that prices typically fall when a product has been on the market for a time. Because producers know that the price will fall, they supply as many of the current models as possible before the next wave of innovation cuts the price that they can charge.

ECONOMICS IN THE REAL WORLD

Why Do the Prices of New Electronics Always Drop?

The first personal computers released in the 1980s cost as much as $10,000. Today, you can purchase a laptop computer for less than $500. When a new technology emerges, prices are initially very high and then tend to fall rapidly. The first PCs profoundly changed the way people could work with information. Before the PC, complex programming could be done only on large mainframe computers that often took up an entire room. But at first only a few people could afford a PC. What makes emerging technology so expensive when it is first introduced and so inexpensive later in its life cycle? Supply and demand tell the story.

In the case of PCs and other recent technologies, both demand and supply increase through time. Demand increases as consumers find more uses for the new technology. An increase in demand, by itself, would ordinarily drive the price up. However, producers are eager to supply this new market and therefore ramp up production quickly. When the supply expands more rapidly than the demand, there is both an increase in the quantity sold and a lower price.

Differences in expectations account for some of the difference between the increase in supply and the increase in demand. Both parties expect the price to fall, and they react accordingly. Suppliers try to get their new products to market as quickly as possible—before the price starts to fall appreciably. Therefore, the willingness to supply the product expands quickly. Consumer demand is slower to pick up because consumers expect the price to fall. This expectation tempers consumers' desire to buy the new technology immediately. The longer they wait, the lower the price will be. Therefore, demand does not increase as fast as the supply. ✳

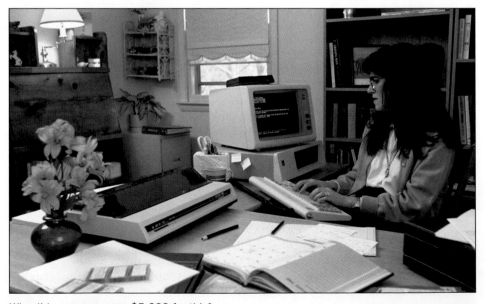

Why did consumers pay $5,000 for this?

PRACTICE WHAT YOU KNOW

Ice Cream: Supply and Demand

Question: Which one of the following will increase the demand for ice cream?

a. A decrease in the price of the butterfat used to make ice cream

b. A decrease in the price of ice cream

c. An increase in the price of the milk used to make ice cream

d. An increase in the price of frozen yogurt, a substitute for ice cream

I scream, you scream, we all scream for ice cream.

Answer: If you answered b, you made a common mistake. A change in the price of a good cannot change overall market demand; it can only cause a movement along an existing curve. So, as important as price changes are, they are not the right answer. Instead, you need to look for an event that shifts the entire curve.

Choices a and c refer to the prices of butterfat and milk. Because these are the inputs of production for ice cream, a change in their prices will shift the supply curve, not the demand curve. That leaves choice d as the only possibility. Choice d is correct because the increase in the price of frozen yogurt will cause consumers to substitute away from frozen yogurt and toward ice cream. This shift in consumer behavior will result in an increase in the demand for ice cream even though its price remains the same.

Question: Which one of the following will decrease the supply of chocolate ice cream?

a. A medical report finding that consuming chocolate prevents cancer

b. A decrease in the price of chocolate ice cream

c. An increase in the price of chocolate, an ingredient used to make chocolate ice cream

d. An increase in the price of whipped cream, a complementary good

Answer: We know that b cannot be the correct answer because a change in the price of the good cannot change supply; it can only cause a movement along an existing curve. Choices a and d would both cause a change in demand without affecting the supply curve. That leaves choice c as the only possibility. Chocolate is a necessary ingredient in the production process. Whenever the price of an input rises, profits are squeezed. The result is a decrease in supply at the existing price.

How Do Supply and Demand Interact to Create Equilibrium?

We have examined supply and demand separately. Now it is time to see how the two interact. The real power of supply and demand analysis is in how well it predicts prices and output in the entire market.

Supply, Demand, and Equilibrium

Let's consider the market for salmon again. This example meets the conditions for a competitive market because the salmon sold by one vendor is essentially the same as the salmon sold by another, and there are many individual buyers.

In Figure 3.9, we see that when the price of salmon fillets is $10 per pound, consumers demand 500 pounds and producers supply 500 pounds. This situation is represented graphically at point E, known as the point of **equilibrium**, where the demand curve and the supply curve intersect. At this point, the two opposing forces of supply and demand are perfectly balanced.

Notice that at $10 per pound, the quantity demanded equals the quantity supplied. At this price, and only this price, the entire supply of salmon in the market is sold. Moreover, every buyer who wants salmon is able to find some and every producer is able to sell his or her entire stock. We say that $10 is the **equilibrium price** because the quantity supplied equals the quantity demanded. The equilibrium price is also called the *market-clearing price*,

Equilibrium occurs at the point where the demand curve and the supply curve intersect.

The **equilibrium price** is the price at which the quantity supplied is equal to the quantity demanded. It is also known as the *market-clearing price*.

FIGURE 3.9

The Salmon Market

At the equilibrium point, E, quantity supplied and quantity demanded are perfectly balanced. At prices above the equilibrium price, a surplus exists. At prices below the equilibrium price, a shortage exists.

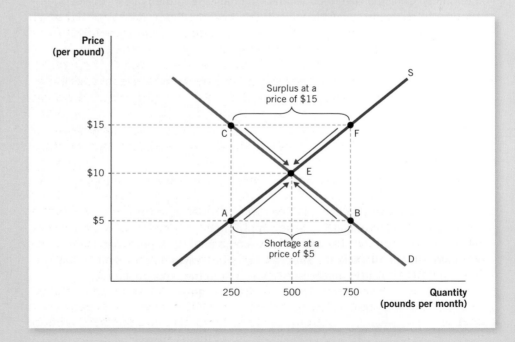

because this is the only price at which no surplus or shortage of the good exists. Similarly, there is also an **equilibrium quantity** at which the quantity supplied equals the quantity demanded (in this example, 500 pounds). When the market is in equilibrium, we sometimes say that *the market clears* or that *the price clears the market*.

The equilibrium point has a special place in economics because movements away from that point throw the market out of balance. The equilibrium process is so powerful that it is often referred to as the **law of supply and demand**, the idea that market prices adjust to bring the quantity supplied and the quantity demanded into balance.

The **equilibrium quantity** is the amount at which the quantity supplied is equal to the quantity demanded.

The **law of supply and demand** states that the market price of any good will adjust to bring the quantity supplied and the quantity demanded into balance.

Shortages and Surpluses

How does the market respond when it is not in equilibrium? Let's look at two other prices for salmon shown on the *y* axis in Figure 3.9: $5 per pound and $15 per pound.

At a price of $5 per pound, salmon is quite attractive to buyers but not very profitable to sellers. The quantity demanded is 750 pounds, represented by point B on the demand curve (D). However, the quantity supplied, which is represented by point A on the supply curve (S), is only 250 pounds. So at $5 per pound there is an excess quantity of $750 - 250 = 500$ pounds demanded. This excess demand creates disequilibrium in the market.

When there is more demand for a product than sellers are willing or able to supply, we say there is a shortage. A **shortage**, or *excess demand*, occurs whenever the quantity supplied is less than the quantity demanded. In our case, at a price of $5 per pound of salmon, there are three buyers for each pound. New shipments of salmon fly out the door, providing a strong signal for sellers to raise the price. As the market price increases in response to the shortage, sellers continue to increase the quantity that they offer. You can see the increase in quantity supplied on the graph in Figure 3.9 by following the upward-sloping arrow from point A to point E. At the same time, as the price rises, buyers demand an increasingly smaller quantity, represented by the arrow from point B to point E along the demand curve. Eventually, when the price reaches $10 per pound, the quantity supplied and the quantity demanded are equal. The market is in equilibrium.

A **shortage** occurs whenever the quantity supplied is less than the quantity demanded. A shortage is also called *excess demand*.

What happens when the price is set above the equilibrium point—say, at $15 per pound? At this price, salmon is quite profitable for sellers but not very attractive to buyers. The quantity demanded, represented by point C on the demand curve, is 250 pounds. However, the quantity supplied, represented by point F on the supply curve, is 750 pounds. In other words, sellers provide 500 pounds more than buyers wish to purchase. This excess supply creates disequilibrium in the market. Any buyer who is willing to pay $15 for a pound of salmon can find some because there are 3 pounds available for every customer. A **surplus**, or *excess supply*, occurs whenever the quantity supplied is greater than the quantity demanded.

When there is a surplus, sellers realize that salmon has been oversupplied, giving them a strong signal to lower the price. As the market price decreases in response to the surplus, more buyers enter the market and purchase salmon. Figure 3.9 represents this situation on the demand side by the downward-sloping arrow moving from point C to point E along the demand curve. At

A **surplus** occurs whenever the quantity supplied is greater than the quantity demanded. A surplus is also called *excess supply*.

FIGURE 3.10

Price and Quantity When Either Supply or Demand Changes

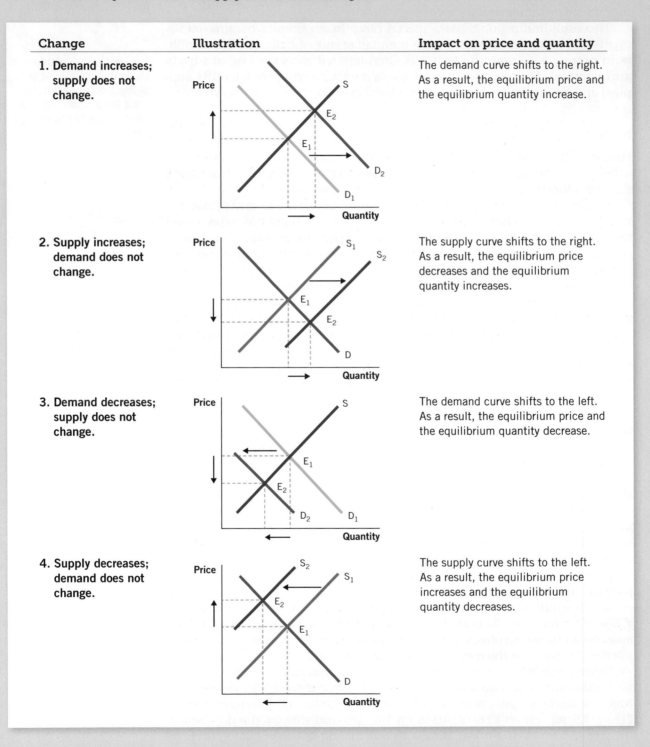

Change	Illustration	Impact on price and quantity
1. Demand increases; supply does not change.		The demand curve shifts to the right. As a result, the equilibrium price and the equilibrium quantity increase.
2. Supply increases; demand does not change.		The supply curve shifts to the right. As a result, the equilibrium price decreases and the equilibrium quantity increases.
3. Demand decreases; supply does not change.		The demand curve shifts to the left. As a result, the equilibrium price and the equilibrium quantity decrease.
4. Supply decreases; demand does not change.		The supply curve shifts to the left. As a result, the equilibrium price increases and the equilibrium quantity decreases.

the same time, sellers reduce output, represented by the arrow moving from point F to point E on the supply curve. As long as the surplus persists, the price will continue to fall. Eventually, the price reaches $10 per pound. At this point, the quantity supplied and the quantity demanded are equal and the market is in equilibrium again.

In competitive markets, surpluses and shortages are resolved through the process of price adjustment. Buyers who are unable to find enough salmon at $5 per pound compete to find the available stocks; this competition drives the price up. Likewise, businesses that cannot sell their product at $15 per pound must lower their prices to reduce inventories; this desire to sell all inventory drives the price down.

Every seller and buyer has a vital role to play in the market. Venues like the Pike Place Market bring buyers and sellers together. Amazingly, market equilibrium occurs without the need for government planning to ensure an adequate supply of the goods that consumers want or need. You might think that a decentralized system would create chaos, but nothing could be further from the truth. Markets work because buyers and sellers can rapidly adjust to changes in prices. These adjustments bring balance. When markets were suppressed in communist countries during the twentieth century, shortages were commonplace, in part because there was no market price system to signal that additional production was needed.

In summary, Figure 3.10 provides four examples of what happens when either the supply curve or the demand curve shifts. As you study these examples, you should develop a sense for how price and quantity are affected by changes in supply and demand. When one curve shifts, we can make a definitive statement about how price and quantity will change. In Appendix 3A, we consider what happens when supply and demand change at the same time. There you will discover the challenges in simultaneously determining price and quantity when more than one variable changes.

Conclusion

Do sellers determine the price of goods? As you learned in this chapter, the answer is no. Demand and supply contribute equally to the functioning of markets. Five years from now, if someone asks you what you remember about your first course in economics, you will probably respond with two words: "supply" and "demand." These two forces allow us to model market behavior through prices. Supply and demand help establish the market equilibrium, or the price at which quantity supplied and quantity demanded are in balance. At the equilibrium point, every good and service produced has a corresponding buyer who wants to purchase it. When the market is out of equilibrium, a shortage or surplus exists. This condition persists until buyers and sellers have a chance to adjust the quantity they demand and the quantity they supply, respectively.

In the next chapter, we extend our understanding of supply and demand by examining how sensitive, or responsive, consumers and producers are to price changes. With this knowledge, we can determine whether price changes have a big effect on behavior or not.

Bringing Supply and Demand Together: Advice for Buying Your First Home

There is an old adage in real estate: "location, location, location." Why does location matter so much? Simple. Supply and demand. There are only so many places to live in any given location—that is the supply. The most desirable locations have many buyers who'd like to purchase in that area—that is the demand.

Consider for a moment all of the variables that can influence where you want to live. As you're shopping for your new home, you may want to consider proximity to where you work and your favorite restaurants, public transportation, and the quality of the schools. You'll also want to pay attention to the crime rate, differences in local tax rates, traffic concerns, noise issues, and zoning restrictions. In addition, many communities have *restrictive covenants* that limit how owners can use their property. Smart buyers determine how the covenants work and whether they would be happy to give up some freedom in order to maintain an attractive neighborhood. Finally, it is always a good idea to visit the neighborhood in the evening or on the weekend to meet your future neighbors before you buy. All of these variables determine the demand for any given property.

Once you've done your homework and settled on a neighborhood, you will find that property values can vary tremendously across very short distances. A home along a busy street may sell for half the price of a similar property a few blocks away that backs up to a quiet park. Properties near a subway line command a premium, as do properties with views or close access to major employers and amenities (such as parks, shopping centers, and places to eat). Here is the main point to remember, even if some of these things aren't important to you: when it comes time to sell, the location of the home will always matter. The number of potential buyers depends on the characteristics of your neighborhood and the size and condition of your property. If you want to be able to sell your home easily, you'll have to consider not only where you want to live now but who might want to live there in the future.

All of this discussion brings us back to supply and demand. The best locations are in short supply and high demand. The combination of low supply and high demand causes property values in those areas to rise. Likewise, less desirable locations have lower property values because demand is relatively low and the supply is relatively high. Because first-time buyers often have wish lists that far exceed their budgets, considering the costs and benefits will help you find the best available property.

There is a popular HGTV show called *Property Virgins* that follows first-time buyers through the process of buying their first home. If you have never seen the show, watching an episode is one of the best lessons in economics you'll ever get. Check it out, and remember that even though you may be new to buying property, you still can get a good deal if you use some basic economics to guide your decision.

Where you buy is more important than *what* you buy.

ANSWERING THE BIG QUESTIONS

What are the fundamentals of markets?

* A market consists of a group of buyers and sellers for a particular product or service.
* A competitive market exists when there are so many buyers and sellers that each has only a small (negligible) impact on the market price and output.
* Not all markets are competitive. When firms have market power, markets are imperfect.

What determines demand?

* The law of demand states that, all other things being equal, quantity demanded falls when the price rises, and rises when the price falls.
* The demand curve is downward sloping.
* A price change causes a movement along the demand curve, not a shift of the curve.
* Changes in something other than price (including changes in income, the price of related goods, changes in tastes and preferences, price expectations, the number of buyers, and taxes) shift the demand curve.

What determines supply?

* The law of supply states that, all other things being equal, the quantity supplied of a good rises when the price of the good rises, and falls when the price of the good falls.
* The supply curve is upward sloping.
* A price change causes a movement along the supply curve, not a shift of the curve.
* Changes in something other than price (the cost of inputs, changes in technology or the production process, taxes and subsidies, the number of firms in the industry, and price expectations) shift the original supply curve.

How do supply and demand interact to create equilibrium?

* Supply and demand work together in a market-clearing process that leads to equilibrium, the balancing point between the two forces. The market-clearing price and output are determined at the equilibrium point.
* When the price is above the equilibrium point, a surplus exists and inventories build up. Suppliers lower their price in an effort to sell the unwanted goods. The process continues until the equilibrium price is reached.
* When the price is below the equilibrium point, a shortage exists and inventories are depleted. Suppliers raise the price until the equilibrium point is reached.

CONCEPTS YOU SHOULD KNOW

competitive market (p. 73)
complements (p. 81)
demand curve (p. 76)
demand schedule (p. 76)
equilibrium (p. 94)
equilibrium price (p. 94)
equilibrium quantity (p. 95)
imperfect market (p. 74)
inferior good (p. 81)
inputs (p. 90)

invisible hand (p. 72)
law of demand (p. 76)
law of supply (p. 85)
law of supply and demand
(p. 95)
market demand (p. 77)
market economy (p. 72)
market power (p. 74)
market supply (p. 87)
monopoly (p. 74)

normal good (p. 80)
purchasing power (p. 80)
quantity demanded (p. 75)
quantity supplied (p. 85)
shortage (p. 95)
subsidy (p. 91)
substitutes (p. 81)
supply curve (p. 85)
supply schedule (p. 85)
surplus (p. 95)

QUESTIONS FOR REVIEW

1. What is a competitive market, and why does it depend on the existence of many buyers and sellers?

2. Why does the demand curve slope downward?

3. Does a price change cause a movement along a demand curve or a shift of the entire curve? What factors cause the entire demand curve to shift?

4. Describe the difference between inferior goods and normal goods. Give an example of each type of good.

5. Why does the supply curve slope upward?

6. Does a price change cause a movement along a supply curve or a shift of the entire curve? What factors cause the entire supply curve to shift?

7. Describe the process that leads a market toward equilibrium.

8. What happens in a competitive market when the price is above the equilibrium price? Below the equilibrium price?

9. What roles do shortages and surpluses play in the market?

STUDY PROBLEMS (*solved at the end of the section)

1. In the song "Money, Money, Money" by ABBA, one of the lead singers, Anni-Frid Lyngstad, is tired of the hard work that life requires and plans to marry a wealthy man. If she is successful, how will this marriage change her demand for goods? How will it change her supply of labor? Illustrate both changes with supply and demand curves. Be sure to explain what is happening in the diagrams. (*Note*: The full lyrics for the song can be found by Googling the song title and ABBA. For inspiration, try listening to the song while you solve the problem.)

2. For each of the following scenarios, determine if there is an increase or a decrease in demand for the good in *italics*.
   a. The price of *oranges* increases.
   b. The cost of producing *tires* increases.
   c. Samantha Brown, who is crazy about *air travel*, gets fired from her job.
   d. A local community has an unusually wet spring and a subsequent problem with mosquitoes, which can be deterred with *citronella*.
   e. Many motorcycle enthusiasts enjoy riding without *helmets* (in states where this is not prohibited by law). The price of new motorcycles rises.

3. For each of the following scenarios, determine if there is an increase or a decrease in supply for the good in *italics*.
   a. The price of *silver* increases.
   b. Growers of *tomatoes* experience an unusually good growing season.
   c. New medical evidence reports that consumption of *organic products* reduces the incidence of cancer.
   d. The wages of low-skilled workers, a resource used to help produce *clothing*, increase.
   e. The price of movie tickets, a substitute for *Netflix video rentals*, goes up.

4. Are laser pointers and cats complements or substitutes? (Not sure? Search for videos of cats and laser pointers online.) Discuss.

✳ 5. The market for ice cream has the following demand and supply schedules:

Price (per quart)	Quantity demanded (quarts)	Quantity supplied (quarts)
$2	100	20
$3	80	40
$4	60	60
$5	40	80
$6	20	100

   a. What are the equilibrium price and equilibrium quantity in the ice cream market? Confirm your answer by graphing the demand and supply curves.
   b. If the actual price is $3 per quart, what would drive the market toward equilibrium?

6. Starbucks Entertainment announced in a 2007 news release that Dave Matthews Band's *Live Trax* CD was available only at the company's coffee shops in the United States and Canada. The compilation features recordings of the band's performances dating back to 1995. Why would Starbucks and Dave Matthews have agreed to partner in this way? To come up with an answer, think about the nature of complementary goods and how both sides can benefit from this arrangement.

7. The Seattle Mariners baseball team wishes to determine the equilibrium price for seats for each of the next two seasons. The supply of seats at the ballpark is fixed at 45,000.

Price (per seat)	Quantity demanded in year 1	Quantity demanded in year 2	Quantity supplied
$25	75,000	60,000	45,000
$30	60,000	55,000	45,000
$35	45,000	50,000	45,000
$40	30,000	45,000	45,000
$45	15,000	40,000	45,000

Draw the supply curve and each of the demand curves for years 1 and 2.

✳ 8. Demand and supply curves can also be represented with equations. Suppose that the quantity demanded, Q_D, is represented by the following equation:

$$Q_D = 90 - 2P$$

The quantity supplied, Q_S, is represented by the equation

$$Q_S = P$$

   a. Find the equilibrium price and quantity. **Hint:** Set $Q_D = Q_S$ and solve for the price, P, and then plug your result back into either of the original equations to find Q.
   b. Suppose that the price is $20. Determine Q_D and Q_S.
   c. At a price of $20, is there a surplus or a shortage in the market?
   d. Given your answer in part (c), will the price rise or fall in order to find the equilibrium point?

✳ 9. Let's take a look at two real-world episodes in the market for gasoline and try to figure out why the price fluctuates so much.
   a. In the summer of 2008, the price of regular gasoline in the United States soared to over $4 per gallon. Then, in the fall of that year, the U.S. economy fell into a deep recession that significantly reduced consumers' income. Use the supply and demand model to determine which curve shifted and what happened to the equilibrium price of gasoline. For this part of the question, assume no other changes in the market for gasoline.

b. By the summer of 2014, the price of regular gasoline in the United States was hovering around $3.50 per gallon. But innovations in oil extraction technology, such as hydraulic fracking, reduced the price of crude oil significantly. Crude oil is the primary input for gasoline production. Use the supply and demand model to determine which curve shifted and then what happened to the equilibrium price of gasoline. For this part of the question, assume no other changes in the market for gasoline.

✳ 10. If the price of alcohol decreases, what happens to the demand for red Solo (plastic) cups?

SOLVED PROBLEMS

5a. The equilibrium price is $4, and the equilibrium quantity is 60 quarts. The next step is to graph the curves, as shown here.

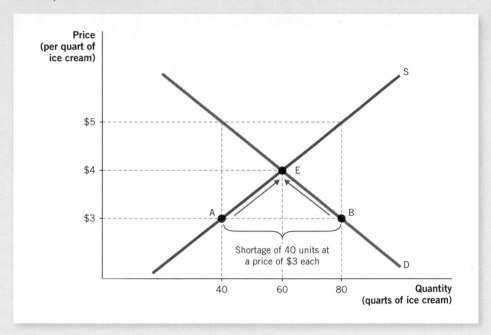

b. A shortage of 40 quarts of ice cream exists at $3 (quantity demanded is 80 and the quantity supplied is 40); therefore, there is excess demand. Ice cream sellers will raise their price as long as excess demand exists—that is, as long as the price is below $4. It is not until $4 that the equilibrium point is reached and the shortage is resolved.

8.a. The first step is to set $Q_D = Q_S$. Doing so gives us $90 - 2P = P$. Solving for price, we find that $90 = 3P$, or $P = 30$. Once we know that $P = 30$, we can plug this value back into either of the original equations, $Q_D = 90 - 2P$ or $Q_S = P$. Beginning with Q_D, we get $90 - 2(30) = 90 - 60 = 30$, or we can plug it into $Q_S = P$, so $Q_S = 30$. Because we get a quantity of 30 for both Q_D and Q_S, we know that the price of $30 is correct.

b. In this part, we plug $20 into Q_D. Doing so yields $90 - 2(20) = 50$. Now we plug $20 into Q_S. Doing so yields 20.

c. Because $Q_D = 50$ and $Q_S = 20$, there is a shortage of 30 quarts.

d. Whenever there is a shortage of a good, the price will rise in order to find the equilibrium point.

9a. The reduction in consumer income led to a negative, or leftward, shift in the demand curve for gasoline. Because this is the only change, the equilibrium price of gasoline fell. In fact, by the end of 2008, the price of gasoline had fallen to under $2 per gallon in the United States.

b. The significant drop in the cost of production led to a large increase, or rightward, shift in the supply of gasoline. This increase in supply led to a decrease in price. In fact, by early 2015, the average price of a gallon of regular gasoline in the United States fell to under $2 per gallon.

Looking at parts (a) and (b) together, you can see that very different causes led to steep drops in the price of gasoline. In 2008 the cause was a decline in demand; in 2014 it was an increase in supply.

10. Because alcohol and Solo cups are complements, the key here is to recall that a change in the price of a complementary good shifts the demand curve for the related good. Lower alcohol prices will cause consumers to purchase more alcohol and therefore demand more Solo cups. In other words, the entire demand curve for Solo cups shifts to the right.

APPENDIX 3A | Changes in Both Demand and Supply

We have considered what would happen if supply *or* demand changes. But life is often more complex than that. To provide a more realistic analysis, we need to examine what happens when supply and demand both shift at the same time.

Suppose that a major drought hits the northwestern United States. The water shortage reduces both the amount of farmed salmon and the ability of wild salmon to spawn in streams and rivers. Figure 3A.1a shows the ensuing decline in the salmon supply, from S_1 progressively leftward, represented by the dotted supply curves. At the same time, a medical journal reports that people who consume at least 4 pounds of salmon a month live five years longer than those who consume an equal amount of cod. Figure 3A.1b shows the ensuing rise in the demand for salmon, from D_1 progressively rightward, represented by the dotted demand curves. This scenario leads to a twofold change. Because of the water shortage, the supply of salmon shrinks. At the same time, new information about the health benefits of eating salmon causes demand for salmon to increase.

It is impossible to predict exactly what happens to the equilibrium point when both supply and demand are shifting. We can, however, determine a region where the resulting equilibrium point must reside.

In this situation, we have a simultaneous decrease in supply and increase in demand. Since we do not know the magnitude of the supply reduction or demand increase, the overall effect on the equilibrium quantity cannot be determined. This result is evident in Figure 3A.1c, as illustrated by the purple region. The points where supply and demand cross within this area represent the set of possible new market equilibria. Because each of the possible points of intersection in the purple region occurs at a price greater than $10 per pound, we know that the price must rise. However, the left half of the purple region produces equilibrium quantities that are lower than 500 pounds of salmon, while the right half of the purple region results in equilibrium quantities that are greater than 500. Therefore, the equilibrium quantity may rise, fall, or stay the same if both shifts are of equal magnitudes.

The world we live in is complex, and often more than one variable will change simultaneously. In such cases, it is not possible to be as definitive as when only one variable—supply or demand—changes. You should think of the new equilibrium not as a single point but as a range of outcomes represented by the purple area in Figure 3A.1c. Therefore, we cannot be exactly sure at what point the new price *and* new quantity will settle. For a closer look at four possibilities, see Figure 3A.2, where E_1 equals the original equilibrium point and the new equilibrium (E_2) lies somewhere in the purple region.

FIGURE 3A.1

A Shift in Supply and Demand

When supply and demand both shift, the resulting equilibrium can no longer be identified as an exact point. We can see this effect in (c), which combines the supply shift in (a) with the demand shift in (b). When supply decreases and demand increases, the result is that the price must rise, but the equilibrium quantity can either rise or fall, or stay the same if both shifts are of equal magnitudes.

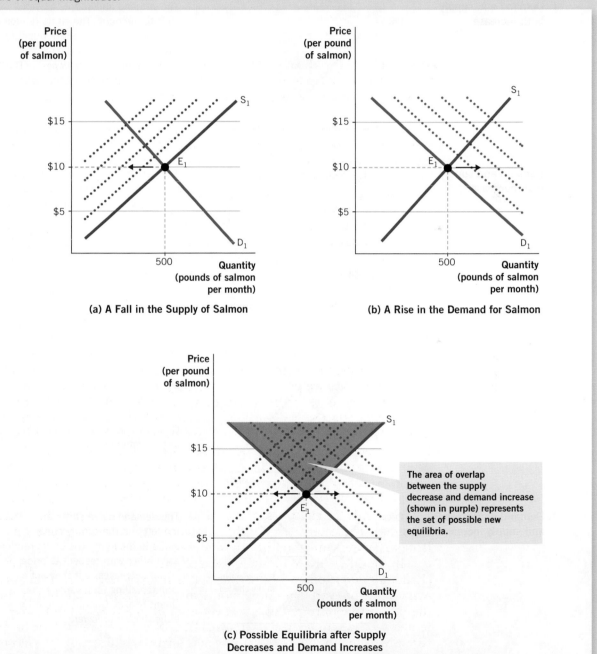

(a) A Fall in the Supply of Salmon

(b) A Rise in the Demand for Salmon

The area of overlap between the supply decrease and demand increase (shown in purple) represents the set of possible new equilibria.

(c) Possible Equilibria after Supply Decreases and Demand Increases

FIGURE 3A.2

Price and Quantity When Demand and Supply Both Change

Change	Illustration	Impact on price and quantity
1. **Demand and supply both increase.**		The demand and supply curves shift to the right. The shifts reinforce each other with respect to quantity, which increases, but they act as countervailing forces along the Price axis. Price could be either higher or lower.
2. **Demand and supply both decrease.**		The demand and supply curves shift to the left. The shifts reinforce each other with respect to quantity, which decreases, but they act as countervailing forces along the Price axis. Price could be either higher or lower.
3. **Demand increases and supply decreases.**		The demand curve shifts to the right and the supply curve shifts to the left. The shifts reinforce each other with respect to price, which increases, but they act as countervailing forces along the Quantity axis. Quantity could be either higher or lower.
4. **Demand decreases and supply increases.**		The demand curve shifts to the left and the supply curve shifts to the right. The shifts reinforce each other with respect to price, which decreases, but they act as countervailing forces along the Quantity axis. Quantity could be either higher or lower.

PRACTICE WHAT YOU KNOW

When Supply and Demand Both Change: Hybrid Cars

Question: At lunch, two friends are engaged in a heated argument. Their exchange goes like this:

The first friend begins, "The supply of hybrid cars and the demand for hybrid cars will both increase. I'm sure of it. I'm also sure the price of hybrids will go down."

The second friend replies, "I agree with the first part of your statement, but I'm not sure about the price. In fact, I'm pretty sure that hybrid prices will rise."

They go back and forth endlessly, each unable to convince the other, so they turn to you for advice. What do you say to them?

Answer: Either of your friends could be correct. In this case, supply and demand both shift out to the right, so we know that the quantity bought and sold will increase. However, an increase in supply would normally lower the price, and an increase in demand would typically raise the price. Without knowing which of these two effects on price is stronger, you can't predict how price will change. The overall price will rise if the increase in demand is larger than the increase in supply. However, if the increase in supply is larger than the increase in demand, prices will fall. But your two friends don't know which condition will be true—so they're locked in an argument that neither can win!

Hybrid cars are becoming increasingly common.

ECONOMICS IN THE REAL WORLD

Polar Vortex Economics

Every few years, the jet stream buckles and the polar vortex drops into the eastern United States. When the vortex descends, temperatures plummet, the demand for propane skyrockets, and supplies of propane are tight. The economic effects of the polar vortex provide a textbook example of a positive demand shock and negative supply shock hitting at the same time. Let's consider the effects of the polar vortex that hit the United States in the winter of 2013–2014.

First, the positive demand shock. It is easy to understand. Bitter cold dramatically increases (that's why we say "positive") the demand for propane, because much more propane than usual is needed to heat homes.

Second, the negative supply shock. There are actually two negative shocks. It turns out that farmers used more propane than usual in the fall of 2013 to dry out their grain crops, thus lowering (that's why we say "negative") supplies of propane for heating homes. Then, during the first cold snap, pipelines across the Midwest froze, disrupting the delivery of propane to holding tanks and then to homes. The frozen pipes were the second negative supply shock.

Third, the complication. Because of the booming supply of natural gas (propane is made from natural gas) in the United States, the price had dropped so low (again, basic supply and demand at work) that very large quantities of propane were exported to markets where suppliers could get a higher price. The supplies that were exported out of the country could have been used in the United States in the winter of 2013–2014, but because they were not here, the shortage was exacerbated. ✳

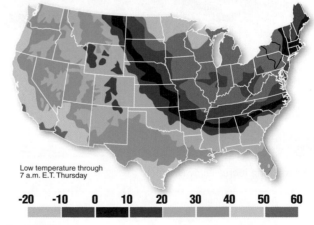

Bitter cold to continue all week

The unusually cold weather is forecast to continue through much of the week for the eastern U.S. Some places from the Carolinas to the Mid-Atlantic may see some of the coldest weather since the mid-1990s. Numerous record low temperatures are expected.

Low temperature through
7 a.m. E.T. Thursday

| -20 | -10 | 0 | 10 | 20 | 30 | 40 | 50 | 60 |

Source: NOAA
Graphic: Tribune News Service

The polar vortex is coming. Do you have enough propane?

QUESTIONS FOR REVIEW

1. What happens to price and quantity when supply and demand change at the same time?

2. Is there more than one potential equilibrium point when supply and demand change at the same time? Explain.

STUDY PROBLEMS (✳ *solved at the end of the section*)

✳ 1. Assume that, over time, consumer incomes generally increase but also that technological advancements in oil extraction lead to lower prices of crude oil (the primary input for gasoline).
   a. If consumer incomes increase by significantly more than input prices fall, what happens to both the price and quantity of gasoline?
   b. If, instead, consumer incomes increase relatively less than input prices fall, what happens to the price and quantity of gasoline?

2. Every Valentine's Day, the price of roses spikes. Using your understanding of the factors that shift both demand and supply, draw the equilibrium in the rose market on January 31 and then draw the new equilibrium that occurs on February 14.

SOLVED PROBLEM

1a. The increase in consumer income increases demand and shifts the demand curve to the right. The decrease in input prices increases supply and shifts the supply curve to the right. Equilibrium quantity unequivocally increases. The demand shift is relatively larger, so price also increases.

  b. Again, we see that the increase in consumer income increases demand and shifts the demand curve to the right; and the decrease in input prices increases supply and shifts the supply curve to the right. Equilibrium quantity increases. But in this question, the demand shift is relatively smaller, so price falls. This example provides a good description of events in the gasoline market at the end of 2014, when price was falling even though consumer incomes were rising.

Sellers charge the highest price possible.

Many students believe that sellers charge the highest price possible for their product or service—that if sellers can get one more penny from a

> **MIS CONCEPTION**

customer, they will, even if it makes the customer angry. It turns out that this belief is wrong. What *is* accurate is that producers charge the highest price they can while maintaining the goodwill of most of their customers.

In the previous chapter, we learned that demand and supply regulate economic activity by balancing the interests of buyers and sellers. We also observed how that balance is achieved through prices. A higher price causes the quantity supplied to rise and the quantity demanded to fall. In contrast, a lower price causes the quantity supplied to fall and the quantity demanded to rise. In this chapter, we examine how decision-makers respond to differences in price and also to changes in income.

The concept of *elasticity*, or responsiveness to a change in market conditions, is a concept that we need to grasp if we are to fully understand supply and demand. Understanding elasticity helps us to determine the impact of government policy on the economy, to vote more intelligently, and even to make wiser day-to-day decisions. Elasticity also helps us understand the faulty logic behind the misconception that sellers charge the highest possible price.

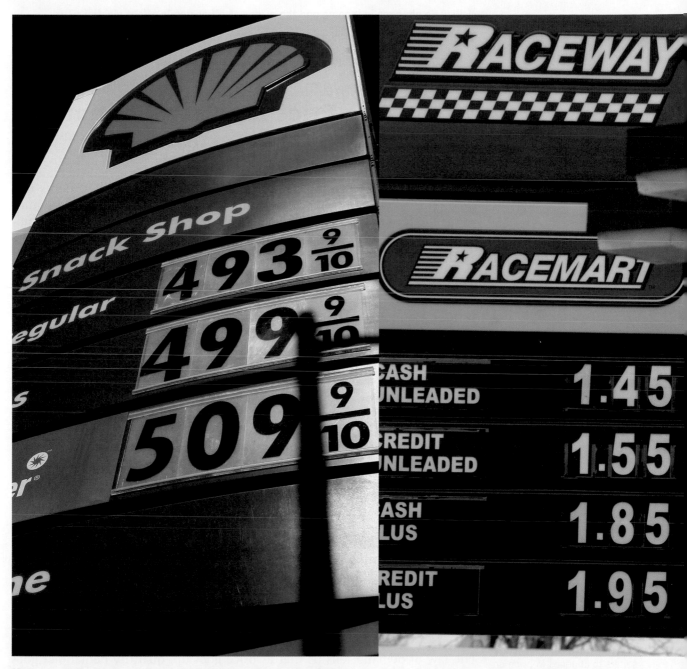

How much do higher prices affect the quantity demanded?

BIG QUESTIONS

* ✳ What is the price elasticity of demand, and what are its determinants?
* ✳ How do changes in income and the prices of other goods affect elasticity?
* ✳ What is the price elasticity of supply?
* ✳ How do the price elasticities of demand and supply relate to each other?

What Is the Price Elasticity of Demand, and What Are Its Determinants?

Trade-offs

Many things in life are replaceable, or have substitutes: boyfriends come and go, people stream videos instead of going out to a movie, and students ride their bikes to class instead of taking the bus. Pasta fans may prefer linguini to spaghetti or angel hair, but all three taste about the same and can be substituted for one another in a pinch. With goods like pasta, where consumers can easily purchase a substitute, we think of demand as being *responsive*. That is, a small change in price will likely cause many people to switch from one good to another.

In contrast, many things in life are irreplaceable or have few good substitutes. Examples include electricity and a hospital emergency room visit. A significant rise in price for either of these items would probably not cause you to consume a smaller quantity. If the price of electricity goes up, you might try to cut your usage somewhat, but you would probably not start generating your own power. Likewise, you could try to treat a serious medical crisis without a visit to the ER—but the consequences of making a mistake would be enormous. In these cases, we say that consumers are *unresponsive*, or unwilling to change their behavior, even when the price of the good or service changes.

Elasticity is a measure of the responsiveness of buyers and sellers to changes in price or income. Elasticity is a useful concept because it allows us to measure *how much* consumers and producers change their behavior when prices or income changes. In the next section, we look at the factors that determine the price elasticity of demand.

Your "average"-looking boyfriend is replaceable.

Determinants of the Price Elasticity of Demand

Elasticity is a measure of the responsiveness of buyers and sellers to changes in price or income.

The law of demand tells us that as price goes up, quantity demanded goes down, and as price goes down, quantity demanded goes up. In other words, there is a negative relationship between the price of a good and the quantity demanded. Elasticity allows us to measure how much the quantity demanded changes in response to a change in price. If the quantity demanded changes significantly as a result of a price change, then demand is *elastic*. If the quantity demanded changes a small amount as a result of a price change, then demand is *inelastic*.

The price elasticity of demand measures the responsiveness of quantity demanded to a change in price. For instance, if the price of a sweatshirt with a college logo rises by $10 and the quantity demanded falls by a large amount (say, half), we'd say that the demand for those sweatshirts is elastic. But if the $10 rise in price results in very little or no change in the quantity demanded, the demand for the sweatshirts is inelastic.

Five determinants play a crucial role in influencing whether demand will be elastic or inelastic: the existence of substitutes, the share of the budget spent on a good, whether the good is a necessity or a luxury good, how broadly defined the market is, and time.

> The **price elasticity of demand** measures the responsiveness of quantity demanded to a change in price.

The Existence of Substitutes

The most important determinant of price elasticity is the number of substitutes available. When substitutes are plentiful, market forces tilt in favor of the consumer. For example, imagine that an unexpected freeze in Florida reduces the supply of oranges. As a result, the supply of orange juice shifts to the left (picture the supply curves we discussed in Chapter 3). Because demand remains unchanged, the price of orange juice rises. However, the consumer of orange juice can find many good substitutes. Because cranberries, grapes, and apple crops are unaffected by the Florida freeze, prices for juices made from those fruits remain constant. This situation leads to a choice: a consumer can continue to buy orange juice at a higher price or choose to pay a lower price for a fruit juice that may not be his first choice but is nonetheless acceptable. Faced with higher orange juice prices, some consumers will switch. How quickly this switch takes place, and to what extent consumers are willing to replace one product with another, determines whether demand is elastic or inelastic. Because many substitutes for orange juice exist, the demand for orange juice is elastic, or responsive to price changes.

What if there are no good substitutes? There is no amusement park quite like Disney. Where else can you see all your favorite Disney characters? Nowhere! Because the experience is unique, the number of close substitutes is small. Therefore, demand is more inelastic, or less responsive to price changes.

To some degree, the price elasticity of demand depends on consumer preferences. For instance, sports fans are often willing to shell out big bucks to follow their passions. Amateur golfers can play the same courses that professional golfers do. But the opportunity to golf where the professionals play does not come cheaply. A round of golf at the Tournament Players Club at Sawgrass, a famous course in Florida, costs close to $300. Why are some golfers willing to pay that much? For an avid golfer with the financial means, the experience of living out the same shots seen on television tournaments is worth $300. In this case, demand is inelastic—the avid golfer does not view other golf courses as good substitutes. However, a less enthusiastic golfer, or one without the financial resources, is happy to golf on a less expensive course even if

Beyoncé is irreplaceable.

the pros don't play it on TV. When less expensive golf courses serve as good substitutes, the price tag makes demand elastic. Ultimately, whether demand is inelastic or elastic depends on the buyer's preferences and resources.

The Share of the Budget Spent on the Good

Despite our example of an avid and affluent golfer willing to pay a premium fee to play at a famous golf course, in most cases price is a critical element in

determining what we can afford and what we choose to buy. If you plan to purchase a 70-inch-screen TV, which can cost as much as $3,000, you will probably be willing to take the time to find the best deal. Because of the high price, even a small discount can cause a relatively large change in consumer demand. A 10% off sale may not sound like much, but when purchasing a big-ticket item like a TV, it can mean hundreds of dollars in savings. In this case, the will-

Saving 10% on this purchase amounts to a few pennies.

ingness to shop for the best deal indicates that the price matters, so demand is elastic.

Incentives

Demand is much more inelastic for inexpensive items on sale. For example, if a candy bar is discounted 10%, the price falls by pennies. The savings from switching candy bars is not enough to make a difference in what you can afford elsewhere. Therefore, the incentive to switch is small. Most consumers still buy their favorite candy because the price difference is so insignificant. In this case, demand is inelastic because the savings gained by purchasing a less desirable candy bar are small in comparison to the consumer's budget.

Necessities versus Luxury Goods

A big-screen TV and a candy bar are both luxury goods. You don't need to have either one. But some goods are necessities. For example, you have to pay your rent and water bill, purchase gasoline for your car, and eat. When consumers purchase a necessity, they are generally thinking about the need, not the price. When the need trumps the price, we expect demand to be relatively inelastic. Therefore, the demand for things like cars, textbooks, and heating oil all tend to have inelastic demand.

Whether the Market Is Broadly or Narrowly Defined

The more broadly we define a market for a good, the harder it is to live without. For instance, demand for housing in general is quite inelastic because without some form of housing you'd be living on the street. However, the demand for a particular apartment or house is much more price sensitive because you don't need to live in *that* exact place. Therefore, a good falling into a narrowly defined category, such as Crest

Saving 10% on this purchase adds up to hundreds of dollars.

toothpaste, will have more elastic demand than a broadly defined category, such as toothpaste, which has more inelastic demand.

Time and the Adjustment Process

When the market price changes, consumers and sellers respond. But that response does not remain the same over time. As time passes, both consumers and sellers are able to find substitutes. To understand these different market responses, when considering elasticity economists consider time in three distinct periods: the *immediate run*, the *short run*, and the *long run*.

In the **immediate run**, there is no time for consumers to adjust their behavior. Consider the demand for gasoline. When the gas tank is empty, you have to stop at the nearest gas station and pay the posted price. Filling up as soon as possible is more important than driving around searching for the lowest price. Inelastic demand exists whenever price is secondary to the desire to attain a certain amount of the good. So in the case of an empty tank, the demand for gasoline is inelastic.

This is *not* the time to try and find cheap gas.

But what if your tank is not empty? The **short run** is a period of time when consumers can partially adjust their behavior (in this case, can search for a good deal on gas). In the short run, we make decisions that reflect our immediate or short-term wants, needs, or limitations. When consumers have some time to make a purchase, they gain flexibility. They can shop for lower prices at the pump, carpool to save gas, or even change how often they drive. In the short run, flexibility reduces the demand for expensive gasoline and makes consumer demand more elastic.

Finally, if we relax the time constraint completely, it is possible to use even less gasoline. The **long run** is a period of time when consumers have time to fully adjust to market conditions. In the long run, we make decisions that reflect our wants, needs, and limitations over a long time horizon. If gasoline prices are high in the long run, consumers can relocate closer to work and purchase fuel-efficient cars. These changes further reduce the demand for gasoline. As a result of the flexibility that additional time gives the consumer, the demand for gasoline becomes more elastic.

We have looked at five determinants of elasticity—substitutes, the share of the budget spent on the good, necessities versus luxury goods, whether the market is broadly or narrowly defined, and time. Each is significant, but the number of substitutes tends to be the most influential factor and dominates the others. Table 4.1 will help you develop your intuition about how different market situations influence the overall elasticity of demand.

In the **immediate run**, there is no time for consumers to adjust their behavior.

The **short run** is a period of time when consumers can partially adjust their behavior. In the short run, we make decisions that reflect our immediate or short-term wants, needs, or limitations.

The **long run** is a period of time when consumers have time to fully adjust to market conditions. In the long run, we make decisions that reflect our wants, needs, and limitations over a long time horizon.

Computing the Price Elasticity of Demand

Until this point, our discussion of elasticity has been descriptive. However, to apply the concept of elasticity in decision-making, we need to view it more quantitatively. For example, if the owner of a business is trying to decide whether to put a good on sale, he or she needs to estimate how many new customers would purchase it at the sale price. If a government is considering a new tax, it needs to know how much revenue that tax will generate. These are questions about elasticity that we can evaluate by using a mathematical formula.

TABLE 4.1

Developing Intuition for the Price Elasticity of Demand

Example	Discussion	Overall elasticity
Football tickets for a true fan	Being able to watch a game live and go to pregame and postgame tailgates is a unique experience. For many fans, the experience of going to the game has few close substitutes. In addition, this is a narrowly defined experience. Therefore, the demand is relatively inelastic.	Tends to be relatively inelastic
Assigned textbooks for a class	The information inside a textbook is valuable. Substitutes such as older editions and free online resources are not exactly the same. As a result, most students buy the required course materials. Acquiring the textbook is more important than the price paid; therefore, the demand is inelastic. The fact that a textbook is needed in the short run (for a few months while taking a class) also tends to make the demand inelastic.	Tends to be inelastic
A slice of pizza from Domino's	In most locations, many pizza competitors exist, so there are many close substitutes. The presence of so much competition tends to make the demand for a narrowly defined brand of pizza elastic.	Tends to be elastic
A Yellow Kia Soul	There are many styles, makes, and colors of cars to choose from. With large purchases, consumers are sensitive to smaller percentages of savings. Moreover, people typically plan their car purchases many months or years in advance. The combination of all these factors makes the demand for any narrowly defined model relatively elastic.	Tends to be relatively elastic

The Price Elasticity of Demand Formula

Let's begin with an example of a pizza shop. Consider an owner who is trying to attract more customers. For one month, he lowers the price of a pizza by 10% and is pleased to find that sales jump by 30%.

Here is the formula for the price elasticity of demand (E_D):

(Equation 4.1) $$\text{price elasticity of demand} = E_D = \frac{\text{percentage change in the quantity demanded}}{\text{percentage change in price}}$$

Using the data from the example, we calculate the price elasticity of demand as follows:

$$\text{price elasticity of demand} = E_D = \frac{30\%}{-10\%} = -3$$

The price elasticity of demand, −3 in this case, is expressed as a coefficient (3) with a specific sign (it has a minus sign in front of it). The coefficient tells us how much the quantity demanded has changed (30%) compared with the price change (10%). In this case, the percentage change in the quantity demanded is three times the percentage change in the price. Whenever the

Price Elasticity of Demand

The Big Bang Theory

The Mystic Warlords of Ka'a (an obvious spoof of Magic: The Gathering) is a fictional trading card game that Sheldon, Leonard, Raj, and Howard all enjoy playing. Howard complains about the release of a new expansion pack called Wild West Witches:

Raj: Hey, look, the new Warlords of Ka'a expansion pack is out.

Howard: A new one? Unbelievable. They just keep making up more cheesy monsters, slapping them on cards, and selling them at 25 bucks a pop.

Raj: Stuart, settle an argument for us. Who would win, Billy the Kid or the White Wizard?

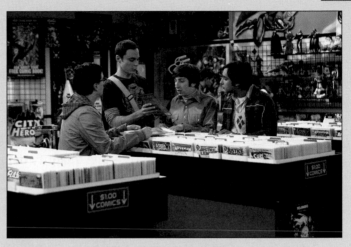

Howard considers buying an expansion pack.

Stuart: If I tell you that, I'm robbing you of the hours of fun you could have for the magical, rootin' tootin' low price of $24.95.

Raj: I'll take one.

Howard: Mmm, make it two.

Leonard: I hate all of you and myself. Three.

Stuart: I'll ring it up. Like shooting nerds in a barrel.

Analysis: Expansion packs allow players of Mystic (and other role playing games) the opportunity to improve the deck of cards with which they play the game. Because all of the guys are smart and competitive, new expansion packs make Mystic more challenging to play and also increases the chance of winning when you play against others who do not have the latest cards. The demand for new expansion packs is quite inelastic because the purchase is made in the short run, the share of the budget that each guy spends on the item ($25) is relatively small, and the number of available substitutes for cards with new powers is effectively zero.

percentage change in the quantity demanded is larger than the percentage change in price, the demand is elastic. In other words, the price drop made a big difference in how much pizza consumers purchased from the pizza shop. If the opposite occurs and a price drop makes a small difference in the quantity that consumers purchase, demand is inelastic.

The negative (minus) sign in front of the coefficient is equally important. Recall that the law of demand describes a negative relationship between the price of a good and the quantity demanded; when price rises, the quantity demanded falls. The E_D coefficient reflects this negative relationship with a negative sign. In other words, the pizza shop drops its price and consumers buy more pizza. Because the price of pizza and consumer purchases of pizza generally move in opposite directions, the sign of the price elasticity of demand is almost always negative.

The Midpoint Method

Our earlier calculation was simple because we looked at the change in price and the change in the quantity demanded from only one direction—that is, from a high price to a lower price and from the corresponding lower quantity demanded to the higher quantity demanded. However, the complete—and proper—way to calculate elasticity is from both directions. Consider the following demand schedule for pizza:

Price	Quantity demanded
$12	20
$ 6	30

Let's calculate the elasticity of demand. If the price drops from $12 to $6—a drop of 50%—the quantity demanded increases from 20 to 30—a rise of 50%. Plugging the percentage changes into the E_D formula yields

$$\text{price elasticity of demand} = E_D = \frac{50\%}{-50\%} = -1.0$$

But if the price rises from $6 to $12—an increase of 100%—the quantity demanded falls from 30 to 20, or decreases by 33%. Plugging the percentage changes into the E_D formula yields

$$\text{price elasticity of demand} = E_D = \frac{-33\%}{100\%} = -0.33$$

This result occurs because percentage changes are usually calculated by using the initial value as the base, or reference point. In this example, we worked the problem two ways: by using $12 as the starting point and dropping the price to $6, and then by using $6 as the starting point and increasing the price to $12. Even though we are measuring elasticity over the same range of values, the percentage changes are different.

To avoid this problem, economists use the *midpoint method*, which gives the same answer for the elasticity no matter what point you begin with. Equation 4.2 uses the midpoint method to express the price elasticity of demand. While this equation looks more complicated than Equation 4.1, it is not. The midpoint method merely specifies how to plug in the initial and ending values for price and quantity to determine the percentage changes. Q_1 and P_1 are the initial values, and Q_2 and Q_2 are the ending values.

(Equation 4.2)

$$E_D = \frac{\text{change in Q} \div \text{average value of Q}}{\text{change in P} \div \text{average value of P}}$$

$$= \frac{(Q_2 - Q_1) \div [(Q_1 + Q_2) \div 2]}{(P_2 - P_1) \div [(P_1 + P_2) \div 2]}$$

The change in the quantity demanded, $(Q_2 - Q_1)$, and the change in price, $(P_2 - P_1)$, are each divided by the average of the initial and ending values, or $[(Q_1 + Q_2) \div 2]$ and $[(P_1 + P_2) \div 2]$.

The midpoint method is the preferred method for solving elasticity problems. To see why, let's return to our pizza demand example.

If the price rises from \$6 to \$12, the quantity demanded falls from 30 to 20. Here the initial values are $P_1 = \$6$ and $Q_1 = 30$. The ending values are $P_2 = \$12$ and $Q_2 = 20$. Using the midpoint method,

$$E_D = \frac{(20 - 30) \div [(30 + 20) \div 2]}{(\$12 - \$6) \div [(\$6 + \$12) \div 2]} = \frac{-10 \div 25}{\$6 \div \$9} = -0.60$$

If the price falls from \$12 to \$6, quantity demanded rises from 20 to 30. This time, the initial values are $P_1 = \$12$ and $Q_1 = 20$. The ending values are $P_2 = \$6$ and $Q_2 = 30$. Using the midpoint method,

$$E_D = \frac{(30 - 20) \div [(20 + 30) \div 2]}{(\$6 - \$12) \div [(\$12 + \$6) \div 2]} = \frac{-10 \div 25}{-\$6 \div \$9} = -0.60$$

When we calculated the price elasticity of demand from \$6 to \$12 using \$6 as the initial point, $E_D = -0.33$. Moving in the opposite direction, from \$12 to \$6, made \$12 the initial reference point and $E_D = -1.0$. The midpoint method splits the difference and uses \$9 and 25 pizzas as the midpoints. This approach makes the calculation of the elasticity coefficient the same, -0.60, no matter what direction the price moves. Therefore, economists use the midpoint method to standardize the results.

So, using the midpoint method, we arrive at an elasticity coefficient of -0.60, which is between 0 and -1. What does that number mean? In this case, the percentage change in the quantity demanded is less than the percentage change in the price. Whenever the percentage change in the quantity demanded is smaller than the percentage change in price, we say that demand is inelastic. In other words, the price drop does not make a big difference in how much pizza consumers purchase from the pizza shop. When the elasticity coefficient is less than -1, the opposite is true, and demand is elastic.

Graphing the Price Elasticity of Demand

Visualizing elasticity graphically helps us understand the relationship between elastic and inelastic demand. Figure 4.1 shows elasticity graphically. As demand becomes increasingly elastic, or responsive to price changes, the demand curve flattens. The range of elasticity runs from perfectly inelastic through perfectly elastic.

Perfectly Inelastic Demand

Figure 4.1, panel (a), depicts the price elasticity for pet care. Many pet owners report that they would pay any amount of money to help their sick or injured pet get better. For these pet owners, the demand curve is a vertical line. If you look along the quantity axis in panel (a), you will see that the quantity of pet care demanded (Q_D) remains constant no matter what it costs. At the same time, the price increases from P_0 to P_1. We can calculate the price elasticity coefficient as follows:

$$E_{\text{pet care}} = \frac{\text{percentage change in } Q_D}{\text{percentage change in P}} = \frac{0}{\text{percentage change in P}} = 0$$

For many pet owners, the demand for veterinary care is perfectly inelastic.

FIGURE 4.1

Elasticity and the Demand Curve

For any given price change across two demand curves, demand will be more elastic on the flatter demand curve than on the steeper demand curve. In (a), the demand is perfectly inelastic, so the price does not matter. In (b), the demand is relatively inelastic, so the price is less important than the quantity purchased. In (c), the demand is relatively elastic, so the price matters more than quantity. In (d), the demand is perfectly elastic, so price is all that matters.

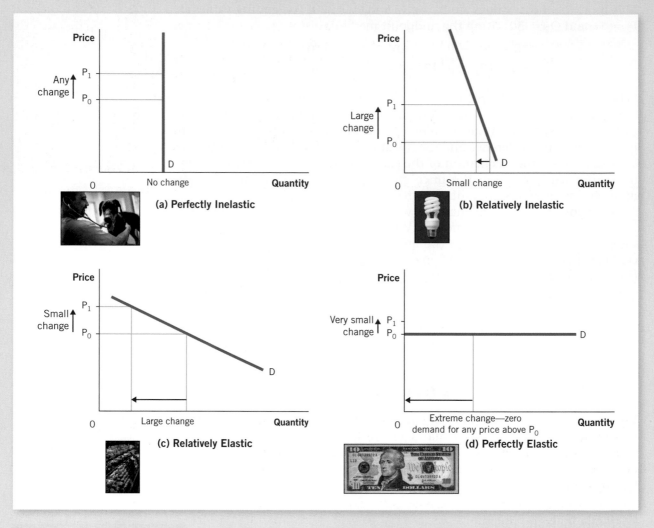

(a) Perfectly Inelastic

(b) Relatively Inelastic

(c) Relatively Elastic

(d) Perfectly Elastic

When zero is in the numerator, we know that the answer will be zero no matter what we find in the denominator. This conclusion makes sense. Many pet owners will try to help their pet feel better no matter what the cost, so we can say that their demand is *perfectly inelastic*. This means that the value of E_D will always be zero. (Of course, pet care is not perfectly inelastic, because there is certainly a price beyond which some pet owners would not or could not pay; but for illustrative purposes, let's say that pet care *is* perfectly elastic.) As you continue reading this section, refer to Table 4.2 on page 123 to help you keep track of the different types of elasticity.

Relatively Inelastic Demand

Moving on to panel (b) of Figure 4.1, we consider the demand for electricity. Whereas many pet owners will not change their consumption of health care for their pet no matter what the cost, consumers of electricity will modify their use of electricity in response to price changes. When the price of electricity goes up, they will use less, and when the price goes down, they will use more. Because living without electricity is not practical, using less is a matter of making relatively small lifestyle adjustments—buying energy-efficient light bulbs or adjusting the thermostat a few degrees. As a result, the demand curve in panel (b) is relatively steep, but not completely vertical as in panel (a).

When the change on the quantity axis is small compared with the change on the price axis, the price elasticity is *relatively inelastic*. Plugging these changes into the elasticity formula, we get

$$E_{electricity} = \frac{\text{percentage change in } Q_D}{\text{percentage change in } P} = \frac{\text{\small small } \text{change}}{\text{\large large } \text{change}}$$

Recall that the law of demand describes a negative relationship between price and quantity demanded. Therefore, the changes along the price and quantity axes will always be in opposite directions. A price elasticity of zero tells us there is no change in the quantity demanded when price changes. So when demand is relatively inelastic, the price elasticity of demand must be relatively close to zero. The easiest way to think about this scenario is to consider how a 10% increase in electric rates affects most households. How much less electricity would you use? The answer for most people would be a little less, but not 10% less. You can adjust your thermostat, but you still need electricity to run your appliances and lights. When the price changes more than quantity changes, there is a larger change in the denominator. Therefore, the price elasticity of demand is between 0 and −1 when demand is relatively inelastic.

The demand for electricity is relatively inelastic.

Relatively Elastic Demand

In Figure 4.1, panel (c), we consider apples. Because there are many good substitutes for apples, the demand for apples is *relatively elastic*. The flexibility of consumer demand for apples is illustrated by the degree of responsiveness we see along the quantity axis relative to the change exhibited along the price axis. We can observe this responsiveness by noting that a relatively elastic demand curve is flatter than an inelastic demand curve. So, whereas perfectly inelastic demand shows no change in demand with an increase in price, and relatively inelastic demand shows a small change in quantity demanded with an increase in price, relatively elastic demand shows a relatively large change in quantity demanded with an increase in price. Placing this information into the elasticity formula gives us

$$E_{apples} = \frac{\text{percentage change in } Q_D}{\text{percentage change in } P} = \frac{\text{\large large } \text{change}}{\text{\small small } \text{change}}$$

Now the numerator—the percentage change in $_Q D$—is large, and the denominator—the percentage change in P—is small.

The demand for apples is relatively elastic.

E_D is less than -1. Recall that the sign must be negative, because there is a negative relationship between price and the quantity demanded. As the price elasticity of demand moves farther away from zero, the consumer becomes more responsive to a price change. Because many other fruits are good substitutes for apples, a small change in the price of apples will have a large effect on the quantity demanded.

Perfectly Elastic Demand

Figure 4.1, panel (d), provides an interesting example: the demand for a $10 bill. Would you pay $11.00 to get a $10 bill? No. Would you pay $10.01 for a $10 bill? Still no. However, when the price drops to $10.00, you will probably become indifferent (that is, you will be equally satisfied with paying $10.00 for the $10 bill or not making the trade). The real magic here occurs when the price drops to $9.99. How many $10 bills would you buy if you could buy them for $9.99 or less? The answer: as many as possible! This is exactly what happens in currency markets, where small differences among currency prices around the globe motivate traders to buy and sell large quantities of currency and clear a small profit on the difference in exchange rates. This extreme form of price sensitivity is illustrated by a perfectly horizontal demand curve, which means that demand is *perfectly elastic*. Solving for the elasticity yields

The demand for a $10 bill is perfectly elastic.

$$E_{\$10\,\text{bill}} = \frac{\text{percentage change in } Q_D}{\text{percentage change in P}} = \frac{\text{nearly infinite change}}{\text{very small (\$0.01) change}}$$

We can think of this very small price change, from $10.00 to $9.99, as having essentially an unlimited effect on the quantity of $10 bills demanded. Traders go from being uninterested in trading at $10.00 to seeking to buy as many $10 bills as possible when the price drops to $9.99. As a result, the price elasticity of demand approaches negative infinity $(-\infty)$.

Unitary Elasticity

There is a fifth type of elasticity, not depicted in Figure 4.1. *Unitary elasticity* describes the situation in which elasticity is neither elastic nor inelastic. This situation occurs when E_D is exactly -1, and it happens when the percentage change in price is exactly equal to the percentage change in quantity demanded. This characteristic of unitary elasticity will be important when we discuss the connection between elasticity and total revenue later in this chapter. You're probably wondering what an example of a unitary good would be. Relax. It is impossible to find a good that has a price elasticity of exactly -1 at all price points. It is enough to know that unitary demand represents the crossover from elastic to inelastic demand.

Price Elasticity of Demand: A Summary

Now that you have had a chance to look at all four panels in Figure 4.1, here is a handy trick that you can use to keep the difference between inelastic and elastic demand straight.

$$\text{I} = \text{inelastic and } \text{E} = \text{elastic}$$

The "I" in the word "inelastic" is vertical, just like the inelastic relationships we examined in Figure 4.1. Likewise, the letter "E" has three horizontal lines to remind us that elastic demand is flat.

Finally, it is possible to pair the elasticity coefficients with an interpretation of how much price matters. Table 4.2 provides a convenient summary. When price does not matter, demand is perfectly inelastic (denoted by the coefficient of zero). Conversely, when price is the only thing that matters, demand becomes perfectly elastic (denoted by $-\infty$). Between these two extremes, the extent to which price matters determines whether demand is relatively inelastic, unitary, or relatively elastic.

Time, Elasticity, and the Demand Curve

We have already seen that increased time makes demand more elastic. Figure 4.2 shows this result graphically. When the price rises from P_1 to P_2, consumers cannot avoid the price increase in the immediate run, and demand is represented by the perfectly inelastic demand curve D_1. For example, if your gas tank is almost empty, you must purchase gas at the new, higher price. Over a slightly longer time horizon—the short run—consumers are more flexible and drive less in order to buy less gasoline. Demand shifts to D_2, and in the short run consumption declines to Q_2. In the long run, when consumers

TABLE 4.2

The Relationship between Price Elasticity of Demand and Price

Elasticity	E_D coefficient	Interpretation	Example in Figure 4.1
Perfectly inelastic	$E_D = 0$	Price does not matter.	Saving your pet
Relatively inelastic	$0 > E_D > -1$	Price is less important than the quantity purchased.	Electricity
Unitary	$E_D = -1$	Price and quantity are equally important.	
Relatively elastic	$-1 > E_D > -\infty$	Price is more important than the quantity purchased.	Apples
Perfectly elastic	$E_D \rightarrow -\infty$	Price is everything.	A $10 bill

FIGURE 4.2

Elasticity and the Demand Curve over Time

Demand becomes more elastic over time. When the price rises from P_1 to P_2, consumers are unable to avoid the price increase in the immediate run (D_1). In the short run (D_2), consumers become more flexible and consumption declines to Q_2. Eventually, in the long run (D_3), there is time to make lifestyle changes that further reduce consumption. As a result, the demand curve continues to flatten and the quantity demanded falls to Q_3 in response to the higher price.

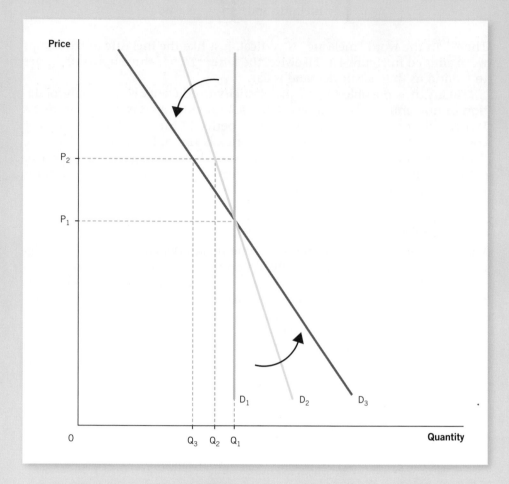

have time to purchase a more fuel-efficient vehicle or move closer to work, demand shifts to D_3 and gas purchases fall even further. As the demand curve continues to flatten, the quantity demanded falls to Q_3.

Slope and Elasticity

In this section, we pause to make sure that you understand what you are observing in the figures. The demand curves shown in Figures 4.1 and 4.2 are straight lines, and therefore they have a constant slope, or steepness. (A refresher on slope is found in the appendix to Chapter 2.) So, looking at Figures 4.1 and 4.2, you might think that slope is the same as the price elasticity. But slope does not equal elasticity.

Consider, for example, a trip to Starbucks. Would you buy a tall skinny latte if it costs $10? How about $7? What about $5? Say you decide to buy the skinny latte because the price drops from $5 to $4. In this case, a small price change, a drop from $5 to $4, causes you to make the purchase. You can say that the demand for skinny lattes is relatively elastic. Now look at Figure 4.3,

FIGURE 4.3

The Difference between Slope and Elasticity

Along any straight demand curve, the price elasticity of demand (E_D) is not constant, as you can see by noting how the price elasticity of demand changes from highly elastic near the top of the demand curve to highly inelastic near the bottom of the curve. In the table, note that all the numbers in the third, fourth, and fifth columns are based on the midpoint formula.

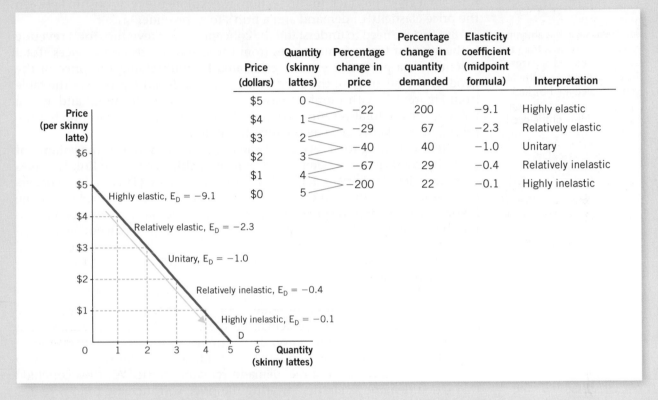

Price (dollars)	Quantity (skinny lattes)	Percentage change in price	Percentage change in quantity demanded	Elasticity coefficient (midpoint formula)	Interpretation
$5	0	−22	200	−9.1	Highly elastic
$4	1	−29	67	−2.3	Relatively elastic
$3	2	−40	40	−1.0	Unitary
$2	3	−67	29	−0.4	Relatively inelastic
$1	4	−200	22	−0.1	Highly inelastic
$0	5				

which shows a demand curve for skinny lattes. At $5 the consumer purchases zero lattes, at $4 she purchases one latte, at $3 she purchases two, and she continues to buy one additional latte with each $1 drop in price. As you progress downward along the demand curve, price becomes less of an inhibiting factor, and as a result, the price elasticity of demand slowly becomes more inelastic. Notice that the slope of a linear demand curve is constant. However, when we calculate the price elasticity of demand between the various points in Figure 4.3, it becomes clear that demand is increasingly inelastic as we move down the demand curve. You can see this in the change in E_D; it steadily decreases from −9.1 to −0.1.

Perfectly inelastic demand would exist if the elasticity coefficient reached zero. Recall that a value of zero means that there is no change in the quantity demanded as a result of a price change. Therefore, values close to zero reflect inelastic demand, while those farther away from zero reflect more elastic demand.

Price Elasticity of Demand and Total Revenue

Understanding the price elasticity of demand for the product you sell is important when running a business. Consumer responsiveness to price changes determines whether a firm would be better off raising or lowering its price for a given product. In this section, we explore the relationship between the price elasticity of demand and a firm's total revenue.

Total revenue is the amount that a firm receives from the sale of goods and services. Total revenue for a particular good is calculated by multiplying the price of the good by the quantity of the good that is sold.

But first we need to understand the concept of total revenue. **Total revenue** is the amount that a firm receives from the sale of goods and services. Total revenue for a particular good is calculated by multiplying the price of the good by the quantity of the good that is sold. Table 4.3 reproduces the table from Figure 4.3 (with numbers based on the midpoint formula) and adds a column for the total revenue. We find the total revenue by multiplying the price of a tall skinny latte by the quantity purchased.

Trade-offs

After calculating total revenue at each price, we can look at the column of elasticity coefficients to determine the relationship. When we link revenues with the price elasticity of demand, a trade-off emerges. (This trade-off occurs because total revenue and elasticity relate to price differently. Total revenue involves multiplying the price by the quantity, while elasticity involves dividing the percentage change in quantity demanded by the percentage change in price.) Total revenue is zero when the price is too high ($5 or more) and when the price is $0. Between these two extremes, prices from $1 to $4 generate positive total revenue.

Consider what happens when the price drops from $5 to $4. At $4, the first latte is purchased. Total revenue is $4 × 1 = $4. This is also the range at which the price elasticity of demand is highly elastic. As a result, lowering the price increases revenue. Revenue continues to increase when the price drops from $4 to $3. Now two lattes are sold, so the total revenue rises to $3 × 2 = $6. At the same time, demand remains elastic. We thus conclude that when demand is elastic, lowering the price will increase total revenue. This relationship is shown in panel (a) of Figure 4.4. By lowering the price from $4 to $3, the business has generated $2 more in revenue. But to generate

---

TABLE 4.3

The Price Elasticity of Demand and Total Revenue

Price (P) (per skinny latte)	Quantity (Q) (skinny lattes)	Total revenue P × Q	Percentage change in price	Percentage change in quantity	Elasticity coefficient	Interpretation
$5	0	$0				
			−22	200	−9.1	Highly elastic
$4	1	$4				
			−29	67	−2.3	Relatively elastic
$3	2	$6				
			−40	40	−1.0	Unitary
$2	3	$6				
			−67	29	−0.4	Relatively inelastic
$1	4	$4				
			−200	22	−0.1	Highly inelastic
$0	5	$0				

FIGURE 4.4

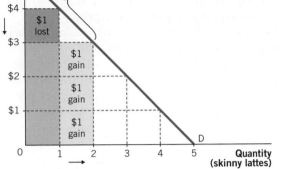

(a) The Total Revenue Trade-off When Demand Is Elastic

In the elastic region of the demand curve, lowering the price will increase total revenue. The gains from increased purchases, shown in the light green area, are greater than the losses from a lower purchase price, shown in the red area. The green area is part of the total revenue that exists at both prices.

(b) . . . When Demand Is Unitary

When demand is unitary, lowering the price will no longer increase total revenue. The gains from increased purchases, shown in the light green area, are equal to the losses from a lower purchase price, shown in the red area.

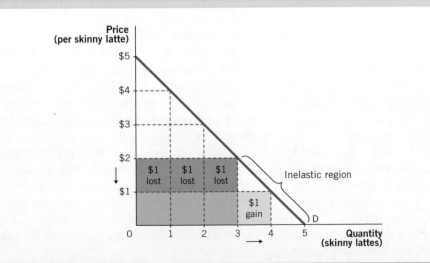

(c) . . . When Demand Is Inelastic

In the inelastic region of the demand curve, lowering the price will decrease total revenue. The gains from increased purchases, shown in the light green area, are smaller than the losses from a lower purchase price, shown in the red area.

this extra revenue, the business has lowered the price from $4 to $3 and therefore has given up $1 for each unit it sells. This lost revenue is represented by the red area under the demand curve in panel (a).

When the price drops from $3 to $2, the total revenue stays at $6. This result occurs because demand is unitary, as shown in panel (b). This special condition exists when the percentage price change is exactly offset by an equal percentage change in the quantity demanded. In this situation, revenue remains constant. At $2, three lattes are purchased, so the total revenue is $2 × 3, which is the same as it was when the price was $3. As a result, we can see that total revenue has reached a maximum. Between $3 and $2, the price elasticity of demand is unitary. This finding does not necessarily mean that the firm will operate at the unitary point. Maximizing profit, not revenue, is the ultimate goal of a business, and we have not yet accounted for costs in our calculation of profits.

ECONOMICS IN THE MEDIA

Elasticity and Total Revenue

D'oh! The Simpsons and Total Revenue

In the episode "Bart Gets an Elephant," the Simpsons find that their pet elephant, Stampy, is eating them out of house and home. So Bart devises a plan to charge admission for people to see the elephant. He begins by charging $1. However, the revenue collected is not enough to cover Stampy's food bill. When Homer discovers that they are not covering the costs of keeping Stampy, he raises the price to see the elephant to $100. However, Homer is not the smartest businessman in the world, and all of the customers who would have paid Bart's $1 admission stay away. We can use our understanding of elasticity to explain why Homer's plan backfires.

Homer's plan is to increase the price. This strategy would work if the demand to see the elephant were inelastic, but it is not. For $100 you could see a concert, attend a major sporting event, or eat at a very nice restaurant. You'd have to really want to see the elephant to be willing to pay $100. It doesn't help that you can also go to any of the best zoos in the country and see hundreds of other animals as well, for much less money. Homer's plan is doomed to fail because no one is willing to pay $100. Remember that total revenue = price × quantity purchased. If the quantity demanded falls to zero,

The Simpsons cannot afford Stampy. What should they do?

zero times anything is still zero. So Homer's plan does not generate any revenue.

In contrast, Bart's admission price of $1 brings in $58 in revenue. This is a good start, but it is not enough to cover Stampy's $300 food bill. Homer actually had the right idea here. Raising the price above $1 would generate more revenue up to a point. Would most of the customers pay $2 to see the elephant? Most likely. $5? Possibly. $10? Maybe. $100? Definitely not. Why not? There is a trade-off dictated by the law of demand. A higher price reduces the quantity demanded. Therefore, the trick to maximizing total revenue is to balance an increase in price against the decrease in the quantity purchased.

PRACTICE WHAT YOU KNOW

Price Elasticity of Demand

The following two questions ask you to compute price elasticity of demand. Before we do the math, ask yourself whether the price elasticity of demand for sandwiches or the antibiotic amoxicillin is elastic.

Question: A deli manager decides to lower the price of a featured sandwich from $3 to $2, and she finds that sales during the week increase from 240 to 480 sandwiches. Is demand elastic?

Answer: Consumers were flexible and bought significantly more sandwiches in response to the price drop. Let's calculate the price elasticity of demand (E_D) using Equation 4.2. Recall that

$$E_D = \frac{(Q_2 - Q_1) \div [(Q_1 + Q_2) \div 2]}{(P_2 - P_1) \div [(P_1 + P_2) \div 2]}$$

Is the demand for a sandwich elastic or inelastic?

Plugging in the values from the question yields

$$E_D = \frac{(480 - 240) \div [(240 + 480) \div 2]}{(\$2 - \$3) \div [(\$3 + \$2) \div 2]} = \frac{240 \div 360}{-\$1 \div \$2.50}$$

Therefore, $E_D = -1.67$.

Whenever the price elasticity of demand is less than -1, demand is elastic: the percentage change in the quantity demanded is greater than the percentage change in price. This outcome is exactly what the store manager expected. But sandwiches are just one option for a meal; there are many other choices, such as salads, burgers, and chicken—all of which cost more than the now-cheaper sandwich. Therefore, we should not be surprised that there is a relatively large percentage increase in sandwich purchases by price-conscious customers.

Question: A local pharmacy manager decides to raise the price of a 50-pill prescription of amoxicillin (an antibiotic) from $8 to $10. The pharmacy tracks the sales of amoxicillin over the next month and finds that sales decline from 1,500 to 1,480 boxes. Is demand elastic?

Is the demand for amoxicillin elastic or inelastic?

Answer: First, let's consider the potential substitutes for amoxicillin. To be sure, it's possible to substitute other drugs, but they might not be as effective. Therefore, most patients prefer to use the drug prescribed by their doctor. Also, in this case the cost of the drug is relatively small. Finally, patients' need for amoxicillin is a short-run consideration. They want the medicine now so they will get better! All three factors would lead us to believe that the demand for amoxicillin is relatively inelastic. Let's find out if the data confirm that intuition.

(CONTINUED)

(CONTINUED)

The price elasticity of demand using the midpoint method is

$$E_D = \frac{(Q_2 - Q_1) \div [(Q_1 + Q_2) \div 2]}{(P_2 - P_1) \div [(P_1 + P_2) \div 2]}$$

Plugging in the values from the question yields

$$E_D = \frac{(1480 - 1500) \div [(1500 + 1480) \div 2]}{(\$10 - \$8) \div [(\$8 + \$10) \div 2]}$$

Simplifying produces this equation:

$$E_D = \frac{-20 \div 1490}{\$2 \div \$9}$$

Therefore, $E_D = -0.06$.

Recall that an E_D near zero indicates that the price elasticity of demand is highly inelastic, which is what we suspected. The price increase does not cause consumption to fall very much. If the store manager was hoping to bring in a little extra revenue from the sales of amoxicillin, his plan is successful. Before the price increase, the business sold 1,500 units at $8, so total revenue was $12,000. After the price increase, sales decrease to 1,480 units, but the new price is $10, so total revenue is now $14,800. Raising the price of amoxicillin has helped the pharmacy make an additional $2,800 in total revenue.

Once we reach a price below unitary demand, we move into the realm of inelastic demand, shown in panel (c). When the price falls to $1, total revenue declines to $4. This result occurs because the price elasticity of demand is now relatively inelastic, or price insensitive. Even though the price is declining by $1, price is increasingly unimportant; as you can see by the blue square, lowering the price to $1 does not spur a large increase in consumption.

As we see in panel (c), at a price of $2, three units are sold and total revenue is $2 × 3 = $6. When the price falls to $1, four units are sold, so the total revenue is now $4 × 1 = $4. By lowering the price from $2 to $1, the business has lost $2 in extra revenue because it does not generate enough extra revenue from the lower price. Lowering the price from $2 to $1 causes a loss of $3 in existing sales revenue (the red boxes). At the same time, it generates only $1 in new sales (the blue box).

In this analysis, we see that once the demand curve enters the inelastic area, lowering the price decreases total revenue. This outcome is unambiguously bad for a business. The lower price brings in less revenue and requires the business to produce more goods. Because making goods is costly, it does not make sense to lower prices into the region where revenues decline. We can be sure that no business will intentionally operate in the inelastic region of the demand curve.

Price Elasticity of Demand

Determining the price elasticity of demand for a product or service involves calculating the responsiveness of quantity demanded to a change in the price. The chart below gives the actual price elasticity of demand for ten common products and services. Remember, the number is always negative because of the negative relationship between price and the quantity demanded. Why is price elasticity of demand important? It reveals consumer behavior and allows for better pricing strategies by businesses.

INELASTIC

Business travel ✈ −.1

Medical care −.17

Coffee −.25

Tobacco products −.45

Movies −.9

−1

−1.1 Private education

−1.6 Restaurant meals

−2.4

Leisure travel ✈

−3.7

−4 Fresh vegetables

Honda automobiles

ELASTIC

There are two very different elasticity values for airline travel. The relatively inelastic type of travel includes business travel and travel for an emergency, and the relatively elastic type is travel for pleasure.

An inelastic product or service is not highly responsive to a price change and has an elasticity value between 0 and -1. Between the inelastic and elastic regions, demand is unitary and equal to -1. A relatively elastic product or service is highly responsive to a price change and has an elasticity value less than -1.

REVIEW QUESTIONS

- Why is demand for coffee relatively inelastic?

- For business owners, why is it important to understand whether demand for their products is elastic or inelastic?

How Do Changes in Income and the Prices of Other Goods Affect Elasticity?

We have seen how consumer demand responds to changes in the price of a single good. In this section, we examine how responsive demand is to changes in income and to price changes in other goods.

Income Elasticity

The **income elasticity of demand** measures how a change in income affects spending.

Changes in personal income can have a large effect on consumer spending. After all, the money in your pocket influences not only how much you buy, but also the types of purchases you make. A consumer who is low on money may opt to buy a cheap generic product, while someone with a little extra cash can afford to upgrade. The grocery store aisle reflects different shoppers' budgets. Store brands and name products compete for shelf space. Lower-income shoppers can choose the store brand to save money, while more affluent shoppers can choose their favorite brand-name product without worrying about the purchase price. The **income elasticity of demand** (E_I) measures how a change in income affects spending. It is calculated by dividing the change in the quantity demanded by the change in personal income:

(Equation 4.3)

$$E_I = \frac{\text{percentage change in the quantity demanded}}{\text{percentage change in income}}$$

Unlike the price elasticity of demand, which is negative, the income elasticity of demand can be positive or negative. When a higher level of income enables the consumer to purchase more, the goods that are purchased are *normal goods*, a term we learned in Chapter 3. Because the demand for normal goods goes up with income, they have a positive income elasticity; a rise in income causes a rise in the quantity demanded. For instance, if you receive a 20% pay raise and you decide to pay an extra 10% on your cable TV bill to add HBO, the resulting income elasticity is positive, because 10% divided by 20% is 0.5. Whenever a good is normal, the result is a positive income elasticity of demand, and purchases of the good rise as income expands and purchases of the good fall as income falls.

Normal goods fall into two categories: *necessities* and *luxuries*. Goods that people consider necessities generally have income elasticities between 0 and 1. For example, expenditures on items such as clothing, electricity, and gasoline are unavoidable, and consumers at any income level must buy them no matter what. Although purchases of necessities will increase as income rises, they do not rise as fast as the increase in income does. Therefore, as income increases, spending on necessities will expand at a slower rate than the increase in income.

Rising income enables consumers to enjoy significantly more luxuries, producing an income elasticity of demand greater than 1 for luxuries. For instance, a family of modest

Clothing purchases expand with income.

means may travel almost exclusively by car. However, as the family's income rises, they can afford air travel. A relatively small jump in income can cause the family to fly instead of drive.

In Chapter 3, we saw that *inferior goods* are those that people will choose not to purchase when their income goes up. Inferior goods have a negative income elasticity, because as income expands, the demand for these goods declines. We see this effect in Table 4.4 with the example of macaroni and cheese, an inexpensive meal. As a household's income rises, it is able to afford healthier food and more variety in its meals. Consequently, the number of times that mac and cheese is purchased declines. The decline in consumption indicates that mac and cheese is an inferior good, as reflected in the negative sign of the income elasticity.

Air travel is a luxury good.

Cross-Price Elasticity

Now we will look at how a price change in one good can affect the demand for a related good. For instance, if you enjoy pizza, the choice between ordering from Domino's or Pizza Hut is influenced by the price of both goods. The **cross-price elasticity of demand** (E_C) measures the responsiveness of the quantity demanded of one good to a change in the price of a related good:

The **cross-price elasticity of demand** measures the responsiveness of the quantity demanded of one good to a change in the price of a related good.

$$E_C = \frac{\text{percentage change in the quantity demanded of one good}}{\text{percentage change in the price of a related good}}$$

(Equation 4.4)

Consider how two goods are related. If the goods are substitutes, a price rise in one good will cause the quantity demanded of that good to decline. At the same time, because consumers can purchase the substitute good for the same price as before, demand for the substitute good will increase. When the price of Domino's pizza rises, consumers will buy more pizza from Pizza Hut.

TABLE 4.4

Income Elasticity

Type of good	Subcategory	E_I coefficient	Example	
Inferior		$E_I < 0$	Macaroni and cheese	
Normal	Necessity	$0 < E_I < 1$	Milk	
Normal	Luxury	$E_I > 1$	Diamond ring	

TABLE 4.5

Cross-Price Elasticity

Type of good	E_C coefficient	Example	
Substitutes	$E_C > 0$	Pizza Hut and Domino's	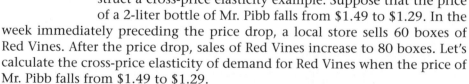
No relationship	$E_C = 0$	A basketball and bedroom slippers	
Complements	$E_C < 0$	Turkey and gravy	

The opposite is true if the goods are complements. In that case, a price increase in one good will make the joint consumption of both goods more expensive. Therefore, the consumption of both goods will decline. For example, a price increase for turkeys will cause the quantity demanded of both turkey and gravy to decline, and a price decrease for turkeys will cause the quantity demanded of both turkey and gravy to increase. This means that the cross-price elasticity of demand is negative.

What if there is no relationship between two goods? For example, if the price of basketballs goes up, that price increase probably will not affect the quantity demanded of bedroom slippers. In this case, the cross-price elasticity is neither positive nor negative; it is zero. Table 4.5 lists cross-price elasticity values according to type of good.

Have you tried Mr. Pibb and Red Vines together?

To learn how to calculate cross-price elasticity, let's consider an example from the skit "Lazy Sunday" on *Saturday Night Live*. The skit features Chris Parnell and Andy Samberg rapping about going to see *The Chronicles of Narnia* and eating cupcakes. In one inspired scene, they describe enjoying the soft drink Mr. Pibb with Red Vines candy and call the combination "crazy delicious." From this scenario, we can construct a cross-price elasticity example. Suppose that the price of a 2-liter bottle of Mr. Pibb falls from $1.49 to $1.29. In the week immediately preceding the price drop, a local store sells 60 boxes of Red Vines. After the price drop, sales of Red Vines increase to 80 boxes. Let's calculate the cross-price elasticity of demand for Red Vines when the price of Mr. Pibb falls from $1.49 to $1.29.

The cross-price elasticity of demand using the midpoint method is

$$E_C = \frac{(Q_{RV2} - Q_{RV1}) \div [(Q_{RV1} + Q_{RV2}) \div 2]}{(P_{MP2} - P_{MP1}) \div [(P_{MP1} + P_{MP2}) \div 2]}$$

Notice that there are now additional subscripts to denote that we are measuring the percentage change in the quantity demanded of good RV (Red Vines) in response to the percentage change in the price of good MP (Mr. Pibb).

Plugging in the values from the example yields

$$E_C = \frac{(80 - 60) \div [(60 + 80) \div 2]}{(\$1.29 - \$1.49) \div [(\$1.49 + \$1.29) \div 2]}$$

Simplifying produces

$$E_C = \frac{20 \div 70}{-\$0.20 \div \$1.39}$$

Solving for E_C gives us a value of -1.99. The result's negative value confirms our intuition that two goods that go well together ("crazy delicious") are complements, since the decrease in the price of Mr. Pibb causes consumers to buy more Red Vines.

ECONOMICS IN THE REAL WORLD

Tennis, Anyone?

Are you a casual tennis player or passionate about your game? The answer to that question helps us understand a real-life elasticity experiment.

In 2011, the New York City Parks Department doubled the prices paid by tennis players between the ages of 18 and 61. Single-pay passes for an hour of court time jumped from $7 to $15, while season passes rose from $100 to $200.

Far fewer tennis permits were sold under the new prices, according to data from the Parks Department. Sales of season passes for most players slipped by 40%, with 7,400 sold in 2011 as compared to 12,400 in 2010. Sales of one-day passes took a big hit as well, dropping by nearly a third from more than 40,000 for the 2010 season to 27,000.

How much would you be willing to pay for court time?

As good economists we can use the given data to help us understand whether the city's price increase raised or lowered total revenue.

Type of pass	Price in 2010	Price in 2011	Passes sold in 2010	Passes sold in 2011	Total revenue in 2010 (in millions)	Total revenue in 2011 (in millions)	E_D
One-day	$7	$15	40,000	27,000	$0.28	$0.41	−0.53
Annual	$100	$200	12,400	7,400	$1.24	$1.48	−0.75
Total					**$1.52**	**$1.89**	

We calculated the price elasticity of demand, E_D, using the midpoint formula. Because the coefficients for the one-day and annual passes are between 0 and −1, we know that demand is relatively inelastic at these prices. We also know that when demand is inelastic and prices increase, total revenue should increase, and that is exactly what happened. Tennis court revenues increased from $1.52 million in 2010 to $1.89 million in 2011.

As you might guess, many tennis players in New York City were quite upset with the sudden price increase. However, the data show that many tennis players decided to keep playing rather than quit. This result shouldn't surprise you too much. Tennis is good exercise, a social experience, and a hobby that many people enjoy. While the price increases were dramatic on a percentage basis (they doubled!), the increase in price is a relatively small part of most New Yorkers' budgets. Because there are not many good substitutes for tennis available in New York City, we'd expect many to continue playing, as the data confirmed. ✳

Sources: Author's calculations. Data from Matt McCue, "Tennis Fees Ace Out Many," *Wall Street Journal*, August 5, 2012. http://www.wsj.com/articles/SB10000872396390443687504577564933033308176

PRACTICE WHAT YOU KNOW

Income Elasticity

Question: A college student eats ramen noodles twice a week and earns $300 a week working part-time. After graduating, the student earns $1,000 a week and eats ramen noodles once every other week , or 0.5 time a week. What is the student's income elasticity?

Yummy, or all you can afford?

Answer: The income elasticity of demand using the midpoint method is

$$E_I = \frac{(Q_2 - Q_1) \div [(Q_1 + Q_2) \div 2]}{(I_2 - I_1) \div [(I_1 + I_2) \div 2]}$$

Plugging in the values from the question yields

$$E_I = \frac{(0.5 - 2.0) \div [(2.0 + 0.5) \div 2]}{(\$1000 - \$300) \div [(\$300 + \$1000) \div 2]}$$

Simplifying yields

$$E_I = \frac{-1.5 \div 1.25}{\$700 \div \$650}$$

Therefore, $E_I = -1.1$.

The income elasticity of demand is positive for normal goods and negative for inferior goods. Therefore, the negative coefficient indicates that ramen noodles are an inferior good over this person's range of income—in this example, between $300 and $1,000 per week. This result should confirm your intuition. The higher postgraduation income enables the student to substitute away from ramen noodles and toward other meals that provide more nourishment and enjoyment.

What Is the Price Elasticity of Supply?

Like consumers, sellers are sensitive to price changes. However, the determinants of the price elasticity of supply are substantially different from the determinants of the price elasticity of demand. The **price elasticity of supply** (sometimes called simply *elasticity of supply* or *supply elasticity*) is a measure of the responsiveness of the quantity supplied to a change in price.

In this section, we examine how much sellers respond to price changes. For instance, if the market price of gasoline increases, how will oil companies respond? The answer depends on the elasticity of supply. Oil must be refined into gasoline. If it is difficult for oil companies to increase their output of gasoline significantly, the quantity of gasoline supplied will not increase much even if the price increases a lot. In this case, we say that supply is inelastic, or unresponsive. However, if the price increase is small and suppliers respond by offering significantly more gasoline for sale, then supply is elastic. We would expect to observe this outcome if it is easy to refine oil into gasoline.

When supply is not able to respond to a change in price, we say it is inelastic. Think of an oceanfront property in Southern California. The amount of land next to the ocean is fixed. If the price of oceanfront property rises, the supply of land cannot adjust to the price increase. In this case, the supply is perfectly inelastic and the price elasticity of supply is zero. Recall that a price elasticity coefficient of zero means that quantity supplied does not change as price changes.

When the supplier's ability to make quick adjustments is limited, the elasticity of supply is less than 1. For instance, when a cellular network becomes congested, it takes suppliers a long time to provide additional capacity. They have to build new cell towers, which requires the purchase of land and additional construction costs. In contrast, a local hot dog vendor can easily add another cart in relatively short order. As a result, for the hot dog vendor, supply is elastic, with an elasticity coefficient that is greater than 1.

What would it take to own a slice of paradise?

Table 4.6 examines the price elasticity of supply (E_S). Recall the law of supply, which states that there is a direct relationship between the price of a good and the quantity that a firm supplies. As a result, the percentage change in the quantity supplied and the percentage change in price move in the same direction. The E_S coefficient reflects this direct relationship with a positive sign.

> The **price elasticity of supply** (sometimes called *elasticity of supply* or *supply elasticity*) is a measure of the responsiveness of the quantity supplied to a change in price.

Determinants of the Price Elasticity of Supply

When we examined the determinants of the price elasticity of demand, we saw that consumers have to consider the number of substitutes, how expensive the item is compared to their overall budget, whether the good is a necessity or a luxury, and the amount of time they have to make a decision. Time and the adjustment process are also key elements in determining the price

TABLE 4.6			
A Closer Look at the Price Elasticity of Supply			
Elasticity	E_S coefficient		Example
Perfectly inelastic	$E_S = 0$	Oceanfront land	
Relatively inelastic	$0 < E_S < 1$	Cell phone tower	
Relatively elastic	$E_S > 1$	Hot dog vendor	

elasticity of supply. However, there is a critical difference: the degree of flexibility that producers have in bringing their product to the market quickly.

The Flexibility of Producers

When a producer can quickly ramp up output, supply tends to be elastic. One way to maintain flexibility is to have spare production capacity. Extra capacity enables producers to quickly meet changing price conditions, so supply is more responsive, or elastic. The ability to store the good is another way to stay flexible. Producers who have stockpiles of their products can respond more quickly to changes in market conditions. For example, De Beers, the international diamond conglomerate, stores millions of uncut diamonds. As the price of diamonds fluctuates, De Beers can quickly change the quantity of diamonds it offers to the market. Likewise, hot dog vendors can relocate quickly from one street corner to another or add carts if demand is strong. However, many businesses cannot adapt to changing market conditions quickly. For instance, a golf course cannot easily add nine new holes to meet additional demand. This constraint limits the golf course owner's ability to adjust quickly, preventing the owner from quickly increasing the supply of golfing opportunities as soon as the fee changes.

Time and the Adjustment Process

In the immediate run, businesses are stuck with what they have on hand. For example, a pastry shop that runs out of chocolate glazed doughnuts cannot bake more instantly. As we move from the immediate run to the short run and a price change persists through time, supply—just like demand—becomes more elastic. For instance, a golf resort may be able to squeeze extra production out of its current facility by staying open longer hours or moving tee times closer together, but those short-run efforts will not match the production potential of adding another golf course in the long run.

Figure 4.5 shows how the two determinants of supply elasticity are mapped onto the supply curve. In the immediate run, the supply curve is vertical (S_1). A vertical curve tells us that there is no responsiveness when the price changes. As producers gain additional time to make adjustments, the supply curve rotates from S_1 (the immediate run) to S_2 (the short run) to S_3 (the long run). Like the demand curve, the supply curve becomes flatter through time. The only difference is that the supply curve rotates clockwise; in contrast, as we saw in Figure 4.2, the demand curve rotates counterclockwise. With both supply and demand, the most important thing to remember is that more time allows for greater adjustment, so the long run is always more elastic.

Calculating the Price Elasticity of Supply

We can use a simple formula to calculate the price elasticity of supply. Doing so is useful when a business owner must decide how much to produce at various prices. The elasticity of supply measures how quickly the producer is able to change production in response to changes in price. When supply is elastic, producers are able to quickly adjust production. If supply is inelastic, production tends to remain roughly constant, despite large swings in price.

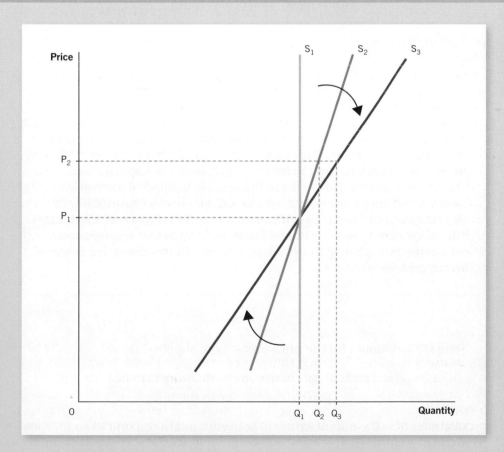

FIGURE 4.5

Elasticity and the Supply Curve

Increased flexibility and more time make supply more elastic. When price rises from P_1 to P_2, producers are unable to expand output immediately and the supply curve remains at Q_1 in the immediate run. In the short run (S_2), the firm becomes more flexible and output expands to Q_2. Eventually, in the long run (S_3), the firm is able to produce even more, and it moves to Q_3 in response to higher prices.

PRACTICE WHAT YOU KNOW

The Price Elasticity of Supply

Question: Suppose that the price of a barrel of oil increases from $50 to $100. The new output is 2 million barrels a day, and the old output is 1.8 million barrels a day. What is the price elasticity of supply?

Answer: The price elasticity of supply using the midpoint method is

$$E_S = \frac{(Q_2 - Q_1) \div [(Q_1 + Q_2) \div 2]}{(P_2 - P_1) \div [(P_1 + P_2) \div 2]}$$

Plugging in the values from the example yields

$$E_S = \frac{(2.0M - 1.8M) \div [(1.8M + 2.0M) \div 2]}{(\$100 - \$50) \div [(\$50 + \$100) \div 2]}$$

Simplifying yields

$$E_S = \frac{0.2M \div 1.9M}{\$50 \div \$75}$$

Oil companies cannot quickly respond to rising prices.

Therefore, $E_S = 0.16$.

Recall that the law of supply specifies a direct relationship between the price and the quantity supplied. Because E_S in this case is positive, we see that output rises as price rises. However, the magnitude of the output increase is quite small, as reflected in the coefficient 0.16. Because oil companies cannot easily change their production process, they have a limited ability to respond quickly to rising prices. That inability is reflected in a coefficient that is relatively close to zero. A zero coefficient would mean that suppliers could not change their output at all. Here suppliers are able to respond, but only in a limited capacity.

Here is the formula for the price elasticity of supply (E_S):

(Equation 4.5) $$E_S = \frac{\text{percentage change in the quantity supplied}}{\text{percentage change in the price}}$$

Consider how the manufacturer of Solo cups might respond to an increase in demand that causes the cups' market price to rise. The company's ability to change the amount it produces depends on the flexibility of the manufacturing process and the length of time needed to ramp up production. Suppose that the price of the cups rises by 10%. The company can increase its production by 5% immediately, but it will take many months to expand production by 20%. What can we say about the price elasticity of supply in this case? Using Equation 4.5, we can take the percentage change in the quantity supplied immediately (5%) and divide that by the percentage change in price (10%). This calculation gives us $E_S = 0.5$, which signals that supply is relatively inelastic. However, with time the firm is able to increase the quantity supplied by 20%. If we divide 20% by the percentage change in the price (10%), we get $E_S = 2.0$, which indicates that supply is relatively elastic in the long run.

How would the manufacturer of Solo cups respond to a price increase in the short run and in the long run?

How Do the Price Elasticities of Demand and Supply Relate to Each Other?

The interplay between the price elasticity of supply and the price elasticity of demand allows us to explain more fully how the economy operates. With an understanding of elasticity at our disposal, we can conduct a much richer and deeper analysis of the world around us.

For instance, suppose that we are concerned about what will happen to the price of oil as economic development spurs additional demand in China and India. An examination of the determinants of the price elasticity of supply quickly confirms that oil producers have a limited ability to adjust production in response to rising prices. Oil wells can be uncapped to meet rising demand, but it takes years to bring the new capacity online. Moreover, storing oil reserves, while possible, is expensive. Therefore, the short-run supply of oil is quite inelastic. Figure 4.6 shows the combination of inelastic supply-side production constraints in the short run and the inelastic short-run demand for oil (D_1).

An increase in global demand from D_1 to D_2 will create significantly higher prices (from \$50 to \$90 per barrel) in the short run. This result occurs because increasing oil production is difficult in the short run. Therefore, the short-run supply curve (S_{SR}) is relatively inelastic. In the long run, though, oil producers are able to bring more oil to the market when prices are higher, so the supply curve rotates clockwise (to S_{LR}), becoming more elastic, and the market price falls to \$80 per barrel (point E_3). (Note that we are using an arbitrary price for a barrel of oil. The price of oil has swung widely over the last decade, making it difficult to predict.)

What does this example tell us? It reminds us that the interplay between the price elasticity of demand and the price elasticity of supply determines the magnitude of the resulting price change. We cannot observe demand in isolation without also considering how supply responds. Similarly, we cannot simply think about the short-run consequences of demand and supply shifts; we also must consider how prices and quantity will vary in the long run. Armed with this knowledge, you can begin to see the power of the supply and demand model to explain the world around us.

FIGURE 4.6

A Demand Shift and the Consequences for Short- and Long-Run Supply

When an increase in demand causes the price of oil to rise from $50 to $90 per barrel, initially producers are unable to expand output very much—production expands from Q_1 to Q_2. However, in the long run, as producers expand their production capacity, the price will fall to $80 per barrel.

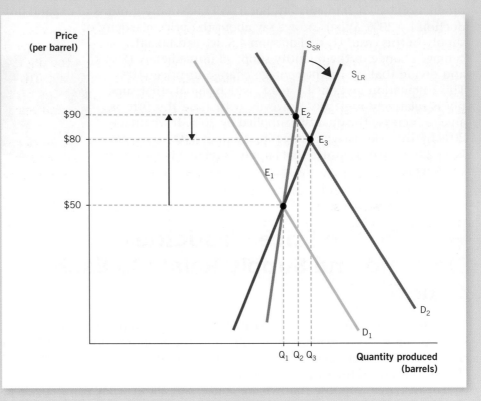

PRACTICE WHAT YOU KNOW

Elasticity: Trick or Treat Edition

Question: An unusually bad growing season leads to a small pumpkin crop. What will happen to the price of pumpkins as Halloween approaches? Use elasticity to explain your answer.

How much would you spend on a Halloween pumpkin?

Answer: The demand for pumpkins peaks in October and rapidly falls after Halloween. Purchasing a pumpkin is a short-run decision to buy a unique product that takes up a relatively small share of the consumer's budget. As a result, the price elasticity of demand for pumpkins leading up to Halloween tends to be quite inelastic. At the same time, a small crop causes the entire supply curve to shift left. As a result, the market price of pumpkins rises. Because the demand is relatively inelastic in the short run and the supply of pumpkins is fixed, we expect the price to rise significantly. After Halloween, the price of any remaining pumpkins falls, because demand declines dramatically.

Conclusion

Do sellers charge the highest price possible? We can now address this misconception definitively: no. Sellers like higher prices in the same way consumers like lower prices, but that does not mean that sellers will charge the highest price possible. At very high prices, consumer demand is quite elastic. Therefore, a seller who charges too high a price will not sell much. As a result, firms learn that they must lower their price to attract more customers and maximize their total revenue.

The ability to determine whether demand and supply are elastic or inelastic enables economists to calculate the effects of personal, business, and policy decisions. When you combine the concept of elasticity with the supply and demand model from Chapter 3, you get a very powerful tool. In subsequent chapters, we use elasticity to refine our models of economic behavior and make our results more realistic.

ECONOMICS FOR LIFE

Price Elasticity of Supply and Demand: Buying Your First Car

When you buy a car, your knowledge of price elasticity can help you negotiate the best possible deal.

Recall that three of the determinants of price elasticity of demand are (1) the share of the budget, (2) the number of available substitutes, and (3) the time you have to make a decision.

Let's start with your budget. You should have one in mind, but don't tell the salesperson what you are willing to spend; that is a vital piece of personal information you want to keep to yourself. If the salesperson suggests that you look at a model that is too expensive, just say that you are not interested. You might reply, "Buying a car is a stretch for me; I've got to stay within my budget." If the salesperson asks indirectly about your budget by inquiring whether you have a particular monthly payment in mind, reply that you want to negotiate over the invoice price once you decide on a vehicle. Never negotiate on the sticker price, which is the price you see in the car window, because it includes thousands of dollars in markup. You want to make it clear to the salesperson that the price you pay matters to you—that is, your demand is elastic.

Next, make it clear that you are gathering information and visiting other dealers. That is, reinforce that you have many available substitutes. Even if you really want a Honda, do not voice that desire to the Honda salesperson. Perhaps mention that you are also visiting the Toyota, Hyundai, and Ford showrooms. Compare what you've seen on one lot versus another. Each salesperson you meet should hear that you are seriously considering other options, which indicates to each dealership that your demand is elastic and that getting your business will require the dealership to offer you a better price.

Taking your time to decide is also important. Never buy a car the first time you walk onto a lot. If you convey the message that you want a car immediately, you are saying that your demand is inelastic. If the dealership thinks that you have no flexibility, the staff will not give you their best offer. Instead, tell the salesperson that you appreciate the help and that you will be deciding over the next few weeks. A good salesperson will know you are serious and will ask for your phone number or email address and contact you. The salesperson will sweeten the deal if you indicate you are narrowing down your choices and his or her dealership is in the running. You wait. You win.

Also know that salespeople and dealerships have times when they want to move inventory. August is an especially good month to purchase. The price elasticity of supply is at work here as well. A good time to buy is when the dealer is trying to move inventory to make room for new models, because prices fall for end-of-the-model-year closeouts. Likewise, many sales promotions and sales bonuses are tied to the end of the month, so salespeople will be more eager to sell at that time.

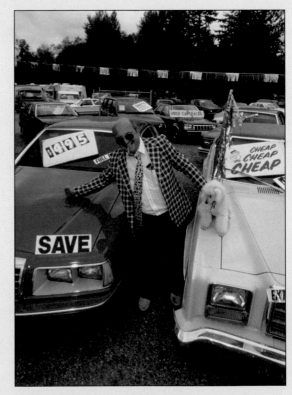

Watch out for shady negotiation practices!

ANSWERING THE BIG QUESTIONS

What is the price elasticity of demand, and what are its determinants?

✳ The price elasticity of demand is a measure of the responsiveness of quantity demanded to a change in price.

✳ Demand will generally be more elastic if there are many substitutes available, if the item accounts for a large share of the consumer's budget, if the item is a luxury good, if the market is more narrowly defined, or if the consumer has plenty of time to make a decision.

✳ Economists categorize time in three distinct periods: (1) the immediate run, when there is no time for consumers to adjust their behavior; (2) the short run, when consumers can adjust, but only partially; and (3) the long run, when consumers have time to fully adjust to market conditions.

✳ The price elasticity of demand is calculated by dividing the percentage change in the quantity demanded by the percentage change in price. A value of zero indicates that the quantity demanded does not respond to a price change; if the price elasticity is zero, demand is said to be perfectly inelastic. When the price elasticity of demand is between 0 and −1, demand is inelastic. If the price elasticity of demand is less than −1, demand is elastic. When price elasticity is exactly −1, the item has unitary elasticity.

How do changes in income and the prices of other goods affect elasticity?

✳ The income elasticity of demand measures how a change in income affects spending. Normal goods have a positive income elasticity. Inferior goods have a negative income elasticity.

✳ The cross-price elasticity of demand measures the responsiveness of the quantity demanded of one good to a change in the price of a related good. Positive values for the cross-price elasticity mean that the two goods are substitutes, while negative values indicate that the two goods are complements. If the cross-price elasticity is zero, then the two goods are not related to each other.

What is the price elasticity of supply?

✳ The price elasticity of supply is a measure of the responsiveness of the quantity supplied to a change in price. Supply will generally be more elastic if producers have flexibility in the production process and ample time to adjust production.

✳ The price elasticity of supply is calculated by dividing the percentage change in the quantity supplied by the percentage change in price. A value of zero indicates that the quantity supplied does not respond to a price change; if the price elasticity of supply is zero, supply is said to be perfectly inelastic. When the price elasticity of supply is between 0 and 1, demand is relatively inelastic. If the price elasticity of supply is greater than 1, supply is elastic.

How do the price elasticities of demand and supply relate to each other?

✳ The interplay between the price elasticity of demand and the price elasticity of supply determines the magnitude of the resulting price change.

CONCEPTS YOU SHOULD KNOW

cross-price elasticity of demand (p. 133)

elasticity (p. 112)

immediate run (p. 115)

income elasticity of demand (p. 132)

long run (p. 115)

price elasticity of demand (p. 113)

price elasticity of supply (p. 137)

short run (p. 115)

total revenue (p. 126)

QUESTIONS FOR REVIEW

1. Define the price elasticity of demand.

2. What are the four determinants of the price elasticity of demand?

3. Give an example of a good that has elastic demand. What is the value of the price elasticity if demand is elastic? Give an example of a good that has inelastic demand. What is the value of the price elasticity if demand is inelastic?

4. What is the connection between total revenue and the price elasticity of demand? Illustrate this relationship along a demand curve.

5. Explain why slope is different from elasticity.

6. Define the price elasticity of supply.

7. What are the two determinants of the price elasticity of supply?

8. Give an example of a good that has elastic supply. What is the value of the price elasticity if supply is elastic? Give an example of a good that has an inelastic supply. What is the value of the price elasticity if supply is inelastic?

9. Give an example of a normal good. What is the income elasticity of a normal good? Give an example of a luxury good. What is the income elasticity of a luxury good? Give an example of a necessity. What is the income elasticity of a necessity? Give an example of an inferior good. What is the income elasticity of an inferior good?

10. Define the cross-price elasticity of demand. Give an example of a good with negative cross-price elasticity, another with zero cross-price elasticity, and a third with positive cross-price elasticity.

STUDY PROBLEMS (∗solved at the end of the section)

∗ 1. If the government decided to impose a 50% tax on gray T-shirts, would this policy generate a large increase in tax revenues or a small increase? Use elasticity to explain your answer.

∗ 2. College logo T-shirts priced at $15 sell at a rate of 25 per week, but when the bookstore marks them down to $10, it finds that it can sell 50 T-shirts per week. What is the price elasticity of demand for the logo T-shirts?

3. Black Friday, the day after Thanksgiving, is the largest shopping day of the year. Do the early shoppers, who often wait in line for hours in the cold to get doorbuster sale items, have elastic or inelastic demand? Explain your response.

4. If a 20% increase in price causes a 10% drop in the quantity demanded, is the price elasticity of demand for this good elastic, unitary, or inelastic?

5. Characterize the demand for each of the following goods or services as perfectly elastic, relatively elastic, relatively inelastic, or perfectly inelastic.
   a. a lifesaving medication
   b. photocopies at a copy shop, when all competing shops charge 10 cents per copy
   c. a fast-food restaurant located in the food court of a shopping mall
   d. the water you buy from your local utility company

6. A local paintball business receives a total revenue of $8,000 a month when it charges $10 per person and $9,600 in total revenue when it charges $6 per person. Over that range of prices, does the business face elastic, unitary, or inelastic demand?

7. At a price of $200, a cell phone company manufactures 300,000 phones. At a price of $150, the company produces 200,000 phones. What is the price elasticity of supply?

8. Do customers who visit convenience stores at 3 a.m. have a price elasticity of demand that is more elastic or less elastic than those who visit at 3 p.m.?

✳ 9. A worker eats at a restaurant once a week. He then gets a 25% raise. As a result, he decides to eat out twice as much as before and cut back on the number of frozen lasagna dinners from one frozen dinner a week to one every other week. Determine the income elasticity of demand for eating at a restaurant and for having frozen lasagna dinners.

10. The cross-price elasticity of demand between American Eagle and Hollister is 2.0. What does that coefficient tell us about the relationship between these two stores?

11. A local golf course is considering lowering its fees in order to increase its total revenue. Under what conditions will the fee reduction achieve its goal?

12. A private university notices that in-state and out-of-state students seem to respond differently to tuition changes.

Tuition	Quantity demanded (in-state applicants)	Quantity demanded (out-of-state applicants)
$10,000	6,000	12,000
15,000	5,000	9,000
20,000	4,000	6,000
30,000	3,000	3,000

As the price of tuition rises from $15,000 to $20,000, what is the price elasticity of demand for in-state applicants and also for out-of-state applicants?

13. The TV show *Extreme Couponing* features coupon users who go to extraordinary measures to save money on their weekly purchases. The show follows these coupon users throughout the week as they assemble coupons and scout out stores to see which have the best deals, and then follows them to the store for the big buy. Do extreme couponers have extremely elastic demand or extremely inelastic demand? Explain. (*Note:* If you are unfamiliar with the show, you can Google it and watch a segment.)

14. Suppose a hotel raises the price of the bottled water in the minibar in each room from $3 to $5. The hotel tracks the number of customers who buy the bottled water and finds that consumption drops from 1,000 bottles a week to 900 bottles. Is demand elastic or inelastic? Explain.

SOLVED PROBLEMS

1. To answer this question, we need to consider the price elasticity of demand. The tax is only on gray T-shirts. This means that T-shirt customers who buy other colors can avoid the tax entirely—which means that the demand for gray T-shirts is relatively elastic. Not many gray T-shirts will be sold, so the government will generate only a small increase in revenues from the tax.

2. Plugging into the formula for E_D gives us

$$E_D = \frac{(50 - 25) \div [(25 + 50) \div 2]}{(10 - 15) \div [(15 + 10) \div 2]} = -1.67$$

9. In this question a worker gets a 25% (or 0.25) raise, so we can use this information in the denominator when determining the income elasticity of demand. We are not given the percentage change for the meals out, so we need to plug in how often the worker ate out before (once a week) and the amount he eats out after the raise (twice a week) into the numerator.

Plugging into E_I gives us

$$E_I = \frac{(2 - 1) \div [(1 + 2) \div 2]}{0.25}$$

Simplifying yields

$$E_I = \frac{1 \div 1.5}{0.25}$$

Therefore, $E_I = 2.67$

The income elasticity of demand for eating at a restaurant is positive for normal goods. Therefore, eating at a restaurant is a normal good. This result should confirm your intuition.

Let's see what happens with frozen lasagna once the worker gets the 25% raise. Now he cuts back on the number of lasagna dinners from once a week to once every other week. This information is plugged into the numerator, while the 25% change in income, or 0.25, is plugged into the denominator.

Plugging into E_I gives us

$$E_I = \frac{(0.5 - 1) \div [(1 + 0.5) \div 2]}{0.25}$$

Simplifying yields

$$E_I = \frac{-0.5 \div 0.75}{0.25}$$

Therefore, $E_I = -2.67$.

The income elasticity of demand for having frozen lasagna is negative. Therefore, frozen lasagna is an inferior good. This result should confirm your intuition.

Market Outcomes and Tax Incidence

Taxes on firms do not affect consumers.

Many people believe that when the government taxes businesses, consumers catch a break because firms pay the tax. If only life worked that

 way! As this chapter explains, who actually pays the tax often is quite different from the party that is legally responsible for making the tax payment.

Gasoline prices are a common and visible sign of the market at work. It is hard not to notice when gasoline prices rise or fall because every gas station posts its prices prominently. But there are a few things you might not know. First, gasoline taxes vary significantly from state to state, and they vary wildly from country to country. In many places, taxes add a significant amount to the price. For example, the price of gasoline throughout Europe is often double that in the United States, largely because of much higher gasoline taxes. At the same time, the governments of certain oil-rich countries, such as Venezuela and Saudi Arabia, subsidize gasoline so that their citizens pay less than the market price. In countries where gasoline is subsidized, consumers drive their cars everywhere, mass transportation is largely unavailable, and there is less concern for fuel efficiency. As you might imagine, the opposite is true in countries with high gasoline taxes, where consumers drive less, use public transportation more often, and tend to purchase fuel-efficient vehicles.

What do gasoline taxes and subsidies around the world have in common? They are all folded into the price you see at the pump, which might lead you to believe that the seller is paying all of the tax or receiving the entire subsidy. Nothing could be further from the truth. The firm

In states with high gasoline taxes, approximately $20 of every fill-up is for taxes.

will try to pass along the tax to consumers in the form of higher prices. Likewise, in countries with subsidies, the firm must pass along lower prices to consumers. After reading this chapter, you will understand how this process works.

We begin this chapter by discussing consumer and producer surplus, two concepts that illustrate gains from trade. These concepts help us measure the efficiency of markets and the effects of taxation. Then we examine how taxation creates distortions in economic behavior by altering the incentives that people and firms face when consuming and producing goods that are taxed.

BIG QUESTIONS

* What are consumer surplus and producer surplus?
* When is a market efficient?
* Why do taxes create deadweight loss in otherwise efficient markets?

What Are Consumer Surplus and Producer Surplus?

Welfare economics is the branch of economics that studies how the allocation of resources affects economic well-being.

Trade
creates
value

Markets create value by bringing together buyers and sellers so that consumers and producers can mutually benefit from trade. **Welfare economics** is the branch of economics that studies how the allocation of resources affects economic well-being. In this section, we develop two concepts that help us measure the value that markets create: *consumer surplus* and *producer surplus*.

In competitive markets, the equilibrium price is simultaneously low enough to attract consumers and high enough to encourage producers. This balance between demand and supply enhances the *welfare* (well-being) of society. That is not to say that society's welfare depends solely on markets. People also find satisfaction in many nonmarket settings, including spending time with their families and friends and doing hobbies and charity work. We incorporate aspects of personal satisfaction into our economic model in Chapter 16. For now, let's focus on how markets enhance human welfare.

Consumer Surplus

Consider three students: Frank, Beanie, and Mitch (you may recognize these names from the movie *Old School*). Like students everywhere, each one has a maximum price he is willing to pay for a new economics textbook. Beanie owns a successful business, so for him the cost of a new textbook does not present a financial hardship. Mitch is a business major who really wants to do well in economics. Frank is not serious about his studies. Table 5.1 shows the value that each student places on the textbook. This value, called the **willingness to pay**, is the maximum price a consumer will pay for a good or service. The willingness to pay is also known as the *reservation price*. In an auction or a negotiation, the willingness to pay, or reservation price, is the price beyond which the consumer decides to walk away from the transaction.

How much will they pay for an economics textbook?

Consider what happens when the price of the book is $151. If Beanie purchases the book at $151, he pays $49 less than the $200 maximum he was willing to pay. He values the textbook at $49 more than the purchase price, so buying the book makes him better off.

Consumer surplus is the difference between the willingness to pay for a good (or service) and the price that is paid to get it. While Beanie gains $49 in consumer surplus, a price of $151 is more than either Mitch or Frank is willing to pay. Because Mitch is willing to pay only $150, if he purchases the book he will experience a consumer loss of $1. Frank's willingness to pay is $100, so if he buys the book for $151 he will experience a consumer loss of $51. Whenever the price is greater than the willingness to pay, a rational consumer will decide not to buy.

Willingness to pay is the maximum price a consumer will pay for a good or service. Also known as the *reservation price*.

Consumer surplus is the difference between the willingness to pay for a good (or service) and the price that is paid to get it.

Using Demand Curves to Illustrate Consumer Surplus

In the previous section, we discussed consumer surplus as a dollar amount. We can illustrate it graphically with a demand curve. Figure 5.1 shows the demand curve drawn from the data in Table 5.1. Notice that the curve looks

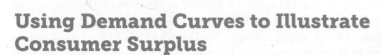

Buyer	Willingness to pay
Beanie	$200
Mitch	150
Frank	100

Willingness to Pay for a New Economics Textbook

FIGURE 5.1

Demand Curve for an Economics Textbook

The demand curve has a step for each additional textbook purchase. As the price goes down, more students buy the textbook.

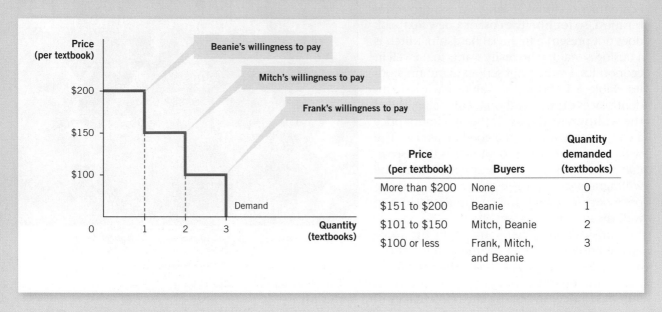

Price (per textbook)	Buyers	Quantity demanded (textbooks)
More than $200	None	0
$151 to $200	Beanie	1
$101 to $150	Mitch, Beanie	2
$100 or less	Frank, Mitch, and Beanie	3

like a staircase with three steps—one for each additional textbook purchase. Each point on a market demand curve corresponds to a specific number of units sold.

At any price above $200, none of the students wants to purchase a textbook. This relationship is evident on the *x* axis where the quantity demanded is 0. At any price between $151 and $200, Beanie is the only buyer, so the quantity demanded is 1. At prices between $101 and $150, Beanie and Mitch are both willing to buy the textbook, so the quantity demanded is 2. Finally, if the price is $100 or less, all three students are willing to buy the textbook, so the quantity demanded is 3. As the price falls, the quantity demanded increases.

We can measure the total extent of consumer surplus by examining the area under the demand curve for each of our three consumers, as shown in Figure 5.2. In panel (a), the price is $175, and only Beanie decides to buy. Because his willingness to pay is $200, he is better off by $25, which is his consumer surplus. The light blue area under the demand curve and above the price represents the benefit Beanie receives from purchasing a textbook at a price of $175. When the price drops to $125, as shown in panel (b), Mitch also decides to buy a textbook. Now the total quantity demanded is 2. Mitch's willingness to pay is $150, so his consumer surplus, represented by the darker blue area, is $25. However, since Beanie's willingness to pay is $200, his consumer surplus rises from $25 to $75. So a textbook price of $125 raises the

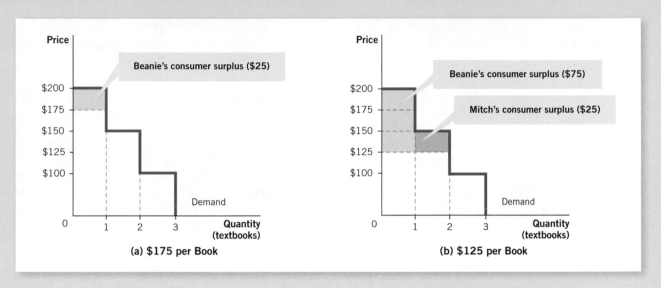

FIGURE 5.2

Determining Consumer Surplus from a Demand Curve

(a) At a price of $175, Beanie is the only buyer, so the quantity demanded is 1. (b) At a price of $125, Beanie and Mitch are both willing to buy the textbook, so the quantity demanded is 2.

total consumer surplus to $75 + $25 = $100. In other words, lower prices create more consumer surplus in this market—and in any other.

Producer Surplus

Sellers also benefit from market transactions. In this section, our three students discover that they are good at economics and decide to go into the tutoring business. They do not want to provide this service for free, but each has a different minimum price. The **willingness to sell** is the minimum price a seller will accept to sell a good or service. Table 5.2 shows each tutor's willingness to sell his services.

Consider what happens at a tutoring price of $25 per hour. Because Frank is willing to tutor for $10 per hour, every hour that he tutors at $25 per hour earns him $15 more than his willingness to sell. This extra $15 per hour is his producer surplus. **Producer surplus** is the difference between the willingness to sell a good or service and the price that the seller receives. Mitch is willing to tutor for $20 per hour and earns a $5 producer surplus for every hour he tutors at $25 per hour. Finally, Beanie's willingness to tutor, at $30 per hour, is more than the market price of $25. If he tutors, he will have a producer loss of $5 per hour.

How do producers determine their willingness to sell? They must consider two factors: the direct costs of producing the good and the indirect costs, or opportunity costs. Students who are new to economics often mistakenly

Willingness to sell is the minimum price a seller will accept to sell a good or service.

Producer surplus is the difference between the price that the seller receives and the price at which the seller is willing to sell the good or service.

TABLE 5.2

Willingness to Sell Tutoring Services

Seller	Willingness to sell
Beanie	$30/hr
Mitch	$20/hr
Frank	$10/hr

Opportunity cost

assume that the cost of producing an item is the only cost to consider in making the decision to produce. But producers also have opportunity costs. Beanie, Mitch, and Frank each has a unique willingness to sell because each has a different opportunity cost. Beanie owns his own business, so for him the time spent tutoring is time that he could have spent making money elsewhere. Mitch is a business student who might otherwise be studying to get better grades. Frank is neither a businessman nor a serious student, so the $10 he can earn in an hour of tutoring is not taking the place of other earning opportunities or studying more to get better grades.

Using Supply Curves to Illustrate Producer Surplus

Continuing our example, the supply curve in Figure 5.3 shows the relationship between the price for an hour of tutoring and the number of tutors who are willing to work. As you can see on the supply schedule (the table within the figure), at any price less than $10 per hour, no one wants to tutor. At prices between $10 and $19 per hour, Frank is the only tutor, so the quantity supplied is 1. Between $20 and $29 per hour, Frank and Mitch are willing to tutor, so the quantity supplied rises to 2. Finally, if the price is $30 or more, all three friends are willing to tutor, so the quantity supplied is 3. As the price they receive for tutoring rises, the number of tutors increases from 0 to 3.

What do these relationships between price and quantity supplied tell us about producer surplus? Let's turn to Figure 5.4. By examining the area above the supply curve, we can measure the extent of producer surplus. In panel (a), the price of an hour of tutoring is $15. At that price, only Frank decides to tutor. Since he would be willing to tutor even if the price were as low as $10 per hour, he is $5 per hour better off tutoring. Frank's producer surplus is represented by the light red area between the supply curve and the price of $15. Because Beanie and Mitch do not tutor when the price is $15 per hour, they do not receive any producer surplus. In panel (b), the price for tutoring is $25 per hour. At this price, Mitch also decides to tutor. His willingness to tutor is $20, so when the price is $25 per hour, his producer surplus is $5 per hour, represented by the darker red area. Since Frank's willingness to tutor is $10, at $25 per hour his producer surplus rises to $15 per hour. By looking at the shaded boxes in panel (b), we see that an increase in the rates for tutoring raises the combined producer surplus of Frank and Mitch to $15 + $5 = $20 per hour.

FIGURE 5.3

Supply Curve for Economics Tutoring

The supply curve has three steps, one for each additional student who is willing to tutor. Progressively higher prices will induce more students to become tutors.

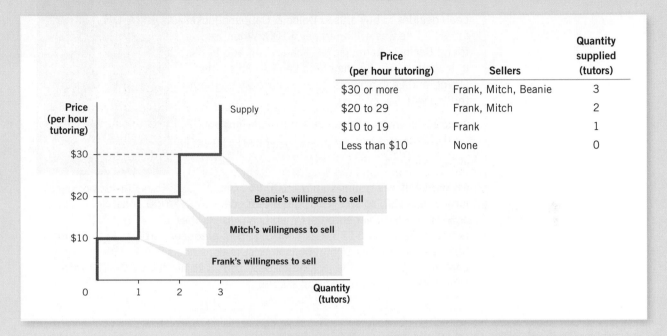

Price (per hour tutoring)	Sellers	Quantity supplied (tutors)
$30 or more	Frank, Mitch, Beanie	3
$20 to 29	Frank, Mitch	2
$10 to 19	Frank	1
Less than $10	None	0

FIGURE 5.4

Determining Producer Surplus from a Supply Curve

(a) The price of an hour of tutoring is $15. At this price, only Frank decides to tutor. (b) The price for tutoring is $25 per hour. At this price, Mitch also decides to tutor.

(a) $15 per Hour

(b) $25 per Hour

PRACTICE WHAT YOU KNOW

Consumer and Producer Surplus: Trendy Fashion

Leah decides to buy a used Dolce & Gabbana jacket for $80. She was willing to pay $100. When her friend Becky sees the jacket, she loves it and thinks it is worth $150. So she offers Leah $125 for the jacket, and Leah accepts. Leah and Becky are both thrilled with the exchange.

Question: Determine the total surplus from the original purchase and the additional surplus generated by the resale of the jacket.

Answer: Leah was willing to pay $100 and the jacket cost $80, so she keeps the difference, or $20, as consumer surplus. When Leah resells the

Rachel Bilson wearing a D&G jacket

jacket to Becky for $125, Leah earns $25 in producer surplus. At the same time, Becky receives $25 in consumer surplus, since she was willing to pay Leah up to $150 for the jacket but Leah sells it to her for $125. The resale generates an additional $50 in surplus.

When Is a Market Efficient?

We have seen how consumers benefit from lower prices and how producers benefit from higher prices. When we combine the concepts of consumer and producer surplus, we can build a complete picture of the welfare of buyers and sellers. Adding consumer and producer surplus gives us **total surplus**, also known as **social welfare**, because it measures the well-being of all participants in a market, absent any government intervention. Total surplus is the best way economists have to measure the benefits that markets create.

Figure 5.5 illustrates the relationship between consumer surplus and producer surplus for a slice of coconut cream pie. The demand curve shows that some customers are willing to pay more for a slice of pie than others. Likewise, some sellers (producers) are willing to sell pie for less than others.

Let's say that Russ is willing to pay $7.00 for a slice of pie, but when he gets to the store he finds it for $4.00. The difference between the price he is willing to pay, represented by point A, and the price he actually pays, represented by E (the equilibrium price), is $3.00 in consumer surplus, as indicated by the blue arrow showing the distance from $4.00 to $7.00. Russ's friend Audrey is willing to pay $5.00 for a slice of pie, but, like Russ, she finds it for $4.00. Therefore, she receives $1.00 in consumer surplus, as indicated by the blue arrow at point B showing the distance from $4.00 to $5.00. In

Total surplus, also known as **social welfare**, is the sum of consumer surplus and producer surplus. It measures the well-being of all participants in a market, absent any government intervention.

FIGURE 5.5

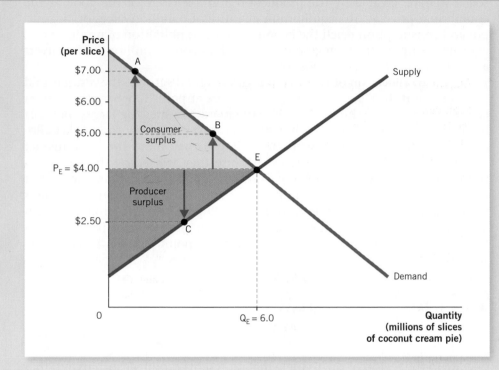

Consumer and Producer Surplus for Coconut Cream Pie

Consumer surplus is the difference between the willingness to pay along the demand curve and the equilibrium price, P_E. It is illustrated by the blue triangle. Producer surplus is the difference between the willingness to produce along the supply curve and the equilibrium price. It is illustrated by the red triangle.

fact, all consumers who are willing to pay more than $4.00 are better off when they purchase the slice of pie at $4.00. We can show this total area of consumer surplus on the graph as the blue triangle bordered by the demand curve, the y axis, and the equilibrium price (P_E). At every point in this area, consumers who are willing to pay more than the equilibrium price for pie are better off.

Trade creates value

Continuing with Figure 5.5, to identify producer surplus we follow a similar process. Suppose that Ellen's Bakery is willing to sell coconut pie for $2.50 per slice, represented by point C. Because the equilibrium price is $4.00, the business makes $1.50 per slice in producer surplus, as indicated by the red arrow at point C showing the distance from $4.00 to $2.50. If we think of the supply curve as representing the costs of many different sellers, we can calculate the total producer surplus as the red triangle bordered by the supply curve, the y axis, and the equilibrium price. The blue triangle (consumer surplus) and the red triangle (producer surplus) describe the increase in total surplus, or

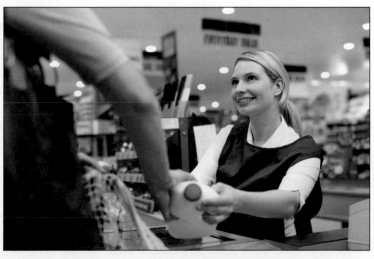

The buyer and seller each benefit from this exchange.

social welfare, created by the production and exchange of the good at the equilibrium price. At the equilibrium quantity of 6 million slices of pie, output and consumption reach the largest possible combination of producer and consumer surplus. In the region of the graph beyond 6 million units, buyers and sellers will experience a loss of surplus.

An outcome is **efficient** when an allocation of resources maximizes total surplus.

When an allocation of resources maximizes total surplus, the result is said to be **efficient**. In Figure 5.5, efficiency occurs at point E, where the market is in equilibrium. To think about why the market creates the largest possible total surplus, or social welfare, it is important to recall how the market allocates resources. Consumers who are willing to pay more than the market equilibrium price will buy the good because they will enjoy the consumer surplus. Producers who are willing to sell the good for less than the market equilibrium price will enjoy the producer surplus. In addition, consumers with a low willingness to buy (less than $4.00 per slice) and producers with a high willingness to sell (more than $4.00 per slice) do not participate in the market. Therefore, the equilibrium output at point E maximizes the total surplus and is also an efficient allocation of resources.

The Efficiency-Equity Debate

When modeling behavior, economists assume that participants in a market are rational decision-makers. That is, we assume that producers will always operate in the region of the triangle that represents producer surplus and that consumers will always operate in the region of the triangle that represents consumer surplus. We do not, for example, expect Russ to pay more than $7.00 for a slice of pie or Ellen's Bakery to sell pie for less than $2.50 per slice. In other words, for the market to work efficiently, voluntary instances of consumer loss must be rare. We assume that self-interest helps to ensure that all participants benefit from an exchange.

Equity refers to the fairness of the distribution of benefits among the members of a society.

However, the fact that both parties benefit from an exchange does not mean that both parties benefit equally. Economists are also interested in the distribution of the gains. **Equity** refers to the fairness of the distribution of benefits among the members of a society. In a world where no one cared about equity, only efficiency would matter and no particular division would be preferred. Another way of thinking about fairness versus efficiency is to consider a pie. If our only concern is efficiency, we will simply want to make sure that none of the pie goes to waste. But if we care about equity, we will also care about how the pie is allocated, perhaps making sure that everyone gets a bite of the pie or at least has access to the pie.

In our first look at consumer and producer surplus, we have assumed that markets produce efficient outcomes. But in the real world, efficient outcomes are not guaranteed. Markets also fail; their efficiency can be compromised in a number of ways. We discuss market failure in much greater detail in subsequent chapters. For now, all you need to know is that failure can occur.

Efficiency only requires that the pie get eaten. Equity is a question of how the pie gets divided.

Efficiency

Old School

In the 2003 movie *Old School*, Frank tries to give away a bread maker he received as a wedding present. First he offers it to a friend as a housewarming gift, but it turns out that this is the friend who originally gave him the bread maker. Ouch! Later in the movie, we see Frank giving the bread maker to a small boy at a birthday party. Both efforts at regifting fail miserably.

From an economic perspective, giving the wrong gift makes society worse off. If you spend $50 on a gift and give it to someone who thinks it is worth only $30, you've lost $20 in value. Whenever you receive a shirt that is the wrong size or style, a fruitcake you won't eat, or something that is worth less to you than what the gift giver paid, an economic inefficiency has occurred. Until now, we have thought of the market as enhancing efficiency by increasing the total surplus in society. But we can also think of the billions of dollars spent on mismatched gifts as a failure to maximize the total surplus involved in exchange. In other words, we can think of the efficiency of the gift-giving process as less than 100%.

Given what you have learned so far about economics, you might be tempted to argue that cash is the best gift you can give. When you give cash, it is never the wrong size or color, and the recipients can use it to buy whatever they want. However, very few people actually give cash (unless it is requested). Considering the advantages of cash, why don't more people give it instead of gifts? One reason is that cash seems impersonal. A second reason is that cash communicates exactly how much the giver spent. To avoid both problems, most people rarely give cash. Instead, they buy personalized gifts to communicate how much they care, while making it hard for the recipient to determine exactly how much they spent.

One way that society overcomes inefficiency in gifting is through the spread of information. For instance, wedding registries provide a convenient way for people who may not know the newlyweds very well to give them what they want. Similarly, prior to holidays many people tell each other what they would

Frank regifts a bread maker.

like to receive. By purchasing gifts that others want, givers can exactly match what the recipients would have purchased if they had received a cash transfer. This system eliminates any potential inefficiency. At the same time, the giver conveys affection—an essential part of giving. To further reduce the potential inefficiencies associated with giving, many large families practice holiday gift exchanges. Another interesting mechanism for eliciting information involves Santa Claus. Children throughout the world send Santa Claus wish lists for Christmas, never realizing that the parents who help to write and send the lists are the primary beneficiaries.

To economists, the strategies of providing better information, taking part in gift exchanges, and sending wish lists to Santa Claus are just a few examples of how society tries to get the most out of the giving process—and that is something to be joyful about!

PRACTICE WHAT YOU KNOW

Total Surplus: How Would Lower Consumer Income Affect Urban Outfitters?

Does less consumer income affect total surplus?

Question: If a drop in consumer income occurs, what will happen to the consumer surplus that customers enjoy at Urban Outfitters? What will happen to the amount of producer surplus that Urban Outfitters receives? Illustrate your answer by shifting the demand curve appropriately and labeling the new and old areas of consumer and producer surplus.

Answer: Because the items sold at Urban Outfitters are normal goods, a drop in income shifts the demand curve (D) to the left. The black arrow shows the leftward shift in the second graph below. When you compare the area of consumer surplus (in blue) before and after the drop in income—that is, graphs (a) and (b)—you can see that consumer surplus shrinks. Producer surplus (in red) also shrinks.

Your intuition might already confirm what the graphs tell us. Because consumers have less income, they buy fewer clothes at Urban Outfitters—so consumer surplus falls. Likewise, because fewer customers buy the store's clothes, Urban Outfitters sells less—so producer surplus falls. This result is also evident in graph (b), because $Q_2 < Q_1$.

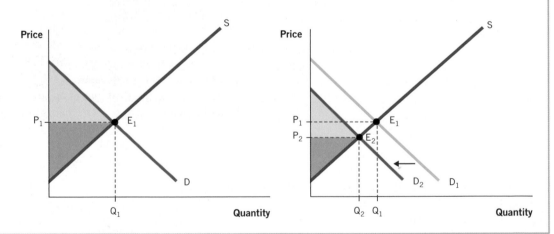

Why Do Taxes Create Deadweight Loss in Otherwise Efficient Markets?

Taxes provide many benefits. Taxes help to pay for many of society's needs—public transportation, schools, police, the court system, and the military, to name just a few. Most of us take these services for granted, but without taxes it would be impossible to pay for them. How much do all of these services cost? When you add all the federal, state, and local government budgets in the United States, you get over $6 trillion a year in taxes!

Spending tax dollars incurs opportunity costs, because the money could have been used in other ways. In this section, we use the concepts of consumer and producer surplus to explain the effect of taxation on social welfare and market efficiency. Taxes come in many sizes and shapes. There are taxes on personal income, payroll, property, corporate profits, sales, and inheritance, for example. Fortunately, we do not have to examine the entire tax code all at once. In the pages that follow, we explore the impact of taxes on social welfare by looking at one of the simplest taxes, the *excise tax*.

Opportunity cost

Tax Incidence

Economists want to know how taxes affect the choices that consumers and producers make. When a tax is imposed on an item, do buyers switch to alternative goods that are not taxed? How do producers respond when the products they sell are taxed? Because taxes cause prices to rise, they can affect how much of a good or service is bought and sold. This outcome is especially evident with **excise taxes**, which are taxes levied on a particular good or service. For example, all 50 states levy excise taxes on cigarettes, but the amount assessed varies tremendously. In New York, cigarette taxes are over $4.00 per pack, while in a handful of tobacco-producing states (including Virginia and North Carolina), the excise tax is less than $0.50 per pack. Overall, excise taxes, such as those on cigarettes, alcohol, and gasoline, account for less than 4% of all tax revenues. But because we can isolate changes in consumer behavior that result from taxes on one item, excise taxes help us understand the overall effect of a tax.

Excise taxes are taxes levied on a particular good or service.

In looking at the effect of a tax, economists are also interested in the **incidence** of taxation, which refers to the burden of taxation on the party who pays the tax. To understand this idea, consider a $1.00 tax on milk purchases. We consider two cases: a tax placed directly on buyers and a tax placed directly on sellers.

Incidence refers to the burden of taxation on the party who pays the tax through higher prices, regardless of whom the tax is actually levied on.

Example 1: Tax on Buyers

Each time a consumer buys a gallon of milk, the cash register adds $1.00 in tax. This means that to purchase the milk, the consumer must be willing to pay the price of the milk plus the $1.00 tax.

The result of the $1.00 tax on milk is shown in Figure 5.6. Because of the tax, consumers' willingness to pay for milk goes down, and the demand curve shifts left from D_1 to D_2. Why does the demand curve shift? The extra cost makes consumers less likely to buy milk at every price, which causes the entire demand curve to shift left. The intersection of the new demand curve (D_2) with the existing supply curve (S) creates a new equilibrium price of $3.50 ($E_2$), which is $0.50 lower than the original price of

Why do we place excise taxes on cigarettes . . .

. . . and gasoline?

FIGURE 5.6

A Tax on Buyers

After the tax, the new equilibrium price (E_2) is $3.50, but the buyer must also pay $1.00 in tax. Therefore, despite the drop in equilibrium price, the buyer still pays more for a gallon of milk: $4.50 instead of the original equilibrium price of $4.00. A similar logic applies to the producer. Because the new equilibrium price after the tax is $0.50 lower, the producer shares the tax incidence equally with the buyer in this example. The consumer pays $0.50 more, and the seller nets $0.50 less.

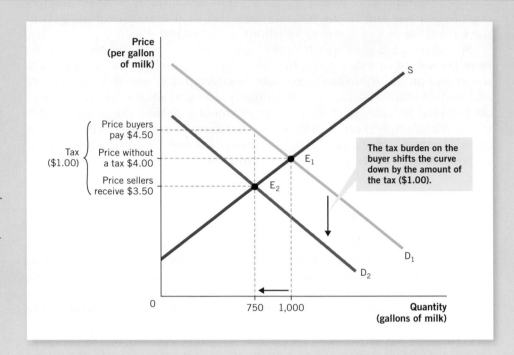

Price (per gallon of milk)

Tax ($1.00) {
  Price buyers pay $4.50
  Price without a tax $4.00
  Price sellers receive $3.50
}

The tax burden on the buyer shifts the curve down by the amount of the tax ($1.00).

E_1

E_2

S

D_1

D_2

0   750   1,000

Quantity (gallons of milk)

$4.00 per gallon. But even though the base price is lower, consumers are still worse off. Because they must also pay part of the $1.00 tax, the total price to them rises to $4.50 per gallon.

At the same time, because the new equilibrium price after the tax is $0.50 lower than it was before the tax, the producer splits the tax incidence with the buyer. The producer receives $0.50 less, and the buyer pays $0.50 more.

The tax on milk purchases also affects the amount sold in the market, which we also see in Figure 5.6. Because the after-tax equilibrium price (E_2) is lower, producers of milk reduce the quantity they sell to 750 gallons. Therefore, the market for milk becomes smaller than it was before the good was taxed.

Excise taxes are rarely levied on consumers because these taxes are highly visible. If you were reminded that you have to pay a $1.00 tax every time you buy a gallon of milk, it would be hard for you to ignore the tax. As a result, politicians often prefer to place the tax on the seller.

Example 2: Tax on Sellers

Now let's look at what happens when the $1.00 tax on milk is placed on sellers. Figure 5.7 shows the result. First, look at the shift in the supply curve. Why does it shift? The $1.00-per-gallon tax on milk lowers willingness to sell, which causes producers to offer less milk at every price level. As a result, the entire supply curve shifts left in response to the tax that milk producers owe the government. The intersection of the new supply curve (S_2) with

FIGURE 5.7

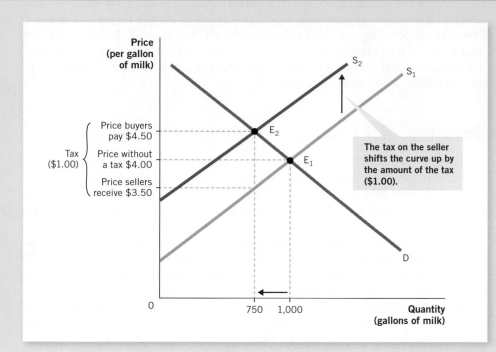

A Tax on Sellers

After the tax, the new equilibrium price (E₂) is $4.50, but $1.00 must be paid in tax to the government. Therefore, despite the rise in price, the seller nets only $3.50. Similar logic applies to the consumer. Because the new equilibrium price after the tax is $0.50 higher, the consumer shares the $1.00-per-gallon tax incidence equally with the seller. The consumer pays $0.50 more, and the seller nets $0.50 less.

the existing demand curve creates a new equilibrium price (E₂) of $4.50 per gallon—which is $0.50 higher than the original equilibrium price of $4.00 (E₁). This higher equilibrium price occurs because the seller passes part of the tax increase along to the buyer in the form of a higher price. However, the seller is still worse off. After the tax, the new equilibrium price is $4.50 per gallon, but $1.00 goes as tax to the government. Therefore, despite the rise in price, the seller nets only $3.50 per gallon, which is $0.50 less than the original equilibrium price.

The tax also affects the amount of milk sold in the market. Because the new equilibrium price after the tax is higher, consumers reduce the quantity demanded from 1,000 gallons to 750 gallons.

So Who Bears the Incidence of the Tax?

It's important to notice that the result in Figure 5.7 looks much like that in Figure 5.6 because it does not matter whether a tax is levied on the buyer or the seller. The tax places a wedge of $1.00 between the price that buyers ultimately pay ($4.50) and the net price that sellers ultimately receive ($3.50), regardless of who is actually responsible for paying the tax.

Continuing with our milk example, when the tax was levied on sellers, they were responsible for collecting the entire tax ($1.00 per gallon), but they transferred $0.50 of the tax to the consumer by raising the market price to $4.50. Similarly, when the tax was levied on consumers, they were responsible for paying the entire tax, but they essentially transferred $0.50 of it to producers, because the market price fell to $3.50. Therefore, we can say that the incidence of a tax is independent of whether it is levied on the buyer or the seller. However, depending on the price elasticity of supply and demand, the tax incidence need not be shared equally, as we will see later. All of this means that the government doesn't get to determine whether consumers or producers bear the tax incidence—the market does!

Deadweight Loss

Deadweight loss is the decrease in economic activity caused by market distortions.

Recall that economists measure economic efficiency by looking at total consumer and producer surplus. We have seen that a tax raises the total price consumers pay and lowers the net price producers receive. For this reason, taxes reduce the amount of economic activity. **Deadweight loss** is the decrease in economic activity caused by market distortions.

In the previous section, we observed that the tax on milk caused the amount purchased to decline from 1,000 to 750 gallons—a reduction of 250 gallons sold in the market. In Figure 5.8, the yellow triangle represents the deadweight loss caused by the tax. When the price rises to $4.50 per gallon, consumers who would have paid between $4.01 and $4.50 will no longer purchase milk. Likewise, the reduction in the price the seller can charge means that producers who were willing to sell a gallon of milk for between $3.50 and $3.99 will no longer do so. The combined reductions in consumer and producer surplus equal the deadweight loss produced by a $1.00 tax on milk.

FIGURE 5.8

The Deadweight Loss from a Tax

The yellow triangle represents the deadweight loss caused by the tax. When the price rises, all consumers who would have paid between $4.01 and $4.50 no longer purchase milk. Likewise, the reduction in revenue the seller receives means that producers who were willing to sell a gallon of milk for between $3.50 and $3.99 will no longer do so.

Taxing Inelastic Goods

"Taxman," by the Beatles

"Taxman" was inspired by the theme song from the popular 1960s television series *Batman*. The Beatles—especially George Harrison, who wrote the song—had grown quite bitter about how much they were paying in taxes. In the beginning of the song, Harrison sings, "Let me tell you how it will be. There's one for you, nineteen for me." This lyric refers to the fact that the British government taxed high-wage earners £19 out of every £20 they earned. (£ is the symbol for the pound, the British currency unit.) Because the Beatles' considerable earnings placed them in the top income tax bracket in the United Kingdom, a part of the group's earnings was subject to the 95% tax introduced by the government in 1965. As a consequence, the Beatles became tax exiles, living in the United States and other parts of Europe, where tax rates were lower.

The inevitability of paying taxes is a theme that runs throughout the song. The lyrics mention that when you drive a car, the government can tax the "street"; if you try to sit, the government can tax "your seat"; if you are cold, the government can tax "the heat"; and if you decide to take a walk, it

The Beatles avoided high taxes by living outside the United Kingdom.

can tax your "feet"! The only way to avoid paying high taxes on these things is to leave the country—which is precisely what the Beatles did. All these examples (streets, seats, heat, and walking) are necessary activities, which makes demand highly inelastic. Anytime demand is highly inelastic, the government can more easily collect the tax revenue it desires.

In the next sections, we examine how differences in the price elasticity of demand lead to varying amounts of deadweight loss. We evaluate what happens when the demand curve is perfectly inelastic, somewhat elastic, and perfectly elastic.

Tax Revenue and Deadweight Loss When Demand Is Inelastic

In Chapter 4, we saw that necessary goods and services—for example, water, electricity, and phone service—have highly inelastic demand. These goods and services are often taxed. For example, consider all the taxes associated with your cell phone bill: sales tax, city tax, county tax, federal excise tax, and annual regulatory fees. In addition, many companies add surcharges, including activation fees, local-number portability fees, telephone number pooling charges, emergency 911 service, directory assistance, telecommunications

How do phone companies get away with all the added fees per month? Answer: inelastic demand.

relay service surcharges, and cancellation fees. Of course, there is a way to avoid all these fees: don't use a cell phone! However, many people today feel that cell phones are a necessity. Cell phone providers and government agencies take advantage of consumers' strongly inelastic demand by tacking on these extra charges.

Figure 5.9 shows the result of a tax on products with almost perfectly inelastic demand, such as phone service—something people feel they need to have no matter what the price. The demand for access to a phone (either a landline or a cell phone) is perfectly inelastic. Recall that whenever demand is perfectly inelastic, the demand curve is vertical. Panel (a) shows the market for phone service before the tax. The blue rectangle represents consumer surplus (C.S.), and the red triangle represents producer surplus (P.S.). Now imagine that a tax is levied on the seller, as shown in panel (b). The supply curve shifts from S_1 to S_2. The shift in supply causes the equilibrium point to move from E_1 to E_2 and the price to rise from P_1 to P_2, but the quantity supplied, Q_1, remains the same. We know that when demand is perfectly inelastic, a price increase does not alter how much consumers purchase. So the quantity demanded remains constant at Q_1 even after the government collects tax revenue equal to the green rectangle.

FIGURE 5.9

A Tax on Products with Almost Perfectly Inelastic Demand

(a) Before the tax, the consumer enjoys the consumer surplus (C.S.) shaded in blue, and the producer enjoys the producer surplus (P.S.) shaded in red. (b) After the tax, the incidence, or the burden of taxation, is borne entirely by the consumer. A tax on a good with almost perfectly inelastic demand, such as phone service, represents a transfer of welfare from consumers to the government, as reflected by the reduced size of the blue rectangle in (b) and the creation of the green tax revenue rectangle between P_1 and P_2.

(a) Before the Tax

(b) After the Tax

There are two reasons why the government may favor excise taxes on goods with almost perfectly (or highly) inelastic demand. First, because these goods do not have substitutes, the tax will not cause consumers to buy less. Thus, the revenue from the tax will remain steady. Second, because the number of transactions, or quantity demanded (Q_1), remains constant, there will be no deadweight loss. As a result, the yellow triangle we observed in Figure 5.8 disappears in Figure 5.9 because the tax does not alter the efficiency of the market. Looking at Figure 5.9, you can see that the same number of transactions exist in panels (a) and (b); the total surplus, or social welfare, is equal in both panels. You can also see this equality by comparing the full shaded areas in both panels. The sum of the blue area of consumer surplus and the red area of producer surplus in panel (a) is equal to the sum of the consumer surplus, producer surplus, and tax revenue in panel (b). The green area in panel (b) is subtracted entirely from the blue rectangle in panel (a), which indicates that the surplus is redistributed from consumers to the government. But society overall enjoys the same total surplus (even though some of this surplus is now in the form of a tax). Thus, we see that when demand is perfectly inelastic, the incidence, or the burden of taxation, is borne entirely by the consumer. A tax on a good with almost perfectly inelastic demand represents a transfer of welfare from consumers of the good to the government, reflected by the reduced size of the blue rectangle in panel (b).

Tax Revenue and Deadweight Loss When Demand Is More Elastic

Now consider a tax on a product with more elastic demand, such as milk, the subject of our earlier discussion. The demand for milk is price sensitive, but not overly so. This elasticity is reflected in a demand curve with a typical slope as shown in Figure 5.10. Let's compare the after-tax price, P_2, in panel (b) of Figures 5.9 and 5.10. When demand is almost perfectly inelastic, as it is in panel (b) of Figure 5.9, the price increase from P_1 to P_2 is absorbed entirely by consumers. But in panel (b) of Figure 5.10, because demand is flatter and therefore more sensitive to price, suppliers must absorb part of the tax themselves (from P_1 to P_3). Thus, the net price they charge, P_3, is less than what they received when the good was not taxed. In addition, the total tax revenue generated (the green area) is not as large in panel (b) of Figure 5.10 as in panel (b) of Figure 5.9 because as the price of the good rises to P_2, some consumers no longer buy it and the quantity demanded falls from Q_1 to Q_2.

Notice that both consumer surplus (C.S., the blue triangle) and producer surplus (P.S., the red triangle) in Figure 5.10, panel (b), are smaller after the tax. Because the price rises after the tax increase (from P_1 to P_2), those consumers with a relatively low willingness to pay for the good are priced out of the market. Likewise, sellers with relatively high costs of production will stop producing the good, because the price they net after paying the tax drops to P_3. The total reduction in economic activity, the change from Q_1 to Q_2, is the deadweight loss (D.W.L.) indicated by the yellow triangle.

A tax on a good for which demand and supply are both somewhat elastic will cause a transfer of welfare from consumers and producers of the good to the government. At the same time, because the quantity bought and sold in the market declines, deadweight loss is created. Another way of seeing this result is to compare the red and blue areas in Figure 5.10, panel (a), with the red and blue areas in panel (b) of Figure 5.10. The sum of the consumer surplus and producer surplus in panel (a) is greater than the sum of the consumer surplus, tax revenue, and producer surplus in panel (b) because the deadweight loss in panel (b) is no longer a part of the surplus. Therefore, the total surplus is lower, which means that the efficiency of the market is smaller. The tax is no longer a pure transfer from consumers to the government, as was the case in Figure 5.9.

Tax Revenue and Deadweight Loss When Demand Is Highly Elastic

We have seen the effect of taxation when demand is inelastic and somewhat elastic. What happens when demand is highly elastic? For example, a customer who wants to buy fresh lettuce at a produce market will find many local growers charging the same price and many varieties to choose from. If one of the vendors decides to charge $1 per pound above the market price, consumers will stop buying from that vendor. They will be unwilling to pay more when they can get the same product from another grower at a lower price. In other words, their demand is highly elastic.

Figure 5.11 shows the result of a tax on lettuce, a good with highly elastic demand. After all, when lettuce is taxed, consumers can switch to other greens such as spinach, cabbage, or endive and completely avoid the tax. In this market, consumers are so price sensitive that they are unwilling to accept any price increase. And because sellers are unable to raise the equilibrium price,

FIGURE 5.10

A Tax on Products with More Elastic Demand

(a) Before the tax, the consumer enjoys the consumer surplus (C.S.) shaded in blue, and the producer enjoys the producer surplus (P.S.) shaded in red. (b) A tax on a good for which demand and supply are both somewhat elastic will cause a transfer of welfare from consumers and producers to the government, the revenue shown as the green rectangle. It will also create deadweight loss (D.W.L.), shaded in yellow, because the quantity bought and sold in the market declines (from Q_1 to Q_2).

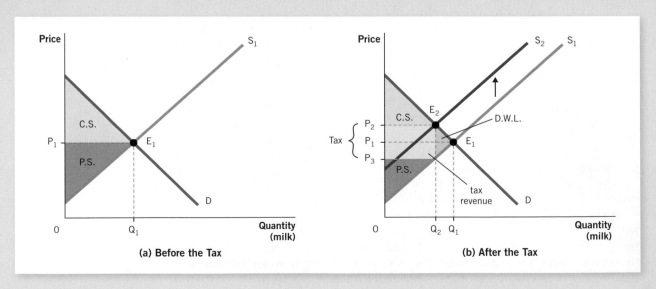

FIGURE 5.11

A Tax on Products with Highly Elastic Demand

(a) Before the tax, the producer enjoys the producer surplus (P.S.) shaded in red. (b) When consumer demand is highly elastic, consumers pay the same price after the tax as before. But they are worse off because less is produced and sold; the quantity produced moves from Q_1 to Q_2. The result is deadweight loss (D.W.L.), as shown by the yellow triangle. The total surplus, or efficiency of the market, is much smaller than before. The size of the tax revenue (shaded in green) is also noticeably smaller in the market with highly elastic demand.

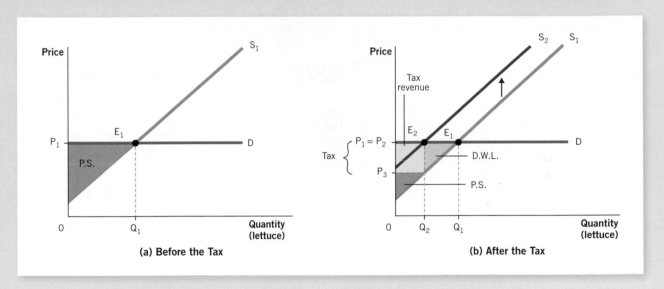

(a) Before the Tax

(b) After the Tax

they bear the entire incidence of the tax. There are two effects. First, producers are less willing to sell the product at all prices, and the supply curve shifts from S_1 to S_2. Because consumer demand is highly elastic, consumers pay the same price as before ($P_1 = P_2$). However, the tax increase causes the producers to net less, or P_3. Because P_3 is substantially lower than the price before the tax, or P_2, producers offer less for sale after the tax is implemented. (Specifically, they offer the amount shown on supply curve S_2 at price P_2.) Panel (b) of Figure 5.11 shows the movement of quantity demanded from Q_1 to Q_2. Because Q_2 is significantly smaller than Q_1, there is deadweight loss. Comparing the green areas of panel (b) in Figures 5.10 and 5.11, you see that the size of the tax revenue continues to shrink. There is an important lesson here for policymakers. They should tax goods with relatively inelastic demand (if the goal is to generate tax revenue or minimize efficiency losses). Doing so will not only lessen the deadweight loss of taxation, but also generate larger tax revenues for the government.

Interaction of Demand Elasticity and Supply Elasticity

So far, we have varied the elasticity of the demand curve while holding the elasticity of the supply curve constant. What would happen if we did the reverse and varied the elasticity of the supply curve while keeping the elasticity

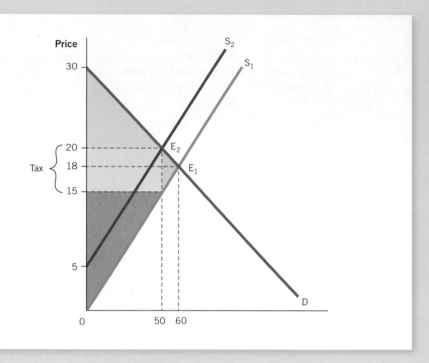

FIGURE 5.12

A Realistic Example
A $5-per-pound tax is placed on mushroom suppliers, driving the equilibrium price up from E_1 ($18) to E_2 ($20). Notice that the price rises by only $2. Consumers therefore pick up $2 of the $5 tax and the seller must pay the remaining $3. Therefore, most of the incidence is borne by the seller.

of the demand curve constant? It turns out that there is a simple method for determining the incidence and deadweight loss in this case. The incidence of a tax is determined by the relative steepness of the demand curve compared with the supply curve. When the demand curve is steeper (more inelastic) than the supply curve, consumers bear more of the incidence of the tax. When the supply curve is steeper (more inelastic) than the demand curve, suppliers bear more of the incidence of the tax. Also, whenever the supply and/or demand curves are relatively steep, deadweight loss is minimized.

Let's explore an example in which we consider how the elasticity of demand and elasticity of supply interact. Suppose that a $5-per-pound tax is placed on shiitake mushrooms, an elastic good. Given the information in Figure 5.12, we will compute the incidence, deadweight loss, and tax revenue from the tax.

Let's start with the incidence of the tax. After the tax is implemented, the market price rises from $18 per pound (at E_1) to $20 per pound (at E_2). But since sellers must pay $5 per pound to the government, they keep only $15. Tax incidence measures the share of the tax paid by buyers and sellers, so we need to compare the incidence of the tax paid by each party. Because the market price rises by $2 (from $18 to $20), buyers are paying $2 of the $5 tax, or $\frac{2}{5}$. Because

How much would you pay per pound for these mushrooms?

the amount the seller keeps falls by $3 (from $18 to $15), sellers are paying $3 of the $5 tax, or $\frac{3}{5}$. Notice that the demand curve is slightly more elastic (flatter) than the supply curve; therefore, sellers have a limited ability to raise their price.

Now let's determine the deadweight loss caused by the tax—that is, the decrease in economic activity. Deadweight loss is represented by the decrease in the total surplus found in the yellow triangle in Figure 5.12. To compute the amount of the deadweight loss, we need to determine the area of the triangle:

$$\text{area of a triangle} = \frac{1}{2} \times \text{base} \times \text{height} \qquad \text{(Equation 5.1)}$$

The triangle in Figure 5.12 is sitting on its side, so its height is $60 - 50 = 10$, and its base is $\$20 - \$15 = \$5$.

$$\text{deadweight loss} = \frac{1}{2} \times 10 \times \$5 = \$25$$

This means that $25 worth of mushroom sales will not take place because of the tax.

Finally, what is the tax revenue generated by the tax? In Figure 5.12, the tax revenue is represented by the green-shaded area, which is a rectangle. We can calculate the tax revenue by determining the area of the rectangle:

$$\text{area of a rectangle} = \text{base} \times \text{height} \qquad \text{(Equation 5.2)}$$

The height of the tax revenue rectangle is the amount of the tax ($5), and the number of units sold after the tax is 50 (the base).

$$\text{tax revenue} = \$5 \times 50 = \$250$$

ECONOMICS IN THE REAL WORLD

The Short-Lived Luxury Tax

The Budget Reconciliation Act of 1990 established a special luxury tax on the sale of new aircraft, yachts, automobiles, furs, and jewelry. The act established a 10% surcharge on new purchases as follows: aircraft over $500,000; yachts over $100,000; automobiles over $25,000; and furs and jewelry over $10,000. The taxes were expected to generate approximately $2 billion a year. However, revenue fell far below expectations, and thousands of jobs were lost in each of the affected industries. Within three years, the tax was repealed. Why was the luxury tax such a failure?

When passing the Budget Reconciliation Act, lawmakers failed to consider basic demand elasticity. Because the purchase of a new aircraft, yacht, car, fur, or jewelry is highly discretionary, many wealthy consumers decided that they would buy substitute products that fell below the tax threshold or buy a used product and refurbish it. Therefore, the demand for these luxury goods turned out to be highly elastic. We have seen that when goods with elastic demand are taxed, the resulting tax revenues are small. Moreover, in this example, the resulting decrease in purchases was significant. As a result, jobs were lost in

If you were rich, would this be your luxury toy?

the middle of an economic downturn. The combination of low revenues and crippling job losses was enough to convince Congress to repeal the tax in 1993.

The failed luxury tax is a reminder that the populist idea of taxing the rich is far more difficult to implement than it appears. In simple terms, it is nearly impossible to tax the toys that the rich enjoy because wealthy people can spend their money in so many different ways. In other words, they have options about whether to buy or lease, as well as many good substitutes to choose from. In other words, in many cases, they can avoid paying luxury taxes. ✴

Balancing Deadweight Loss and Tax Revenues

Up to this point, we have kept the size of the tax increase constant. Doing so enabled us to examine the impact of the elasticity of demand and supply on deadweight loss and tax revenues. But what happens when a tax is high enough to significantly alter consumer or producer behavior? For instance, in 2002, the Republic of Ireland instituted a tax of 15 euro cents on each plastic bag in order to curb litter and encourage recycling. Since the cost of production of each plastic bag is just a few pennies, a 15-euro-cent tax is enormous by comparison. As a result, consumer use of plastic bags quickly fell by over 90%. Thus, the tax was a major success because the government achieved its goal of curbing litter. In this section, we consider how consumers respond to taxes of different sizes, and we determine the relationship between the size of a tax, the deadweight loss, and tax revenues.

Incentives

Figure 5.13 shows the market response to a variety of tax increases. The five panels in the figure begin with a reference point, panel (a), where no tax is levied, and progress toward panel (e), where the tax rate becomes so extreme that it curtails all economic activity.

As taxes rise, so do prices. You can trace this price rise from panel (a), where there is no tax and the price is P_1, all the way to panel (e), where the extreme tax causes the price to rise to P_5. At the same time, deadweight loss (D.W.L.) also rises. You can see this increase by comparing the sizes of the yellow triangles. The trade-off is striking. Without any taxes, deadweight loss does not occur. But as soon as taxes are in place, the market equilibrium quantity demanded begins to decline, moving from Q_1 to Q_5. As the number of transactions (quantity demanded) declines, the area of deadweight loss rapidly expands.

Trade-offs

When taxes are small, as in panel (b), the tax revenue (green rectangle) is large relative to the deadweight loss (yellow triangle). However, as we progress through the panels, this relationship slowly reverses. In panel (c), the size of the tax revenue remains larger than the deadweight loss. In panel (d), however, the magnitude of the deadweight loss is far greater than the tax revenue. The size of the tax in panel (d) is creating a significant cost in terms

FIGURE 5.13

Examining Deadweight Loss and Tax Revenues

The panels show that increased taxes result in higher prices. Progressively higher taxes lead to more deadweight loss (D.W.L.), but higher taxes do not always generate more tax revenue, as evidenced by the reduction in tax revenue that occurs when tax rates become too large in panels (d) and (e).

(a) No Tax

(b) Small Tax

(c) Moderate Tax

(d) Large Tax

(e) Extreme Tax

Unusual Taxes

Governments tax their citizens for a variety of reasons. Often it's to raise revenue. Sometimes, taxes are levied to influence citizens' behavior. Occasionally, both of these reasons are in play. These two motivations have led to some creative tax initiatives, as seen below.

Flush Tax

Maryland's "flush tax," a fee added to sewer bills, went up from $2.50 to $5.00 a month in 2012. The tax is paid only by residents who live in the Chesapeake Bay Watershed, and it generates revenue for reducing pollution in Chesapeake Bay.

Bagel Tax

New Yorkers love their bagels and cream cheese from delis. In the state, any bagel that has been sliced or has any form of spread on it (like cream cheese) is subject to an 8-cent tax. Any bagel that is purchased "unaltered" is classified as unprepared and is not taxed.

Playing Card Tax

The state of Alabama really doesn't want you playing solitaire. Buyers of playing cards are taxed ten cents per deck, while sellers must pay a $2 annual licensing fee.

Tattoo Tax

Arkansas imposes a 6% tax on tattoos and body piercings, meaning that the people of Arkansas pay extra when getting inked or pierced.

Window Tax

England passed a tax in 1696 targeting wealthy citizens—the more windows in one's house, the higher the tax. Many homeowners simply bricked over their windows. But they could not seal all of them, and the government did indeed collect revenue.

Blueberry Tax

Maine levies a penny-and-a-half tax per pound on anyone growing, handling, processing, selling, or purchasing the state's delicious wild blueberries. The tax is an effort to make sure that the blueberries are not overharvested.

Maine produces 99% of the wild blueberries consumed in the USA, meaning that blueberry lovers have few substitutes available to avoid paying the tax and that demand is therefore inelastic.

Marylanders are being taxed on a negative externality, which we cover in Chapter 7.

REVIEW QUESTIONS

- Suppose that because of Alabama's playing card tax, fewer consumers purchase cards and fewer store owners sell them. What is this loss of economic activity called?

- Do you think the New York bagel tax is an effective tool to raise government revenue? Think about how the tax may or may not affect the purchasing behavior of New Yorkers.

PRACTICE WHAT YOU KNOW

Deadweight Loss of Taxation:
The Politics of Tax Rates

Imagine that you and two friends are discussing the politics of taxation. One friend, who is fiscally conservative, argues that tax rates are too high. The other friend, who is more progressive, argues that tax rates are too low.

What is the optimal tax rate?

Question: Is it possible that both friends are right?

Answer: Surprisingly, the answer is yes. When tax rates become extraordinarily high, the amount of deadweight loss dwarfs the amount of tax revenue collected. We observed this result in our discussion of the short-lived luxury tax. Fiscal conservatives often note that taxes inhibit economic activity. They advocate lower tax rates and limited government involvement in the market, preferring to minimize the deadweight loss on economic activity—see panel (b) in Figure 5.13. However, progressives prefer somewhat higher tax rates than fiscal conservatives, because a moderate tax rate—see panel (c)—generates more tax revenue than a small tax does. The additional revenues that moderate tax rates generate can fund more government services. Therefore, a clear trade-off exists between the size of the public (government) sector and market activity. Depending on how you view the value created by markets versus the value added through government provision, there is ample room for disagreement about the best tax policy.

Trade-offs

of economic efficiency. Finally, panel (e) shows an extreme case in which all market activity ceases as a result of the tax. Because nothing is produced and sold, there is no tax revenue.

Conclusion

Let's return to the misconception we started with: taxes on firms do not affect consumers. This misconception is almost entirely false. The government largely taxes goods that have inelastic demand, which means that firms are able to transfer most of the tax incidence to consumers through higher prices.

In the first part of this chapter, we learned that society benefits from unregulated markets because they generate the largest possible total surplus. However, society also needs the government to provide an infrastructure for the economy. The taxation of specific goods and services gives rise to a form of market failure called deadweight loss, which reflects reduced economic activity. Thus, any intervention in the market requires a deep understanding of how society will respond to the incentives created by the legislation. In addition, unintended consequences can affect the most well-intentioned

Incentives

Trade-offs

tax legislation and, if the process is not well thought through, can cause inefficiencies with far-reaching consequences. None of this means that taxes are undesirable. Rather, society must balance (1) the need for tax revenues and the programs those revenues help fund with (2) trade-offs in the market.

ANSWERING THE BIG QUESTIONS

What are consumer surplus and producer surplus?

* Consumer surplus is the difference between the willingness to pay for a good or service and the price that is paid to get it. Producer surplus is the difference between the price that the seller receives and the price at which the seller is willing to sell the good or service.

* Total surplus (social welfare) is the sum of consumer and producer surplus that exists in a market.

When is a market efficient?

* Markets maximize consumer and producer surplus, provide goods and services to buyers who value them most, and reward sellers who can produce goods and services at the lowest cost. As a result, markets create the largest amount of total surplus possible.

* Whenever an allocation of resources maximizes total surplus, the result is said to be efficient. However, economists are also interested in the distribution of the surplus. Equity refers to the fairness of the distribution of the benefits within the society.

Why do taxes create deadweight loss in otherwise efficient markets?

* Deadweight loss occurs because taxes increase the purchase price, which causes consumers to buy less and producers to supply less. Deadweight loss can be lessened by taxing goods or services that have inelastic demand or supply.

* Economists are also concerned about the incidence of taxation. Incidence refers to the burden of taxation on the party who pays the tax through higher prices, regardless of whom the tax is actually levied on. The incidence is determined by the balance between the elasticity of supply and the elasticity of demand.

Excise Taxes Are Almost Impossible to Avoid

The federal government collected $62 billion in excise taxes in 2014. Excise taxes are placed on many different products, making them almost impossible to avoid. They also have the added advantages of being easy to collect, hard for consumers to detect since the producer is responsible for paying the tax, and easier to enact politically than other types of taxes. You'll find federal excise taxes on many everyday household expenses—what you drink, the gasoline you purchase, plane tickets, and much more. Let's add them up over the course of a typical year.

1. **Gasoline.** 18.4 cents per gallon, generating $25 billion to help finance the interstate highway system.

2. **Cigarettes.** $1.01 per pack, generating $14 billion for the general federal budget.

3. **Air travel.** 7.5% of the base price of the ticket plus $4 per flight segment, generating $13 billion for the Transportation Security Administration and the Federal Aviation Administration.

Data from Jill Barshay, "The $240-a-Year Bill You Don't Know You're Paying," *Fiscal Times*, Sept. 7, 2011. Author's note: data updated in 2014.

4. **Alcohol.** 5 cents per can of beer, 21 cents per bottle of wine, and $2.14 per bottle of spirits, generating $9 billion for the general federal budget.

These four categories account for $61 billion in excise taxes. You could still avoid the taxman with this simple prescription: don't drink, don't travel, and don't smoke. Where does that leave you? Way out in the country somewhere far from civilization. Since you won't be able to travel to a grocery store, you'll need to live off the land, grow your own crops, and hunt or fish.

But there is still one last federal excise tax to go.

5. **Hunting and fishing.** Taxes range from 3 cents for fishing tackle boxes to 11% for archery equipment, generating over $1 billion for fish and wildlife services.

Living off the land and avoiding taxes just got much harder, and that's the whole point. The government taxes products with relatively inelastic demand because most people will still purchase them after the tax is in place. As a result, avoiding excise taxes isn't practical.

ECONOMICS FOR LIFE

Excise taxes are everywhere.

CONCEPTS YOU SHOULD KNOW

consumer surplus (p. 153)
deadweight loss (p. 166)
efficient (p. 160)
equity (p. 160)

excise taxes (p. 163)
incidence (p. 163)
producer surplus (p. 155)
social welfare (p. 158)

total surplus (p. 158)
welfare economics (p. 152)
willingness to pay (p. 153)
willingness to sell (p. 155)

QUESTIONS FOR REVIEW

1. Explain how consumer surplus is derived from the difference between the willingness to pay and the market equilibrium price.

2. Explain how producer surplus is derived from the difference between the willingness to sell and the market equilibrium price.

3. Why do economists focus on consumer and producer surplus and not on the possibility of consumer and producer loss? Illustrate your answer on a supply and demand graph.

4. How do economists define efficiency?

5. What type of goods should be taxed in order to minimize deadweight loss?

6. Suppose that the government taxes a good that has very elastic demand. Illustrate what will happen to consumer surplus, producer surplus, tax revenue, and deadweight loss on a supply and demand graph.

7. What happens to tax revenues as tax rates increase?

STUDY PROBLEMS (*solved at the end of the section)

1. A college student enjoys eating pizza. Her willingness to pay for each slice is shown in the following table:

Number of pizza slices	Willingness to pay (per slice)
1	$6
2	5
3	4
4	3
5	2
6	1
7	0

a. If pizza slices cost $3 each, how many slices will she buy? How much consumer surplus will she enjoy?
b. If the price of slices falls to $2, how much consumer surplus will she enjoy?

2. A cash-starved town decides to impose a $6 excise tax on T-shirts sold. The following table shows the quantity demanded and the quantity supplied at various prices.

Price per T-shirt	Quantity demanded	Quantity supplied
$19	0	60
16	10	50
13	20	40
10	30	30
7	40	20
4	50	10

a. What are the equilibrium quantity demanded and the quantity supplied before the tax is implemented? Determine the consumer and producer surplus before the tax.

b. What are the equilibrium quantity demanded and quantity supplied after the tax is implemented? Determine the consumer and producer surplus after the tax.

c. How much tax revenue does the town generate from the tax?

3. Andrew pays $30 to buy a potato cannon, a cylinder that shoots potatoes hundreds of feet. He was willing to pay $45. When Andrew's friend Nick learns that Andrew bought a potato cannon, he asks Andrew if he will sell it for $60, and Andrew agrees. Nick is thrilled, since he would have paid Andrew up to $80 for the cannon. Andrew is also delighted. Determine the consumer surplus from the original purchase and the additional surplus generated by the resale of the cannon.

4. If the government wants to raise tax revenue, which of the following items are good candidates for an excise tax? Why?

a. granola bars   d. automobile tires
b. cigarettes   e. bird feeders
c. toilet paper

✳ 5. If the government wants to minimize the deadweight loss of taxation, which of the following items are good candidates for an excise tax? Why?

a. bottled water
b. prescription drugs

c. oranges
d. batteries
e. luxury cars

6. A new medical study indicates that eating blueberries helps prevent cancer. If the demand for blueberries increases, what will happen to the size of the consumer surplus and producer surplus? Illustrate your answer by shifting the demand curve appropriately and labeling the new and old areas of consumer and producer surplus.

7. Use the following graph to answer questions a–f.

a. What area represents consumer surplus before the tax?
b. What area represents producer surplus before the tax?
c. What area represents consumer surplus after the tax?
d. What area represents producer surplus after the tax?
e. What area represents the tax revenue after the tax?
f. What area represents the deadweight loss after the tax?

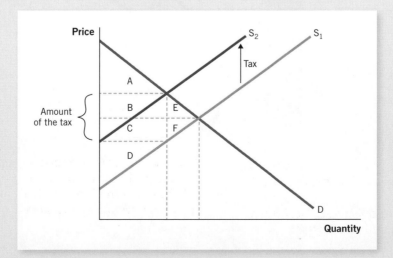

8. The cost of many electronic devices has fallen appreciably since they were first introduced. For instance, computers, cell phones, microwave ovens, and calculators not only provide more functions but also do so at a lower cost. Illustrate the impact of lower production costs on the supply curve. What happens to the size of the consumer surplus and producer surplus? If consumer demand for cell phones is relatively elastic, who is likely to benefit the most from the lower production costs?

9. Suppose that the demand for a concert, Q_D, is represented by the following equation, where P is the price of concert tickets and Q is the number of tickets sold:

$$Q_D = 2500 - 20P$$

The supply of tickets, Q_S, is represented by the equation

$$Q_S = -500 + 80P$$

a. Find the equilibrium price and quantity of tickets sold. (**Hint:** Set $Q_D = Q_S$ and solve for the price, P, and then plug the result back into either of the original equations to find Q_E.)

b. Carefully graph your result from part a.

c. Calculate the consumer surplus at the equilibrium price and quantity. (**Hint:** Because the area of consumer surplus is a triangle, you will need to use the formula for the area of a triangle, $\frac{1}{2} \times$ base $\times$ height, to solve the problem.)

10. In this chapter, we focused on the effect of taxes on social welfare. However, governments also subsidize goods, making them cheaper to buy or sell. How would a $2,000 subsidy on the purchase of a new hybrid car impact the consumer surplus and producer surplus in the hybrid-car market? Use a supply and demand diagram to illustrate your answer. Does the subsidy create deadweight loss?

＊ 11. Suppose that a new $50 tax is placed on each new cell phone sold. Use the information in the following graph to answer these questions.

a. What is the incidence of the tax?

b. What is the deadweight loss of the tax?

c. What is the amount of tax revenue generated?

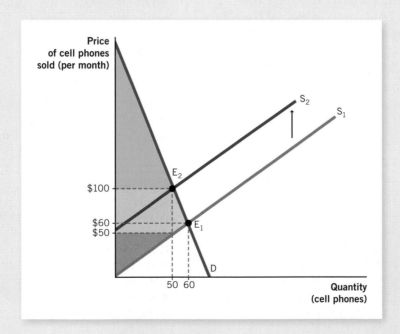

✴ 12. A well-known saying goes, "Honesty is not only morally right, it is also highly efficient." Explain why firms that practice honesty lead to more social welfare than firms that practice dishonesty.

13. We defined deadweight loss as the decrease in economic activity caused by market distortions. One place where we see deadweight loss is during Halloween's trick-or-treat. Children of all ages return home with bags of candy, some of which they love and others that they don't care for. A lot of candy ends up uneaten. In this context, we can think of uneaten candy as not being distributed effectively by the market; therefore, deadweight loss occurs. What ways can you think of to improve how candy is given away during trick-or-treat so that children would receive more candies that they enjoy? Provide three possible solutions.

SOLVED PROBLEMS

5.a. Many good substitutes are available: consumers can drink tap water, filtered water, or other healthy beverages instead of bottled water. Therefore, bottled water is not a good candidate for an excise tax.

b. Taxing prescription drugs will generate significant revenues without reducing sales much, if at all. There is almost no deadweight loss because consumers have few, if any, alternatives. Thus, prescription drugs are a good candidate for an excise tax.

c. Consumers can select many other fruits to replace oranges. The deadweight loss will be quite large. Therefore, oranges are not a good candidate for an excise tax.

d. Without batteries, many devices won't work. The lack of substitutes makes demand quite inelastic, so the deadweight loss will be small. Thus, batteries are an excellent candidate for an excise tax.

e. Wealthy consumers can spend their income in many ways. They do not have to buy luxury cars. As a result, the tax will create a large amount of deadweight loss. Therefore, luxury cars are a poor candidate for an excise tax.

11.a. After the tax is implemented, the market price rises from \$60 to \$100; but because sellers must pay \$50 to the government, they net only \$50. Tax incidence measures the share of the tax paid by buyers and sellers. Because the market price rises by \$40 (from \$60 to \$100), buyers are paying \$40 of the \$50 tax, or $\frac{4}{5}$. Because the net price falls by \$10 (from \$60 to \$50), sellers are paying \$10 of the \$50 tax, or $\frac{1}{5}$.

b. The deadweight loss is represented by the decrease in the total surplus found in the yellow triangle. To compute the amount of the deadweight loss, we need to determine the area inside the triangle. The area of a triangle is found by taking $\frac{1}{2} \times$ base $\times$ height. The triangle is sitting on its side, so the height of the triangle is 10 (60 − 50) and the base is \$50 (\$100 − \$50). Hence the deadweight loss is $\frac{1}{2} \times 10 \times \$50 = \$250$.

c. The tax revenue is represented by the green area. You can calculate the tax revenue by multiplying the amount of the tax (\$50) by the number of units sold after the tax (50), which equals \$2,500.

12. For markets to benefit both the buyer and the seller, both parties must have accurate information about the good. We learned that an efficient allocation maximizes total surplus. Think about how dishonesty disrupts trade. Suppose a seller misrepresents the qualities of the good she is selling. A consumer buys the good and finds it to be defective or undesirable. As a result, the consumer does not get any consumer surplus from the transaction. In this case, total surplus is less than it otherwise would be. In addition, the consumer will no longer purchase from the dishonest seller, which means that potential gains from trade in the future will be lost as well.

Rent controls help make housing more affordable for everyone.
You are probably familiar with rent controls, which is an example of
a *price control* set by the government. If you have ever looked for an

apartment in an expensive location, you probably think that
stabilizing rents is a great idea. You may support rent control
legislation because you believe it will help struggling workers
make ends meet. After all, it seems reasonable that rents should be low
enough so that workers can cover the necessities of life.

Price controls are not a new idea. The first recorded attempt to
control prices was 4,000 years ago in ancient Babylon, when King
Hammurabi decreed how much corn a farmer could pay for a cow. Similar attempts to control prices occurred in ancient Egypt, Greece, and
Rome. Each attempt ended badly. In Egypt, farmers revolted against
tight price controls and intrusive inspections, eventually causing the
economy to collapse. In Greece, the Athenian government set the price
of grain at a very low level. Predictably, the quantity of grain supplied
dried up. In 301 CE, the Roman government under Emperor Diocletian
prescribed the maximum price of beef, grains, clothing, and many other
items. Almost immediately, markets for these goods disappeared.

History has shown us that price controls generally do not work. Why?
Because they disrupt the normal functioning of the market. By the end
of this chapter, you will understand why price controls are rarely the
win-win propositions that legislators often claim. To help you understand why price controls lead to disequilibrium in markets, this chapter
focuses on the two most common types of price controls: *price ceilings*
and *price floors*.

The Code of Hammurabi established the first known price controls.

BIG QUESTIONS

* When do price ceilings matter?
* What effects do price ceilings have on economic activity?
* When do price floors matter?
* What effects do price floors have on economic activity?

When Do Price Ceilings Matter?

Price controls attempt to set prices through government involvement in the market.

A **price ceiling** is a legally established maximum price for a good or service.

Price controls attempt to set prices through government involvement in the market. In most cases, and certainly in the United States, price controls are enacted to ease perceived burdens on society. A **price ceiling** creates a legally established maximum price for a good or service. In the next section, we consider what happens when a price ceiling is in place. Price ceilings create many unintended effects that policymakers rarely acknowledge.

Understanding Price Ceilings

To understand how price ceilings work, let's try a simple thought experiment. Suppose that most prices are rising as a result of *inflation*, an overall increase in prices. The government is concerned that people with low incomes will not be able to afford to eat. To help the disadvantaged, legislators pass a law stating that no one can charge more than $0.50 for a loaf of bread. (Note that this price ceiling is about one-third the typical price of a loaf of generic white bread.) Does the new law accomplish its goal? What happens?

The law of demand tells us that if the price drops, the quantity that consumers demand will increase. At the same time, the law of supply tells us that the quantity supplied will fall because producers will be receiving lower profits for their efforts. This combination of increased quantity demanded and reduced quantity supplied will cause a shortage of bread.

On the demand side, consumers will want more bread than is available at the legal price. There will be long lines for bread, and many people will not be able to get the bread they want. On the supply side, producers will look for ways to maintain their profits.

Empty shelves signal a shortage of products.

They can reduce the size of each loaf they produce. They can also use cheaper ingredients, thereby lowering the quality of their product, and they can stop making fancier varieties.

In addition, *black markets* will develop. For instance, in 2014 Venezuela instituted price controls on flour, which has led to severe shortages of bread. In this real-life example, many people who do not want to wait in line for bread or who do not obtain it despite waiting in line will resort to illegal means to obtain it. In other words, sellers will go "underground" and charge higher prices to customers who want bread. **Black markets** are illegal markets that arise when price controls are in place.

Table 6.1 summarizes the likely outcomes of price controls on bread.

Incentives

Black markets are illegal markets that arise when price controls are in place.

TABLE 6.1

A Price Ceiling on Bread

Question	Answer / Explanation	Result	
Will there be more bread or less bread for sale?	Consumers will want to buy more because the price is lower (the law of demand), but producers will manufacture less (the law of supply). The net result will be a shortage of bread.		Empty shelves.
Will the size of a typical loaf change?	Because the price is capped at $0.50 per loaf, manufacturers will try to maintain profits by reducing the size of each loaf.		No more giant loaves.
Will the quality change?	Because the price is capped, producers will use cheaper ingredients, and many expensive brands and varieties will no longer be profitable to produce. Thus the quality of available bread will decline.		Focaccia bread will disappear.
Will the opportunity cost of finding bread change?	The opportunity cost of finding bread will rise. Consumers will spend significant resources going from store to store to see if a bread shipment has arrived and waiting in line for a chance to get some.		Bread lines will become the norm.
Will people have to break the law to buy bread?	Because bread will be hard to find and people will still need it, a black market will develop. Those selling and buying on the black market will be breaking the law.		Black-market bread dealers will help reduce the shortage.

If you can touch the ceiling, you can't go any higher. A binding price ceiling stops prices from rising.

The Effect of Price Ceilings

Now that we have some understanding of how a price ceiling works, we can transfer that knowledge into the supply and demand model for a deeper analysis of how price ceilings affect the market. To explain when price ceilings matter in the short run, we examine two types of price ceilings: nonbinding and binding.

Nonbinding Price Ceilings

The effect of a price ceiling depends on the level at which it is set. When a price ceiling is above the equilibrium price, we say it is *nonbinding*. Figure 6.1 shows a price ceiling of $2.00 per loaf in a market where $2.00 is above the equilibrium price (P_E) of $1.00. All prices at or below $2.00 (the green area) are legal. Prices above the price ceiling (the red area) are illegal. But because the market equilibrium (E) occurs in the green area, the price ceiling does not influence the market; it is nonbinding. As long as the equilibrium price remains below the price ceiling, price will continue to be regulated by supply and demand.

Binding Price Ceilings

When a price ceiling is below the market price, it creates a binding constraint that prevents supply and demand from clearing the market. In Figure 6.2, the

---

FIGURE 6.1

A Nonbinding Price Ceiling

The price ceiling ($2.00) is set above the equilibrium price ($1.00). Because market prices are set by the intersection of supply (S) and demand (D), as long as the equilibrium price is below the price ceiling, the price ceiling is nonbinding and has no effect.

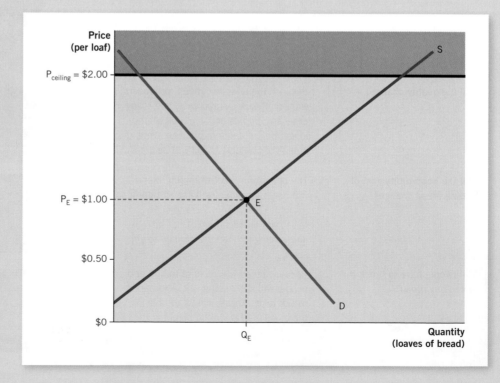

price ceiling for bread is set at $0.50 per loaf. Because $0.50 is well below the equilibrium price of $1.00, the price ceiling is *binding*. Notice that at a price of $0.50, the quantity demanded (Q_D) is greater than the quantity supplied (Q_S); in other words, a shortage exists. Shortages typically cause prices to rise, but the imposed price ceiling prevents that from happening. A price ceiling of $0.50 allows only the prices in the green area. The market cannot reach the equilibrium point E at $1.00 per loaf because it is located above the price ceiling, in the red area.

The black-market price is also set by supply and demand. Because prices above $0.50 are illegal, sellers are unwilling to produce more than Q_S. Because a shortage exists, an illegal market will form in response to the shortage. In the black market, purchasers can illegally resell what they have just bought at $0.50 for far more than what they just paid. Because the supply of legally produced bread is Q_S, the intersection of the vertical dashed line that reflects Q_S with the demand curve D_{SR} at point $E_{black\ market}$ establishes a black-market price ($P_{black\ market}$) at $2.00 per loaf for illegally sold bread. The black-market price is substantially more than the market equilibrium price (P_E) of $1.00, so illegal suppliers (underground bakers) will enter the market to satisfy demand. As a result, the black-market price eliminates the shortage caused by the price ceiling. However, the price ceiling has created two unintended consequences: a smaller quantity of bread supplied (Q_S is less than Q_E), and a higher price for those who purchase it on the black market.

Incentives

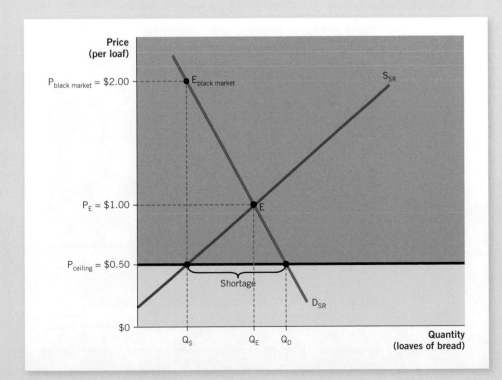

FIGURE 6.2

The Effect of a Binding Price Ceiling in the Short Run

A binding price ceiling prevents sellers from increasing the price and causes them to reduce the quantity they offer for sale. As a consequence, prices no longer signal relative scarcity. Consumers desire to purchase the product at the price ceiling level, which creates a shortage in the short run (SR); many will be unable to obtain the good. As a result, those who are shut out of the market will turn to other means to acquire the good, establishing an illegal market for the good at the black-market price.

Price Ceilings in the Long Run

In the long run, supply and demand become more elastic, or flatter. Recall from Chapter 4 that when consumers have additional time to make choices, they find more ways to avoid high-priced goods and more ways to take advantage of low prices. Additional time also gives producers the opportunity to produce more when prices are high and less when prices are low. In this section, we consider what happens if a binding price ceiling on bread remains in effect for a long time. We have already observed that binding price ceilings create shortages and black markets in the short run. Are the long-run implications of price ceilings more problematic or less problematic than the short-run implications? Let's find out by looking at what happens to both supply and demand.

Figure 6.3 shows the result of a price ceiling that remains in place for a long time. Here the supply curve is more elastic than its short-run counterpart in Figure 6.2. The supply curve is flatter because producers respond in the long run by producing less bread and converting their facilities to make similar products that are not subject to price controls and that will bring them a reasonable return on their investments—for example, bagels and rolls. Therefore, in the long run the quantity supplied (Q_S) shrinks even more.

The demand curve is also more elastic (flatter) in the long run. In the long run, more people will attempt to take advantage of the price ceiling by changing their eating habits to consume more bread. Even though consumers will

FIGURE 6.3

The Effect of a Binding Price Ceiling in the Long Run

In the long run (LR), increased elasticity on the part of both producers and consumers makes the shortage larger than it was in the short run. Consumers adjust their demand to the lower price and want more bread. Producers adjust their supply and make less of the unprofitable product. As a result, the product becomes progressively harder to find.

Price Ceilings

Moscow on the Hudson

This 1984 film starring Robin Williams chronicles the differences between living in the United States and living in the former Soviet Union. In the film, we see hundreds of people in Moscow waiting in line to receive essentials like bread, milk, and shoes. In the Soviet Union, production was controlled and prices were not allowed to equalize quantity supplied and quantity demanded. As a result, shortages were common. Waiting in line served as a rationing mechanism in the absence of price adjustments.

This film is memorable because of the reactions that Robin Williams's character has once he immigrates to the United States. In one inspired scene, he walks into a supermarket to buy coffee. He asks the manager where the coffee aisle is located, and

Soviet-era food-rationing coupon

Soviet-era bread line

when he sees that the aisle is not crowded, he asks the manager where the coffee line is located. The manager responds that there is no coffee line, so Williams walks down the coffee aisle slowly, naming each variety. We see his joy at being able to buy coffee without waiting and at having so many options to choose from. This scene nicely showcases the differences between the market system of the United States and the controlled economy of the former Soviet Union.

often find empty shelves in the long run, the quantity demanded of cheap bread will increase. The flatter demand curve means that consumers are more flexible. As a result, the quantity demanded (Q_D) expands and bread is harder to find at $0.50 per loaf. The shortage will become so acute that consumers will turn to bread substitutes, like bagels and rolls, that are more plentiful because they are not price controlled.

Increased elasticity on the part of producers and consumers magnifies the unintended consequences we observed in the short run. Therefore, products subject to a price ceiling become progressively harder to find in the long run

PRACTICE WHAT YOU KNOW

Price Ceilings: Concert Tickets

Question: Suppose that fans of Calvin Harris persuade Congress to impose a price ceiling of $25 for every Calvin Harris concert ticket. Would this policy affect the number of people who attend his concerts?

How deep is your love for Calvin?

Answer: The price that makes quantity supplied equal to quantity demanded is now illegal as a result of this binding price ceiling. As a result, at $25 there is a shortage of tickets. Because Calvin controls when and where he tours, he will choose to tour less in the United States and more in countries that do not regulate ticket prices. Calvin's choice of venues will make it more difficult for his U.S. fans to see him perform live, so the answer to the question is yes: the policy will influence the number of people who attend Calvin Harris concerts (fewer in the United States and more abroad).

and the black market continues to operate. However, in the long run our bread consumers will choose substitutes for expensive black-market bread, leading to somewhat lower black-market prices in the long run.

What Effects Do Price Ceilings Have on Economic Activity?

We have seen the logical repercussions of a hypothetical price ceiling on bread and the incentives it creates. Now let's use supply and demand analysis to examine two real-world price ceilings: *rent control* and *price gouging laws*.

Rent Control

Rent control is a price ceiling that applies to the market for apartment rentals.

Under **rent control**, a local government caps the price of apartment rentals to keep housing affordable. While this goal may be laudable, rent control doesn't work. In fact, it doesn't help the poor residents of a city find affordable housing or gain access to housing at all. In addition, these policies contribute to dangerous living conditions.

Mumbai, India, provides a chilling example of what can happen when rent controls are applied over an extended period. In Mumbai, many rent-controlled buildings have become dilapidated. Every monsoon season, several of these buildings fall—often with tragic consequences. Because the rent that property owners are permitted to charge is so low, they have less income to use for maintenance on the buildings. They cannot make a reasonable profit and afford to maintain the buildings properly. As a result, rent control policies have led to the decay of many apartment buildings. Similar controls have caused the same problem in cities worldwide.

Many apartment buildings in Mumbai, India, are dilapidated as a result of rent control laws.

To understand how a policy can backfire so greatly, let's look at the history of rent control in New York City. In 1943, in the midst of World War II, the federal government established the Emergency Price Control Act. The act was designed to keep inflation in check during the war, when many essential commodities were scarce. After the war, the federal government ended price controls, but New York City continued rent control. Today, there are approximately 1 million rent-controlled units in New York City. Rent controls limit the price a landlord can charge a tenant for rent. They also require that the landlord provide certain basic services; but not surprisingly, landlords keep maintenance to a minimum.

Does the presence of so many rent-controlled apartments mean that less affluent households can easily find a cheap place to rent? Hardly. When a rent-controlled unit is vacated, the property is generally no longer subject to rent control. Laws allow the tenants of rent-controlled apartments to pass those apartments from generation to generation, which keeps the apartments in the rent control program. Because so many rent-controlled apartments are inherited, rent control no longer even remotely serves its original purpose of helping low-income households. Clearly, the law was never intended to subsidize fancy vacation homes, but that's what it does! This outcome has happened, in part, because some tenants who can afford to live elsewhere choose not to. Their subsidized rent enables them to afford a second or third home in places such as upstate New York, Florida, or Europe.

Incentives

The attempt to make housing more affordable in New York City has, ironically, made housing harder to obtain. It has encouraged the building of upscale properties rather than low-income units, and it has created a set of behaviors among landlords that is inconsistent with the affordability that rent control was designed to address. Figure 6.4 shows why rent control fails. As with any price ceiling, rent control causes a shortage because the quantity demanded in the short run ($Q_{D_{SR}}$) is greater than the quantity supplied in the short run ($Q_{S_{SR}}$).The combination of fewer available units and more consumers looking for rent-controlled units leads to a larger shortage in the long run.

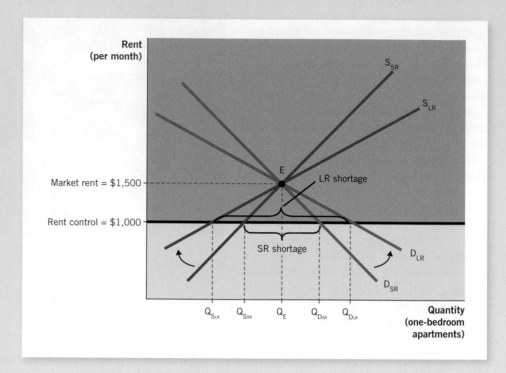

FIGURE 6.4

Rent Control in the Short Run and the Long Run

Because rent-controlled apartments are vacated slowly, the quantity supplied contracts in the short run and the supply curve become more elastic in the long run. Demand also becomes more elastic in the long run, causing the quantity demanded to rise. The combination of fewer units available to rent and more consumers looking to find rent-controlled units leads to a larger shortage in the long run.

Price Gouging

Price gouging laws place a temporary ceiling on the prices that sellers can charge during times of emergency.

Another kind of price control, **price gouging laws**, places a temporary ceiling on the prices that sellers can charge during times of emergency until markets function normally again. Over 30 U.S. states have laws against price gouging. Like all price controls, price gouging laws have unintended consequences. These consequences became very apparent after Superstorm Sandy in 2012.

When Hurricane Sandy hit New Jersey in October, a state of emergency activated price gouging laws. The statute makes it illegal to charge an "excessive" price immediately following a natural disaster. The law is designed to prevent the victims of natural disasters from being exploited in a time of need. But does it work?

Suppose that an entrepreneur from North Carolina is interested in delivering generators to the affected area. He can purchase generators for $530 where he lives and he hopes to sell them for $900 when he arrives in New Jersey. However, he finds out that under New Jersey law he can be fined up to $10,000 for each sale he makes above the legal price during a state of emergency. Facing this prospect, he decides to stay in North Carolina, where the generators are not needed, rather than incur the risk. As a result, the residents of New Jersey never get the opportunity to decide for themselves whether they wish to voluntarily pay $900 for a generator or not.

Prices act to ration scarce resources. When the demand for generators or other necessities is high, the price rises to ensure that the available units are distributed to those who value them the most. More important, the ability

Incentives

to charge a higher price provides sellers with an incentive to make more units available. If laws limit the ability for the price to change when demand increases, the result will be a shortage. Therefore, price gouging legislation means that devastated communities must rely exclusively on the goodwill of others and the slow-moving machinery of government relief efforts. In addition, price gouging laws close off entrepreneurial activity, which would otherwise be a means to alleviate dire conditions.

Large generator: Demand increased after Superstorm Sandy hit.

Figure 6.5 shows how price gouging laws work and the shortage they create. If the demand for gas generators increases immediately after a disaster (D_{after}), the market price rises from \$530 to \$900. But because \$900 is considered excessive, sales at that price are illegal. The result is a binding price ceiling for as long as a state of emergency is in effect. A binding price ceiling creates a shortage. You can see the shortage in Figure 6.5 in the difference between quantity demanded and quantity supplied at the price ceiling mandated by the law. In this case, the normal ability of supply and demand to ration the available generators is short-circuited. Because more people demand generators after the disaster than before it, those who do not get to the store soon enough are out of luck. When the emergency is lifted and the market returns to normal, the temporary shortage created by price gouging laws is eliminated.

FIGURE 6.5

Price Gouging

Price gouging laws serve as a nonbinding price ceiling during normal times. However, when a natural disaster strikes, price gouging laws go into effect. In our example, the demand curve for generators shifts to the right as a result of the natural disaster, causing the new equilibrium price (E_{after}) to rise above the legal limit. The result is a shortage. When the emergency is lifted, the market demand returns to normal, and the temporary shortage created by price gouging legislation is eliminated.

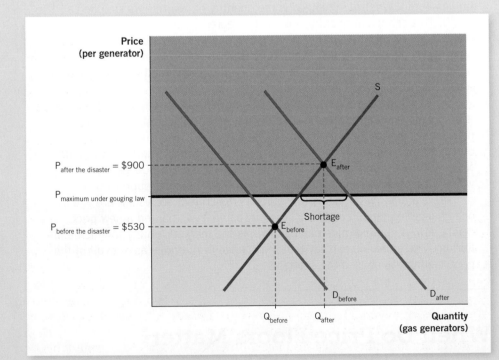

PRACTICE WHAT YOU KNOW

Price Ceilings: Student Rental Apartments

Here is a question that often confuses students.

Question: Imagine that a city council decides that the market price for student rental apartments is too high. It passes a law that establishes a rental price ceiling of $600 per month. The result of the price ceiling is a shortage. Which of the following has caused the shortage of apartments?

a. Both suppliers and demanders. Landlords will reduce the supply of apartments, and the demand from renters will increase.

b. A spike in demand from many students who want to rent cheap apartments

c. The drop in supply caused by apartment owners pulling their units off the rental market and converting them into condos for sale

d. The change in price as a result of the price ceiling set by the city council

Answer: Many students think that markets are to blame when shortages (or surpluses) exist. The first reaction is to find the culpable party—either the supplier or the demander, or both. For this reason, many students believe that choice (a) is correct. But be careful. Supply and demand have not changed—they are exactly the same as they were before the price ceiling was implemented. What *has* changed is the quantity of apartments supplied at $600. This change in quantity supplied is represented by a movement along the existing supply curve. The same type of analysis applies to renters. The quantity demanded at $600 is much larger than it was when the price was not controlled. Therefore, the change in quantity demanded is represented by a movement along the demand curve.

    The same logic applies to choices (b) and (c). Choice (b) states that there is a spike in student demand caused by the lower price. But price cannot cause a shift in the demand curve; it can only cause a movement along a curve. Likewise, choice (c) states that apartment owners supply fewer units for rent. The fact that fewer apartments are available at $600 per month would be represented by a movement along the apartment supply curve.

    So we are left with choice (d), which is the correct answer. There is only one change in market conditions: the city council has passed a new price ceiling law. A binding price ceiling disrupts the market's ability to reach equilibrium. Therefore, we can say that the change in the price as a result of the price ceiling has caused the shortage.

When Do Price Floors Matter?

A **price floor** is a legally established minimum price for a good or service.

A **price floor** creates a legally established minimum price for a good or service. The minimum wage law is an example of a price floor in the market for labor. Like price ceilings, price floors create many unintended effects that policymakers rarely acknowledge. However, unlike price ceilings, price floors result from the political pressure of suppliers to keep prices high. Most consumers prefer lower prices when they shop, so the idea of a law that keeps prices high may sound like a bad one to you. However, if you are selling a product or service, you might think that legislation to keep prices high is a very good idea. For instance, many states establish minimum prices for milk. As a result, milk prices are higher than they would be if supply and demand set the price.

In this section, we follow the same progression that we did with price ceilings. We begin with a simple thought experiment. Once we understand how price floors work, we use supply and demand analysis to examine the short- and long-run implications for economic activity.

Understanding Price Floors

To understand how price floors affect the market, let's try a thought experiment. Suppose that a politician suggests we should encourage dairy farmers to produce more milk so that supplies will be plentiful and everyone will get enough calcium. To accomplish these goals, the government sets a price floor of $6 per gallon—about twice the price of a typical gallon of fat-free milk—to make production more attractive to milk producers. What repercussions should we expect?

First, more milk will be available for sale because the higher price will cause dairies to increase the quantity that they supply. At the same time, because consumers must pay more, the quantity demanded will fall. The result will be a surplus of milk. Because every gallon of milk that is produced but not sold hurts the dairies' bottom line, sellers will want to lower their prices enough to get as many sales as possible before the milk goes bad. But the price floor will not allow the market to respond, and sellers will be stuck with milk that goes to waste. They will be tempted to offer illegal discounts in order to recoup some of their costs.

What happens next? Because the surplus cannot be resolved through lower prices, the government will try to help equalize the quantity supplied and the quantity demanded through other means. It can do so in one of two ways: by restricting the supply of the good or by stimulating additional demand. Both solutions are problematic. If production is restricted, dairy farmers will not be able to generate a profitable amount of milk. Likewise, stimulating additional demand is not as simple as it sounds. Let's consider how these government programs work with other crops.

In many cases, the government purchases surplus agricultural production, most notably with corn, soybeans, cotton, and rice. Once the government buys the surplus production, it often sells the surplus below cost to developing countries to avoid wasting the crop. This strategy has the unintended consequence of making it cheaper for consumers in these developing nations to buy excess agricultural output from developed nations like the United States than to have local farmers grow the crop. International treaties ban the practice of dumping surplus production, but it continues under the guise of humanitarian aid. This practice makes little economic sense. Table 6.2 summarizes the result of our price floor thought experiment using milk.

The Effect of Price Floors

We have seen that price floors create unintended consequences. Now we will use the supply and demand model to analyze how price floors affect the market. We look at the short run first.

If you're doing a handstand, you need the floor for support. A binding price floor keeps prices from falling.

Got milk? Maybe not, if there's a price floor.

TABLE 6.2

A Price Floor on Milk

Question	Answer / Explanation		Result
Will the quantity of milk for sale change?	Consumers will purchase less because the price is higher (the law of demand), but producers will manufacture more (the law of supply). The net result will be a surplus of milk.		There will be a surplus of milk.
Would producers sell below the price floor?	Yes. A surplus of milk would give sellers a strong incentive to undercut the price floor to avoid having to discard leftover milk.	REDUCED MILK AHEAD	Illegal discounts will help reduce the milk surplus.
Will dairy farmers be better off?	Not if they have trouble selling what they produce.	not for Sale no good.	There might be a lot of spoiled milk.

Nonbinding Price Floors

Like price ceilings, price floors can be binding or nonbinding. Figure 6.6 illustrates a nonbinding price floor of $2 per gallon on milk. As you can see, at $2 the price floor is below the equilibrium price (P_E), so the price floor is nonbinding. Because the actual market price is above the legally established minimum price (P_{floor}), the price floor does not prevent the market from reaching equilibrium at point E. Consequently, the price floor has no impact on the market. As long as the equilibrium price remains above the price floor, price is determined by supply and demand.

Full shelves signal a market at equilibrium.

Binding Price Floors

For a price floor to have an impact on the market, it must be set above the market equilibrium price. In that case, it is a binding price floor. With a binding price floor, the quantity supplied will exceed the quantity demanded. Figure 6.7 illustrates a binding price floor in the short run. Continuing our example of milk prices, at $6 per gallon the price floor is above the equilibrium price of $3. Market forces always attempt to restore the equilibrium between supply and demand at point E. So we know that there is downward pressure on the price. At a price floor of $6, we see that

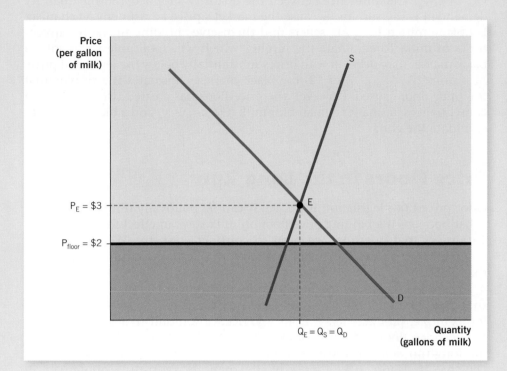

FIGURE 6.6

A Nonbinding Price Floor

Under a nonbinding price floor, price is regulated by supply and demand. Because the price floor ($2) is below the equilibrium price ($3), the market will voluntarily charge more than the legal minimum. Therefore, this nonbinding price floor will have no effect on sales and purchases of milk.

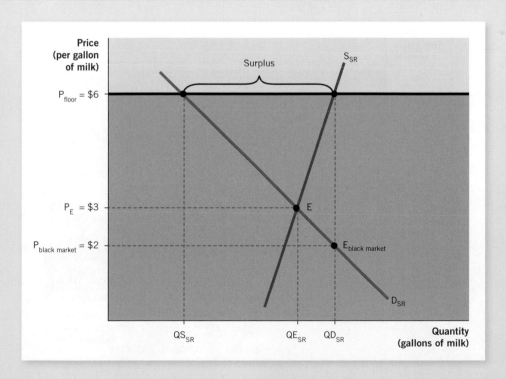

FIGURE 6.7

A Binding Price Floor in the Short Run

A binding price floor creates a surplus, which has two unintended consequences: (1) a smaller quantity demanded than the equilibrium quantity ($Q_{D_{SR}} < Q_{E_{SR}}$) and (2) a lower black-market price to eliminate the glut of the product.

$QS_{SR} > QD_{SR}$. The difference between the quantity supplied and the quantity demanded is the surplus. Because the market's price adjustment mechanism is not permitted to work, sellers find themselves holding unwanted inventories of milk. To eliminate the surplus, which will spoil unless it is sold, a black market may develop with prices substantially below the legislated price. At a price ($P_{black\ market}$) of $2, the black market eliminates the surplus that the price floor caused. However, the price floor has created two unintended consequences: a smaller demand for milk ($Q_{D_{SR}} < Q_{E_{SR}}$) and a black market to eliminate the glut.

Incentives

Price Floors in the Long Run

Once price floor legislation is passed, it can be politically difficult to repeal. What happens if a binding price floor on milk stays in effect for a long time? To answer that question, we need to consider elasticity. We have already observed that in the short run, binding price ceilings cause shortages and that black markets follow.

Figure 6.8 shows a price floor for milk that remains in place well past the short run. The long run gives consumers a chance to find milk substitutes—for example, products made from soy, rice, or almond that are not subject to the price floor—at lower prices. This added consumer flexibility makes the long-run demand for milk more elastic. As a result, the demand curve depicted in Figure 6.8 is more elastic than its short-run counterpart in

FIGURE 6.8

The Effect of a Binding Price Floor in the Long Run

When a price floor is left in place over time, supply and demand both become more elastic. The result is a larger surplus ($Q_{S_{LR}} > Q_{D_{LR}}$) in the long run. Because sellers are unable to sell all that they produce at $6 per gallon, a black market develops to eliminate the glut of milk.

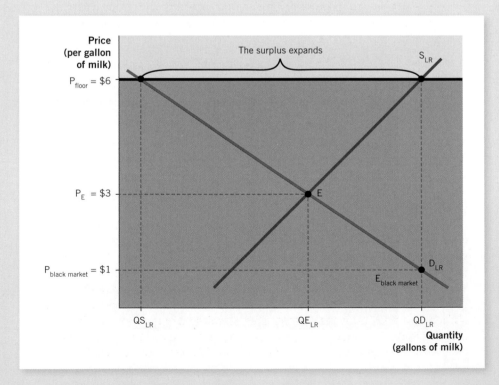

Figure 6.7. The supply curve also becomes flatter (more elastic) because firms (dairy farms) are able to produce more milk by acquiring additional land and production facilities. Therefore, a price floor ($6) that remains in place over time causes the supply and demand curves to become more elastic, magnifying the surplus.

What happens to supply? In the long run, producers are more flexible and therefore supply is more elastic. The pool of potential milk producers rises as other closely related businesses retool their operations to supply more milk. The flatter supply curve in Figure 6.8 reflects this flexibility. As a result, $Q_{S_{LR}}$ expands and becomes much larger than it was in Figure 6.7. The increased elasticity on the part of both producers and consumers makes the surplus larger in the long run and magnifies the unintended consequences we observed in the short run.

PRACTICE WHAT YOU KNOW

Price Floors: Fair-Trade Coffee

Fair-trade coffee is sold through organizations that purchase directly from growers. The coffee is usually sold for a higher price than standard coffee. The goal is to promote more humane working conditions for the coffee pickers and growers. Fair-trade coffee has become more popular but still accounts for a small portion of all coffee sales, in large part because it is substantially more expensive to produce.

Question: Suppose that the price of a 1-pound bag of standard coffee is $8 and the price of a 1-pound bag of fair-trade coffee is $12. Congress decides to impose a price floor of $10 per pound on all 1-pound bags of coffee. Will this policy cause more or fewer people to buy fair-trade coffee?

Answer: Fair-trade producers typically sell their product at a higher price than mass-produced coffee brands. Therefore, a $10 price floor is binding for inexpensive brands like Folgers but nonbinding for premium coffees, which include fair-trade sellers. The price floor will reduce the price disparity between fair-trade coffee and mass-produced coffee.

To see how the market will respond, consider a fair-trade coffee producer who charges $12 per pound and a mass-produced brand that sells for $8 per pound. A price floor of $10 reduces the difference between the price of fair-trade coffee and the inexpensive coffee brands, which now must sell for $10 instead of $8. The consumer's opportunity cost of choosing fair-trade coffee is now lower. Therefore, some consumers of the inexpensive brands will opt for fair-trade coffee instead. As a result, fair-trade producers will benefit indirectly from the price floor. Thus, the answer to the question is that more people will buy fair-trade coffee as a result of this price floor policy.

Would fair-trade coffee producers benefit from a price floor?

Opportunity cost

What Effects Do Price Floors Have on Economic Activity?

We have seen the logical repercussions of a hypothetical price floor on milk and the incentives it creates. Now let's use supply and demand analysis to examine two real-world price floors: *minimum wage laws* and *sugar subsidies*.

The Minimum Wage

The **minimum wage** is the lowest hourly wage rate that firms may legally pay their workers.

The **minimum wage** is the lowest hourly wage rate that firms may legally pay their workers. Minimum wage workers can be skilled or unskilled and experienced or inexperienced. The common thread is that these workers, for a variety of reasons, lack better prospects. A minimum wage functions as a price floor. Figure 6.9 shows the effect of a binding minimum wage. Note that the wage, or the cost of labor, on the *y* axis ($10 per hour) is the price that must be paid. However, the market equilibrium wage ($7), or W_E, is below the minimum wage. The minimum wage prevents the market from reaching W_E at E (the equilibrium point) because only the wages in the green area are legal. The minimum wage raises the cost of hiring workers. Therefore, a higher minimum wage will lower the quantity of labor demanded. At the

FIGURE 6.9

Price Floors and a Binding Minimum Wage Market in the Short Run and Long Run

A binding minimum wage is a price floor above the current equilibrium wage, W_E. At $10 per hour, the number of workers willing to supply their labor (S_{SR}) is greater than the demand for workers (D_{SR}). The result is a surplus of workers (which we recognize as unemployment). Because the supply of workers and demand for workers both become more elastic in the long run, unemployment expands ($Q_{S_{LR}} > Q_{D_{LR}}$).

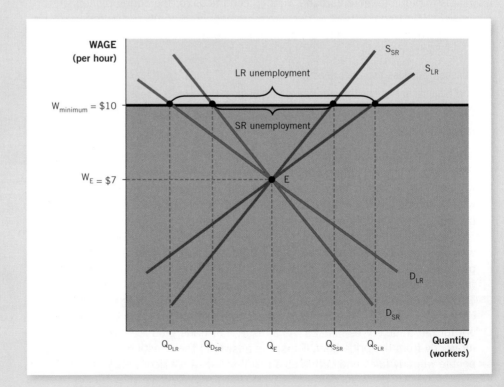

same time, firms will look for ways to substitute capital for workers. As a result, a binding minimum wage results in unemployment in the short run because $Q_{S_{SR}} > Q_{D_{SR}}$.

Businesses generally want to keep costs down, so in the long run they will try to reduce the amount they spend on labor. They might replace workers with machinery, shorten work hours, offer reduced customer service, or even relocate to countries that do not have minimum wage laws. As we move past the short run, more people will attempt to take advantage of higher minimum wages. Like firms, workers will adjust to the higher minimum wage over time. Some workers who might have decided to go to school full-time or remain retired or who simply want some extra income will enter the labor market because the minimum wage is now higher. As a result, minimum wage jobs will become progressively harder to find and unemployment will increase. The irony is that in the long run, the minimum wage, just like any other price floor, has created two unintended consequences: a smaller demand for workers by employers ($Q_{D_{LR}}$ is significantly less than Q_E) and a larger supply of workers ($Q_{S_{LR}}$) looking for jobs.

Proponents of minimum wage legislation are aware that it often creates unemployment. To address this problem, they support investment in training, education, and the creation of government jobs programs to provide more work opportunities. While jobs programs increase the number of minimum wage jobs, training and additional education enable workers to acquire skills needed for jobs that pay more than the minimum wage. Economists generally believe that education and training programs have longer-lasting benefits to society as a whole because they enable workers to obtain better-paying jobs on a permanent basis.

ECONOMICS IN THE REAL WORLD

Wage Laws Squeeze South Africa's Poor

Consider this story, which originally appeared in the *New York Times*. We have updated the data to reflect recent events.[*]

In South Africa, the minimum wage is above the market equilibrium wage. To prevent clothing companies from ignoring the minimum wage, South African law-enforcement officers routinely shut down factories that violate the minimum wage law. You might expect workers to celebrate these shutdowns, but the workers begged the authorities to keep the factory open. South Africa has a huge unemployment problem (an excess supply of labor), and approximately a quarter of South Africans are jobless. The workers in the factories shut down by the government were being paid just $36 a week (far less than the minimum wage). However, the factory workers needed the job to support their families. Workers viewed having a job, even at a very low wage, as better than no job. This vivid example is the downside of binding minimum wage that creates unemployment.

Trade-offs

Since the end of apartheid, the South African economy has struggled to grow fast enough to reduce one of the worst employment crises in the

---

[*] Celia W. Dugger, "Wage Laws Squeeze South Africa's Poor," *New York Times*, September 27, 2010.

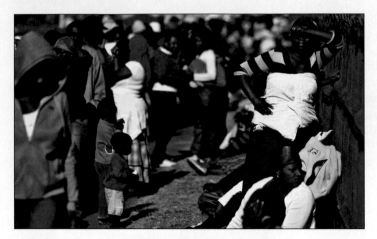

South Africans wait in line for unemployment benefits.

world. A long-term unemployment rate near 25% has led to increased crime, social unrest, and staggering income inequality in Africa's richest country. The global economic downturn of 2007–2010 only made matters worse, effectively destroying over a million jobs. The unemployment problem is especially acute among the young minorities, whose unemployment rate exceeds 50%.

In the United States, where the unemployment rate hovers near 5%, it is hard to fully appreciate difficulties facing South African workers. Many U.S. states and local governments have raised the minimum wage substantially above the federal minimum. Those efforts were possible because the United States has a healthy economy and the federal minimum wage is largely nonbinding. If the United States had a huge unemployment problem, efforts to raise the minimum wage would likely be met with the same worker resistance that we see in South Africa. ✷

The Minimum Wage Is Often Nonbinding

Most people believe that raising the minimum wage is a simple step that the government can take to improve the standard of living of the working poor. However, in most places the minimum wage is nonbinding and therefore has no impact on the market. Why would we have a minimum wage if it is largely nonbinding?

To help us answer this question, consider the two nonbinding minimum wage rates ($7 and $9) shown in Figure 6.10. A minimum wage of $7 per hour is far below the equilibrium wage of $10 ($W_E$), so at that point supply and demand push the equilibrium wage up to $10. Suppose that politicians decide to raise the minimum wage to $9. This new minimum wage of $9 would remain below the market wage, so there would be no impact on the labor market for workers who are willing to accept the minimum wage. Therefore, an increase in the minimum wage from $7 to $9 an hour will not create unemployment. Unemployment will occur only when the minimum wage rises above $10.

Politicians know that most voters have a poor understanding of basic economics. As a result, a politician can seek to raise the minimum wage with great fanfare. Voters would support the new rate because they do not know that it is likely to be nonbinding; they expect wages to rise. In reality, nothing will change, but the perception of a benevolent action will remain. In fact, since the inception of the minimum wage in 1938, increases in the U.S. minimum wage have generally trailed the market wage and therefore have avoided creating unemployment. The minimum wage adjusts sporadically upward every few years but rarely rises enough to cause the market wage to fall below it. This situation creates the illusion that the minimum wage is lifting wages. However, it does not cause any of the adverse consequences of a binding minimum wage.

Minimum Wage: Always the Same?

A minimum wage is a price floor, a price control that doesn't allow prices—in this case the cost of labor—to fall below an assigned value. Although the media and politicians often discuss the minimum wage in the United States as if there is only one minimum wage, there are numerous minimum wages in the USA. In states where the state minimum wage is not the same as the federal minimum wage, the higher of the two wage rates takes effect.

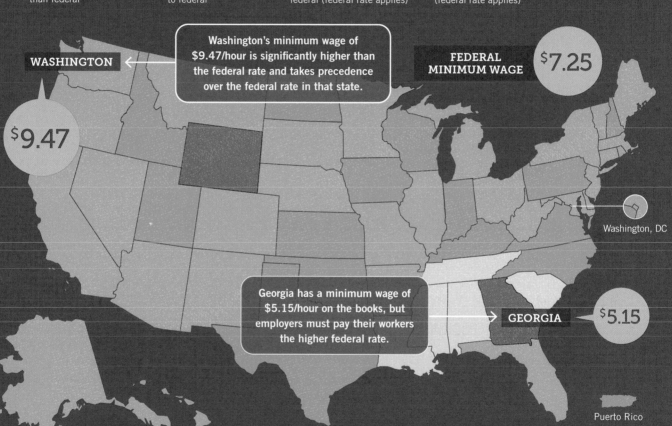

■ Minimum wage higher than federal

■ Minimum wage equal to federal

■ Minimum wage lower than federal (federal rate applies)

■ No minimum wage (federal rate applies)

WASHINGTON

Washington's minimum wage of $9.47/hour is significantly higher than the federal rate and takes precedence over the federal rate in that state.

$9.47

FEDERAL MINIMUM WAGE $7.25

Washington, DC

Georgia has a minimum wage of $5.15/hour on the books, but employers must pay their workers the higher federal rate.

GEORGIA $5.15

Puerto Rico

Highest Minimum Wages, 2016

1. Washington, DC	$10.50
2. California	$10.00
3. Washington	$9.47
4. Oregon	$9.25
5. Connecticut	$9.15

REVIEW QUESTIONS

• Suppose you live in Arkansas and are looking for a job. The state minimum wage rate is $7.50/hour, the federal minimum wage rate is $7.25/hour, and the market equilibrium wage for the job is $8.00/hour. What wage will you be paid? Are the state and national minimum wages binding or non-binding price floors?

• Suppose Wisconsin increases its minimum wage from $7.25/hour, which is below the market wage for low-skill labor, to $11.00/hour, which is above the market wage. Using supply and demand curves, show how this might increase the number of employed workers.

Source: U.S. Department of Labor.

FIGURE 6.10

A Nonbinding Minimum Wage

An increase in the minimum wage from $7 to $9 remains nonbinding. Therefore, it will not change the demand for labor or the unemployment rate. If the minimum wage rises above the market wage, unemployment will occur.

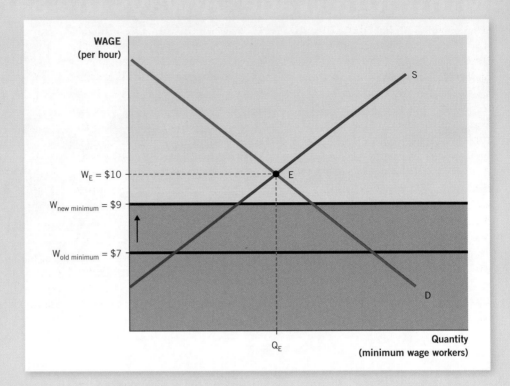

WAGE (per hour)

$W_E = \$10$

$W_{new\ minimum} = \$9$

$W_{old\ minimum} = \$7$

Q_E

Quantity (minimum wage workers)

ECONOMICS IN THE REAL WORLD

A Sweet Deal, If You Can Get It

Incentives

Sugar is one of life's small pleasures. It can be extracted and refined from sugarcane and sugar beets, two crops that can be grown in a variety of climates around the world. Sugar is both plentiful and cheap. As a result, Americans enjoy a lot of it—an average of over 50 pounds of refined sugar per person each year!

We would consume a lot more sugar if it were not subject to price controls. After the War of 1812, struggling sugarcane producers asked the government to pass a tariff (tax) that would protect domestic production. Over the years, price supports of all kinds have served to keep domestic sugar production high. The result is an industry that depends on a high price to survive. Under the current price-support system, the price of U.S.-produced sugar is roughly two to three times the world price. This situation has led to a bizarre set of incentives whereby U.S. farmers grow more sugar than they should and use land that is not well suited to the crop. For instance, sugarcane requires a subtropical climate, but most of the U.S. crop is grown in Louisiana, a region that is prone to hurricanes in the summer and killing freezes in the late fall. As a result, many sugarcane crops there are completely lost.

Why do farmers persist in growing sugarcane in Louisiana? The answer lies in the political process: sugar growers have effectively lobbied to keep prices high through tariffs on foreign imports. Because lower prices would put many U.S. growers out of business and cause the loss of many jobs, politicians have given in to their demands.

Meanwhile, the typical sugar consumer is largely oblivious to the political process that sets the price floor. It has been estimated that the sugar subsidy program costs consumers over $1 billion a year. To make matters worse, thanks to corn subsidies, high-fructose corn syrup has become a cheap alternative to sugar and is often added to processed foods and soft drinks. In 1980, Coca-Cola replaced sugar with high-fructose corn syrup in its U.S. factories to reduce production costs. However, Coca-Cola continues to use sugarcane in many Latin American countries because it is cheaper there. Research shows that high-fructose corn syrup causes a metabolic reaction that makes people who ingest it more inclined to obesity. This is an example of an unintended consequence that few policymakers could have imagined. There is no reason why the United States must produce its own sugarcane. Ironically, sugar is cheaper in Canada than in the United States primarily because Canada has no sugar growers—and thus no trade restrictions or government support programs. ✳

Which of these is the *real* thing? The Coke on the right, with high-fructose corn syrup, was made in the United States; the other, with sugar, was made in Mexico.

PRACTICE WHAT YOU KNOW

Price Ceilings and Price Floors: Would a Price Control on Internet Access Be Effective?

A recent study found the following demand and supply schedule for high-speed Internet access:

In today's Internet age, four degrees of separation are all that stand between you and the rest of the world.

Price of Internet	Connections demanded (millions of units)	Connections supplied (millions of units)
$60	10.0	62.5
$50	20.0	55.0
$40	30.0	47.5
$30	40.0	40.0
$20	50.0	32.5
$10	60.0	25.0

Question: What are the equilibrium price and equilibrium quantity of Internet service?

Answer: First, look at the table to see where quantity supplied and quantity demanded are equal. At a price of $30, consumers purchase 40 million units and producers supply 40 million units. Therefore, the equilibrium price is $30 and the equilibrium quantity is 40 million. At any price above $30, the

(CONTINUED)

(CONTINUED)

quantity supplied exceeds the quantity demanded, so there is a surplus. The surplus gives sellers an incentive to cut the price until it reaches the equilibrium point, E. At any price below $30, the quantity demanded exceeds the quantity supplied, so there is a shortage. The shortage gives sellers an incentive to raise the price until it reaches the equilibrium point, E.

Question: Suppose that providers convince the government that maintaining high-speed access to the Internet is an important element of technology infrastructure. As a result, Congress approves a price floor at $10 above the equilibrium price to help companies provide Internet service. How many people are able to connect to the Internet?

Answer: Adding $10 to the market price of $30 gives us a price floor of $40. At $40, consumers demand 30 million connections. Producers provide 47.5 million connections. The result is a surplus of 17.5 million units (shown in the graph). A price floor means that producers cannot cut the price below that point to increase the quantity that consumers demand. As a result, only 30 million units are sold. So only 30 million people connect to the Internet.

Question: When consumers realize that fewer people are purchasing Internet access, they demand that the price floor be repealed and a price ceiling be put in its place. Congress acts immediately to remedy the problem, and a new price ceiling is set at $10 below the market price. Now how many people are able to connect to the Internet?

Answer: Subtracting $10 from the market price of $30 gives us a price ceiling of $20. At $20 per connection, consumers demand 50 million connections. However, producers provide only 32.5 million connections. The result is a shortage of 17.5 million units (shown in the graph). A price ceiling means that producers cannot raise the price, which will cause an increase in the quantity supplied. As a result, only 32.5 million units are sold, so only 32.5 million people connect to the Internet.

Question: Which provides the greatest access to the Internet: free markets, price floors, or price ceilings?

Answer: With no government intervention, 40 million connections are sold. Once the price floor is established, 30 million people have an Internet connection. Under the price ceiling, 32.5 million people have an Internet connection. Despite legislative efforts to satisfy both producers and consumers of Internet service, the best solution is to allow free markets to allocate the good.

Conclusion

The policies presented in this chapter—rent control, price gouging laws, the minimum wage, and agricultural price controls—create unintended consequences. Attempts to control prices should be viewed cautiously. When the price signal is suppressed through a binding price floor or a binding price ceiling, the market's ability to allocate goods and services is diminished, surpluses and shortages develop and expand through time, and obtaining goods and services becomes difficult.

The role of markets in society has many layers, and we've only just begun our analysis. In the next chapter, we consider two cases—externalities and public goods—in which the unregulated market produces an output that is not socially desirable.

ANSWERING THE BIG QUESTIONS

When do price ceilings matter?

* A price ceiling is a legally imposed maximum price. When the price is set below the equilibrium price, the quantity demanded will exceed the quantity supplied. The result is a shortage. Price ceilings matter when they are binding (below the equilibrium price).

What effects do price ceilings have on economic activity?

* Price ceilings create two unintended consequences: a smaller quantity supplied of the good (Q_S) and a higher price for consumers who turn to the black market.

When do price floors matter?

* A price floor is a legally imposed minimum price. The minimum wage is an example of a price floor. If the minimum wage is set above the equilibrium wage, a surplus of labor will develop. However, if the minimum wage is nonbinding, it will have no effect on the market wage. Thus, price floors matter when they are set above the equilibrium price.

What effects do price floors have on economic activity?

* Price floors lead to many unintended consequences, including surpluses, the creation of black markets, and artificial attempts to bring the market back into balance. For example, proponents of a higher minimum wage are concerned about finding ways to alleviate the resulting surplus of labor, or unemployment.

ECONOMICS FOR LIFE

Price Gouging: Disaster Preparedness

During a disaster, shortages of essential goods and services become widespread. In the more than 30 states where price gouging laws are on the books, merchants are prevented from charging unusually high prices. If you live in one of these states, cash alone can't save you. You will have to survive on your own for a time before help arrives and communication channels are restored.

Taking measures to prepare for a disaster reduces the likelihood of injury, loss of life, and property damage far more than anything you can do after a disaster strikes. An essential part of disaster planning should include financial planning. Let's begin with the basics. Get adequate insurance to protect your family's health and property; plan for the possibility of job loss or disability by building a cash reserve; and safeguard your financial and legal records. It is also important to set aside extra money in a long-term emergency fund. Nearly all financial experts advise saving enough money to cover your expenses for six months. Most households never come close to reaching this goal, but don't let that stop you from trying.

Preparing a simple disaster supply kit is also a must. Keep enough water, nonperishable food, sanitation supplies, batteries, medications, and cash on hand for three days. Often, the power is out after a disaster, so you cannot count on ATMs or banks to be open. These measures will help you to weather the immediate impact of a disaster.

Finally, many documents are difficult to replace. Consider investing in a home safe or safe deposit box to ensure that your important records survive. Place your passports, Social Security cards, copies of drivers' licenses, mortgage and property deeds, car titles, wills, insurance records, and birth and marriage certificates out of harm's way.

Will you be ready if disaster strikes?

CONCEPTS YOU SHOULD KNOW

black markets (p. 187)
minimum wage (p. 202)
price ceiling (p. 186)

price controls (p. 186)
price floor (p. 196)
price gouging laws (p. 194)

rent control (p. 192)

QUESTIONS FOR REVIEW

1. Does a binding price ceiling cause a shortage or a surplus? Provide an example to support your answer.

2. Does a nonbinding price floor cause a shortage or a surplus? Provide an example to support your answer.

3. Will a surplus or a shortage caused by a price control become smaller or larger over time? Explain.

4. Are price gouging laws an example of a price floor or a price ceiling?

5. What will happen to the market price when a price control is nonbinding?

6. Why do most economists oppose attempts to control prices? Why does the government attempt to control prices anyway in a number of markets?

STUDY PROBLEMS (＊solved at the end of the section)

1. In the song "Minimum Wage," the punk band Fenix TX comments on the inadequacy of the minimum wage for making ends meet. Using the poverty thresholds provided by the Census Bureau,* determine whether the federal minimum wage of $7.25 an hour provides enough income for a single full-time worker to escape poverty.

＊ 2. Imagine that the community you live in decides to enact a rent control of $700 per month on every one-bedroom apartment. Using the following table, determine the market price and equilibrium quantity without rent control. How many one-bedroom apartments will be rented after the rent control law is passed?

Monthly rent	Quantity demanded	Quantity supplied
$600	700	240
700	550	320
800	400	400
900	250	480
1,000	100	560

*See: www.census.gov/hhes/www/poverty/data/threshld/index.html

3. Suppose that the federal government places a binding price floor on chocolate. To help support the price floor, the government purchases all of the leftover chocolate that consumers do not buy. If the price floor remains in place for a number of years, what do you expect to happen to each of the following?

   a. quantity of chocolate demanded by consumers
   b. quantity of chocolate supplied by producers
   c. quantity of chocolate purchased by the government

4. Suppose that a group of die-hard sports fans are upset about the high price of tickets to many games. As a result of their lobbying efforts, a new law caps the maximum ticket price to any sporting event at $50. Will more people be able to attend the games? Explain your answer. Will certain teams and events be affected more than others? Provide examples.

5. Many local governments use parking meters on crowded downtown streets. However, the parking spaces along the street are typically hard to find because the metered price is often set below the market price. Explain what happens when local governments set the meter

price too low. Why do you think the price is set below the market-clearing price?

6. Imagine that local suburban leaders decide to enact a minimum wage. Will the community lose more jobs if the nearby city votes to increase the minimum wage to the same rate? Discuss your answer.

✳ 7. Examine the following graph, showing the market for low-skilled laborers.

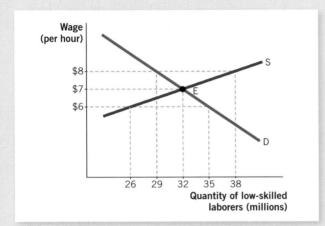

How many low-skilled laborers will be unemployed when the minimum wage is $8 an hour? How many low-skilled workers will be unemployed when the minimum wage is $6 an hour?

8. Demand and supply curves can be represented with equations. Suppose that the demand for low-skilled labor, Q_D, is represented by the following equation, where W is the wage rate:

$$Q_D = 53{,}000{,}000 - 3{,}000{,}000W$$

The supply of low-skilled labor, Q_S, is represented by the equation

$$Q_S = -10{,}000{,}000 + 6{,}000{,}000W$$

a. Find the equilibrium wage. (**Hint**: Set $Q_D = Q_S$ and solve for the wage, W.)
b. Find the equilibrium quantity of labor. (**Hint**: Now plug the value you got in part (a) back into Q_D or Q_S. You can double-check your answer by plugging the answer from part (a) into both Q_D and Q_S to see that you get the same result.)
c. What happens if the minimum wage is $8? (**Hint**: Plug W = 8 into both Q_D and Q_S.) Does this minimum wage cause a surplus or a shortage?
d. What happens if the minimum wage is $6? (**Hint**: Plug W = 6 into both Q_D and Q_S.) Does this minimum wage cause a surplus or a shortage?

9. Most of us would agree that movie theater popcorn is outrageously priced. Why don't price gouging laws result in arrests and prosecutions of theater operators and other firms that charge prices far beyond the actual cost of production?

✳ 10. Approximately 4,000 people in the United States die each year because they cannot find a suitable kidney donor. Under U.S. law, citizens cannot sell their spare kidney, which effectively means that there is a price ceiling on the sale of kidneys equal to $0. What do you think would happen to the number of deaths caused by kidney failure each year if the law prohibiting the sale of kidneys were repealed?

SOLVED PROBLEMS

2. The equilibrium price occurs where the quantity demanded is equal to the quantity supplied. This equilibrium occurs when $Q_D = Q_S = 400$. When the quantity is 400, the monthly rent is $800. Next, the question asks how many one-bedroom apartments will be rented after a rent control law limits the rent to $700 a month. When the rent is $700, the quantity supplied is 320 apartments. It is also worth noting that the quantity demanded when the rent is $700 is 550 units, so there is a

shortage of 550 − 320 = 230 apartments once the rent control law goes into effect.

7. The first question asks how many low-skilled laborers will be unemployed when the minimum wage is $8 an hour. The quantity demanded is 29 million, and the quantity supplied is 38 million. The result is 38 million − 29 million = 9 million unemployed low-skilled workers.

   The next question asks how many low-skilled workers will be unemployed when the minimum wage is $6 an hour. Because $6 an hour is below the market equilibrium wage of $7, it has no effect. In other words, a $6 minimum wage is nonbinding, and therefore no unemployment is caused.

10. Despite the repugnant nature of organ sales, there is no doubt that a price exists that would alleviate the kidney shortage and save lives. Under the current system, market prices are unable to identify people who would sell their spare kidney and match those sellers with the people who would be willing to buy a kidney. In the absence of a legal market, black markets have arisen to bring buyers and sellers together. The black-market price for a kidney ($250,000) is far higher than the market equilibrium price ($20,000) that economists estimate would exist if organ sales were legal.

CHAPTER 7

Market Inefficiencies
Externalities and Public Goods

Pollution should always be eliminated, no matter the cost.

We would all agree that it's important to protect the environment. So when we face pollution and other environmental degradation, should

MIS CONCEPTION

we eliminate it? If your first thought is "yes, always," you're not alone. After all, there's only one Earth, and we'd better get tough on environmental destruction wherever we find it, whatever it takes. Right?

It's tempting to think this way, but the prescription comes up short as a useful social policy. No one wants to go back to the way it was when businesses were free to dump their waste anywhere they chose, but it is also impractical to eliminate all pollution. Some amount of environmental damage is inevitable whenever we extract resources, manufacture goods, fertilize croplands, or power our electrical grid—all activities that are integral to modern society. But how do we figure out what the "right" level of pollution is, and how do we get there? The answer is to examine the tension between social costs and benefits and to ensure that participants in markets are fully accounting for both.

In the preceding chapters, we saw that markets provide many benefits and that they work because participants pursue their own self-interests. But sometimes markets need a helping hand. For example, some market exchanges harm innocent bystanders, and some trades are not efficient because the ownership of property is not clearly defined or actively enforced. To help explain why markets do not always operate efficiently, this chapter explores two important concepts: externalities and the differences between private and public goods.

What is the most efficient way to deal with pollution?

BIG QUESTIONS

✳ **What are externalities, and how do they affect markets?**

✳ **What are private goods and public goods?**

✳ **What are the challenges of providing nonexcludable goods?**

What Are Externalities, and How Do They Affect Markets?

Externalities are the costs or benefits of a market activity that affect a third party.

Market failure occurs when there is an inefficient allocation of resources in a market.

We have seen that buyers and sellers benefit from trade. But what about the effects that trade might have on bystanders? **Externalities**, or the costs and benefits of a market activity that affect a third party, often lead to undesirable consequences. **Market failure** occurs when there is an inefficient allocation of resources in a market. Externalities are a type of market failure. For example, in 2010, an offshore oil rig in the Gulf of Mexico operated by British Petroleum (BP) exploded, causing millions of barrels of oil to spill into the water and resulting in over $40 billion in damage. Even though both BP and its customers benefit from the production of oil, others along the Gulf Coast had their lives severely disrupted. Industries dependent on high environmental quality, like tourism and fishing, were hit particularly hard by the costs of the spill.

Internal costs are the costs of a market activity paid only by an individual participant.

For a market to work as efficiently as possible, two things must happen. First, each participant must be able to evaluate the **internal costs** of participation—the costs that only the individual participant pays. For example, when we choose to drive somewhere, we typically consider our internal (also known as personal) costs—the time it takes to reach our destination, the amount we pay for gasoline, and what we pay for routine vehicle maintenance. Second, for a market to work efficiently, the external costs must also be paid. **External costs** are the costs of a market activity imposed on people who are not participants in that market. In the case of driving, the congestion and pollution that our cars create are external costs. Economists define **social costs** as the sum of the internal costs and external costs of a market activity.

External costs are the costs of a market activity imposed on people who are not participants in that market.

Social costs are the sum of the internal costs and external costs of a market activity.

In this section, we consider some of the mechanisms that encourage consumers and producers to account for the social costs of their actions.

The Third-Party Problem

An externality exists whenever a private cost (or benefit) diverges from a social cost (or benefit). For example, manufacturers who make vehicles and consumers who purchase them benefit from the transaction, but making and using those vehicles lead to externalities—including air pollution and traffic congestion—that adversely affect others. A **third-party problem** occurs when those not directly involved in a market activity experience negative or positive externalities.

If a third party is adversely affected, the externality is negative. For example, a negative externality occurs when the number of vehicles on the roads causes air pollution. Negative externalities present a challenge to society because it is difficult to make consumers and producers take responsibility for the full costs of their actions. For example, drivers typically consider only the internal costs (their own costs) of reaching their destination. Likewise, manufacturers generally prefer to ignore the pollution they create, because addressing the problem would raise their costs without providing them with significant direct benefits.

In general, society would benefit if all consumers and producers considered both the internal and external costs of their actions. Because this expectation is not reasonable, governments design policies that create incentives for firms and people to limit the amount of pollution they emit.

An effort by the city government of Washington, D.C., shows the potential power of this approach. Like many communities throughout the United States, the city instituted a 5-cent tax on every plastic bag a consumer picks up at a store. While 5 cents may not sound like much of a disincentive, shoppers have responded by switching to cloth bags or reusing plastic ones. In Washington, D.C., the number of plastic bags used every month fell from 22.5 million in 2009 to 9 million in 2014, significantly reducing the amount of plastic waste entering landfills in the process.

Not all externalities are negative, however. Positive externalities also exist. For instance, education creates a large positive externality for society beyond the benefits to individual students, teachers, and support staff. A more knowledgeable workforce benefits employers looking for qualified employees and is more efficient and productive than an uneducated workforce. And because local businesses experience a positive externality from a well-educated local community, they have a stake in the educational process. A good example of the synergy between local business and higher education is California's Silicon Valley, which is home to many high-tech companies and Stanford University. As early as the late nineteenth century, Stanford's leaders felt that the university's mission should include fostering the development of self-sufficient local industry. After World War II, Stanford encouraged faculty and graduates to start their own companies, which led to the creation of Hewlett-Packard, Bell Labs, and Xerox. A generation later, this nexus of high-tech firms gave birth to leading software and Internet firms like 3Com, Adobe, and Facebook, and—more indirectly—Cisco, Apple, and Google.

Recognizing the benefits that they received, many of the most successful businesses associated with Stanford have donated large sums to the university. For instance, the Hewlett Foundation gave $400 million to Stanford's endowment for the humanities and sciences and for undergraduate education—an act of generosity that highlights the positive externality that Stanford University had on Hewlett-Packard.

A **third-party problem** occurs when those not directly involved in a market activity experience negative or positive externalities.

Incentives

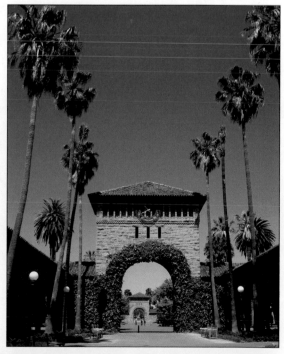

Many of the most successful businesses associated with Stanford have made large donations to the university.

When oil refineries are permitted to pollute the environment without any limitations, they are likely to overproduce.

The **social optimum** is the price and quantity combination that would exist if there were no externalities.

Correcting for Negative Externalities

In this section, we explore ways to correct for negative externalities. To do so, we use supply and demand analysis to understand how the externalities affect the market. Let's begin with supply and compare the difference between what market forces produce and what is best for society in the case of an oil refinery. A refinery converts crude oil to gasoline. This complex process generates many negative externalities, including the release of pollutants into the air and the dumping of waste by-products.

Figure 7.1 illustrates the contrast between the market equilibrium and the social optimum in the case of an oil refinery. The **social optimum** is the price and quantity combination that would exist if there were no externalities. The supply curve $S_{internal}$ represents how much the oil refinery will produce if it does not have to pay for the negative consequences of its activity. In this situation, the market equilibrium, E_M, accounts only for the internal costs of production.

FIGURE 7.1

Negative Externalities and Social Optimum

When a firm is required to internalize the external costs of production, the supply curve shifts to the left, pollution is reduced, and output falls to the socially optimal level, Q_S. The deadweight loss that occurs from overproduction is eliminated.

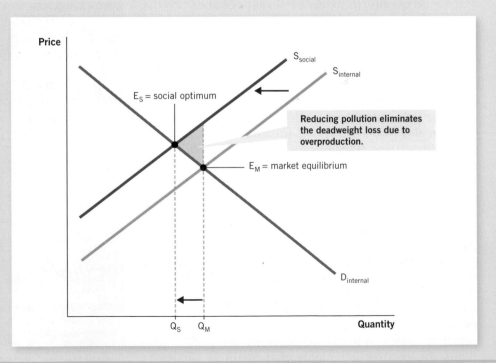

Reducing pollution eliminates the deadweight loss due to overproduction.

When a negative externality occurs, the government may be able to restore the social optimum by requiring externality-causing market participants to pay for the cost of their actions. In this case, there are three potential solutions. First, the refinery can be required to install pollution abatement equipment or change production techniques to reduce emissions and waste by-products. Second, the government can levy a tax on the refinery as a disincentive to produce. Finally, the government can require the firm to pay for any environmental damage it causes. Each solution forces the firm to **internalize** the externality, meaning that the firm must take into account the external costs (or benefits) to society that occur as a result of its actions.

Having to pay the costs of imposing pollution on others reduces the amount of the pollution-causing activity. This result is evident in the shift of the supply curve to S_{social}. The new supply curve reflects a combination of the internal and external costs of producing the good. Because each corrective measure requires the refinery to spend money to correct the externality and therefore increases overall costs, the willingness to sell the good declines, or shifts to the left. The result is a social optimum at a lower quantity, Q_S, than at the market equilibrium quantity demanded, Q_M. The trade-off is clear. We can reduce negative externalities by requiring producers to internalize the externality. However, doing so does not come without cost. Because the supply curve shifts to the left, the quantity produced is lower and the price rises. In the real world, there is always a cost.

In addition, when an externality occurs, the market equilibrium creates deadweight loss, as shown by the blue triangle in Figure 7.1. In Chapter 5, we considered deadweight loss in the context of government regulation or taxation. These measures, when imposed on efficient markets, create deadweight loss, or an undesirable amount of economic activity. In the case of a negative externality, the market is not efficient because it is not fully capturing the cost of production. Once the government intervenes and requires the firm to internalize the external costs of its production, output falls to the socially optimal level, Q_S, and the deadweight loss from overproduction is eliminated.

Table 7.1 outlines the basic decision-making process that guides private and social decisions. Private decision-makers consider only their internal costs, but society as a whole experiences both internal and external costs. To align the incentives of private decision-makers with the interests of society, we must find mechanisms that encourage the internalization of externalities.

Incentives

Firms **internalize** an externality when it takes into account the external costs (or benefits) to society that occur as a result of its actions.

Trade-offs

TABLE 7.1			
Private and Social Decision-Making			
Personal decision	**Social optimum**	**The problem**	**The solution**
Based on internal costs	Social costs = internal costs plus external costs	To get consumers and producers to take responsibility for the externalities they create	Encourage consumers and producers to *internalize* externalities

ECONOMICS IN THE REAL WORLD

Express Lanes Use Dynamic Pricing to Ease Congestion

Metro Washington, D.C., is notorious for traffic, especially on the Capital Beltway (Interstate 495), but new express lanes keep traffic moving by using dynamic pricing, which adjusts tolls based on real-time traffic conditions. Dynamic pricing helps manage the quantity demanded and keeps motorists moving at highway speeds. I-495 express-lane tolls can range from as low as $0.20 per mile during less busy times to approximately $1.25 per mile in some sections during rush hour. The higher rush-hour rates are designed to ensure that the express lanes do not become congested. Motorists thus have a choice: pay more to use the express lanes and arrive faster, or use the regular lanes and arrive later. The decision about whether to use the express lanes is all about opportunity cost. High-opportunity-cost motorists regularly drive the express lanes, while others with lower opportunity costs avoid the express lanes.

Opportunity cost
Marginal thinking

Because dynamic prices become part of a motorist's internal costs, they cause motorists to weigh the costs and benefits of driving into congested areas. In addition, the dynamic pricing of express lanes causes motorists to make marginal adjustments in terms of the time when they drive. High-demand times, such as the morning and evening rush, see higher tolls for using the express lanes and also longer waits in the regular lanes. Faced with either sitting in traffic (if they don't pay the toll) or being charged more to enter the express lanes at peak-demand times, many motorists attempt to use the Beltway at off-peak times. As drivers internalize the external costs even more precisely, the traffic flow spreads out. ✳

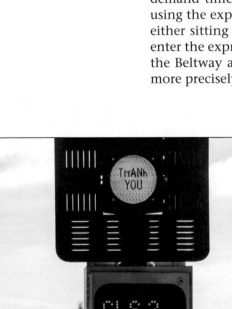

How much would you pay to avoid sitting in traffic?

Correcting for Positive Externalities

Positive externalities, such as vaccines, are the result of economic activities that have benefits for third parties. As with negative externalities, economists use supply and demand analysis to compare the efficiency of the market with the social optimum. This time, we focus on the demand curve. Consider a person who gets a flu shot. When the vaccine is administered, the recipient is immunized, which creates an internal benefit. But there is also an external benefit. Because the recipient likely will not come down with the flu, fewer other people will catch the flu and become contagious, which helps to protect even those who do not get flu shots. Therefore, we can say that vaccines provide a positive externality to the rest of society.

Why do positive externalities exist in the market? Using our example of flu shots, there is an incentive for people in high-risk groups to get vaccinated for the sake of their own health. In Figure 7.2, we capture this internal benefit in the demand curve labeled $D_{internal}$. However, the market equilibrium, E_M, only accounts for the internal benefits of individuals deciding whether to get vaccinated. To maximize the health benefits for everyone, public health officials need to find a way to encourage people to consider the external benefit of their vaccination, too. One way is to issue school vaccination laws, which require that all children entering school provide proof of vaccination against a variety of diseases. This requirement creates a direct incentive for vaccination and produces positive benefits for all members of society by internalizing the externality. The overall effect is that more people get vaccinated early in life, helping to push the market toward the socially optimal number of vaccinations. Despite the benefits, however, vaccination rates in the United States have been steadily falling for years. The lower vaccination rate led to an outbreak of measles at Disneyland in California in late 2014, where it was believed a foreign visitor introduced the disease and unvaccinated children

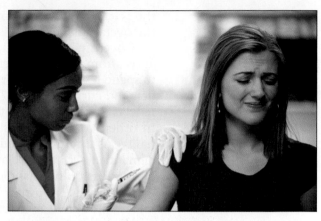

Vaccines offer both individual and social benefits.

were exposed to it. The outbreak eventually spread to six U.S. states, Mexico, and Canada—demonstrating just how quickly measles can spread when the vaccination rate is not 100%.

Government can also promote the social optimum by encouraging economic activity that helps third parties. For example, it can offer a subsidy, or price break, to encourage more people to get vaccinated. The subsidy lowers

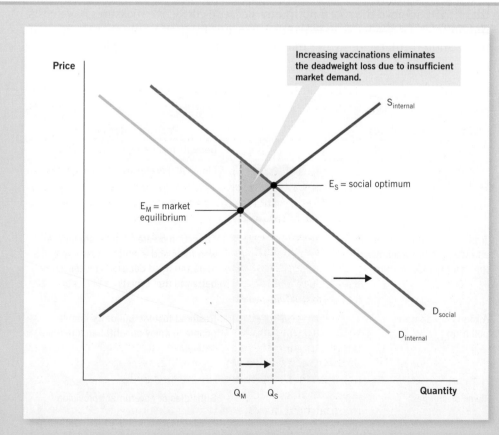

FIGURE 7.2

Positive Externalities and Social Optimum

The subsidy encourages consumers to internalize the externality. As a result, consumption moves from the market equilibrium (Q_M) to a social optimum at a higher quantity (Q_S), vaccinations increase, and the deadweight loss from insufficient market demand is eliminated.

the price to individuals but increases the demand for vaccines, which raises the overall market price.

Governments routinely provide free or reduced-cost vaccines to those most at risk from flu and to their caregivers. Because the subsidy enables consumers to spend less money, their willingness to get the vaccine increases, shifting the demand curve in Figure 7.2 from $D_{internal}$ to D_{social}. The social demand curve reflects the sum of the internal and social benefits of getting the vaccination. In other words, the subsidy encourages consumers to internalize the externality. As a result, the output moves from the market equilibrium quantity demanded, Q_M, to a social optimum at a higher quantity, Q_S.

Incentives

Markets do not handle externalities well. With a negative externality, the market produces too much of a good. But in the case of a positive externality, the market produces too little. In both cases, the market equilibrium creates dead-weight loss. When positive externalities are present, the private market is not efficient because it is not fully capturing the social benefits. In other words, the market equilibrium does not maximize the gains for society as a whole. When positive externalities are internalized, the demand curve shifts outward and output rises to the socially optimal level, Q_S. The deadweight loss that results from insufficient market demand, and therefore underproduction, is eliminated.

Table 7.2 summarizes the key characteristics of positive and negative externalities and presents additional examples of each type.

Before moving on, it is worth noting that not all externalities warrant corrective measures. There are times when the size of the externality is negligible and does not justify the cost of increased regulations, charges, taxes, or subsidies that might achieve the social optimum. Because corrective measures have costs, the presence of negligible externalities does not by itself imply that the government should intervene in the market. For instance, some people have strong

TABLE 7.2

A Summary of Externalities

	Negative externalities		Positive externalities
Definition	Costs borne by third parties		Benefits received by third parties
Examples		Oil refining creates air pollution.	Flu shots prevent the spread of disease.
		Traffic congestion causes all motorists to spend more time on the road waiting.	Education creates a more productive workforce and enables citizens to make more informed decisions for the betterment of society.
		Airports create noise pollution.	Restored historic buildings enable people to enjoy beautiful architectural details.
Corrective measures	Taxes or charges		Subsidies or government provision

PRACTICE WHAT YOU KNOW

Externalities: Fracking

In 2003, energy companies began using a process known as hydraulic fracturing, or fracking, to extract underground reserves of natural gas in certain states, including Pennsylvania, Texas, West Virginia, and Wyoming. Fracking involves injecting water, chemicals, and sand into rock formations more than a mile deep. The process releases the natural gas that is trapped in those rocks, allowing it to escape up the well. The gas comes to the surface along with much of the water and chemical mixture, which now must be disposed of. Unfortunately, the chemicals in the mix make the water toxic. Consequently, as fracking has expanded to more areas, controversy has grown about the potential environmental effects of the process.

What the frack?

Question: What negative externalities might fracking generate?

Answer: People who live near wells worry about the pollutants in the water mixture and their potential to leach into drinking-water supplies. Additionally, the drilling of a well is a noisy process. Drilling occurs 24 hours a day for a period of a few weeks. This noise pollution affects anyone who lives close by. Another issue is that the natural gas has to be trucked away from the well. Additional truck traffic can potentially damage local roads and cause even more pollution.

Question: What positive externalities might fracking generate?

Answer: Fracking has brought tremendous economic growth to the areas where it is occurring. The resulting jobs have employed many people, providing them with a good income. Local hotels and restaurants have seen an increase in business as temporary employees move from one area to another. As permanent employees take over the operation of a well, housing prices climb as a result of increasing demand, which benefits local homeowners.

body odor. This does not mean that the government needs to force everyone to shower regularly. Persons with bad body odor are the exception and they have every reason to shower, use extra-strength deodorant, or use cologne to mask the smell on their own. If they choose not to avail themselves of these options, they'll be ostracized in many social situations. Because the magnitude of the negative externality is small and government regulations to completely eliminate the externality would be quite onerous, it is best to leave well enough alone.

What Are Private Goods and Public Goods?

Property rights give the owner the ability to exercise control over a resource.

The presence of externalities reflects a divide between the way markets operate and the social optimum. What creates this divide? The answer is often related to property rights. **Property rights** give the owner the ability to exercise control over a resource. When property rights are not clearly defined, resources can be mistreated. For instance, because no one owns the air, manufacturing firms often emit pollutants into it.

Incentives

To understand why firms sometimes overlook their actions' effects on others, we need to examine the role of property rights in market efficiency. When property rights are poorly established or not enforced effectively, the wrong incentives come into play. The difference is apparent when we compare situations in which people do have property rights. Private owners have an incentive to keep their property in good repair because they bear the costs of fixing what they own when it breaks or no longer works properly. For instance, if you own a personal computer, you will probably protect your investment by treating it with care and dealing with any problems immediately. However, if you access a public computer terminal in a campus lab or library and find that it is not working properly, you will most likely ignore the problem and simply look for another computer that is working. The difference between solving the problem and ignoring it is crucial to understanding why property rights matter.

Private Property

Private property provides an exclusive right of ownership that allows for the use, and especially the exchange, of property.

One way to minimize externalities is to establish well-defined private property rights. **Private property** provides an exclusive right of ownership that allows for the use, and especially the exchange, of property. This right creates incentives to maintain, protect, and conserve property and to trade with others. Let's consider these four incentives in the context of automobile ownership.

Incentives

Opportunity costs

1. *The incentive to maintain property.* Car owners have an incentive to maintain their vehicles. Routine maintenance, replacement of worn parts, and repairs keep the vehicle safe and reliable. In addition, a well-maintained car can be sold for more than one in poor condition.
2. *The incentive to protect property.* Owners have an incentive to protect their vehicles from theft or damage. They protect their property by using alarm systems, locking the doors, and parking in well-lit areas.
3. *The incentive to conserve property.* Car owners also have an incentive to extend the usable life of their automobiles by limiting the number of miles they put on their cars each year.
4. *The incentive to trade with others.* Car owners have an incentive to trade with others because they may profit from the transaction. Suppose someone offers to buy your car for $5,000 and you think it is worth only $3,000. Because you own the car, you can do whatever you want with it. If you decline to sell, you will incur an opportunity cost: you will be giving up $5,000 to keep something you value at $3,000. There is no law requiring you to sell your vehicle, so you *could* keep the car—but you probably won't. Why? Because private property gives you as the owner an incentive to trade for something better in the market.

The incentives to maintain, protect, and conserve property help to ensure that owners keep their private property in good shape. The fourth incentive, to trade with others, helps to ensure that private property is held by the person with the greatest willingness to pay for it.

The Coase Theorem

In 1960, economist Ronald Coase argued that establishing private property rights can close the gap between internal costs and social costs.

Consider an example involving two adjacent landowners, one who raises cattle and another who grows wheat. Because neither landowner has built a fence, the cattle wander onto the neighboring land to eat the wheat. Coase concluded that in this situation, both parties are responsible for the dilemma. He arrived at that conclusion by considering two possible scenarios.

The first scenario supposes that the wheat farmer has the legal right to expect cattle-free fields. In this scenario, the cattle rancher is liable for the damage caused to the wheat farmer. If the damage is costly and the rancher is liable, the rancher will build a fence to keep the cattle in rather than pay for the damage they cause. The fence internalizes the negative externality and forces the rancher to bear the full cost of the damage. If the cost of the damage to the crop is much smaller than the cost of building a fence, then the rancher is more likely to compensate the wheat farmer for his losses rather than build the fence.

Selling a car, an exchange of private property, benefits both the owner and the buyer.

What if the wheat farmer does not have the legal right to expect cattle-free fields? In this scenario, the cattle rancher is not liable for any damages that his cattle cause to the wheat farmer. If the

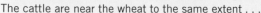

The cattle are near the wheat to the same extent . . .

. . . that the wheat is near the cattle.

damage to the nearby wheat field is large and the rancher is *not* liable, the wheat farmer will build a fence to keep the cattle out. The fence internalizes the negative externality and forces the wheat farmer to bear the full cost of the damage. If the amount of damage is smaller than the cost of a fence, the farmer may accept occasional damage as the lower-cost option.

From comparing these two scenarios, Coase determined that whenever the externality is large enough to justify the expense, the externality gets internalized. As long as the property rights are fully specified (and there are no barriers to negotiations), either the cattle rancher or the wheat farmer will build a fence. The fence will keep the cattle away from the wheat, remove the externality, and prevent the destruction of property.

> The **Coase theorem** states that if there are no barriers to negotiations, and if property rights are fully specified, interested parties will bargain to correct externalities.

With these scenarios in mind, we can now appreciate the **Coase theorem**, which states that if there are no barriers to negotiations, and if property rights are fully specified, interested parties will bargain privately to correct externalities. As a result, the assignment of property rights under the law gives each party an incentive to internalize any externalities. If it is difficult to bargain (because the costs of reaching an agreement are too high), private parties will be unable to internalize the externality between themselves. Therefore, the Coase theorem also suggests that private solutions to externality problems are not always possible, implying a role for government in solving complex externality issues.

A fence internalizes the externality.

To think about the case for a government role, consider the difference between the example of a rancher and a farmer with adjacent land and the example of a community-wide problem such as pollution. With two landowners, a private solution should be possible because the parties can bargain with each other at a low cost. With pollution, though, so many individuals are affected that the polluting company cannot afford to bargain with each one. Because bargaining costs are high in the case of pollution, an intermediary, like the government, may be necessary to ensure that externalities are internalized.

Private and Public Goods

When we think of private goods, most of us imagine something that we enjoy, like a slice of pizza or a favorite jacket. When we think of public goods, we think of goods provided by the government, like roads, the post office, and the military. The terms "private" and "public" typically imply ownership or production, but that is not the criterion economists use to categorize private and public goods. To understand the difference between private and public goods, you need to know whether a good is excludable, rival in consumption, or both. An **excludable good** occurs when it is possible to prevent consumers who have not paid for it from having access to it. A **rival good** is one that cannot be enjoyed by more than one person at a time.

> An **excludable good** occurs when it is possible to prevent consumers who have not paid for it from having access to it.

> A **rival good** is a good that cannot be enjoyed by more than one person at a time.

Private Goods

A **private good** is both excludable and rival in consumption. For instance, a slice of pizza is excludable because you must purchase it before you can eat it. Also, a slice of pizza is rival; only one person can eat it. These two characteristics, excludability and rivalry, allow the market to work efficiently in the absence of externalities. Consider a pizza business. The pizzeria bakes pizza pies because it knows it can sell them to consumers. Likewise, consumers are willing to buy pizza because it is a food they enjoy. Because the producer gets to charge a price and the consumer gets to acquire a rival good, the stage is set for mutual gains from trade.

A **private good** has two characteristics: it is excludable and rival in consumption.

Gains from trade

Public Goods

Markets have no difficulty producing purely private goods, like pizza, because in order to enjoy them you must first purchase them. But when was the last time you paid to see a fireworks display? Hundreds of thousands of people view many of the nation's best fireworks displays, but only a small percentage of them pay admission to get a preferred seat. Fireworks displays are a **public good** because (1) they can be jointly consumed by more than one person and (2) it is difficult to exclude non-payers. Because consumers cannot be easily forced to pay to observe fireworks, they may desire more of the good than is typically supplied. As a result, a market economy underproduces fireworks displays and many other public goods.

A **public good** can be jointly consumed by more than one person, and nonpayers are difficult to exclude.

Pizza is a private good.

Public goods are often underproduced because people can get them without paying for them. This means that public goods, like externalities, also result in market failure. Consider Joshua Bell, one of the most famous violinists in the world. The day after giving a concert in Boston for which patrons paid $100 a ticket, he decided to reprise the performance in a Washington, D.C., subway station and just ask for donations.* Any passerby could listen to the music—it did not need to be purchased to be enjoyed. In other words, it was nonexcludable and nonrival in consumption. But because it is impossible for a street musician to force bystanders to pay, it is difficult for the musician—even one as good as Joshua Bell—to make a living. Suppose he draws a large crowd and the music creates $500 worth of enjoyment among the audience. At the end of the performance, he receives a loud round of applause and then motions to the donation basket. A number of people come up and donate, but when he counts up the contributions, he finds only $30— the actual amount he earned while playing in the Metro.

Why did Joshua Bell receive $30 when he created many times that amount in value? This phenomenon, known as a **free-rider problem**, occurs whenever people receive a benefit they do not pay for. A street musician provides a public good and must rely on the generosity of the audience to contribute. If very few people contribute, many potential musicians will not find it worthwhile to perform. We tend to see very few street performances because free-riding

A **free-rider problem** occurs whenever someone receives a benefit without having to pay for it.

---

* This really happened! The *Washington Post* and Bell conducted an experiment to test the public's reaction to performances of "genius" in unexpected settings. Our discussion here places the event in a hypothetical context. For the real-life result, see Gene Weingarten, "Pearls before Breakfast," *Washington Post*, April 8, 2007.

Concerned about security? Only the government is capable of provide adequate national defense.

lowers the returns to performing, and the private equilibrium amount of street performances is undersupplied in comparison to the social optimum. When payment cannot be linked to production or consumption, the efficient quantity is not produced.

Street performances are just one example of a public good. National defense, lighthouses, streetlights, clean air, and open-source software such as Mozilla Firefox are other examples. Let's examine national defense because it is a particularly clear example of a public good that is subject to a free-rider problem. All citizens value security, but consider the difficulty of trying to organize and provide adequate national defense through private contributions alone. How could you get enough people to voluntarily coordinate a missile defense system or pay for an aircraft carrier and the personnel to operate it? Society would be underprotected because many people would not voluntarily contribute their fair share of the expense. For this reason, defense expenditures are normally provided by the government and funded by tax revenues. Because most people pay taxes, the free-rider problem is almost eliminated in the context of national defense.

Most people agree that government should provide certain public goods for society, including national defense, the interstate highway system, and medical and science-related research to fight pandemics. In each case, public-sector provision helps to eliminate the free-rider problem and create the socially optimal level of activity.

ECONOMICS IN THE REAL WORLD

Group Work

Perhaps you've taken a class where group work is required. These assignments are valuable opportunities to develop a skill that businesses are looking for in potential employees: the ability to work as a team to accomplish a task. However, group work in class or in the workplace creates an environment for the free-rider problem. In many groups, one of the members doesn't put in the time or effort to complete the project. This person realizes that he or she will get the benefit of the group grade without incurring the full cost. You may think that this behavior is lazy or inconsiderate, and it is, but it is nonetheless quite rational. The question for the free-rider is whether his or her actions will marginally affect the group's grade. Does the cost of completing part of the project justify what is likely to be only a small change in the grade earned by every member in the group? If the work raises the group's grade from a B– to a B, the free-rider may find that it is too costly to participate. To avoid the free-rider problem, teachers often ask the group to grade each group member's contribution to the group's overall output. The hope is that this system will give free-riders the incentive to pull their own weight. ✳

Incentives
Marginal
thinking

Club Goods and Common-Resource Goods

There are two additional types of goods that we have not yet introduced. Because club goods and common-resource goods have characteristics of both private and public goods, the line between private provision and public provision is often blurred.

A **club good** is nonrival in consumption and excludable. Satellite television is an example. It is excludable because you must pay to receive the signal, but it is nonrival in consumption because more than one customer can receive the signal at the same time. Because customers who wish to enjoy club goods can be excluded, markets typically provide these goods. However, once a satellite television network is in place, the cost of adding customers is low. Firms are motivated to maximize profits, not the number of people they serve, so the market price is higher and the output is lower than what society desires.

A **common-resource good** is rival in consumption but nonexcludable. King crab in the Bering Sea off Alaska is an example. Because any particular crab can be caught by only one boat crew, the crabs are a rival resource. At the same time, exclusion is not possible because any boat crew that wants to brave the elements can catch crab.

We have seen that the market generally works well for private goods. In the case of public goods, the market generally needs a hand. In between, club and common-resource goods illustrate the tension between the private and public provision of many goods and services. Table 7.3 summarizes the four types of goods we have discussed.

A **club good** has two characteristics: it is nonrival in consumption and excludable.

A **common-resource good** has two characteristics: it is rival in consumption and nonexcludable.

© 2006 Bil Keane, Inc.
Dist. by King Features Synd.
www.familycircus.com

"How much would it cost to see a sunset if God decided to charge for it?"

Satellite television is a club good.

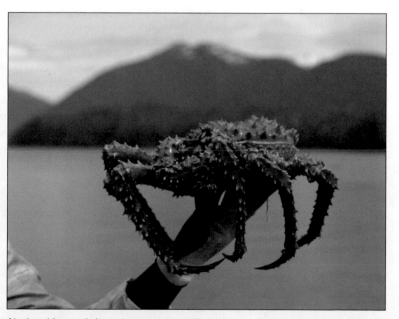

Alaskan king crab is a common-resource good.

TABLE 7.3

The Four Types of Goods

		Consumption	
		Rival	**Nonrival**
Excludable?	**Yes**	*Private goods* are rival and excludable: pizza, watches, automobiles.	*Club goods* are nonrival and excludable: satellite television, education, country clubs.
	No	*Common-resource goods* are rival and nonexcludable: Alaskan king crab, a large shared popcorn at the movies, congested roads.	*Public goods* are nonrival and nonexcludable: street performers, national defense, tsunami warning systems.

PRACTICE WHAT YOU KNOW

Public Goods: Are Parks Public Goods?

Many goods have the characteristics of a public good, but few goods meet the exact definition.

Question: Are parks public goods?

Answer: We tend to think of public parks as meeting the necessary requirements to be a public good. But not so fast. Have you been to any of America's top national parks on a peak summer weekend? Parks are subject to congestion, which makes them rival. In addition, most national and state parks require an admission fee—translation: they are excludable. Therefore, public parks do not meet the exact definition of a public good.

Not surprisingly, there are many good examples of private parks that maintain, protect, and conserve the environment alongside their public counterparts. For instance, Natural Bridge is a privately owned and operated park in Virginia that preserves a rare natural arch over a small stream. The East Coast is dotted with private parks that predate the establishment of the national park system. Like their public counterparts, private parks are also not public goods.

Natural Bridge in Virginia

What Are the Challenges of Providing Nonexcludable Goods?

Understanding the four types of goods provides a solid foundation for understanding the role of markets and the government in society. Next, we consider some of the special challenges that arise in providing nonexcludable goods.

Cost-Benefit Analysis

To help make decisions about providing public goods, economists turn to **cost-benefit analysis**, a process used to determine whether the benefits of providing a public good outweigh the costs. Costs are easier to quantify than benefits. For instance, if a community puts on a Fourth of July celebration, it will have to pay for the fireworks and labor involved in setting up the event. The costs are a known quantity. But benefits are difficult to quantify. Because people do not need to pay to see the fireworks, it is hard to determine how much benefit the community receives. If asked, people might misrepresent the social benefit in two ways. First, some residents who value the celebration highly might claim that the fireworks bring more benefit than they actually do, because they want the community fireworks to continue. Second, those residents who dislike the crowds and noise might understate the benefit of the fireworks, because they want the fireworks to cease. Since there is no way to know how truthful people are when responding to a questionnaire, the actual social benefit of a fireworks show is hard to measure.

Because people do not pay to enjoy public goods, and because the government provides them without charging a direct fee, determining the socially optimal amount typically takes place through the political system. Generally speaking, elected officials do not get reelected if the populace believes that they have not done a good job with their cost-benefit analyses.

Cost-benefit analysis is a process that economists use to determine whether the benefits of providing a public good outweigh the costs.

Figuring out the social benefit of a fireworks display is quite difficult.

ECONOMICS IN THE REAL WORLD

Internet Piracy

The digitization of media, along with the speed with which it can be transferred across the Internet, has made the protection of *intellectual property rights* (that is, the protection of patents, copyrights, and trademarks) very difficult to enforce. Many countries either do not have strict copyright standards or fail to enforce them. The result is a black market filled with bootlegged copies of movies, music, and other media.

Because digital "file sharing" is so common these days, you might not fully understand the harm that occurs. Piracy is an illegal form of free-riding. Every song and every movie that is transferred takes away royalties that would have gone to the original artist or the studio. After all, producing content is expensive, and violations of copyright law prevent businesses from making a fair return on their investments. However, consumers of content don't often see it this way. Some believe that breaking the copyright encryption is fair game because they "own" the object in question or bought it legally or got it from a friend. The reality is different. One reason copyright law exists is to limit free-riding. When copyrights are fully specified and enforced across international boundaries, content creators receive compensation for their efforts. But if copyrights are routinely violated, revenues to private businesses will decline and the amount of music and movies produced will decrease. In the long run, artists will produce less and society will suffer. (For other benefits of copyright law, see Chapter 10.)

Incentives

Think about the relationship between artists and the public as reciprocal: each side needs the other. In that sense, the music you buy or the movie you watch is not a true public good, but more of a club good. Copyright laws make the good excludable but nonrival. For this reason, some people will always have an incentive to violate copyright law, artists and studios will insist on ever more complicated encryption methods to protect their interests, and for the betterment of society as a whole, the government will have to enforce copyright law to prevent widespread free-riding. ✳

Common Resources and the Tragedy of the Commons

Tragedy of the commons occurs when a good that is rival in consumption but nonexcludable becomes depleted.

Common resources often give rise to the **tragedy of the commons**, a situation that occurs when a good that is rival in consumption but nonexcludable becomes depleted. The term "tragedy of the commons" refers to a phenomenon that ecologist Garrett Hardin wrote about in the magazine *Science* in 1968. Hardin described the hypothetical use of a common pasture shared by local herders in a pastoral community. Herders know that intensively grazed land will be depleted and that this depletion is very likely to happen to common land. Knowing that the pasture will be depleted creates a strong incentive for individual herders to bring their animals to the pasture as much as possible

Incentives

while it is still green, because every other herder will be doing the same thing. Each herder has the same incentive to overgraze, which quickly makes the pasture unusable. The overgrazing is a negative externality brought about by poorly designed incentives and the absence of clearly defined private property rights.

Even though the concept of common ownership sounds ideal, it can be a recipe for resource depletion and economic disaster. Common ownership, unlike private ownership, leads to overuse. With a system of private property rights, an owner can seek damages in the court system if his property is damaged or destroyed. But the same cannot be said for common property, because joint ownership allows any party to use the resource as he or she sees fit. This situation creates incentives to use the resource now rather than later and to neglect it. In short, common property leads to abuse and depletion of the resource.

Consider global warming. Scientific evidence clearly links increasing amounts of CO_2 (carbon dioxide) in the atmosphere and global warming. This negative externality is caused by some but borne jointly by everyone. Because large CO_2 emitters consider only the internal costs of their actions and ignore the social costs, the amount of CO_2 released, and the corresponding increase in global warming, is larger than optimal. The air, a common resource, is being "overused" and degraded.

Private property rights give owners an incentive to maintain, protect, and conserve their property and to transfer it if someone else values it more than they do. How are those incentives different under a system of common ownership? Let's examine a real-world example of the tragedy of the commons: the collapse of cod populations off Newfoundland, Canada, in the 1990s. Over the course of three years, cod hauls fell from over 200,000 tons annually to close to zero. Why did the fishing community allow this to happen? The answer: incentives. Let's consider the incentives associated with common property in the context of the cod industry.

Incentives

1. *The incentive to neglect.* No one owns the ocean. As a result, fishing grounds in international waters cannot be protected. Even fishing grounds within territorial waters are problematic because fish do not adhere to political borders. Moreover, the fishing grounds in the North Atlantic cannot be maintained in the same way that one can, say, check the oil in an automobile. The grounds are too large, and the cod population depends on variations in seawater temperature, salinity, and availability of algae and smaller fish to eat. The idea that individuals or communities could "maintain" a population of cod in this wild environment is highly impractical.

2. *The incentive to overuse.* Each fishing boat crew would like to maintain a sustainable population of cod to ensure future harvests. However, conservation on the part of one boat is irrelevant because other boats would catch whatever the first boat leaves behind. Because cod are a rival and finite resource, boats have an incentive to harvest as much as they can before another vessel does. With common resources, no one has the authority to define how much of a resource can be used. Maintaining economic activity at a socially optimal level would require the coordination of thousands of vested interests, each of which could gain by free-riding. For instance, if a socially responsible boat crew (or country) limits its catch in order to protect the species from depletion, this action does not guarantee that rivals will follow suit. Instead, rivals who disregard the socially optimal behavior stand to benefit by overfishing what remains.

Because cod are a common resource, the incentives we discussed under a system of private ownership do not apply. With common property, resources are neglected and overused.

Possible Solutions to the Tragedy of the Commons

Preventing the tragedy of the commons requires planning and coordination. Unfortunately, in our cod example, officials were slow to recognize that there was a problem with Atlantic cod until it was too late to prevent the collapse. Ironically, just as they placed a moratorium on catching northern cod, the collapse of the fish population became an unprecedented disaster for all of Atlantic Canada's fisheries. Cod populations dropped to 1% of their former sizes. The collapse of cod and many other species led to the loss of 40,000 jobs and over $300 million in income annually. Because the communities in the affected region relied almost exclusively on fishing, this outcome crippled their economies.

Common resources, such as cod, encourage overuse (in this case, overfishing).

The lesson of the northern cod is a powerful reminder that efforts to avoid the tragedy of the commons must begin before a problem develops. For example, king crab populations off the coast of Alaska have fared much better than cod, thanks to proactive management. To prevent the collapse of the king crab population, the state and federal governments enforce several regulations. First, the length of the fishing season is limited so that populations have time to recover. Second, there are regulations that limit how much fishing boats can catch. Third, to promote sustainable populations, only adult males are harvested. It is illegal to harvest females and young crabs, because these are necessary for repopulation. It is important to note that without government enforcement of these regulations, the tragedy of the commons would result.

Trade-offs

What is the best way to curb global warming?

Cap and trade is an approach used to curb pollution by creating a system of emissions permits that are traded in an open market.

Can the misuse of a common resource be foreseen and prevented? If predictions of rapid global warming are correct, our analysis points to a number of solutions to minimize the tragedy of the commons. Businesses and individuals can be discouraged from producing emissions through carbon pricing. This policy encourages parties to internalize the negative externality, because carbon pricing acts as an internal cost that must be considered before creating carbon pollution.

Another solution, known as **cap and trade**, is an approach to emissions reduction that has received much attention lately. The idea behind cap and trade policy is to encourage carbon producers to internalize the externality by establishing markets for tradable emissions permits. As a result, a profit motive is created for some firms to purchase, and others to sell, emissions permits. Under cap and trade, the government sets a *cap*, or limit, on the amount of CO_2 that can be emitted. Businesses and individuals are then issued permits to emit a certain amount of carbon each year. Also, permit owners may *trade* permits. In other words, companies that produce fewer carbon emissions can sell the permits they do not use. By establishing property rights that control emissions permits, cap and trade causes firms to internalize externalities and to seek out methods that lower emissions. Global warming is an incredibly complex process, but cap and trade policy is one tangible step that minimizes free-riding, creates incentives for action, and promotes a socially efficient outcome.

Cap and trade is a good idea, but there are issues that must be overcome to make it work effectively. For example, cap and trade presumes that nations can agree on and enforce emissions limits, but international agreements have proved difficult to negotiate. Without binding international agreements, nations that adopt cap and trade policies will experience higher production costs, while nations that ignore them—and free-ride in the process—will benefit.

ECONOMICS IN THE REAL WORLD

Deforestation in Haiti

Nothing symbolizes the vicious cycle of poverty in Haiti more than the process of deforestation. Haiti was once a lush tropical island covered with pines and broadleaf trees. Today, only about 3% of the country has tree cover. A number of factors have contributed to this environmental catastrophe: shortsighted logging and agricultural practices, demand for charcoal, rapid population growth, and increased competition for land. Widespread deforestation caused soil erosion, which in turn caused the fertile topsoil layer to wash away. As a result, land that was once lush and productive became desert-like. Eventually, nearly all remaining trees were cut down. Not enough food could be produced on this impoverished land, which contributed to widespread poverty.

Haiti is an extreme example of the tragedy of the commons. Its tragedy is especially striking because Haiti shares the island of Hispaniola with the Dominican Republic. One of the starkest differences between the two countries is the contrast between the lush tropical landscape of the Dominican Republic and the eroded, deforested Haitian land. In Haiti, the land was a semipublic resource that was overused and abused and therefore subject to the tragedy of the commons. In the Dominican Republic, property rights preserved the environment. All of this means that Haiti would not be as poor today if it had relied more on private property rights. ✳

Haiti, seen on the left in this aerial photo, is deforested. The Dominican Republic, seen on the right, has maintained its environment.

PRACTICE WHAT YOU KNOW

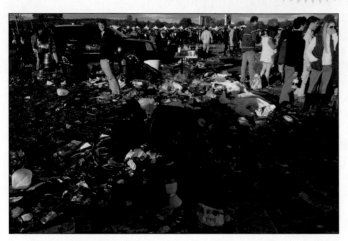

Why don't these tailgaters make a "concerted" effort to clean up?

Common Resources: Why Do Tailgaters Trash Parking Lots?

Tailgating can be one of the best parts of attending a big game or concert. You enjoy a great time with your friends and take in the action, leaving quickly afterward with little concern about the trash left behind. Consider this example: In 2014, country artist Luke Bryan played at Heinz Field in Pittsburgh. His fans care about the environment as much as you and I do, but check out this photo! The parking lot at Heinz Field was trashed.

Question: What economic concept explains why so many people left so much trash behind?

Answer: Tailgaters brought snacks, drinks, cups, napkins, and all kinds of things to party before the concert, so a lot of trash was generated. Would you throw your trash on your driveway? Of course not. But otherwise conscientious individuals often don't demonstrate the same concern for public property. As a public space, the Heinz Field parking lot is subject to the tragedy of the commons. No one person can keep the lot clean, so overuse and littering occur. The effects of littering can be especially apparent when 50,000 people fill a stadium at one time.

ECONOMICS IN THE MEDIA

Tragedy of the Commons

South Park and Water Parks

If you have ever been to a water park or community pool, you know that the staff checks the pH of the water regularly to make sure it is clean. However, in a 2009 episode of *South Park*, everyone is peeing in Pi Pi's water park. The resulting pee concentration ends up being so high that it triggers a disaster-movie-style cataclysm, unleashing a flood of pee that destroys the place.

Why did this happen? Because each person looked at all the water and thought it wouldn't matter if *he* or *she* peed in it. But when *everyone* thought the same way, the water quality was affected. This led to the tragedy of the commons, in which the overall water quality became degraded. Pee-ew.

Thankfully, the real world is cleaner than South Park!

Buying Used Is Good for Your Wallet and for the Environment

Many people waste their hard-earned money buying new. We could do our wallets, and the environment, a favor by opting to buy used instead. Some customers are willing to pay a premium for that "new" feeling—but if you avoid that price markup, you'll save money *and* extend the usable life of a product. Here are a few ideas.

1. **Jewelry**. Would you buy something that immediately drops in value by 70%? When you buy jewelry at a retail store, you'll rarely get even a third of it back if you need to sell. If you are comfortable with the risk, search Craigslist or a local pawn shop instead. Just be sure to get an appraisal before buying.

2. **Sports equipment**. Let the enthusiasts buy the latest equipment. When they tire of it and switch to the newest golf clubs or buy a new kayak, you can swoop in and save big bucks.

3. **Video game consoles and games**. You can buy used and pay half price or less. The catch is you'll have to wait. But the good news is that you'll never find out that your expensive new system isn't as exciting as advertised. Waiting means better information *and* lower prices. That's how you find a good deal.

4. **Automobiles**. The average new car can lose as much as 20% of its value during the first year

after purchase. For a $30,000 car, that means $6,000 in lost value. Let someone else take that hit and buy a used vehicle instead.

5. **Tools and yard equipment**. Think twice before heading to the hardware store. Many tools like hammers and shovels are designed to last. Used tools might not look shiny-new, but they work just as well.

Every time you buy used, you extend the usable life of a product, which helps maximize the value society gets from its resources. These examples also illustrate the benefit of private property: recall that owners have incentives to (1) maintain, (2) protect, and (3) conserve the products they own so that they can (4) maximize the value when they sell them.

Buying used can save you thousands.

Conclusion

Although it's tempting to believe that the appropriate response to pollution is always to eliminate it, this belief is a misconception. As with all things, there are trade-offs. When pollution is taxed or regulated, business activity declines. It's possible to eliminate too much pollution, forcing businesses to shut down, creating undesirably high prices for anything from groceries to gasoline to electronics, and all in all creating an enormous deadweight loss to society. When you think about pollution like an environmental economist, you realize that eliminating pollution would create benefits and also costs. A truly "green" environment without any pollution would leave most people without enough "green" in their wallets. Therefore, the goal for pollution isn't zero because the cost of attaining zero pollution outweighs the benefit.

Trade-offs

In this chapter, we have considered two types of market failure: externalities and public goods. When externalities and public goods exist, the market does not provide the socially optimal amount of the good or service. One solution is to encourage businesses to internalize externalities. The government can aid the process through taxes and regulations that force producers to account for the negative externalities that they create. Similarly, subsidies can spur the production of activities that generate positive externalities.

Likewise, public goods present a challenge for the market. Free-riding leads to the underproduction of goods that are nonrival and nonexcludable. Because not enough is produced privately, one solution is to eliminate free-riding by making involvement compulsory through taxation or regulation. A second problem occurs whenever goods are nonexcludable, as is the case with common-resource goods. This condition gives rise to the tragedy of the commons and can lead to the overuse of valuable resources.

ANSWERING THE BIG QUESTIONS

What are externalities, and how do they affect markets?

* An externality exists whenever an internal cost (or benefit) diverges from a social cost (or benefit). Third parties can experience negative or positive externalities from market activity. Externalities are a type of market failure, which occurs when there is an inefficient allocation of resources in a market.
* Social costs are the sum of an activity's internal costs and external costs.
* When a negative externality exists, government can restore the social optimum by discouraging economic activity that harms third parties. When a positive externality exists, government can restore the social optimum by encouraging economic activity that benefits third parties.
* An externality is internalized when decision-makers must pay for the externality created by their participation in the market.

What are private goods and public goods?

* Private goods (or private property) ensures that owners have an incentive to maintain, protect, and conserve their property and also to trade it with others.
* A public good has two characteristics: it is nonexcludable and nonrival in consumption. Public goods give rise to the free-rider problem and result in the underproduction of the good in the market. Public goods give rise to market failure.

What are the challenges of providing nonexcludable goods?

* Economists use cost-benefit analysis to determine whether the benefits of providing a particular good outweigh the costs, but benefits can be hard to determine.
* Under a system of common property, the incentive structure encourages neglect and overuse.

CONCEPTS YOU SHOULD KNOW

cap and trade (p. 234)
club good (p. 229)
Coase theorem (p. 226)
common-resource good (p. 229)
cost-benefit analysis (p. 231)
excludable good (p. 226)
external costs (p. 216)
externalities (p. 216)

free-rider problem (p. 227)
internal costs (p. 216)
internalize (p. 219)
market failure (p. 216)
private good (p. 227)
private property (p. 224)
property rights (p. 224)
public good (p. 227)

rival good (p. 226)
social costs (p. 216)
social optimum (p. 218)
third-party problem (p. 217)
tragedy of the commons
  (p. 232)

QUESTIONS FOR REVIEW

1. Does the market overproduce or underproduce when third parties enjoy positive externalities? Show your answer on a supply and demand graph.

2. Is it possible to use bargaining to solve externality problems involving many parties? Explain your reasoning.

3. Describe all of the ways in which externalities can be internalized.

4. Does cost-benefit analysis apply to public goods only? If yes, why? If not, name situations in which economists would use cost-benefit analysis.

5. What is the tragedy of the commons? Give an example that is not in the chapter.

6. What are the four incentives of private property? How do they differ from the incentives found in common property?

7. Give an example of a good that is nonrival in consumption and nonexcludable. What do economists call goods that share these characteristics?

STUDY PROBLEMS (*solved at the end of the section*)

1. Many cities have noise ordinances that impose especially harsh fines and penalties for early-morning and late-evening disturbances. Explain why these ordinances exist.

2. Indicate whether the following activities create a positive or negative externality:

   a. Late-night road construction begins on a new bridge. As a consequence, traffic is rerouted past your house while the construction takes place.

   b. An excavating company pollutes a local stream with acid rock.

   c. A homeowner whose property backs up on a city park enjoys the sound of kids playing soccer.

   d. A student uses her cell phone discreetly during class.

   e. You and your friends volunteer to plant wildflowers along the local highway.

3. Indicate whether the following are private goods, club goods, common-resource goods, or public goods:

   a. a bacon double cheeseburger

   b. an NHL hockey game between the Detroit Red Wings and Boston Bruins

   c. a Fourth of July fireworks show

   d. a swimming pool

   e. a vaccination for the flu

   f. streetlights

4. Can you think of a reason why making cars safer would create negative externalities? Explain.

5. Which of the following activities give rise to the free-rider problem?

   a. recycling programs
   b. biking
   c. studying for an exam
   d. riding a bus

✱ 6. The students at a crowded university have trouble waking up before 10 a.m., and most work jobs after 3 p.m. As a result, there is a great deal of demand for classes between 10 a.m. and 3 p.m., and classes before and after those hours are rarely full. To make matters worse, the university has a limited amount of classroom space and faculty. As a result, not every student can take classes during the most desirable times. Building new classrooms and hiring more faculty are not options. The administration asks for your advice about the best way to solve the problem of demand during the peak class hours. What advice would you give?

7. Two roommates are opposites. One enjoys playing Modern Warfare with his friends all night. The other likes to get to bed early for a full 8 hours of sleep. If Coase is right, the roommates have an incentive to solve the noise externality issue themselves. Name at least two solutions that will internalize, or eliminate, the externality.

✱ 8. Two companies, Toxic Waste Management and Sludge Industries, both pollute a nearby lake. Each firm dumps 1,000 gallons of goo into the lake every day. As a consequence, the lake has lost its clarity and the fish are dying. Local residents want to see the lake restored. But Toxic Waste's production process depends heavily on being able to dump the goo into the lake. It would cost Toxic Waste $10 per gallon to clean up the goo it generates. Sludge can clean up its goo at a cost of $2 per gallon.

   a. If the local government cuts the legal goo emissions in half for each firm, what are the costs to each firm to comply with the law?

   What is the total cost to both firms in meeting the goo-emissions standard?
   b. Another way of cutting goo emissions in half is to assign each firm tradable pollution permits that allow 500 gallons of goo to be dumped into the lake every day. Under this approach, will each firm still dump 500 gallons of goo? Would the firms be willing to trade permits with one another?

9. A study finds that leaf blowers make too much noise, so the government imposes a $10 tax on the sale of every unit to correct for the social cost of the noise pollution. The tax completely internalizes the externality. Before the corrective tax, Blown Away Manufacturing regularly sold blowers for $100. After the tax is in place, the consumer price for leaf blowers rises to $105.

   a. Describe the impact of the tax on the number of leaf blowers sold.
   b. What is the socially optimal price to the consumer?
   c. What is the private market price?
   d. What net price is Blown Away receiving after it pays the tax?

10. In most areas, developers are required to submit an environmental impact study before work can begin on a new construction project. Suppose that a commercial developer wants to build a new shopping center on an environmentally protected piece of property that is home to a rare three-eyed toad. The shopping complex, if approved by the local planning commission, will cover 10 acres. The planning commission wants the construction to go forward because the shopping complex means additional jobs for the local community, but it also wants to be environmentally responsible. One member of the commission suggests that the developer relocate the toads. She describes the relocation process as follows: "The developer builds the shopping mall and agrees to create 10 acres of artificial toad habitat elsewhere." Will this proposed solution make the builder internalize the externality? Explain.

✱ 11. Describe the difference between the way an environmental economist thinks about policy and the way an environmentalist thinks about policy. (**Hint:** Recall the difference between positive economics and normative economics from Chapter 1.)

12. If a company pollutes the water and transactions costs are high, which of the following makes the most economic sense?

   a. All parties connected with the pollution should negotiate.

   b. The company should be allowed to pollute.
   c. The company should be liable for the damages it causes.
   d. The company should go out of business.

SOLVED PROBLEMS

6. A flat-fee congestion charge is a good start, because this charge would reduce the quantity demanded between 10 a.m. and 3 p.m., but such a fee is a blunt instrument. Making the congestion charge dynamic (or varying the price by the hour) will encourage students to move outside the window with the most popular class times in order to pay less. For instance, classes between 11 a.m. and 2 p.m. would have the highest fee. Classes between 10 and 11 a.m. and between 2 and 3 p.m. would be slightly discounted. Classes between 9 and 10 a.m. and between 3 and 4 p.m. would be cheaper still, and those earlier than 9 a.m. and after 4 p.m. would be the cheapest. By altering the price of different class times, the university would be able to offer classes at less popular times and fill them up regularly, thus efficiently using its existing resources.

8.a. If the local government cuts the legal goo emissions in half for each firm, Toxic Waste will cut its goo by 500 gallons at a cost of $10 per gallon, for a total cost of $5,000. Sludge Industries will also cut its goo by 500 gallons; at $2 per gallon, the cost is $1,000. The total cost to both firms in meeting the goo-emissions standard is $5,000 + $1,000 = $6,000.

   b. It costs Toxic Waste $10 per gallon to clean up its goo. It is therefore more efficient for Toxic to buy all 500 permits from Sludge—which enables Toxic to dump an additional 500 gallons in the lake and saves the company $5,000 minus the price it pays to Sludge for its permits. At the same time, Sludge could decide not to dump any goo in the lake. Because it costs Sludge $2 per gallon to clean up its goo, it will have to pay $1,000 unless it sells its permits to Toxic, in which case it might actually make a profit. Because Toxic is saving more than it costs Sludge to clean up the goo, the two sides have an incentive to trade the permits.

11. Thinking like an economist requires one to consider the marginal benefits and the marginal costs of every policy. This perspective allows environmental economists to assess whether a particular policy will create enough benefits to outweigh the costs. It is this positive (dispassionate) perspective that causes an environmental economist to argue that the optimal rate of pollution is above zero. In contrast, an environmentalist sees policy solutions through a normative lens. Environmentalists weigh the benefits of protecting the environment much more heavily than the costs and therefore advocate for policies that protect the environment even when the costs are quite high.

PART

3

The Theory of
THE FIRM

CHAPTER 8 | Business Costs and Production

Larger firms have lower costs than their smaller competitors do. Walmart, the nation's largest retailer, leverages its size to get price breaks on bulk purchases from its suppliers. People commonly

believe that this kind of leverage enables larger firms to operate at lower costs than smaller firms do. It is true that large firms have broader distribution networks, and they benefit from more specialization and automation compared with their smaller competitors. However, not all industries enjoy lower costs with additional sales the way retailers do. Even Walmart, known for its very low prices, can be undercut by online outlets that have lower costs and therefore lower prices. In other words, larger firms do not always have the lowest costs.

More generally, in any industry where transportation and advertising costs are high, smaller localized firms are not always at a disadvantage in terms of pricing. In fact, they often have the edge. For instance, in most college towns you will find many pizza shops—the national brands (Pizza Hut, Papa John's, Domino's) and the local shops. Often, the local shop is the one with the cheapest pizza special, while the name brands charge more. By the end of this chapter, you will appreciate the importance of cost and understand why smaller and more nimble firms are sometimes able to undercut the prices of larger companies.

We begin the chapter with an examination of costs and how they relate to production. After we understand the basics, we consider how firms can keep their costs low in the long run by choosing a scale of operation that best suits their needs.

A Walmart distribution center speeds goods to its stores.

BIG QUESTIONS

A **profit** results when total revenue is higher than total cost.

A **loss** results when total revenue is less than total cost.

Total revenue is the amount a firm receives from the sale of goods and services.

Total cost is the amount a firm spends to produce and/ or sell goods and services.

* **How are profits and losses calculated?**
* **How much should a firm produce?**
* **What costs do firms consider in the short run and the long run?**

How Are Profits and Losses Calculated?

To determine the potential profits of a business, the first step is to look at how much it will cost to run it. Consider a McDonald's restaurant. While you are probably familiar with the products McDonald's sells, you may not know how an individual franchise operates. For one thing, the manager at a McDonald's must decide how many workers to hire and how many to assign to each shift. Other managerial decisions involve the equipment needed and what supplies to have on hand each day—everything from hamburger patties to paper napkins. In fact, behind each purchase a consumer makes at McDonald's, there is a complicated symphony of delivery trucks, workers, and managers.

For a company to be profitable, it is not enough to provide products that consumers want. It must simultaneously manage its costs. In this section, we discuss how profits and costs are calculated.

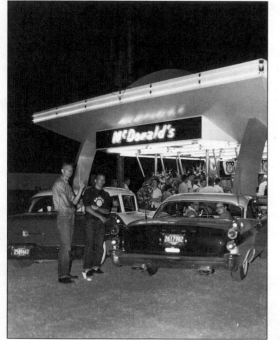

The first McDonald's—much like the one pictured here—opened in San Bernardino, California, in 1940.

Calculating Profit and Loss

The simplest way to determine profit or loss is to calculate the difference between expenses (costs) and total revenue. A **profit** occurs whenever total revenue is higher than total cost. A **loss** occurs whenever total revenue is less than total cost. The **total revenue** of a business is the amount the firm receives from the sale of goods and services. In the case of McDonald's, the total revenue is determined by the number of items sold and their prices. **Total cost** is the amount that a firm spends to produce and/or sell goods and services. To determine total cost, the firm adds the individual costs of the resources used in producing and/or selling the goods. We can express this relationship as an equation:

(Equation 8.1)   **profit (or loss)** = total revenue − total cost

To calculate total revenue, we look at the dollar amount that the business takes in over a specific period. For instance, suppose that in a given day McDonald's sells 1,000 hamburgers for $1.00 each, 500 orders of large fries for $2.00 each, and 100 shakes for $2.50 each. The total revenue is the sum of all of these values, or $2,250. The profit is therefore $2,250 (total revenue) minus the total cost.

Calculating costs, however, is a little more complicated than calculating revenue; we don't simply tally the cost of making each hamburger, order of large fries, and shake. Total cost has two parts—one that is visible and one that is largely invisible. In the next section, we will see that determining total costs is part art and part science.

Explicit Costs and Implicit Costs

Economists break costs into two components: explicit costs and implicit costs. **Explicit costs** are tangible out-of-pocket expenses. To calculate explicit costs, we add every expense incurred to run the business. For example, in the case of a McDonald's franchise, the weekly supply of hamburger patties is one explicit cost; the owner receives a bill from the meat supplier and has to pay it. **Implicit costs** are the costs of resources already owned, for which no out-of-pocket payment is made. Implicit costs are also opportunity costs because the use of owned resources means that the next-best alternative use is forgone.

Let's consider an example. Purchasing a McDonald's franchise costs about $1 million; this is an explicit cost. However, there is also a high opportunity cost—the next-best possibility for investing $1 million. That money could have earned interest in a bank, been used to start a different business, or been invested in the stock market. Each alternative is an implicit cost.

Implicit costs are hard to calculate and easy to miss. For example, it is difficult to determine how much an investor could have earned from an alternative activity. Is the opportunity cost the 3% interest he might have earned by placing the money in a bank, the 10% he might have hoped to earn in the stock market, or the 15% he might have gained by investing in a different business? We can be sure that there is an opportunity cost for owner-provided capital, but we can never know exactly how much that might be.

Explicit costs are tangible out-of-pocket expenses.

Implicit costs are the costs of resources already owned, for which no out-of-pocket payment is made.

Opportunity costs

TABLE 8.1

Examples of a Firm's Explicit and Implicit Costs

Explicit costs	Implicit costs
The electricity bill	The labor of an owner who works for the company but does not draw a salary
Advertising in the local newspaper	The opportunity cost of the capital invested in the business
Employee wages	The use of the owner's car, computer, or other personal equipment to conduct company business

In addition to the opportunity cost of capital, implicit costs include the opportunity cost of the owner's labor. Often, business owners do not pay themselves a direct salary. However, because they could have been working somewhere else, it is reasonable to consider the fair value of the owner's time—income the owner could have earned by working elsewhere—as part of the business's costs.

To fully account for all the costs of doing business, we must calculate the explicit costs, determine the implicit costs, and add them together:

(Equation 8.2)   **total cost** = explicit costs + implicit costs

A simple way of thinking about the distinction between explicit costs and implicit costs is to consider someone who wants to build a bookcase. Suppose that John purchases $30 in materials and takes half a day off from work, where he normally earns $12 an hour. After 4 hours, he completes the bookcase. His explicit cost is $30, but his total cost is much higher because he also gave up 4 hours of work at $12 an hour. His implicit cost is therefore $48. When we add the explicit cost ($30) and the implicit cost ($48), we get John's total cost ($78).

Table 8.1 shows examples of a firm's implicit and explicit costs.

Accounting Profit versus Economic Profit

Now that you know about explicit and implicit costs, we can refine our definition of profit. In fact, there are two types of profit—accounting profit and economic profit.

Accounting profit is calculated by subtracting the explicit costs from total revenue.

A firm's **accounting profit** is calculated by subtracting only the explicit costs from total revenue. Accounting figures permeate company reports, quarterly and annual statements, and the media.

(Equation 8.3)   **accounting profit** = total revenues − explicit costs

Economic profit is calculated by subtracting both the explicit costs and the implicit costs of business from total revenue.

As you can see, accounting profit does not take into account the implicit costs of doing business. To calculate the full cost of doing business, we need to consider both implicit and explicit costs. Doing so yields a firm's economic profit. **Economic profit** is calculated by subtracting both the explicit and the implicit costs of doing business from total revenue. Economic profit gives a more complete assessment of how a firm is doing.

$$\textbf{economic profit} = \text{total revenues} - (\text{explicit costs} + \text{implicit costs})$$ (Equation 8.4)

Simplifying Equation 8.4 gives us

$$\textbf{economic profit} = \text{accounting profit} - \text{implicit costs}$$ (Equation 8.5)

Therefore, economic profit is always less than accounting profit.

The difference in accounting profits among various types of firms can be misleading. For instance, if a company with $1 billion in assets reports an annual profit of $10 million, we might think it is doing well. After all, wouldn't you be happy to make $10 million in a year? However, that $10 million is only 1% of the $1 billion the company holds in assets. As Table 8.2 shows, a 1% return is far less than the typical return available in a number of other places, including the stock market, bonds, or a savings account at a financial institution.

If the return on $1 billion in assets is low compared with what an investor can expect to make elsewhere, the firm with the $10 million accounting profit actually has a negative economic profit. For instance, if the firm had invested the $1 billion in a savings account, according to Table 8.2 it would have earned 2% on $1 billion—that is, $20 million. In that case,

$$\begin{aligned}
\textbf{economic profit} &= \text{accounting profit} - \text{implicit costs} \\
&= \$10 \text{ million} - \$20 \text{ million} \\
&= -\$10 \text{ million}
\end{aligned}$$

As you can see, economic profit can be negative, since the minus dollar amount is a loss. If a business has an economic profit, its revenues are larger than the combination of its explicit costs and implicit costs. Likewise, a business has an economic loss when its revenues are smaller than the combination of its explicit and implicit costs. The difficulty in determining economic profit lies in calculating the tangible value of implicit costs.

TABLE 8.2

Historical Rates of Return in Stocks, Bonds, and Savings Accounts, 1928–2015

Financial instrument	Historical average rate of return since 1928 (adjusted for inflation)
Stocks	7%
Bonds	3%
Savings account at a financial institution	2%

Source: Federal Reserve database in St. Louis (FRED) and author's adjustments. Data from 1928–2015.

PRACTICE WHAT YOU KNOW

Accounting Profit versus Economic Profit: Calculating Summer Job Profits

Kyle is a college student who works during the summer to pay for tuition. Last summer he worked at a fast-food restaurant and earned $2,500. This summer he is working as a painter and will earn $4,000. To do the painting job, Kyle had to spend $200 on supplies.

How much economic profit do you make from painting?

Question: What is Kyle's accounting profit?

Answer: accounting profit = total revenues − explicit cost
= $4,000 − $200 = $3,800

Question: If working at the fast-food restaurant was Kyle's next-best alternative, how much economic profit will Kyle earn from painting?

Answer: To calculate economic profit, we need to subtract the explicit and implicit costs from the total revenue. Kyle's total revenue from painting will be $4,000. His explicit costs are $200 for supplies, and his implicit cost is $2,500—the salary he would have earned in the fast-food restaurant. So

economic profit = total revenue − explicit cost + implicit cost
= $4,000 − ($200 + $2,500) = $1,300

Kyle's economic profit will be $1,300.

Question: Suppose that Kyle can get an internship at an investment bank. The internship provides a stipend of $3,000 and tangible work experience that will help him get a job after graduation. Should Kyle take the painting job or the internship?

Answer: The implicit costs have changed because Kyle now has to consider the $3,000 stipend and the increased chance of securing a job after graduation versus what he can make painting houses. Calculation of economic profit from painting is now

economic profit = $4,000 − ($200 + $3,000) = $800

So at this point, Kyle's economic profit from painting would be only $800. But this number is incomplete. There is also the value of the internship experience. If Kyle wants to work in investment banking after graduation, then this decision is a no-brainer. He should take the internship—that is, unless some investment banks value painting houses more than work experience!

How Much Should a Firm Produce?

Every business must decide how much to produce. In this section, we describe the factors that determine output, and we explain how firms use inputs to maximize their production. Because it is possible for a firm to produce too little or too much, we must also consider when a firm should stop production.

The Production Function

For a firm to earn an economic profit, it must produce a product that consumers want. This product is the firm's **output**. A firm should produce an output that is consistent with the largest possible economic profit.

    The firm must also control its costs. To do so, the firm must use resources efficiently. There are three primary **factors of production**: labor, land, and capital. Each factor of production is an *input*, or a resource used in the production process to generate the firm's output. *Labor* consists of workers, *land* consists of the geographical location used in production, and *capital* consists of all the resources that the workers use to create the final product. Consider McDonald's as an example. The labor input includes managers, cashiers, cooks, and janitorial staff. The land input includes the land on which the McDonald's building sits. The capital input includes the building itself, the equipment used, the parking lot, the signs, and all the hamburger patties, buns, fries, ketchup, and other foodstuffs.

    To keep costs down in the production process, a firm needs to find the right mix of these inputs. The **production function** describes the relationship between the inputs a firm uses and the output it creates. As we saw at the beginning of the chapter, the manager of a McDonald's must make many decisions about inputs. If she hires too little labor, some of the land and capital will be underutilized. Likewise, with too many workers and not enough land or capital, some workers will not have enough to do to stay busy. For example, suppose that only a single worker shows up at McDonald's one day. This employee will have to do all the cooking; bag up the meals; handle the register, the drive-through, and the drinks; and clean the tables. This single worker, no matter how productive, will not be able to keep up with demand. Hungry customers will grow tired of waiting and take their business elsewhere—maybe for good!

    When a second worker shows up, the two employees can begin to specialize in what they do well. Recall that specialization and comparative advantage lead to higher levels of output (see Chapter 2). Therefore, individual workers will be assigned to tasks that match their skills. For example, one worker can take the orders, fill the bags, and get the drinks. The other can work the grill area and drive-through. When a third worker comes on,

Output is the product that the firm creates.

Factors of production are the inputs (labor, land, and capital) used in producing goods and services.

The **production function** describes the relationship between the inputs a firm uses and the output it creates.

McDonald's needs the correct amount of labor to maximize its output.

the specialization process can extend even further. Specialization and division of labor are key to the way McDonald's operates. Production per worker expands as long as additional workers become more specialized and there are enough capital resources to keep each worker occupied.

When only a few workers share capital resources, the resources that each worker needs are readily available. But what happens when the restaurant is very busy? The manager can hire more staff for the busiest shifts, but the amount of space for cooking and the number of cash registers, drink dispensers, and tables in the seating area are fixed. Because the added employees have less capital to work with, beyond a certain point the additional labor will not continue to increase the restaurant's output at the same rate as it did at first. You might recognize this situation if you have ever gone into a fast-food restaurant at lunchtime. Even though the space behind the counter bustles with busy employees, they can't keep up with the orders. Only so many meals can be produced in a short time and in a fixed space; some customers have to wait.

The restaurant must also maintain an adequate supply of materials. If a shipment is late and the restaurant runs out of hamburger patties, sales (and total revenue) will decrease. The manager must therefore (1) decide how many workers to hire for each shift and (2) manage the inventory of supplies.

Let's look more closely at the manager's decision about how many workers to hire. On the left side of Figure 8.1, we see what happens when workers are added, one by one. When the manager adds one worker, output goes from 0 meals to 5 meals. Going from one worker to two workers increases total output to 15 meals. The second worker has increased the number of meals produced from 5 to 15, an increase of 10 meals. This increase in output is the **marginal product**, which is the change in output associated with one additional unit of an input. In this case, the change in output (10 additional meals) divided by the increase in input (1 worker) gives us a marginal product of 10 ÷ 1, or 10. Because the table in Figure 8.1 adds one worker at a time, the marginal product is just the increase in output shown in the third column.

Looking down the three columns, we see that the total output continues to expand, and it keeps growing through eight workers. But after the first three workers, the rate of increase in the marginal product slows down. Why? The gains from specialization are slowly declining. With the ninth worker (going from 8 to 9), we see a negative marginal product. Once the cash registers, drive-through, grill area, and other service stations are fully staffed, there is not much for an extra worker to do. Eventually, extra workers will get in the way or distract other workers from completing their tasks.

The graphs on the right side of Figure 8.1 show (a) total output and (b) marginal product of labor. The graph of total output in (a) uses data from the second column of the table. As the number of workers goes from 0 to 3 on the *x* axis, total output rises at an increasing rate from 0 to 30. The slope of the total output curve rises until it reaches three workers at the first dashed vertical line. Between three workers and the second dashed vertical line at eight workers, the total output curve continues to rise, though at a slower rate; the slope of the curve is still positive, but the curve becomes progressively flatter. Finally, once we reach the ninth worker, total output begins to fall and the slope becomes negative. At this point, it is not productive to have so many workers.

Marginal thinking

Marginal product is the change in output associated with one additional unit of an input.

FIGURE 8.1

The Production Function and Marginal Product

(a) Total output rises rapidly in the green zone from zero to three workers, rises less rapidly in the yellow zone between three and eight workers, and falls in the red zone after eight workers. (b) The marginal product of labor rises in the green zone from zero to three workers, falls in the yellow zone from three to eight workers but remains positive, and becomes negative after eight workers. Notice that the marginal product becomes negative after total output reaches its maximum at eight workers. As long as marginal product is positive, total output rises. Once marginal product becomes negative, total output falls.

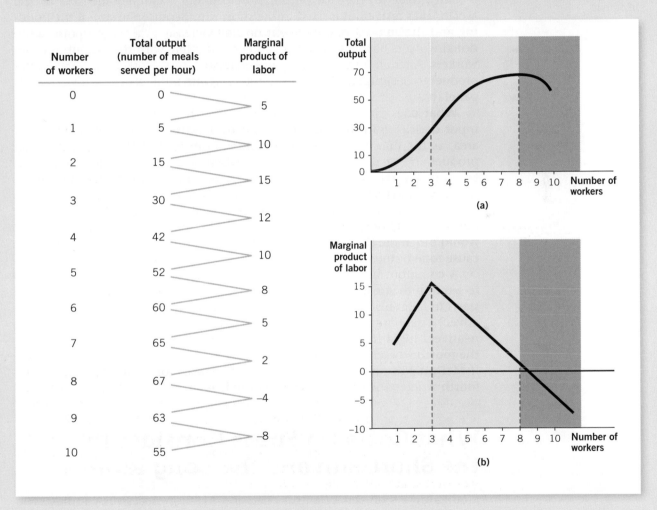

Number of workers	Total output (number of meals served per hour)	Marginal product of labor
0	0	
		5
1	5	
		10
2	15	
		15
3	30	
		12
4	42	
		10
5	52	
		8
6	60	
		5
7	65	
		2
8	67	
		−4
9	63	
		−8
10	55	

Diminishing Marginal Product

The marginal product curve in panel (b) of Figure 8.1 explains the shape of the total output curve in panel (a). Consider that each worker's marginal productivity either adds to or subtracts from the firm's overall output. Marginal product increases from 5 meals served per hour with the first worker to

15 meals per hour with the third worker. From the first worker to the third, each additional worker leads to increased specialization and teamwork, which explains the rapid rise—from 0 to 30 meals—in the total output curve. By the fourth worker, marginal product begins to decline. Looking back to the table, you can see that the fourth worker produces 12 extra meals—3 fewer than the third worker. The point at which successive increases in inputs are associated with a slower rise in output is known as the point of **diminishing marginal product**.

Why does the rate of output slow? In our example, the size of the McDonald's restaurant is fixed in the short run. Because the size of the building and the amount of equipment do not increase, at a certain point additional workers have less to do or can even interfere with the output of other workers. After all inputs are fully utilized, additional workers cause marginal product to decline, which we see in the marginal product curve in Figure 8.1, panel (b).

What does diminishing marginal product tell us about the firm's labor input decision? Turning again to the two graphs, we see that in the green area, as the number of workers increases from zero to three, the marginal product and total output also rise. But when we enter the yellow zone with the fourth worker, we reach the point of diminishing marginal product where the curve starts to decline. Total output continues to rise, though at a slower rate. Finally, in the red zone, which we enter with the ninth worker, marginal product becomes negative and total output declines. No rational manager would hire more than eight workers in this scenario, because doing so would cause total output to drop.

A common mistake when considering diminishing marginal product is to assume that a firm should stop production as soon as marginal product starts to fall. This is not necessarily true. "Diminishing" does not mean "negative." There are many times when marginal product is declining but still relatively high. In our example, diminishing marginal product begins with the fourth worker. However, that fourth worker still produces 12 extra meals. If McDonald's can sell those 12 additional meals for more than it pays the fourth worker, the company's profits will rise.

Diminishing marginal product occurs when successive increases in inputs are associated with a slower rise in output.

Marginal thinking

What Costs Do Firms Consider in the Short Run and the Long Run?

Production is one part of a firm's decision-making process. If you have run even a simple business—for example, mowing lawns—you know that it requires decision-making. How many lawns do you want to be responsible for? Should you work on different lawns at the same time or specialize by task, with one person doing all the mowing and another taking care of the trimming? These are the kinds of production-related questions every firm must address. The other major component of production is cost. Should you invest in a big industrial-size mower? How much gasoline will you need to run your mowers? What does it cost to hire someone to help get the work done? These are some of the cost-related concerns that firms face. Each one may seem like a small decision, but the discovery process that leads to the answers is crucial.

PRACTICE WHAT YOU KNOW

Diminishing Returns: Snow Cone Production

It's a hot day, and customers are lined up for snow cones at your small stand. The following table shows your firm's short-run production function for snow cones.

Number of workers	Total output of snow cones per hour
0	0
1	20
2	50
3	75
4	90
5	100
6	105
7	100
8	90

How many workers are too many? Use marginal product to decide.

Question: When does diminishing marginal product begin?

Answer: You have to be careful when calculating this answer. Total output is maximized when you have six workers, but diminishing marginal return begins before you hire that many workers. Look at the following table, which includes a third column showing marginal product.

Number of workers	Total output of snow cones per hour	Marginal product
0	0	0
1	20	20
2	50	30
3	75	25
4	90	15
5	100	10
6	105	5
7	100	−5
8	90	−10

The marginal product is highest when you hire the second worker. After that, each subsequent worker you hire has a lower marginal product. Therefore, the answer to the question is that diminishing marginal product begins after the second worker.

Every firm, whether just starting out or already well established and profitable, can benefit by assessing how much to produce and how to produce it more efficiently. In addition, production and cost considerations are different in the short run and in the long run. We begin with the short run because the majority of firms are most concerned with making the best short-run decisions, and then we extend our analysis to the long run, where planning ahead plays a central role.

Costs in the Short Run

All firms experience some costs that are unavoidable in the short run. These unavoidable costs—for example, a lease on space or a contract with a supplier—are a large part of short-run costs. In the short run, costs can be variable or fixed.

Variable costs change with the rate of output. Let's see what this means for a McDonald's and further simplify our example by assuming that the McDonald's produces only Big Macs. In this case, the variable costs include the number of workers the firm hires; the electricity the firm uses; the all-beef patties, special sauce, lettuce, cheese, pickles, onions, and sesame seed buns needed to create the Big Macs; and the packaging. These items are variable costs because the restaurant doesn't need them unless it has customers. The amount of these resources varies with the amount of output the restaurant produces. You might be thinking that a firm should decide to produce at an output where its average variable costs are lowest; but be careful—you don't have all the facts yet. In Chapter 9, we add demand to our analysis to determine how much the firm should produce. For now, we stay focused on the cost side.

Fixed costs are unavoidable; they do not vary with output in the short run. For instance, no matter how many Big Macs the McDonald's sells, most of the costs associated with the building remain the same and the business must pay for them. These fixed costs—also known as *overhead*—include rent, insurance, and property taxes.

> **Variable costs** change with the rate of output.

> **Fixed costs** are unavoidable; they do not vary with output in the short run. Fixed costs are also known as overhead.

Interpreting Tabular Data

Every business must be able to determine how much it costs to provide the products and services it sells. Table 8.3 lists many different ways to measure the costs associated with business decisions.

Let's begin with total variable cost (TVC) in column 2 and total fixed cost (TFC) in column 3. Notice that when output—the quantity (Q) of Big Macs produced per hour—is 0, total variable cost starts at $0 and rises with production at an uneven rate, depending on output and the cost of the ingredients that go into each Big Mac. We attribute this increase in TVC to the simple fact that additional workers and other inputs are needed to generate additional output. In contrast, total fixed cost starts at $100, even when output is 0, and remains constant as output rises. As already noted, fixed costs include overhead expenses such as rent, insurance, and property taxes. For simplicity, we assume that this amount is $100 a day. When we add fixed cost and variable cost together, we get total cost (TC), listed in column 4: TC = TVC + TFC.

Columns 5 and 6 enable us to determine the cost of producing a Big Mac by examining the average cost of production. **Average variable cost (AVC)**, in column 5, is the total variable cost divided by the output produced: AVC = TVC ÷ Q. Notice that the average variable cost declines until 60 Big Macs are produced at an average variable cost of $1.67, which is the lowest average variable cost. Why should we care about AVC? Because it can be a useful signal. In this case, total variable costs in column 2 always rise, but the average variable cost falls until 60 Big Macs are produced.

Average variable cost (AVC) is determined by dividing total variable cost by the output.

Average fixed cost (AFC), listed in column 6, is calculated by dividing total fixed cost by the output: AFC = TFC ÷ Q. Because total fixed cost is constant, dividing these costs by the output means that as the output rises, the average fixed cost declines. In other words, higher output levels spread out the total fixed cost across more units. As Table 8.3 shows, average fixed cost is lowest at an output of 100 Big Macs, where

Average fixed cost (AFC) is determined by dividing total fixed cost by the output.

$$AFC = TFC \div Q$$
$$AFC = \$100 \div 100$$
$$AFC = \$1$$

What does this example tell a business that wants to lower its costs? Because overhead costs such as rent cannot be changed, the best way to lower average fixed costs is to raise output.

TABLE 8.3

Measuring Costs

(1) Quantity (Q = Big Macs produced per hour)	(2) Total Variable Cost	(3) Total Fixed Cost	(4) Total Cost	(5) Average Variable Cost	(6) Average Fixed Cost	(7) Average Total Cost	(8) Marginal Cost
Abbreviation:	TVC	TFC	TC	AVC	AFC	ATC	MC
Formula:			TVC + TFC	TVC ÷ Q	TFC ÷ Q	TC ÷ Q or AVC + AFC	ΔTVC ÷ ΔQ or ΔTC ÷ ΔQ
0	$0.00	$100.00	$100.00				
10	30.00	100.00	130.00	$3.00	$10.00	$13.00	$3.00
20	50.00	100.00	150.00	2.50	5.00	7.50	2.00
30	65.00	100.00	165.00	2.17	3.33	5.50	1.50
40	77.00	100.00	177.00	1.93	2.50	4.43	1.20
50	87.00	100.00	187.00	1.74	2.00	3.74	1.00
60	100.00	100.00	200.00	1.67	1.67	3.34	1.30
70	120.00	100.00	220.00	1.71	1.43	3.14	2.00
80	160.00	100.00	260.00	2.00	1.25	3.25	4.00
90	220.00	100.00	320.00	2.44	1.11	3.55	6.00
100	300.00	100.00	400.00	3.00	1.00	4.00	8.00

Average total cost (ATC) is the sum of average variable cost and average fixed cost.

Average total cost (ATC), shown in column 7, is calculated by adding the AVC and AFC. It can also be calculated by dividing total cost by quantity (TC ÷ Q). Let's look at the numbers to get a better understanding of what average total cost tells us. Even though the average variable cost rises from $1.67 to $1.71 after 60 Big Macs are produced, the average fixed cost is still falling, from $1.67 to $1.43. The decline in average fixed cost is enough to pull the average total cost down to $3.14. Eventually, increases in variable cost overwhelm the cost savings achieved by spreading fixed cost across more production. We can see this result if we compare the average total costs of making 70 Big Macs and 80 Big Macs.

For 70 Big Macs:

$$ATC = AVC + AFC$$
$$ATC = \$1.71 + \$1.43 = \$3.14$$

For 80 Big Macs:

$$ATC = AVC + AFC$$
$$ATC = \$2.00 + \$1.25 = \$3.25$$

At 80 Big Macs, the average variable cost rises from $1.71 to $2.00. And the average fixed cost falls from $1.43 to $1.25. Therefore, the rise in average variable cost—$0.29—is higher than the fall in average fixed cost—$0.18. ATC therefore rises, removing the benefit of higher output.

Interpreting Data Graphically

Now that we have walked through the numerical results in Table 8.3, it is time to visualize the cost relationships with graphs. Figure 8.2 shows a graph of total cost curves (a) and the relationship between the marginal cost curve and the average cost curves (b).

In panel (a) of Figure 8.2, we see that although the total cost curve continues to rise, the rate of increase in total cost is not constant. For the first 50 Big Macs, the total cost rises at a decreasing rate, reflecting the gains of specialization and comparative advantage that come from adding workers who concentrate on specific tasks. After 50 Big Macs, diminishing marginal product causes the total cost curve to rise at an increasing rate. Because a McDonald's restaurant has a fixed capacity, producing more than 50 Big Macs requires a significantly higher investment in labor, and those workers do not have any additional space to work in—a situation that makes the total cost curve rise more rapidly at high production levels. The total cost (TC) curve is equal to the sum of the total fixed cost and total variable cost curves, as shown in panel (a). Total fixed cost (TFC) is constant, so it is the total variable cost (TVC) that gives the TC curve its shape.

Marginal thinking

But that is not the most important part of the story. Any manager at McDonald's can examine total costs. Likewise, she can look at the average cost and compare that information with the average cost at other local businesses. But neither the total cost of labor nor the average cost will tell her anything about the cost of making additional units—that is, Big Macs.

FIGURE 8.2

The Cost Curves

(a) The total variable cost (TVC) dictates the shape of the total cost (TC) curve. After 50 Big Macs, diminishing marginal product causes the total cost curve to rise at an increasing rate. Notice that the total fixed cost curve (TFC) stays constant, or flat. (b) The marginal cost curve (MC) reaches its minimum before average variable cost (AVC) and average total cost (ATC). Marginals always lead the average variable and average total costs either up or down. Average fixed cost (AFC), which has no variable component, continues to fall with increased quantity, because total fixed costs are spread across more units.

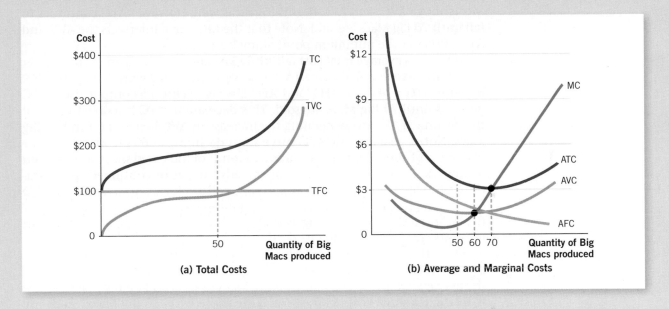

(a) Total Costs

(b) Average and Marginal Costs

A manager can make even better decisions by looking at marginal cost. The **marginal cost (MC)** is the increase in cost that occurs from producing one additional unit of output. (In column 8 of Table 8.3, this relationship is shown as the change in TVC divided by the change in quantity produced, where "change" is indicated by Δ, the Greek letter delta.) For example, in planning the weekly work schedule, the manager has to consider how many workers to hire for each shift. She wants to hire additional workers when the cost of doing so is less than the expected boost in profits. In this situation, it is essential to know the marginal cost, or extra cost, of hiring one more worker.

In Table 8.3, marginal cost (MC) falls to a minimum of $1.00 when between 40 and 50 Big Macs are produced. Notice that the minimum MC occurs at a lower output level than average variable cost (AVC) and average total cost (ATC) in panel (b) of Figure 8.2. When output is less than 50 Big Macs, marginal cost is falling because over this range of production the marginal product of labor is increasing due to better teamwork and more specialization. After the fiftieth Big Mac, MC rises, acting as an early warning that

Marginal cost (MC) is the increase in cost that occurs from producing one additional unit of output.

Marginal thinking

average variable and total costs will soon follow suit. Why would a manager care about the marginal cost of the last few units being produced more than the average total cost of producing all the units? Because marginal cost helps the manager decide if making one more unit of output will increase profits or not!

The MC curve reaches its lowest point before the lowest point of the AVC and ATC curves. For this reason, a manager who is concerned about rising costs would look to the MC curve as a signal that average total cost will eventually increase as well. Once marginal cost begins to increase, it continues to pull down average variable cost until sales reach 60 Big Macs. After that point, MC is above AVC, and AVC begins to rise as well. However, ATC continues to fall until 70 Big Macs are sold. Note that the MC curve intersects the AVC and ATC curves at the minimum point along both curves.

Why does average total cost fall while MC and AVC are rising? The answer lies in the average fixed cost (AFC) curve shown in Figure 8.2, panel (b). Because ATC = AVC + AFC, and AFC always declines as output rises, ATC declines until 70 Big Macs are sold. This decrease in ATC is a direct result of the decline in AFC overwhelming the increase in AVC between 60 and 70 Big Macs. Notice also that the AVC curve stops declining at 60 Big Macs. Average variable cost should initially decline as a result of increased specialization and teamwork. However, at some point the advantages of continued specialization are overtaken by diminishing marginal product, and average variable cost begins to rise. The transition from falling costs to rising costs is of particular interest because as long as average total cost is declining, the firm can lower its costs by increasing its output.

Once the marginal cost in Table 8.3 rises above the average total cost, the average total cost begins to rise as well. This result is evident if we compare the average total cost of making 70 Big Macs ($3.14) and 80 Big Macs ($3.25) with the marginal cost ($4.00) of making those extra 10 Big Macs. Since the marginal cost ($4.00) of making Big Macs 71 through 80 is higher than the average total cost at 70 ($3.14), the average total cost of making 80 Big Macs goes up (to $3.25).

Marginal cost always leads (or pulls) average variable cost and average total cost along. The MC eventually rises above the average total cost because of diminishing marginal product. Because the firm has to pay a fixed wage in our McDonald's example, the cost to produce each hamburger increases as each worker's output decreases.

Note that there is one "average" curve that the marginal cost does not affect: average fixed cost. Notice that the AFC curve in panel (b) of Figure 8.2

Costs in the Short Run

The Office

The popular TV series *The Office* had an amusing episode devoted to the discussion of costs. The character Michael Scott establishes his own paper company to compete with both Staples and his former company, Dunder Mifflin. He then outcompetes his rivals by keeping his fixed and variable costs low.

In one inspired scene, we see the Michael Scott Paper Company operating out of a single room and using an old church van to deliver paper. Thus, the company has very low *fixed costs*, which enables it to charge unusually low prices. In addition, Michael Scott keeps *variable costs* to a minimum by hiring only essential employees and not paying any benefits, such as health insurance. But this is a problem, because Michael Scott does not fully account for the cost of the paper he is selling. In fact, he is selling below unit cost!

As we will discover in upcoming chapters, firms with lower costs have many advantages in the market. Such firms can keep their prices lower to attract additional customers. Cost matters because price matters.

Michael Scott doesn't fully understand fixed and variable costs.

continues to fall even though marginal cost eventually rises. The AFC curve declines with increased output. Because McDonald's has $100.00 in fixed costs each day, we can determine the average fixed cost by dividing the total fixed cost ($100.00) by the number of Big Macs sold. When 10 Big Macs are sold, the average fixed cost is $10.00 per Big Mac, but this value falls to $1.00 per Big Mac if 100 burgers are sold. Because McDonald's is a high-volume business that relies on low costs to compete, being able to produce enough Big Macs to spread out the firm's fixed costs is essential.

Costs in the Long Run

We have seen that in the short run, businesses have fixed costs and fixed capacities. In the long run, all costs are variable and can be renegotiated. Thus, firms have more control over their costs in the long run, which enables them to reach their desired level of production. One way that firms can adjust in the long run is by changing the **scale**, or size, of the production process.

Scale refers to the size of the production process.

If the business is expected to grow, the firm can ramp up production. If the business is faltering, it can scale back its operations. This flexibility enables firms to avoid a situation of negative marginal product. Economists refer to the quantity of output that minimizes the average total cost in the long run as the **efficient scale**.

The **efficient scale** is the output level that minimizes average total cost in the long run.

A long-run time horizon allows a business to choose a scale of operation that best suits its needs. For instance, if a local McDonald's is extremely popular, in the short run the manager can only hire more workers or expand the restaurant's hours to accommodate more customers. However, in the long run all costs are variable; the manager can add drive-through lanes, increase the number of registers, expand the grill area, and so on.

The absence of fixed factors in the long-run production process means that we cannot explain total costs in the long run in the same way that we explained short-run costs. Short-run costs are a reflection of diminishing marginal product, whereas long-run costs are a reflection of scale and the cost of providing additional output. Because diminishing marginal product is no longer relevant in the long run, one might assume that costs would fall as output expands. However, this is not necessarily the case. Depending on the industry and the prevailing economic conditions, long-run costs can rise, fall, or stay approximately the same.

Three Types of Scale

In this section, we describe three different scenarios for a firm in the long run. A firm may experience *economies of scale*, *diseconomies of scale*, or *constant returns to scale*. Let's consider each of these in turn.

Economies of scale occur when long-run average total costs decline as output expands.

Diseconomies of scale occur when long-run average total costs rise as output expands.

If output expands and long-run average total costs decline in the long run, a business experiences **economies of scale**. National homebuilders, such as Toll Brothers, provide a good example of economies of scale. All builders, whether they are local or national, do the same thing—they build houses. Each builder needs lumber, concrete, excavators, electricians, plumbers, roofers, and many more specialized workers or subcontractors. A big company, such as Toll, is able to hire many specialists and also buy the equipment it needs in bulk. As a result, Toll can manufacture the same home as a local builder but at a much lower cost.

But bigger isn't always better! Sometimes a company grows so large that coordination problems make costs rise. For example, as an enterprise expands its scale, it might require more managers, highly specialized workers, and a coordination process to pull everything together. As the layers of management expand, the coordination process can break down. For this reason, a larger firm can become less effective at holding down long-run average total costs and experience **diseconomies of scale**, or higher costs as output expands in the long run.

Building more than one house at a time would represent economies of scale.

The problem of diseconomies of scale is especially relevant in the service sector of the economy. For example, large regional hospitals have many layers of bureaucracy. These added management costs and infrastructure expenses can make medical care more expensive beyond a certain point. If you are not convinced, ask yourself why large cities have many smaller competing hospitals rather than one centralized hospital. The answer becomes obvious: bigger doesn't always mean less expensive (or better)!

When long-run average total costs remain constant even as output expands in the long run, we say that the firm has **constant returns to scale**. For example, large national restaurant chains like Olive Garden, which specializes in Italian cuisine, compete with local Italian restaurants. In each case, the local costs to hire workers and build the restaurant are the same. Olive Garden does have a few advantages; for example, it can afford to advertise on national television and buy food in bulk. But Olive Garden also has more overhead costs for its many layers of management. Constant returns to scale in the bigger chain mean that a small local Italian restaurant will have approximately the same menu prices as its bigger rivals.

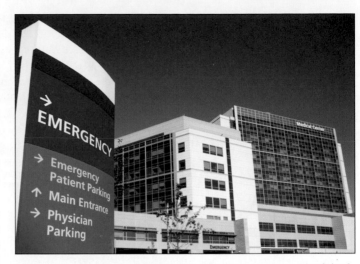

Would you rather see the ER's doctor du jour or your own physician?

Constant returns to scale occur when long-run average total costs remain constant as output expands.

Long-Run Cost Curves

Now it is time to illustrate the long-run nature of cost curves. We have seen that increased output may not always lead to economies of scale. Average total costs can decline, be constant, or rise with output. Figure 8.3 illustrates

Will you find lower prices at the Olive Garden or your local Italian restaurant?

FIGURE 8.3

Costs in the Long Run

In the long run, there are three distinct possibilities: the long-run average total cost curve (LRATC) can exhibit economies of scale (the green curve), constant returns to scale (the purple curve), or diseconomies of scale (the orange curve).

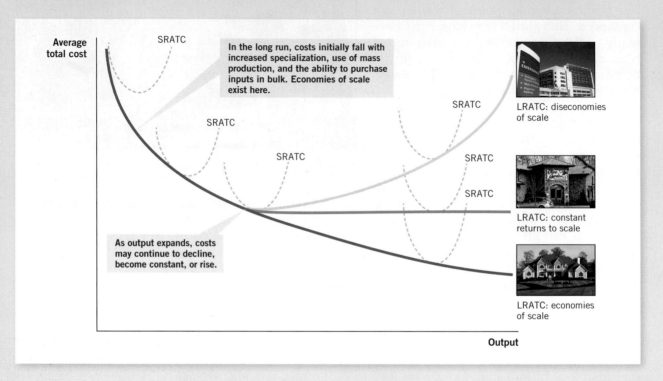

each of the three scale possibilities graphically. The long-run average total cost curve (LRATC) is actually a composite of many short-run average total cost curves (SRATC), which appear as the faint U-shaped dashed curves drawn in gray. By visualizing the short-run cost curves at any given output level, we can develop a composite of them to create the LRATC curve, which comprises all the short-run cost curves that the firm may choose to deploy in the long run. In the long run, the firm is free to choose any of its short-run curves, so it always picks the output/cost combination that minimizes costs.

In the long run, there are three distinct possibilities: economies of scale, constant returns to scale, and diseconomies of scale. At first, each LRATC curve exhibits economies of scale as a result of increased specialization, the utilization of mass production, bulk purchasing power, and increased automation. The main question in the long run is whether the cost curve will continue to decline, level off, or rise. In an industry with economies of scale at high output levels—for example, homebuilding—the cost curve continues to decline, and the most efficient output level is always the largest output: the green curve in Figure 8.3. In this situation, we would expect only

Bigger Is Not Always Better

Large firms take advantage of economies of scale in many ways, such as buying their inputs at discounted prices. But bigger is not always better. One major problem that confronts large firms is becoming "top-heavy"—that is, having a labor force that requires a large number of managers whose only job is to manage. This lowers the overall productivity of the labor force and increases costs.

■ Owner / Executive manager   ■ Division manager   ■ Line manager   ■ Supervisor   ■ Worker

Small Business

10% Reduced productivity

A typical small business might consist of 1 owner and 9 workers.

Mid-Sized Business

12.2% Reduced productivity

A typical mid-sized business might consist of 41 employees, including 1 executive manager and 4 supervisors who oversee 9 workers each.

Large Business

14.9% Reduced productivity

A typical large company might consist of 127 employees: 1 executive manager, 2 division managers, 4 line managers, 12 supervisors, and 108 workers.

REVIEW QUESTIONS

- Calculate the reduced productivity in a company of 1,000 employees when there are 2 executive managers, 6 line managers, and 12 supervisors for every 80 workers.

- Your friend owns a business and is looking to expand. Describe the risks and rewards of such a move using economies of scale and costs.

Economies of Scale

The Big Bang Theory: The Work Song Nanocluster

In an episode of the long-running TV series *The Big Bang Theory*, Penny decides to make flower barrettes in her spare time to supplement her pay as a waitress. Because Penny is not very good at math, when Sheldon stops by she seeks his advice about how she can earn more money. What transpires can only be described as the best explanation of business costs you'll ever see.

As Sheldon explains to Penny: "If you took advantage of modern marketing techniques and optimized your manufacturing process, you might make this a viable business." They get to work and Sheldon starts timing how long it takes Penny to make a flower barrette. It takes her 12 minutes and 17 seconds, and Penny seems quite happy until Sheldon says, "That's 4.9 Penny Blossoms per hour. Based on your cost of materials and your wholesale selling price, you'll effectively be paying yourself $5.19 a day. There are children in a sneaker factory in Indonesia who outearn you." To increase Penny's productivity, he suggests that they create an assembly line to lower the cost of manufacturing the barrettes, and they begin working together to make the Penny Blossoms, even singing a rhythmic work song

Creating flower barrettes by hand in your apartment misses out on economies of scale.

to increase their productivity. Together they can now make each Penny Blossom in under 3 minutes!

At this point, Leonard, Howard, and Raj enter Penny's apartment and start to ask questions about what is going on. Everyone quickly realizes that they will have to expand the scale of the operation to fully optimize the production process to lower costs even further. The result is that you see the production process evolve from a small-scale operation in Penny's apartment in the short run to a sophisticated large-scale enterprise in the long run. All of this is done in one very funny 22-minute episode.

one large firm to dominate the industry because large firms have significant cost advantages. However, in an industry with constant returns to scale—for example, restaurants—the cost curve flattens out: the purple line. Once the curve becomes constant, firms of varying sizes can compete equally with one another because they have the same costs. Finally, in the case of diseconomies of scale—for example, big-city hospitals—bigger firms have higher costs: the orange curve.

Conclusion

Do larger firms have lower costs? Not always. When diseconomies of scale occur, average total costs will rise with output. This result contradicts the common misconception that bigger firms have lower costs than their smaller

PRACTICE WHAT YOU KNOW

Marginal Cost: The True Cost of Admission to Universal Studios

You and your family visit Orlando for a week. While there, you decide to go to Universal Studios. When you arrive, you notice that each family member can buy a day pass for $100 or a two-day pass for $150. Your parents are concerned about spending too much, so they decide to calculate the average cost of a two-day pass to see if it is a good value. The average cost is $150 ÷ 2, or $75 per day. Their math is correct, but something you learned in economics tells you that they are not thinking about this situation in the correct way.

Is one day enough to do it all?

Question: What concept can you apply to make the decision more clear?

Answer: Tell your parents about *marginal cost*. The first day costs $100, but the marginal cost of going back to the park on the second day is only the extra cost per person, or $150 – $100, which equals $50. Your parents still might not want to spend the extra money, but spending only an extra $50 for a second day makes it an attractive value. Someone who does not appreciate economics might think the second day costs an extra $75 because that is the average cost but the average cost is misleading. Looking at marginal cost is the best way to weigh these two options. By the way, if you want a three-day pass the price is $160, making the marginal cost of the third day just $160 – $150, which equals $10. That sounds ridiculously low but the incremental increase in the price is low because no matter how much you like Harry Potter, a third straight day in the same theme park becomes repetitive quickly.

competitors. Simply put, sometimes a leaner firm with less overhead can beat its larger rivals on cost.

Costs are defined in a number of ways, but marginal cost plays the most crucial role in a firm's cost structure. By observing what happens to marginal cost, you can understand changes in average cost and total cost. This simple fact explains why economists place so much emphasis on marginal cost. Going forward, a solid grasp of marginal analysis will help you understand many of the most important concepts in microeconomics.

Marginal
thinking

You now understand the cost, or supply side, of business decisions. However, to provide a complete picture of how firms operate, we still need to examine how markets work. Costs are only part of the story, and in the next chapter we take a closer look at profits.

ANSWERING THE BIG QUESTIONS

How are profits and losses calculated?

* Profits and losses are determined by calculating the difference between expenses (total cost) and total revenue.

* There are two types of profit: economic profit and accounting profit. If a business has an economic profit, its revenue is larger than the combination of its explicit and implicit costs.

* Economists break costs into two components: explicit costs, which are easy to calculate, and implicit costs, which are hard to calculate. Because economic profit accounts for implicit costs, the economic profit is always less than the accounting profit.

How much should a firm produce?

* A firm should produce an output that is consistent with the largest possible economic profit.

* To maximize profit, firms must effectively combine land, labor, and capital in the right quantities.

* In any short-run production process, a point of diminishing marginal product will occur at which additional units of a variable input no longer generate as much output as before. Diminishing marginal product is a result of fixed inputs (such as capital and land) in the short run.

* Marginal cost (MC) is the key variable in determining a firm's cost structure. The MC curve always leads the average total cost (ATC) and average variable cost (AVC) curves up or down.

What costs do firms consider in the short run and the long run?

* In the short run, firms consider variable and fixed costs, as well as marginal cost. Firms also consider average variable cost (AVC), average fixed cost (AFC), and average total cost (ATC).

* With the exception of the average fixed cost (AFC) curve, which always declines, short-run cost curves are U-shaped. All variable costs initially decline due to increased specialization. At a certain point, the advantages of continued specialization give way to diminishing marginal product, and the MC, AVC, and ATC curves begin to rise.

* Long-run costs are a reflection of scale. Firms can experience diseconomies of scale, economies of scale, or constant returns to scale, depending on the industry.

How Much Does It Cost to Raise a Child?

Trade-offs
Opportunity
cost

Raising a child is one of life's most rewarding experiences, but it can be very expensive. According to the U.S. Department of Agriculture, the cost for a middle-income, two-parent family to raise a child from birth to age 18 is more than $250,000 (not including college). To determine this number, the government considers all the costs related to raising a child, such as food, clothing, medical care, and entertainment. In addition, the government apportions a share of the costs of the family home and vehicles to each child in the household. To put the cost of raising a child in perspective, the median home value in 2015 was $178,000. Talk about opportunity cost!

What if a family has more than one child? You wouldn't necessarily multiply the cost by 2 or 3, because there are economies of scale in raising more children. For example, some things can be shared: the children might share a bedroom and wear hand-me-downs. Also, the family can purchase food in bulk. As a result, families that have three or more children can manage to spend an average of 22% less on each child.

The cost of raising children also forces families to make trade-offs. In many households, both parents must work or work longer hours. When one parent steps out of the workforce, the household loses a paycheck. While leaving the workforce may save in expenses associated with working, including certain clothes, transportation, and childcare, there are also hidden costs. For example, the lack of workplace continuity lowers the stay-at-home parent's future earning power.

Raising a child is an expensive proposition in both the short run and the long run. But don't let this discourage you; it is also one of the most rewarding investments you will ever make.

Daddy Day Care? Childcare expenses add up.

CONCEPTS YOU SHOULD KNOW

accounting profit (p. 248)
average fixed cost (AFC) (p. 257)
average total cost (ATC) (p. 258)
average variable cost (AVC)
    (p. 257)
constant returns to scale
    (p. 263)
diminishing marginal product
    (p. 254)

diseconomies of scale (p. 262)
economic profit (p. 248)
economies of scale (p. 262)
efficient scale (p. 262)
explicit costs (p. 247)
factors of production (p. 251)
fixed costs (p. 256)
implicit costs (p. 247)
loss (p. 246)

marginal cost (MC) (p. 259)
marginal product (p. 252)
output (p. 251)
production function (p. 251)
profit (p. 246)
scale (p. 261)
total cost (p. 246)
total revenue (p. 246)
variable costs (p. 256)

QUESTIONS FOR REVIEW

1. What is the equation for the profit (or loss) of a firm?

2. Why is economic profit a better measure of profitability than accounting profit? Give an example.

3. What role does diminishing marginal product play in determining the ideal mix of labor and capital a firm should use?

4. Describe what happens to the total product of a firm when marginal product is increasing, decreasing, and negative.

5. Explain why marginal cost is the glue that connects average variable cost and average total cost.

6. Compare the short-run and long-run cost curves. In a few sentences, explain their differences.

7. Name examples of industries that illustrate each of the following: economies of scale, constant returns to scale, and diseconomies of scale. Think creatively; do not use the textbook examples.

STUDY PROBLEMS (*solved at the end of the section*)

1. Go to www.lemonadegame.com. This free online game places you in the role of a lemonade seller. Nothing could be simpler, right? Not so fast! You still need to control costs and ensure that you have the right ingredients on hand to be able to sell lemonade. You will need to manage your supply of lemons, sugar, ice, and cups. You will also have to set a price and decide how many lemons and how much sugar and ice to put in each glass of lemonade you produce. This is not a trivial process, so play the game. Your challenge is to make $20 in profit over the first five days. (Your business starts with $20, so you need to have $40 in your account by the end of day 5 to meet the challenge. Are you up to it?)

2. The following table shows a short-run production function for laptop computers. Use the data to determine where diminishing product begins.

Number of workers	Total output of laptop computers
0	0
1	40
2	100
3	150
4	180
5	200
6	205
7	200
8	190

3. A pizza business has the cost structure described below. The firm's fixed costs are $25 per day. Calculate the firm's average fixed costs, average variable costs, average total costs, and marginal costs.

Output (pizzas per day)	Total cost of output
0	$25
10	75
20	115
30	150
40	175
50	190
60	205
70	225
80	250

＊ 4. A firm is considering changing its plant size, so it calculates the average cost of production for various plant sizes, shown below. If the firm is currently using plant size C, is the firm experiencing economies of scale, diseconomies of scale, or constant returns to scale?

Plant size	Average total cost
A (smallest)	$10,000
B	9,500
C	9,000
D	8,800
E	8,800
F (largest)	8,900

5. True or false?
   a. The AFC curve can never rise.
   b. Diminishing marginal product is a long-run constraint that prevents lower costs.
   c. The MC curve intersects the AVC and ATC curves at the minimum point along both curves.
   d. Accounting profit is smaller than economic profit.
   e. Total cost divided by output is equal to marginal cost.

6. Digital media distributed over the Internet often have marginal costs of zero. For instance, people can download music and movies instantly through many providers. Do these products exhibit economies, diseconomies, or constant returns to scale?

7. An airline has a marginal cost per passenger of $30 on a route from Boston to Detroit. At the same time, the typical fare charged is $300. The planes that fly the route are usually full, yet the airline claims that it loses money on the route. How is this possible?

8. Many amusement parks offer two-day passes at dramatically discounted prices. If a one-day pass costs $40 but the two-day pass costs $50, what is the average cost for the two-day pass? What is the marginal cost of the second day pass?

＊ 9. Suppose that you own a yard care business. You have your own mower, flatbed truck, and other equipment. You are also the primary employee. Why might you have trouble calculating your profits? (**Hint:** Think about the difference between accounting profits and economic profits.)

10. Use the information provided in the following table to fill in the blanks.

Output	Total fixed cost	Total variable cost	Total cost	Average fixed cost	Average variable cost	Average total cost	Marginal cost
0	$500	$0	$500	___	___	___	
1	500	200	___	___	___	___	___
2	___	___	800	___	___	___	___
3	___	___	875	___	___	___	___
4	___	___	925	___	___	___	___
5	___	___	___	$100	___	___	$25
6	___	450	___	___	___	___	___

11. If you are a fan of cold dessert treats, you'll recognize that the production process at Cold Stone Creamery differs a great deal from frozen yogurt places. At Cold Stone you give the server your order and the mix-ins you want, and the server creates your treat for you. This process is labor intensive. At a frozen yogurt place, you pick up a cup, choose your flavor from the self-serve machine, serve it yourself, and add in your own mix-ins. You put your creation on a scale and the worker then rings you up. This process is capital intensive. Given this information, which type of frozen dessert business will have the lower marginal cost of production?

✳ **12.** Watch the Reebok commercial on "Terry Tate, Office Linebacker" (www.youtube.com /watch?v=tbSpAsJSZPc). Is the firm that hires Terry Tate experiencing economies, constant returns, or diseconomies of scale? Explain your answer.

SOLVED PROBLEMS

4. The key to solving this problem is recognizing the direction of change in the average total cost. If the firm were to switch to a smaller plant, like B, its average total cost would rise to $9,500. Because the smaller plant would cost more, plant C is currently enjoying economies of scale. When we compare the average total cost of C ($9,000) to D ($8,800), it continues to fall. Because the average total cost is falling from B to D, we again know that the firm is experiencing economies of scale.

9. When calculating your costs for the mower, truck, and other expenses, you are computing your explicit costs. Subtracting the explicit costs from your total revenue will yield the accounting profit you have earned. However, you still do not know your economic profit because you haven't determined your implicit costs. Because you are the primary employee, you also have to add in the opportunity cost of the time you invest in the business. You may not know exactly what you might have earned doing something else, but you can be sure it exists—this is your implicit cost. Implicit costs are the reason you may have trouble computing your profits. You might show an accounting profit only to discover that what you thought you made was less than you could have made by doing something else. If that is the case, your true economic profit is actually negative.

12. Terry Tate enforces company policies and helps to reduce the amount of slacking, making the workforce more productive. However, at the same time, the company needs to hire Terry Tate to reduce slacking, and this is costly, which means that the company is experiencing diseconomies of scale.

Firms in a Competitive Market

Firms control the prices they charge.

Many people believe that firms set the prices for their products with little concern for the consumer. This misconception occurs because

many people think that only the firm is central to the functioning of the market. However, market forces are much stronger than individual firms. Under the right conditions, markets produce high-quality goods at remarkably low prices, to the benefit of both buyers and sellers. Competition drives prices down, which limits the firm's ability to charge as much as it would like.

In this chapter and the next four, we look in more detail at how markets work, the profits firms earn, and how market forces determine the price that a firm can charge for its product or service. We begin our examination of *market structure*, or how individual firms are interconnected, by looking at the conditions necessary to create a competitive market. Although few real markets achieve the ideal market structure described in this chapter, this model provides a good starting point for understanding other market structures.

Our analysis of competitive markets shows that when competition is widespread, firms have little or no control over the price they can charge, and they make little or no economic profit. Thus, in competitive markets, firms are completely at the mercy of market forces that set the price. Let's find out why.

Individual vendors in a flower market face stiff competition.

BIG QUESTIONS

✳ How do competitive markets work?

✳ How do firms maximize profits?

✳ What does the supply curve look like in perfectly competitive markets?

How Do Competitive Markets Work?

Competitive markets exist when there are so many buyers and sellers that each one has only a small impact on the market price and output. Recall that in Chapter 3 we used the example of the Pike Place Market, where each fish vendor sells similar products. Because each fish vendor is small relative to the whole market, no single firm can influence the market price. It doesn't matter where you buy salmon because the price is the same or very similar at every fish stall. When buyers are willing to purchase a product anywhere, sellers have no control over the price they charge. These two characteristics—similar goods and many participants—create a highly competitive market where the price and quantity sold are determined by the market conditions rather than by any one firm.

In competitive markets, buyers can expect to find consistently low prices and a wide availability of the good that they want. Firms that produce goods in competitive markets are known as price takers. A **price taker** has no control over the price set by the market. It "takes"—that is, accepts—the price determined by the overall supply and demand conditions that regulate the market. One of the reasons why firms are price takers is that each seller is small compared to the overall market. This means that any individual seller's decision (to either increase or decrease production) has no impact on the market price.

Competitive markets have another important feature: new competitors can easily enter the market. If you want to open a copy shop, all you have to do is rent store space and several copy machines. There are no licensing or regulatory obstacles in your way. Likewise, there is very little to stop competitors from leaving the market. If you decide to shut down your business, you can lock the doors, return the equipment you rented, and move on to do

A **price taker** has no control over the price set by the market. It "takes" (accepts) the price determined from the overall supply and demand conditions that regulate the market.

TABLE 9.1

Characteristics of Competitive Markets

- Many sellers
- Similar products
- Free entry and exit
- Price taking
- Every firm is small

something else. When barriers to entry into a marketplace are low, new firms are free to compete with existing businesses, which ensures the existence of competitive markets and low prices. Table 9.1 summarizes the characteristics of competitive markets.

Real-life examples of competitive markets usually fall short of perfection. Markets that are almost perfectly competitive, shown in Table 9.2, include the stock market, farmers' markets, online ticket auctions, and

TABLE 9.2

Almost Perfect Markets

Example	How it works	Reality check
Stock market	Millions of shares of stocks are traded every day on various stock exchanges, and generally the buyers and sellers have access to real-time information about prices. Because most of the traders represent only a small share of the market, they have little ability to influence the market price.	Because of the volume of shares that they control, large institutional investors, like Pacific Investment Management Company (PIMCO), manage billions of dollars in funds. As a result, they are big enough to influence the market price.
Farmers' markets	In farmers' markets, sellers are able to set up at little or no cost. Many buyers are also present. The gathering of numerous buyers and sellers of similar products causes the market price for similar products to converge toward a single price.	Many produce markets do not have enough sellers to achieve a perfectly competitive result. With fewer vendors, individual sellers can often set their prices higher.
Online ticket auctions	The resale market for tickets to major sporting events and concerts involves many buyers and sellers. The prices for seats in identical sections end up converging quickly toward a narrow range.	Some ticket companies and fans get special privileges that enable them to buy and sell blocks of tickets before others can enter the market.
Currency trading	Hundreds of thousands of traders around the globe engage in currency buying and selling on any given day. Because all traders have very good real-time information, currency trades in different parts of the world converge toward the same price.	Currency markets are subject to intervention on the part of governments that want to strategically alter the prevailing price of their currency.

currency trading. Of all the market structures, perfect competition is the most beneficial to society because it creates the maximum combined consumer surplus and producer surplus (as we saw in Chapter 5). The more imperfectly competitive a market is, the lower is the total of the two types of surplus and the less beneficial it is to society overall.

In the next section, we examine the profits that competitive firms make. After all, profits motivate firms to produce a product, so knowing how a business can make the most profit is central to understanding how competitive markets work.

ECONOMICS IN THE REAL WORLD

Aalsmeer Flower Auction

The world's largest flower auction takes place in Aalsmeer, a small town in the Netherlands. Each week, producers sell over 100 million flowers there. In

The Aalsmeer flower market is almost perfectly competitive.

fact, over one-third of all the flowers sold in the world pass through Aalsmeer. Because the Aalsmeer market serves thousands of buyers and sellers, it is one of the best examples of a competitive market you will ever find. The supply comes from approximately 6,000 growers worldwide. More than 2,000 buyers attend the auction to purchase flowers.

Aalsmeer uses a method known as a Dutch auction to determine the price for each crate of flowers sold. Most people think of an auction as a situation in which two or more individuals try to outbid each other. However, in Aalsmeer that process is reversed. As each crate of flowers goes on sale, the price on a huge board starts at 100 euros and then goes down until the lot is sold. This special kind of auction was invented here, and it is a very efficient way of getting the highest price out of the buyer who wants the lot the most.

At Aalsmeer, individual buyers and sellers are small compared with the overall size of the market. In addition, the flowers offered by one seller are almost indistinguishable from those offered by the other sellers. As a result, individual buyers and sellers have no control over the price set by the market. ✳

How Do Firms Maximize Profits?

All firms, whether they are active in a competitive market or not, attempt to maximize profits. Making a profit requires that a firm have a thorough grasp of its costs and revenues. In the previous chapter, we learned about the firm's cost structure. In this section, we examine its revenues. Combining

PRACTICE WHAT YOU KNOW

Price Takers: Mall Food Courts

Your instructor asks you to find an example of a competitive market nearby. Your friend suggests that you visit the food court at a nearby mall.

Question: Does each restaurant in a food court meet the definition of a price taker, thereby signaling a competitive market?

Answer: Most food courts contain many sellers. Customers can choose among burgers, sandwiches, salads, pizza, and much more. Everywhere you turn, there is another place to eat and the prices at each place are comparable. Is this enough to make each restaurant a price taker? Not quite. Each restaurant has some market power because it serves different food, enabling the more popular places to charge somewhat more.

Are the restaurants in a food court price takers?

While the restaurants in the court are not price takers, the drinks (both fountain drinks and bottled water) that they sell are essentially the same. Any customer who is only interested in getting something to drink has a highly competitive market to choose from.

the firm's revenues with its costs enables us to determine how much profit the firm makes.

Profits are a key goal of almost every firm, but they don't always materialize. Sometimes, firms experience losses instead of profits, so we also explore whether a firm should shut down or continue to operate in order to minimize its losses. Once we fully understand the firm's decision-making process, we will better comprehend how the entire market functions. To make this process easier, throughout this section we refer to Mr. Plow (from the *Simpsons* episode mentioned in the Economics in the Media box on p. 282) to examine the choices every business must make. We look at the price Mr. Plow (Homer Simpson) charges and how many driveways he clears, and then we compare his revenues to his costs to determine whether he is maximizing his profit.

The Profit-Maximizing Rule

Let's imagine how much revenue Mr. Plow will make if the competitive price is $10 for each driveway he clears. Table 9.3 shows how much profit he might make if he clears up to 10 driveways. As we learned in Chapter 8,

TABLE 9.3

Calculating Profits for Mr. Plow

(1)	(2)	(3)	(4)	(5)	(6)	(7)
Quantity (Q = driveways cleared)	Total revenue	Total cost	Total profit	Marginal revenue	Marginal cost	Change (Δ) in profit
Abbreviation:	TR	TC	∏	MR	MC	Δ∏
Formula:	P × Q		TR − TC	ΔTR	ΔTC	MR − MC
0	$0	$25	−$25			
1	10	34	−24	$10	$9	$1
2	20	41	−21	10	7	3
3	30	46	−16	10	5	5
4	40	49	−9	10	3	7
5	50	51	−1	10	2	8
6	60	54	6	10	3	7
7	70	60	10	10	6	4
8	80	70	**10**	**10**	**10**	**0**
9	90	95	−5	10	25	−15
10	100	145	−45	10	50	−40

total profit (column 4) is determined by taking the total revenue (column 2) and subtracting the total cost (column 3). Mr. Plow's profits start out at −$25 because even if he does not clear any driveway, he incurs a fixed cost of $25 to rent a snow plow each day. To recover the fixed cost, he needs to generate revenue by clearing driveways. As Mr. Plow clears more driveways, the losses (the negative numbers) shown in column 4 gradually contract; he begins to earn a profit by the time he plows 6 driveways.

What does Table 9.3 tell us about Mr. Plow's business? Column 4 shows the company's profits at various output (Q) levels. Profit reaches a maximum of $10 at 7 or 8 driveways. From looking at this table, you might suppose that the firm can make a production decision based on the data in the profit column. However, firms don't work this way. The total profit (or loss) is typically determined after the fact. For example, Homer may have to fill up with gas at the end of the day, buy new tires for his plow, or purchase liability insurance. His accountant will take his receipts and deduct each expense to determine his accounting profit. This process takes time. An accurate understanding of Homer's profits may have to wait until the end of the quarter, or even the year, in order to fully account for all the irregular expenses associated with running a business. This means that the information found in the profit column is not available until long after the business decisions have been made. So, in day-to-day operations, the firm needs another way to make production decisions.

The key to determining Mr. Plow's profits comes from understanding the relationship between marginal revenue (column 5) and marginal

Marginal thinking

cost (column 6). The **marginal revenue** is the change (Δ) in total revenue when the firm produces one additional unit of output. So, looking down column 5, we see that for every driveway Mr. Plow clears, he makes $10 in extra revenue. The marginal cost (column 6) is the change (Δ) in total cost when the firm produces one additional unit. Column 7 calculates the difference between the marginal revenue (column 5) and marginal cost (column 6).

In Chapter 8, we saw that to understand cost structure, a firm focuses on marginal cost. The same is true on the revenue side. To make a good decision on the level of investment, Mr. Plow must use marginal analysis. Looking at column 7, we see that where total profit equals $10, the change in profit, MR − MC, is equal to $0. (See the numbers in red in columns 4 and 7.) At output levels at or below 7, MR − MC is positive, as indicated by the numbers in green. Expanding output to 7 driveways adds to profits. But as Mr. Plow services more driveways, the marginal cost rises dramatically. For instance, Mr. Plow may have to seek driveways that are farther away and thus incur higher transportation costs for those additional customers. Whatever the cause, increased marginal cost (column 6) eventually overtakes the constant marginal revenue (column 5).

Recall that we began our discussion by saying that a firm can't wait for the yearly, or even quarterly, profit statements to make production decisions. By examining the marginal impact, shown in column 7, a firm can make good day-to-day operational decisions. Each time it snows, Mr. Plow has to decide whether or not to clear more driveways. For instance, if he is plowing 4 driveways, he may decide to work a little harder the next time it snows and plow one more. At 5 driveways, his profits increase by $8. Since he enjoys making this extra money, he could expand again from 5 to 6 driveways. This time, he makes an extra $7 in profit. From 6 to 7 driveways, he earns $4 more in profit. However, when Mr. Plow expands from 7 to 8 driveways, he discovers that he does not earn any additional profit, and at 9 driveways he loses $15. This loss would cause him to scale back his efforts to a more profitable level of output.

Marginal thinking helps Mr. Plow discover the production level at which his profits are maximized. The **profit-maximizing rule** states that profit maximization occurs when a firm expands output until marginal revenue is equal to marginal cost, MR = MC. (This is the point at which 10 = 10 in columns 5 and 6 of Table 9.3.) The profit-maximizing rule may seem counterintuitive, because at MR = MC (where marginal revenue is equal to the extra cost of production), there is no additional profit. However, according to the MR = MC rule, production should stop at the point at which profit opportunities no longer exist. Suppose that Mr. Plow chooses a point at which MR > MC. At this point, the cost of producing additional units adds more to revenue than to costs, so production should continue. However, if MR < MC, the cost of producing additional units is more than the additional revenue those units bring in. At that point, production is not profitable. The point at which MR = MC is the exact level of production at which no further profitable opportunities exist and losses have not yet occurred. This is the optimal point at which to stop production. In the case of Mr. Plow, he should stop adding new driveways once he reaches 8.

Marginal revenue is the change in total revenue a firm receives when it produces one additional unit of output.

The **profit-maximizing rule** states that profit maximization occurs when a firm chooses the quantity of output that equates marginal revenue and marginal cost, or MR = MC.

If you already own a truck and a plow, starting your own snowplow business is inexpensive.

Marginal
thinking

ECONOMICS IN THE MEDIA

Competitive Markets

The Simpsons: "Mr. Plow"

In this episode, Homer buys a snowplow and goes into the snow removal business. After a few false starts, his business, Mr. Plow, becomes a huge success. Every snowy morning, he looks out the window and comments about "white gold."

The episode illustrates each of the factors that go into making a competitive market. Businesses providing snow removal all offer the same service. Because there are many buyers (homeowners) and many businesses (the "plow people"), the market is competitive.

However, Homer's joy, profits, and notoriety are short-lived. Soon his friend Barney buys a bigger plow and joins the ranks of the "plow people." Barney's entry into the business shows how easy it is for competitors to enter the market. Then Homer, who has begun to get lazy and rest on his success, wakes

Homer's great idea is about to melt away.

up late one snowy morning to find all the driveways in the neighborhood already plowed. A nasty battle over customers ensues.

When firms can easily enter the market, any positive economic profit that a firm enjoys in the short run will dissipate in the long run due to increased competition. As a result, we can say that this *Simpsons* episode shows a market that is not just competitive; it is perfectly competitive.

Deciding How Much to Produce in a Competitive Market

We have observed that a firm in a highly competitive market is a price taker; it has no control over the price set by the market. Because all snow removal companies provide the same service, they must charge the price that is determined from the overall supply and demand conditions that regulate that particular market.

To better understand these relationships, we can look at them visually. In Figure 9.1, we use the MR and MC data from Table 9.3 to illustrate the profit calculation. For reference, we also include the average total cost curve. Recall from Chapter 8 that the marginal cost curve (MC, shown in orange) always crosses the average total cost curve (ATC) at the lowest point. Figure 9.1 illustrates the relationship between the marginal cost curve (MC) and the marginal revenue curve (MR). Because the price (P) Mr. Plow charges is constant at $10, marginal revenue is horizontal. Unlike MR, MC at first decreases and then rises due to diminishing marginal product. Therefore, the firm wants to expand production as long as MR is greater than MC, and it will stop production at the quantity where MR = MC = $10. When Q = 8, MR = MC and profits are maximized. At quantities beyond 8, the MC curve is above the MR curve. Marginal cost is higher than marginal revenue, and the firm's profits fall.

FIGURE 9.1

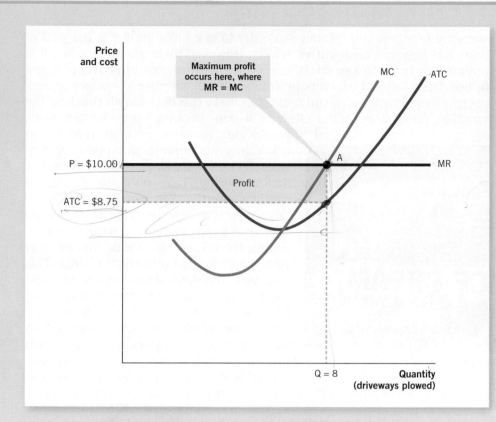

Price and cost

Maximum profit occurs here, where MR = MC

MC   ATC

A   MR

P = $10.00

ATC = $8.75

Profit

Q = 8   **Quantity (driveways plowed)**

Profit Maximization
Mr. Plow uses the profit-maximizing rule to locate the point at which marginal revenue equals marginal cost, or MR = MC. This point determines the ideal output level, Q. The firm takes the price from the market; price is shown as the horizontal MR curve at P = $10.00. Because the price charged is higher than the average total cost curve along the dashed line at quantity Q, the firm makes the economic profit shown in the green rectangle.

Note that we can use the profit-maximizing rule, MR = MC, to identify the most profitable output in a two-step process:

1. Locate the point at which the firm will maximize its profits: MR = MC. This is the point labeled A in Figure 9.1.
2. Look for the profit-maximizing output: move down the vertical dashed line to the *x* axis at point Q. Any quantity greater than or less than Q would result in lower profits.

Once we know the profit-maximizing quantity, we can determine the average cost of producing Q units. From Q, we move up along the dashed line until it intersects with the ATC curve. From that point, we move horizontally until we come to the *y* axis. Doing so tells us the average cost of making 8 units. Because the total cost in Table 9.3 is $70 when 8 driveways are plowed, dividing 70 by 8 gives us $8.75 for the average total cost. We can calculate Mr. Plow's profit rectangle from Figure 9.1 as follows:

profit = (price − ATC [along the dashed line at quantity Q]) × Q

This equation gives us $(10 − 8.75) × 8 = 10, which is the profit we see in Table 9.3, column 4, in red numbers. Because the MR is the price, and because the price is higher than the average total cost, the firm makes the profit visually represented in the green rectangle.

The Firm in the Short Run

Deciding how much to produce in order to maximize profits is the goal of every business in a competitive market. However, there are times when it is not possible to make a profit. When revenue is insufficient to cover cost, the firm suffers a loss—at which point it must decide whether to operate or temporarily shut down. Successful businesses make this decision all the time. For example, retail stores often close by 9 p.m. because operating overnight would not generate enough revenue to cover the costs of remaining open. Or consider the Ice Cream Float, which crisscrosses Smith Mountain Lake in Virginia during the summer months. You can hear the music announcing its arrival at the public beach from over a mile away. By the time the float arrives, there is usually a long line of eager customers waiting for the float to dock. This is a very profitable business on hot and sunny summer days. However, during the late spring and early fall, the float operates on weekends only. Eventually, colder weather forces the business to shut down until the crowds return the following season. This shutdown decision is a short-run

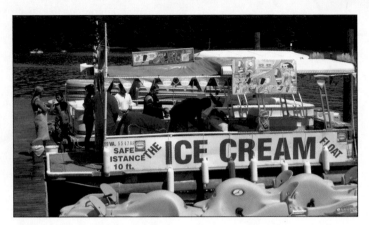

The Ice Cream Float, a cool idea on a hot day at the lake.

calculation. If the float were to operate during the winter, it would need to pay for employees and fuel. Incurring these variable costs when there are so few customers would result in greater total costs than simply dry-docking the boat. When the float is dry-docked over the winter, only the fixed cost of storing the boat remains.

Fortunately, a firm can use a simple, intuitive rule to decide whether to operate or shut down in the short run: if the firm would lose less by shutting down than by staying open, it should shut down. Recall that costs are broken into two parts—fixed and variable. Fixed costs must be paid whether the business is open or not. Because variable costs are incurred only when the business is open, if it can make enough to cover its variable costs—for example, employee wages and the cost of the electricity needed to run the lighting—it will choose to remain open. Once the variable costs are covered, any extra money goes toward paying the fixed costs.

A business should operate if it can cover its variable costs, and it should shut down if it cannot. Figure 9.2 illustrates the decision using cost curves. As long as the firm's marginal revenue curve (MR) is greater than the minimum point on the average variable cost curve (AVC)—the green and yellow areas—the firm will choose to operate. (Note that the MR curve is not shown in Figure 9.2. The shaded areas in the figure denote the range of potential MR curves that are profitable or that cause a loss.) Recalling our example of the Ice Cream Float, you can think of the green area as the months during the summer when the business makes a profit and the yellow area as the times during spring and fall when the float operates even though it is incurring a loss (because the loss is less than if the float were to shut down entirely). Finally, if the MR curve falls below the AVC curve—the red area—the firm should shut down. Table 9.4 summarizes these decisions.

FIGURE 9.2

When to Operate and When to Shut Down

If the MR (marginal revenue) curve is above the minimum point on the ATC (average total cost) curve, the Ice Cream Float will make a profit (shown in green). If the MR curve is below the minimum point on the ATC curve ($2.50) but above the minimum point on the AVC (average variable cost) curve ($2.00), the float will operate at a loss (shown in yellow). If the MR curve is below the minimum point on the AVC curve ($2.00), the float will temporarily shut down (shown in red).

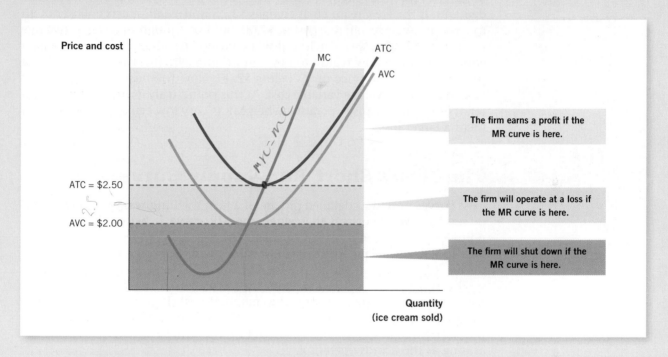

TABLE 9.4

Profit and Loss in the Short Run

Condition	In words	Outcome
$P > ATC$	The price is greater than the average total cost of production.	The firm makes a profit.
$ATC > P > AVC$	The average total cost of production is greater than the price the firm charges, but the price is greater than the average variable cost of production.	The firm will operate to minimize loss.
$AVC > P$	The price is less than the average variable cost of production.	The firm will temporarily shut down.

To make the shutdown decision more concrete, imagine that the Ice Cream Float's minimum ATC (average total cost) is $2.50 and its minimum AVC is $2.00. During the summer, when many customers line up on the dock waiting for it to arrive, it can charge more than $2.50 and earn a substantial profit. However, as the weather cools, fewer people want ice cream. The Ice Cream Float still has to crisscross the lake to make sales, burning expensive gasoline and paying employees to operate the vessel. If the Ice Cream Float is to keep its revenues high, it needs customers; but cooler weather suppresses demand. If the Ice Cream Float charges $2.25 in the fall, it can make enough to cover its average variable cost of $2.00, but not enough to cover its average total cost of $2.50. Nevertheless, it will continue to operate because it makes enough in the yellow region to pay part of its fixed cost. Finally, it reaches a point at which the price drops below $2.00. Now the business is no longer able to cover its average variable cost. At this point, it shuts down for the winter. It does this because operating when MR is very low causes the business to incur a larger loss.

The Firm's Short-Run Supply Curve

Marginal thinking

Cost curves provide a detailed picture of a firm's willingness to supply a good or service. We have seen that when the MR curve is below the minimum point on the AVC curve, the firm shuts down and production, or output, falls to zero. In other words, when revenues are too low, no supply is produced. For example, during the winter, the Ice Cream Float is dry-docked, so the supply curve does not exist. However, when the firm is operating, it bases its output decisions on the marginal cost. Recall that the firm uses the profit-maximizing rule, or MR = MC, to determine how much to produce. The marginal cost curve is therefore the firm's short-run supply curve as long as the firm is operating.

Figure 9.3 shows the Ice Cream Float's short-run supply curve. In the short run, diminishing marginal product causes the firm's costs to rise as the quantity produced increases. This is reflected in the shape of the firm's short-run supply curve, shown in red. The supply curve is upward sloping above the minimum point on the AVC curve. Below the minimum point on the AVC curve, the short-run supply curve is vertical at a quantity of zero, indicating that a willingness to supply the good does not exist below a price of $2.00. At prices above $2.00, the firm will offer more for sale as the price increases.

The Firm's Long-Run Supply Curve

In the long run, a competitive firm's output decision is directly tied to profits. Because the firm is flexible in the long run, all costs are variable. As a result, the firm's long-run supply curve exists only when the firm expects to cover its total costs of production (because otherwise the firm would go out of business—that is, exit the market).

Returning to the Ice Cream Float example, recall that the boat shuts down over the winter instead of going out of business because demand is low but is expected to return. If for some reason the crowds do not come back, the float would go out of business. Turning to Figure 9.4, we see that at any point

FIGURE 9.3

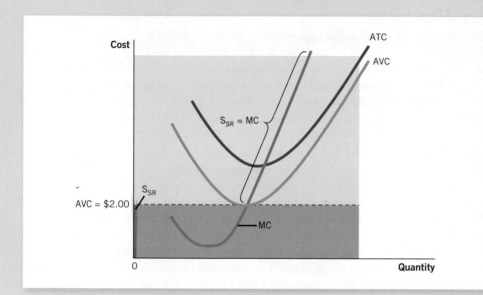

The Firm's Short-Run Supply Curve

The short-run supply curve (S_{SR}) and marginal cost curve (MC) are equivalent when the price is above the minimum point on the average variable cost curve (AVC). Below that point, the firm shuts down and no supply exists.

FIGURE 9.4

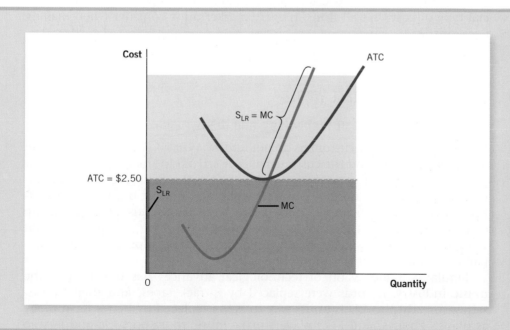

The Firm's Long-Run Supply Curve

The long-run supply curve (S_{LR}) and marginal cost curve (MC) are equivalent when the price is above the minimum point on the average total cost curve (ATC). Below that point, the firm shuts down and no supply exists.

below the minimum point, $2.50 on the ATC curve, the float will experience a loss. Because firms are free to enter or exit the market in the long run, no firm will willingly produce in the market if the price is less than average total cost (P < ATC). As a result, no supply exists below $2.50. However, if price is greater than average total cost (P > ATC), the float expects to make a profit and thus will continue to produce.

TABLE 9.5		
The Long-Run Shutdown Criteria		
Condition	In words	Outcome
P > ATC	The price is greater than the average total cost of production.	The firm makes a profit.
P < ATC	The price is less than the average total cost of production.	The firm should shut down.

The firm's long-run supply curve, shown in Figure 9.4 in red, is upward sloping above the minimum point on the ATC curve, which is denoted by ATC on the *y* axis. The supply curve is vertical at a quantity of zero, indicating that a willingness to supply the good does not exist below a price of $2.50. In the long run, a firm that expects price to exceed ATC will continue to operate, because the conditions for making a profit seem favorable. In contrast, a firm that does not expect price to exceed ATC should cut its losses and exit the market. Table 9.5 outlines the long-run decision criteria.

So far, we have examined the firm's decision-making process in the short run in the context of revenue versus cost, which has enabled us to determine the profit each firm makes. But now we pause to consider *sunk costs*, a special type of cost that all firms in every market must consider when making decisions.

ECONOMICS IN THE REAL WORLD

Blockbuster, Changes in Technology, and the Dynamic Nature of Change

What happens if your customers do not return? What if you simply had a bad idea to begin with, and the customers never arrived in the first place?

When the long-run profit outlook is bleak, the firm is better off shutting down. This is a normal part of the ebb and flow of business in a market economy. For example, once there were thousands of buggy whip companies. Today, as technology has improved and we no longer rely on horse-drawn carriages, few buggy whip makers remain. However, many companies now manufacture automobile parts.

Similarly, a succession of technological advances has transformed the music industry. Records were replaced by 8-track tapes, and then by cassettes. Already, the CD is on its way to being replaced by better technology as iPods, iPhones, and MP3 players make music more portable and as web sites such as Pandora, Spotify, and the Apple music service allow streaming of almost any selection a listener wants to hear. However, there was a time when innovation meant playing music on the original Sony Walkman. What was cool in the early 1980s is antiquated today. Any business engaged in distributing music has had to adapt or shut down.

Similar changes are taking place in the video rental industry. Blockbuster was founded in 1982 and experienced explosive growth, becoming the nation's largest video store chain by 1988. The chain's growth was fueled by its large selection and use of a computerized tracking system that made the checkout process faster than the one at competing video stores. At its zenith in 2004, Blockbuster had 60,000 employees in 9,000 stores. But even then, it was clear that the company's days were numbered. By the early 2000s, Blockbuster faced stiff competition from online providers like Netflix and Amazon and in-store dispensers like Redbox. As a result, Blockbuster filed for bankruptcy and closed its remaining stores in 2013.

In addition to changes in technology, other factors such as downturns in the economy, changes in tastes, demographic factors, and migration can all force businesses to close. These examples remind us that the long-run decision to go out of business has nothing to do with the short-term profit outlook. ✳

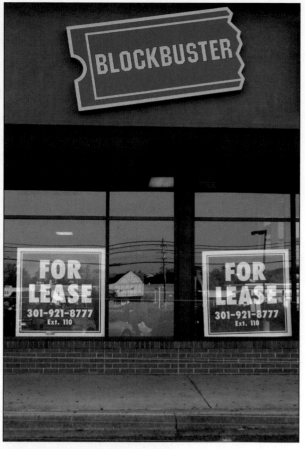

Blockbuster once had 9,000 stores.

Sunk Costs

Unrecoverable costs that have been incurred as a result of past decisions are known as **sunk costs**. For example, the decision to build a new sports stadium is a good application of the principle of sunk costs. Many professional stadiums have been built in the past few years, even though the arenas they replaced were built to last much longer. For example, Three Rivers Stadium in Pittsburgh and Veterans Stadium in Philadelphia were built in the early 1970s as multiuse facilities for both football and baseball, each with an expected life span of 60 or more years. However, in the early 2000s, both were replaced. Each city built two new stadiums with features such as luxury boxes and better seats that generate more revenue than Veterans and Three Rivers did. The additional revenue makes the new stadiums financially attractive even though the old stadiums were still structurally sound.

Sunk costs
are unrecoverable costs that have been incurred as a result of past decisions.

Demolishing a structure that is still in good working order may sound like a waste, but it can be good economics. When the extra benefit of a new stadium is large enough to pay for the cost of imploding the old stadium and constructing a new one, a city will do just that. In fact, because Pittsburgh and Philadelphia draw significantly more paying spectators with the new stadiums, the decision to replace the older stadiums has made the citizens in both cities better off because the new stadiums have created increased ticket sales, higher tax revenues, and a more enjoyable experience for fans.

Opportunity costs can lead to stadium implosions.

PRACTICE WHAT YOU KNOW

The Profit-Maximizing Rule: Show Me the Money!

Here is a question that often confuses students.

Question: At what point does a firm maximize profits?

a. where the profit per unit is greatest

b. where total revenue is maximized

c. where the total revenue is equal to the total cost

d. where marginal revenue equals marginal cost

Answer: Each answer sounds plausible, so the key is to think about each one in a concrete way. To help do that, we will refer back to the Mr. Plow data in Table 9.3.

What is the rule for making the most profit?

a. Incorrect. Making a large profit per unit sounds great. However, if the firm stops production when the increase in profit is the greatest—$8 in column 7—it will fail to realize the additional profits—$7 and $4 in column 7—that come from continuing to produce until MR = MC.

b. Incorrect. Recall that total revenue is only half of the profit function: Profit = TR − TC. No matter how much revenue a business brings in, if total costs are higher than total revenue, the firm will experience a loss. Therefore, the firm wishes to maximize profits, not revenue. For example, looking at column 2, we see that at 10 driveways Mr. Plow earns a total revenue of $100. But column 3 tells us that the total cost of plowing 10 driveways is $145. With a total profit of −$45, this level of output would not be a good idea.

c. Incorrect. If total revenue and total cost are equal, the firm makes no profits.

d. Correct. A firm maximizes profits where MR = MC, because at this point all profitable opportunities are exhausted. If Mr. Plow clears 7 or 8 driveways, his profit is $10. If he clears 9 driveways, his profits fall from $10 to −$5 because the marginal cost of clearing that ninth driveway, $25, is greater than the marginal revenue he earns of $10.

Opportunity cost

Continuing to use an out-of-date facility has an opportunity cost. Those who do not understand sunk costs might point to the benefits of getting maximum use out of what already exists. But good economists learn to ignore sunk costs and focus on marginal value. They compare marginal benefits and marginal costs. If a new stadium and the revenue it brings in will create more value than the old stadium, the decision should be to tear the old one down.

Sunk Costs: If You Build It, They Will Come

Replacing an old stadium with a new one is sometimes controversial. People often misunderstand sunk costs and argue for continuing with a stadium until it's completely worn down. But economics tells us not to focus on the sunk costs of the old stadium's construction. Instead, we should compare the marginal benefit of a new stadium to the marginal cost of demolition and new construction.

Old Stadium · **New Stadium**

10,000 Seats · Capacity · % Attendance · % Attendance

62,000
44,000 — 93%
42% — VETERANS STADIUM (1971–2003)
CITIZENS BANK PARK (2004–2012)

46,000
37,500
39% — DOLPHINS (SUN LIFE) STADIUM (2005–2011)
60% — MARLINS BALLPARK (2012–2015)

53,000
42,000
47% — CINERGY FIELD (1970–2002)
62% — GREAT AMERICAN BALLPARK (2003–2012)

PHILADELPHIA PHILLIES

MIAMI MARLINS

CINCINNATI REDS

 The three new stadiums shown are considered successes. Higher attendance (especially in Philadelphia) and higher revenue per ticket—thanks to luxury boxes and better concessions—make the franchises happy.

 An economist's analysis of the stadiums would go beyond attendance, however. The additional revenue generated by the new stadiums must be weighed against the costs of imploding the old stadiums and building new venues.

REVIEW QUESTIONS

- What effect do you think the reduced seating capacities of the new stadiums has on ticket prices, and why?

- Use the idea of sunk costs to analyze switching majors in college.

What Does the Supply Curve Look Like in Perfectly Competitive Markets?

We have seen that a firm's willingness to supply a good or service depends on whether the firm is making a short-run or long-run decision. In the short run, a firm may choose to operate at a loss to recover a portion of its fixed costs. In the long run, there are no fixed costs, so a firm is willing to operate only if it expects the price it charges to cover total costs.

However, the supply curve for a single firm represents only a small part of the overall supply in a competitive market. We now turn to market supply and develop the short-run and long-run market supply curves.

The Short-Run Market Supply Curve

A competitive market consists of a large number of identical sellers. Because an individual firm's supply curve is equal to its marginal cost curve, if we add together all the individual supply curves in a market, we arrive at the short-run market supply curve. Figure 9.5 shows the short-run market supply curve in a two-firm model consisting of Mr. Plow and the Plow King. At a price of $10, Mr. Plow is willing to clear 8 driveways (Q_A) and the Plow King is willing to clear 20 driveways (Q_B). When we sum the output of the two firms, we get a total market supply of 28 driveways (Q_{market}), seen in the third graph.

FIGURE 9.5

Short-Run Market Supply

The market supply is determined by summing the individual supplies of all the firms in the market. Although we have only shown this process for two firms, Mr. Plow and Plow King, the process extends to any number of firms in a market.

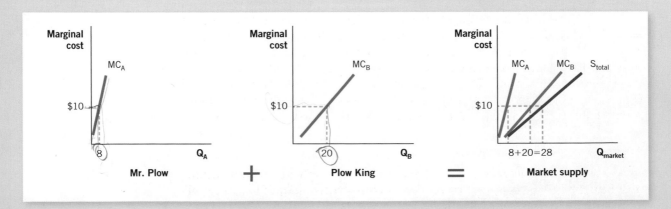

The Long-Run Market Supply Curve

Recall that a competitive market is one in which a large number of buyers seek a product that many sellers offer. Competitive markets are also characterized by easy entry and exit. Existing firms and entrepreneurs decide whether to enter and exit a market based on incentives. When existing firms are enjoying profits, there is an incentive for them to produce more and also for entrepreneurs to enter the market. The result is an increase in the quantity of the good supplied. Likewise, when existing firms are experiencing losses, there is an incentive for them to exit the market; then the quantity supplied decreases.

Incentives

Entry and exit have the combined effect of regulating the amount of profit a firm can hope to make in the long run. As long as profits exist, the quantity supplied will increase because existing firms expand production or other firms enter the market. When losses exist, the quantity supplied will decrease because existing firms reduce production or other firms exit the market. So both profits and losses signal a need for an adjustment in market supply. In other words, profits and losses act as signals for resources to enter or leave a market. **Signals** convey information about the profitability of various markets.

The only time an adjustment does not take place is when participants in the market make zero economic profit. In that case, the market is in long-run equilibrium. Existing firms and entrepreneurs are not inclined to enter or exit the market; the adjustment process that occurs through price changes ends.

The benefit of a competitive market is that profits guide existing firms and entrepreneurs to produce more goods and services that society values. Losses encourage firms to exit and move elsewhere. Without profits and losses acting as signals for firms to enter or exit the market, resources will be misallocated and surpluses and shortages will occur.

Figure 9.6 captures how entry and exit determine the market supply. The profit-maximizing point of the individual firm in panel (a), MR = MC, is located at the minimum point on the ATC curve. The price (P = min. ATC) that existing firms receive is just enough to cover costs, so profits are zero. As a result, new firms have no incentive to enter the market and existing firms have no reason to leave. At all prices above P = min. ATC, firms will earn a profit (the green area), and at all prices below P = min. ATC, firms will experience a loss (the red area). This picture is consistent for all markets with free entry and exit; zero economic profit occurs at only one price, and that price is the lowest point of the ATC curve.

At this price, the supply curve in panel (b) must be a horizontal line at P = min. ATC. If the price were any higher, firms would enter, supply would increase, and price would be forced back down to P = min. ATC. If the price were any lower, firms would exit, supply would decrease, and price would be forced up to P = min. ATC. Because we know that these adjustments will have time to take place in the long run, the long-run supply curve must also be equal to P = min. ATC to satisfy the demand that exists at this price.

> The **signals** of profits and losses convey information about the profitability of various markets.

A Reminder about Economic Profit

Now that you have learned how perfect competition affects business profits in the long run, you may not think that a competitive market is a desirable environment for businesses seeking to earn profits. After all, if a firm cannot expect to make an economic profit in the long run, why bother? It's easy to

FIGURE 9.6

The Long-Run Market Supply Curve and Entry and Exit

Entry into the market and exit from it force the long-run price to be equal to the minimum point on the average total cost curve (ATC). At all prices above P = min. ATC, firms will earn a profit (the green area), and at all prices below P = min. ATC, firms will experience a loss (the red area). For this reason, the long-run supply curve (S_{LR}) must be horizontal at price P = min. ATC. If the price was any higher or lower, firms would enter or exit the market, and the market could not be in a long-run equilibrium.

(a) Individual Firm
(b) Market

Opportunity cost

forget the distinction between accounting profit and economic profit. Firms enter a market when they expect to be reasonably compensated for their investment. And they leave a market when the investment does not yield a satisfactory result. Economic profit is determined by deducting the explicit and implicit costs from total revenue. The remaining examples (graphs) in this chapter focus on our benchmark, economic profit. Therefore, firms are willing to stay in perfectly competitive markets in the long run when they are breaking even because they are being reasonably compensated for the explicit expenses they have incurred and also for the implicit expenses—like the opportunity costs of other business ventures—that they would expect to make elsewhere.

For example, if Mr. Plow has the explicit and implicit costs shown in Table 9.6, we can see the distinction between accounting profit and economic profit more clearly. Mr. Plow has a revenue of $25,000 during the year.

If Mr. Plow asks his accountant how much the business earned during the year, the accountant adds up all of Mr. Plow's explicit costs and subtracts them from his revenue. The accountant reports back that Mr. Plow earned $25,000 − $10,000, or $15,000 in profit. Now $15,000 in profit would sound good to a lot of firms, so we would expect many new entrants in the plowing

TABLE 9.6

Mr. Plow's Economic Profit and the Entry or Exit Decision

Explicit costs per year	
Payment on the loan on his snowplow	$7,000
Gasoline	2,000
Miscellaneous equipment (shovels, salt)	1,000
Implicit costs	
Forgone salary	$10,000
The forgone income that the $50,000 invested in the business could have earned if invested elsewhere	5,000
Total cost	**$25,000**

business. But not so fast! We have not accounted for the implicit costs—the money Mr. Plow could have earned by working another job instead of plowing and also the money he invested in the business ($50,000) that could have yielded a return ($5,000) elsewhere. If we add in the implicit costs, we find that the economic profit is $25,000 − $10,000 − $15,000 = $0. Zero profit sounds unappealing, but it is not. It means that Mr. Plow covered his forgone salary and also his next-best investment alternative. If you could not make any more money doing something else with your time or your investments, you might as well stay in the same place. So Mr. Plow is content to keep on plowing, while others, outside the market, do not see any likely profit from entering the market.

How the Market Adjusts in the Long Run: An Example

We have seen that profits and losses may exist in the short run; in the long run, the best the competitive firm can do is earn zero economic profit. This section looks in more detail at the adjustment process that leads to long-run equilibrium.

We begin with the market in long-run equilibrium, shown in Figure 9.7. Panel (a) represents an individual firm operating at the minimum point on its ATC curve. In long-run equilibrium, all firms are operating as efficiently as possible. Because the price is equal to the average cost of production, economic profit for the firm is zero. In panel (b), the short-run supply curve (S_{SR}) and the short-run demand curve (D_{SR}) intersect along the long-run supply curve (S_{LR}), so the market is also in equilibrium. But if the short-run supply curve and demand curve happened to intersect above the long-run supply curve, then the price would be higher than the minimum point on the ATC curve. The result would be short-run profits, indicating that the market is not in long-run equilibrium. And if the short-run supply curve and demand curve intersected below the long-run supply curve, then the price would be lower than the

FIGURE 9.7

A Competitive Market in Long-Run Equilibrium

When a market is in long-run equilibrium, the short-run supply curve (S_{SR}) and short-run demand curve (D_{SR}) intersect along the long-run supply curve (S_{LR}). At this point, the price that the firm charges is equal to the minimum point along the average total cost curve (ATC). The existing firms in the market earn zero economic profit, and there is no incentive for firms to enter or exit the market.

(a) Individual Firm

(b) Market

minimum point on the ATC curve. In that case, the result would be short-run losses.

Now suppose that demand declines, as shown in Figure 9.8. In panel (b), we see that the market demand curve shifts from D_1 to D_2. When demand falls, the equilibrium point moves from point A to point B. The price drops to P_2 and the market output drops to Q_2. The firms in this market take their price from the market, so the new marginal revenue curve shifts down from MR_1 to MR_2 at P_2 in panel (a). Because the firm maximizes profits where $MR_2 = MC$, the firm will produce an output of q_2. When the output is q_2 the firm's costs, C_2, are higher than the price it charges, P_2, so it experiences a loss equal to the red area in panel (a). In addition, because the firm's output is lower, it is no longer producing at the minimum point on its ATC curve, so the firm is not as efficient as before.

Firms in a competitive market can exit the market easily. Some will do so to avoid further losses. Figure 9.9 continues the example from Figure 9.8. It shows that as firms exit, the market supply contracts from S_{SR1} to S_{SR2} and the market equilibrium moves from point B to point C. At point C, the price rises back to P_1 and the market output drops to Q_3. The firms that remain in the market no longer experience a short-run loss, because MR_2 returns to MR_1 and costs fall from C_2 to C_1. The end result is that the firm is once again efficient, and economic profit returns to zero.

FIGURE 9.8

The Short-Run Adjustment to a Decrease in Demand

A decrease in demand causes the price to fall in the market, as shown by the movement from D_1 to D_2 in panel (b). Because the firm is a price taker, the price it can charge falls to P_2. As we see in panel (a), the intersection of MR_2 and MC occurs at q_2. At this output level, the firm incurs the short-run loss shown by the red area in (a).

(a) Individual Firm

(b) Market

For example, suppose there is a decline in demand for mangoes due to a false rumor that links the fruit to a salmonella outbreak. The decline in demand causes the price of mangoes to drop. As a consequence, mango producers experience negative economic profit—generating curves like the ones shown in Figure 9.8. In response to the negative profit, some mango growers will exit the market, the mango trees will be sold for firewood, and the land will be converted to other uses. With fewer mangoes being produced, the supply will contract. Eventually, the smaller supply will cause the price of mangoes to rise until a new long-run equilibrium is reached at a much lower level of output, as shown in Figure 9.9.

More on the Long-Run Supply Curve

To keep the previous example as simple as possible, we assumed that the long-run supply curve was horizontal. However, this is not always the case. There are two reasons why the long-run supply curve may slope upward. First, some resources needed to produce the product may only be available in limited supplies. As firms try to expand production, they must bid to acquire those resources—a move that causes the average total cost curve to rise. For instance, a mango grower who wants to plant more trees must acquire more land. Because mangoes grow in tropical areas with warm, wet summers, not all land is perfectly suited to growing them. The limited supply of land will cause the price of

What does it take to produce more mangoes?

FIGURE 9.9

The Long-Run Adjustment to a Decrease in Demand

Short-run losses cause some firms to exit the market. Their exit shifts the market supply curve to the left in panel (b) until the price returns to long-run equilibrium at point C. Price is restored to P_1 and the MR_2 curve in panel (a) shifts up to MR_1. At P_1 the firm is once again earning zero economic profit.

(a) Individual Firm

(b) Market

producing more mangoes to rise, which will cause the supply curve to be positively sloped.

A second reason the long-run supply curve may be upward sloping is the opportunity cost of the labor used in producing the good. If you want to produce more mangoes, you will need more workers to pick the fruit. Hiring extra workers will mean finding people who are both willing and capable. Some workers are better than others at picking mangoes, and some workers have higher opportunity costs. As your firm attempts to expand production, it must increase the wage it pays to attract additional help or accept new workers who are not quite as capable. Either way you slice it, the result is higher costs, which would be reflected in an upward-sloping long-run supply curve.

Opportunity cost

This discussion simply means that higher prices are necessary to induce suppliers to offer more for sale. None of it changes the basic ideas we have discussed throughout this section. The entry and exit of firms ensure that the market supply curve is much more elastic in the long run than in the short run.

Entry and Exit

I Love Lucy

I Love Lucy was the most watched television comedy of the 1950s. The show featured two couples who are best friends, the Ricardos and the Mertzes, who find themselves in the most unlikely situations.

One episode finds Ricky Ricardo disillusioned with show business. After some conversation, Ricky and Fred Mertz decide to go into business together and start a diner. Fred and Ethel Mertz have the experience to run the diner, and Ricky plans to use his name and star power to help get the word out about the restaurant, which they name A Little Bit of Cuba.

If you have seen any of the *I Love Lucy* episodes, you already know that the business venture is destined to fail. Sure enough, the Mertzes get tired of doing all of the hard work—cooking and serving the customers—while Ricky and Lucy Ricardo meet and greet the guests. Things quickly deteriorate, and the two couples decide to part ways. The only problem is that they are both part owners, and neither can afford to buy out the other. So they decide to split the diner in half right down the middle!

The result is absurd and hilarious. On one side, guests go to A Little Bit of Cuba. On the other side, the Mertzes set up Big Hunk of America. Because both restaurants use the same facilities and sell the same food, the only way they can differentiate themselves is by lowering their prices. The result is a hamburger price war to attract customers:

> **Ethel:** "Three!"
> **Lucy:** "Two!"
> **Ethel:** "One-cent hamburgers."
> **Fred:** "Ethel, are you out of your mind?" *[Even in the 1950s, a penny was not enough to cover the marginal cost of making a hamburger.]*
> **Ethel:** "Well, I thought this could get 'em."
> **Fred:** "One-cent hamburgers?"

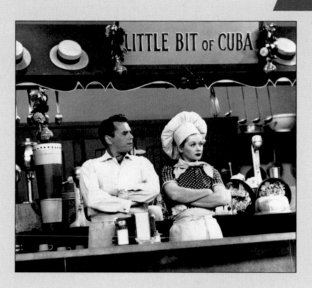

After the exchange, Lucy whispers in a customer's ear and gives him a dollar. He then proceeds to Big Hunk of America and says, "I'd like 100 hamburgers!"

Fred Mertz replies, "We're all out of hamburgers."

How do the falling prices described here affect the ability of the firms in this market to make a profit?

The exchange is a useful way of visualizing how perfectly competitive markets work. Competition forces the price down, but the process of entry and exit takes time and is messy. The Ricardos and Mertzes can't make a living selling one-cent hamburgers—one cent is below their marginal cost—so one of the couples will end up exiting. At that point, the remaining couple would be able to charge more. If they end up making a profit, that profit will encourage entrepreneurs to enter the market. As the supply of hamburgers expands, the price that can be charged will be driven back down. Because we live in an economically dynamic world, prices are always moving toward the long-run equilibrium.

PRACTICE WHAT YOU KNOW

Long-Run Profits: How Much Can a Firm Expect to Make?

Fill in the blank: In the long run, a firm in a perfectly competitive market earns _____ profits.

(Caution: there may be more than one right answer!)

a. positive accounting
b. zero accounting
c. positive economic
d. zero economic

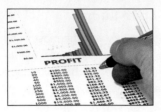

Calculating profits

Answers:

a. **Correct**. Accounting profits cover only the explicit costs of doing business, so they are positive. But they do not include the implicit costs; once those implicit costs are taken into account, the economic profit will be lower than the accounting profit. If the implicit costs are exactly equal to the accounting profit, the firm will earn zero economic profit, and the long-run equilibrium will be reached.

b. **Incorrect**. If a firm earns zero accounting profit, the implicit costs will make the economic profit negative. When economic profit is negative, firms will exit the market.

c. **Incorrect**. When a firm earns an economic profit, that profit sends a signal to firms outside the market to enter. The long-run equilibrium occurs when there is no incentive to enter or exit the market.

d. **Correct**. This answer makes sense only when you recall that *zero* does not mean *nothing*. Zero economic profit means that the firm can cover its explicit (accounting) and implicit (opportunity) costs. It also means that firms inside the market are content to stay and that firms outside the market do not see the value of entering. In the long run, the only condition that would not signal firms to enter or exit would be zero economic profit.

Opportunity costs

Conclusion

It is tempting to think that firms control the prices they charge. This is not true in competitive markets, where firms are at the mercy of market forces that set the price charged throughout the market. Individual firms have no control over the price because they sell the same products as their competitors. In addition, profits and losses help regulate economic activity in competitive markets and promote economic efficiency. Profits reward producers for producing a good that is valued more highly than the resources used to produce it. Profits encourage entry into a market. Likewise, losses penalize producers who operate inefficiently or produce goods that consumers do not want. Losses encourage exit from the market. The process of entry and exit ensures that resources flow into markets that are undersupplied and away from markets where too many firms exist.

In this chapter, we studied competitive markets to establish a benchmark that will help us understand how other market structures compare with this ideal. In the next few chapters, we explore imperfect markets, which provide a significant contrast with the results we have just seen. The closer a market is to meeting the criteria of perfect competition, the better the result for consumers and society in general.

ANSWERING THE BIG QUESTIONS

How do competitive markets work?

* The firms in competitive markets sell similar products. Firms are also free to enter and exit the market whenever they wish.
* A price taker has no control over the price it receives in the market.
* In competitive markets, the price and quantity produced are determined by market forces instead of by the firm.

How do firms maximize profits?

* A firm maximizes profits by expanding output until marginal revenue is equal to marginal cost (MR = MC, or the profit-maximizing rule). The profit-maximizing rule is a condition for stopping production at the point where profit opportunities no longer exist.
* The firm should shut down in the short run if the price it receives does not cover its average variable costs. Because variable costs are incurred only when operating, if a firm can make enough to cover its variable costs in the short run, it will choose to continue to operate.
* In the long run, the firm should go out of business if it cannot cover its average total costs.

What does the supply curve look like in perfectly competitive markets?

* Profits and losses act as signals for firms to enter or leave a market. As a result, perfectly competitive markets drive economic profit to zero in the long run.
* The entry and exit of firms ensure that the market supply curve in a competitive market is much more elastic in the long run than in the short run.

ECONOMICS FOR LIFE

Tips for Starting Your Own Business

Before you go into business for yourself, you need to devise a plan. Over 80% of all small businesses fail within five years because the businesses were ill conceived or relied on unrealistic sales projections. You don't need a hugely detailed plan as long as it covers these essential points:

Do a cost-benefit analysis, and determine how long it will take you to break even. If you don't break even, you could run out of money and have to close your doors before you start to make a profit. Reaching the break-even point is different from earning an economic profit. Breaking even requires that you cover your explicit expenses with your revenue. This condition is especially important if you enter a perfectly competitive market where long-run profits are not possible. You need to be lean and efficient just to survive.

Keep your start-up costs as low as possible. Consider investing as much of your own money as possible. It can be very tempting to take out loans to cover your start-up costs, but if you expect to start immediately paying back your loans with the profits from your new business, think again. It can take years to become profitable. To lessen this problem, you can invest more of your own capital into the business to ensure that loans don't sink you. Also, start small and grow your business slowly to avoid overreaching.

Protect yourself from risk. If you are a sole proprietor, you are liable for business debts and judgments, and your creditors can come after your personal assets—like your home and savings accounts. To protect against this possibility, you can incorporate into what

Make sure your business plan covers the essential points.

is known as a limited liability corporation, which helps shield business owners from personal liability.

Realize that you need a competitive advantage to attract customers. It could be price, better service, a better product—but it has to be something. Don't expect to be successful unless you can do something better than your rivals!

Hire the right people to help you. Remember what you learned about specialization. Embrace it. You don't have to be an expert tax accountant, manager, and marketer. Offload some of these tasks on others who are better at them, and focus on doing what you do best. However, once you find the right people to help, treat them well and provide an environment in which they will thrive and give their all.

CONCEPTS YOU SHOULD KNOW

marginal revenue (p. 281)   profit-maximizing rule (p. 281)   sunk costs (p. 289)
price taker (p. 276)   signals (p. 293)

QUESTIONS FOR REVIEW

1. What are the necessary conditions for a perfectly competitive market to exist?

2. Describe the two-step process used to identify the profit-maximizing level of output.

3. Under what circumstances will a firm have to decide whether to operate or to shut down?

4. What is the difference between the decision to go out of business and the decision to shut down?

5. How do profits and losses act as signals that guide producers to use resources to make what society wants most?

6. What are sunk costs? Give an example from your own experience.

7. Why do competitive firms earn zero economic profit in the long run?

STUDY PROBLEMS (*solved at the end of the section*)

1. Using the definition of a price taker as your guide, explain why each of the following industries does not meet the definition.
   a. the pizza delivery business
   b. the home improvement business
   c. cell phone companies
   d. cereal producers

2. A local snow cone business sells snow cones in one size for $3 each. It has the following cost and output structure per hour:

Output (cones per hour)	Total cost (per hour)
0	$60
10	90
20	110
30	120
40	125
50	135
60	150
70	175
80	225

   a. Calculate the total revenue for the business at each rate of output.
   b. Calculate the total profit for the business at each rate of output.
   c. Is the business operating in the short run or the long run?
   d. Calculate the profit-maximizing rate of output using the MR = MC rule. (**Hint:** First compute the marginal revenue and marginal cost from the table.)

3. Determine whether the following statements are true or false. Explain your answers.
   a. A firm will make a profit when the price it charges exceeds the average variable cost of the chosen output level.
   b. To maximize profits in the short run, a firm must minimize its costs.
   c. If economic profit is positive, firms will exit the market in the short run.
   d. A firm that receives a price greater than its average variable cost but less than its average total cost should shut down.

4. In the following table, fill in the blanks. After you have completed the entire table, determine the profit-maximizing output.

Output	Price	Total revenue	Marginal revenue	Total cost	Marginal cost	Total profit
1	$20	___	___	$40	___	−$20
2	___	___	___	50	___	___
3	___	___	___	60	___	___
4	___	___	___	65	$5	___
5	___	___	___	85	___	___
6	___	$120	___	120	___	___

5. Use the graph to answer the questions that follow.

a. At what prices is the firm making an economic profit, breaking even, and experiencing an economic loss?

b. At what prices would the firm shut down?

c. At what prices does the firm's short-run supply curve exist? At what prices does the firm's long-run supply curve exist?

✳ 6. Identify as many errors as you can in the following graph.

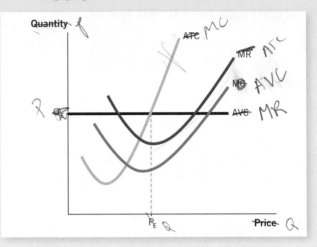

7. A firm is experiencing a loss of $5,000 per year. The firm has fixed costs of $8,000 per year.

a. Should the firm operate in the short run or shut down?

b. If the situation persists into the long run, should the firm stay in the market or go out of business?

c. Now suppose that the firm's fixed costs are $2,000. How would this level of fixed costs change the firm's short-run and long-run decisions?

8. Three students at the same school hear about the success of cookie delivery businesses on college campuses. Each student decides to

open a local service. The individual supply schedules are shown below.

Delivery charge	Quantity supplied		
	Esra	Remzi	Camilo
$1	2	3	6
2	4	6	7
3	6	9	8
4	8	12	9
5	10	15	10
6	12	18	11

a. Draw the individual supply curves.
b. Sum the individual supply schedules to compute the short-run market supply schedule.
c. Draw the market supply curve.

9. Do you agree or disagree with the following statement? "A profit-maximizing, perfectly competitive firm should select the output level at which the difference between the marginal revenue and marginal cost is the greatest." Explain your answer.

10. Barney's snow removal service is a profit-maximizing, competitive firm. Barney clears driveways for $10 each. His total cost each day is $250, and half of his total costs are fixed. If Barney clears 20 driveways a day, should he continue to operate or shut down? If this situation persists, will Barney stay in the market or exit?

* 11. Suppose you are the owner of a firm producing jelly beans. Your production costs are shown in the following table. Initially, you produce 100 boxes of jelly beans per time period. Then a new customer calls and places an order for an additional box of jelly beans, requiring you to increase your output to 101 boxes. She offers you $1.50 for the additional box. Should you produce it? Why or why not?

Jelly Bean Production

Number of boxes	Average cost per box
100	$1.00
101	1.01
102	1.02
103	1.03

12. You pay $10 to see *Furious 10*, but realize 15 minutes into the film that the plot and acting are truly terrible. What economic concept should you use to help you decide whether to leave or stay through the remainder of the film?

* 13. Determine the profit-maximizing output level from the following table. The firm has no fixed costs in this example, only variable costs.

Output	Marginal revenue	Marginal cost
1	$10	$13
2	10	10
3	10	8
4	10	7
5	10	9
6	10	11
7	10	14

SOLVED PROBLEMS

6. Here is the corrected graph with the errors struck out and some explanation below.

Also, the ATC and AVC curves did not intersect the MC curve at their minimum points. That is corrected here.

11. This problem requires marginal thinking. We know the profit-maximizing rule, MR = MC. Here all we need to do is compare the additional cost, or MC, against the additional revenue, or MR, to see if the deal is a good idea. We know that MR = $1.50, because that is what the customer is offering to pay for another box of jelly beans. Now we need to calculate the marginal cost of producing the additional box.

Jelly Bean Production

Number of boxes	Average cost per box	Total cost	Marginal cost
100	$1.00	$100.00	—
101	1.01	102.01	$2.01
102	1.02	104.04	2.03
103	1.03	106.09	2.05

First we compute the total cost. To do this, we multiply the number of boxes, listed in the first column, by the average cost, shown in the second column. The results are shown in the third column.

Next we find the marginal cost. Recall that the marginal cost is the amount that it costs to produce one more unit. So we subtract the total cost of producing 101 boxes from the total cost of producing 100 boxes. For 101 boxes, MC = $102.01 − $100.00, or $2.01. Because MR − MC is $1.50 − $2.01, producing the 101st box would create a loss of $0.51. Therefore, at a price of $1.50, your firm should not produce the 101st box.

13. This problem confounds many students because if you've memorized only one thing from this chapter, it is the profit-maximizing rule, MR = MC, and it is clear that this condition is satisfied when the output is 2 (where MR and MC are both $10). But the answer 2 would be incorrect. A second part of the profit-maximizing rule is often overlooked: MR = MC, but MC must also be increasing. To see why 2 is not the profit-maximizing output, you should calculate the profit in a fourth column, as in the following table:

Output	Marginal revenue	Marginal cost	Profit (MR − MC)
1	$10	$13	−$3
2	10	10	0
3	10	8	+2
4	10	7	+3
5	10	9	+1
6	10	11	−1
7	10	14	−4

Profit is maximized at an output of 5, but why is this the case? Marginal cost is declining until output reaches 4, at which point the MR = $10 and MC = $7. So when the fourth unit is sold, it generates $3, and the firm is profitable for the first time. By the fifth unit, MC is rising but remains less than MR, so the profit rises. However, MC is higher than MR for the sixth unit, which causes profits to decline. The reason 2 is *not* the profit-maximizing output is that MC is falling, which means that the firm is at the point where additional output is just becoming profitable.

Understanding Monopoly

Monopolists always make a profit.

In this chapter, we explore another market structure: monopoly. Many people mistakenly believe that monopolists always make a profit. This

MIS CONCEPTION

is not true. Monopolists enjoy market power for their specific product, but they cannot force consumers to purchase what they are selling. The law of demand regulates how much a monopolist can charge. When a monopolist charges more, people buy less. If demand is low, a monopolist may experience a loss instead of a profit.

While pure monopolies are unusual, it is important to study this market structure because many markets exhibit some form of monopolistic behavior. Google, the National Football League, the United States Postal Service (for first-class mail), and some small-town businesses are all examples of monopoly. In this chapter, we explore the conditions that give rise to monopolies and also the ways in which monopoly power can erode.

The typical result of monopoly is higher prices and less output than we find in a competitive market. Once we understand the market conditions that give rise to a monopoly, we consider how governments try to address the problems that monopolies present and also how governments can be the cause of monopolies.

A small town's sole veterinarian functions as a monopolist.

BIG QUESTIONS

* **How are monopolies created?**
* **How much do monopolies charge, and how much do they produce?**
* **What are the problems with, and solutions for, monopoly?**

How Are Monopolies Created?

As we explained in Chapter 3, a monopoly exists when a single seller supplies the entire market for a particular good or service. Two conditions enable a single seller to become a monopolist. First, the firm must have something unique to sell—that is, something without close substitutes. Second, it must have a way to prevent potential competitors from entering the market.

Monopolies occur in many places and for several different reasons. For example, companies that provide natural gas, water, and electricity are all examples of monopolies that occur naturally because of economies of scale. But monopolies can also occur when the government regulates the amount of competition. For example, trash pickup, street vending, taxicab rides, and ferry service are often licensed by local governments. These licenses have the effect of limiting competition and creating **monopoly power**, which is a measure of a monopolist's ability to set the price of a good or service.

A monopoly operates in a market with high **barriers to entry**, which are restrictions that make it difficult for new firms to enter a market. As a result, monopolists have no competition nor any immediate threat of competition. High barriers to entry insulate the monopolist from competition, which means that many monopolists enjoy long-run economic profits. There are two types of barriers to entry: natural barriers and government-created barriers. Let's look at each.

> **Monopoly power** is a measure of a monopolist's ability to set the price of a good or service.

> **Barriers to entry** are restrictions that make it difficult for new firms to enter a market.

Natural Barriers

Some barriers exist naturally within the market. These include control of resources, problems in raising capital, and economies of scale.

Control of Resources

The best way to limit competition is to control a resource that is essential in the production process. This extremely effective barrier to entry is hard to accomplish. But if you control a scarce resource, other competitors will not be able to find enough of it to compete. For example, in the early twentieth century, the Aluminum Company of America (ALCOA) made a concerted effort to buy bauxite mines around the globe. Within a decade, the company owned 90% of the world's bauxite, an essential element in making aluminum.

This strategy enabled ALCOA to eliminate potential competitors and achieve dominance in the aluminum market.

Problems in Raising Capital

Monopolists are usually very big companies that have grown over an extended period. Even if you had a wonderful business plan, it is unlikely that a bank or a venture-capital company would lend you enough money to start a business that could compete effectively with a well-established company. For example, if you wanted to design a new operating system to compete with Microsoft and Apple, you would need tens of millions of dollars to fund your start-up. Lenders provide capital for business projects when the chance of success is high, but the chance of a new company successfully competing against an entrenched monopolist is not high. Consequently, raising capital to compete effectively is difficult.

Economies of Scale

In Chapter 8, we saw that economies of scale occur when long-run average costs fall as production expands. Low unit costs and the low prices that follow give some larger firms the ability to drive rivals out of business. For example, imagine a market for electric power where companies compete to generate electricity and deliver it through their own grids. In such a market, it would be technically possible to run competing sets of wire to every home and business in the community, but the cost of installation and the maintenance of separate lines to deliver electricity would be both prohibitive and impractical. Even if a handful of smaller electric companies could produce electricity at the same cost, each would have to pay to deliver power through its own grid. This system would be highly inefficient.

In an industry that enjoys large economies of scale, production costs per unit continue to fall as the firm expands. Smaller rivals then have much higher average costs that prevent them from competing with the larger company. As a result, firms in the industry tend to combine over time. These mergers lead to the creation of a **natural monopoly**, which occurs when a single large firm has lower costs than any potential smaller competitor.

A **natural monopoly** occurs when a single large firm has lower costs than any potential smaller competitor.

Government-Created Barriers

The creation of a monopoly can be either intentional or an unintended consequence of a government policy. Government-enforced statutes and regulations, such as laws and regulations covering licenses and patents, limit the scope of competition by creating barriers to entry.

Licensing

In many instances, it makes sense to give a single firm the exclusive right to sell a good or service. To minimize negative externalities, governments occasionally establish monopolies, or near monopolies, through licensing requirements. For example, in some communities trash collection is licensed to a single company. The rationale usually involves economies of scale, but there are additional factors to consider. Because firms cannot collect trash without a government-issued operating license, opportunities to enter the business are limited, which leaves consumers with a one-size-fits-all level of service. This outcome is the opposite of what we'd expect to see in a competitive market, where there would be many varieties of service at different price points.

Licensing also creates an opportunity for corruption. In fact, in many parts of the world, bribery is so common that it often determines which companies receive the licenses in the first place.

Patents and Copyright Law

Another area in which the government fosters monopoly is that of patents and copyrights. For example, when musicians create a new song and copyright their work, they earn royalties over the life of the copyright. The copyright is the government's assurance that no one else can play or sell the work without the artist's permission. Similarly, when a pharmaceutical company develops a new drug, the company receives a patent under which it has the exclusive right to market and sell the drug for as long as the patent is in force.

Incentives

By granting patents and copyrights to developers and inventors, the government creates monopolies. Patents and copyrights create stronger incentives to develop new drugs and produce new music than would exist if market competitors could immediately copy inventions. As a result, pharmaceutical companies invest heavily in developing new drugs and musicians devote their time to writing new music. At least in theory, these activities make our society a healthier and culturally richer place. After the patent or copyright expires, rivals can mimic the invention. This new competition opens up the market and provides dual benefits: wider access to the innovation and more sellers—both of which are good for consumers in the long run.

Taylor's fans wanted her to *stay, stay, stay* but now there is a *blank space* on Spotify.

Nonetheless, many economists wonder if patents and copyrights are necessary or have unintended consequences. Sometimes copyright holders benefit more from exposure than from exercising their right to charge consumers. For example, when a music video goes viral on YouTube, the exposure causes many people to buy the original artist's work. Consider Justin Bieber. He managed to leverage his YouTube fame into a successful album launch, concert tours, and appearance fees that might never have occurred if a music studio had tightly controlled his sound while he was an emerging artist. Conversely, Taylor Swift refuses to allow her music on Spotify because she feels the service doesn't properly compensate her and all the other people involved in creating the music. The point to remember is that copyright protection gives artists the right to decide how to distribute their work and what price to charge. It also gives them the ability to litigate when their work is stolen, illegally downloaded, or improperly used.

Though market-created and government-created barriers occur for different reasons, they have the same effect—they create monopolies. Table 10.1 summarizes the key characteristics of monopolies. In the next section, we examine how the monopolist determines the price it charges and how much to produce, explaining the term "price making" listed in Table 10.1.

TABLE 10.1

The Characteristics of Monopolies

- One seller

- A unique product without close substitutes

- High barriers to entry

- Price making

ECONOMICS IN THE REAL WORLD

Merck's Zocor

In 1985, the pharmaceutical giant Merck released Zocor, the first statin drug for treating high cholesterol. The company spent millions of dollars developing the drug and bringing it to the market. Zocor is highly effective and has saved or extended millions of lives. It was also highly profitable for Merck, generating over $4 billion in annual revenues before the patent ran out in 2006. Zocor is now available in an inexpensive generic formulation at a price that is 80% to 90% lower than the original patent-protected price. Even after the patent expired, many customers continued to ask for Zocor—not the generic—so brand recognition and customer loyalty represent another entry barrier.

Would Zocor have been developed without patent protection? Probably not. Merck would have had little incentive to incur the cost of developing a cholesterol treatment if other companies could immediately copy the drug. In this case, society benefits because of the twofold nature of patents: they give firms the incentive to innovate, but they also limit the amount of time the patent is in place (20 years from the time of filing), thereby guaranteeing that competitive forces will govern long-run access to the product. ✳

Do you want fries with that cholesterol medication?

Incentives

How Much Do Monopolies Charge, and How Much Do They Produce?

Both monopolists and firms in a competitive market seek to earn a profit. However, a monopolist is the sole provider of a product and holds market power. Thus, monopolists are price makers. A **price maker** has some control over the price it charges. As you learned in Chapter 9, a firm in a competitive market is a price taker.

We can see the difference between price takers and price makers graphically in Figure 10.1. The demand curve for the product of a firm in a competitive market, shown in panel (a), is horizontal. When individual firms are price takers, they have no control over what they charge. In other words, demand is perfectly elastic—or horizontal—because every firm sells the same

A **price maker** has some control over the price it charges.

PRACTICE WHAT YOU KNOW

Monopoly profits!

Monopoly: Can You Spot the Monopolist?

Here are three questions to test your understanding of the conditions necessary for monopoly power to arise.

Question: Is LeBron James (an NBA superstar) a monopolist?

Answer: LeBron is a uniquely talented basketball player. Because of his physical gifts, he can do things that other players can't. But that does not mean there are no substitutes for him around the league. So no, LeBron is not a monopolist. Perhaps more important, his near-monopoly power is limited because younger players (like Steph Curry) are always entering the league and trying to establish themselves as the best.

Question: Is the only hairdresser in a small town a monopolist?

Answer: For all practical purposes, yes. He or she sells a unique service with inelastic demand. Because the nearest competitor is in the next town, the local hairdresser enjoys significant monopoly power. At the same time, the town's size limits potential competitors from entering the market, because the small community may not be able to support two hairdressers. Once one hairdresser is in place, a potential rival looks at the size of the market in the small town, calculates how many people he or she could expect to serve, and deduces that the potential revenue is too small to justify entrance into this market.

Question: Is Amazon a monopolist?

Answer: Amazon is the nation's largest bookseller, with sales that dwarf those of its nearest retail rival, Barnes & Noble. In 2015, Amazon's market value surpassed that of Walmart. Amazon is by far the nation's leader in e-commerce with online sales that exceed the combined total of Walmart, Apple, Macy's, Home Depot, Best Buy, Costco, Nordstrom, Gap, and Target! Despite Amazon's market share, that does not make it a monopolist. It still faces intense competition.

product. Demand for an individual firm's product exists only at the price determined by the market, and each firm is such a small part of the market that it can sell its entire output without lowering the price.

In contrast, because a monopolist is the only firm—the sole provider—in the industry, the demand curve for its product, shown in panel (b), constitutes the market demand curve. But the demand curve is downward sloping, which limits the monopolist's ability to make a profit. The monopolist would like to exploit its market power by charging a high price to many customers. However, the law of demand, which identifies a negative relationship between price and quantity demanded, dictates otherwise. Unlike the horizontal demand curve of a firm in a competitive market, the downward-sloping demand curve of the monopolist has many price-output combinations. If market demand is inelastic, a monopolist will choose a comparatively

Barriers to Entry

Forrest Gump

In this 1994 movie, Tom Hanks's character, Forrest Gump, keeps his promise to his deceased friend, Bubba, to go into the shrimping business after leaving the army. Forrest invests $25,000 in an old shrimp boat, but the going is tough—he catches only a handful of shrimp because of the competition for space in the shrimping waters. So Forrest tries naming his boat for good luck and brings on a first mate, Lieutenant Dan, who unfortunately is less knowledgeable and resourceful than Forrest. The fledgling enterprise continues to struggle, and eventually Forrest decides to pray for shrimp. Soon after, Forrest's boat, the *Jenny*, is caught out in the Gulf of Mexico during a hurricane. Miraculously, the *Jenny* makes it through the storm while the other shrimp boats, all anchored in the harbor, are destroyed.

Forrest recounts the events to some strangers while sitting on a park bench:

Forrest: After that, shrimping was easy. Since people still needed them shrimps for shrimp cocktails and barbecues and all, and we were the *only* boat left standing, Bubba-Gump shrimp's what they got. We got a whole bunch of boats. Twelve *Jennys*, big old warehouse. We even have hats that say "Bubba-Gump" on them. Bubba-Gump Shrimp. A household name.

Man on the bench: Hold on there, boy. Are you telling me you're the owner of the Bubba-Gump Shrimp Corporation?

Forrest: Yes. We got more money than Davy Crockett.

Man on the bench: Boy, I heard some whoppers in my time, but that tops them all. We were sitting next to a millionaire.

The film suggests that Forrest's good luck—being in the right place at the right time—explains how he became a millionaire. But is Forrest's case realistic? Let's leave the movie's storyline for a moment and consider the situation in real-world economic terms.

If shrimping were easy, everyone would do it.

Remember, Forrest was able to enter the business simply by purchasing a boat. To be sure, he would catch more shrimp in the short run while the other boats were docked for repairs. However, once the competitors' boats returned, they would catch shrimp and Forrest's short-run profits will disappear. The reason we can be so confident of this result is that shrimping, with low barriers to entry and an undifferentiated product, is an industry that closely mirrors a perfectly competitive market. So when profits exist, new entrants will expand the supply produced and profits will return to the break-even level. Having Forrest become a "millionaire" makes for a good movie, but none of the elements are in place to suggest that he could attain a permanent monopoly. Forrest does not control an essential resource; the other shrimp captains will have little difficulty raising capital to repair their boats; and the economies of scale in this situation are small. ✷

FIGURE 10.1

Comparing the Demand Curves of Perfectly Competitive Firms and Monopolists

(a) Firms in a competitive market face a horizontal demand curve. (b) Because the monopolist is the sole provider of the good or service, the demand for its product constitutes the industry—or market—demand curve, which is downward sloping. So while the perfectly competitive firm has no control over the price it charges, the monopolist gets to search for the profit-maximizing price and output.

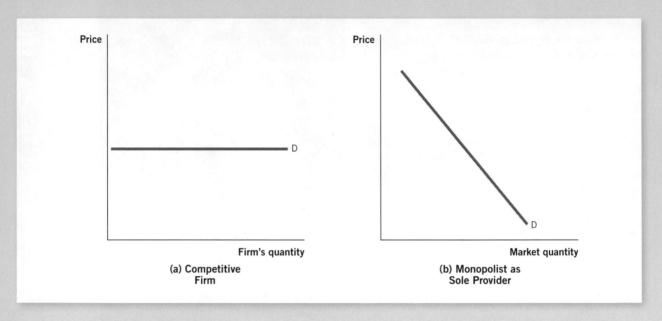

higher price. When market demand is more elastic, a monopolist will choose a comparatively lower price. As a result, monopolists must search for the profit-maximizing price and output.

The Profit-Maximizing Rule for the Monopolist

Marginal thinking

A competitive firm can sell all it produces at the existing market price. But a monopolist, because of the downward-sloping demand curve, must search for the most profitable price. To maximize profits, a monopolist can use the profit-maximizing rule we introduced in Chapter 9: MR = MC. But the monopolist's marginal revenue is computed differently.

Table 10.2 shows the marginal revenue for a cable company that serves a small community. Notice the negative relationship between output (quantity of customers) and price in columns 1 and 2: as the price goes down, the quantity of customers goes up. Total revenue is calculated by multiplying output by price (TR = Q × P). At first, total revenue rises as the price falls. Once the price becomes too low ($40), total revenue begins to fall. As a result, the

TABLE 10.2

Calculating the Monopolist's Marginal Revenue

(1) Quantity of customers (Q) Formula:	(2) Price of service (P)	(3) Total revenue (TR) (Q) × (P)	(4) Marginal revenue per 1,000 customers (MR) Δ (TR)
0	$100	$0.00	
			$90,000
1,000	$90	90,000	
			70,000
2,000	$80	160,000	
			50,000
3,000	$70	210,000	
			30,000
4,000	$60	240,000	
			10,000
5,000	$50	250,000	
			−10,000
6,000	$40	240,000	
			−30,000
7,000	$30	210,000	
			−50,000
8,000	$20	160,000	
			−70,000
9,000	$10	90,000	
			−90,000
10,000	$0	0.00	

total revenue in column 3 initially rises to $250,000 before it begins to fall off. The final column, marginal revenue, shows the change (Δ) in total revenue. Here we see positive (though falling) marginal revenue associated with prices between $100 and $50 (see the green dollar amounts in column 4). Below $50, marginal revenue becomes negative (see the red dollar amounts in column 4).

The change in total revenue reflects the trade-off that a monopolist encounters in trying to attract additional customers. To gain additional sales, the firm must lower its price. But the lower price is available to both new and existing customers. The impact on total revenue therefore depends on how many new customers buy the good because of the lower price.

Trade-offs

Figure 10.2 uses the linear demand schedule from Table 10.2 to illustrate the two separate effects that determine marginal revenue. First, there is a *price effect*, which reflects how the lower price affects revenue. If the price of service drops from $70 to $60, each of the 3,000 existing customers saves $10, and the firm loses $10 × 3,000, or $30,000 in revenue, represented by the red area on the graph. But dropping the price also has an *output effect*, which reflects how the lower price affects the number of customers. Because 1,000 new customers buy the product (that is, cable service) when the price drops to $60, revenue increases by $60 × 1,000, or $60,000, represented by the green area. The output effect ($60,000) is greater than the price effect ($30,000). When we subtract the $30,000 in lost revenue (the red rectangle) from the $60,000 in revenue gained (the green rectangle), the result is $30,000 in marginal revenue at an output level between 3,000 and 4,000 customers.

Lost revenues associated with the price effect are always subtracted from the revenue gains created by the output effect. Now let's think of this data at the individual level. Because the firm adds 1,000 new customers, the marginal revenue per customer—$30,000 ÷ 1,000 new customers—is $30. Notice that this marginal revenue is less than the price, $60, that the firm charges. Because there is a price effect whenever the price drops, the marginal revenue curve lies below the demand curve. Therefore, in Figure 10.2, the y intercept is the same for the demand and marginal revenue curves and the x intercept of the MR curve is half of the demand curve's.

At high price levels—where demand is elastic—the price effect is small relative to the output effect. As the price drops, demand slowly becomes more inelastic. The output effect diminishes and the price effect increases. In other words, as the price falls, it becomes harder for the firm to acquire enough new customers to make up for the difference in lost revenue. Eventually, the price effect becomes larger than the output effect. This means that the marginal revenue curve will have the same y intercept as the demand curve and be twice as steep. As a result, marginal revenue becomes negative and dips below the x axis, as shown by the MR curve in Figure 10.2. When the marginal revenue is negative, the firm cannot maximize profit. This outcome

Marginal
thinking

FIGURE 10.2

The Marginal Revenue Curve and the Demand Curve

A price drop has two effects. (1) Existing customers now pay less—this is the price effect. (2) New customers decide to purchase the good for the first time—this is the output effect. The relative size of the two effects, as shown by the red and green rectangles, determines whether the firm is able to increase its revenue by lowering its price. In this case, marginal revenue increases by $30,000.

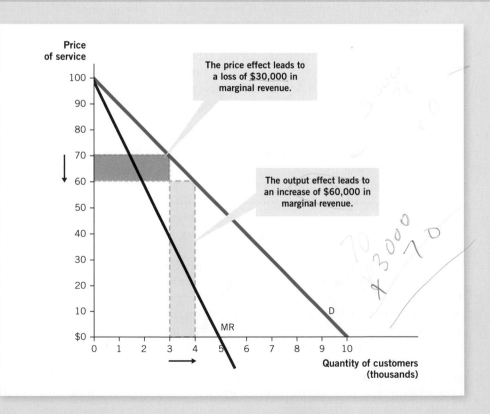

puts an upper limit on the amount that the firm will produce. This outcome is evident in Table 10.2: once the price becomes too low, the firm's marginal revenue is negative.

Deciding How Much to Produce

In Chapter 9, we explored the profit-maximizing rule for a firm in a competitive market. This rule also applies to a monopolist: marginal revenue should be equal to marginal cost. However, there is one big difference: a monopolist does not charge a price equal to marginal revenue.

Figure 10.3 illustrates the profit-maximizing decision-making process for a monopolist. We use a two-step process to determine the monopolist's profit:

1. Locate the point at which the firm will maximize its profits: MR = MC.
2. Set the price: from the point at which MR = MC, determine the profit-maximizing output, Q. From Q, move up along the dashed line

FIGURE 10.3

The Monopolist's Profit Maximization

The firm uses the profit-maximizing rule to locate the point at which MR = MC. This condition determines the ideal output level, Q. Because the price (which is determined by the demand curve) is higher than the average total cost curve (ATC) along the dashed line at quantity Q, the firm makes the profit shown in the green area.

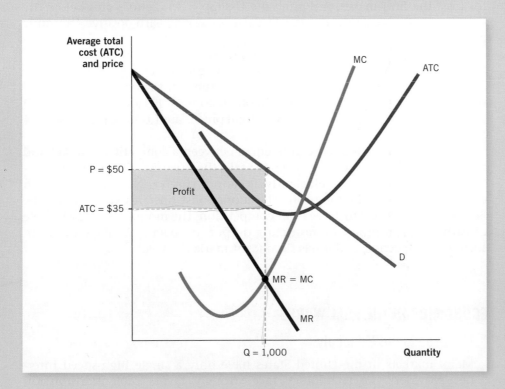

TABLE 10.3	
The Major Differences between a Monopoly and a Competitive Market	
Competitive market	**Monopoly**
Many firms	One firm
Cannot earn long-run economic profits	May earn long-run economic profits
Has no market power (is a price taker)	Has significant market power (is a price maker)
Produces an efficient level of output (because P = MC)	Produces less than the efficient level of output (because P > MC)

until it intersects with the demand curve (D). From that point, move horizontally until you come to the y axis. This point on the y axis tells us the price (P) the monopolist should charge. Notice that the monopolist's price (P) is greater than MC (P > MC). This result differs from the competitive outcome, where P = MC.

Using this two-step process, we can determine the monopolist's profit. Locate the average total cost, ATC, of making Q units along the vertical dashed line. From that point, move horizontally until you come to the y axis. This point tells us the average total cost of making Q units. The difference between the price and the average total cost multiplied by Q tells us the profit (or loss) the firm makes. Any time the U-shaped ATC curve dips below the downward-sloping demand curve, D, there is a way to earn positive economic profits.

Because the price (P = $50) is higher than the average total cost (ATC = $35), the firm makes the profit shown in the green rectangle. For example, a profit-maximizing veterinarian will choose the point where MR = MC, and that means that the vet will serve 1,000 customers. Because the price at Q is $50 and the average total cost is $35, total profits are 1,000 × ($50 − $35) = $15,000.

Table 10.3 summarizes the differences between a competitive market and a monopoly. The competitive firm must take the price established in the market. If it does not operate efficiently, it cannot survive. Nor can it make an economic profit in the long run. The monopolist operates very differently. Because high barriers to entry limit competition, the monopolist may be able to earn long-run profits by restricting output. It operates inefficiently from society's perspective, and it has significant market power.

 ECONOMICS IN THE REAL WORLD

The Broadband Monopoly

Many markets in the United States have only a single high-speed Internet provider. The technology race strongly favors cable transmission over competing telephone lines. Internet access is provided by telephone

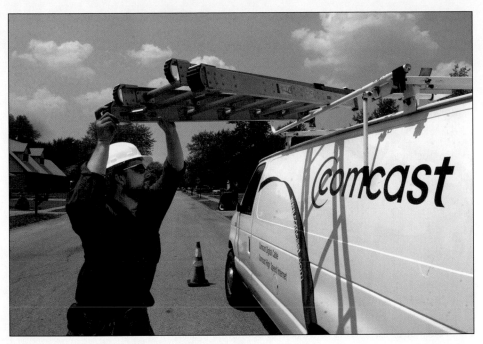

Does Comcast own the Internet in your area?

companies using aging copper wiring, whereas cable companies use the latest fiber-optic technology. When it comes to truly high-speed Internet access, cable companies benefit from considerable barriers to entry. In many places, Comcast effectively owns access to the Internet and can price its service accordingly.

The cable monopoly on high-speed Internet access affects both consumers and businesses. First, consumers increasingly need more bandwidth to stream movies, view YouTube, and load media-rich web sites. A slow connection can make surfing the Internet a chore. In other words, consumer demand is high and very inelastic. Second, businesses rely on bandwidth to maintain web sites and provide services to customers. Companies such as Netflix, Amazon Prime, and Hulu Plus, which deliver streaming content over the Internet, rely on access to a relatively affordable broadband Internet connection. Therefore, businesses also have high demand that is quite inelastic. For this reason, many people argue that relatively inexpensive access to the Internet is crucial if it is to continue as an engine of economic growth. Without competition, access will remain expensive.

Our dependence on the Internet invites a larger question. Where the bandwidth is controlled by only one provider, should the government have a role in providing the infrastructure, or cables, in order to allow greater (or less expensive) access? This is a concern in metropolitan areas served by only one Internet provider. Meanwhile, small rural communities may have no Internet access at all. For example, it is estimated that more than 25 million people in rural areas remain off the grid. Cable companies wouldn't make enough profit to connect these low-density areas, making it more difficult for their residents to participate in today's economy. ✳

PRACTICE WHAT YOU KNOW

Monopoly Profits: How Much Do Monopolists Make?

Question: A monopolist always earns _____ economic profit.

a. a positive

b. zero

c. a negative

d. We cannot be sure about the profit a monopolist makes.

Is there a key profit takeaway?

Answers:

a. Incorrect. A monopolist is a price maker with considerable market power. This situation usually, but not always, leads to a positive economic profit.

b. Incorrect. Zero economic profit exists in competitive markets in the long run. Because a monopolist, by definition, does not operate in competitive markets, it is protected from additional competition that would drive its profit to zero.

c. Incorrect. Whoa there! Negative profit? There is absolutely no reason to think that would happen. Monopolists sell a unique product without close substitutes in a market that is insulated from competitive pressures.

d. Correct. Because a monopolist benefits from barriers that limit the entry of competitors into the market, we would expect an economic profit. However, this outcome is not guaranteed. Monopolies do not control the demand for the product they sell. Consequently, in the short run the monopolist may experience either a profit (if demand is high) or a loss (if demand is low).

What Are the Problems with, and Solutions for, Monopoly?

Monopolies can adversely affect society by restricting output and charging higher prices than sellers in competitive markets do. This activity causes monopolies to operate inefficiently, provide less choice, promote an unhealthy form of competition known as *rent seeking* (see below), and make economic profits that fail to guide resources to their highest-valued use. Recall that **market failure** occurs when there is an inefficient allocation of resources in a market. Once we have examined the problems with monopoly, we will turn to the potential solutions to the problems of monopoly.

Market failure
occurs when there is an inefficient allocation of resources in a market.

The Problems with Monopoly

Monopolies result in an inefficient level of output, provide less choice to consumers, and encourage monopoly firms to lobby for government protection. Let's look at each of these concerns.

Inefficient Output and Price

From an efficiency standpoint, the monopolist charges too much and produces too little. This result is evident in Figure 10.4, which shows what happens when a competitive market (denoted by the subscript C) ends up being controlled by a monopoly (denoted by the subscript M).

First, imagine a competitive fishing industry in which each boat catches a small portion of the fish, as shown in panel (a). Each firm is a price taker that must charge the market price. In contrast, panel (b) depicts pricing and output decisions for a monopoly fishing industry when it confronts the same cost structure as presented in panel (a). When a single firm controls the entire fishing ground, it is the sole supplier, so the supply curve becomes the monopolist's marginal cost curve. To set its price, it considers the downward-sloping

FIGURE 10.4

When a Competitive Industry Becomes a Monopoly

(a) In a competitive industry, the intersection of supply and demand determines the price (P_C) and quantity (Q_C). (b) When a monopoly controls an entire industry, the supply curve becomes the monopolist's marginal cost curve. The monopolist uses MR = MC to determine its price (P_M) and quantity (Q_M). As a result, the monopolist charges a higher price and produces a smaller output than when an entire industry is populated with competitive firms.

(a) Competitive Industry

(b) Monopoly as Sole Provider

demand and marginal revenue curves that serve the entire market. Therefore, it sets marginal revenue equal to marginal cost. The result is a smaller output than the competitive industry ($Q_M < Q_C$) and a higher price ($P_M > P_C$). The smaller output level is not efficient. In addition, the price the monopolist charges, P_M, is significantly above the marginal cost at the profit-maximizing level of output.

Figure 10.5 captures the deadweight loss (see Chapter 5) of the monopoly. The monopolist charges too high a price and produces too little of the product, so some consumers who would benefit from a competitive market lose out. Because the demand curve (the willingness to pay) is greater than the marginal cost between output levels Q_M and Q_C, society would be better off if output expanded to Q_C. But a profit-maximizing monopolist will limit output to Q_M. The result, a deadweight loss equal to the area of the yellow triangle, is inefficient for society. Consumer surplus is also transferred to the monopolist, as shown in the blue rectangle.

Marginal thinking

Few Choices for Consumers

Another problem associated with monopoly is the lack of choice. Have you ever wondered why cable companies offer their services in bundles? You can buy basic, digital, and premium packages, but the one thing you cannot do is buy just the cable channels you want. This situation prevails because cable companies function like monopolies, and monopolies limit consumer choice. Because the monopolist sells a good with few close substitutes, it can leverage its market power to offer product features that benefit the monopoly at the expense of consumer choice. With a monopolist, there is only one

FIGURE 10.5

The Deadweight Loss of Monopoly

Because the profit-maximizing monopolist produces an output of Q_M, an amount that is less than Q_C, the result is the deadweight loss shown in the yellow triangle. The blue rectangle is the consumer surplus that is transferred to the monopolist.

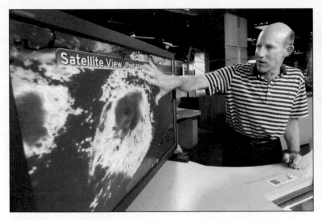

Would you rather watch the Weather Channel . . .

. . . or SportsCenter?

outlet: if you do not like the design, features, price, or any other aspect of the good provided, you have few (or no) other options. For example, in many communities there is only one cable television provider. In a hypothetical competitive market, we would expect each company to provide more options to satisfy consumer preferences. For instance, in a competitive market you should be able to find a firm willing to sell only ESPN and the Weather Channel. In a monopoly situation, though, the cable company forces you to choose between buying more cable than you really want or going without cable altogether. Because the cable company has a good deal of market power, it can restrict your options and force you to buy more in order to get what you want. This is a profitable strategy for the company but a bad outcome for consumers.

Rent Seeking

The attempt to gain monopoly power encourages **rent seeking**, which occurs when resources are used to secure monopoly rights through the political pro-

Rent seeking occurs when resources are used to secure monopoly rights through the political process.

cess. Throughout this text, we have seen the desirable effects of competition: lower prices, increased efficiency, and enhanced service and quality. However, rent seeking is a form of competition that produces an undesirable result. When firms compete to become monopolists, there is one winner without any of the benefits usually associated with competition. Consider the U.S. steel industry, which has been in decline for many years and has lost market share to steel firms in China, Japan, and Europe. If a U.S. steel company is losing money because of foreign competition, it can address the situation in one of two ways. It can modernize by building new facilities and using the latest equipment and techniques. (In other words, it can become

A former steel plant in Bethlehem, Pennsylvania.

PRACTICE WHAT YOU KNOW

Problems with Monopoly: Coffee Consolidation

A community has many competing coffee shops.

Question: How can we use the market demand curve to illustrate the consumer surplus and producer surplus created by a competitive market?

Answer:

When companies compete, consumers win.

In a competitive market, supply and demand determine the price and quantity. In the figure, consumer surplus is represented by the blue area. Producer surplus is represented by the red area.

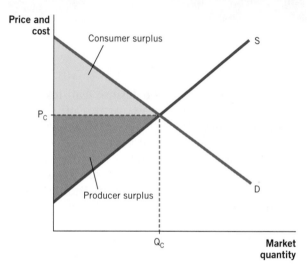

Question: Now imagine that all the independent coffee shops combine under one fictional franchise, known as Harbucks. How can we create a new graph that illustrates the consumer surplus, producer surplus, and deadweight loss that occur when a monopoly takes over the market?

Answer:

In this figure, we see that the consumer surplus has shrunk, the producer surplus has increased, and the higher price charged by Harbucks creates deadweight loss. Allowing a monopolist to capture a market does not benefit consumers and is inefficient for society.

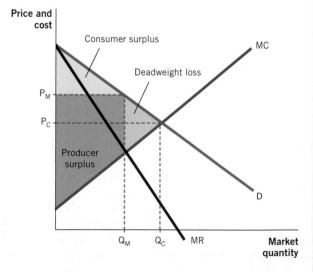

competitive with the overseas competition.) Or it can lobby the government to limit imports. The domestic steel industry chose to lobby, and in 2002 the George W. Bush administration imposed tariffs of up to 30% on imported steel. Here is the danger: when lobbying is less expensive than building a new factory, the company will choose to lobby! If politicians give in and the lobbying succeeds, society is adversely affected because the gains from trade are smaller.

Supply and demand tell us that steel prices will rise in the absence of competition. This outcome is inefficient. Also, instead of pushing for legislation that grants market power, the lobbying resources could have gone into the production of useful products. As a result, the process of rent seeking potentially benefits the rent seeker but yields little direct benefit for society.

Trade
creates
value

ECONOMICS IN THE REAL WORLD

New York City Taxis

In 1932, during the depths of the Great Depression, New York City decided to license taxicabs. The goal was to standardize fares, operating procedures, and safety requirements. At that time, a taxicab license, or medallion, was available at no cost. Today, if you find one on the resale market, it costs over $500,000. The medallions are worth so much because the owners often make six-figure incomes from leasing and operating taxis in New York City.

The city did not intend to create an artificial monopoly, but it did. From 1932 until the 1990s, the number of medallions, which represents the supply of taxis, was fixed at approximately 12,000. During the same 60-year period, population growth and an increase in tourism caused the demand for taxi services to rise steeply. The number of medallions would have had to quadruple to keep up with demand.

In recent years, the city of New York has offered three auctions to introduce more medallions into the market. These auctions have netted the city over $100 million in revenue and have raised the number of medallions to slightly more than 13,000. Each of the current medallion holders owns a small part of an artificially created government monopoly. Collectively, the holders of medallions own a monopoly on taxi services worth about $8 billion.

Imagine what would happen if the city lifted restrictions on the number of available medallions and gave them out to any qualified applicant. Applications for licenses would increase, and profits for cab drivers and cab companies would fall until quantity supplied equaled quantity demanded. Conversely, if taxicab drivers experienced economic losses, the number of taxis operating would decline until the losses disappeared.

Medallion owners in New York City are protected from competition.

Owning and operating a taxi has all the makings of an industry with low barriers to entry. The only reason that medallions are worth so much is the artificially created barrier to entry, which protects medallion holders from competition. Restoring competitive markets would make each current medallion holder worse off by reducing the existing barriers to entry into the industry. As a result, the medallion owners' profits would fall. Therefore, it is not surprising that they seek to keep the number of medallions as low as possible and to keep out Uber, Lyft, and other rivals. Because monopolists make profits by charging higher prices than firms in competitive markets do, no one who already has a medallion wants the supply to expand.

Despite medallion owners' efforts to restrict the supply, Uber and other ride-sharing companies are having a big impact in the medallion market. The added competition has driven down medallion prices from slightly more than $1 million in 2013 to $600,000 today. Competition, it seems, may yet save the day for consumers. ✳

Solutions to the Problems of Monopoly

We have learned that monopolies do not produce as much social welfare as competitive markets do. As a result, public policy approaches attempt to address this problem. The policy solutions include breaking up the monopoly, reducing trade barriers, and regulating markets.

ECONOMICS IN THE MEDIA

The Problems of Monopoly

One-Man Band

This Pixar short animation from 2005 tells the story of two street musicians competing for the gold coin of a young peasant girl who wants to make a wish in the town square's fountain.

When the short opens, there is only one street musician in the plaza. He performs a little bit and almost coaxes the girl to place her coin in his tip basket. Just as she is about to give it to him, another street musician starts playing. Because there is no longer a single performer, a spirited rivalry develops between the two very eager musicians vying to win the little girl's attention and money.

This clever story illustrates monopoly and competition in a number of compelling ways. The first street musician plays only halfheartedly in the beginning, when he does not face any competition. Indeed, lack

A little competition goes a long way to reduce monopoly.

of choice is one of the major criticisms of monopoly. But then the second musician's arrival changes the dynamic, inspiring a spirited competition for the gold coin. The "one-man band" is not really a monopolist, however; he is providing a service that has many good substitutes, and he lacks the ability to keep imitators from entering the market.

Breaking Up the Monopoly

Eliminating deadweight loss and restoring efficiency can be as simple as promoting competition. From 1913 until 1982, AT&T had a monopoly on the delivery of telephone services in the United States. As the years passed, however, it became progressively harder for AT&T to defend its position that having a single provider of phone services was good for consumers. By the early 1980s, AT&T was spending over $300 million to fend off antitrust lawsuits from the states, the federal government, and many private firms. The AT&T monopoly ended in 1982, when enormous pressure from the government led the company to split into eight smaller companies. Suddenly, AT&T had to compete to survive. The newly competitive phone market forced each of the phone companies to expand the services it offered—and sometimes even lower its prices—to avoid losing customers. For example, rates on long-distance calls, which were quite high before the break-up, plummeted.

Incentives

From this example, we see that the government can help to limit monopoly outcomes and restore a competitive balance. The government can accomplish this goal through antitrust legislation. Antitrust laws are designed to prevent monopoly practices and promote competition. The government has exercised control over monopoly practices since the passage of the Sherman Act in 1890, and the task currently falls to the Department of Justice. We discuss these regulations at greater length in Chapter 13.

Reducing Trade Barriers

Countries use *tariffs*, which are taxes on imported goods, as a trade barrier to prevent competition and protect domestic business. However, any barrier—whether a tariff, a quota, or a prohibition—limits the possible gains from trade. For monopolists, trade barriers prevent rivals from entering their territory. For example, imagine that Florida could place a tariff on California oranges. For every California orange sold in Florida, the seller would have to pay a fee. Florida orange producers might like this tariff because it would limit competition from California. But California growers would cry foul and reciprocate with a tariff on Florida oranges. Growers in both states would be happy, but consumers would be harmed. For example, if a damaging freeze in Florida depleted the crop, Florida consumers would have to pay more than the demand-driven price for imported oranges from California. If, in contrast, Florida had a bumper crop, the tariff would keep prices artificially high, and much of the extra harvest would go to waste.

The United States has achieved tremendous growth by limiting the ability of individual states to place import and export restrictions on goods and services. The Constitution reads, "No State shall, without the consent of Congress, lay any imposts or duties on imports or exports." Rarely have so few words been more profound. With this simple law in place, states must compete on equal terms.

Reducing trade barriers creates more competition, lessens the influence of monopoly, and promotes the efficient use of resources. For example, prior to 1994, private air carriers accounted for less than 0.5% of the air traffic in India. In 1994, Indian airspace was opened to allow private airlines to operate scheduled service. This move forced the state-owned Air India to become more competitive. These changes in Indian aviation policies had the effect

Trade
creates
value

of raising the share of private airline operators in domestic passenger carriage to over 80% by 2015. Two private companies, Jet Airways and IndiGo, are now the largest carriers in India, while Air India—which once controlled the market—has fallen to third place.

Regulating Markets

In the case of a natural monopoly, it is not practical to harness the benefits of competition. Consider the economies of scale that utility companies experience. Breaking up a company that provides natural gas, water, or elec-

Since 1994, reduced barriers to competition have transformed India's airline industry.

tricity would result in higher production costs. For instance, a second water company would have to build infrastructure to each residence or business in a community. Having redundant water lines with only a fraction of the customers would make the delivery of water extremely expensive, such that the final price to the consumer, even with competition, would be higher. Therefore, keeping the monopoly intact is the best option. In this situation, policymakers might attempt to create a more efficient outcome and maximize society's welfare by regulating the monopolist's prices. Theoretically, this process would be straightforward. However, the reality is that few regulators are experts in the fields of electricity, natural gas, water, and other regulated industries, so they often lack sufficient knowledge to make the regulations work as designed.

When a natural monopoly exists, the government may choose to use the marginal cost pricing rule $P = MC$ to generate the greatest welfare for society. Because the price is determined along the demand curve, setting $P = MC$ guarantees that the good or service will be produced as long as the willingness to pay exceeds the additional cost of production. Figure 10.6 shows the difference in pricing and profits for a regulated monopoly and an unregulated natural monopoly.

Marginal
thinking

To maximize profits, an unregulated monopolist sets $MR = MC$ and produces quantity Q_M at a price of P_M. Because P_M is greater than the average total cost of producing Q_M units, or C_M, the monopolist earns the profit shown in the green rectangle. If the firm is regulated and the price is set at marginal cost, regulators can set $P = MC$, and the output expands to Q_R. (The subscript R denotes the regulated monopolist.) In this example, because the cost of production is subject to economies of scale, the cost falls from C_M to C_R and generates a large improvement in efficiency. The regulated price, P_R, is lower than the unregulated monopolist's price, P_M, and production increases. As a result, consumers are better off.

But what happens to the monopolist? It loses money in the amount of the red rectangle because the average total costs under the marginal cost pricing solution, C_R, are higher than the price allowed by regulators, P_R. This outcome is problematic because a firm that suffers losses will go out of business. That outcome is not desirable from society's standpoint, because the consumers of the product will be left without it. There are three possible solutions. First, to make up for the losses incurred at the higher output level, C_R, the government

The Demise of a Monopoly

A monopoly can be broken up by the courts or by market forces. In the case of Microsoft, only one has worked. In November 1999, a federal judge declared Microsoft a monopoly of computer operating systems. The original decision underwent appeals that continue to this day, making the ruling largely ineffective in breaking up the monopoly. But market forces have had more success. What ended Microsoft's stranglehold on the operating systems/PC market was something that no one foresaw—the explosive popularity of smartphones.

Legend:
- PC / Windows
- Apple Devices
- Android Devices

In the early 2000s, Microsoft controlled nearly 100% of the operating system market (through PC sales), but Apple sold enough of its Mac computers to remain in business.

Since 2007, the explosive growth of smartphone and tablet sales has tilted the operating system market toward Android (owned by Google) and Apple, eating into Microsoft's market share.

Y-axis: Unit Sales (millions) — 200, 400, 600, 800, 1,000, 1,200, 1,400, 1,600, 1,800, 2,000

X-axis: 2002, 2003, 2004, 2005, 2006, 2007, 2008, 2009, 2010, 2011, 2012, 2013, 2014

Fast forward from 1999 to 2016. The European Union filed an antitrust case against Google for controlling nearly the entire search-engine market and engaging in practices that hamper its competitors. Does this situation sound familiar to you? So, Google might lose its lofty perch if simply left alone.

REVIEW QUESTIONS

- About what percentage of the operating system market did Microsoft (PC) control in 2014?

- Describe the demise of the Microsoft operating system monopoly using the following terms: competition, innovation, and market power.

could subsidize the monopolist. Second, the regulated price could be set so that
P = ATC at Q_R and the monopoly breaks even. (Remember that ATC is the
average total cost.) Third, the government could own and operate the business
in lieu of the private firm. This solution, however, has its own challenges, as we
explore in the next section.

A Caveat about Government Oversight

Incentives

Firms with a profit motive have an incentive to minimize the costs of production, because lower costs translate directly into higher profits. If a firm's
managers do a poor job reining in costs, they will be fired. The same cannot
be said about government managers, or bureaucrats. Government employees
are rarely let go, regardless of their performance. As a result, the government
oversight and management of monopolies is problematic because there are
fewer incentives to keep costs in check.

Consequently, the marginal cost pricing rule is not as effective as it first
seems. Regulated firms and government-owned businesses do not have the
same incentives to keep costs down. Without the correct incentives in place,
we would expect cost inefficiencies to develop.

Public policy can mitigate the power of monopolies. But this outcome is
not guaranteed. While monopolies are not as efficient as firms in competitive markets, this comparison is not always relevant. We need to ask how the
inefficiency of monopoly compares with the inefficiencies associated with
government involvement in the market. Good economists assess the benefits
as well as the costs, so when the costs of government involvement are greater
than the efficiency gains that can be realized, the best solution to the problem of monopoly might be to do nothing.

FIGURE 10.6

**The Regulatory
Solution for Natural
Monopoly**

An unregulated monopolist
uses the profit-maximizing
rule MR = MC and earns
a small profit, shown in
the green rectangle. If the
monopolist is regulated
using the marginal cost
pricing rule, P = MC, it
will experience the loss
shown in the red rectangle.

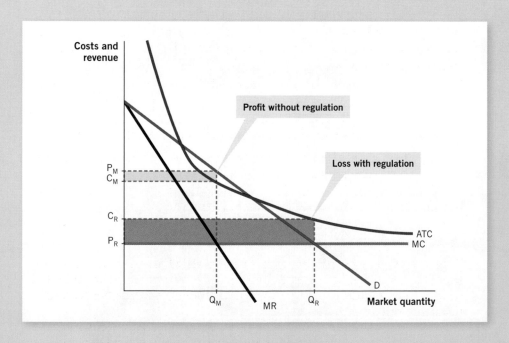

Conclusion

It is tempting to believe that monopolies always earn a profit, but that is a misconception. The monopolist controls the supply, not the demand, so monopolies occasionally suffer losses despite the advantages they enjoy. Still, many monopolists do make economic profits.

In this chapter, we examined the monopoly model and, along the way, compared the results under monopoly with the results of the competitive model that we developed in the previous chapter. While competitive markets generally yield welfare-enhancing outcomes for society, monopolies often do the opposite. Because monopolists do not produce an efficient outcome, government often seeks to limit monopoly outcomes and promote competitive markets.

Competitive markets and monopoly are market structures at opposite extremes. Indeed, we rarely encounter the conditions necessary for either a pure monopoly or a perfectly competitive market. Most economic activity takes place between these two alternatives. In the upcoming chapters, we examine monopolistic competition and oligopoly—two markets that constitute the bulk of the economy. Fortunately, if you understand the market structures at the extremes, understanding the middle ground is straightforward. As we move forward, we will deploy the same tools we used to examine monopoly in order to understand monopolistic competition (Chapter 12) and oligopoly (Chapter 13).

ANSWERING THE BIG QUESTIONS

How are monopolies created?

* Monopoly is a market structure characterized by a single seller that produces a well-defined product with no good substitutes.
* Monopolies operate in a market with high barriers to entry, the chief source of market power.
* Monopolies are created when a single seller supplies the entire market for a particular good or service.

How much do monopolies charge, and how much do they produce?

* Monopolists are price makers who may earn long-run economic profits.
* Like perfectly competitive firms, a monopoly tries to maximize its profits. To do so, it uses the profit-maximizing rule, MR = MC, to select the optimal price and quantity combination of a good or service.

What are the problems with, and solutions for, monopoly?

* From an efficiency standpoint, the monopolist charges too much and produces too little. Because the monopolist's output is smaller than the output that would exist in a competitive market, monopolies lead to deadweight loss.
* Government grants of monopoly power encourage rent seeking, or the use of resources to secure monopoly rights through the political process.

✳ There are three potential solutions to the problem of monopoly. First, the government may break up firms that gain too much market power in order to restore a competitive market. Second, the government can promote open markets by reducing trade barriers. Third, the government can regulate a monopolist's ability to charge excessive prices.

✳ When the costs of government involvement in regulating a monopoly are greater than the efficiency gains that can be realized, it is better to leave the monopolist alone.

ECONOMICS FOR LIFE

Playing Monopoly Like an Economist

In the game Monopoly, you profit only by taking from other players. The assets of its world are fixed in number. The best player drives others into bankruptcy and is declared the winner only after gaining control of the entire board.

Here is some advice on how to play the game like an economist.

- Remember that a monopoly is built on trade. You are unlikely to acquire a monopoly by landing on the color groups you need. Instead, you have to trade properties in order to acquire the ones you need. Because every player knows this, acquiring the last property to complete a color group is nearly impossible. Your competitors will never willingly hand you a monopoly unless they get something of great value in return.

- Don't wait to trade until it is obvious what you need. Instead, try to acquire as many properties as you can in order to gain trading leverage as the game unfolds. Always pick up available properties if no other player owns one of the same color group; purchase properties that will give you two or three of the same group; or purchase a property if it blocks someone else from completing a set.

- Think about probability. Mathematicians have determined that Illinois Avenue is the property most likely to be landed on and that B&O is the best railroad to own. Know the odds, and you can weigh the risks and rewards of trade better than your opponents. This is just like doing market research before you buy. Being informed matters in Monopoly and in business.

Apply some basic economic principles, and you can win big.

- When you get a monopoly, develop it quickly. Build as many houses as you can. That's sound advice in the board game and in life. Monopoly power is fleeting—you must capitalize on your advantages as soon as possible.

- Finally, if you gain the upper hand and have a chance to bankrupt a player from the game, do it. Luck plays a key role in Monopoly, as it does in life. Although it may sound harsh, eliminating a competitor moves you one step closer to winning the game.

The decisions you make while playing Monopoly are all about cost-benefit analysis. You have limited resources and only so many opportunities to use them to your advantage. The skilled player understands how to weigh the values of tradable properties, considers the risk-return proposition of every decision, manages money effectively, and eliminates competitors when given a chance.

CONCEPTS YOU SHOULD KNOW

barriers to entry (p. 310)
market failure (p. 322)

monopoly power (p. 310)
natural monopoly (p. 311)

price maker (p. 313)
rent seeking (p. 325)

QUESTIONS FOR REVIEW

1. Describe the difference between a monopoly and a natural monopoly.

2. What are barriers to entry, and why are they crucial to the creation of potential long-run monopoly profits? Give an example of a barrier that can lead to monopoly.

3. Explain why a monopoly is a price maker but a perfectly competitive firm is a price taker.

4. Why is a monopolist's marginal revenue curve less than the price of the good it sells?

5. What is the monopolist's rule for determining the profit-maximizing output? What two steps does the monopolist follow to maximize profits?

6. Why does a monopolist operate inefficiently? Draw a demand curve, a marginal revenue curve, and a marginal cost curve to illustrate the deadweight loss from monopoly.

7. Why is it difficult to regulate a natural monopoly?

STUDY PROBLEMS (✳ *solved at the end of the section*)

1. In the figure below, identify the price the monopolist will charge and the output the monopolist will produce. How do these two decisions on the part of the monopolist compare with the efficient price and output?

2. Which of the following could be considered a monopoly?
   a. your local water company
   b. Boeing, a manufacturer of airplanes
   c. Brad Pitt
   d. Walmart
   e. the only gas station along a 100-mile stretch of road

3. A monopolist has the following fixed and variable costs:

Price	Quantity	Fixed cost	Variable cost
$10	0	$8	$0
$9	1	8	5
$8	2	8	8
$7	3	8	10
$6	4	8	11
$5	5	8	13
$4	6	8	16
$3	7	8	20
$2	8	8	25

At what level of output will the monopolist maximize profits?

4. The year is 2278, and the starship *Enterprise* is running low on dilithium crystals, which are used to regulate the matter-antimatter reactions that propel the ship across the universe. Without the crystals, space-time travel is not possible. If there is only one known source of dilithium crystals, are the necessary conditions met to establish a monopoly? If the crystals are government owned or regulated, what price should the government set for them?

✳ 5. If demand falls, what is likely to happen to a monopolist's price, output, and economic profit?

✳ 6. A new musical group called The Incentives cuts a debut single. The record company determines a number of price points for the group's first single, "The Big Idea."

Price per download	Quantity of downloads
$2.99	25,000
$1.99	50,000
$1.49	75,000
$0.99	100,000
$0.49	150,000

The record company can produce the song with fixed costs of $10,000 and no variable cost.

a. Determine the total revenue at each price. What is the marginal revenue as the price drops from one level to the next?
b. What price would maximize the record company's profits? How much would the company make?
c. If you were the agent for The Incentives, what signing fee would you request from the record company? Explain your answer.

7. Recalling what you have learned about elasticity, what can you say about the connection between the price a monopolist chooses to charge and whether or not demand is elastic, unitary, or inelastic at that price? (**Hint:** Examine the marginal revenue curve of a monopolist. The fact that marginal revenue becomes negative at low prices implies that a portion of the demand curve cannot possibly be chosen.)

8. A small community is served by five independent gas stations. Gasoline is a highly competitive market. Use the market demand curve to illustrate the consumer surplus and producer surplus created by the market. Now imagine that the five independent gas stations are all combined under one franchise. Create a new graph that illustrates the consumer surplus, producer surplus, and deadweight loss after the monopoly enters the market.

9. A local community bus service charges $2.00 for a one-way fare. The city council is thinking of raising the fare to $2.50 to generate 25% more revenue. The council has asked for your advice as a student of economics. In your analysis, be sure to break down the impact of the price increase into the price effect and the output effect. Explain why the city council's estimate of the revenue increase is likely to be overstated. Use a graph to illustrate your answer.

10. Suppose that a monopolist's marginal cost curve shifts upward. What is likely to happen to the price the monopolist charges, the quantity it produces, and the profit it makes? Use a graph to illustrate your answer.

✳ **11.** Go to www.economicsoftheoffice.com and watch the two short clips from *The Office* episode "Moroccan Christmas." How is Dwight able to establish a monopoly in this market? Discuss.

SOLVED PROBLEMS

5. The following graph shows a monopolist making a profit:

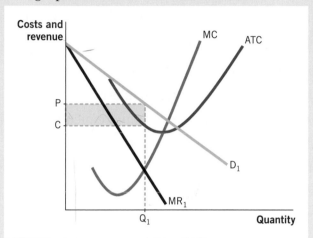

Now we show what happens if demand falls:

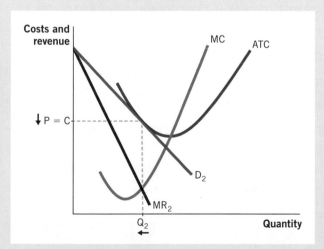

Lower demand causes the price to fall, the output to decline, and the profit to disappear.

6.a.

Price per download	Downloads	Total revenue	Marginal revenue
$2.99	25,000	$74,750	$74,750
$1.99	50,000	99,500	24,750
$1.49	75,000	111,750	12,250
$0.99	100,000	99,000	−12,750
$0.49	150,000	73,500	−25,500

b. Because marginal costs are $0, the firm would maximize its profits at $1.49. The company would make $111,750 − $10,000, or $101,750.

c. The company makes $101,750 from production, so as the agent you could request any signing fee up to that amount. Because determining a fee is a negotiation and both sides have to gain from trade, as the agent you should argue for a number close to $100,000, and you should expect the firm to argue for a much smaller fee.

11. Dwight corners the market on Princess Unicorn dolls right before Christmas by buying all of the dolls in the Scranton area. Dwight knows that the demand for these dolls will become more inelastic as Christmas approaches, allowing him to mark up the original market price to the profit-maximizing price for a monopolist. Ultimately, Dwight's monopoly is short-lived because suppliers can bring in more dolls after Christmas, but since most of the demand is in the short run, Dwight's temporary monopoly is all he needs to earn a large profit.

Charging different prices to different people is unfair and harmful.

Have you ever wondered why private colleges have high sticker prices and then offer tuition discounts to some students but not others?

Maybe you have noticed that many nightclubs or bars let women in without a cover charge but require men to pay. And why do theaters charge more for adults and less for children when everyone sees the same movie? In each of these examples, some customers pay more and others pay less. Is this practice unfair and harmful? Not really. When a firm can charge more than one price, markets work more efficiently.

In this chapter, we examine many real-life pricing situations and how businesses can make additional profits if they charge different prices to different groups of customers. The study of *price discrimination* adds a layer of complexity to the simple models of perfect competition and monopoly. A thorough understanding of how price discrimination works is especially useful as we complete our study of market structure with monopolistic competition and oligopoly in the next two chapters.

Why do some night clubs let women in for free but hit men with a cover charge? (See the answer in the conclusion to the chapter.)

BIG QUESTIONS

✳ **What is price discrimination?**

✳ **How is price discrimination practiced?**

What Is Price Discrimination?

Price discrimination
occurs when a firm sells
the same good or service at
different prices to different
groups of customers.

Price discrimination occurs when a firm sells the same good or service at different prices to different groups of customers. The difference in price is not related to differences in cost. Although "price discrimination" sounds like something illegal, in fact it is beneficial to both sellers and buyers. When a firm can charge more than one price, markets work more efficiently. Because price-discriminating firms typically charge a "high" and a "low" price, some consumers are able to buy the product at a low price. Of course, firms are not in business to provide goods at low prices; they want to make a profit. Price discrimination enables them to make more money by dividing their customers into at least two groups: those who get a discount and others who pay more.

We have seen that in competitive markets, firms are *price takers*. If a competitive firm attempts to charge a higher price, its customers will likely buy elsewhere. To practice price discrimination, a firm must be a *price maker*; it must have some market power before it can charge more than one price. Both monopolies and nonmonopolistic companies use price discrimination to earn higher profits. Common examples of price discrimination are movie theater tickets, restaurant menus, college tuition, airline reservations, discounts on academic software, and coupons.

Conditions for Price Discrimination

For price discrimination to take place, two conditions must be met. First, there must be at least two different types of buyers. Second, the firm must be able to prevent resale of the product or service. Let's look at each in turn.

Distinguishing Groups of Buyers

To price-discriminate, the firm must be able to distinguish groups of buyers with different price elasticities of demand. Firms can generate additional revenues by charging more to customers with inelastic demand and less to customers with elastic demand. For instance, many restaurants offer lower prices, known as "early-bird specials," to people who eat dinner early. Who are these customers? Many, such as retirees and families with children, are on a limited budget. These early diners not only have lower demand but also represent demand that is more elastic; they eat out only if the price is low enough.

Early-bird specials work for restaurants by separating customers into two groups: one that is price sensitive and another that is willing to pay full price. This strategy enables the restaurants to serve more customers and generate additional revenue.

Trade-offs

Preventing Resale

For price discrimination to be a viable strategy, a firm must also be able to prevent resale of the product or service. In some cases, preventing resale is easy. For example, airlines require that electronic tickets match the passenger's government-issued photo ID. This system prevents a passenger who received a discounted fare from reselling it to another passenger who would be willing to pay more. The process works well for airlines and enables them to charge more to groups of flyers with more inelastic demand, such as business travelers. It also works well for restaurants offering early-bird specials, because the restaurants can easily distinguish between customers who arrive in time for the specials and those who arrive later.

One Price versus Price Discrimination

A business that practices price discrimination would prefer to differentiate every customer by selling the same good or service at a price unique to that customer—a situation known as **perfect price discrimination**. To achieve this result, a business would have to know exactly what any particular customer would be willing to pay and charge him or her exactly that price. Many jewelry stores and automobile dealerships attempt to practice perfect price discrimination by posting high sticker prices and then bargaining with each customer to reach a deal. When you enter a jewelry store or a vehicle showroom, the salesperson tries to determine the highest price you are willing to pay. Then he or she bargains with you until that price is reached.

Perfect price discrimination occurs when a firm sells the same good or service at a unique price to every customer.

In practice, perfect price discrimination is hard to implement. To see why, let's look at a hypothetical example. Consider two small airlines, Flat Earth Air and Discriminating Fliers. Each airline has a monopoly on the route it flies, and each faces the same market demand curves and marginal costs. The costs of running a flight—fuel, pilots, flight attendants, ground crew, and so on—are about the same no matter how many passengers are on board. Both firms fly the same model of airplane, which seats 200 passengers. So the marginal cost of adding one passenger—the extra weight and the cost of a can of soda or two—is very small, almost negligible. What happens if one of the airlines price-discriminates but the other does not?

In Figure 11.1, Flat Earth Air charges the same price to every passenger, while Discriminating Fliers uses two different price structures. To keep our example easy to work with, the marginal cost (MC) is set at $100, shown as a horizontal line.

Flat Earth Air sets its price by using the profit-maximizing rule, $MR = MC$. It charges $300 for every seat and serves 100 customers (that is, passengers). Because the marginal cost is $100, every passenger who gets on the plane generates $200 in producer surplus. The profit, represented by the green rectangle in panel (a), is $200 × 100, or $20,000. At 100 passengers, this airline has done everything it can to maximize profits at a single price. At the

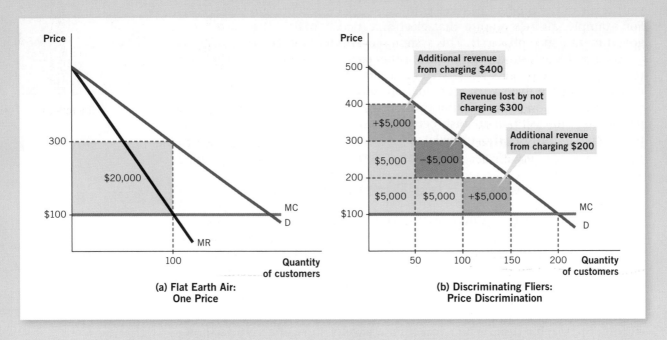

FIGURE 11.1

One Price versus Price Discrimination

(a) A firm that charges a single price uses MR = MC to earn a profit. (b) When a firm price-discriminates, it takes in more profit than a firm that charges a single price. The discriminating firm increases its revenue by charging some customers more and other customers less, as shown in the green areas. The increase in profit is partly offset by the loss of revenue from existing customers who receive a lower price, as shown in the red area.

Marginal thinking

same time, there are plenty of unsold seats in the plane, which holds 200 passengers. Those unfilled seats represent a lost opportunity to earn additional revenue. As a result, airlines typically try to fill the plane by discounting the price of some seats. And this is precisely what Discriminating Fliers does.

Discriminating Fliers experiments with two prices, as shown in panel (b). Let's look at the reasoning behind these two prices. Because the firm faces a downward-sloping demand curve, the airline cannot sell every seat on the plane at the higher price. So it saves a number of seats, in this case 50, for last-minute bookings to capture customers with less flexibility who are willing to pay $400. These are travelers with inelastic demand, such as those who travel for business. The airline offers the rest of the seats at a low price, in this case $200, to capture customers with more elastic demand. The challenge for the airline is to make sure that the people who are willing to pay $400 do not purchase the $200 seats. So it makes the low fare available to customers who book far in advance, because these customers are typically more flexible and shop for the best deal. It is common for a businessperson who needs to visit a client to make flight arrangements just days before the meeting, which precludes purchasing a $200 ticket weeks in advance. The customers who book early fill the seats that would otherwise be empty if the airline had charged only one price, as Flat Earth Air does. We can see this outcome by comparing the total number of passengers under the two strategies. Discriminating Fliers, with its two-price strategy, serves 50 passengers who pay $400 and 100 additional passengers who pay $200. Flat Earth Air's single price of $300 brings in only 100 passengers.

The net effect of price discrimination is apparent in the shaded areas of panel (b). By charging two prices, Discriminating Fliers generates more profit. The high price, $400, generates additional revenue equal to the upper green rectangle—$5,000—from passengers who must pay more than the $300 charged by Flat Earth Air. Discriminating Fliers also gains additional revenue with its low price of $200. The less expensive tickets attract passengers with more elastic demand, such as college students, vacationers, and retirees. The low-price tickets generate $5,000 in revenue, as shown by the lower green rectangle.

Airlines offer lower fares if you are willing to take the red-eye.

Some customers would have paid Discriminating Fliers more if the airline had charged a single price. The group of customers willing to pay $300 is able to acquire tickets on Discriminating Fliers for $200. The red rectangle represents the lost profit, equal to $5,000. The $10,000 in revenue represented by the darker green rectangles more than offsets the $5,000 in lost profit represented by the red rectangle. The airline that price-discriminates, depicted in panel (b), generates a profit of $25,000. The airline that charges a single price, depicted in panel (a), generates a profit of $20,000.

In reality, airlines often charge many prices. For example, you will find higher prices for travel on Friday and for midday flights. If your stay includes a Saturday night or if you choose a red-eye flight, prices are lower. Airlines charge more for last-minute bookings and less to customers who book in advance. Airlines also change prices from day to day and even from hour to hour. All of these price changes reflect efforts to price-discriminate.

Because passengers cannot resell their tickets or easily change their plans, airlines can effectively price-discriminate. In fact, if an airline could charge unique prices for every passenger booking a flight, it would transform the entire area under the demand curve and above the marginal cost curve into more profit.

The Welfare Effects of Price Discrimination

Price discrimination is profitable for the companies that practice it. But it also increases the welfare of society. How, you might ask, can companies make more profit and also benefit consumers? The answer: because a price discriminator charges a high price to some and a low price to others, more consumers are able to buy the good.

To illustrate this point, let's imagine an airline, Perfect Flights, that is able to perfectly price-discriminate. Perfect Flights charges each passenger a price exactly equal to what that passenger is willing to pay. As a result, some customers pay more and others pay less than they would under a single-price system. This outcome is evident in Figure 11.2, where a profit-maximizing firm charges $300. At this price, the firm captures the profit in the light green rectangle, B. However, Perfect Flights charges each passenger a price based on his or her willingness to pay. Therefore, it earns significantly more profit. By charging higher prices (P_{high}) to those willing to pay more than $300, the firm is able to capture the additional profit in the upper green triangle, A. Likewise, by charging lower prices (P_{low}) to those not willing to pay $300, the firm is able to capture the additional profit in the lower green triangle, C. As a result, Perfect Flights is making more money and serving more customers.

By charging a different fare to every customer, Perfect Flights can also increase the quantity of tickets sold to 200. This strategy yields two results worth noting. First, in the long run, a perfectly competitive firm would

FIGURE 11.2

Perfect Price Discrimination

If the firm charges one price, the most it can earn is the profit in the light green rectangle. However, if a firm is able to perfectly price-discriminate, it can pick up the additional profit represented by the green triangles.

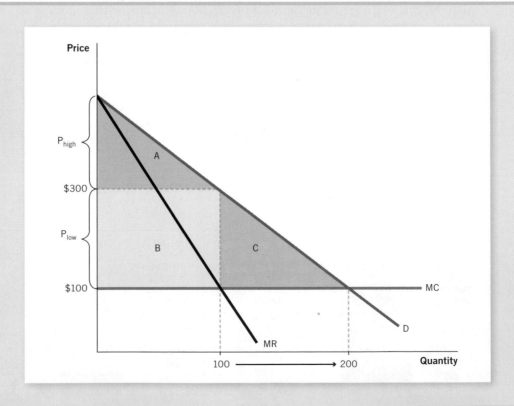

charge a price just equal to marginal cost. In the case of Perfect Flights, the last customer who gets on the plane will pay an extraordinarily low price of $100—the price you might find in a competitive market. Second, this outcome mirrors the result of a government-regulated monopolist that uses the marginal cost pricing rule, P = MC, to enhance social welfare. Perfect Flights is therefore achieving the efficiency of a competitive market while also producing the output that a regulated monopolist would choose. This strategy provides the firm with the opportunity to convert the area consisting of the two green triangles into more profit. In other words, the process maximizes the quantity sold. The efficiency of the market improves, and the firm generates more profit.

Marginal
thinking

ECONOMICS IN THE REAL WORLD

Santa Fe, New Mexico: Using Negative Incentives as Price Discrimination

If you live in an arid climate, water rationing is the norm. Tiered pricing is one way to encourage water conservation. In most markets, bulk purchases get a volume discount. But as a way of encouraging water rationing, those who use more water pay much more for it.

Santa Fe, New Mexico, decided to use economics to address the issue of water conservation. Fifteen years ago, facing an acute water shortage (the city literally almost ran out of water), Santa Fe's city government introduced a tiered pricing system. The tiered system makes the heaviest users of water pay a premium for water used beyond a minimum. The heaviest users pay four times more per gallon than modest users.

Incentives

An article in the *New York Times* summarized the program's effects: "The tiered approach has worked as intended. Since 2001, Santa Fe's total water consumption has dropped by a fifth, even as the high desert city's population has increased more than 10%. When water costs more as its consumption increases, people respond exactly as an economics textbook would dictate: They use less."* This policy is truly economics in action, with a 20% reduction in water use even as the population increases!

The tiered pricing system involves several important economic concepts that we have already learned about:

1. *Incentives matter* (Chapter 1). The people of Santa Fe have responded to the negative incentive of being penalized for using too much water.
2. *Internalizing the externality* (Chapter 7). Before 2001, heavy water users were affecting everyone in Santa Fe by creating periodic water shortages, but they did not have to pay extra for their actions. By paying much more for their water now, the heavy users are internalizing (paying for) the externality.
3. *Tragedy of the commons* (Chapter 7). Santa Fe has avoided a tragedy-of-the-commons scenario where all the water runs dry.

Tiered pricing encourages water conservation.

---

*Nelson D. Schwartz, "Water Pricing in Two Thirsty Cities: In One, Guzzlers Pay More, and Use Less," *New York Times*, May 6, 2015.

In contrast, Fresno, California—which has not implemented a tiered pricing system but is facing a situation similar to Santa Fe's in 2001—is heading for trouble.

4. *The welfare effects of price discrimination* (this chapter). Dividing groups by their willingness to pay is beneficial to society, and that is what the Santa Fe water pricing system has achieved. ✳

Comparing Perfect Price Discrimination with Perfect Competition and Monopoly

To understand the welfare effects of perfect price discrimination, we can compare the consumer and producer surplus in three scenarios: a competitive market, a market in which a monopolist charges a single price, and a market characterized by perfect price discrimination. The results, shown in Table 11.1, are derived by examining Figure 11.2.

Marginal thinking

In a perfectly competitive market, there are no barriers to entry and no firm has market power. In the long run, the price will be equal to the marginal cost. In our example of airline ticket prices, the price is driven down to $100. At this price, 200 tickets are sold. The entire area above the marginal cost curve (A + B + C) is consumer surplus, because the willingness to pay—as determined along the demand curve—is at least as great as the price. Because the ticket price is the same as the marginal cost, the producer surplus is zero. Because every customer who is willing to pay $100 or more can find a ticket, there is no deadweight loss. Under perfect competition, the market structure clearly favors consumers.

A monopoly holds substantial market power, so the firm in this scenario sets a price using the profit-maximizing rule, MR = MC, without having to worry about competition driving the price down to marginal cost. The monopolist's profit-maximizing price, or $300 in Figure 11.2, is higher than the $100 price under perfect competition. This higher price reduces the amount of consumer surplus to triangle A and creates a producer surplus equal to rectangle B. In addition, because the number of tickets sold falls to 100, there is now deadweight loss equal to triangle C. Economic activity associated with triangle C no longer exists, and the total welfare of society is now limited to A + B. From this analysis, we see that monopoly causes a partial transfer of consumer surplus to producers and a reduction in total welfare for society.

TABLE 11.1

The Welfare Effects of Perfect Price Discrimination

	Perfect competition	A monopolist that charges a single price	Perfect price discrimination
Consumer surplus	A + B + C	A	0
Producer surplus	0	B	A + B + C
Deadweight loss	0	C	0
Total welfare	A + B + C	A + B	A + B + C

In our third scenario, a firm that can practice perfect price discrimination is able to charge each customer a price exactly equal to the price that customer is willing to pay. This strategy enables the firm to convert the entire area of consumer surplus that existed under perfect competition into producer surplus (A + B + C). For the firm to capture the entire area of available consumer surplus, it must lower some prices all the way down to marginal cost. At that point, the number of tickets sold returns to 200, the market is once again efficient, and the deadweight loss disappears. Perfect price discrimination transfers the gains from trade from consumers to producers, but it also yields maximum efficiency.

Marginal cost

Note that these examples give us a better understanding of what economists mean when they use the word "perfect" in connection with a market.

Perfect Price Discrimination

Legally Blonde

In this 2001 film, Reese Witherspoon stars as Elle Woods, a sun-washed sorority girl who defies expectations. Believing that her boyfriend is about to propose to her, Elle and two friends go shopping to find the perfect dress for the occasion. They enter an exclusive boutique and start trying on dresses.

The saleswoman comments to another associate, "There's nothing I love more than a dumb blonde with daddy's plastic." She grabs a dress off the clearance sale rack and removes the "half price" tag. Approaching Elle, she says, "Did you see this one? We just got it in yesterday." Elle fingers the dress, then the price tag, and looks at the saleswoman with excitement.

> **ELLE:** "Is this a low-viscosity rayon?"
> **SALESWOMAN:** "Uh, yes—of course."
> **ELLE:** "With half-loop topstitching on the hem?"
> **SALESWOMAN** (smiling a lie): "Absolutely. It's one of a kind."
> (Elle hands the dress back to her, no longer pretending to be excited.)
> **ELLE:** "It's impossible to use a half-loop topstitch on low-viscosity rayon. It would snag the fabric. And you didn't just get this in, because I remember it from the June *Vogue* a year ago, so if you're trying to sell it to me at full price, you picked the wrong girl."

Do you know how to look good for the right price?

The scene is a wonderful example of an attempt at price discrimination gone wrong. Unbeknownst to the saleswoman, Elle is majoring in fashion merchandising in college and knows more about fashion than the saleswoman does. Her effort to cheat Elle fails miserably.

What makes the scene powerful is the use of stereotypes. When merchants attempt to price-discriminate, they look for clues to help them decide whether the buyer is willing to pay full price or needs an incentive, or discount, to make a purchase. In this case, Elle's appearance suggests that she is an uninformed buyer with highly inelastic demand. Consequently, the saleswoman's strategy backfires. ✳

ECONOMICS IN THE MEDIA

It can mean that consumer surplus is maximized, as it is under perfect competition, or that producer surplus is maximized, as it is under perfect price discrimination. It does not specify an outcome from a particular perspective; instead, *perfect* describes any market process that produces no deadweight loss. If society's total welfare is maximized, economists do not distinguish whether the benefits accrue to consumers or producers.

ECONOMICS IN THE REAL WORLD

Outlet Malls—If You Build It, They Will Come

Have you ever noticed that outlet malls along major roadways are often located a considerable distance from large population centers? Moreover,

How far would you drive to visit an outlet mall?

every item at an outlet mall can be found closer to home. The same clothes, shoes, and kitchenware are available nearby.

Logic tells us that it would be more convenient to shop locally and forgo the time and hassle of getting to an outlet center. But that is not how many shoppers feel.

Discount shopping is a big deal. How big? Here are a few statistics. Potomac Mills, 30 miles south of Washington, D.C., is Virginia's most popular attraction, with nearly 23 million visitors a year. (That figure rivals the number of annual visitors to Disney World's Magic Kingdom!) But Potomac Mills is not unique. Two adjacent outlet malls in San Marcos, Texas, attract over 6 million visitors a year—many more than the number that visit the Alamo. And in Pigeon Forge, Tennessee, over 10 million shoppers go to the outlets annually—more than the number of visitors to nearby Great Smoky Mountains National Park.

Outlet shopping is an example of price discrimination at work. Traditional malls are usually situated in urban settings and offer a wide variety of choices, but not necessarily low prices. If you want convenience, the local shopping mall is right around the corner. But if you want a bargain, shopping at a traditional local mall is not the best way to go.

Incentives

What makes outlets so attractive are the discounts. Bargain hunters have much more elastic demand than their traditional mall-shopping counterparts who desire convenience. Moreover, the difference in the price elasticity of demand between these two groups means that traditional malls can more easily charge full price, while outlets must discount their merchandise to attract customers. The difference between these two groups of customers gives merchants a chance to price-discriminate on the basis of location—which is another way of separating customers into two groups and preventing resale at the same time. Retailers can therefore earn additional profits through price discrimination, while price-sensitive consumers can find lower prices at the outlets.

It is noteworthy that the convenience of finding discounts online threatens not only the traditional malls but also the outlets. When savvy shoppers can simply click to find the best deal, will they continue to drive to the outlets? ✳

Opportunity cost

PRACTICE WHAT YOU KNOW

Price Discrimination: Taking Economics to New Heights

Consider the table below, which shows seven potential customers who are interested in taking a 30-minute helicopter ride. The helicopter has room for eight people, including the pilot. The marginal cost of taking on additional passengers is $10.

Customer	Maximum willingness to pay	Age
Amelia	$80	66
Orville	70	34
Wilbur	40	17
Neil	50	16
Charles	60	9
Chuck	100	49
Buzz	20	9

How much would you pay to fly in a helicopter?

Question: If the company can charge only one price, what should it be?

Answer: First, create an ordered array of the customers, from those willing to pay the most to those willing to pay the least.

Customer	Maximum willingness to pay	Price	TR	MR
Chuck	$100	$100	$100	$100
Amelia	80	80	160	60
Orville	70	70	210	50
Charles	60	60	240	30
Neil	50	50	250	10
Wilbur	40	40	240	−10
Buzz	20	20	140	−100

(CONTINUED)

If the firm charges $100, only Chuck will take the flight. When the firm drops the price to $80, Chuck and Amelia both buy tickets, so the total revenue (TR) is $80 × 2, or $160. Successively lower prices result in higher total revenue from the first five customers. Because the marginal cost is $10, the firm will benefit from lowering its price as long as the increase in marginal revenue is greater than, or equal to, the marginal cost. When the price is $50, five customers get on the helicopter, for a total of $250 in revenue. Adding the fifth passenger brings in exactly $10 in marginal revenue, so $50 is the best possible price to charge. Because each of the five passengers has a marginal cost of $10, the company makes $250 − (5 × $10), or $200 in profit.

Question: If the company could charge two prices, what should they be, and who would pay them?

Answer: First, arrange the customers in two distinct groups: adults and children.

Adult customers	Willingness to pay	Age	Price	TR	MR
Chuck	$100	49	$100	$100	$100
Amelia	80	66	80	160	60
Orville	70	34	70	210	50

Young customers	Willingness to pay	Age	Price	TR	MR
Charles	$60	9	$60	$60	$60
Neil	50	16	50	100	40
Wilbur	40	17	40	120	20
Buzz	20	9	20	80	−40

As you can see, two separate prices emerge. For adults, profits are maximized at a price of $70. For children, total profits are maximized at $40. The company should charge $70 to the adult customers, which brings in $70 × 3, or $210 in total revenue. The company should charge $40 for each child under the age of 18, which brings in $40 × 3, or $120.

Price discrimination earns the company $210 + $120 − (6 × $10), or $270 in profit. This is a $70 improvement over charging a single price. In addition, six passengers are now able to get on the helicopter instead of only five under the single-price model.

How Is Price Discrimination Practiced?

Price discrimination is one of the most interesting topics in economics because each example is slightly different from the others. In this section, we take a closer look at real-world examples of price discrimination at movie theaters and on college campuses. As you will see, price discrimination takes many forms, some that are easy to describe and others that are more nuanced.

Price Discrimination at the Movies

Have you ever gone to the movies early so you can pay less for tickets? Movie theaters price-discriminate based on the time of day, age, student status, and whether or not you buy snacks. Let's examine these pricing techniques to see if they are effective.

Pricing Based on the Time of the Show

Why are matinees priced less than evening shows? To encourage customers to attend movies during the afternoon, theaters discount ticket prices for matinees. This strategy makes sense because customers who can attend matinees (retirees, people on vacation, and those who do not work during the day) either have less demand or are more flexible, or price elastic. Work and school limit the options for many other potential customers. As a result, theaters discount matinee prices to encourage moviegoers who have elastic demand and are willing to watch at a less crowded time. Movie theaters also discount the price of matinee shows because they pay to rent films on a weekly basis, so it is in their interest to show a film as many times as possible. Because the variable cost of being open during the day is essentially limited to paying a few employees relatively low wages, the theater can make additional profits even with a relatively small audience. On weekends, matinees also offer a discount to families that want to see a movie together—adding yet another layer of price discrimination.

Once the doors open, matinee prices bring in moviegoers with elastic demand.

Theaters charge two different prices based on showtime because they can easily distinguish between high-demand customers and price-sensitive customers who have the flexibility to watch a matinee. Those with higher demand or less-flexible schedules must pay higher ticket prices to attend in the evening.

Pricing Based on Age or Student Status

Why are there different movie prices for children, seniors, students, and everyone else? This is a complex question. Income does not fully explain the discounts that the young, the old, and students receive. Movie attendance is highest among 13- to 24-year-olds and declines thereafter with age. Given the strong demand among teenagers, it is not surprising that "child" discounts are phased out at most theaters by age 12. But did you know that most "senior" discounts begin before age 65? In some places, senior discounts start at age 50. Now you might think that because people in their 50s tend to be at the peak of their earning power, discounting ticket prices for them would be a bad move. However, because interest in going to the movies declines with age, the "senior" discount actually provides an incentive for a population that might not otherwise go to a movie theater. However, as we have seen, age-based price discrimination does not always work perfectly. Theaters do not usually ask for proof of age, and it may be hard to tell the difference between a child who is just under 12 and one who is over 12. Nonetheless, price discrimination works well enough to make age or student status a useful revenue-generating tool.

Concession Pricing

Have you ever wondered why it is so expensive to purchase snacks at the movie theater? The concession area is another arena in which movie theaters practice price discrimination. To understand why, we need to think of two groups of customers: those who want to eat while they watch movies and those who do not. By limiting outside food and drink, movie theaters push people with inelastic demand for snacks to buy from the concession area. Of course, that does not stop some customers with elastic demand from sneaking food into the theater. But as long as some moviegoers are willing to buy concession fare at exorbitant prices, the theater will generate more revenue. Movie theaters cannot prevent smuggling in of snacks, and they don't have to. All they really want to do is separate their customers into two groups: a price-inelastic group of concession-area snackers and a price-elastic group of nonsnackers and smugglers who fill up the remaining empty seats. This situation is very similar to the problem we examined with airlines. Empty seats represent lost revenue, so it makes sense to price-discriminate through a combination of high and low prices.

If you have ever smuggled food into a movie theater, it is because your demand for movie theater concessions is elastic.

Price Discrimination on Campus

Colleges and universities are experts at price discrimination. Think about tuition. Some students pay the full sticker price, while others enjoy a free ride. Some students receive the in-state rate, while out-of-state students pay substantially more. And once you get to campus, discounts for students are everywhere. In this section, we consider the many ways in which colleges and universities differentiate among their students.

Tuition

Price discrimination begins before you ever set foot on campus, with the Free Application for Federal Student Aid (known as the FAFSA) that most families complete. The form determines eligibility for federal aid. Families that qualify are eligible for grants and low-interest loans, which effectively lower the tuition cost for low- and medium-income families. Therefore, the FAFSA enables colleges to separate applicants into two groups based on income. Because many colleges also use the FAFSA to determine eligibility for their own institutional grants of aid, the FAFSA makes it possible for colleges to precisely target grants and loans to the students who need the most financial help.

Many state institutions of higher education have a two-tiered pricing structure. In-state students get a discount on the tuition, while out-of-state students pay a much higher rate. Part of the difference is attributable to state subsidies that are intended to make in-state institutions more affordable for residents. In-state students pay less because their parents have been paying taxes to the state, often for many years, and the state then uses some of those tax dollars to support its system of higher education. However, in-state subsidies only partially explain the difference in pricing. Out-of-state tuition is higher than it would be if all students paid the same price because out-of-state students are generally less sensitive to price than in-state students.

This two-tiered pricing structure creates two separate groups of customers with distinctly different elasticities of demand. Students choose an out-of-state college or university because they like what that institution has to offer more than the institutions in their home state. It might be that a particular major or program is more highly rated or simply that they prefer the location of the out-of-state school. Whatever the reason, they are willing to pay more for the out-of-state school. Therefore, out-of-state students have a much more inelastic demand. Colleges know this and price their tuition accordingly. Conversely, in-state students often view the opportunity to attend a nearby

Resort or college? Sky-high tuition and room and board are one way to help pay for a beautiful campus.

college as the most economical decision. Because price is a big factor in choosing an in-state institution, it is not surprising that in-state demand is more elastic.

Selective private colleges also play the price discrimination game by advertising annual tuition and room and board fees that exceed $60,000. With price discrimination, the "sticker" price is often discounted. Depending on how much the college wants to encourage a particular student to attend, it can discount the tuition all the way to zero. This strategy enables selective private colleges to price-discriminate by offering scholarships based on financial need, while also guaranteeing placements for the children of wealthy alumni and others willing to pay the full sticker price.

Student Discounts

The edge of campus is a great place to look for price discrimination. Local bars, eateries, and shops all want college students to step off campus, so student discounts are the norm. Why do establishments offer student discounts? Think about the average college student. Price matters to that student. Knowing this, local merchants in search of college customers can provide student discounts without lowering their prices across the board. This means they can charge more to their regular clients while providing the necessary discounts to get college students to make the trek off campus.

Now Playing: Economics!

Have you ever gone to the movies early so you can pay less for tickets? Movie theaters price-discriminate based on the time of the movie and the age of the customer. In order to practice price discrimination, theaters must be able to identify different groups of moviegoers, where each group has a different price elasticity of demand.

MATINEE $9

Demand for matinees is typically low. These showings attract groups with relatively elastic demand, like families and those on a budget, who decide to attend matinees because of lower prices.

EVENING $13

Evening movie showings attract larger crowds that consist mainly of adults and couples on dates. This group has relatively inelastic demand, so price is not the determining factor of when and where they see a movie.

The concession counter also generates profit for the movie theater. The high prices mean that patrons who are price–conscious (having relatively elastic demand) skip the counter or smuggle in their own snacks, while those who are more concerned about convenience than price (having relatively inelastic demand) buy snacks at the counter.

REVIEW QUESTIONS

- Does price discrimination hurt all consumers? Think about the example of movie theaters as you craft your response.

- Your local movie theater is thinking about increasing ticket prices for just the opening day of a blockbuster movie. How would you explain the economics behind this price increase?

PRACTICE WHAT YOU KNOW

Price Discrimination in Practice: Everyday Examples

Question: Test your understanding by thinking about the examples below. Are they examples of price discrimination?

a. **Retail coupons.** Programs such as discount coupons, rebates, and frequent-buyer plans appeal to customers willing to spend time pursuing a deal.

b. **Using Priceline to make hotel reservations.** "Naming your price" on Priceline.com is a form of haggling that enables users to get hotel rooms at a discount. Hotels negotiate with Priceline to fill unused rooms while still advertising the full price on their web sites.

c. **$6 footlong subs at Subway.** Customers who buy a $6 footlong get more sub at a substantially lower price per inch than a $4 6-inch sub.

d. **The McPick 2 Menu at McDonald's.** Customers who order off the McPick 2 Menu get a variety of smaller menu items for $1 each.

e. **Discounts for early shoppers on Black Friday.** Customers who line up in the early-morning hours after Thanksgiving get first dibs on a limited quantity of reduced-price items at many retailers.

Price discrimination or not?

Answers:

a. **Retail coupons.** Affluent customers generally do not bother with the hassle of clipping, sending in, and keeping track of coupons because they value their time more than the small savings. However, customers with lower incomes usually take the time to get the discount. This means that coupons, rebates, and frequent-buyer programs do a good job of price-discriminating.

b. **Using Priceline to make hotel reservations.** Priceline enables hotels to divide their customers into two groups: those who don't want to be bothered with haggling and those who value the savings enough to justify the time spent negotiating. This is a good example of price discrimination.

c. **$6 footlong subs at Subway.** The $6 price is available to anyone anytime. Therefore, the $6 footlong is catchy marketing, but it does not strictly meet the definition of price discrimination. However, to get the deal, customers must buy a 12-inch sub. Anyone could conceivably get the deal, but only those with big appetites or a willingness to eat leftovers will choose a footlong. Those with smaller appetites are stuck paying $4 for a 6-inch sub.

d. **The McPick 2 Menu at McDonald's.** Anyone can buy off the McPick 2 Menu at any time. Because McDonald's does not force customers to buy a large serving in order to get the deal, this is not price discrimination.

e. **Discounts for early shoppers on Black Friday.** The discounts are time sensitive. Shoppers who arrive before the deadline get a lower price; shoppers who arrive after the deadline do not. This is a clear-cut example of price discrimination.

ECONOMICS IN THE MEDIA

Price Discrimination

Extreme Couponing

Most of us use coupons from time to time, when it is convenient. The TV show *Extreme Couponing* showcases a small number of shoppers who plan their trips to the store with military precision. They clip coupons, scout out the stores that offer the best deals, and buy products in enormous quantities to save money. The returns are typically hundreds of dollars in savings each time they visit the store.

While these couponers often get groceries for practically nothing and appear to beat the system, they go to a lot of trouble to secure a deal. Some dive in dumpsters to get the discarded Sunday newspaper coupon sections. Others keep food stashes that take up most of the space in their homes. They use spreadsheets, folders, and calculators to determine how to save as much as possible.

As good economists, we know that getting a really good deal on something doesn't make it free. The amount of time it takes to be an extreme couponer is staggering—equivalent to a part-time job. Clearly, the participants do not fully account

Would you dumpster-dive to get coupons?

for the time they spend on couponing. Saving $200 at the store sounds great unless it takes you 20 hours to do so; that's the equivalent of only $10 an hour. Many of the people on the show might find that they could earn substantially more by putting their organizational skills to use in the workforce. It is for this very reason that many households do not clip coupons in the first place. After all, time is money. ✳

Opportunity cost

Price discrimination also occurs on campus. For example, students typically receive discounts for campus activities like concerts and sporting events. Because students generally have elastic demand, price discrimination provides greater student access to on-campus events than charging a single price does.

Conclusion

The word "discrimination" has negative connotations, but not when combined with the word "price." Charging different prices to different groups of customers results in more economic activity and is more efficient than charging a single price across the board. Under price discrimination, many consumers pay less than they would if a firm had charged a single price, while other consumers will pay more because their demand is more inelastic. But overall, total social welfare increases, and the amount of deadweight loss in society is reduced.

Price discrimination also helps us understand how many markets actually function, because instances of perfectly competitive markets and monopoly are rare.

Finally, we answer the question we posed in the caption at the start of the chapter: Why do some nightclubs let women in for free and charge a cover to men? Clubs need the right balance of men and women to create buzz. Because demand among women is more elastic, they often can get in without a cover charge. However, demand among men is more inelastic, so they have to pay the cover charge. As we learned in the chapter, the result is win/win for all involved. The club increases its profit by price discriminating and social welfare increases because the club is more crowded when women get in for free.

ANSWERING THE BIG QUESTIONS

What is price discrimination?

* Price discrimination occurs when firms can identify different groups of customers with varying price elasticities of demand and can prevent resale among their customers.
* A firm must have some market power before it can charge more than one price.

How is price discrimination practiced?

* Under price discrimination, some consumers pay a higher price and others receive a discount. Price discrimination is profitable for the firm, reduces deadweight loss, and leads to a higher output level.

Outsmarting Grocery Store Tactics

Throughout this chapter, we considered the shopping experience in the context of price discrimination. Here we focus on how the typical grocery store is set up to manipulate buyers into spending more. Grocery stores carefully cultivate an enticing, multisensory experience—from the smell of the bread in the bakery, to the colorful cut flowers and fresh produce, to the eat-in restaurants and coffee bars, to the tens of thousands of other items to purchase. You need to be on your game so as not to overspend your budget. Here is some advice to help you save a few dollars.

Understand how grocery stores route you through the store. Have you ever wondered why the produce is displayed in a certain area? Or why most of the stuff you really need is at the back of the store? The grocery store has set things up to entice you to purchase more than you really need. Suppose that you are there to pick up a gallon of milk. In most stores, the refrigerated section is in the back, so that you have plenty of opportunities to impulsively grab something else that looks good.

Notice that popular items are placed at eye level. Believe it or not, supermarkets make more profits from manufacturers than from consumers. Manufacturers pay "slotting fees" to have their products placed in desirable locations. But the product you actually want may be on a higher or lower shelf—so it pays to look up and down.

Beware of sales. Stores know that shoppers gravitate to markdowns and sales. However, many shoppers are not very diligent in determining if the sale is a good value. Don't buy something simply because it is "on sale" and located at the end of the aisle. This is one way that groceries make extra money: you end up buying stuff you don't really need.

Find the loss leaders. To draw traffic to the store, groceries compete by offering a few fantastic promotions. Sometimes the sale items are priced so low that the store actually loses money by selling them. But the store's management is counting on mak-

Grocery stores try to tempt you to buy more than you need.

ing up the difference when you buy other items throughout the store. The deal you get on one item should not cause you to let down your guard on other purchases.

Beware of coupons! Coupons aren't always a good deal. Stores know which manufacturer coupons their customers have, so they rarely reduce the price on those products. If you have to pay full price to use a coupon, is it really a good deal? Consider store brands or other brands of the same product before you use a coupon.

Try the store brands. Generally, store brands are cheaper than name brands. The store brand is often exactly the same product as the name brand—it is just repackaged at the manufacturing plant and sold for less. When this is the case, you can save a lot of money by buying store brands.

Finally, get a smaller shopping cart. When their carts fill up, most shoppers instinctively ration the remaining space and become far more selective about what they pick up.

If you are aware of the tactics that grocery stores deploy, you can start beating them at their own game.

CONCEPTS YOU SHOULD KNOW

perfect price discrimination (p. 341)

price discrimination (p. 340)

QUESTIONS FOR REVIEW

1. What two challenges must a price maker overcome to effectively price-discriminate?

2. Why does price discrimination improve the efficiency of the market?

3. Why is preventing resale a key to successful price discrimination?

4. If perfect price discrimination reduces consumer surplus to zero, how can this situation lead to the most socially desirable level of output?

STUDY PROBLEMS (✳ *solved at the end of the section*)

1. Seven potential customers are interested in seeing a movie. Because the marginal cost of admitting additional customers is zero, the movie theater maximizes its profits by maximizing its revenue.

Customer	Maximum willingness to pay	Age
Allison	$8	66
Becky	11	34
Charlie	6	45
David	7	16
Erin	6	9
Franco	10	28
Grace	9	14

a. What price would the theater charge if it could charge only one price?

b. If the theater could charge two prices, what prices would it choose? Which customers would pay the higher price, and which would pay the lower price?

c. How much profit does the theater make when it charges only one price? How much profit does the theater make if it price-discriminates?

2. Which of the following are examples of price discrimination? Explain your answers.
   a. A cell phone carrier offers unlimited calling on the weekends for all of its customers.
   b. Tickets to the student section for all basketball games are $5.
   c. A restaurant offers a 20% discount for customers who order dinner between 4 and 6 p.m.
   d. A music store has a half-price sale on last year's guitars.
   e. A well-respected golf instructor charges each customer a fee just under the customer's maximum willingness to pay for lessons.

3. At many amusement parks, customers who enter after 4 p.m. receive a steep discount on the price of admission. Explain how this practice is a form of price discrimination.

4. Name three products for which impatience on the part of the consumer enables a firm to price-discriminate.

✱ 5. Prescription drug prices in the United States are often substantially higher than in Canada, the United Kingdom, and India. Today, pharmacies in these countries fill millions of low-cost prescriptions through the mail to U.S. citizens. Given that the pharmaceutical industry cannot prevent the resale of these drugs, are the industry's efforts to price-discriminate useless? Explain your answer.

✱ 6. Metropolitan Opera tickets are the most expensive on Saturday night. There are often a very limited number of "student rush tickets," with which a lucky student can wind up paying $20 for a $250 seat. The student rush tickets are available first-come, first-served. Why does the opera company offer these low-cost tickets? How does it benefit from this practice? Why are students, and not other groups of customers, offered the discounted tickets?

✱ 7. Have you ever tipped a restaurant host in order to bypass a long wait and get a table more quickly? Would this be an example of price discrimination? Why or why not? Discuss.

8. Orbitz, the travel web site, routinely offers PC and Apple users different search results. Apple users typically have higher-priced hotels show up on the top page of the results, while PC users are presented with somewhat lower prices. Is Orbitz practicing price discrimination? Discuss.

SOLVED PROBLEMS

5. Buying prescription drugs outside the United States is increasingly common. Because the pharmaceutical companies charge three to four times more for drugs sold domestically than they do in most other countries, it would seem that the drug industry's efforts to price-discriminate aren't working, but that is not true. Not everyone fills their prescriptions from foreign sources; only a small fraction of U.S. customers go to that much effort. Because most U.S. citizens still purchase the more expensive drugs here, the pharmaceutical companies are benefiting from price discrimination, even though some consumers manage to navigate around their efforts.

6. The Met hopes to sell all of its $250 tickets, but not every show sells out and some tickets become available at the last minute. The student rush tickets benefit both the opera company and the students: the company can fill last-minute seats, and the students, who have elastic demand and low income, get a steep discount. The Met is able to perfectly price-discriminate, because the rush tickets require a student ID. Other groups of operagoers are therefore unable to buy the rush tickets. This practice effectively separates the customer base into two groups: students and nonstudents. Students make ideal rush customers because they are more willing to change their plans in hopes of obtaining last-minute tickets than other groups. Some opera companies also open up the rush tickets to seniors, another group that is easy to identify and generally has significant flexibility.

7. As a college student you probably don't have a lot of money to tip the restaurant host. But if you do have the money, it would make sense to tip the host. Here is why: First, your tip gets you seated sooner and avoids the wait time.

Time is money, so you save right there. Second, the host has an incentive to let tippers in sooner, and that's not just good for the host. It is also good for the business because tippers have much more inelastic demand, which translates into customers who spend more while dining. So the host is actually separating customers into two groups: tippers with inelastic demand and nontippers with much more elastic demand. Third, the restaurant wins because when tippers with inelastic demand get tables faster, the restaurant makes more revenue.

Monopolistic Competition and Advertising

Advertising increases the price of products without adding value for the consumer.

If you drive down a busy street, you will find many competing businesses, often right next to one another. For example, in most places a consumer in search of a quick meal has many choices, and more fast-food restaurants appear all the time. These competing firms advertise heavily. The temptation is to see advertising as driving up the price of a product without any benefit to the consumer. However, this misconception doesn't account for why firms advertise. In markets where competitors sell slightly differentiated products, advertising enables firms to inform their customers about new products and services. Yes, costs rise, but consumers also gain information to help make purchasing decisions. Consumers also benefit from added variety, and we all get a product that's pretty close to our vision of a perfect good—and no other market structure delivers that outcome.

In this chapter, we look at *monopolistic competition*, a widespread market structure that has features of both competitive markets and monopoly. We also explore the benefits and disadvantages of advertising, which is prevalent in markets with monopolistic competition.

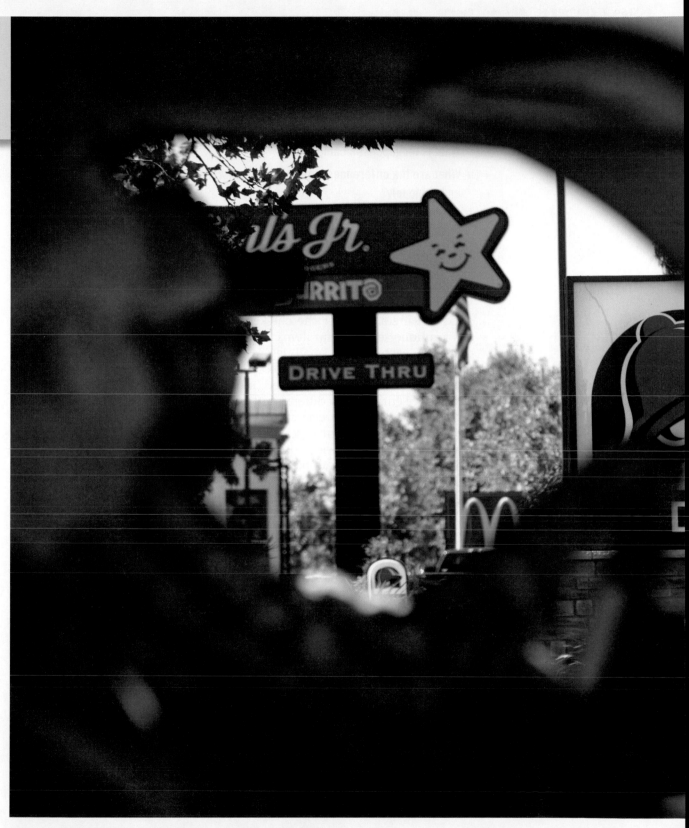

Want something to eat quickly? There are many choices.

BIG QUESTIONS

* What is monopolistic competition?
* What are the differences between monopolistic competition, competitive markets, and monopoly?
* Why is advertising prevalent in monopolistic competition?

What Is Monopolistic Competition?

Some consumers prefer the fries at McDonald's, while others may crave a salad at Panera Bread or the chicken at KFC. Each fast-food establishment has a unique set of menu items. The different products in fast-food restaurants give each seller a small degree of market power. This combination of market power and competition is typical of the market structure known as monopolistic competition. Indeed, **monopolistic competition** is characterized by free entry, many different firms, and product differentiation. **Product differentiation** is the process firms use to make a product more attractive to potential customers. Firms use product differentiation to contrast their product's unique qualities with competing products. The differences, which we will examine in detail, can be minor and can involve subtle changes in packaging, quality, availability, and promotion. Or the differences can be very significant. For example, some soup companies specialize in organic soups, which the consumers they are targeting would find an extremely important characteristic.

How does monopolistic competition compare with other market structures we have studied? As Table 12.1 shows, monopolistic competition falls between competitive markets and monopoly in terms of the number of sellers, the types of products sold, and competing firms' ability to enter and exit the market.

Monopolistic competition
is a type of market structure characterized by free entry, many different firms, and product differentiation.

Product differentiation
is the process that firms use to make a product more attractive to potential customers.

TABLE 12.1

Competitive Markets, Monopolistic Competition, and Monopoly

Competitive markets	Monopolistic competition	Monopoly
Many sellers	Many sellers	One seller
Similar products	Differentiated products	A unique product without close substitutes
Free entry and exit	Low barriers to entry and exit	Significant barriers to entry and exit

We have seen that firms in competitive markets do not have any market power. As a result, buyers can expect to find consistently low prices and wide availability. And we have seen that monopolies charge more and restrict the availability of a good or service. In markets that are monopolistically competitive, firms sell differentiated products. This differentiation gives the monopolistic competitor some market power, though not as much as a monopolist, which controls the entire market. Monopolistically competitive firms have a small amount of market power that enables them to search for the price that is most profitable.

To understand how monopolistic competition works, we begin with a closer look at product differentiation.

Product Differentiation

Monopolistically competitive firms create some market power through product differentiation. Differentiation can occur in a variety of ways, including style or type, location, and quality.

Style or Type

A trip to a mall is a great way to see product differentiation firsthand. For example, you will find many clothing stores, each offering a unique array of styles and types of clothing. Some stores, such as Abercrombie & Fitch, carry styles that attract younger customers. Others, such as Ann Taylor, appeal to older shoppers. Clothing stores can also vary by the type of clothing they sell, specializing in apparel such as business clothing, plus sizes, or sportswear. Each store hopes to attract a specific type of customer.

When you're ready for lunch at the mall, you can go to the food court, where many different places to eat offer a wide variety of choices. Where you decide to eat is a matter of your personal preferences and the price you are willing to pay. Like most consumers, you will select the place that gives you what you want while providing the best value for your money. Consumers' differing tastes make it possible for a wide range of food vendors to compete side by side with rivals who provide many good substitutes.

Location

Many businesses attract customers because of their convenient location. Gasoline stations, dry cleaners, barber shops, and car washes provide products and services that customers tend to choose on the basis of convenience of location rather than price. When consumers prefer to save time and to avoid the inconvenience of shopping for a better deal, a firm with a more convenient location will have some pricing power. As a result, producers who sell very similar products can generate some market power by locating their businesses along routes to and from work or in other areas where customers frequently travel.

Quality

Firms also compete on the basis of quality. For instance, if you want Mexican food, you can go to Taco Bell, which is inexpensive and offers food cooked in

Would you like your Mexican food cheaper . . .   . . . or fresher?

advance. In contrast, at Chipotle the food is freshly prepared and as a result more expensive. This form of product differentiation serves consumers quite well. Budget-conscious consumers can feast at Taco Bell, while those with a larger budget and a taste for higher-quality Mexican food can consider Chipotle as another option.

PRACTICE WHAT YOU KNOW

Product Differentiation: Would You Recognize a Monopolistic Competitor?

Is Hollister a monopolistic competitor?

Question: Which of the following is a monopolistic competitor?

a. a local apple farm that grows Red Delicious apples

b. Hollister, an apparel store

c. your local water company

Answers:

a. Because Red Delicious apples are widely available at grocery stores, this local apple farm does not have a differentiated product to sell. In addition, it has many competitors that grow exactly the same variety of apples. This apple farm is part of a competitive market; it is not a monopolistic competitor.

b. Hollister has a slightly different mix of clothes than competitors Abercrombie & Fitch and American Eagle Outfitters. This differentiation gives the brand some pricing power. Hollister is a good example of a monopolistically competitive firm.

c. Because water is essential and people cannot easily do without it, the local water company has significant monopoly power. Moreover, purifying and distributing water are subject to economies of scale. Your local water company is definitely a monopolist, not a monopolistic competitor.

What Are the Differences among Monopolistic Competition, Competitive Markets, and Monopoly?

Monopolistic competition occupies a place between competitive markets, which produce an efficient output at low prices, and monopoly, which produces an inefficient output at high prices. To help explain whether monopolistic competition is desirable or not, we consider the outcomes that individual firms can achieve when facing monopolistic competition in the short run and in the long run. Once you understand how monopolistic competition works, we will be able to compare the long-run equilibrium result with that of competitive markets and then determine if monopolistic competition is efficient.

Monopolistic Competition in the Short Run and the Long Run

A monopolistically competitive firm sells a differentiated product and for this reason has some market power. Recall that in perfect competition, each firm sells the same product, so competitors' products are perfect substitutes, which means that demand is perfectly elastic (flat). In monopolistic competition, each competitor provides a differentiated product, so competitors' products are imperfect substitutes for one another, which means that demand is relatively elastic (less flat), but still flatter (more elastic) than monopoly. Like a monopolist, the monopolistic competitor uses the profit-maximizing rule, MR = MC, and locates the corresponding point on its demand curve to determine the best price to charge and the best quantity to produce. Whether the firm earns a profit, experiences a loss, or breaks even is a function of other firms entering and exiting the market. Recall that entry and exit do not take place in the short run. In the long run, however, firms are free to enter an industry when they see a potential for profits or leave if they are making losses. Therefore, entry and exit regulate how much profit a firm can make in the long run.

Marginal thinking

Suppose you own a Hardee's fast-food restaurant in Asheville, North Carolina. Your business is doing well and making a profit. Then one day a Five Guys opens up across the street. Some of your customers will try Five Guys and switch, while others will still prefer your fare. But your profit will take a hit. Whether or not you stay in business will depend on how much business you lose. To understand how a business owner makes the decision to keep operating or to shut down, we now turn to the short-run and long-run implications of monopolistic competition.

Monopolistic Competition in the Short Run

Figure 12.1 depicts a firm, like Hardee's, in a monopolistically competitive environment. In panel (a), the firm makes a profit. Panel (b) shows the same firm incurring a loss after a new competitor, like Five Guys, opens nearby. In each case, the firm uses the profit-maximizing rule to determine the best price

FIGURE 12.1

The Monopolistically Competitive Firm in the Short Run

In this figure, we see how a single monopolistically competitive firm may make a profit or incur a loss depending on the demand conditions it faces. Notice that the marginal cost curve (MC) and average total cost curve (ATC) are identical in both panels because we are considering the same firm. The only functional difference is the location of the demand curve (D) and marginal revenue curve (MR). The demand in (a) is high enough for the firm to make a profit. In (b), however, there is not enough demand, so the firm experiences a loss.

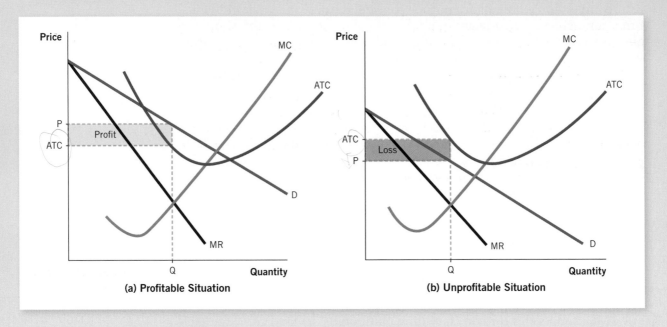

(a) Profitable Situation   (b) Unprofitable Situation

to charge by locating the point at which marginal revenue equals marginal cost. This calculation establishes the profit-maximizing output (Q) along the vertical dashed line. The firm determines the best price to charge (P) by following the dashed horizontal line from the demand curve to the vertical axis.

In panel (a), we see that because price is greater than average total cost (P > ATC), the firm makes a short-run economic profit. The situation in panel (b) is different. Because P < ATC, the firm experiences a short-run economic loss. What accounts for the difference? Because we are considering the same firm, the marginal cost (MC) and average total cost (ATC) curves are identical in both panels. The only functional difference is the location of the demand (D) and marginal revenue (MR) curves. The demand in panel (a) is high enough for the firm to make a profit. In panel (b), however, there is not enough demand; perhaps too many customers have switched to the new Five Guys. So even though the monopolistic competitor has some market power, if demand is too low, the firm may not be able to price its product high enough to make a profit.

Monopolistic Competition in the Long Run

In the long run, when firms can easily enter and exit a market, competition will drive economic profit to zero. This dynamic should be familiar to you from our previous discussions of competitive markets. If a firm is making an economic profit, that profit attracts new entrants to the business. Then the larger supply of competing firms will cause the demand for an individual firm's product to contract. Eventually, as more firms enter the market, it is no longer possible for existing firms to make an economic profit. A reverse process unfolds in the case of a market that is experiencing a loss. In this case, some firms exit the industry. Then consumers have fewer options to choose from, and the remaining firms experience an increase in demand. Eventually, demand increases to the point at which firms no longer experience a loss.

Figure 12.2 shows the market after the long-run adjustment process takes place. Price (P) is just equal to the average total cost of production (ATC) at the profit-maximizing rate of output (Q). At this point, firms are earning zero economic profit, as noted by P = ATC along the vertical axis; the market reaches a long-run equilibrium at the point where there is no reason for firms to enter or exit the industry. Note that the demand curve is drawn *tangent* to the average total cost curve (touching at one place). If demand were any larger, the result would look like panel (a) in Figure 12.1 and firms would experience an economic profit. Conversely, if demand were any lower, the result would look like panel (b) in Figure 12.1 and firms would experience an economic loss. Where entry and exit exist, profits and losses are not possible in the long run. In this way, monopolistic competition resembles a competitive market.

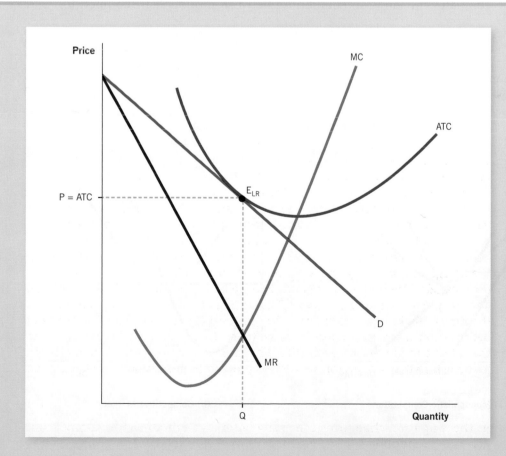

FIGURE 12.2

The Monopolistically Competitive Firm in the Long Run

Entry and exit cause short-run profits and losses to disappear in the long run, which means that the price charged (P) must be equal to the average total cost (ATC) of production. At this point, firms are earning zero economic profit, as noted by P = ATC along the vertical axis. The market reaches a long-run equilibrium (E_{LR}) at the point where there is no reason for firms to enter or exit the industry.

Returning to our example of Hardee's, the firm's success will attract attention and encourage rivals, like Five Guys, to enter the market. As a result, the short-run profits that Hardee's enjoys will erode. As long as profits occur in the short run, other competitors will be encouraged to enter, while short-run losses will prompt some existing firms to close. The dynamic nature of competition guarantees that long-run profits and losses are not possible.

Incentives

Monopolistic Competition and Competitive Markets

We have seen that monopolistic competition and competitive markets are similar; both market structures drive economic profit to zero in the long run. But monopolistic competitors enjoy some market power, which is a crucial difference. In this section, we compare pricing and output decisions in these two market structures. Then we look at issues of scale and output.

The Relationship between Price, Marginal Cost, and Long-Run Average Cost

Monopolistically competitive firms have some market power, which enables them to charge slightly more than firms in competitive markets. Figure 12.3 compares the long-run equilibrium between monopolistic competition and

FIGURE 12.3

The Long-Run Equilibrium in Monopolistic Competition and Competitive Markets

There are two primary differences between the long-run equilibrium in monopolistic competition (a) and a competitive market (b). First, monopolistic competition produces markup, because P is greater than MC. In a competitive market, P = MC. Second, the output in monopolistic competition is smaller than the efficient scale. In a competitive market, the firm's output is equal to the most efficient scale.

(a) **Monopolistic Competition**

(b) **Competitive Market**

a competitive market. Turning first to the firm in a market characterized by monopolistic competition, shown in panel (a), notice that the price (P) is greater than the marginal cost (MC) of making one more unit. The difference between P and MC is known as the markup. **Markup** is the difference between the price the firm charges and the marginal cost of production.

A markup is possible when a firm enjoys some market power. Products such as bottled water, cosmetics, prescription medicines, eyeglass frames, brand-name clothing, restaurant drinks, and greeting cards all have hefty markups. Let's focus on bottled water. In most cases, it costs just pennies to produce a bottle of water, but you're unlikely to find it for less than $1; there is a lot of markup on every bottle! Some firms differentiate their product by marketing their water as the "purest" or the "cleanest." Other companies use special packaging. While the marketing of bottled water is unquestionably a successful business strategy, the markup means that consumers pay more. You can observe this result in panel (a) of Figure 12.3, where the price under monopolistic competition is higher than the price in a competitive market, shown in panel (b).

Next, look at the ATC curves in both panels. Because a monopolistic competitor has a downward-sloping demand curve, the point of tangency between the demand curve and the ATC curve is different from the point of tangency in a competitive market. The point where P = ATC is higher under monopolistic competition. Panel (b) shows the demand curve just tangent to the ATC curve at ATC's lowest point in a competitive market. Consequently, we can say that monopolistic competition produces higher prices than a competitive market does. If this result seems odd to you, recall that entry and exit do not ensure the lowest possible price, only that the price is equal to the average total cost of production. In a competitive market, where the demand curve is horizontal, the price is always the lowest possible average total cost of production. This is not the case under monopolistic competition. However, the price in monopolistic competition often reflects quality; cheap food is cheap for a reason. Firms may charge more for higher-quality food, but there will still be zero economic profit.

Scale and Output

When a firm produces at an output level that is smaller than the output level needed to minimize average total costs, we say it has **excess capacity**. Turning back to panel (a) of Figure 12.3, we see excess capacity in the difference between Q and the efficient scale.

This result differs from what we see in panel (b) of Figure 12.3 for a competitive market. In a competitive market, the profit-maximizing output is equal to the most efficient scale of operation. This result is guaranteed because each firm sells an identical product and must therefore set its price equal to the minimum point on the average total cost curve. If, for instance, a corn farmer tried to sell a harvest for more than the prevailing market price, the farmer would not find any customers. In contrast, a monopolistic competitor in a food court enjoys market power because some customers prefer its product, which enables food court vendors to charge more than the lowest average total cost. Therefore, under monopolistic competition, the profit-maximizing output is less than the minimum efficient scale. Monopolistically competitive firms have the capacity to produce more output at a lower cost. But if they

Markup is the difference between the price the firm charges and the marginal cost of production.

Excess capacity occurs when a firm produces at an output level that is smaller than the output level needed to minimize average total costs.

Perrier has a distinctive look—but how different is it from other mineral water?

produced more, they would have to lower their price. Because a lower price decreases the firm's marginal revenue, it is more profitable for the monopolistic competitor to operate with excess capacity.

Monopolistic Competition, Inefficiency, and Social Welfare

Monopolistic competition produces a higher price and a lower level of output than a competitive market does. Recall that we looked at efficiency as a way to determine whether a firm's decisions are consistent with an output level that is beneficial to society. Does monopolistic competition display efficiency?

In Figure 12.3, panel (a), we observed that a monopolistic competitor has costs that are slightly above the lowest possible cost. So the average total costs of a monopolistically competitive firm are higher than those of a firm in a competitive market. This result is not efficient. To achieve efficiency, the monopolistically competitive firm could lower its price to what we would find in competitive markets. However, because a monopolistic competitor's goal is to make a profit, there is no incentive for the firm to lower its price. Every monopolistic competitor has a downward-sloping demand curve, so the demand curve cannot be tangent to the minimum point along the average total cost curve, as seen in panel (a).

Markup is a second source of inefficiency. We have seen that for a monopolistically competitive firm at the profit-maximizing output level, P > MC by an amount equal to the markup. The price reflects the consumer's willingness to pay, and this amount exceeds the marginal cost of production. A reduced markup would benefit consumers by lowering the price and decreasing the spread between the price and the marginal cost. If the firm did away with the markup entirely and set P = MC, the output level would benefit the greatest number of consumers. However, this result would not be practical. At the point where the greatest efficiency occurs, the demand curve would be below the average total cost curve and the firm would lose money. It is unreasonable to expect a profit-seeking firm to pursue a pricing strategy that would benefit its customers at the expense of its own profit.

What if the government intervened on behalf of the consumer? Increased efficiency could be achieved through government regulation. After all, the government regulates monopolists to reduce market power and restore social welfare. Couldn't the government do the same in monopolistically competitive markets? Yes and no! It is certainly possible, but not desirable. Monopolistically competitive firms have a limited amount of market power, so they cannot make a long-run economic profit like monopolists do. In addition, regulating the prices that firms in a monopolistically competitive market can charge would put many of them out of business. Bear in mind that we are talking about firms in markets like the fast-food industry. Doing away with a significant percentage of these firms would mean fewer places for consumers to grab a quick bite. The remaining restaurants would be more efficient, but with fewer restaurants the trade-off for consumers would be less convenience and fewer choices.

Regulating monopolistic competition through marginal cost pricing, or setting P = MC, would also create a host of problems like those we discussed for monopoly. A good proportion of the economy consists of monopolistically

Trade-offs

competitive firms, so the scale of the regulatory effort would be enormous. And because implementing marginal cost pricing would result in widespread losses, the government would need to find a way to subsidize the regulated firms to keep them in business. Because the only way to fund these subsidies would be higher taxes, the inefficiencies present in monopolistic competition do not warrant government action.

Varying Degrees of Product Differentiation

We have seen that products sold under monopolistic competition are more differentiated than those sold in a competitive market and less differentiated than those sold under monopoly. At one end of these two extremes we have competitive markets where firms sell identical products, have no market power, and face a perfectly elastic demand curve. At the other end we have a monopolist that sells a unique product without good substitutes and faces a steep downward-sloping demand curve indicative of highly inelastic demand. What about the firm that operates under monopolistic competition?

Figure 12.4 illustrates two monopolistic competitors with varying degrees of product differentiation. Firm A enjoys significant differentiation. High

FIGURE 12.4

Product Differentiation, Excess Capacity, and Efficiency

Firm A enjoys more product differentiation. As a result, it has more excess capacity and is less efficient. Firm B sells a product that is only slightly different from its competitors'. In this case, consumers have only weak preferences about which firm to buy from, and consumer demand is elastic. The results are a small amount of excess capacity and a more efficient result.

Firm A: More Product Differentiation

Firm B: Less Product Differentiation

Would you want to dress like this every day? Product variety is something consumers are willing to pay for.

levels of differentiation occur when the firm has an especially attractive location, style, type, or quality of product that is in high demand among consumers and that competitors cannot easily replicate. H&M, Urban Outfitters, and Abercrombie & Fitch are good examples. Consumers have strong brand loyalty for the clothes these firms sell, so the demand curve is quite inelastic. The relatively steep slope of the demand curve means that the point of tangency between the demand curve (D) and the average total cost curve (ATC) occurs at a high price, which produces a large amount of excess capacity. In contrast, firm B sells a product that is only slightly different from its competitors'. Here we can think of T.J.Maxx, Ross, and Marshalls—three companies that primarily sell discounted clothes. In this case, consumers have only weak preferences for a particular firm and

PRACTICE WHAT YOU KNOW

Markup: Punch Pizza versus Pizza Hut

Question: Punch Pizza is a small upscale chain in Minnesota that uses wood-fired ovens. In contrast, Pizza Hut is a large national chain. Which pizza chain would have a greater markup on each pizza?

Punch Pizza uses wood-fired ovens.

Answer: If you ask people in the Twin Cities about their favorite pizza, you will find a cultlike following for Punch Pizza. That loyalty translates into inelastic demand. Punch Pizza claims to make the best Neapolitan pie. Fans of this style of pizza gravitate to Punch Pizza for the unique texture and flavor. In contrast, Pizza Hut competes in the middle of the pizza market and has crafted a taste that appeals to a broader set of customers. Pizza Hut's customers can find many other places that serve a similar product, so these customers are much more price sensitive.

   The marginal cost of making pizza at both places consists of the dough, the toppings, and wages for labor. At Pizza Hut, pizza assembly is streamlined for efficiency. Punch Pizza is more labor intensive, but its marginal cost is still relatively low. The prices at Punch Pizza are much higher than at Pizza Hut. As a result, the markup—or the difference between the price charged and the marginal cost of production—is greater at Punch Pizza than at Pizza Hut.

consumer demand is elastic. The relatively flat nature of the demand curve means that the point of tangency between demand (D) and average total cost (ATC) occurs at a relatively low price, which produces a small amount of excess capacity.

Monopolistic competition leads to substantial product variety and greater selection and choice, all of which are beneficial to consumers. Therefore, any policy efforts that attempt to reduce inefficiency by lowering the prices that monopolistically competitive firms can charge will have the unintended consequence of limiting the product variety in the market. That sounds like a small price to pay for increased efficiency. But not so fast! Imagine a world without any product differentiation in clothes. One reason fashions go in and out of style is the desire among consumers to express their individuality. Therefore, consumers are willing to pay a little more for product variety in order to look different from everyone else.

Why Is Advertising Prevalent in Monopolistic Competition?

Advertising is a fact of daily life. It is also a means by which companies compete and therefore a cost of doing business in many industries. In the United States, advertising expenditures account for approximately 2% of all

Advertising

Super Bowl Commercials

The be-all and end-all of advertising spots is the televised Super Bowl. Because commercial time costs more than $4.5 million for a 30-second spot, examining the companies that advertise provides a useful barometer of economic activity. In 2015, three of the most popular commercials were by T-Mobile, Esurance, and Anheuser-Busch. They joined the usual suspects Coca-Cola and Pepsi (soft drinks), Tide (detergent), Paramount (motion pictures), and Volkswagen, Audi, Toyota, Mercedes-Benz, Kia, and Hyundai (autos) in buying advertising time.

Super Bowl ads highlight sectors of the economy that are thriving. In addition, firms that advertise during the Super Bowl build brand recognition,

Lost puppy meets Clydesdale: Anheuser-Busch created the top-rated Super Bowl commercial of 2015.

which helps to differentiate their product from the competition.

economic output annually. Worldwide, advertising expenses are a little less—about 1% of global economic activity. While the percentages are small in relative terms, in absolute terms worldwide advertising costs are over half a trillion dollars each year. Is this money well spent? Or is it a counterproductive contest that increases cost without adding value for the consumer? In this section, we will find that the answer is a little of both. Let's start by seeing who advertises.

Why Firms Advertise

No matter the company or slogan, the goal of advertising is to drive additional demand for the product being sold. Advertising campaigns use a variety of techniques to stimulate demand. In each instance, advertising is designed to highlight an important piece of information about the product. Table 12.2 shows how this process works. For instance, the FedEx slogan, "When it absolutely, positively has to be there overnight," conveys reliability and punctual service. Some customers who use FedEx are willing to pay a premium for overnight delivery because the company has differentiated itself from its competitors—UPS, DHL, and (especially) the United States Postal Service.

A successful advertising campaign will change the demand curve in two dimensions: it will shift the demand curve to the right and alter its shape. Turning to Figure 12.5, we see this change. First, the demand curve shifts to the right in response to the additional demand created by the advertising. Second, the demand curve becomes more inelastic, or slightly more vertical. This change in shape happens because advertising has highlighted features that make the product attractive to specific customers who are now more likely to want it. Because demand is more inelastic after advertising, the firm increases its market power and can raise its price.

In addition to increasing demand, advertising conveys information that consumers may find helpful in matching their preferences. Advertising tells us about the price of the goods offered, the location of products, and the introduction of new products. Firms also use advertising as a competitive mechanism to underprice one another. Finally, an advertising campaign signals quality. Firms that run expensive advertising campaigns are making a significant investment in their product. It is highly unlikely that a firm would spend a great deal on advertising if it did not think the process would yield a positive return. So a rational consumer can infer that firms spending a great deal on advertising are likely to have a higher-quality product than a competitor who does not advertise.

Advertising in Different Markets

Many firms engage in advertising, but advertising is not equally productive in all market structures. In our continuum from competitive markets to monopoly, markets that function under monopolistic competition invest the most in advertising.

TABLE 12.2

Advertising and Demand

Company / Product	Advertising slogan	How it increases demand
Convention and Visitors Authority / Las Vegas	*What happens here stays here.*	The slogan attempts to convince travelers that they will have a better vacation than anywhere else.
John Deere / tractors	*Nothing runs like a Deere.*	The emphasis on quality and performance appeals to buyers who desire a high-quality tractor.
Frito-Lay / Lay's potato chips	*Betcha can't eat just one.*	The message that one potato chip is not enough to satisfy your craving appeals to chip buyers who choose better taste over lower-priced generics.
Energizer / batteries	*He keeps going and going and going.*	The campaign focuses attention on longevity in order to justify the higher prices of top-quality batteries.
FedEx / delivery service	*When it absolutely, positively has to be there overnight.*	Reliability and timeliness are crucial attributes of overnight delivery.
Visa / credit card	*It's everywhere you want to be.*	Widespread acceptance and usability are two of the major reasons for carrying a credit card.
Avis / rental cars	*We're number two; we try harder.*	The emphasis on service encourages people to use the company.

FIGURE 12.5

Advertising and the Demand Curve

A successful advertising campaign increases demand. Advertising also makes the demand curve more inelastic, or vertical, by informing consumers about differences that they care about. After advertising, consumers desire the good more intensely, which makes the demand curve for the firm's product somewhat more vertical.

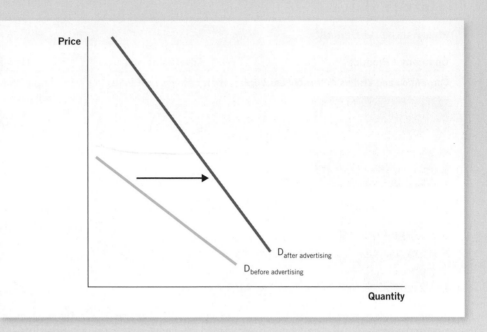

Advertising in Competitive Markets

As you know by now, competitive firms sell nearly identical products at an identical price. For this reason, advertising raises a firm's costs without directly influencing its sales. Advertising for a good that is undifferentiated functions like a public good for the industry as a whole: the benefits flow to every firm in the market through increased market demand for the product. However, each firm sells essentially the same good, so consumers can find the product at many competing locations at the same price. An individual firm that advertises in this market is at a competitive disadvantage because it will have higher costs that it cannot pass on to the consumer.

This does not mean that we never see advertising in competitive markets. Although individual firms do not benefit from advertising, competitive industries as a whole can. For example, you have probably heard the slogan "Beef—it's what's for dinner." The campaign, which began in 1992, is recognized by over 80% of Americans and has been widely credited with increasing the demand for beef products. The campaign was funded by the National Cattlemen's Beef Association, an organization that puts millions of dollars a year into advertising. In fact, industrywide marketing campaigns such as "It's not just for breakfast anymore" by the Florida Orange Juice Growers Association or "Got milk?" by the National Milk Processor Board generally indicate that competitive firms have joined forces to advertise in an effort to increase demand. Other examples include "the incredible, edible egg" and "pork—the other white meat."

Advertising

E.T.: The Extra-Terrestrial

The movie *E.T.* (1982) contains one of the most famous examples of product placement. In the movie, a boy leaves a trail of candy to bring E.T. closer to him. Originally, the filmmakers offered Mars the chance to have M&Ms used in the movie. Mars said no thanks. The filmmakers instead approached Hershey's, the manufacturers of Reese's Pieces—at that time a rival product of M&Ms that was not terribly successful. When *E.T.* became a blockbuster, the demand for Reese's Pieces suddenly tripled and firmly established the product in the minds of many Americans. How much did Hershey's pay for the product placement? It paid $1 million—not bad, considering how successful Reese's Pieces have become.

This is a great example of how firms must think beyond their advertising budgets and consider the strategic repercussions of possibly losing market share to a rival. Mars failed to protect its position in the market. ✳

Hungry for a snack?

Advertising under Monopolistic Competition

Advertising is widespread under monopolistic competition because firms have differentiated products. Let's look at the advertising behavior of pizza companies. Television commercials by national chains such as Domino's, Pizza Hut, Papa John's, and Little Caesars are widespread, as are flyers and advertisements for local pizza places. Because each pizza is slightly different, each firm's advertising increases the demand for its product. In short, the gains from advertising go directly to the firm spending the money. These benefits generate a strong incentive to advertise to gain new customers or to keep customers from switching to other products. Because each firm feels the same way, advertising becomes the norm among monopolistically competitive firms.

Incentives

Advertising and the Super Bowl

Super Bowl commercials are watched at least as closely as the football game itself. Fans love these usually creative and comedic ads. But economists pay close attention for different reasons. Who's advertising and what does it say about those industries? Are the ads money well spent, or do they increase business costs without making a noticeable difference in profits? Here we examine advertising over thirteen recent Super Bowls.

| | Amount Spent (2002–2014) | # of Super Bowls Advertised In | Average # of Ads per Super Bowl |

ANHEUSER-BUSCH
$337.4M — 13 — 8.3

Anheuser-Busch spends more than any other company on Super Bowl advertising to differentiate its product and create brand awareness.

PEPSI CO
$269.5M — 13 — 7.1

Coca-Cola has spent significantly less than PepsiCo on Super Bowl ads, yet it remains the market-leading soft drink brand. Coke has ramped up its Super Bowl efforts in the past few years to maintain this lead, however.

HYUNDAI
$148.5M — 9 — 5.6

COCA-COLA
$97M — 8 — 3.8

REVIEW QUESTIONS

- Draw what happens to a brand's demand curve when it successfully achieves product differentiation through advertising.

- Describe the risks and rewards of advertising from the perspective of both the brand and the consumer.

Some of these companies, especially Coca-Cola and Pepsi, are considered oligopolists rather than monopolistic competitors. We'll discuss oligopoly in the next chapter.

ECONOMICS IN THE REAL WORLD

What Happened to Sears?

Sears, JCPenney, Kohl's, and The Gap are all famous brick-and-mortar retailers. Depending on how old you are, at some point in your life you probably spent a lot of time in one of these stores. Kohl's and The Gap appear to be back on course for growth and viability. JCPenney might make it, too. But, after three straight years of posting a loss, it looks like Sears might be in a death spiral.

A few generations ago, a Sears credit card was as important as American Express. Sears is also historically important because it was the Sears catalog, first mailed in 1893, that allowed non–city dwellers access to products previously available only in cities.

So what has happened to Sears? Online giant Amazon and bad management have had major impacts since the mid-2000s. But Sears started losing business in the early 1990s. What happened then was the rapid rise of Walmart, which gave consumers significantly lower prices because of its sophisticated inventory control. By then, Sears had diversified into many areas, which caused it to lose focus on its main retail business. The rise of Walmart meant that Sears had to become more efficient (lower its markup) to survive, but because of the way Sears had expanded, its cost structure was higher than Walmart's.

What is the economics lesson that we extract from the Sears saga? A business must never take its success for granted, and you never know where your most fierce competitor will emerge from. Ever hear of Bentonville, Arkansas? That's where Walmart started (and is still headquartered). ✳

Source: Hiroko Tabuchi and Rachel Abrams, "4 Different Turnaround Tales at Retailers Sears, Kohl's, Gap and J.C. Penney," *New York Times*, Feb. 26, 2015.

Advertising as a Monopolist

The monopolist sells a unique product without close substitutes. The fact that consumers have few, if any, good alternatives when deciding to buy the good makes the monopolist less likely to advertise than a monopolistic competitor. When consumer choice is limited, the firm does not have to advertise to get business. In addition, the competitive aspect is missing, so there is no need to advertise to prevent consumers from switching to rival products. However, that does not mean that the monopolist never advertises.

The monopolist may wish to advertise to inform the consumer about its product and stimulate demand. This strategy can be beneficial as long as the gains from advertising are enough to cover the cost of advertising. For example, De Beers, the giant diamond cartel, controls most of the world's supply of rough-cut diamonds. The company does not need to advertise to fend off competitors, but it advertises nevertheless because it is interested in creating more demand for diamonds. De Beers created the famous "A diamond is forever" campaign.

The Negative Effects of Advertising

We have seen the benefits of advertising, but there are also drawbacks. Two of the most significant drawbacks are that advertising raises costs and can be deceitful.

Advertising and Costs

Advertising costs are reflected in the firm's average total cost curve. Figure 12.6 shows the paradox of advertising for most firms. When a firm advertises, it hopes to increase demand for the product and sell more units—say, from point 1 at Q_1 to point 2 at the higher quantity Q_2. If the firm can sell enough additional units, it will enjoy economies of scale, and the average total cost will fall from ATC_1 to ATC_2. This return on the advertising investment looks like a good business decision.

However, the reality of advertising is much more complex. Under monopolistic competition, each firm is competing with many other firms selling somewhat different products. Rival firms will respond with advertising of their own. This dynamic makes advertising the norm in monopolistic competition. Each firm engages in competitive advertising to win new customers and keep the old ones. As a result, the impact on each individual firm's demand largely cancels out. This result is evident in the movement from point 1 to point 3 in Figure 12.6. Costs rise from ATC_1 to ATC_3 on the higher LRATC curve, but demand (that is, quantity produced) may remain at Q_1. The net result is that advertising creates higher costs. In this case, we can think of advertising as causing a negative *business-stealing externality* whereby no individual firm can easily gain market share but feels compelled to advertise to protect its customer base.

We have seen that advertising raises costs for the producer. It also raises prices for consumers. In fact, consumers who consistently favor a particular brand of a product have more inelastic demand than those who are willing

FIGURE 12.6

Advertising Increases Cost

By advertising, the firm hopes to increase demand (or quantity) from point 1 to point 2. In this scenario, the increase in demand from Q_1 to Q_2 is large enough to create economies of scale even though advertising causes the long-run average total cost curve (LRATC) to rise. Because monopolistically competitive firms each advertise, the advertising efforts often cancel one another out. As a result, long-run average total costs rise without demand increasing much, so the firm may move from point 1 to point 3 instead.

Pearl ear studs are a nice gift, but they are even better when they come in a . . .

. . . blue box.

to switch from one product to another. Therefore, brand loyalty often means higher prices. Let's look at an example.

Suppose that you buy all your jewelry at Tiffany's. One day, you enter the store to pick up pearl ear studs. You can get a small pair of pearl studs at Tiffany's for $300. But it turns out that you can get studs of the same size, quality, and origin (freshwater) at Pearl World for $43, and you can find them online at Amazon for $19. There are no identifying marks on the jewelry that would enable you, or a seasoned jeweler, to tell the ear studs apart! Why would you buy them at Tiffany's when you can purchase them for far less elsewhere? The answer, it turns out, is that buying ear studs is a lot like consuming many other goods: name recognition matters. So do perception and brand loyalty. Many jewelry buyers also take cues from the storefront, how the staff dress, and how the jewelry is packaged. Spending $300 total is a lot of money for the privilege of getting Tiffany's blue box. Consumers believe that Tiffany's jewelry is better, when all that the store is doing is charging more markup.

PRACTICE WHAT YOU KNOW

Advertising: Brands versus Generics

Why do some frozen pizzas cost more than others when brands that offer similar quality are only a few feet away in the frozen foods aisle? To answer that question, consider the following questions:

Question: What would graphs showing price and output look like for DiGiorno and for a generic pizza? What is the markup for DiGiorno?

DiGiorno or generic?

(CONTINUED)

(CONTINUED)

Answer: Here is the graph for DiGiorno.

And here is the graph for the generic pizza.

Question: Which company has a stronger incentive to maintain strict quality control in the production process, DiGiorno or a generic brand? Why?

Answer: DiGiorno has a catchy slogan: "It's not delivery. It's DiGiorno!" This statement tries to position the product as being just as good as a freshly delivered pizza. Some customers who buy frozen pizzas will opt for DiGiorno over comparable generics because they are familiar with the company's advertising claim about its quality. Therefore, DiGiorno has a stronger incentive to make sure that the product delivers as advertised. Because generic, or store-name, brands are purchased mostly on the basis of price, the customer generally does not have high expectations about the quality.

Truth in Advertising

Finally, many advertising campaigns are not just informative—they are designed to produce a psychological response. When an ad moves you to buy or act in a particular way, it becomes manipulative. Because advertising can be such a powerful way to reach customers, there is a temptation to lie about a product. To prevent firms from spreading misinformation about their products, the Federal Trade Commission (FTC) regulates advertising and promotes economic efficiency. At the FTC, the Division of Advertising Practices protects consumers by enforcing truth-in-advertising laws. While the commission does not have enough resources to track down every violation, it does pay particular attention to claims involving food, nonprescription drugs, dietary supplements, alcohol, and tobacco. Unsubstantiated claims are particularly prevalent on the Internet, and they tend to target vulnerable populations seeking quick fixes to a variety of medical conditions.

Of course, even with regulatory oversight, consumers must still be vigilant. At best, the FTC can remove products from the market and levy fines against companies that make unsubstantiated claims. However, the damage is often already done. The Latin phrase *caveat emptor*, or "buyer beware," sums up the dangers of false information.

ECONOMICS IN THE REAL WORLD

The Federal Trade Commission versus Kevin Trudeau

Channel flippers will surely recognize Kevin Trudeau, who was a staple of infomercials for over a decade. Trudeau has a formula: he writes books about simple cures for complex medical conditions. He is an engaging smooth talker. The infomercial is usually a "conversation" between Trudeau and a good-looking woman who seems very excited to learn more about the product. Unfortunately, Trudeau's claims are often unsubstantiated.

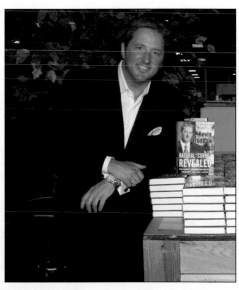

In 2009, a federal judge ordered Trudeau to pay more than $37 million for misrepresenting the content of his book *The Weight Loss Cure "They" Don't Want You to Know About* and banned him from appearing in infomercials for three years. This was not the first time that the FTC had taken Trudeau to task. The commission first filed a lawsuit against him in 1998, charging him with making false and misleading claims in infomercials for products that he claimed could cause significant weight loss, cure drug addictions, and improve memory.

Do you trust this guy?

After failing to pay the fines levied against him, Trudeau was sent to federal prison in 2014. ✳

ECONOMICS FOR LIFE

Product Differentiation: Would You Buy a Franchise?

Franchises are valuable in markets where product differentiation matters. McDonald's, Panera Bread, and KFC all have a different take on serving fast food. But what does it mean to own a franchise?

Franchises are sold to individual owners, who operate subject to the terms of their agreement with the parent company. For instance, purchasing a McDonald's franchise, which can cost as much as $2 million, requires the individual restaurant owner to charge certain prices and offer menu items selected by the parent corporation. As a result, customers who prefer a certain type and quality of food know that the dining experience at each McDonald's will be similar. Most franchises also come with noncompete clauses that guarantee that another franchise will not open nearby. This guarantee gives the franchise owner the exclusive right to sell a differentiated product in a given area.

Suppose that you want to start a restaurant. Why would you, or anyone else, be willing to pay as much as $2 million just for the right to sell food? For that amount, you could open your own restaurant with a custom menu and interior, create your own marketing plan, and locate anywhere you like. For example, Golden Corral and Buffalo Wild Wings are two restaurants with high franchising fees that exceed $1 million. Golden Corral is the largest buffet-style restaurant in the country, and Buffalo Wild Wings is one of the top locations to watch sporting events. You might think that it would make more sense to avoid the franchising costs by opening your own buffet

How much do different franchises cost?

or setting up a bank of big-screen TVs. However, failures in the restaurant industry are high. With a franchise, the customer knows what to expect. Translation: high franchise fees enable firms to charge a higher markup because consumer demand is more inelastic.

Franchise owners are assured of visibility and a ready supply of customers. Purchasing a franchise means that more potential customers will notice your restaurant, and that drives up revenues. Is that worth $2 million? Yes, in some cases. Suppose that you'll do $1 million in annual sales as part of a franchise, but only $0.5 million on your own. That half-million difference over 20 years means $10 million more in revenue, a healthy chunk of which will turn into profits. This is the magic of franchising.

Conclusion

We began this chapter by discussing the misconception that advertising increases the price of goods and services without adding value for the consumer. Advertising does cost money, but that does not mean it is harmful. Firms willingly spend on advertising because it can increase demand, build brand loyalty, and provide consumers with useful information about differences in products. Monopolistic competitors advertise and mark up their products like monopolists, but, like firms in a competitive market, they cannot earn long-run profits. While an economic profit is possible in the short run in all three types of market structure (perfect competition, monopolistic competition, and monopoly), only the monopolist, whose business has significant barriers to entry, can earn an economic profit in the long run. Entry and exit cause long-run profits to equal zero in competitive and monopolistically competitive firms.

Monopolistic competitors are price makers who fail to achieve the most efficient welfare-maximizing output for society. But this observation does not tell the entire story. Monopolistic competitors do not have as much market power or create as much excess capacity or markup as monopolists. Consequently, the monopolistic competitor lacks the ability to exploit consumers. The result is not perfect, but widespread monopolistic competition generally serves consumers and society well.

In the next chapter, we continue our exploration of market structure with *oligopoly*, which produces results that are much closer to monopoly than monopolistic competition.

ANSWERING THE BIG QUESTIONS

What is monopolistic competition?

✳ Monopolistic competition is a market structure characterized by free entry and many firms selling differentiated products.

✳ Differentiation of products takes three forms: differentiation by style or type, location, and quality.

What are the differences between monopolistic competition, competitive markets, and monopoly?

✳ Monopolistic competitors, like monopolists, are price makers that have downward-sloping demand curves. Whenever the demand curve is downward sloping, the firm is able to mark up the price above marginal cost. The results are excess capacity and an inefficient level of output.

✳ In the long run, barriers to entry enable a monopoly to earn an economic profit. This is not the case for monopolistic competition or competitive markets.

Why is advertising prevalent in monopolistic competition?

✳ Advertising performs useful functions under monopolistic competition: it conveys information about the price of the goods offered for sale, the location of products, and new products. It also signals differences in quality. However, advertising also encourages brand loyalty, which makes it harder for other businesses to successfully enter the market. Advertising can be manipulative and misleading.

CONCEPTS YOU SHOULD KNOW

excess capacity (p. 371)
markup (p. 371)

monopolistic competition
(p. 364)

product differentiation (p. 364)

QUESTIONS FOR REVIEW

1. Why is product differentiation necessary for monopolistic competition? What are three types of product differentiation?

2. How is monopolistic competition like competitive markets? How is monopolistic competition like monopoly?

3. Why do monopolistically competitive firms produce less than those operating at the most efficient scale of production?

4. Draw a graph that shows a monopolistic competitor making an economic profit in the short run and a graph that shows a monopolistic competitor making no economic profit in the long run.

5. Monopolistic competition produces a result that is inefficient. Does this outcome mean that monopolistically competitive markets should be regulated? Discuss.

6. Draw a typical demand curve for competitive markets, monopolistic competition, and monopoly. Which of these demand curves is the most inelastic? Why?

7. How does advertising benefit society? In what ways can advertising be harmful?

STUDY PROBLEMS (*solved at the end of the section)

* 1. At your high school reunion, a friend describes his plan to take a break from his florist shop and sail around the world. He says that if he continues to make the same economic profit for the next five years, he will be able to afford the trip. Do you think your friend will be able to achieve his dream in five years? What do you expect to happen to his firm's profits in the long run?

2. Which of the following could be considered a monopolistic competitor?

   a. a local corn farmer
   b. the Tennessee Valley Authority, a large electricity producer
   c. pizza delivery
   d. a grocery store
   e. Kate Spade, fashion designer

3. Which of the following are the same under monopolistic competition and in a competitive market in the long run?

   a. the markup the firm charges
   b. the price the firm charges to consumers
   c. the firm's excess capacity
   d. the average total cost of production
   e. the amount of advertising

   f. the firm's profit
   g. the efficiency of the market structure

4. In competitive markets, price is equal to marginal cost in the long run. Explain why this statement is not true for monopolistic competition.

5. Econoburgers, a fast-food restaurant in a crowded local market, has reached a long-run equilibrium.

   a. Draw a diagram showing demand, marginal revenue, average total cost, and marginal cost curves for Econoburgers.
   b. How much profit is Econoburgers making?
   c. Suppose that the government decides to regulate burger production to make it more efficient. Explain what would happen to the price of Econoburgers and the firm's output.

* 6. Consider two different companies. The first manufactures cardboard, and the second sells books. Which firm is more likely to advertise?

7. In the diagram below, identify the demand curve consistent with a monopolistic competitor making zero long-run economic profit. Explain why you have chosen that demand curve and why the other two demand

curves are not consistent with monopolistic competition.

8. Titleist has an advertising slogan: "the #1 ball in golf." Consumers can also buy generic golf balls. The manufacturers of generic golf balls do not engage in any advertising. Assume that the average total cost of producing Titleist and generic golf balls is the same.
   a. Create a graph showing the price and the markup for Titleist.
   b. In a separate graph, show the price and output for the generic firms.
   c. Who has a stronger incentive to maintain strict quality control in the production process—Titleist or the generic firms? Why?

9. Taste of India is a small restaurant in a small town. The owner of Taste of India marks up his dishes by 300%. Indian Cuisine is a small restaurant in a large city. The owner of Indian Cuisine marks up her dishes by 200%. Explain why the markup is higher in the small town.

✱ 10. Read the following online article: http://20somethingfinance.com/why-eyeglasses-are-so-expensive-how-you-can-pay-less/. Using your understanding of monopolistic competition and markup, explain why retail customers pay so much more for eyeglasses than online customers.

SOLVED PROBLEMS

1. The florist business is monopolistically competitive. This means that firms are free to enter and exit at any time. Firms will enter because your friend's shop is making an economic profit. As new florist shops open, the added competition will drive prices down, causing your friend's profits to fall. In the long run, this means that he will not be able to make an economic profit. He will earn only enough to cover his opportunity costs, or what is known as a *fair return* on his investment. That is not to say that he won't be able to save enough to sail around the world, but it won't happen as fast as he would like because other firms will enter the market and limit his profits going forward.

6. The cardboard firm manufactures a product that is a component used mostly by other firms that need to package final products for sale. As a result, any efforts at advertising will only raise costs without increasing the demand for cardboard. This situation contrasts with that of the bookseller, who advertises to attract consumers to the store. More traffic means more purchases of books and other items sold in the store. The bookstore has some market power and markup. In this case, it pays to advertise. A cardboard manufacturing firm sells exactly the same product as other cardboard producers, so it has no market power, and any advertising expenses will only make its cost higher than its rivals'.

10. There are many retailers (LensCrafters, Pearle, Sears, Target), but the brands that they sell all come from Italian eyeglass manufacturer Luxottica. Luxottica prevents these major retailers from discounting the frames and will pull their brands if they do. However, if you don't care about the brand of eyeglasses that you wear, you can find a pair online for well under $100. Online retailers aren't selling a brand, so they attract customers with much more elastic demand compared with customers who want their frames to be fashionable. This scenario fits perfectly with the idea of markup. Firms with brand-loyal customers have much higher markup than firms with customers who do not care about the brand they purchase.

Oligopoly and Strategic Behavior

Cell phone companies are highly competitive.

If you have a cell phone, chances are that you receive service from one of four major cell phone carriers in the United States: AT&T, Verizon,

MIS CONCEPTION

Sprint, or T-Mobile. Together, these firms control 95% of all cellular service. In some respects, this market is very competitive. For example, cell phone companies advertise intensely, and they offer a variety of phones with voice and data plans. Also, there are differences in network coverage and in the number of applications users can access. But despite outward appearances, the cell phone companies do not do business in a competitive or even a monopolistically competitive market. How can we explain this misconception? An important factor is the expense of building and maintaining a cellular network. The largest cell phone companies have invested billions of dollars in infrastructure. Therefore, the cost of entry is very high. As we learned in Chapter 10, barriers to entry are a key feature of monopolies.

The cell phone industry has features of both competition and monopoly: competition is fierce, but smaller firms and potential entrants into the market find it difficult to enter and compete. This mixture of characteristics represents another form of market structure—*oligopoly*. In this chapter, we examine oligopoly by comparing it with other market structures that are already familiar to you. We then look at some of the strategic behaviors that firms in an oligopoly employ, an examination that leads us into the fascinating topic of game theory.

Lots of advertising and regular promotions lead most people to view cell phone carriers as highly competitive firms. But are these companies really competitive or even monopolistically competitive?

BIG QUESTIONS

* What is oligopoly?
* How does game theory explain strategic behavior?
* How do government policies affect oligopoly behavior?
* What are network externalities?

What Is Oligopoly?

Oligopoly is a form of market structure that exists when a small number of firms sell a differentiated product in a market with high barriers to entry.

Oligopoly is a form of market structure that exists when a small number of firms sell a product in a market with significant barriers to entry. An oligopolist is like a monopolistic competitor in that it often sells a differentiated product. But like pure monopolists, oligopolists enjoy significant barriers to entry. Table 13.1 compares the differences and similarities between the four market structures.

We have seen that firms in monopolistically competitive markets usually have a limited amount of market power. As a result, buyers often find low prices and wide availability. In contrast, an oligopolist sells in a market with significant barriers to entry and fewer rivals. Thus, the oligopolist has more market power than a firm operating under monopolistic competition. However, because an oligopolistic market has more than one seller, no single oligopolist has as much market power as a monopolist.

Our study of oligopoly begins with a look at how economists measure market power in an industry. We then work through a simplified model of oligopoly to explore the choices that oligopolists make.

Measuring the Concentration of Industries

In markets with only a few sellers, industry output is highly concentrated among a few large firms. Economists use *concentration ratios* as a measure of the oligopoly power present in an industry. The most common measure, known as the four-firm concentration ratio, expresses the sales of the four largest firms in an industry as a percentage of that industry's total sales.

TABLE 13.1

Comparing Oligopoly to Other Market Structures

Competitive market	Monopolistic competition	Oligopoly	Monopoly
Many sellers	Many sellers	A few sellers	One seller
Similar products	Differentiated product	Differentiated product (most of the time)	Unique product without close substitutes
Free entry and exit	Easy entry and exit	Barriers to entry	Significant barriers to entry

TABLE 13.2

Highly Concentrated Industries in the United States

Industry	Concentration ratio of the four largest firms (%)	Top firms
Search engines	98.5	Google, Yahoo, Microsoft
Wireless telecommunications	94.7	Verizon, AT&T, Sprint Nextel, T-Mobile
Satellite TV providers	94.5	DIRECTV, DISH Network
Soda production	93.7	Coca-Cola, PepsiCo, Dr Pepper Snapple
Sanitary paper products	92.7	Kimberly-Clark, Procter & Gamble, Georgia-Pacific
Lighting and bulb manufacturing	91.9	General Electric, Philips, Siemens
Tire manufacturing (domestic)	91.3	Goodyear, Michelin, Cooper, Bridgestone
Major household appliances	90.0	Whirlpool, Electrolux, General Electric, LG
Automobile manufacturing (domestic)	87.0	General Motors, Toyota, Ford, Daimler-Chrysler

Source: *Highly Concentrated: Companies That Dominate Their Industries*, www.ibisworld.com. Special Report, February 2012.

Table 13.2 lists the four-firm concentration ratios for highly concentrated industries in the United States. This ratio is determined by taking the output of the four largest firms in an industry and dividing that output by the total production in the entire industry.

In highly concentrated industries like search engines, wireless telecommunications, and satellite TV providers, the market share held by the four largest firms approaches 100%. At the bottom of our list of most concentrated industries is domestic automobile manufacturing. General Motors, Chrysler Group, Ford, and Toyota (which has seven manufacturing plants in the United States) dominate the domestic automobile industry. These large firms have significant market power.

However, when evaluating market power in an industry, it is important to be aware of international activity. In several industries, including automobile and tire manufacturing, intense global competition keeps the market power of U.S. companies in check. For instance, domestic manufacturers that produce automobiles also must compete globally against cars that are produced elsewhere. This means that vehicles produced by Honda, Nissan, Volkswagen, Kia, and Volvo, to name just a few companies, limit the market power of domestic producers. As a result, the concentration ratio is a rough gauge of oligopoly power—not an absolute measure.

Competition from foreign car companies keeps the market power of the U.S.-based automobile companies in check.

Collusion and Cartels in a Simple Duopoly Example

In this section, we explore the two conflicting tendencies found in oligopoly: oligopolists would like to act like monopolists, but they often end up competing like monopolistic competitors. To help us understand oligopoly behavior, we start with a simplified example: an industry consisting of only two firms, known as a *duopoly*. Duopolies (such as Boeing and Airbus in the wide-body jet market) are rare in national and international markets, but not that uncommon in small, local markets. For example, in many small communities, the number of cell phone carriers is limited. Imagine a small town where only two providers have cell phone towers. In this case, the cell towers are a sunk cost (see Chapter 9); both towers were built to service all of the customers in the town, so each carrier has substantial excess capacity when the customers are divided between the two carriers. Also, because there is extra capacity on each network, the marginal cost of adding additional customers is zero.

Table 13.3 shows the community's demand for cell phones. Because the prices and quantities listed in the first two columns are negatively related, the data are consistent with a downward-sloping demand curve.

TABLE 13.3

The Demand Schedule for Cell Phones

Here we assume that 1 customer = 1 cell phone = 1 purchase of cell phone service.

(1) Price/month (P)	(2) Number of customers (Q)	(3) Total revenue (TR) (P) × (Q)
$180	0	$0
165	100	16,500
150	200	30,000
135	300	40,500
120	400	48,000
105	500	52,500
90	600	54,000
75	700	52,500
60	800	48,000
45	900	40,500
30	1,000	30,000
15	1,100	16,500
0	1,200	0

Column 3 calculates the total revenue from columns 1 and 2. With Table 13.3 as our guide, we will examine the output in this market under three scenarios: competition, monopoly, and duopoly.

Duopoly sits between the two extremes. Competition still exists, but it is not as extensive as you would see in competitive markets, which ruthlessly drive the price down to cost. Nor does the result always mirror that of monopoly, where competitive pressures are completely absent. In an oligopoly, a small number of firms feel competitive pressures and also enjoy some of the advantages of monopoly.

Competitive Outcome

Marginal thinking

Recall that competitive markets drive prices down to the point at which marginal revenue is equal to the marginal cost. So if the market is highly competitive and the marginal cost is zero, we would expect the final price of cell phone service to be zero and the quantity supplied to be 1,200 customers—the number of people who live in the small town. At this point, anyone who desires cell phone service would be able to receive it without cost. Because efficiency exists when the output is maximized, and because everyone who lives in the community would have cell phone service, the result would be socially efficient. However, it is unrealistic to expect this outcome. Cell phone companies provide a good that is nonrival and also excludable; in other words, they sell a club good (see Chapter 7). Because these firms are in business to make money, they will not provide something for nothing.

Monopoly Outcome

At the other extreme of the market structure continuum, a monopolist faces no competition, and price decisions do not depend on the activity of other firms. A monopolist can search for the price that brings it the most profit. Looking at Table 13.3, we see that total revenue peaks at $54,000. At this point, the price is $90 per month, and 600 customers sign up for cell phone service. The total revenue is the monopolist's profit because the marginal cost is zero. Notice that the monopolist's price, $90, is more than the marginal cost of $0. In this case, the monopolist's marginal revenue is $1,500. The marginal revenue is determined by looking at column 3 and observing that total revenue rises from $52,500 to $54,000—an increase of $1,500. Because the firm serves 100 additional customers, the marginal revenue is $15 per customer. When the price drops to $75, marginal revenue is −$1,500, because total revenue falls from $54,000 to $52,500. Dividing −$1,500 by 100 yields a marginal revenue of −$15 per customer. The monopolist will maximize profit where MC = MR = 0, and the point closest to this in Table 13.3 is somewhere between P = $90 and P = $75, but we will use P = $90 for simplicity's sake. Compared with a competitive market, the monopoly price is higher and the quantity sold is lower. The result is a loss of efficiency.

Duopoly Outcome

In a duopoly, the two firms can decide to cooperate—even though this practice is illegal in the United States, as we will discuss shortly. If the duopolists cooperate, we say that they collude. **Collusion** is an agreement between rival firms that specifies the price each firm charges and the quantity it produces.

Collusion is an agreement among rival firms that specifies the price each firm charges and the quantity it produces.

A **cartel** is a group of two or more firms that act in unison.

Antitrust laws attempt to prevent oligopolies from behaving like monopolies.

Incentives

Mutual interdependence is a market situation where the actions of one firm have an impact on the price and output of its competitors.

The firms that collude can act like a single monopolist to maximize their profits. In this case, the monopolist would maximize its profit by charging $90 and serving 600 customers. If the duopolists divide the market equally, they will each have 300 customers who pay $90, for a total of $27,000 in revenue.

When two or more firms act in unison, economists refer to them as a **cartel**. Many countries prohibit cartels. In the United States, **antitrust laws** prohibit collusion. However, even if collusion were legal, it would probably fail more often than not. Imagine that two theoretical cell phone companies, AT-Phone and Horizon, have formed a cartel and agreed that each will serve 300 customers at a price of $90 per month per customer. But AT-Phone and Horizon each have an incentive to earn more revenue by cheating while the rival company keeps the agreement. Suppose that AT-Phone believes that Horizon will continue to serve 300 customers per their collusive agreement, and AT-Phone lowers its price to $75. Looking at Table 13.3, we see that at this price the total market demand rises to 700 customers. So AT-Phone will be able to serve 400 customers, and its revenue will be 400 × $75, or $30,000. This is an improvement of $3,000 over what AT-Phone made when the market price was $90 and the customers were equally divided.

How would Horizon react? First, it would be forced to match AT-Phone's lower price, which would lower the revenue from its 300 customers to $22,500. In this position, there's no reason for Horizon to sit on the sideline and do nothing. If it decides to match AT-Phone's market share of 400 customers by lowering its price to $60, it would increase its revenue to 400 × $60, or $24,000. AT-Phone would match that price and make the same revenue, leaving each firm making $3,000 less than when they served only 600 customers total. From what we know about competitive markets, we might expect the competition between the two firms to cause a price war in which price eventually falls to zero. Duopolists are unlikely to participate in an all-out price war because both firms would no longer be making any profit, but we cannot be sure to what extent competitive pressures will determine each firm's decision.

Table 13.4 summarizes the different results under competition, duopoly, and monopoly using our cell phone example. From this example, we see that a market with a small number of sellers is characterized by **mutual interdependence**, which is a market situation in which the actions of one firm have an impact on the price and output of its competitors. As a result, a firm's market share is determined by the products it offers, the price it charges, and the actions of its rivals.

Oligopolists want to emulate the monopoly outcome, but the push to compete with their rivals often makes it difficult to maintain a cartel. Yet the idea that cartels are unstable is not guaranteed. In the appendix to this chapter, we explore two alternative theories that oligopolists will form long-lasting cartels. When a stable cartel is not achieved, firms in oligopoly fall short of fully maximizing profits. But they do not compete to the same degree as firms in competitive markets either. Therefore, when a market is an oligopoly, output is likely to be higher than under monopoly and lower than within a competitive market. As you would expect, the amount of output affects the prices. The higher output (compared with monopoly) makes oligopoly prices generally lower than monopoly prices, and the lower output (compared with a competitive market) makes oligopoly prices higher than those found in competitive markets.

TABLE 13.4

Outcomes under Competition, Duopoly, and Monopoly

	Competitive markets	Duopoly	Monopoly
Price	$0	$0–90	$90
Output	1,200	600–1200	600
Socially Efficient?	Yes	Only when the price is $0 and output is 1200	No
Explanation	Because the marginal cost of providing cell phone service is zero, the price is eventually driven to zero. Since firms are in business to make a profit, it is unrealistic to expect this result.	Because each firm is mutually interdependent, it adopts a strategy based on the actions of its rival. The two firms may decide to collude and charge $90, or competitive pressures may lead them to charge a much lower price.	The monopolist is free to choose the profit-maximizing output. In the cell phone example, it maximizes its total revenue. As a result, the monopolist charges $90 and serves 600 customers.

ECONOMICS IN THE REAL WORLD

OPEC: An International Cartel

The best-known cartel is the Organization of the Petroleum Exporting Countries, or OPEC, a group of oil-exporting countries that have a significant influence on the world price of crude oil and the output of petroleum. To maintain relatively high oil prices, the member nations collude to limit the overall supply of oil. While OPEC's activities are legal under international law, collusion is illegal under U.S. antitrust law.

OPEC controls almost 60% of the world's known oil reserves and accounts for almost one-third of the world's crude production, giving the cartel's 12 member nations significant control over the world price of oil. OPEC's production is dominated by Saudi Arabia, which accounts for approximately 40% of OPEC's reserves and production. As is the case within any organization, conflict inevitably arises. In the 50 years that OPEC has existed, there have been embargoes (government prohibitions on the trade of oil), oil gluts, production disputes, and periods of falling prices. As a result, OPEC has been far from perfect in consistently maintaining high prices. In addition, OPEC has been careful to keep the price of oil below the cost of alternative energy options. Despite the limitations on OPEC's pricing power, OPEC has effectively acted as a cartel during the periods when it adopted output rationing to maintain price. In 2014, however, oil prices fell dramatically as a result of the oil shale boom in the United States and Canada. Shale technology has significantly reduced OPEC's control over worldwide oil production and price. ✳

What would oil prices be like if OPEC didn't exist?

Nash Equilibrium

A Brilliant Madness and *A Beautiful Mind*

A Brilliant Madness (2002) is the story of a mathematical genius, John Nash, whose career was cut short by a descent into madness. At the age of 30, Nash began claiming that aliens were communicating with him. He spent the next three decades fighting paranoid schizophrenia. Before this time, while he was a graduate student at Princeton, Nash wrote a proof about noncooperative equilibrium. The proof established the Nash equilibrium and became a foundation of modern economic theory. In 1994, Nash was awarded a Nobel Prize in Economics. The documentary features interviews with John Nash, his wife, his friends and colleagues, and experts in both economics and mental illness. Nash died in 2015.

The 2001 film *A Beautiful Mind*, directed by Ron Howard, is based on the life of Nash but does not adhere strictly to the facts. If you watch *A Brilliant Madness* and then watch the famous bar scene in *A Beautiful Mind*, you'll see that Ron Howard attempts to depict a Nash equilibrium when we see the men and women dancing together. *A Beautiful Mind* won the Academy Award for Best Picture, but the film's most famous scene is infamous among economists because it does not depict a Nash equilibrium. If

Russell Crowe plays John Nash, who revolutionized modern microeconomics.

you are curious about why this is the case, read the section on the Nash equilibrium and then read the spoiler in the conclusion of this chapter. ✳

The Nash Equilibrium

In oligopoly, the process that leads to equilibrium may take on a special form referred to as a *Nash equilibrium*, named for mathematician John Nash.

A **Nash equilibrium** occurs when all economic decision-makers opt to keep the status quo. The theoretical phone example we just explored was an example of a Nash equilibrium. The best strategy for AT-Phone and Horizon is to increase their output to 400 customers each. When both firms reach that level of output, neither has an incentive to change. Bear in mind that the rivals can do better if they collude. Under collusion, each rival serves 300 customers and their combined revenues rise. However, as we saw, if one rival is willing to break the cartel, it will make more revenue if it serves 400 customers ($30,000) while the other firm continues to serve only 300 ($22,500). The firms continue to challenge each other until they reach a combined output

*A **Nash equilibrium** occurs when all economic decision-makers opt to keep the status quo.*

level of 800 customers. At this point, the market reaches a Nash equilibrium and neither firm has a reason to change its short-term profit-maximizing strategy.

Oligopoly with More Than Two Firms

We have seen how firms behave in a duopoly. What happens when more firms enter the market? The addition of a third firm complicates efforts to maintain a cartel and increases the possibility of a more competitive result.

We can see this interaction in the cell phone market. The four major companies are not all equal. AT&T and Verizon are significantly larger than Sprint and T-Mobile. If AT&T and Verizon were the only two providers, the market might have very little competition. However, the smaller Sprint and T-Mobile play a crucial role in changing the market dynamic. Even though Sprint and T-Mobile have significantly less market share, they still have developed extensive cellular networks in order to compete. Because Sprint and T-Mobile have networks with smaller subscriber bases and significant excess capacity, they both aggressively compete on price. As a result, in many (but not all) respects, the entire cell phone industry functions competitively.

To see why, consider what the addition of a third firm will do to the market. When the third firm enters the market, there are two effects to consider—price and output. For example, if the third firm builds a cell tower, it will increase the overall capacity to provide cell phone service. As we observed in the duopoly example, if the total number of cell phone contracts (the supply)

PRACTICE WHAT YOU KNOW

Oligopoly: Can You Recognize the Oligopolist?

Question: Which firm is the oligopolist?

a. Firm A is in retail. It is one of the largest and most popular clothing stores in the country. It also competes with many rivals and faces intense price competition.

b. Firm B is in the airline industry. It is not the largest carrier, but significant barriers to entry enable it to serve a number of very profitable routes.

c. Firm C is a restaurant in a small, isolated community. It is the only local eatery. People drive from miles away to eat there.

Is an airline a good example of an oligopolist?

Answer: Firm A sells clothing, a product with many competing brands and outlets. The competition is intense, which means that the firm has little market power. As a result, firm A is a player in a competitive market. It is not an oligopolist. Firm B has market power on a number of routes it flies. Because barriers to entry prevent new carriers from securing gate space, even smaller airlines are oligopolists—as is firm B. Firm C is a monopolist. It is the only place to eat out in the isolated community, and no other restaurant is nearby. It is not an oligopolist.

A **price effect** reflects how a change in price affects the firm's revenue.

increases, all the firms must charge a lower price. This is the **price effect**, and it reflects how a change in price affects the firm's revenue. But because the marginal cost of providing cell phone service is essentially zero, the price that each firm charges is substantially higher than the marginal cost of adding a new customer to the network. When the firm sells an additional unit, it generates additional revenues for the firm. This **output effect** occurs when a change in price affects the number of customers in a market.

An **output effect** occurs when a change in price affects the number of customers in a market.

The price effect and output effect make it difficult to maintain a cartel when there are more than two firms. Generally, as the number of firms grows, each individual firm becomes less concerned about its impact on the overall price, because any price above marginal cost creates a profit. Therefore, individual firms are more willing to lower prices because doing so creates a large output effect for the individual firm and only a small price effect in the market.

Of course, not all firms are the same size. Therefore, smaller and larger firms in an oligopolistic market react differently to the price and output effects. Increased output at smaller firms will have a negligible impact on overall prices because small firms represent only a tiny fraction of the market supply. But the same is not true for firms with a large market share. Decisions at these firms will have a substantial impact on price and output because the overall amount supplied in the market will change appreciably. In other words, in an oligopoly, the decisions of one firm directly affect other firms.

How Does Game Theory Explain Strategic Behavior?

Decision-making under oligopoly can be complex. Recall that with a Nash equilibrium, participants make decisions based on the behavior of others around them. **Game theory** is a branch of mathematics that economists use to analyze the strategic behavior of decision-makers. In particular, game theory can help us determine what level of cooperation is most likely to occur. A game consists of a set of players, a set of strategies available to those players, and a specification of the payoffs for each combination of strategies. The game is usually represented by a payoff matrix that shows the players, strategies, and payoffs. It is presumed that each player acts simultaneously or without knowing the actions of the other.

Game theory is a branch of mathematics that economists use to analyze the strategic behavior of decision-makers.

In this section, we will learn about the prisoner's dilemma, an example from game theory that helps us understand how dominant strategies often frame short-run decisions. (The prisoner's dilemma is a game that is played only once.) We will use the idea of the dominant strategy to explain why oligopolists often choose to advertise. Finally, we will come full circle and argue that the dominant strategy in a game may be overcome in the long run through repeated interactions.

Strategic Behavior and the Dominant Strategy

We have seen that in oligopoly there is mutual interdependence: a rival's business choices affect the earnings that the other rivals can expect to make. To learn more about the decisions firms make, we will explore a fundamental problem in game theory known as the *prisoner's dilemma*. The dilemma takes its name from a famous scenario devised by pioneer game theorist Al Tucker soon after World War II.

The scenario goes like this: Two prisoners are being interrogated separately about a crime they both participated in, and each is offered a plea bargain to cooperate with the authorities by testifying against the other. If both suspects refuse to cooperate with the authorities, neither can be convicted of a more serious crime, though they will both have to spend some time in jail. But the police have offered full immunity if one cooperates and the other does not. This means that each suspect has an incentive to betray the other. The rub is that if they both confess, they will spend more time in jail than if they had both stayed quiet. When decision-makers face incentives that make it difficult to achieve mutually beneficial outcomes, we say they are in a **prisoner's dilemma**. This situation makes the payoff for cooperating with the authorities more attractive than the result of keeping quiet.

We can understand the outcomes of the prisoner's dilemma by looking at the payoff matrix in Figure 13.1. Starting with the white box in the upper left corner, we see that if both suspects testify against each other, they each get 10 years in jail. If one suspect testifies while his partner remains quiet—the upper right and lower left boxes—he goes free and his partner gets 25 years in jail. If both keep quiet—the result in the lower right corner—they each get off with 1 year in jail. This result is better than the outcome in which both prisoners testify.

Because each suspect is interrogated separately, the decision about what to tell the police cannot be made cooperatively; thus, each prisoner faces a

The **prisoner's dilemma** occurs when decision-makers face incentives that make it difficult to achieve mutually beneficial outcomes.

Incentives

FIGURE 13.1

The Prisoner's Dilemma

The two suspects know that if they both keep quiet, they will spend only 1 year in jail. The prisoner's dilemma occurs because the decision to testify results in no jail time for the one who testifies if the other does not testify. However, this outcome means that both are likely to testify and get 10 years.

		Tony Montana	
		Testify	**Keep quiet**
Manny Ribera	**Testify**	10 years in jail 10 years in jail	25 years in jail goes free
	Keep quiet	goes free 25 years in jail	1 year in jail 1 year in jail

dilemma. The interrogation process makes the situation a noncooperative "game" and changes the incentives that each party faces.

Under these circumstances, what will our suspects choose? Let's begin with the outcomes for Tony Montana. Suppose that he testifies. If Manny Ribera also testifies, Tony will get 10 years in jail (the upper left box). If Manny keeps quiet, Tony will go free (the lower left box). Now suppose that Tony decides to keep quiet. If Manny testifies, Tony can expect 25 years in jail (the upper right box). If Manny keeps quiet, Tony will get 1 year in jail (the lower right box). No matter what choice Manny makes, Tony is always better off choosing to testify. If his partner testifies and he testifies, he gets 10 years in jail as opposed to 25 if he keeps quiet. If his partner keeps quiet and he testifies, Tony goes free as opposed to spending a year in jail if he also keeps quiet. The same analysis applies to the outcomes for Manny.

When a player always prefers one strategy, regardless of what his opponent chooses, we say it is a **dominant strategy**. We can see a dominant strategy at work in the case of our two suspects. They know that if they both keep quiet, they will spend one year in jail. The dilemma occurs because both suspects are more likely to testify and get 10 years in jail. This choice is obvious for two reasons. First, neither suspect can monitor the actions of the other after they are separated. Second, once each suspect understands that his partner will save jail time if he testifies, he realizes that the incentives are not in favor of keeping quiet.

Incentives

The dominant strategy in our example is a Nash equilibrium. If each suspect reasons that the other will testify, the best response is also to testify. Each suspect may wish that he and his partner could coordinate their actions and agree to keep quiet. However, without the possibility of coordination, neither has an incentive to withhold testimony. So they both think strategically and decide to testify.

> A **dominant strategy** exists when a player will always prefer one strategy, regardless of what his opponent chooses.

Duopoly and the Prisoner's Dilemma

The prisoner's dilemma example suggests that cooperation can be difficult to achieve. To get a better sense of the incentives that oligopolists face when trying to collude, we will use game theory to evaluate the outcome of our cell phone duopoly example.

Figure 13.2 puts some of the information from Table 13.3 into a payoff matrix and highlights the revenue that AT-Phone and Horizon could earn at various production levels.

Incentives

Looking at the bottom two boxes, we see that at a high production level, Horizon can earn either $30,000 or $24,000 in revenue, depending on what AT-Phone does. At a low production level (the top two boxes), it can earn either $27,000 or $22,500. The same reasoning is true for AT-Phone. Now look at the right-hand boxes, and you will see that AT-Phone can earn either $30,000 or $24,000, depending on what Horizon does. At a low production level (the left-hand boxes), it can earn either $27,000 or $22,500. So the high production levels dominate. The two companies have an incentive to serve more customers because this strategy yields the most revenue. A high level of production leads to a Nash equilibrium; both firms make $24,000. However, if the companies operate as a cartel with low production, they can both earn $27,000.

FIGURE 13.2

The Prisoner's Dilemma in Duopoly

Each company has a dominant strategy to serve more customers because it makes more revenue even if its competitor also expands production. A high level of production leads to a Nash equilibrium at which both firms make $24,000.

		AT-Phone	
		Low production: 300 customers	High production: 400 customers
Horizon	Low production: 300 customers	$27,000 revenue $27,000 revenue	$30,000 revenue $22,500 revenue
	High production: 400 customers	$22,500 revenue $30,000 revenue	$24,000 revenue $24,000 revenue

Prisoner's Dilemma

Murder by Numbers

There is an especially compelling example of the prisoner's dilemma at work in *Murder by Numbers* (2002). In this scene, the district attorney's office decides to interrogate two murder suspects. Without a confession, they don't have enough evidence and the two murderers are likely to go free. Each is confronted with the prisoner's dilemma by being placed in a separate room and threatened with the death penalty. To get the confession, the detective tells one of the suspects, "Just think of it as a game. Whoever talks first is the winner." The detective goes on to tell one of the suspects that his partner in the other room is "rolling over" (even though the partner is not actually talking) and that the partner will get a lighter

Would you rat on your partner in crime?

sentence because he is cooperating. This interrogation method places added pressure on the suspect.

ECONOMICS IN THE MEDIA

Advertising and Game Theory

We have seen that oligopolists function like monopolistic competitors in that they sell differentiated products. We know that advertising is commonplace in markets with a differentiated product. In the case of an oligopoly, mutual interdependence means that advertising can create a contest between firms trying to gain customers. The result may be skyrocketing advertising budgets and little, or no, net gain of customers. Therefore, oligopolists have an incentive to scale back their advertising, but only if their rivals also agree to scale back. Like all cooperative action among competitors, this is easier said than done.

Incentives

Figure 13.3 highlights the advertising choices of Coca-Cola and PepsiCo, two fierce rivals in the soft-drink industry. Together, Coca-Cola and PepsiCo account for 72% of the soft-drink market, with Coca-Cola being the slightly larger of the two firms. Both companies are known for their advertising campaigns, which cost hundreds of millions of dollars. To determine if they gain anything by spending so much on advertising, let's look at the dominant strategy. In the absence of cooperation, each firm will choose to advertise, because the payoffs under advertising ($100 million or $150 million) exceed those of not advertising ($75 million or $125 million). When each firm chooses to advertise, it generates a profit of $100 million. This is a second-best outcome compared with the $125 million profit each could earn if neither firm advertises. The dilemma is that each firm needs to advertise to market its product and retain its customer base, but most advertising expenditures end up canceling each other out and costing the companies millions of dollars.

FIGURE 13.3

The Prisoner's Dilemma and Advertising

The two companies each have a dominant strategy to advertise. We can see this strategy by observing that Coca-Cola and PepsiCo each make $25 million more profit by choosing to advertise. As a result, they both end up in the upper left box earning $100 million profit when they could have each made $125 million profit in the lower right box if they had agreed not to advertise.

		Coca-Cola	
		Advertises	**Does not advertise**
PepsiCo	**Advertises**	$100 million profit $100 million profit	$75 million profit $150 million profit
	Does not advertise	$150 million profit $75 million profit	$125 million profit $125 million profit

Airlines in the Prisoner's Dilemma

American Airlines and Delta Airlines once found themselves in a classic prisoner's dilemma. It all started when Delta wanted to expand its share of the lucrative Dallas-to-Chicago route, where American was the dominant carrier. Delta offered a substantial fare cut on that route to attract new travelers. American threatened a price war by offering its own fare cut on the Delta-dominated Dallas-to-Atlanta route.

Both airlines had a dominant strategy to cut their fare on the targeted route. Why? If one airline cut its fares and the other did not, the airline that did would earn a large profit ($100,000) while the other suffered a large loss (-$200,000). This was each airline's best possible outcome.

Even if the rival cut its fare too, lowering the price was still the right move—the dominant strategy—for each airline. Why? Because if an airline failed to match the fare of its rival, it would make less profit than before.

American

	Discount	**No Discount**
Delta — Discount	-$100,000 / -$100,000	-$200,000 (Chicago) / $100,000 (Dallas)
Delta — No Discount	$100,000 / -$200,000	$50,000 / $50,000 (Atlanta)

The hallmark of a prisoner's dilemma is when two rivals follow their dominant strategy and the result is not the best result for both. It would have been better if no fare discounts were ever considered.

What happened? Fortunately for both airlines, they posted their planned fare cuts on a computer system that allowed them to see what their rival was doing. They each saw the price war starting, backed down, and escaped the prisoner's dilemma!

REVIEW QUESTIONS

- Which expected outcome in the matrix reflects the outcome of this American/Delta pricing war?

- Explain how the ability to communicate can allow two parties to escape a prisoner's dilemma.

ECONOMICS IN THE REAL WORLD

The Cold War

The idea that companies benefit from spending less on advertising has an analogue in warfare. Countries benefit from a "peace dividend" whenever war ends. There is no better example than the Cold War between the Soviet Union and the United States that began in the 1950s. By the time the Cold War ended in the late 1980s, both countries had amassed thousands of nuclear warheads in an effort to deter aggression.

This buildup put enormous economic pressure on each country to keep up with the other. During the height of the Cold War, each country found itself in a prisoner's dilemma in which spending more in an arms race was the dominant strategy. When the Soviet Union ultimately dissolved, the United States was able to spend less money on deterrence. In the post–Cold War world of the 1990s, the U.S. military budget fell from 6.5% to 3.5% of gross domestic product (GDP) as the nation reaped a peace dividend. Of course, the prisoner's dilemma cannot account for all military spending: following the terrorist attacks of 2001, U.S. military spending increased again. ✳

The Cold War created a prisoner's dilemma for the United States and the Soviet Union.

Escaping the Prisoner's Dilemma in the Long Run

We have seen how game theory can be a useful tool for understanding strategic decision-making in noncooperative environments. However, the dominant strategy does not consider the possible long-run benefits of cooperation.

Game theorist Robert Axelrod decided to examine the choices that participants make in a long-run setting. He ran a sophisticated computer simulation in which he invited scholars to submit strategies for securing points in a prisoner's dilemma tournament over many rounds. All the submissions were collected and paired, and the results were scored. After each simulation, Axelrod eliminated the weakest strategy and reran the tournament with the remaining strategies. This evolutionary approach continued until the best strategy remained. Among all strategies, including those that were solely cooperative or noncooperative, tit-for-tat dominated. **Tit-for-tat** is a long-run strategy that promotes cooperation among participants by mimicking the opponent's most recent decision with repayment in kind. As the name implies, a tit-for-tat strategy is one in which you do whatever your opponent does. If your opponent breaks the agreement, you break the agreement, too. If the opponent behaves properly, then you behave properly, too.

Because the joint payoffs for cooperation are high in a prisoner's dilemma, tit-for-tat begins with the players cooperating. In subsequent rounds, the tit-for-tat strategy mimics whatever the other player did in the

Tit-for-tat is a long-run strategy that promotes cooperation among participants by mimicking the opponent's most recent decision with repayment in kind.

previous round. The genius behind tit-for-tat is that it changes the incentives and encourages cooperation. Turning back to our example in Figure 13.3, suppose that Coca-Cola and PepsiCo want to save on advertising expenses. The companies expect to have repeated interactions, so they both know from past experience that any effort to start a new advertising campaign will be immediately countered by the other firm. Because the companies react to each other's moves in kind, any effort to exploit the dominant strategy of advertising will ultimately fail. This dynamic can alter the incentives that the firms face in the long run and lead to mutually beneficial behavior.

Incentives

Tit-for-tat makes it less desirable to advertise by eliminating the long-run benefits. Advertising is still a dominant strategy in the short run because the payoffs with advertising ($100 million or $150 million) exceed those of not advertising ($75 million or $125 million). In the short run, the firm that advertises could earn $25 million extra, but in every subsequent round—if the rival responds in kind—the firm should expect profits of $100 million because its rival will also be advertising. As a result, there is a large long-run opportunity cost for not cooperating. If one firm stops advertising and the other follows suit, they will each find themselves making $125 million in the long run. Why hasn't this outcome happened in the real world? Because Coke and PepsiCo don't trust each other enough to earn the dividend that comes from an advertising truce.

Opportunity cost

The prisoner's dilemma nicely captures why cooperation is so difficult in the short run. But most interactions in life occur over the long run. For example, scam artists and sketchy companies take advantage of short-run opportunities that cannot last because relationships in the long run—with businesses and with people—involve mutual trust. Cooperation is the default because you know that the other side is invested in the relationship. Under these circumstances, the tit-for-tat strategy works well.

Prisoner's Dilemma

The Dark Knight

In *The Dark Knight* (2008), the Joker (played by the late Heath Ledger) always seems to be one step ahead of the law. The strategic interactions between the police and the conniving villain illustrate game theory in action.

Near the end of the movie, the Joker rigs two full passenger ferries to explode at midnight and tells the passengers that if they try to escape, the bomb will detonate earlier. To complicate matters, one of the ferries is carrying civilian passengers, including a number of children, while the other ferry is transporting prisoners. Each ferry can save itself by hitting a detonator button attached to the other ferry.

The Joker's plan sets up a prisoner's dilemma between the two boats that is also an ethical experiment. Are the lives of those on the civilian boat worth more than those of the prisoners? The Joker's intention is to have one of the ferries blow up the other and thereby create chaos in Gotham City.

In the payoff matrix, the dominant strategy is to detonate the other boat. Failing to detonate the other boat results in death—either the ferry blows up at midnight or the other boat detonates it first.

In this scenario, the only chance of survival is if one ferry detonates the other ferry first. As the scene unfolds and the tension builds, the passengers on both boats realize their plight and wrestle with the consequences of their decisions. Gradually, everyone becomes aware that the dominant strategy is to detonate the other boat. What is interesting is how the civilians and prisoners react to this information.

What actually happens? Passengers on each boat decide that they would rather be detonated than willingly participate in the Joker's experiment. Watching the scene as a game theorist will give you a new appreciation for the film. ✳

		Prisoner ferry	
		Detonate other boat	**Do not detonate other boat**
Civilian ferry	**Detonate other boat**	Cannot simultaneously happen / Cannot simultaneously happen	Die / Survive
	Do not detonate other boat	Survive / Die	Die / Die

Sequential Games

Not all games involve simultaneous decisions. Sometimes one player must move first and then the other player responds to the first move. In this case it is possible for the first player to utilize **backward induction** to get the best possible result. Backward induction in game theory is the process of deducing backward from the end of a scenario to infer a sequence of optimal actions.

To help visualize this situation, look at Figure 13.4. The payoff matrix summarizes the payoffs that Iggy and Azalea face in a noncooperative game. Neither Iggy nor Azalea has a dominant strategy, so it is impossible to predict what the final outcome will be.

However, if we let one player go first, the game has a predictable conclusion. To see this process at work, look at Figure 13.5. This type of diagram is known as a **decision tree**; it illustrates all of the possible outcomes in a sequential game. Let's imagine that Azalea goes first and Iggy chooses second.

In a sequential game, the first player can restrict the set of outcomes to one of the branches at the top of the decision tree. When Azalea chooses Agree, Iggy works off the lower left set of branches and must choose between making $20,000 if she agrees or $75,000 if she disagrees. Of course, Iggy chooses to disagree. In this case, the final outcome is $50,000 for Azalea and $75,000 for Iggy. If Azalea instead choses Disagree to start, Iggy would be faced with the payoffs on the lower right side of the decision tree. Here Iggy would get $50,000 if she agrees and $25,000 if she disagrees, so this time she agrees. Now the final outcome is $35,000 for Azalea and $50,000 for Iggy.

Backward induction in game theory is the process of deducing backward from the end of a scenario to infer a sequence of optimal actions.

A decision tree illustrates all of the possible outcomes in a sequential game.

FIGURE 13.4

To Cooperate or Not
Iggy and Azalea do not have dominant strategies, so the outcome of this game cannot be determined.

		Iggy	
		Agree	Disagree
Azalea	Agree	$20,000 / $60,000	$75,000 / $50,000
	Disagree	$50,000 / $35,000	$25,000 / $75,000

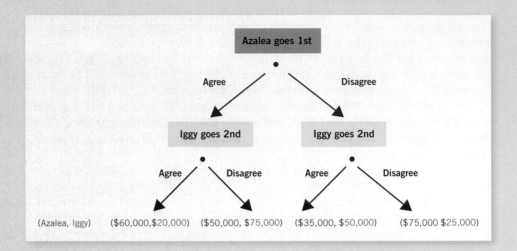

FIGURE 13.5

Decision Tree for a Sequential Game

Azalea will agree, knowing that Iggy will disagree. This game guarantees Azalea $50,000 and Iggy $75,000.

Azalea goes 1st

Agree — Disagree

Iggy goes 2nd — Iggy goes 2nd

Agree / Disagree — Agree / Disagree

(Azalea, Iggy) — ($60,000,$20,000) — ($50,000, $75,000) — ($35,000, $50,000) — ($75,000 $25,000)

Because Azalea has full information about all of the payoffs in the matrix, she knows what Iggy will choose at the end of each set of branches. This knowledge allows her to use backward induction to earn $50,000 for herself by selecting Agree with the full knowledge that Iggy will choose Disagree.

There are many examples of sequential games in life. Chess and checkers are two popular board games that utilize backward induction. Likewise, many business decisions are also sequential in nature, and once a particular path is taken, it becomes easier to predict how future decisions will unfold. For instance, when a firm decides to launch a new advertising campaign, it is easier for the firm to predict how a rival will react by examining the remaining choices along a decision tree.

A Caution about Game Theory

Game theory is a decision-making tool, but not all games have dominant strategies that make player decisions easy to predict. Perhaps the best example is the game known as rock-paper-scissors. This simple game has no dominant strategy: paper beats rock (because the paper will cover the rock) and rock beats scissors (because the rock will break the scissors), but scissors beats paper (because the scissors will cut the paper). The preferred choice is strictly a function of what the other player selects. Many situations in life and business are more like rock-paper-scissors than the prisoner's dilemma. Winning at business in the long run often occurs because you are one step ahead of the competition, not because you deploy a strategy that attempts to take advantage of a short-run opportunity.

Consider two friends who enjoy playing racquetball together. Both players are of equal ability, so each point comes down to whether the players guess correctly about the direction the other player will hit. Take a look at Figure 13.6. The success of Joey and Rachel depends on how well each one guesses where the other will hit.

Rock-paper-scissors is a game without a dominant strategy.

PRACTICE WHAT YOU KNOW

Dominant Strategy: To Advertise or Not—That Is the Question!

Question: University Subs and Savory Sandwiches are the only two sandwich shops in a small college town. If neither runs a special 2-for-1 promotion, both are able to keep their prices high and earn $10,000 a month. However, when both run promotions, their profits fall to $1,000. Finally, if one runs a promotion and the other does not, the shop that runs the promotion earns a profit of $15,000 and the other loses $5,000. What is the dominant strategy for University Subs? Is there a Nash equilibrium in this example?

How much should a sandwich shop in a small college town charge for this sandwich?

	University Subs	
	Runs a 2-for-1 promotion	**Keeps price high**
Savory Sandwiches — Runs a 2-for-1 promotion	Makes $1,000 Makes $1,000	Loses $5,000 Makes $15,000
Savory Sandwiches — Keeps price high	Makes $15,000 Loses $5,000	Makes $10,000 Makes $10,000

Answer:

If University Subs runs the 2-for-1 promotion, it will make either $1,000 or $15,000, depending on its rival's actions. If University Subs keeps the price high, it will either lose $5,000 or make $10,000, depending on what Savory Sandwiches does. Suppose that Savory Sandwiches decides to run a 2-for-1 promotion. In this case, University Subs's best response is also to run a 2-for-1 promotion because $1,000 > –$5,000. Now imagine that Savory Subs uses the strategy of keeping the price high. University Subs's best response remains running the 2-for-1 promotion because $15,000 > $10,000. So regardless of what Savory Subs does, University Subs's best response—and therefore its dominant strategy—is to run a 2-for-1 promotion. Savory Sandwiches has the same dominant strategy and the same payoffs. Therefore, both companies will run the promotion and each will make $1,000. Neither firm has a reason to switch to the high-price strategy because it would lose $5,000 if the other company runs the 2-for-1 promotion. A Nash equilibrium occurs when both companies run the promotion.

FIGURE 13.6

No Dominant Strategy Exists

Neither Rachel nor Joey has a dominant strategy that guarantees winning the point. Any of the four outcomes are equally likely on successive points, and there is no way to predict how the next point will be played. As a result, there is no Nash equilibrium here.

		Rachel	
		Guesses to the left	**Guesses to the right**
Joey	**Hits to the left**	Rachel wins the point Joey loses the point	Rachel loses the point Joey wins the point
	Hits to the right	Rachel loses the point Joey wins the point	Rachel wins the point Joey loses the point

In this competition, neither Rachel nor Joey has a dominant strategy that guarantees success. Sometimes Joey wins when hitting to the right; at other times he loses the point. Sometimes Rachel wins when she guesses to the left; at other times she loses. Each player guesses correctly only half the time. Because we cannot say what each player will do from one point to another, there is no Nash equilibrium. Any of the four outcomes are equally likely on successive points, and there is no way to predict how the next point will be played. In other words, we cannot expect every game to include a prisoner's dilemma and produce a Nash equilibrium. Game theory, like real life, has many different possible outcomes.

How Do Government Policies Affect Oligopoly Behavior?

When oligopolists in an industry form a cooperative alliance, they function like a monopoly. Competition disappears, which is not good for society. One way to improve the social welfare of society is to restore competition and limit monopoly practices through policy legislation.

Antitrust Policy

Efforts to curtail the adverse consequences of oligopolistic cooperation began with the **Sherman Antitrust Act** of 1890, the first federal law to place limits on cartels and monopolies. The Sherman Act was created in response to the increase in concentration ratios in many leading U.S. industries, including steel, railroads, mining, textiles, and oil. Prior to passage of the Sherman Act, firms were free to pursue contracts that created mutually beneficial outcomes. Once the act took effect, however, certain cooperative actions became criminal. Section 2 of the Sherman Act reads, "Every person who shall monopolize, or attempt to monopolize, or combine or conspire with any other person or persons, to monopolize any part of the trade or commerce among the several States, or with foreign nations, shall be deemed guilty of a felony."

The **Clayton Act** of 1914 targets corporate behaviors that reduce competition. Large corporations had been vilified during the presidential election of 1912, and the Sherman Act was seen as largely ineffective in curbing monopoly power. To strengthen antitrust policy, the Clayton Act added to the list of activities that were deemed socially detrimental, including:

1. *price discrimination* if it lessens competition or creates monopoly
2. *exclusive dealings* that restrict a buyer's ability to deal with competitors
3. *tying arrangements* that require the buyer to purchase an additional product in order to purchase the first
4. *mergers and acquisitions* that lessen competition, or situations in which a person serves as a director on more than one board in the same industry

As the Clayton Act makes clear, there are many ways to reduce competition.

Over the past hundred years, lawmakers have continued to refine antitrust policy. Additional legislation along with court interpretations of existing antitrust law have made it difficult to determine whether a company has violated the law. The U.S. Justice Department is charged with oversight, but it often lacks the resources to fully investigate every case. Antitrust law is complex, and cases are hard to prosecute, but these laws are essential to maintain a competitive business environment. Without effective restraints on excessive market power, firms would organize into cartels more often or would find other ways to restrict competition. Table 13.5 briefly describes the most influential antitrust cases in history.

> The **Sherman Antitrust Act** (1890) was the first federal law limiting cartels and monopolies.

> The **Clayton Act** (1914) targets corporate behaviors that reduce competition.

Predatory Pricing

While firms have a strong incentive to cooperate in order to keep prices high, they also want to keep potential rivals out of the market. **Predatory pricing** is the practice of setting prices deliberately below average variable costs with the intent of driving rivals out of the market. The firm suffers a short-run loss in order to prevent rivals from entering the market or to drive rival firms out of business in the long run. Once the rivals are gone, the firm should be able to act like a monopolist.

Predatory pricing is illegal, but it is difficult to prosecute. Neither the court system nor economists have a simple rule that helps to determine when a firm steps over the line. Predatory pricing can look and feel like spirited competition. Moreover, the concern is not the competitive aspect or lower prices,

> **Predatory pricing** occurs when firms deliberately set their prices below average variable costs with the intent of driving rivals out of the market.

TABLE 13.5

Influential Antitrust Cases in U.S. History

Defendant	Year	Description
Standard Oil	1911	Standard Oil was founded in 1870. By 1897, the company had driven the price of oil down to 6 cents a gallon, which put many of its competitors out of business. Subsequently, Standard Oil became the largest company in the world. In 1906, the U.S. government filed suit against Standard Oil for violating the Sherman Antitrust Act. Three years later, the company was found guilty and forced to break up into 34 independent companies.
ALCOA	1944	The Aluminum Company of America (ALCOA), founded in 1907, maintained its position as the only producer of aluminum in the United States for many years. To keep that position, the company acquired exclusive rights to all U.S. sources of bauxite, the base material from which aluminum is refined. It then acquired land rights to build and own hydroelectric facilities in both the United States and Canada. By owning both the base materials and the only sites where refinement could take place, ALCOA effectively barred other firms from entering the U.S. aluminum market. In 1937, the Department of Justice filed suit against ALCOA. Seven years later, the Supreme Court ruled that ALCOA had taken measures to restrict trade and functioned as a monopoly. ALCOA was not broken apart because two rivals, Kaiser and Reynolds, emerged soon after.
AT&T	1982	In 1974, the U.S. Attorney General filed suit against AT&T for violating antitrust laws. It took seven years before a settlement was reached to split the company into seven new companies, each serving a different region of the United States. However, five of the seven have since merged to become AT&T Incorporated, which is now one of the largest companies in the world.
Microsoft	2001	When Internet Explorer was introduced in 1995, Microsoft insisted that it was a feature rather than a new Windows product. The U.S. Department of Justice did not agree and filed suit against Microsoft for illegally discouraging competition to protect its software monopoly. The government argued that Microsoft leveraged its monopoly power from the operating systems market into the browser market by strong-arming personal computer manufacturers like Dell into favoring Internet Explorer over Netscape. After a series of court decisions and appeals, a settlement ordered Microsoft to share application programming interfaces with third-party companies. Today, Internet Explorer has largely been replaced by Chrome and Firefox.
Google	2015	The European Union began investigating whether Google used its dominant market share as a search engine to gain an unfair advantage over competitors. As of 2015, Google was the search engine of choice in 92% of all searches in Europe. The regulators have focused on accusations that Google search results divert traffic away from search results that favor its rivals and toward results that favor Google's own products.

but the effect on the market when all rivals fail. To prove that predatory pricing has occurred, the courts need evidence that the firm's prices increased significantly after its rivals failed.

Walmart is often cited as a firm that engages in predatory pricing because its low prices effectively drive many smaller companies out of business. However, there is no evidence that Walmart has ever systematically raised prices after a rival failed. Therefore, its price strategy does not meet the legal standard for predatory pricing. Similarly, Microsoft came under intense scrutiny in the 1990s for giving away its browser, Internet Explorer, in order to undercut Netscape, which also ended up giving away its browser. Microsoft understood that the key to its long-term success was the dominance of

PRACTICE WHAT YOU KNOW

Predatory Pricing: Price Wars

You've undoubtedly encountered a price war at some point. It could be two gas stations, clothing outlets, or restaurants that are charging prices that seem unbelievably low.

Question: Is a price war between two adjacent pizza restaurants evidence of predatory pricing?

Predatory pricing? Check out the competing signs in the photo!

Answer: One essential element for proving predatory pricing is evidence of the intent to raise prices after others are driven out of business. That is a problem in this example. Suppose one of the pizza places closes. The remaining firm could then raise its price substantially. But barriers to entry in the restaurant industry are low in most metropolitan areas, so any efforts to maintain high prices for long will fail. Customers will vote with their feet and wallets by choosing another pizza place a little farther away that offers a better value. Or a new competitor will sense that the victor is vulnerable because of the high prices and will open a new pizza parlor nearby. Either way, the market is monopolistically competitive, so any market power created by driving out one rival will be fleeting.

The aggressive price war is not evidence of predatory pricing. Instead, it is probably just promotional pricing to protect market share. Firms often price some items below their variable costs to attract customers. These firms hope to make up the difference and then some with high profit margins on other items, such as beverages and side dishes.

the Windows platform. Bundling Internet Explorer with Microsoft Office enabled the company not only to gain over 80% of the browser market but also to keep its leadership with the Windows operating system. Eventually, Microsoft was prosecuted by the government—but not for predatory pricing, which could not be proved because Microsoft never significantly raised the price of Internet Explorer. Instead, the government prosecuted Microsoft for tying the purchase of Internet Explorer to the Windows operating system in order to restrict competition. The Microsoft case lasted over four years, and it ended in a settlement that placed restrictions on the firm's business practices.

Because Walmart keeps its prices low, there is no evidence that it engages in predatory pricing.

What Are Network Externalities?

A **network externality** occurs when the number of customers who purchase or use a good influences the quantity demanded.

We end this chapter by considering a special kind of externality that often occurs in oligopoly. A **network externality** occurs when the number of customers who purchase or use a good influences the demand. When a network externality exists, firms with many customers often find it easier to attract new customers and to keep their regular customers from switching to other rivals. In the early days of social networking, for example, MySpace had many more users than Facebook. How did Facebook gain over 2.2 billion users when it had to play catch-up? Facebook built a better social network, and MySpace was slow to respond to the threat. By the time MySpace did respond, it was too late: Facebook was on its way. Now the tables are turned, as Facebook is the dominant social networking platform. Moreover, among most demographics, the sheer size of Facebook makes it a better place to do social networking than Google+, Twitter, and LinkedIn. However, even though Facebook now enjoys significant network externalities, it must be mindful to keep innovating or else it might end up irrelevant like MySpace.

Most network externalities involve the introduction of new technologies. For instance, some technologies need to reach a critical mass before consumers can effectively use them. Consider that today everyone seems to have a cell phone. However, when cell phones were introduced in the United States in 1983, coverage was quite limited. The first users could not surf the Internet, roam, text, or use many of the applications we enjoy today. Moreover, the phones were large and bulky. How did we get from that situation in 1983 to today? As additional people bought cell phones, networks expanded and manufacturers and telephone companies responded by building more cell towers and offering better phones. The expansion of networks brought more users, and the new adopters benefited from the steadily expanding customer base.

Other technologies have gone through similar transformations. The Internet, fax machines, and apps all depend on the number of users. If you were the only person on the Internet or the only person with the ability to send and receive a fax, your technical capacity would have little value. In a world with ever-changing technology, first adopters pave the way for the next generation of users.

Switching costs are the costs incurred when a consumer changes from one supplier to another.

In addition to the advantages of forming a larger network, customers may face significant switching costs if they leave. **Switching costs** are the costs incurred when a consumer changes from one supplier to another. For instance, the transition from listening to music on CDs to using digital music files involved a substantial switching cost for many users. Today, there are switching costs among the many digital music options. Once a consumer has established a library of MP3s or uses iTunes, the switching costs of transferring the music from one format to another create a significant barrier to change. When consumers face switching costs, the demand for the existing product becomes more inelastic. As a result, oligopolists not only leverage the number of customers they maintain in their network, but also try to make switching to another network more difficult. For instance, firms promote customer loyalty through frequent flier benefits, hotel reward points, and credit card reward programs to create higher switching costs.

An excellent example of the costs of switching are the costs associated with cell phone services. First, contract termination fees apply to many cell phone

Users of the first-generation cell phone, the Motorola DynaTAC 8000X, created a positive network externality for future users.

PRACTICE WHAT YOU KNOW

Examples of Network Externalities

Question: In which two of these examples are network externalities important?

a. college alumni

b. Netflix

c. a local bakery that sells fresh bread

Does Netflix benefit from network externalities?

Answers:

a. Colleges and universities that have more alumni are able to raise funds more easily than smaller schools, so the size of the alumni network matters. The number of alumni also matters when graduates look for jobs, because alumni are often inclined to hire individuals who went to the same school. For example, Penn State University has the nation's largest alumni base. This means that each PSU graduate benefits from network externalities.

b. Netflix's size enables it to offer a vast array of DVDs, downloads, and streaming video. If it were smaller, Netflix would be unable to make as many obscure titles available. This means that Netflix customers benefit from network externalities by having more DVDs to choose from.

c. The local bakery is a small company. If it attracts more customers, each one will have to compete harder to get fresh bread. Because the bakery's supply of bread is limited, additional customers create congestion, and network externalities do not exist.

agreements if the contract is broken. Second, many providers do not charge for calls inside the network or among a circle of friends. This means that if you switch and your friends do not, you will end up using more minutes on a rival network. These two tactics create high switching costs for many cell phone customers. To reduce switching costs, the Federal Communications Commission in 2003 began requiring that phone companies allow customers to take their cell phone numbers with them when they change to a different provider. This change in the law has reduced the costs of switching from one provider to another and has made the cell phone market more competitive.

Oligopolists are keenly aware of the power of network externalities. As new markets develop, the first firm into an industry often gains a large customer base. When there are positive network externalities, the customer base enables the firm to grow quickly. In addition, consumers are often more comfortable purchasing from an established firm. These two factors favor the formation of large firms and make it difficult for smaller competitors to gain customers. As a result, the presence of significant positive network externalities causes small firms to be driven out of business or forces them to merge with larger competitors.

Should You Buy Now or Wait?

If you are like a lot of people, when you hear about something new and cool, you check it out. There is no harm in doing that. But what happens when you decide to purchase the latest gadget or join a new social media web site? You've made an investment of money or time. The fruitfulness of that investment often depends on how many other people do the same thing.

Consider the first people to get a 3D television. The first purchasers paid well over $5,000 for the new technology, but what exactly could they watch? The amount of 3D programming to start was tiny. Those early purchasers had very expensive TVs that they could rarely use to watch 3D because the content was playing catch-up. In contrast, consumers who waited could buy a 3D unit with greater clarity at a lower price, and more content was available to watch. That meant a win-win-win for procrastinators. The early adopters got penalized for paving the way.

The same is true today with many social media sites. Waiting for a web site to gain traction will save you from setting up a profile and investing your time and effort only to find out that other people are not nearly as excited about the features as you are. You end up wasting a lot of time, and because other online users never show up, you don't get the benefits that come from network externalities. If you wait until a platform is already established, then you can be fairly confident that your return on your

The Apple Watch: Should you buy the newest gadget when it comes out?

investment will be rewarded. This was certainly true with Facebook, Twitter, and LinkedIn—all of which have come to dominate segments of the social media market.

Network externalities are also important on dating sites. Just consider the overwhelming number of choices in this market: Match, Zoosk, eHarmony, OurTime, Tinder, and many other sites. You could sign up for dozens of dating sites or simply choose the largest site, Match.com, because it offers the biggest database. Because dating sites charge membership fees, waiting to see which sites are more popular is one way to use network externalities to improve your odds of success.

Conclusion

We opened this chapter with the misconception that cell phone companies are highly competitive—that is, that they compete like firms in competitive markets or monopolistically competitive markets do. The reality is that cell phone companies are oligopolists. Firms in oligopoly markets can compete or collude to create monopoly conditions. The result is often hard to predict. In many cases, the presence of a dominant short-run strategy causes firms to compete on price and advertising even though doing so yields a lower economic profit. In contrast, the potential success of a tit-for-tat strategy suggests that oligopolistic firms are capable of cooperating to jointly maximize their long-run profits. Whether oligopoly mirrors the result found in monopolistic competition or monopoly matters a great deal because society's welfare is higher when more competition is present. Because oligopoly is not a market structure with a predictable outcome, each oligopolistic industry must be assessed on a case-by-case basis by examining data and utilizing game theory. For these reasons, the study of oligopoly is one of the most fascinating parts of the theory of the firm.

Revisiting *A Beautiful Mind*: Recall that a Nash equilibrium exists when all economic decision-makers opt to keep the status quo. In *A Beautiful Mind*, the famous bar scene is not a Nash equilibrium. If the most beautiful woman in the bar was without a dance partner, each of the gentlemen would have had an incentive to change his behavior and switch to her.

ANSWERING THE BIG QUESTIONS

What is oligopoly?

* Oligopoly is a type of market structure that exists when a small number of firms sell a differentiated product in a market with significant barriers to entry. An oligopolist is like a monopolistic competitor in that it sells differentiated products. It is like a monopolist in that it enjoys significant barriers to entry. The small number of sellers in oligopoly leads to mutual interdependence.

* Oligopolists have a tendency to collude and to form cartels in the hope of achieving monopoly-like profits.

* Oligopolistic markets are socially inefficient because price and marginal cost are not equal. The result under oligopoly falls somewhere between the competitive market and monopoly outcomes.

How does game theory explain strategic behavior?

* Game theory helps to determine when cooperation among oligopolists is most likely to occur. In many cases, cooperation fails to occur because decision-makers have dominant strategies that lead them to be uncooperative. As a result, firms compete with price or advertising when they could potentially earn more profit by curtailing these activities.

* Games become more complicated when they are played multiple times, so short-run dominant strategies often disappear. Whenever repeated interaction occurs, decision-makers fare better under tit-for-tat, an approach that maximizes the long-run profit.

How do government policies affect oligopoly behavior?

✳ Antitrust law is complex, and cases are hard to prosecute. Nevertheless, these laws are essential in providing oligopolistic firms an incentive to compete rather than collude.

✳ Antitrust policy limits price discrimination, exclusive dealings, tying arrangements, mergers and acquisitions that limit competition, and predatory pricing.

What are network externalities?

✳ A network externality occurs when the number of customers who purchase or use a good influences the quantity demanded. The presence of significant positive network externalities can cause small firms to go out of business.

CONCEPTS YOU SHOULD KNOW

antitrust laws (p. 396)
backward induction (p. 409)
cartel (p. 396)
Clayton Act (p. 413)
collusion (p. 395)
decision tree (p. 409)
dominant strategy (p. 402)

game theory (p. 400)
mutual interdependence (p. 396)
Nash equilibrium (p. 398)
network externality (p. 416)
oligopoly (p. 392)
output effect (p. 400)
predatory pricing (p. 413)

price effect (p. 400)
prisoner's dilemma (p. 401)
Sherman Antitrust Act (p. 413)
switching costs (p. 416)
tit-for-tat (p. 406)

QUESTIONS FOR REVIEW

1. Compare the price and output under oligopoly with that of monopoly and monopolistic competition.

2. How does the addition of another firm affect the ability of the firms in an oligopolistic industry to form an effective cartel?

3. What is predatory pricing?

4. How is game theory relevant to oligopoly? Does it help to explain monopoly? Give reasons for your response.

5. What does the prisoner's dilemma indicate about the longevity of collusive agreements?

6. What is a Nash equilibrium? How does it differ from a dominant strategy?

7. What practices do antitrust laws prohibit?

8. What are network externalities? Explain why network externalities matter to an oligopolist.

STUDY PROBLEMS (✳solved at the end of the section)

1. Some places limit the number of hours that alcohol can be sold on Sunday. Is it possible that this sales restriction could help liquor stores? Use game theory to construct your answer. (**Hint:** Even without restrictions on the hours of operation, individual stores could still limit Sunday sales if they wanted to.)

2. Which of the following markets are oligopolistic?
   a. passenger airlines
   b. cereal
   c. fast food
   d. wheat
   e. golf equipment
   f. the college bookstore on your campus

✳3. Imagine that your roommate's alarm goes off at 4:30 every morning, and she hits snooze every 10 minutes until 6:00, when you both need to get up. She insists that this maddening procedure is the only way she is able to wake up. How would you respond? Is there

a nonviolent way you can convince her to change her morning wake-up routine? (**Hint:** Think about a tit-for-tat strategy.)

4. After teaching a class on game theory, your instructor announces that if every student skips the last question on the next exam, everyone will receive full credit for that question. However, if one or more students answer the last question, all responses will be graded and those who skip the question will get a zero on that question. Will the entire class skip the last question? Explain your response.

5. For which of the following are network externalities important?
   a. gas stations
   b. American Association of Retired Persons (AARP)
   c. eHarmony, an Internet dating site

6. Your economics instructor is at it again (see question 4). This time, you have to do a two-student project. Assume that you and your

partner are both interested in maximizing your grade, but you are both very busy and get more happiness if you can get a good grade with less work.

	Your partner	
	Work hard	**Work less hard**
You **Work hard**	Grade = A, but your partner had to work 10 hours. Happiness = 7/10.	Grade = A, and your partner only worked 5 hours. Happiness = 9/10.
	Grade = A, but you had to work 10 hours. Happiness = 7/10.	Grade = A, but you had to work 15 hours. Happiness = 4/10.
Work less hard	Grade = A, but your partner had to work 15 hours. Happiness = 4/10.	Grade = B, but your partner only worked 5 hours. Happiness = 6/10.
	Grade = A, and you only worked 5 hours. Happiness = 9/10.	Grade = B, but you only worked 5 hours. Happiness = 6/10.

a. What is your dominant strategy? Explain.
b. What is your partner's dominant strategy? Explain.
c. What is the Nash equilibrium in this situation? Explain.
d. If you and your partner are required to work together on a number of projects throughout the semester, how might this requirement change the outcome you predicted in parts (a), (b), and (c)?

7. Suppose that the marginal cost of mining gold is constant at $300 per ounce and the demand schedule is as follows:

Price (per oz.)	Quantity (oz.)
$1,000	1,000
900	2,000
800	3,000
700	4,000
600	5,000
500	6,000
400	7,000
300	8,000

a. If the number of suppliers is large, what would be the price and quantity?

b. If there is only one supplier, what would be the price and quantity?
c. If there are only two suppliers and they form a cartel, what would be the price and quantity?
d. Suppose that one of the two cartel members in part (c) decides to increase its production by 1,000 ounces while the other member keeps its production constant. What will happen to the revenues of both firms?

✷ 8. Trade agreements encourage countries to curtail tariffs (taxes on imports) so that goods may flow across international boundaries without restrictions. Using the following payoff matrix, determine the best policies for China and the United States.

	China	
	Low tariffs	**High tariffs**
United States **Low tariffs**	China gains $50 billion	China gains $100 billion
	U.S. gains $50 billion	U.S. gains $10 billion
High tariffs	China gains $10 billion	China gains $25 billion
	U.S. gains $100 billion	U.S. gains $25 billion

a. What is the dominant strategy for the United States?
b. What is the dominant strategy for China?
c. What is the Nash equilibrium for these two countries?
d. Suppose that the United States and China enter into a trade agreement that simultaneously lowers trade barriers in both countries. Is this agreement a good idea? Explain your response.

9. A small town has only one pizza place, The Pizza Factory. A small competitor, Perfect Pies, is thinking about entering the market. The profits of these two firms depend on whether Perfect Pies enters the market and whether The Pizza Factory—as a price leader—decides

to set a high price or a low price. Use the payoff matrix below to answer the questions that follow.

	Perfect Pies	
	Enter	**Stay out**
High price	Perfect Pies makes $10,000 The Pizza Factory makes $20,000	Perfect Pies makes $0 The Pizza Factory makes $50,000
Low price	Perfect Pies loses $10,000 The Pizza Factory makes $10,000	Perfect Pies makes $0 The Pizza Factory makes $25,000

(Row label: **The Pizza Factory**)

a. What is the dominant strategy of The Pizza Factory?
b. Does Perfect Pies have a dominant strategy?
c. What is the Nash equilibrium in this situation?
d. The combined profit for both firms is highest when The Pizza Factory sets a high price

and Perfect Pies stays out of the market. If Perfect Pies enters the market, how will this entry affect the profits of The Pizza Factory? Would The Pizza Factory be willing to pay Perfect Pies not to enter the market? Explain.

10. Two brands of coffee makers, Keurig and Tassimo, are vying for the convenience market. Keurig is the market-share leader and has the largest variety of cups that are used to make coffees and teas. Tassimo makes a smaller machine that brews faster, but it lacks the variety of coffees and teas sold by Keurig. To complicate matters, Keurig and Tassimo users cannot easily switch from one manufacturer to the other because the cups that each manufacturer uses are a different size. Which manufacturer is likely to dominate the market in the long run?

✱ 11. On the TV show *The Big Bang Theory*, the characters have an interesting way of resolving disputes. Watch this link: www.youtube.com /watch?v=cSLeBKT7-sM. Is there a dominant strategy in rock-paper-scissors-lizard-Spock? Why do the guys always answer with Spock?

SOLVED PROBLEMS

3. If your roommate does not wake up immediately, a tit-for-tat response would be for you to get up. Once up, you should turn on the lights, get dressed, and make enough noise that your roommate cannot easily sleep. If you use this approach, it won't take long for your roommate to realize that she should set the alarm for a more reasonable time and *not* hit the snooze button. When your roommate no longer relies on the snooze button to wake up, you can return to your normal sleeping pattern and stay in bed for as long as you wish.

8.a. The dominant strategy for the United States is to impose high tariffs, because it always earns more from that strategy than if it imposes low tariffs, no matter what policy China pursues.

b. The dominant strategy for China is to impose high tariffs, because it always earns more from that strategy than if it imposes low tariffs, no matter what policy the United States pursues.

c. The Nash equilibrium for both countries is to levy high tariffs. Each country will earn $25 billion.

d. China and the United States would each benefit from cooperatively lowering trade barriers. In that case, each country would earn $50 billion.

11. There is not a dominant strategy in this variation of rock-paper-scissors, but the guys can't bring themselves to answer with paper, even though it disproves Spock, because they respect him so much.

Two Alternative Theories of Pricing Behavior

Two alternative theories argue that oligopolists will form long-lasting cartels. These are the kinked demand curve and price leadership.

The Kinked Demand Curve

Imagine that a group of oligopolists have established an output level and price designed to maximize economic profit. The **kinked demand curve** theory states that oligopolists have a greater tendency to respond aggressively to rivals' price cuts but will largely ignore price increases. When a rival raises prices, the other firms all stand to benefit by holding their prices steady in order to capture those customers who do not want to pay more. In this scenario, the firm that raises its price will see a relatively large drop in sales. However, if any of the rivals attempts to lower the price, other firms in the industry will immediately match the price decrease. The price match policy means that the firm that lowers its price will not gain many new customers. In practice, because a price drop by one firm will be met immediately by a price drop from all the competitors, no one firm will be able to attract many new customers. This is the case at any price below the agreed-to price.

The firms' behavior creates a demand curve that is more elastic (or flatter) at prices above the cartel price and more inelastic (or steeper) at prices below the cartel price. The junction of the elastic and inelastic segments on the demand curve creates a "kink" that we see in Figure 13A.1.

This illustration begins with each of the firms in the industry charging P and producing Q. Because demand is more elastic above P and less elastic below P, the marginal revenue curve (MR) is discontinuous. The gap is illustrated by the dark dotted black vertical line. The presence of the gap in marginal revenue means that more than one marginal cost curve intersects marginal revenue at output level Q. This fact is evident in marginal cost curves MC_1 and MC_2. As a consequence, small changes in marginal cost, like those shown in Figure 13A.1, will not cause the firms to deviate from the established price (P) and quantity (Q).

The **kinked demand curve** theory states that oligopolists have a greater tendency to respond aggressively to rivals' price cuts but will largely ignore price increases.

Price Leadership

The kinked demand curve explains why oligopolistic firms generally keep the same price, but it cannot explain how prices change. In that regard, the theory of price leadership provides some insight.

FIGURE 13A.1

The Kinked Demand Curve

At prices above P, demand is relatively elastic. At prices below P, demand is relatively inelastic. The result is a kink in the demand curve that causes the marginal revenue curve to become discontinuous. Thus, small changes in marginal cost do not cause firms to change their pricing and output. Therefore, firms are generally slow to adjust to changes in cost.

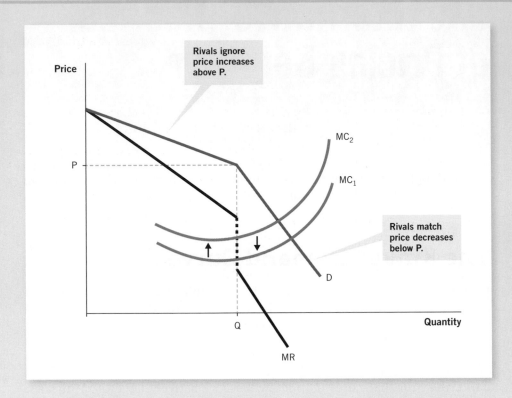

Price leadership occurs when a dominant firm in an industry sets the price that maximizes profits and the smaller firms in the industry follow by setting their prices to match the price leader.

In many industries, smaller firms may take a cue from the decisions made by the price leader. **Price leadership** occurs when a single firm, known as the price leader, produces a large share of the total output in the industry. The price leader sets the price and output level that maximizes its own profits. Smaller firms then set their prices to match the price leader. Because the impact on price is small to begin with, it makes sense that smaller rivals tend to follow the price leader.

Price leadership is not illegal because it does not involve collusion. Rather, it relies on an understanding that an effort to resist changes implemented by the price leader will lead to increased price competition and lower profits for every firm in the industry. Because the firms act in accordance with one another, this practice is commonly known as *tacit collusion*.

One well-known example of price leadership is pricing patterns in the airline industry. On almost any route with multiple-carrier options, a price search for flights will reveal almost identical prices on basic economy-class flights. This similarity of prices happens even though the firms do not collude to set a profit-maximizing price. Rather, when one firm sets a fare, the other carriers feel compelled to match it. Price leadership works best when the largest firm in an industry raises or lowers its price and smaller rivals follow suit.

CONCEPTS YOU SHOULD KNOW

kinked demand curve (p. 425)   price leadership (p. 426)

STUDY PROBLEMS

1. A parking garage charges $10 a day. Whenever it tries to raise its price, the other parking garages in the area keep their prices constant and it loses customers to the cheaper garages. However, when the parking garage lowers its price, the other garages almost always match the price reduction. Which type of oligopoly behavior best explains this situation? If the parking garage business has marginal costs that generally vary only a small amount, should the parking garage change the price it charges when its marginal costs change a little?

2. Most large banks charge the same or nearly the same interest rate. When market conditions require an adjustment, one of the major banks announces a change in its rate and other banks quickly follow suit. Is this an example of price leadership or the kinked demand curve? Explain.

Labor Markets and
EARNINGS

The Demand and Supply of Resources

Outsourcing is bad for the economy.

When U.S. jobs are outsourced (sent to other countries), workers in the United States lose their jobs. People commonly think that outsourc-

ing is bad for the U.S. economy, but the situation is not that simple. Outsourced jobs are relocated from high-labor-cost areas to low-labor-cost areas. Often, a U.S. job lost to out-

sourcing creates more than one job in another country. In addition, outsourcing lowers the cost of manufacturing goods and providing services. Those lower costs translate into lower prices for U.S. consumers and streamlined production processes for U.S. businesses. The improved efficiency helps U.S. firms compete in the global economy. In this chapter, we examine the demand and supply of resources throughout the economy. The outsourcing of jobs is a very visible result of these resource flows and an essential part of the market economy.

In earlier chapters, we saw that profit-maximizing firms must decide how much to produce. For production to be successful, firms must combine the right amounts of labor and capital to maximize output while simultaneously holding down costs. Because labor often constitutes the largest share of the costs of production, we begin by looking at the labor market. We use supply and demand to illustrate the role of the labor market in the U.S. economy. We then extend the lessons learned about labor into the markets for land and capital. In Chapter 15, we expand our understanding of the labor market by examining income inequality, unemployment, discrimination, and poverty.

If U.S. jobs are relocated to low-labor-cost areas like rural India, is it good or bad for the U.S. economy?

* **What are the factors of production?**
* **Where does the demand for labor come from?**
* **Where does the supply of labor come from?**
* **What are the determinants of demand and supply in the labor market?**
* **What role do land and capital play in production?**

What Are the Factors of Production?

Wages and salaries account for two-thirds of all the income generated by the U.S. economy. The remaining one-third of income goes to the owners of land and capital. Together, labor, land, and capital make up the *factors of production*, or the *inputs* used in producing goods and services. (For a review of these terms, see Chapter 8.)

For instance, let's imagine that Sophia wants to open a Mexican restaurant named Agaves. Sophia will need a dining room staff, cooks, dishwashers, and managers to coordinate everyone else; these are the labor inputs. She also will need a physical location; this is the land input. Finally, she will need a building in which to operate, along with ovens and other kitchen equipment, seating and tableware, and a cash register; these are the capital inputs.

Of course, Sophia's restaurant won't need any inputs if there is no demand for the food she plans to sell. The demand for each of the factors of production that go into her restaurant (land, labor, and capital) is said to be a *derived demand* because the factors are inputs the firm uses to supply a good in another market—in this case, the market for Mexican cuisine. Let's say that Sophia secures the land, builds a building, and hires employees to produce the food she will serve. She is willing to spend a lot of money up front to build and staff the restaurant because she expects there to be demand for the food her restaurant will prepare and serve.

Derived demand—the demand for an input used in the production process—is not limited to the demand for a certain type of cuisine. For example, consumer demand for iPads causes Apple to demand the resources needed to make them. The switches, glass, memory, battery, and other parts have little value alone, but when assembled into an iPad, they become a device that many people find very useful. Therefore, when economists speak of derived demand, they are differentiating between the

Derived demand is the demand for an input used in the production process.

A lack of customers is an ominous sign for restaurant workers.

PRACTICE WHAT YOU KNOW

Derived Demand: Tip Income

Your friend waits tables 60 hours a week at a small restaurant. He is discouraged because he works hard but can't seem to make enough money to cover his bills. He complains that the restaurant does not have enough business and that is why he has to work so many hours just to make ends meet.

Question: As an economist, what advice would you give him?

Answer: Because labor is a derived demand, he should apply for a job at a more popular restaurant. Working at a place with more customers will help him earn more tip income.

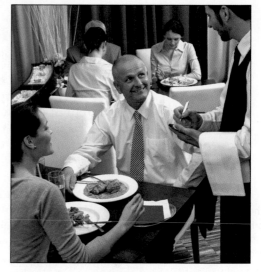

Want more tip income? Follow the crowd.

demand for a product or service and the demand for the resources used to make or produce that product or service.

Where Does the Demand for Labor Come From?

As a student, you are probably hoping that one day your education will translate into tangible skills that employers will seek. As you choose a major, you might be thinking about potential earnings in different occupations. Have you ever wondered why there is so much variability in levels of salary and wages? For instance, economists generally earn more than elementary school teachers but less than engineers. Workers on night shifts earn more than those who do the same job during the day. And professional athletes and successful actors make much more for jobs that are not as essential as the work performed by janitors, construction workers, and nurses. In one respect, the explanation is surprisingly obvious: demand helps to regulate the labor market in much the same way that it helps to determine the prices of goods and services sold in the marketplace.

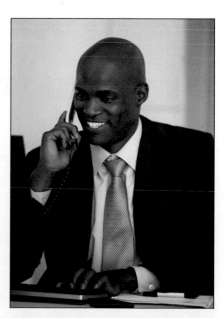

Why do economists generally earn more than elementary school teachers?

To understand why some people get paid more than others, we need to explore each worker's output at the margin, or the *marginal product of labor*. In fact, the value that each worker creates for a firm is highly correlated with the demand for labor. Then, to develop a more complete understanding of how the labor market works, we will examine the factors that influence labor demand.

The Marginal Product of Labor

To gain a concrete appreciation for how labor demand is determined, let's look at the restaurant business—a market that is highly competitive. In Chapter 8, we saw that a firm determines how many workers to hire by comparing the output of labor with the wages the firm must pay. We will apply this analysis of production to the labor market in the restaurant business. Table 14.1 should look familiar to you; it highlights the key determinants of the labor hiring process.

The **marginal product of labor** is the change in output associated with adding one additional worker.

Marginal
thinking

Let's work our way through the table. Column 1 lists the number of laborers, and column 2 reports the daily numbers of meals that can be produced with differing numbers of workers. Column 3 shows the **marginal product of labor**, or the change (Δ, Greek delta) in output associated with adding one additional worker. For instance, when the firm moves from three employees to four, output expands from 120 meals to 140 meals. The increase of 20 meals is the marginal product of labor for the fourth worker. Note that the values in column 3 decline as additional workers are added. Recall from Chapter 8 that each successive worker adds less value, a phenomenon known as *diminishing marginal product*.

It is useful to know the marginal product of labor, which tells us how much each additional worker adds to the firm's output. Combining the marginal product of labor with the price the firm charges gives us a tool that we can use to explain how many workers the firm will hire. Suppose that Agaves charges $10 for each meal. When the firm multiplies the marginal product

TABLE 14.1

Deciding How Many Laborers to Hire

(1) Labor (number of workers)	(2) Output (daily meals produced)	(3) Marginal product of labor	(4) Value of the marginal product of labor	(5) Wage (daily)	(6) Marginal profit
		Δ Output	Price ($10) × marginal product of labor		Value of the marginal product of labor − wage
0	0				
		50	$500	$100	$400
1	50				
		40	400	100	300
2	90				
		30	300	100	200
3	120				
		20	200	100	100
4	140				
		10	100	100	**0**
5	150				
		0	0	100	**− 100**
6	150				

of labor in column 3 by the price it charges, $10 per meal, we see the value of the marginal product in column 4. The **value of the marginal product (VMP)** is the marginal product of an input multiplied by the price of the output it produces. The firm compares the gain in column 4 with the cost of achieving that gain—the wage that must be paid—in column 5. This process reduces the hiring decision to a simple cost-benefit analysis in which the wage (column 5) is subtracted from the value of the marginal product (column 4) to determine each worker's marginal profit (column 6).

You can see from the green numbers that the marginal profit is positive for the first four workers. You might be tempted to argue that the firm should quit hiring once it has four workers because the marginal profit is zero for the fifth worker, shown in black. However, this argument is not valid because the firm can hire part-time workers. If the firm hires four full-time workers plus a fifth part-time worker, the fifth worker's VMP is greater than the wage the firm pays. The firm would be indifferent (neutral) about hiring the fifth worker if he or she were full-time because the marginal cost of hiring that employee is equal to the marginal benefit. Because the marginal profit is negative for the sixth worker, shown in red, the firm would not hire the sixth worker.

Figure 14.1 plots the value of the marginal product (VMP) from Table 14.1. Look at the curve: What do you see? Does it remind you of a demand curve? The VMP is the firm's willingness to pay for each laborer. In other words, it is the firm's labor demand curve.

The VMP curve slopes downward due to diminishing marginal product—which we see in column 3 of Table 14.1. As long as the value of the marginal product is higher than the market wage, shown in column 5 as $100 a day, the firm will hire more workers. For example, when the firm hires the first worker,

The **value of the marginal product (VMP)** is the marginal product of an input multiplied by the price of the output it produces.

Marginal thinking

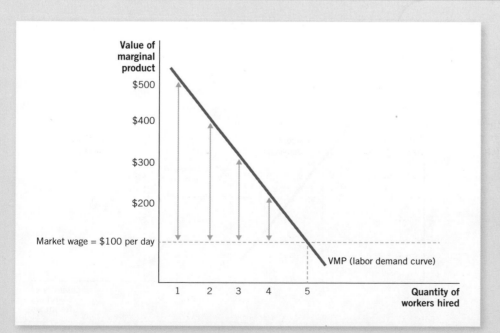

FIGURE 14.1

The Value of the Marginal Product

The value of the marginal product (VMP) is the firm's labor demand curve. When the value of the marginal product is higher than the market wage, the firm will hire more workers. However, because labor is subject to diminishing marginal product, eventually the value created by hiring additional labor falls below the market wage.

the VMP is $500. This amount easily exceeds the market wage of hiring an extra worker and creates a marginal profit of $400. Figure 14.1 illustrates this additional profit with the longest green arrow under the demand curve and above the market wage. The second, third, and fourth workers generate additional profit of $300, $200, and $100, respectively, represented by the progressively shorter green arrows. As the value of the marginal product declines, there will be a point at which hiring additional workers will cause profits to fall. Because labor is subject to diminishing marginal product, the value created by hiring additional labor eventually falls below the market wage.

Changes in the Demand for Labor

We know that customers desire good food and that restaurants like Agaves hire workers to satisfy their customers. Figure 14.2 illustrates the relationship between the demand for restaurant meals and the demand for restaurant workers. Notice that the demand for labor is downward sloping; at high wages Agaves will use fewer workers; at lower wages it will hire more workers. We illustrate the law of demand with the blue arrow that moves along the original demand curve (D_1). Recall from Chapter 3 that a change in price results in a change in the quantity demanded. In addition, the demand for workers depends on, or is derived from, the number of customers who place orders. So changes in the restaurant business as a whole can shift the original demand curve and influence the number of workers that the restaurant hires. For example, if the number of customers increases, the demand for workers will increase, or shift to the right to D_2. Likewise, if the number of customers decreases, the demand for workers will decrease, or shift to the left to D_3.

FIGURE 14.2

The Labor Demand Curve

When the wages of workers change, the quantity of workers demanded, shown by the blue arrow moving along the demand curve D_1, also changes. Changes that shift the entire labor demand curve, shown by the gray horizontal arrows, include changes in demand for the product that the firm produces and changes in cost.

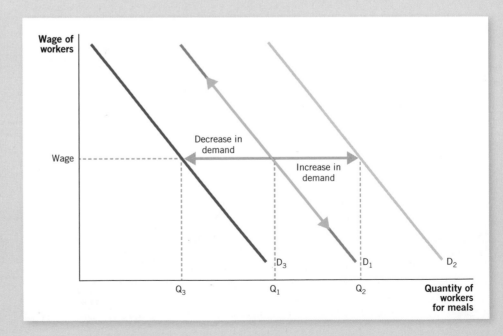

Two primary factors shift labor demand: (1) a change in demand for the product that the firm produces and (2) a change in the cost of producing that product.

Changes in Demand for the Product the Firm Produces

Because a firm is primarily interested in making a profit, it hires workers only when the value of the marginal product of labor is higher than the cost of hiring labor. Consider Agaves. If a rival Mexican restaurant closes down, many of its customers will likely switch to Agaves. Then Agaves will need to prepare more meals, which will cause the entire demand curve for cooks, table clearers, and waitstaff to shift outward to D_2 in Figure 14.2.

A machine at McDonald's helps to fill the drink orders.

Changes in Cost

A change in the cost of production can sometimes be positive, such as when a new technology makes production less expensive. It can also be negative, such as when an increase in the cost of a needed raw material makes production more expensive.

In terms of a positive change for the firm, technology can act as a substitute for workers. For example, microwave ovens enable restaurants to prepare the same number of meals with fewer workers. The same is true with the growing trend of using conveyor belts and automated systems to help prepare meals or even serve them. Therefore, changes in technology can lower a firm's demand for workers.

In the short run, substituting technology for workers may seem like a bad outcome for the workers and for society in general. However, in the long run that is not typically the case. Consider how technological advances affect the demand for lumberjacks in the forestry business. As timber companies invest in new harvesting technology, they can replace traditional logging jobs, which are dangerous and inefficient, with equipment that is safer and more efficient. By deploying the new technology, the lumber companies can cut down trees faster and more safely, and the workers are freed up to work in other parts of the economy. In the short run, the result is fewer timber jobs; those workers must find employment elsewhere. Admittedly, this adjustment is painful for the workers involved, and they often have difficulty finding jobs that pay as well as the job that they lost. However, the new equipment requires trained, highly skilled operators who can fell more trees in a

One John Deere 1270D harvester can replace 10 lumberjacks.

PRACTICE WHAT YOU KNOW

Value of the Marginal Product of Labor: Flower Barrettes

Question: Penny can make five flower barrettes each hour. She works 8 hours each day. Penny is paid $75.00 a day. The firm can sell the barrettes for $1.99 each. What is Penny's value of the marginal product of labor? What is the barrette firm's marginal profit from hiring her?

Answer: In 8 hours, Penny can make 40 barrettes. Because each barrette sells for $1.99, her value of the marginal product of labor, or VMP_{labor}, is $40 \times \$1.99$, or $79.60. Her VMP_{labor} is greater than the daily wage she receives, so the marginal profit from hiring her is $79.60 − $75.00, or $4.60.

How many flower barrettes could you make in an hour?

shorter period than traditional lumberjacks can. As a result, harvester operators have a higher marginal product of labor and can command higher wages.

For every harvester operator employed at a higher wage, there are perhaps 10 traditional lumberjacks displaced and in need of a job. But consider what happens after the short-run job losses. Overall production rises because while 1 worker harvests trees, the 9 other workers are forced to move into related fields or do something entirely different. It might take some of these displaced workers many years to find new work, but when they eventually do, society benefits in the long run. What once required 10 workers to produce now takes only 1, and the 9 other workers are able to work in other jobs and grow the economy in different ways.

To summarize, if labor becomes more productive, the VMP curve shifts to the right, driving up both wages and employment, which is exactly what occurs with the demand for harvester operators. There is the potential for substitution as well, causing the demand for traditional labor to fall. This is what has happened to traditional lumberjack jobs, leading to a decrease in those workers' wages.

Where Does the Supply of Labor Come From?

In this section, we examine the connection between the wage rate and the number of workers who are willing to supply their services to employers. Because workers also value leisure, the supply curve is not always directly related to the wage rate. Indeed, at high wage levels, some workers may desire to cut back the number of hours that they work. Other factors that influence the labor supply include other employment opportunities, the changing composition of the workforce, migration, and immigration; we explore these factors as well.

The Labor-Leisure Trade-Off

People work because they need to earn a living. While it is certainly true that many workers enjoy their jobs, this does not mean they would work for nothing. In other words, while many people experience satisfaction in their work, most of us have other interests, obligations, and goals. As a result, the supply of labor depends both on the wage that is offered and on how individuals want to use their time. We call this relationship the *labor-leisure trade-off.*

In our society today, most individuals must work to meet their basic needs. However, once those needs are met, a worker might be more inclined to use his or her time in leisure. Would higher wages induce an employee to give up leisure and work more hours? The answer is both yes and no!

At higher wage rates, workers may be willing to work more hours, or substitute labor for leisure. This effect is known as the **substitution effect**. One way to think about the substitution effect is to note that higher wages make leisure time more expensive, because the opportunity cost of enjoying more leisure means giving up more income. For instance, suppose that Emeril is a short-order cook at Agaves. He works 40 hours at $10 per hour and can also work 4 hours overtime at the same wage. If Emeril decides to work the overtime, he ends up working 44 hours and earns $440. In that case, he substitutes more labor for less leisure.

But at higher wage rates, some workers may work fewer hours, or substitute leisure for labor. This effect is known as the **income effect**. Leisure is a normal good (see Chapter 3), so as income rises, some workers may use their additional income to demand more leisure. As a consequence, at high income levels the income effect may outweigh the substitution effect and cause the supply curve to bend backward. For example, suppose that Rachael chooses to work overtime for $10 per hour. Her total pay (like Emeril's) will be $10 × 44, or $440. If her wage rises to $11, she may continue to work the overtime at a higher wage. However, if she does not work overtime, she will earn as much as she earned before the wage increase ($11 × 40 = $440), and she might choose to discontinue the overtime altogether or work fewer overtime hours. The income effect is at work when Rachael's wage goes up and she chooses to work fewer hours.

Figure 14.3 shows what can happen to the labor supply curve when the supply of labor responds directly to wage increases. When the wage rises progressively from W_1 to W_2 to W_3, the number of hours worked increases from Q_1 to Q_2 to Q_3, along the curve labeled S_{normal}. However, at high wage rates the number of hours worked is large. As a result, workers might experience diminishing marginal utility from the additional income and thus might value increased leisure time more than increased income. In this situation, workers might choose to work less, and the normal supply curve bends backward between W_2 and W_3 because as the wage goes up, the hours worked go down.

Trade-offs

The **substitution effect** occurs when laborers work more hours at higher wages, substituting labor for leisure.

Opportunity cost

The **income effect** occurs when laborers work fewer hours at higher wages, using their additional income to demand more leisure.

The Labor Supply Curve

At high wage levels (in this figure, above W_2), the income effect may become larger than the substitution effect and cause the labor supply curve to bend backward. The backward-bending supply curve occurs when additional leisure time becomes more valuable than additional income.

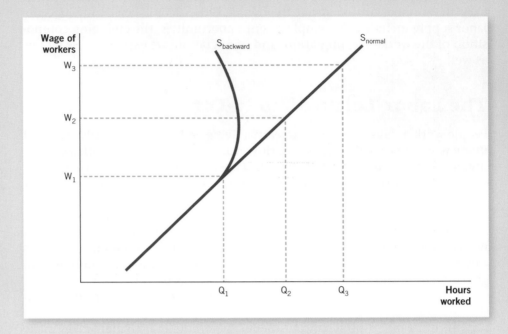

A **backward-bending labor supply curve** occurs when workers value additional leisure more than additional income.

The **backward-bending labor supply curve** occurs when workers value additional leisure more than additional income. The labor supply curve bends backward when the income effect is large enough to offset the substitution effect that typically causes individuals to work more when the wage rate is higher. Because most workers in the real world do not reach wage level W_2 (that is, a wage at which they might begin to value leisure more than labor), we will draw the supply curve as upward sloping throughout the chapter. Nevertheless, it is important to recognize that the direct relationship we normally observe does not always hold.

Changes in the Supply of Labor

If we hold the wage rate constant, a number of additional factors determine the supply of labor. In this section, we look beyond the wage rate to other forces that govern the supply of labor.

Turning to Figure 14.4, the red arrow along S_1 shows that the quantity of workers increases when the wage rate rises. But what will cause a shift in the supply curve? Three primary factors affect the supply curve: other employment opportunities, the changing composition of the workforce, and migration and immigration.

Other Employment Opportunities

The supply of workers for any given job depends on the employment opportunities and prevailing wage in related labor markets. Let's consider the supply of labor at Agaves. Notice that the supply curve for labor in Figure 14.4 is

FIGURE 14.4

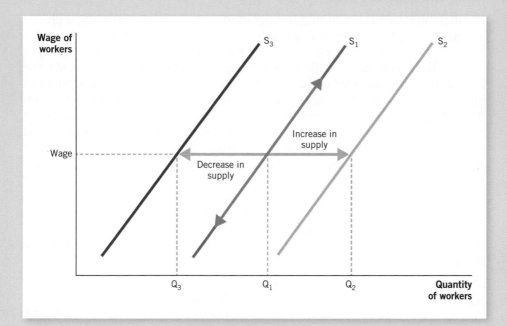

The Labor Supply Curve

A change in the quantity supplied occurs when wages change, causing a movement along the supply curve S_1, shown by the red arrow. Changes in the supply of labor (the quantity of workers), shown by the gray horizontal arrows, can occur due to other employment opportunities, the changing composition of the workforce, immigration, and migration.

upward sloping; if Agaves offers higher wages, more workers, such as table clearers, will be willing to work there. We illustrate this situation with the red arrow that moves along the original supply curve (S_1).

The supply of table clearers also depends on a number of nonwage factors. Because table clearers are generally young and largely unskilled, the number of laborers willing to work is influenced by the prevailing wages in similar jobs. For instance, if the wages of baggers at local grocery stores increase, some of the table clearers at Agaves will decide to bag at local grocery stores instead. The supply of table clearers will decrease and cause a leftward shift to S_3. If the wages of baggers were to fall below the wages of table clearers, the supply of table clearers would increase, or shift to the right to S_2. These shifts reflect the fact that when jobs that require comparable skills have different wage rates, the number of workers willing to supply labor for the lower-wage job will shrink and the number willing to supply labor for the better-paid job will grow.

The Changing Composition of the Workforce

Over the last 30 years, the labor force participation rate (as measured by the female/male ratio) has increased significantly in most developed countries. Among that group, as measured by the United Nations Development Programme, the United States saw its female/male ratio rise from 66% to 82%, Switzerland from 67% to 81%, and New Zealand from 65% to 84%. Overall, there are many more women employed in the workforce today than there were a generation ago, and the supply of workers in many occupations has expanded significantly as a result.

Immigration and Migration

Demographic factors, including immigration and migration, also play a crucial role in the supply of labor. For example, immigration—both legal and illegal—increases the available supply of workers by a significant amount each year.

In 2015, over half a million people from foreign countries entered the United States through legal channels and gained permission to seek employment. There are over 40 million legal immigrants in the United States. In addition, illegal immigrants account for close to 10 million workers in the United States, many of whom enter the country to work as hotel maids, janitors, and fruit pickers. Often when states suggest or pass a tough immigration law, businesses in food and beverage, agriculture, and construction protest because they need inexpensive labor to remain competitive, and U.S. citizens are reluctant to work these jobs. Many states have wrestled with the issue, but policies that address illegal immigration remain controversial, and the solutions are difficult. The states need the cheap labor but don't want to pay additional costs such as medical care, as well as the cost of schooling the illegal immigrants' children.

ECONOMICS IN THE MEDIA

Immigration

A Day without a Mexican

This offbeat film from 2004 asks a simple question: What would happen to California's economy if all the Mexicans in the state suddenly disappeared? The answer: the state economy would come to a halt.

Indeed, the loss of the Mexican labor force would have a dramatic impact on California's labor market. For example, the film makes fun of affluent Californians who must do without low-cost workers to take care of their yards and homes. It also showcases a farm owner whose produce is ready to be picked without any migrant workers to do the job.

In addition, the film adeptly points out that migrants from Mexico add a tremendous amount of value to the local economy through their purchases as well as their labor. One inspired scene depicts a television commercial for a "disappearance sale" put on by a local business after it realizes that most of its regular customers are gone.

A Day without a Mexican illustrates both sides of the labor relationship at work. Because demand and supply are inseparably linked, the disappearance of all of the Mexican workers creates numerous voids that require serious adjustments for the economy. ✳

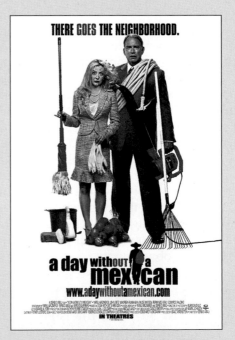

What would happen to an economy if one-third of the workers suddenly disappeared? Hispanics hold 35% of California's jobs.

For the purposes of this discussion, we consider migration to be the process of moving from one place to another within the United States. Although the U.S. population grows at an annual rate of approximately 1%, there are significant regional differences. Indeed, large population influxes lead to marked regional changes in the demand for labor and the supply of people looking for work. According to the U.S. Census Bureau, in 2010 the 10 fastest-growing states were in the South or West, with some states adding as much as 4% to their population in a single year. States in these areas provided 84% of the nation's population growth from 2000 to 2010, with Nevada, Utah, North Carolina, Idaho, and Texas all adding at least 20% to their populations.

It is worth noting that statewide data can hide significant localized changes. For example, census data from 2010 indicate that a number of counties experienced 50% or more population growth between 2000 and 2010. The biggest population gain was in Kendall County, Illinois, a far-flung suburb of Chicago that grew by nearly 100% between censuses. The county has been transitioning from an agricultural area to a bedroom community. Most of the fastest-growing counties are, like Kendall, relatively distant suburbs of major metropolitan areas. These are areas where new homes are available at comparatively reasonable prices.

PRACTICE WHAT YOU KNOW

The Labor Supply Curve: What Would You Do with a Big Raise?

Question: Your friend is concerned about his uncle, who just received a big raise. Your friend doesn't understand why his uncle wants to take time off from his job to travel. Can you help him understand why his uncle might want to cut back on his hours?

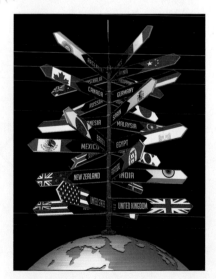

If you got a big raise, would you travel the world?

Answer: Ordinarily, we think of the labor supply curve as upward sloping, in which case higher wages translate into more hours worked and less leisure time. However, when the wage rate becomes high enough, some workers choose to substitute leisure for labor because they feel that enjoying free time is more valuable than earning more money. In this case, the labor supply curve bends backward, and the worker spends fewer hours working as his wage rises. Your friend's uncle is reflecting this tendency.

What Are the Determinants of Demand and Supply in the Labor Market?

In earlier chapters, we saw how markets reconcile the forces of demand and supply through pricing. Now that we have considered the forces that govern demand and supply in the labor market, we are ready to see how the equilibrium wage is established. We can then examine the labor market in greater detail and identify what causes shortages and surpluses of labor, why outsourcing occurs, and what happens when there is a single buyer of labor. The goal of this section is to provide a rich set of examples that help you become comfortable using demand and supply curves to understand how the labor market operates.

How Does the Market for Labor Reach Equilibrium?

We can think about wages as the price at which workers are willing to "rent" their time to employers. Turning to Figure 14.5, we see that at wages above equilibrium (W_E), the supply of workers willing to rent their time

FIGURE 14.5

Equilibrium in the Labor Market

At high wages (W_{high}), a surplus of workers exists. The wage rate is driven down until the supply of workers and the demand for workers reach equilibrium. At low wages (W_{low}), a shortage occurs. The shortage forces the wage rate up until the equilibrium wage is reached and the shortage disappears.

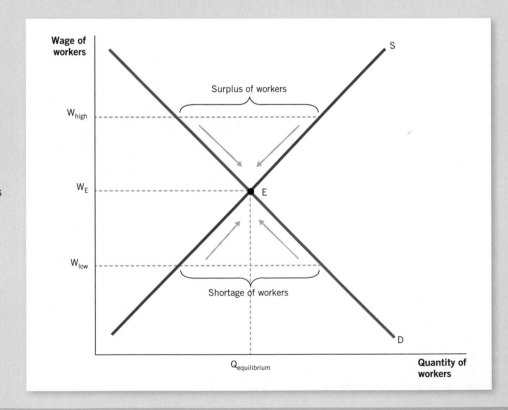

exceeds the demand for that time. The result is a surplus of available workers. The surplus, in turn, places downward pressure on wages. As wages drop, fewer workers are willing to rent their time to employers. When wages drop to the equilibrium wage, the surplus of workers is eliminated. At that point, the number of workers willing to work in that profession at that wage is exactly equal to the number of job openings that exist at that wage.

A similar process guides the labor market toward equilibrium from low wages. At wages below the equilibrium, the demand for labor exceeds the available supply. The shortage forces firms to offer higher wages to attract workers. As a result, wages rise until the shortage is eliminated at the equilibrium wage.

ECONOMICS IN THE REAL WORLD

Where Are the Nurses?

The United States is experiencing a shortage of nurses. A stressful job with long hours, nursing requires years of training. As baby boomers age, demand for nursing care is expected to rise. At the same time, the existing pool of nurses is rapidly aging and nearing retirement. According to the Bureau of Labor Statistics, the shortage of nurses in America will approach 1 million by 2025, making nursing the number 1 job in the country in terms of growth prospects.

However, economists are confident that the shortage of nurses will disappear long before 2025. After all, a shortage creates upward pressure on wages. In this case, rising wages also signal that nursing services are in high demand and that wages will continue to rise. This situation has led to a surge in nursing school applications and caused some practicing nurses to postpone retirement.

Because the training process takes two or more years to complete, the labor market for nurses won't return to equilibrium immediately. The nursing shortage will persist for a few years until the quantity of nurses supplied to the market increases. During that time, many of the tasks that nurses traditionally carry out—such as taking patients' vital signs—will likely be shifted to nursing assistants or technicians.

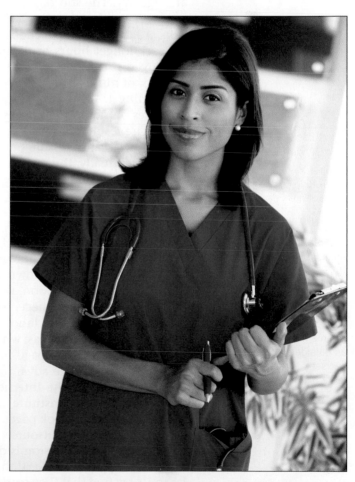

Entering an occupation with a shortage of workers will result in higher pay.

Economics tells us that the combination of more newly trained nurses entering the market and the transfer of certain nursing services to assistants and technicians will eventually cause the nursing shortage to disappear. Remember that when a market is out of balance, forces are acting on it to restore it to equilibrium. ✴

Change and Equilibrium in the Labor Market

Now that we have seen how labor markets find an equilibrium, let's see what happens when the demand or supply changes. Figure 14.6 contains two graphs. Panel (a) shows a shift in labor demand, and panel (b) shows a shift in labor supply. In both cases, the equilibrium wage and the equilibrium quantity of workers employed adjust accordingly.

Let's start with a shift in labor demand, shown in panel (a). Imagine that the demand for medical care increases due to an aging population and that, as a result, the demand for nurses increases, causing a shift in the demand curve from D_1 to D_2. The result is a shortage of workers equal to $Q_3 - Q_1$ at wage W_1. The shortage places upward pressure on wages, which increase from W_1 to W_2. As wages rise, nursing becomes more attractive as a profession. Additional people choose to enter the field, and existing nurses decide to work longer hours or postpone retirement. Thus, the number of nurses employed rises from Q_1 to Q_2. Eventually, the wage settles at W_2, and the number of nurses employed reaches Q_2.

Turning to panel (b), we see what happens when the supply of nurses increases. As additional nurses are certified, the overall supply shifts from S_1 to S_2. The result is a surplus of workers equal to $Q_3 - Q_1$ at wage W_1, which places downward pressure on wages. As a result, the wage rate falls from W_1 to W_2. Eventually, the market wage settles at W_2, the new equilibrium point is E_2, and the number of nurses employed reaches Q_2.

Outsourcing

Why would a firm hire someone from outside if it has a qualified employee nearby? This practice, known as *outsourcing*, has gotten a lot of attention in recent years. In this section, we explain how outsourcing works, why companies do it, and how it affects the labor market for workers.

Outsourcing of labor occurs when a firm shifts jobs to an outside company, usually overseas, where the cost of labor is lower.

The **outsourcing of labor** occurs when a firm shifts jobs to an outside company, usually overseas, where the cost of labor is lower. In the publishing industry, for example, page make-up (also known as composition) is often done overseas to take advantage of lower labor costs. This outsourcing has been facilitated by the Internet, which eliminates the shipping delays and costs that used to constitute a large part of the business. Today, a qualified worker can lay out book pages anywhere in the world.

When countries outsource, their pool of potential workers expands. But whether a labor expansion is driven by outsourcing or by an increase in the domestic supply of workers, those who are already employed in that particular industry find that they earn less. Moreover, a rise in unemployment occurs in the occupation that can be outsourced.

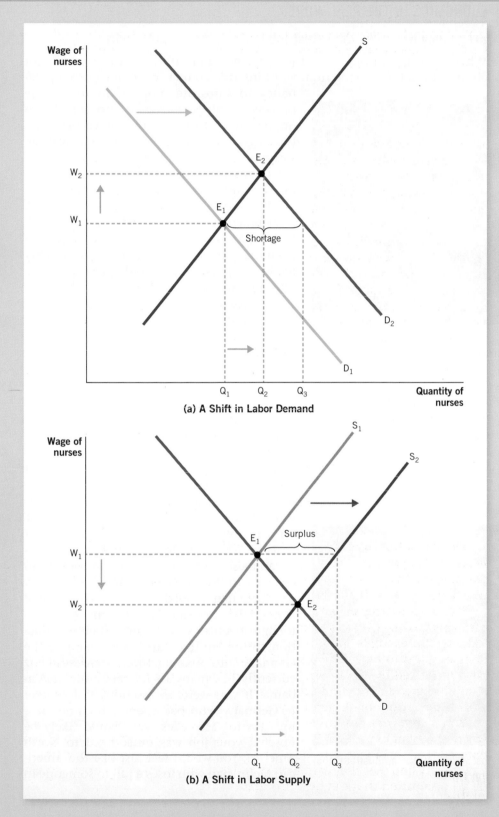

(a) A Shift in Labor Demand

(b) A Shift in Labor Supply

FIGURE 14.6

Shifting the Labor Market Equilibrium

In panel (a), the demand for nurses increases, creating a shortage of workers equal to $Q_3 - Q_1$, which leads to a higher equilibrium wage (W_2) and a higher quantity of nurses employed (Q_2) than before. In panel (b), the supply of nurses increases. The result is a surplus of workers equal to $Q_3 - Q_1$, causing the equilibrium wage to fall (to W_2) and the number of nurses employed to rise (to Q_2).

ECONOMICS IN THE REAL WORLD

Pregnancy Becomes the Latest Job to Be Outsourced to India

When we think of outsourced jobs, we generally think of call centers, not childbirth. But a growing number of infertile couples have outsourced pregnancy to surrogate mothers in India. The process involves surrogate mothers being impregnated with eggs that have been fertilized in vitro. While often controversial, surrogacy is a growing practice in India, and has been legal in India since 2002, as it is in many other countries, including the United States. While no reliable numbers track such pregnancies nationwide, doctors work with surrogates in virtually every major city in India. Surrogate mothers earn roughly $5,000 for a nine-month commitment. This amount is the equivalent of what low-skilled workers in India earn in 10 or more years. Couples typically pay approximately $10,000 for all of the costs associated with the pregnancy. ✳

Kaival Hospital in Anand, India, matches infertile couples with local women, such as these surrogate mothers.

The Global Implications of Outsourcing in the Short Run

Recall our chapter-opening misconception that outsourcing is bad for the economy. Many people hold that opinion because when they think of outsourcing, they immediately imagine the jobs that are lost in the short run. However, the reality is more complex. Outsourced jobs are not lost; they are relocated from high-labor-cost areas to low-labor-cost areas. Outsourcing also creates benefits for firms in the form of lower production costs. The lower costs translate into lower prices for consumers and also help the firms that outsource to compete in the global economy.

Outsourcing need not cost the United States jobs. Consider what happens when foreign countries outsource their production to the United States. For example, the German auto manufacturer Mercedes-Benz currently has many of its cars built in Alabama. If you were an assembly-line worker in Germany who had spent a lifetime making cars for Mercedes, you would likely be upset if your job was outsourced to North America. You would feel just like the American technician who loses a job to someone in

The Mercedes-Benz plant near Tuscaloosa, Alabama, illustrates that outsourcing is more than just a one-way street.

India or the software writer who is replaced by a worker in China. Outsourcing always produces a job winner and a job loser. In the case of foreign outsourcing to the United States, employment in this country rises. In fact, the Mercedes-Benz plant in Alabama employs more than 3,000 workers. Those jobs were transferred to the United States because the company felt that it would be more profitable to hire American workers and make the vehicles in the United States rather than construct them in Germany and shipping them across the Atlantic.

Figure 14.7 shows how outsourcing by foreign firms helps to increase U.S. labor demand. In panel (a), we see the job loss and lower wages that occur in Germany when jobs are outsourced to the United States. As the demand for labor in Germany falls from D_1 to D_2, wages drop to W_2 and employment declines to Q_2. Panel (b) illustrates the corresponding increase in demand for U.S. labor in Alabama. As demand shifts from D_1 to D_2, wages rise to W_2 and employment rises to Q_2.

Because each nation will experience outsourcing flows out of and into the country, it is impossible to say anything definitive about the overall impact of outsourcing on labor in the short run. However, it is highly unlikely that workers who lose high-paying jobs toward the end of their working lives will be able to find other jobs that pay equally well.

The Global Implications of Outsourcing in the Long Run

Although we see mixed results for outsourcing in the short run, we can say that in the long run outsourcing benefits domestic consumers and producers. In fact, outsourcing is a key component in international trade. Throughout this book, we have seen that trade creates value. When companies and even countries specialize, they become more efficient. The efficiency gains, or cost savings, help producers to expand production. In the absence of trade barriers, lower costs benefit consumers in domestic and international markets through lower prices, and the outsourcing of jobs provides the income for foreign workers to purchase domestic imports. Therefore, the mutually interdependent nature of international trade enhances overall social welfare.

Trade creates value

FIGURE 14.7

Shifting the Labor Market Equilibrium

Outsourcing creates more demand in one market at the expense of the other. In panel (a), the demand for German labor declines from D_1 to D_2, leading to lower wages and less employment. Panel (b) shows the increase in the demand for labor from D_1 to D_2 in Alabama. The results are higher wages and more employment.

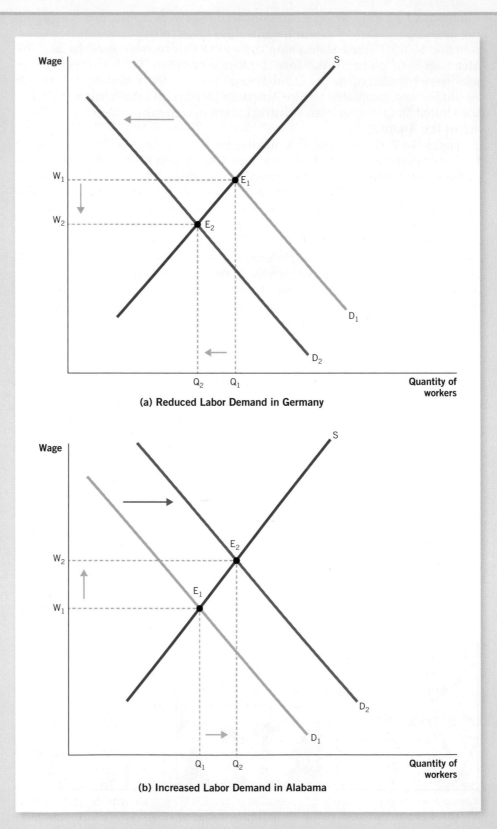

(a) Reduced Labor Demand in Germany

(b) Increased Labor Demand in Alabama

Monopsony

In looking at supply, demand, and equilibrium in the labor market, we have assumed that the market for labor is competitive. But that is not always the case. Sometimes the labor market has only a few buyers or sellers who are able to capture market power. One extreme form of market power is **monopsony**, which occurs when only a single buyer exists. Like a monopolist, a monopsonist has a great deal of market power. As a consequence, the output in the labor market will favor a monopsonist whenever one is present.

In Chapter 10, we examined how a monopolist behaves. Compared with a firm in a competitive market, the monopolist charges a higher price for the product it sells. Likewise, a monopsonist in the labor market can leverage its market power. Because it is the only firm hiring, it can pay its workers less. Isolated college towns are a good example. Workers who wish to live in such college towns often find that almost all the available jobs are through the college. Because it is the chief provider of jobs, the college has a monopsony in the labor market. It can use its market power to hire many local workers at low wages.

Monopsony is a situation in which there is only one buyer.

ECONOMICS IN THE REAL WORLD

Pay and Performance in Major League Baseball

Gerald Scully was the first sports economist. In his seminal work, "Pay and Performance in Major League Baseball," published in 1974 in the *American Economic Review*, Scully used economic analysis to determine the value of the marginal product that each player produced during the season. Scully's work was important because at that time each player's contract had a "reserve clause" stating that the player belonged to the team for his entire career unless he was traded or released.

If a player was unhappy with his contract, his only option was to withdraw from playing. Because most players could not make more than they were earning as baseball players in their next-most-productive job, the teams knew that the players would stay for the wage that the team was willing to pay. Therefore, under the reserve clause each team was a monopsonist. The teams used their market power to suppress wages and increase their profits.

In this context, Scully's work changed everything. He used two baseball statistics—slugging percentage for hitters and the strikeout-to-walk ratio for pitchers—to evaluate the player performance and then estimate how much player performance affected winning. Next he examined the correlation between winning and revenues, which enabled him to estimate how many dollars of revenue each player generated for his team. The results were stunning. The top players at that time earned about $100,000 per season but generated nearly $1 million in revenue for their teams, approximately 10 times more than they were being paid. But because each player was tied to a particular team through the reserve clause, no matter how good the player was, he lacked the leverage to bargain for higher wages.

Scully's work played a key role in the court decisions of two players, Andy Messersmith and Dave McNally, whose cases led to the repeal of the reserve clause in 1975. The reserve clause was struck down because the practice was deemed anticompetitive. Today, because players have gained limited free agency, salaries have steadily increased. Top professional baseball players can earn over $30 million a year, and the average salary is slightly more than $4 million. ✳

What is the correlation between winning and revenues?

TABLE 14.2

Why Some Workers Make More than Others

Question	Answer
Why do economists generally earn more than elementary school teachers?	Supply is the key. There are fewer qualified economists than certified elementary school teachers. Therefore, the equilibrium wage in economics is higher than it is in elementary education. It's also important to note that demand factors may be part of the explanation. The value of the marginal product of labor of economists is generally higher than that of most elementary school teachers because many economists work in industry, which pays higher wages than the public sector.
Why do people who work the night shift earn more than those who do the same job during the day?	Again, supply is the key. Fewer people are willing to work at night, so the wage necessary to attract labor to perform the job must be higher. (That is, night shift workers earn what is called a *compensating differential*, which we discuss in Chapter 15.)
Why do professional athletes and successful actors make so much when what they do is not essential?	Demand and supply both play important roles here. The paying public is willing, even eager, to spend a large amount of income on entertainment. Thus, demand for entertainment is high. On the supply end of the equation, the number of individuals who capture the imagination of the paying public is small, and they are therefore paid handsomely. Since the value of the marginal product that they create is incredibly high, and the supply of workers with these skills is quite small, accomplished athletes and actors earn huge incomes.
Why do janitors, construction workers, and nurses—whose jobs are essential—have salaries that are a tiny fraction of celebrities' salaries?	Demand again. The value of the marginal product of labor created in these essential jobs is low, so their employers are unable to pay high wages.

Why Do Some Workers Make More Than Others?

While most workers generally spend 35 to 40 hours a week at work, the amount they earn varies dramatically. Table 14.2 presents a number of simple questions that answer the larger question "Why do some workers make more than others?"

The table shows how demand and supply determine wages in a variety of settings. Workers with a high-value marginal product of labor invariably earn more than those with a lower-value marginal product of labor. It is important to note that working an "essential" job does not guarantee a high income. Instead, the highest incomes are reserved for jobs that have high demand and a low supply of workers. In other words, our preconceived notions of fairness take a backseat to the underlying market forces that govern pay. In the next chapter, we consider many additional factors that determine wages, including wage discrimination.

What Role Do Land and Capital Play in Production?

In addition to labor, firms need land and capital to produce goods and services. In this section, we complete our analysis of the resource market by considering how land and capital enter into the production process. Returning to the restaurant Agaves, we know that the business hires labor to make

PRACTICE WHAT YOU KNOW

Labor Supply: Changes in Labor Supply

Question: A company builds a new facility that doubles its workspace and equipment. How is labor affected?

Answer: The company has probably experienced additional demand for the product it sells. Therefore, it needs additional employees to staff

Labor is always subject to changes in demand.

the facility, causing a positive shift in the demand curve. When the demand for labor rises, wages increase and so does the number of people employed.

Question: A company decides to outsource 100 jobs from a facility in Indiana to Indonesia. How is labor affected in the short run?

Answer: This situation leads to two changes. First, a decrease in demand for labor in Indiana results in lower wages there and fewer workers hired. Second, an increase in demand for labor in Indonesia results in higher wages there and more workers hired.

meals. But to do their jobs, the workers need equipment, tables, chairs, cash registers, and a kitchen. Without a physical location and a host of capital resources, labor would be irrelevant.

The Market for Land

Like the demand for labor, the demand for land is determined by the value of the marginal product that it generates. However, unlike the supply of labor, the supply of land is ordinarily fixed. We can think of it as nonresponsive to prices, or perfectly inelastic.

In Figure 14.8, the vertical supply curve reflects the inelastic supply. The price of land is determined by the intersection of supply and demand. Notice the label on the vertical axis, which reflects the price of land as the rental price necessary to use it, not the price necessary to purchase it. When evaluating a firm's economic situation, we do not count the entire purchase price of the land it needs. To do so would dramatically overstate the cost of land in the production process because the land is not used up, but only occupied for a certain period. For example, consider a car that you buy. You drive it for a year and put 15,000 miles on it. Counting the entire purchase price of the car would overstate the true operating cost for one year of service. The true cost of operating the vehicle includes wear and tear along with operating expenses such as gasoline, maintenance, and service visits. A similar process is at work with land. Firms that own land consider the rent they could have

ECONOMICS IN THE MEDIA

Value of the Marginal Product of Labor

Moneyball

Moneyball (2011), a film based on Michael Lewis's 2003 book of the same name, details the struggles of the Oakland Athletics, a major-league baseball team. The franchise attempts to overcome some seemingly impossible obstacles with the help of its general manager, Billy Beane, by applying innovative statistical analysis, known as sabermetrics, pioneered by Bill James.

Traditional baseball scouts use experience, intuition, and subjective criteria to evaluate potential players. However, Beane, formerly a heavily recruited high school player who failed to have a successful professional career, knows firsthand that this method of scouting does not guarantee success. The Oakland A's lack the financial ability to pay as much as other teams. While trying to negotiate a trade with the Cleveland Indians, Beane meets Peter Brand, a young Yale economist who has new ideas about applying statistical analysis to baseball in order to build a better team. Brand explains that evaluating a player's marginal product would be a better tool for recruitment.

In the key scene in the movie, Brand briefly explains his methodology for evaluating players and how the A's can build a championship team:

> It's about getting things down to one number. Using the stats the way we read them, we'll find value in players that no one else can see. People are overlooked for a variety of biased reasons and perceived flaws: age, appearance, and personality. Bill James and mathematics cut straight through that. Billy, of the 20,000 notable players for us to consider, I believe that there is a championship team of 25 people that we can afford, because everyone else in baseball undervalues them.

The A's go on to have a remarkable season by picking up "outcasts" that no other team wanted.

Can a young economist's algorithm save the Oakland A's?

Thanks to Kim Holder (the University of West Georgia).

Opportunity cost

earned if they had rented the land out for the year. This method nicely captures the opportunity cost of using the land.

Because the supply of land is usually fixed, changes in demand determine the rental price. When demand is low—say, at D_1—the rental price received, P_1, is also low. When demand is high—say, at D_2—the rental price of land is high, at P_2. Apartment rentals near college campuses provide a good example of the conditions under which the demand for land is high. Because students and faculty want to live near campus, the demand for land is often much higher there than even a few blocks away. Like labor, the demand for land is derived from the demand for the products that it is used to produce. In this case, the demand for apartments, homes, and retail space near campus is very high. The high demand drives up the rental price of land closer to campus because the marginal product of land there is higher.

Marginal thinking

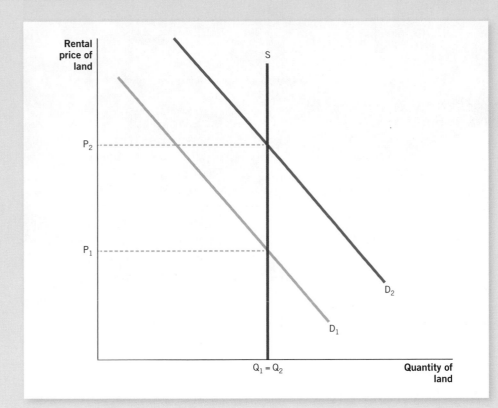

FIGURE 14.8

Supply and Demand in the Market for Land
Because the supply of land is fixed, the price it commands depends on demand. If demand increases from D_1 to D_2, the price will rise from P_1 to P_2. Note that "price" here reflects the rental price of the land, not the purchase price.

When we see the term "rent," most of us think of the rental price of an apartment or house. But when economists talk about an **economic rent**, they mean the difference between what a factor of production earns and what it could earn in the next-best alternative. Economic rent is different from *rent seeking*. Recall from Chapter 10 that rent seeking occurs when firms compete to seek a monopoly position. In contrast, economic rent refers to investors' ability to beat their opportunity cost. For instance, in the case of housing near college campuses, a small studio apartment generally commands a much higher rent than a similar apartment located 10 miles away. Why? The rent near campus must be high enough to compensate the property owners for using their land for an apartment instead of in other ways that might also be profitable in the area—for example, for a single residence, a business, or a parking lot. Once you move 10 miles farther out, the number of people interested in using the land for these purposes declines.

More generally, in areas where many people would like to live or work, rental prices are often very high. Many places in the United States have high rental prices, but none of those compare with Tokyo, where an average two-bedroom apartment rents for almost $4,500 a month. That staggering amount makes most apartment rental prices in the United States seem downright inexpensive. Similarly, owners of property in Moscow, Hong Kong, London, and New York all receive more economic rent on properties than those who own similar two-bedroom apartments in Peoria, Idaho Falls, Scranton, or Chattanooga. The ability to earn a substantial economic rent comes back

Economic rent is the difference between what a factor of production earns and what it could earn in the next-best alternative.

A satellite photo shows manufactured islands in Dubai, United Arab Emirates—an exception to our assumption that the amount of land is fixed.

Opportunity
costs

to opportunity costs: because there are so many other potential uses of property in densely populated areas, rents are correspondingly higher.

The Market for Capital

Capital, or the equipment and materials needed to produce goods, is a necessary factor of production. The demand for capital is determined by the value of the marginal product that it creates. Like the demand for land and labor, the demand for capital is a derived demand: a firm requires capital only if the product it produces is in demand. The demand for capital is also downward sloping, reflecting the fact that the value of the marginal product associated with its use declines as the amount used rises.

When to Use More Labor, Land, or Capital

Firms must evaluate whether hiring additional labor, utilizing more land, or deploying more capital will constitute the best use of their resources. To do this, they compare the value of the marginal product per dollar spent across the three factors of production.

Let's consider an example. Suppose that a company pays its employees $15 per hour, the rental rate of land is $5,000 per acre per year, and the rental rate of capital is $1,000 per year. The company's manager determines that the value of the marginal product of labor is $450, the value of the marginal product of an acre of land is $125,000, and the value of the marginal product of capital is $40,000. Is the firm using the right mix of resources? Table 14.3 compares the ratios of the value of the marginal product (VMP) of each factor of

Outsourcing

Outsourcing, though painful for those whose jobs are outsourced, is simply the application of a fundamental economic principle—keep costs as low as possible. Labor is usually the most expensive input for a business, so all managers must seek to pay the lowest wage that still ensures an effective workforce. Firms seek the right balance of costs and relevant skills when outsourcing jobs. Here is a look at three representative jobs in the United States, Mexico, China, and India, with salaries measured as a percentage of the typical U.S. salary.

■ U.S. salary   China   ■ India   Mexico

Information technology project manager
30%   38%   64%
0%   50%   100%

Software engineer
11%   22%   36%
0%   50%   100%

Customer service representative
18%   42%   55%
0%   50%   100%

The communications and transportation revolutions, along with the increasing skill level of foreign labor, have created conditions for the outsourcing of millions of U.S. jobs to China, India, and Latin America.

Outsourcing is about comparative advantage. Firms hire foreign workers who hold a comparative advantage and can produce a good or service more cheaply and at a lower opportunity cost than domestic workers.

REVIEW QUESTIONS

- Software engineering jobs are outsourced from the United States to India. Use supply and demand curves to sketch the effects on the U.S. and Indian labor forces.

- Outsourcing is controversial. Explain why by citing effects to the economy both in the short run and long run.

TABLE 14.3

Determining the Bang per Buck for Each Resource

(1) Factor of production	(2) Value of the marginal product	(3) Wage or rental price	(4) Bang per buck
Labor	$450	$15	$450 ÷ 15 = $30
Land	125,000	5,000	125,000 ÷ 5,000 = 25
Capital	40,000	1,000	40,000 ÷ 1,000 = 40

production with the cost of attaining that value (this calculation gives us the "bang per buck" for each resource, or the relative benefit of using each resource).

Looking at these results, we see that the highest bang per buck (column 4) is the value $40 created by dividing the VMP of capital by the rental price of capital. When we compare this value with the bang per buck for labor and land, we see that the firm is getting more benefit per dollar spent on capital than from labor ($30) or land ($25). Therefore, the firm would benefit from using capital more intensively. As it does so, the VMP of capital in column 2 will fall due to diminishing returns, and the bang per buck for capital will drop from $40 in column 4 to a number that is more in line with bang per buck for labor and land. Conversely, the firm is using land ($25) too intensively, and it would benefit from using less. Doing so will raise the VMP it produces and increase its bang per buck for land. By using less land and more capital and by tweaking the use of labor as well, the firm will eventually bring the value created by all three factors to a point at which the bang per buck spent is equal for each of the factors. At that point, the firm will be utilizing its resources efficiently.

Why does all this matter? Because the world is always changing: wages rise and fall, as do property values and the cost of acquiring capital. A firm must constantly adjust the mix of land, labor, and capital it uses to get the largest return. Moreover, the markets for land, labor, and capital are connected. The amount of labor a firm uses depends not only on the marginal product of labor, but also on the marginal product of land and capital. Therefore, a change in the supply of one factor will alter the returns of all factors. For instance, if wages fall, firms will be inclined to hire more labor. But if they hire more labor, they will use less capital. Capital itself is not any more, or less, productive. Rather, lower wages reduce the demand for capital. In this situation, the demand curve for capital would shift to the left, lowering the rental price of capital as well as the quantity of capital deployed.

Marginal
thinking

ECONOMICS IN THE REAL WORLD

Skilled Work without the Worker

While the many robots in auto factories typically perform only one function, at the Tesla electric automobile factory in Fremont, California, a robot might perform up to four tasks. And it does it all without a coffee break—three shifts a day, 365 days a year. This is the future. A new wave of robots, far more adept than those now commonly used by automakers and other heavy manufacturers, are replacing workers around the world in both manufacturing and distribution. Factories like Tesla's are a striking counterpoint to those used by Apple and other consumer electronics giants, which employ hundreds of thousands of low-skilled workers.

Tesla factory in California. Where are the workers?

The falling costs and growing sophistication of robots have touched off a renewed debate among economists and technologists over how quickly jobs will be lost. MIT economists Erik Brynjolfsson and Andrew McAfee argue that the transformation will be rapid: "The pace and scale of this encroachment into human skills is relatively recent and has profound economic implications." In their minds, the advent of low-cost automation foretells changes similar to those of the revolution in agricultural technology over the last century, which decreased farming employment in the United States from 40% of the workforce to about 2% today.

Robot manufacturers in the United States say that in many applications, robots are already more cost-effective than humans. In one example, a robotic manufacturing system initially cost $250,000 and replaced two machine operators, each earning $50,000 a year. Over the 15-year life of the system, the machines yielded $3.5 million in labor savings.

Some jobs are still beyond the reach of automation: construction jobs that require workers to move in unpredictable settings and perform different tasks that are not repetitive; assembly work that requires tactile feedback like placing fiberglass panels inside airplanes, boats, or cars; and assembly jobs where only a limited quantity of the product is made or where there are many versions of each product, which would require expensive reprogramming of robots.

But that list is growing shorter. Older robots cannot do such work because computer vision systems were costly and limited to carefully controlled environments where the lighting was just right. But thanks to an inexpensive stereo camera and software that lets the system see shapes with the same ease as humans, new types of robot can quickly discern the irregular dimensions of randomly placed objects.

"We're on the cusp of completely changing manufacturing and distribution," says Gary Bradski, a machine-vision scientist. "I think it's not as singular an event, but it will ultimately have as big an impact as the Internet." ✳

Adapted from "Skilled Work, Without the Worker" by John Markoff, *New York Times*, August 18, 2012.

Conclusion

We began this chapter with the misconception that outsourcing is bad for the economy. It is true that outsourcing destroys some jobs in high-labor-cost areas, but it also creates jobs in low-labor-cost areas. As a result, it lowers the cost of manufacturing goods and providing services. This improved efficiency helps firms that outsource by enabling them to better compete in the global economy.

PRACTICE WHAT YOU KNOW

Bang for the Buck: When to Use More Capital or More Labor

Suppose that Agaves is considering the purchase of a new industrial dishwasher. The unit cleans faster and uses less labor and less water, but it costs $10,000. Should the restaurant make the capital expenditure, or would it be better off saving the money and incurring higher operating costs? To help decide what Agaves should do, consider this information: the dishwasher has a usable life of five years before it will need to be replaced. It will save the restaurant $300 a year in water and 10 hours of labor each week. Human dishwashers are currently paid $8 per hour.

How are all those dishes going to get clean?

Question: Should Agaves purchase the new dishwasher?

Answer: This is the kind of question every business wrestles with on a regular basis. And the way to answer it is very straightforward. A firm should invest in new capital when the value of the marginal product it creates per dollar spent is greater than the value of the marginal product per dollar spent on the next-best alternative. In other words, a firm should invest in new capital when the bang per buck exceeds that of labor and other investments.

Let's compare the total cost of purchasing the dishwasher with the total savings. The total cost of the dishwasher is $10,000, but the savings are larger.

Item	Amount saved	Total for five years
Water	$300/year	$1,500
Labor	10 hours per week × $8/hour = $80/week × 52 weeks = $4,160/year	20,800
Total		22,300

The total savings over five years is $22,300. This makes the investment in the dishwasher the best choice!

Throughout this chapter, we learned that the compensation for factor inputs depends on the interaction between demand and supply. Resource demand is derived from the demand for the final product a firm produces, and resource supply depends on the other opportunities and compensation level that exist in the market. As a result, the equilibrium prices and outputs in the markets for land, labor, and capital reflect, in large part, the forces of demand and supply.

In the next chapter, we examine income and poverty. As you will discover, there are many factors beyond the demand for and supply of workers that explain why some workers make more than others. For instance, wages also depend on the amount of human capital required for a job, as well as location, lifestyle choices, union membership, and the riskiness of the profession. Understanding these elements will deepen your understanding of why workers earn what they do.

ANSWERING THE BIG QUESTIONS

What are the factors of production?

* Labor, land, and capital are the factors of production, or the inputs used in producing goods and services.

Where does the demand for labor come from?

* The demand for each factor of production is a derived demand that stems from a firm's desire to supply a good in another market. Labor demand is contingent on the value of the marginal product that is produced, and the value of the marginal product is equivalent to the firm's labor demand curve.

Where does the supply of labor come from?

* The supply of labor comes from the wage rate that is offered. Each worker faces the labor-leisure trade-off. At high wage levels, the income effect may become larger than the substitution effect and cause the labor supply curve to bend backward. Changes in the supply of labor can result from other employment opportunities, the changing composition of the workforce, immigration, and migration.

What are the determinants of demand and supply in the labor market?

* Labor markets bring the forces of demand and supply together in a wage signal that conveys information to both sides of the market. At wages above the equilibrium, the supply of workers exceeds the demand for labor. The result is a surplus of available workers that places downward pressure on wages until they reach the equilibrium wage, at which point the surplus is eliminated. At wages below the equilibrium, the demand for labor exceeds the available supply of workers, and a shortage develops. The shortage forces firms to offer higher wages to attract workers. Wages rise until they reach the equilibrium wage, at which point the shortage is eliminated.
* There is no definitive result for outsourcing of labor in the short run. In the long run, outsourcing moves jobs to workers who are more productive and enhances overall social welfare.

What role do land and capital play in production?

* Land and capital (as well as labor) are the factors of production across which firms compare the value of the marginal product per dollar spent. Firms seek to equalize the revenue per dollar spent on each input, thereby maximizing their efficiency.

Will Your Future Job Be Outsourced?

When you select an academic major and learn a set of skills, you hope they will enable you to find stable employment. Finding stable employment becomes more challenging in an environment where labor is easily outsourced. So as you seek employment, you need to consider the long-term likelihood that your job could be replaced. To help you think about your future career, let's consider jobs that are likely to be outsourced and jobs that are more likely to remain in the United States.

Jobs with a high risk of outsourcing

Let's begin with computer programmers, who typically earn $70,000 per year. Programming is not location specific; that is, it can be done from anywhere. For this reason, programmers are susceptible to outsourcing. Similarly, insurance underwriters, who earn approximately $60,000 per year, are increasingly being outsourced because the mathematical algorithms involved in estimating risk can be analyzed from any location. Also at risk are financial analysts. When we think of financial analysts, who make roughly $70,000 per year, we typically think of Wall Street. However, crunching numbers and evaluating prospective stock purchases do not require residence in New York City. As a result, financial positions are increasingly being outsourced. The same is true of biochemists, who make $85,000, and physicists, who make $95,000. Even jobs in architecture, management, and law are under pressure. Having a high-paying job does not guarantee that it is safe from outsourcing.

Jobs with a low risk of outsourcing

Conversely, it is good to be a dentist because fillings, crowns, and root canals have to be done locally. Most jobs in medical care are also safe. Physicians, nurses, technicians, and support staff are all part of the medical delivery process. More broadly, most service-sector jobs are safe from outsourcing because they require

someone to be nearby to assist the client. Real estate and construction jobs function in the same way: houses must be built and sold in the local community, so outsourcing is not possible. Also, despite the increase in online courses, education remains primarily a brick-and-mortar enterprise. Likewise, public-sector jobs such as police protection and administration of government programs cannot be outsourced.

More important, the best way to ensure that your future job is not outsourced is to be valuable to your organization. Developing new skills and knowledge is integral to maintaining and increasing the value of the marginal product of your labor. When you are highly valued, it will be difficult to replace you, especially by someone overseas.

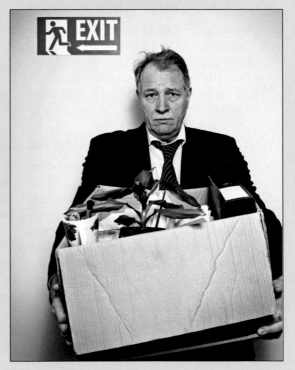

Might your future job be outsourced? Then what would you do?

CONCEPTS YOU SHOULD KNOW

backward-bending labor supply
  curve (p. 440)
derived demand (p. 432)
economic rent (p. 455)

income effect (p. 439)
marginal product of labor
  (p. 434)
monopsony (p. 451)

outsourcing of labor (p. 446)
substitution effect (p. 439)
value of the marginal product
  (VMP) (p. 435)

QUESTIONS FOR REVIEW

1. Why is the demand for factor inputs a derived demand?

2. What rule does a firm use when deciding to hire an additional worker?

3. What are the two shifters of labor demand? What are the four shifters of labor supply?

4. What can cause the labor supply curve to bend backward?

5. If wages are below the equilibrium level, what would cause them to rise?

6. What would happen to movie stars' wages if all major film studios merged into a single firm, creating a monopsony for film actors?

7. If workers became more productive (that is, produced more output in the same amount of time), what would happen to the demand for labor, the wages of labor, and the number of workers employed?

8. How is economic rent different from rent seeking?

9. How does outsourcing affect wages and employment in the short run and the long run?

STUDY PROBLEMS (✱ *solved at the end of the section*)

1. Maria is a hostess at a local restaurant. When she earned $8 per hour, she worked 35 hours per week. When her wage increased to $10 per hour, she decided to work 40 hours per week. However, when her wage increased again to $12 per hour, she decided to cut back to 37 hours per week. Draw Maria's supply curve. How would you explain her actions to someone who is unfamiliar with economics?

2. Would a burrito restaurant hire an additional worker for $10.00 an hour if that worker could produce an extra 30 burritos and each burrito made added $0.60 in revenues?

✱ 3. Pam's Pretzels has a production function shown in the following table. It costs Pam's Pretzels $80 per day per worker. Each pretzel sells for $3.

Quantity of labor	Quantity of pretzels
0	0
1	100
2	180
3	240
4	280
5	310
6	330
7	340
8	320

a. Compute the marginal product and the value of the marginal product that each worker creates.

b. How many workers should Pam's Pretzels hire?

4. Jimi owns a music school that specializes in teaching guitar. Jimi has a limited supply of rooms for his instructors to use for lessons. As a result, each successive instructor adds less to Jimi's output of lessons. The following table lists Jimi's production function. Guitar lessons cost $25 per hour.

Quantity of labor	Quantity of lessons (hours)
0	0
1	10
2	17
3	23
4	28
5	32
6	35
7	37
8	38

a. Construct Jimi's labor demand schedule at each of the following daily wage rates for instructors: $75, $100, $125, $150, $175, $200.
b. Suppose that the market price of guitar lessons increases to $35 per hour. What does Jimi's new labor demand schedule look like at the daily wage rates listed in part (a)?

5. In an effort to create a healthcare safety net, the government requires employers to provide healthcare coverage to all employees. What impact will this increased coverage have in the following labor markets in the short run?

a. the demand for doctors
b. the demand for medical equipment
c. the supply of hospital beds

6. A million-dollar lottery winner decides to quit working. How can you explain this behavior using economics?

7. Illustrate each of the following changes with a labor supply and demand diagram. (Use a sepa-

rate diagram for each part.) Diagram the new equilibrium point, and note how the wage and quantity of workers employed changes.

a. There is a sudden migration out of an area.
b. Laborers are willing to work more hours.
c. Fewer workers are willing to work the night shift.
d. The demand for California wines suddenly increases.

✳ 8. A football team is trying to decide which of two running backs (A or B) to sign to a one-year contract.

Predicted statistics	Player A	Player B
Touchdowns	7	10
Yards gained	1,200	1,000
Fumbles	4	5

The team has done a statistical analysis to determine the value of each touchdown, yard gained, and fumble to the team's revenue. Each touchdown is worth an extra $250,000, each yard gained is worth $1,500, and each fumble costs $75,000. Player A costs $3.0 million and player B costs $2.5 million. Based on their predicted statistics in the table above, which player should the team sign?

9. Farmers in Utopia experience perfect weather throughout the entire growing season, and as a result their crop is double its normal size. How will this bumper crop affect each of the following ?

a. the price of the crop
b. the marginal product of workers who harvest the crop
c. the demand for the workers who harvest the crop

10. What will happen to the equilibrium wage of crop harvesters in Dystopia if the price of the crop falls by 50% and the marginal product of the workers increases by 25%?

11. Suppose that the current wage rate is $20 per hour, the rental rate of land is $10,000 per acre, and the rental rate of capital is $2,500. The manager of a firm determines that the value of the marginal product of labor is $400, the value of the marginal product of an acre of land is $200,000, and the value of the marginal product of capital is $4,000. Is the firm maximizing profit? Explain your response.

✳ 12. What country made the shirt you are wearing? Go ahead and check the tag and write down your answer. Even though we can't predict the exact country your shirt is from, there is a surprising answer in the Solved Problems section that you should check out.

13. Why are most iPhones manufactured and assembled in China and then shipped to the United States, even though Apple was founded in California and most of Apple's workforce still reside in this country?

SOLVED PROBLEMS

3.a.

Quantity of labor	Quantity of pretzels	Marginal product	Value of the marginal product
0	0	0	$0
1	100	100	300
2	180	80	240
3	240	60	180
4	280	40	120
5	310	30	90
6	330	20	60
7	340	10	30
8	320	−20	−60

b. The VMP of the fifth worker is $90 and each worker costs $80, so Pam should hire five workers. Hiring the sixth worker would cause her to lose $20.

8.

Predicted statistics	Player A	VMP of Player A	Player B	VMP of Player B
Touchdowns	7	$1,750,000	10	$2,500,000
Yards gained	1,200	1,800,000	1,000	1,500,000
Fumbles	4	−300,000	5	−375,000
Total value		3,250,000		3,625,000

Player A has a predicted VMP of $3.25 million and a cost of $3.0 million. Player B has a predicted VMP of $3.625 million and a cost of $2.5 million. Since player B's predicted VMP exceeds his salary by $1.125 million and player A's predicted VMP exceeds his salary by only $0.25 million, the team should sign player B.

12. Forget the country of origin on your tag—that is just where the final product was assembled. Your shirt is actually a product of a global supply chain that includes cotton seeds that were engineered in the United States, cotton grown in India, sewing machines manufactured in Germany, a collar lining from Brazil, and inexpensive labor from the place on your tag (where all the pieces were sewn together). The tag chronicles the end of your shirt's journey, so it gets the credit; but behind the scenes it takes a planet to make every shirt, and that is the surprising answer to the question.

Working hard and performing well at your job leads to good pay.
Many people believe that the structure of compensation in the working world is unfair. After all, why should someone who does backbreaking

work digging holes for fence posts make so much less than someone who works as an attorney? Why do such large differences in income exist? You may be an outstanding babysitter or short-order cook, but because these jobs are considered unskilled, many other workers can easily replace you. And neither occupation will ever earn much more than the minimum wage. In contrast, even an average neurosurgeon gets paid very well, because few individuals have the skill and training to perform neurosurgery. In addition, society values neurosurgeons more than babysitters because the neurosurgeons are literally saving lives.

If you wish to earn a sizable income, it is not enough to be good at something; that "something" needs to be an occupation that society values highly. What matters are your skills, what you produce, and the supply of workers in your chosen profession. Therefore, how hard you work often has little to do with how much you get paid.

In this chapter, we continue our exploration of labor by examining income and inequality in labor markets, including the characteristics of successful wage earners and the impediments the poor face when they try to escape poverty. Examining those at the top and the bottom of the income ladder helps us explain the many forces that determine income. In addition, we explore the incidence of poverty, poverty trends, and measurement issues. Examining the poverty statistics, and understanding the causes of poverty, allows society to craft economic policies that more effectively help those in need.

Why do neurosurgeons earn more than short-order cooks?

BIG QUESTIONS

✳ **What are the determinants of wages?**

✳ **What causes income inequality?**

✳ **How do economists analyze poverty?**

What Are the Determinants of Wages?

The reasons why some workers get paid more than others are complex. We learned in Chapter 14 that the forces of supply and demand explain a large part of wage inequality. However, numerous additional factors contribute to differences in earnings. Various nonmonetary factors cause some occupations to pay higher or lower wages than supply and demand would seem to dictate. In other contexts, discrimination on the basis of gender, race, or other characteristics is an unfortunate but very real factor in wages. And in some markets, a "winner-take-all" structure can lead to a small number of workers capturing a large majority of the total earnings.

A **compensating differential** is the difference in wages offered to offset the desirability or undesirability of a job.

The Nonmonetary Determinants of Wages

Some jobs have characteristics that make them more desirable or less desirable. Also, no two workers are exactly alike. Differences in jobs and worker ability affect the supply and demand of labor. In this section, we examine the nonmonetary determinants of wages, including compensating differentials, education and human capital, location and lifestyle, unions, and efficiency wages.

Incentives

Compensating Differentials

Some jobs are more unpleasant, risky, stressful, inconvenient, or monotonous than others. If the characteristics of a job make it unattractive, firms must offer more to attract workers. For instance, roofing, logging, and deep-sea fishing are some of the most dangerous occupations in the world. Workers who do these jobs must be compensated with higher wages to offset the higher risk of injury. A **compensating differential** is the difference in wages offered to offset the desirability or undesirability of a job. If a job's characteristics make it unattractive, the compensating wage differential must be positive.

In contrast, some jobs are highly desirable. For example, restaurant critics sample a lot of great food, radio DJs spend the day playing their favorite music, and video game testers try beta versions before they are released. Some jobs are simply more fun, exciting, prestigious, or stimulating than others. In these cases, the compensating differential is negative and the firm offers

Are you being paid enough to risk a fall?

TABLE 15.1

The Relationship between Education and Pay

Education level	Median annual earnings in 2014 (persons age 25 and over)
Advanced (master's or doctoral) degree	$83,980
Bachelor's degree	57,252
Some college or associate degree	39,884
High school degree (includes GED)	34,736
Less than high school diploma	25,376

Source: Bureau of Labor Statistics, Current Population Survey, April 2015.

lower wages. For example, newspaper reporters and radio DJs earn low pay. Video game testing is so desirable that most people who do it are not paid at all.

Education and Human Capital

Many complex jobs require substantial education, training, and industry experience. Qualifying to receive the specialized education required for certain occupations—for example, getting into medical school—is often very difficult. Relatively few students are able to pursue these degrees. In addition, such specialized education is expensive, in terms of both tuition and forgone income.

Opportunity cost

The set of skills that workers acquire on the job and through education are collectively known as **human capital.** Unlike other forms of capital, investments in human capital accrue to the employee. As a result, workers who have high human capital can market their skills among competing firms. Engineers, doctors, and members of other professions that require extensive education and training can command high wages in part because the human capital needed to do those jobs is high. In contrast, low-skilled workers such as ushers, baggers, and sales associates earn less because the human capital required to do those jobs is quite low; it is easy to find replacements.

Human capital is the set of skills that workers acquire on the job and through education.

Table 15.1 shows the relationship between education and pay. Increased human capital (education) qualifies a worker for jobs paying higher wages. Workers who earn advanced degrees have a higher marginal product of labor because their extra schooling has presumably given them additional skills for the job. But they also have invested heavily in education. Higher wages are a compensating differential that rewards additional education.

ECONOMICS IN THE REAL WORLD

Does Education *Really* Pay?

An alternative perspective on the value of education argues that the returns to increased education are not the product of what a student learns, but rather a signal to prospective employers. In other words, the degree itself (specifically,

Is it the amount of education you obtain or other traits that determine your financial success?

the classes taken to earn that degree) is not evidence of a set of skills that makes a worker more productive. Rather, earning a degree and attending prominent institutions is a signal of a potential employee's quality. Prospective employers assume that a student who gets into college must be intelligent and willing to work hard. Students who have done well in college send another signal: they are able to learn quickly and perform well under stress.

It is possible to test the importance of signaling by looking at the returns to earning a college degree, controlling for institutional quality. At many elite institutions, the four-year price tag has reached extraordinary levels. For example, to attend New York University in New York City, the most expensive institution in the country, it cost $62,930 in 2014–2015. Over four years, that adds up to slightly more than a quarter of a million dollars! What type of return do graduates of such highly selective (and expensive) institutions make on their sizable investments? And are those returns the result of a rigorous education or a result of the institution's reputation? It is difficult to answer this question because the students who attend more selective institutions are more likely to have higher earnings potential regardless of where they attend college. These students enter college as high achievers, a trait that carries forward into the workplace no matter where they attend school.

Economists Stacy Dale and Alan Krueger examined the financial outcomes for over 6,000 students who were accepted or rejected by a comparable set of colleges. They found that 20 years after graduation, students who had been accepted at more selective colleges but decided to attend a less selective college earned the same amount as their counterparts from more selective colleges. This finding indicates that actually attending a prestigious school is less important for future career success than the qualities that enable students to get *accepted* at a prestigious school.

Although Table 15.1 shows that additional education pays, the reason is not simply an increase in human capital. There is also a signal that employers can interpret about other, less observable qualities. For instance, Harvard graduates presumably learn a great deal in their time at school, but they were also highly motivated and likely to be successful even before they went to college. Part of the increase in income attributable to completing college depends on a set of other traits that the student already possessed independent of the school or the degree. ✳

Location and Lifestyle

For most people, sipping margaritas in Key West, Florida, sounds more appealing than living in Eureka, Nevada, along the most isolated stretch of road in the continental United States. Likewise, being able to see a show, visit a museum, or go to a Yankees game in New York City constitutes a different lifestyle from what you'd experience in Dodge City, Kansas. People find some places more desirable than others. So how does location affect wages? Where the climate is more pleasant, all other things being equal, people are willing to accept lower wages because the nonmonetary benefits of enjoying the weather act as a compensating differential. Similarly, jobs in metropolitan areas—where the cost of living is significantly higher than in most other places—pay higher wages as a cost-of-living adjustment. The higher wage helps employees afford a quality of life similar to what they would enjoy if they worked in less expensive areas.

How much more would you pay to live near here?

Choice of lifestyle is also a major factor in determining wage differences. Some workers are not particularly concerned with maximizing their income; instead, they care more about working for a cause. This is true for many employees of nonprofits or religious organizations or even for people who take care of loved ones. Others follow a dream of being a musician, writer, or actor. And still others are guided by a passion such as skiing or surfing. Indeed, many workers view their pay as less important than doing something they are passionate about. For these workers, lower pay functions as a compensating differential.

Unions

A **union** is a group of workers who bargain collectively for better wages and benefits. Unions are able to secure increased wages by creating significant market power over the supply of labor available to a firm. A union's ability to achieve higher wages depends on a credible threat of a work stoppage, known as a **strike**. In effect, unions can raise wages because they represent labor, and labor is a key input in the production process. Because firms cannot do without labor, an effective union can use the threat of a strike to negotiate higher wages for its workers.

A **union** is a group of workers who bargain collectively for better wages and benefits.

A **strike** is a work stoppage designed to aid a union's bargaining position.

U.S. law prohibits some unions from going on strike, including those that represent many transit workers, some public school teachers, law enforcement officers, and workers in other essential services. If workers in one of these industries reach an impasse in wage and benefit negotiations, the employee union is required to submit to the decision of an impartial third party, a process known as *binding arbitration*. The television show *Judge Judy* is an example of binding arbitration in action: two parties with a small claims grievance agree in advance to accept the verdict of Judith Sheindlin, a noted family court judge.

The effect of unions in the United States has changed since the early days of unionization in the late 1800s. Early studies of the union wage premium found wages to be as much as 30% higher for unionized workers. At the height of unionization approximately 60 years ago, one in three jobs was a unionized position. Today, only about one in eight workers belongs to a union. Today, most empirical studies find the wage premium to be between 10% and 20%. The demise of many unions has coincided with the transition of the U.S. economy from a manufacturing base to a greater emphasis on the service sector, which is less centralized.

Efficiency Wages

In terms of paying wages, one approach stands out as unique. Ordinarily, we think of wages being determined in the labor market at the intersection of supply and demand. When the labor market is in equilibrium, the wage guarantees that every

Does going on strike result in higher wages?

Efficiency wages are wages higher than equilibrium wages, offered to increase worker productivity.

Productivity is the effectiveness of effort as measured in terms of the rate of output per unit of input.

Incentives

qualified worker can find employment. However, some firms willingly pay more than the equilibrium wage. **Efficiency wages** exist when an employer pays its workers more than the equilibrium wage. Why would a business do that? Surprisingly, the answer is to make *more* profit. That outcome hardly seems possible when a firm that uses efficiency wages pays its workers more than its competitors do. But think again. Above-equilibrium wages (1) provide an incentive for workers to reduce slacking, (2) decrease turnover, and (3) increase productivity. **Productivity** is the effectiveness of effort as measured in terms of the rate of output per unit of input. If the gains in overall labor productivity are higher than the increased cost, the result is greater profit for the firm.

Automaker Henry Ford used efficiency wages to generate more productivity on the Model T assembly line. In 1914, Ford decided to more than double the pay of assembly-line workers to $5 a day—an increase that his competitors did not match. He also decreased the workday from 9 hours to 8 hours. Ford's primary goal was to reduce worker turnover, which was frequent because of the monotonous nature of assembly-line work. By making the job so lucrative, he hoped that most workers would not quit so quickly. He was right. The turnover rate plummeted from over 10% per day to less than 1%. As word of Ford's high wages spread, workers flocked to Detroit. The day after the wage increase was announced, over 10,000 eager job seekers lined up outside Ford's Highland Park, Michigan, plant. From this crowd, Ford hired many temporary workers and gave each a 30-day trial. At the end of the trial period, he permanently hired the most productive workers and let the others go. The resulting productivity increase per worker was more than enough to offset the wage increase. In addition, reducing the length of each shift enabled Ford to add an extra shift, which increased productivity even more.

We have seen that wages are influenced by factors that include compensating differentials, human capital, location and lifestyle, union membership, and the presence of efficiency wages. Table 15.2 summarizes these nonmonetary determinants of income differences.

Wage discrimination occurs when workers with the same ability as others are not paid the same because of their race, ethnic origin, sex, age, religion, or some other group characteristic.

Wage Discrimination

When workers with the same ability as others are not paid the same because of their race, ethnic origin, sex, age, religion, or some other group characteristic, we say they are experiencing **wage discrimination**. Because of its importance for individuals and for policymakers, economists study the topic of wage discrimination by trying to understand its effects in the past and to help address wage discrimination today. In this section, we explore some of their observations. While most economists acknowledge that bias plays a role in wage discrimination, they believe that broader factors related to human capital play the major roles.

Looking at the Data

Table 15.3 presents median annual earnings in the United States by sex, race or ethnic group, age and experience, and location. Looking at the data, we see large earnings differences across many groups in U.S. society. In particular, female workers earn

Henry Ford developed a visionary assembly process and also implemented efficiency wages at his plants.

TABLE 15.2

The Key Nonmonetary Determinants of Wage Differences

Determinant	Impact on wages	In pictures
Compensating differentials	Some workers are eager to have jobs that are more fun, exciting, prestigious, or stimulating than others. As a result, they are willing to accept lower wages. Conversely, jobs that are unpleasant or risky require higher wages.	
Human capital	Many jobs require substantial education, training, and experience. As a result, workers who acquire additional amounts of human capital can command higher wages.	
Location and lifestyle	When the location is desirable, the compensating wage will be lower. Similarly, when employment is for a highly valued cause, wage is less important. In both situations, the compensating wage will be lower.	
Unions	Because firms cannot do without labor, unions can threaten a strike to negotiate higher wages.	
Efficiency wages	The firm pays above-equilibrium wages to help reduce slacking, decrease turnover, and increase productivity.	

PRACTICE WHAT YOU KNOW

Efficiency Wages: Which Company Pays an Efficiency Wage?

You are considering two job offers. Company A is well known and respected. This company offers a year-end bonus based on your productivity relative to other workers that can substantially boost your income, but its base wage is relatively low. Company B is not as well known, but its wages are higher than the norm in your field. This company does not offer a year-end bonus.

Question: Which company, A or B, is the efficiency wage employer?

Answers: Efficiency wages are a mechanism that some companies use to reduce turnover, encourage teamwork, and create loyalty. Company A's bonus plan will reward the best producers, but the average and less-than-average workers will become frustrated and leave. Company A is not paying efficiency wages; it is simply using incentives tied to productivity. Company B is the efficiency wage employer because it pays every worker somewhat higher wages to reduce turnover.

Forbes magazine calls Google the best company to work for—and not just because you can bring your dog to work.

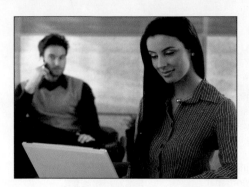

For every $1 men make, women make, on average, 82 cents.

18% less than their male counterparts. While most of us would like to believe that employers no longer pay men more than women for doing the same job, wage discrimination does still exist. In 2009, President Obama signed the Lilly Ledbetter Fair Pay Act, which gives victims of wage discrimination more time to file a complaint with the government. The act is named after a former Goodyear employee who sued the company in 2007. The courts determined that she was paid 15% to 40% less than her male counterparts. The fact that a major U.S. corporation was violating the Equal Pay Act of 1963 almost 50 years after its passage was a poignant reminder that wage discrimination still occurs in our society.

But economists try to study the topic of wage discrimination further by examining the data. For example, women and men often hold different types of jobs, and certain jobs pay more than others. Higher wages in jobs such as road work and construction reflect in part a compensating differential for exposure to extreme temperatures, bad weather, and other dangers, and men are more likely to work in these jobs. Additionally, more women than men take time off from work to raise a family, meaning that women ultimately have fewer years of work experience, put in fewer paid work hours per year, are less likely to work a full-time schedule, and leave the labor force for longer periods. In contrast, men normally take less, if any, time off to raise children. In the long term, these differences tend to lead to lower levels of human capital and overall lower wages for women.

Similarly, differences in human capital can help explain wide gaps in earnings data by race or ethnic group. Asian Americans (55% of whom have a bachelor's degree or higher) have higher education levels than whites (43%), who in turn generally have much higher levels than Blacks (22%) and Hispanics (18%). Economists expect the wage disparities between groups to decrease as these educational differences (and the resulting differences in human capital) become less pronounced. Socioeconomic factors also play a significant role in these disparities. For instance, the low quality of some inner-city schools can limit the educational attainment of students, many of whom are minorities.

Human Capital and the Life-Cycle Wage Pattern

The earnings gap between mid-career workers and others also reflects differences in human capital. After all, workers who are just starting out have limited experience. As these workers age, they accumulate on-the-job training and experience that make them more productive and enable them to obtain higher wages. However, for older workers the gains from increased experience are eventually offset by diminishing returns. Consequently, wages peak when these workers are in their early 60s and then slowly fall thereafter. This pattern, known as the **life-cycle wage pattern**, refers to the predictable effect that age has on earnings over a person's working life.

As we noted earlier, location is also a source of wage differentials. Workers who live outside metropolitan areas make, on average, 24% less than their counterparts who live in cities (see again Table 15.3). This gap occurs because the cost of living is much higher in metropolitan areas.

The **life-cycle wage pattern** refers to the predictable effect that age has on earnings over the course of a person's working life. Wages peak for people in their early 60s and then slowly fall thereafter.

TABLE 15.3

Median Annual Earnings by Group

Group	Median earnings in 2013	Percentage difference within each group
Males	$49,192	–
Females	40,383	−18%
White	45,874	–
Black	35,978	−22
Asian	53,081	16
Hispanic	33,061	−28
Early-career workers (25–34)	40,497	−22
Mid-career workers (35–54)	50,221	−3
Late-career workers (55–64)	51,709	–
Inside a metropolitan area	51,651	–
Outside a metropolitan area	39,354	−24

Source: U.S. Bureau of Labor Statistics, 2014. Authors' adjustments.

ECONOMICS IN THE REAL WORLD

The Effects of Beauty on Earnings

According to research that spans the labor market from the law profession to college teaching and in countries as different as the United States and China, beauty matters. How much? You might be surprised. As related by economist Daniel S. Hamermesh in his book *Beauty Pays*, beautiful people make as much as 10% more than people with average looks, while those whose looks

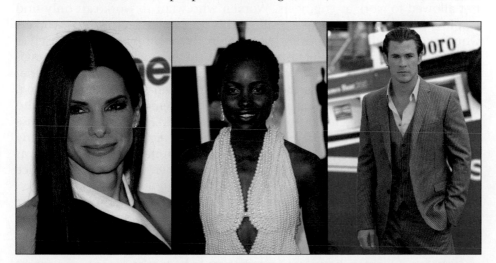

Sandra Bullock, Lupita Nyong'o, Chris Hemsworth—three of the decade's most beautiful people.

are considered significantly below average may make as much as 25% below normal.

The influence of beauty on wages can be viewed in two ways. First, beauty can be seen as a marketable trait that has value in many professions. Actors, fashion models, restaurant servers, and litigators all rely on their appearance to make a living, so it is not surprising that beauty is correlated with wages in those professions. If beautiful people are more productive in certain jobs because of their beauty, then attractiveness is simply a measure of the value of the marginal product that they generate. In other words, being beautiful is a form of human capital that the worker possesses.

However, a second interpretation finds evidence of discrimination. If employers prefer "beautiful" people as employees, then part of the earnings increase associated with beauty might reflect that preference. In addition, the success of workers who are more beautiful could also reflect the preferences of customers who prefer to buy products and services from attractive people.

Because it is impossible to determine whether the beauty premium is a compensating differential or the result of overt discrimination, we have to acknowledge the possibility that the truth, in many situations, could be a little bit of both. ✳

Occupational Crowding: How Discrimination Affects Wages

Occupational crowding is the phenomenon of relegating a group of workers to a narrow range of jobs in the economy.

Another factor deserving particular attention is **occupational crowding**–the phenomenon of relegating a group of workers to a narrow range of jobs in the economy. To understand how occupational crowding works, imagine a community named Utopia with only two types of jobs: a small number in engineering and a large number in secretarial services. Furthermore, men and women are equally proficient at both occupations, and everyone in the community is happy to work either job. Under these assumptions, we would expect the wages for engineers and secretaries to be the same.

Now imagine that not everyone in Utopia has the same opportunities. Suppose that we roll back the clock to a time when women in Utopia are not allowed to work as engineers. Women who want to work can only find employment as secretaries. As a result of this occupational crowding, workers who have limited opportunities (women, in this example) find themselves competing with one another, as well as with the men who cannot get engineering jobs, for secretarial positions. As a result, wages fall in secretarial jobs and rise in engineering. Because only men can work in engineering, they are paid more than their similarly qualified female counterparts, who are crowded into secretarial positions and earn less. Furthermore, because women who want to work can only receive a low wage as a secretary, many effectively decide to stay at home and produce nonmarket services, such as child-rearing, which have a higher value to the women who make this choice than the wages they could earn as secretaries.

Of course, women today are not restricted to secretarial jobs, but they still dominate in many of the lower-paying jobs in our society. Table 15.4 shows a number of female-dominated occupations in the United States. Not surprisingly, given the low wages, men have not rushed into these jobs. However, because women have not exited these jobs to the extent one might expect, wages have remained low. Similar forces are at work in traditionally male-dominated jobs, where men have enjoyed higher wages due to a lack of competition from female employees–jobs such as engineers, auto mechanics, and airline pilots.

Why do occupational crowding and wage differentials continue? Rigidity in changing occupations, social customs (including discrimination), and personal preferences are all part of the explanation. However, many economists see a change coming. Because more women than men attend colleges and universities, women are now primarily responsible for expanding the supply of workers in most fields. As the supply of workers expands, the net effect will likely be lower wages in traditionally male-dominated jobs.

A Cautiously Optimistic Outlook

Because no employer will admit to discriminating, researchers can only infer the amount of bias driven discrimination after first correcting for observable differences from compensating differentials and differences in human capital. The unobservable differences that remain are presumed to reflect discrimination. While the number is hotly debated, most economists estimate that discrimination accounts for less than 5% of observed wage differences. They also see many signs of improvement.

Though it is still real, the gender gap is shrinking. In 1960 women in the workforce earned, on average, 60 cents for every dollar that men earned. Today women earn 82 cents for every dollar that men earn, and the gap continues to close by about half a cent each year. In addition, women are no longer clustered in less rigorous academic programs than men, so women are more prepared to get jobs that pay better. In 2013, for example, more women than men in the United States received doctoral degrees. The number of women at every level of academia has been rising for decades. There are now three women for every two men enrolled in postsecondary education. Over time, this education advantage may offset some of the other compensating differentials that have kept men's wages higher than women's.

TABLE 15.4

Where the Men Aren't

Job	Percentage female
Kindergarten teachers	98%
Dental hygienists	98
Secretaries	98
Childcare workers	97
Nurses	93
Bank tellers	87
Librarians	86
Legal assistants	84
Telephone operators	83

Source: Bureau of Labor Statistics, 2010.

ECONOMICS IN THE MEDIA

Wage Discrimination

Anchorman: The Legend of Ron Burgundy

This film from 2004 depicts the television news industry in the early days of women anchors—the 1970s! Stations were diversifying their broadcast teams and beginning to add women and minorities to previously all-white, all-male lineups.

In one scene, Veronica Corningstone, a news anchor, introduces herself: "Hello, everyone. I just want you all to know that I look forward to contributing to this news station's already sterling reputation."

The added competition for airtime does not sit well with Ron Burgundy and his male colleagues: "I mean, come on, Ed! Don't get me wrong. I love the ladies. They rev my engine, but they don't belong in the newsroom! It is anchorman, not anchor lady! And that is a scientific fact!"

Veronica overhears the conversation, and after leaving the office she begins a monologue: "Here we go again. Every station it's the same. Women ask me how I put up with it. Well, the truth is, I don't really have a choice. This is definitely a man's world. But while they're laughing and carrying on, I'm chasing down leads and practicing my nonregional diction. Because the only way to win is to be the best."

Fortunately, society has changed a great deal since the 1970s, and women are seeing gains, especially by obtaining more human capital through education. For instance, women comprised 30% of pharmacists in 1985; today the number is 54%. Likewise, women held 25% of purchasing manager jobs in the 1980s; today that number is 51%. Women make up 44% of all chemists today, but that number was just 21% thirty years ago.

"You stay classy, San Diego."

Winner-Take-All

In 1930, baseball legend Babe Ruth demanded and received a salary of $80,000 from the New York Yankees. This would be approximately $1 million in today's dollars. Babe Ruth earned a lot more than the other baseball players of his era. When told that President Herbert Hoover earned less than he was asking for, Ruth famously said, "I had a better year than he did." In fact, the annual salary of the president of the United States is far less than that of top professional athletes, movie stars, college presidents, and many corporate CEOs.

Why does the most important job in the world pay less than jobs with far less value to society? Part of the answer involves compensating differentials. Being president of the United States means being the most powerful person in the world, so paid compensation is only a small part of the benefit of holding that office. The other part of the answer has to do with the way labor markets function. Pay at the top of most professions is subject to a form of competition known as **winner-take-all**, which occurs when extremely small differences in ability lead to sizable differences in compensation. This compensation structure has been common in professional sports and in the entertainment industry for many years, but it also exists in the legal profession, medicine, journalism, investment banking, fashion design, and corporate management.

In a winner-take-all market, being a little bit better than one's rivals can be worth a tremendous amount. For example, in 2015, baseball player Clayton Kershaw earned $31.5 million. As good as Kershaw is, he is not eight times better than an average major-league baseball player, who makes $4 million. Nor

Clayton Kershaw has 31.5 million reasons a year to practice, but not all professional baseball players are as fortunate.

is he a thousand times better than a typical minor-league player, who earns a few thousand dollars a month. In fact, it is hard to tell the difference between a baseball game played by major- and minor-leaguers. Minor-league pitchers throw just about as hard, the players run almost as fast, and the fielding is almost as good. Yet major-league players make hundreds of times more.

Winner-take-all occurs when extremely small differences in ability lead to sizable differences in compensation.

Paying so much to a relatively small set of workers may seem unfair, but the prospect of much higher pay or bonuses motivates many ambitious employees to exert maximum effort. If we look beyond the amount of money that some people earn, we can see that winner-take-all creates incentives that encourage supremely talented workers to maximize their abilities.

Incentives

What Causes Income Inequality?

Income inequality occurs when some workers earn more than others. Compensating differentials, discrimination, corruption, and differences in the marginal product of labor all lead to inequality of income. In this section, we first examine why income inequality exists. Once we understand the factors that lead to income inequality, we examine how it is measured. Because income inequality is difficult to measure and easy to misinterpret, we explain how observed income inequality statistics are constructed and what they mean. We end by discussing income mobility, a characteristic in many developed nations that can lessen the impact of income inequality on the life-cycle wage pattern.

Factors That Lead to Income Inequality

To illustrate the nature of income inequality, we begin with a simple question: what would it take to equalize wages? For all workers to get the same wages, three conditions would have to be met. First, every worker would have to have the same skills, ability, and productivity. Second, every job would have to be equally attractive to potential employees. Third, all workers would have to be perfectly mobile. In other words, perfect equality of income would require that workers be clones who perform the same job. Needless to say, we do not live in such a world. In the real world, some people work harder than others and are more productive. Some people, such as humanitarian aid workers, missionaries, teachers, and even ski bums, choose occupations where they know they will earn less. In fact, our traits, our desires, and our differences all help to explain income inequality, which is the natural result of a market economy.

Next we look at five factors that can contribute to income inequality: ability, training and education, discrimination, wealth, and corruption.

Ability

Workers who have more ability (for example, mental acuity, physical strength, fortitude) than less-able workers generally earn higher wages. Differences in ability can lead to large differences in wages because more-able workers have the potential to create much larger marginal products than their less-able counterparts.

Training and Education

More ability is a necessary but not sufficient condition for high wages. Workers of all ability levels benefit from receiving additional training and education. The acquisition of specific skills through training and additional education enhances each worker's human capital. More human capital often makes workers more valuable in the marketplace, helping them earn higher wages.

Discrimination

Discrimination harms the workers who are discriminated against, and it makes the overall distribution of income in a country more unequal. Workers who are passed over for promotions or job openings because of their gender, race, age, religion, or other traits earn lower wages that do not reflect their ability, training or education. Discrimination in this context acts as a price ceiling that limits some workers' ability to earn more. Since discriminated workers are concentrated among women and minorities, the net effect is that discriminated groups end up concentrated among the lowest-paid groups– leading to more income inequality.

The Role of Wealth

How much does a privileged background matter? According to controlled studies, children born into wealthy households earn about 10% more than children born into low-income households. Wealth gives a child from an affluent home access to better education, private tutoring, a healthier diet, and many other intangible benefits that provide a head start in life. These early advantages often lead to higher levels of human capital that translate into higher wages.

The Role of Corruption in Income Inequality

All economic systems require trust in order to achieve gains from trade. However, some societies value the rule of law more than others. Many less developed countries suffer from widespread corruption. Consider Somalia, a country without a functional central government. This situation has led to lawlessness in which clans, warlords, and militia groups fight for control. The situation is so dire that international aid efforts often require the bribing of government officials to ensure that the aid reaches those in need.

Corruption can play a large role in income inequality. In societies where corruption is common, working hard or being innovative is not enough; getting ahead often requires bribing officials to obtain business permits or to ward off competitors. Moreover, when investors cannot be sure that their assets are safe from government seizure or criminal activity, they are less likely to develop a business. Under political systems that are subject to bribery and other forms of corruption, dishonest people benefit at the expense of the poor. Corruption drives out legitimate business opportunities and magnifies income inequality.

ECONOMICS IN THE REAL WORLD

5th Pillar

Recognizing the damage that corruption causes has prompted some people to fight back. For example, 5th Pillar, an independent organization, has developed zero-rupee notes in India, where corruption is rampant. The notes provide a way for persons who are asked for a bribe to indicate that they are unwilling to participate. Presenting a zero-rupee note lets the other person know that you refuse to give or take any money for services required by law or to give or take money for an illegal activity. Because 5th Pillar reports attempted bribery to the authorities, individuals who are brave enough to use the zero-rupee notes know that they are not alone in fighting corruption. ✳

Widespread corruption leads to more income inequality.

Measuring Income Inequality

How do we measure income inequality in a country? To answer this question, we begin by looking at income inequality in the United States. Economists study the distribution of household income in the United States by quintiles, or five groups of equal size, ranging from the poorest fifth (20%) of households to the top fifth. Figure 15.1 shows the data from the last census in 2010.

According to the U.S. Bureau of the Census, the poorest 20% of households makes just 3.2% of all income earned in the United States. The next quintile, the second fifth, earns 8.4% of income. In other words, fully 40% of U.S. households (the bottom two quintiles) account for only 11.6% of earned income. The middle quintile earns 14.3%, the second-highest quintile

The **income inequality ratio** is calculated by dividing the top quintile's income percentage by the bottom quintile's income percentage.

23.0%, and the top quintile 51.1%. Being a pie chart, Figure 15.1 vividly shows the wide disparity between the percentage of total U.S. income earned by the poorest households (3.2%) and by the richest households (51.1%). If we divide the percentage of income earned by households in the top fifth (51.1%) by the percentage of income earned by households in the bottom fifth (3.2%), we get an **income inequality ratio** of about 16. Looking at the numbers this way, we can say that households in the top fifth have approximately 16 times the income of those in the bottom fifth. Viewing that number in isolation makes the amount of income inequality in the United States seem large. However, we have not yet adjusted the data to reflect disposable income. When taxes and subsidies are included the U.S. income inequality ratio drops to 9.8.

To provide some perspective, Table 15.5 compares the income inequality in various other countries using disposable income. The countries above the line are more developed, and those below are less developed.

As you can see, the U.S. income inequality ratio of 9.8 after controlling for taxes and subsides is high compared with that of other highly developed nations but relatively low compared with that of less developed nations. In general, highly developed nations have lower degrees of income inequality. Why? More developed countries have less poverty, so those individuals who are at the bottom of the income ladder in the developed countries earn more than those at the bottom in less developed countries.

Understanding Observed Inequality

Translating income inequality into a number, as we've done with the income quintiles, can mask the true nature of income inequality. In this section, we step back and consider what the income inequality ratio can tell us and what it cannot tell us.

Because the income inequality ratio measures the success of top earners against that of bottom earners, if the bottom group is doing relatively well, then the inequality ratio will be smaller, which explains why many highly

FIGURE 15.1

The Distribution of Income in the United States by Quintile

The top fifth of income earners makes 51.1% of all income, an amount greater than the combined incomes of the four remaining quintiles. Income declines across the quintiles, falling to 3.2% in the lowest fifth.

Source: U.S. Census Bureau.

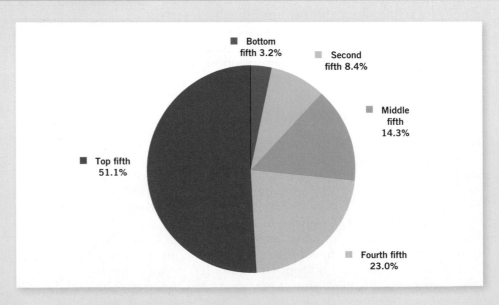

TABLE 15.5

Income Inequality Ratios (after controlling for taxes and subsidies) in Selected Countries

Country	Inequality ratio (richest 20% ÷ poorest 20%)
Japan	5.4
Germany	4.7
Canada	5.8
United Kingdom	7.6
United States	9.8
Mexico	11.1
Brazil	16.9
Bolivia	15.2
Namibia	19.6

Source: Adapted from United Nations Development Programme, *Human Development Report,* 2009, Table M.

developed countries have ratios under 6. However, the United States has an inequality ratio that is close to 10. What is driving the difference? The United States has many highly successful workers and a poverty rate that is similar to those found in other highly developed countries. The **poverty rate** is the percentage of the population whose income is below the poverty threshold. The **poverty threshold** is the income level below which a person or family is considered impoverished.

According to the Organization for Economic Cooperation and Development (OECD), the United States has a poverty rate that is quite similar to that of Japan, a country with a markedly lower inequality ratio. Given that the poverty rate in the United States is not unusually large compared with Japan's, we cannot explain the higher inequality ratio by pointing to the percentage of poor people. Rather, it is the relative success of the top income earners in the United States that causes the markedly higher inequality ratio. In other words, there are more high-income earners in the United States than in Japan.

High levels of income inequality also occur when the poorest are *really* poor. For example, there are many successful people in Mexico, Brazil, Bolivia, and Namibia. The problem in these countries is that the success of some people is benchmarked against the extreme poverty of many others. Therefore, high inequality ratios can be a telltale sign of a serious poverty problem. Suppose that the poorest quintile of the population in Bolivia has an average disposable income of $4,000, while those in the top quintile have a disposable income of $60,800. The income inequality ratio is $60,800/$4,000 = 15.2. By comparison, consider Canada. If the poorest quintile of the population in Canada has an average disposable income of $10,500, while those in the top quintile have an average of $60,800, the income inequality ratio there is $60,800/$10,500 = 5.8. In both countries, the top quintile is doing equally well, but the widespread poverty in Bolivia produces an alarming income inequality ratio. In this example, the inequality ratio signals a significant poverty problem.

The **poverty rate** is the percentage of the population whose income is below the poverty threshold.

The **poverty threshold** is the income level below which a person or family is considered impoverished.

In sum: A high income inequality ratio can occur if people at the bottom earn very little or if the income of high-income earners is much greater than the income of others. The key point to remember is that even though income inequality ratios give us some idea about the degree of inequality in a society, a single number cannot fully reflect the sources of the underlying differences in income.

The Gini Index

The **Gini index** is a measurement of the income distribution of a country's residents.

An alternative way of representing income inequality across countries is to use the **Gini index**, which represents the income distribution of a nation's residents. Its value fluctuates between 0 (no income inequality) and 100 (extreme income inequality). If every individual's income is equal in a society, the Gini index (or Gini coefficient) is 0. A nation where one individual gets all the income, while everyone else gets nothing, would have a Gini index of 100. The average Gini index is approximately 40 (Figure 15.2).

The **Lorenz curve** is a visual representation of the Gini index.

The **Lorenz curve** is a visual way of representing the Gini index. A perfectly equal distribution of income is represented by the green 45-degree line in Figure 15.3. As the income distribution becomes more unequal, the Lorenz curve, represented by the orange line in Figure 15.3, shifts downward and to the right. The Gini index is calculated by taking the area between the two curves (shaded and labeled A in Figure 15.3) and dividing that amount by area A plus area B. Area A represents the amount of income *inequality* in society,

FIGURE 15.2

The Gini Index Across the World, 2014

All countries color-coded in green have a Gini index lower than 40, while those in shades of red have a Gini index above 45.

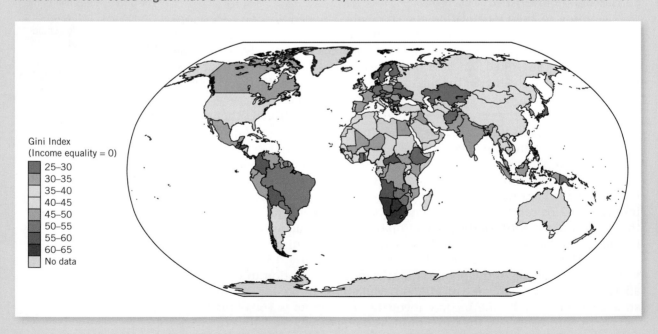

Gini Index
(Income equality = 0)
- 25–30
- 30–35
- 35–40
- 40–45
- 45–50
- 50–55
- 55–60
- 60–65
- No data

FIGURE 15.3

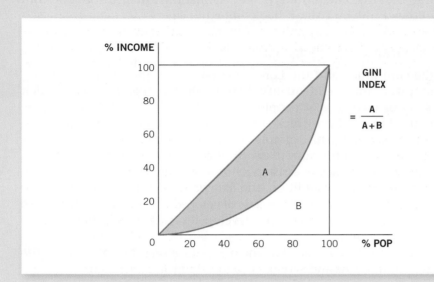

The Gini Index and the Lorenz Curve

The green curve indicates complete income equality. As income inequality increases, the curve shifts down and to the right.

Source: M. Tracy Hunter, https://commons.wikimedia .org/wiki/File:2014_Gini _Index_World_Map,_income _inequality_distribution_by _country_per_World_Bank.svg

while area B represents the amount of income *equality* in society. Calculating the Gini index gives us a number between 0 and 1. Economists multiply this number by 100 to represent the score as a whole number between 1 and 100.

The Lorenz curve is especially helpful for seeing how income inequality has changed over time. Income inequality has become greater in the United States over the last 50 years. The blue line in Figure 15.4 shows the Lorenz curve in 1968. The red line shows the Lorenz curve in 2010 (at the time of the most recent Census). Notice that the red Lorenz curve from 2010 shifted

FIGURE 15.4

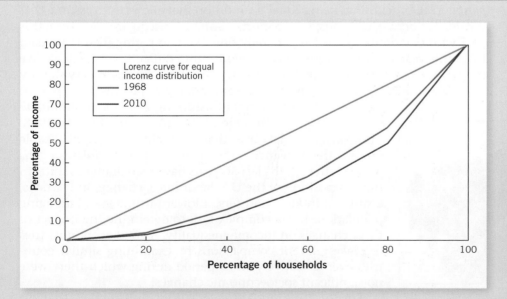

Lorenz Curves for the United States, 1968 and 2010

The Gini index in the United States was 39 in 1968. By 2010, it had climbed to 44, indicating an increase in income inequality.

down and to the right, away from the perfect income equality line. The Gini index in 1968 was 39; by 2010, it had climbed to 44.

Difficulties in Measuring Income Inequality

In-kind transfers are transfers (mostly to the poor) in the form of goods or services instead of cash.

Because the Gini index and the Lorenze curve reflect income before taxes, these indicators of income inequality do not reflect *disposable income*, which is the portion of income that people actually have to spend. Nor does the data account for **in-kind transfers**—that is, goods and services that are given to the poor instead of cash. Examples of in-kind services are government-subsidized housing and the Subsidized Nutrition Assistance Program (SNAP) that provides food-purchasing assistance for low- and no-income people living in the United States. In addition, the data do not account for unreported or illegally obtained income. Because less developed countries generally have larger **underground economies** than developed countries do, their income data are even less reliable.

Underground economies are composed of markets in which goods or services are traded illegally.

Many economists also note that income data alone do not capture the value created from goods and services produced in the household. For example, if you mow your own lawn or grow your own vegetables, those activities have a positive value that is not expressed in your income data. In less developed countries, many households engage in very few market transactions and produce a large portion of their own goods and services. If we do not count these, our comparison of data with other countries will overstate the amount of inequality present in the less developed countries. Finally, the number of workers per household and the median age of each worker differ from country to country. When households contain more workers or those workers are, on average, older and therefore more experienced, comparing inequality across countries is more likely to be misleading.

Individually, none of these shortcomings poses a serious measurement issue from year to year. However, if we try to measure differences in income across generations, the changes can be significant enough to invalidate the *ceteris paribus* ("all other things being equal") condition that allows us to assume that outside factors are held constant. In short, comparing inequality data from this year with data from last year is generally fine, but comparing inequality data from this year with data from 50 years ago is more difficult. For instance, we might note that income inequality in the United States increased very slightly from 2014 to 2015. However, because we are looking at just two data points, we must be cautious about assuming a trend. To eliminate that problem, we can extend the time frame back to 1968. Comparing the data over that range shows an unmistakable upward trend in income inequality but also violates *ceteris paribus*; after all, the last 50 years have seen dramatic shifts in the composition of the U.S. labor force, changes in tax rates, a surge in in-kind transfers, a lower birthrate, and an aging population. It is a complex task to determine the impact of these changes on income inequality. A good economist tries to make relevant comparisons by examining similar countries over a relatively short period during which there were no significant socioeconomic changes.

Growing your own vegetables is an activity that is not counted in official income data.

Finally, the standard calculations and models that we have discussed assume that the income distribution is a direct reflection of a society's well-being. However, we must be very careful not to infer too much about how well people are living based on their income alone. Indeed, income analysis does not offer a complete picture of human welfare. In Chapter 16, we will see that income is only one factor that determines human happiness and well-being. People also value leisure time, non-wage benefits, a sense of community, safety from crime, and social networks, among other things.

Income Mobility

When workers have a realistic chance of moving up the economic ladder, each person has an incentive to work harder and invest in human capital. **Income mobility** is the ability of workers to move up or down the economic ladder over time. Think of it this way: if today's poor must remain poor 10 years from now, income inequality remains high. However, if someone in the lowest income category can expect to experience enough economic success to move to a higher income quintile, being poor is a temporary condition. In other words, economic mobility reduces inequality over long periods of time.

Income mobility is the ability of workers to move up or down the economic ladder over time.

The dynamic nature of the U.S. economy is captured by income mobility data. Table 15.6 reports the income mobility in the United States over a series

| TABLE 15.6 |

Income Mobility in the United States, 1970–2010				
(1) Ten-year period	(2) % Poorest quintile that move up at least one quintile	(3) % Highest quintile that move down at least one quintile	(4) % Poorest quintile that move up at least two quintiles	(5) % Highest quintile that move down at least two quintiles
1970–1980	43.2	48.8	19.1	22.8
1975–1985	45.3	50.9	20.6	24.8
1980–1990	45.2	47.6	21.3	25.7
1985–1995	41.8	45.8	17.8	21.5
1990–2000	41.7	46.7	15.2	20.7
1995–2005	41.9	45.0	15.4	20.2
2000–2010	41.8	44.8	14.9	19.9

Source: Katharine Bradbury, *Trends in U.S. Family Income Mobility, 1969–2006*, Working Paper, Federal Reserve Bank of Boston, No. 11-10. Data for 1990–2005 was interpolated. Author's adjustments.

Income Inequality around the World

"The rich get richer, and the poor get poorer" is a simple yet profound way to think about income inequality. As top earners make more and bottom earners make less, the inequality rate increases. It's a combination of these factors, not just extreme wealth or extreme poverty, that leads to huge gaps between those at the very top and those at the very bottom.

$$\text{Quintile ratio} = \frac{\text{Income earned by top 20\%}}{\text{Income earned by bottom 20\%}}$$

- Income earned by top 20%
- Income earned by bottom 20%
- Inequality ratio
- Poverty rate

Namibia 19.6

Brazil 16.9

Less developed countries, like Namibia, have high rates of inequality. Why? Because the poor are extremely poor and earn just a fraction of the income of the affluent.

United States 9.8

15.1%

Poverty is not the only factor of inequality, however. When the top earners are highly successful, the gap between rich and poor grows. The United States has a poverty rate similar to Japan's but a top 20% who earn more than Japan's top class.

Japan 5.4

16.1%

REVIEW QUESTIONS

- Suppose the top 20% of Brazilian earners make, on average, the equivalent of $100,000 a year. What does the average earner in the bottom 20% make?

- A friend tells you he wants to live in a world without income inequality. Discuss the pros and cons using at least one of the five foundations of economics from Chapter 1.

Sources: United Nations Development Programme, Human Development Reports 2015; CIA World Factbook

PRACTICE WHAT YOU KNOW

Income Inequality: The Beginning and End of Inequality

Consider two communities, Alpha and Omega. Alpha has 10 residents, 5 who earn $90,000 and 5 who earn $30,000. Omega also has 10 residents, 5 who earn $250,000 and 5 who earn $50,000.

Question: What is the income inequality ratio in each community?

Answer: To answer this question, we must use quintile analysis. Because there are 10 residents in Alpha, the top 2 earners represent the top quintile and the lowest 2 earners represent the bottom quintile. Therefore, the degree of income inequality in Alpha using quintiles analysis is $90,000 ÷ $30,000, or 3. In Omega, the top 2 earners represent the top quintile and the lowest 2 earners represent the bottom quintile. Therefore, the degree of income inequality in Omega is $250,000 ÷ $50,000, or 5.

The good life: so near, yet so far.

Question: Which community has the more unequal distribution of income, and why?

Answer: Omega has the more unequal distribution of income because the quintile analysis yields an income inequality ratio of 5, versus 3 for Alpha.

Question: Can you think of a reason why someone might prefer to live in Omega?

Answer: Each rich citizen of Omega earns more than each rich citizen of Alpha, and each poor citizen of Omega earns more than each poor citizen of Alpha. Admittedly, there is more income inequality in Omega, but there is also more income across the entire income distribution. Thus, one might prefer Omega if the absolute amount of income is what matters more, or one might prefer Alpha if relative equality is what matters more.

of 10-year periods from 1970 to 2010. We can see that mobility increased through the late 1980s, but thereafter declined for both the poorest and the highest quintiles. Columns 4 and 5 show the percentage of households that moved up or down at least two quintiles.

Mobility data enable us to separate those at the bottom of the economic ladder into two groups: (1) the *marginal poor*, or people who are poor at a particular point in time but have the skills necessary to advance up the ladder, and (2) the *long-term poor*, or people who lack the skills to advance to the next quintile. The differences in income mobility between these two groups provide a helpful way of understanding how income mobility affects poverty.

For the marginal poor, low earnings are the exception. Because most young workers expect to enjoy higher incomes as they get older, many are willing to borrow in order to make a big purchase—for example, a car or a home. Conversely, middle-aged workers know that a comfortable retirement

Income Inequality

Capital in the Twenty-First Century

Capital in the Twenty-First Century, by Thomas Piketty, focuses on wealth and income inequality in Europe and the United States since the eighteenth century. The book quickly became a best seller, selling over a million copies in 2014.

Piketty used historical data to examine income inequality beginning with the Industrial Revolution. He found that high levels of income inequality were the norm during the 18th and 19th centuries. Wealth and income were highly concentrated among rich households. During the 20th century this pattern changed. Higher tax rates, increased government provision of services, and turbulent economic times caused the concentration of wealth to decline dramatically by the late 1960s. However, Piketty's data show a marked increase in income inequality beginning in the late 20th century.

Piketty developed a theory that in normal times wealth grows faster than economic output. This means that the world's natural state is a highly unequal distribution of wealth unless economic calamities (such as war or depressions) or government intervention reduce the impact of inherited wealth on the rest of society. For this reason, Piketty recommends that governments increase tax rates on accumulated wealth with the goal of reducing income inequality.

Not all economists are convinced by Piketty's argument. Will the future really look like the past? The answer is not clear. Over time, technological progress could lead to a more equal income distribution, not a less equal one.

More generally, standard economic theory holds that any asset (wealth included) is subject to diminishing returns. Therefore, the more wealth there is, the harder it is for the wealthy to earn an above-normal return on their investments. In other words, wealth cannot grow faster than economic output indefinitely. Also, inherited wealth accounts for only about 10% of income inequality.

Despite these criticisms, many skeptics have kind words for Piketty because he succeeded in bringing rising income inequality to the forefront of public discussion and debate.

will be possible only if they save now for the future. As a result, workers in their 50s have much higher savings rates than young workers and retirees. On reaching retirement, earnings fall; but if the worker has saved enough, retirement need not be a period of low consumption. The life-cycle wage pattern argues that changes in borrowing and saving patterns over one's life smooth out the consumption pattern. In other words, for many people, a low income at a point in time does not necessarily reflect a low standard of living.

When we examine how people live in societies with substantial income mobility, we see that the annual income inequality data can create a false

Marginal
thinking

impression about the spending patterns of young and old. The young are generally upwardly mobile, so they spend more than one might expect by borrowing. The middle-aged, who have relatively high incomes, spend less than one might expect because they are saving for retirement. And the elderly, who have lower incomes, spend more than one might expect because they are drawing down their retirement savings.

In the next section, we turn our attention to the long-term poor, who do not escape the lowest quintile. Members of this group spend their entire lives near or below the poverty threshold.

How Do Economists Analyze Poverty?

Poverty remains an ongoing challenge in the United States. According to the Census Bureau, close to 15% of all households are below the poverty threshold. To help us understand the issues, we begin with poverty statistics. Then, once we understand the scope of the problem, we examine possible policy solutions.

The Poverty Rate

For the last 50 years, the U.S. Bureau of the Census has been tracking the poverty rate, or the percentage of the population whose income is below the poverty threshold. To keep up with inflation, the poverty threshold is adjusted each year for changes in the overall level of prices in the economy. However, an individual family's threshold is calculated to include only the money that represents income earned by family members in the household. It does not include in-kind transfers, nor are the data adjusted for cost-of-living differences in the family's specific geographical area. For these reasons, poverty thresholds are a crude yardstick. Figure 15.5 shows the poverty rate for households in the United States from 1959 to 2013.

In 1964, Congress passed the Equal Opportunity Act and a number of other measures designed to fight poverty. Despite those initiatives, the rate of poverty today is slightly higher than it was 50 years ago. This result is surprising, because the U.S. economy's output has roughly doubled in that time. One would have hoped that the economy's progress could be enjoyed at the bottom of the economic ladder as well as at the top. Unfortunately, the stagnant poverty rate suggests that the gains from economic growth over that period have accrued to households in the middle and upper quintiles, rather than to the poor. Poverty has remained persistent, in part, because many low-income workers lack the necessary skills to earn a living wage and, at the same time, investments by firms in automation and technology have reduced the demand for these workers.

Table 15.7 illustrates that children, female heads of household, and certain minorities disproportionately feel the incidence of poverty. When we combine at-risk groups—for example, black or Hispanic women who are heads of household—the poverty rate can exceed 50%.

Those below the poverty threshold are unable to make ends meet.

FIGURE 15.5

Poverty Rate for U.S. Households, 1959–2013

Poverty rates for households fluctuated from 1959 through 2013.

Source: U.S. Bureau of the Census.

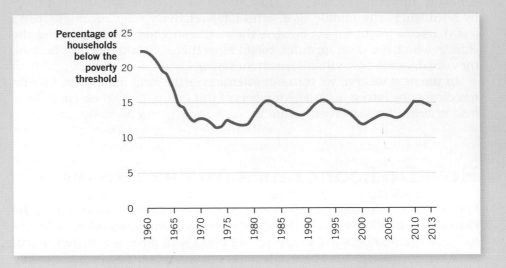

TABLE 15.7

The Poverty Rate for Various Groups, 2013	
Group	**Poverty rate (percentage)**
Age	
Children (under 18)	19.5
Adults (18–64)	14.4
Elderly (65 or older)	9.5
Race/Ethnicity	
White	9.5
Asian	10.1
Hispanic	30.4
Black	30.2
Type of household	
Married couple	6.3
Male head only	16.4
Female head only	30.9

Source: U.S. Bureau of the Census, 2013.

Poverty Policy

Trade-offs

In this section, we outline a number of policies related to the problem of poverty. These policies are hotly debated because each policy carries both associated costs and assumed benefits, and assumptions about the benefits differ widely.

Welfare

"Welfare" is not the name of a specific government program, but rather a term that describes a series of initiatives designed to help the poor by supplementing their income. The term "welfare" in this section should not be confused with our earlier discussions of "social welfare." Here we focus on how government assistance programs ("welfare") operate and the incentives that these programs create.

Welfare can take a variety of forms, such as monetary payments, subsidies and vouchers, health services, or subsidized housing. Welfare is provided by the government and by other public and private organizations. It is intended to help the unemployed, those with illnesses or disabilities that prevent them from working, the elderly, veterans, and households with dependent children. An individual's eligibility for welfare is often limited to a set amount of time and is valid only as long as the recipient's income remains below the eligibility cutoff. Examples of welfare programs include Temporary Assistance for Needy Families (TANF), which provides financial support to families with dependent children; the Supplemental Security Income (SSI) program, which provides financial support to those who are unable to work; and the Subsidized Nutrition Assistance Program (SNAP), which gives financial assistance to those who need help to purchase basic foods.

In-Kind Transfers

In addition to financial assistance, the poor can receive direct assistance in the form of goods and services. The government provides health care to the poor through Medicaid. **Medicaid** is a joint federal and state program that helps low-income individuals and households pay for the costs associated with long-term medical care. Communities or cities often provide organized assistance like shelters, and local community food banks, religious organizations, and private charities like Habitat for Humanity and Toys for Tots all provide in-kind benefits to the poor.

The idea behind in-kind transfers is that they protect recipients from the possibility of making poor decisions if they receive cash instead. For example, some recipients may use cash transfers to support drug or alcohol addictions, to gamble, or to buy unnecessary goods and services. To limit the likelihood of such poor decisions, in-kind transfers can be targeted at essential services. However, not everyone agrees that in-kind transfers are a good idea. Skeptics view them as paternalistic, inefficient, and disrespectful, and they argue that cash payments allow recipients to make the choices that best fit their needs.

Medicaid is a joint federal and state program that helps low-income individuals and households pay for the costs associated with long-term medical care.

The Earned Income Tax Credit (EITC)

The Earned Income Tax Credit (EITC) is a tax credit designed to encourage low-income workers to work more. At very low income levels, EITC offers an incentive to work by supplementing earned income with a tax credit of approximately $6,000 a year. The amount is determined, in part, by the number of dependent children in the household and the location. Once a family reaches an income level above its earnings threshold, EITC is phased out, and workers gradually lose the tax credit. Under many welfare and in-kind transfer programs, the qualifying income is a specific cutoff point; an individual

Poverty

The Hunger Games (2008–2010)

The *Hunger Games* series of dystopian-themed books written by Suzanne Collins (and later made into feature films) chronicles the life of Katniss Everdeen, a teenager living in the post-apocalyptic country of Panem, which has been divided into twelve districts. Life in each district is unique, with vast differences in wealth, resources, and production. The wealthy Capitol district governs the economy by heavily regulating all aspects of life in the other poverty-stricken districts. One of the methods of control is the annual Hunger Games, where a boy and a girl are chosen from each district to battle to the death. The survivor earns extra food and a life of luxury.

Katniss Everdeen lives in District 12, an area with striking similarities to the coal mining Appalachian region of the United States. In District 12, inhabitants work in the mines. They struggle to make ends meet, often go hungry, and have a permeating sense of desolation because there is no escape.

The rising income inequality we see in the United States is not as extreme as we find in *The Hunger Games*, but it does remind us that we need to pay

Where would you rather live, the Capitol district or District 12?

attention to income inequality in our society. When an income distribution becomes too unequal, the result is often political and social instability. *The Hunger Games* challenges us to think about economic freedom, the role of institutions in creating growth, the extent to which governments should regulate economic activity, and how policy decisions made today will shape the future world.

or household is either eligible or not. In contrast, EITC is gradually reduced, which means that workers do not face a sizable disincentive to work as the program is phased out.

Incentives

EITC, which was established in 1975, helps over 25 million families, making it the largest poverty-fighting tool in the United States. The government estimates that EITC payments are sufficient to lift more than 5 million households out of poverty each year. In addition, EITC creates stronger work incentives than those found under traditional antipoverty programs that critics argue discourage recipients from working.

The Minimum Wage

Trade-offs

The minimum wage is often viewed as an antipoverty measure. However, we learned in Chapter 6 that the minimum wage creates trade-offs. Predictably, firms respond to higher minimum wages by hiring fewer workers and utilizing more capital-intensive production processes, such as self-checkout lanes and robotic production. Because the minimum wage does not guarantee employment, the most it offers to a low-skill worker is a slightly larger pay-check. At the same time, a higher minimum wage makes those jobs more difficult to find.

Problems with Traditional Aid

While trying to be well meaning, many welfare programs can create unintended work disincentives, especially when we examine the combined effects of welfare and in-kind transfer programs.

As an example, consider a family of five with a combined income of $30,000 a year. Suppose that the family qualifies for public assistance that amounts to another $10,000 in benefits. The family's combined income from employment and benefits thus rises to $40,000. What happens if another family member gets a part-time job and income from wages rises from $30,000 to $40,000? Under the current law, an income of $40,000 disqualifies the family from receiving most of the financial assistance it had been getting. As a result, the family's benefits fall from $10,000 to $2,000 per year. Now the family nets $42,000 total. The person who secured part-time employment may feel that working isn't worth it because even though the family earned an additional $10,000, they lost $8,000 in welfare benefits. Because the family is able to raise its net income by only $2,000, it has effectively returned $8,000. The loss of those benefits as they are phased out feels like an 80% tax, which creates a large disincentive to work.

This is a basic dilemma that poverty-reducing programs face: those that provide substantial benefits can discourage participation in the workforce because a recipient who starts to work, in many cases, no longer qualifies for the benefits and loses them.

While few people dispute that welfare programs are well intentioned, many economists are concerned about the programs' unintended consequences. A society that establishes a generous welfare package for the poor will find that it faces a Samaritan's dilemma. A **Samaritan's dilemma** occurs when an act of charity creates disincentives for recipients to take care of themselves. President Bill Clinton's 1996 vow "to end welfare as we know it" and for welfare to be "a second chance, not a way of life" attempted to address this dilemma by providing benefits for only a limited period of time. Clinton changed the payout structure for federal assistance and encouraged states to require employment searches as a condition for receiving aid. In addition, the TANF program imposed a five-year maximum for the time during which a recipient can receive benefits. This strategy changed welfare from an entitlement under the law into a temporary safety net, thereby reducing the Samaritan's dilemma.

Incentives

A **Samaritan's dilemma** occurs when an act of charity creates disincentives for recipients to take care of themselves.

Incentives

ECONOMICS IN THE REAL WORLD

Muhammad Yunus and the Grameen Bank

In 2006, economist Muhammad Yunus received the Nobel Peace Prize for his work helping poor families in Bangladesh. What did Yunus do to win that honor? He founded the Grameen Bank, which was instrumental in creating

In 2006, Yunus received the Nobel Peace Prize.

a new type of loan that has loaned more than $10 billion to poor people in Bangladesh in an effort to eliminate extreme poverty.

The Grameen Bank gives out very small loans, known as *microcredit*, to poor Bangladeshis who are unable to qualify for conventional loans from traditional lenders. The loans are provided without collateral, and repayment is based on an honor system. By conventional standards that sounds preposterous, but it works! The Grameen Bank reports a 97% repayment rate, and according to one survey, over 50% of the families of Grameen borrowers have moved above the poverty line.

It all started with just a few thousand dollars. In 1974, Yunus, who was trained as an economist in the United States, returned to Bangladesh and lent $27 to each of 42 villagers who made bamboo furniture. The loans, which were all paid back, enabled the villagers to cut out middlemen and purchase their own raw materials. A few years later, Yunus won government approval to open the Grameen Bank, named for the Bengali word for "rural."

Yunus had a truly innovative idea. To receive a loan, applicants must belong to a five-member group. Once the first two members begin to pay back their loans, the others can get theirs. While there is no group responsibility for returning the loans, the Grameen Bank believes that it creates a sense of social responsibility, ensuring that all members will pay back their loans. More important, Yunus trusted that people would honor their commitments, and he was proved right. ✳

PRACTICE WHAT YOU KNOW

Welfare is an economic means of lending a helping hand.

Incentives

Samaritan's Dilemma: Does Welfare Cause Unemployment?

The state you live in is considering two different welfare programs. The first plan guarantees $8,000 for each person. The second plan does not guarantee any payments, but it doubles any income earned up to $12,000.

Question: Which program creates the lesser amount of unemployment?

Answer: Think about incentives. Under the first plan, recipients' benefits are not tied to work. The $8,000 is guaranteed. However, the second plan will pay more if recipients do work. This policy acts as a positive incentive to get a job. For instance, someone who works 20 hours a week and earns $10 per hour would make $200 per week, or about $10,000 a year. Under the second plan, that person would receive an additional $10,000 from the government. Therefore, we can say that the second program reduces the amount of unemployment.

Donating to Charity More Effectively

The Samaritan's dilemma is not unique to public assistance; it also applies to private charitable donations. Here the dilemma occurs with the stewardship of the donations. Donors want their gifts to benefit the largest possible set of needs. However, charitable organizations have overhead expenses that limit how much of the gift actually reaches the hands of the needy. In addition, not all charities are aboveboard. Here are a few tips to ensure that your donations make a difference.

1. Ask for a copy of the organization's financial report. Find out how much of your money actually will be used for charitable programs. If the organization is reluctant to share this information, walk away.
2. Be careful of charities with copycat names. Some organizations use names similar to those of well-known organizations in order to confuse donors.
3. Be wary of emotional appeals that talk about problems but do not explain how donated money will be spent. Do not succumb to high-pressure tactics or solicitations made over the phone; donating should be a reasoned and thoughtfully considered process. Step back, and ask for written materials containing information about the charity.
4. Ask if donations are tax deductible. Do not pay in cash, but instead pay by check so you have proof that you gave if you are ever audited.
5. Finally, after you have done your due diligence, give confidently and generously.

How can you make sure your donation gets to those that need it?

Conclusion

Income and work have long been a subject of discussion and contention. We find that some jobs pay much more than others, and working hard and performing well at one's job do not guarantee good pay. People and jobs differ in many dimensions, and wages usually respond accordingly, though wages are affected by compensating differentials, location, education and human capital, union membership, and efficiency wages, all of which create significant income inequality.

This chapter is ultimately about trade-offs and incentives–two of our five foundations of economics. The debate about how society should handle income, poverty, and inequality is complex, and passions run deep. Depending on your perspective, you can point to data that show that society is improving (the narrowing wage gap between females and males) or worsening (increased levels of income inequality). In economics there are always trade-offs. Policies designed to reduce income inequality may cause highly productive workers to work less. Poverty initiatives may have unintended consequences as well. Unfortunately, good intentions alone won't close the wage gap or decrease income inequality, but the judicious use of incentives just might.

ANSWERING THE BIG QUESTIONS

What are the determinants of wages?

* Supply and demand play a key role in determining wages, along with a number of nonmonetary determinants of earnings, such as compensating differentials, education and human capital, location, lifestyle, union membership, and efficiency wages.

* Economic studies estimate that wage discrimination accounts for less than 5% of wage differences.

* Despite recent gains, women still earn significantly less than men. Occupational crowding partially explains the wage gap. As long as supply imbalances remain in traditional male and female jobs, significant wage differences will persist.

What causes income inequality?

* Five factors can contribute to income inequality: ability, training and education, discrimination, wealth, and corruption. The income inequality ratio is sometimes used to measure a nation's level of inequality. Another measure of income inequality is the Gini index.

* Economic mobility reduces income inequality over long periods. Due to the life-cycle wage pattern, distinct borrowing and saving patterns over an individual's life smooth out his or her spending pattern. Therefore,

in societies with substantial income mobility, the annual income inequality data overstate the amount of inequality.

How do economists analyze poverty?

* Economists determine the poverty rate by establishing a poverty threshold.

* The poverty rate in the United States is now slightly higher than it was 50 years ago, despite many efforts (welfare, in-kind transfers, and EITC) to reduce it.

* Efforts to reduce poverty are subject to the Samaritan's dilemma because they can create disincentives for recipients to support themselves.

CONCEPTS YOU SHOULD KNOW

compensating differential
   (p. 468)
efficiency wages (p. 472)
Gini index (p. 484)
human capital (p. 469)
income mobility (p. 487)
income inequality ratio (p. 482)
in-kind transfers (p. 486)

life-cycle wage pattern (p. 474)
Lorenz curve (p. 484)
Medicaid (p. 493)
occupational crowding (p. 476)
poverty rate (p. 483)
poverty threshold (p. 483)
productivity (p. 472)
samaritan's dilemma (p. 495)

strike (p. 471)
underground economies
   (p. 486)
union (p. 471)
wage discrimination (p. 472)
winner-take-all (p. 479)

QUESTIONS FOR REVIEW

1. Why do garbage collectors sometimes make more than furniture movers?

2. What are efficiency wages? Why are some employers willing to pay them?

3. Why is it difficult to determine the amount of wage discrimination in the workplace?

4. Discuss some of the reasons why full-time working women make, on average, 82% as much as full-time working men.

5. How does the degree of income inequality in the United States compare with that in similarly developed countries? How does U.S. income inequality compare with that in less developed nations?

6. Why do high rates of income mobility mitigate income inequality?

7. Which antipoverty program (welfare, in-kind transfers, or EITC) creates the strongest incentive for recipients to work? Why?

STUDY PROBLEMS (✳*solved at the end of the section*)

1. Suppose that society restricted the economic opportunities of right-handed persons to jobs in construction, while left-handed persons can work any job.
   a. Would wages in construction be higher or lower than wages for other jobs?
   b. Would left-handed workers make more or less than right-handed workers?
   c. Now suppose that right-handers are allowed to work any job they like. What effect would this change have on the wages of right-handers and left-handers over time?

2. Internships are considered a vital stepping-stone to full-time employment after college, but not all internship positions are paid. Why do some students take unpaid internships when they could be working summer jobs and earning an income? Include a discussion of human capital in your answer.

3. Consider two communities. In Middletown, two families earn $40,000 each, six families

earn $50,000 each, and two earn $60,000 each. In Polarity, four families earn $10,000 each, two earn $50,000 each, and four earn $90,000 each. Which community has the more unequal distribution of income as measured by the income inequality ratio? Explain your response.

4. The United States has attracted many highly productive immigrants who work in fields such as education, health, and technology. How do these immigrants affect income inequality in the United States? Is this type of immigration good or bad for the United States, and why? What impact is this type of immigration having on the countries that are losing some of their best workers?

✳ 5. Suppose that a wealthy friend asks for your advice on how to reduce income inequality. Your friend wants to know if it would be better to give $100 million to poor people who will never attend college or to offer $100 million in financial aid to students who could not otherwise afford to attend college. What advice would you give, and why?

6. What effect would doubling the minimum wage have on income inequality? Explain your answer.

✳ 7. Suppose that a company has 10 employees. It agrees to pay each worker on the basis of productivity. The individual workers' output is 10, 14, 15, 16, 18, 19, 21, 23, 25, and 30 units. However, some of the workers complain that they are earning less than the other workers, so they appeal to management to help reduce the income inequality. As a result, the company decides to pay each worker the same salary. But the next time the company measures each worker's output, they find that 6, 7, 7, 8, 10, 10, 11, 11, 12, and 12 units are produced. Why did this happen? Would you recommend that the company continue the new compensation system? Explain your response.

8. The government is considering three possible welfare programs:
   a. Give each low-income household $10,000.
   b. Give each low-income household $20,000 minus the recipient's income.
   c. Match the income of each low-income household, where the maximum it can receive in benefits is capped at $10,000.

   Which program will do the most to help the poor? Describe the work incentives under each program.

9. A number of very famous people (Ellen DeGeneres, Brad Pitt, Mark Zuckerberg, Bill Gates) all dropped out of college. Why would anyone drop out of college when college graduates typically make significantly more than college dropouts?

✳ 10. Tracy Chapman's song "Fast Car" reminds us how difficult it is to escape poverty. Identify the reasons in the song that keep Tracy trapped in poverty. (To listen to the song, visit https://www.youtube.com/watch?v=uTIB10eQnA0.)

SOLVED PROBLEMS

5. The return on your wealthy friend's investment will be higher if the money is given to students with the aptitude, but not the income, to go to college. After all, college students earn substantially more than high school graduates do. Therefore, an investment in additional education will raise the marginal revenue product of the poor students' labor. With the higher earning power that a college degree provides, more people will be lifted out of poverty, thereby reducing the amount of income inequality in the future.

7. Begin by calculating the average output when each worker's wage is based on the amount that he or she produces: 10 + 14 + 15 + 16 + 18 + 19 + 21 + 23 + 25 + 30 = 191, and 191 ÷ 10 = 19.1. Then compute the average output when the company decides to pay each worker the same wage: 6 + 7 + 7 +

8 + 10 + 10 + 11 + 11 + 12 + 12 = 94, and 94 ÷ 10 = 9.4. The output has dropped by approximately one-half! Why? The company forgot about incentives. In this case, an attempt to create equal pay caused a disincentive problem (because hard work is not rewarded), and the workers all reduced their work effort. The new compensation system should be scrapped.

10. Tracy's condition is difficult because she lives in the country and the jobs are in the city—which is why she wants a "fast car" to drive away in. She also comes from a broken family; her mother left her father because he had a drinking problem. The lack of nearby job opportunities and the necessity of caring for her father prevents Tracy from taking advantage of economic opportunities elsewhere.

Special Topics in
MICROECONOMICS

Consumer Choice

The more money you have, the happier you'll be.

Did having more money make Ebenezer Scrooge satisfied? How about Montgomery Burns from *The Simpsons*? Or Mr. Potter from *It's a Won-*

derful Life? The answer is no. All three fatally flawed charac-ters hoarded money and, in the process, missed out on many of the good things that life has to offer. Then there is Jack Whittaker, a real-life millionaire who won a $315 million Powerball jackpot in 2002. He is now completely broke, is divorced from his wife, has been arrested for DUI, and was robbed on two separate occasions while carrying $500,000. (Who carries *that much* money?) Worst of all, he lost his daughter and granddaughter to drug overdoses.

Money can be used in ways that lift the spirit. For one thing, more money means more opportunities to strengthen your connections with others and contribute to your community. It also means you can afford to travel, experience the diverse wonders of nature, and spend more time with family and friends instead of working all the time. Moreover, saving money for a goal, such as a special trip, can make the experience more rewarding. So can more money buy more satisfaction? We say yes, but only if you are careful about how you spend it and do not become consumed by the pursuit of money.

In this chapter, we use our understanding of income constraints, price, and personal satisfaction to determine which economic choices yield the greatest benefits.

Can money really buy satisfaction?

BIG QUESTIONS

* How do economists model consumer satisfaction?
* How do consumers optimize their purchasing decisions?
* What is the diamond-water paradox?

How Do Economists Model Consumer Satisfaction?

Trade-offs

Utility is a measure of the level of satisfaction that a consumer enjoys from the consumption of goods and services.

A **util** is a personal unit of satisfaction used to measure the enjoyment from consumption of a good or service.

Do you prefer a slice of apple pie . . .

. . . or a fudge brownie?

Imagine that it is a hot afternoon and you decide to stop at a convenience store for a cold drink. While you're there, you decide to get a snack as well. Brownies are your favorite, but apple pie is on sale and you choose that instead. You may not think about these purchases very carefully, but they involve several trade-offs, including the time you could use to do something else and the money that you could be spending on something else. If brownies are your favorite snack, why do you sometimes choose to eat apple pie? Why do many people pay thousands of dollars for diamond jewelry, which is not essential for life, and yet pay only pennies for water, which is essential for life? These are the kinds of questions we must answer if we are to understand how people make personal buying decisions.

To better understand the decisions that consumers make, economists attempt to measure the satisfaction that consumers get when they make purchases. **Utility** is a measure of the level of satisfaction that a consumer enjoys from the consumption of goods and services. Utility theory seeks to measure contentment, or satisfaction. To understand why people buy the goods and services they do, we need to recognize that some products produce more utility than others and that everyone receives different levels of satisfaction from the same good or service. In other words, utility varies from individual to individual. To quantify this idea of relative satisfaction, economists measure utility with a unit they refer to as a **util**.

There is tremendous value in modeling decisions this way. When we understand utility, we can predict what people are likely to purchase. We model consumer behavior in a manner similar to the way we model how a firm makes decisions or how the labor market works. We expect the firm to maximize profits, the laborer to accept the best offer, and the consumer to find the combination of goods that gives the most utility. For example, a brownie lover may get 25 utils from her favorite snack, but someone who is less susceptible to the pleasures of chewy, gooey chocolate may rate the same brownie at 10 utils. However, these are not completely accurate measurements of relative utility. Who can say whether one person's 25 utils represents more actual satisfaction than another person's 10? Even if you and a friend agree that you each receive 10 utils from eating brownies, you cannot say that you both experience the same amount of satisfaction; each of you has a unique personal scale. However, the level of enjoyment one receives can be internally consistent. For example, if you rate a brownie at 25 utils and a slice of apple pie at 15 utils, we know that you like brownies more than apple pie.

Utility, or what most of us think of as satisfaction, is a balance between economic and personal factors. Even though there is an inherent problem with equating money and satisfaction, this has not stopped researchers from exploring the connection.

In the next section, we explore the connection between total utility and marginal utility. This connection will help us understand why more money does not necessarily bring more satisfaction.

ECONOMICS IN THE REAL WORLD

Happiness Index

Since 2006, the Organisation for Economic Co-operation and Development (OECD) has published the Better Life Index—popularly called the "happiness index"—which compiles social and economic data for 34 highly developed countries. The OECD measures well-being across these countries, based on 11 topics it has identified as essential in the areas of material living conditions and quality of life.

Which countries are happiest? The OECD doesn't rank them, and the results depend on the relative importance assigned to the different measurements. Giving each category equal weight, Australia currently comes in first, followed closely by Norway and the United States. What makes Aus-

"Down under" is a satisfying place to live!

tralians so happy? It's not their income, which averages only $26,000 per year. However, Australians live to an average age of 82 (two years longer than typical in developed countries), experience low amounts of pollution, display a high degree of civic engagement, and enjoy a very high life satisfaction rating.

In contrast, the OECD identifies the United States as having the highest income, but it scores substantially lower in work-life balance than many of the other top countries do. At the opposite end of the list, we find Mexico, where safety concerns, poor education, and low levels of income combine to produce a very low rating. ✳

Total Utility and Marginal Utility

Thinking about choices that consumers make can help us understand how to increase total utility. Consider a person who really likes brownies. In this case, the **marginal utility** is the additional satisfaction enjoyed from consuming one more brownie. In the table on the left-hand side of Figure 16.1, we see that the first brownie eaten brings 25 total utils. Eating additional brownies increases total utility until it reaches 75 utils after eating five brownies.

The graph in panel (a) of Figure 16.1 reveals that while the total utility (the green curve) rises until it reaches 75, the rate of increase (that is, the

Marginal utility is the additional satisfaction derived from consuming one more unit of a good or service.

Marginal thinking

FIGURE 16.1

Total Utility and Marginal Utility

The relationship between total utility and marginal utility can be seen by observing the dashed line that connects panels (a) and (b). Because the marginal utility becomes negative after five brownies are consumed, the total utility eventually falls after a certain number of brownies are eaten. To the left of the dashed line, the marginal utility is positive in panel (b) and the total utility is rising in panel (a). Conversely, to the right of the dashed line, the marginal utility is negative and the total utility is falling.

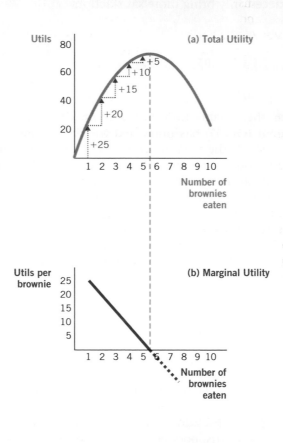

increase in marginal utility) falls from 25 utils for the first brownie down to 5 additional utils for the fifth. The marginal utility values from the table are plotted in panel (b), which shows that marginal utility declines steadily as consumption rises.

The relationship between total utility and marginal utility is evident when we observe the dashed line that connects panels (a) and (b). Because the marginal utility becomes negative after five brownies are consumed, the total utility eventually falls. To the left of the dashed line, the marginal utility is positive in panel (b) and the total utility is rising in panel (a). Conversely, to the right of the dashed line, the marginal utility is negative and the total utility is falling.

When marginal utility becomes negative, the consumer is tired of eating brownies. At that point, the brownies are no longer adding to the consumer's utility, and he or she will stop eating them.

Diminishing Marginal Utility

As you can see in panel (b) of Figure 16.1, the satisfaction that a consumer derives from consuming a good or service declines with each additional unit consumed. Consider what happens when you participate in a favorite activity for an hour and then decide to do something else. **Diminishing marginal utility** occurs when marginal utility declines as consumption increases. The concept of diminishing marginal utility is so universal that it is one of the most widely held ideas in all of economics.

In rare cases, marginal utility can rise—but only temporarily. Consider running. Many people choose to run for recreation because it is both healthy and pleasurable. Often, the first mile is difficult as the runner's body gets warmed up. Thereafter, running is easier—for a while. No matter how good you are at distance running, eventually the extra miles become more exhausting and less satisfying, and you stop. This does not mean that running is not healthy or pleasurable. Far from it! But it does mean that forcing yourself to do more running after you have already pushed your limit yields less utility. Your own intuition should confirm this theory. If increasing marginal utility were possible, you would find that with every passing second you would enjoy what you were doing more and never want to stop. Because economists do not observe this behavior among rational consumers, we can be highly confident that diminishing marginal utility has tremendous explanatory power.

Diminishing marginal utility occurs when marginal utility declines as consumption increases.

Running is fun for only so long.

PRACTICE WHAT YOU KNOW

Diminishing Marginal Utility

Question: A friend confides to you that a third friend has gradually lost interest in watching *The Big Bang Theory* with her and has begun saying she's too busy. How would you advise your friend to handle the situation?

Would you watch a *Big Bang Theory* marathon?

Answer: Tell your friend about diminishing marginal utility! Even the best television show runs its course. After a while, the same humor or drama that once made the show interesting no longer seems as interesting. Then suggest to your friend that they mix it up and do something different together. If that doesn't work, it may not be *The Big Bang Theory* that is the problem—it may be that your friend's friend has grown tired of her.

TABLE 16.1

Examples of Diminishing Marginal Utility

Example	Explanation using diminishing marginal utility
Discounts on two-day passes to amusement parks	The excitement on the first day is palpable. You run to rides, don't mind waiting in line, and experience the thrill for the first time. By the second day, the enthusiasm has worn off and the lower price entices you to return.
Discounts on season tickets	Over the course of any season, people anticipate some games and concerts more highly than other games and concerts. To encourage patrons to buy the entire season package, venues must discount the total price.
All-you-can-eat buffet	All-you-can-eat buffets offer the promise of unlimited food, but the average diner has a limited capacity. Eating more eventually leads to negative marginal utility. Restaurants assume that diminishing utility will limit how much their customers eat.
Unlimited night and weekend minutes on cell phone plans	Cell phone companies rely on the diminishing marginal utility of conversation. Cell phone companies offer "unlimited" plans because they know that consumers will not stay on their phones indefinitely.
Newspaper vending machines	A person rarely wants a second copy of the same newspaper. Because the value of the second paper is close to zero, most people do not steal additional copies from vending machines. (Sunday papers with money-saving coupons are a possible exception.)
Nathan's Famous Hot Dog Eating Contest	Many people enjoy eating a hot dog or two or three, but Nathan's Eating Contest is very difficult to watch. The idea of eating so many hot dogs makes a lot of people queasy.

Table 16.1 highlights how diminishing marginal utility can serve to explain a number of interesting real-world situations. Do not skip this table! It is very useful in helping you understand the concept of diminishing marginal utility.

How Do Consumers Optimize Their Purchasing Decisions?

Maximizing utility requires that consumers get the most satisfaction out of every dollar they spend, or what is commonly called "getting the biggest bang for the buck." When a consumer gets the most bang for the buck, we say that the consumer has *optimized* his or her purchasing decisions. However, optimization is easier said than done. Over the course of the year, each of us will make thousands of purchases of different amounts. Our budgets are generally not unlimited, and we try to spend in a way that enables us to meet both our short-run and our long-run needs. The combination of goods and services that maximizes the satisfaction, or utility, we get from our income or budget is the **consumer optimum**. In this section, we examine the decision process that leads to the consumer optimum. We start with two goods and then generalize those findings across a consumer's entire income or budget.

> The **consumer optimum** is the combination of goods and services that maximizes the consumer's utility for a given income or budget.

Consumer Purchasing Decisions

Let's begin by imagining a world with only two goods: Pepsi and pizza. This example will help us focus on the opportunity cost of purchasing Pepsi instead of pizza, or pizza instead of Pepsi.

Opportunity cost

Pepsi is available for $1 per can, and each pizza slice costs $2. Suppose that you have $10 to spend. How much of each good should you buy in order to maximize your satisfaction? Before we can answer that question, we need a rule for making decisions. To reach your consumer optimum, you must allocate your available money by choosing goods that give you the most utility per dollar spent. By getting the biggest bang for your buck, you will end up optimizing your choices. This relationship, shown below in terms of marginal utility (MU), helps quantify the decision. So if you get more for your money by purchasing Pepsi rather than pizza, then you should buy Pepsi—and vice versa.

$$\frac{MU_{Pepsi}}{Price_{Pepsi}} \quad \textbf{Which is larger?} \quad \frac{MU_{Pizza}}{Price_{Pizza}}$$

If we divide the marginal utility of a good by its price, we get the utility per dollar spent. Because you wish to optimize your utility, a direct comparison of the marginal utility per dollar spent on Pepsi versus pizza gives you a road map to your consumer satisfaction. Table 16.2 shows the marginal

TABLE 16.2

The Consumer Optimum with Pepsi and Pizza

(1) Pepsi consumed (cans)	(2) Marginal utility (MU Pepsi)	(3) MU Pepsi / Price Pepsi (Pepsi $1/can)	(4) Pizza consumed (slices)	(5) Marginal utility (MU pizza)	(6) MU pizza / Price pizza (pizza $2/slice)
1	9	9/1 = 9	1	20	20/2 = 10
2	8	8/1 = 8	2	16	16/2 = 8
3	7	7/1 = 7	3	12	**12/2 = 6**
4	6	**6/1 = 6**	4	8	8/2 = 4
5	5	5/1 = 5	5	4	4/2 = 2
6	4	4/1 = 4	6	0	0/2 = 0
7	3	3/1 = 3	7	−4	−4/2 = −2
8	2	2/1 = 2	8	−8	−8/2 = −4
9	1	1/1 = 1	9	−12	−12/2 = −6
10	0	0/1 = 0	10	−16	−16/2 = −8

utility for each can of Pepsi (column 2) and the marginal utility for each slice of pizza (column 5).

To decide what to consume first, look at column 3, which lists the marginal utility per dollar spent for Pepsi, and column 6, which lists the marginal utility per dollar spent for pizza. Now it's time to make your first spending decision—whether to drink a Pepsi or eat a slice of pizza. Because the marginal utility per dollar spent for the first slice of pizza (10) is higher than the marginal utility for the first can of Pepsi (9), you order a slice of pizza, which costs $2. You have $8 left.

After eating the first slice of pizza, you can choose between having a second slice of pizza, which brings 8 utils per dollar spent, and having the first can of Pepsi, which brings 9 utils per dollar spent. This time you order a Pepsi, which costs $1. You have $7 left.

Now you can choose between having a second slice of pizza, representing 8 utils per dollar spent, and having a second can of Pepsi, also 8 utils per dollar spent. Because both choices yield the same amount of utility per dollar spent and you have enough money to afford both, we'll assume you would probably purchase both at the same time. Your purchase costs another $3, which leaves you with $4.

Your next choice is between the third slice of pizza at 6 utils per dollar spent and the third can of Pepsi at 7 utils per dollar spent. Pepsi is the better value, so you buy that. You are left with $3 for your final choice: between the third slice of pizza at 6 utils per dollar spent and the fourth can of Pepsi at 6 utils per dollar spent. Since you have exactly $3 left and the items are of equal utility, you buy both, and you have no money left.

Let's see how well you have done. Looking at column 2 in Table 16.2, we calculate that the four Pepsis you consumed yielded a total utility of 9 + 8 + 7 + 6 = 30 utils. Looking at column 5, we see that three slices of pizza yielded a total utility of 20 + 16 + 12 = 48. Adding the two together (30 + 48) gives 78 total utils of satisfaction. This is the most utility you can afford with $10. To see why, look at Table 16.3, which reports the maximum utility for every affordable combination of Pepsi and pizza.

The optimum combination of Pepsi and pizza is highlighted in orange. This is the result we found by comparing the marginal utilities per dollar spent in Table 16.2. Notice that Table 16.3 confirms that this process results in the highest total utility. All other affordable combinations of Pepsi and

TABLE 16.3

The Maximum Utility from Different Combinations of Pepsi and Pizza

Affordable combination of pizza and Pepsi	Total utility
5 pizza slices (20 + 16 + 12 + 8 + 4)	60 utils
2 Pepsis (9 + 8) and 4 pizza slices (20 + 16 + 12 + 8)	73 utils
4 Pepsis (9 + 8 + 7 + 6) and 3 pizza slices (20 + 16 + 12)	**78 utils**
6 Pepsis (9 + 8 + 7 + 6 + 5 + 4) and 2 pizza slices (20 + 16)	75 utils
8 Pepsis (9 + 8 + 7 + 6 + 5 + 4 + 3 + 2) and 1 pizza slice (20)	64 utils
10 Pepsis (9 + 8 + 7 + 6 + 5 + 4 + 3 + 2 + 1 + 0)	45 utils

The OECD Better Life Index

The OECD Better Life Index attempts to measure 11 key factors of material well-being in each of its 34 member countries. The goal of the index is to provide member governments with a snapshot of how their citizens are living, thus providing a road map for future policy priorities. Some factors are objectively measured, such as average household income. Others are more subjective, such as "life satisfaction," and are measured from survey responses. Below is a look at the results in three countries.

Legend:
- Housing
- Income
- Jobs
- Community
- Education
- Environment
- Health
- Life satisfaction
- Safety
- Work-life balance
- Civic engagement

Australia
4.9
7.4 / 5.2
8.1 / 8.3
8.2 / 8.6
9.2 / 9.2
9.6 / 9.5

Italy
4.1
4.5 / 4.6
4.6 / 4.9
5.2 / 5.2
7.5 / 7.2
8.4 / 7.7

Mexico
0.4
0.4 / 0.5
1.9 / 1.8
3.5 / 3.5
5.3 / 4.7
5.5 / 7.0

10.0

Each factor is ranked on a scale of zero to 10, with 10 being the highest. One to three indicators go into each measurement. For instance, "Jobs" is measured through the unemployment rate, job security, and personal earnings.

What do these numbers say about a nation's quality of life? It depends on which factors you think are most important. At www.oecdbetterlifeindex.org you can weight the different categories, create an index, and see how nations compare.

REVIEW QUESTIONS

- Mexico has five glaring challenges to the well-being of its citizens. What are they?

- Visit the OECD website and create your own index. Are any of the pizza produce less utility. Table 16.3 also illustrates diminishing marginal utility. If you select either pizza or Pepsi exclusively, you would have a much lower total utility: 60 utils with pizza and 45 utils with Pepsi. In addition, the preferred outcome of four Pepsis and three pizza slices corresponds to a modest amount of each good; this outcome avoids the utility reduction associated with excessive consumption of either good.

By thinking at the margin about which good provides the highest marginal utility, you also maximize your total utility. Of course, most people rarely think this way. But as consumers we make marginal choices all the time. Instead of adding up utils, we think "that isn't worth it" or "that's a steal." Consumer choice is not so much a conscious calculation as an instinct to seek the most satisfaction. Next we extend our analysis by generalizing the two-good example.

Marginal Thinking with More Than Two Goods

Marginal thinking

The idea of measuring utility makes our instinctive sense more explicit and enables us to solve simple optimization problems. For instance, when you travel without the aid of GPS, you instinctively make choices about which route to take to save time. The decision to turn left or right when you come to a stop sign is a decision at the margin: one route will be better than the other. If you consistently make the best choices about which way to turn, you will arrive at your destination sooner. This is why economists focus on marginal thinking.

In reality, life is more complex than the simple two-good model implies. When you have $10 to spend, you may choose among many goods. Because you buy many items at all kinds of prices over the course of a year, you must juggle hundreds (or thousands) of purchases so that you enjoy roughly the same utility per dollar spent. Consumer optimum captures this idea by comparing the utility gained with the price paid for every item a consumer buys. In other words, a consumer's income or budget is balanced so that the ratio of the marginal utility (MU) per dollar spent on every item, from good A to good Z, is equal. In mathematical terms:

Left or right? One way will get you to your destination sooner.

$$\frac{MU_A}{Price_A} = \frac{MU_B}{Price_B} = \cdots = \frac{MU_Z}{Price_Z}$$

In the next section, we explore the relationship between changes in price and changes in the consumer optimum.

Price Changes and the Consumer Optimum

Recall our example of pizza and Pepsi: you reached an optimum when you purchased four Pepsis and three slices of pizza. At that point, the marginal utility per dollar spent for Pepsi and pizza was equal:

$$\frac{MU_{pizza} \text{ (12 utils)}}{\$2} = \frac{MU_{Pepsi} \text{ (6 utils)}}{\$1}$$

In the earlier example, the prices of a slice of pizza ($2) and a can of Pepsi ($1) were held constant. But suppose that the price of a slice of pizza drops to $1.50. This new price causes the ratio of $MU_{pizza} \div Price_{pizza}$ to change from 12 ÷ 2, or 6 utils per dollar, to 12 ÷ 1.5, or 8 utils per dollar. The lower price for pizza increases the quantity of slices that the consumer will buy:

$$\frac{MU_{pizza} \ (12 \ utils)}{\$1.50} > \frac{MU_{Pepsi} \ (6 \ utils)}{\$1}$$

As a result, we can say that lower prices increase the marginal utility per dollar spent and cause consumers to buy more of a good. Higher prices have the opposite effect by lowering the marginal utility per dollar spent. If that conclusion sounds an awful lot like the law of demand, it is! We have just restated the law of demand in terms of marginal utility.

We know that according to the law of demand (see Chapter 3), the quantity demanded falls when the price rises, and the quantity demanded rises when the price falls—all other things being equal. If we think of consumer desire for a particular product as demand, it makes sense to find a connection between the prices that consumers pay, the quantity that they buy, and the marginal utility that they receive.

A lower price has two effects. First, because the marginal utility per dollar spent is now higher, consumers substitute the product that has become relatively less expensive—this is the **substitution effect**. Second, at the same time, a lower price can also change the purchasing power of income—this is the **real-income effect**. (For a basic discussion of the trends behind these effects, see Chapter 3.)

Let's go back to our Pepsi and pizza example to separate these two effects. A lower price for a slice of pizza makes it more affordable. If slices are $2.00 each, a consumer with a budget of $10.00 can afford five slices. If the price drops to $1.50 per slice, the consumer can afford six slices and still have $1.00 left over.

When the price of a slice of pizza is $2.00, your optimum is three slices of pizza and four Pepsis. If we drop the price of a slice of pizza to $1.50, you save 50 cents per slice. Because you are purchasing three slices, you save $1.50—which is enough to buy another slice. Looking back at column 5 in Table 16.2, we see that the fourth slice of pizza yields an additional 8 utils. Alternatively, you could use the $1.50 you saved on pizza to buy a fifth can of Pepsi—which has a marginal utility of 5—and still have 50 cents left over.

The lower price of pizza may cause you to substitute pizza for Pepsi because pizza has become relatively less expensive. This is the substitution effect at work. In addition, you have more purchasing power through the money you save from the lower-priced pizza. This is the real-income effect.

The real-income effect matters only when prices change enough to cause a measurable effect on the purchasing power of the consumer's income or budget. For example, suppose that a 10% price reduction in peanut butter cups occurs. Will there be a substitution effect, a real-income effect, or both? The key to answering this question is to consider how much money is saved. Most candy bars cost less than a dollar, so a 10% reduction in price would be less than 10 cents. The lower price will motivate some consumers to switch to peanut butter cups—a substitution effect that can be observed through increased purchases of peanut butter cups. However, the real-income effect is negligible. The consumer has saved less than 10 cents. The money saved could be used to purchase other goods; but very few goods cost so little, and the enhanced purchasing power is effectively zero. Thus, the answer to the question is that there will be a modest substitution effect and essentially no real-income effect.

The **substitution effect** occurs when consumers substitute a product that has become relatively less expensive as the result of a price change.

The **real-income effect** occurs when there is a change in purchasing power as a result of a change in the price of a good.

ECONOMICS IN THE REAL WORLD

Would You Pay More Than $50 for a Drink at Starbucks?

Your favorite Starbucks creation typically costs about $5. Now just imagine how it would taste if you spent over $50 on extra shots, add-ins, and flavors. Would the drink be better? Perhaps. But would it taste 10 times better? Not a chance. How do we know this? The law of diminishing marginal utility tells us that additional units of the same good will eventually bring less marginal utility. In addition, substantial income and substitution effects are at work when you consider what $50 could buy instead of coffee. For many people, $50 is enough to purchase a week's worth of groceries. It is hard to imagine that a single Starbucks drink could provide more utility than you would experience from the variety of food you would eat over the course of a week. If you are interested in learning more about the curious obsession some people have with purchasing a superexpensive Starbucks creation, check out this link: http://www.caffeineinformer.com/what-is-the-most-expensive-starbucks-drink. ✳

What is the most you would pay for your favorite drink?

PRACTICE WHAT YOU KNOW

Consumer Optimum

Question: Suppose your favorite magazine, *The Economist*, costs $6 per issue and *People* magazine costs $4 per issue. If you receive 20 utils when you read *People*, how many additional utils would you need to get from reading *The Economist* to cause you to spend the extra $2 it costs to purchase it?

Answer: To answer the question, you first need to equate the marginal utility (MU) per dollar spent for both magazines and solve for the missing variable, the utility from *The Economist*:

$$\frac{MU_{The\ Economist}\ (X\ utils)}{\$6} = \frac{MU_{People}\ (20\ utils)}{\$4}$$

$$\frac{X}{\$6} = \frac{20}{\$4}$$

$$X = \frac{\$120}{\$4}$$

$$X = 30$$

When the $MU_{The\ Economist}$ is equal to 30 utils, you are indifferent between purchasing either of the two magazines (that is, each magazine would bring you equal satisfaction). Because the question asks how many *additional* utils are needed to justify purchasing *The Economist*, you should subtract the utils from *People*, or 20, to get the difference, which is 30 − 20, or 10 utils.

What Is the Diamond-Water Paradox?

Now that you understand the connection between prices and utility, we can tackle one of the most interesting puzzles in economics—the **diamond-water paradox**. First described by Adam Smith in 1776, the diamond-water paradox explains why water, which is essential to life, is inexpensive, while diamonds, which do not sustain life, are expensive. Many people of Smith's era found the paradox perplexing. Today, we can use consumer choice theory to answer the question.

Essentially, the diamond-water paradox unfairly compares the amount of marginal utility a person receives from a small quantity of something rare (the diamond) with the marginal utility received from consuming a small amount of additional water after already consuming a large amount.

We know that marginal utility is captured in the law of demand and therefore by the price of a good. For example, when the price of diamonds increases, the quantity demanded declines. We learned in Chapter 5 that in graphical terms, the consumer surplus is the area under the demand curve and above the price, or the gains from trade that a consumer enjoys. Therefore, if the price of diamonds rises, consumers will enjoy less surplus when buying them.

Figure 16.2 contrasts the demand and supply equilibrium in both the market for water and the market for diamonds. Notice that the consumer surplus is the area highlighted in blue for water and the triangular area highlighted with dots for diamonds. The blue area of total utility for water (TU_w) is much larger than the dotted area of total utility for diamonds (TU_d) because water is essential for life. Therefore, water creates significantly more total utility than diamonds do. However, in most places in the United States, water is very plentiful, so people take additional units of it for granted. In fact, it is so plentiful that if someone were to offer you a gallon of water right now, you would probably hesitate to take it. But what if someone offered you a gallon-size bucket of diamonds? You bet you would take that! Therefore, it should not surprise you that something quite plentiful, water, would yield less marginal utility than something rare, diamonds ($MU_w < MU_d$). However, if water were as rare as diamonds, there is no doubt that the price of water would exceed the price of diamonds.

Let's consider how we use water. We bathe in it, cook with it, and drink it. Each of those uses has high value, so the marginal utility of water is high. But we also use it to water our lawns and fill our fish tanks. Those uses are not nearly as essential, so the marginal utility of water for these uses is much lower. The reason we use water in both essential and nonessential ways is that its price is relatively low, so low-value uses, like filling fish tanks, yield enough utility to justify the cost. Because water is abundant in most places, the price (P_{water}) is low. In contrast, diamonds are rare, and their price ($P_{diamond}$) is high. The cost of obtaining a diamond means that a consumer must get a great deal of marginal utility from the purchase of a diamond to justify the expense, which explains why diamonds are given as gifts for extremely special occasions.

The **diamond-water paradox** explains why water, which is essential to life, is inexpensive, while diamonds, which do not sustain life, are expensive.

FIGURE 16.2

The Diamond-Water Paradox

The diamond-water paradox exists because people fail to recognize that demand and supply are equally important in determining the value a good creates in society. The demand for water is large, while the demand for diamonds is small. If we look at the amount of consumer surplus, we observe that the blue area (TU_w, which represents the consumer surplus for water) is much larger than the dotted area (TU_d, which represents the consumer surplus for diamonds) because water is essential for life. As a result, water creates significantly more total utility (TU) than diamonds. However, because water is abundant in most places, the price, P_{water}, is low. In contrast, diamonds are rare and the price, $P_{diamond}$, is high.

ECONOMICS IN THE MEDIA

The Diamond-Water Paradox

Super Size Me

What would happen if you ate all your meals at McDonald's for an entire month—without ever exercising? *Super Size Me*, a 2004 documentary by Morgan Spurlock, endeavored to find out. It is the absurd nature of Spurlock's adventure that pulls viewers in. No one would *actually* eat every meal at the same restaurant for a month, because diminishing marginal utility would cause the utility from the meals to plunge. (This is especially true with McDonald's, which is not known for high-quality cuisine.)

A Big Mac a day for 30 days! What could possibly go wrong?

Why did Spurlock take aim at McDonald's and more generally the fast-food industry? His aim was to reveal how unhealthy fast food really is, but the documentary also happens to unintentionally offer a modern parallel to the diamond-water paradox.

The key is the business model that many fast-food restaurants follow. These restaurants provide filling food at low prices, a combination that encourages consumers to eat more than they would if the price was higher. Eating a lot of food causes diminishing marginal utility; often, the last bite of a sandwich or fries or the last gulp of a 32-ounce drink brings very little additional utility, so it is not uncommon for consumers to discard the excess.

In contrast, consider fine dining. Fancy establishments serve smaller portions by design. A five-course meal is meant to be savored, and the experience trumps price. What makes someone willing to pay significantly more when dining out at such places? Upscale restaurants are creating high marginal utility by making every bite mouthwatering. They do not want to diminish the marginal value through overeating.

To summarize, McDonald's is a lot like water in the diamond-water paradox. It is easy to find a McDonald's restaurant almost anywhere, and the chain serves close to 70 million customers a day. Therefore, the total utility the chain creates is high, despite the fact that the marginal utility of an individual bite is low. Upscale restaurants are a lot like diamonds: they are uncommon, and the number of customers they serve is small. The total utility that upscale restaurants create is low compared with McDonald's, but the marginal utility of an individual bite at an upscale restaurant is quite high.

Conclusion

Does having more money make people more satisfied? The answer is no. More money enables people to buy more goods, but because of diminishing marginal utility, the increases in satisfaction from being able to buy more goods or higher-quality goods become progressively smaller with rising income. So we could say that having more money makes people somewhat more satisfied. But it seems appropriate to add that the relationship between quality of life and money is not direct. More money sometimes leads to more utility, and at other times more money means more problems.

As we have seen in this chapter, price plays a key role in determining utility. Because consumers face a budget and wish to maximize their utility, the prices they pay determine their marginal utility per dollar spent. Comparing the marginal utility per dollar spent across many goods helps us understand individuals' consumption patterns. Diminishing marginal utility also helps to describe consumer choice. Because marginal utility declines with additional consumption, consumers do not exclusively purchase their favorite products. Instead, they diversify their choices in order to gain more utility. In addition, changes in prices have two different effects: one on real income and a separate substitution effect that determines the composition of the bundle of goods that are purchased.

In the next chapter, we question how much individuals use consumer choice theory to make their decisions. The approach known as behavioral economics argues that decision-makers are not entirely rational about the choices they make.

Finally, in the appendix that follows, we refine consumer theory by discussing indifference curves. Please read the appendix to get a glimpse into how economists model consumer choice in greater detail.

ANSWERING THE BIG QUESTIONS

How do economists model consumer satisfaction?

＊ Economists model consumer satisfaction by examining utility, which is a measure of the level of satisfaction that a consumer enjoys from the consumption of goods and services.

＊ Utility diminishes with additional consumption. This property limits the amount of any particular good or service that a person will consume.

How do consumers optimize their purchasing decisions?

＊ Consumers optimize their purchasing decisions by finding the combination of goods and services that maximizes the level of satisfaction from a given income or budget. The consumer optimum occurs when a consumer maximizes the utility from his or her income or budget, so that the marginal utility per dollar spent on every item purchased is equal to that of every other item purchased.

＊ Changes in price have two distinct effects on consumer behavior. If the price falls, the marginal utility per dollar spent will be higher. As a result, consumers will substitute the product that has become relatively less expensive. This is the substitution effect. If the lower price also results in substantial savings, it causes an increase in purchasing power, known as the real-income effect.

What is the diamond-water paradox?

✳ The diamond-water paradox explains why water, which is essential to life, is inexpensive, while diamonds, which do not sustain life, are expensive. Many people of Adam Smith's era, in the eighteenth century, found the paradox perplexing. We can solve the diamond-water paradox by recognizing that the price of water is low because its supply is abundant, and the price of diamonds is high because their supply is small. If water were as rare as diamonds, there is no doubt that the price of water would exceed the price of diamonds.

ECONOMICS FOR LIFE

The Economics of Romance: When Do You Know You've Found the "Right" Person?

We all know that finding your soul mate can create more satisfaction in your life than anything else. Being with the right person can bring you joy, meaning, and a sense of personal strength. But—if you'll forgive us for being a bit unromantic—isn't there also something to say about all this satisfaction in terms of utility? Here we give some "economic" advice about love and marriage.

1. Recognize that your choice in a partner is being made in a market (the dating market), but the market doesn't use money. Instead, it uses barter. You offer someone the qualities that he or she is looking for—love, support, shared life goals—and hope that he or she is willing to trade those things back to you (and that the person doesn't get a better offer from someone else!). You find someone you want who feels the same way about you.

2. Partnerships often work best when the partners have different characteristics and skills. Maybe one person manages the household finances, while the other takes care of the yard. In other words, a couple can make gains from trade by using their comparative advantage in the production of household services.

3. Consumption complementarities also exist in a strong relationship. When doing things together makes them more enjoyable than doing them alone, you've found someone special. These activities can be as simple as taking walks, making dinner together, having a common passion for animals, or belonging to the same religious organization. A beneficial partnership isn't just about getting more done through gains from trade. It's also about having more fun because each partner enjoys "consuming" life more when the other one is around.

4. Finally, when you think of marriage, think of a business contract between two people about how they will organize their lives together. As with any contract, you'll need to set some terms. Will you both need to work to support your lifestyle together? Where will you live, and will you plan to have children? How will you organize your financial affairs—will you use separate or joint bank accounts? How much will you set aside for retirement? The effort you make to understand decisions like these is time and energy well spent, because you can avoid serious conflicts later.

There you have it. All you need to do is to find someone who is willing to enter into a binding contract with you. Or in the words of this chapter, you just need to find someone with a consumer optimum that matches yours!

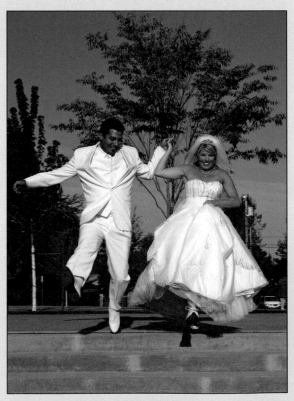

Do you suppose this couple has found their consumer optimum in the market for romance?

CONCEPTS YOU SHOULD KNOW

consumer optimum
  (p. 511)
diamond-water paradox
  (p. 517)

diminishing marginal utility
  (p. 509)
marginal utility (p. 507)
real-income effect (p. 515)

substitution effect
  (p. 515)
util (p. 506)
utility (p. 506)

QUESTIONS FOR REVIEW

1. After watching a movie, you and your friend both indicate that you liked it. Does this mean that each of you received the same amount of utility? Explain your response.

2. What is the relationship between total utility and marginal utility?

3. How is diminishing marginal utility reflected in the law of demand?

4. What does it mean when we say that the marginal utility per dollar spent is equal for two goods?

STUDY PROBLEMS (✳ *solved at the end of the section*)

1. A local pizza restaurant charges full price for the first pizza but offers 50% off on a second pizza. Using marginal utility, explain the restaurant's pricing strategy.

2. Suppose that the price of trail mix is $4 per pound and the price of cashews is $6 per pound. If you get 30 utils from the last pound of cashews you consume, how many utils would you have to get from the last pound of trail mix to be in consumer equilibrium?

3. Fill in the missing information in the table below:

Number of cookies	Total utility of cookies	Marginal utility of cookies	Number of pretzels	Total utility of pretzels	Marginal utility of pretzels
0	0	—	0	0	—
1	—	25	1	10	—
2	—	15	2	18	—
3	—	10	3	24	6
4	—	5	4	—	4
5	55	—	5	—	2
6	50	—	6	—	0

4. Use the table in problem 3. Suppose that you have a budget of $8 and that cookies and pretzels cost $1 each. What is the consumer optimum?

5. Use the table in problem 3. What is the consumer optimum if the price of cookies rises from $1 to $1.50 and the price of pretzels remains at $1.00?

6. You are considering either dining at Cici's, an all-you-can-eat pizza chain, or buying pizza by the slice at a local pizzeria for $2 per slice. At which restaurant are you likely to obtain the most marginal utility from the last slice you eat? Explain your response.

7. In consumer equilibrium, a person buys four cups of coffee at $2 per cup and two muffins at $2 per muffin each day. If the price of a cup of coffee rises to $3, what would you expect to happen to the amount of coffee and muffins this person consumes?

8. How do dollar stores survive when *none* of the items sold brings a high amount of total utility to consumers?

✳ 9. Imagine that the total utility from consuming five tacos is 10, 16, 19, 20, and 17 utils, respectively. When does marginal utility begin to diminish?

10. You and your friends are considering vacationing in either Cabo San Lucas or Cancun for spring break. When you first researched the cost of your hotel and flights, the total price was $1,000 to each destination. However, a sale has lowered the total cost of going to Cancun to $800. Does this change create a substitution effect, a real-income effect, or both? Explain.

✳ 11. Everyone wears underwear, but comparatively few people wear ties. Why are ties so much more expensive than underwear if the demand for underwear is so much greater than the demand for ties?

12. Do you agree with Henry David Thoreau's quote, "Happiness is like a butterfly; the more you chase it, the more it will elude you, but if you turn your attention to other things, it will come and sit softly on your shoulder"? Explain your answer using diminishing marginal utility.

✳ 13. A health study found that patients who experience severe pain may feel better if they curse as a coping mechanism. Based on what you have learned about economics, would you expect to see a difference in pain relief between people who normally use profanity and those who do not normally use profanity?

SOLVED PROBLEMS

9. The key to answering this question is to realize that the data are expressed in total utils. The first taco brings the consumer 10 utils. Consuming the second taco yields $16 - 10$, or 6 additional utils. Since there are fewer extra utils from the second taco (6) than the utils from the first taco (10), diminishing marginal utility begins after the first taco.

11. Recall that demand is only half of the market. The other half is supply. Far fewer ties are produced than items of underwear. The supply of ties also plays a role in determining the price. In addition, ties are a fashion statement, which makes ties a luxury good. Underwear is a necessity. As a result, ties are a lot like diamonds: there is a small overall market, and prices are high. Underwear is a lot like water: there is a very large overall market, and prices are low. The fact that ties generally cost more does not mean that ties are more valuable to society. Rather, people get more marginal utility from purchasing the "perfect" tie as opposed to finding the "perfect" underwear.

13. The researchers found that patients who infrequently cursed in their daily lives experienced more pain relief when they were in severe pain. Those who regularly cursed in their daily lives experienced almost no pain relief from cursing. This result is not surprising when you recall the law of diminishing marginal utility. For additional information, see http://www.ncbi.nlm.nih.gov/m/pubmed/22078790/.

16A | Indifference Curve Analysis

There is much more to economic analysis than the simple supply and demand model can capture. Chapter 16 considered how consumers can get the biggest bang for their buck, or the greatest utility out of their purchases. Here we explore the question in more detail, using the tool of indifference curve analysis. The purpose of this appendix is to get you thinking at a deeper level about the connections between price changes and consumption decisions.

Indifference Curves

Indifference curves are a tool that economists use to describe the trade-offs that exist when consumers make decisions.

An **indifference curve** represents the various combinations of two goods that yield the same level of satisfaction, or utility. The simplest way to think about indifference curves is to envision a topographical map on which each line represents a specific elevation. When you look at a topographical map, you see ridges, mountains, valleys, and the subtle flow of the land. An indifference curve conveys the same complex information about personal satisfaction. Indifference curves visually rise to a peak called the **maximization point**, or the point at which utility is maximized. The only limitation of this analysis is that this book is a two-dimensional space that we use to illustrate a three-dimensional concept. Let's set this concern aside and focus on achieving the maximization point, where total utility is highest.

Returning to our example of pizza and Pepsi, recall that you had $10 to spend and only two items to purchase: Pepsi at $1 per can and pizza at $2 per slice. Like all consumers, you will optimize your utility by maximizing the marginal utility per dollar spent, so you select four Pepsis and three slices of pizza. But what happens if your budget is unlimited? If you're free to spend as much you like, how much pizza and Pepsi would you want?

Economic "Goods" and "Bads"

To answer the question we just posed, we'll start with another question. Are Pepsi and pizza always economic "goods"? This may seem like a strange question, but think about your own consumption habits. Do you keep eating something after you feel full? Do you continue to eat even if your stomach aches? At some point, we all stop eating and drinking. In this sense, economic goods, like Pepsi and pizza, are "good" only

An indifference curve represents the various combinations of two goods that yield the same level of personal satisfaction, or utility.

A maximization point is the point at which a certain combination of two goods yields the most utility.

A topographical map and indifference curve analysis share many of the same properties.

up to a point. Once we are full, however, the utility from attaining another unit of the good becomes negative—a "bad."

Each indifference curve represents lines of equal satisfaction. For simplicity, Figure 16A.1 shows the indifference curve as circles around the point of maximum satisfaction. The closer the indifference curve is to the maximization point, the higher the consumer's level of satisfaction.

Indifference curves are best seen as approaching the maximization point from all directions (like climbing up a mountain on four different sides). In any hike, some paths are better than others. Figure 16A.1 illustrates four separate ways to reach the maximization point. However, only one of the paths makes any sense. In quadrants II, III, and IV, either pizza or Pepsi is a "bad" or both are "bads" (because at those levels of consumption one or both of them make the consumer feel too full or sick). Because the consumer must pay to acquire pizza and Pepsi, and because at least one of them is reducing the

FIGURE 16A.1

Indifference Curves

The maximization point indicates where a consumer attains the most utility. In quadrant I, both Pepsi and pizza are "goods" (because their consumption involves the reactions of either tasting great or getting full), so attaining more of each will cause utility to rise toward the maximization point. In quadrants II, III, and IV, either pizza or Pepsi is a "bad" or both are (because at those levels of consumption they make the consumer feel either too full or sick). Because the consumer must pay to acquire pizza and Pepsi, and because at least one of the items is reducing the consumer's utility in quadrants II, III, and IV, the most affordable path to the highest utility—that is, the maximization point—is quadrant I. (Notice that the labels are qualitative and reflect decreasing utility with additional consumption.)

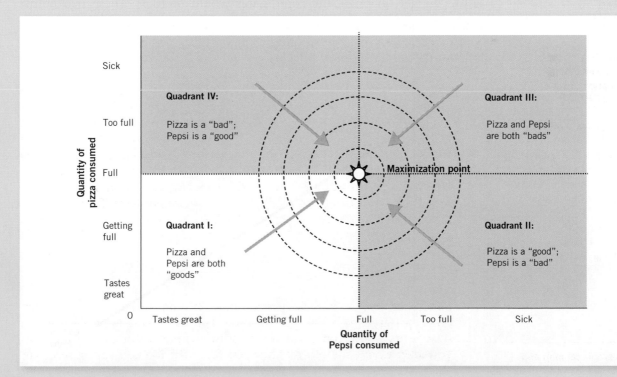

consumer's utility, the consumer's satisfaction will increase by purchasing less of the "bad." In other words, why would anyone willingly pay to feel worse? Quadrants II, III, and IV are highlighted in orange because people are unlikely to choose an option that makes them feel too full or sick. That leaves quadrant I as the preferred path to the highest utility. In quadrant I, increasing amounts of pizza and Pepsi produce more utility. (Notice that the labels in Figure 16A.1 are qualitative and reflect decreasing utility with additional consumption.)

The Budget Constraint

Figure 16A.1 illustrates the choices facing a consumer with an unlimited budget and no opportunity costs. However, in real life we need to account for a person's budget and the cost of acquiring each good. The amount a person has to spend is the **budget constraint**, or the set of consumption bundles that represent the maximum amount the consumer can afford. If you have $10 to spend on pizza ($2 per slice) and Pepsi ($1 per can), you could choose to purchase 10 cans of Pepsi and forgo the pizza. Alternatively, you could purchase 5 slices of pizza and do without the Pepsi. Or you could choose a number of different combinations of pizza and Pepsi, as we saw in Chapter 16. The budget constraint line in Figure 16A.2 delineates the affordable combinations of pizza and Pepsi.

There are many different affordable combinations of the two goods. Let's take the pairs along the budget constraint line first. If you spend your entire $10 on Pepsi, the combination of coordinates would be the point (10,0), which represents 10 cans of Pepsi and 0 slices of pizza. If you spend your entire budget on pizza, the coordinates would be (0,5). These two points

> The **budget constraint** is the set of consumption bundles that represent the maximum amount the consumer can afford.

FIGURE 16A.2

The Budget Constraint

The budget constraint line shows the set of affordable combinations of Pepsi and pizza with a budget of $10. Any point inside the budget constraint—for example (2,2)—is also affordable. Points beyond the budget constraint—for example (10,5)—are not affordable.

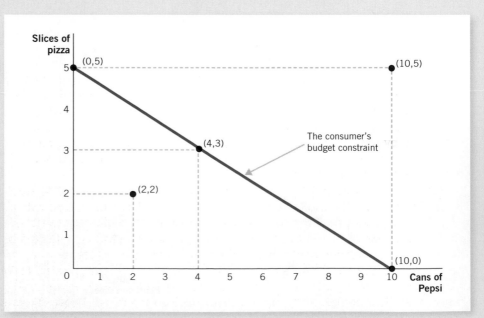

are the extreme outcomes. By connecting these two points with a line—the budget constraint—we can see the many combinations that would fully exhaust $10. As a consumer, your goal is to pick the combination that maximizes your satisfaction, subject to your budget constraint. One possibility would be to spend the $10 on four cans of Pepsi and three slices of pizza (4,3), which happens to be the point of utility maximization we discovered in the chapter (see Table 16.3).

What about the points located below and above the budget constraint? For example, looking again at Figure 16A.2, at the point (2,2) you would be spending $6—that is, $2 on Pepsi and $4 on pizza. You would still have $4 to spend on more of either good. Because both goods are desirable, spending the leftover money in your budget will increase your level of satisfaction. So the combination (2,2) represents a failure to maximize utility. On the other side of the budget constraint line, we find the point (10,5). This combination, which would cost you $20 to attain, represents a combination of items that you cannot afford. From this example, you can see that the budget constraint is a limiting set of choices, or a constraint imposed by scarcity.

In the next section, we examine indifference curves in greater detail. Once we fully understand the properties that characterize indifference curves, we can join them with the budget constraint to better describe how consumers make choices.

Properties of Indifference Curves

It is useful to keep in mind several assumptions about indifference curves. The properties described in this section help ensure that our model is logically consistent.

Indifference Curves Are Typically Bowed Inward

A rational consumer will operate only in quadrant I in Figure 16A.1. Within that quadrant, the higher indifference curves (those nearer the utility maximization point) are bowed inward (convex) and are preferred to the lower ones (nearer the origin). Our model eliminates any outcome in quadrants II through IV by requiring that goods be "good," not "bad." Because quadrants II through IV result in less utility and greater expenditures, no rational consumer would ever willingly operate in these regions.

Figure 16A.3 shows an indifference curve that reflects the trade-off between two goods. Because the indifference curve bows inward, the **marginal rate of substitution (MRS)**, or the rate at which a consumer is willing to trade one good for another along the indifference curve, varies. The MRS is reflected in the slope of the indifference curve in the figure. Points A and B are both on the same indifference curve, so the consumer finds the combinations (1,5) and (2,3) to be equally attractive. Between points A and B, the consumer must receive two slices of pizza to compensate for the loss of a can of Pepsi. We can see this in the figure by observing that the consumer chooses only two cans of Pepsi and three slices of pizza at (2,3). Because the marginal utility from

Trade-offs

The **marginal rate of substitution (MRS)** is the rate at which a consumer is willing to trade one good for another along an indifference curve.

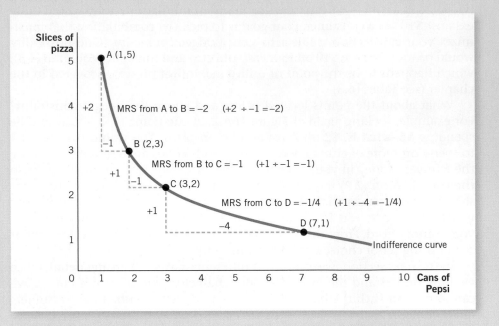

FIGURE 16A.3

The Marginal Rate of Substitution

The marginal rate of substitution (MRS) along an indifference curve varies, as reflected in the slope of the indifference curve. Because Pepsi and pizza are both subject to diminishing marginal utility, it takes more of the plentiful good to keep the consumer indifferent when giving up another good that is in short supply.

Marginal thinking

consuming Pepsi is high when the amount consumed is low, giving up an additional Pepsi requires that the consumer receive back two slices of pizza to reach the point (1,5). Therefore, the marginal rate of substitution (MRS) is -2 (because $+2 \div -1 = -2$).

However, if we examine the same indifference curve between points C and D, we see that the consumer is also indifferent between the combinations (3,2) and (7,1). However, this time the consumer is willing to give up four cans of Pepsi to get one more slice of pizza, so the MRS is -4 (because $+1 \div -4 = -1/4$). Why is there such a big difference between (3,2) and (7,1) compared with (2,3) and (1,5)? At (7,1), the consumer has a lot of Pepsi and very little pizza to enjoy it with. As a result, the marginal utility of the second slice of pizza is so high that it is worth four Pepsis! We can see the change in the marginal rate of substitution visually, because the slope between points A and B is steeper than it is between points C and D.

What explains why Pepsi is more valuable between points A and B? The consumer starts with only two cans. Pizza is more valuable between points C and D because the consumer starts with only two slices of pizza. Because Pepsi and pizza are both subject to diminishing marginal utility, it takes more of the plentiful good to keep the consumer indifferent when giving up another good that is in short supply.

Indifference Curves Cannot Be Thick

Another property of indifference curves is that they cannot be thick. If they could be thick, then it would be possible to draw two points inside an indifference curve where one of the two points was preferred to the other. Therefore, a consumer could be indifferent between those points. In Figure 16A.4, points A, B, and C are all located on the same (impossible) indifference curve. However, points B and C are both strictly preferred to point A. Why? Because point B has one extra slice of pizza compared with point A, and point C has two extra cans of Pepsi compared with point A. Because more pizza and Pepsi adds to the consumer's utility, the consumer cannot be indifferent between these three points.

Indifference Curves Cannot Intersect

Indifference curves, by their very nature, cannot intersect. To understand why, let's look at a hypothetical case. Figure 16A.5 shows two indifference curves crossing at point A. Points A and B are both located along the light orange curve (IC_1), so we know that those two points bring the consumer the same utility. Points A and C are both located along the darker orange curve (IC_2), so those two points also yield the same utility for the consumer. Therefore, the utility at point A equals the utility at point B, and the utility at point A also equals the utility at point C. This means that the utility at point B should also equal the utility at point C, but that cannot be true. Point B is located at (1,3), and point C is located at (2,4). Because (2,4) strictly dominates (1,3), point C is preferred to point B. Therefore, we can say that indifference curves cannot intersect without violating the assumption that consumers are rational utility maximizers.

We have seen that indifference curves have three properties: they are bowed inward toward the origin (convex); they cannot be thick; and they cannot intersect. These properties guarantee that they take the general levels shown in quadrant I of Figure 16A.1.

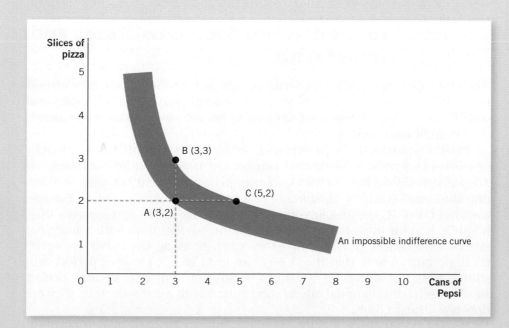

Indifference Curves Cannot Be Thick

If indifference curves could be thick, it would be possible to draw two points inside the curve in a way that indicates that one of the two points is preferred to the other. Point B has one extra slice of pizza and point C has two extra cans of Pepsi compared with point A. Therefore, the consumer cannot be indifferent between these three points, and the indifference curve cannot be thick.

Indifference Curves Cannot Intersect

The utility at point B should equal the utility at point C, but that cannot be true even though the utility at point B is equal to the utility at point A (along IC_1) and the utility at point C is equal to the utility at point A (along IC_2). Point B is located at (1,3) and point C is located at (2,4). Because (2,4) strictly dominates (1,3), point C is preferred to point B. Indifference curves cannot intersect.

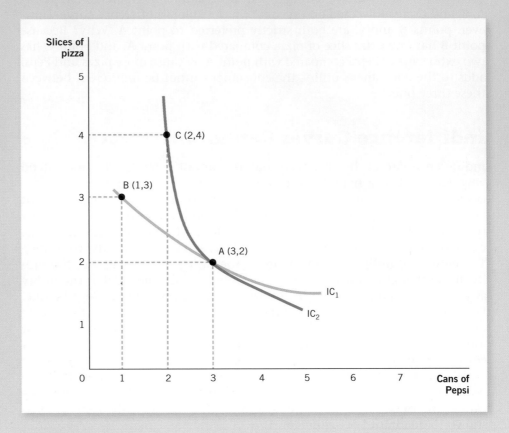

Extreme Preferences: Perfect Substitutes and Perfect Complements

As we have just seen, indifference curves typically are convex and bow inward toward the origin. However, there are two exceptions: *perfect substitutes* and *perfect complements*. These are found on either side of the standard-shaped, convex indifference curve.

Perfect substitutes exist when a consumer is completely indifferent between two goods. Suppose that you cannot taste any difference between Aquafina and Evian bottled water. You would be indifferent between drinking one additional bottle of Aquafina or one additional bottle of Evian. Turning to panel (a) of Figure 16A.6, you can see that the indifference curves (IC_1, IC_2, IC_3, IC_4) for these two goods are straight, parallel lines with a marginal rate of substitution, or slope, of −1 everywhere along the curve. However, it's important to note that the slope of an indifference curve of perfect substitutes need not always be −1; it can be any constant rate. Because perfect substitutes have a marginal rate of substitution with a constant rate, they are drawn as straight lines.

Perfect complements exist when a consumer is interested in consuming two goods in fixed proportions. Shoes are an excellent example. We buy shoes in pairs because the left or right shoe is not valuable by itself; we need

Perfect substitutes exist when the consumer is completely indifferent between two goods, resulting in a straight-line indifference curve with a constant marginal rate of substitution.

Perfect complements exist when the consumer is interested in consuming two goods in fixed proportions, resulting in a right-angle indifference curve.

(a) Perfect Substitutes

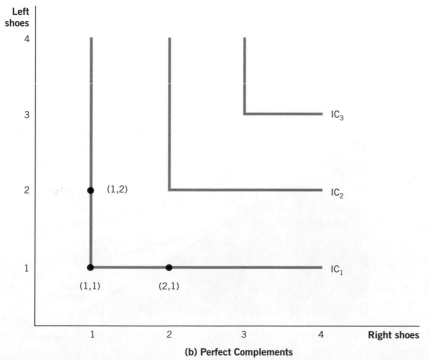

(b) Perfect Complements

FIGURE 16A.6

Perfect Substitutes and Perfect Complements

(a) Because perfect substitutes have a marginal rate of substitution that is constant, they are drawn as straight lines. In this case, the MRS, or slope, is -1 everywhere along the lines, or curves.

(b) Perfect complements are drawn as right angles. A typical indifference curve that reflects the trade-off between two goods that are not perfect substitutes or perfect complements has a marginal rate of substitution that falls between these two extremes.

both shoes to be able to walk comfortably. This explains why shoes are not sold individually. An extra left or right shoe has no marginal value to the consumer, so the indifference curves are right angles. For instance, left and right shoes are needed in a 1:1 ratio. Let's look at indifference curve IC_1 in panel (b) of Figure 16A.6. This curve forms a right angle at the point (1,1) where the person has one left and one right shoe. Now notice that the points (1,2) and (2,1) are also on IC_1. Because an extra left or right shoe by itself does not add utility, the points (1,2), (1,1), and (2,1) are all connected, since the individual has only one pair of usable shoes.

Perfect complements can also occur in combinations other than 1:1. For instance, an ordinary chair needs four legs for each seat. In that case, the indifference curve is still a right angle, but additional chair legs do not enhance the consumer's utility unless they come in groups of four.

Using Indifference Curves to Illustrate the Consumer Optimum

Figure 16A.7 shows the relationship between indifference curves and the budget constraint. As the indifference curves move higher, the consumer moves progressively closer to the consumer optimum. At some point, the consumer will run out of money. Therefore, the area bounded by the budget constraint (shaded in purple) represents the set of possible choices. The highest indifference curve that can be attained within the set of possible choices is IC_3, where the budget constraint is just tangent to (that is, just touches) IC_3. Even though all the points on IC_4 are more desirable than those on IC_3, the

FIGURE 16A.7

Consumer Optimum

Progressively higher indifference curves bring the consumer closer to the maximization point. Because the budget constraint limits what the consumer can afford, the tangency of the budget constraint with the highest indifference curve represents the highest level of affordable satisfaction—that is, the consumer optimum. In this case, the point (4,3) represents the consumer's preferred combination of Pepsi and pizza.

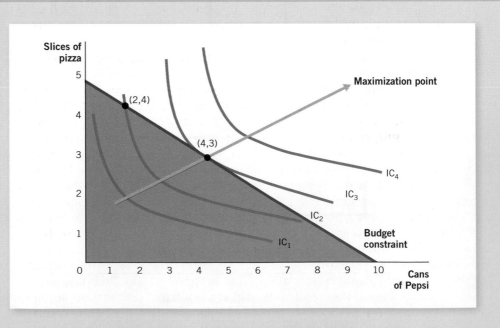

consumer lacks the purchasing power to reach the level of satisfaction represented by IC_4. Moreover, the point (4,3) is now clearly the preferred choice among the set of possible decisions. Other choices that are also affordable—for example, the combination (2,4)—fall on a lower (and hence less preferable) indifference curve.

Progressively higher indifference curves bring the consumer closer to the maximization point. Because the budget constraint limits what the consumer can afford, the tangency of the budget constraint with the highest indifference curve represents the highest affordable level of satisfaction—that is, the consumer optimum.

Using Indifference Curves to Illustrate the Real-Income and Substitution Effects

The power of indifference curve analysis is its ability to display how price changes affect consumption choices. Part of the intuition behind the analysis involves understanding when the substitution effect is likely to dominate the real-income effect, and vice versa.

In our example, you have only $10, so when the price of Pepsi increases from $1 to $2 per can, it represents a financial burden that significantly lowers your real purchasing power. However, we can easily think of cases in which a change in the price of Pepsi wouldn't matter. Suppose yours is a typical American household with a median annual income of $50,000. While out shopping, you observe that a local Toyota car dealer is offering 10% off new cars and a nearby grocery store is selling Pepsi at a 10% discount. Because of the substitution effect, more people will buy Toyotas instead of Hondas, and more people will buy Pepsi instead of Coca-Cola. However, the real-income effects will be quite different. Saving 10% on the price of a new car could easily amount to a savings of $3,000 or more. In contrast, saving 10% on a 2-liter bottle of Pepsi will save only a couple of dimes. In the case of the new car, there is a substantial real-income effect, while the amount you save on the Pepsi is almost immaterial.

As we have just seen, changes in prices can have two distinct effects. The first is a substitution effect, under which changes in price will cause the consumer to substitute toward a good that becomes relatively less expensive. In our Pepsi/pizza example, suppose that the price of Pepsi rises to $2 per can. This price increase reduces your marginal utility per dollar of consuming Pepsi. As a result, you would probably buy fewer Pepsis and use the remaining money to purchase more pizza. In effect, you would substitute the relatively less expensive good (pizza) for the relatively more expensive good (Pepsi).

However, this is not the only effect at work. The change in the product price will also alter the purchasing power of your money, or income. And a change in purchasing power generates a real-income effect. In this case, your $10 will not go as far as it used to. In Figure 16A.8, we can see that the inward rotation of the budget constraint along the x axis from BC_1 to BC_2 is a result of the rise in the price of Pepsi. At $2 per can, you can no longer afford to buy 10 cans; the most you can purchase is 5. Therefore, the budget constraint moves inward along the x axis to 5 units while remaining constant along the y axis (because the price of pizza did not change). As a result, the combination (4,3) is no longer affordable. The higher price of Pepsi produces a new

FIGURE 16A.8

How a Change in Price Rotates the Budget Constraint

The inward rotation of the budget constraint along the *x* axis from BC_1 to BC_2 is a result of the rise in the price of Pepsi. At the price of $2 a can, you can no longer afford to buy 10 cans; the most you can purchase is 5. Therefore, the budget constraint moves inward along the *x* axis to 5 units (causing utility to fall from IC_3 to IC_2) while remaining constant along the *y* axis (because the price of pizza slices did not change).

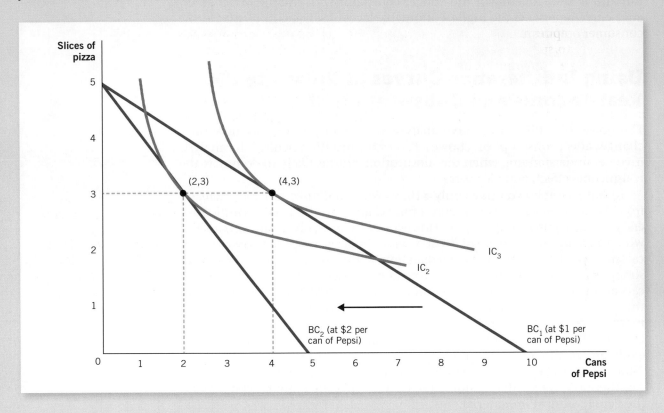

consumer optimum at (2,3) along IC_2. The end result is predictable: a rise in the price of Pepsi causes you to purchase less Pepsi and yields a lower level of satisfaction at IC_2 than your former point on IC_3 did, which is no longer possible.

Separating the Substitution Effect from the Real-Income Effect

Sometimes the substitution effect and the real-income effect reinforce each other; at other times, they work against each other. In this section, we separate the substitution effect from the real-income effect.

Breaking down the movement from IC_3 to IC_2 into the separate real-income effect and substitution effect enables us to see how each effect impacts the consumer's choice. Imagine that you were given just enough money to attain IC_2 in Figure 16A.9 with the original prices of pizza and Pepsi intact. The new budget constraint ($BC_{real\ income}$) will now be parallel to BC_1 but just tangent to IC_2. The change from BC_1 to $BC_{real\ income}$ separates the real-income effect from the substitution effect. Because the slope of the new budget constraint, $BC_{real\ income}$, is less steep than that of BC_2, the point of tangency between $BC_{real\ income}$ and IC_2, point A, is lower. Furthermore, because the slopes of $BC_{real\ income}$ and BC_1 are equal, we can think of the movement from (4,3) to point A as a function of the real-income effect alone. This result occurs because we have kept the slope of the budget constraint constant. Keeping the slope constant reflects the fact that the consumer has less money to spend, while the prices of Pepsi and pizza are held constant, hence the only difference between BC_1 and $BC_{real\ income}$ is the money available to spend. The subsequent movement along IC_2 from point A to (2,3) results from the substitution effect exclusively, and it occurs because the price of Pepsi is now higher. This outcome causes BC_2 to become steeper.

FIGURE 16A.9

Separating the Substitution Effect from the Real-Income Effect

Breaking down the movement from IC_3 to IC_2 into the real-income effect and the substitution effect enables us to see how each effect impacts the consumer's choice. The real-income effect causes the budget constraint to shift to $BC_{real\ income}$, and the loss of purchasing power lowers the consumption of both Pepsi and pizza, as noted by the green arrows. At the same time, the substitution effect reduces the amount of Pepsi consumed and increases the consumption of pizza, as noted by the blue arrows.

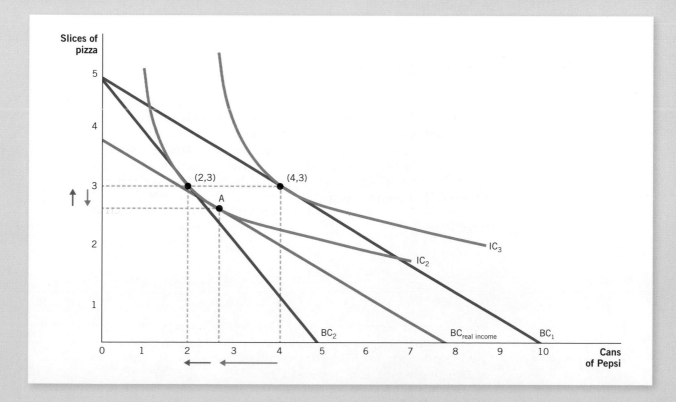

Beginning with the real-income effect, we see that the impact of a loss of purchasing power lowers consumption of both Pepsi and pizza. The green arrows in Figure 16A.9 highlight this outcome. At the same time, the substitution effect reduces the amount of Pepsi consumed and increases the consumption of pizza. The blue arrows in the figure highlight this outcome. Because Pepsi is now relatively more expensive, you reallocate your consumption toward pizza. Overall, your consumption of Pepsi falls dramatically while your consumption of pizza remains constant.

More generally, whenever the price of a good increases (as the price of Pepsi does in this example), the result will be a reduction in the amount consumed because both the real-income and substitution effects (as represented by the blue and green arrows along the x axis) move in the same direction. However, because the real-income effect and substitution effect move in opposite directions with respect to the good whose price has not changed (pizza in this example), the result is ambiguous for that good (pizza), and any change in consumption depends on which effect—the substitution effect or the real-income effect—is greater.

In our example, when the price of Pepsi rose to $2 per can, it produced a large real-income effect (the green arrow along the x axis). Prior to the price increase, you were spending $4 out of your $10 budget on Pepsi, so Pepsi expenditures represented 40% of your budget. Because Pepsi is a big component of your budget, a doubling of its price causes a sizable real-income effect. This is not always the case, however. For example, if the price of a candy bar were to double, the typical household would barely notice this change. In that case, the real-income effect is negligible and the substitution effect tends to dominate.

Conclusion

Economists use indifference curve analysis to gain additional insights into consumer behavior. This analysis extends the basic understanding found in supply and demand analysis by incorporating utility theory. Because indifference curves are lines of equal utility, we can impose a budget constraint to describe the bundle of goods that maximizes utility. This framework enables us to illustrate the effect of price changes and budget constraints on the decisions that consumers make.

CONCEPTS YOU SHOULD KNOW

budget constraint (p. 528)
indifference
curve (p. 526)

marginal rate of substitution
(MRS) (p. 529)
maximization point (p. 526)

perfect complements
(p. 532)
perfect substitutes (p. 506)

QUESTIONS FOR REVIEW

1. If your budget increases, what generally happens to the amount of utility you experience?

2. If your budget increases, is it possible for your utility to fall? Explain your response.

3. What is the difference between an economic "good" and an economic "bad"?

4. Describe what happens to your budget constraint if the price of one item in your budget decreases. Show the result on a graph.

5. A friend mentions to you that the campus coffee shop offers a 10% discount each Thursday morning before 10 a.m. Is this discount more likely to cause a significant substitution effect or a significant real-income effect? Explain.

STUDY PROBLEMS (✳ *solved at the end of the section*)

1. Kate has $20. Fish sandwiches cost $5, and a cup of espresso costs $4. Draw Kate's budget constraint. If espresso goes on sale for $2 a cup, what does her new budget constraint look like?

2. When you head home for dinner, your mother always sets the table with one spoon, two forks, and one knife. Draw her indifference curves for forks and knives.

✳ 3. Frank's indifference curves for movies and bowling look like the figure to the right.

    Each game of bowling costs $4, and each movie costs $8. If Frank has $24 to spend, how many times will he go bowling? How many times will he go to the movies?

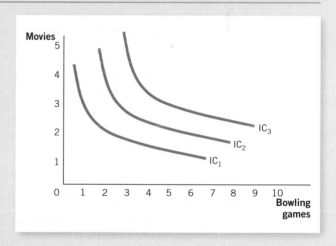

SOLVED PROBLEM

3. Because Frank has $24 to spend, he can afford $24 ÷ $4, or six games of bowling. If he spends his money instead on movies, he can afford $24 ÷ $8, or three movies. Because Frank's budget constraint (BC) is just tangent to IC_1 at the point (2,2), Frank will go to two movies and bowl two games.

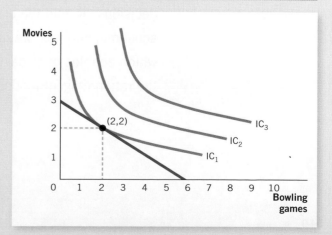

CHAPTER
17 | Behavioral Economics and Risk Taking

People always make rational decisions.

In this textbook, we have proceeded as if every person were *Homo economicus*, or a rationally self-interested decision-maker. *Homo economicus* is acutely aware of opportunities in the environ-

ment and strives to maximize the benefits received from each course of action while minimizing the costs. What does *Homo economicus* look like? If you are a fan of *Star Trek,* you'll recall Spock, the Vulcan with perfect logic. Spock eschewed human emotion and didn't face many of the complications that it creates in making decisions.

We don't want to leave you with the misconception that we're all like this! As human beings, we love, laugh, and cry. Sometimes, we seek revenge; at other times, forgiveness. We can be impulsive and short-sighted, and we can fail to see the benefits of pursuing long-run gains. Each of these behaviors is real, although they do not fit squarely within our economic models. Human decision-making is far more complex than the standard economic model of behavior implies. In this chapter, we step back and consider why people don't always make rational decisions. To fold the broadest possible set of human behavior into economic analysis, we must turn to the field of *behavioral economics*, which enables us to capture a wider range of human motivations than the rational-agent model alone affords.

Vulcans, like Spock, make decisions using logic. However, humans, like James Kirk, are subject to many behavioral biases.

BIG QUESTIONS

✳ **How do economists explain irrational behavior?**

✳ **What is the role of risk in decision-making?**

How Do Economists Explain Irrational Behavior?

Behavioral economics is the field of economics that draws on insights from experimental psychology to explore how people make economic decisions.

Bounded rationality (also called limited reasoning) proposes that although decision-makers want a good outcome, either they are not capable of performing the problem solving that traditional economic theory assumes or they are not inclined to do so.

Like economics, psychology endeavors to understand the choices that people make. One key difference is that psychologists do not assume that people always behave in a fully rational way. As a result, psychologists have a much broader toolbox at their disposal to describe human behavior. **Behavioral economics** is the field of economics that draws on insights from experimental psychology to explore how people make economic decisions.

Until relatively recently, economists have ignored many human behaviors that do not fit their models. For example, because traditional economic theory assumed that people make optimal decisions, economic theorists did not try to explain why people might make an impulse purchase. Behavioral economists, however, understand that many behaviors contradict standard assumptions about rationality. They employ the idea of **bounded rationality**, which proposes that although decision-makers want a good outcome, either they are not capable of performing the problem-solving that traditional economic theory assumes or they are not inclined to do so.

Bounded rationality, or limited reasoning, can be explained in three ways. First, the information that the individual uses to make the decision may be limited or incomplete. Second, the human brain has a limited capacity to process information. Third, there is often a limited amount of time in which to make a decision. These limitations prevent the decision-maker from reaching the results predicted under perfect rationality.

For example, suppose you're about to get married and find yourself at Kleinfeld Bridal with your bridesmaids. You enter the store to begin your search for the perfect wedding dress. You find a dress that you like, but its price is higher than you were planning to spend. Do you make the purchase or not? The decision to buy depends on whether you believe that the value is high enough to justify the price. But there is a problem: you have a limited amount of information. In a fully rational world, you would check out alternatives in other stores and on the Internet and then make the decision to purchase the dress only after you were satisfied that it is the best possible choice. Full rationality also assumes that your brain is able to recall

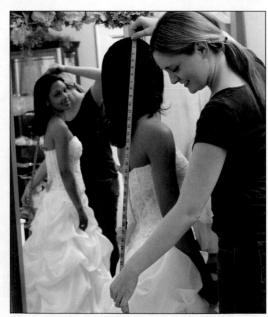

Will you say yes to the dress?

the features of every dress. However, a dress you tried on at one location often blurs into another dress you tried on elsewhere. Wedding dresses are selected under a binding deadline. This deadline means that you, the bride, must reach a decision quickly. Collectively, these three reasons often prevent a bride from achieving the result that economists' rational models predict. In reality, you walk into a store, see something you love, and make the purchase using partial information. Whenever people end up making decisions without perfect information, the decisions reflect bounded rationality.

We will continue our discussion of behavioral economics by examining various behaviors that do not fit assumptions about fully rational behavior. These include misperceptions of probabilities, inconsistencies in decision-making, and judgments about fairness when making decisions. The goal in this section is to help you recognize and understand many of the behaviors that lead to contradictions between what economic models predict and what people actually do.

Misperceptions of Probabilities

Economic models that assume rationality in decision-making do not account for the way people perceive the probability of events. Low-probability events are often overanticipated, and high-probability events are often underanticipated. To understand why, we consider several familiar examples, including games of chance, difficulties in assessing probabilities, and seeing patterns where none exist.

Games of Chance

Playing games of chance—for example, a lottery or a slot machine—is generally a losing proposition. Yet even with great odds against winning, millions of people spend money to play games of chance. How can we explain this behavior?

For some people, the remote chance of winning a lottery offers hope that they will be able to purchase something they need but cannot afford or even to escape from poverty. In many cases, people have incomplete information about the probabilities and prize structures. Most lottery players do not calculate the exact odds of winning. Lottery agencies typically highlight winners, as if the game has a positive expected value, which gets people excited about playing. Imagine how sobering it would be if every headline trumpeting the newest lottery millionaire was followed by all the names of people who lost. In fact, almost all games of chance have *negative expected values* for the participants, meaning that players are not likely to succeed at the game.

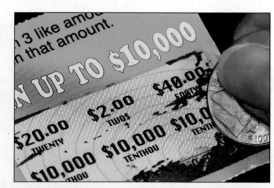

Players often operate under the irrational belief that they have control over the outcome. They are sure that playing certain numbers or patterns (for example, birthdays, anniversaries, or other lucky numbers) will bring success. Many players also feel that they must stick with their favorite numbers to avoid regret; everyone has heard stories about players who changed from their lucky pattern only to watch it win.

In contrast, some gaming behaviors are rational. For example, the film *21* depicts how skilled blackjack players,

Many games of chance return only about 50 cents for every dollar played.

working in tandem, can beat the casinos by betting strategically and paying close attention to the cards on the table. In fact, some individuals are able to win at blackjack by counting the cards that have been dealt. Anytime the expected value of a gamble is positive, there is an incentive to play. For instance, if a friend wants to wager $10.00 on the flip of a coin and promises you $25.00 if you guess right, the expected value is half of $25.00, or $12.50. (There are only 2 possible outcomes, heads or tails, so your chances of winning are 1 in 2, or 1/2. So 1/2 × $25.00 = $12.50.) Because $12.50 is greater than the $10.00 you are wagering, we say that the gamble has a *positive expected value*. When the expected value of a gamble is positive, we actually expect that the more you play, the more likely it is that your earnings will be larger than your losses.

Incentives

Gambles can also make sense when you have very little to lose or no other options. And some people find the thrill of gambling enjoyable as entertainment, whether they win or lose. However, most gambling behaviors do not have rational motivations. Gambling often creates addictions that lead players to make poor financial decisions.

The Difficulties in Assessing Probabilities

In our discussion of games of chance, we saw that people who gamble do not usually evaluate probabilities in a rational way. But this irrational decision-making also happens with many other behaviors besides gambling. For example, on a per-mile basis, traveling by airplane is approximately 10 times safer than traveling by automobile. However, millions of people who refuse to fly because they are afraid of a crash do not hesitate to get into a car. Driving seems to create a false sense of control over one's surroundings.

The 1970s television game show *Let's Make a Deal* provides a well-known example of the difficulties in assessing probabilities accurately. At the end of the show, the host would ask a contestant to choose one of three curtains. Behind each curtain was one of three possible prizes: a car, a nice but less expensive item, or a worthless joke item. Contestants could have maximized their chances of winning the car if they had used probability theory to make a selection. However, contestants rarely chose in a rational way.

Suppose that you are a contestant on a game show like *Let's Make a Deal*. You pick curtain number 3. The host, who knows what is behind the curtains, opens a different one—say, curtain number 1, which has a pen filled with chickens (the joke prize). He then offers you the opportunity to switch your choice to curtain number 2. According to probability theory, what is the right thing to do? Most contestants would stay with their original choice because they figure that now they have a 50/50 chance of winning the car. But the probability of winning with your original choice remains 1/3 because the chance that you guessed correctly the first time is unchanged. Equally, the chance that one of the other curtains contains the car is still 2/3. But with curtain number 1 revealed as the joke prize, that 2/3 probability now belongs entirely to curtain number 2. Therefore, the contestant should take the switch, because it upgrades the chance of winning the car from 1/3 to 2/3. Few

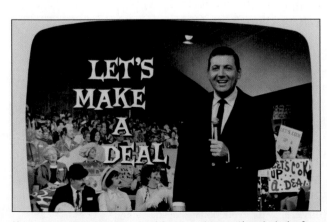

If you were a contestant, would you make a rational choice?

contestants make the switch, though. Almost all contestants think that each of the two remaining unopened curtains has an equal probability of holding the car, so they decide not to switch for fear of regretting their decision. Not switching indicates a failure to understand the opportunity costs involved in the decision.

Opportunity cost

The difficulty in recognizing the true underlying probabilities, combined with an irrational fear of regret, leads to many poor decisions. Understanding these tendencies helps economists to evaluate why some decisions are difficult to get right.

Seeing Patterns Where None Exist

Two fallacies, or false ways of thinking, help explain how some people make decisions: the *gambler's fallacy* and the *hot hand fallacy*.

The **gambler's fallacy** is the belief that recent outcomes are unlikely to be repeated and that outcomes that have not occurred recently are due to happen soon. For example, studies examining state lotteries find that bets on recent winning numbers decline. Because the selection of winning numbers is made randomly, just like flipping coins, the probability that a certain number will be a winner in one week is not related to whether the number came up in the previous week. In other words, someone who uses the gambler's fallacy believes that if many "heads" have occurred in a row, then "tails" is more likely to occur next.

The **hot hand fallacy** is the belief that random sequences exhibit a positive correlation (relationship). The classic study in this area examined perceptions about the game of basketball. Most sports enthusiasts believe that a player who has scored several baskets in a row—one with a "hot hand"—is more likely to score a basket with his next shot than he might be at another time. However, the study found no positive correlation between success in one shot and success in the next shot.

The **gambler's fallacy** is the belief that recent outcomes are unlikely to be repeated and that outcomes that have not occurred recently are due to happen soon.

The **hot hand fallacy** is the belief that random sequences exhibit a positive correlation (relationship).

ECONOMICS IN THE REAL WORLD

How Behavioral Economics Helps to Explain Stock Price Volatility

Let's examine some of the traps that people fall into when they invest in the stock market. In a fully rational world, the gambler's fallacy and the hot hand fallacy would not exist. In the real world, however, people are prone to seeing patterns in data even when there are none. Investors, for example, often believe that the rise and fall of the stock market is driven by specific events and by underlying metrics such as profitability, market share, and return on investment. But, in fact, investors often react with a herd mentality by rushing into stocks that appear to be doing well—reflecting the hot hand fallacy—and selling off stocks when a downward trend seems to be occurring. Similarly, there are times when investors believe the stock market has run up or down too rapidly and they expect its direction to change soon—reflecting the gambler's fallacy.

Some segments of the market are driven by investor psychology instead of metrics that measure valuation. Research has also shown that mood matters: believe it or not, there is a small correlation between the weather and how the stock market trades on a particular day. The market is more likely to move higher when it is sunny on Wall Street than when it is cloudy! The very fact that the weather in Lower Manhattan could have anything to do with how the overall stock market performs is strong evidence that some market participants are not rational. ✳

The stock market can give investors a wild ride.

PRACTICE WHAT YOU KNOW

Gambler's Fallacy or Hot Hand Fallacy? Patterns on Exams

Your instructor is normally conscientious and makes sure that exam answers are randomly distributed. However, you notice that the first five answers on the multiple-choice section are all C. Unsure what this pattern means, you consider the next question. You do not know the answer and are forced to guess. You decide to avoid C because you figure that C cannot happen six times in a row.

Do you ever wonder what it means when the same answer comes up many times in a row?

Question: Which is at work: the gambler's fallacy or the hot hand fallacy?

Answer: According to the gambler's fallacy, recent events are less likely to be repeated again in the near future. So it is the gambler's fallacy at work here in your decision to avoid marking another C. If you had acted on the hot hand fallacy, you would have believed that random sequences exhibit a positive correlation and therefore would have marked the next answer as C.

Inconsistencies in Decision-Making

Trade-offs

If people were entirely rational, they would always be consistent. So the way a question is asked should not alter our responses, but research has shown that it does. Likewise, rational decision-making requires the ability to take the long-run trade-offs into account: if the returns are large enough, people should be willing to sacrifice current enjoyment for future benefits. Yet many of us make shortsighted decisions. In this section, we examine a variety of decision-making mistakes, including framing effects, priming effects, status quo bias, and intertemporal decision-making.

Framing Effects and Priming Effects

The **framing effect** occurs when people change their answer depending on how the question is asked (or change their decision depending on how alternatives are presented).

We have seen a number of ways in which economic models do not entirely account for the behavior of real people. One common mistake that people make involves the **framing effect**, which occurs when an answer is influenced by the way a question is asked or a decision is influenced by the way alternatives are presented. Consider an employer-sponsored retirement plan. Companies can either (1) ask employees if they want to join or (2) use an automatic enrollment system and ask employees to let them know if they do not wish to participate. Studies have shown that workers who are asked if they want to join tend to participate at a much lower rate than those who are automatically enrolled and must say they want to opt out. Surely, a rational

Misperceptions of Probabilities

π

This psychological thriller from 1998 tries to make sense out of chaos. The title refers to the mathematical constant π (pi). In the film, Max Cohen is using his supercomputer to find predictable patterns within the stock market. What makes the film especially interesting are the three assumptions that rule Max's life:

1. Mathematics is the language of nature.
2. Everything around us can be represented and understood from numbers.
3. If you graph the numbers in any system, patterns emerge.

Based on these assumptions, Max attempts to identify a mathematical pattern that will predict the behavior of the stock market. As he gets closer to uncovering the answer, he is pursued by two parties: a Wall Street firm that wishes to use Max's discovery to manipulate the market and a religious person who believes that the pattern is a code sent from God.

Can we use mathematical patterns to predict what will happen next?

Max's quest reminds us that the average investor lacks full information, but nevertheless irrationally believes that he or she knows more than others. As a result, widespread investor misperceptions about the true probability of events can lead to speculative bubbles and crashes in the stock market.

---

economic decision-maker would determine whether to participate by evaluating the plan itself, not by responding to the way the employer presents the option to participate. However, people are rarely that rational!

Another decision-making pitfall, known as the **priming effect**, occurs when the order of the questions influences the answers. For example, consider two groups of college students. The first group is asked "How happy are you?" followed by "How many dates have you had in the last year?" The second group is asked "How many dates have you had in the last year?" followed by "How happy are you?" The questions are the same, but they are presented in reverse order. In the second group, students who had gone out on more dates reported being much happier than similar students in the first group! In other words, because they were reminded of the number of dates first, those who had more dates believed they were happier.

> The **priming effect** occurs when the order of the questions influences the answers.

Status Quo Bias

When people want to maintain their current choices, they may exhibit what is known as the **status quo bias**. This bias leads decision-makers to try to protect what they have, even when an objective evaluation of their circumstances suggests that a change would be beneficial.

> **Status quo bias** exists when decision-makers want to maintain their current choices.

Are you on Team Dollar Bill or Team Dollar Coin?

The status quo bias causes people to behave conservatively. The cost of this behavior is missed opportunities that could potentially enhance welfare. For example, an individual with status quo bias would maintain a savings account with a low interest rate instead of actively shopping for better rates elsewhere. This person would lose the potential benefits from higher returns on savings.

Status quo bias also explains why new products and ideas have trouble gaining traction: many potential customers prefer to leave things the way they are, even if something new might make more sense. Consider the $1 coin. It is far more durable than the $1 bill. It is also easier to tell the $1 coin apart from the other coins and bills in your wallet, and if people used the coin, the government would save about $5 billion in production costs over the next 30 years. That sounds like a slam-dunk policy change, but it is not. Americans like their dollar bills and rarely use the $1 coins in circulation even though they repeatedly use nickels, dimes, and quarters to make change, to feed parking meters, and to buy from vending machines. Introducing more of the $1 coin and eliminating the $1 bill would be rational, but the status quo bias has prevented the change from happening.

ECONOMICS IN THE REAL WORLD

Are You an Organ Donor?

More than 25,000 organ transplants take place every year in the United States, with the vast majority coming from deceased donors. Demand greatly exceeds supply. Over 100,000 people are currently on organ donation waiting lists. Most Americans are aware of the need, and 90% of all Americans say they support donation. But only 30% know the essential steps to take to become a donor.

There are two main donor systems: the "opt-in" system and the "opt-out" system. In an opt-in system, individuals must give explicit consent to be a donor. In an opt-out system, anyone who has not explicitly refused is considered a donor.

In the United States, donors are required to opt in. Because opting in generally produces fewer donors than opting out, many states have sought to raise donation awareness by allowing consent to be noted on individual driver's licenses.

In the United Kingdom, organ donors must opt in.

In Europe, many countries have opt-out systems, where consent is presumed. The difference is crucial. After all, in places with opt-in systems, many people who would be willing to donate organs never actually take the time to complete the necessary steps to opt in. In countries like France and Poland, where people must opt out, over 90% of citizens do not explicitly opt out, which means they give consent. This strategy yields organ donation rates that are significantly higher than those of opt-in programs.

According to traditional economic analysis, opting in or opting out should not matter—the results should be the same. The fact that we find strong evidence to the contrary is a compelling illustration of the framing effect. ✳

Opt-Out Is Optimal

Some of the most successful applications of behavioral economics are "opt-out" programs, which automatically enroll eligible people unless they explicitly choose not to participate. The incentives and freedom of choice are exactly the same as in "opt-in" programs, where members must choose to participate, but enrollments are significantly higher under opt-out. Here's a look at three remarkable results.

■ Participation Rate

401(k)

Opt-Out — 76% — Austria
Opt-In — 20% — Germany

You can never start saving soon enough, and sending part of your paycheck into a 401(k) retirement account is a great way to do it. Opt-out programs are far more successful than opt-in programs at encouraging young workers to participate.

Organ Donor Consent

Opt-Out — 99% — Austria
Opt-In — 12% — Germany

Tragically, thousands of people die each year waiting for an organ transplant. Opt-out organ donor consent programs lead to higher participation and more saved lives.

HIV Testing

Opt-Out — 69.4% — Austria
Opt-In — 51.2% — Germany

HIV screening remains a crucial public health need. Evidence from one study indicates that opt-out consent at emergency rooms leads to substantially more individuals agreeing to be tested.

REVIEW QUESTIONS

- How would a behavioral economist explain the disparity in 401(k) enrollments among young employees between opt-out and opt-in programs?

- Opt-in and opt-out programs ask us to make the same decisions, but achieve different results. Use the concepts of the framing effect and non-rational behavior to explain why.

Intertemporal Decision-Making

Intertemporal decision-making involves planning to do something over a period of time, which requires valuing the present and the future consistently.

Can you resist eating one marshmallow now in order to get a second one later?

Intertemporal decisions occur across time. **Intertemporal decision-making—** that is, planning to do something over a period of time—requires the ability to value the present and the future consistently. For instance, many people, despite their best intentions, do not end up saving enough for retirement. The temptation to spend money today ends up overwhelming the willpower to save for tomorrow. In a perfectly rational world, a person would not need outside assistance to save enough for retirement. In the real world, however, workers depend on 401(k) plans and other work-sponsored retirement programs to deduct funds from their paycheck so that they don't spend that portion of their income on other things. It may seem odd that people would need an outside agency to help them do something that is in their own long-term interest, but as long as their intertemporal decisions are likely to be inconsistent, the additional commitment helps them to achieve their long-run objectives.

The ability to resist temptation is illustrated by a classic research experiment conducted at a preschool at Stanford University in 1972. One at a time, individual children were led into a room devoid of distractions and were offered a marshmallow. The researchers explained to each child that he or she could eat the marshmallow right away or wait for 15 minutes and be rewarded with a second marshmallow. Very few of the 600 children in the study ate the marshmallow immediately. Most tried to fight the temptation. Of those who tried to wait, approximately one-third held out long enough to earn the second marshmallow. That finding is interesting by itself, but what happened next is truly amazing. Many of the parents of the children in the original study noticed that the children who had delayed gratification seemed to perform better as they progressed through school. Researchers have tracked the participants over the course of 40 years and found that the delayed-gratification group had higher SAT scores, more savings, and larger retirement accounts.

Judgments about Fairness

The pursuit of fairness is another common behavior that is important in economic decisions but that standard economic theory cannot explain. For example, fairness is one of the key drivers in determining tax rate structure for income taxes. Proponents of fairness believe in progressive taxation, whereby the rich pay a higher tax rate on their income than those in lower income brackets do. Likewise, some people object to the high pay of chief executive officers or the high profits of some corporations because they believe there should be an upper limit to what constitutes fair compensation.

While fairness is not normally modeled in economics, behavioral economists have developed experiments to determine the role of fairness in personal decisions. The **ultimatum game** is an economic experiment in which two players decide how to divide a sum of money. The game shows how fairness enters into the rational decision-making process. In the game, player 1 is given a sum of money and is asked to propose a

The **ultimatum game** is an economic experiment in which two players decide how to divide a sum of money.

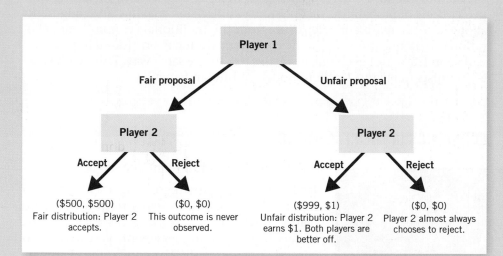

FIGURE 17.1

The Decision Tree for the Ultimatum Game

The decision tree for the ultimatum game has four branches. If player 1 makes a fair proposal, player 2 will accept the distribution and both players will earn $500. However, if player 1 makes an unfair proposal, player 2 may reject the distribution even though this rejection means receiving nothing.

way of splitting it with player 2. Player 2 can either accept or reject the proposal. If player 2 accepts, the sum is split according to the proposal. However, if player 2 rejects the proposal, neither player gets anything. The game is played only once, so the first player does not have to worry about reciprocity.

Consider an ultimatum game that asks player 1 to share $1,000 with player 2. Player 1 must decide how fair to make the proposal. The decision tree in Figure 17.1 highlights four possible outcomes to two very different proposals—a fair proposal and an unfair proposal.

Traditional economic theory presumes that both players are fully rational and wish to maximize their income. Player 1 should therefore maximize his gains by offering the minimum, $1, to player 2. The reasoning is that player 2 values $1 more than nothing and so will accept the proposal, leaving player 1 with $999. But real people are not always economic maximizers because they generally believe that fairness matters. Most of the time, player 2 would find such an unfair division infuriating and reject it.

Player 1 knows that player 2 will definitely accept an offer of $500; this division of the money is exactly equal and therefore fair. Thus, the probability of a 50/50 agreement is 100%. In contrast, the probability of player 2 accepting an offer of $1 is close to 0%. Offering increasing amounts from $1 to $500 will continue to raise the probability of an acceptance until it reaches 100% at $500.

Player 2's role is simpler: her only decision is whether to accept or reject the proposal. Player 2 desires a fair distribution but has no direct control over the division. To punish player 1 for being unfair, player 2 must reject the proposal altogether. The trade-off of penalizing player 1 for unfairness is a complete loss of any prize. So while player 2 may not like any given proposal, rejecting it would cause a personal loss. Player 2 might therefore accept a number of unfair proposals because she would rather get something than nothing.

Trade-offs

Each of the ideas that we have presented in this section, including mis-perceptions of probability, inconsistency in decision-making, and judgments about fairness, represent a departure from the traditional economic model of rational maximization. In the next section, we focus on risk-taking. As you will soon learn, not everyone evaluates risk in the same way. This fact has led economists to reconsider their models of human behavior.

 ECONOMICS IN THE REAL WORLD

Unfair Pay Matters to Capuchin Monkeys

Traditional economic theory suggests that when two traders each expect gains from a trade, no matter how unequal those gains may be, the traders will reach an agreement. Researchers on fairness disagree with that conclusion. Frans de Waal, a primatologist, uses capuchin monkeys to argue that fairness matters throughout the animal kingdom. All you have to do is watch a short TED talk that is equal parts *America's Funniest Home Videos* and Econ 101. https://www.youtube.com/watch?v=meiU6TxysCg ✳

Sour grapes? A capuchin monkey throws away cucumber to protest unfairness.

What Is the Role of Risk in Decision-Making?

In this section, we examine the role that risk plays in decision-making. The standard economic model of consumer choice assumes that people are consist-ent in their risk-taking preferences. However, people's risk tolerances actually vary widely and are subject to change. Thus, risk-taking behavior is not nearly as simple or predictable as economists once believed. We begin with a phe-nomenon known as *preference reversal*. We then consider how negative sur-prises can cause people to take more risk, which is explained by *prospect theory*.

Risk-averse people prefer a sure thing over a gamble with a higher expected value.

Risk-neutral people choose the highest expected value regardless of the risk.

Risk-takers prefer gambles with lower expected values, and potentially higher win-nings, over a sure thing.

Preference Reversals

As you know, trying to predict human behavior is not easy. Maurice Allais, the recipient of the 1988 Nobel Prize in Economics, noticed that people's tolerance for risk appeared to change in different situations. This observa-tion did not agree with the standard economic model, which assumes that an individual's risk tolerance is constant and places the individual into one of three distinct groups: **risk-averse people**, who prefer a sure thing over a gamble with a higher expected value; **risk-neutral people**, who choose the highest expected value regardless of the risk; and **risk-takers**, who prefer gambles with lower expected values, and potentially higher winnings, over a sure thing.

TABLE 17.1

The Allais Paradox

Choose gamble A or B

Gamble A	Gamble B
No gamble—receive $1 million in cash 100% of the time	A lottery ticket that pays $5 million 10% of the time, $1 million 89% of the time, and nothing 1% of the time

Choose gamble C or D

Gamble C	Gamble D
A lottery ticket that pays $5 million 10% of the time and nothing 90% of the time	A lottery ticket that pays $1 million 11% of the time and nothing 89% of the time

Allais developed a means of assessing risk behavior by presenting the set of choices (known as the Allais paradox) depicted in Table 17.1. Individuals were asked to choose their preferred options between gambles A and B and then again between gambles C and D.

Economic science predicts that people will choose consistently according to their risk preference. As a result, economists understood that risk-averse individuals would choose the pair A and D. Likewise, the pair B and C makes sense if the participants are risk-neutral and wish to maximize the expected value of the gambles. Let's see why.

1. *Risk-Averse People:* People who select gamble A over gamble B take the sure thing. If they are asked to choose between C and D, we would expect them to try to maximize their chances of winning something by selecting D, because it has the higher probability of winning.

2. *Risk-Neutral People:* Gamble B has a higher expected value than gamble A. We know that gamble A always pays $1 million because it occurs 100% of the time. Calculating gamble B's expected value is more complicated. The expected value is computed by multiplying each outcome by its respective probability. For gamble B, this means that the expected value is ($5 million $\times$ 0.10) + ($1 million $\times$ 0.89), which equals $1.39 million. So a risk-neutral player will select gamble B. Likewise, gamble C has a higher expected value than gamble D. Gamble C has an expected value of ($5 million $\times$ 0.10), or $0.5 million. Gamble D's expected value is ($1 million $\times$ 0.11), or $0.11 million. Therefore, a risk-neutral player who thinks at the margin will choose gambles B and C in order to maximize potential winnings from the game.

3. *Risk-Takers:* Because risk-takers prefer risk, they would choose gambles B and C even if they were not already the gambles with the highest expected values.

Marginal Thinking

While we would expect people to be consistent in their choices, Allais found that approximately 30% of his research population selected gambles A and C, which are contrasting pairs. Gamble A is the sure thing; however, Gamble C, even though it has the higher expected value, carries more risk. This scenario illustrates a *preference reversal*. A **preference reversal** occurs

A **preference reversal** occurs when risk tolerance is not consistent.

Preference Reversals

"Mine"

The music video for Taylor Swift's 2010 hit begins with Swift walking into a coffee shop. When she sits down, she notices a couple arguing at a nearby table. This reminds Swift about her parents arguing when she was very young. Just then, the waiter drops by to take Swift's order. She looks up and dreams of what life would be like with him. We see them running together in the waves at the beach, then unpacking boxes as they move in together. Later, the two argue, resulting in Swift running away from their house and crying, just like she did when she was young and saw her parents arguing. Her boyfriend follows her, and they reconcile. They get married and have two sons. The video ends with Swift reemerging from her dream and ordering her food at the coffee shop.

In the song's refrain, Swift sings, "You made a rebel of a careless man's careful daughter." Think about that line, keeping in mind that a "rebel" is a risk-taker. Does that remind you of a concept from this chapter? It should—this is a preference reversal. The entire song is about someone (Swift) who is normally risk-averse but falls for this guy so hard that she lets her guard down and acts differently. Instead

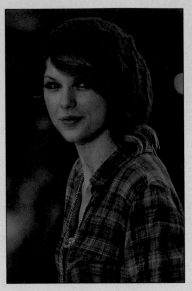

Taylor's dream illustrates one version of a preference reversal.

of running away when it comes time to fall in love, she stays in the relationship. In other words, the song is about finding someone who makes you believe in love so much that you are willing to take a chance for the first time in your life.

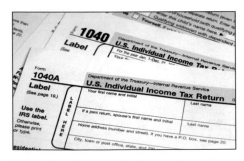

Withholding too much in the previous year and then paying your accountant to file for a rapid refund is a good example of a preference reversal.

when risk tolerance is not consistent. Allais argued that a person's risk tolerance depends on his or her financial circumstances. Someone who chooses gamble A over gamble B prefers the certainty of a large financial prize—the guarantee of $1 million over the uncertainty of the larger prize. Choosing gamble A could be seen as similar to purchasing insurance: you pay a fee, known as a *premium*, to protect your winnings. In this case, you forfeit the chance to win $5 million. In contrast, gambles C and D offer small chances of success, and therefore the choice is more like playing the lottery.

People who play games of chance are more likely to participate in games with large prizes—for example, Powerball—because the winnings will measurably improve their financial status. Allais showed that people care about how much they might win and also how much they stand to lose. This distinction causes people to choose gambles A and C. By establishing that many people behave this way, Allais reshaped the traditional economic view of risk-taking behavior.

It turns out that preference reversals are more common than economists once believed. For example, almost 80% of all income tax filers expect to get a refund because they overpaid in the previous year. This behavior is odd, since there is an opportunity cost of waiting to get money back from the government when it didn't need to be paid in the first place. Employees could have asked their employers to withhold less and enjoyed their money sooner. Individuals who choose to wait to receive their money later are said to have a time preference that is weakly positive. In most circumstances, people have strongly positive time preferences: they prefer to have what they want sooner rather than later. So what do these taxpayers do when they learn the amount of their refund? In many cases, they pay their tax preparers an additional fee to have their refunds sent to their bank accounts electronically so they can receive the money sooner! Traditional economic analysis is unable to explain this behavior; but armed with Allais's insights, we now see this behavior as a preference reversal.

Opportunity Cost

Prospect Theory

The television game show *Deal or No Deal* (2005—2010) provided an opportunity for economists to examine the risk choices that contestants make in a high-stakes setting. *Deal or No Deal* created particular excitement among researchers who study game shows because it involved no skill whatsoever. Taking skill out of the equation made it easier to analyze the contestants' strategy choices. Other TV game shows, such as *Jeopardy!*, require skill to win prizes. Highly skilled players may have different risk tolerances than their less skilled counterparts. As a result, part of the beauty of studying *Deal or No Deal* is that the outcome is a pure exercise in probability theory.

Deciding when to take the "deal" makes the show compelling.

For those who are unfamiliar with *Deal or No Deal,* here is how the show worked. Each of 26 models held a briefcase containing a sum of money, varying from 1 cent to $1 million. The contestant would pick one briefcase as her own and then begin to open the other 25 briefcases one at a time, slowly revealing a little more about what her own case might hold. Suspense would build, and the contestant's chance of a big payoff grew as small sums were eliminated and the $1 million case and other valuable cases remained unopened. As cases were eliminated, a "banker" periodically called the host to offer the contestant a "deal" in exchange for quitting the game.

At the start of the game, the expected value (EV) of the chosen briefcase was determined as follows:

$$\text{EV}_{\text{briefcase}} = \$.01 \times (1/26) + \$1 \times (1/26) + \$5 \times (1/26) + \cdots + \$1\text{M} \times (1/26)$$

This value computes to approximately $131,000. As the game progressed and cases were opened, the "banker" offered a settlement based on whether the expected value of the briefcase had increased or decreased.

Some contestants behaved as the traditional model of risk behavior predicted: they maximized the expected value of the briefcase while remaining risk-neutral. Because contestants who are risk neutral don't make for

PRACTICE WHAT YOU KNOW

Risk Aversion: Risk-Taking Behavior

Question: You have a choice between selecting heads or tails. If your guess is correct, you earn $2,000. But you earn nothing if you are incorrect. Alternatively, you can simply take $750 without the gamble. You decide to take the $750. Is your choice evidence of risk aversion or risk-taking?

Answer: The expected value of a 50/50 outcome worth $2,000 is $1,000. Therefore, the decision to take the sure thing, which is $250 less, is evidence of risk aversion.

Question: You have a choice between (a) predicting the roll of a six-sided die, with a $3,000 prize for a correct answer, or (b) taking a sure $750. You decide to roll the die. Is your choice evidence of risk aversion or risk-taking?

Answer: The expected value of the roll of the die is 1/6 × $3,000, or $500. Therefore, the $750 sure thing has an expected value that is $250 more. By rolling the die, you are taking the option with the lower expected value and also more risk. Therefore, you are a risk-taker.

How do you handle risky decisions?

---

exciting television, the "banker" typically offered a "deal" that was far less than the expected value of the remaining cases throughout the early part of the game. This move encouraged contestants to play longer so that the excitement and tension had a chance to build.

But not all contestants did what the traditional model expected them to do. For example, some contestants took more risks if they suffered setbacks early in the game, such as opening the $1 million briefcase. This behavior is consistent with *prospect theory* from psychology. **Prospect theory**, developed by Daniel Kahneman and Amos Tversky, suggests that people weigh decisions according to subjective utilities of gains and losses. The theory implies that people evaluate the risks that lead to gains separately from the risks that lead to losses. This concept is useful because it explains why some investors try to make up for losses by taking more chances rather than by maximizing the utility they receive from money under a rigid calculation of expected value.

Prospect theory suggests that individuals weigh the utilities and risks of gains and losses differently.

ECONOMICS IN THE REAL WORLD

Why Are There Cold Openings at the Box Office?

Movie studios generally make a film available for review if the screenings are expected to generate a positive buzz. Also, access to movie reviews provides moviegoers with a measure of a film's quality. So a rational moviegoer should infer that if a movie studio releases a film without reviews, it is signaling that the movie is not very good: the studio didn't want to risk negative reviews, so it didn't show the movie to reviewers.

Economists Alexander L. Brown, Colin F. Camerer, and Dan Lovallo studied 856 widely released movies and found that cold openings—movies withheld from critics (that is, not screened) before their release—produced a significant increase (15%) in domestic box office revenue compared with poor films that were reviewed and received predictably negative reviews. Most movie openings are accompanied by a marketing campaign to increase consumer demand. As a consequence, cold openings provide a natural field setting to test how rational moviegoers are. Their results are consistent with the hypothesis that some moviegoers do not infer low quality from a cold opening as they should.

The researchers showed that cold-opened movies earned more than prescreened movies after a number of characteristics were controlled for in the study. An important point is that the researchers also found that cold-opened films did not fare better than expected once they reached foreign film or video rental markets. In both of those cases, movie reviews were widely available, which negated any advantage from cold-opening the films. This finding is consistent with the hypothesis that some moviegoers fail to realize that no advance review is a signal of poor quality. The fact that moviegoer ratings from the Internet Movie Database are lower for movies that were cold-opened also suggests that in the absence of information, moviegoers overestimate the expected quality.

The line for tickets is long. Do you suppose this movie was cold-opened?

Over time, distributors have learned that there is a certain amount of moviegoer naiveté, especially among teenagers. As a result, distributors have overcome their initial reluctance and have cold-opened more movies in recent years.

These findings provide evidence that the best movie distribution strategy does not depend entirely on generating positive movie reviews. Cold openings work because some people are unable to process the negative signal implied by incomplete information, despite what traditional economic analysis would lead us to expect. ✳

Conclusion

Behavioral economics helps to dispel the misconception that people always make rational decisions. Indeed, behavioral economics challenges the traditional economic model and invites a deeper understanding of human behavior. Armed with the insights from behavioral economics, we can answer questions that span a wider range of behaviors. We have seen behavioral economics at work in the examples in this chapter, which include the "opt-in" or "opt-out" debate, the economics of risk-taking, the effects of question design, and the status quo bias. These ideas do not fit squarely into traditional economic analysis. You have learned enough at this point to question the assumptions we have made throughout this book. In the next chapter, we apply all of the tools we have acquired to examine one of the most important sectors of the economy—health care and health insurance.

ECONOMICS FOR LIFE

Bounded Rationality: How to Guard Yourself Against Crime

Suppose that a recent crime wave has hit your community and you are concerned about your family's security. Determined to make your house safe, you consider many options: an alarm system, bars on your windows, deadbolts for your doors, better lighting around your house, and a guard dog. Which of these solutions will protect you from a criminal at the lowest cost? All of them provide a measure of protection—but there's another solution that provides deterrence at an extremely low cost.

The level of security you need depends, in part, on how rational you expect the burglar to be. A fully rational burglar would stake out a place, test for an alarm system before breaking in, and choose a home that is an easy target. In other words, the burglar would gather full information. But what if the burglar is not fully rational?

Because criminals look for the easiest target to rob, they will find a house that is easy to break into without detection. If you trim away the shrubs and install floodlights, criminals will realize that they can be seen approaching your home. A few hundred dollars spent on better lighting will dramatically lower your chances of being robbed. However, if you believe in bounded rationality, there is an even better answer: a criminal may not know what is inside your house, so a couple of prominently displayed "Beware of dog!" signs would discourage the burglar for less than $10! In other words, the would-be thief has incomplete information

Beware of dog!

and only a limited amount of time to select a target. A quick scan of your house would identify the "Beware of dog!" signs and cause him to move on.

This is an example of bounded rationality because only limited, and in this case unreliable, information is all that is easily available regarding possible alternatives and their consequences. Knowing that burglars face this constraint can be a key to keeping them away.

ANSWERING THE BIG QUESTIONS

How do economists explain irrational behavior?

* Economists use a number of concepts from behavioral economics to explain how people make choices that display irrational behavior. These concepts include bounded rationality, misperceptions of probabilities, framing effects and priming effects, the status quo bias, intertemporal decision-making, judgments about fairness, preference reversals, and prospect theory.

＊ Folding the behavioral approach into the standard model makes economists' predictions about human behavior much more robust.

What is the role of risk in decision-making?

＊ Risk influences decision-making because people can be risk-averse, risk-neutral, or risk-takers.

＊ In the traditional economic model, risk tolerances are assumed to be constant. If an individual is a risk-taker by nature, he or she will take risks in any circumstance. Likewise, if an individual does not like to take chances, he or she will avoid risk.

＊ Maurice Allais proved that many people have inconsistent risk preferences, or what are known as preference reversals. Moreover, he showed that simply because some people's preferences are not constant does not necessarily mean that their decisions are irrational.

＊ Prospect theory suggests that individuals weigh the utilities and risks of gains and losses differently and are therefore willing to take on additional risk to try to recover losses caused by negative shocks.

CONCEPTS YOU SHOULD KNOW

behavioral economics (p. 542)
bounded rationality (p. 542)
framing effect (p. 546)
gambler's fallacy (p. 545)
hot hand fallacy (p. 545)

intertemporal decision-making (p. 550)
preference reversal (p. 554)
priming effect (p. 547)
prospect theory (p. 556)

risk-averse people (p. 552)
risk-neutral people (p. 552)
risk-takers (p. 552)
status quo bias (p. 547)
ultimatum game (p. 550)

QUESTIONS FOR REVIEW

1. What is bounded rationality? How is this concept relevant to economic modeling?

2. What are the hot hand fallacy and the gambler's fallacy? Give an example of each.

3. How does the status quo bias reduce the potential utility that consumers enjoy?

4. Economists use the ultimatum game to test judgments of fairness. What result does economic theory predict?

5. What is prospect theory? Have you ever suffered a setback early in a process (for example, seeking a job or applying for college) that caused you to alter your behavior later on?

STUDY PROBLEMS (✷ solved at the end of the section)

✷ 1. You have a choice between two jobs. The first job pays $50,000 annually. The second job has a base pay of $40,000 with a 30% chance that you will receive an annual bonus of $25,000. You decide to take the $50,000 job. On the basis of this decision, can we tell if you are risk-averse or a risk-taker? Explain your response.

2. Suppose that Danny Ocean decides to play roulette, one of the most popular casino games. Roulette is attractive to gamblers because the house's advantage is small (less than 5%). If Danny Ocean plays roulette and wins big, is this evidence that Danny is risk-averse or a risk-taker? Explain.

3. Many voters go to the polls every four years to cast their ballot for president. The common refrain from those who vote is that their vote "counts" and that voting is important. A skeptical economist points out that with over 100 million ballots cast, the probability that any individual's vote will be decisive is close to 0%. What idea, discussed in this chapter, explains why so many people actually vote?

4. Your instructor is very conscientious and always makes sure that exam answers are randomly distributed. However, you notice that the first five answers on the true/false section are all "true." Unsure what this pattern means, you consider the sixth question. However, you do not know the answer. What answer would you give if you believed in the gambler's fallacy? What answer would you give if you believed in the hot hand fallacy?

✷ 5. Suppose that a university wishes to maximize the response rate for teaching evaluations. The administration develops an easy-to-use online evaluation system that each student can complete at the end of the semester. However, very few students bother to complete the survey. The registrar's office suggests that the online teaching evaluations be linked to course scheduling. When students access the course scheduling system, they are redirected to the teaching evaluations. Under this plan, each student can opt out and go directly to the course scheduling system. Do you think this plan will work to raise the response rate on teaching evaluations? What would traditional economic theory predict? What would a behavioral economist predict?

6. Ray likes his hamburgers with American cheese, lettuce, and ketchup. Whenever he places an order for a burger, he automatically orders these three toppings. What type of behavior is Ray exhibiting? What does traditional economic theory say about Ray's preferences? What would a behavioral economist say?

7. Many people give to charity and leave tips. What prediction does traditional economic theory make about each of these activities? (**Hint:** Think of the person's narrow self-interest.) What concept from behavioral economics explains this behavior?

8. Given a choice of an extra $1,000 or a gamble with the same expected value, a person prefers the $1,000. But given a choice of a loss of $1,000 or a gamble with the same expected value, the same person prefers the gamble. How would a behavioral economist describe this decision?

✱ 9. A researcher asks you the following question: "Would you rather have a 10% chance of mortality or a 90% chance of survival?" What concept from behavioral economics is illustrated here? What is the difference between the two choices, if any? Which choice do you think most people make?

SOLVED PROBLEMS

1. The first job pays $50,000 annually, so it has an expected value of $50,000. The second job has a base pay of $40,000 with a 30% chance that you will receive an annual bonus of $25,000. To determine the expected value of the second job, the calculation looks like this: $40,000 + (0.3 × $25,000) = $40,000 + $7,500 = $47,500. Since you decided to take the job with higher expected value, we cannot tell if you are a risk-taker or risk-averse.

5. Because students who access the course scheduling system are redirected to the teaching evaluations, they are forced to opt out if they do not wish to evaluate the instructors. As a result, a behavioral economist would predict that the new system will raise the teaching evaluation response rate. Traditional economic theory would predict that the response rate will not change simply based on whether or not students opt in or opt out.

9. According to behavioral economics, how the question is framed, which should not matter according to traditional economic theory, affects how people respond. When asked to choose which of the two outcomes they prefer, a significant majority chooses "a 90% chance of survival," even though this statement is equivalent to "a 10% chance of mortality."

Health Insurance and Health Care

Providing national health care would be a simple solution to the healthcare crisis.

We have come a long way in our exploration of microeconomics. In this chapter, we apply our economic toolkit to one particular industry— health care. The goal of this chapter is not to sway your opinion but to provide you with a simple set of tools to focus your thinking about how medical care can best serve individuals and society as a whole.

The debate over healthcare spending is at the core of the healthcare crisis in the United States. Many people believe that national health care (also called universal health care) would be the solution to the healthcare crisis because it would help to control costs. For example, the Affordable Care Act passed under President Obama (the federal healthcare law often called "Obamacare") argues that expanding healthcare coverage will lower healthcare costs. But can we really get more coverage for less? Supporters and opponents vehemently disagree.

The healthcare debate is about trade-offs. In this chapter, we describe how the healthcare industry works and how the government and the market can each make the delivery of health care more efficient. We consider how health care is delivered, who pays, and what makes the provision of medical care unlike the delivery of services in any other sector of the economy. Then we use supply and demand analysis to look at how the medical market functions. One important aspect of medical care is the role that information plays in the incentive structure for patients and providers. Finally, we examine a number

The healthcare debate has many sides.

Trade-offs

of case studies to pull all this information together so you can decide for yourself where you stand on one of the most important issues of the twenty-first century.

BIG QUESTIONS

* **What are the important issues in the healthcare industry?**
* **How does asymmetric information affect healthcare delivery?**
* **How do demand and supply contribute to high medical costs?**
* **How do incentives influence the quality of health care?**

What Are the Important Issues in the Healthcare Industry?

Health care is big business. If you add the education and automobile sectors together, they represent about 10% of national economic output. But health care alone accounts for more than 17% of the nation's economic output. That's 1 out of every 6 dollars spent annually in the United States—almost $3 trillion, or over $8,000 for every citizen. No matter how you slice it, that is a lot of money.

In this section, we examine the key issues in health care: how much is spent on it, where the money goes, and who the key players in the industry are. The goal is to give you a sense of how the sector functions. Then we turn our attention to supply and demand. First, though, we take a brief look at how health care has changed over the past hundred or so years.

The History of U.S. Health Care

At the start of the twentieth century, life expectancy in the United States was slightly less than 50 years. Now life expectancy is close to 80 years—a longevity gain that would have been unthinkable a few generations ago. Let's go back in time to examine the way medical care was delivered and see some of the advances that have improved the human condition.

Early in the twentieth century, infectious diseases were the most common cause of death in the United States. Typhoid, diphtheria, gangrene, gastritis, smallpox, and tuberculosis were major killers. Today, because of antibiotics, they

Cutting-edge medical equipment: then . . .   . . . and now.

have either been completely eradicated or are extremely rare. Moreover, the state of medical knowledge was so dismal that a cure was often far worse than the condition it was supposed to treat. For instance, tobacco was recommended for the treatment of bronchitis and asthma, and leeches were used to fight laryngitis. Throughout the first half of the twentieth century, a trip to the doctor was painful, and it rarely produced positive results.

Since 1950, advances in cellular biology and discoveries in biochemistry have led to a better understanding of diseases and more precise diagnostic tests. In addition, discoveries in biomedical engineering have led to the widespread use of imaging techniques such as ultrasound, computerized axial tomography (CAT scans), and nuclear magnetic resonance imaging (MRI). These and other technological innovations have replaced the medical practices of the past and made medical care safer, gentler, and more effective. In addition, pharmaceutical companies have developed a number of "miracle" drugs for fighting many conditions, including high blood pressure, leukemia, and bad cholesterol, thereby limiting the need for more invasive treatments. Each of these amazing medical advances costs money—sometimes, lots of money. As a society, we have made a trade-off: in exchange for a dramatically longer life expectancy, we now devote much more of our personal and government budgets to health care.

Trade-offs

Healthcare Expenditures

We have noted that healthcare expenditures in the United States are more than 17% of economic output. As you can see in Table 18.1, this total is quite a bit higher than similar expenditures in Canada and Mexico. Canada spends about 11% of its economic output on health care, and Mexico spends slightly more than 6%.

The United States spends significantly more on health care than our neighbors to the north and south, but life expectancy in the United States is lower than in Canada. How does Canada achieve a higher life expectancy while spending less money? And why doesn't Mexico, which spends only about one-tenth of what we do on health care per capita (see Table 18.1), trail farther behind the United States than it does? To answer those questions, consider

TABLE 18.1

Selected Healthcare Facts

Country	Total expenditure on health (percentage of economic output)	Per capita expenditure on health (in U.S. dollars)	Life expectancy at birth, total population (in years)
Mexico	6.2	916	75.5
Canada	11.4	4,445	80.8
U.S.	17.6	8,223	78.7

Source: OECD Health Division, *Health Data 2012: Frequently Requested Data.*

the usual assumption of *ceteris paribus*, or other things being constant. We all agree that increased healthcare expenditures are making people healthier, probably happier (because they feel better), and more productive—this is true for most countries. However, longevity is also a function of environmental factors, genetics, and lifestyle choices—variables that are not constant across countries. The question we should be asking is not how much money we are spending, but whether we are getting our money's worth. In other words, in this context economists are most concerned with the impediments to the efficient delivery of medical care.

Why does health care take up so much of our budget? There are a number of reasons. Health insurance plays a contributing role. When private insurance covers most treatment costs, many patients agree to tests or medical visits that they wouldn't be willing to pay for out of pocket. Also, doctors are more willing to order tests that might not be necessary if they know the patient isn't paying directly. Medicare and Medicaid, the two government-sponsored forms of health insurance, add to the overall demand for medical services by providing medical coverage to the elderly and poor. And we know that anytime there is more demand for services, the market price rises in response, as long as supply remains constant.

Another reason for high healthcare costs is the number of uninsured people in the United States—approximately 35 million in 2015. When uninsured people need immediate medical treatment, they often seek care from emergency rooms and clinics, which raises costs in two ways. First, emergency care is extraordinarily expensive—much more so than routine care. Second, waiting until one has an acute condition that requires immediate attention often requires more treatment than would occur with preventive care or an early diagnosis. For example, an insured person who develops a cough with fever is likely to see a physician. If the patient has bronchitis, a few days of medicine and rest will be all it takes to feel better. However, an uninsured person who develops bronchitis is less likely to seek medical help and risks the possibility of a worsening condition, such as pneumonia, which can be difficult and costly to treat.

Medical demand is quite inelastic, so when competition is absent (which is usually the case), hospitals and other providers can charge what they want, and patients will have to pay. In addition, many people are not proactive about their health. Many health problems could be dramatically reduced and costs contained if people curbed habits such as cigarette use, excessive alcohol consumption, and overeating and if they exercised more. Finally, heroic end-of-life efforts are extraordinarily expensive. These efforts may extend life for a few months, days, or hours, and they come at a steep price.

Diminishing Returns

In the United States, it has become the norm to spare no expense in the effort to extend life for even a few days. However, providing more medical care is subject to diminishing returns, as we can see in Figure 18.1. The orange curve shows a society's aggregate health production function, a measure of health reflecting the population's longevity, general health, and quality of life. This function initially rises rapidly when small amounts of health care are provided, but the benefits of additional care are progressively smaller. To understand why, compare points A and B. At point A, only a small amount of medical care is provided (Q_A), but this care has a large impact on health. The slope at point A represents the marginal product of medical care. However, by the time we reach point B at a higher amount of care provided (Q_B), the marginal product of medical care (the slope) is much flatter, indicating that diminishing returns have set in.

Marginal Thinking

Higher medical care expenditures, beyond some point, are unlikely to measurably improve longevity and quality of life because many other factors—for example, disease, genetics, and lifestyle—also play a key role in determining health, quality of life, and longevity. As we move out along the

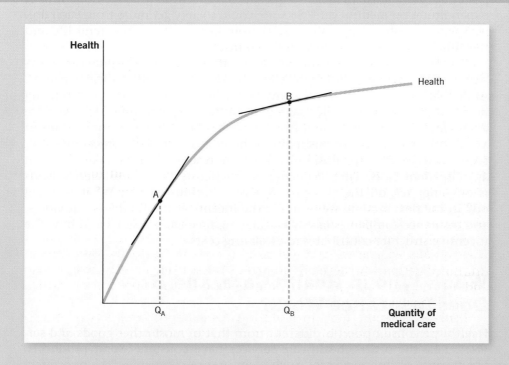

FIGURE 18.1

Health Production Function

The marginal product of medical care, indicated by the slope of the health production function, is higher at point A than at point B.

FIGURE 18.2

The Nation's Health Dollar

Hospital care, physicians, and clinics make up over half of all healthcare expenditures, which totaled $2.9 trillion in 2012. (Total does not add to 100% due to rounding.)

Source: Centers for Medicare and Medicaid Services, Office of the Actuary, National Health Statistics Group. See "National Health Expenditure Data," cms.gov.

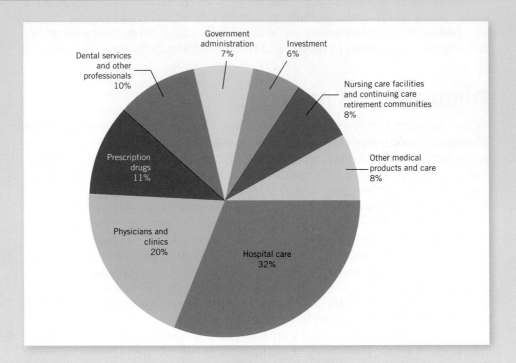

medical production function, extending life becomes progressively more difficult, so it is not surprising that medical costs rise appreciably. Given this pattern, society must answer two questions. First, what is the optimal mix of expenditures on medical care? Second, could society get more from each dollar spent by reallocating dollars away from heroic efforts to extend life and toward prevention and medical research instead?

Figure 18.2 shows where the typical health dollar goes. Hospital care, physicians, and clinics account for a little more than half of all medical expenses. After that, prescription drugs, dental care, home health care, and nursing homes each represent smaller parts of healthcare expenditures. Here we note a paradox. On the one hand, medical care has become much more efficient as medical records are increasingly computerized and many procedures that required days of hospitalization a generation ago can now take place on an outpatient basis. Thus, reducing medical costs through efficiency gains is ongoing. Yet, on the other hand, costs continue to rise. What is going on? In the next section, we examine the incentives that patients, providers, and insurance companies face when making medical decisions and how the incentive structure contributes to escalating costs.

Who's Who in Health Care, and How Does Insurance Work?

Healthcare consumption is different from that of most other goods and services. Like the others, healthcare services have consumers and producers; but because of intermediaries, such as insurance companies, the two rarely interact directly. This situation generates a unique set of incentives and leads to distortions in the standard supply and demand analysis. It is important to understand how medical care is delivered and paid for, as well as the incentives that patients, medical providers, and insurers face when making decisions.

Incentives

Consumers

The two biggest consumers of medical care are patients and the government. Patients demand medical care to prevent and treat illness. The federal government runs Medicare, a program that provides medical assistance to the elderly, and Medicaid, a program that provides medical assistance to the poor. Medicare and Medicaid are social insurance programs that each serve over 40 million enrollees. The two programs account for approximately one-third of all medical spending in the United States and represent about one-fourth of all U.S. government expenditures.

Producers

The medical care industry employs millions of workers, including doctors, nurses, psychologists, technicians, and many more. There are also over 500,000 medical facilities in this country, including small medical offices, large regional hospitals, nursing homes, pharmacies, and stores that supply medical equipment. In addition, pharmaceutical companies generate over $300 billion in annual sales in the United States.

Intermediaries

Intermediaries—for example, insurance companies—cover certain medical expenses in exchange for a set monthly fee, known as a *premium*. Medical insurance enables consumers to budget their expenses and limit what they will have to pay out of pocket in the event of a serious condition.

In addition to the premium, a *copayment* or deductible is typically required. **Copayments** (sometimes called "copays") are fixed amounts that the insured pays when receiving a medical service or filling a prescription. Insurance companies use copayments in part to share expenses with the insured. In addition to covering a small portion of the costs, the copay serves to prevent most people from seeking care for common conditions that are easy to treat at home. **Deductibles** are fixed amounts that the insured must pay before most of the policy's benefits can be applied. Deductibles are sometimes subject to exceptions, such as a necessary visit to the emergency room or preventive physician visits and tests. Some policies also require **coinsurance payments**, a percentage that the insured pays after the insurance policy's deductible is exceeded up to the policy's contribution limit. These services vary with each type of plan. Like coinsurance, copayments and deductibles work to encourage consumers to use medical services judiciously.

Insurance companies use the premiums, copayments, deductibles, and coinsurance they receive from their customers to pay medical suppliers. For example, you may not need an appendectomy this year, but a predictable number of insured customers will. Using statistical techniques, an insurance company with millions of customers can accurately predict how many of its

Copayments are fixed amounts that the insured must pay when receiving a medical service or filling a prescription.

Deductibles are fixed amounts that the insured must pay before most of the policy's benefits can be applied.

Coinsurance payments are a percentage of costs that the insured must pay after exceeding the insurance policy's deductible up to the policy's contribution limit.

customers will visit the doctor and require hospitalization and other services. This statistical analysis enables the company to estimate its costs in advance and set premiums that generate a profit for the company.

Many people receive medical care through *health maintenance organizations*, or HMOs—another example of an intermediary. HMOs provide managed care for their patients by assigning them a primary care physician (PCP) who oversees their medical care. The HMO then monitors the primary care provider to ensure that unnecessary care is not prescribed. HMOs earn revenue from premiums, copayments, deductibles, and coinsurance. Many insurance plans allow the insured to make choices. *Preferred provider organizations*, or PPOs, are a type of health insurance arrangement that gives plan participants relative freedom to choose the doctors and hospitals they want to visit.

Another kind of insurance company sells insurance against medical malpractice, or negligent treatment on the part of doctors. The doctor pays a set fee to the insurer, which in turn pays for the legal damages that arise if the doctor faces a malpractice claim. By analyzing statistics about the number of malpractice cases for each type of medical procedure performed each year, insurers can estimate the probability that a particular physician will face a malpractice claim; the insurers then incorporate that risk into the premium they charge to doctors.

Pharmaceutical Companies

Constituting another major player in the healthcare industry are the many pharmaceutical companies that develop the drugs used to treat a wide variety of conditions. Global pharmaceutical sales are almost $1 trillion. The United States accounts for about 30% of this $1 trillion—that's a lot of prescriptions! Pharmaceutical companies spend billions of dollars developing and testing potential drugs. One drug can take years or decades to develop. Once a drug is developed, it must receive approval by the Federal Drug Administration (FDA) before it can be sold. The development cost, time required, and risk that a drug may turn out to be problematic or ineffective combine to make the development of new drugs an expensive proposition.

Medical Costs

To understand why medical costs are so high, we must look at the incentives that drive the decisions of the major players. Consumers want every treatment to be covered, providers want a steady stream of business and don't want to be sued for malpractice, and the insurance companies and pharmaceutical companies want to make profits. These market dynamics showcase the inherent conflict that exists between consumers, producers, and intermediaries, and it helps explain the difficulty of providing medical care at a reasonable cost.

Incentives

Because patient copayments are only a tiny fraction of the total cost of care, the effective marginal cost of seeking medical treatment is quite low. As a result, consumers increase the quantity of medical care they demand. Some physicians prescribe more care than is medically necessary in order to earn more income and to avoid malpractice lawsuits. Meanwhile, insurance

PRACTICE WHAT YOU KNOW

Physical Fitness

Question: You go in for a physical, and your doctor suggests that you get more exercise. So you decide to start working out. The increased physical activity has a big payoff and soon you feel much better, so you decide to double your efforts and get in even better shape. However, you notice that the gains from doubling your workout effort do not make you feel much better. What economic concept explains this effect?

"I work out . . ."

Answer: More of a good thing isn't always better. Physical activity extends longevity and increases quality of life up to a point. However, working out is subject to *diminishing returns*. In other words, a small amount of physical activity has a big payoff, but lifting more weights or running more miles, after a certain point, does not increase your overall health—it simply maintains your health.

companies, which are caught in the middle between patients and medical providers, do their best to contain costs, but they find that controlling the behavior of patients and providers is difficult. Consequently, escalating costs result from a system with poorly designed incentive mechanisms. In the case of Medicare and Medicaid, the government attempts to control costs by setting caps on the reimbursements that are paid to providers for medical treatments. An unintended consequence of government price setting is that it forces physicians and medical centers to raise prices for other procedures that are not covered by Medicare and Medicaid.

How Does Asymmetric Information Affect Healthcare Delivery?

We have seen that incentives play an important role in the delivery of medical care. Another important element is the information and lack of information available to participants. Imbalances in information, known as **asymmetric information**, occur whenever one party knows more than the other. Asymmetric information has two forms: *adverse selection* and the *principal-agent problem.*

Asymmetric information is an imbalance in information that occurs when one party knows more than the other.

Adverse Selection

Most of us know very little about medicine. We know when we don't feel well and that we want to feel better, so we seek medical attention. Because we know very little about the service we are buying, we are poor judges of quality. For example, how can you know if your doctor is qualified or better than another doctor? **Adverse selection** exists when one party has information about some aspect of product quality that the other party does not have. As a result, the party with the limited information should be concerned that the other party will misrepresent information to gain an advantage.

When one side knows more than the other, the only way to avoid an adverse outcome is to gather better information. Suppose that you are new in town and need medical care. You haven't had a chance to meet anyone and find out whom to see or where to go for care. Fortunately, there is a way to avoid the worst doctors: websites like ratemds.com provide patient feedback on the quality of care that they have received. Armed with knowledge from sources like these, you can request to be treated by doctors whom you know to be competent and have strong reputations. Conducting this research helps new residents avoid below-average care. More generally, it is important for patients to take charge of their own health care and learn all they can about a condition and its treatment so they are prepared to ask questions and make better decisions about treatment options. When patients are better informed, adverse selection is minimized.

Adverse selection also applies when buyers are more likely to seek insurance if they are more likely to need it. Consider a life insurance company. The company wants to avoid selling an inexpensive policy to someone who is likely to die prematurely, so before selling a policy to that applicant, the insurance company has to gather additional information about the person. It can require a medical exam and delay eligibility for full benefits until it can determine that the applicant has no preexisting health conditions. The process of gathering information about the applicant is crucial to minimizing the risk associated with adverse selection. In fact, the process is similar for automobile insurance, in which drivers with poor records pay substantially higher premiums and safe drivers pay substantially lower ones.

Adverse selection exists when one party has information about some aspect of product quality that the other party does not have.

The Principal-Agent Problem

Patients generally trust doctors to make good treatment decisions. A **principal-agent problem** arises when a principal entrusts an agent to complete a task and the agent does not do so in a satisfactory way. Some nonmedical examples will be familiar to you. Parents (the principal) hire a babysitter (the agent) to watch their children, but the babysitter might talk on the phone instead. A company manager (the agent) might try to maximize his own salary instead of working to increase value for the shareholders (the principal). Finally, a politician (the agent) might be more likely to grant favors to interest groups than to focus on the needs of his or her constituents (the principal).

In a medical setting, the principal-agent problem occurs whenever patients cannot directly observe how medical providers and insurers are managing their patients' interests. The lack of oversight on the part of patients gives their agents, the physicians and insurance companies, some freedom

A **principal-agent problem** arises when a principal entrusts an agent to complete a task and the agent does not do so in a satisfactory way.

to pursue other objectives that do not directly benefit patients. In the case of medicine, doctors and hospitals may order more tests, procedures, or visits to specialists than are medically necessary. The physician or the hospital may be more concerned about making profits or avoiding medical malpractice lawsuits than ensuring the patient's health and well-being. At the same time, insurance companies may want to save on treatment costs in order to maximize profit. In both cases, the patient's desire for the best medical care conflicts with the objectives of the agents who deliver their care.

Moral Hazard

Moral hazard is the lack of incentive to guard against risk where one is protected from its consequences. Moral hazard does not necessarily refer to behavior that is "immoral" or "unethical." But it does imply that some people will change their behavior when their risk exposure is reduced and an "it's insured" mentality sets in. This mentality can lead to inefficient outcomes, such as visiting the doctor more often than necessary.

In the example mentioned, there is a moral hazard problem that can be lessened by restructuring the incentives. For the patient, a higher copayment will discourage unnecessary visits to the doctor.

To solve a moral hazard problem in medical care, it is necessary to fix the incentive structure. Many health insurance companies address moral hazard by encouraging preventive care, which lowers medical costs. They also impose payment limits on treatments for preventable conditions, such as gum disease and tooth decay.

Moral hazard is the lack of incentive to guard against risk where one is protected from its consequences.

Incentives

Moral Hazard

"King-Size Homer"

In this episode of *The Simpsons*, a new corporate fitness policy is intended to help the power plant workers become healthier. Morning exercises are instituted, and the employees are whipped into shape. But Homer hates working out, so he decides to gain a lot of weight in order to claim disability and work at home. To qualify, he must weigh at least 300 pounds. To get to that weight, he must go on an eating binge. Of course, his behavior is not what the designers of the fitness policy had in mind.

This amusing episode is a good example of moral hazard, and it showcases how well-intentioned policies can often be abused.

Moral hazard makes Homer decide to gain weight.

ECONOMICS IN THE MEDIA

PRACTICE WHAT YOU KNOW

Asymmetric Information

Question: Your sister's regular tutor is out of town, so you hire a substitute tutor and agree to pay $40 up front for one intense tutoring session. Later, you find out that the substitute tutor spent more time texting on his phone than helping your sister. Is adverse selection, the principal-agent problem, moral hazard, or some combination of these at work?

Answer: Since you paid up front for a one-time session, the substitute tutor has much less incentive to help compared with your sister's regular tutor, who expects repeat business and a tip. The poor outcome reflects the moral hazard problem. The substitute tutor does not have the same incentives that your regular tutor has and is therefore more likely to slack off.

Question: You decide to use an online dating site, but you are not entirely sure if the posted picture of someone is accurate. Is adverse selection, the principal-agent problem, moral hazard, or some combination of these at work?

Answer: Adverse selection is at work. The person you are interested in knows more about herself than you do. She can, and probably would, post a flattering picture of herself. When you finally meet her, you are likely to be disappointed.

Question: You hire a friend to feed your cat and change the litter twice a day while you are on spring break. However, your friend only visits your apartment every other day, and your cat shows his disapproval by using your bedspread as a litter box. Is adverse selection, the principal-agent problem, moral hazard, or some combination of these at work?

Answer: This is a great example of the principal-agent problem. Because you are out of town, there is no way to tell how often your friend goes to your house. Your friend knows that cats are largely self-sufficient and figures that you won't be able to tell how often she changed the litter.

How Do Demand and Supply Contribute to High Medical Costs?

Now that we have a basic understanding of how the healthcare industry functions and who the key players are, we can examine the way demand and supply operate in the market for health care. On the demand side, we consider what makes healthcare demand stubbornly inelastic. Health care, when you need it, is not about the price—it is about getting the care you need. When you consider this fact and the presence of third-party payments, or payments made by insurance companies, you can begin to understand why medical expenses have risen so rapidly. On the supply side, medical licensing requirements help explain why the supply of medical services is limited. The combination of strongly inelastic demand and limited supply pushes up prices for medical services.

Healthcare Demand

Health care is usually a necessity, and it doesn't have many good alternatives. These two facts explain why the demand for health care is typically inelastic. For example, going without a heart transplant when you need one isn't an option. In fact, a 2002 RAND Corporation study found that health care has an average price elasticity coefficient of -0.17. This means that a 1% increase in the price of health care will lead to a 0.17% reduction in healthcare expenditures. Recall that as an elasticity coefficient approaches zero, demand becomes more inelastic. So we can say that the demand for medical care is quite inelastic. (For a refresher on elasticity, see Chapter 4.)

But there are some situations in which healthcare expenditures can be reduced. For example, otherwise healthy people with minor colds and other viruses can use home remedies, such as drinking fluids and resting, rather than make an expensive visit to the doctor. So the price elasticity of demand depends on the severity of the medical need and the sense of urgency involved in treatment. Urgent needs have the most inelastic demand. As the time horizon expands from the short run to the long run, the demand for health care becomes progressively more elastic. Nonemergency long-term treatments have the greatest price elasticity. For instance, a significant portion of the adult population postpones routine dental visits, despite the obvious benefits. Later, when a tooth goes bad, some people choose extractions, which are less expensive (though less attractive) than root canals and crowns.

In recent years, demand for health care has grown. As people live longer, demand rises for expensive medical goods and services, including hearing aids, replacement joints, and assisted living and nursing home facilities. In an aging population, the incidence of certain illnesses and conditions—for example, cancer and Alzheimer's disease—rises. In addition, new technologies have made it possible to treat medical conditions for which there previously was no treatment. While these medical advances have improved the quality of life for many consumers, they drive up demand for more advanced medical procedures, equipment, and specialty drugs.

People who are risk averse (see Chapter 17) generally choose to purchase health insurance because it protects them against the possibility of extreme financial hardship in the case of severe illness or other medical problems. But insurance may distort their idea of costs and cause them to change their behavior, which creates a moral hazard problem. For example, if an insurance policy does not require the patient to pay anything, or requires very little, to see the doctor, the patient may wind up seeing the doctor more often than necessary.

ECONOMICS IN THE MEDIA

Inelastic Healthcare Demand

John Q

The 2002 feature film *John Q* follows John Quincy Archibald's quest to help his son receive a heart transplant. His son suddenly collapses while playing baseball and is rushed to the emergency room. Doctors inform John Q (played by Denzel Washington) that his son's only hope is a transplant. Because the child will die without the transplant, John Q's demand for this surgery is perfectly inelastic. Unfortunately, John Q's insurance won't cover his son's transplant.

The tagline of the film is "give a father no options and you leave him no choice." This statement summarizes the dilemma that many people without adequate insurance face. However, it does not stop the uninsured from demanding medical care when the situation is life-threatening. This situation is problematic on two fronts. First, when those without insurance turn to the emergency room as their only source of medical care, their medical conditions are treated in the most expensive manner possible. Second, hospitals transfer the cost of treating the uninsured by raising fees for the other services that they provide. As a result, society picks up the tab for the uninsured indirectly through higher insurance premiums.

The film is also about a fixed supply because someone has to die to provide a heart for transplant.

Inelastic demand for his son's heart transplant drives John Q to take desperate steps.

No one wants to risk a child possibly dying because his family lacks health insurance. After exploring every available financial option, John Q takes matters into his own hands and takes the emergency room staff hostage until the hospital agrees to do the transplant. Of course, this plot line sensationalizes the problem, but it also makes a very powerful point about the costs and benefits of lifesaving care.

Consider how this situation affects two patients. Abigail does not have insurance and therefore must pay the full cost of medical care out of pocket. Brett has an insurance policy that requires a small copayment for medical care. Figure 18.3 illustrates the difference between how Abigail (point A) and Brett (point B) might react. Let's suppose that they both get sick five times during the year. Because Abigail pays the full cost of seeking treatment ($100 per physician office visit), she will go to the doctor's office only three times. She ends up paying $300. Brett pays $10 per visit, so he will go to the doctor's office five times for a total cost to him of $50. The insurance company picks up the rest of the cost for Brett, or $90 per visit.

The overall impact of a $10 copayment on healthcare costs is large. In the Abigail/Brett scenario, since each visit costs $100, total healthcare costs

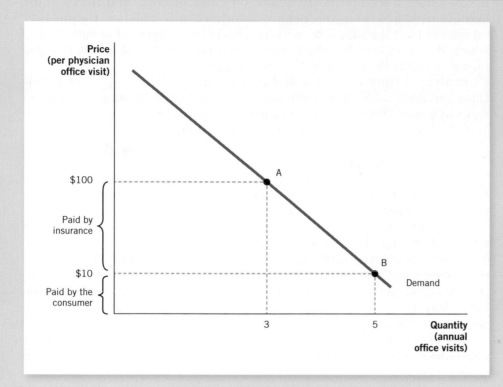

FIGURE 18.3

Price and the Quantity Demanded of Medical Care Services

Without insurance, the consumer bears the entire cost of an office visit, or $100. At this amount, the consumer (Abigail) might think twice about whether the medical care is truly necessary. As a result of these costs, Abigail makes three office visits per year, represented by point A. However, when a consumer has insurance and pays only a $10 copayment per visit, the marginal price drops and the quantity demanded increases. This insured consumer, Brett, makes five office visits per year, represented by point B.

for the office visits are only $300 when a patient is uninsured, but $500 with healthcare coverage—a $200 increase in total healthcare costs. Because in our example the insurance companies are paying 90% of the cost, the consumer has little reason not to seek medical attention, even for minor problems that will respond to home treatment. The two extra visits per year illustrate a change in consumer behavior as a result of the lower copayment, helping to explain why insurance costs are so high.

Healthcare Supply

While consumers worry about the price, or premium, they pay for health insurance, producers are concerned about profits. As much as we might like to think that medical providers care only about our health, we must acknowledge that they are providing a service for which they expect to be paid. Therefore, it is more accurate to think of healthcare providers in the same way we think of any other producers: when the price rises, they are willing to supply additional health care. Producers of medical care such as physicians and hospitals also enjoy significant market power. In this section, we consider how licensing requirements limit the supply of certain healthcare providers and thereby impact the market.

Becoming a skilled medical provider is a lengthy process that requires extensive training, education, and certification. Physicians must secure licenses from a medical board before they can practice, and nurses must become registered. Thus, restrictions associated with entering the medical profession limit the supply of workers. This point is captured in Figure 18.4, which illustrates how barriers to entry limit the number of physicians and nurses and the associated effect on their wages.

Barriers to entry in the medical profession restrict the supply of physicians and nurses. The subsequent decrease in the quantity supplied of these medical workers (from Q_1 to Q_2) causes their wages to increase (from W_1 to W_2). In addition, many medical facilities do not face direct competition. For example, many small communities have only one hospital. In these cases, familiarity, the need for immediate care, and convenience make the nearest hospital the default option for most patients. Because economies of scale are important in the provision of medical care, even large metropolitan areas tend to have only a few large hospitals rather than many smaller competitors. As the population base expands, larger hospitals can afford to offer a wider set of services than smaller hospitals do. For instance, the need for pediatric care units, oncology centers, organ transplant centers, and a host of other services require that the hospital develop a particular expertise. The availability of specialized care is, of course, a good thing. However, as hospitals become larger and more highly specialized, competitive pressures subside and they are able to charge higher fees.

The market power of suppliers is held in check to some extent by insurance companies and by the Medicare and Medicaid programs. Also, some

FIGURE 18.4

Barriers to Entry Limit the Supply of Certain Medical Workers

Restrictions associated with entering the medical profession limit the supply of certain workers. These restrictions cause a decrease in the quantity supplied of physicians and nurses from Q_1 to Q_2 and an increase in wages from W_1 to W_2.

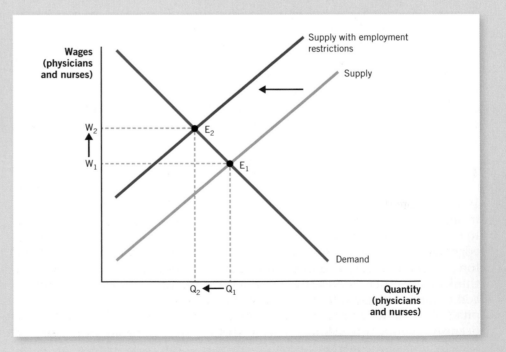

services are not reimbursed by insurance. And the insurance companies push back against certain other medical charges by limiting the amount they reimburse, as do Medicare and Medicaid for certain treatments. In addition, elective medical services, such as Lasik eye surgery, are typically not reimbursed by insurance plans. As a result, consumer demand is quite elastic for some services. Still, overall medical costs have continued to rise.

ECONOMICS IN THE REAL WORLD

Medical Tourism

Medical tourism has grown explosively over the last 20 years as the quality of medical care around the globe has improved rapidly and international travel has become more convenient. Today, it is possible for a patient to have cardiac surgery in India, a hip replacement in Egypt, and a face-lift in Rio de Janeiro. Supply and demand helps explain the rapid growth of medical tourism. The United States attracts its share of wealthy medical tourists looking for better outcomes than they can expect in their home country. However, the majority of people who seek medical care abroad do so for two reasons: cost and wait times.

Recovery from surgery doesn't get any better than this!

First, the cost of medical care is as much as 90% lower in a developing country than in a developed country such as the United States. This price differential is a function of lower costs of living, less administrative overhead, a favorable currency exchange rate, lower physician wages, and lower malpractice premiums in developing countries. Also, health insurance is not readily available in many locations within developing countries, which leads to a policy of cash payment for healthcare services and also suppresses demand. Second, there are long wait times for certain procedures in countries with universal health care. Avoiding long wait times is the leading factor for medical tourism from the United Kingdom and Canada.

In the United States, the main reason for medical tourism is the lower cost. Indeed, many procedures performed abroad cost a fraction of the price in developed countries. For example, a liver transplant in the United States can cost more than $250,000, but it costs less than $100,000 in Taiwan. Some insurance plans offer incentives to have orthopedic surgery, such as knee and hip replacements, performed in Panama and Costa Rica, where the cost of the surgery is a quarter of the cost in the United States. Patients agree to leave the country for this type of surgery because their insurance company will pay all their travel-related expenses and waive the typical out-of-pocket expenses that would be incurred from copays and deductibles.

Medical tourism has even led to the creation of medical "safaris," where patients go to South Africa or South America for cosmetic surgery, stay in luxurious accommodations, and take in the savanna or rain forest while recuperating. ✳

PRACTICE WHAT YOU KNOW

A increase in the quantity of medical care demanded for services might mean that "hurry up and wait" becomes a common experience for most patients.

Demand for Health Care: How Would Universal Health Care Alter the Demand for Medical Care?

Question: Suppose that the United States scraps its current healthcare system, and citizens are 100% covered for all medical care with no copayments or deductibles. How would the new system affect the demand for medical care? Illustrate your answer on a graph.

Answer: Without any copayment or deductibles, each patient's out-of-pocket expense would be zero. Society would pick up the tab through taxes. As a result, the quantity of medical care demanded by each patient would increase from point A to point B.

At point B, demand is no longer contingent on price, so this represents the largest potential quantity of care demanded.

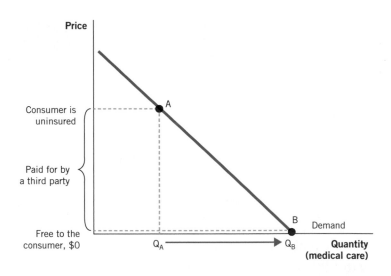

How Do Incentives Influence the Quality of Health Care?

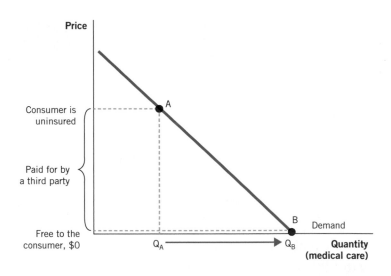

Incentives

In this section, we apply what we've learned about health care. First, we look at the universal healthcare debate by comparing the healthcare systems in the United States and Canada. Then we examine the shortage of human organs available for transplant. By considering these two issues, we can see how incentives influence the quality of health care that patients receive.

Single-Payer versus Private Health Care

Rationing is a fact of life because we live in a world of scarcity. The simplest way of thinking about the healthcare issue is to understand how different rationing mechanisms are used in medical care. In the United States, the primary rationing mechanism is the consumer's ability to pay. One consequence of using prices to ration medical care is that close to 35 million U.S. citizens forgo some medical care because they lack insurance or the means to pay for care on their own. In Canada, no citizen lacks the means to pay because medical care is paid for by taxes. This does not mean that medical care there is unlimited, however. In Canada, rationing occurs through wait times, fewer doctors, and limited availability of certain drugs.

Which country has better health care, the United States or Canada?

As in almost all things economic, there is a trade-off. No medical system creates the perfect set of incentives. In the United States, a large majority of citizens have the means to pay for medical care, have access to some of the best medical facilities in the world, and face relatively short wait times. However, under the current U.S. system, access to the best facilities is limited, and longer wait times exist for the poorest members of society. The Affordable Care Act has reduced some of the disparities between the rich and the poor, but a system of private health care makes those differences impossible to eliminate.

Trade-offs

In Canada, each citizen is treated equally, but access to immediate medical treatment is more restricted. We saw in Table 18.1 that Canada spends far less than the United States per capita ($4,445 versus $8,223). How does Canada provide medical care to every citizen at approximately half the price of the U.S. system? There are several ways. First, the government sets the rates that are paid to medical providers. Second, physicians are not permitted to have private practices. Third, hospitals receive grants from the government to cover the costs of providing care. This system, in which there is only a *single payer*, makes the government the single buyer, or monopsonist, of most medical care. (See Chapter 14 for a discussion of monopsony.) In other words, in a **single-payer system**, the government covers the cost of providing most health care, and citizens pay their share through taxes.

In a **single-payer system**, the government covers the cost of providing most health care, and citizens pay their share through taxes.

The Canadian government uses its leverage as a monopsonist to set compensation levels for physicians below the competitive market wage rate. Under Canada's Health Act, government funding is required for medically necessary care, but only if that care is delivered in hospitals or by certified physicians. This means that the Canadian government funds about 70% of all medical expenses, with the remaining 30% of costs being generated by prescription medications, long-term care, physical therapy, and dental care. In these areas, private insurance operates in much the same way it does in the United States.

Patients seeking medical care in Canada are far more likely to seek additional care in the United States than U.S. patients are to seek care in Canada. This fact might strike you as odd. After all, Canada has national health care, and health services there are covered under the Canadian Health Act. However, there is a difference between access and availability. Because Canada keeps tight control over medical costs, people with conditions that are not life-threatening often face extended waits. Services that are not regulated—for example, veterinarian

Health: United States vs. Canada

Is the healthcare dollar being spent as efficiently as possible to maintain the health of Americans? To answer this question, it's helpful to compare our situation to other countries, such as Canada. The United States and Canada have very different healthcare systems. Canada's is primarily a publicly funded, single-payer system with the government paying 70% of all health-related expenses. The United States' is primarily a privately funded, multi-payer system with the government paying approximately 48% of all health-related expenses.

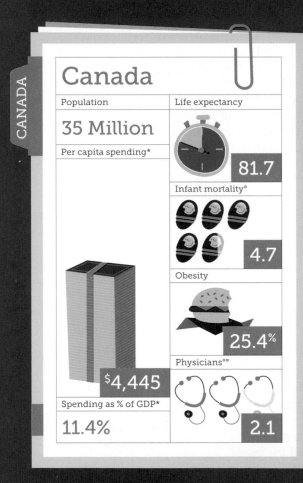

Canada

CANADA

Population	Life expectancy
35 Million	81.7
Per capita spending*	
	Infant mortality° 4.7
	Obesity 25.4%
$4,445	Physicians°° 2.1
Spending as % of GDP* 11.4%	

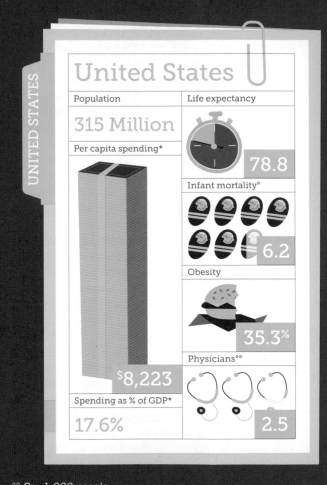

United States

UNITED STATES

Population	Life expectancy
315 Million	78.8
Per capita spending*	
	Infant mortality° 6.2
	Obesity 35.3%
$8,223	Physicians°° 2.5
Spending as % of GDP* 17.6%	

Total expenditure, public and private   °Per 1,000 live births   °°Per 1,000 people

Both countries achieve similar health outcomes, but health care is a clear example of trade-offs. The Canadian system cuts costs, while patients in the United States benefit from shorter wait times for care and the best medical facilities in the world.

REVIEW QUESTIONS

- How do you think the obesity level in the United States contributes to healthcare costs?

- What are the benefits and costs of a private versus a public healthcare system?

Sources: OECD, World Health Organization, CIA World Factbook.

visits—provide access to medical care without waiting. Dogs in Canada have no trouble getting MRIs and chemotherapy quickly—unlike their human counterparts, who have to wait—but of course the pet owner has to pay the full expense.

ECONOMICS IN THE REAL WORLD

Health Care in France

In 2000, the World Health Organization (WHO) ranked every country's healthcare system. France came in first. The United States finished 37 out of 191 nations. In a second study, conducted in 2008, researchers looked at health care in 19 industrialized nations. France, again, finished first. The United States was last. More recent studies, with some variations, continue to confirm these findings.

What separates the United States from France? Not as much as you might think. The French balk at any notion that they have socialized health care. France, like the United States, relies on both private insurance and government insurance. In both countries, people generally get private insurance through their employer. Both healthcare systems value choice, and patients can choose preferred providers and specialists. One major difference is that 99.9% of French citizens have health insurance, as opposed to 88% of people in the United States (in 2015). The reason for this difference is clear: in France there is mandatory national health insurance, alongside supplemental private insurance that most people purchase. France's mandatory national health insurance takes care of 70% of patient needs, and supplemental private insurance (which is quite affordable) makes up the remaining 30%. This arrangement differs from medical care in the United States, where the federal government pays only approximately 25% of medical expenses and the remainder is picked up by privately funded insurance (which is quite expensive).

France is number 1 in health care, according to the World Health Organization.

Another difference between the French and U.S. systems is in the way coverage works for the sickest patients. In France, the most serious conditions are 100% covered. In contrast, in the United States, patients' out-of-pocket expenses for the most serious conditions often require supplemental insurance, and experimental procedures and drugs are rarely covered. As a result, the French report that they are quite satisfied with their healthcare system, while similar surveys in the United States find a much more mixed reaction, with roughly half the population happy and the other half concerned.

Of course, none of this is inexpensive. In France, the average person pays slightly over 20% of his or her income to support the national healthcare system. Because French firms must pick up a large chunk of the healthcare tab through payroll taxes, they are reluctant to hire workers. In the United States, workers do not pay as much in taxes, but they do pay more for medical care than the French do when we add in the costs of private insurance and higher out-of-pocket expenses.

The lower overall costs of providing medical care in France can be traced to the government control of the amount of compensation that hospitals and providers receive. In other words, the French do a better job of using monopsony power to control costs. Nevertheless, healthcare costs in France have risen rapidly, which has led to cuts in services in order to keep the system solvent. ✳

The Human Organ Shortage

Many altruistic people donate blood each year to help save the lives of tens of thousands of other people. Their generosity makes transplants and other surgeries possible. Unfortunately, the same level of generosity does not apply to organ donations. The quantity of replacement organs demanded exceeds the quantity of replacement organs supplied each year, resulting in thousands of deaths. Many of these deaths would be preventable if people were allowed to sell organs. However, the National Organ Transplant Act of 1984 makes it illegal to do so in the United States. Restrictions do not cover the entire body: people can sell platelets, sperm, and ova (the female reproductive cell). In those markets, prices determine who donates. With blood, kidneys, livers, and lungs, the donors are not paid. This discrepancy has created two unintended consequences. First, many people die unnecessarily: in the United States, more than 7,000 patients on transplant waiting lists die each year. Second, the demand for human organs has created a billion-dollar-a-year black market.

Let's consider the market for kidneys. Figure 18.5 illustrates how the supply of and demand for human kidneys works. Almost everyone has two kidneys, and a person's life can continue almost normally with only one healthy kidney. Of course, there are risks associated with donation, including complications from the surgery and during recovery, as well as no longer having a backup kidney. However, since there are roughly 300 million "spare" kidneys in the United States (because the population is 300 million), there is a large pool of potential donors who are good matches for recipients awaiting a transplant.

Because kidneys cannot be legally bought and sold, the supply curve shown in Figure 18.5 does not respond to price. As a result, the curve becomes a vertical line at point Q_S (quantity supplied). Notice that the quantity supplied is not zero because many people donate kidneys to friends and family members in need. Others participate in exchange programs under which they donate a kidney to someone they don't know in exchange for someone else agreeing to donate a kidney to their friend or family member. (Exchange programs help to provide better matches so that the recipient is less likely to reject the kidney transplant.) Moreover, a few altruistic persons donate their kidneys to complete strangers. Nevertheless, the quantity supplied still falls short of the quantity demanded, because $Q_D > Q_S$ at a price of $0.

Trade creates value

Markets would normally reconcile a shortage by increasing prices. In Figure 18.5, an equilibrium market price of $15,000 is shown ($E_1$). Economists have estimated that this would be the market price if the sale of kidneys were legal in the United States. Because such sales are illegal, the nation faces the shortage illustrated in Figure 18.5. Over 4,000 people die each year in this country waiting for a kidney transplant. Many others have a low quality of life while waiting to receive a kidney. Because patients waiting for human organs eventually die without a transplant, a black market for kidney transplants has developed outside the United States. However, the price—typically

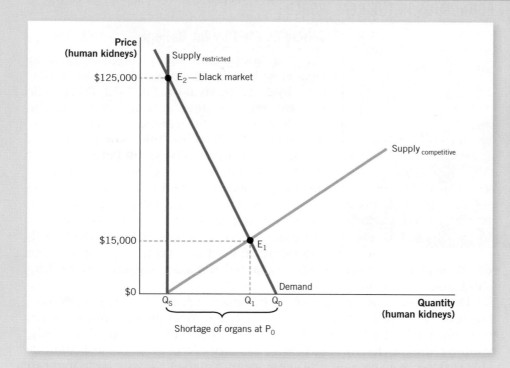

FIGURE 18.5

The Supply and Demand for Human Kidneys

Restrictions on selling kidneys limit the supply of organs as shown by Supply$_{restricted}$ and cause the shortage noted between Q_D and Q_S. A black market develops with an illegal price of $125,000.

$125,000 or greater—requires doctors, hospitals, staff, and patients to circumvent the law. As a consequence, the black market price (at E_2) is much higher than it would be if a competitive market for human kidneys existed.

In its simplest form, the issue is essentially this: why should the affluent, who can afford to pay for organ transplants, continue to live, while the poor, who also need organ transplants, die? That hardly seems fair. Unfortunately, altruism alone has not provided enough organs to meet demand, leading to a shortage of many vital organs. Because we continue to experience shortages of human organs, the supply must be rationed. Whether the rationing takes place through markets, waiting in line, or via some other mechanism is a matter of efficiency. As a result, using markets, in some form, may be one way to prevent avoidable deaths. However, the ethical considerations are significant. For example, if organs can be bought and sold, what would prevent the use of coercion to force people to sell their organs?

Of course, the ethical dilemma becomes moot if viable artificial organs can be created. And in fact, in this regard medical science is making progress toward someday solving the organ shortage. In the meantime, if you are uncomfortable with markets determining the price, remember that relying solely on altruism is not enough. If we really want to increase the supply of organs, we need to try incentives and harness behavioral economics. Some proposals along this line include allowing people to receive tax deductions, college scholarships, or guaranteed health care in exchange for donating an organ. A behavioral solution (see Chapter 17) would require people to opt out of organ donations in the event of their death. All these suggestions would reduce the ethical dilemma while still harnessing the power of economics to save lives.

Incentives

ECONOMICS IN THE REAL WORLD

Selling Ova to Pay for College

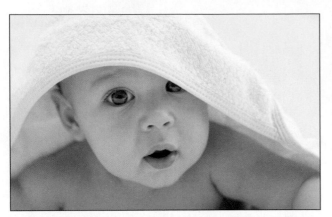

"Baby, baby, baby, oh."

Did you know that young, bright, American women with college loans can help pay off their debts by donating their ova? In 2012, *The Atlantic* reported on this phenomenon, exploring the donation process and experience. The donor is paid to travel to a fertility clinic, and several weeks of hormone treatments begin. Afterward, pairs of the donor's ova are removed surgically, then fertilized in a laboratory and implanted inside the womb of a woman who is infertile. With careful lab work and a little luck, the procedure works. The donor receives between $5,000 and $15,000, depending on her track record as a donor. Those whose ova have been successfully implanted and led to the birth of a healthy child are in high demand.

The procedure is not without risks, including rare but potentially serious complications for donors and a high incidence of multiple births among recipients; additionally, long-term risks are not well understood. And, clearly, volunteering for elective surgery isn't a choice everyone would feel comfortable making. But that said, the existence of a market allows a trade that can greatly benefit both the donor and the recipient. ✳

PRACTICE WHAT YOU KNOW

Human Organ Shortage: Liver Transplants

Most liver transplants make use of organs from cadavers. However, liver transplants are also possible with live donors, who give a portion of their liver to a needy recipient. Donating a live liver involves major surgery that lasts between 4 and 12 hours. The complication rate for the donor is low, but the recovery time is typically two to three months. Not surprisingly, there is still a shortage of live livers for transplant.

Question: What solutions can you think of that would motivate more people to donate part of their liver to help save the life of someone else?

Answer: One answer would be to repeal the National Organ Transplant Act. This move would create a market for livers and establish a price that would eliminate the shortage. Other ways to increase donations would be to allow donors to claim a tax deduction equal to the value of the portion of the liver donated or to receive scholarships for themselves or members of their family.

The Human Organ Black Market

Law & Order: Special Victims Unit

In one episode of *Law & Order: Special Victims Unit*, the officers try to track down a sleazy kidney dealer. What makes the episode compelling is the tension between doing what the law requires—stopping an illegal kidney transplant mid-surgery—and subsequently wrestling with watching the patient suffer as a result. In addition, the officers interview the dealer, the physician, patients on kidney waiting lists, and an administrator of the national kidney wait list. Their opinions, which run a wide gamut, allow the viewer to experience all of the emotions and arguments for and against the purchase of kidneys.

Each character tugs on viewers' emotions in a different way. The sleazy dealer proudly proclaims that he is making his customers happy and that the officers wouldn't be so judgmental if one of their own family members needed a kidney. The physician who does the transplant explains that he is not driven by making money but by saving lives. The patients all know where they can get an illegal kidney, but most accept their fate within the current system.

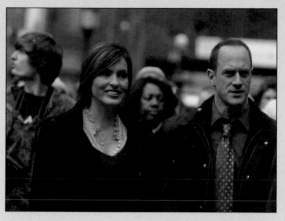

On the track of a black-market kidney dealer.

The administrator of the wait list argues that "they have enough trouble getting people to volunteer as it is. What would happen if donors learned that we had made an exception and approved the transplant of an illegally purchased kidney?" By the end of the episode, we see that the economic and ethical dimensions of the issue are not clear-cut.

Conclusion

When people speak about health care, they often debate the merits of universal health care versus private medical care as if the issue involves just those two factors. That misconception, which frames the political debate about health care, obscures the important economic considerations at work on the micro level. The reality is that the healthcare debate exists on many margins and requires complex trade-offs. The way the various participants deal with different healthcare issues affects how well our nation's overall healthcare system functions. Supply and demand works just fine in explaining the incentives that participants face when considering healthcare options; what complicates the analysis is the impact of third parties on the incentives that patients face.

Health care straddles the boundary between microeconomic analysis, which focuses on individual behavior, and macroeconomics, in which society's overarching concern is how to best spend so large an amount of money. Moreover, health decisions are an unavoidable part of our individual lives.

Obamacare: A Primer

Formally called the Affordable Care Act (ACA), Obamacare is a federal law that provided fundamental reform of the U.S. healthcare and health insurance system, signed by President Barack Obama in 2010. To help you understand the Affordable Care Act, we have created this primer for you.

1. The ACA does not create health insurance. The legislation regulates the health insurance industry and it is designed to increase the quality, affordability, and availability of private insurance.

2. Young adults can stay on their parents' plan until age 26. Before the ACA was passed, it was common for young adults to fall off their parents' plans and, due to low income, forgo health care. Under the ACA, most young adults qualify for federal subsidies or Medicaid through the Health Insurance Marketplace.

3. The ACA created new health insurance exchanges to promote increased enrollment, deliver subsidies, and help spread risk to ensure that the costs associated with expensive medical treatments are shared more broadly across large groups of people, rather than spread across just a few beneficiaries. If you don't have coverage, you can use the Health Insurance Marketplace (healthcare.gov) to buy a private insurance plan. However, if you don't obtain coverage and maintain coverage throughout each year or get an exemption, you must pay a per-month fee on your federal income tax return for every month you are without health insurance. The fee acts as a negative incentive and encourages people to sign up for insurance. The cost of your marketplace health insurance works on a sliding scale. Those who make less pay less. Poorer

Learn about the Affordable Care Act.

Americans are eligible for premium tax credits through the marketplace. These tax credits subsidize the cost of insurance premiums.

4. All new plans sold on or off the marketplace must include a wide range of new benefits. These include wellness visits and preventive tests and treatments at no additional out-of-pocket cost. Preventive care is much cheaper than addressing serious medical issues too late, so this provision of the ACA is intended to lower overall costs.

5. The ACA does away with discrimination based on preexisting conditions and gender, so these factors no longer affect the cost of insurance on or off the marketplace. You can't be denied health coverage based on health status. You can't be dropped from coverage when you are sick. These changes spread risk more evenly and encourage people to get medical care sooner.

Medical expenditures account for one out of every six dollars spent in the United States. Therefore, micro forces that lead to fundamental changes to the healthcare system will have a large impact—a macro effect—on our economy.

ANSWERING THE BIG QUESTIONS

What are the important issues in the healthcare industry?

* The healthcare debate is about efficiency and cost containment. Increases in longevity and quality of life are subject to diminishing returns and require choices with difficult trade-offs.

* The widespread use of insurance alters the incentives that consumers and producers face when making healthcare decisions. Consumers pay premiums up front and much smaller deductibles and copayments when seeking medical care. Producers receive the bulk of their revenue from intermediaries such as insurance companies. The result is a system in which consumers demand more medical care because they are insured and many providers have an incentive to order additional tests or procedures that may not be absolutely necessary.

How does asymmetric information affect healthcare delivery?

* Asymmetric information (adverse selection, the principal-agent problem, and moral hazard) affects incentives in healthcare delivery. Insurance companies try to structure their plans to encourage patients to seek care only when it is needed and also to seek preventive care. The companies can achieve these goals by making many preventive care visits free and establishing deductibles and copayments that are high enough to discourage unnecessary trips to the doctor or a demand for additional procedures.

* Inelastic demand for many medical services, combined with third-party payments that significantly lower out-of-pocket expenses to consumers, gives rise to a serious moral hazard problem in which patients demand more medical care than is medically advisable. To solve a moral hazard problem, it is necessary to fix the incentive structure. Moral hazard explains why many insurance companies encourage preventive care: it lowers medical costs. It also explains why insurance companies impose payment limits on preventable conditions.

How do demand and supply contribute to high medical costs?

* Inelastic demand and third-party payments help explain why medical expenses have risen so rapidly. The combination of third-party payments and inelastic demand for medical care increases the quantity of medical care demanded; both factors also result in increased expenditures. As we learned previously, more demand means higher prices, all else equal.

* In addition, licensing requirements limit the supply of key healthcare providers. Licensing requirements provide a supply-side explanation for increased medical expenditures. In addition, hospital charges are rarely subject to competitive pressures. In many small communities, there is only one local hospital, clinic, or specialist nearby. Providers therefore have market power, which they can use in setting prices.

How do incentives influence the quality of health care?

⁎ A single-payer system makes the government the single buyer, or monopsonist, of most medical care. The government uses its leverage as a monopsonist to set compensation levels for providers below the competitive market wage rate.

⁎ Single-payer systems ration medical services through increased wait times, whereas private healthcare systems ration medical care through prices.

⁎ The demand for many replacement organs exceeds the supply made available each year. However, because of the National Organ Transplant Act of 1984, it is illegal to sell most organs in the United States. This restriction results in thousands of deaths annually, many of which would be preventable if people were allowed to sell organs in legal markets.

CONCEPTS YOU SHOULD KNOW

adverse selection (p. 572)

asymmetric information
  (p. 571)

coinsurance payments (p. 569)

copayments (p. 569)

deductibles (p. 569)

moral hazard (p. 573)

principal-agent problem (p. 572)

single-payer system (p. 581)

QUESTIONS FOR REVIEW

1. What is asymmetric information? How is it relevant to medical care?

2. Give one example each of adverse selection, moral hazard, and the principal-agent problem.

3. For each of the examples you gave in question 2, discuss a solution that lessens the asymmetric information problem.

4. Describe why the marginal product of medical care declines as medical expenditures rise.

5. What are two primary reasons healthcare demand has increased dramatically over the last 20 years?

6. What is a supply-related reason for high medical care costs?

7. What are the two primary ways in which health care is rationed?

STUDY PROBLEMS (✳ solved at the end of the section)

1. Suppose that a medical specialist charges $300 per consultation. If your insurance charges you a $25 copay, what is the marginal cost of your consultation? Suppose that a second patient has a different policy that requires a 25% co-insurance payment, but no copay. What is the second patient's marginal cost of the consultation? Which patient is more likely to see the specialist?

✳ 2. Newer automobiles have many safety features, including antilock brakes, side air bags, traction control, and rear backup sensors, to help prevent accidents. Do these safety features lead the drivers of newer vehicles to drive more safely? In your answer, consider how an increased number of safety features affects the problem of moral hazard.

3. A customer wants a new life insurance policy. Even though the customer's medical records indicate a good health history, the insurance company requires a physical exam before coverage can be extended. Why would the insurance company insist on a physical exam?

4. Indicate whether the following medical services have elastic or inelastic demand.

   a. an annual physical for someone between the ages of 20 and 35
   b. an MRI used to detect cancer
   c. the removal of a noncancerous mole on your back
   d. seeing a physician when your child has a temperature of 104°F

5. Most people have two working kidneys, but humans need only one working kidney to survive. If the sale of kidneys were legalized, what would happen to the price and the number of kidneys sold in the market? Would a shortage of kidneys continue to exist? Explain your response.

✳ 6. An isolated community has one hospital. The next closest hospital is 2 hours away. Given what you have learned about monopoly, what prices would you expect the hospital to charge? How much care would you expect it to provide? Compare the prices and amount of care provided to those of a comparably sized hospital in a major metropolitan area where competition is prevalent.

7. One insurance plan costs $100 a month and has a $50 copayment for all services. Another insurance plan costs $50 a month and requires patients to pay a 15% coinsurance. A consumer is trying to decide which plan to purchase. Which plan would the consumer select with an anticipated $200 per month in medical bills? What about $600 per month in medical bills? Set up an equation to determine the monthly amount of medical expenses at which the consumer would be indifferent between the two plans.

8. For each of the following situations, determine whether adverse selection, moral hazard, or the principal-agent problem is at work.

a. You decide to buy a scalped ticket before a concert, but you are not entirely sure the ticket is legitimate.

b. A contractor takes a long time to finish the construction work he promised after you gave him his final payment.

c. You hire a neighborhood teenager to mow your grass once a week over the summer while you are traveling. The teenager mows your grass every three weeks instead.

✳ 9. "To economists, human life is not of infinite value." Explain this statement and its economic implications for end-of-life care.

10. What characteristics make the market for health care different from other markets?

SOLVED PROBLEMS

2. When drivers feel safer, they drive faster—not more safely. The higher speed offsets the safety gain from safety features that help prevent accidents or make them survivable. Drivers of vehicles who feel especially safe are more likely to take on hazardous conditions and become involved in accidents. In other words, they alter their behavior when driving a safer car. The change in behavior is evidence of a moral hazard problem.

6. Because the demand for medical care is quite inelastic, an isolated hospital with significant monopoly power will charge more and offer fewer services. In contrast, a comparably sized hospital in a major metropolitan area where competition is prevalent is forced to charge the market price and offer more services to attract consumers.

9. Human life is not of infinite value because we live in a world of trade-offs. An "infinite value" implies that the value is so high that all medical paths are worth pursuing. However, one must be mindful of the marginal cost of care versus the amount of additional life that end-of-life care buys. This consideration is especially important at the end of life when extraordinary medical efforts might mean only a few extra days of low-quality life. The law of diminishing returns applies, and the application of this economic principle suggests that resources should be redirected from end-of-life care to preventive care with larger returns.

Macroeconomic BASICS

Introduction to Macroeconomics and Gross Domestic Product

There is no reliable way to gauge the health of an economy.
You may notice that people often disagree on how the economy is doing. This might give you the impression that we aren't able to measure the economy's performance very well. But in fact, there is a reliable and objective measure of a country's economic performance. This measure is the primary focus of this chapter.

How can you tell if you have a good day at work or school? The answer is often tied to your productivity—how much you get done. Or the answer may be related to how much income you earn. Productivity and income are also useful measures for evaluating the performance of an entire economy, because a productive economy is a healthy economy that generates income for its workers. This chapter describes how economists measure the health of an economy using a measure of both output and income. This measure, called gross domestic product, or GDP, is the primary focus of this chapter.

The U.S. economy produces almost one-fifth of all goods and services in the world.

BIG QUESTIONS

* ✳ **How is macroeconomics different from microeconomics?**
* ✳ **What does GDP tell us about the economy?**
* ✳ **How is GDP computed?**
* ✳ **What are some shortcomings of GDP data?**

How Is Macroeconomics Different from Microeconomics?

Macroeconomics is the study of the economy of an entire nation or society. This is different from microeconomics, which considers the behavior of individual people, firms, and industries. In microeconomics, you study what people buy, what jobs they take, and how they distribute their income between purchases and savings; you also examine the decisions of firms and how they compete with other firms. In macroeconomics, you consider what happens when the *national* output of goods and services rises and falls, when overall *national* employment levels rise and fall, and when the *overall* price level goes up and down.

Here's a more specific example. In microeconomics, you study the markets for salmon fillets (an example from Chapter 3). You study the behavior of people who consume salmon and firms that sell salmon—demanders and suppliers. Then you bring them together to see how the equilibrium price depends on the behavior of both demanders and suppliers.

Macroeconomics is the study of the broader economy. It looks at the big picture created by all markets in the economy—the markets for salmon, coffee,

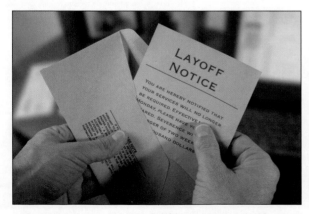

A pink slip for one person is a microeconomic issue . . .

. . . but widespread unemployment is a macroeconomic issue.

TABLE 19.1		
Comparing the Perspectives of Microeconomics and Macroeconomics		
Topic	**Microeconomics**	**Macroeconomics**
Income	The income of a person or the revenue of a firm	The income of an entire nation or a national economy
Output	The production of a single worker, firm, or industry	The production of an entire economy
Employment	The job status and decisions of an individual or firm	The job status of a national population, particularly the number of people who are unemployed
Prices	The price of a single good	The combined prices of all goods in an economy

computers, cars, haircuts, and health care, to name just a few. In macroeconomics, we examine *total* output in an economy rather than just a single firm or industry. We look at *total* employment across the economy rather than employment at a single firm. We consider *all* prices in the economy rather than the price of just one product, such as salmon. To illustrate these differences, Table 19.1 compares a selection of topics from the different perspectives of microeconomics and macroeconomics.

What Does GDP Tell Us about the Economy?

Economists measure the total output of an economy as a gauge of its overall health. An economy that produces a large amount of valuable output is a healthy economy. If output falls for a certain period, there is something wrong in the economy. The same is true for individuals. If you have a fever for a few days, your output goes down—you don't go to the gym, you study less, and you might call in sick for work. We care about measuring our nation's economic output because it gives us a good sense of the overall health of the economy, much like a thermometer that measures your body temperature can give you an indication of your overall health. In this section, we introduce and explain our measure of an economy's output.

Production Equals Income

This chapter is about the measurement of a nation's output, but it's also about the measurement of a nation's income. There's a good reason to cover output and income together: they are essentially the same thing. Nations and individuals that produce large amounts of highly valued output are relatively wealthy. Nations and individuals that don't produce much highly valued output are relatively poor. This is no coincidence.

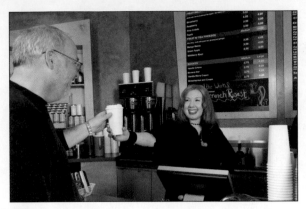

Adding up dollar sales is a way of measuring both production and income.

Gross domestic product (GDP) is the market value of all final goods and services produced within a country during a specific period.

Let's say you open a coffee shop in your college town. You buy or rent the supplies and equipment you need to produce coffee—everything from coffee beans and espresso machines to electricity. You hire the workers you need to keep the business running. Using these resources, you produce output such as cappuccinos, espressos, and draft coffee. On the first day, you sell 600 coffee drinks at an average price of $4 each, for a total of $2,400. This dollar figure is a measure of your firm's production, or output, on that day, and it is also a measure of the income received. You use the income to pay for your resources and to pay yourself. If you sell even more coffee on the second day, the income generated increases. If you sell less, the income goes down.

The same holds true for nations. **Gross domestic product (GDP)** is the market value of all final goods and services produced within a nation during a specific period of time—typically, a year. GDP is the primary measure of a nation's output.

GDP is the sum of all the output from coffee shops, doctor's offices, software firms, fast-food restaurants, and all the other firms that produce goods and services within a nation's borders. The sale of this output becomes income to the firms' owners and the resource suppliers. This dual function of GDP is part of the reason we focus on GDP as a barometer of the economy. When GDP goes up, national output and income are both higher. When GDP falls, the economy is producing less than before, and total national income is falling.

Three Uses of GDP Data

Before analyzing the components of GDP, let's see why GDP is such an important indicator. In this section, we briefly explain the three primary uses of GDP data: to measure living standards, to measure economic growth, and to determine whether an economy is experiencing recession or expansion.

Measuring Living Standards

Imagine two very different nations. In the first nation, people work long hours in physically taxing labor, and yet their pay enables them to purchase only life's barest necessities—meager amounts of food, clothing, and shelter. In this nation, very few individuals can afford a high school education or health care from a trained physician. In the second nation, virtually no one starves, people tend to work in an air-conditioned environment, almost everyone graduates from high school, and many receive college degrees. The first nation experiences life similar to that in the United States two centuries ago; the second describes life in the United States today. Everyone would agree that living standards are higher in the United States today, because most people can afford more of what they generally desire: goods, services, and leisure.

We can see these differences in living standards in GDP data. Indeed, GDP in the modern United States is much higher than it was in nineteenth-century America. Both output and income are higher, which indicates that living standards are also higher. While not perfect, GDP offers us a way of estimating living standards across both time and place.

Let's look at the nations with highest GDP in the world. Table 19.2 lists the world's largest economies by GDP in 2013. Column 3 shows GDP for the top 11 economies, giving a picture of each nation's overall output and income. Total world GDP in 2013 was $76 trillion, which means that the United States alone produced almost 20% of all final goods and services in the world. The most significant recent movement on this list has occurred in China: in 1999, China ranked seventh, but by 2013, it had moved into second place.

Although total GDP is important, it is not the best indicator of living standards for a typical person. Table 19.2 reveals that in 2013, China produced about twice as much GDP as Japan, yet China's population was about 10 times the population of Japan. If we divide each nation's GDP by its population, we find that in Japan there was over $38,000 of GDP (or income) for every person, and in China only about $6,800 per person.

When we want to gauge living standards for an average person, we compute **per capita GDP**, which is GDP per person. That is, we divide the country's total GDP by its population. Per capita GDP is listed in the last column of Table 19.2.

Per capita GDP is GDP per person.

TABLE 19.2

World's Largest Economies by GDP, 2013

(1) Rank	(2) Country	(3) 2013 GDP (billions of U.S. dollars)	(4) Per capita GDP (U.S. dollars)
1	United States	$16,768	$53,042
2	China	9,240	6,807
3	Japan	4,920	38,634
4	Germany	3,730	46,269
5	France	2,806	42,503
6	United Kingdom	2,678	41,787
7	Brazil	2,246	11,208
8	Italy	2,149	35,926
9	Russia	2,097	18,783
10	India	1,877	1,499
11	Canada	1,827	51,958

Source: World Bank. All data are in 2013 U.S. dollars.

Measuring Economic Growth

We also use GDP data to measure economic growth. You can think of *economic growth* as changes in living standards over time. When economies grow, living standards rise, and this outcome is evident in GDP data.

Figure 19.1 shows the change in real per capita GDP in the United States from 1965 to 2015. The overall positive slope of the curve indicates that U.S. living standards rose over the last 50 years, even though growth was not positive in every year. The data show that income for the average person in 2015 was more than double what it was in 1965. So the typical person can now afford about twice as much education, food, vacations, air-conditioning, houses, and cars as the average person in 1965.

You might notice that in this section we have added the word "real" to our discussion of GDP. Figure 19.1 plots *real* per capita GDP. Because we are now looking at data over several years, we have to adjust the GDP data for price changes that occur over time. Prices of goods and services almost always rise through time because of inflation. **Inflation** is the growth in the overall level of prices in an economy. Because GDP is calculated using market values (prices) of goods and services, inflation causes GDP to go up even if there is no change in the quantity of goods and services produced. Therefore, when we look at GDP data over time, we have to adjust it for the effects of inflation. **Real GDP** is GDP adjusted for changes in prices. We discuss how to compute real GDP later in this chapter. For now, just note that any time we evaluate GDP figures across different time periods, we must use real GDP to account for inflation.

Economic growth is measured as the percentage change in real per capita GDP. Notice that this measure starts with GDP data but then adjusts for both population growth and inflation. Given this definition, you should view

Inflation is the growth in the overall level of prices in an economy.

Real GDP is GDP adjusted for changes in prices.

Economic growth is measured as the percentage change in real per capita GDP.

FIGURE 19.1

U.S. Real Per Capita GDP, 1965–2015

The positive slope in this graph indicates increased living standards in the United States since 1965. It shows that the average person earns significantly more income today, even after adjusting for inflation. Over this period, real GDP per person increased by an average of 2% per year.

Source: U.S. Bureau of Economic Analysis; U.S. Census Bureau.

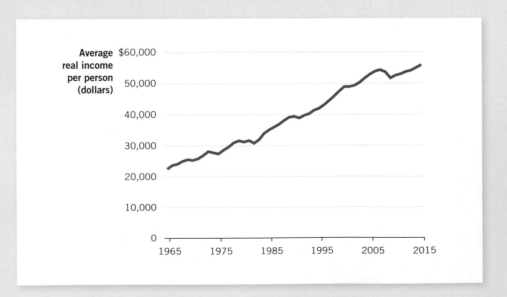

Figure 19.1 as a picture of economic growth in the United States. But despite what you see in the U.S. GDP data, you should not presume that economic growth is automatic or even typical. Figure 19.2 shows the experience of six other nations with six distinct experiences. The real per capita GDP in Poland, Turkey, and Mexico rose significantly, more than doubling between 1950 and 2008. India's remained very low for many years and then recently began to grow. Sadly, the data for Nicaragua and Somalia indicate that citizens in these nations are poorer now than they were in 1950.

Economic growth is one of the primary topics that macroeconomists study. In Chapters 24 and 25, we consider the factors that lead to the type of growth that the United States, Poland, Turkey, Mexico, and, more recently, India have enjoyed. We also consider why economies like those of Nicaragua and Somalia struggle to grow. Because real per capita GDP measures living standards, these issues are critical to real people's lives around the globe.

Measuring Business Cycles

We have seen that GDP data are used to measure living standards and economic growth. GDP is also used to determine whether an economy is expanding or contracting in the short run. In recent years, this use of GDP has received a lot of media attention because of concerns about recessions. A **recession** is a short-term economic downturn that typically lasts about 6 to 18 months. Even the mere threat of recession strikes fear in people's hearts because income levels fall and many individuals lose their jobs or cannot find work during recessions. The U.S. recession that began in December 2007

A **recession** is a short-term economic downturn.

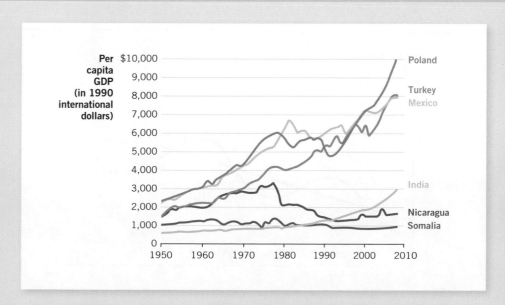

FIGURE 19.2

Real Per Capita GDP in Six Nations, 1950–2008

Growth in real per capita GDP in six nations shows that growth is not guaranteed. The levels for Poland, Turkey, and Mexico more than doubled since 1950. And while India began to grow more recently, both Nicaragua and Somalia have lost ground.

Source: The Maddison-Project, http://www.ggdc.net/maddison/maddison-project/home.htm, 2013 version.

The **Great Recession** was the U.S. recession lasting from December 2007 to June 2009.

A **business cycle** is a short-run fluctuation in economic activity.

An **economic expansion** is a phase of the business cycle during which economic activity is increasing.

An **economic contraction** is a phase of the business cycle during which economic activity is decreasing.

and lasted until June 2009 has been dubbed the **Great Recession** because of its length and depth. It lasted for 19 months, and real GDP fell by more than 8% in the last three months of 2008. In addition, the recovery from the Great Recession was very slow.

Even if an economy is expanding in the long run, it is normal for it to experience temporary downturns. A **business cycle** is a short-run fluctuation in economic activity. Figure 19.3 illustrates a theoretical business cycle in relationship to a long-term trend in real GDP growth. The straight line represents the long-run trend of real GDP. The slope of the trend line is the average long-run growth of real GDP. For the United States, this is about 3% per year. But real GDP doesn't typically grow at exactly 3% per year. Instead of tracking exactly along the trend line, the economy experiences fluctuations in output. The wavy line represents the actual path of real GDP over time. It climbs to peaks when GDP growth is positive and falls to troughs when output growth is negative.

The peaks and troughs divide the business cycle into two phases: expansions and contractions. An **economic expansion** occurs from the bottom of a trough to the next peak, when economic activity is increasing. After a certain period, the economy enters a recession, or an **economic contraction**—the period extending from the peak downward to the trough. During this phase, economic activity is declining. During expansions, jobs are relatively easy to find and average income levels climb. During contractions, more people lose their jobs and income levels often fall.

Figure 19.3 makes it look like business cycles are uniform and predictable, but the reality is very different. Figure 19.4 plots U.S. real GDP over time, with contractionary periods—the recessions—shaded. GDP consistently declines during these recessionary periods, but they don't occur in a consistent, predictable pattern. You can easily spot the Great Recession, which began in December 2007 and lasted through June 2009.

FIGURE 19.3

The Business Cycle

The long-run trend of GDP shows consistent growth. The business cycle reflects the fluctuations that an economy typically exhibits. Economic activity increases during the expansion period of the business cycle, but declines during the contraction phase. In real life, the cycle is not nearly as smooth and easy to spot as pictured here.

FIGURE 19.4

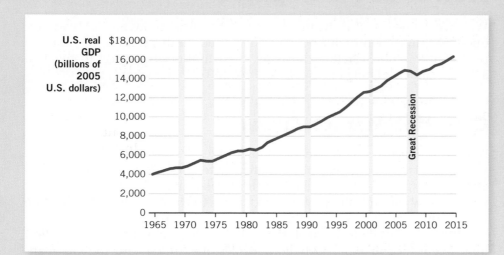

U.S. Real GDP and Recessions, 1965–2015

Over time, U.S. real GDP fluctuates. The shaded areas indicate periods of recession, when real GDP declines. The Great Recession, which began in December 2007 and lasted through June 2009, was a particularly deep and lengthy modern recession.

Source: U.S. Bureau of Economic Analysis.

PRACTICE WHAT YOU KNOW

Three Uses of GDP Data: GDP as an Economic Barometer

Question: Which of the three uses of GDP data was applied in each case described below?

a. In 2011, many analysts claimed that the economy of India began slowing as GDP growth declined from 8.4% in 2010 to 6.9% in mid-2011.

b. Nicaragua and Haiti are the poorest nations in the Western Hemisphere, with annual 2013 per capita GDP of only $1,851 and $820, respectively.

c. The economy of Italy has slowed considerably over the past two decades, as evidenced by an average growth of real GDP of only 1.25% per year from 1990 to 2010.

What does GDP data tell us about Haiti?

Answers:

a. This case reflects the use of GDP data to identify and measure business cycles and indicates a potential recession. The statement describes a short-run window of data.

b. This statement uses data to show living standards. The numbers indicate that average Nicaraguans and Haitians have to live on very small amounts of income each year.

c. This observation considers growth rates over 20 years, which means that GDP was applied to look at long-run economic growth.

How Is GDP Computed?

We have defined GDP as the market value of all final goods and services produced within a country during a specific period. In this section, we examine the definition more carefully, breaking the definition into pieces to give you a deeper understanding of what is counted in GDP and what is not.

Counting Market Values

Nations produce a wide variety of goods and services, which are measured in various units. Computation of GDP literally requires the addition of apples and oranges, as well as every other final good and service produced in a nation. How can we add everything from cars to corn to haircuts to gasoline to prescription drugs in a way that makes sense? Certainly, we can't just add quantities. For example, in 2014, the United States produced about 8 million motor vehicles and about 12 billion bushels of corn. Looking only at quantities, one might conclude that because the nation produced about 1,500 bushels of corn for every car, corn production is much more important to the U.S. economy. But of course this conclusion is wrong; a bushel of corn is not worth nearly as much as a car.

To add corn and cars and the other goods and services in GDP, economists use market values. That is, we include not only the quantity data but also the price of the good or service. Figure 19.5 offers an example with fairly realistic data. If corn production is 12 billion bushels and these bushels sell for $5 each, the contribution of corn to GDP is $60 billion. If car production

FIGURE 19.5

Using Market Values to Compute GDP

GDP reflects market values added together for many types of goods. In this simple example, the contribution to GDP from corn production is $60 billion, and the contribution from car production is $240 billion.

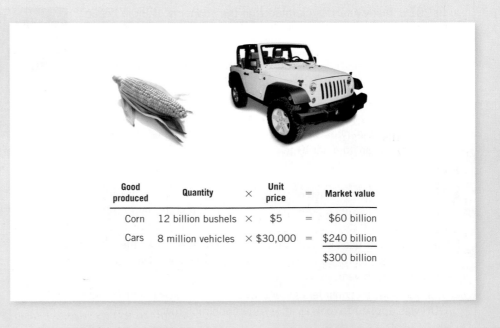

Good produced	Quantity	×	Unit price	=	Market value
Corn	12 billion bushels	×	$5	=	$60 billion
Cars	8 million vehicles	×	$30,000	=	$240 billion
					$300 billion

is 8 million vehicles and cars sell for $30,000 each, the contribution of cars to GDP is $240 billion. If these were the only goods produced in a given year, GDP would be $60 billion + $240 billion = $300 billion.

As we have said, GDP reflects market values, and these values include both price and quantity information. Remember that one purpose of GDP data is to evaluate the health of an economy. A nation's economic health depends on the total quantities of goods and services produced, as represented in the Quantity column of Figure 19.5. Market values allow us to add together many types of goods. At the same time, market values rely on prices, which can rise when inflation occurs. What if the prices of both cars and corn rise but the quantities produced remain unchanged? In that case, GDP will rise even though the production level stays the same. This is why we compute real GDP by adjusting for inflation (we discuss how to adjust for inflation later in this chapter).

Including Goods and Services

Physical goods are easy to visualize, but less than half of U.S. GDP comes from goods; the majority comes from services. **Services** are outputs that provide benefits without producing a tangible product. Consider a service like a visit to your doctor for a physical. The doctor examines you and offers some medical advice, but you leave with no tangible output.

Services are outputs that provide benefits without producing a tangible product.

When considering the proportion of goods and services in U.S. GDP, it is important to note that the composition of U.S. GDP has evolved over time. In the past, the dominant U.S. industries were manufactured goods such as autos, steel, and household goods. Today, a majority of U.S. GDP is service output such as medical, financial, transportation, education, and technology services. Figure 19.6 shows services as a share of U.S. GDP since 1950. As you can see, service output now accounts for about two-thirds of all U.S. output.

Most economists are not concerned about this move toward a service-dominated economy, but others lament this shift. These others remember that manufacturing industries were a source of prosperity for the U.S. economy and then assume they are still necessary for future growth. This is not a partisan issue; politicians from both major parties take this stand. However, this argument does not allow for the nature of modern economic growth.

A century ago, the significant economic growth in the United States came from manufacturing output. But two centuries ago, U.S. economic growth came from agricultural output. Economies evolve. The fact that innovations in manufacturing spurred past growth does not mean that future growth should not occur through services.

When you visit the grocery store, you often purchase both goods (groceries) and services (clerking and bagging).

FIGURE 19.6

Services as a Share of U.S. GDP, 1950–2013

A century ago, the U.S. economy produced mostly manufactured goods. This trend has shifted in recent decades, and now services account for about two-thirds of U.S. output.

Source: U.S. Bureau of Economic Analysis.

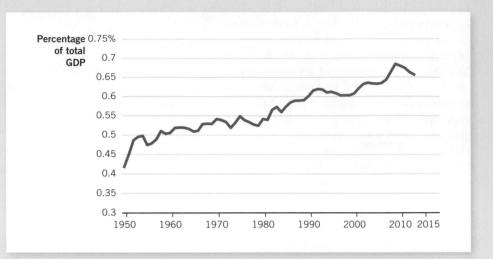

Including Only Final Goods and Services

As we have said, GDP is the summation of spending on goods and services. However, not *all* spending is included. To see why, consider all the spending involved in building a single good—a cell phone. Table 19.3 outlines some intermediate steps required to produce a cell phone that sells for $199. In the process of producing this phone, the manufacturer uses many intermediate goods. **Intermediate goods** are goods that firms repackage or bundle with other goods for sale at a later stage. For example, the cell phone's outer case and keyboard are intermediate goods because the phone manufacturer combines them with other intermediate goods, such as the operating system, to produce the cell phone, which is the final good. **Final goods** are goods that are sold to final users. The sale of the cell phone is included as part of GDP, but the value of the intermediate goods is not.

Intermediate goods are goods that firms repackage or bundle with other goods for sale at a later stage.

Final goods are goods sold to final users.

What happens if we count the value added during each intermediate step in making a cell phone? We start with the outer case and keyboard, which costs $5 to produce. Once the case and keyboard have been purchased, the component hardware, which costs $10, must be installed, bringing the value of the phone to $15. The operating system software, which costs $15, is then installed, raising the cost to $30. Next, a service provider purchases the phone and connects it to a cellular network; this costs another $49, raising the phone's cost to $79. Finally, the phone is sold to the consumer for $199. The final value in this string of events, the retail price, is the true value that the cell phone creates in the economy. If we counted the value of each intermediate step, we would arrive

This Intel processor is an intermediate good, buried inside your computer.

TABLE 19.3

Intermediate Steps in Cellphone Production

Steps	Value added during step	Prices of completed steps
1. Assemble outer case and keyboard.	$5	$5
2. Prepare internal hardware.	10	15
3. Install operating system.	15	30
4. Connect to network.	49	79
5. Transact retail sale.	120	199
Total	$199	$338

at a total of $338, which would overstate the phone's value in the economy because it sells for only $199.

We cannot get an accurate measure of GDP by summing all the sales made throughout the economy during the year, because many of them reflect intermediate steps in the production process. It is possible to get an accurate measurement of GDP by taking the sale price of the final good or by taking the value added at each step along the way, but not both; that would be double counting. For example, the operating system (OS) is part of the phone, and its value is included as part of the phone in the final sale. If we counted the sale of the OS to the phone manufacturer and then again as a part of the phone, we would be double counting and thus overstating GDP.

Within a Country

The word "domestic" in the phrase "gross domestic product" is important. GDP includes only goods and services produced domestically, or within a nation's physical borders. The output of foreign-owned firms that is produced inside the United States is included in U.S. GDP, but the output of U.S. firms that is produced overseas is included in the GDP of the overseas nation. For example, Nike is a U.S. firm that produces shoes in Thailand. Thus, all the shoes produced in Thailand count as GDP for Thailand.

Gross national product (GNP), an alternative measure of national output, is the output produced by workers and resources owned by residents of the nation. Thus, shoes produced by Nike in Thailand would count as part of U.S. GNP, since the owners of Nike are citizens (and residents) of the United States. Many nations prefer GDP to GNP because much of their domestic output is produced by

Gross national product (GNP) is the output produced by workers and resources owned by residents of the nation.

Nike shoes produced in Thailand count as GDP for Thailand.

foreign-owned firms (like Nike shoes produced in Thailand). For these nations, GDP is larger than GNP. These countries prefer GDP because it measures the production that takes place within their borders. Thus, GDP has become the standard measure of international output. As national economies have become more globalized with more production taking place outside the home country, GDP is now used more often than GNP to measure a nation's overall production.

Including Only Production from a Particular Period

GDP only counts goods and services that are produced during a given period. Goods or services produced in earlier years do not count in the current year's GDP. For instance, when a new car is produced, it adds to GDP in the year it is sold. However, a used car that is resold does not count in current GDP because it was already counted in GDP for the year when it was first produced and sold. If we counted the used car when it was resold, we would be counting that car as part of GDP twice—double counting—even though it was produced only once.

In addition, sales of financial assets such as stocks and bonds do not count toward GDP. After all, these kinds of sales, which we will discuss in Chapter 23, do not create anything new; they simply transfer ownership from one person to another. In this way, they are like used goods. However, brokerage fees do count as payment for the brokerage service, and they are included in GDP.

We have now examined the GDP definition in greater detail. In the next section, we consider the way GDP is actually measured by adding together different types of expenditures.

Ice cream cones count as nondurable consumption goods.

Looking at GDP as Different Types of Expenditures

In this section, we look more closely at the different categories of goods and services included in GDP. The Bureau of Economic Analysis (BEA) is the U.S. government agency that tallies GDP data in a process called *national income accounting*. The BEA breaks GDP into four major categories: consumption (C), investment (I), government purchases (G), and net exports (NX). Using this framework, it is possible to express GDP as the following equation:

(Equation 19.1)

$$GDP = C + I + G + NX$$

Table 19.4 details the composition of U.S. GDP in 2015. For that year, total GDP was $17,937.8 billion, or almost $18 trillion. To get a sense of what that amount represents, imagine laying 18 trillion one-dollar bills from end to end. That would be enough to cover every U.S. highway, street, and county road more than twice!

Looking at Table 19.4, you can see that consumption is by far the largest component of GDP, followed by government purchases and then by investment. Note that the value of net exports is negative. This negative value occurs because the United States imports more goods than it exports. Let's take a closer look at each of these four components of GDP.

TABLE 19.4

Composition of U.S. GDP, 2015

Category	Individual expenditures (billions of dollars)	Total expenditures per category (billions of dollars)	Percentage of GDP
Consumption (C)		**$12,267.9**	68.4%
Durable goods	$1,328.8		
Non-durable goods	2,649.8		
Services	8,289.3		
Investment (I)		**3,017.8**	16.8%
Fixed investment	2,911.3		
Change in business inventories	106.5		
Government purchases (G)		**3,184**	17.8%
Federal	1,224.7		
State and local	1,959.3		
Net exports (NX)		**−531.9**	−3.0%
Exports	2,253		
Imports	−2,784.9		
Total GDP		**$17,937.8**	100.0%

Source: U.S. Bureau of Economic Analysis.

Refrigerators count as durable consumption goods.

Consumption

Consumption (C) is the purchase of final goods and services by households, with the exception of new housing. Most people spend a large majority of their income on consumption goods and services. Consumption goods include everything from groceries to automobiles. You can see in Table 19.4 that services are a very big portion of consumption spending. They include things such as haircuts, doctor's visits, and help from a real estate agent.

Consumption goods can be divided into two categories: nondurable and durable. *Nondurable* consumption goods are consumed over a short period, and *durable* consumption goods are consumed over a long period. This distinction is important when the economy swings back and forth between good times and bad times. Sales of durable goods—for example, automobiles, appliances, and computers—are subject to significant cyclical fluctuations that correspond to the health of the economy. Because durable goods are generally designed to last for many years, consumers tend to purchase more

Consumption is the purchase of final goods and services by households, excluding new housing.

When firms buy tools to aid in production, they are making an investment.

Investment is private spending on tools, plant, and equipment used to produce future output.

Government spending includes spending by all levels of government on final goods and services.

of these goods when the economy is strong. In contrast, when the economy is weak, they put off purchases of durables and make what they already have last longer—for example, working with an old computer for another year rather than replacing it with a new model right away. However, nondurables don't last very long, so consumers must often purchase them regardless of economic conditions.

Investment

When you hear the word "investment," you likely think of savings or stocks and bonds. But in macroeconomics, **investment** (I) refers to private spending on tools, plant, and equipment used to produce future output. Investment can be something as simple as the purchase of a shovel, a tractor, or a personal computer to help a small business produce goods and services for its customers. But investment also includes more complex endeavors, such as the construction of large factories. For example, when Pfizer builds a new factory to manufacture a new drug, it is making an investment. When Walmart builds a new warehouse, that expense is an investment. And when a family purchases a newly built house, that expense also counts as an investment. This way of accounting for house purchases may seem odd, since most of us think of a home purchase as something that is consumed; but in the national income accounts, such a purchase counts as an investment.

Investment also includes all purchases by businesses that add to their inventories. For example, in preparation for the Christmas buying season, an electronics retailer will order more TVs, cameras, and computers. GDP rises when business inventories increase. GDP is calculated this way because we want to measure output in the period it is produced. Investment in inventory is just one more way that firms spend today to increase output in the future.

Government Spending

National, state, and local governments purchase many goods and services. These purchases are included in GDP as **government spending** (G), which includes spending by all levels of government on final goods and services. For example, every government employee receives a salary, which is considered a part of GDP. Similarly, governments spend money purchasing buildings, equipment, and supplies from private-sector firms. Governments also make expenditures on public works projects, including national defense, highway construction, schools, and post offices. *Transfer payments* that the government makes to households, such as welfare payments, social security, and unemployment insurance, do not count as GDP, since they are not direct purchases of new goods and services.

Net Exports

The United States produces some goods and services that are exported to other countries, and it imports some goods and services that are produced elsewhere. Only exports are counted in GDP because they are produced in the United States. In contrast, imports are produced elsewhere but are used domestically within the United States. Because our goal is to measure domestic production accurately, GDP includes only **net exports** (NX), which are total exports of final goods and services minus total imports of final goods and services. We can write the calculation of net exports in equation form as

$$\text{net exports}(NX) = \text{exports} - \text{imports}$$

When spending on imports is larger than spending on exports, net exports are negative. Net exports are typically negative for the United States.

Notice that imports enter the GDP calculations as a negative value: GDP = C + I + G + (exports − imports). From this equation, it would be easy to conclude that imports are harmful to an economy because they seem to reduce GDP. However, adding the different components together (C, I, G, and NX) in the process of national income accounting really is just that—accounting. The primary goal of the national income accounts is to keep a record of how people are buying the goods and services produced in the United States. More imports coming in means more goods and services for people in the United States. All other things being equal, imports do not make us worse off.

Real GDP: Adjusting GDP for Price Changes

According to the Bureau of Economic Analysis, in 2009, the U.S. economy produced GDP of $14.4 trillion. Just six years later, in 2015, it produced almost $18 trillion. That's a 24% increase in just six years. Is that really possible? Think about this question in long-run historical terms. Is it possible that the nation's economy grew to $14.4 trillion over more than two centuries, but then just six years later grew to $18 trillion? If we look more closely, we'll see that much of the recent increase in GDP is actually due to inflation.

The raw GDP data, based on market values, is computed on the basis of the prices of goods and services current at the time GDP is calculated. Economists refer to these prices as the *current prices*. The GDP calculated from current prices is called **nominal GDP**. Figure 19.7 compares U.S. nominal and real GDP from 2009 to 2015. Notice that nominal GDP rises much faster than real GDP. While nominal GDP rose by 24%, real GDP increased by 13%. The difference between these percentages reflects inflation.

Computing nominal GDP is straightforward: we add the market values (actual prices) of all final goods and services. But to compute real GDP, we also need a measure of overall prices, known as a price level. A **price level** is an index of the average prices of goods and services throughout the economy. It goes up when prices generally rise, and it falls when prices across the economy fall. Chapter 21 explores prices and the calculation of price levels. For now, just take the price data as given, and think of the price level as an indicator of changes in the general level of all prices across the economy.

The price level we use to adjust GDP data, the **GDP deflator**, includes the prices of the final goods and services counted in GDP. The GDP deflator "deflates" all the price inflation out of nominal GDP so that we can see real

Net exports are total exports of final goods and services minus total imports of final goods and services.

(Equation 19.2)

Nominal GDP is GDP measured in current prices and not adjusted for inflation.

A **price level** is an index of the average prices of goods and services throughout the economy.

The **GDP deflator** is a measure of the price level that is used to calculate real GDP.

FIGURE 19.7

U.S. Nominal and Real GDP, 2009–2015

Nominal GDP typically rises faster than real GDP because nominal GDP reflects both growth in real production and growth in prices (inflation). From 2009 to 2015, nominal GDP in the United States rose by 24%, but nearly half of that increase was due to inflation. The increase in real GDP during the same period was 13%.

Source: U.S. Bureau of Economic Analysis.

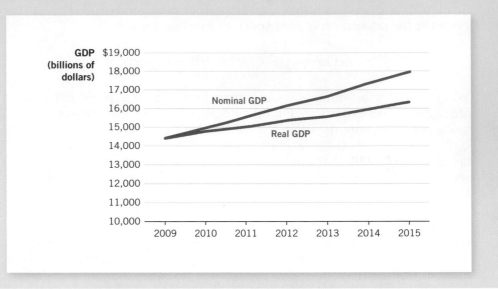

GDP. Let's look at some actual data. Table 19.5 shows U.S. nominal GDP and price level data from 2006 to 2015. Looking at just two lines, for example, we can see that the price level was set at 100.0 in 2009 and rose to 101 in 2010. These numbers indicate that, on average, prices across the economy rose by 1% (101 − 100) between 2009 and 2010.

To compute real GDP, we use the current prices of goods and services and then adjust them to prices from an agreed-upon common time period, or *base period*. We do this in two steps:

1. Divide nominal GDP by the price level.
2. Multiply the result by the price level (100) from the base period.

TABLE 19.5

U.S. Nominal GDP and Price Level, 2006–2015

Year	Nominal GDP (billions of dollars)	Price Level (GDP deflator)
2006	$13,855.9	95
2007	14,477.6	97
2008	14,718.6	99
2009	14,418.7	100
2010	14,964.4	101
2011	15,517.9	103
2012	16,155.3	105
2013	16,663.2	107
2014	17,348.1	109
2015	17,937.8	110

Source: U.S. Bureau of Economic Analysis.

Putting these two steps together, we compute real GDP for any time period (t) as

$$\text{real GDP}_t = \underbrace{\frac{\text{nominal GDP}_t}{\text{price level}_t}}_{\text{Step 1}} \underbrace{\times\ 100}_{\text{Step 2}}$$

(Equation 19.3)

For example, nominal GDP in 2015 was $17,938 billion, and the price level was 110. To convert nominal GDP to real GDP, we divide by 110 and then multiply by 100:

$$\text{real GDP}_{2015} = \frac{\$17{,}938}{110} \times 100 = \$16{,}307 \text{ billion}$$

Table 19.6 illustrates both steps of this conversion.

The figure $16,307 billion is the U.S. real GDP in 2015, adjusted for inflation. Economists and the financial media use other terms for real GDP; sometimes they might say "GDP in 2009 prices" or "GDP in constant 2009 dollars." Whenever you consider changes in GDP over time, you should look for these terms to ensure that the data are not biased by price changes.

Growth Rates

For many macroeconomic applications, it is useful to calculate growth rates. For example, let's say you read that the GDP in Mexico in 2013 was about $1.3 trillion. You might consider this information to be troubling for the future of the Mexican economy, since $1.3 trillion is very small compared with U.S. GDP. But maybe you also read that Mexico's GDP grew by 6.3% in 2013 (it did!). In that case, you will probably get a different, and more positive, impression. In general, growth rates often convey additional illuminating information.

TABLE 19.6

Converting Nominal GDP into Real GDP

Data for 2015:
Nominal GDP = $17,938 billion
Price level (GDP deflator) = 110

General steps	Our example
Step 1: Filter out current prices.	$17,938 ÷ 110 = $163.07
Step 2: Input base-period prices.	$163.07 × 100 = $16,307

Growth rates are calculated as percentage changes in a variable. For example, the growth of U.S. nominal GDP in 2015 is computed as

(Equation 19.4)

$$\text{nominal GDP growth in 2015} = \frac{\text{GDP}_{2015} - \text{GDP}_{2014}}{\text{GDP}_{2014}} \times 100$$

Unless noted otherwise, the data come from the end of the period. Therefore, the nominal GDP growth computed by Equation 19.4 tells us the percentage change in U.S. GDP from the end of 2014 to the end of 2015, or over the course of 2015. Using actual data, the calculation is

nominal GDP growth in 2015 = % change in nominal GDP

$$= \frac{17{,}937.8 - 17{,}348.1}{17{,}348.1} \times 100 = 3.4\%$$

We can also compute the growth rate of the price level (GDP deflator) for 2015:

price level growth rate = % change in price level

$$= \frac{110 - 109}{109} \times 100 = 1.0\%$$

This means that throughout the U.S. economy in 2015, inflation was 1%.

Armed with these two computations, we can derive one more useful formula for evaluating GDP data. Recall that nominal GDP, which is the raw GDP data, includes information on both the price level and real GDP. When either of these factors changes, nominal GDP is affected. In fact, the growth rate of nominal GDP is approximately equal to the sum of the growth rates of these two factors:

(Equation 19.5)   growth of nominal GDP ≈ growth of real GDP + growth of price level

Since growth rates are calculated as percentage changes, we can rewrite equation 19.5 as

(Equation 19.6)   % change in nominal GDP ≈ % change in real GDP

+ % change in price level

Equation 19.6 gives us a simple way of dissecting GDP growth into its respective parts. For example, since we know that nominal GDP grew by 3.4% in 2015 and the price level grew by 1%, the remaining nominal GDP growth of 2.4% (3.4% − 1%) is the result of growth in real GDP.

PRACTICE WHAT YOU KNOW

Computing Real and Nominal GDP Growth: GDP Growth in Mexico

The table at the bottom of this page presents GDP data for Mexico.

Use the data from the table to answer the following questions.

How much is Mexico's economy growing?

Question: What was the rate of growth of real GDP in Mexico in 2010?

Answer: Using equation 19.6,

$$\% \text{ change in real GDP} + \% \text{ change in price level} \approx \% \text{ change in nominal GDP}$$

Rewriting the equation, we can solve for real GDP growth as

$$\% \text{ change in real GDP} \approx \% \text{ change in nominal GDP} - \% \text{ change in price level}$$

For 2010, we have

$$\% \text{ change in real GDP} \approx 18 - 4.4 \approx 13.6$$

That's impressive.

Question: How would you compute real GDP growth in Mexico in 2009?

Answer: Using the 2009 data in the same equation, we get

$$\% \text{ change in real GDP} \approx -19 - 4 \approx -23$$

This means that 2009 was a pretty rough year for the Mexican economy.

Year	Nominal GDP growth rate	Price-level growth rate
2007	9%	6%
2008	6	6
2009	−19	4
2010	18	4.4

Source: World Bank.

Looking at GDP in the United States

Gross domestic product (GDP) is the single most important indicator of macroeconomic performance. It gives us a snapshot of the overall health of the economy because it measures both output and income. These graphics illustrate the four pieces of GDP—consumption, investment, government spending, and net exports—and how these pieces changed from 1965 to 2015. On the bottom left, you can also see how real GDP has more than tripled since 1965.

(In billions of 2015 dollars)	1965	2015
TOTAL GDP	$4,365.1	$17,937.8
Consumption	$2,603.7	$12.267.9
Investment	$760.7	$3,017.8
Government	$967.9	$3,184.0
Net Exports	$32.9	-$531.9

-4.3%

16.8%

17.8%

68.4%

1.3%

22.2%   17.4%

59.6%

1965

2015

Real GDP (in billions of 2015 dollars)

Period of Recession

Despite seven recessions, real GDP grew by 3% on average per year from 1965 to 2015.

Between December 2007 and June 2009, GDP declined by 4.7%.

$20,000

$15,000

$10,000

$5,000

$0

1965 1970 1975 1980 1985 1990 1995 2000 2005 2010 2015

Percentage Breakdowns, 1965 vs. 2015

By measuring the components of each piece of GDP, we can see how the makeup of the U.S. economy has changed over time.

1965
2015

Consumption

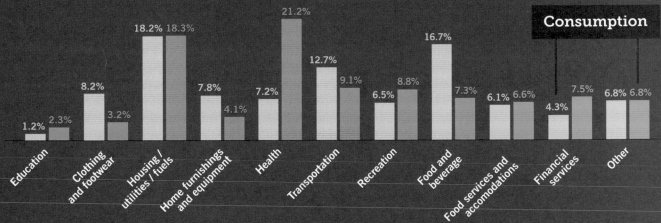

	1965	2015
Education	1.2%	2.3%
Clothing and footwear	8.2%	3.2%
Housing / utilities / fuels	18.2%	18.3%
Home furnishings and equipment	7.8%	4.1%
Health	7.2%	21.2%
Transportation	12.7%	9.1%
Recreation	6.5%	8.8%
Food and beverage	16.7%	7.3%
Food services and accomodations	6.1%	6.6%
Financial services	4.3%	7.5%
Other	6.8%	6.8%

Government*

	1965	2015
National defense	40.0%	23.7%
General public service	5.5%	8.4%
Public order and safety	4.3%	11.8%
Transportation	11.1%	9.5%
Education	20.3%	27.1%
Health	0.8%	7.6%
Housing and community services	2.6%	1.7%
Other	15.3%	10.2%

*Data for government spending are for 2014

Investments

	1965	2015
Structures (non-residential)	23.5%	17.1%
Equipment and intellectual property products (non-residential)	47.2%	66.9%
Structures (residential)	28.7%	21.7%
Equipment and software (residential)	0.6%	0.4%

Net Exports

	1965	2015
Export goods	74.7%	66.2%
Export services	25.1%	33.8%
Import goods	69.7%	82.2%
Import services	30.6%	17.8%

(% of total exports)   (% of total imports)

REVIEW QUESTIONS

- What component of consumption do we spend a much greater percentage on now than in 1965?

- Why do economists stress real GDP rather than nominal GDP when looking at GDP changes over time?

What Are Some Shortcomings of GDP Data?

We began this chapter with a claim that GDP is the single best measure of economic activity. Along the way, we have learned that nominal GDP fails to account for changes in prices and that real GDP is a better measure of economic activity. We also talked about how real GDP per capita accounts for population differences. You will be relieved to learn that by now we have finished introducing new variations of GDP! However, there are some problems with relying on GDP data as a measure of a nation's well-being. In this section, we highlight four shortcomings that limit the effectiveness of GDP as a measure of the health of an economy. We also look at the relationship between GDP and happiness. At the end of this section, we consider why economists continue to rely on GDP.

Nonmarket Goods

Many goods and services are produced but not sold. Those goods and services are not counted in GDP data even though they create value for society. For instance, work done at home such as an individual caring for their children, washing their dishes, mowing their lawn, or washing their car are services produced but not counted in GDP. When the nonmarket segment of an economy is large, the result can be a dramatic undercounting of the annual output being produced. In less developed societies where many households live off the land and produce goods for their own consumption, GDP—the measure of market activity—is a less reliable measure of economic output.

Underground Economy

The underground, or shadow, economy encompasses transactions that are not reported to the government and therefore are not taxed. Usually, these transactions are settled in cash. Many of these exchanges are for illegal goods and services, such as narcotics and illegal gambling. However, some transactions are for legal goods and services, but these activities are not reported in order to avoid taxes. Legal activities that go unreported include tips for waiting tables and tending bar, lawn services, and even home renovations. Because underground transactions are not reported, they are not easily measured and so they are not included in U.S. GDP calculations. However, as we explain in Economics in the Real World, many European nations now include illegal underground activities when calculating their GDP.

How big is the underground economy? No one is exactly sure. Economist Friedrich Schneider has estimated that for wealthy developed economies it is

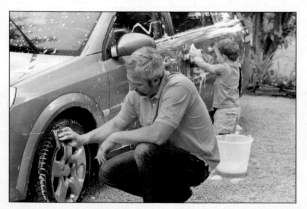

Not counted in GDP: washing your own car.

roughly 15% of GDP and that in transitioning economies the percentage rises to between 21% and 30% of GDP. However, in the world's most underdeveloped economies, like those of Nigeria or Armenia, the underground economy can be as much as 40% of GDP.

The United States is widely believed to have one of the smallest shadow economies in the world, with less than 10% of GDP unaccounted for in the official measurement. Why is the underground economy so small in the United States? The simple answer is that in the United States and in many other developed economies, most citizens can earn more by legitimately participating in the economy than by engaging in illegal activities. In short, a strong economy that generates jobs and opportunities for advancement helps to reduce the size of the underground economy. In addition, corruption is much less common. This means that participants in the economy rarely face demands for bribes or kickbacks from authorities or organized crime. This is not the case in many developing nations. For example, Somalia, which ranks last on Transparency International's corruption index, has widespread piracy and virtually no formal economy that escapes bribery and thuggery.

ECONOMICS IN THE REAL WORLD

Sex, Drugs, and GDP in Europe

In September 2014, the GDP for the European Union (EU)* increased by 3.53% overnight. That is a full year's worth of very solid growth. But it didn't make Europeans any wealthier because it was actually just the result of a new way of defining and calculating GDP. Eurostat (the economic statistics office of the European Commission) redefined GDP to include many transactions that were previously uncounted and are actually illegal across much of Europe.

The new GDP definition includes illegal drug deals, prostitution, and even sales of stolen goods. Specifically, it includes illegal transactions as long as both parties agree to the transaction.

Ostensibly, Eurostat is trying to capture part of the shadow economy that is typically not measured in GDP. Unfortunately, the process becomes even more complicated when the legality of goods and services varies across nations. For example, Figure 19.8 shows how cannabis laws vary across Europe. Cannabis is essentially legal in some nations (the Netherlands) but strictly illegal in others (France, for example).

Normalizing the accounting standards across nations makes sense. But illegal activities are difficult to measure. In addition, if the illegal activities are a relatively stable portion of GDP, then there is really no bias when they are not included. In fact, the new estimates, in an attempt to provide a more complete measure, may actually introduce more error into GDP measurement due to the difficulty of estimating illegal trade.

So why the change in definition? Many European nations are dealing with high deficit- (and debt-) to-GDP ratios, and some of these new measurements

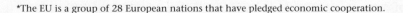

*The EU is a group of 28 European nations that have pledged economic cooperation.

FIGURE 19.8

Legality of Cannabis in the European Union

The legality of cannabis varies drastically across the European Union. For example, cannabis is essentially legal in the Netherlands but strictly illegal in France. Previously, only legal transactions were counted as part of GDP in the European Union. However, the new standards adopted in 2014 include illegal transactions in European nations, so long as both parties agree to the transaction. Therefore, illegal trades in France are now counted as part of GDP so that French GDP and Dutch GDP both include transactions for the same goods and services.

Source: Wikimedia Commons.

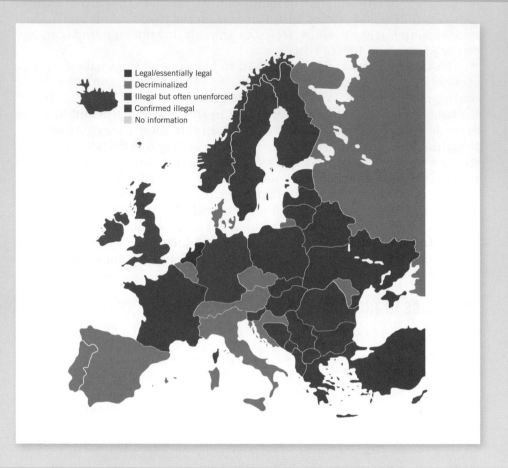

Legend:
- Legal/essentially legal
- Decriminalized
- Illegal but often unenforced
- Confirmed illegal
- No information

(in a backhanded way) help lower these ratios. The European Commission has explicit rules regarding these budget measures: a nation's deficit in a given fiscal year is not to exceed 3% of its GDP, and the national debt is not to exceed 60% of GDP. When nations exceed these bounds, the governing council is directed to use coercive measures called excessive deficit procedures (EDRs). The council has been lax in enforcing EDRs in recent years. However, increasing GDP by simply redefining how it is measured automatically lowers deficit and debt ratios and helps nations that have higher government debt levels.

Figure 19.9 shows the effect of the new GDP definition on each nation's GDP level in 2013 (along with the overall EU and Euroarea). The countries are ordered according to their GDP gains from the new GDP measurements. (ESA 2010 stands for European System Accounts.)

As you can see, GDP for Cyprus jumped 9.8% due to the accounting change, shrinking the country's debt-to-GDP ratio by a full half of a percentage point in 2013—from 5.4% to 4.9%. Clearly, the new accounting rule exaggerates debt reduction in Cyprus as the country tries to move closer to the EU goal of 3%.

FIGURE 19.9

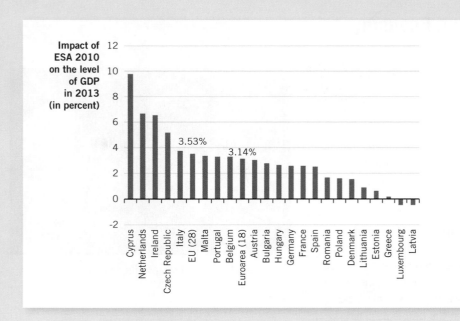

Impact of ESA 2010 on the level of GDP in 2013 (in percent)

3.53%

3.14%

Cyprus · Netherlands · Ireland · Czech Republic · Italy · EU (28) · Malta · Portugal · Belgium · Euroarea (18) · Austria · Bulgaria · Hungary · Germany · France · Spain · Romania · Poland · Denmark · Lithuania · Estonia · Greece · Luxembourg · Latvia

Increase in GDP Due to Accounting Change

This data shows how the GDP of each European nation changed as a result of the new GDP accounting rules (ESA). The overall average for the EU was a 3.53% increase in GDP, but the GDP of Cyprus jumped 9.8%.

Source: Eurostat.

In short, while new GDP accounting rules in Europe may normalize national income accounting across the Eurozone, they are particularly helpful to nations that have high government debt levels. ✳

Quality of the Environment

GDP measures the final amount of goods and services produced in a given period, but it does not distinguish how those goods and services are produced. In particular, it does not account for negative environmental side effects that sometimes occur in production. Imagine two economies, both with the same real GDP per capita. One economy relies on clean energy for its production, and the other has lax environmental standards. Citizens in both countries enjoy the same standard of living, but their well-being is not the same. The lax environmental standards in the second economy lead to air and water pollution as well as health problems for its citizens. Since there is more to quality of life than the goods and services we buy, using GDP to infer that both places are equally desirable would be inaccurate.

Leisure Time

Because GDP only counts market activity, it fails to capture how long laborers work to produce goods and services. For most developed nations, according to the OECD (Organization for Economic Cooperation

Not counted in GDP: a clean environment.

The Underground Economy

Traffic

Traffic, a crime film from 2000, looks at America's war on drugs through the lives of the people involved in it. The characters offer a fascinating range: from the nation's drug czar, to his cocaine-using daughter, to the cops who fight the war on both sides of the U.S./Mexican border, to the drug dealers who profit from trafficking the drugs.

In one scene, two agents from the Drug Enforcement Agency are interrogating a suspected drug trafficker. The suspect explains that the cocaine flow from Mexico into the United States cannot be stopped because there is too much demand in the United States and because Mexican dealers are willing to "throw supply at the problem." That is, the Mexican drug lords recognize that some of their shipments will be seized but that enough will get through to reach their customers in the United States to make the risks worthwhile.

One of the ironies about measuring GDP is that even though the drug trades are not part of GDP—because those illegal market transactions are not formally recorded—the people involved in fighting the war on drugs, as well as the sales of drug paraphernalia, are included in GDP.

How does more illegal drug traffic lead to higher GDP?

The movie also traces the life of a successful businessman who has made millions selling drugs. We see his estate, luxury cars, trophy wife, and all the accoutrements of success. His purchases, made from illegal sales, are counted in GDP because it measures the sales of final goods and services. Thus, while GDP cannot measure the economic activity in the underground economy, it can indirectly capture some of those transactions when the gains from selling drugs are used to purchase legal products.

and Development), the average workweek is slightly over 35 hours. However, there are wide variations from country to country. At the high end, laborers in South Korea average 46 hours per week. In contrast, laborers in the Netherlands average fewer than 28 hours per week. This means that comparisons of GDP across countries are problematic because they do not account for the extra time available to workers in countries with substantially fewer hours worked. For example, in the United States the average workweek is 36 hours. A comparison with Japan, which also averages 36 hours per workweek, would be valid; but a comparison of U.S. GDP with that of Sweden (31-hour workweek) or Greece (41-hour workweek) would be misleading.

GDP and Happiness

Throughout this chapter, we have presented real per capita GDP as a measure of living standards. But let's be careful; economists do not generally claim that money can buy happiness. However, it is a fact that, *ceteris paribus*, greater wealth does make it easier to afford conveniences, experiences, and even health and well-being that contribute to life satisfaction or happiness. Per capita GDP is positively correlated with many human welfare outcomes that nearly everybody finds desirable: higher life expectancy, higher levels of education, and reduced infant mortality. This probably doesn't surprise you; income allows people to buy better health care, medicines, and education, among other purchases.

Recent research done by economists Betsey Stevenson and Justin Wolfers seems to support these assumptions. Their research has found a consistently positive relationship between self-reported life satisfaction and income. In their research, Stevenson and Wolfers asked questions similar to those found on other surveys used to study happiness and life satisfaction:

> "Here is a ladder representing the 'ladder of life.' Let's suppose that the top of the ladder represents the best possible life for you, and the bottom, the worst possible life for you. On which step of the ladder do you feel you personally stand at the present time? [0–10 steps]?"

You can see now what the data might look like. People and nations with relatively low life satisfaction will produce survey results in the 3–4 range, but people and nations with relatively high life satisfaction will produce survey results in the 6–8 range.

Here are two key results from the Stevenson/Wolfers research:

1. Wealthier individuals report greater life satisfaction than poorer people in the same country.

Figure 19.10 shows how life satisfaction varies across varying income levels in the 10 most populous countries. The vertical axis measures the life satisfaction variable, and the horizontal axis measures income on a log scale. Clearly,

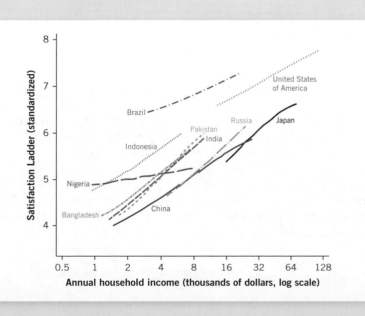

FIGURE 19.10

Life Satisfaction and Income by Country

The data shows a positive relationship between self-reported life satisfaction (happiness) and household income in ten nations. Wealthier people inside each nation express greater happiness than poorer people in the same nation.

Source: Betsey Stevenson and Justin Wolfers, "Subjective Well-Being and Income: Is There Any Evidence of Satiation?" NBER Working Paper 18992, April 2013.

life satisfaction climbs with income: all the lines have a positive and similar slope. Even though Mexicans are especially happy for their given income levels, the general relationship for Mexicans is similar to that for Indians, Iranians, and Thais.

In addition, they point out the importance of paying attention to percentage changes in that variable, rather than absolute changes. For example, an income change from $400 to $500 is a 25% change, but a change from $40,000 to $50,000 is also a 25% change.

Why do percentage changes matter in this study? Basic economics assumes a diminishing utility of income, which means that increases in life satisfaction (utility) per dollar should decline as income increases. This study demonstrates that percentage changes do matter: the data indicate that a doubling of income leads to about a 0.35 unit increase on the life satisfaction ladder.

2. Wealthier nations report greater life satisfaction than poorer nations.

Figure 19.11 plots the cross-country data. Each dot represents an individual nation, and the dots together tell a consistent story. First, it shows a clear positive relationship between life satisfaction and income around the globe. Second, there really is a lot of variation in happiness, even at a given income level. For example, compare Mexico and Bulgaria.

In conclusion, survey data from around the globe and across time indicate that increases in income level lead to higher life satisfaction, or happiness. Money may not be able to buy happiness, but there is significant evidence that more income presents more opportunities to "pursue happiness."

FIGURE 19.11

Life Satisfaction and Income around the Globe

Individuals in nations with higher income levels (GDP per capita) report greater happiness on the life satisfaction ladder.

Source: Betsey Stevenson and Justin Wolfers, "Subjective Well-Being and Income: Is There Any Evidence of Satiation?" NBER Working Paper 18992, April 2013.

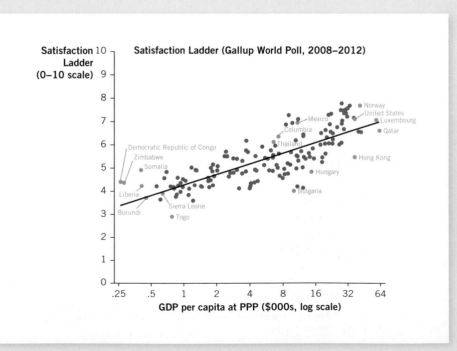

Why Do Economists Continue to Rely on GDP Data?

In addition to the production of goods and services, there are many other measurements that economists might use to determine a country's standard of living: life expectancy, educational levels, access to health care, crime rates, and so on. One problem with including these additional factors in GDP is that they are difficult to measure. Moreover, the combined statistic that we would generate would be even more challenging to understand. Therefore, we limit GDP to measuring economic production, knowing that it is not a

Not counted in GDP: extra time to relax.

perfect measure of well-being. In addition, GDP is actually correlated with many of the variables we care about. In other words, higher levels of GDP are highly correlated with a better environment, higher-quality and better access to health care, more education, more leisure time, and lower crime rates.

PRACTICE WHAT YOU KNOW

Shortcomings of GDP Data: Use Caution in Interpreting GDP as an Economic Barometer

In many parts of the world, a significant amount of effort goes into nonmarket production in the household, such as stay-at-home parenting. For example, Zimbabwe has a very high rate of nonmarket household production. In contrast, Canada has a low rate of nonmarket household production.

Question: How does the difference in nonmarket household production affect a comparison of GDP between Zimbabwe and Canada?

Answer: The GDP statistics for Zimbabwe are biased downward more than the statistics for Canada, since a larger portion of Zimbabwe's actual production goes unreported. While Zimbabwe is actually a poorer nation than Canada, official statistics exaggerate the difference slightly, making Zimbabwe seem poorer than it is.

Some nations have more stay-at-home parents than others. How does this affect GDP comparisons?

Conclusion

We began this chapter with the misconception that there is no reliable way to determine how well an economy is performing. But GDP is a measure that works well. In the short run, it helps us recognize business cycles, including the ups of an expansion and the downs of a recession. GDP also serves as a reasonably good indicator of living standards around the globe and over time. Nations with better living conditions are also nations with higher GDP. Thus, even though it has some shortcomings, GDP is a sound indicator of the overall health of an economy.

In the next chapter, we look at another macroeconomic indicator—the unemployment rate. The unemployment rate and other job indicators give us an additional dimension on which to consider the health of an economy.

ANSWERING THE BIG QUESTIONS

How is macroeconomics different from microeconomics?

* Microeconomics is the study of individuals and firms, but macroeconomics considers the entire economy.
* Many of the topics in both areas of study are the same; these topics include income, employment, and output. But the macro perspective is much broader than the micro perspective.

What does GDP tell us about the economy?

* GDP measures both output and income in a macroeconomy.
* It is a gauge of productivity and the overall level of wealth in an economy.
* We use GDP data to measure living standards, economic growth, and business cycle conditions.

How is GDP computed?

* GDP is the total market value of all final goods and services produced in an economy in a specific time period, usually a year.
* Economists typically compute GDP by adding four types of expenditures in the economy: consumption (C), investment (I), government spending (G), and net exports (NX). Net exports are total exports minus total imports.
* For many applications, it is also necessary to compute real GDP, adjusting GDP for changes in prices (inflation).

What are some shortcomings of GDP data?

* GDP data do not include the production of nonmarket goods, the underground economy, production effects on the environment, or the value placed on leisure time.

Economic Growth Statistics: Deciphering Data Reports

ECONOMICS FOR LIFE

Economics is all around us, and the topics of economics are constantly reported in the media. In addition to monthly reports on unemployment and inflation, there are monthly releases and revisions of GDP data for the United States and other nations. These updates often get a lot of attention. Unfortunately, media reports are not as careful with their economics terminology as we would like. Because they are not worded carefully, the reports can be misleading.

After learning about historical experiences with economic growth, you might find new interest in the economic growth reports that appear almost every month in the mainstream media. However, you must carefully evaluate the data they present. Now that you have perspective on growth statistics, you can determine for yourself whether economic news is positive or negative. For example, a *New York Times* article from April 2009 offers the following synopsis of economic growth in China for the previous quarter:

> China's economic output was 6.1 percent higher in the first quarter than a year earlier . . . . China's annual growth rate appeared slow in the first quarter after the 6.8 percent rate in the fourth quarter of 2008, partly because it was being compared with the economy's formidable output in the first quarter of last year.*

Economic reports in the media are often misleading.

China's economy grew at over 6%, and yet this rate is described as "slow." By now, you know that 6% is an incredibly fast rate of growth.

Good economists are very careful with language, and certain terms have very specific meanings. For example, we know that "economic growth" always refers to changes in real *per capita* GDP, not simply GDP or real GDP. But economic reports in mainstream media outlets often blur this distinction. That is exactly the case with the report in the *New York Times* article cited above.

Even though the author uses the term "annual growth rate," additional research reveals that he is talking about real GDP growth, but not adjusting the data for population changes. This mistake is fairly common, so you should watch for it when you read economic growth reports. It turns out that the population growth rate in China was about 0.6% in 2009. This means that the growth rate of real per capita GDP in China was actually about 5.5%, which is still very impressive.

---

*Keith Bradsher, "China's Economic Growth Slows in First Quarter," *New York Times,* April 16, 2009.

CONCEPTS YOU SHOULD KNOW

business cycle (p. 604)
consumption (p. 611)
economic contraction (p. 604)
economic expansion (p. 604)
economic growth (p. 602)
final goods (p. 608)
GDP deflator (p. 613)
government spending (p. 612)

Great Recession (p. 604)
gross domestic product (GDP)
 (p. 600)
gross national product (GNP)
 (p. 609)
inflation (p. 602)
intermediate goods (p. 608)
investment (p. 612)

net exports (p. 613)
nominal GDP (p. 613)
per capita GDP (p. 601)
price level (p. 613)
real GDP (p. 602)
recession (p. 603)
services (p. 607)

QUESTIONS FOR REVIEW

1. Explain the relationship between output and income for both an individual and an entire economy.

2. What is the largest component (C, I, G, or NX) of GDP? Give an example of each component.

3. A farmer sells cotton to a clothing company for $1,000, and the clothing company turns the cotton into T-shirts that it sells to a store for a total of $2,000. How much did GDP increase as a result of these transactions?

4. A friend of yours is reading a financial blog and comes to you for some advice about GDP. She wants to know whether she should pay attention to nominal GDP or real GDP. Which one do you recommend, and why?

5. Is a larger GDP always better than a smaller GDP? Explain your answer with an example.

6. If Max receives an unemployment check, would we include that transfer payment from the government in this year's GDP? Why or why not?

7. Phil owns an old set of golf clubs that he purchased for $1,000 seven years ago. He decides to post them on Craigslist and quickly sells the clubs for $250. How does this sale affect GDP?

8. Real GDP for 2015 is less than nominal GDP for that year. But real GDP for 2000 is more than nominal GDP for that year. Why?

9. What are the four shortcomings with using GDP as a measure of well-being?

STUDY PROBLEMS (*solved at the end of the section)*

1. A friend who knows of your interest in economics comes up to you after reading the latest GDP data and excitedly exclaims, "Did you see that nominal GDP rose from $19 trillion to $19.5 trillion?" What should you tell your friend about this news?

2. In the following situations, explain what is counted (or is not counted) in this year's GDP.
   a. You bought a new Wii at GameStop last year and resold it on eBay this year.
   b. You purchase a new copy of *Investing for Dummies* at Barnes & Noble.
   c. You purchase a historic home using the services of a real estate agent.
   d. You detail your car so it is spotless inside and out.
   e. You purchase a new hard drive for your old laptop.
   f. Your physical therapist receives $300 for physical therapy but reports only $100.
   g. Apple buys 1,000 motherboards for use in making new computers.
   h. Toyota produces 10,000 new Camrys that remain unsold at the end of the year.

3. To which component of GDP expenditure (C, I, G, or NX) does each of the following belong?
   a. Swiss chocolates imported from Europe
   b. a driver's license you receive from the Department of Motor Vehicles
   c. a candle you buy at a local store
   d. a new house

4. A mechanic builds an engine and then sells it to a customized body shop for $7,000. The body shop installs the engine in a car and sells the car to a dealer for $20,000. The dealer then sells the finished vehicle for $35,000. A consumer drives off with the car. By how much does GDP increase? What is the value added at each step of the production process? How does the total value added compare with the amount by which GDP increased?

5. In this chapter, we used nominal GDP data from Table 19.5 to compute 2015 GDP in 2009 dollars. Using the same steps, use the data from Table 19.5 to compute 2014 GDP in 2009 dollars.

6. Many goods and services are illegally sold or legally sold but not reported to the government. How would increased efforts to count those goods and services affect GDP data?

7. Leisure time is not included in GDP, but what would happen if it was included? Would high-work countries like South Korea fare better in international comparisons of well-being, or worse?

*8. Fill in the missing data in the following table.

Year	Nominal GDP (thousands of $)	Real GDP (thousands of $)	GDP Deflator
2013	$100	_____	100.0
2014	_____	$110	108.0
2015	$130	$117	_____
2016	$150	_____	120.0
2017	_____	$136	125.0

*9. Consider an economy that only produces two goods: strawberries and cream. Use the table below to compute nominal GDP, real GDP, and the GDP deflator for each year. (Year 2015 is the base year.)

Year	Price of strawberries (per pint)	Quantity of strawberries (pints)	Price of cream (per pint)	Quantity of cream (pints)
2015	$3.00	100	$2.00	200
2016	$4.00	125	$2.50	400
2017	$5.00	150	$3.00	500

*10. The table below presents GDP data for an imaginary economy.

a. Fill in the blanks.

Year	Nominal GDP (in billions)	GDP Deflator (2010 = base year)	Real GDP (billions of 2010 dollars)
1970	$500	20	_____
1980	$1,000	25	_____
1990	$3,000	_____	$6,000
2000	_____	80	$7,500
2010	_____	100	$9,000

b. Compute both nominal and real GDP growth rates from the end of 1960 to the end of 1970. Note that your result is not an annual growth rate; it is the total growth rate over the entire decade.

SOLVED PROBLEMS

8.

Year	Nominal GDP (thousands of $)	Real GDP (thousands of $)	GDP Deflator
2013	$100	$100	100.0
2014	$118.8	$110	108.0
2015	$130	$117	111.1
2016	$150	$125	120.0
2017	$170	$136	125.0

To solve for the missing data, use the following equation (and 2013 as the base year):

$$\text{real GDP}_{\text{year}} = \frac{\text{nominal GDP}_{\text{year}}}{\text{price level}_{\text{year}}} \times \text{base year price level}$$

For 2013: real GDP$_{2013}$ = ($100 ÷ 100.0)
$\times 100.0 = \underline{\$100}$

For 2014: $110,000 = (\text{nominal GDP}_{2014}$
$÷ 108.0) \times 100.0$

nominal GDP$_{2014}$ = ($110 ÷ 100.0)
$\times 108.0 = \underline{\$118.8}$

For 2015: $117,000 = ($130,000 ÷ GDP
deflator$_{2015}$) × 100.0

GDP deflator$_{2015}$ = ($130 ÷ $117)
× 100.0

GDP deflator$_{2015}$ = $\underline{111.1}$

For 2016: real GDP$_{2016}$ = ($150,000 ÷ 120.0)
× 100.0

real GDP$_{2016}$ = $\underline{\$125}$

For 2017: $136,000 = (\text{nominal GDP}_{2017}$
÷ 125.0) × 100.0

nominal GDP$_{2017}$ = ($136,000 ÷ 100.0)
× 125.0

nominal GDP$_{2017}$ = $\underline{\$170,000}$

9.

Year	Nominal GDP	Real GDP	GDP Deflator
2015	$700	$700	100.0
2016	$1,500	$1,175	127.7
2017	$2,250	$1,450	155.2

First, let's calculate nominal GDP for each of the three years by adding up the market values of the strawberries and cream produced during that year.

For 2015: nominal GDP$_{2015}$ = ($3.00 × 100) +
($2.00 × 200) = $700

For 2016: nominal GDP$_{2016}$ = ($4.00 × 125) +
($2.50 × 400) = $1,500

For 2017: nominal GDP$_{2017}$ = ($5.00 × 150)
+ ($3.00 × 500) = $2,250

Now, let's calculate real GDP in 2010 dollars by multiplying the quantities produced in each year by the 2010 prices.

For 2015: real GDP$_{2015}$ = ($3.00 × 100)
+ ($2.00 × 200) = $700

For 2016: real GDP$_{2016}$ = ($3.00 × 125)
+ ($2.00 × 400) = $1,175

For 2017: real GDP$_{2017}$ = ($3.00 × 150)
+ ($2.00 × 500) = $1,450

Finally, using the nominal GDP and real GDP numbers we calculated above, let's calculate the GDP deflator by using the following formula:

$$\text{GDP deflator}_{\text{year}} = \frac{\text{nominal GDP}_{\text{year}}}{\text{real GDP}_{\text{year}}} \times 100.0$$

GDP deflator$_{2015}$ = 100.0. Since 2010 is given as the base year, the GDP deflator must be 100.0.

For 2016: GDP deflator$_{2016}$ = ($1,500 ÷ $1,175)
× 100 = 127.7

For 2017: GDP deflator$_{2017}$ = ($2,250 ÷ $1,450)
× 100 = 155.2

10.a. Recall equation 19.3:

$$\text{real GDP}_t = \frac{\text{nominal GDP}_t}{\text{price level}_t} \times 100$$

Year	Nominal GDP (in billions)	GDP Deflator (2010 = base year)	Real GDP (billions of 2010 dollars)
1970	$500	20	$2,500
1980	$1,000	25	$4,000
1990	$3,000	50	$6,000
2000	$6,000	80	$7,500
2010	$9,000	100	$9,000

Since we know that the GDP deflator is used as the price level, for 1970 we use equation 19.3 to solve for real GDP:

$$\text{real GDP}_{1970} = (\$500/20) \times 100 = \$2,500$$

For 1980, we use equation 19.3 to solve for real GDP:

$$\text{real GDP}_{1980} = (\$1,000/25) \times 100 = \$4,000$$

For 1990, we use equation 19.3 to solve for the GDP deflator:

$$\$6,000 = (\$3,000/\text{price level}_t) \times 100 = 50$$

For 2000, we use equation 19.3 to solve for nominal GDP:

$$\$7,500 = (\text{nominal GDP}_t/80) \times 100 = \$6000$$

For 2010, we know that nominal GDP is equal to real GDP because this is the base year.

b. nominal GDP growth rate =
(nominal GDP in 1970 − nominal GDP in 1960)/nominal GDP in 1960 =
($1,000 − $500)/$500 = 1.0 = 100%

real GDP growth rate =

(real GDP in 1970 − real GDP in 1960)/real GDP in 1960 =

($4,000 − $2,500)/$2,500 =
$1,500/$2,500 = 3/5 = 60%

CHAPTER 20 | Unemployment

We should aim for zero unemployment.

Many people believe that even a small amount of unemployment is a sign of problems. This isn't true. On the one hand, it is never fun for any

person to search unsuccessfully for work. On the other hand, some unemployment is the result of positive changes in the economy that make us all better off in the long run. For this reason, economists agree that we can never eliminate unemployment entirely and that attempts to do so are misguided.

In this chapter, we take a closer look at unemployment. After GDP, the unemployment rate is the second most important indicator of economic health. We examine the causes of unemployment and explain how it is measured. By looking at some historical data in context, we will begin to understand when unemployment is a matter of concern.

While some macroeconomic unemployment is natural, on the micro level unemployment is not fun.

BIG QUESTIONS

* What are the major reasons for unemployment?
* What can we learn from the employment data?

What Are the Major Reasons for Unemployment?

Perhaps you know someone who has lost his or her job—a parent or a friend. Losing a job is particularly difficult when a person is unable to transition easily to another one. After all, many of us depend on our jobs just to survive. Being willing and able to work, but unable to find a job—there are few greater frustrations than this in a modern economy. **Unemployment** occurs when a worker who is not currently employed is searching for a job without success. Unfortunately, the level of unemployment in the United States has been relatively high since the beginning of the Great Recession, which began at the end of 2007.

People leave their jobs for many reasons. Some do so voluntarily: they may return to school, take another job, or decide to leave the workforce to care for their children. Others lose a job they wish to keep: an employee might be fired for poor performance or let go because the company is downsizing. When macroeconomists consider unemployment, they explicitly look at workers who seek employment but are unable to secure it. We use the unemployment rate to monitor the level of unemployment in an economy. The **unemployment rate** (u) is the percentage of the labor force that is unemployed. Figure 20.1 plots the U.S. unemployment rate from 1960 to 2015. This graph is one way of quickly measuring national economic frustration. As the unemployment rate climbs, people are more likely to be disappointed in their pursuit of a job.

Economists distinguish three types of unemployment: structural, frictional, and cyclical. You can think of each type as deriving from a different source. As it turns out, structural and frictional unemployment occur even when the economy is healthy and growing. For this reason, they are often called *natural unemployment*. We consider them first.

Structural Unemployment

Unemployment is difficult on households, and resources are wasted when idle workers sit on the sidelines. However, a dynamic, growing economy is an economy that adapts and changes. No one would consider it an improvement to return to the economy of early America, where 90% of Americans toiled in manual farmwork and earned meager subsistence wages that just

Unemployment occurs when a worker who is not currently employed is searching for a job without success.

The **unemployment rate** is the percentage of the labor force that is unemployed.

FIGURE 20.1

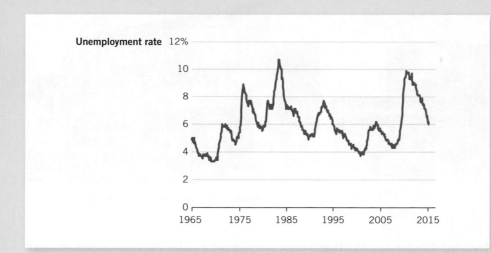

U.S. Unemployment Rate, 1965–2015
The unemployment rate is an important indicator of the economy's health. Since 1965, the average unemployment rate in the United States has been about 6%.

Source: U.S. Bureau of Labor Statistics.

barely covered the cost of food and shelter. The transformation to our modern economy has brought new jobs but also has required completely different skills. This has made some jobs obsolete, which has led inevitably to a certain amount of unemployment, even if just temporarily. And herein lies the dilemma. Dynamic, growing economies are also evolving economies. If we want an economy that adapts to changes in consumer demands and technology, we must accept some unemployment, at least temporarily, as a by-product of the growth.

Consider that in the past we produced no computers, cell phones, or polio vaccines, and the invention of these products led to great job creation. Improving technologies in these fields enabled us to produce more and better output with fewer resources or fewer employees. Over time, we also produced less of some other things—such as black and white televisions, cassette tapes, and typewriters. These structural changes left some workers unemployed, even if just temporarily.

Creative Destruction

As new industries are created, some old ones are destroyed. The economist Joseph Schumpeter coined the term *creative destruction* to describe this process of economic evolution. **Creative destruction** occurs when the introduction of new products and technologies leads to the end of other industries and jobs. As some jobs become obsolete, the result is **structural unemployment**, which is caused by changes in the industrial makeup (structure) of the economy. Although structural unemployment can cause transitional problems, it is often a sign of a healthy, growing economy.

The retail book market provides a good example. In the 1980s and 1990s, the Borders book retailer grew from a small Ann Arbor, Michigan, bookseller to a national chain with 1,249 total locations. Borders' success came from innovation: the stores were physically much larger than earlier bookstores, offered four to five times as many titles, had comfortable reading areas, and

Creative destruction occurs when the introduction of new products and technologies leads to the end of other industries and jobs.

Structural unemployment is unemployment caused by changes in the industrial makeup (structure) of the economy.

Creative destruction in the retail book market means that when new products and jobs are created, other jobs are destroyed.

featured in-store cafés. These innovations led to the closure of many small independent booksellers, causing some temporary job shifts.

But innovations in the book market didn't end in the 1990s. The following decade saw greater competition from online booksellers like Amazon .com and the introduction of e-readers like the Kindle, Nook, and iPad. These changes led to the decline of Borders, which had 19,000 employees when it declared bankruptcy in 2011. At that point, Borders's employees found themselves structurally unemployed: they lost their jobs as a result of market innovations.

From these examples, we can begin to understand why there is unemployment even in a healthy economy. For instance, in 2014, real GDP in the United States increased by nearly 2.4%, and 3.1 million new jobs were created overall. Yet even then, there were more than 55 million job separations (workers who quit or were laid off). In a dynamic economy, job turnover is normal.

An Evolving Economy

In the long run, the evolving economy has led to drastic changes in the type of work Americans do. Figure 20.2 shows how jobs in the United States have evolved over the past two centuries. In 1800, over 90% of Americans worked in agriculture, either as farmers or as farm laborers. A century later, in 1900, only about half of U.S. workers were employed in farming. The rest were split between manufacturing (industry) jobs and service-related jobs. In 1900, manufacturing jobs may have been in railroad or steel production, while service jobs included teaching and accounting. Today, five out of six American workers are employed in service-related jobs. Since 1979, U.S. manufacturing employment has fallen from almost 20 million jobs to just 12 million in 2014. Over the same period, employment in service industries has risen from 65 million jobs to 120 million. While we still need teachers and accountants, there are many new service jobs in fields such as engineering, finance, transportation, health, and government.

The trends presented in Figure 20.2 illustrate creative destruction: the structure of the economy evolves, which leads to different types of jobs. This long view presents the most positive angle on this process. After all, most of

FIGURE 20.2

The Evolution of Jobs in the United States

Over the past two centuries, jobs in the United States have evolved from being primarily agricultural to industrial (manufacturing) and then to service.

Source: Federal Reserve Bank of Dallas.

us would prefer working at modern jobs rather than toiling with simple farm tools in a field all day. But along the way, as jobs shift, some temporary structural unemployment inevitably occurs.

While structural unemployment can't be eliminated, it can be reduced in a number of ways. Workers must often retrain, relocate, or change their expectations in some way before they can work elsewhere. Lumberjacks may need to become computer repair specialists, or autoworkers may need to relocate from Michigan to Kentucky. Government can also enact policies to alleviate the pain of structural unemployment, such as by establishing job training programs and relocation subsidies (that is, paying part of workers' moving costs).

ECONOMICS IN THE REAL WORLD

Americans Don't Appear to Want Farmwork

In September 2010, Garance Burke, of the Associated Press, wrote an article about the frustration of U.S. farmers trying to find American workers to harvest fruit and vegetables. Even though the unemployment rate at the time was very high, Americans did not apply for available farm jobs. Burke noted that the few Americans who do take such jobs usually don't stay in the fields

Why don't Americans want a career picking grapes?

for long. The AP analysis showed that from January to June 2010, California farmers advertised 1,160 farm-worker jobs available to U.S. citizens and legal residents; only 36 were hired. One farmer named Steve Fortin noted problems with American workers: "A few years ago when domestic workers were referred here, we saw absentee problems, and we had people asking for time off after they had just started. Some were actually planting the plants upside down."

Comedian Stephen Colbert partnered with the United Farm Workers (UFW) union in a "Take Our Jobs" campaign, aimed at getting farm jobs filled with American workers. Colbert even spent a day picking beans in a field, concluding that farmwork is "really, really hard."

Ironically, during the 2007–2009 recession, many migrant farm jobs were available, but unemployed Americans refused to apply for them. This lack of interest contrasts with worker attitudes during the Great Depression more than 80 years earlier, when displaced farmers from the Great Plains flooded California looking for work. So when some people today claim that immigrants are taking jobs away from U.S. citizens, we can say that in the heart of the nation's biggest farming state, this is certainly not true. In addition, when we look at the long-run trend in U.S. jobs, which shows a movement away from agricultural work and into service-sector jobs, we probably shouldn't be too alarmed. ✳

Frictional Unemployment

Frictional unemployment is unemployment caused by delays in matching available jobs and workers.

Even when jobs are available and qualified employees live nearby, it takes time for workers and employers to find one another and agree to terms. **Frictional unemployment** is caused by delays in matching available jobs and workers. Frictional unemployment is another type of natural unemployment: no matter how healthy the economy may be, there is always some frictional unemployment.

Consider how a successful new product launch at McDonald's affects Burger King. Suppose that McDonald's introduces a new product called the "Quad-stack," which is really just four Quarter Pounders stacked on top of one another. Also suppose that customers can't get enough of the new burger. Because of the spike in new business, McDonald's needs to hire more employees. At the same time, Burger King loses customers to McDonald's and decides to lay off some of its workers. Of course, the laid-off Burger King workers will take some time searching for new jobs. And McDonald's will take time deciding how many new workers it needs and which applicants to hire. Because some workers are unemployed during this transition, frictional unemployment results.

Frictional unemployment occurs even in the healthiest economy. Because we live in a world of imperfect information, there are incentives for employees to keep searching for the perfect job or for employers to search longer for the best employees. For example, as you approach graduation from college, you will probably take some time to search for a job and determine which offer to accept. Similarly, employers rarely hire the first applicant they see, even though it may be costly to leave a position vacant. Even if there is a perfect job available for every worker, it will still take time to match workers and jobs. These time lags create friction in the labor market, and the result is temporary, frictional unemployment.

Even though frictional unemployment is natural, its level can rise or fall over time. Let's look at two factors that affect frictional unemployment: information availability and government policies.

Information Availability

Imagine looking for a job in a world without the Internet. You'd read a lot of newspaper ads, make dozens or hundreds of phone calls, and probably make several in-person visits to firms where you think you might like to work. Yet after all that, you'd still have a great deal of uncertainty about the complete set of your job prospects.

Today, most job searches are conducted online. For example, let's say you graduate with a degree in accounting and pass the CPA (certified public accountant) exam. You decide to search for a job online at Indeed.com. Even in 2015, with high overall unemployment, a nationwide search for job opportunities for CPAs yields over 4,000 potential matches. Even narrowing this search to, say, the state of Virginia nets 186 potential jobs. The point is that the vast pool of information available through the Internet enables workers and companies to find one another more quickly and to make better matches with substantially lower costs. The result is lower frictional unemployment.

Searching for a job has never been easier.

Government Policies

Any factors that lengthen the job search process increase frictional unemployment. These factors include government policies such as unemployment compensation and government regulations related to the hiring and firing of employees.

Unemployment Insurance and Incentives **Unemployment insurance**, also known as *federal jobless benefits*, is a government program that reduces the hardship of joblessness by guaranteeing that unemployed workers receive a percentage of their former income while they are unemployed. Governments provide unemployment insurance for many reasons. The benefit cushions the economic consequences of being laid off, and it provides workers time to search for new employment. In addition, unemployment insurance can help contain macroeconomic problems before they spread to other industries. Consider what happens if the auto industry is struggling and workers are laid off: the unemployed autoworkers will not be able to pay for some of the goods and services they used to buy, and the reduction in their overall spending will hurt other industries. For example, if unemployed workers can't pay their mortgages, lenders will suffer and the downturn will spread to the financial industry. Viewed in this way, unemployment insurance serves to reduce the severity of the overall economic contraction.

However, unemployment insurance also creates unintended consequences. For one thing, receiving the cushion of unemployment benefits makes some

Unemployment insurance, also known as federal jobless benefits, is a government program that reduces the hardship of joblessness by guaranteeing that unemployed workers receive a percentage of their former income while unemployed.

Incentives

people feel less inclined to search for and take a job. These workers spend more time unemployed when they have insurance; without unemployment insurance, they are much more motivated to seek immediate employment. For example, in late 2007, the U.S. economy entered the Great Recession, which ended in mid-2009. But several years after GDP growth resumed and the recession was declared over, the level of unemployment has remained high. Why? One reason might be the frictional unemployment that occurred from unprecedented extensions to unemployment insurance benefits. In particular, the federal government offered extensions of up to 47 weeks after state benefits ran out. These extensions meant that many places offered benefits of up to 99 weeks—nearly two years. Economists Marcus Hagedorn, Iourii Manovskii, and Kurt Mitman estimated that 1.8 million new jobs opened up in 2014, when the extensions of federal benefits were allowed to expire. So while it certainly seems appropriate to help the jobless during recessions, this policy likely created an incentive to search longer for a new job, which in turn contributed to frictional unemployment.

Regulations on Hiring and Firing Government regulations on hiring and firing also contribute to frictional unemployment. Regulations on hiring include restrictions on who can and must be interviewed, paperwork that employers must complete for new hires, and additional tax documents that must be filed for new employees. Regulations on firing include mandatory severance pay, written justification, and government fines. While these regulations may be instituted to help workers by giving them greater job security, they have unintended consequences. When it is difficult to hire employees, firms take longer to do so, which increases frictional unemployment. When it is difficult to fire employees, firms take greater care in hiring them. Again, the longer search time increases frictional unemployment.

The United States has relatively few labor market regulations. However, many European nations have especially stringent regulations. Consider Spain, where mandated severance pay is particularly generous. Until 2012, any Spanish firm that wished to fire a worker was required to pay that worker for 45 days for every year the worker had been employed with the company. Thus, if a firm wanted to fire a 10-year employee, it had to pay that person for 450 days after his or her employment ended. (In 2012, the required severance pay was reduced to 20 days of pay for every year of employment.) This regulation makes it very difficult for young workers to break into the labor force. In fact, unemployment rates for workers aged 24 and younger were over 50% in 2015! These regulations also incentivize firms to search longer for the right workers to fill open positions, thereby increasing frictional unemployment. Another regulation seen in Spain is mandated annual increases in wages and benefits. That is, firms are required by law to give pay and benefits raises every year. Think about this regulation as if you were the manager of a Spanish business firm: before you ever hire and retain a worker for more than a year, you will want to make sure that this individual is worthy of the current pay plus raises. Like mandatory severance pay, this regulation increases the time firms spend searching for just the right match, again increasing frictional unemployment. Figure 20.3 plots the unemployment rates for Spain and the United States from 1995 to 2015. Notice how much higher the Spanish unemployment rate is. Even in 2014 and 2015, when the Spanish economy was growing briskly, the unemployment rate remained above 20%. Much of this unemployment is due to frictional unemployment

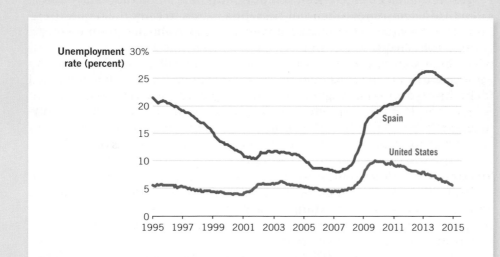

FIGURE 20.3

Unemployment Rate in the United States and Spain, 1995–2015

From 1995 to 2015, the unemployment rate in Spain was much higher than the unemployment rate in the United States. This difference is largely a result of Spanish labor-market regulations, many of which were put in place to help workers. But the reality is that these regulations increase frictional unemployment.

caused by labor market regulations. These regulations were put in place to help workers, but economics tells us that incentives affect behavior, and these regulations change firms' hiring incentives.

ECONOMICS IN THE REAL WORLD

Employment, Italian Style

Labor market restrictions may be intended to help workers, but often workers bear the costs themselves, as fewer jobs are created. Consider regulations in Italy, as reported in the *Wall Street Journal*.* The key point of the article relates to the government's inability to draw the Italian economy out of stagnation in 2012. The authors point to hiring regulations as one significant problem impeding employment:

> Imagine you're an ambitious Italian entrepreneur, trying to make a go of a new business. You know you will have to pay at least two-thirds of your employees' social security costs. You also know you're going to run into problems once you hire your 16th employee, since that will trigger provisions making it either impossible or very expensive to dismiss a staffer.
>
> But there's so much more. Once you hire employee 11, you must submit an annual self-assessment to the national authorities outlining every possible health and safety hazard to which your employees might be subject. These include stress that is work related or caused by age,

Italian firms like Fiat would hire many more employees if hiring regulations weren't so stringent.

---

*"Employment, Italian Style," *Wall Street Journal*, June 25, 2012.

gender and racial differences. You must also note all precautionary and individual measures to prevent risks, procedures to carry them out, the names of employees in charge of safety, as well as the physician whose presence is required for the assessment.

Now say you decide to scale up. Beware again: Once you hire your 16th employee, national unions can set up shop. As your company grows, so does the number of required employee representatives, each of whom is entitled to eight hours of paid leave monthly to fulfill union or works-council duties. Management must consult these worker reps on everything from gender equality to the introduction of new technology.

Hire No. 16 also means that your next recruit must qualify as disabled. By the time your firm hires its 51st worker, 7% of the payroll must be handicapped in some way, or else your company owes fees in-kind. During hard times, your company may apply for exemptions from these quotas—though as with everything in Italy, it's a toss-up whether it's worth it after the necessary paperwork.

Once you hire your 101st employee, you must submit a report every two years on the gender dynamics within the company. This must include a tabulation of the men and women employed in each production unit, their functions and level within the company, details of compensation and benefits, and dates and reasons for recruitments, promotions and transfers, as well as the estimated revenue impact.

From one view, regulations like these can be seen as helpful to employees. After all, we all want greater job benefits and protections. But such highly complex regulations clearly reduce an employer's incentives for hiring. The result is greater frictional unemployment. ✳

Cyclical Unemployment

Cyclical unemployment is unemployment caused by economic downturns.

The third type of unemployment, **cyclical unemployment**, is caused by recessions, or economic downturns. This type of unemployment generates the greatest concern among economists and policymakers. It is the most serious type of unemployment because it means that jobs are not available for many people who want to work. And while both structural and frictional unemployment are consistent with a growing, evolving economy, the root cause of cyclical unemployment is an unhealthy economy. Unlike structural unemployment and frictional unemployment, cyclical unemployment is not considered a natural type of unemployment.

Although all three types of unemployment are temporary and disappear when workers are matched with jobs, the duration of cyclical unemployment is open-ended. No one knows how long a general macroeconomic downturn might last. Fortunately, many recent recessions in the United States have been fairly short. However, the Great Recession of 2007–2009 lasted for 19 months and led to more cyclical unemployment than at any time in the previous 30 years.

During the Great Depression, almost all unemployment was cyclical.

The Natural Rate of Unemployment

We have seen that there are three types of unemployment: structural, frictional, and cyclical. Figure 20.4 illustrates the relationship between these types of unemployment and both recessionary and healthy macroeconomic conditions. Notice that structural and frictional unemployment are always present, even when the economy is healthy and growing. During these healthy periods, cyclical unemployment disappears. During recessionary periods, cyclical unemployment appears. It is also possible for structural and frictional unemployment to increase in economic slowdowns. Structural unemployment might increase if the slowdown leads to changes in the structure of the economy: some jobs or industries may shrink permanently. Frictional unemployment might increase if government policies are adopted to aid the unemployed while they search for work.

This chapter began with the misconception that we should aim for zero unemployment. However, we have seen that some unemployment remains even during periods of economic expansion. Thus, zero unemployment is not attainable. Further, if policymakers consistently strive for zero unemployment, they may take actions that harm the economy. For example, in the 1970s, policymakers tried to push unemployment down past natural levels by putting more and more money into the economy. This strategy led to other complications like inflation, but it failed to reduce unemployment.

When we acknowledge a certain level of natural unemployment, we must also recognize a natural rate of unemployment. The **natural rate of unemployment** (u^*) is the typical unemployment rate that occurs when the economy is growing normally. Maintaining this natural rate is a more appropriate goal for policymakers. Economists never know the exact numerical value of the natural rate, in part because it changes over time. Currently, most economists feel that the natural rate of unemployment in the United States is near 5%.

The **natural rate of unemployment** is the typical unemployment rate that occurs when the economy is growing normally.

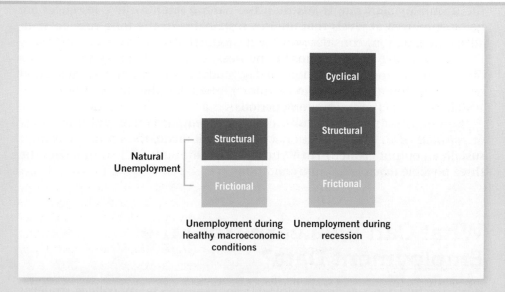

FIGURE 20.4

Three Types of Unemployment

Even during healthy economic periods, both structural and frictional unemployment are present. During recessions, cyclical unemployment appears. At the same time, structural and frictional unemployment may grow. As a result, the natural rate of unemployment increases.

Natural Unemployment

Structural

Frictional

Unemployment during healthy macroeconomic conditions

Cyclical

Structural

Frictional

Unemployment during recession

TABLE 20.1			
The Natural Rate of Unemployment and Full Employment Output			
	Healthy economy	**Recession**	**Exceptional expansion**
Where is the unemployment rate (u) relative to the natural rate of unemployment (u*)?	u = u*	u > u*	u < u*
Where is economic output (Y) relative to full employment output (Y*)?	Y = Y*	Y < Y*	Y > Y*
What is the level of cyclical unemployment?	Cyclical unemployment is zero.	Cyclical unemployment is positive.	Cyclical unemployment is negative.

Full-employment output, also called potential output or potential GDP, is the output level produced in an economy when the unemployment rate is equal to the natural rate. Also called potential output or potential GDP.

When the unemployment rate is equal to its natural rate—that is, when no cyclical unemployment exists—the output level produced in the economy is called **full-employment output** (Y*). Recall from Chapter 19 that we measure economic output with real GDP. For the rest of the book, our shorthand notation is this: real GDP = Y. An unemployment rate that is above the natural rate indicates cyclical unemployment, and at that point we say that the economy is producing at less than full-employment output levels (Y < Y*).

Sometimes, the actual unemployment rate is less than the natural rate (u < u*). This can happen temporarily when the economy is expanding beyond its long-run capabilities. What conditions might bring about a lower-than-natural unemployment rate? Demand for output might be so high that firms keep their factories open for an extra shift and pay their workers overtime. When output is at greater-than-full-employment output (Y > Y*) and the unemployment rate is less than the natural rate (u < u*), resources are being employed at levels that are not sustainable in the long run. To visualize this situation, consider your own productivity as deadlines approach. Perhaps you have several exams in one week, so you decide to set aside most other activities and study 15 hours a day. Studying this much may yield good results, and you may be able to do it for a little while, but most of us cannot sustain such an effort over a long period.

Economists also refer to full-employment output (Y*) as *potential output* or *potential GDP*. Unless additional changes are made, the economy cannot sustain an output greater than Y* in the long run. Table 20.1 summarizes the three possible macroeconomic conditions.

What Can We Learn from the Employment Data?

Who exactly counts as "unemployed"? For example, many college students don't have jobs, but that doesn't mean they are officially unemployed. Before examining historical unemployment rates in detail, we need to understand

PRACTICE WHAT YOU KNOW

Three Types of Unemployment: Which Type Is It?

Question: In each of the following situations, is the unemployment that occurs a result of cyclical, frictional, or structural changes? Explain your responses.

How long will you search for work?

a. Workers in a high-end restaurant are laid off when the establishment experiences a decline in demand during a recession.

b. Two hundred automobile workers lose their jobs as a result of a permanent reduction in the demand for automobiles.

c. A new college graduate takes three months to find his first job.

Answers:

a. *Cyclical changes.* Short-run fluctuations in the demand for workers often result from the ebb and flow of the business cycle. When the economy picks up, the laid-off workers may be rehired.

b. *Structural changes.* Since the changes described here are long-run in nature, these workers cannot expect their old jobs to return. Therefore, they must engage in retraining to reenter the labor force. Because they will be unable to find work until the retraining process is complete, the lost jobs represent a fundamental shift in the demand for labor.

c. *Frictional changes.* The recent college graduate has skills that the economy values, but finding an employer still takes time. This short-run job search process is a perfectly natural part of finding a job.

how unemployment is measured in the official employment statistics. In this section, we also look at some challenges of measuring unemployment.

The **labor force** includes people who are already employed or actively seeking work and are part of the work-eligible population (civilian, non-institutionalized, and age 16+).

The Unemployment Rate

Earlier in this chapter, we defined the unemployment rate (u) as the percentage of the labor force that is unemployed. We measure the unemployment rate as follows:

$$\text{unemployment rate} = u = \frac{\text{number unemployed}}{\text{labor force}} \times 100$$

(Equation 20.1)

Let's look at this definition more closely. To be officially unemployed, a person has to be in the labor force. A member of the **labor force** is defined as someone who is already employed or actively seeking work. If a jobless person has not sought a job in four weeks, that person is not counted in the labor force. In addition, only *work-eligible* people are counted. People who are institutionalized, children under the age of 16, and military workers are not considered in the official work-eligible population. Thus, individuals not included in the labor force include retirees, stay-at-home parents, people who are in jail, military personnel, children under age 16, and many full-time students.

Figure 20.5 provides recent data for the different groups. Starting with the relevant U.S. population (249,027,000), we find that approximately two-thirds of it is counted in the labor force (156,129,000). Of this number, in December 2014, fully 8,688,000 were unemployed. Plugging these numbers into equation 20.1 yields

$$u = \frac{8,688,000}{156,129,000} = 5.6\%$$

Historical Unemployment Rates

We now turn to historical data. One of our goals is to give you a good sense of normal conditions. It's also helpful to examine periods when particularly high unemployment rates prevailed. In Chapter 26, we discuss possible reasons for

---

FIGURE 20.5

Unemployment in the United States, December 2014

To compute the unemployment rate, we divide the work-eligible population between those who are in the labor force and those who are not. To be counted in the labor force, a person must either have a job or be actively seeking work. The unemployment rate is the percentage of the labor force that is unemployed.

Source: U.S. Bureau of Labor Statistics.

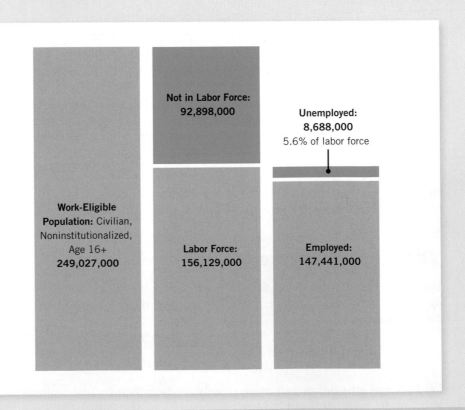

Not in Labor Force: 92,898,000

Unemployed: 8,688,000
5.6% of labor force

Work-Eligible Population: Civilian, Noninstitutionalized, Age 16+ 249,027,000

Labor Force: 156,129,000

Employed: 147,441,000

these difficult periods. Figure 20.6 shows the U.S. unemployment rate from 1965 to 2015, with the blue vertical bars representing periods of recession.

The average U.S. unemployment rate since 1960 has been about 6%. On average, there is a small amount of cyclical unemployment, so this number is above the natural rate of about 5%. But 6% is a good reference point to use when comparing unemployment rates across time and across nations. Rates above 6% are high by historical U.S. standards; rates under 6% are low.

Notice how the U.S. unemployment rate consistently spikes during recessions. This pattern vividly illustrates cyclical unemployment. Also note how long it takes for unemployment to return to the natural level of about 5% after a recession ends. As you can see, some unemployment always remains, no matter how significant or prolonged the economic expansion. Unemployment always exists because structural and frictional unemployment are always positive. For example, in early 2000, real GDP for the United States was expanding at a very significant 6.4%, and the unemployment rate (as Figure 20.6 shows) was 3.8%. That's the lowest U.S. unemployment rate since 1970—but still above zero.

Shortcomings of the Unemployment Rate

The unemployment rate, released monthly, is a timely and consistent indicator of the health of the macroeconomy. However, it has two shortcomings as an economic indicator. Let's look at each in turn.

FIGURE 20.6

U.S. Unemployment Rate and Recessions, 1965–2015

The U.S. unemployment rate consistently spikes during recessions, which are indicated here by the blue-shaded bars. During recessions, cyclical unemployment rises. During nonrecessionary periods, the unemployment rate drops toward the natural rate of approximately 5%, and only structural and frictional unemployment remain.

Source: U.S. Bureau of Labor Statistics.

ECONOMICS IN THE MEDIA

Structural Unemployment

The Office

In the TV show *The Office*, Angela, Kevin, and Oscar are accountants at the Scranton branch office of Dunder-Mifflin, a paper company. In one episode, a representative from the corporate office (which oversees all branches) unveils a new accounting system. Ryan, from corporate, explains to Angela, Kevin, and Oscar that the new system automates most of the billing process, so that when a customer places an order, it gets emailed to the warehouse and a copy goes directly to the customer's inbox.

Angela then asks, "How do we bill them?" and Ryan responds, "You don't. The invoicing, account reconciliation, and all the follow-up claims just go right to your BlackBerry." At this point, Oscar says, "So what do the accountants do?" Ryan responds, "Well, unless there is a real problem client, nothing."

Angela and Oscar immediately understand that their jobs are becoming obsolete. But Kevin still doesn't understand. So after Ryan has left the room, he crows, "This is the greatest thing that has ever happened to us!" Angela responds, "No, it's not." Kevin still doesn't get it, jumping in with, "Are you kidding me?" Oscar then delivers the bad news: "It

Is technical progress always good news?

was already a stretch that they needed three of us. Now they don't even need one."

In this story, Angela, Oscar, and Kevin are seeing the effects of structural unemployment, as technological advances are making their jobs redundant. This is true in the short run because less labor is needed to complete the billing process. However, the structural unemployment that is about to occur is a by-product of a dynamic and growing economy, and most economists would assume that with possibly some additional retraining they will find work elsewhere.

The first shortcoming of the unemployment rate is related to exclusions. People who are unemployed for a long time may just stop looking for work—not because they don't want a job, but because they get discouraged. When they stop looking for work, they fall out of the labor force and no longer count as unemployed; in other words, they are excluded from the statistics. **Discouraged workers** are defined as those who are not working, have looked for a job in the past 12 months and are willing to work, but have not sought employment in the past 4 weeks.

Another group not properly accounted for is composed of **underemployed workers**, defined as workers who have part-time jobs but who would like to have full-time jobs. These workers are not counted as unemployed. In fact, the official unemployment rate includes only workers who have no job and who are actively seeking work. This definition excludes both discouraged and underemployed workers, groups that increase during economic downturns. Figure 20.7 shows the official U.S. unemployment rate for the period 1995–2015 versus an alternative measure that includes discouraged and

Discouraged workers are those who are not working, have looked for a job in the past 12 months and are willing to work, but have not sought employment in the past 4 weeks.

Underemployed workers are those who have part-time jobs but who would prefer to work full-time.

underemployed workers. Not only is the alternative measure much higher than the unemployment rate, but the difference expands significantly during and after recessions (the blue vertical bars).

The second shortcoming of the official measurement of unemployment is that it does not specify who is unemployed or how long they have been out of work. Are people unemployed for short spells, or is their joblessness long-term? If most unemployment is short-term, we might not be as concerned with a higher unemployment rate, because it indicates that unemployment is temporary rather than a long-term problem for workers. To help fill in this part of the unemployment picture, the Bureau of Labor Statistics keeps an alternative measure of unemployment that tracks how long workers have been unemployed.

Table 20.2 shows the duration of unemployment in the United States in 2007 and 2015. The year 2007 came at the end of a long expansionary period in the U.S. economy. At that time, more than two-thirds of total unemployment was short-term (14 weeks or less), and just 17.6% of those unemployed

FIGURE 20.7

A Broader Measure of U.S. Labor Market Problems, 1995–2015

The blue line includes workers who are officially unemployed, discouraged workers who have given up the job search, and workers who are underemployed (that is, working part-time when they would rather work full-time). The gap between this broader measure and the official unemployment rate, shown by the orange line, grows when the economy enters a recession. Notice how the gap between the two series widens during the Great Recession, which began at the end of 2007.

Source: U.S.Bureau of Labor Statistics.

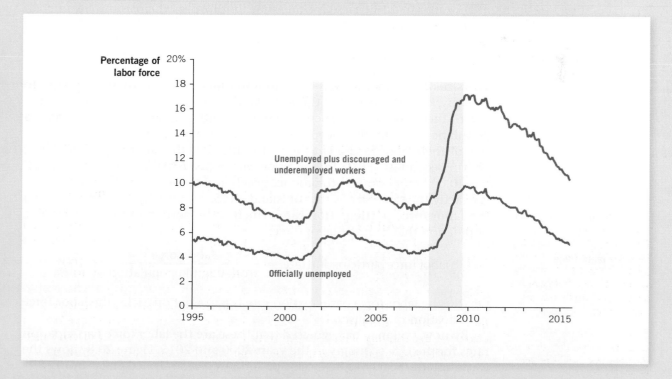

TABLE 20.2

Duration of Unemployment in the United States, 2007 and 2015

| | Percentage of total unemployed | |
Duration	2007	2015
Short-term	67.4%	58.5%
Less than 5 weeks	35.9	30.7
5–14 weeks	31.5	27.8
Long-term	32.6	41.5
15–26 weeks	15.0	14.6
27 weeks or longer	17.6	26.9

Source: U.S. Bureau of Labor Statistics.

were out of work for 27 weeks or longer. In contrast, consider 2015, which was, of course, after the Great Recession. Even six years after the Great Recession had ended, those unemployed for the very long term (27 weeks or more) accounted for 26.9% of total unemployment in 2015.

Other Labor Market Indicators

Macroeconomists use several other indicators to get a more complete picture of the labor market. These include the labor force participation rate and statistics on gender and race.

Labor Force Participation

The size of the labor force is itself an important macroeconomic statistic. To see why, consider two hypothetical island economies that differ only in the size of their labor forces. These two islands, called 2K and 2K15, each have a population of 1 million people and are identical in every way except in the size of their labor forces. On the first island, 2K, the labor force is 670,000. On the second island, 2K15, the labor force is just 630,000 workers. Island 2K has 40,000 more workers to produce goods and services for a population that is exactly the same size as that of island 2K15. This is why economists watch the **labor force participation rate**, which is the portion of the work-eligible population that is in the labor force:

The **labor force participation rate** is the percentage of the work-eligible population that is in the labor force.

$$\text{labor force participation rate} = \frac{\text{labor force}}{\text{work-eligible population}} \times 100$$

On 2K, the labor force participation rate is 67%; but on 2K15, the labor force participation rate is just 63%.

By now, you may have guessed that these are the labor force participation rates for the U.S. economy in the years 2000 and 2015. Figure 20.8 shows the evolution of the labor force participation rate in the United States from 1995 to 2015. You can see that it peaks at 67.3% in 2000 but then falls to 62.6% in

FIGURE 20.8

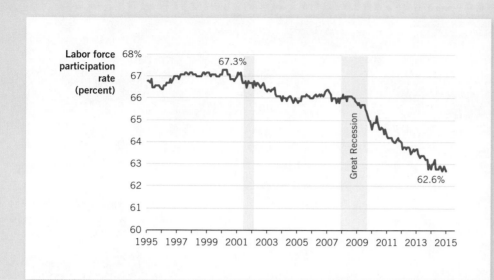

**U.S. Labor Force
Participation Rate,
1995–2015**

The labor force participation rate in the United States peaked at 67.3% in 2000, but it has subsequently fallen below 63%.

Source: U.S. Bureau of Labor Statistics.

2015. All else equal, this means that in 2015 there were fewer people working relative to the overall U.S. population than in any of the previous years shown in the graph, including the year 2000.

The changing demographics of the U.S. population is likely to reduce the labor force participation rate even further over the coming decades. The term "baby boom" refers to the period after World War II when U.S. birthrates temporarily rose dramatically. The U.S. Census Bureau pegs this period at 1946–1964. So there is now a bubble in the U.S. population known as the "baby boomers." (This group most likely includes your parents.) But now, as the oldest baby boomers begin to retire, the labor force participation rate will fall. All else being equal, fewer workers will produce less GDP. At the same time, federal expenses allocated toward retirees—for example, Social Security and Medicare—will rise. As you can see in Figure 20.8, these demographic changes are coming at a time when the U.S. labor force participation rate is declining.

Gender and Race Labor Force Statistics

As Figure 20.9 indicates, the composition of the U.S. labor force today is markedly different from that of two generations ago. Not only are more women working (from 32% in 1948 to 56.7% in 2015), but male labor force participation has fallen dramatically (from over 87% to just 69% in 2015). Men still remain more likely to participate in the labor force than women, but the participation gap has significantly narrowed.

How do we explain the fact that fewer males are working? A number of reasons account for the

Men are more likely to stay at home today than they were two generations ago.

Unemployment and the Labor Force

The unemployment rate is a primary economic indicator. Many people view it as particularly important because it measures a level of hardship that is not necessarily conveyed in GDP statistics. Every 1% jump in the U.S. unemployment rate means an additional 1.5 million jobs are lost. These effects are not spread equally over society, and there can be great variation across races and other demographic categories. For an example of a demographic comparison, rates are shown here for white and black (African American) men and women.

The labor force participation rate tells a vivid story about the United States over the course of the twentieth and early twenty-first centuries. As more and more women have entered, men have also exited, so that the two rates have converged.

Unemployment Rate by Demographic, 1972–2015

During and after recessionary periods, the unemployment rate rises.

The unemployment rate for black (African American) workers is consistently higher than that for white workers, and tough economic times affect them more.

Key

— White men
— White women
— Black men
— Black women
▉ Period of recession

Source: Bureau of Labor Statistics.

REVIEW QUESTIONS

- In the Great Recession of the late 2000s, roughly how many percentage points did the unemployment rate of black (African American) men rise?

- How do you explain the labor force participation rate changes between men and women?

Labor Force Participation Rate by Demographic, 1972–2015

Over the past 40 years, the percentage of white and black (African American) men in the work force has witnessed a substantial decline.

In one generation (between 1972 and 1990) the labor-force participation rate for women jumped dramatically.

FIGURE 20.9

Trends in U.S. Labor Force Participation, 1940–2015

Over the past 75 years, the composition of the U.S. labor force has shifted drastically. While more women have entered the labor force, the percentage of men in the labor force has dropped from almost 90% to under 70%.

Source: U.S. Bureau of Labor Statistics.

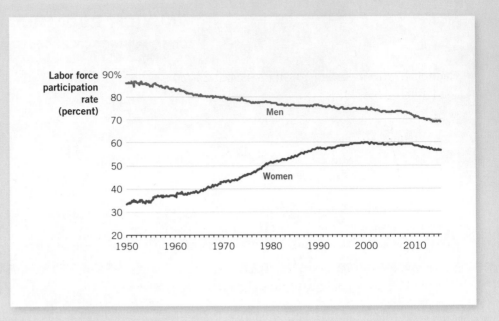

TABLE 20.3

U.S. Unemployment and Labor Force Participation Rates by Gender and Race, July 2015		
Group	Unemployment rate	Labor force participation rate
Overall	5.3%	62.6%
Adults (age 20+)		
Black males	8.8	67.0
Black females	8.0	62.1
White males	4.3	72.1
White females	4.3	57.4
Teenagers (age 16–19)		
Black males	30.1	24.9
Black females	27.6	31.2
White males	15.6	35.9
White females	12.5	35.8

Source: U.S. Bureau of Labor Statistics.

decline. Men are living longer, acquiring more education, and spending more time helping to raise families. Because men who are retired, in school, or staying at home to care for children are not counted as part of the labor force, the labor force participation rate for males is lower.

Unemployment rates also vary widely across age and race. Table 20.3 breaks down these statistics by age, race, and gender. Looking first at unem-

PRACTICE WHAT YOU KNOW

Unemployment and Labor Force Participation Rates: Can You Compute the Rates?

The following data are from Germany in 2013:

> Working-age population = 71,711,000
> Labor force = 44,451,000
> Employed = 42,269,000

This German worker is employed at a textile plant.

Question: Using the data, how would you compute the number of unemployed workers, the unemployment rate, and the labor force participation rate for Germany in 2013?

Answer: The unemployment rate is the total number of unemployed as a percentage of the labor force. First, determine the number of unemployed as the total labor force minus the number of employed:

$$\text{unemployed} = \text{labor force} - \text{employed} = 2,182,000$$

Use this information to determine the unemployment rate, which is the number of unemployed divided by the labor force:

$$\text{unemployed} \div \text{labor force} = 4.91\%$$

Finally, the labor force participation rate is the labor force as a percentage of the work-eligible population:

$$
\begin{aligned}
\text{labor force participation rate} &= \text{labor force} \div \text{working-eligible population} \\
&= 44,451,000 \div 71,711,000 \\
&= 61.99\%
\end{aligned}
$$

ployment rates, in July 2015, the overall unemployment rate was 5.3%. But the rate ranges from a low of 4.3% for both white males and white females (over 20 years old) to a high of 30.1% for black teenage males. Notice also that labor force participation rates are very low among teenagers, with white teenagers at about 36% but black males at 24.9%.

Conclusion

This chapter began with the misconception that we should aim for zero unemployment. However, you have learned that even a growing economy has some unemployment. We considered why policymakers shouldn't aim for zero unemployment—mainly because some unemployment is natural. People pay attention to the unemployment rate because it can affect them personally, but economists monitor the unemployment rate as an important macroeconomic indicator. In addition to real GDP, we use the unemployment rate to assess the position of the economy relative to the business cycle. Because employment data are released more frequently than GDP data, they offer a timely snapshot of current conditions. For this reason, the first Friday of every month, when the employment data are released, tends to be a nervous day, especially during turbulent economic times.

In the next chapter, we will look more closely at a third important macroeconomic indicator—inflation.

ANSWERING THE BIG QUESTIONS

What are the major reasons for unemployment?

* There are three types of unemployment: structural unemployment, frictional unemployment, and cyclical unemployment.
* Structural unemployment is caused by changes in the structure of the economy that make some jobs obsolete.
* Frictional unemployment is affected by information availability and government policies.
* Cyclical unemployment is caused by recessionary conditions that eliminate jobs during a downturn in the business cycle.

What can we learn from the employment data?

* The unemployment rate, one of the most reliable indicators of an economy's health, reflects the portion of the labor force that is not working and is unsuccessfully searching for a job.
* The labor force participation rate reflects the portion of the work-eligible population that is working or searching for work.
* Unemployment data enable economists to examine economic trends and identify where the labor market conditions are particularly strong or weak.
* Unemployment data also help to evaluate current conditions in a long-run historical perspective. For example, the case study in this chapter helps us view the recent Great Recession in the context of earlier economic downturns.

Finish Your Degree!

College students often fret over which major will increase their chances of getting a good job. Your major certainly matters for getting the job you want, and it may also affect your future income. But the figure below shows just how important it is to finish your degree, no matter what your major may be.

The chart plots unemployment rates by level of educational attainment. The data shown here are from April 2015, but you can find current data by visiting the Bureau of Labor Statistics (BLS) at www .bls.gov. Notice how the unemployment rate drops as the level of educational attainment increases. This pattern holds true across all majors. In particular, look at the big drop in the unemployment rate for those who complete a bachelor's degree or higher. The unemployment rate is about half that of those who have some college but do not complete a bachelor's degree. It turns out that the most important major is the one that holds your interest long enough to guarantee that you graduate!

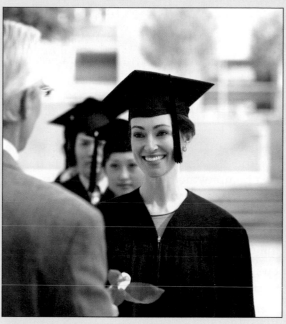

Want to give yourself the best chance of getting a job?

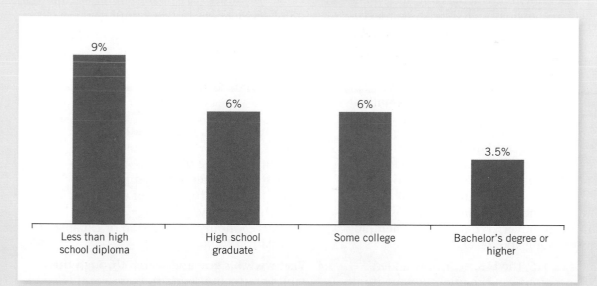

U.S. unemployment rate by educational attainment, April 2015

CONCEPTS YOU SHOULD KNOW

creative destruction (p. 637)
cyclical unemployment (p. 644)
discouraged workers (p. 650)
frictional unemployment
   (p. 640)
full-employment output
   (p. 646)

labor force (p. 647)
labor force participation rate
   (p. 652)
natural rate of unemployment
   (p. 645)
structural unemployment
   (p. 637)

underemployed workers (p. 650)
unemployment (p. 636)
unemployment insurance
   (p. 641)
unemployment rate (p. 636)

QUESTIONS FOR REVIEW

1. Until the late 1960s, most economists assumed that less unemployment was always preferable to more unemployment. Define and explain the two types of unemployment that are consistent with a dynamic, growing economy.

2. Is there any unemployment when an economy has "full employment"? If so, what type(s)?

3. The news media almost always bemoans the current state of the U.S. economy. How does the most recent unemployment rate relate to the long-run average?

4. What type of unemployment is affected when online job search engines reduce the time necessary for job searches? Does this outcome affect the natural rate of unemployment? If so, how?

5. What groups does the Bureau of Labor Statistics count in the labor force? Explain why the official unemployment rate tends to underestimate the level of labor market problems.

6. Does the duration of unemployment matter? Explain your answer.

7. What does an increase in the natural rate of unemployment imply about each of the three types of unemployment?

8. What can cause an increase in frictional unemployment? Give at least one example. What can cause an increase in structural unemployment? Give at least one example.

STUDY PROBLEMS (*solved at the end of the section*)

1. In his song "Allentown," Billy Joel sings about the demise of the steel and coal industries in Pennsylvania. Why do you think the loss of manufacturing jobs was so difficult on the workers in areas like Allentown and parts of the Midwest where manufacturing was once the largest employer? What type of unemployment is the song about?

2. In January 2015, the U.S. economy added 257,000 new jobs. Yet the unemployment rate rose from 5.6% to 5.7%. How is this possible?

3. A country with a civilian (work-eligible) population of 90,000 (all over age 16) has 70,000 employed and 10,000 unemployed persons. Of the unemployed, 5,000 are frictionally unemployed and another 3,000 are structur-

ally unemployed. On the basis of these data, answer the following questions.
a. What is the size of the labor force?
b. What is the unemployment rate?
c. What is the natural rate of unemployment for this country?
d. Is this economy in recession or expansion? Explain.

4. Visit www.bls.gov and search through the tables on unemployment to answer the following questions.
a. What is the current national unemployment rate for the United States?
b. What is the current unemployment rate among people of your age, sex, and race?

5. Consider a country with 300 million residents, a labor force of 150 million, and 10 million unemployed. Answer the following questions.
   a. What is the labor force participation rate?
   b. What is the unemployment rate?
   c. If 5 million of the unemployed become discouraged and stop looking for work, what is the new unemployment rate?
   d. Suppose instead that 30 million jobs are created, attracting 20 million new people into the labor force. What would be the new rates for labor force participation and unemployment?

✳ 6. Consider the following hypothetical data from the peaceable nation of Adirolf, where there is no military, the entire population is over the age of 16, and no one is institutionalized for any reason. Then answer the questions.

Classification	Number of people
Total population	200 million
Employed	141 million
Full-time students	10 million
Homemakers	25 million
Retired persons	15 million
Seeking work but without a job	9 million

   a. What is the unemployment rate in Adirolf?
   b. What is the labor force participation rate in Adirolf?

For questions c through f: assume that 15 million Adirolfian homemakers begin seeking jobs and that 10 million find jobs.

   c. Now what is the rate of unemployment in Adirolf?
   d. How does this change affect cyclical unemployment in Adirolf?
   e. What will happen to per capita GDP?
   f. Is the economy of Adirolf better off after the homemakers enter the labor force? Explain your response.

✳ 7. In each of the following situations, determine whether or not the person would be considered unemployed.
   a. A 15-year-old offers to pet-sit, but no one hires her.
   b. A college graduate spends the summer after graduation touring Europe before starting a job search.
   c. A part-time teacher works only two days a week, even though he would like a full-time job.
   d. An automobile worker becomes discouraged about the prospects for future employment and decides to stop looking for work.

✳ 8. The table below presents real data from the U.S. labor market in January 2015. Fill in any numbers that are missing.

Civilian, noninstitutionalized, 16+ population	
Labor force	
Employed	148,201,000
Unemployed	
Labor force participation rate	62.9%
Unemployment rate	5.7%

SOLVED PROBLEMS

6a. The unemployment rate in Adirolf is 6%. To calculate the unemployment rate, use:

unemployment rate = u = (number unemployed ÷ labor force) × 100

- The number of unemployed: 9 million
- Labor force can be calculated in two ways:
  - Employed plus unemployed: 141 million + 9 million = 150 million
  - Total population minus those not in labor force (students, homemakers, retirees):

200 million − (10 million + 25 million + 15 million) = 150 million

Note: Because the total population is only composed of noninstitutionalized civilians over the age of 16, we can use this number (200 million) as the relevant population.

unemployment rate = u = (number unemployed ÷ labor force) × 100 = (9 ÷ 150) × 100 = 6%

b. The labor force participation rate in Adirolf is 75%. To calculate the labor force participation rate, use:

labor force participation rate =
(labor force ÷ population) × 100

- Labor force (calculated above): 150 million
- Population: 200 million

labor force participation rate =
(labor force ÷ population) × 100
= (150 ÷ 200) × 100 = 75%

c. Now the rate of unemployment in Adirolf is 8.5%. To calculate the new unemployment rate, use the same equation as above. However, the figures have changed with new entrants to the labor force:

- The new number of unemployed:
  9 million + 5 million = 14 million
- The new number of employed:
  141 million + 10 million = 151 million
- The new labor force can be calculated in three ways:
  - Previous labor force plus new entrants:
    150 million + 15 million = 165 million
  - Employed plus unemployed:
    151 million + 14 million = 165 million
  - Total population minus those not in labor force (students, homemakers, retirees):

200 million − (10 million +
10 million + 15 million) = 165 million

unemployment rate = u
= (number unemployed ÷ labor force) × 100
= (14 ÷ 165) × 100 = 8.5%

Note: Even though the number of employed increased, because the size of the labor force increased by more, the unemployment rate has increased.

d. The change does not affect cyclical unemployment, which is generally associated with economic downturns. Instead, the entrance of new workers into the labor force represents a change in the labor force participation rate. In general, the entry of new workers to the labor force is associated with good economic times. Because most of the homemakers were able to find jobs, we can conclude that the economy of Adirolf is growing.

e. With an increase in the number of employed workers, total output in the economy will increase. However, the size of the population has not changed. Thus, per capita GDP will increase as a result of the change.

f. Adirolf has a stronger economy with more working homemakers. Even though the unemployment rate has increased as a result of many homemakers entering the labor force, the increase in unemployment is not the result of economic downturn; rather, it is a sign of a growing economy. Adirolf has a stronger economy with higher GDP per capita and a greater labor force participation rate as a result of this change.

7a. No. The relevant population used to measure unemployment and the labor force comprises work-eligible individuals 16 years of age or older. This 15-year-old is not part of the relevant population, so she is not considered unemployed.

b. No. To be counted in the unemployment statistics, an individual must have made efforts to get a job in the past four weeks. This college graduate is not actively seeking work during the summer, so he is not counted as an unemployed individual.

c. No. This part-time teacher is underemployed because he would prefer a full-time position, but under the unemployment rate measurements he is considered to be employed.

d. No. The automobile worker is a discouraged worker if he has searched for work in the past year but stopped looking for work over four weeks ago. However, since he is not actively looking for work now, he is no longer considered part of the labor force.

8. First, determine the number in the labor force.
   We know that the labor force is composed of the employed and the unemployed. We also know that the unemployment rate is 5.7% of the labor force, so

100% = 5.7% + portion of the labor
force that is employed

This means that the portion employed is 94.3%.

If 94.3% of the labor force is employed, and the number employed is 148,201,000, then we can determine the size of the labor force as

$$\frac{148,201,000}{\text{labor force}} = 0.943$$

Therefore,

labor force = <u>157,159,067</u> (rounding to the nearest whole number)

Next, we find the size of the civilian, noninstitutional, 16+ population (pop). We know that

$$\text{labor force participation rate} = \frac{\text{labor force}}{\text{pop}}$$

and we already know the labor force participation rate and the labor force. Therefore,

$$62.9\% = \frac{157,159,067}{\text{pop}}$$

$$\text{pop} = \frac{157,159,067}{0.629}$$

population = <u>249,855,432</u>

Finally, we can now solve for the number unemployed because we know the total size of the labor force and the number employed:

labor force = employed + unemployed

157,159,067 = 148,201,000 + unemployed

unemployed = <u>8,958,067</u>.

The Price Level and Inflation

Inflation is no big deal.

For the last 30 years, inflation has been under control in the United States. As a college student, you have probably never experienced

significant inflation. Sure, you may notice that many prices rise from year to year, but these are slow, steady, often pre-dictable increases. However, as recently as the early 1980s, the annual inflation rate in the United States was close to 15%—about seven times the average inflation rate over the last two decades. And 15% is low by international standards. So it may appear that inflation is not a significant problem. But it certainly has been in the past, and there is no guarantee that we are safe from it in the future.

Moreover, looking around the world, we can see that inflation is still an important issue for many countries. In Zimbabwe, for example, the rate of inflation was so high in 2008 that prices were doubling every day! Zimbabwean dollars became worthless by the thousand, million, and even billion before the currency was effectively abandoned in 2009. High inflation can cause the destruction of wealth across an entire economy, and equally important, unpredictable inflation can wreak havoc within an economy—as we will see in the pages ahead.

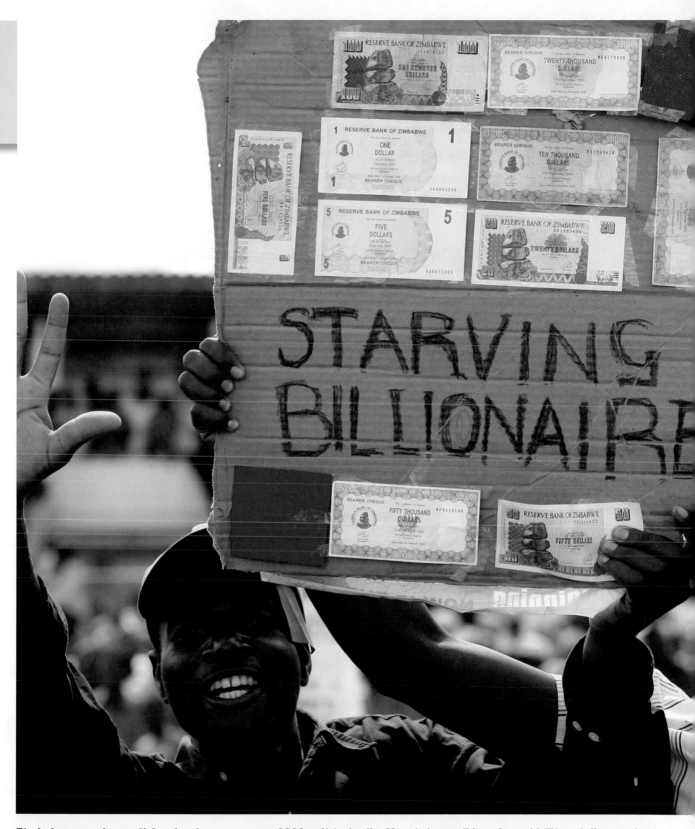

Zimbabweans show off devalued currency at a 2008 political rally. How is it possible to have 1 billion dollars and not be able to afford dinner?

BIG QUESTIONS

* How is inflation measured?
* What problems does inflation bring?
* What is the cause of inflation?

How Is Inflation Measured?

You might notice inflation on a routine shopping trip or especially when you see a reference to prices in an old book or movie. For example, in the 1960 movie *Psycho*, a hotel room for one night was priced at just $10. In Chapter 19, we defined inflation as the growth in the overall level of prices in an economy; so inflation occurs when prices rise throughout the economy. When overall prices rise, this affects our budget; it limits how much we can buy with our income. On the other hand, when overall prices fall, our income goes farther and we can buy more goods.

Imagine an annual inflation rate of 100%. At this rate, prices would double every year. How would this affect your life? Would it change what you buy? Would it change your savings plans? Would it change the salary you negotiate with your employer? Yes, it would change your life on a daily basis. Now imagine that prices double *every day*. This was the situation in Zimbabwe in 2008, when the inflation rate reached almost 80 billion percent per month! This is an example of what economists call *hyperinflation*, an extremely high rate of inflation, and it completely stymies economic activity. In Zimbabwe, for example, average citizens could barely afford necessities like bread and eggs.

Figure 21.1 shows inflation in the United States from 1965 to 2015. The long-run average inflation rate over this period was 4%, a good benchmark for evaluating current inflation rates. In the 1970s and early 1980s, there were periods of very high inflation. At one point in 1980, the inflation rate was almost 15%. But since the early 1980s, inflation seems well controlled in the United States. Looking again at Figure 21.1, you might notice a brief spell of deflation in 2009. **Deflation** occurs when overall prices fall; it is negative inflation.

Deflation occurs when overall prices fall.

Measuring inflation is straightforward but requires great care. First, prices don't all move together; some prices fall even when most others rise. Second, some prices affect consumers more than others. For example, a 10% increase in the price of housing is significantly more painful than a 10% increase in the price of hot dogs. Before we arrive at a useful measure of inflation, we have to agree on what prices to monitor and how much weight we'll give to each price. In the United States, the Bureau of Labor Statistics (BLS) measures and reports inflation data. In this section, we describe how the BLS estimates the overall price level. (Remember from Chapter 19 that the price level is an index of the average prices of goods and services throughout an economy.)

The BLS's goals are to (1) determine the prices of all the goods and services that a typical consumer buys and (2) identify how much of a typical consumer's budget is spent on these particular items.

The **consumer price index (CPI)** is a measure of the price level based on the consumption patterns of a typical consumer.

The Consumer Price Index (CPI)

We start by looking at the most common price level used to compute inflation. The **consumer price index (CPI)** is the measure of the price level based on the consumption patterns of a typical consumer. When you read or hear about inflation in the media, the report almost certainly focuses on this measure. The CPI is essentially the price of a typical "basket" of goods and services purchased by a representative consumer in the United States. What's in that basket? In addition to groceries, there is clothing, transportation, housing, medical care, education, and many other goods and services. The idea is to include everything a typical consumer buys. This gives us a realistic measure of a typical consumer's cost of living.

Figure 21.2 displays how the CPI was allocated among major spending categories in July 2015. There are prices for very specific goods and services inside these categories. For example, "Food and beverages" includes prices for everything from potato chips to oranges (both Valencia and navel) to flour (white, all purpose, per pound). These are goods in a "basket" that typical American consumers buy.

While the CPI is the predominant measure of the general price level, it is not the only one. In Chapter 19, for example, we saw that when computing real GDP data, the best choice is the GDP deflator, which includes prices from all the final goods and services that constitute GDP. Remember that GDP includes not only consumer goods and services, but also

The CPI is based on prices from a typical "basket" of all consumer goods and services.

FIGURE 21.1

Inflation in the United States, 1965–2015

From 1965 to 2015, inflation rates in the United States averaged 4%. This number is high because of excessive inflation in the 1970s. The inflation rate peaked at over 14% in 1980. More recently, inflation rates have averaged less than 3%.

Source: U.S. Bureau of Labor Statistics.

FIGURE 21.2

The Pieces of the Consumer Price Index, July 2015

The weights assigned to the different categories of expenditures are based on the spending patterns of a typical American. For example, 16% of a typical American's spending is on transportation; this includes car payments and fuel, among other expenses.

Source: U.S. Bureau of Labor Statistics.

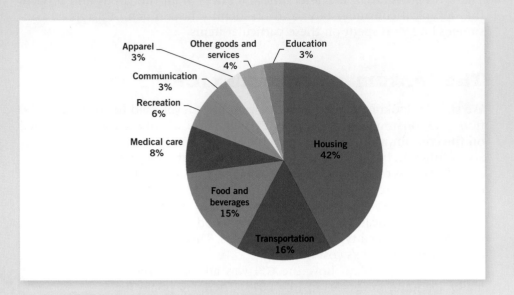

goods and services that consumers never actually purchase, like large farm equipment and wind turbines. The GDP deflator is too broad for our purposes here, because we are focusing on the prices of goods and services purchased by typical American consumers.

Of course, none of us is exactly typical in our spending. College students allocate significantly more than average to spending on education; senior citizens spend a lot more than average on medical care; a fashionista spends more than average on clothing; and those with lengthy commutes spend more than average on transportation. The CPI reflects the overall rise in prices for consumers *on average*.

Computing the CPI

Each month, the BLS conducts surveys by sending employees into stores in 38 geographical locations to gather and input price information on over 8,000 goods. The BLS estimates prices on everything from apples in Chicago, Illinois, to electricity in Scranton, Pennsylvania, to gasoline in San Diego, California. In addition to inputting price information, the BLS surveyors estimate how each good and service affects a typical consumer's budget. Once they do this, they attach a weight to the price of each good or service in the consumer's "basket." For example, Figure 21.2 indicates that the typical consumer spends 16% of his or her budget on transportation. Therefore, transportation prices receive 16% of the total weight in the typical consumer's basket of goods and services. Once the BLS has compiled the prices and budget allocation weights, it can construct the CPI.

To illustrate how this works, let's build a price index using just three goods. Imagine that when you go to the movies you notice that you are spending more for that outing than you did last year. You decide to construct a price index to see exactly how the price increases are affecting your budget. You decide to name your index the EPI (entertainment price index). For the sake

FIGURE 21.3

Calculating a Simple Price Index

In calculating this entertainment price index (EPI), we use the same steps that the Bureau of Labor Statistics does when calculating the CPI. First, we determine the typical basket of goods. Then we calculate the total price of the basket in a base year, 2016 in this example, and set that base year at 100 (creating an index). For subsequent years, we add up the new prices for the same basket of goods, then divide by the basket price in the base year, and then multiply by 100 to determine the new index number.

Good	Quantity	2016 Unit price	2016 Total cost	2017 Unit price	2017 Total cost
Popcorn	1	$6	$6	$8	$8
Coke	2	$5	$10	$5	$10
Movie ticket	2	$12	$24	$13	$26
Basket price			$40		$44
Index (EPI)			$\frac{\$40}{\$40} \times 100 = 100$		$\frac{\$44}{\$40} \times 100 = 110$

of this example, assume that a typical night at the movie theater includes two movie tickets, one box of popcorn, and two medium Cokes. This is the basket of goods (the popcorn and Cokes) and service (movie) included in your EPI.

The first four columns in Figure 21.3 show your EPI data for the first year, 2016. The second column shows the respective quantities of goods and service in your basket, and the third column displays the unit prices of these goods and service. The price of popcorn is $6 per box, the Cokes are $5 each, and the movie tickets are $12 each. The fourth column shows how much you pay in total for each good or service; this number is price multiplied by quantity. For example, in 2016, the price of a ticket was $12, so you paid a total of $24 for two tickets. Adding up, we get the total price for your basket of goods and service in 2016, which was $40. This is how much you spent for all goods and service in your EPI in 2016.

Let's now move to 2017. First, note that your consumption pattern hasn't changed; you still buy the same basket of goods and service. But some of the prices did change in 2017. Popcorn is now priced at $8 per box, and the movie ticket costs $13. But note that not all prices have changed. The cost of a Coke remains the same.

To see how the new 2017 prices affect your spending, we compute the total cost required to consume the same goods and service in the same quantities. The last column shows the costs of each component in your basket. The sum of these is now $44.

The final step is to create an index. You need an index because in the real world, adding a lot of prices together yields a huge number that would be difficult to work with. So we create an index that is equal to 100 at a fixed point in time—your base year. In our example, 2016 can be your base year. To convert to your index, we divide the basket price in each year by the basket price value from the base year and multiply by 100:

(Equation 21.1)
$$\text{price index} = \frac{\text{basket price}}{\text{basket price in base year}} \times 100$$

Using this formula, you can confirm that the EPI for 2017 is 100 and that the EPI for 2017 is 110 (see the last line of Figure 21.3).

When the Bureau of Labor Statistics computes the CPI for the United States, it follows the same basic steps:

1. Define the basket of goods and services and their appropriate weights.
2. Determine the prices of goods across periods.
3. Convert to the index number for each period.

ECONOMICS IN THE REAL WORLD

Sleuthing for Prices

The government considers paper towels to be a typical consumer item.

Tracking the prices in the CPI requires a great deal of effort and precision. The Bureau of Labor Statistics (BLS) is the U.S. government agency that is responsible for estimating the consumer price index. As of 2015, the BLS employed 428 "economic assistants." Their job is to fan out around the nation and determine the actual prices of goods and services—every month. This is no easy task because the items in the market basket are constantly changing. In September 2015, Emily Wax-Thibodeaux of the *Washington Post* followed one of these economic assistants on a typical day's work. The BLS employee, Caren Gaffney, drove all around the state of Virginia for more than 8 hours tracking prices on gasoline, sugar, and beer.

The items to be priced were very specific. For the gas price alone, Gaffney needed to determine the octane grade, whether the quoted prices depended on the day of the week, and whether the customer paid with cash or credit. The BLS tracks 200 different price categories, and each category includes the prices of several hundred goods and services. For example, the BLS tracks the prices of four types of margarine (sticks, soft, vegetable blend sticks, and vegetable blend soft). Paper towels may seem like a pretty standard item, but it turns out that there are 31 different varieties of some brands.

In macroeconomics, we generally see one number that indicates how much prices have changed. But it's important to remember that thousands of prices are tracked each month by government workers like Caren Gaffney. ✳

Source: https://www.washingtonpost.com/politics/the-governments-human-price-scanners/2013/11/11/a4225dc2-4576-11e3-bf0c-cebf37c6f484_story.html

Measuring Inflation Rates

Once the CPI is computed, economists use it to measure inflation rates. The inflation rate (i) is calculated as the percentage change in the price level (P). Using the CPI as the price level, the inflation rate from period 1 to period 2 is

$$\text{inflation rate (i)} = \frac{P_2 - P_1}{P_1} \times 100 \qquad \text{(Equation 21.2)}$$

Note that this is a growth rate, computed just like the growth rate of GDP in Chapter 19. In our entertainment price index example, the CPI rose from 100 to 110 in one year. So the inflation rate for that year was 10%, computed as

$$\text{inflation rate (i)} = \frac{110 - 100}{100} \times 100 = 10\%$$

The BLS releases CPI estimates every month. Normally, inflation rates are measured over the course of a year, showing how much the price level grows in 12 months. Figure 21.4 shows the historical relationship between the U.S. inflation rate and the CPI. Panel (a) plots the U.S. CPI from 1965 to 2015. The base period for the CPI is set for 1982–1984, so it goes through

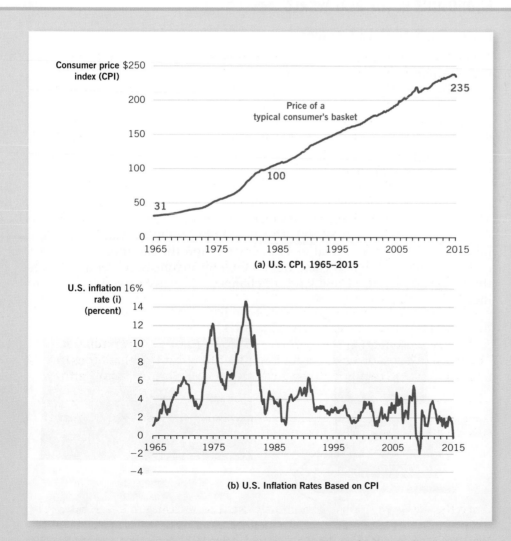

FIGURE 21.4

The CPI and Inflation, 1965–2015

Panel (a) shows the CPI since 1965. The index of prices for a typical consumer's basket of goods was at 31 in 1965 but rose to 235 by 2015. Panel (b) shows the U.S. inflation rate, computed as the growth rate of the CPI. A rapidly rising CPI, like we see in panel (a) during the 1970s, is reflected in the high inflation rate.

Source: U.S. Bureau of Labor Statistics.

100 in mid-1983. The CPI was just 31 in 1965 and rose to 235 by 2015. This means that the typical basket of consumer goods and services cost almost eight times as much in 2015 as it did 50 years earlier.

Panel (b) of Figure 21.4 plots inflation rates based on the CPI data in panel (a). The inflation graph reveals a number of historical observations that are important to our study of macroeconomics. For example, when you look at the graph, you might wonder what was going on in the 1970s. Before and after the 1970s, inflation was relatively stable, and the rate averaged less than 3%. But from 1970 to 1981, the inflation rate averaged 8%, including the year between April 1979 and March 1980, when it was over 14.5%. We'll explain the reasons for these historically high rates in Chapter 31. For now, in comparing the two graphs in Figure 21.4, notice that the CPI increased more rapidly from 1979 to 1980 than in any other period shown. Overall, the long-run average rate of inflation in the United States is about 4%.

ECONOMICS IN THE REAL WORLD

Prices Don't All Move Together

While it's clear that prices generally rise, not all prices go up. When the CPI rises, it indicates that the price of the overall consumer basket rises. However, some individual prices stay the same or even fall. For example, consumer electronic prices almost always fall. When flat-panel plasma TVs were introduced in the late 1990s, a 40-inch model cost more than $7,000. Fifteen years later, 50-inch flat-panel TVs are available for less than $500. This is the result of technological advancements: as time passes, it often takes fewer resources to produce the same item or something better.

Computers are another example. In 1984, Apple introduced the Macintosh computer at a price of $2,495. The CPU for the Macintosh ran at 7.83 MHz, and the 9-inch monitor was black and white. Today, you can buy an Apple iMac for less than $2,000. This new Apple computer has a quad-core processor that runs at a total of 11,200 MHz, and the monitor is 27 inches (color, of course). The new computer is better by any measure, yet it costs less than the early model. These kinds of changes in quality make it difficult to measure the CPI over time. ✳

The 1984 Macintosh price was $2,495 . . .   . . . but this 2011 Apple iMac cost just $1,999.

Using the CPI to Equate Dollar Values over Time

Prices convey a lot of information, but prices from different periods can be quite confusing. For example, in 1924, a consumer could buy a fully constructed, 1,600-square-foot home through a physical catalog distributed by Sears at a price of just $1,969. But how does that price compare with today's prices? In addition to measuring inflation rates, we can use the CPI to answer these types of questions.

To compare the prices of goods over time, we convert all prices to today's prices, or "prices in today's dollars." Here is the formula:

$$\text{price in today's dollars} = \text{price in earlier time} \times \frac{\text{price level today}}{\text{price level in earlier time}}$$ (Equation 21.3)

Following this formula, we can compute the 2015 price of the 1924 Sears home. The CPI in 2015 was 235, and the CPI in 1924 was 17, so the computation is

$$\text{price in 2015} = \$1{,}969 \times \frac{235}{17} = \$27{,}566$$

In fact, the 1924 Sears price would be pretty low even today.

Table 21.1 takes past prices from some iconic foods and converts them to today's dollars. For example, the price of a 1-pound bag of Oreo cookies was 32 cents in 1922. Using Equation 21.3, we multiply $0.32 by the modern price level (235) and divide by the 1922 price level (17) to determine the old price in today's dollars. It turns out that, once converted, the old price is $4.48, which is much higher than today's actual price of $2.99. The price in today's dollars corrects for the overall amount of inflation since 1922, helps make sense of historical prices, and dispels the notion that everything was less expensive in the past. This observation is nominally true but not especially interesting. Adjusting for inflation provides a real comparison, which is what good economists always look for.

TABLE 21.1

Converting Past Prices into Modern Dollar Values

	Product	Year	Price	Conversion	Today's dollars (2015)	Today's actual price
	Coca-Cola (12 oz.)	1942	$0.05	**$0.05 × (235 ÷ 16)**	$0.73	$0.63
	Hershey's chocolate bar (1 oz.)	1921	0.05	**$0.05 × (235 ÷ 18)**	0.65	0.69
	McDonald's hamburger	1955	0.15	**$0.15 × (235 ÷ 27)**	1.31	0.89
	Nabisco's Oreo cookies (1 lb.)	1922	0.32	**$0.32 × (235 ÷ 17)**	4.42	2.99

Inflation and the Consumer Price Index

Inflation is a concern for everyone, not just economists. When inflation occurs, the purchasing power of a dollar's worth of income falls, so inflation can eat into the real purchasing power of an individual's income. If unexpected, or significantly different from what was expected, inflation can cause serious harm to an economy. The inflation rate is measured as the percentage change in the overall price level. The price level we often use to measure inflation is the Consumer Price Index (CPI), which is driven by the prices paid by a typical American consumer.

Rate of Inflation and CPI, 1960–2015

Although inflation varied quite a bit over the last 50, the price of the typical consumer basket rose gradually and consistently.

—— Rate of inflation   —— Price of typical consumer basket   ▨ Period of recession

The inflation rate peaked at 14.8% in 1980 after a long buildup that began in the 1960s. In the early 1980s, the Fed got serious about fighting inflation, and since then rates have been much lower.

Time periods when the CPI is increasing most rapidly correspond to time periods when the inflation rate is at its highest.

In 2008 and 2009, there was a period of deflation, marked by a negative inflation rate and a decline in the CPI.

The Pieces of the CPI, September 2015

The data below shows the various categories in which U.S. citizens spend their income.

PIECES OF THE CPI
SEPTEMBER 2015

HOUSING	**42.4%**
TRANSPORTATION	**15.3%**
FOOD AND BEVERAGES	**15.1%**
MEDICAL CARE	**7.7%**
EDUCATION AND COMMUNICATION	**7.0%**
RECREATION	**5.7%**
APPAREL	**3.3%**
OTHER	**3.4%**

Source: Bureau of Labor Statistics

HOUSING	42.4%
Shelter	33.0%
Fuels and utilities	5.3%
Furnishings and other	4.1%

TRANSPORTATION	15.3%
Private transportation	14.2%
Public transportation	1.1%

FOOD AND BEVERAGE	15.1%
Food at home	8.3%
Food away from home	5.8%
Alcoholic beverages	1.0%

MEDICAL CARE	7.7%
Medical care services	5.9%
Drugs and supplies	1.8%

EDUCATION AND COMMUNICATION	7.0%
Communication	3.6%
Tuition and supplies	3.4%

RECREATION	5.7%
Video and audio	1.8%
Pets and pet care	1.0%
Other	2.9%

APPAREL	3.3%
Women's / girls' apparel	1.4%
Men's / boys' apparel	0.8%
Footwear and other	1.1%

OTHER	3.4%
Personal care	2.7%
Tobacco products	0.7%

REVIEW QUESTIONS

- When was the last time the inflation rate exceeded 5% in the United States?

- Explain why television and computer prices continue to fall but we still observe increases in the CPI.

ECONOMICS IN THE REAL WORLD

Which Movies Are Most Popular?

After a successful new movie comes out, the film industry totals up box office receipts and other revenue to see how well the movie has done. But since the receipt data are tied to the period in which the movie was released, they are nominal receipts, not receipts adjusted for inflation.

For example, *Avatar* is now the highest-grossing film of all time, meaning that it earned more revenue than any film from the past. *Titanic* held the top spot from 1998 to 2009, and *Star Wars* held the top spot from 1977 to 1997. Table 21.2 ranks the top eight movies of all time first by total worldwide receipts. The list of movies may not surprise you—there are several modern movies there that you've probably seen. However, you may find it odd to think of *Furious 7* as the fifth most popular movie of all time.

The second-to-last column shows total receipts adjusted for inflation in 2015. After this adjustment, you can see that *Avatar* is no longer number 1 and in fact produced only just more than the original *Star Wars* movie, which was released in 1977. The last column shows the rank of these movies once inflation is accounted for. Notice that *Avatar* falls to number 14 and *Furious 7* falls to number 140. So what is the absolute top movie of all time, based on total inflation-adjusted receipts? The answer is *Gone with the Wind*, released in 1939, with inflation-adjusted receipts of over $3.4 billion. ✳

Is *Avatar* really the most successful movie of all time?

The Accuracy of the CPI

We have seen that computing the CPI is not simple. Yet to understand what is happening in the macroeconomy, it is important that the CPI be accurate. For example, sometimes a rapid fall in inflation signals a recession, as it did in 1982 and 2008. Like real GDP and the unemployment rate, inflation is an indicator of national economic conditions.

But there is another reason the CPI needs to be accurate: when employers adjust wages for inflation, they generally use the CPI. For example, when the United Auto Workers (UAW) union signs a wage agreement with General Motors, the agreement specifies wages for autoworkers several years in advance. Since future inflation is unknown and the UAW wants to protect its workers from excess inflation, the agreement stipulates that wages will be tied to the CPI. Therefore, when the CPI rises, the wages of UAW workers rise; when the CPI falls, the wages of UAW workers fall. So if the CPI overstates inflation, the miscalculation can cost companies millions of dollars. If the CPI understates inflation, this hurts workers, since their wages will not rise as much as they should.

How accurate is the CPI? If consumers always bought the same goods and services from the same suppliers, it would be extremely accurate, and economists would be able to compare the changes in price from one year to the next very easily. But this is not realistic. Consumers buy different goods and services from different stores at different locations, and the quality of goods and services changes over time. Because the typical basket keeps changing,

Wage contracts for over 200,000 UPS employees are adjusted for inflation in reference to the CPI.

TABLE 21.2

Top Movies of All Time, Ranked by Total Worldwide Receipts

	Movie	Year	Receipts	Receipts adjusted for inflation 2015	Adjusted rank
	1. *Avatar*	2009	$2,787,965,087	$3,046,110,002	2
	2. *Titanic*	1997	2,186,772,302	3,205,455,051	5
	3. *Star Wars: The Force Awakens*	2015	2,068,178,000	2,068,178,000	9
	4. *Jurassic World*	2015	1,637,179,580	1,637,179,580	29
	5. *The Avengers*	2012	1,519,557,910	1,566,007,278	27
	6. *Furious 7*	2015	1,511,726,205	1,511,726,205	140
	7. *Avengers: Age of Ultron*	2015	1,401,213,387	1,401,213,387	89
	8. *Harry Potter and the Deathly Hallows—Part 2*	2011	1,341,511,219	1,413,377,891	110

it is difficult to measure its price. The most common concern is that the CPI overstates true inflation. There are three reasons for this concern: the substitution of different goods and services, changes in quality, and the availability of new goods, services, and locations.

Substitution

When the price of a good rises, consumers instinctively look to substitute less expensive alternatives. This makes CPI calculations difficult because the typical consumer basket changes. Earlier, when we calculated an entertainment price index, we assumed that you always bought the same quantities of all goods and services, even when the price of popcorn rose and the price of

Equating Dollar Values through Time

Austin Powers: International Man of Mystery

The Austin Powers series is a hilarious spoof of the James Bond films. In *International Man of Mystery*, we are introduced to British secret agent Austin Powers, who was cryofrozen at the end of the 1960s. Thirty years later, Austin Powers is thawed to help capture his nemesis, Dr. Evil, who was cryofrozen at the same time as Austin and has now stolen a nuclear weapon to hold the world hostage.

Being frozen for 30 years causes Dr. Evil to underestimate how much he should ask for in ransom money: "Gentlemen, it's come to my attention that a breakaway Russian republic called Kreplachistan will be transferring a nuclear warhead to the United Nations in a few days. Here's the plan. We get the warhead, and we hold the world ransom . . . FOR ONE MILLION DOLLARS!"

There is an uncomfortable pause.

Dr. Evil's Number Two speaks up: "Don't you think we should ask for more than a million dollars? A million dollars isn't that much money these days. Virtucon alone makes over nine billion dollars a year."

Dr. Evil responds (pleasantly surprised): "Oh, really? ONE HUNDRED BILLION DOLLARS!"

"ONE HUNDRED BILLION DOLLARS!"

International Man of Mystery takes place in 1997, and Dr. Evil was frozen in 1967. How much did the price level rise over those 30 years? The CPI was 33.4 in 1967 and 160.5 in 1997. Dividing 160.5 by 33.4 yields a ratio of 4.8. So if Dr. Evil thought that $1 million was a lot of money in 1967, an equivalent amount in 1997 would be $4.8 million. Dr. Evil does not let that stop him from asking for more!

Coke remained the same. However, it is more realistic to assume that if the price of popcorn rises, then some people will choose a less expensive snack. In other words, they find a substitute for popcorn. But when consumers substitute less expensive goods, that change alters the weights of all the goods and services in the typical consumption basket. Without acknowledging the substitution of less expensive items, the CPI would exaggerate the effects of the price increase, leading to upward bias (the reported CPI would be too high). Since 1999, the BLS has used a formula that accounts for both the price increase and the shift in goods and services consumption.

Changes in Quality

Over time, the quality of goods and services generally improves. For example, the movie theater you frequent may soon begin to offer all movies in 3D. Because this technology is more expensive than the older technology, the price of a ticket might rise from $10 to $12. The increase will seem like inflation, since ticket prices will go up. And yet, consumers will be getting "more" movie for their buck, because the quality will have improved. If the CPI did not account for quality changes, it would have an upward bias in the true cost of living. But the BLS uses an adjustment method to account for quality changes.

New Goods, Services, and Locations

In a dynamic, growing economy, new goods and services are introduced and new buying options become available. For example, tablet computers, flash drives, and even cell phones weren't in the typical consumer's basket 20 years ago. In addition, Amazon.com and eBay weren't options for consumers to make purchases before the 1990s.

Traditionally, the BLS updated the CPI basket of goods and services only after long time delays. This strategy biased the CPI in an upward direction for two reasons. First, the prices of new products typically drop in the first few years after their introduction. If the CPI basket doesn't include the latest prices, this price drop is lost. Second, new retail outlets such as Internet stores typically offer lower prices than traditional retail stores. If the BLS continued to check prices only at traditional retail stores, it would overstate the price that consumers actually pay for goods and services.

In an effort to measure this upward bias, the BLS began computing a chained CPI in 2000. The **chained CPI** is a measure of the CPI in which the typical consumer's basket of goods and services is updated monthly. While it's more difficult to measure and takes longer to estimate, the chained CPI is a better indicator of inflation for the typical consumer. Figure 21.5 shows the two CPI measures together. The vertical distance between the two lines indicates the upward bias of the traditional CPI, which updates the basket of goods and services less often. Notice that the distance grows over time.

The **chained CPI** is a measure of the CPI in which the typical consumer's "basket" of goods and services considered is updated monthly.

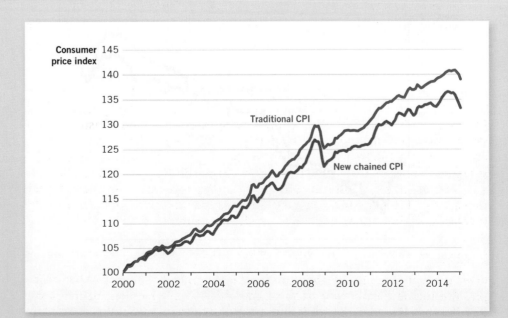

FIGURE 21.5

The Chained CPI versus the Traditional CPI

The chained CPI reduces the upward bias of the traditional CPI by updating the consumer's basket of goods and services every month. This single correction accounts for price reductions that typically occur during the first few years after a new product has been introduced.

Source: U.S. Bureau of Labor Statistics.

Consumer price index

Traditional CPI

New chained CPI

ECONOMICS IN THE REAL WORLD

The Billion Prices Project

The Billion Prices Project (BPP) is an academic initiative at the Massachusetts Institute of Technology that monitors daily price fluctuations of approximately 5 million items sold by roughly 300 online retailers in more than 70 countries. The BPP is different from the CPI in that it only tracks the prices of goods and services that are sold online, and it does not weight those prices to reflect their importance in a typical consumer basket. However, even given these differences, the BPP coincides with the CPI rather closely. Figure 21.6 shows the BPP index along with the CPI. Obviously, they look very similar, but the BPP index often estimates slightly more inflation than the CPI.

Why would researchers create an alternative measure to the CPI? The answer, in part, is because having access to the Internet makes the gathering of real-time price data extremely easy. With time, researchers hope to be able to examine over a billion prices each day across every major sector of the economy. Because the BPP is based only on online sales, there are limitations in generalizing its findings to the entire economy. In relatively stable environments with low inflation, the BPP and CPI are not likely to be very different. But that is not likely to be the case in high-inflation environments and certainly not when hyperinflation is present. When inflation is high (or highly variable), the BPP has the potential to point out meaningful trends in prices long before the CPI data can capture those changes. ✳

FIGURE 21.6

The Billion Prices Project

The Billion Prices Project is an independent index that tracks prices across the Internet as an alternative to the CPI. As the data lines indicate, the BPP index looks very similar to the CPI; however, it is compiled exclusively from online retail prices and requires no input from government workers.

Source: BPP - PriceStats - State Street, http://bpp.mit .edu/usa/.

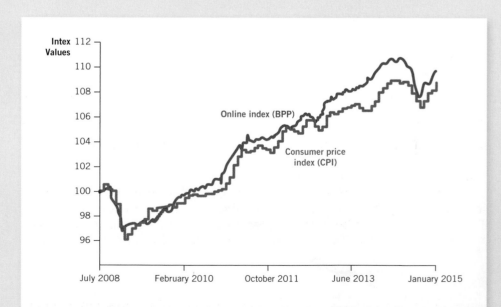

PRACTICE WHAT YOU KNOW

Using the CPI to Equate Prices over Time: How Cheap Were the First Super Bowl Tickets?

Ticket prices to America's premier sporting event, the Super Bowl, were much lower when it was first played in 1967. In fact, you could have bought a ticket for as little as $6. This seems very low by today's prices. In 2015, many seats sold for more than $5,000 each.

Question: If the CPI from 1967 was 33 and the CPI for 2015 was 238, how would you convert the price of a $6 ticket in 1967 to 2015 dollars?

Answer: For this question, we need to use equation 21.3:

$$\text{price in today's dollars} = \text{price in earlier time} \times \frac{\text{price level today}}{\text{price level in earlier time}}$$

The earlier price was $6, so we substitute this price and the two price levels from above to get

$$\text{price in today's dollars} = \$6 \times \frac{238}{33} = \$43.27$$

It turns out that the old Super Bowl tickets were indeed cheap—you'd be lucky to get a hot dog and a soda at a modern Super Bowl for $43.27.

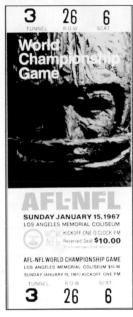

A 1967 Super Bowl ticket.

What Problems Does Inflation Bring?

Many people believe that inflation is most harmful because it reduces the purchasing power of their income. For example, consider that prices were much lower in the 1970s; therefore, it's easy to think that an annual salary of $10,000 at that time could buy a lot more than it can today. Well, this would be true if all else were equal. But salaries are prices, too (prices for labor), and inflation causes them to rise as well. Remember: inflation is an overall rise in prices throughout the economy.

But this does not mean that inflation is harmless. Indeed, inflation does impose many costs on an economy. In this section, we discuss these costs. They include shoe-leather costs, money illusion, menu costs, uncertainty over future price levels, wealth redistribution, price confusion, and tax distortions.

Shoe-Leather Costs

Inflation is costly for society when it causes people to do things they wouldn't do in an environment of price stability. After all, the higher the rate of inflation, the more likely people are to change their normal patterns of spending

When inflation reaches the levels witnessed in Zimbabwe in 2008, shoe-leather costs are significant.

Shoe-leather costs are the resources that are wasted when people change their behavior to avoid holding money.

Money illusion occurs when people interpret nominal changes in wages or prices as real changes.

and money-holding. The reason is that inflation is essentially a tax on holding money. As the prices of goods and services rise with inflation, the value of dollars in people's wallets falls. This problem is not currently severe in the United States because inflation rates are very low. But in hyperinflation, the value of dollars falls daily.

To avoid the "tax" on holding money, people hold less money, which means more trips to the bank to make withdrawals. **Shoe-leather costs** are the resources that are wasted when people change their behavior to avoid holding money. In times past, these costs referred to the actual expense of replacing shoes that might get worn out as a result of making many trips to the bank. Today, these include fuel costs and the time and effort that people expend when they make multiple trips to a bank or ATM.

Money Illusion

The second problem that inflation imposes is among the least understood. Even when people know that inflation has occurred, they do not always react rationally. So although wages and prices might rise because of inflation, people frequently respond as if the prices are higher in real terms. For example, if the price of a movie goes up by 10% but our wages and all other prices go up by a similar amount, nothing has changed in real terms. But many people mistakenly conclude that movies have become more expensive. If they treat a price increase from inflation as a change in relative price, they may go see fewer movies or make other decisions based on the new price. Economists call this *money illusion*. **Money illusion** occurs when people interpret nominal changes in wages or prices as real changes.

Money illusion is an easy trap to fall into. Let's see if we can trick you into it. Consider the cost-of-living data presented in Table 21.3. The index scores show relative living costs for an average inhabitant of various U.S. cities. The index is set so that 100 is the cost of living in an average U.S. city.

For this example, let's focus on two particular cities: Philadelphia, Pennsylvania, and Charlotte, North Carolina. The index score for Philadelphia is 126.5; for Charlotte, it is 93.2. These index scores imply that a salary of $93,200 for a person living in Charlotte is equivalent to a salary of $126,500 for a person living in Philadelphia. The difference is more than $30,000.

Now imagine that you are living in Charlotte and earning $93,200, but your firm offers to relocate you to Philadelphia at a pay rate of $100,000. Doesn't that seem like a pretty large raise? You might be excited to call your parents and tell them you'll be making "six figures." But, in fact, it is actually a real pay cut, since you can buy less with $100,000 in Philadelphia than you can with $93,200 in Charlotte. Money illusion makes it feel like a raise.

A worker's **nominal wage** is his or her wage expressed in current dollars.

The **real wage** is the nominal wage adjusted for changes in the price level.

The key distinction in this situation is between real wages and nominal wages. The nominal wage is similar to nominal GDP. A worker's **nominal wage** is his or her wage expressed in current dollars, like $60 per hour or $120,000 per year. The **real wage** is the nominal wage adjusted for changes in the price level. The real wage is more informative because it describes what the worker earns in terms of purchasing power. So while a salary of $100,000 a year may sound high, if the CPI doubles, that salary will not go very far.

Significant macroeconomic problems arise if workers fall victim to money illusion when they interpret the value of their wages, because the illusion

TABLE 21.3

The Cost of Living in Selected U.S. Cities

City	Cost-of-living index number
New York (Manhattan)	216.7
San Francisco, CA	164.0
Washington, DC	140.1
Los Angeles, CA	136.4
Boston, MA	132.5
Philadelphia, PA	**126.5**
Seattle, WA	121.4
Chicago, IL	116.9
Richmond, VA	104.5
Phoenix, AZ	100.7
Detroit, MI	99.4
Atlanta, GA	95.6
Charlotte, NC	**93.2**
Dallas, TX	91.9

Source: U.S Census, Annual Average 2010.

causes them to focus on their nominal wage instead of their real wage. For example, when prices fall, any given nominal wage is worth more in real terms. In Chapter 26, we'll see that macroeconomic adjustments can depend on whether workers are willing to let wages fall when other prices fall. Money illusion causes these adjustments to take longer than they should, and this delay tends to lengthen economic downturns.

Menu costs are the costs of changing prices.

Menu Costs

The act of physically changing prices is also costly. **Menu costs** are the costs of changing prices. While some businesses can change prices easily—for example, gas pumps and signs at gas stations are designed for this purpose—businesses such as restaurants can find it expensive to print new menus when their prices change.

Other costs considered in this category are not directly related to menus. For example, changing prices can make regular customers angry enough to take their business elsewhere. Think about your favorite lunch spot. Perhaps you regularly buy a bagel and an iced tea for $4 at Bodo's Bagels. What

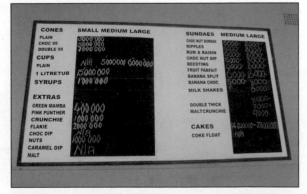

Chalk menus are one way to limit menu costs. This menu is from an ice cream parlor in Zimbabwe during its 2008 hyperinflation. Notice that the price of a small chocolate cone is 5 million Zimbabwean dollars.

if the price for this combination suddenly increases to $5? You might be annoyed enough to go somewhere else next time.

Menu costs discourage firms from adjusting prices quickly. When some prices are slow to respond, the effects of macroeconomic disturbances are magnified.

Future Price Level Uncertainty

Imagine you decide to open a new coffee shop in your college town. You want to produce espressos, café mochas, and cappuccinos. Of course, you hope to sell these for a profit. But before you can sell a single cup of coffee, you have to spend funds on your resources. You have to buy (that is, invest in) capital goods like an espresso bar, tables, chairs, and a cash register. You also have to hire workers and promise to pay them. All firms, large and small, face this situation. Before any revenue arrives from the sales of output, firms have to spend on resources. This also applies to the overall macroeconomy: to increase GDP in the future, firms must invest today. The funds required to make these investments are typically borrowed from others.

Output is the product that the firm creates.

The timeline of production shown in Figure 21.7 illustrates how this process works. At the end, the firm sells its output. **Output** is the product that the firm creates. The important point is that in a normal production process, funds must be spent today and then repaid in the future—after the output sells. But for this sequence of events to occur, businesses must make promises to deliver payments in the future: these include payments to workers and lenders. Thus, two types of long-term agreements form the foundation for production: wage and loan contracts. Both of these involve agreements for dollars to be delivered in future periods.

But inflation affects the real value of these future dollars. When inflation confuses workers and lenders, these essential long-term agreements seem risky and people are less likely to enter into them. Chapter 22 focuses on the market for loans in an economy, and we cover this topic at a deeper level there. For now, we note that inflation can cripple loan markets because peo-

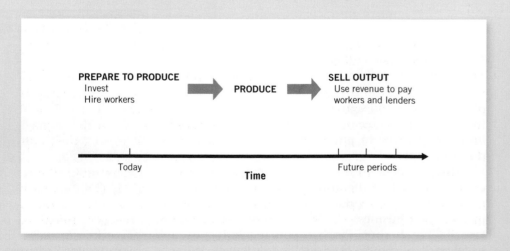

FIGURE 21.7

The Timeline of Production

The way output is typically produced begins with preparation that includes purchases of equipment, labor, and other resources. Actual output and revenue from the sale of output come later. Thus, the firm can only begin production with promises of future payments to resource suppliers.

PREPARE TO PRODUCE
Invest
Hire workers

PRODUCE

SELL OUTPUT
Use revenue to pay workers and lenders

Today   **Time**   Future periods

ple don't know what future price levels will be. When firms cannot borrow money or hire long-term workers, future production is limited. Thus, inflation risk can lead to lower economic output, which is GDP.

Wealth Redistribution

Inflation can also redistribute wealth between borrowers and lenders. Returning to our coffee shop example, imagine that you borrow $50,000 to start your business. You borrow this sum from a bank with the promise of paying back $60,000 in five years. Now if inflation unexpectedly rises during those five years, the inflation will devalue your future payment to the bank. As a result, you will be better off, but the bank will be worse off. Thus, surprise inflation redistributes wealth from lenders to borrowers.

If both you and the bank fully expect the inflation to occur, the bank will require more in return for the loan, so the inflation will be less of a problem. In the United States, inflation has been low and steady since the early 1980s. Therefore, surprises are rare. But nations with higher inflation rates also have a higher variability of inflation, which makes it difficult to predict the future. This is one more reason why high inflation increases the risk of making the loans that are an important source of funding for business ventures.

You might assume that deflation, or falling prices, brings only positive side effects for the economy. After all, wouldn't it be great if the prices of the goods and services you purchase began falling? But unexpected deflation redistributes from borrowers to lenders. Consider again the $50,000 loan with promised repayment of $60,000 in five years. Now, if prices fall unexpectedly over the course of the five years, the real value of the $60,000 loan repayment increases. This helps the lender but harms the borrower. In response, fewer of these loans will be made and this is not helpful to the economy as a whole.

Price Confusion

Market prices are signals to consumers and firms—signals that help allocate resources in a market economy. For example, if demand increases, prices rise and firms have an incentive to increase the quantity of output that they supply. All else equal, firms take rising prices as a signal to increase output and falling prices as a signal to decrease output. But inflation also shows up as rising prices. If firms cannot determine which price changes are due to inflation, resources may be misdirected in the economy.

Figure 21.8 illustrates the dilemma that firms face in this context. Initially, it may appear that output prices are rising as a result of an increase in demand. But if the cause is inflation, then prices throughout the economy will rise and the optimal output for the firm should remain at the original output level. If firms always react to price increases by increasing their output, they run the risk of overbuilding. This can be painful later.

The housing market in the United States provides a good example of price confusion. In 2005, housing prices were high and rising. We can look back now and recognize a price bubble that did not reflect real long-run increases in demand. It appears now that rising housing prices reflected inflation. However, high prices at the time spurred many builders to develop more properties. When housing prices later fell, many of those builders declared

FIGURE 21.8

"Why Did My Price Change?"

Price changes send information, or signals, to businesses. However, higher prices can be the result of either a real increase in demand or inflation. If upward pressure on prices is the result of greater demand, the profit-maximizing firm should increase its output. But if the price increase is the result of inflation, the firm should not change its level of output.

bankruptcy. The crash in housing prices was one of the contributing factors to the Great Recession, which began at the end of 2007.

Tax Distortions

Even if inflation caused all prices to rise uniformly, there would still be distortionary effects. These would occur because tax laws do not typically account for inflation. One area in which particularly distortionary effects occur is capital gains taxes.

Capital gains taxes are taxes on the gains realized by selling an asset for more than its purchase price. For example, if your parents bought a house in 1980 for $80,000 and then sold it in 2012 for $230,000, they made a $150,000 capital gain on the sale of the house, and this capital gain is taxed. However, it turns out that the CPI rose by exactly the same amount between 1980 and 2012: the CPI was 80 in 1980 and climbed to 230 by 2012. Therefore, the value of your parents' house just kept pace with inflation. In real terms, the value of their house did not climb. But they would still be required to pay a significant tax on the sale of their home. As it turns out, the amount of their tax was determined by inflation and not by the tax laws; if there had been no inflation, your parents would have owed no tax.

Capital gains are realized on more than just home sales. Capital gains also arise with the sales of stocks, bonds, and other financial securities. As we will discuss in Chapter 23, these securities are a crucial ingredient to a growing and expanding economy. But inflation combined with a capital gains tax means that most people will be less likely to make these kinds of purchases. One possible solution is to rewrite the tax laws to take account of inflation's effects.

As the previous discussion points out, inflation imposes specific costs on an economy. Table 21.4 summarizes these costs.

Capital gains taxes are taxes on the gains realized by selling an asset for more than its purchase price.

TABLE 21.4

The Costs of Inflation

Cost of inflation	Description
Shoe-leather costs	Time and resources are spent to guard against the effects of inflation.
Money illusion	Consumers misinterpret nominal changes as real changes.
Menu costs	Firms incur extra costs to change their output prices.
Future price level uncertainty	Long-term agreements may not be signed if lenders, firms, and workers are unsure about future price levels.
Wealth redistribution	Surprise inflation redistributes wealth from lenders to borrowers.
Price confusion	Inflation makes it difficult to read price signals, and this confusion can lead to a misallocation of resources.
Tax distortions	Inflation makes capital gains appear larger and thus increases tax burdens.

PRACTICE WHAT YOU KNOW

Problems with Inflation: How Big Is Your Raise in Real Terms?

Your boss calls you into his office and tells you he has good news. Because of your stellar performance and hard work, you have earned a 3% raise for next year. But when you think about your future pay, you should also know how much inflation has eroded your current pay. For example, if the inflation rate is 3% per year, then you need a 3% raise just to keep pace with inflation. Note that you can see inflation rates for yourself by visiting the Bureau of Labor Statistics web site (www.bls.gov). Once there, look up inflation rates based on the CPI.

Question: In what situation would a 3% raise signify a lower real wage?

Answer: If the inflation rate is greater than 3%, then a 3% raise would actually be a decline in your real wage.

Question: What inflation problem must you overcome to correctly see the value of your raise?

Answer: Money illusion. You must evaluate the real, rather than the nominal, value of your pay.

The printing press: the cause of inflation.

What Is the Cause of Inflation?

Because inflation presents such serious macroeconomic costs, you might assume that there is significant debate about its cause. But that assumption would be incorrect. Economist Milton Friedman famously said, "Inflation is always and everywhere a monetary phenomenon." What he meant is that inflation is consistently caused by increases in a nation's money supply relative to the quantity of real goods and services in the economy.

Figure 21.9 shows average inflation rates and the money supply growth rates across 160 nations for the years 1991–2011. For practically all nations, the relationship appears to be almost one-to-one. The blue line is a hypothetical one-to-one line, where a nation's average inflation rate is exactly equal to the average money supply growth rate. It is difficult to distinguish all 160 nations, because almost all of the data points are right on this one-to-one line, with inflation rates of less than 75%. In contrast, the few nations with even higher average inflation rates are easy to pick out. For example, in this sample, the average inflation rates in Brazil were 323% per year (this is not a typo!), and that inflation stemmed from monetary growth rates of about 331%.

In Chapter 31, we will address this question more formally; we will use a macroeconomic model to show how monetary expansion translates into

FIGURE 21.9

Inflation and Money Growth Rates in 160 countries, 1991–2011

The relationship between inflation rates and money growth rates is virtually one-to-one for many countries over long periods of time. This relationship applies to nations with low inflation rates and to nations with high inflation rates.

Source: World Bank.

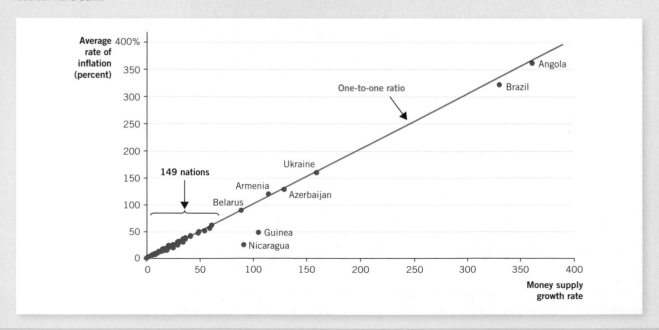

inflation. But the intuition is straightforward: when the supply of money in an economy grows *relative to the quantity of goods and services*, then it takes more money to buy any particular good or service. Money then becomes less valuable relative to goods and services—and this relationship constitutes inflation. The principle holds true regardless of the type of money used. For example, when Spanish conquistadors brought gold back to Europe from Latin America in the sixteenth century, the supply of money (gold) in Europe increased, and this led to inflation.

The Equation of Exchange

The data presented in the last section show that more money in an economy generally leads to higher prices. Theoretically, this relationship makes sense. For example, if you have a given level of real GDP in an economy and the money supply doubles, you have twice as many dollars chasing the same quantity of final goods and services. Eventually, it will take about twice as many dollars to buy any particular good or service—which means that prices double.

We can summarize that long-run relationship between the price level and the quantity of money with a simple relationship known as the **equation of exchange**. The equation of exchange specifies the long-run relationship between the money supply, the price level, real GDP, and the velocity of money. The actual equation is

$$M \times V = P \times Y$$

The right side of the equation is nominal GDP, or real GDP (Y) times the price level (P). The left side includes the quantity of money in the economy (M) and the velocity of money (V). The **velocity of money** is the number of times a unit of money exchanges hands in a given year. The equation of exchange represents the fact that GDP in a given year is purchased with money, but that money can (and does) turn over more than once in a given year. We'll define money (M) very carefully in Chapter 30, but for now you should know that money includes more than paper currency and coins. Money includes whatever we use in exchange for goods and services. For this reason, the equation of exchange is actually an identity—it is true by definition.

The equation of exchange gives a direct relationship between prices and the size of the money supply, especially if velocity doesn't change much. To see this relationship, consider another version of the equation of exchange, this time in growth rates:

$$\%\triangle M + \%\triangle V \approx \%\triangle P + \%\triangle Y$$

This equation uses several mathematical symbols that may be new to you. First that $\triangle$ is the Greek letter delta, and it means "change in." So $90\%\triangle V$ means "percent change in velocity" and $90\%\triangle P$ means "change in the price level." Also $\approx$ means "is approximately equal to," so the value on one side of the equation is very close but not the same as the other.

This form of the equation is a helpful approximation because we often think in terms of growth rates. Let's consider four cases, all of which are summarized in Table 21.5.

The **equation of exchange** specifies the long-run relationship between the money supply, the price level, real GDP, and the velocity of money.

The **velocity of money** is the number of times a unit of money exchanges hands in a given year.

First, consider a case where velocity and real GDP are constant, that is, $\%\triangle V = 0$ and $\%\triangle Y = 0$. In this case, it is clear that the growth rate of the money supply ($\%\triangle M$) will translate exactly to the growth rate of the price level ($\%\triangle P$), which is the definition of inflation. If money grows by 2%, inflation will also be 2%. As shown in case 1 in Table 21.5, the quantity of goods and services does not change but the money supply grows. As a result, you have 2% more money to use to purchase the same quantity of goods and services, so prices must rise by 2%.

Now consider a more realistic case in which real GDP is growing. Let's continue the assumptions that the money supply grows at 2% and velocity does not change. In this case, if real GDP grows at 2% in a given year, then there is no change in the price level ($\%\triangle P = 0$). In this scenario, presented as case 2 in Table 21.5, the money supply grows at exactly the same rate as real GDP, so there is no effect on the price level.

Consider a third, even more realistic case. A typical year brings both real GDP growth and some inflation. In this case, if velocity is constant, the money supply is growing at a greater rate than real GDP growth. Case 3 in Table 21.5 presents such a scenario: real GDP grows at 2% and inflation is also 2%. In this case, with constant velocity, the growth rate of the money supply must be 4%.

Finally, let's consider a case where velocity changes (case 4 in Table 21.5). Changes in velocity occur when those that hold money (for example, individuals and banks) decide to change their spending habits. If people and banks decide to spend their dollars at faster rates, velocity rises. When people and banks decide to hold on to money longer, velocity falls. Let's consider this last possibility, since it is related to changes in the macroeconomy over the past decade. What if velocity falls by 5% ($\%\triangle V = -5$)? Let's assume that real GDP rises by 2% and that the money supply grows by 9%. However, the result is not a lot of inflation. We can see that the implied change in the price level ($\%\triangle P$) is just 2%. Inflation is low because people and banks have decided to hold on to their money longer.

In fact, this last scenario is what seems to have occurred in the U.S. economy over the past decade. Since 2006, the annual velocity of money has fallen by almost 25%. Over this same period, real GDP and prices have risen modestly, but there was also a rapid monetary expansion over the same period, which we will discuss fully in Chapter 30. Many casual observers consistently

TABLE 21.5

Four Scenarios for the Equation of Exchange

	$\%\triangle M$	+	$\%\triangle V$	=	$\%\triangle P$	+	$\%\triangle Y$
	Money growth		Velocity growth		Inflation		Real GDP growth
Case 1	2	+	0	=	2	+	0
Case 2	2	+	0	=	0	+	2
Case 3	4	+	0	=	2	+	2
Case 4	9	+	−5	=	2	+	2

predicted high levels of inflation because they failed to account for the drop in velocity. The equation of exchange helps us see that changes in all four of these variables—money, velocity, the price level, and real GDP—must be accounted for.

The Reasons Why Governments Inflate the Money Supply

In this chapter, we discussed several problems that stem from inflation: shoe-leather costs, money illusion, menu costs, future price level uncertainty, wealth redistribution, price confusion, and tax distortions. And yet we know what causes inflation. Thus, it is reasonable to wonder why inflation is often still a macroeconomic problem. We point to two reasons: large government debts and short-term gains.

First, large government debts often spur governments to choose to increase the money supply rapidly. When a government owes large sums and also controls the supply of money, there is a natural urge to print more money to pay off debts. After World War I, the German government owed billions of dollars to other nations and to its workers, so it resorted to printing more money—and this action led to inflation rates of almost 30,000% in late 1923.

Second, surprise increases in the money supply can temporarily stimulate an economy toward more rapid growth rates. We'll look at this issue very closely in Chapter 31, but it is a constant temptation for governments that can be shortsighted. The problems from inflation are often long-term and difficult to overcome. But the short-term economic boost can be very tempting for governments. Unfortunately, to realize any benefits from inflation, the government has to keep surprising people in the economy. As a result of the government's attempts to stay ahead of expectations, inflation can spiral out of control.

Conclusion

This chapter began with a common misconception—that inflation is no big deal. But we have seen that inflation and the problems it imposes can be severe. And while inflation rates have been low in the United States for several years now, at times in the past they have been very high—such as during the 1970s. In addition, inflation rates in some other nations remain high.

Inflation, along with the unemployment rate and changes in real GDP, is an important indicator of overall macroeconomic conditions. Now that we have covered these three, we move next to savings and the determination of interest rates.

ECONOMICS FOR LIFE

Inflation Devalues Dollars: Preparing Your Future for Inflation

In this chapter, we talked about how inflation devalues the money you currently hold and the money you've been promised in the future. One problem you may encounter is how to prepare for retirement in the face of inflation. Perhaps you are not worried about this, since the inflation rate in the United States over the past 50 years has averaged 4%, and more recently the average has been only 2%. But even these low rates mean that dollars will be worth significantly less 40 years from now.

One way to think about the effect of inflation on future dollars is to ask what amount of future dollars it will take to match the real value of $1.00 today. The graph below answers this question based on a retirement date of 40 years in the future. The different inflation rates are specified at the bottom.

Thus, if the inflation rate averages 4% over the next four decades, you'll need $4.80 just to buy the same goods and services you can buy today for $1.00.

What does this mean for your overall retirement plans? Let's say you decide you could live on

How many nest eggs will you need to put aside to keep pace with inflation?

$50,000 per year if you retired today. If the inflation rate is 4% between now and your retirement date, you would need enough savings to supply yourself with 50,000 × $4.80, or $240,000 per year, just to keep pace with inflation.

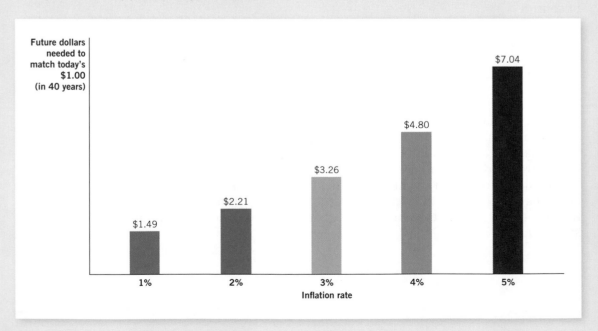

Future dollars needed to match today's $1.00 (in 40 years)

- 1%: $1.49
- 2%: $2.21
- 3%: $3.26
- 4%: $4.80
- 5%: $7.04

Inflation rate

ANSWERING THE BIG QUESTIONS

How is inflation measured?

* The inflation rate is calculated as the percentage change in the overall level of prices.
* Economists use the consumer price index (CPI) to determine the general level of prices in the economy.
* Determining which prices to include in the CPI can be challenging for several reasons: consumers change what they buy over time; the quality of goods and services changes; and new goods, services, and sales locations are introduced.

What problems does inflation bring?

* Inflation imposes shoe-leather costs: it causes people to waste resources as they seek to avoid holding money.
* Inflation can cause people to make decisions based on nominal rather than real monetary values, a problem known as money illusion.
* Inflation adds menu costs, as sellers need to physically change prices.
* Inflation introduces uncertainty about future price levels. Because uncertainty makes it difficult for consumers and producers to plan, it impedes economic progress.
* Unexpected inflation redistributes wealth from lenders to borrowers.
* Inflation creates price confusion: that is, it makes it difficult for producers to read price signals correctly. The result may be a misallocation of resources.
* Inflation distorts people's tax obligations.

What is the cause of inflation?

* Inflation is caused by increases in a nation's money supply relative to the quantity of real goods and services in the economy.
* Governments often increase the money supply too quickly when they are in debt or when they desire a short-run stimulus for the economy.
* The equation of exchange offers a simple summary of the long-run relationship between the inflation rate and quantity of money in an economy.

CONCEPTS YOU SHOULD KNOW

capital gains taxes (p. 686)
chained CPI (p. 679)
consumer price index (CPI)
  (p. 667)
deflation (p. 666)

equation of exchange (p. 689)
menu costs (p. 683)
money illusion (p. 682)
nominal wage (p. 682)
output (p. 684)

real wage (p. 682)
shoe-leather costs (p. 682)
velocity of money (p. 689)

QUESTIONS FOR REVIEW

1. The price of a typical laptop computer has fallen from $2,000 in 1985 to $800 today. At the same time, the consumer price index has risen from 100 to 238. Adjusting for inflation, how much did the price of laptops change? Does this answer seem right to you, or is it missing something? Explain your response.

2. What three issues are at the center of the debate regarding the accuracy of the CPI? Give an example of each issue.

3. If the prices of homes go up by 5% and the prices of concert tickets rise by 10%, which will have the larger impact on the CPI? Why?

4. If a country is experiencing a relatively high rate of inflation, what impact will this have on the country's long-term rate of economic growth?

5. In a sentence or two, evaluate the accuracy of the following statement, including a clear and precise statement of historical comparison: Inflation in the United States last year was 0%. This is close to the historical level.

6. Wage agreements and loan contracts are two types of multiperiod agreements that are important for economic growth. Suppose you sign a two-year job contract with Wells Fargo stipulating that you will receive an annual salary of $93,500 plus an additional 2% over that in the second year to account for expected inflation.
   a. If the inflation rate turns out to be 3% rather than 2%, who will be hurt? Why?
   b. If the inflation rate turns out to be 1% rather than 2%, who will be hurt? Why?

   Suppose that you also take out a $1,000 loan at the Cavalier Credit Union. The loan agree-

ment stipulates that you must pay it back with 4% interest in one year, and again, the inflation rate is expected to be 2%.
   c. If the inflation rate turns out to be 3% rather than 2%, who will be hurt? Why?
   d. If the inflation rate turns out to be 3% rather than 2%, who will be helped? Why?

7. What are the seven problems caused by inflation? Briefly explain each one.

8. Following is a list of potential problems that inflation might cause. Use the space on the left to name each of these with the terms used in this chapter.
   a. _____ Lenders and workers are reluctant to help firms produce output because the real value of future dollar payoffs is unclear.
   b. _____ Workers make decisions on the basis of nominal rather than real wage changes.
   c. _____ Unexpected inflation reduces the real value of loan repayments.
   d. _____ Firms cannot distinguish whether there is a change in the relative price of their good or a change in the overall price level.
   e. _____ Restaurants need to spend resources to alter the prices on their menus.
   f. _____ Individuals own stock shares for many years and then sell them and are required to pay taxes on the nominal capital gain.
   g. _____ People leave work early to shop before inflation changes prices.

9. Inflation causes a lot of problems for the macroeconomy.
   a. What is the key misconception people have about inflation, and why does this problem generally not accompany inflation?

b. In this chapter, we discussed the problem of price confusion and the problem of future price uncertainty. Explain the difference between these two problems.

c. Wealth redistribution is another problem caused by inflation. What is this problem, and how is it related to the future price uncertainty?

STUDY PROBLEMS (✳ *solved at the end of the section*)

1. In 1991, the Barenaked Ladies released their hit song "If I Had a Million Dollars." How much money would the group need in 2015 to have the same amount of real purchasing power they had in 1991? Note that the consumer price index in 1991 was 136.2 and in 2015 it was 238.

2. Visit the Bureau of Labor Statistics web site for the CPI (www.bls.gov/cpi), and find the latest news release. Table 1 in that release presents CPI data for all items and also for many individual categories.
   a. How much has the entire index changed (in percentage terms) in the past year?
   b. Now identify and list the five individual categories that have increased the most in the past year.

3. While rooting through the attic, you discover a box of old tax forms. You find that your grandmother made $75 working part-time during December 1964, when the CPI was 31.3. How much would you need to have earned in January of this year to have at least as much real income as your grandmother did in 1964? To determine the CPI for January of this year, you can visit the Bureau of Labor Statistics web site (www.bls.gov).

✳ 4. Suppose that the residents of Greenland play golf incessantly. In fact, golf is the only thing that they spend their money on. They buy golf balls, clubs, and tees. In 2016, they bought 1,000 golf balls for $2.00 each, 100 clubs for $50.00 each, and 500 tees for $0.10 each. In 2017, they bought 1,000 golf balls for $2.50 each, 100 clubs for $75.00 each, and 500 tees for $0.12 each.

a. What was the CPI for each year?
b. What was the inflation rate in 2017?

✳ 5. If healthcare costs make up 10% of total expenditures and they rise by 15% while the other components in the consumer price index remain constant, by how much will the price index rise?

✳ 6. The equation of exchange is helpful for determining the effect of money supply changes on the price level. Use the equation of exchange to answer each of the following questions.
   a. Real GDP grows at 3% and inflation is equal to 2%, but there is no change in velocity. What can you conclude about the change in the money supply?
   b. Real GDP falls by 3% and there is no inflation, but the money supply grew by 5%. What is the implied change in velocity?
   c. Real GDP increases by 3%, velocity does not change, and the money supply grows by 10%. What is the implied rate of inflation?
   d. The money supply grows at 6%, velocity is constant, and inflation is 3%. What can you conclude about the rate of real GDP growth?

7. Let's say you graduate from college and accept a job in 2018. You decide to compare your starting salary with your grandfather's and mother's starting salaries. The salaries you compare are:

   • You: $80,000 per year beginning in 2018
   • Your mother: $50,000 per year beginning in 1983
   • Your grandfather: $20,000 per year beginning in 1965

To compare these salaries, you decide to use the CPI, using 1983 as the base year.

a. Why is the CPI a good price index to use for this comparison?

b. Fill in the missing data point in the following table:

Year	CPI
1965	30
1983	
2015	238
2018	240

c. Convert both your mother's salary and your grandfather's salary to 2018 dollars. Enter your answers in the table below.

Grandfather's 1965 salary in 2018 dollars	
Mother's 1983 salary in 2018 dollars	

✳ **8.** In the following chart, which of these prices would be included in the CPI? Which would be included in the GDP deflator? Which would be included in both or neither? Mark the correct option for each price.

		GDP		
PRICE OF	CPI	DEFLATOR	BOTH	NEITHER
Toothpaste	☐	☐	☐	☐
Industrial coolant	☐	☐	☐	☐
Milk you bought in a grocery store	☐	☐	☐	☐
Milk bought by Starbucks from a food distributor	☐	☐	☐	☐
An Intel computer chip bought by Dell to put into a laptop computer	☐	☐	☐	☐
Bus fare for a trip to a shopping mall	☐	☐	☐	☐
A doctor's appointment, to get a physical	☐	☐	☐	☐

SOLVED PROBLEMS

4.a. We'll use the quantities from the first year to designate the weights. To build a price index, we first need to choose which year we will use as the base year. Let 2016 be the base year. Next we define our basket as the goods consumed in 2016: 1,000 golf balls, 100 clubs, and 500 tees.

In 2016, this basket cost as follows:

$$(1,000 \times \$2) + (100 \times \$50) + (500 \times \$0.10)$$
$$= \$7,050$$

In 2017, this basket cost as follows:

$$(1,000 \times \$2.50) + (100 \times \$75) + (500 \times \$0.12)$$
$$= \$10,060$$

Dividing the cost of the basket in each year by the cost of the basket in the base year and multiplying by 100 gives us the CPI for each year.

For 2016, the CPI is calculated as

$$(\$7,050 \div \$7,050) \times 100 = 100$$

For 2017, the CPI is calculated as

$$(\$10,060 \div \$7,050) \times 100 = 142.7$$

b. The inflation rate is defined as $[(CPI_2 - CPI_1) \div CPI_1] \times 100$. Plugging the values from part (a) into the formula, we get an inflation rate of 42.7%:

$$[(142.7 - 100) \div 100] \times 100 = 42.7$$

5. The CPI will rise by 1.5%. Suppose the CPI in the first year is 100. If healthcare costs are 10% of total expenditures, then they account for 10 of the 100 points, with the other 90 points falling in other categories. If healthcare costs rise by 15% in the second year, then those 10 points become 11.5 points. Since the prices of the other categories have not changed, the CPI now stands at 101.5, since 11.5 + 90 = 101.5.

Using our formula for calculating the inflation rate, the rise in healthcare costs has raised the overall price level by 1.5%:

$$[(101.5 - -100) \div 100] \times 100 = 1.5$$

6. Using the equation of exchange in rates of growth, we know that

$$\%\triangle M + \%\triangle V \approx \%\triangle P + \%\triangle Y$$

a. $\%\triangle M + 0 \approx 2\% + 3\%$

Thus, $\%\triangle M \approx 5\%$.

b. $5\% + \%\triangle V \approx 0 + -3\%$

Thus, $\%\triangle V \approx -8\%$.

c. $10\% + 0 \approx \%\triangle P + 3\%$

Thus, $\%\triangle P \approx 7\%$.

d. $6\% + 0 \approx 3\% + \%\triangle Y$

Thus, $\%\triangle Y \approx 3\%$.

8.

PRICE OF	CPI	GDP DEFLATOR	BOTH	NEITHER
Toothpaste	☐	☐	■	☐
Industrial coolant	☐	■	☐	☐
Milk you bought in a grocery store	☐	☐	■	☐
Milk bought by Starbucks from a food distributor	☐	☐	☐	■
An Intel computer chip bought by Dell to put into a laptop computer	☐	☐	☐	■
Bus fare for a trip to a shopping mall	☐	☐	■	☐
A doctor's appointment, to get a physical	☐	☐	■	☐

CHAPTER 22

Savings, Interest Rates, and the Market for Loanable Funds

The government sets interest rates.

Just about anything you read or hear about interest rates in the popular media leaves you with the impression that the government sets interest rates. This isn't exactly true. For sure, the government can influence many rates. But almost all interest rates in the U.S. economy are determined privately—by the market forces of supply and demand. In fact, you can understand why interest rates rise and fall by applying supply and demand analysis to the market for loans. That's what we do in this chapter. Along the way, we also consider the many factors that influence savers and borrowers.

MIS CONCEPTION

In this chapter, we discuss many of the same topics you might study in a course on banking or financial institutions, but our emphasis is different. We are interested in studying how financial institutions and markets affect the macroeconomy. When we are finished, you will understand why interest rates rise and fall, and you will also appreciate the necessity of the loanable funds market in the larger macroeconomy.

The loanable funds market is the bridge between savers and borrowers, and it is also the bridge to economic growth.

BIG QUESTIONS

⁂ What is the loanable funds market?

⁂ What factors shift the supply of loanable funds?

⁂ What factors shift the demand for loanable funds?

⁂ How do we apply the loanable funds market model?

What Is the Loanable Funds Market?

Financial markets are where firms and governments obtain funds, or *financing*, for their operations. These funds come primarily from household savings across the economy. In economics, we analyze financial markets in the context of a loanable funds market. The **loanable funds market** is the market where savers supply funds for loans to borrowers.

The **loanable funds market** is the market where savers supply funds for loans to borrowers.

This market is not a single physical location but includes places like stock exchanges, investment banks, mutual fund firms, and commercial banks. In this section, we explain the particular characteristics of the loanable funds market and the significant role it plays in the overall economy.

Figure 22.1 illustrates the role of the loanable funds market. Savings flow in and become loans for borrowers. We could call it the market for savings or even the market for loans. The term "loanable funds" captures the information in both.

On the left side of the figure, the suppliers of funds—those who save—include households and foreign entities. Households are private individuals

FIGURE 22.1

The Role of the Loanable Funds Market

The market for loanable funds is where savers bring funds and make them available to borrowers. Households (private individuals and families) are the primary suppliers of loanable funds. Firms are the primary demanders, or borrowers, of loanable funds. When this market is functioning well, firms get the funds necessary for production and savers are paid for lending.

and families. Foreign entities include foreign governments, firms, and private citizens that choose to save in the United States. For most of the applications we discuss, we focus on households as the primary suppliers of loanable funds. If you have a checking or savings account at a bank, you are a supplier of loanable funds. You deposit funds into your bank account, but these funds don't just sit in a vault; banks loan out the majority of these funds. Household savings in retirement accounts, stocks, bonds, and mutual funds are other big sources of loanable funds.

The demanders, or borrowers, of loanable funds include firms and governments. In this chapter, we focus on firms as the primary borrowers of loanable funds. To reinforce the significance of this market, think about why borrowing takes place: firms borrow to invest, to buy tools and equipment and build factories. Firms looking to produce output in the future must borrow to pay their expenses today.

Figure 22.2 shows the production timeline that we introduced in Chapter 21. At the end of the timeline is output, or GDP. When this output is sold, it produces revenue for the firms, and the revenue serves to pay bills. But future GDP depends on spending today for necessary resources. This spending comes before any revenue is gained from the sale of output. Therefore, firms must borrow in order to generate future GDP—that's how important the loanable funds market is to the entire economy. Without a well-functioning loanable funds market, future GDP dries up.

Imagine that you are an entrepreneur who decides to start a company that will produce and sell college apparel. If you succeed, you will contribute to national GDP. But you don't really think of it this way; you simply hope that you have discovered a great business opportunity. Now before you ever sell your first shirt, hat, or sweatpants, you have to spend money on the resources you'll use in the production process. For example, if you plan on silk-screening your college logo onto hooded sweatshirts, you have to buy sweatshirts, ink, and a screen printing press. Here is where the loanable funds

FIGURE 22.2

The Timeline of Production

The production timeline illustrates that GDP depends critically on the loanable funds market. At the end of the production timeline we see output, or GDP. But before a firm can produce output, it must purchase resources. Since these purchases occur before the revenue comes in, firms must borrow at the beginning of the timeline.

Before you can sell college apparel, you have to buy equipment and other supplies.

market comes into play: since you have no revenue yet, you need to borrow in order to make these investments.

Borrowing fuels investment, which creates future output. But notice that *every dollar borrowed requires a dollar saved*. Without savings, we cannot sustain future production. If you want to borrow to buy the resources you need to produce college apparel, someone else has to save. Working backward, the chain of crucial relationships looks like this: output (GDP) requires investment; investment requires borrowing; borrowing requires savings. And all the links in this chain require a loanable funds market that efficiently channels funds from savers to borrowers.

We will study this crucial market from the perspective of prices, quantities, supply, and demand—like any other market. The good in this market is loanable funds. The demanders (or consumers) are borrowers who want to invest; the suppliers are savers. Figure 22.3 presents a picture of supply (savings) and demand (investment) for loanable funds, along with a summary of the distinctions of the loanable funds market.

One advantage of this demand and supply approach is that it clarifies the role of interest rates. An **interest rate** is a price of loanable funds. It is like the price of toothpaste or computers or hoodies; it is simply quoted differently—as a percentage of the original loan amount. People who are thinking about planning for retirement or making a big purchase such as a house or a car worry about interest rate fluctuations but do not necessarily understand why interest rates rise and fall. If we acknowledge that an interest rate is just the price of loanable funds, we can use supply and demand to reveal the factors that make interest rates rise and fall.

We now turn to the two different views of interest rates: the saver's view and the borrower's view.

An **interest rate** is a price of loanable funds, quoted as a percentage of the original loan amount.

FIGURE 22.3

The Loanable Funds Market

Savings (S) is channeled into investment (D) in the loanable funds market. In this market, loanable funds are the goods that are bought and sold. The price is an interest rate. This price, like any other market-determined price, is determined by the interaction between supply and demand.

Good	Loanable funds: savings available for a loan
Price	Interest rate
Seller/Suppliers	Savers
Buyers/Demanders	Borrowers

Interest Rates as a Reward for Saving

If you are a saver, the interest rate is the return you get for supplying funds. For example, let's say your parents gave you some cash when you left for college this term. After buying textbooks, groceries, and other supplies, you have $1,000 left, which you consider saving. You go to a bank near campus and inquire about opening a new account. In this transaction, the bank is the buyer, and it offers a certain price for the use of your savings. When it does offer a price, it is not in dollars. The bank quotes a price in an interest rate, or as a percentage of how much you save. But the interest rate communicates the same information. So if you are saving $1,000, the bank might tell you, "We'll pay you 6% if you save that money for a year." Because 6% of $1,000 is $60, this is equivalent to saying, "We'll pay you $60 if you save that money for a year."

If you save $1,000 for one year with an interest rate of 6%, your total amount of savings is $1,060 at the end of the year, which is computed as

$$\$1,000 + (6\% \text{ of } \$1,000) = \$1,000 + \$60 = \$1,060$$

For savers, the interest rate is a reward. Every dollar saved today returns more in the saver's account in the future. The higher the interest rate, the greater the return will be in the future. Table 22.1 illustrates how interest rates affect $1,000 worth of savings. An interest rate of 4% yields $1,040 one year later; an interest rate of 10% yields $1,100.

Think of the interest rate as the opportunity cost of consumption. With a 4% interest rate and a $1,000 purchase today, you are giving up the $40 you would make by saving that $1,000. But at an interest rate of 10%, using the $1,000 for consumption today means giving up an additional $100 next year. Interest rates on savings accounts in the United States today are typically less than 2%. But imagine an interest rate of 10% for a savings account. This was actually the situation in the United States in the 1980s. With an interest rate that high, even college students find a way to save.

As we have mentioned, savings constitutes the supply of loanable funds. The higher the interest rate, the greater is the incentive to save. This is the loanable funds version of the law of supply: the quantity of savings rises when the interest rate rises. This positive relationship between interest rate and savings is reflected in the slope of the supply curve (S), illustrated in Figure 22.3. When the interest rate is 4%, the quantity of loans supplied is $200 billion per year; at 5% the quantity supplied increases to $250 billion; and at 6% it increases to $300 billion.

Banks are willing to pay you for your savings. The price they pay is the interest rate.

Opportunity cost

Incentives

TABLE 22.1

Higher Interest Rates and Greater Future Returns

Interest rate	Value of $1,000 after one year
4%	$1,040
5	1,050
6	1,060
10	1,100

If you save $1,000 for one year at an interest rate of 6%, this leads to $1,060 next year, computed as

$$\$1,000 + (6\% \text{ of } \$1,000)$$
$$= \$1,000 + (0.06 \times \$1,000)$$
$$= \$1,000 + \$60$$
$$= \$1,060$$

Interest Rates as a Cost of Borrowing

We now turn to the demand, or borrowing, side of the loanable funds market. For this we shift to the firm's perspective and return to your plan to produce college apparel. Recall that you need to buy the sweatshirts, paint, and a screen printing press to produce hoodies and other products with a college logo. Assume that you need $100,000 to start your business. If you borrow $100,000 for one year at an interest rate of 6%, you'll need to repay $106,000 in one year. It makes sense to do this only if you expect to earn more than 6%, or $6,000, on this investment.

For borrowers, the interest rate is the cost of borrowing. Firms borrow only if they expect the return on their investment to be greater than the cost of the loan. For example, at an interest rate of 6%, a firm would borrow only if it expected to make more than a 6% return with its use of the funds. Let's state this as a rule:

Profit-maximizing firms borrow to fund an investment if and only if the expected return on the investment is greater than the interest rate on the loan.

The lower the interest rate, the more likely a business will succeed in earning enough to exceed the interest it will owe at the end of the year. For example, if your firm can borrow at an interest rate of just 4%, you'll need to make a return greater than 4%. There are probably several investments available today that would pay more than a 6% return; but there are even more that would yield returns greater than 4% and more still that would pay greater than 2%. If we apply our rule from above, we'll see a larger quantity of loans demanded as the interest rate drops. This gives us the negative relationship between the interest rate and quantity demanded of loans that is reflected in the slope of the demand curve for loanable funds.

The graph of the loanable funds market in Figure 22.3 illustrates the demand curve (D) for loanable funds across the entire U.S. economy. At an interest rate of 6%, the quantity of loans demanded by all business firms in the economy is $200 billion. This indicates that firms believe that only $200 billion worth of investment will pay returns greater than 6%. At an interest rate of 5%, firms estimate that another $50 billion worth of total loans will earn between 5% and 6%, and the quantity of loans demanded rises to $250 billion. Lower interest rates lead to a greater quantity demanded of loanable funds.

How Inflation Affects Interest Rates

If you save $1,000 for a year at an interest rate of 6%, your reward for saving is $60. But inflation affects the real value of this reward. For example, imagine that the inflation rate is exactly 6% during the year you save. This means that next year it will take $1,060 to buy the same quantity of goods and services that you are able to buy this year for $1,000. In this case, your interest rate of 6% and the inflation rate of 6% cancel each other out. You break even, and that's no reward.

When making decisions about saving and borrowing, people care about the real interest rate, not the nominal interest rate. The **real interest rate** is the interest rate that is corrected for inflation; it is the rate of return in terms of real purchasing power. In contrast, the **nominal interest rate** is the

The **real interest rate** is the interest rate that is corrected for inflation. It is the rate of return in terms of real purchasing power.

The **nominal interest rate** is the interest rate before it is corrected for inflation. It is the stated interest rate.

interest rate before it is corrected for inflation; it is the stated interest rate. In our example, the interest rate of 6% is the nominal interest rate. But with 6% inflation, the real return on your savings disappears, and the real interest rate is zero—or 0%. In general, we can approximate the real interest rate by subtracting the inflation rate from the nominal interest rate in an equation known as the **Fisher equation**:

$$\text{real interest rate} = \text{nominal interest rate} - \text{inflation rate} \qquad \text{(Equation 22.1)}$$

The **Fisher equation** states that the real interest rate equals the nominal interest rate minus the inflation rate.

For example, if the inflation rate this year is 2%, a nominal interest rate of 6% on your savings yields a 4% real interest rate. The Fisher equation is named after Irving Fisher, the economist who formulated the relationship between inflation and interest rates.

Savers and borrowers care about the real rate of interest on a loan because this is the rate that describes how their funds' real purchasing power changes over the course of the loan. Because the interest rate is a result of supply and demand in the market for loanable funds, higher inflation rates lead to higher nominal interest rates to compensate lenders for the loss of purchasing power. We can rewrite the Fisher equation to see how inflation generally increases nominal interest rates:

$$\text{nominal interest rate} = \text{real interest rate} + \text{inflation rate} \qquad \text{(Equation 22.2)}$$

For a given real interest rate, the higher the rate of inflation, the higher the nominal interest rate will be. Table 22.2 shows how the nominal interest rate rises with inflation rates for a given level of the real interest rate. If the real interest rate is 4% and there is no inflation, then the nominal interest rate is also 4%. But if the inflation rate rises to 2%, the nominal interest rate increases to 6%. If the inflation rate rises further to 4%, then the nominal interest rate rises to 8%.

We can picture the Fisher equation by looking at real and nominal interest rates over time. Figure 22.4 plots the real and nominal interest rates in the United States from 1965 to 2015. The difference between them is the inflation rate. Notice that this gap was particularly high during the inflationary 1970s but that it narrowed considerably as inflation rates fell in the 1980s. After 2008, the nominal interest rate in the United States was less than 1%. Because inflation rates were around 2%, the real interest rate was negative.

Unless otherwise stated, in this text we will use the nominal interest rate. We do this for two reasons. First, the nominal interest rate is the stated interest rate—the rate you read about and consider in actual financial transactions. Second, low and steady inflation means that the difference between real and nominal interest rates doesn't fluctuate much. That is, while we recognize that savers and borrowers care about the real interest rate, the current

TABLE 22.2

How Inflation Affects Nominal Interest Rates

Inflation rate		Real interest rate		Nominal interest rate
0%	+	4%	=	4%
2	+	4	=	6
4	+	4	=	8

FIGURE 22.4

Real and Nominal Interest Rates, 1965–2015

The difference between the real interest rate and the nominal interest rate is the rate of inflation. The experience of the 1970s illustrates that the nominal interest rate is historically high when inflation is also high.

Sources: Federal Reserve Bank of St. Louis FRED database; Bureau of Labor Statistics.

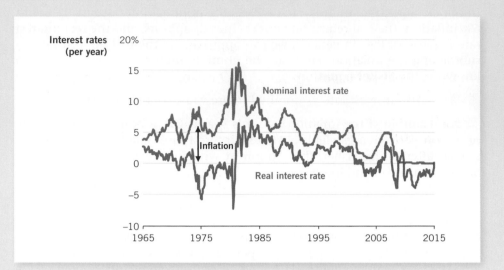

inflationary environment throughout much of the developed world leaves us little to gain by focusing on the real interest rate.

In the next two sections, we consider the factors that cause shifts in the supply of and demand for loanable funds.

As India grows from poor to rich, many of the funds that its citizens save find their way into the U.S. loanable funds market.

What Factors Shift the Supply of Loanable Funds?

Recall that the supply of loanable funds comes from savings. If you have either a savings or a checking account, you are a participant in this market. We turn now to three factors that shift the supply curve for loanable funds: income and wealth, time preferences, and consumption smoothing. When these factors change, the supply curve shifts.

Income and Wealth

Imagine that a distant relative dies and you inherit $20,000. What will you do with these unexpected funds? You might celebrate with a fancy meal and a shopping spree. But most of us would also save some of this newfound wealth. All else equal, people prefer to have more savings. Thus, increases in income generally produce increases in savings. If income declines, people save less. These changes shift the loanable funds supply curve.

The relationship between income and savings is true across the globe. As nations gain wealth, they save more.

PRACTICE WHAT YOU KNOW

Interest Rates and Quantity Supplied and Demanded: U.S. Interest Rates Have Fallen

In 1981, many interest rates in the United States were 15%, but the inflation rate was 10%. In 2015, many interest rates were less than 1%, and the inflation rate was 2%.

Question: What were the real interest rates in 1981 and 2015?

Answer: Using equation 22.1, we compute the real interest rate as

real interest rate = nominal interest rate − inflation rate

For 1981, the real interest rate was 15% − 10% = 5%.

For 2015, the real interest rate was: 1% − 2% = −1%.

Question: All else equal, how does the drop in interest rates between 1981 and 2015 affect the quantity of loanable funds supplied?

Answer: The quantity supplied decreases along the supply curve. Lower interest rates reduce the incentive to save.

Over the past 20 years, the increase in foreign savings has often made its way into the U.S. loanable funds market. For example, a businessman in Mumbai, India, may find himself with extra savings. He will probably put some into an Indian bank and some into Indian stocks and bonds. But there's a good chance he'll also channel some of his savings into the United States. Historically, U.S. financial markets have offered relatively greater returns than markets in other countries. In addition, the U.S. financial markets are often considered less risky than other global markets because of the size and relative robustness of the U.S. economy. Therefore, as global economies have grown, there has been an increase in foreign savings in the United States.

The increase in foreign savings came at a good time for the United States because domestic savings began falling in the 1980s. Without the influx of foreign funds, U.S. firms would have had difficulty funding investment. Of course, there is no guarantee that foreign savings will continue to flow into the United States at the same rates. But as long as some foreign funds still enter the U.S. financial markets, their presence will allow more opportunities for domestic firms to borrow for investment than if firms relied solely on domestic savers.

Time Preferences

Imagine that your parents promised you a cash reward for getting a good grade in economics. Does it matter if they pay immediately or wait until you graduate? Yes, it matters. You want the money as soon as you earn it. This is

The term **time preferences** refers to the fact that people prefer to receive goods and services sooner rather than later.

Do you care when a friend repays your loan?

not unusual. People always prefer to receive funds sooner rather than later, and the same applies to goods and services. The term **time preferences** refers to the fact that people prefer to receive goods and services sooner rather than later. Because people have time preferences, someone must pay them to save. While time preferences are generally stable over time, if the rate of time preference in a society changes, the supply of loanable funds shifts.

While we all prefer sooner to later, some people have greater time preferences than others. Think of those with the strongest time preferences as being the least patient: they *strongly* prefer now to later. Someone with weaker time preferences has more patience. All else equal, people with stronger time preferences save less than people with weaker time preferences.

There are other ways time preferences can be observed. For example, people with very strong time preferences may not go to college, since the returns to getting a college education are not typically realized until years later. Time spent in college is time that could have been spent earning income. The fact that you are a college student demonstrates that you are more patient than some others who choose instead to work for more income now.

Opportunity cost

You'll be happy to know that there is a definite payoff to getting a college education. College graduates earn significantly more than high school graduates. Figure 22.5 shows median annual salary in the United States by educational attainment. Some college dropouts—for example, Mark Zuckerberg (creator of Facebook)—earn millions of dollars a year. But Figure 22.5 shows that the median worker with a basic college degree earns about $15,000 more a year than those who don't graduate from college. Patience pays off!

FIGURE 22.5

Median Annual Salary and Educational Attainment, 2014

It takes patience, or relatively low time preferences, to stay in school. But annual earnings based on years of schooling shows that education pays off for most graduates.

Source: Bureau of Labor Statistics.

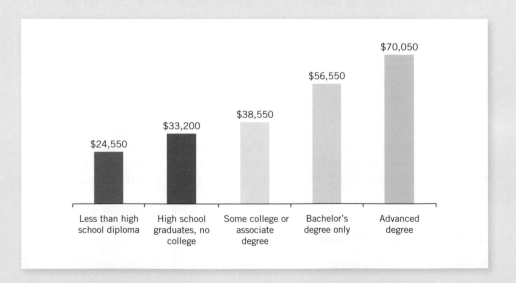

Consumption Smoothing

Over the course of a typical lifetime, income varies drastically. Early in life, income levels are relatively low, but income generally rises through midlife. As people near retirement, their income levels fall again. Figure 22.6 illustrates a typical economic life cycle. Income (the green line) is highest in the middle "prime earning years" and lower at both the beginning and end of an individual's work life.

But no one wants to *consume* according to this pattern over the course of a lifetime; most people prefer to consume in a more consistent way throughout their life. Thus, when we are young, we often borrow and spend more than we are earning. We may borrow for a college education or to buy our first home. And when we retire, our income levels fall, but we don't want our spending to fall by the same amount. So we generally smooth our consumption over the course of our life. The blue line in Figure 22.6 represents a normal consumption pattern, which is smoother than the income pattern. This **consumption smoothing** is accomplished with the help of the loanable funds market.

Early in life, we spend more than we earn. Therefore, we have to borrow. In Figure 22.6, borrowing is the shaded red vertical area between income and consumption in early life. Midlife, or the prime earning years, is the time to repay loans and save for retirement. During this period of the life cycle, the income line exceeds the consumption line, and people save. Later in life, when people retire and their income falls, they tend to live on their savings. Economists call this **dissaving**. Dissaving occurs when people withdraw funds from their previously accumulated savings. Figure 22.6 shows dissavings as the shaded red vertical area between income and consumption in later life.

Consumption smoothing occurs when people borrow and save to smooth consumption over their lifetime.

Dissaving occurs when people withdraw funds from their previously accumulated savings.

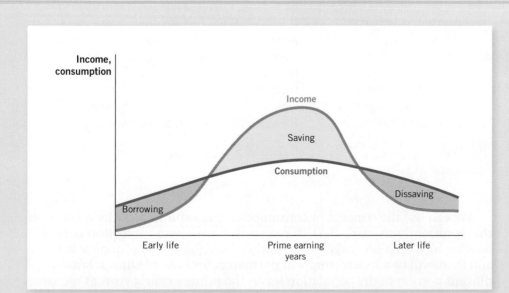

FIGURE 22.6

Savings over a Typical Life Cycle

For most people, income is relatively low in early life, rises in their prime earning years, and falls in later life. But people generally prefer to smooth their consumption over the course of their life. This means that they borrow early in life for items like education and their first home; save during midlife when their income is highest; and finally, draw down savings when they retire.

Time Preferences

Confessions of a Shopaholic

This movie from 2009 follows a shopping junkie, Becky Bloomwood, who must come to terms with her exploding debt. Becky has very strong time preferences: she can't stop spending even though she owes almost $20,000 on her credit cards. When she finally realizes the mess she is in, she attends a Shopaholics Anonymous meeting. This is where the fun really begins.

Becky, like many other first-time visitors to the support group, is reluctant to tell her story. But after listening to others speak of their trials during the past week, the leader turns to Becky, who begins to tell her story. The pure joy she experiences while shopping is immediately obvious to the other members of the support group. As they listen to her describe the fantastic feeling she gets from making new purchases, they long to feel the same way. Her story is not as much about repentance as it is about the need to shop more. This creates a euphoric response from the group. After talking for a short time, Becky has convinced herself—and most of the group—to go on a shopping spree. She bolts from the meeting and races home to her apartment, where she keeps one last credit card in the freezer for emergencies. Gleefully, she takes the card and heads off to find something new to purchase.

This film conveys how easy it is to get into unmanageable debt and how hard it is to break the cycle. Do you know of any friends or relatives— maybe even you yourself—who carry a large amount of credit card debt? Can you imagine how many

Economists would say that Becky has very strong time preferences.

people in the entire United States might be in a similar situation? Now think about how those people prefer to borrow rather than save. This perspective helps us to see that in the nation's macroeconomy, the desire to borrow, driven by time preferences, reduces the supply of loanable funds. You can learn more about the essentials of personal finance from the appendix located at the end of this book.

We can use the concept of consumption smoothing to clarify a situation that is currently affecting the U.S. economy. If we have a steady flow of people moving into each life stage, the amount of savings in the economy is stable and there will be a steady supply in the market for loanable funds. But if a significant portion of the population leaves the prime earning years at the same time, overall savings will fall. As it turns out, this is the current situation in the United States because the baby boomers are now retiring from the labor force. The oldest members of this group reached retirement age in 2011. Over the next 10 to 15 years, U.S. workers will enter retirement in record numbers. This means an exit from the prime earning years and, consequently, much less savings. Furthermore, similar issues are facing other nations, including Japan, Germany, and Italy. We'll come back to this issue later in this chapter.

Figure 22.7 illustrates the effect on the supply of loanable funds when there are changes in income and wealth, time preferences, or consumption smoothing. The initial supply of loanable funds is represented by S_1. The supply of loanable funds increases to S_2 if there is a change that leads to an increase in savings at all levels of the interest rate. For example, an increase in foreign income and wealth will increase the supply of savings. Similarly, if people's time preferences fall—if they become more patient—the supply of loanable funds will increase. Finally, if a relatively large portion of the population moves into midlife, when savings is highest, this will also increase savings from S_1 to S_2.

At other, times, however, the supply of loanable funds might decrease. For example, if income and wealth decline, people will save less across all interest rates. This is illustrated as a shift from S_1 to S_3 in Figure 22.6. And if time preferences increase, people will become more impatient, which will reduce the supply of loanable funds. Finally, if a relatively large population group moves out of the prime earning years and into retirement, the supply of loanable funds will decrease. This last example describes what is happening in the United States right now.

Table 22.3 summarizes our discussion of the factors that either increase or decrease the supply of loanable funds.

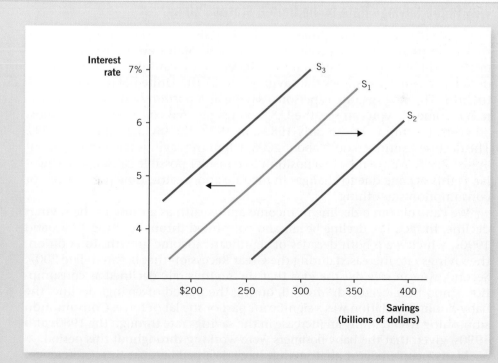

FIGURE 22.7

Shifts in the Supply of Loanable Funds

The supply of loanable funds shifts to the right when there are decreases in time preferences, increases in income and wealth, and more people in midlife, when savings is highest. The supply of loanable funds shifts to the left when there are increases in time preferences, decreases in income and wealth, and fewer people in midlife, when savings is highest.

TABLE 22.3		
Factors That Shift the Supply of Loanable Funds		
Factor	**Direction of effect**	**Explanation**
Income and wealth	• *Increases* in income and wealth *increase* the supply of loanable funds. • *Decreases* in income and wealth *decrease* the supply of loanable funds.	Savings is more affordable when people have greater income and wealth.
Time preferences	• *Increases* in time preferences *decrease* the supply of loanable funds. • *Decreases* in time preferences *increase* the supply of loanable funds.	Lower time preferences indicate that people are more patient and more likely to save for the future.
Consumption smoothing	• If *more* people are in midlife and their prime earning years, savings is *higher*. • If *fewer* people are in midlife, savings is *lower*.	Income varies over the life cycle, but people generally like to smooth their consumption.

ECONOMICS IN THE REAL WORLD

Why Is the Savings Rate in the United States Falling?

Are U.S. citizens becoming increasingly shortsighted? Many people believe that time preferences of people in the United States are indeed climbing, because the personal savings rate has fallen significantly over the past few decades. Figure 22.8 shows the savings rate in the United States from 1965 to 2015. The **savings rate** is personal saving as a portion of disposable (after-tax) income. As you can see, the U.S. savings rate fell consistently for almost 30 years, beginning in the early 1980s. In 1982, the savings rate was 11.5%. The decline continued until about 2005, when the savings rate bottomed out at just 2.5%. We are now in a position to consider possible causes. In particular, is this decline due to changes in income and wealth, time preferences, or consumption smoothing?

The **savings rate** is personal saving as a portion of disposable (after-tax) income.

We can rule out a decline in income and wealth as a cause of the savings decline. In fact, the decline began and continued throughout the 1980s and 1990s, which were both decades of significant income growth. In addition, the savings rate increased during the Great Recession that began in late 2007. Second, we can rule out the idea that the savings rate declined as consumption smoothing occurred. After all, during the period of savings decline, the baby-boom population was a significant part of the labor force. Consumption smoothing would imply an increase in the savings rate through the 1980s and 1990s, given that the baby boomers were working throughout this period.

Many people believe that savings have dropped because time preferences have risen. Perhaps you have heard older Americans talking about the impatience of today's younger workers. If today's working Americans are more focused on instant gratification, they save less. Is this really the cause of the savings decline? If so, why did it happen? Economists don't have consistent answers to these questions.

A closer look at the data indicates that there may be something else behind the decline in personal savings: it could just be a measurement issue. In reality, there are several alternative ways to save for the future, not all of which are counted in the official definition of "personal savings." For example, let's say you buy a house for $200,000 and the value of the house rises to $300,000 in just a few years. This means you now have gained $100,000 in personal wealth. The gain in the value of your house helps

Is your generation too shortsighted?

you prepare for the future just like increased savings would. But gains of this nature are not counted as personal savings. In addition to real estate gains, the gains from purchases of stocks and bonds are also not counted in personal savings.

Here is an alternative view of the recent trends. From 1980 to 2007, real estate and stock market values rose significantly. Recognizing these as alternative paths to future wealth, many people shifted their personal savings into these assets. The result is that the personal savings rate, as officially measured, plummeted. Not convinced yet? Look what happened to the personal savings rate beginning in 2008 as real estate prices fell: the personal savings rate climbed to 6% and higher.

Are today's Americans less patient than earlier generations? Perhaps. But given the way the personal savings rate is measured, it is difficult to determine a clear answer to this question. ✳

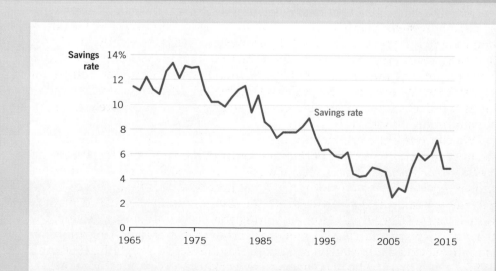

FIGURE 22.8

Savings Rate in the United States, 1965–2015

In the United States, the savings rate (savings as a portion of disposable income) has fallen significantly over the past three decades. In 1982, the savings rate was 11.5%; but it fell to just 2.5% in 2005.

Source: U.S. Bureau of Economic Analysis.

A Map of the Loanable Funds Market

The loanable funds market is really a picture of financial markets. Savers are the sellers in this market, while borrowers are the buyers. Firms borrow to fund investments in buildings, equipment, and inventory. Governments borrow to pay for public goods like roads, bridges, and national defense in addition to wealth transfer programs. Every dollar borrowed requires a dollar saved, so we need savings to fund the private and public sector—investments that help increase GDP in the future.

D Direct Finance   **I** Indirect Finance

$ SAVINGS

STOCK AND BONDS

Borrowers make the investments that help GDP keep growing.

Savers

FOREIGN ENTITIES   HOUSEHOLDS

FIRMS   GOVERNMENTS

Borrowers

REPAYMENT + INTEREST

Savers supply the loanable funds that keep this market working.

$ SAVINGS

REPAYMENT + INTEREST

If financial firms are distressed, they cannot channel funds to borrowers efficiently.

REVIEW QUESTIONS

- Suppose your bank uses your savings to make a loan to a computer company. Is this an example of direct finance or indirect finance?

- Explain why financial markets play a critical role in the macroeconomy.

Banks   LOANS

PRACTICE WHAT YOU KNOW

Time Preferences: War in Syria

In 2010, life expectancy in Syria was 75 years. But then an intense and deadly internal war gripped that nation for many years. In addition to the massive bloodshed and millions of refugees created by the conflict, the economy came to a standstill. According to a report in *The Guardian*, Syria's civil war basically brought the economy to a halt. By 2015, 80% of Syria's population lived in poverty, and the unemployment rate was up to 57.7% by the end of 2014. By 2015, life expectancy in Syria had fallen to just 55 years.

One of the difficult side effects of war is a collapse of loanable funds markets.

Question: How does a drop in life expectancy affect time preferences and the supply of loanable funds in Syria?

Answer: Savings, or the supply of loanable funds, depend critically on people's time preferences. When life expectancy is plummeting, time preferences increase drastically: people have no reason to save for the future. With life expectancy plummeting to under 55 years, people are less likely to plan for the future. As time preferences increase, the supply of loanable funds goes down. Thus, when a nation is hit hard by political instability, war, or even a pandemic, one side effect is lower savings, which means a reduced supply of loanable funds—which in turn leads to lower economic output in the future.

Source: http://www.theguardian.com/world/2015/mar/12/syrias-war-80-in-poverty-life-expectancy-cut-by-20-years-200bn-lost

What Factors Shift the Demand for Loanable Funds?

To look at the demand side, we shift perspective to those who borrow in the loanable funds market. As we have seen, the demand for loanable funds derives from the desire to invest or purchase capital goods that aid in future production. We know that the interest rate matters and that this relationship is reflected in the slope of the demand curve. We now turn to factors that cause shifts in the demand for loanable funds. We focus on two: the productivity of capital and investor confidence.

Productivity of Capital

Consider a firm that is trying to decide whether to borrow for an investment. Perhaps your own firm is trying to decide whether to borrow to buy a new

This manual screwdriver depicts capital . . .

. . . and this electric version of a screwdriver represents an increase in capital productivity.

silk-screening machine, the SS-1000, for your college clothing business. This machine is capital, and its purchase counts as an investment. To determine whether you should take a loan, recall our rule: a firm should borrow to fund an investment only if the expected return is greater than the interest rate on the loan. Therefore, if the interest rate on the loan is 6%, you will borrow to buy the SS-1000 only if you expect to earn more than a 6% return from it.

Let's say that after crunching the numbers on expected costs and sales from the SS-1000, you estimate a return of just 4% from an investment in the SS-1000. You decide not to buy the new machine.

But then something changes. That something is the availability of the brand-new SS-2000. The SS-2000 is an improved machine that prints T-shirts at double the rate of the SS-1000. Given this new machine, which is slightly more expensive, you calculate that your expected return will be 7%, so you decide to take the loan and buy the machine. Thus, your demand for loanable funds has increased as a direct result of the availability of the new machine, which is twice as productive as the earlier machine.

What are the implications for the macroeconomy? Remember that firms borrow to finance capital purchases. Therefore, the level of demand for loans depends on the productivity of capital. Changes in capital productivity shift the demand for loanable funds. If capital is more productive, the demand for loans increases; if capital is less productive, the demand for loans decreases.

Productivity can change for a number of reasons. Consider the impact of the Internet. A connection to the Internet provides quick access to data and networking capabilities that people only dreamed about 25 years ago. The Internet also increases the productivity of computers, which are a major capital expense. Over the past 25 years, an increase in expected returns associated with the Internet has made investment in computer equipment (capital) more attractive. This means that investment in capital yields greater returns, which in turn increases the demand for loans. When capital is more productive, firms are more likely to borrow to finance purchases of this type of capital.

Investor Confidence

Investor confidence is a measure of what firms expect for future economic activity.

The demand for loanable funds also depends on the beliefs or expectations of the investors at business firms. If a firm believes its sales will increase in the future, it invests more today to build for future sales. If, instead, it believes its future sales will fall, it invests less today. **Investor confidence** is a measure of what firms expect for future economic activity. If confidence is high, they are more likely to borrow for investment at any interest rate. Economist John Maynard Keynes referred to an investor's drive to action as "animal spirits," meaning that investment demand may not even be based on rational decisions or real factors in the economy.

Figure 22.9 illustrates shifts in the demand for loanable funds. If capital productivity increases, demand for investment increases from D_1 to D_2—that is, demand is higher across all interest rates. Similarly, if investor confidence rises, demand for loanable funds increases from D_1 to D_2. In contrast, if capital productivity or investor confidence falls, the demand for loanable funds falls from D_1 to D_3.

PRACTICE WHAT YOU KNOW

Demand for Loanable Funds: SpongeBob and Loanable Funds

Question: Which one of the following changes would affect the demand for loanable funds, and how?

a. Research shows that watching the cartoon *SpongeBob SquarePants* can shorten a child's attention span. Now assume that an entire generation of children grows up watching this cartoon, resulting in adults who are less patient (their time preferences have increased).

b. A technological advance leads to greater capital productivity.

c. The interest rate falls.

How dangerous is this sponge?

Answer:

a. This factor would not affect the demand for loanable funds, but it would affect the supply of loanable funds. Less patience means that time preferences increase and the supply of loanable funds declines.

b. This technological advance would increase the demand for loanable funds.

c. The falling interest rate would lead to a movement along the demand curve, rather than a shift in the demand curve for loanable funds. A shift can be caused by an increase in the supply of loanable funds.

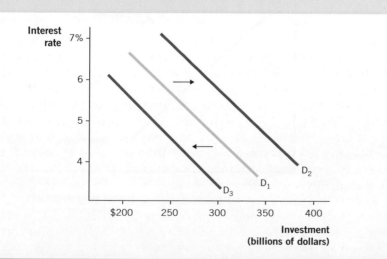

FIGURE 22.9

Shifts in the Demand for Loanable Funds

Increases in capital productivity and investor confidence lead to an increase in the demand for loanable funds at all interest rates, shifting demand from D_1 to D_2. Decreases in capital productivity and investor confidence decrease the demand for loanable funds from D_1 to D_3.

How Do We Apply the Loanable Funds Market Model?

We are now ready to begin using the loanable funds market model to study applications we see in the real world. First, we consider the implications of equilibrium in the loanable funds market. After that, we examine past and future views of the U.S. loanable funds market.

Equilibrium

Equilibrium in the loanable funds market occurs at the interest rate where the plans of savers match the plans of borrowers—that is, where quantity supplied equals quantity demanded. In Figure 22.10, this occurs at an interest rate of 5%, where savers are willing to save $250 billion and borrowers desire $250 billion in loans (in other words, they seek to invest $250 billion). At interest rates above 5%, the quantity of loanable funds supplied exceeds the quantity demanded, and this imbalance leads to downward pressure on the interest rate. At interest rates below 5%, the quantity demanded exceeds the quantity supplied, and this imbalance leads to upward pressure on the interest rate.

The loanable funds market, like other markets, naturally tends to move toward equilibrium, where supply is equal to demand. This equilibrium con-

FIGURE 22.10

Equilibrium in the Market for Loanable Funds

Equilibrium in the loanable funds market occurs where supply equals demand, at an interest rate of 5% and a quantity of $250 billion. Because investment is limited by savings, exactly $250 billion is saved and $250 billion is invested.

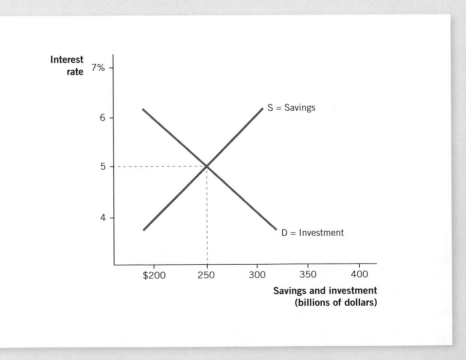

PRACTICE WHAT YOU KNOW

Working with the Loanable Funds Model: Foreign Savings in the United States

Recently, the economies of China and India have begun to grow very rapidly. This increases their citizens' income and wealth. In turn, these citizens increase their savings in their country and also in the United States.

How does foreign economic growth affect the U.S. loanable funds market?

Question: When foreign savings enter the U.S. loanable funds market, which curve is affected—supply or demand? How is this curve affected?

Answer: The supply of loanable funds increases as savings increase.

Question: How would you graph the U.S. loanable funds market both before and after the increase in foreign savings?

Answer:

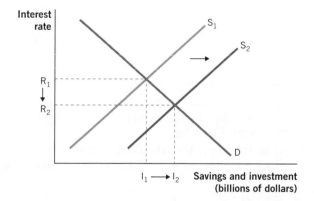

Before the increase in foreign savings, supply is designated as S_1 and demand as D. These imply interest rate R_1 and savings/investment amount I_1. When new foreign savings enter the market, supply increases to S_2, which decreases the interest rate to R_2 and increases the savings/investment amount to I_2.

Question: How does the change in foreign savings affect both investment and future output in the United States?

Answer: When the interest rate falls, the quantity of investment increases. Firms can afford to borrow more to build and expand their businesses. This increase in investment means that future output, or GDP, will be higher in the United States.

dition reinforces a key relationship between savings and investment. Equilibrium occurs when

savings = investment

In Figure 22.10, households and foreign entities have decided to save a combined total of $250 billion at an interest rate of 5%. Subsequently, firms borrow this $250 billion for investment. Thus, dollars that are saved make their way into the loanable funds market and are then channeled to firms for investment purposes.

Equilibrium also helps to clarify an important principle we'll return to often in this text. Investment requires saving because

Every dollar borrowed requires a dollar saved.

If an economy is to grow over time, someone has to invest in capital that helps to produce more in the future. But investment requires savings. Without savings, the economy cannot grow.

Equilibrium is a helpful starting point for understanding how the loanable funds market functions. But in the real world, financial market conditions change frequently. We can account for these changes in our model by using shifts in the supply and demand curves. Let's consider two examples: a decline in investor confidence and a decrease in the supply of loanable funds.

A Decline in Investor Confidence

When the overall economy slows, firms often reduce investment, since they expect reduced sales in future periods; this move reflects a decline in investor confidence. This happened recently in the United States during the Great Recession that began at the end of 2007. Panel (a) of Figure 22.11 shows how a decline in investor confidence affects the loanable funds market. When investment demand declines (shown in the figure as a shift from D_{2007} to D_{2008}), the loanable funds model predicts lower interest rates (a drop from R_1 to R_2) and a lower equilibrium level of investment (a drop from I_1 to I_2). Panel (b) of Figure 22.11 shows that investment fell during both recessions (the blue bars) in the years shown. During the Great Recession, real investment fell from $2.2 trillion to just $1.4 trillion—a 36% drop in less than two years.

A Decrease in the Supply of Loanable Funds

Let's now return to the potential effects of the baby boomers' retirement over the next 10 to 15 years. As we saw in the discussion of consumption smoothing, this will likely lead to a decrease in the supply of loanable funds in the United States. Figure 22.12 illustrates this kind of change. The curve labeled S_{2018} represents the supply of loanable funds in 2018. But as the baby boomers retire, supply may shift back to S_{2028} one decade later.

All else equal, this shift means lower investment (in the figure, a drop from I_1 to I_2) and lower GDP growth going forward. However, many other factors

FIGURE 22.11

A Decline in Investment Demand

(a) When decision-makers at firms lose confidence in the future direction of the economy, investment demand declines and lower investment results. (b) In the United States, real investment declined during both recessions that occurred between 2000 and 2012.

Source: Panel (b): U.S. Bureau of Economic Analysis.

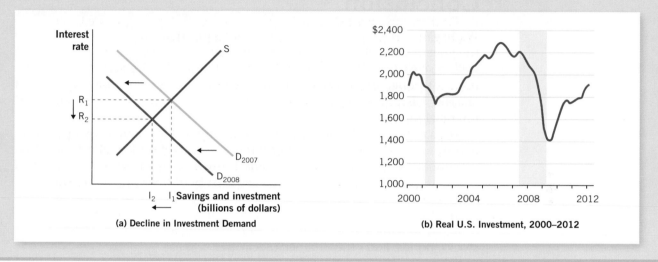

(a) Decline in Investment Demand

(b) Real U.S. Investment, 2000–2012

FIGURE 22.12

The Possible Future of the U.S. Loanable Funds Market

As baby boomers retire and draw down their savings, supply in the loanable funds market will decrease. Then if there are not increases in saving from other sources, interest rates will rise, leading to lower levels of investment.

may change over the next few years to increase savings in the United States. For example, as other nations grow, foreigners may continue to increase their savings in the United States. Or perhaps the savings rate in the United States will continue its recent rise. These increases could offset the effects of the baby boomers' retirement and keep interest rates low for U.S. firms.

Conclusion

We began this chapter with the misconception that interest rates are set by the government. To be sure, the government influences interest rates, a topic we'll discuss further in Chapter 30. But interest rates are actually set in the market through the interaction of supply and demand. The discussion in this chapter has provided the foundation we need to discuss interest rates and financial markets further.

In macroeconomics, few topics are more important than investment. And investment is the result of equilibrium in the market for loanable funds. Savers supply the funds that support loans; borrowers are investors who demand the loans. Equilibrium determines the quantity of investment and the interest rate in an economy.

In the next chapter, we extend our analysis of the market for loanable funds by looking at other methods for borrowing and lending. These include stocks, bonds, and other financial securities.

Compound Interest: When Should You Start Saving for Retirement?

When you graduate from college, get a job, and start earning a steady income, you'll have several choices to make. Should you buy or lease a car? Should you buy or rent a home? Should you donate money or time to charity? Regardless of your decisions on issues such as these, you should always make room in your budget for savings.

We know that everyone has positive time preferences, so all else equal, you probably would rather consume now than later. But all else is not equal. That is, a little less consumption now will lead to a lot more consumption later, even under assumptions of very reasonable interest rates. The return to savings is like an exponential function: the longer you save, the greater the return to your savings, even at a constant interest rate. The reason is based on compound interest, which implies that the interest you earn becomes savings—which also bears interest. Let's see how this works.

Consider two people who choose alternate paths. Dirk understands the power of compound interest and chooses to start saving $100 per month when he is 25 years old. Lee has stronger time preferences and decides to wait until age 45 to start saving $100 per month. If both Dirk and Lee work until they are 65 years old, Dirk saves for 40 years and Lee saves for 20.

You might guess that Dirk will end up with twice as much in his retirement account, since he saves twice as long. But you'd be wrong. It turns out that Lee's retirement savings will increase to $53,988. That's not too bad, considering he will have saved just $100 per month over 20 years, or 240 months—the interest payments certainly helped. But what about Dirk? His retirement savings will be worth $281,767! That's more than five times the size of Lee's, and Dirk only made twice as many payments.

What did we assume to get these returns? We assumed a 7% interest rate, which is the long-run

Compound interest produces more interest income.

historical real rate of return on a diversified stock portfolio. But any interest rate would illustrate the key point here: compound interest increases the value of your savings exponentially. So even with very strong time preferences, it makes sense to start saving early.

The graph illustrates the returns to saving $100 per month at an average annual return of 7% until retirement. The only difference is when you start saving. Notice that as you move along the horizontal axis, for each additional five years' worth of savings, the amount by which total savings grows will increase.

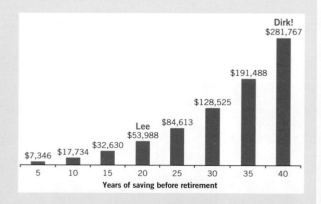

ANSWERING THE BIG QUESTIONS

What is the loanable funds market?

* The loanable funds market connects savers with borrowers.
* Savers are suppliers of loanable funds, and they earn interest as a reward for saving.
* Borrowers are the buyers of loanable funds, and they pay interest as the cost of borrowing.

What factors shift the supply of loanable funds?

* Changes in income and wealth shift the supply of loanable funds.
* Changes in time preferences also affect the supply of loanable funds.
* Consumption smoothing is another factor that shifts the loanable funds supply.

What factors shift the demand for loanable funds?

* Capital productivity affects the demand for loanable funds.
* Investor confidence also affects the demand for loanable funds.

How do we apply the loanable funds market model?

* We can use the loanable funds market model to examine real-world changes in both supply and demand for loanable funds.
* The loanable funds model also clarifies the important conclusion that every dollar borrowed requires a dollar saved.

CONCEPTS YOU SHOULD KNOW

consumption smoothing
    (p. 709)
dissaving (p. 709)
Fisher equation (p. 705)

interest rate (p. 702)
investor confidence (p. 716)
loanable funds market (p. 700)
nominal interest rate (p. 704)

real interest rate (p. 704)
savings rate (p. 712)
time preferences (p. 708)

QUESTIONS FOR REVIEW

1. Explain the importance of the loanable funds market to basic GDP in a macroeconomy.

2. All else equal, what does a lower interest rate mean for firms? What does a lower interest rate mean for savers?

3. Consider two alternatives to prepare for retirement: (1) saving in a bank where your funds earn interest and (2) buying fine art that rises in value over time. Each grows your retirement account over time.
   a. If the rates of return on fine art purchases fall, how would you expect the allocation of retirement funds to change across the macroeconomy?
   b. If the national savings rate is based only on the first option (saving in a bank), then what happens to the national savings rate when the allocation of retirement funds shifts as you describe in your response to part (a)?
   c. In addition to art, people often purchase real estate, stocks, and/or bonds as part of their savings, even though these assets are also not counted in the official data on personal savings. Discuss how these purchases

affect the official data on a nation's savings rate.

4. List the factors that affect the supply side of the loanable funds market. Which factors shift the curve?

5. List the factors that affect the demand side of the loanable funds market. Which factors shift the curve?

6. Why does inflation have a positive effect on the nominal interest rate?

7. Many people believe that a high interest rate is bad for the economy. Of course, all else equal, a higher interest rate means greater borrowing costs for firms. But a high interest rate is also helpful to some people in the economy.
   a. What group of people benefits from a higher interest rate? Explain how they benefit.
   b. A high interest rate can also indicate that something positive is happening in the economy. Describe how positive factors can lead to an increase in the demand for loanable funds and then an increase in the interest rate.

STUDY PROBLEMS (✳ solved at the end of the section)

1. Assume that the residents of a nation become more patient (experience a reduction in their time preferences).
   a. What will happen to the interest rate in that nation? What will happen to the equilibrium level of investment in that nation? Explain your answers.
   b. In the long run, how will the lower time preferences affect the levels of capital and income growth in that nation?

2. Many interest rates in the United States have fallen over the past couple of decades. Which of the following factors could have been the cause?
   a. increase in the demand for loanable funds
   b. decrease in the demand for loanable funds
   c. increase in the supply of loanable funds
   d. decrease in the supply of loanable funds

3. Use the Fisher equation to fill in the blanks in the following table:

Inflation rate	Real interest rate	Nominal interest rate
___	2%	7%
___	0%	7%
2%	___	6%
9%	___	6%
2%	2%	___
10%	2%	___

✳ 4. Consider two hypothetical nations: Wahooland and Wildcat Island. Initially, these nations are identical in every way. In particular, they are the same with regard to population size and age, income and wealth, and time preferences. They also have the same interest rate, savings, and investment.
   a. Suddenly, in the year 2015, the interest rate in Wahooland rises. After some investigating, economists determine that nothing has happened to the supply of loanable funds. Therefore, what are the possible reasons for this rise in the interest rate in Wahooland?
   b. Given your answer to part (a), what can you say about the level of investment in Wahooland relative to that in Wildcat Island in 2015? What can you say about future income levels in Wahooland versus Wildcat Island?
   c. Often, we think of a lower interest rate as always being preferable to a higher interest rate. What has this question taught us about that idea?

✳ 5. Some people have proposed an increase in the retirement age for U.S. citizens. Consider the effects of this proposed new policy.
   a. How would this change affect supply and demand in the market for loanable funds?
   b. How would this change affect the equilibrium interest rate and investment?
   c. In the long run, how would this change affect real GDP in the United States?

6. The Ragged Mountain Running Shop (RMRS) sells running shoes and apparel in Charlottesville, Virginia. The owners of RMRS are considering the possibility of opening new retail locations. After careful market analysis, they estimate the expected returns at five new potential locations. These estimates are listed in the following table, along with the amount RMRS would need to borrow in order to open each location:

Crozet	6%	$100,000
Downtown Charlottesville	4%	$100,000
Harrisonburg	11%	$80,000
Waynesboro	2%	$60,000
West End of Richmond	8%	$200,000

   a. RMRS approaches the Virginia National Bank (VNB) with hopes of borrowing to expand into other locations. Which locations will RMRS open if VNB offers them a loan at an interest rate of 7%? What if VNB offers loans at a lower interest rate of 5%?
   b. What is the total dollar amount of loans that RMRS takes at an interest rate of 7%? At an interest rate of 5%?
   c. Use the information in the table to graph the demand curve for investment for RMRS.

SOLVED PROBLEMS

4.a. If supply does not change, the rise in the interest rate must be due to a change in demand. If the rate went up, then demand must have increased. An increase in the demand for loanable funds occurs from an increase in the productivity of capital and/or an increase in investor confidence.

b. Investment will be higher in Wahooland than in Wildcat Island. Future GDP will be higher in Wahooland, and this means that income will be higher.

c. A higher interest rate can be caused by very productive capital. Thus, an innovative nation that tends to have new productive ideas and then high capital productivity might also have a higher interest rate. A higher interest rate can indicate very high returns to capital investment, which is certainly not bad for an economy.

5.a. The key is to examine how the policy change would affect savings through people's preferences for consumption smoothing. If U.S. workers start working longer, this would delay the dissaving period in their life and increase their savings. So supply would increase (shift outward). Demand would not change.

b. The equilibrium interest rate would fall, and investment would increase.

c. Real GDP would be greater, all else equal, due to the increase in investment. Basically, the new savings would become investment in capital. Thus, in the future there would be more tools for production in the United States, and output would be higher.

MIS CONCEPTION

Borrowing from foreign countries is harmful to the economy.

Many people are concerned that foreign nations own significant amounts of U.S. national debt. China, in particular, owns more U.S. debt than any other foreign nation. The worry is that since we owe them money, these nations can control us. But think of the situation in terms of loanable funds. From this perspective, the Chinese are lenders who are sending their savings into the United States. These Chinese savings keep our interest rates lower than they would otherwise be, helping both our government and private firms in the United States.

The financial vehicles that we discuss in this chapter are necessary for economic growth and development. These include stocks, bonds, home mortgages, and other financial instruments. Even though we are covering financial topics, macroeconomics is the common thread that weaves throughout them; each helps you gain a more detailed understanding of the factors that impact the overall economy. We can minimize the negative effects of recessions and experience economic growth only when financial markets function efficiently. When there are problems in financial markets, economic growth is impossible.

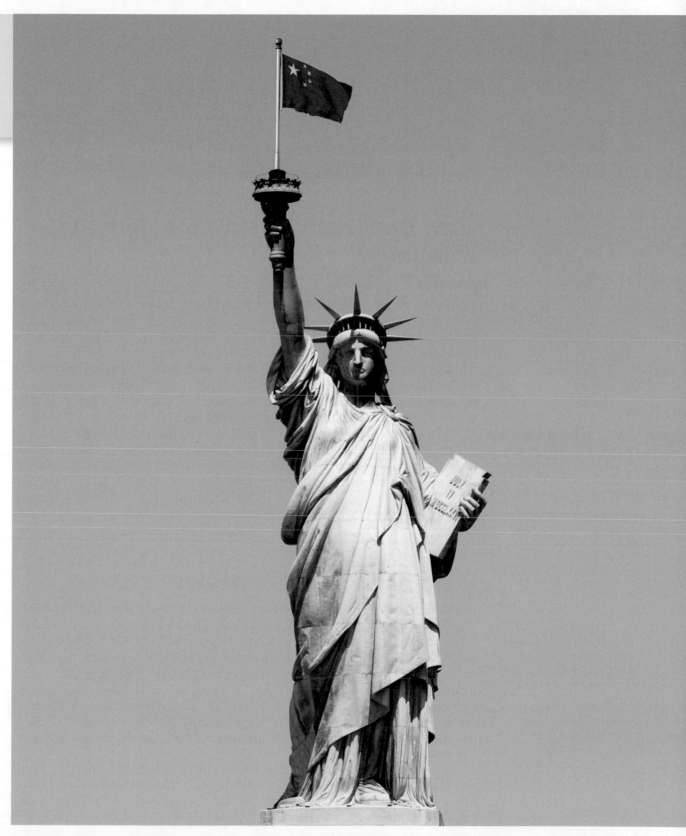

Would we ever have to sell U.S. landmarks to China to help pay the debt?

BIG QUESTIONS

* ✳ How do financial markets help the economy?
* ✳ What are the key financial tools for the macroeconomy?

How Do Financial Markets Help the Economy?

In financial markets, borrowers and lenders come together. The buyers (or borrowers) in financial markets are firms and governments in search of funds to undertake their daily operations. The sellers (or lenders) are savers looking for opportunities to earn a return on their savings. In Chapter 22, we introduced the loanable funds market as a way of thinking about financial markets through the lens of supply and demand. In this chapter, we present an *institutional* view of financial markets. That is, we consider what types of firms operate in the middle of financial markets and what types of tools they use to facilitate the exchanges between savers and borrowers.

The major players in the middle of financial markets are called financial intermediaries. **Financial intermediaries** are firms that help to channel funds from savers to borrowers. Banks are one example of a financial intermediary. **Banks** are private firms that accept deposits and extend loans. Banks and other financial intermediaries are important for the macroeconomy because they are at the center of financial markets: they help connect borrowers with savers.

Financial intermediaries are firms that help to channel funds from savers to borrowers.

Banks are private firms that accept deposits and extend loans.

Direct and Indirect Financing

When firms seek funding to pay for resources for production, they go to the loanable funds market. There are two different paths through the loanable funds market: indirect finance and direct finance. **Indirect finance** occurs when savers lend funds to financial intermediaries, which then loan these funds to borrowers. In this case, savers are indirectly financing the investments of firms.

Direct finance occurs when borrowers go directly to savers for funds. If you want a loan to start or expand a small business, you might go to a bank. But large established firms can skip financial intermediaries and go directly to the lenders when they need funds.

Figure 23.1 shows the two alternate routes through the loanable funds market. The top half illustrates indirect finance, in which banks and other financial intermediaries facilitate the exchanges between lenders (that is, savers) and borrowers. If you have a savings or checking account at a bank, you

Indirect finance occurs when savers deposit funds into banks, which then loan these funds to borrowers.

Direct finance occurs when borrowers go directly to savers for funds.

participate in the loanable funds market as a lender. Banks package together the savings of many depositors like you to extend loans. The bottom half of Figure 23.1 illustrates direct finance, in which borrowers bypass financial intermediaries and go directly to lenders for funds.

To undertake direct finance, firms need a contract that specifies the terms and conditions of the loan. These contracts usually take the form of a security. A **security** is a tradable contract that entitles its owner to certain rights. For example, a **bond** is a security that represents a debt to be paid. If you own a bond, it means that someone owes you money—it is a formal IOU. Bonds are a tool of direct finance because they enable borrowers to go directly to savers for funds. If a firm sells a bond to an individual, it is borrowing funds that will be repaid at a later date. For example, in 2015 the Target Corporation had $12 billion in bonds outstanding. This means that the Target Corporation owed $12 billion to the owners of those bonds.

A **security** is a tradable contract that entitles its owner to certain rights.

A **bond** is a security that represents a debt to be paid.

The Importance of Financial Markets

Financial markets play a vital role in the macroeconomy. Macroeconomic growth is based on the production of GDP across the economy. This production comes from individual firms such as cupcake shops, department

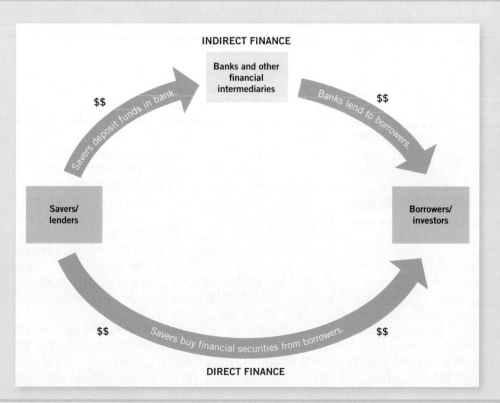

FIGURE 23.1

Direct versus Indirect Finance

Funds make their way through the loanable funds market through two distinct paths. Indirect finance occurs when savers and borrowers utilize banks or other financial intermediaries. Alternatively, direct finance occurs when borrowers go directly to savers for their funds.

stores, computer producers, and airplane manufacturers. But these firms need funding to build and buy the resources they use to produce their goods and services. These funds come from financial markets.

Consider what happens when financial markets break down. In 2007, several U.S. financial institutions began faltering. In September 2008, Lehman Brothers, a financial intermediary with over $600 billion in assets, went bankrupt. As a result, financial intermediaries all over the world became less inclined to extend loans. Because firms found it more difficult to borrow, economic contraction was inevitable. This contraction was the Great Recession that lasted through mid-2009.

ECONOMICS IN THE REAL WORLD

Should We Bail Out Big Banks?

In September 2008, Lehman Brothers, one of the largest financial firms, went bankrupt as many of the real estate loans they were holding went sour. After the Lehman Brothers bankruptcy (which had followed an earlier bankruptcy of Bear Stearns), it appeared there might be a domino effect that would lead to the collapse of many large banks. To avoid this potential disaster, the U.S. government implemented the Troubled Asset Relief Program—which came to be known as TARP—in October 2008. TARP allocated $700 billion to keep banks from failing. The money was used to aid banks that had made bad loans.

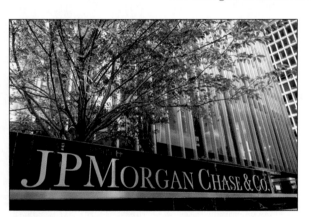

Do America's wealthiest banks really need taxpayer-funded bailouts?

TARP was very controversial from the beginning. On the one hand, the government was clearly bailing out big banks after many had made poor business decisions, and people from all walks of life question why the government would use taxpayer funds to help banks that seemed to contribute to the recession, especially since most people in the general population were still struggling financially.

Others, including both the outgoing and incoming presidents and their secretaries of Treasury, argued in favor of TARP. They considered these large financial intermediaries the bridge to future GDP. When the bridge is strong and safe, savers can lend to borrowers and then firms can invest in future GDP. But if the bridge collapses, output grinds to a halt. If firms aren't producing, they certainly don't need workers. GDP falls and unemployment rises. That's how important the bridge is.

Even today, economists (and politicians) are not in complete agreement about the need for TARP; though many feel this act spared the economy from falling into an even more dire situation, others feel that it was misguided and that no institution should be "too big to fail." While economists do agree on the necessity of healthy financial institutions, bank bailouts and the rules, regulations, and policies affecting financial institutions will likely remain topics of debate. ✳

PRACTICE WHAT YOU KNOW

Direct versus Indirect Finance: Which Is It?

Your friend Krista wants to open a cupcake shop. She needs to buy many resources before she can sell cupcakes and earn revenue. She is uncertain as to whether she should use direct or indirect financing.

Question: For each of the following alternatives, is the financing considered direct or indirect?

a. Krista borrows money from a friend.

b. Krista takes a loan from her small local bank.

c. Krista arranges a loan from a large national bank.

d. Krista issues bonds and sells them to people in her neighborhood.

These are some of the resources necessary to produce Lemon Bliss cupcakes.

Answers:

a. This is direct finance: Krista, the borrower, goes directly to the lender without the aid of a financial intermediary.

b. This is indirect finance: the bank makes the loan to Krista from the funds of various savers.

c. This is also indirect finance; the size of the bank does not matter.

d. This is direct finance: Krista goes directly to the lenders. It doesn't matter if the bonds are sold to people she happens to know.

What Are the Key Financial Tools for the Macroeconomy?

In this section, we explore tools used in financial markets to help fund investment. We focus on tools that matter for the macroeconomy, including bonds, stocks, Treasury securities, home mortgages, and private-sector securities created by the process of securitization. We start with bonds.

Bonds

Firms issue several types of securities to raise funds, but we can view them all as variations of a basic corporate bond.

Let's say your friend Kara wants to open a new website design business. But first she needs a loan to buy computers and software. Initially, Kara goes to a bank for a loan, but it turns her away because her company is new and viewed as very risky. So Kara comes to you and asks for a one-year loan. You know Kara well, so you agree to loan her some money with the understanding that she will repay the funds plus interest exactly one year later.

To formalize your agreement, you decide to draw up an IOU contract like the one presented in Figure 23.2. When you "buy" this contract from Kara, you are lending her funds with the promise that she'll pay you $10,000 in one year. The contract is essentially the same as a corporate or government bond, and it serves the same purpose. This is an example of direct finance, with the borrower going directly to the lender.

Like any bond, your contract contains three important pieces of information: the name of the borrower, the repayment date, and the amount due at repayment. In this example, the name of the borrower is Kara Alexis; the repayment date is February 20, 2018. The date on which the loan repayment is due is the **maturity date**. Finally, every bond contract also specifies the face value, or par value, of the bond. The bond's **face value**, or **par value**, is the bond's value at maturity—the amount due at repayment. For notation purposes, we'll call the face value p_m because it is the price, or value, of the bond at maturity.

Perhaps you noticed that Figure 23.2 shows the bond's face value, but not the amount of the initial loan. In fact, you and Kara must come to an agreement about how much you will loan her. But with a bond agreement, the face value is typically set at a round number like $10,000. When you and Kara settle on the initial loan amount, you are agreeing to the dollar price of the bond (p). The price of the bond is the original dollar amount of the loan. For example, if you agree on a price of $8,000 for Kara's bond, that is the amount you loan her. From your perspective, you loan her $8,000 today for the promise that she'll pay you $10,000 in one year. From Kara's perspective, she now has $8,000 she can use to buy computers and software for her website design business, and she can begin producing GDP. But one year from now she has to repay you $10,000.

The **maturity date** of a bond is the date on which the loan repayment is due.

A bond's **face value**, or **par value**, is the bond's value at maturity—the amount due at repayment.

FIGURE 23.2

A Basic Bond Security

A simple IOU contract between two friends is like a bond. It specifies three things: (1) the name of the borrower (here, Kara Alexis); (2) the repayment date (February 20, 2018); (3) the amount due at repayment ($10,000).

I, <u>Kara Alexis,</u> owe you <u>$10,000.</u>

I will pay you on <u>February 20, 2018.</u>

Today's date: February 20, 2017.

Kara Alexis

That's how a basic bond security works. Many bonds also include *coupons* that specify periodic interest payments to the bond owner. That distinction is not important for our purposes, so we focus on bonds that entail a single payment when the bond matures.

We now build on this foundation by discussing how interest rates relate to bond prices and how default risk affects the price of a bond.

The Bond Dollar Price and Interest Rate

In the previous discussion, we described Kara's bond in dollar prices. But loan prices are generally quoted in interest rates. Therefore, we need to consider how the bond's dollar price (p) is related to its interest rate (R). To determine the interest rate on this bond, we have to find the rate of return on the dollars that are loaned. For example, you "buy" Kara's bond for $8,000, and one year later the bond is worth $10,000. In percentage terms, the value of the bond increases by 25%. Thus, the rate of return, or interest rate, is computed as a growth rate, where the price of the bond is growing from its initial value (p_0):

$$\text{interest rate} = R = \frac{\text{face value} - \text{initial price}}{\text{initial price}} = \frac{p_m - p_0}{p_0} \qquad \text{(Equation 23.1)}$$

If the price of the bond is $8,000, the interest rate is computed as

$$R = \frac{p_m - p_0}{p_0} = \frac{\$10,000 - \$8,000}{\$8,000} = 25\%$$

We used growth rates when we discussed GDP growth and inflation. Here, the interest rate is computed as a growth rate; it is the growth rate of the original funds invested.

With bonds, the face value is fixed—it is printed on the front of the bond. Thus, *the dollar price of a bond determines the bond's interest rate.* If you know the dollar price of a given bond, you can determine the interest rate. Table 23.1 shows several alternative prices for a $10,000 bond. Notice that the lower the price, the higher the interest rate, because it takes fewer dollars for the lender to earn $10,000 one year later.

Each price implies a different interest rate. For example, if Kara sells you the $10,000 bond for only $7,500, the interest rate rises to 33%. This is much better for you, since you buy the bond for $7,500 and are repaid that amount plus $2,500 in interest only one year later. But this is worse for Kara because she is getting just $7,500 this year, with the same promise to repay you $10,000 next year.

Notice that as the price of the bond drops, the interest rate on the bond rises. If the bond price drops to $5,000, the interest rate climbs to 100%. This relationship holds by definition: *the dollar price and interest rate of a bond have a negative relationship.*

In Chapter 22, we saw that the interest rate on a loan is the cost of borrowing and the reward for saving. Higher interest rates (lower dollar prices) hurt borrowers and help lenders. As a lender, you want to buy bonds for the lowest price possible because you want the highest possible interest rate on your

TABLE 23.1

Dollar Price and Interest Rate for a $10,000 One-Year Bond

Dollar price (p_0)	Interest rate (R)
$9,000	11%
8,000	25
7,500	33
5,000	100

savings. The borrower wants to sell bonds for the highest price possible so that she can pay the lowest possible interest rate.

A primary factor in determining the interest rate on bonds is the borrower's default risk, a topic to which we now turn.

Default Risk

Default risk is the risk that the borrower will not pay the face value of a bond on the maturity date.

Some financial transactions are very complex and potentially lead to many different outcomes. But bonds are fairly straightforward. If the bond owner holds the bond until maturity, there are only two possible outcomes: the borrower pays the maturity value of the bond, or the borrower defaults on the loan. These possibilities are illustrated in Figure 23.3. For the bond owner, then, the risk of default is the primary concern. **Default risk** is the risk that the borrower will not pay the face value of the bond on the maturity date.

All else equal, the greater the default risk, the lower the price of a bond. Consider the bond that Kara is selling to finance her start-up website design company. If you really trust Kara and believe that her business will succeed, you might buy her $10,000 bond for $9,500. At this price, she promises to pay you about 5.25% interest for the use of your funds for a year. However, if you are skeptical about either Kara's integrity or the prospects for her business success, you may be willing to pay only $8,000 for the bond. At this price, she will pay 25% interest for the loan instead. This scenario illustrates an important bond price principle: a *bond's interest rate rises with default risk*.

Consider bonds offered by the Target Corporation. Target is a large company with many capital investments. As mentioned earlier, the Target Corporation had $12 billion in bonds outstanding in 2015. Clearly, there is a significant market for Target bonds. Consider the hypothetical supply and demand for one-year $100,000 Target bonds illustrated in Figure 23.4. Initially, with the demand curve at D_1 and supply at S, the equilibrium price is $98,000.

FIGURE 23.3

Two Possible Outcomes with a Bond

With a bond, both the maturity date and the face value are certain. Thus, there are only two possible outcomes if a bond owner holds the bond until maturity: either the borrower will pay the face value, or she will default. Because these are the only two possible outcomes, default risk is the primary concern of a bond owner.

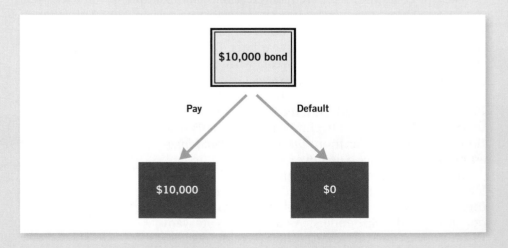

Now let's assume that something negative happens to the future prospects of Target's business. Perhaps Walmart attracts customers away from Target. This news reduces the probability that Target will pay off its bonds as they mature; in other words, it increases Target's default risk. As such, the demand for Target bonds declines from D_1 to D_2. As demand declines, the market price of Target bonds falls from \$98,000 to \$97,000, which means that the interest rate rises (because the dollar price and interest rate on a bond always move in opposite directions). As a result, we can generalize to say that increases in default risk (1) cause a drop in the price that firms can charge for their bonds and (2) cause an increase in their bonds' interest rate.

Bond Ratings

Default risk is important to bondholders, and it helps to determine the price of the bond. But typical individuals have difficulty judging the default risk of any one company, let alone the thousands of firms that sell bonds in a developed economy. To address this problem, private rating agencies evaluate and then grade the default risk of borrowing entities. They give a grade that reflects the likelihood of default. Three ratings agencies are particularly prominent in the United States: Moody's, Standard and Poor's, and Fitch. The ratings systems are similar for all three firms, so we'll choose Standard and Poor's (S&P) for explanatory purposes.

The most stable firms, those most likely to pay their debts, are given a rating of AAA. In the recent past, firms like Johnson & Johnson and Microsoft have achieved AAA ratings. A high rating is desirable because it directly translates into higher prices and lower interest rates on the firm's bonds. Moreover, the firm's operating costs are directly affected by its bond rating, because the interest rate is the cost of a key resource for its production. If Microsoft's bond rating falls from AAA to AA, this change increases the company's cost in the same way that its costs would rise if its employees negotiated higher wages or if another key resource became more expensive.

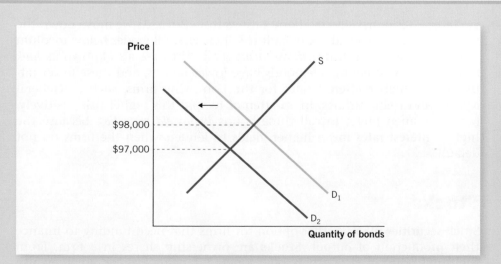

FIGURE 23.4

How Increased Default Risk Affects the Market for \$100,000 Target Bonds

The initial price in the market for Target bonds is \$98,000. But an increase in default risk reduces the demand for Target bonds, resulting in a lower price and a higher interest rate. This outcome drives up the borrowing costs for Target.

TABLE 23.2		
Sample Bond Ratings		
S&P*	**Grade**	**Examples**
AAA	Prime	Harvard University, Johnson & Johnson, Microsoft, University of Virginia
AA	High	Berkshire Hathaway, Coca-Cola, Duke University, Toyota, Walmart
A	Upper medium	Anheuser-Busch, Goldman Sachs, Home Depot, Intel, Lowes, Nike, Target
BBB	Lower medium	Brazil, EBady, Ford, Hewlett-Packard, Mattel, McDonald's, Spain
BB	Non-investment or speculative	Deli, Delta Airlines, Dillard's, General Motors, Goodyear, Nokia, Washington Post
B	Highly speculative	Dave & Buster's Egypt, New York Times, Nicaragua, Pakistan, Sprint
CCC	Extremely speculative	Belarus, Greece, Jamaica, JCPenney, Sears, Venezuela
CC	In or near default	Argentina

*As of January 2016.

Table 23.2 shows selected bond ratings from 2016. As we move down the table, the grade falls and the default risk increases. All grades below medium (BB and lower) are called *noninvestment grade*. They are also known as *junk bonds*. Noninvestment-grade bonds have lower ratings, and these lower ratings mean higher interest rates for the borrowing firms, such as General Motors and Delta Airlines. In an attempt to spin this higher risk positively, bond salesmen prefer to call these bonds *high-yield securities*, because the higher interest rates mean higher yields to lenders when the firms do not default.

Stocks

Stocks are ownership shares in a firm.

Stock securities offer another option for firms that need funding to finance their production of output. **Stocks** are ownership shares in a firm. From the firm's point of view, stocks offer a new financing avenue, but they also involve ceding some ownership of the firm. In this important sense, stocks are very different from bank loans or bonds: owners of stock securities are actual owners of the firm. In contrast, when a firm sells bonds, it does not cede direct control of the firm to new owners.

Why would a firm sell stocks instead of bonds? One reason is that bond financing leaves the firm with a lot of bills that must be paid. For example, when IBM sells $10 million worth of 10-year bonds, the company takes on the obligation to pay $10 million in 10 years. If the firm cannot pay this debt, the owners may need to declare bankruptcy and lose the firm altogether. With stocks, however, the owners can sell shares of the firm to others and move forward without the burden of debt.

You can own part of Microsoft! To see its current share price, type its ticker symbol (MSFT) into a search engine.

From the lender's perspective, stock ownership is also different from bond ownership. Because stock owners (shareholders) are owners of the firm, they have some influence on the firm's operations. In fact, a shareholder who owns more than 50% of the shares of the firm is the majority shareholder and controls more than 50% of the ownership votes. A majority shareholder can determine the direction of the company, an influence that is not available to bondholders.

Secondary Markets

Most people who purchase stocks and bonds use brokers, who buy the stocks and bonds in secondary markets. **Secondary markets** are markets in which securities are traded after their first sale. Secondary markets are like used-car markets, but the "used" assets are securities. There's nothing wrong with a used security; it just means that the buyer is not purchasing the security directly from the firm whose name is on it. You probably recognize the names of some important secondary stock markets. They include the New York Stock Exchange (NYSE) and NASDAQ (the National Association of Securities Dealers Automated Quotations).

Secondary markets are markets in which securities are traded after their first sale.

The existence of a secondary market for a given security increases the demand for that security. Consider the difference between a Target Corporation bond and the hypothetical bond you bought from Kara Alexis to help fund her website design company. Whoever buys the Target bond can sell it with a quick call to a broker or with the click of a mouse. The ease of resale is valuable and therefore worth a higher price. But when you buy Kara's bond, you have to hold on to it until you can personally locate another buyer. This sort of complication greatly limits the demand for bonds that cannot be resold in secondary markets, which lowers the price (that is, raises the interest rate).

Figure 23.5 illustrates the impact that secondary markets have on security prices. If a secondary market exists for a security, then the demand for the security increases (from D_1 to D_2); in turn, the increased demand causes the price of the security to rise (from p_1 to p_2), all else being equal. For the firm, the existence of a secondary market is helpful because it lowers the interest rate the firm pays on its bonds and therefore its cost of borrowing.

The NYSE is the largest secondary stock market in the world.

Secondary markets are a valuable institution of market economies because they lower the cost of borrowing. This is true of secondary markets for any

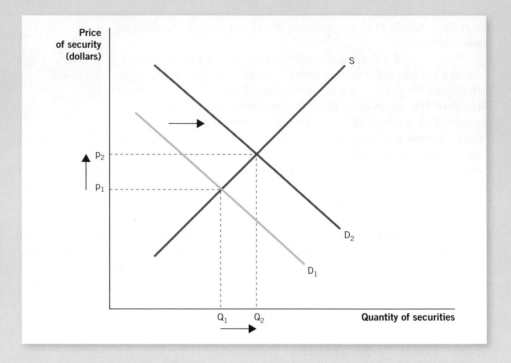

The Effect of Secondary Markets on Security Prices

The existence of secondary markets increases the demand for securities. When demand increases, the price rises (and the interest rate falls). Secondary markets allow firms to borrow at lower interest rates.

asset, not just stocks and bonds. For example, let's say you are considering buying a particular house. Your real estate agent tells you that the price is very reasonable, but there is one unusual stipulation: you can never sell the house after you buy it. Of course, this is not a realistic stipulation, but think about how it would affect your willingness to buy the home. The purchase would be more risky, and no buyer would pay as much for that house as for one that could be resold. Secondary markets, by offering future sale opportunities for securities, increase the demand for them.

ECONOMICS IN THE REAL WORLD

Stock Market Indices: Dow Jones versus S&P

Media reports about the stock market tend to focus on stock price indices like the Dow Jones Industrial Average and the Standard and Poor's 500 (S&P 500). Just as the consumer price index (CPI) tracks general consumer prices, these stock market indices track overall stock prices. Recall that the CPI is a weighted average of all consumer prices, where the weights are determined by the portion of the typical consumer budget that is spent on any given item. An increase in the CPI indicates a corresponding rise in the general level of consumer prices. Similarly, the rise and fall of stock indices indicate a corresponding rise and fall in the general level of stock prices.

The best-known stock index is the Dow Jones Industrial Average (the Dow). When the Dow was first published in 1896, it tracked 12 companies.

Is it good news when the Dow Jones Industrial Average goes up?

Today, it tracks 30 companies selected by the editors of the *Wall Street Journal*. The editors maintain the index so that it represents companies in all the important sectors of the economy. To stay up to date, the Dow must occasionally change the companies it indices. For example, when the technology sector came to the forefront in the late 1990s, Intel and Microsoft were added. And in March 2015, Apple replaced AT&T in the Dow.

One of the advantages of the Dow is that it provides historical data all the way back to May 26, 1896. At that time, the calculation was very simple: an investor added the price of all 12 stocks and divided the sum by 12 to compute a simple average. Today, the Dow incorporates 30 stock prices in the average, but it is essentially computed in the same way. This means that the Dow tracks only the price of the stock, not the overall value of a company or the relative values of the companies in the stock market.

The S&P 500 index weights the stock prices by the *market value* of the companies it tracks. The market value is the total number of stock shares multiplied by the price per share. Under a market value–weighted index, the stock prices of large companies have a greater impact than those of smaller companies. For instance, Apple (with a market value of $636 billion in 2015) weighs much more heavily than Facebook (with a market value of $248 billion in 2015). Moreover, there is another difference between the S&P 500 and the Dow Jones index: while the Dow tracks only 30 companies, the S&P 500 tracks 500 companies, thus providing a much broader representation of the stock market.

In many respects, the Dow is an artifact of simpler times, when computing a broadly based index was time intensive. Today, spreadsheets can crunch all the stock price data in milliseconds. Nevertheless, the Dow has been a very reliable measure of market performance, and it also provides a continuous record of historical information that cannot be replaced by more recent indices. In addition, investors are accustomed to the Dow, and its simplicity makes it easy to understand and follow. ✳

Treasury Securities

So far in our discussion, we have considered firms as the major borrowing entity in an economy. But governments are significant borrowers, too. According to the U.S. Treasury Department, the U.S. federal government has about $18 trillion worth of debt—that's more than $50,000 per citizen. All this borrowing takes place through bond sales. **Treasury securities** are the bonds sold by the U.S. government to pay for the national debt.

Treasury securities are sold through auctions to large financial firms. The auction price determines the interest rate. After a Treasury security is sold the

Treasury securities are the bonds sold by the U.S. government to pay for the national debt.

The Dow Jones Industrial Average

The Dow Jones Industrial Average is perhaps the most closely watched financial market indicator. The Dow tracks average stock prices of 30 firms that represent major industries in the U.S. economy; these include Coca-Cola, Walmart, Disney, Microsoft, Apple, Visa, and Boeing. Since the Dow represents a broad array of industries, movements indicate changes in private investors' expectations about the future direction of the macroeconomy. Increases in the Dow generally reflect confidence in the future of the U.S. economy; decreases mean people are pessimistic. While other economic indicators take months to measure, the Dow is an instantaneous indicator of how private investors view future economic conditions.

The DJIA is shown here in a logarithmic graph, which means the vertical scale measures changes in percentage terms. For example, the distance between 100 and 110 is the same as the distance between 10,000 and 11,000, since both are 10% changes.

October 1929: In the stock market crash of October 1929, the DJIA plummeted 24% over five days.

The corporations included in the DJIA change over time, in an effort to reflect the U.S. economy. Some past and present companies are shown here with the year they were added to the DJIA.

Chrysler · Eastman Kodak · Paramount Pictures · United Airlines · Westinghouse · Standard Oil · Coca-Cola · General Electric · AT&T · DuPont · IBM · U.S. Steel · General Motors · Sears · Proctor & Gamble

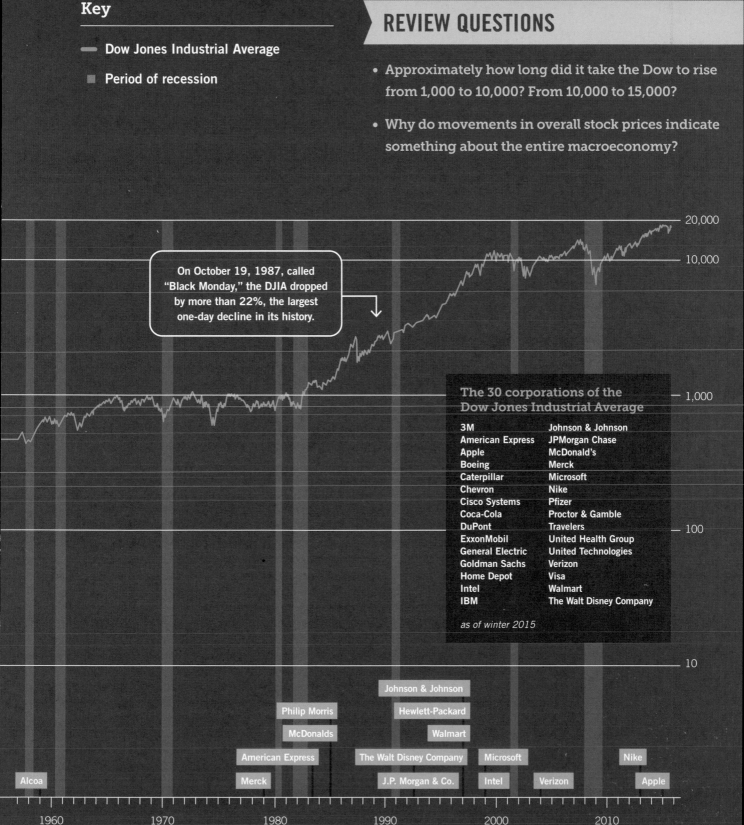

Key

— Dow Jones Industrial Average

■ Period of recession

REVIEW QUESTIONS

- Approximately how long did it take the Dow to rise from 1,000 to 10,000? From 10,000 to 15,000?

- Why do movements in overall stock prices indicate something about the entire macroeconomy?

On October 19, 1987, called "Black Monday," the DJIA dropped by more than 22%, the largest one-day decline in its history.

The 30 corporations of the Dow Jones Industrial Average

3M	Johnson & Johnson
American Express	JPMorgan Chase
Apple	McDonald's
Boeing	Merck
Caterpillar	Microsoft
Chevron	Nike
Cisco Systems	Pfizer
Coca-Cola	Proctor & Gamble
DuPont	Travelers
ExxonMobil	United Health Group
General Electric	United Technologies
Goldman Sachs	Verizon
Home Depot	Visa
Intel	Walmart
IBM	The Walt Disney Company

as of winter 2015

20,000

10,000

1,000

100

10

Johnson & Johnson

Philip Morris

Hewlett-Packard

McDonalds

Walmart

American Express

The Walt Disney Company

Microsoft

Nike

Alcoa

Merck

J.P. Morgan & Co.

Intel

Verizon

Apple

1960   1970   1980   1990   2000   2010

U.S. Treasury securities are used to pay for government spending when tax revenue falls short.

first time, anyone can buy it in the large and active secondary market for U.S. Treasury securities.

U.S. Treasury securities are generally considered less risky than any other bond, because borrowers don't expect the U.S. government to default on its debts. Even when politicians threaten actions that could lead to default, the values of U.S. securities have stayed historically steady because borrowers on the whole have felt a U.S. loan default is highly unlikely.

Because Treasury bonds are safe, firms and governments from all over the world buy U.S. Treasury securities as a way to limit risk. In 2013, approximately $5.3 trillion (about 30%) of U.S. federal debt was held by foreigners. Figure 23.6 shows the breakdown of foreign ownership of U.S. Treasury securities.

As we noted in this chapter's opening "misconception" statement, a common concern is that nations like China will exert undue influence on the U.S. government if we owe them money. But this perspective does not consider a key point: foreign savings keep interest rates lower in the United States than they would otherwise be. This means that U.S. firms and governments can undertake their activities at lower costs. In turn, lower interest rates mean more investment and greater future GDP. That is a clear benefit of foreign investment in the United States.

Treasury securities play many roles in the macroeconomy. For example, they are used when the government alters the supply of money in the economy, which we discuss in Chapter 30. In addition, if the government decides to increase spending without raising taxes, it must pay for the additional spending by borrowing—by selling bonds. We will explore this role of Treasury securities in Chapter 28.

FIGURE 23.6

Major Foreign Holders of U.S. Treasury Securities, 2013 (in billions of dollars)

Of the $18 trillion of U.S. government debt, foreigners hold approximately 30%. China alone owns almost $1.3 billion of our national debt, but this represents about 7% of the total outstanding.

Source: U.S. Treasury Department.

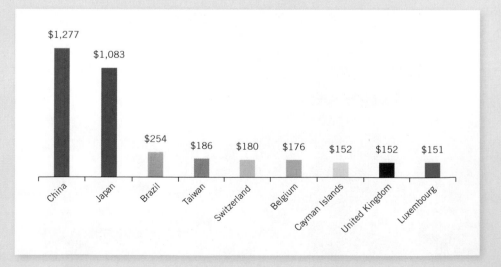

Home Mortgages

Another important borrowing tool in the United States is the home mortgage loan, which individuals use to pay for homes. The most common mortgage loan lasts 30 years from inception and is paid off with 360 monthly payments. These mortgages are really just variations on the basic bond security we have described in this chapter. When a family wants to buy a home, they take on a mortgage loan, which is a contract that states their willingness to repay the loan over several years—just like a firm signing a bond contract.

The macroeconomic significance of home mortgages has grown over time as more and more people own homes. Figure 23.7 shows the growth in the U.S. mortgage market from 1983 to 2014. The graph plots the total size of the U.S. mortgage market in real (2014) dollars. The U.S. home mortgage market expanded greatly, leading up to the recession in 2008. In 1983, there was about $2.7 trillion in home mortgages in the United States. By 2007, the market had expanded to over $12 trillion. However, as you can see in the figure, the U.S. home mortgage market has declined since 2007 and, as of 2015, is still only about three-fourths the size of its peak in 2007.

Securitization

Since the 1980s, bonds, stocks, and other financial securities, including home mortgages, have been bundled together to create new financial assets in a process called securitization. **Securitization** is the creation of a new security by combining otherwise separate loan agreements. These agreements are then bought and sold like any other agreement on secondary markets.

For example, consider two common personal loans: home mortgages and student loans. The United States has secondary markets in which home

Incentives

Securitization is the creation of a new security by combining otherwise separate loan agreements.

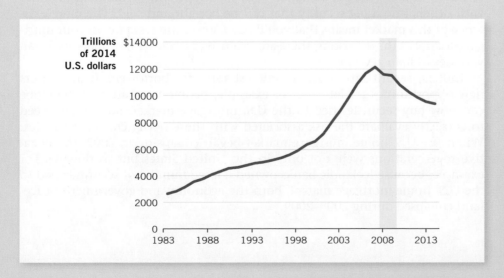

Total Size of U.S. Mortgage Market, 1983–2014

The home mortgage market in the United States expanded greatly, leading up to the recession in 2008. In 1983, there was about $2.7 trillion worth of home mortgages in the United States. But by 2007, this amount had expanded to over $12 trillion.

Source: Federal Reserve.

FIGURE 23.8

Securitization

Securitization is the creation of a new security by combining otherwise separate loan agreements. For example, it is possible to create a $1 million mortgage-backed security by buying five separate $200,000 mortgages and then selling them together as a bundle.

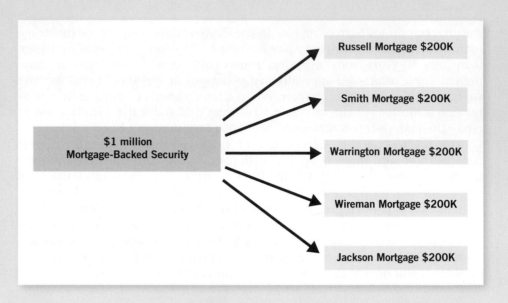

mortgages and student loans are bought and sold daily. Figure 23.8 illustrates how mortgage-backed securities are created. Each mortgage-backed security (MBS) is a combination, or bundle, of mortgages. The new security is then available for resale in secondary markets.

Most economists believe that these tools are important because opportunities for firms and individuals expand when credit is available. More credit leads to lower borrowing costs, which certainly help borrowers. When interest rates are lower, investment opportunities expand for everything from factories to roads to homes to education. And as we noted earlier, secondary markets reduce borrowing costs. In a few years, you may take out a mortgage to buy a home. There is a chance your mortgage will be bundled together with others into a big security that can be bought and sold. The mere existence of this market means that you'll pay a lower interest rate on your mortgage loan. For these reasons, there are incentives to create new markets for all varieties of loan agreements.

Indeed, securitization lowers interest rates for borrowers. It also offers new opportunities for lenders. For example, people from all over the globe can now buy securities tied to the U.S. mortgage market. But lenders need to correctly evaluate the risk associated with these newly created securities. When the U.S. home mortgage market began collapsing in 2007, the negative reverberations were not only in the United States but worldwide. For example, because Icelandic banks owned a large number of securities tied to the U.S. home mortgage market, both the economy and government of Iceland collapsed during 2008–2009.

PRACTICE WHAT YOU KNOW

The Effects of Foreign Investment: What If We Limit Foreign Ownership of Our National Debt?

Imagine that a new law significantly limits foreign ownership of U.S. Treasury bonds.

Question: How would you graph the market for Treasury bonds showing how the new law will affect demand?

Answer: Demand will decline because the new law limits foreign demand.

Could both of these flags fly over Washington someday?

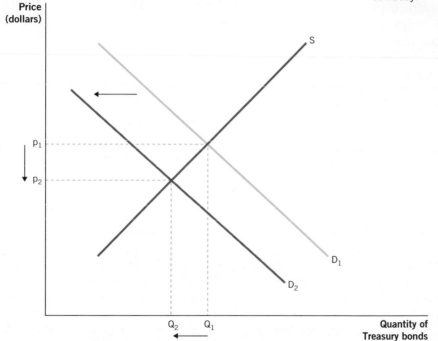

Question: What will happen to Treasury bond prices?

Answer: The price of Treasury bonds will decline. When demand falls, the new equilibrium price will be lower.

Question: What will happen to the interest rate on Treasury bonds?

Answer: The interest rate on Treasury bonds will increase, because dollar price and the interest rate move in opposite directions. A lower price means that the government will sell each bond for fewer dollars, so it will be paying higher interest to the bond owner.

In the end, restrictions on foreign investment will lead to higher domestic interest rates.

Direct Finance

The Big Short

The Big Short (2016) is based on the book with the same title by Michael Lewis. The movie is essentially a documentary that doesn't feel like a documentary as the actors carefully explain the details of the financial collapse that led to the Great Recession in 2007.

The movie introduces Mark Baum (played by Steve Carrell) and Michael Burry (played by Christian Bale), who were among the few people who recognized the dangers in the economy's rampant reliance on overvalued mortgage-backed securities.

In the movie, Baum and Burry travel to Florida to interview real borrowers. They knock on home doors and visit local businesses. These interviews help them see what almost nobody at the big banks sees: that the borrowers will not have the income to repay their loans when their low introductory interest rates increase. When these borrowers stop paying, their securitized mortgages being sold to investors will become worthless. When Baum realizes that he can make a lot of money by betting that these losses will happen (a process called "shorting" the mortgages), he recognizes that the economy will take a nosedive when other financial insiders finally reach the same conclusion. In the meantime, he determines, the very biggest invest-

In the movie *The Big Short*, we get a look at the complicated world of finance.

ment banks (including Goldman Sachs and Lehman Brothers) are in over their heads, have no idea about the dangers that are brewing, and do not realize how dangerous subprime loans are to the economy.

At the end of the day, *The Big Short* helps you understand secondary markets, securitization, and mortgage-backed securities. In addition, it provides a good look at some of the perverse incentives and dangers that lurk inside the real-world loanable funds market.

Conclusion

We began this chapter with the misconception that borrowing from foreign countries—that is, foreign ownership of the national debt—is harmful to the economy. However, we have seen that this is not the case. Funds flowing into the U.S. loanable funds market help lead to economic expansion, no matter where they originate. One of the themes throughout this chapter has been the importance of saving and lending to the macroeconomy. With indirect finance, banks and financial intermediaries help channel funds from savers to borrowers. With direct finance, firms sell securities such as stocks and bonds directly to savers. These securities enable savers to earn returns on their savings while also giving firms access to funds for investment.

In the chapters that follow, we'll see that these financial institutions play a major role in the macroeconomy.

Long-Run Returns for Stocks versus Bonds

In this chapter, we focused on the importance of stocks and bonds for financing the activities of firms and governments. But you may be wondering which of these instruments would best serve your own personal savings.

Let's begin by looking at the historical returns for stocks versus bonds. The bar graph below, based on data from the Bureau of Labor Statistics, shows that from 1960 to 2011, the average inflation-adjusted return for long-term Treasury bonds was 3.18%. But over the same period, stocks yielded 6.67%. Thus, the return on stocks was more than twice the return on bonds.

Perhaps this doesn't seem like a huge difference to you. After all, 3% and 6% both seem small. But think of it this way: what if your grandparents had put $100 into both stocks and bonds for you in 1960? After adjusting for inflation, by 2011 your savings in bonds would have yielded $2,735.63, but the $100 in stocks would have generated a return of $10,027.78. These alternatives are plotted in the graph.

Which should you choose: stocks or bonds?

To be sure, stocks are riskier. Just look at how the value of your savings would have fluctuated over the years. With stocks, the value of your savings would have sometimes climbed or fallen by more than $1,000 a year. With bonds, the fluctuations would have been much smaller. Therefore, if you are extremely averse to risk, you might choose bonds. But in the long run, taking more risk with stocks has historically been more lucrative.

Average Real Return, 1960–2011

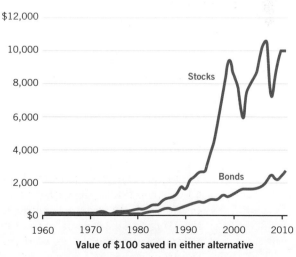

Value of $100 saved in either alternative

ECONOMICS FOR LIFE

ANSWERING THE BIG QUESTIONS

How do financial markets help the economy?

* Financial markets help channel funds to investment opportunities throughout the economy.
* Direct finance occurs when savers lend directly to borrowers; indirect finance occurs when savers and borrowers go through financial intermediaries.

What are the key financial tools for the macroeconomy?

* Bonds serve as a basic instrument of direct finance: they provide a tool with which firms and governments can finance their activities.
* Stocks are an additional source of funds for firms. They give the security holder an ownership share in the firm.
* Secondary markets make securities more valuable and offer more avenues for funds to flow to investors.
* Treasury securities are the bonds sold by the U.S. government to finance the national debt. They play a prominent role in macroeconomic policy.
* Home mortgages are the contracts that people sign to borrow for the purchase of a home. Because the mortgage market is so large, the entire macroeconomy is affected by its condition.

CONCEPTS YOU SHOULD KNOW

banks (p. 730)
bond (p. 731)
default risk (p. 736)
direct finance (p. 730)
face value (p. 734)

financial intermediaries (p. 730)
indirect finance (p. 730)
maturity date (p. 734)
par value (p. 734)
secondary markets (p. 739)

securitization (p. 745)
security (p. 731)
stocks (p. 738)
Treasury securities (p. 741)

QUESTIONS FOR REVIEW

1. What is the difference between direct and indirect finance? Discuss the reasons why a firm (a borrower) might choose each method. Discuss the reasons why a saver might choose each method.

2. What is securitization? Discuss how securitization benefits borrowers.

3. One principle we learned in this chapter is that the dollar price and the interest rate on a bond move in opposite directions. Why is this always the case?

4. What is the primary use of U.S. Treasury securities? Why are the interest rates on Treasury securities so low? If people worried about the United States defaulting on the national debt, what would you expect to happen to interest rates on U.S. Treasury securities? Why?

5. Why might a firm prefer to finance its investments with bonds rather than stocks? Alternatively, why might a firm prefer stocks to bonds?

6. What is a mortgage-backed security (MBS)? Why is it difficult for ratings agencies to determine the risk of an MBS? Describe how the existence of MBSs helps homebuyers in the United States. Describe how MBS markets spread financial troubles around the world when U.S. home prices dropped in 2008.

7. What is a U.S. Treasury bond? Why are Treasury bonds such a popular asset in world markets?

STUDY PROBLEMS (✳solved at the end of the section)

1. Toyota bonds are currently rated AA, and Ford bonds are rated BB. Suppose the price of a $1,000 one-year Toyota bond is $970.
   a. What is the rate of return on the one-year Toyota bond?
   b. The price of a $1,000 one-year Ford bond must be:
      i. less than $970
      ii. greater than $970
      iii. $970
      iv. There is insufficient information to answer this question.
   c. The rate of return on a $1,000 one-year Ford bond must be:
      i. less than the return on the Toyota bond
      ii. greater than the return on the Toyota bond

   iii. the same as the return on the Toyota bond
   iv. There is insufficient information to answer this question.

✳2. In 2008, when the U.S. automobile industry was struggling, the price of Ford Motor Company bonds rose. In this question, you need to calculate how the price increase also affected the interest rate.
   a. What was the interest rate on a one-year Ford bond with a face value of $5,000 and a price of $4,750?
   b. What was the new interest rate on a one-year Ford bond with a face value of $5,000 and a price of $4,950?

✳3. Let's say you own a firm that produces and sells Ping-Pong tables. The name of your company is iPong because your tables have a plug-in jack for all Apple products. To finance a new factory, you decide to sell bonds. Your bonds are rated BBB.

a. Draw supply and demand curves for your iPong bonds. (The quantity of bonds is measured along the x axis and the price along the y axis.) Label the supply curve S, the demand curve D, and the equilibrium price p.

b. How will the demand for iPong bonds be affected if a new secondary market agrees to buy and sell iPong bonds? Illustrate the new demand curve in the graph from part (a), and label it D_{SM}. What are the effects on the price and interest rate on iPong bonds?

4. This question involves the hypothetical iPong firm from question 3.

a. How will demand be affected if a ratings agency upgrades your bond rating to AA?

b. How will the ratings upgrade affect the price of your bond?

c. How will the ratings upgrade affect your cost of borrowing?

5. Use supply and demand curves to illustrate how default risk affects both the price and the interest rate of a bond.

6. In this chapter, we discussed Target Corporation bonds to illustrate the effect of default risk on the price of a bond. In particular, when the default risk rises, the demand for a bond falls and then the equilibrium price falls. In our example, the price of a $100,000 Target bond fell from $98,000 to $97,000.

a. What is the interest rate on a one-year $100,000 bond that sells for $98,000?

b. What is the interest rate on a one-year $100,000 bond that sells for $97,000?

✳ 7. The following table presents partial information for several different bonds that each mature in one year. Use the information given along with Equation 23.1 to fill in the blank cells in the table.

Bond	Face Value p_m	Initial Price p_0	Interest Rate R
A	$10,000	$9,000.00	_____
B	$10,000	_____	10%
C	_____	$98,039.22	2%

SOLVED PROBLEMS

2.a. Use the formula

$$R = \frac{p_m - p_0}{p_0}$$

Then compute: $R = (\$5,000 - \$4,750) \div \$4,750 = \$250 \div \$4,750 = 5.26\%$

b. $R = (\$5,000 - \$4,950) \div \$4,950 = \$50 \div \$4,950 = 1.01\%$

Therefore, when the price of the bond rose by $200, the interest rate decreased from 5.26% to just 1.01%.

3.a.

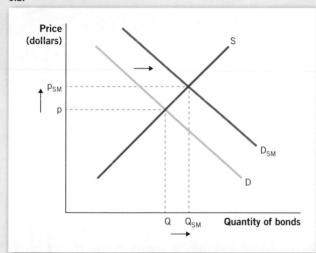

b. If a secondary market is available to sell bonds, the demand for the bonds will increase because the bonds will become more attractive to buyers. When a secondary market exists, you can always resell any bond you own. If there is no secondary market, you are stuck with it once you have it.

In the graph, demand increases and price rises. The result is lower interest rates for your iPong firm.

7.a. For bond A, we are given both the initial price (p_0) and the face value (p_m). We can insert these values into Equation 23.1 and then solve for the interest rate:

$$R = \frac{p_m - p_0}{p_0} = \frac{\$10,000 - \$9,000}{\$9,000}$$

$$= \frac{\$1,000}{\$9,000} = \frac{1}{9} = 11.1\%$$

b. For bond B, we are given the face value (p_m) and the interest rate (R), which we can insert into Equation 23.1 to solve for the initial price (p_0):

$$10\% = 0.10 = \frac{\$10,000 - p_0}{p_0}$$

$$0.10p_0 = \$10,000 - p_0$$

$$0.10p_0 + p_0 = \$10,000$$

$$p_0 = \frac{\$10,000}{1.10} = \$9,090.91$$

$$p_0 = \frac{\$10,000}{1.10} = \$9,090.91$$

c. For bond C, we are given the initial price (p_0) and the interest rate R, which we can plug into Equation 23.1 and solve for the price at maturity (p_m):

$$2\% = 0.02 = \frac{p_m - \$98,039.22}{\$98,039.22}$$

$$0.02 \times \$98,039.22 = p_m - \$98,039.22$$

$$\$1,960.78 = p_m - \$98,039.22$$

$$p_m = \$100,000$$

PART

7

The Long and Short of
MACROECONOMICS

Economic Growth and the Wealth of Nations

Natural resources are the key to economic prosperity.

Many people believe that natural resources, such as trees, oil, and farmland, are the primary sources of economic growth. They believe that

nations like the United States and Australia are prosperous because they have vast natural resources that can be used to produce goods and services. A variation on this idea emphasizes geography—that nations with the best shipping locations and the mildest climates have more prosperous economies. But what about the two Koreas? North Korea and South Korea have the same natural resources, yet the two economies are as different as night and day. Over the course of this chapter and the next, we explore what economics has to say about differences in economic growth across nations.

Striving for economic growth is not only about accumulating more wealth. Yes, economic growth brings iPads and Jet Skis, but it's much more important than that. Economic growth offers the potential for more women and infants to survive childbirth, more people to have access to clean water and better sanitation, and more people to live healthier, longer, and more educated lives.

In this chapter, we begin by looking at the implications of economic growth for human welfare. We then consider the impact of an economy's resources and technology on economic growth. Finally, we discuss the key elements that an economy needs in order to grow.

The two Koreas at night: South Korea, bursting with light, and North Korea, mired in economic darkness.

BIG QUESTIONS

* Why does economic growth matter?
* How do resources and technology contribute to economic growth?
* What institutions foster economic growth?

Why Does Economic Growth Matter?

In 1900, life expectancy in the United States was 47 years. Income—adjusted for inflation—was less than $5,000 per person. About 140 of every 1,000 children died before their first birthday. Only about one-third of American homes had running water. Most people lived less than a mile from their job, and almost nobody owned an automobile. Yes, this is a description of life in the United States in 1900, but it is also a description of life in many poor countries today. What happened in the United States since 1900? Economic growth.

In this section, we examine how economic growth impacts the lives of average people around the world. We also examine the historical data on economic growth and explain some mathematics of growth rates.

Some Ugly Facts

Economic growth is measured as the percentage change in real per capita GDP.

Before looking at data on growth, we need to recall how economists measure economic growth. In Chapter 19, we defined **economic growth** as the percentage change in real per capita GDP. We know that real per capita GDP measures the average level of income in a nation. For most people, life is not all about the pursuit of more income. However, economic growth does alleviate human misery and lengthen lives. Wealthier societies provide better living standards, which include better nutrition, educational opportunities, health care, freedom, and even sources of entertainment.

Let's look around the world and compare life in poor countries with life in rich countries. Table 24.1 presents human welfare indicators for a selection of rich and poor countries. Among the poor nations are Bangladesh, Haiti, North Korea, Niger, Liberia, Tanzania, Nepal, Ethiopia, and Zimbabwe. The wealthy nations include Australia, Denmark, Israel, Japan, Germany, South Korea, and the United States, among others.

Consider the first group of indicators, which are related to mortality. In poor countries, 53 out of every 1,000 babies die at birth or in the first year of life, while in rich nations the number is only 4 out of every 1,000. This means that infants are 13 times more likely to die in poor nations. Those that survive one year in poor nations are about 15 times more likely to die before their fifth birthday, as indicated by the under-5 mortality rates. Overall, life expectancy in poor nations is 62 years, while in wealthy nations it is 81 years.

TABLE 24.1		
Living Conditions in Poor Nations versus Rich Nations		
Life indicators*	**Poor**	**Rich**
GDP per capita, PPP (2011 international $)	$1,872	$40,651
Infant mortality rate (per 1,000 live births)	53	4
Under-5 mortality rate (per 1,000)	76	5
Life expectancy at birth (years)	62	81
Physicians (per 10,000 people)	2.1	29.3
Access to improved water (%)	68.7%	99.6%
Access to improved sanitation (%)	37.1%	99.9%
Access to electricity (%)	31.2%	99.7%
Mobile cellular subscriptions (per 100 people)	55	113
Secure Internet servers (per million people)	1.43	1,181.03
Literacy rate, adult male (%)	68%	99%
Literacy rate, adult female (%)	53%	99%
Female/male secondary enrollment (ratio)	0.89	0.99
Female/male postsecondary enrollment (ratio)	0.65	1.24

Source: World Bank, World Development Indicators. Poor nations are 40 poorest; rich nations are 31 high-income OECD nations.

*Data are generally from 2013 but some individual observations are from 2011 and 2012.

Just being born in a wealthy nation adds almost 20 years to an individual's life.

The second group of indicators in Table 24.1 helps to explain the mortality data. Rich nations have about 14 times as many doctors per person: 29 physicians per 10,000 people versus 2 per 10,000. Clean water and sanitation are available to only a fraction of people in poor nations, while these are generally available to all in rich nations. Children in poor nations die every year because they can't get water as clean as the water that comes out of virtually any faucet in the United States. This leads to common ailments like tapeworms and diarrhea that are life-threatening in poor nations. In fact, in 2010, the World Health Organization estimated that 3.6 million people died each year from waterborne diseases.

The last group of indicators in Table 24.1 tells the sobering story about education. First, notice that literacy rates in poor countries are significantly lower than literacy rates in wealthy countries. But there is also a significant difference in literacy rates between men and women in poor nations. Furthermore, women have less access to both secondary and postsecondary education than men in poor nations; equal access would imply an enrollment ratio of 100%. So while educational opportunities are rarer for all people in poor nations, women fare the worst.

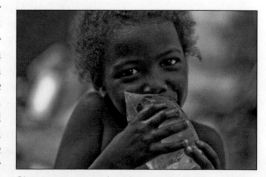

Clean water, even in a bag, saves lives.

The data in Table 24.1 support the contention that per capita GDP matters—not for the sake of more income per se, but because it correlates with better human welfare conditions, which matter to everyone.

Learning from the Past

We can learn a lot about the roots of economic growth by looking at historical experiences. Until very recently, the common person's existence was devoted to subsistence, which involved simply trying to find enough shelter, clothing, and nourishment to survive. As we saw in the previous section, even today many people still live on the margins of subsistence. What can history tell us about how rich nations achieved economic development? The answer will help to clarify possible policy alternatives going forward.

We Were All Poor Once

When you look around the globe today, you see rich nations and poor nations. You can probably name many rich nations: the United States, Japan, Taiwan, and the Western European nations, among others. You might also know the very poor nations: almost all of Africa, parts of Latin America, and significant parts of Asia. But the world was not always this way. If we consider the longer history of humankind, only recently did the incomes of common people rise above subsistence level. The Europe of 1750, for instance, was not noticeably richer than Europe at the time of the birth of Jesus of Nazareth.

Consider the very long run. Angus Maddison, a noted economic historian, estimated GDP levels for many nations and for the whole world back to the year AD 1. This remarkable data set is now available at the Maddison Project web site. Figure 24.1 plots Maddison's estimates of real per capita GDP in 2010 U.S. dollars. Clearly, there was a historical break around 1800 that dramatically changed the path of average world living standards.

Maddison estimated that the average level of income in the world in 1820 was about $1,100. Given that the number is adjusted to 2010 prices, this would be comparable to you having an annual income of about $1,100 in 2010. If you had to live on $1,100 for an entire year, it's clear that your solitary focus would be on basic necessities like food, clothing, and shelter. Of course, there were certainly rich individuals over the course of history, but until relatively recently, the average person's life was essentially one of subsistence living. Consider Alice Toe, the Liberian girl profiled in the Economics in the Real World feature on p. 341. This type of life, where even meals are uncertain, was the basic experience for the average person for nearly all of human history.

Of course, there were global variations in income before 1700. For example, average income in Western Europe in 1600 was about $1,400, while in Latin America it was less than $700. This means that Western Europeans were twice as wealthy as Latin Americans in 1600. But average Europeans were still very poor!

The Industrial Revolution, during which many economies moved away from agriculture and toward manufacturing in the 1800s, is at the very center of the big increase in world income growth. Beginning with the Industrial Revolution, the rate of technical progress became so rapid that it was able to outpace population growth. The foundation for the Industrial Revolution was laid in the preceding decades, and these foundations included private property protection and several technological innovations. We don't claim that the Industrial Revolution was idyllic for those who lived through it, but the legal and technological innovations of that era paved the way for the unprecedented gains in human welfare that people have experienced since.

These data do not imply that life is always easy and predictably comfortable for everyone in the modern world. But the opportunities afforded to the average person alive today are very different from those afforded to the average person in past centuries. Table 24.2 lists a sampling of some of the major innovations that have taken place in the past 150 years. Try to imagine life without any of these, and you'll get a sense of the gains we've made since the Industrial Revolution.

Some Got Rich, Others Stayed Poor

Although wealth has increased over the past two centuries, it is not evenly distributed around the globe. Figure 24.2 shows real per capita GDP (in 2010 U.S. dollars) for various world regions. In 1800, the income of the average U.S. citizen was just less than $2,000 (in 2010 dollars). Imagine trying

FIGURE 24.1

Long-Run World Real Per Capita GDP (in 2010 U.S. dollars)

Historical accounts often focus on monarchs and other wealthy people. But for the average person, living standards across the globe didn't change considerably from the time of Jesus to the time of Thomas Jefferson. The data plotted here show per capita GDP in 2010 U.S. dollars, which is adjusted for prices across both time and place.

Source: Angus Maddison, *Statistics on World Population, GDP and Per Capita GDP, 1–2008 AD.* All figures converted to 2010 U.S. dollars.

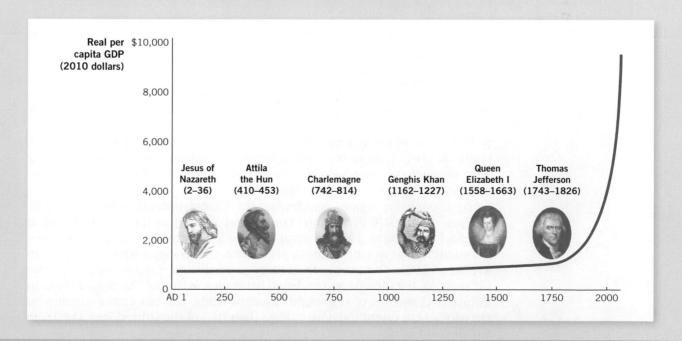

TABLE 24.2			
Important Inventions since the U.S. Civil War			
Typewriter	1867	Electron microscope	1939
Sheep shears	1868	Electric clothes dryer	1940
Telephone	1876	Nuclear reactor	1942
Phonograph	1877	Microwave oven	1945
Milking machine	1878	Cruise control	1945
Two-stroke engine	1878	Computer	1946
Blowtorch	1880	Xerography	1946
Slide rule	1881	Videotape recorder	1952
Arc welder	1886	Airbags	1952
Diesel engine	1892	Satellites	1958
Electric motor (AC)	1892	Laser	1960
X-ray machine	1895	Floppy disk	1965
Electric drill	1895	Microprocessor	1971
Radio	1906	Personal computer	1975
Assembly line	1908	Fiber-optic cables	1977
Cash register	1919	Fax machine	1981
Dishwasher	1924	Camcorder	1982
Rocket	1926	Cell phone	1983
Television	1926	Compact disk	1983
Antilock brakes	1929	GPS	1989
Radar	1934	Laser eye surgery	1989
Tape recorder	1935	Internet	1991
Jet engine	1939		

Source: Michael Cox and Richard Alm, *Myths of Rich and Poor* (New York: Basic Books, 1999), and miscellaneous other sources.

to live on $5.50 per day in today's world—that is, $5.50 to buy all the food, clothing, shelter, education, transportation, and anything else you might need to purchase. That was life in the United States in 1800, and it's comparable to life in many nations today.

By 1900, some regions had broken the stranglehold of poverty. In 1900, real per capita GDP in Western Europe was $4,701; in the United States, it was $6,153. Prior to 1900, general income levels this high had never been experienced. But in China, India, and Africa, the averages were still less than $1,000 in 1900. The twentieth century proved to be even more prosperous for some, as the income gap widened between the United States and Western Europe and the rest of the world. Unfortunately, real per capita income on the African continent today is still less than that of the United States in 1850, which was $2,768.

FIGURE 24.2

Real Per Capita GDP over 200 Years (in 2010 U.S. dollars)

Two hundred years ago, all regions and nations were poor. The modern differences in wealth that we see around the world today began to emerge before 1900. But the twentieth century saw unprecedented growth take hold in the United States and Western Europe. Unfortunately, some parts of the globe today are no better off than the United States and Western Europe were in 1800.

Source: Angus Maddison, *Statistics on World Population, GDP and Per Capita GDP, 1–2008 AD.* All figures converted to 2010 U.S. dollars.

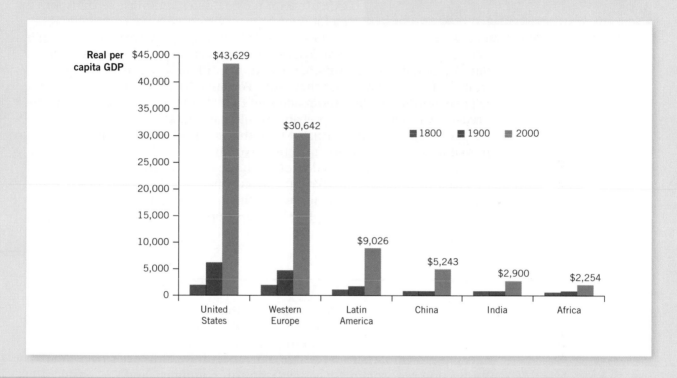

While many of the current disparities between nations began about 200 years ago, some nations have moved from poor to rich as recently as the past few decades. In 1950, for example, South Korea, with real per capita GDP of just $1,309, was poorer than Liberia, at $1,617. Today, South Korea is one of the wealthiest countries in the world, with a per capita income of more than $30,000, while Liberia is near $1,200 in per capita income.

ECONOMICS IN THE REAL WORLD

One Child Who Needs Economic Progress

This is a true story about a girl named Alice Toe, who is 4 years old. In her photo, you can see from her eyes that she is mischievous and has a sparkling personality. When this picture was taken, she was digging for crabs for the sole purpose of frightening a visiting American economist.

Alice and her brother Reuben search for crabs in Monrovia, Liberia.

Alice lives in Monrovia, the capital of Liberia, an impoverished country in West Africa about the size of the state of Virginia. She was 3 years old when she contracted tapeworms by drinking water from the neighborhood well. Unfortunately, her family could not afford to send her to a doctor. Her stomach became enlarged and her hair bleached—indicators of malnutrition caused by tapeworms. Filtered water, which costs about $3 per gallon in Liberia, is too expensive for most families and must be transported by foot.

Tapeworm infection is easily treated with a pill that costs less than 25 cents and lasts for six months. But Alice and her grandfather could not afford even this inexpensive treatment—that's how poor they were. Fortunately, an American missionary happened to meet Alice and made sure that she received the treatment she needed. Without help, she probably would have died.

Alice's story is not unusual. Many thousands of children die each year from illnesses like tapeworm infection. Worldwide, 76 of every 1,000 children born in the poorest nations do not reach the age of 5, although many could be saved with treatments that literally cost pennies. The good news is that economic growth can bring improvements in quality of life. For the sake of Alice Toe and other children like her, let's hope that economic progress will take root in Liberia. ✳

Measuring Economic Growth

Overall, people today are much wealthier than they were 200 years ago. However, this prosperity did not occur overnight. Rather, income grew a little bit each year. There is a striking mathematical truth about growth: small differences in growth rates lead to large differences in wealth levels over time. In this section, we explain how growth rates are computed, and we consider the level of growth a nation needs for its population to experience significant improvements in living standards.

The Mathematics of Growth Rates

The big break out of poverty began during the nineteenth century. Table 24.3 shows data on world economic growth in different periods. From 1800 to 1900, average world GDP growth was only 0.64% per year. From 1900 to 1950, world economic growth increased to 1.04%. The difference between 0.64% and 1.04% might seem trivial. After all, it certainly doesn't seem like much if your exam grade increases by half a percentage point. But when economic growth increases by 0.4% and is sustained for many years, it makes a big difference. In this section, we show how growth is calculated.

TABLE 24.3

World Economic Growth for Different Historical Eras	
Years	Annual Growth rate
AD 1–1800	0.02%
1800–1900	0.64
1900–1950	1.04
1950–2000	2.12

Source: Angus Maddison, *Statistics on World Population, GDP and Per Capita GDP, 1–2008 AD.* All figures converted to 2010 U.S. dollars.

We have seen that economic growth is the annual growth rate of real per capita GDP. It is our measure of how an average person's income changes over time, including an allowance for price changes. But the government reports overall GDP data in nominal terms. Therefore, to get an accurate growth rate, we need to account for both inflation and population growth. We can use the following equation to approximate economic growth, where %Δ indicates the percentage change in a variable:

economic growth ≈ %Δ in nominal GP − %Δ price level − %Δ population   (Equation 24.1)

Let's walk through the equation for economic growth using actual U.S. data as shown in Table 24.4. Starting with nominal GDP data for 2013 and 2014, we compute nominal GDP growth as 3.9%. But part of the increase in nominal GDP is due to inflation. In 2014, the price level, as measured by the GDP deflator, grew by 1.5%. We subtract this inflation rate from nominal GDP growth to get real GDP growth of 2.4%. This number applies to the entire nation, but population also increased by 0.7% in 2014. When we subtract population growth, we are left with 1.7% as the rate of economic growth for the United States in 2014. This growth rate was slightly lower than normal: since 1950, average economic growth in the United States has been about 2%.

A word of caution about terminology is in order. There's a big difference between nominal GDP growth, real GDP growth, and real per capita GDP growth. (In Table 24.4, these terms appear in orange.) But sloppy economic reporting sometimes confuses the terms. You may read something like "the U.S. economy grew by 2.4% in 2014," which refers to real GDP growth and is not calculated on a per capita basis. It would be an even bigger mistake to claim that U.S. economic growth in 2014 was 3.9%, a number that is not adjusted for either population growth or inflation. Such confusing wording is a common mistake in reports on international economic growth statistics.

Growth Rates and Income Levels

Before we consider policies that might aid economic growth, we need to look more closely at how growth rates affect income levels.

TABLE 24.4

Computing an Economic Growth Rate

U.S. GDP in 2013 (in millions)	$16,768,100	
U.S. GDP in 2014 (in millions)	$17,418,900	
Nominal GDP growth	3.9%	
− Price growth (inflation)	1.5%	
= Real GDP growth	2.4%	
− Population growth	0.7%	
≈ Real per capita GDP growth	1.7%	≈ Economic growth

Source: GDP data, U.S. Bureau of Economic Analysis; population data, U.S. Census Bureau, www.census.gov /popest/states/NST-ann-est.html.

First, consider how significant it is when income doubles, or increases by 100%. If your income doubled today—all else being equal—you could afford twice as much of everything you are currently buying. Now imagine what would happen if income doubled for an entire country or even for all countries. In the United States, real per capita GDP more than doubled in the 40 years between 1970 and 2010. This means that the average person living in the United States in 2010 could afford twice as much food, clothing, transportation, education, and even government services as the average U.S. resident in 1970. That's quite a difference.

But increasing real income by 100% in a single year is not realistic. Let's pick a number closer to reality—say, 2%, which is a normal rate of economic growth for the United States. With a growth rate of 2%, how long would it take to double your income? For example, let's say you graduate and, given your expertise in economics, you get several job offers. One offer is for $50,000 per year with a guaranteed raise of 2% every year. How long would it take for your salary to reach $100,000?

The first answer that pops into your head might be 50 years (based on the idea that 2% growth for 50 years adds up to 100% growth). But this answer would be wrong because it ignores the fact that growth compounds over time. As your salary grows, 2% growth leads to larger and larger dollar increases. Because of this compounding effect, it actually would take only about 35 years to double your income at a 2% growth rate.

Table 24.5 illustrates the process of compounding over time by showing the increase from year to year. Income starts at $50,000 in year 1, and a 2% increase yields $1,000, so that one year of growth results in an income of $51,000 in year 2. Subsequent 2% growth in the second year yields $1,020 of new income (2% of $51,000), so after two years your income is $52,020. Looking at year 3, the 2% increase yields $1,040.40. Each year, the dollar increase in income (the green numbers in the third column) gets larger, as 2% of a growing number continues to grow.

In fact, at a growth rate of 2%, it takes only about 35 years for income to double. This scenario corresponds with the experience of the U.S. economy. Since 1970, real per capita GDP in the United States has more than doubled.

TABLE 24.5

Compound Growth

	Income	2% increase in income	Income in next year
Year 1	$50,000.00	$1,000.00	$51,000.00
Year 2	$51,000.00	$1,020.00	$52,020.00
Year 3	$52,020.00	$1,040.40	$53,060.40
Year 4	$53,060.40	$1,061.21	$54,121.61
Year 5	$54,121.61	$1,082.43	$55,204.04
...			
Year 35	$100,000		

Yet this jump occurred while U.S. economic growth rates averaged "only" about 2%.

The Rule of 70

In the previous example, we saw that when income grows at 2% per year, it doubles in approximately 35 years. A simple rule known as the **rule of 70** determines the length of time necessary for a sum of money to double at a particular growth rate. According to the rule of 70:

If the annual growth rate of a variable is x%, the size of that variable doubles approximately every 70 ÷ x years.

The **rule of 70** states that if the annual growth rate of a variable is *x*%, the size of that variable doubles approximately every 70 ÷ x years.

The rule of 70 is an approximation, but it works well with typical economic growth rates.

Table 24.6 illustrates the rule of 70 by showing how long it takes for a single dollar of income to double in value, given different growth rates. At a growth rate of 1%, each dollar of income will double approximately every 70 ÷ 1 years. If growth increases to 2%, then a dollar of income will double approximately every 70 ÷ 2 = 35 years. Consider the impact of a 4% growth rate. If this rate can be sustained, income doubles approximately every 70 ÷ 4 = 17.5 years. In 70 years, income doubles 4 times, ending up at approximately 16 times its starting value! China has been recently growing at almost 10% per year, and indeed its per capita income has been doubling about every seven years—a remarkable rate of growth.

The rule of 70 shows us that small and consistent growth rates, if sustained for a decade or two, can greatly improve living standards. Over the long course of history, growth rates were essentially zero and the general human condition was poverty. But the past two centuries have seen small, consistent growth rates, and the standard of living for many has increased dramatically.

We can look at actual growth rates of various countries over a long period to see the impact on income levels. Table 24.7 presents growth rates of several countries over the 60 years from 1950 to 2010. Let's start with Nicaragua and Turkey. In 1950, both nations had roughly the same income per person. But Turkey grew at 2.7% annually, and Nicaragua experienced almost no net growth over 60 years. As a result, the average income in Turkey is now almost five times the average income in Nicaragua.

TABLE 24.6

A Dollar of Income at Different Growth Rates

Annual growth rate	Years to double	Value after 70 years (approximate)
0%	Never	$1
1	70	2
2	35	4
3	23.3	8
4	17.5	16

TABLE 24.7

Economic Growth, 1950–2010

Average annual growth rate		Real per capita GDP in 1950		Real per capita GDP in 2010
less than 1% growth	−1.3% Dem. Republic Congo	$863		$394
	−0.7 Haiti	1,591		1,038
	0.1 Nicaragua	2,446		2,534
	0.1 Zimbabwe	1,061		1,135
	0.5 North Korea	1,293		1,698
about 1% growth	1.1 Tanzania	642		1,217
	1.1 Lebanon	3,677		6,741
	1.1 Rwanda	828		1,544
	1.2 El Salvador	2,254		4,452
	1.5 Nigeria	1,140		2,840
about 2% growth	2.0 United States	14,476		46,164
	2.0 Mexico	3,581		11,682
	2.1 Australia	11,221		38,735
	2.1 United Kingdom	10,506		35,999
	2.2 Chile	5,556		21,019
greater than 2% growth	2.7 Turkey	2,454		12,452
	2.9 India	937		5,105
	4.1 Japan	2,908		33,209
	4.4 Singapore	3,360		43,963
	4.9 China	678		12,160
	5.5 South Korea	1,293		32,855

Source: Angus Maddison, *Statistics on World Population, GDP and Per Capita GDP, 1–2008 AD.* All figures converted to 2010 U.S. dollars.

Further down Table 24.7, you see other nations that grew at rates faster even than Turkey. In 1950, Japan's per capita income was just a little higher than Turkey's. Yet 4.1% growth led to income of $33,209 per person by 2010 in Japan. South Korea, with 5.5% growth over the entire period, moved from being among the world's poorest economies to being among the richest.

Perhaps the biggest recent growth story is China's. Only 20 years ago, it was among the world's poorer nations. Over the past 20 years, China has grown at nearly 10% a year. Even if its astonishing growth slows considerably, China will still likely move into the group of the wealthiest nations in the coming decades.

Clearly, economic growth experiences have varied widely across time and place. But relatively small and consistent growth rates are sufficient to

This entire Shanghai skyline was built in the past 25 years, testament to an astonishing rate of growth.

move a nation out of poverty over the period of a few generations. And this movement out of poverty really matters for the people who live in these nations.

ECONOMICS IN THE REAL WORLD

How Does 2% Growth Affect Average People?

We have seen that economic growth in the United States has averaged 2% per year over the past 50 years. What does this economic growth mean for a typical person's everyday life? We've assembled some basic data on economic aspects of life in the United States for an average person in 1960, which may be about the time your grandparents were your age.

In what ways was life different when your grandparents were your age?

Today, average real income is four times the level of 1960. Americans live about 12% longer, have access to about twice as many doctors, live in houses that are more than twice as big, enjoy more education, and own more and better cars and household appliances. We work about 17% fewer hours and hold jobs that are physically less taxing. In 1960, there were no cell phones, and roughly three out of four homes had a single telephone. Today, there are more telephones than there are people in the United States. In addition, many modern amenities were not available in 1960. Can you imagine life without a computer, the Internet, streaming music, microwave ovens, and central air conditioning? Take a look at Table 24.8 to see a striking contrast. *

TABLE 24.8

The United States: 1960 versus 2010

General Characteristics	1960	2010
Life expectancy	69.7 years	78.3 years
Physicians per 10,000 people	14.8	27
Years of school completed	10.5 (median)	12 (average)
Portion of income spent on food	27%	8%
Average workweek	40.9 hours	34 hours
Workforce in agriculture or manufacturing	37%	19%
Home ownership	61.9%	67.4%

New Home

Size	1,200 square feet	2,457 square feet
Bedrooms	2	3
Bathrooms	1	2.5
Central air conditioning?	no	yes

Best-Selling Car

Model	Chevrolet Impala	Toyota Camry
Price (2010 dollars)	$19,753	$26,640
Miles per gallon	13–16	20–29
Horsepower	135	268
Air conditioning?	optional	standard
Automatic transmission?	optional	standard
Airbags?	no	standard
Power locks and windows?	no	standard

TV

Size	23 inches	50 inches
Display	black & white	high-definition color
Price (2010 dollars)	$1,391	$500

Source: U.S. Census Bureau, *Statistical Abstract of the United States*, and U.S. Bureau of Labor Statistics.

PRACTICE WHAT YOU KNOW

Computing Economic Growth: How Much Is Brazil Growing?

After several years of solid growth in real per capita GDP, economic growth in Brazil has slowed recently. The data below are 2014 statistics for Brazil.

Nominal GDP growth rate	GDP deflator growth rate	Population growth rate
6.98%	6.875%	0.87%

Question: What was the rate of economic growth for Brazil in 2010?

Answer: First, recall Equation 24.1:

$$\text{economic growth} \approx \%\Delta \, \text{nominal GDP} - \%\Delta \, \text{price level} - \%\Delta \, \text{population}$$

Now, for Brazil, we have

$$\text{economic growth} \approx 6.98 - 6.87 - 0.87 = -0.76\%$$

How much does inflation affect Brazil's growth data?

Question: If the price level (as measured by the GDP deflator) continues to grow at 6.87% per year, approximately how long will it take for prices to double?

Answer: We use the rule of 70:

$$70 \div 6.87 \approx 10.19 \text{ years}$$

As you can see, once we account for price and population changes, economic growth in Brazil was actually negative in 2014.

Data source: International Monetary Fund, World Economic Outlook, April 2016.

How Do Resources and Technology Contribute to Economic Growth?

At this point, you may wonder what can be done to provide the best opportunity for economic growth. We see economic growth in many, though certainly not all, nations. But even in those that have grown in the past, future growth is not assured. So now we turn to the major sources of economic growth.

Economists continue to debate the relative importance of the factors that lead to economic growth. However, there is a general consensus on the significance of three factors for economic growth: *resources*, *technology*, and *institutions*. In this section, we examine the first two; in the final section of the chapter, we look at institutions.

Economic Growth

Economic growth, measured as the growth rate of per capita real GDP, is the key determinant of living standards in nations across time. The map shows the average annual growth rates of nations across the globe from 1950 to 2010. On the right, we give a snapshot of the differences in living conditions between wealthy nations and poor nations.

⬤ Less than 1% growth
With 0% growth, nations are no better off than they were in 1950.

Dem. Rep. Congo	−1.41
Haiti	−0.73
Liberia	−0.47
Zimbabwe	0.28
Iraq	0.11

⬤ 1% – 1.6% growth
With 1% growth, living standards nearly doubled over 58 years.

Lebanon	1.05
Cuba	1.06
South Africa	1.17
Bangladesh	1.45
Nigeria	1.53

⬤ 1.7% – 2.5% growth
With 2% growth, living standards almost quadrupled over 58 years.

United States	1.95
Mexico	1.99
Canada	2.07
Pakistan	2.28
Chile	2.24

⬤ Greater than 2.5% growth
With 3% growth, some of the poorest nations are now among the richest.

Israel	3.25
Japan	4.14
China	4.93
Taiwan	5.54
South Korea	5.54

⬤ Incomplete Data

All dollar figures are 2010 U.S. dollars.

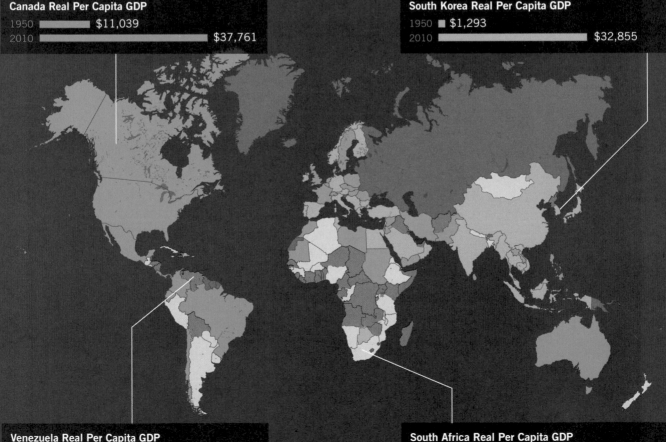

Canada Real Per Capita GDP
1950		$11,039
2010		$37,761

South Korea Real Per Capita GDP
1950		$1,293
2010		$32,855

Venezuela Real Per Capita GDP
1950		$11,297
2010		$14,950

South Africa Real Per Capita GDP
1950		$3,838
2010		$7,691

Human Welfare: Poor vs. Rich Nations

GDP per capita (2005 International $)		Life expectancy at birth		Infant mortality rate (per 1,000 live births)		Under-5 m (per 1
$1,095	$32,971	57	80	76	5	118

Physicians (per 10,000 people)		Access to electricity		Access to improved water source		Acce improved
1.8	29.3	31.2%	99.7%	64%	100%	35%

Female to Male secondary enrollment (ratio)		Female to Male post-secondary enrollment (ratio)		Mobile cell phone subscriptions (per 100 people)		Interne (per 100
0.89	0.99	0.65	1.24	27	108	2.7

Literacy rate (adult male)		Literacy rate (adult female)	
69%	99%	55%	99%

Poor nations are the 40 poorest; rich nations are 31 high-income OECD nations. GDP data is from 2010 and is adjusted for prices across the different nations using a purchasing power parity (PPP) method. Other indicators are from 2008 and 2009.

REVIEW QUESTIONS

- On average, how much longer live in rich versus poor nations

- If a growth rate of 1.17% persis South Africa, how long it will t income to double? Use the Ru

Resources

Resources, also known as **factors of production**, are the inputs used to produce goods and services.

All else equal, the higher the quantity and quality of resources available to a nation, the more output that nation can produce. **Resources**, also known as **factors of production**, are the inputs used to produce goods and services. The discovery or cultivation of new resources is a source of economic growth. Economists divide resources into three major categories: natural resources, physical capital, and human capital.

Natural Resources

Diamonds may be a girl's best friend, but are they essential for economic growth?

Natural resources include physical land and the inputs that occur naturally in or on the land. Coal, iron ore, diamonds, and lumber are examples of natural resources. Less obvious examples are mountains, beaches, temperate weather patterns, and scenic views—resources that residents enjoy consuming and that sometimes lead to tourism as a major industry.

Natural resources are an important source of economic wealth for nations. For example, the United States has fertile farmland, forests, coal, iron ore, and oil; the United States supplied more than 12% of the world's oil in 2014.

Geography, or the physical location of a nation, is also a natural resource that can contribute to economic growth. Geographical location facilitates trade and affects other important variables, such as weather and disease control. The world map in Figure 24.3 shows global GDP per square kilometer. As you can see, locations on coasts or along rivers have developed more rapidly than areas inland. These coastal or waterway-based locations were more naturally suited to trade in the days before railroads, trucks, and airplanes.

Natural resources clearly help to increase economic development, but they are not enough to make a nation wealthy. Many poor nations are rich in natural resources. For example, Liberia has mahogany forests, iron ore deposits, rubber tree forests, diamonds, and a beautiful coastline along the Atlantic

FIGURE 24.3

Global GDP Density

The world's wealthiest areas (shown in darker colors on this map) are often those located near natural shipping lanes along coasts and rivers, where trade naturally flowed. This pattern is evidence that geography matters in economic development.

Source: John Luke Gallup, Jeffrey D. Sachs, and Andrew D. Mellinger, "Geography and Economic Development," Working Paper No. 1, Center for International Development at Harvard University, March 1999.

GDP per square kilometer
$0 – 499
$500 – 1,099
$1,100 – 2,999
$3,000 – 8,099
$8,100 – 21,199
$22,000 – 59,999
$60,000 – 162,999
$163,000 – 441,999
$442,000 – 546,000,000
No data

Ocean. Yet despite all these natural resources, Liberia is still poor. In contrast, think about Hong Kong, which is now part of China. Hong Kong is very small and densely populated with few natural resources. Yet the citizens of Hong Kong are among the wealthiest people in the world.

Physical Capital

The second category of resources is physical capital, or just capital. Recall that capital comprises the tools and equipment used in the production of goods and services. Examples of capital are factories, tractors, roads and bridges, computers, and shovels. The purpose of capital is to aid in the production of future output.

Consider the shipping container, a basic tool that has aided the movement of goods around the globe. The shipping container is a standard-size (20- or 40-foot-long) box used to move goods worldwide. In 1954, a typical cargo ship traveling from New York to Germany might have carried as many as 194,582 individual items. The transportation involved bags, barrels, cartons, and many other different means of packaging and storing goods. Loading and unloading the ship required armies of men working long hours for days on end. Not surprisingly, shipping goods from one country to another was expensive.

The standardized shipping container was first used in 1956. Suddenly, it was possible to move cargo around the globe without repacking every time the mode of transportation changed. Once a cargo ship enters the port, cranes lift the containers 200 feet in the air and unload about 40 large boxes each hour. Dozens of ships can be unloaded at a time, and computers run most of the operation. A container full of iPads can be loaded on the back of a truck in Shenzhen, China, transported to port, and loaded onto a ship that carries 3,000 containers. The ship can bring the iPads to the United States, where the containers are loaded onto a train and, later, a truck. This movement happens without anyone touching the contents. Clearly, the shipping container is a tool that has revolutionized world trade and improved lives.

As the quantity of physical capital per worker rises, so does output per worker. Of course, workers are more productive with more and better tools. Look around the world: the productive nations have impressive roads, bridges, buildings, and factories. In poor nations, paved roads are nonexistent or in disrepair, vehicles are of lower quality, and computers are a luxury. Even public electricity and sewage treatment facilities are rare in many developing nations.

Because of the obvious correlation between tools and wealth, many of the early contributions to growth theory focused on the role of physical capital. As a result, much international aid went into the building of roads and factories, in the hope that prosperity would follow automatically. But today most economists understand that capital alone is not sufficient to produce economic growth. Factories, dams, and other large capital projects bring wealth only when they mesh well with the rest of the economy. A steel factory is of little use in a region better suited for growing corn. Without a good rail network or proper roads, a steel factory cannot get the tools it needs and

This cargo ship, bearing hundreds of individual shipping containers, is arriving in San Francisco with goods from Asia.

cannot easily sell its products. Dams that are not maintained fall into disrepair within years. Water pipes are a wonderful modern invention, but if they are not kept in good shape, human waste from toilets contaminates the water supply. The point is that simply building new capital in a nation does not ensure future sustained economic growth.

Human Capital

Human capital is the resource represented by the quantity, knowledge, and skills of the workers in an economy.

The output of a nation also depends on people to use its natural resources. **Human capital** is the resource represented by the quantity, knowledge, and skills of the workers in an economy. It is possible to expand human capital by increasing the number of workers available, by educating the existing labor force, or both.

We often think in terms of the sheer quantity of workers: all else being equal, a nation with more workers produces more output. But more output

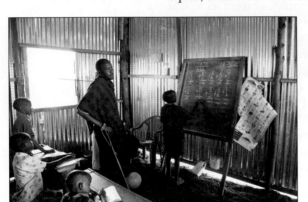

Education enhances human capital, but is it the key ingredient to economic growth?

does not necessarily mean more economic growth. In fact, economic growth requires more output *per capita*. Adding more workers to an economy may increase total GDP without increasing per capita GDP. However, if more workers from a given population enter the labor force, GDP per capita can increase. For example, as we discussed in Chapter 20, women have entered the U.S. labor force in record numbers over the past 50 years as they have moved from home-making services not counted in official GDP statistics to the official labor force. As more women join the official labor force, their formally measured output increases both GDP and per capita GDP.

There is another important dimension of human capital: the knowledge and skills of the workers themselves. In this context, it is possible to increase human capital through education and training. Training includes everything from basic literacy to college education and from software competencies to specific job training.

Not many people would doubt that a more educated labor force is more productive. And certainly, to boost per capita output, educating the labor force is more helpful than merely increasing the quantity of workers. But education alone is not enough to ensure economic progress. For many years, for example, India struggled with economic growth, even while its population was significantly more literate than those of other developing nations.

Technology

Technology is the knowledge that is available for use in production.

A **technological advancement** introduces new techniques or methods so that firms can produce more valuable outputs per unit of input.

We all know that the world would be much poorer without computers, automobiles, electric light bulbs, and other goods that have resulted from productive ideas. **Technology** is the knowledge that is available for use in production. Though technology is often embodied in machines and productive techniques, it is really just knowledge. New technology enables us to produce more while using fewer of our limited resources. A **technological advancement** introduces new techniques or methods so that firms can produce more valuable outputs per unit of input. We can either

PRACTICE WHAT YOU KNOW

Resources: Growth Policy

Many policies have been advocated to help nations escape poverty, and the policies often focus on the importance of resources.

Question: For each policy listed below, which resource is the primary focus: natural resources, physical capital, or human resources?

a. international loans for infrastructure like roads, bridges, and dams

b. mandated primary education

c. restrictions on the development of forested land

d. population controls

e. international aid for construction of a shoe factory

The Akosombo Dam in Ghana was built with international aid funds.

Answers:

a. Infrastructure is physical capital.

b. Education involves human capital.

c. These restrictions focus on maintaining a certain level of natural resources.

d. Population controls often result from a shortsighted focus on physical capital per capita. The fewer people a nation has, the more tools there are per person.

e. The focus here is physical capital.

produce more with the same resources or use fewer resources to produce the same quantity.

For example, the assembly line was an important technological advance. Henry Ford adopted and improved the assembly-line method in 1913 at the Ford Motor Company. In this new approach to the factory, workers focused on well-defined jobs such as screwing on individual parts. The conveyor belt moved the parts around the factory to workers' stations. The workers themselves, by staying put rather than moving around the production floor, experienced a lower rate of accidents and other mishaps.

Agriculture is a sector where technological advances are easy to spot. For example, we know that land resources are necessary to produce corn. But technological advances mean that over time it has become possible to grow and harvest more corn per acre of land. In fact, in the United States, the corn yield per acre is now six times what it was in 1930. In 1930, we produced about 25 bushels of corn per acre, but now the yield is consistently over 150 bushels per acre. Higher yields are a result of technology that has produced hybrid seeds, herbicides, fertilizers, and irrigation techniques.

FIGURE 24.4

Fewer Cows but More Milk

U.S. dairy cow populations continue to decline, but the average cow now produces five times more milk than in 1924. This means that even with fewer cows, farmers produce 2.3 times more milk than they did in 1924.

Source: USDA.

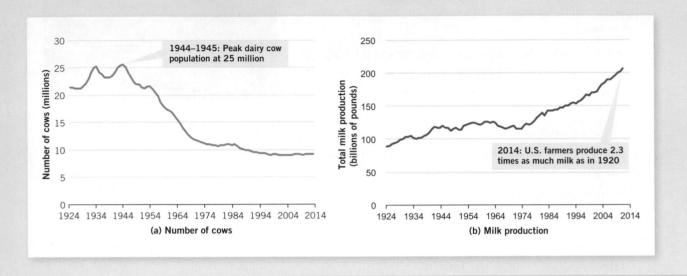

(a) Number of cows

(b) Milk production

Figure 24.4 presents another agricultural example of technological advancement. There are now significantly fewer milk cows in the United States than at any time since 1920. But total milk output is at historic highs because dairy farmers can now get about four times as much milk out of each cow. While strategic breeding has played a large role in this increase, even simple technology has had factored in this change. For example, farmers now line the cows' stalls with 6 to 8 inches of sand. The sand is comfortable to lie on, it offers uniform support, and it stays cooler in the summer. In the end, the cows produce more milk. This is one simple example of how new ideas or technological advancements enable us to produce more while using fewer resources.

Like capital, technology produces value only when it is combined with other inputs. For example, simply carrying plans for a shoe factory to Haiti would not generate much economic value. The mere knowledge of how to produce shoes, while important, is only one piece of the growth puzzle. An economy must have the physical capital to produce shoes, must have the human capital to staff the factory and assembly line, and must create favorable conditions and incentives for potential investors. Economic growth occurs when all these conditions come together. That is one reason why it is incorrect to identify technological innovations as the sole cause of differences in wealth across nations.

Moreover, technological innovations do not occur randomly across the globe. Some places produce large clusters of such innovations. Consider that information technology largely comes from MIT and Silicon Valley, movie and television ideas generally come from Hollywood, and new fashion designs regularly come from Paris, Milan, Tokyo, and New York. Technological innovations tend to breed more innovations. This conclusion leads us to reword an earlier question: Why do some regions innovate (and grow) more than others? A large part of the answer lies in our next topic, institutions.

What Institutions Foster Economic Growth?

In 1950, residents in the African nation of Liberia were wealthier than those on the Southeast Asian island of Taiwan. Today, however, per capita GDP in Taiwan is more than 20 times that of Liberia. Yes, much of this wealth gap stems from obvious current differences in physical capital, human capital, and technology. But we must ask how these differences came about. Without a doubt, the biggest difference between Taiwan and Liberia since 1950 is the final growth factor we consider in this chapter: institutions.

An **institution** is a significant practice, relationship, or organization in a society. Institutions are the official and unofficial conditions that shape the environment in which decisions are made. When we think of institutions, we normally focus on laws, regulations, and the type of government in a nation. But other institutions, such as social mores and work habits, are also important.

Institutions are not always tangible physical items that we can look at or hold. There might be a physical representative of an institution, such as the U.S. Constitution or the building where the Supreme Court meets, but the essence of an institution encompasses expectations and habitual practices. The rules and the mind-set within the Supreme Court are what is important, not the building or the chairs.

In this section, we consider the significant institutions that affect a nation's production and income. These include private property rights, political stability and the rule of law, competitive and open markets, efficient taxes, and stable money and prices. Many of these are examined in detail elsewhere in this book, so we cover them only briefly here.

> An **institution** is a significant practice, relationship, or organization in a society. Institutions are the official and unofficial conditions that shape the environment in which decisions are made.

Private Property Rights

The single greatest incentive for voluntary production is ownership of what you produce. The existence of **private property rights** means that individuals can own property—including houses, land, and other resources—and that when they use their property in production, they own the resulting output.

Think about the differences in private property rights between Liberia and Taiwan. In Liberia, the system of ownership titles is not dependable. As a result, Liberians who wish to purchase land often must buy the land multiple times from different "owners," because there is no dependable record of true ownership. Taiwan, in contrast, has a well-defined system of law and property rights protection. Without such a system, people have very little incentive to improve the value of their assets.

In the past two decades, the government of China has relaxed its laws against private property ownership, a move that has spurred unprecedented

> **Private property rights** are the rights of individuals to own property, to use it in production, and to own the resulting output.

growth. These market reforms stem from a risky experiment in the rural community of Xiaogang. In 1978, the heads of 21 families in Xiaogang signed an agreement that became the genesis of private property rights in China. This remarkable document read:

> December 1978, Mr. Yan's Home. We divide the field (land) to every household. Every leader of the household should sign and stamp. If we are able to produce, every household should promise to finish any amount they are required to turn in to the government, no longer asking the government for food or money. If this fails, even if we go to jail or have our heads shaved, we will not regret. Everyone else (the common people who are not officers and signees of this agreement) also promise to raise our children until they are eighteen years old. First signer: Hong Chang Yan.*

This little Chinese agreement between 21 poor rural families helped to bring private property rights to modern China.

The agreement stipulated that each family would continue to produce the government quota for their agricultural output. But they would begin keeping anything they produced above this quota. They also agreed to stop taking food or money from the government. This agreement was dangerous in 1978—so dangerous that they stipulated that they would raise one another's children if any of the signees were put in jail.

The Xiaogang agreement led to an agricultural boom that other communities copied. Seeing the success of this property rights experiment, Deng Xiaoping and other Chinese leaders subsequently instituted market reforms in agriculture in the 1980s and then in manufacturing in the 1990s. China's economy is growing rapidly today not because the Chinese found new resources or updated their technology. The Chinese are wealthier because they now recognize private property rights in many different industries.

Political Stability and the Rule of Law

To understand the importance of political stability and the rule of law, consider again Liberia and Taiwan. Before 2006, Liberia endured 35 years of political unrest. Government officials assumed office through the use of violence, and national leaders consistently used their power to eradicate their opponents. In contrast, Taiwan's political climate has been relatively stable since 1949. If you were an entrepreneur deciding where to build a factory, would you want to invest millions of dollars in a country with constant violent unrest, or would you choose a peaceful country instead? Which nation would you predict is more likely to see new factories and technological innovation?

Bullet casings litter the street in Monrovia, Liberia, in 2003.

*Literal translation by Chuhan Wang.

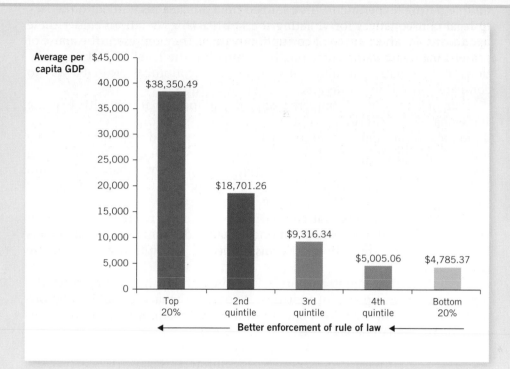

FIGURE 24.5

The Rule of Law and Per Capita Income

Consistent and fair enforcement of a nation's laws pays off with economic growth. The nations with the least corruption have average per capita GDP of $38,350, but the most corrupt nations have average per capita GDP of just $4,785.

Source: World Justice Project, Annual Report 2011. GDP figures are adjusted using PPP (constant 2005 international $), 2005–2009.

Political instability is a disincentive for investment. After all, investment makes sense only if there is a fairly certain payoff at the end. In an environment of political instability, there is no incentive to invest in either human or physical capital because there is no predictable future payoff.

Consistent and trustworthy enforcement of a nation's laws is crucial for economic growth. Corruption is one of the most common and dangerous impediments to economic growth. When government officials steal, elicit bribes, or hand out favors to friends, incentives for private investment are reduced. If individuals from all walks of life cannot count on a fair system and the opportunity to earn returns in their investments in human or physical capital, investment declines. And this decline reduces future growth.

Incentives

The World Justice Project has collected data on the rule of law across the world. Figure 24.5 shows the nations broken down into five groups, based on consistent enforcement of the rule of law. It is no surprise that nations scoring in the top group on this index are also the nations with the highest levels of per capita GDP. The most corrupt nations are also those with the lowest levels of income.

ECONOMICS IN THE REAL WORLD

What Can Parking Violations Teach Us about International Institutions?

Until 2002, diplomatic immunity protected United Nations diplomats in New York City from fines or arrest because of parking violations. This immunity gave economists Raymond Fisman and Edward Miguel the idea for a

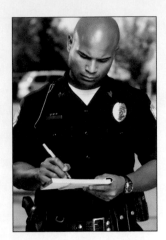

Would you get more parking tickets if you weren't compelled to pay for them?

Incentives

unique natural experiment: they studied how officials responded to the lack of legal consequences for violating the law. Parking violations under these conditions are an example of corruption because they represent the abuse of power for private gain. Therefore, by comparing the level of parking violations of diplomats from different societies, the economists created a way to compare corruption norms among different cultures.

Fisman and Miguel compared unpaid parking violations with existing survey-based indices on levels of corruption across nations. They found that diplomats from high-corruption nations accumulated significantly more unpaid parking violations than those from low-corruption nations. Among the worst offenders were diplomats from Kuwait, Egypt, Chad, Sudan, and Bulgaria. Among those with zero unpaid parking violations were diplomats from Australia, Canada, Denmark, Japan, and Norway.

This finding suggests that cultural or social norms related to corruption are quite persistent: even when stationed thousands of miles away, diplomats behave as if they are at home. Norms related to corruption are apparently deeply ingrained.

In 2002, enforcement authorities acquired the right to confiscate the diplomatic license plates of violators. And guess what? Unpaid violations dropped by almost 98%. This outcome illustrates the power of incentives in influencing human behavior. ✳

Competitive and Open Markets

In this section, we take a quick look at three institutions that are essential for economic growth: competitive markets, international trade, and the flow of funds across borders. These market characteristics are covered in detail elsewhere in this book.

Competitive Markets

In Chapter 3, we explored how competitive markets ensure that consumers can buy goods at the lowest possible prices. When markets aren't competitive, people who want to participate face barriers to entry, which inhibit competition and innovation. Yet many nations monopolize key industries by preventing competition or by establishing government ownership of industries. This strategy limits macroeconomic growth.

International Trade

Trade creates value

Recall from Chapter 2 that trade creates value. In some cases, trade enables nations to consume goods and services that they would not produce on their own. Specialization and trade make all nations better off because each can produce goods for which it enjoys a comparative advantage. Output increases when nations (1) produce the goods and services for which they have the lowest opportunity cost and (2) trade for the other goods and services they wish to consume.

International trade barriers reduce the benefits available from specialization and trade. Chapter 32 is devoted to the study of international trade.

Flow of Funds across Borders

In Chapter 22, we talked about the importance of savings for economic growth. For example, the inflow of foreign savings has helped to keep interest rates low in the United States even as domestic savings rates have fallen. If firms and individuals are to invest in physical or human capital, someone has to save. Opportunities for investment expand if there is access to savings from around the globe. That is, if foreigners can funnel their savings into your nation's economy, your nation's firms can use these funds to expand. However, many developing nations have restrictions on foreign ownership of land and physical capital within their borders. Restrictions on the flow of capital across borders handcuff domestic firms, which are forced to seek funds solely from domestic savers.

Efficient Taxes

On the one hand, taxes must be high enough to support effective government. Political stability, the rule of law, and the protection of private property rights all require strong and consistent government. And taxes provide the revenue to pay for government services. On the other hand, if we tax activities that are fundamental to economic growth, there will be fewer of these activities. In market economies, output and income are strictly intertwined. If we tax income, we are taxing output, and that is GDP. So although taxes are necessary, they can also reduce incentives for production.

Incentives

Before the federal government instituted an income tax, government services were largely funded by taxes on imports. But international trade is also an essential institution for economic growth. So taxes on imports also impede growth.

Efficient taxes are taxes sufficient to fund the activities of government while impeding production and consumption decisions as little as possible. It is not easy to determine the efficient level of taxes or even to determine what activities should be taxed. We will discuss this issue further in Chapter 29, when we discuss fiscal policy.

Stable Money and Prices

High and variable inflation is a sure way to reduce incentives for investment and production. In Chapter 22, we saw that inflation increases uncertainty about future price levels. When people are unsure about future price levels, they are more reluctant to sign contracts that deliver dollar payoffs in the future. Thus, unpredictable inflation diminishes future growth possibilities. In the United States, the Federal Reserve (Fed) is charged with administering monetary policy. The Fed is designed to reduce incentives for politically motivated monetary policy, which typically leads to highly variable inflation rates. We cover the Fed in greater detail in Chapter 30.

Incentives

PRACTICE WHAT YOU KNOW

Institutions: Can You Guess This Country?

Question: The following is a list of characteristics for a particular country. Can you name it?

Hint: The nation's flag is one of those shown here.

1. This country has almost no natural resources.
2. It has no agriculture of its own.
3. It imports water.
4. It is located in the tropics.
5. It has four official languages.
6. It occupies 710 square kilometers.
7. It has one of the world's lowest unemployment rates.
8. It has a literacy rate of 96%.
9. It had a per capita GDP of $56,000 in 2014.
10. It has one of the densest populations per square kilometer on the planet.

Answer: Congratulations if you thought of Singapore! At first blush, it seems almost impossible that one of the most successful countries on the planet could have so little going for it in terms of natural resources.

Question: How could a country with so few natural resources survive, let alone flourish? How can an economy grow without any agriculture or enough fresh water?

Answer: What Singapore lacks in some areas it more than makes up for in others. Singapore has a lot of human capital from a highly educated and industrious labor force. It has been able to attract plenty of foreign financial funds by creating a stable and secure financial system that protects property rights and encourages free trade. Singapore also has a strategically situated deep-water port in Southeast Asia that benefits from proximity to the emerging economies of China and India.

Conclusion

We began this chapter with the misconception that natural resources are the primary source of economic growth. While it doesn't hurt to have more natural resources, they are certainly not sufficient for economic growth. Modern economics points instead to the institutions that frame the environment within which business and personal decisions are made.

Learning More and Helping Alleviate Global Poverty

The information presented in this chapter reveals a picture of significant and persistent poverty across much of the globe. It is possible that this discussion and your classroom lectures have inspired you to learn more about global poverty or even to try to help those who are less fortunate around the globe. Toward those ends, we can give a little advice.

The surest way to learn about world economic reality is to travel to a developing nation. We suggest taking an alternative spring break or even studying abroad for an entire semester in a developing nation. These are costly ventures, but they will almost certainly change your perspective on life. If you get the chance to travel, be sure to speak directly to people on the streets and ask them to share their personal stories with you. Talk to small business owners, parents, and children. If possible, try to speak to people who have nothing to gain by sharing their story.

It is possible that you wish to give financially to help the less fortunate around the globe. There are many international aid charities, but unfortunately, not all are truly helpful or even completely honest. We recommend visiting the website for Givewell (www.givewell.org), which researches charitable organizations from around the world and recommends a few that have proved to be honest and effective.

If you want to study more about growth economics, you should start with two books. The first book is by economist William Easterly, titled *The Elusive Quest for Growth: Economists' Adventures and Misadventures in the Tropics*. In this book, Easterly weaves personal narrative and economic theory together in a unique way to help you understand how economic theories regarding growth have evolved through the years. He both explains past failures and argues compellingly for future policy proposals. The second book, by economists Daron Acemoglu and

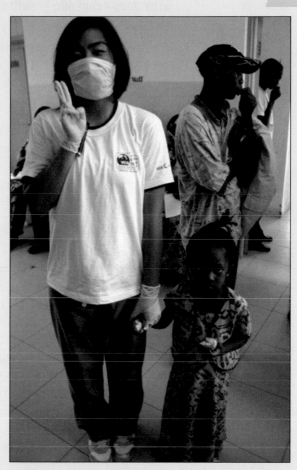

A University of Virginia student helps with eye surgeries in Tema, Ghana.

James Robinson, is called *Why Nations Fail: The Origins of Power, Prosperity, and Poverty*. This book presents the very best arguments for institutions as the primary source of economic growth. Even though this book is written by leading macroeconomists, it is enjoyable reading for mass audiences.

This chapter helps set a framework for thinking about growth policies. Many of the issues we touch on will see deeper treatment in later chapters. In particular, Chapter 25 presents the theory of economic growth.

ANSWERING THE BIG QUESTIONS

Why does economic growth matter?

* Economic growth affects human welfare in meaningful ways.
* Historical data show that sustained economic growth is a relatively modern phenomenon.
* Relatively small but consistent growth rates are an effective path out of poverty.

How do resources and technology contribute to economic growth?

* Natural resources, physical capital, and human capital all contribute to economic growth.
* Technological advancement, which leads to the production of more output per unit of input, also sustains economic growth.

What institutions foster economic growth?

* Private property rights secure ownership of what an individual produces, creating incentives for increased output.
* Political stability and the rule of law allow people to make production decisions without concern for corrupt government.
* Competitive and open markets allow everyone to benefit from global productivity.
* Efficient taxes are high enough to support effective government, but low enough to provide positive incentives for production.
* Stable money and prices allow people to make long-term production decisions with minimal risk.

CONCEPTS YOU SHOULD KNOW

economic growth (p. 758)
factors of production (p. 774)
human capital (p. 776)
institution (p. 779)

private property rights
 (p. 779)
resources (p. 774)
rule of 70 (p. 767)

technological advancement
 (p. 776)
technology (p. 776)

QUESTIONS FOR REVIEW

1. What are the three factors that influence economic growth?

2. What is human capital, and how is it different from the quantity of workers available for work? Name three ways to increase a nation's human capital. Is an increase in the size of the labor force also an increase in human capital? Explain your answer.

3. How is economic growth measured?

4. Describe the pattern of world economic growth over the past 2,000 years. Approximately when did economic growth really take off?

5. List five human welfare conditions that are positively affected by economic growth.

6. Many historical accounts credit the economic success of the United States to its abundance of natural resources.

   a. What is missing from this argument?
   b. Name five poor nations that have significant natural resources.

7. The flow of funds across borders is a source of growth for economies. Use what you learned about loanable funds in Chapter 22 to describe how foreign funds might expand output in a nation.

8. In 2011, when the U.S. unemployment rate was over 9%, President Barack Obama said, "There are some structural issues with our economy where a lot of businesses have learned to become much more efficient with a lot fewer workers. You see it when you go to a bank and you use an ATM, you don't go to a bank teller, or you go to the airport and you're using a kiosk instead of checking in at the gate." Discuss the president's quote in terms of both short-run unemployment and long-run growth.

9. The difference between 1% growth and 2% growth seems insignificant. Explain why it really matters.

10. What do economists mean by the term "institutions"? Name five different laws that are institutions that affect production incentives. Name three social practices that affect production in a society.

STUDY PROBLEMS (✷*solved at the end of the section*)

✷ 1. Real per capita GDP in China in 1959 was about $350, but it doubled to about $700 by 1978, when Deng Xiaoping started market reforms.

   a. What was the average annual economic growth rate in China over the 20 years from 1959 to 1978?
   b. Chinese real per capita GDP doubled again in only seven years, reaching $1,400 by 1986. What was the average annual economic growth rate between 1979 and 1986?

✱ 2. The table below presents long-run macroeconomic data for two hypothetical nations, A and B:

	A	B
Nominal GDP growth	12%	5%
Inflation	10%	2%
Nominal interest	4%	4%
Unemployment rate	12%	5%
Population growth	1.5%	1%

Assume that both nations start with real GDP of $1,000 per citizen. Fill in the blanks in the following table, assuming that the data above apply for every year considered.

	A	B
Economic growth rate	_____	_____
Years required for real per capita GDP to double	_____	_____
Real per capita GDP 140 years later	_____	_____

3. Let's revisit the data from Table 24.3, showing the following world economic growth rates for specific historical eras:

Years	Growth rate
AD 1–1800	0.02%
1800–1900	0.64%
1900–1950	1.04%
1950–2000	2.12%

Approximately how many years will it take for average real per capita GDP to double at each of those growth rates?

4. Use the data in the table below to compute economic growth rates for the United States for 2008, 2009, and 2010. Note that all data are from the end of the year specified.

Date	Nominal GDP (billions of current $)	GDP deflator	Population growth rate
2007	$14,061.8	106.30	1.01%
2008	$14,369.1	108.62	0.93%
2009	$14,119.0	109.61	0.87%
2010	$14,660.4	110.66	0.90%

5. The rule of 70 applies in any growth rate application. Let's say you have $1,000 in savings and you have three alternatives:

- a savings account earning 1% interest per year
- a U.S. Treasury bond earning 3% interest per year
- a stock market mutual fund earning 8% interest per year

Approximately how long would it take to double your savings in each of the three accounts?

6. Assume that you plan to retire in 40 years and are evaluating the three different accounts listed in question 5. How much would your $1,000 be worth in 40 years under each of the three alternatives?

✱ 7. Economic growth is a very particular concept in economics. The term "economic growth" is not always used correctly in media reports.
a. Define economic growth.
b. Consider the following economy:

Year	Nominal GDP (trillions of dollars)	Price level
2014	$18	240
2015	$20	250

Is it possible to calculate the economic growth rate in 2015 given the information above? If so, calculate the economic growth rate. If not, what other information would you need to calculate the economic growth rate?

SOLVED PROBLEMS

1a. The rule of 70 tells us that we can divide 70 by the rate of growth to approximate the number of years it takes for a variable to double. Therefore, if we know the number of years that a variable actually did take to double, we can rearrange the rule of 70 to approximate the average annual growth rate, x:

$$70 \div x = 20$$
$$70 \div 20 = x$$
$$= 3.5$$

Therefore, the Chinese economy grew at an approximate average of 3.5% per year over the 20-year period from 1959 to 1978.

b. Now, with real per capital GDP doubling in approximately seven years, the rule of 70 implies

$$70 \div 7 = 10$$

Therefore, China grew an average of 10% over the seven-year period from 1979 to 1986.

2. To determine economic growth rate, we use the approximations formula:

- Economic growth ≈ %Δ in nominal GDP – %Δ price level – %Δ population
- For nation A: 12% – 10% – 1.5% = 0.5%
- For nation B: 5% – 2% – 1% = 2%

To determine the approximate number of years required for real per capita GDP to double, we use the rule of 70:

- For nation A: 70 ÷ 0.5 = 140
- For nation B: 70 ÷ 2 = 35

To determine real per capita GDP 140 years later, we use the rule of 70 results. Nation A's

level doubles in exactly 140 years, so it will be two times the original level of $1,000, or $2,000. Nation B's level doubles after 35 years and then doubles again after 35 more. So after 70 years, its level of real per capita GDP is four times the original level. It doubles again in 35 years, so after 105 years, it is eight times the original level. Then it doubles again in 35 more years, so after 140 years, its real per capita GDP is $16,000, which is 16 times the original level.

	A	B
Economic growth rate	0.5%	2%
Years required for real per capita GDP to double	140	35
Real per capita GDP 140 years later	$2,000	$16,000

7a. Economic growth is measured as the percentage change in real per capita GDP.

b. It is not possible to calculate the economic growth rate from the data because we also need the growth rate of the population.

The essential ingredient for economic growth is physical capital, such as factories, infrastructure, and other tools.

Looking around the world, you see many rich nations and many poor nations. Rich developed nations have impressive capital, including high-

ways, factories, and office buildings. Poor underdeveloped nations have more unpaved roads and fewer modern factories and buildings. Many people see that capital and wealth seem to go hand in hand and conclude that capital is the source of wealth. From this view, if poor nations could just acquire bigger and better tools, they, too, could be wealthy. But correlation does not prove causation. Modern economic growth theory indicates that capital is the result of growth, rather than the cause of it, and that institutions are the key to economic growth.

In the last chapter, we saw that economic growth can transform lives. Consistent economic growth, even at relatively small rates, can be the pathway out of poverty. In this chapter, we shed light on the causes of economic growth by examining growth theory. We also discuss policies that foster growth.

As the chapter title implies, much of the content of this chapter is theoretical. Yet, because of the relationship between economic growth and human welfare, the theory is never far from the real world. We begin the chapter with a brief description of how economic theories develop. After that, we consider the evolution of growth theory, starting with the Solow growth model, a model created and named for American economist Robert Solow. The Solow model formed the foundation for growth theory beginning in the 1950s. After discussing the theory and implications of the Solow model, we consider modern growth theory and the implied policy prescriptions.

Modern roads speed productivity, but are they a sure route to wealth?

BIG QUESTIONS

* How do macroeconomic theories evolve?
* What is the Solow growth model?
* How does technology affect growth?
* Why are institutions the key to economic growth?

How Do Macroeconomic Theories Evolve?

This chapter marks our first major step into macroeconomic theory, or modeling. In Chapter 2, we discussed the characteristics of good economic models: they are simple, flexible, and useful for making accurate predictions. In this chapter, we present a model of economic growth that simplifies from the real world yet also helps us make powerful predictions about economic growth. The stakes are high: growth theory and policy have significant impacts on human lives. Therefore, it's important to consistently reevaluate growth theory in light of real-world results.

Today, economists agree that economic growth is determined by a combination of resources, technology, and institutions. But this consensus is the result of an evolution in growth theory that started almost 60 years ago with the contributions of economist Robert Solow. Although the theory has changed significantly over the past two decades, Solow's growth model still forms the core of modern growth theory.

In many academic disciplines, new theories are fodder for intellectual debates, with no direct impact on human lives. But in economics, theories are put to the test in the real world, often very soon after they are first articulated. Figure 25.1 illustrates the relationship between economic ideas and real-world events. At the top of the circle, we begin with observations of the real world, which inform a theory as it develops. Once an economic theory is developed, it can influence the policies that are used to pursue certain economic goals. These policies affect the daily lives and well-being of real people. Finally, as economists observe the effects of policy in the real world, they continue to revise economic theory.

Economic growth models affect the welfare of billions of people worldwide. The results can be beneficial. But if growth theory is wrong or incomplete, it can lead to faulty policy prescriptions that result in poverty. We revisit this point toward the end of the chapter.

The Evolution of Growth Theory

In 1776, Adam Smith published his renowned book *An Inquiry into the Nature and Causes of the Wealth of Nations*. This book was the first real economics

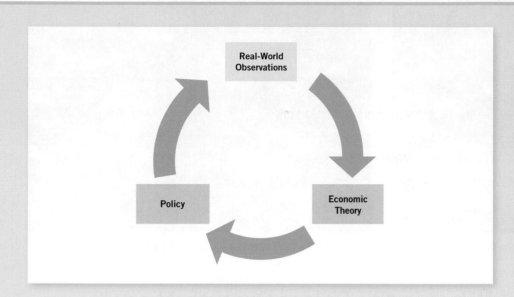

FIGURE 25.1

The Interplay between the Real World and Economic Theory
Observations of the real world shape economic theory. Economic theory then informs policy decisions that are designed to meet certain economic goals. Once these policies are implemented, they affect the real world. Further real-world observations contribute to additional advances in economic theory, and the cycle continues.

textbook, and, as the title indicates, it focused on what makes a nation wealthy. The central question, paraphrased from the title, is this: Why do some nations prosper while others do not? More than two centuries later, we still grapple with the nature and causes of the wealth of nations.

Economists are not alone in their pursuit of answers to this question. Perhaps you or someone you know has visited a developing country. As travel becomes easier and the world economy becomes more integrated, people are more aware of poverty around the globe. Many college students today ask the same questions as economists: Why are so many people poor, and what can be done about it?

This link between economic theory and human welfare is what drives many scholars to study the theory of economic growth. As the Nobel Prize–winning macroeconomist Robert Lucas wrote in 1988:

> Is there some action a government of India could take that would lead the Indian economy to grow like Indonesia's or Egypt's? If so, what exactly? If not, what is it about the "nature of India" that makes it so? The consequences for human welfare involved in questions like these are simply staggering: *Once one starts to think about them it is hard to think of anything else.*

Economic growth has not always been the primary focus of macroeconomics. After the Great Depression in the 1930s, macroeconomics focused on the study of business cycles, or short-run expansions and contractions. Growth theory began with the Solow model in the 1950s and still serves as the foundation for growth theory, both in method and in policy. Therefore, while growth theory has evolved, it is helpful to consider the Solow model as both a starting point and the basis of current theory.

Why are some nations rich, like Malaysia . . .

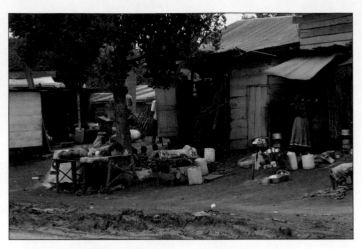

. . . while other nations remain poor, like Uganda?

What Is the Solow Growth Model?

If you travel around the globe and visit nations with different levels of income, you will notice significant differences in the physical tools available for use in production. Wealthy nations have more factories, better roads, more and better computers—that is, they have more capital. Simply viewing the difference in capital, it is easy to conclude that capital automatically yields economic growth.

This was the basic premise of early growth theory: there are rich nations and there are poor nations, and the rich nations are those that have capital. Throughout this chapter, we will often refer to capital as *physical capital* to distinguish it from human capital. Natural resources and human capital are also important in the Solow growth model, but the focus is primarily on physical capital, or what we sometimes call just "capital." We begin by looking at a nation's production function, which describes how changes in capital affect real output.

A Nation's Production Function

A **production function** for a firm describes the relationship between the inputs the firm uses and the output it creates.

The Solow model starts with a *production function* for the entire economy. In microeconomic theory, a firm's **production function** describes the relationship between the inputs a firm uses and the output it creates. (You can refer back to Chapter 22 for a refresher if you like.) For example, at a single McDonald's restaurant, the daily output depends on the number of employees; anything needed to make the final products (hamburger patties, French fries, and so on); and the capital tools that employees have to work with, including space for cooking, cash registers, and drink dispensers. In equation form, the production function for a single firm is

(Equation 25.1)
$$q = f(\text{physical capital, human capital})$$

where q is the firm's output. Equation 25.1 says that output *is a function of* the quantities of physical capital and human capital that the firm uses. For McDonald's, the output is the number of meals produced.

In macroeconomics, we extend the production function to an entire nation or macroeconomy. The **aggregate production function** describes the relationship between all the inputs used in the macroeconomy and the economy's total output, where GDP is output. In its simplest form, the aggregate production function tells us that GDP is a function of three broad types of resources, or factors of production, which are the inputs used in producing goods and services. These inputs are physical capital, human capital, and natural resources. We can state the aggregate production function in equation form as

GDP = Y = F(physical capital, human capital, natural resources)   (Equation 25.2)

> The **aggregate production function** describes the relationship between all the inputs used in the macroeconomy and the economy's total output (GDP).

where Y is real output, or GDP.

We can think about the relationship between input and output in a very simple economy. Consider a situation in which there is only one person in the macroeconomy—for example, the character Chuck Noland (played by Tom Hanks) in the 2000 movie *Cast Away* who finds himself stranded on an island in the South Pacific after his plane crashes. Chuck's individual, or microeconomic, decisions are also macroeconomic decisions, because he is the only person in the economy. The GDP of Chuck's island includes only what he produces with his resources. Let's say that Chuck spends his days harvesting fruit on the island. In this case, GDP is equal to whatever fruit Chuck harvests. Table 25.1 shows Chuck's production function and some of the resources he has available.

In the film *Cast Away*, Chuck Noland's individual, or microeconomic, decisions are also macroeconomic decisions, because he is the only person in the economy.

Chuck's output is the fruit he harvests from around his island. His resources include his human capital, the physical capital of a bamboo ladder, and the island's natural resources, such as bamboo and fruit trees. All else equal, the more Chuck has of any of these resources, the more GDP he can produce. Economic growth occurs if Chuck produces more fruit per week.

In many ways, the production function for a large developed macroeconomy like that of the United States is the same as Chuck Noland's. Output depends on the resources available for production, and the United States has significant natural resources, such as oil, iron ore, coal, timber, and farmland.

TABLE 25.1

Chuck Noland's Production Function

Production function		
GDP = F(physical capital, human capital, natural resources)		
GDP	**Resources**	**Example**
	Physical capital	Bamboo ladder
Fruit	Human capital	Chuck's time and knowledge
	Natural resources	Fruit trees and bamboo

In terms of human capital, the United States has a large labor force composed of over 155 million workers, and of those workers age 25 and over, more than 90% have graduated from high school. Finally, the United States has built up a very large stock of physical capital—highways, factories, ports, machinery, etc. All of these resources enable the nation to produce an annual GDP of more than $18 trillion.

The Focus on Capital Resources

While the Solow model explicitly recognizes contributions from both labor and capital resources, many economists and policy-makers focused on capital goods. As we noted in the chapter opener, early growth theorists saw that capital resources in wealthy nations far exceed those available in developing nations. After all, there are more factories, highways, bridges, and dams in wealthy nations. It seemed logical to conclude that capital is the key to growth.

In addition, periods of investment growth in developed economies are also periods of economic expansion. Figure 25.2 plots U.S. economic growth rates with investment growth rates from 1965 to 2014. The data show a clear positive correlation between real GDP growth and the rate of investment growth. This is another reason to believe that investment and capital are the primary sources of economic growth.

Earlier, we noted the interplay of theory and real-world observations. This is one example. Capital *appears* to cause economic growth because there is such a strong correlation between capital and output. And, certainly, no one would dispute that workers are more productive when they have more tools. For now, we will continue our focus on capital. Later, we will explore some of the missing pieces that contemporary growth theory has contributed.

FIGURE 25.2

U.S. Investment and GDP Growth, 1965–2014

Growth in real investment is positively correlated with growth in real GDP. The big question is whether this correlation implies causation.

Source: Bureau of Economic Analysis.

Diminishing Marginal Products

Marginal thinking

Chuck Noland would be happy if he found a new grove of mangoes on his island, and his newfound resources would increase his GDP. Resources also help actual macroeconomies. For example, the discoveries of natural gas in the United States have increased dramatically over the past two decades. This new energy resource has enabled the United States to produce more with cheaper resources, because natural gas is less expensive than crude oil. To quantify how helpful a resource may be, economists employ the concept of *marginal product*. The **marginal product** of an input is the change in output associated with one additional unit of an input. More resources increase output, so we say the marginal product of each resource is positive.

The **marginal product** of an input is the change in output divided by the change in input.

Diminishing Marginal Product in a One-Person Economy

Let's take a closer look at Chuck Noland's production function. Initially, Chuck produces GDP by climbing trees and picking fruit. With this method, he is able to gather 1 bushel of fruit in a week. He produces this weekly GDP without the aid of any physical capital. Then Chuck decides to build a bamboo ladder. Building the ladder is a costly investment because it takes him away from producing fruit for a whole week. But then, after he has the ladder as physical capital, his weekly output grows to 4 bushels. Using the language we defined earlier, we say that the marginal product (MP) of his ladder is 3 bushels of fruit per week:

$$MP_{capital} = \text{change in output from a one-unit change in capital} = 3$$

Chuck is so happy with his ladder that he builds a second ladder so that he can leave one on each side of the island. Now his weekly output climbs to 6 bushels of fruit. Because he produces 4 bushels with one ladder and 6 bushels with two ladders, the marginal product of the second ladder is 2 bushels. Note that while the marginal product of the second ladder is positive, it is less than the marginal product of the first ladder. The marginal product of the second ladder is not as large because while the first ladder completely altered the way Chuck harvests fruit, the second ladder just makes his job a little easier.

Figure 25.3 shows a hypothetical relationship between Chuck's output and the number of ladders he uses. Looking first at the table on the right, note that the second column shows total output (bushels per week), which depends on the number of ladders. The third column shows the marginal product of each ladder. Notice that the marginal product per ladder declines as more ladders are added. This outcome reflects the principle of **diminishing marginal product**, which states that the marginal product of an input falls as the quantity of the input rises. Diminishing marginal product generally applies across all factors of production at both the microeconomic and the macroeconomic levels.

The left side of Figure 25.3 is a graph of Chuck's production function: it plots the points from the first two columns of the table on the right. With no ladders, the production function indicates 1 bushel of fruit; but then as ladders are added, output climbs along the curve. The slope of the curve flattens out because the marginal product of the added ladders diminishes.

This principle of diminishing marginal productivity is not special to our example of one man alone on an island. It is a phenomenon that holds for

A ladder would help!

Diminishing marginal product occurs when the marginal product of an input falls as the quantity of the input rises.

FIGURE 25.3

Chuck Noland's Production Function

The table shows how output (bushels per week) increases as the number of ladders increases; it describes the relationship between output and capital inputs. The graph is a picture of the production function. Output increases with capital, but each unit of capital yields less additional output. The shape of the production function, in which the slope is declining, illustrates the diminishing marginal product of capital.

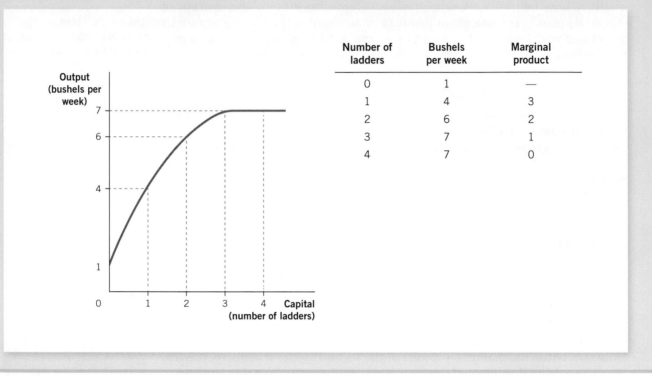

Number of ladders	Bushels per week	Marginal product
0	1	—
1	4	3
2	6	2
3	7	1
4	7	0

resources in a macroeconomy in general, and it is a cornerstone insight of the Solow growth model. Sometimes, this principle is simplified to *diminishing returns*. The following discussion places this concept in the macroeconomic context of the U.S. interstate highway system.

U.S. Interstate Highways and the Aggregate Production Function

In the United States, we have a system of interstate highways that the federal government has built. This highway system is essentially a 50,000-mile capital good that we use to help produce GDP. The network of highways connects the major cities of the United States. These highways increase GDP in the United States because they enhance our ability to transport goods and services across the nation. For example, a couch manufactured in High Point, North Carolina, can be transported exclusively by interstate highway to Cleveland, Ohio, in less than 8 hours. Before the construction of the interstate system, the same trip between High Point and Cleveland would have taken twice as long, required more gasoline due to inefficient speeds, and caused much more wear and tear on the vehicles used.

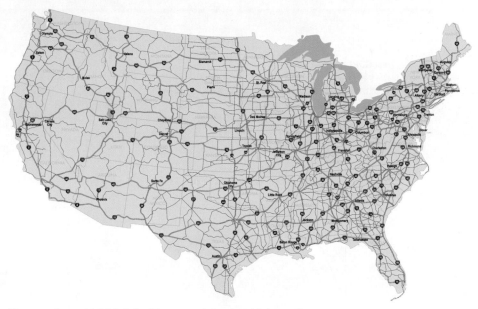

How much would GDP fall without our interstate highways?

Our highway system is a significant resource that contributes to our nation's GDP. If the interstate highway system were somehow to close down completely, GDP would immediately fall. But what would happen to GDP if the government created a second interstate highway system with 50,000 miles of additional roads crisscrossing the United States? That is, what would be the marginal product of an additional interstate highway system? The impact would be positive, but much smaller than that of the original network. This example illustrates diminishing returns: the marginal product of highways declines as more and more become available. The production relationship is just like that of Chuck Noland's ladders.

Figure 25.4 is a graph of the aggregate production function—the production function for the entire economy. On the vertical axis, we have output for the macroeconomy, which is real GDP (Y). If we assume no population growth, then economic growth is represented as movements upward along the vertical axis. On the horizontal axis, capital resources (K) increase from left to right. Notice that the slope of the function is positive, which indicates positive marginal product. But the marginal product of capital also declines as more capital is added. For example, the difference in output from the increase in capital from K_1 to K_2 is larger than the change in output from a change in capital from K_3 to K_4. This outcome illustrates the declining marginal product of capital.

The aggregate production function has formed the basis for most discussions in growth theory since 1956. Economic growth is represented by upward movement along the vertical axis. Indeed, if we focus *only* on this simple formulation, economic growth happens only with investment in capital. Diminishing returns, or declining marginal productivity, is the key assumption of the Solow model. As we shall see, this single assumption leads to striking implications for the macroeconomy.

FIGURE 25.4

The Aggregate Production Function

The aggregate production function graphs the relationship between output (Y, or real GDP) and capital inputs (K). The shape of the production function illustrates two important features of production. First, the marginal production of resources is positive, as indicated by the positive slope. Second, the marginal product of additional resources declines as more resources are added. This result is evident in the declining slope of the function.

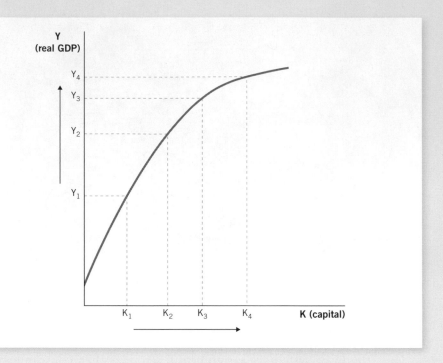

Implications of the Solow Model

We can use the basic framework of the production function with an emphasis on capital and diminishing returns to flesh out the two important implications of the Solow model: the conditions of a *steady state* and *convergence*.

The Steady State

Incentives

How many ladders should Chuck Noland build? It takes a week to build each ladder, and each additional ladder adds less output than the one before. Therefore, at some point Chuck has no incentive to build additional ladders. Perhaps Chuck's incentive declines after he builds two ladders. Looking back at Figure 25.3, you can see that a third ladder yields only 1 more bushel of fruit. Let's assume that Chuck decides it is not worth a week of work (to build a ladder) for 1 more bushel of fruit. Therefore, he builds only two ladders, and his output remains at 6 bushels a week. At this point, economic growth for Chuck stops.

The Solow model implies the same outcome for large macroeconomies. Because the marginal product of capital decreases, at some point there is no reason to build (that is, invest in) more capital. Perhaps this occurs at K_3 in Figure 25.4. This means there is no incentive to build additional capital beyond K_3 because the benefits in terms of additional output no longer

An economy at the steady state is like an airplane at its cruising altitude.

exceed the cost of building capital. Since there is no incentive to build capital past K_3, and since we are assuming that capital is the source of growth, the economy stops growing once it reaches K_3. In this example, K_3 is the economy's **steady state**, the condition of a macroeconomy when there is no new net investment.

Once an economy reaches the steady state, there is no change in either capital or real income. The steady state is a direct implication of diminishing returns: when the marginal return to capital declines, at some point there is no incentive to build more capital. The steady state is not a very encouraging situation. You can think of the steady state as the "stagnant state," because when the economy reaches its steady state, real GDP is no longer increasing and economic growth stops.

It is important to distinguish between *investment* and *net investment*. Over time, capital wears out: roads get potholes, tractors break down, and factories become obsolete. This is known as capital depreciation. **Depreciation** is a decline in the value of a resource over time. Depreciation is natural with capital, and it erodes the capital stock. Without new investment, capital declines over time, so some positive investment is needed to offset depreciation. But if investment is exactly enough to replace depreciated items, the capital stock will not increase—and this means no net investment. **Net investment** is investment minus depreciation. For the capital stock to increase, net investment must be positive.

This distinction between investment and net investment is important when we consider the steady state. In the steady state, net investment equals zero. There may be positive investment, but this is investment to replace worn-out machines and tools. So when an economy reaches its steady state, the capital stock stays constant. For example, if three ladders represent a steady-state condition on Chuck Noland's island, he may repair his ladders periodically. Repairing the ladders to maintain a level of capital counts as investment, but not as net investment.

The **steady state** is the condition of a macroeconomy when there is no new net investment.

Depreciation is a fall in the value of a resource over time.

Net investment is investment minus depreciation.

PRACTICE WHAT YOU KNOW

The Japanese government estimated total damages of $309 billion from the 2011 earthquake and tsunami.

Changes in Resources: Natural Disasters

In 2011, a major earthquake and tsunami in Japan destroyed significant physical capital, including roads, homes, factories, and bridges.

Question: How would you use an aggregate production function to illustrate the way a major destruction of capital affects a macroeconomy in the short run?

Answer:

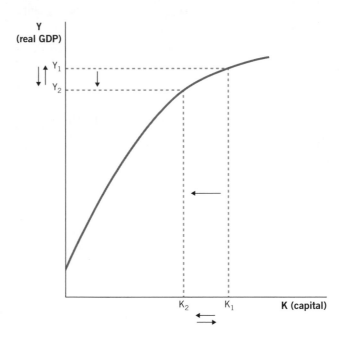

This is an unusual situation in which the level of capital in a nation actually falls. Because capital (K) is on the horizontal axis of the production function, the decline in capital moves Japan back along its production function. This means less GDP for Japan (Y falls) until the nation can get its capital rebuilt.

Question: With no further changes, what happens to real GDP in the long run?

Answer: With no further changes, real GDP returns to the steady-state output level in the long run. At the new level of capital after the earthquake (K_2), the marginal product of additional capital is relatively high, so there is a greater return to building new capital. But in the long run, because there was no shift in the production function, the level of capital returns to the steady-state level (K_1), which means that output also returns to its steady-state level (Y_1).

Convergence

If nations with large stocks of capital stop growing, then nations with less capital can catch up if they are adding to their capital stock. This means that nations all over the globe could potentially converge to the same level of wealth. **Convergence** is the idea that per capita GDP across nations will equalize as nations approach the steady state. Here is the logic of the Solow model: Rich nations are rich because they have more capital. But as these nations approach their steady state, the returns to capital decline and the growth slows. When a nation reaches a steady state, its economic growth stops. But if a nation has not yet reached the steady state, adding capital still leads to growth. Therefore, investment in developing nations should yield relatively greater returns, and this outcome should lead to more capital in developing nations.

Consider the United States and China. In 1980, the United States was wealthy, but China was poor. Figure 25.5 shows both nations as they might have appeared on a production function in 1980. Yet since 1980, growth rates in China have exceeded growth rates in the United States. This blast of growth in China has been accompanied by rapid industrialization—that is, the creation of new physical capital. According to the Solow model, the new capital in China yields greater returns because the nation started with less capital.

If this basic model were always true to reality, new factories would typically yield higher returns in poor nations than in rich nations. Investors seeking to build new factories would turn to nations like Haiti, Nicaragua, and North Korea—nations with relatively small capital stocks.

Convergence is the idea that per capita GDP across nations will equalize as nations approach the steady state.

FIGURE 25.5

Convergence

In 1980, the United States had much more capital than China did; this was one reason why real GDP for the United States was much higher. But in the years since, China has increased its capital stock substantially and has grown much more rapidly than the United States. The Solow model implies that the United States is closer to its steady state and therefore grows more slowly than China.

Convergence argues that the hare and the tortoise will end up at the finish line together.

According to the Solow theory, developing nations should catch up because the older, developed economies have already made new discoveries and have documented mistakes to avoid in the development process. Developing nations can jump right into acquiring the best equipment, tools, and practices. For example, if they are building cars, they don't have to start with a Model T and a basic labor-intensive assembly line; they can immediately establish a modern plant resembling those of, say, Ford, Honda and Volkswagen.

But reality has been much different from what the theory implies. First, although we have seen cases of rapid growth in poor nations, convergence has been rare. In addition to China, the nations of South Korea, Singapore, India, Chile, and others have done well. But they are exceptions. Very recently, it seems that some growth is sprouting in African nations, but for the second half of the twentieth century, most poor nations continued to stagnate, rather than converge to the economic levels of wealthier nations. Second, growth did not seem to slow in wealthy nations over the second half of the twentieth century. Recent decades have brought slower growth in many wealthy nations, like the United States, but the gap between rich countries and poor countries is widening. More often countries have shown patterns of *divergence* (greater differences between the GDPs of countries) instead of the predicted state of convergence.

Given that we have little or no evidence of either a steady state or convergence, economists have reassessed the model, trying to answer the question of why sustained growth continues in wealthy nations. Some economists have pointed to technology as the key driver of this growth, and in the next section, we will examine this concept.

How Does Technology Affect Growth?

In this section, we consider how technological innovations affect the Solow model, and also address assumptions about the way they occur. Recall that *technology* refers to the knowledge that is available for use in production.

Technology and the Production Function

In 1994, Intel introduced a revolutionary computer chip for personal computers—the Pentium chip. The Pentium could perform 188 million instructions per second and was more than three times faster than its predecessor chip. But by 2014, just 22 years later, Intel's new chip, the Core i7 5960x, could perform 238 *billion* instructions per second. The new chip costs less and uses less energy than the old chip, yet it is almost a thousand times faster!

These Intel chips give us a good picture of what technology does. A computer chip is physical capital—it is a tool that helps us produce. When we get faster chips, we can produce more with the same amount of capital.

Now let's see how new technology affects the Solow growth model. First, consider the production function. Figure 25.6 shows two production functions: F_1 is the initial production function, when computers are running on Pentium chips. F_2 is the production function after faster chips become available. Note that the new production function is steeper than the old one. The

FIGURE 25.6

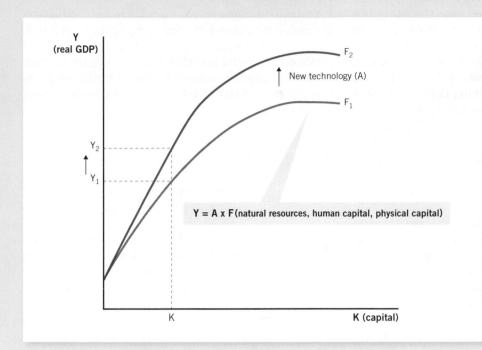

New Technology and the Production Function

New technology increases the slope of the production function as the marginal product of capital increases. The old production function is shown as F_1 and the new production function as F_2. After the technological innovation (represented by A), capital is more productive, and this outcome leads to new economic growth. If technology continues to advance, economic growth can be sustained.

slope is determined by the marginal product of capital, and the new computer chips make capital more productive at all levels. For any given level of capital, real GDP is higher. These are the kinds of technological changes that fuel sustained economic growth.

We can also use an equation to see how the production function is altered. The aggregate production function now includes an allowance for technological advancement:

$$Y = A \times F(\text{physical capital, human capital, natural resources})$$ (Equation 25.3)

where A accounts for technological change. The addition of A to the basic model helps to explain continued economic growth. Without new technology, the economy eventually reaches a steady state, and growth stops. But

Older map technology took lots of time . . .

. . . but the new map technology is faster.

new technology means that output is higher for any given level of capital, because the capital, which embeds the new technology, is more productive. The new technology shifts real output, and therefore income, up to new levels.

Economists and policy-makers of course see this shift as very important, and it has driven many political decisions. Before looking at policy implications that derive from the Solow model, let's first look more closely at how technological change occurs in the model.

Exogenous Technological Change

Why do people innovate? What drives them to create better ways of producing? If technology is the source of sustained growth, then the answer to this question is critical.

In the Solow model, there is no real answer to the question of what causes technological innovation. The model assumes that technological change occurs *exogenously*. Recall from Chapter 2 that exogenous factors are the variables that cannot be controlled for in a model. For our purposes here, the implication is that technological innovations just happen—they are not based on economics. In this sense, technological innovations occur randomly. If technology is exogenous, it is like rainfall: sometimes you get a lot, and sometimes you don't get any. If some nations get more technological innovations than others, then that is just their good fortune.

Exogenous growth is growth that is independent of any factors in the economy.

But if technology is the source of sustained growth, and if technology is exogenous, then economic growth is also exogenous. **Exogenous growth** is growth that is independent of any factors in the economy. When we see innovation occurring in the same places over and over, the Solow model chalks it up to luck. In this view, the innovations are not due to any inherent characteristics of the economies that experience them. Similarly, in this view, poor nations are poor because the random technological innovations happened elsewhere.

If you question the assumption that technological advance is a matter of pure luck, you are not alone, so why did the Solow growth model make this assumption in the first place? First, the model assumes that technological progress is tied to scientific advancements, and at times scientific discoveries seem to happen by chance. One classic example is the invention of Post-it Notes. Researchers at 3M accidentally stumbled onto a formula for glue that made Post-it Notes possible.

Second, this model like most economic models are developed mathematically. Simply put, the assumption of exogenous technological change made the theoretical growth models simpler to solve than an alternative model where technological change is dependent upon multiple factors in the economy.

However, in the 1980s, economists developed other models (or techniques) to help incorporate technological change into the heart of the original model.

The discovery of the glue used for Post-it Notes was accidental. When the notes are used to paper a friend's car, the act is normally premeditated.

PRACTICE WHAT YOU KNOW

Technological Innovations: How Is the Production Function Affected?

When new technology is introduced, it makes capital more productive. For example, modern tractors are faster and more powerful than tractors used a century ago.

This tractor was state-of-the-art technology in 1910.

Question: How does this type of change affect the production function?

Answer: The production function gets steeper at each point. For example, when the level of capital is K, the slope of production function F_2 is steeper than the slope of F_1. The reason is that capital is now more productive at every level. The first unit of capital adds more to output than before, and the 500th unit of capital adds more to output than before. The marginal product of capital, which is embedded in the slope of the production function, is now higher at all levels.

ECONOMICS IN THE MEDIA

Technological Change

Modern Marvels

Modern Marvels is a television series on the History Channel. It often showcases technological innovations that have revolutionized the way goods and services are produced. In Season 13, an episode titled "Harvesters 2" included a look at cranberry harvesting around the globe.

Cranberries are grown on low-lying vines. In the past, cranberry harvesting involved many workers carefully hand-harvesting the berries. But cranberries also have air pockets inside them, and these pockets enable farmers to employ a wet harvest. The big innovation in harvesting occurred when farmers began flooding the fields and then knocking the cranberries off the bushes with water-reel harvesters called beaters. This innovation meant that just a few workers could harvest 10 acres of cranberries in a single day, saving hundreds of hours of labor.

The beaters make the harvest go quickly, but they also tend to damage some of the berries. Recently, Habelman Brothers, a cranberry farm in Tomah, Wisconsin, began using a gentler method than the water-reel so as not to damage the cranberries. Their harvesters use waterwheels with wooden panels to

Cranberries don't grow in water, but they float to the top when farmers flood the fields.

knock the berries off the vines, damaging fewer berries in the process.

These two innovations—water harvesting and the new, gentler waterwheel—are both examples of innovations caused by incentives. The first innovation cut harvesting costs significantly, and the second increased the return from the harvest. The innovators are the farmers—those who have the most to gain. Technology is not random; it is a result of individuals responding to incentives. ✳

Incentives

Policy Implications of the Solow Model

At the beginning of this chapter, we noted that macroeconomic theory has strong implications for policy; it translates into policy recommendations. So what were the policy prescriptions that followed from the Solow growth model? Proponents of this model saw a straightforward relationship where wealth comes from capital and modern technology. For nations to develop they needed the latest technology embedded in capital goods, and wealthy nations and individuals around the globe could help poor nations with aid so they can purchase the latest capital.

Two specific types of aid developed during the 1950s and 1960s to implement this approach. First, actual capital goods were built with aid from developed nations. For example, in 1964, with funding from the United States, Great Britain, and the World Bank, the Akosombo Dam was built in the West

African nation of Ghana to create hydroelectric power and form a lake that could be used for water transportation and a fishing industry.

Second, international aid was sent directly to developing nations to help them fund investment in infrastructure such as highways, bridges, and modern ports, as well as other types of capital. These aid payments were intended to help poor nations build capital infrastructure that would pave the way to economic growth.

While there were of course some successes with both attempts, many economists and policy makers are largely discouraged by these attempts. For example, in Ghana forty-six years after the dam was completed, average income levels in Ghana have risen by just $300 per person, and this is not an isolated story. Similarly, even after billions of dollars in aid, nations such as Zimbabwe, Liberia, Nicaragua, and Haiti are just as poor today as they were in 1960. In contrast, Taiwan, Chile, China, and India received almost no international aid and have grown rapidly.

Clearly, the application of the Solow model via growth policy was not always successful. In fact, most of the twentieth century witnessed policies based on incomplete growth theory that resulted in very few success stories and a series of failures. Consider Africa, where policies based on Solow growth models were applied consistently. Solow's growth model was developed in 1956. Thirty-seven African nations achieved independence from 1956 to 1977, so these newly independent and poverty-stricken nations offered a unique opportunity to apply the Solow model. Yet now, half a century later, it is clear that these policies failed across the continent, as many African nations are no better off now than they were 50 years ago, even while much of the rest of the globe has experienced significant economic gains. These real-world observations led to a reexamination of growth theory in the late twentieth century.

Why Are Institutions the Key to Economic Growth?

Endogenous growth is growth driven by factors inside the economy.

Over the past 20 years, a resurgence in growth theory has been spurred by the belief that some economies grow faster *for reasons particular to those economies*. In some nations, and even in pockets within nations, technological advances arrive more rapidly. Growth is sustained through technological innovation, but these innovations do not occur randomly. Rather, economic growth is endogenous. **Endogenous growth** is growth driven by factors inside the economy. There must be some reason that assembly lines, sewing machines, air conditioning, personal computers, and the Internet were all developed in the United States. These advances spurred economic growth and improved people's lives. Why did they all occur here? Modern growth theory seeks to understand why such innovations occur in one place and not another.

Today, many economists stress the importance of institutions as a key factor in economic growth. We introduced institutions in Chapter 24. In this section, we will examine ideas behind this thinking.

Endogenous growth originates inside an economy, as it does inside an organism.

The Role of Institutions

Consider the city of Nogales, which straddles the border of the United States (in Arizona) and Mexico. Average income in the northern half of the city is three times that in the southern half. The education level on the northern side is much higher, the roads are much better, and infant mortality much lower. The two halves of the city have the same geography, ethnicity, and weather, so why are they so different? According to economist Daron Acemoglu, who wrote about the city in *Esquire* magazine in 2009:

> The key difference is that those on the north side of the border enjoy law and order and dependable government services—they can go about their daily activities and jobs without fear for their life or safety or property rights. On the other side, the inhabitants have *institutions* that perpetuate crime, graft, and insecurity. [emphasis added]

In other words, Acemoglu and many other economists feel that institutions are the final ingredient in the list of factors that affect economic growth. Recall from Chapter 24 that institutions are significant practices, relationships, or organizations in society that frame the incentive structure within which individuals and business firms act. Institutions are the rules of the game, both formal and informal, framing the environment within which production takes place. They help determine the costs and benefits of production. Table 25.2 lists the institutions that are important for growth.

If we include institutions in the aggregate production function, we have

(Equation 25.4) $Y = A \times F(\text{physical capital, human capital, natural resources, } \mathbf{institutions})$

Certain institutions lay the groundwork for natural endogenous growth. With these institutions in place, there are incentives for new technology to emerge and drive growth.

Incentives

Figure 25.7 shows how institutions can affect the production function, causing it to rise from F_1 to F_2. Consider the shift toward private property rights that has occurred in China since the 1980s. As we discussed in Chapter 24, the shift toward private property rights changed incentives for producers, who now get to keep much of their output. This change is behind the exploding growth we now see in China.

Today, most modern growth theory builds on the Solow model, and the aggregate production function is still the core of all growth theory. Resources and technology are also considered important contributors to economic

TABLE 25.2
Institutions That Foster Economic Growth

1. Political stability and the rule of law	5. The flow of funds across borders
2. Private property rights	6. Efficient taxes
3. Competitive markets	7. Stable money and prices
4. International trade	

FIGURE 25.7

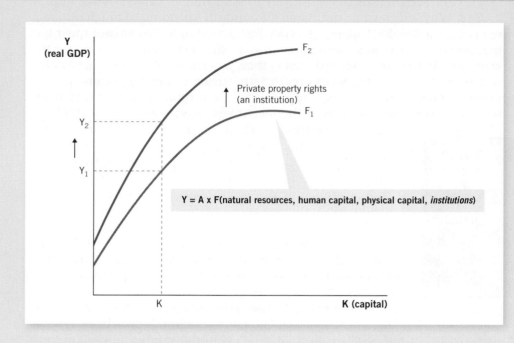

Efficient Institutions and the Production Function

The adoption of efficient institutions shifts a nation's production function upward. Efficient institutions (such as private property rights, shown here) make it possible for nations to produce more with any given level of resources, and they increase incentives for technological innovation.

growth. However, many modern growth economists are focusing more and more on strong institutions as the key to a complicated puzzle.

Institutions Determine Incentives

As you know by now, GDP is production. To determine what leads to endogenous economic growth, we need to consider how institutions affect production decisions, to keep it simple and focus on an individual firm's decision to produce. Imagine that you are considering whether to open a new website design business. You decide that you will start such a business only if you expect to at least break even—that is, your payoff must cover your costs. We can state this common condition as follows:

Incentives

Voluntary investment and production occurs only if *expected payoff ≥ costs.*

The payoffs come later than the costs and are uncertain, which is why we call them *expected payoffs.*

No matter what your output—website design, college gear, cupcakes, or tractors—the payoffs come after production and after sales. The exact time lag depends on the type of output, but the payoffs from all output come sometime after the expenditures on resources. Because of the delay and the resources required, firms need to believe that the sacrifice, patience, and effort will offer a real payoff in the future.

Institutions make a difference: this is how Shanghai, the financial capital of China, looked in 1990 . . .

Or consider your decision to invest in your human capital by attending college. Why are you and your family voluntarily spending so much of your resources on the development of your human capital? The answer must be that you expect the return to be greater than the cost. That is, you expect to gain more from your college education than you pay for it. And you probably will, even if it takes a few years to realize the greatest monetary returns.

Investment and production occur naturally if future payoffs are significant and predictable—that is, if the incentives for investment and production are strong enough. These incentives are determined by a nation's institutions. For example, if people are allowed to own private property and use it for personal gain, they have strong incentives to use their resources wisely. In contrast, if the government or a group owns property, there is less individual incentive to care for the property. For example, consider how you might care for your dorm room compared to a room in a house that you or your parents own. People are generally less careful with rental property than with their own property, which explains why security deposits are standard policy for rentals.

. . . and this is how Shanghai looked, just 20 years later, in 2010. The difference: institutional changes based on economic incentives for production and growth.

Institutions that foster growth are institutions that create incentives for endogenous or natural growth. In Chapter 24, we saw that the institutions most important for growth include private property rights, political stability

FIGURE 25.8

Institutions, Incentives, and Endogenous Growth

The goal is economic growth, but it all starts with institutions. Institutions provide the incentives that motivate choices made by people in an economy. The right institutions provide incentives for people to invent new technology and to invest in human and physical capital. These actions lead to economic growth.

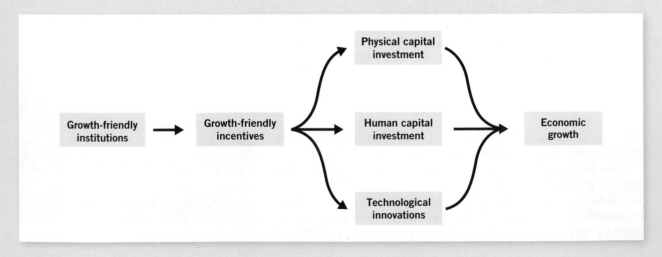

FIGURE 25.9

Institutions That Inhibit Endogenous Growth

People must work and invest today in order to get payoffs from output in the future. Inefficient institutions (such as political instability, corruption, inflation, and high tax rates) reduce the expected future payoffs and thus reduce the incentives for production. Growth-fostering institutions are those that maximize expected future payoffs for producers.

and the rule of law, competitive and open markets, the flow of funds across borders, efficient taxes, and stable money and prices (see Table 25.2). These institutions create incentives for technological innovation and investments in both human and physical capital. Figure 25.8 illustrates this relationship between institutions and economic growth. Institutions create incentives for production and investment. If the right incentives are in place, production and investment occur naturally, and the result is more human capital, more physical capital, and technological advancement—all of which lead to economic growth.

As Acemoglu found in Nogales, institutions can also act to reduce expected payoffs, like corruption, political instability, high and variable inflation, and high tax rates. One of the keys to sustained growth is to eliminate these barriers to natural growth. Figure 25.9 illustrates how inefficient institutions can impede growth. Because payoffs from productive actions come in the future, anything that reduces the likelihood of these payoffs reduces the incentive for investment today.

We can now understand why we don't see convergence across all economies: different institutions lead to different rates of growth. Resources and technology are not enough. Nations grow faster when they have more efficient institutions. Others grow slowly because they don't. Unless institutions are the same across nations, we should not expect to see convergence.

Modern growth theory acknowledges the core truths of the Solow model: resources and technology are sources of economic growth. But it also recognizes the importance of institutions. This emphasis on institutions matters for policy. For example, international aid, even aid that is invested in capital goods, cannot lead to growth if corruption and political instability are rampant in the recipient nation. Institutions are the key ingredient to long-run growth.

ECONOMICS IN THE REAL WORLD

Chile: A Modern Growth Miracle

Several nations, after struggling for centuries with little economic growth, have recently begun to grow at impressive rates. The best-known examples are China and India. Not as well known is the recent economic growth in Chile, a country that saw growth even while being ruled by a harsh military dictator.

Since 1985, the growth of real per capita GDP in Chile has averaged 4.3%. The rule of 70 (see Chapter 24) tells us that it takes approximately 16 years to double living standards at that rate. In fact, real GDP for Chile rose from $7,709 per person to over $20,000 per person in the 23 years from 1985 to 2008. You can see this increase in the real per capita GDP shown in panel (a) of Figure 25.10. This is quite a change from Chile's past experience. Chile grew by less than 1% a year from 1900 to 1985.

As we have seen, economic growth means that many lives change for the better. One vivid indicator of these changes is life expectancy. Panel (b) of Figure 25.10 shows that life expectancy in Chile increased from 57 years in 1960 to 78 years by 2009. This increase of 21 years in average life span moved Chile ahead of many of its Latin American neighbors.

What is the cause of Chile's growth? In a word—institutions. In 1973, Chile began significant economic reforms. In addition to lowering trade barriers and instituting monetary and price stability (inflation was 665% in 1974), the government privatized many state-owned businesses and removed controls on wages and prices. These institutional reforms paved the way for the historic economic growth happening now in Chile. ✳

Chile's recent growth is as breathtaking as the view of Santiago, its capital city.

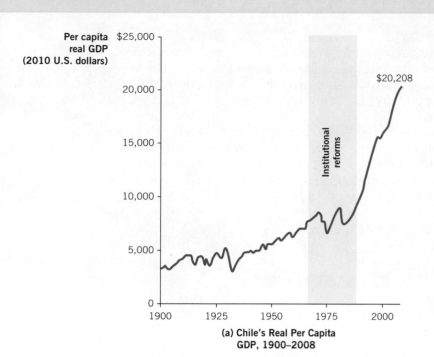

(a) Chile's Real Per Capita GDP, 1900–2008

(b) Life Expectancy, 1960–2009

FIGURE 25.10

Economic Growth and Life Expectancy in Chile

Institutional reforms in Chile have led to historic economic growth, which has helped the people of Chile in many ways. One clear improvement is the increase in life expectancy.

Source: (a) Angus Maddison, *Statistics on World Population, GDP and Per Capita GDP, 1–2008 AD*. All figures converted to 2010 dollars. (b) Gapminder.org.

Institutions and Growth

The three sources of economic growth are resources, technology, and institutions. Institutions provide the framework within which production and work decisions are made. Efficient institutions provide the necessary foundation for natural endogenous growth, leading to better uses of resources and maximizing the incentives for technological innovations.

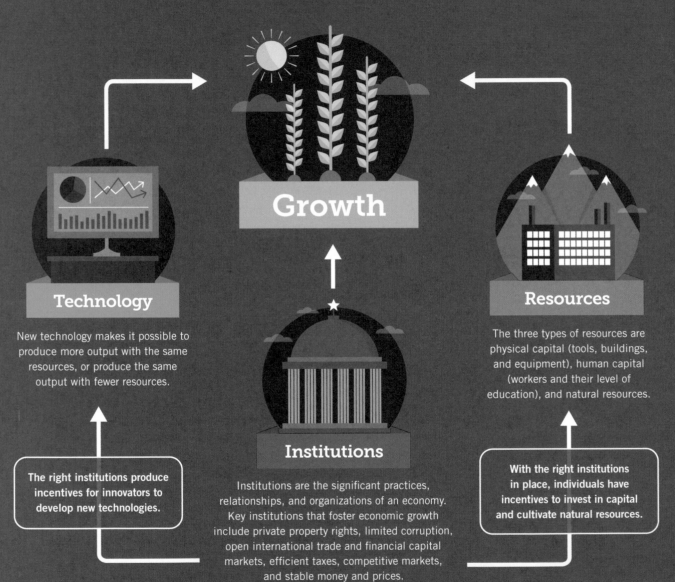

Growth

Technology

New technology makes it possible to produce more output with the same resources, or produce the same output with fewer resources.

The right institutions produce incentives for innovators to develop new technologies.

Institutions

Institutions are the significant practices, relationships, and organizations of an economy. Key institutions that foster economic growth include private property rights, limited corruption, open international trade and financial capital markets, efficient taxes, competitive markets, and stable money and prices.

Resources

The three types of resources are physical capital (tools, buildings, and equipment), human capital (workers and their level of education), and natural resources.

With the right institutions in place, individuals have incentives to invest in capital and cultivate natural resources.

REVIEW QUESTIONS

- How does private property ownership (versus government ownership) affect the incentives for productive use of resources?

- How does technological progress aid resources to promote growth?

PRACTICE WHAT YOU KNOW

Solow Growth Theory versus Modern Growth Theory: What Policy Is Implied?

Question: Below is a list of policy proposals that have been advanced to help the economies of developing nations. Determine whether each proposal is consistent with the Solow model, modern growth theory, neither, or both.

a. unrestricted international aid to help build a power plant

b. aid for a power plant that is dependent on democratic reforms

c. reductions in trade restrictions

Answer:

a. This policy proposal is consistent with the Solow model: physical capital leads to growth.

b. This policy proposal is consistent with both Solow and modern growth theory. The power plant is physical capital, but the aid is dependent on institutional reform.

c. This policy proposal is consistent with modern growth theory. Open trade is institutional reform that leads to greater competition and more options for citizens in developing nations.

This cargo ship brings goods from Asia to the United States. Which growth model would encourage this kind of international trade?

Institutions of Growth: Applying for a Patent

The late Apple CEO Steve Jobs is famous for having his name on well over 300 different patents. In other words, Jobs is credited with participation in 300 new inventions. Inventions are technological innovations, which we've seen are a source of economic growth.

Patent laws are an important institution that has helped to pave the way for many technological advancements. Patents create a 20-year monopoly for the inventor or owner of the patent. This monopoly is an incentive that encourages innovation. Patent laws are thus an institution that encourages new inventions that shift the economy's production function upward.

If you have an idea that you'd like to patent, you need to apply for your patent through the U.S. Patent Office. In addition to a detailed description of your patent, you'll need to create a drawing that specifies exactly how your idea is new and different. Finally, it is a good idea to hire a patent attorney to edit your patent application so you can reduce the chances that someone will copy your idea later.

Steve Jobs was one of the great innovators.

Even if you don't have the resources to capitalize on your invention, you can always try to sell your patent to someone who can.

You may not be as successful as Steve Jobs, but you can be sure that patents are a legal way to make monopoly profit.

Conclusion

We opened this chapter with the misconception that physical capital is the essential ingredient for economic growth. We have seen that while capital is helpful, physical tools are not enough to ensure long-run growth. The same applies to other resources and technology. Without institutions that promote the incentive to produce, sustained endogenous growth does not take root.

Many people think that macroeconomics is all about business cycles and recessions. Our goal in this chapter has been to present the ideas behind long-run growth theory, rather than short-run cycles. In Chapter 26, we present a model that economists use to study short-run business cycles.

ANSWERING THE BIG QUESTIONS

How do macroeconomic theories evolve?

* Macroeconomic theories evolve in relationship to observations in the real world. Policies often follow from theory. Policies produce results, which in turn influence revisions of economic theory.

What is the Solow growth model?

* The Solow growth model is a model of economic growth based on a production function for the economy.
* The key feature of the production function is diminishing returns.
* The Solow growth model posits that diminishing returns lead economies toward a zero-growth steady state.
* The Solow growth model further posits that given steady states, economies tend to converge over time.

How does technology affect growth?

* Technology is a source of sustained economic growth.
* In the Solow model, technology is exogenous.

Why are institutions the key to economic growth?

* Modern growth theory emphasizes institutions as the key source of economic growth.
* Institutions determine incentives for production.
* Efficient institutions can lead to endogenous growth.

CONCEPTS YOU SHOULD KNOW

aggregate production function (p. 795)
convergence (p. 803)
depreciation (p. 801)

diminishing marginal product (p. 797)
endogenous growth (p. 809)
exogenous growth (p. 806)

marginal product (p. 797)
net investment (p. 801)
production function (p. 794)
steady state (p. 801)

QUESTIONS FOR REVIEW

1. Modern economic theory points to three sources of economic growth. What are these three sources? Give an example of each.

2. About 50 years ago, Robert Solow formulated a simple model of economic growth. What are the two key properties of the aggregate production function at the center of Solow's first contribution?

3. Explain why a nation cannot continue to grow forever by just adding more capital.

4. The Solow model assumes that technological changes are exogenous. What does the term "exogenous" mean? Why does the assumption of exogenous technological change matter for growth policy? What does this assumption imply about growth rates across nations over time?

5. China is a land of vast resources. In addition, technology is easily transportable across international borders. If we rule out these two sources of growth, to what can we attribute the economic growth in China since 1979?

6. The basic Solow growth model implies convergence. What is convergence? What key assumption about the marginal product of capital implies convergence?

7. How can an increase in educational opportunities increase growth? Use a graph to illustrate how educational opportunities affect a nation's production function.

8. Robert Solow formulated a model that still serves as the basis for growth theory.
   a. What is the steady state of an economy, and what key piece of the Solow model implies that the steady state is an inevitable outcome?
   b. Explain the concept of convergence in growth theory. What has been the general experience with regard to convergence across the globe in the years since the Solow papers were published?

9. Modern growth theory still uses the basic Solow production function as a starting point, but the emphasis is much different.
   a. What is the key theoretical distinction between modern growth theory and the Solow growth models?
   b. How does this one difference affect policy recommendations?

STUDY PROBLEMS (*solved at the end of the section*)

1. The Solow model focuses on how resources affect output. In this chapter, we focused on capital.
   a. Name the other two major categories of resources.
   b. Draw an aggregate production function with a typical shape; label this function F.
   c. Draw a second production function that indicates a technological advancement; label this new function F_1.

2. Define human capital. Draw a graph that illustrates an increase in effective labor on a production function.

3. Suppose the people in the United States increase their savings rate. How will this change affect the rate of economic growth in the United States?

✳ **4.** Economic growth derives from many sources. Some of these cause a parallel shift in a nation's production function, while others change the slope of the production function. Below is a graph of three different production functions: F_1, F_2, and F_3. Assume that a nation begins with production function F_1. Production function F_2 is a parallel shift upward from F_1. In contrast, F_3 is an increase in the slope from F_1.

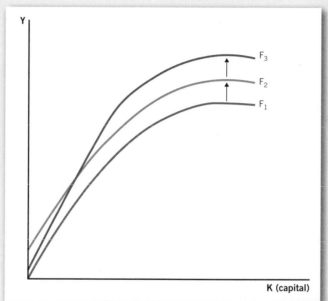

For each of the following scenarios, determine which of the two new production functions, F_2 or F_3, better illustrates how the scenario would affect production.
a. Human capital rises through education.
b. Technological advancement occurs.
c. New natural gas reserves are found.

✳ **5.** The Solow model is still at the core of all modern growth theory.
a. Draw an aggregate production function for a hypothetical nation. Draw the production function as we do in this chapter, with an emphasis on the capital resource. Label both axes and label your production function F_0.
b. Suppose several million new workers enter the nation. Show this change on your graph in part (a), carefully distinguishing the new situation from the old. If you have a new production function, label it F_1.
c. Now suppose the nation invests in new capital, increasing the total capital stock in the nation. Show this change on your graph in part (b), carefully distinguishing the new situation from the old.

✳ **6.** The following list describes policy proposals that have been advanced to help the economies of developing nations. Determine whether each proposal is consistent with the Solow model, modern growth theory, both, or neither. For each proposal, indicate the corresponding theory with the following notation: S for Solow, M for modern growth theory, B for both, or N for neither.
a. microfinance (very small short-term loans for small businesses)
b. a system of private property rights
c. international governmental loans to build a shoe factory
d. international aid for a power plant based on objective corruption controls
e. unrestricted international aid to build roads
f. low tax rates

SOLVED PROBLEMS

4.a. The shift would be to F_2, because it represents more output at all levels of capital.

b. The shift would be to F_3, because the marginal product of capital increases.

c. The shift would be to F_2, because it represents more output at all levels of capital.

5.a. The key here is to label the graph correctly and have a declining slope.

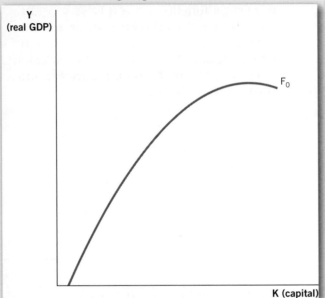

b. The key here is to shift the graph upward in a parallel fashion. More workers mean more total output because the nation now has more resources.

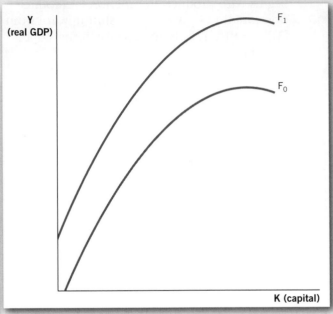

c. The key here is that there is a movement along a given production function, from K_0 to K_1.

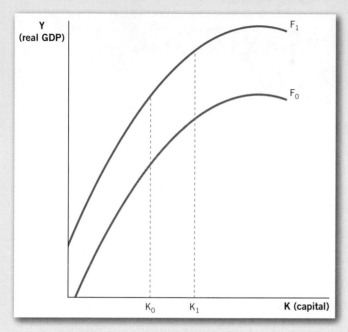

6.a. N or M: Microfinance loans might help small businesses, and it is possible that the introduction of microfinance could be considered an institutional change. However, if other political and economic institutions are not conducive to growth, microfinance will not be enough.

b. M: Private property rights are an institution that has been shown to foster growth but would not have been relevant before institutions were incorporated into modern growth theory.

c. S: Loans for capital development are a direct policy proposal from the Solow growth model.

d. B: Here the focus is on capital *along with* institutional changes.

e. S: Here the emphasis is solely on capital.

f. M: Low tax rates are an institution focused on growth.

The Aggregate Demand–Aggregate Supply Model

Recessions are inevitable and occur every few years.

Many people believe that every few years the economy plunges into a recession and then, after a short period of slow growth, rebounds for a

MIS CONCEPTION

period of expansion. They consider this pattern to be inevitable, with recessions happening every six to eight years.

The term "business cycle" is a popular way to describe the recession-expansion phenomenon because so many people are convinced that the recession-expansion pattern occurs in a regular cycle.

But, in fact, recessions are rarer today than at any other time in our nation's history: while there have been 22 U.S. recessions since 1900, just three occurred after 1982. In addition, no two recessions are exactly alike in either cause or effect.

If you came to macroeconomics with a desire to learn more about recessions and their causes, this is the chapter for you. Chapters 24 and 25 focused on long-run economic growth. In this chapter and the next, we focus on short-run fluctuations in the macroeconomy. We begin by building a model of the economy that we can use to consider the causes of business cycle fluctuations. In this chapter 26, we'll examine historical events in the context of the model and also consider some of the major debates in macroeconomics, which can be framed in terms of our short-run model.

Worldwide recession from 2007 to 2009 left many economic resources underutilized, like these unoccupied homes in Spain.

BIG QUESTIONS

* What is the aggregate demand–aggregate supply model?
* What is aggregate demand?
* What is aggregate supply?
* How does the aggregate demand–aggregate supply model help us understand the economy?

What Is the Aggregate Demand–Aggregate Supply Model?

In macroeconomics, there are two major paths of study. One direction explores long-run growth and development. The second direction examines short-run fluctuations, or business cycles. The two paths are complementary: both study GDP growth, employment, and the people, firms, and governments that impact the economy. But the paths are also different. Growth economics focuses on longer time horizons—say, five to ten years or more. Business cycle theory typically focuses on time horizons of five years or less.

In Chapter 19, we presented the idea of a basic business cycle, in which real GDP increases for a while during the expansionary phase and then decreases during the contractionary, or recessionary, phase. The business cycle is most evident in real GDP growth and unemployment rates. During recessions, real GDP growth slows and the unemployment rate rises. During expansions, real GDP growth expands and the unemployment rate falls.

Panel (a) of Figure 26.1 shows real GDP growth rates by quarter for the United States from 1990 to 2015. The blue vertical bars indicate the three recessions during this period. During each recession, real GDP growth slowed and even turned negative. The fourth quarter of 2008 registered −8.9% growth, making it the worst quarter since 1958. Panel (b) plots the unemployment rate over the same period. The unemployment rate rose sharply during each of the recessions and then slowly fell afterward. The highest unemployment rate during this period was 10% in October 2009.

The model we use to study business cycles is the aggregate demand–aggregate supply model. At the core of the model are the concepts of demand and supply, which are already familiar to you. In earlier chapters, we looked at the demand and supply of a single good, like savings. But now we look at the demand and supply of all final goods and services in an economy—the demand for and supply of GDP. **Aggregate demand** is the total demand for final goods and services in an economy. **Aggregate supply** is the total supply of final goods and services in an economy. The word "aggregate" means total.

Aggregate demand is the total demand for final goods and services in an economy.

Aggregate supply is the total supply of final goods and services in an economy.

We consider each side of the economy separately before bringing them together. The next section explains aggregate demand; after that, we look at aggregate supply.

What Is Aggregate Demand?

We have an experiment for you to try. Ask five people the following question: *How can you personally help our economy?* We predict that most responses will focus on buying something or spending money somewhere. In our model of the economy, this is demand. Aggregate demand is the spending side of the economy. When people spend on goods and services, aggregate demand

FIGURE 26.1

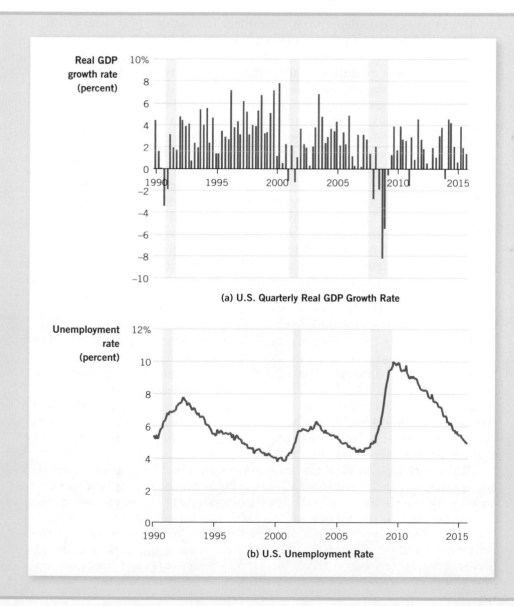

(a) U.S. Quarterly Real GDP Growth Rate

(b) U.S. Unemployment Rate

U.S. Real GDP Growth, Unemployment Rates, and Recessions, 1990–2015

Business cycles are readily observable in real GDP growth and unemployment rates. Panel (a) shows that quarterly real GDP growth often declines during recessionary periods. Panel (b) shows how the unemployment rate spikes during recessions, then gradually falls as the economy expands.

Sources: (a) U.S. Bureau of Economic Analysis; (b) U.S. Bureau of Labor Statistics.

increases, and most people believe that this spending is what drives the economy. We'll see later that this is only partially true.

To determine aggregate demand, we sum up spending from different sources in the economy. These sources include private domestic consumers who buy cars, food, clothing, education, and many other goods and services. Business firms are another major group; they buy resources needed to produce output. The government is a large purchaser of labor and other resources used to produce government services. Finally, foreign consumers buy many goods and services produced in the United States. These four major groups constitute the four pieces of aggregate demand: consumption (C), investment (I), government spending (G), and net exports (NX). The total of these four yields aggregate demand (AD) in a given period:

(Equation 26.1)
$$AD = C + I + G + NX$$

As we study aggregate demand, we consider factors that affect each of these sources. (For a review of C, I, G, and NX, see Chapter 19.)

Figure 26.2 shows a graph of the aggregate demand curve. On the horizontal axis, we plot quantities of all final goods and services, which constitute real GDP. On the vertical axis, we measure the overall price level (P) in the economy. This is not the price of any particular good or service, but rather a general level of prices for the whole economy. Because we are looking at all final goods and services, the correct price index to use is the GDP deflator (see Chapter 19). The GDP deflator is set at 100 in a particular period of time and then fluctuates from that level. A rise in P indicates inflation in the economy.

On the graph in Figure 26.2, we have labeled a particular point where the price level is 100 and the quantity of aggregate demand is $18 trillion, which was the size of the U.S. economy in 2015. The negative slope of the aggregate demand curve means that increases in the price level lead to decreases in the quantity of aggregate demand. Similarly, when the price level falls, the quantity of aggregate demand rises. But be careful here: aggregate demand does not slope downward for the same reason that individual demand curves

FIGURE 26.2

The Aggregate Demand Curve

The aggregate demand curve shows the negative relationship between the quantity demanded of real GDP and the economy's price level (P).

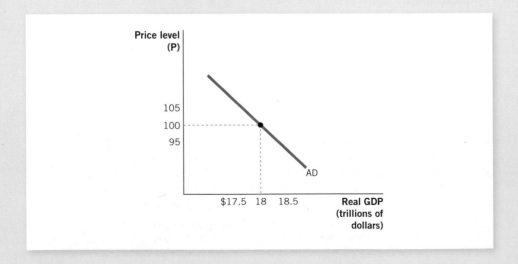

slope downward. In the case of a particular good, an increase in price leads consumers to substitute out of consumption for that good and into consumption for other goods. But the aggregate demand curve indicates demand for all goods and services in an economy, so there is no corresponding substitution effect. In the next section, we explain the reasons for the negative slope.

The Slope of the Aggregate Demand Curve

All else being equal, increases in the economy's price level lead to decreases in the quantity of aggregate demand. You might agree with this statement without closely evaluating it, because it sounds like the relationship between the quantity demanded of a single good and its price. But now we are evaluating the whole economy. Remember that the price level is the general price level of all final goods and services. Aggregate demand and aggregate supply don't just measure the quantity of pizzas demanded and supplied; they measure the production of all the firms in all the markets that constitute the economy. Therefore, substitutions from one market to another have no effect on the total amount of output, or real GDP. Substituting out of pizza and into chicken nuggets doesn't change GDP.

There are three reasons for this negative relationship between the quantity of aggregate demand and the price level: the wealth effect, the interest rate effect, and the international trade effect.

The Wealth Effect

If you wake up tomorrow morning and all prices have suddenly doubled, you'll be poorer, in real terms, than you are today. Your consumption will fall because your wealth has fallen. **Wealth** is the net value of one's accumulated assets. Your wealth is the total net value of everything you own, including the money in your wallet and in your bank accounts. The **wealth effect** is the change in the quantity of aggregate demand that results from wealth changes due to price-level changes.

For example, if you and your friends have $60 to buy pizza, you can afford to buy four $15 pizzas. But if inflation causes the price of a pizza to rise to $20, you can afford only three pizzas. Similarly, a rise in prices all over the economy reduces real wealth in the economy, and then the quantity of aggregate demand falls. In contrast, if prices fall, real wealth increases, and then the quantity of aggregate demand also increases.

The Interest Rate Effect

If the price level rises and real wealth falls, people also save less. Therefore, in addition to the wealth effect, an increase in the price level affects people's savings. Let's say that you are on a budget that allows you to buy groceries and save a little each month. If the price level rises, you'll probably cut back on both areas. When you spend less on groceries, your actions are reflecting the wealth effect. When you cut back on savings, your action leads to the interest rate effect. The **interest rate effect** occurs when a change in the price level leads to a change in interest rates and therefore in the quantity of aggregate demand. Remember that every dollar borrowed requires

Wealth is the net value of one's accumulated assets.

The **wealth effect** is the change in the quantity of aggregate demand that results from wealth changes due to price-level changes.

The **interest rate effect** occurs when a change in the price level leads to a change in interest rates and therefore in the quantity of aggregate demand.

If you hold money as part of your wealth, the price level affects its real value.

a dollar saved. Therefore, when savings declines, the quantity of investment must also decline, which affects aggregate demand.

Figure 26.3 shows the loanable funds market before and after a decrease in savings. Initially, the demand and supply of loanable funds are indicated by curves D and S_1, and the equilibrium interest rate is 5%. If the economy's price level rises, people save less, which shifts supply to S_2. The reduction in supply leads to a higher interest rate of 6%, at which point the quantity of investment falls from I_1 to I_2. Because investment is one piece of aggregate demand, a decrease in investment decreases overall aggregate demand. Thus, a change in the price level initiates a cascade of events with the result that firms invest less at higher interest rates because individuals are saving less.

The **international trade effect** occurs when a change in the price level leads to a change in the quantity of net exports demanded.

The International Trade Effect

In our model, the price level and real GDP represent the domestic market. In the context of the world economy, we must also consider the prices of goods from the United States *relative to* the prices of goods from other countries. When the U.S. price level rises, all else being equal, U.S. goods are relatively more expensive than goods from other countries, and the quantity demanded of U.S. goods falls. The **international trade effect** occurs when a change in the price level leads to a change in the quantity of net exports demanded.

Jeep Wrangler: produced in Toledo, Ohio.

Consider two similar sport utility vehicles: a Jeep Wrangler and a Toyota 4Runner. The Jeep is produced in the United States in Toledo, Ohio. The Toyota is produced in a suburb of Tahara, Aichi, Japan. When the prices of U.S. goods rise relative to the prices of Japanese goods, consumers are more likely to choose the Toyota, so U.S. exports fall and imports rise.

FIGURE 26.3

The Interest Rate Effect in the Loanable Funds Market

If the economy's price level rises, people save less. The decline in savings from S_1 to S_2 leads to an increase in the interest rate from 5% to 6%. At this higher interest rate, the quantity of investment falls from I_1 to I_2 because investment is more costly. Because investment is a component of aggregate demand, a fall in equilibrium investment that occurs with a rise in price level causes the quantity of aggregate demand to fall.

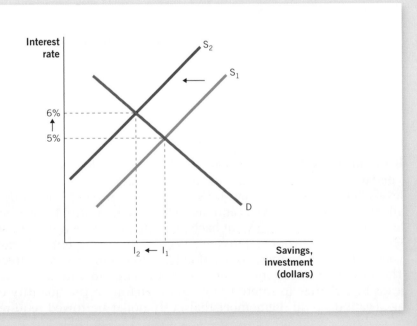

Figure 26.4 shows how the wealth effect, the interest rate effect, and the international trade effect work together to influence the quantity of aggregate demand. Each effect begins with a change in the economy's price level. When the price level rises from 100 to 110, consumption (C) declines from the wealth effect, investment (I) declines via the interest rate effect, and net exports (NX) fall due to the international trade effect. In reality, the three effects do not influence aggregate demand equally. The international trade effect is relatively small because exports are a relatively small part of GDP. Because consumption is by far the largest component of GDP, the wealth effect is the most significant.

Toyota 4Runner: produced in Tahara, Aichi, Japan.

It is important to distinguish between *shifts in* the aggregate demand curve versus *movements along* the aggregate demand curve. In this section, we have identified three effects related to movements along the aggregate demand curve. These three effects originate with a change in the economy's price level. In contrast, shifts in the demand curve occur when people demand more goods and services at a given price level. These shifts can come from any of the components of aggregate demand: consumption, investment, government spending, or net exports. In the next section, we look at four factors that shift aggregate demand.

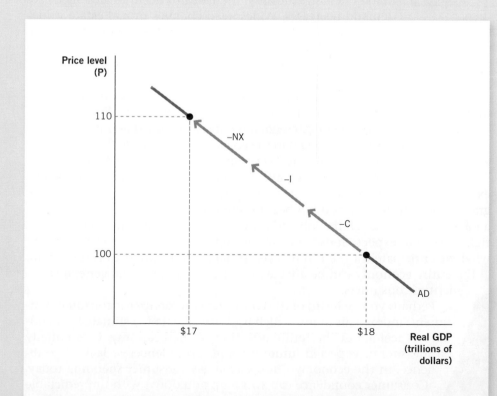

FIGURE 26.4

The Slope of the Aggregate Demand Curve

When the price level rises, the quantity of aggregate demand falls. This negative relationship is due to three different effects: (1) the wealth effect implies a lower quantity of consumption (C) demand because real wealth falls at higher price levels; (2) the interest rate effect implies a lower quantity of investment (I) demand due to higher interest rates; (3) the international trade effect implies a lower quantity of net export (NX) demand due to relatively higher domestic prices. Each effect focuses on a different component of aggregate demand.

Shifts in Aggregate Demand

When people demand more goods and services at all price levels, aggregate demand increases and the AD curve shifts to the right. When people demand fewer goods and services at all price levels, aggregate demand decreases and the AD curve shifts to the left.

In thinking about the many factors that shift aggregate demand, it is helpful to categorize them into the different types of aggregate demand spending: consumption (C), investment (I), government spending (G), and net exports (NX). We begin with factors that cause changes in consumption spending.

Shifts in Consumption

One determinant of people's spending habits is their current wealth. If your great-aunt died and left you $1 million, you'd increase your consumption spending: you'd eat out more often, upgrade your wardrobe, and maybe even shop for some bigger-ticket items. This observation also applies to entire nations. When national wealth increases, the consumption component of aggregate demand increases. When wealth falls, consumption declines.

Median home prices fell from $248,000 to $222,000 between 2007 and 2010. That roughly 10% drop led to a significant decrease in many people's wealth, as well as a decline in aggregate demand.

For example, many people own stocks or mutual funds that are tied to the stock market. So when the stock market fluctuates, the wealth of a large portion of the population is affected. When overall stock values rise, wealth increases, which increases aggregate demand. However, if the stock market falls significantly, then wealth declines and aggregate demand decreases. Widespread changes in real estate values also affect wealth. Consider that for many people a house represents a large portion of their wealth. When real estate values rise and fall, individual wealth follows, and this outcome affects aggregate demand.

Before moving on, let's be clear that here we are talking about changes in individuals' wealth *not* caused by changes in the price level. When we discussed the slope of the aggregate demand curve, we talked about the wealth effect, which is caused by changes in the economy's price level (P). The wealth effect causes a *movement along* the AD curve, not a shift of the AD curve.

Expected future income also affects consumption spending. If people expect higher income in the future, they spend more today. For example, graduating college seniors often begin spending more as soon as they secure a job offer, even though the job and the corresponding income may not start right away. But expectations aren't always right. We consume today based on what we anticipate for the future, even though the future is uncertain. Still, the entire economy can be affected by just a change in the general sentiment of consumers.

How much income does your future hold?

Perhaps you've heard of the consumer confidence (or consumer sentiment) index. This index, which uses survey data to estimate how consumers feel about the future direction of the economy, is essentially a measure of expected future income. Confidence, or lack of confidence, in the economy's future changes consumer spending today. Consumer confidence can swing up and down with unpredictable events such as national elections or international turmoil. When these sentiments change, they change consumption spending and thus shift aggregate demand.

Changes in Wealth

Dumb and Dumber

In this comedy from 1994, two likable but incredibly simpleminded friends, Harry and Lloyd, try to return a suitcase to its owner. For most of the movie, they have no idea that the suitcase is filled with a million dollars.

When they accidentally open the case while en route to Aspen, Colorado, the friends discover the cash and decide to spend the money freely by writing IOUs and placing them in the suitcase to be repaid later. The newfound money creates a change in Harry and Lloyd's wealth. The two friends immediately enjoy their unexpected wealth by staying at a lavish hotel, giving away $100 bills as tips for the staff, and even using money to wipe their noses when they can't find ordinary tissues to do the job.

What kind of tuxedo would you buy if you had a suitcase full of money?

In one sense, Harry and Lloyd are much like the rest of us. If our wealth increases, our demand for goods and services increases (via the wealth effect). But Harry and Lloyd are dumb and dumber in that their spending is completely based on someone else's wealth.

Finally, taxes also affect consumption spending. When consumers pay lower taxes, they can afford to spend more. When taxes rise, consumers have less to spend. In Chapter 29, we cover the effect of taxes on consumption in greater detail. For now, we note that higher taxes lead to lower consumption and lower aggregate demand.

Shifts in Investment

Investment spending shifts when decision-makers at firms decide to increase or decrease spending on capital goods. One possibility is that investor confidence has changed. Keep in mind that "investors" here are firms that spend on plant and equipment used in future production. If firms decide that the future of their industry or the overall economy is positive, they might decide to purchase capital tools so they can increase production and future profits. On the other hand, a decrease in investor confidence might lead to a decrease in investment and thus a decrease in aggregate demand.

Interest rates also affect investment demand. An increase in interest rates makes investment more expensive for firms, and so aggregate demand decreases. In contrast, lower interest rates decrease the cost of borrowing for firms, which increases the investment component of aggregate demand. While we typically focus on investment effects from interest rate changes, consumption is also affected by changes in interest rates. At lower interest rates, the return to savings falls and so consumers are more likely to spend their income.

Increases in the quantity of money in an economy also increase aggregate demand. All else being equal, more money leads to lower interest rates in the economy. Lower interest rates then mean that firms can borrow more

PRACTICE WHAT YOU KNOW

Textile workers in Nicaragua depend on the export economy as a source of jobs.

Aggregate Demand: Shifts in Aggregate Demand versus Movements along the Aggregate Demand Curve

One of the challenges in applying the aggregate demand–aggregate supply model is distinguishing shifts in aggregate demand from movements along the aggregate demand curve. Here we present four scenarios.

Question: Does each scenario below cause a movement along the curve or a shift in the curve? Explain your response each time.

1. Consumers read positive economic news and then expect strong future economic growth.

2. Due to an increase in the price level in the United States, consumers substitute out of clothes made in the United States and into clothes made in Nicaragua.

3. Several European economies go into recession.

4. A decrease in the price level leads to greater real wealth and more savings, which reduces the interest rate and increases investment.

Answers:

1. This scenario involves an increase in expected future income, which increases aggregate demand and causes a positive (rightward) shift in the curve.

2. This scenario begins with a change in the price level, so we know it will involve a movement along the curve. Here the price level rises, so it is a movement back along the curve, signaling a decrease in the quantity of aggregate demand.

3. Foreign recession leads to lower foreign income and wealth, an outcome that decreases the demand for goods and services made in the United States. Less demand for U.S. products causes a decrease in aggregate demand in the United States, leading to a negative (leftward) shift in the aggregate demand curve.

4. Because this scenario involves a change in the price level, it will lead to a movement along the aggregate demand curve. In this case, the lower prices lead to the interest rate effect and an increase in the quantity of aggregate demand.

cheaply. As a result, investment demand expands. On the other hand, if the money supply decreases, interest rates rise and investment demand falls. This relationship between money and aggregate demand is sometimes more complicated than explained here. For this reason, Chapter 31 is devoted to the effects of money changes on the economy.

Shifts in Government Spending

Government spending is the third component of aggregate demand, and it is the piece that policymakers influence most directly. For example, when federal or state governments increase spending to build a new highway, aggregate demand increases. When government spending falls, aggregate demand decreases. Often, these changes are a result of policy decisions made in direct response to economic conditions. For example, if consumption and investment spending fall, the government may increase spending to counteract the decline in aggregate demand. Chapter 29 covers this topic more extensively.

Shifts in Net Exports

When the income of people in foreign nations grows, their demand for U.S. goods increases. The result is an increase in U.S. net exports, which are the final component of aggregate demand. In contrast, if a foreign nation goes into recession, its demand for U.S. goods and services falls. One recent positive example is the growth of large emerging economies and their demand for U.S. goods. As Brazil, China, and India have grown wealthier, their demand for U.S. goods and services has increased.

Exchange rates are another factor that shifts aggregate demand by changing net exports. We cover exchange rates fully in Chapter 33. For now, think in terms of the value of the dollar in world markets. When the value of the dollar rises relative to the currency of other nations, Americans find that imports are less expensive. At the same time, it becomes more expensive for other nations to buy U.S. exports. These two factors combine to reduce net exports, so a stronger dollar leads to a decline in net exports, which reduces aggregate demand.

Figure 26.5 summarizes the effects of the four factors that shift aggregate demand. On the graph, initial aggregate demand is shown as AD_1. Aggregate demand shifts to the right (to AD_2) with *increases* in consumption, investment, government spending, or net exports. In contrast, aggregate demand shifts to the left (to AD_3) with *decreases* in consumption, investment, government spending, or net exports.

ECONOMICS IN THE REAL WORLD

General Motors Sales Up in China, but Down in Europe

General Motors, one of the world's largest car manufacturers, sold more than 3.5 million vehicles in China in 2014. Sales in China are growing at nearly 10% per year thanks in part to the growing incomes of many Chinese citizens. The GM product line Buick does particularly well in China. Buick now sells about four times as many cars in China as in the United States. In 2014, Buick sold 919,582 cars in China and 228,963 in the United States. ✳

Buick: more popular in China than in the United States.

FIGURE 26.5

Factors That Shift the Aggregate Demand Curve

The aggregate demand curve shifts to the right with *increases* in real wealth, expected income, expected future prices, and foreign income and wealth or with a *decrease* in the value of the dollar. The aggregate demand curve shifts to the left with *decreases* in real wealth, expected income, expected future prices, and foreign income and wealth or with an *increase* in the value of the dollar.

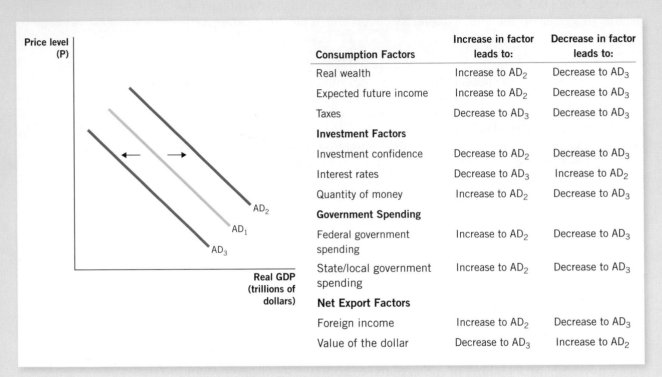

	Increase in factor leads to:	Decrease in factor leads to:
Consumption Factors		
Real wealth	Increase to AD_2	Decrease to AD_3
Expected future income	Increase to AD_2	Decrease to AD_3
Taxes	Decrease to AD_3	Decrease to AD_3
Investment Factors		
Investment confidence	Decrease to AD_2	Decrease to AD_3
Interest rates	Decrease to AD_3	Increase to AD_2
Quantity of money	Increase to AD_2	Decrease to AD_3
Government Spending		
Federal government spending	Increase to AD_2	Decrease to AD_3
State/local government spending	Increase to AD_2	Decrease to AD_3
Net Export Factors		
Foreign income	Increase to AD_2	Decrease to AD_3
Value of the dollar	Decrease to AD_3	Increase to AD_2

What Is Aggregate Supply?

We have seen that aggregate demand embodies the spending desires of an economy. It tells us how many goods and services people want at different price levels. But peoples' wants and desires alone do not determine GDP. We must also consider the supply side of the economy, which tells us about the willingness and ability of producers to supply GDP.

Most of us relate easily to the demand side because we are used to buying things on a daily basis. To understand the supply side of the economy, we need to think from the perspective of those who produce and sell goods and services. For example, imagine you own a coffee shop where you produce drinks such as espressos, lattes, and iced coffee. Your inputs include workers, coffee beans, milk, water, and espresso machines. You buy inputs and combine them in a particular way to produce your output.

Figure 26.6 presents an overview of the basic function of the firm. In the middle is the firm, where inputs are turned into output. The input prices, such as wages and interest rates on loans, help to determine the firm's costs. The output prices, such as the cost of an espresso, determine the firm's revenue.

FIGURE 26.6

The Function of the Firm

The firm uses inputs, or factors of production, to produce its output in a particular way. Input prices, such as wages for workers, affect the firm's costs. Output prices affect the firm's revenue.

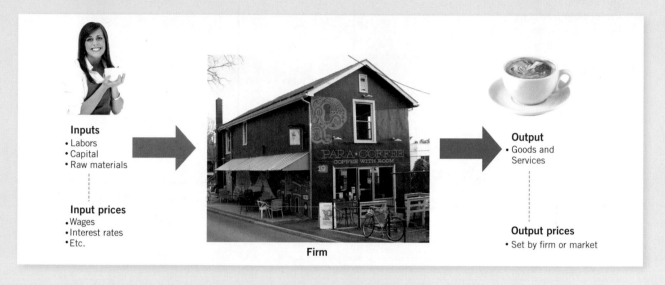

Inputs
• Labors
• Capital
• Raw materials

Input prices
• Wages
• Interest rates
• Etc.

Firm

Output
• Goods and
  Services

Output prices
• Set by firm or market

To understand aggregate supply, we need to consider how changes in the overall price level (P) affect the supply decisions of the firm. But the influence of the price level on aggregate supply depends on the time frame we are considering. The **long run** in macroeconomics is a period of time sufficient for all prices to adjust. The long run doesn't arrive after a set period of time; it arrives when all prices have adjusted. However, in the **short run**, only some prices can change. In macroeconomics, the short run is the period of time in which some prices have not yet adjusted.

In macroeconomics, the **long run** is a period of time sufficient for all prices to adjust.

In macroeconomics, the **short run** is the period of time in which some prices have not yet adjusted.

Long-Run Aggregate Supply

As we've discussed several times in this text, the long-run output of an economy depends on resources, technology, and institutions. In the short run there may be fluctuations in real GDP, but in the long run the economy moves toward full-employment output (Y*). The price level does not affect long-run aggregate supply. Think of it this way: in the long run, the number of paper dollars we exchange for our goods and services does not impact our ability to produce.

Figure 26.7 plots the economy's long-run aggregate supply curve (LRAS). Notice that since we plot LRAS with the economy's price level (P) on the vertical axis and real GDP (Y) on the horizontal axis, long-run aggregate supply is a vertical line at Y*, which is full-employment output. In Chapter 20, we defined full-employment output as the output produced in the economy when unemployment (u) is at the natural rate (u*). This is the output level that is sustainable for the long run in the economy. Because prices don't affect full-employment output, the LRAS curve is a vertical line at Y*. If the

FIGURE 26.7

The Long-Run Aggregate Supply Curve

The LRAS curve is vertical at Y* because in the long run the price level does not affect the quantity of aggregate supply. Y* is full-employment output, where the unemployment rate (u) is equal to the natural rate (u*).

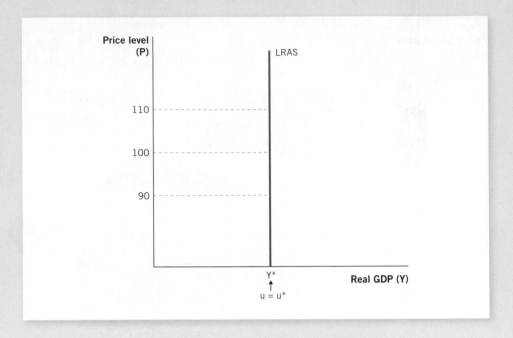

price level is 100, the quantity of aggregate supply is equal to Y*. If the price level rises to 110 or falls to 90, output in the long run is still Y*.

Shifts in Long-Run Aggregate Supply

The long-run aggregate supply curve shifts when there is a long-run change in a nation's ability to produce output, or a change in Y*. The factors that shift long-run aggregate supply are the same factors that determine economic growth: resources, technology, and institutions.

For example, new technology leads to increases in long-run aggregate supply. Consider what would happen if a firm develops safe, effective, and affordable driverless cars that enable people to travel more quickly and free up congestion on the roads. This new technology would lead to an increase in long-run aggregate supply because it would increase productivity in the economy: we would now produce more with our limited resources.

Figure 26.8 illustrates a shift in long-run aggregate supply. Initially, the LRAS curve is vertical at Y*, which depends on resources, technology, and institutions. After the new driverless technology is introduced, $LRAS_1$ shifts to the right (to $LRAS_2$) because now the full-employment output in the economy is greater than before. Notice that both before and after the shift, the unemployment rate is at the natural rate (u*). The new technology does not reduce the unemployment rate, but workers in the economy are more productive. The new output rate, Y**, is designated with two asterisks because it represents a new full-employment output rate.

If driverless cars improve traffic conditions and allow people to enjoy work or leisure during their commute, the economy's LRAS curve will shift to the right.

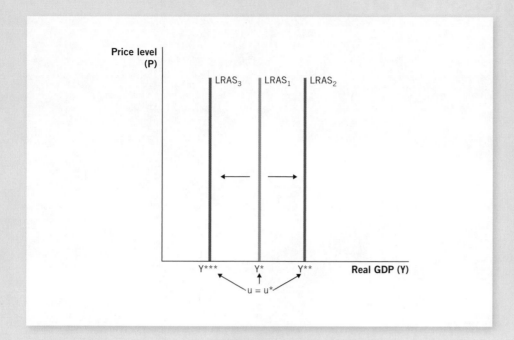

FIGURE 26.8

Shifts in Long-Run Aggregate Supply

Shifts in the long-run aggregate supply curve occur when there is a change in an economy's resources, technology, or institutions. A technological advance moves an economy from $LRAS_1$ to $LRAS_2$. This is a picture of economic growth. When the LRAS curve shifts to the right, this shift also indicates a change in the economy's full-employment output level from Y^* to Y^{**}. The unemployment rate does not change, but workers are more productive.

We can illustrate economic growth by using the long-run aggregate supply curve. As the economy grows over time, full-employment output increases, shifting the LRAS curve to the right. But $LRAS_1$ can also shift to the left (to $LRAS_3$). This shift would occur with a permanent decline in the economy's resources or with the adoption of inefficient institutions. For example, if political instability leads to the overthrow of the government of a nation, LRAS would shift to the left.

Short-Run Aggregate Supply

We just saw that the price level does not affect aggregate supply in the long run. However, in the short run there is a positive relationship between the price level and the quantity of aggregate supply. There are three reasons for this relationship: inflexible input prices, menu costs, and money illusion.

First, consider input prices. At your coffee shop, you pay the baristas a particular wage, and this wage is set for a period of time. In addition, interest rates for your loans are normally fixed. Economists say that these input prices are *sticky*, because they "stick" at a certain level and take time to change. In contrast, output prices tend to be more flexible. Whereas input prices are typically set in a written contract, output prices are often easy to change. For example, coffee shop prices are often written on a chalkboard, which makes it pretty easy to change them from day to day.

The distinction between sticky input prices and flexible output prices is at the center of our discussion of aggregate supply because it affects the way firms react when prices do move. Think about your coffee shop. You

The Business Cycle

Since 1970, the U.S. economy has experienced seven recessions. These business cycle fluctuations are most visible in observations of real GDP growth and the unemployment rate. During recessions, real GDP typically falls and the unemployment rate climbs. During expansions, real GDP expands and the unemployment rate falls back toward the natural rate.

— Unemployment rate   ■ Real GDP growth   ■ Period of recession

1978 Q2 **16.7%**

The unemployment rate peaked at 10.8% in November and December of 1982.

Long-run average 6.0%

Long-run average 3.0%

Real GDP grew by 8% or more for four consecutive quarters in 1983 and 1984, including an amazing 9.3% growth rate in mid-1983.

The recession in 1981 and 1982 marked the fourth recession in just 13 years, the end of a very rough period for the U.S. economy.

12%

10%

8%

6%

4%

2%

0%

−2%

−4%

−6%

−8%

−10%

1970   1975   1980   1985   1990

REVIEW QUESTIONS

- Looking at the year immediately following each recession, can you determine which economic recovery was most difficult? On what do you base your answer?

- If the unemployment rate was below the natural rate in 2000, what does this imply about aggregate demand?

In 2000, the unemployment rate dropped under 4%, which is below what economists believe to be the natural rate.

After the Great Recession, the unemployment rate remained stubbornly high.

The Great Recession lasted from December 2007 to June 2009.

The expansion from April 1991 to March 2001 lasted a full ten years, the longest expansion in U.S. history.

Real GDP plunged 8.2% in the fourth quarter of 2008.

FIGURE 26.9

The Short-Run Aggregate Supply Curve

The positive slope of the short-run aggregate supply curve indicates that increases in the economy's price level lead to an increase in the quantity of aggregate supply in the short run. For example, if the price level rises from 100 to 110, the quantity of aggregate supply rises from $18 trillion to $19 trillion in the short run. The reason is that some prices are sticky in the short run.

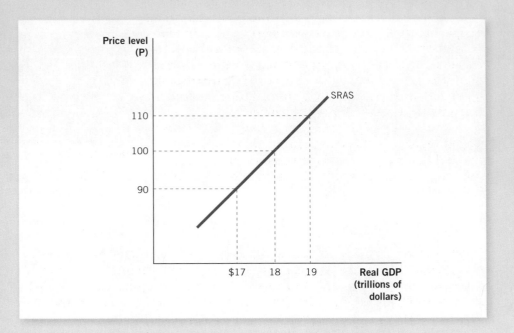

negotiate one-year contracts with your workers. Your coffee bean suppliers fix their prices for a certain period as well. If inflation begins to push up all prices in the macroeconomy, you pull out your chalkboard eraser and raise the price of lattes, espressos, and mochas; these are output prices, and they are very flexible. But your input prices are sticky (the coffee beans still cost the same, and you have to pay your employees the same amount)—at least for a while. Therefore, your costs remain the same. And here is the link to aggregate supply: because your costs don't rise but your revenues do, it makes sense for you to increase output. When you and other firms raise output, GDP rises.

The dynamic between sticky input prices and flexible output prices explains the positive slope of the short-run aggregate supply curve. Figure 26.9 shows the short-run aggregate supply curve, labeled as SRAS. When the price level rises from 100 to 110, firms produce more in the short run because input prices are sticky, and real GDP rises from $18 trillion to $19 trillion. When the price level falls to 90, firms produce less in the short run because flexible output prices fall but sticky input prices stay relatively high. The result is a decrease in real GDP to $17 trillion.

There are other reasons why aggregate supply might be positively related to the price level in the short run. Menu costs, which we introduced in Chapter 21, are another factor that affects short-run aggregate supply. If the general price level is rising but a firm decides not to adjust its prices because of menu costs, customers will want more of its output. If firms decide to increase output rather than print new menus, the quantity of aggregate supply increases. So again, output is positively related to the price level in the short run.

We also talked about the problem of money illusion in Chapter 21. Recall that *money illusion* occurs when people interpret nominal values as real values. In terms of aggregate supply, if output prices are falling but workers are reluctant to accept nominal pay decreases, they reinforce the stickiness of input prices. If input prices don't fall with output prices, firms reduce output in response to general price-level changes.

Any type of price stickiness leads to a positively sloped aggregate supply curve in the short run. But keep in mind that since all prices can change in the long run, the long-run aggregate supply curve is vertical at the full-employment output level.

These output prices are very flexible—they can be changed with the push of a button.

Shifts in Short-Run Aggregate Supply

When the long-run aggregate supply curve shifts, it signals a permanent change that affects the long run and the short run. Therefore, all long-run aggregate supply curve shifts (caused by changes in resources, technology, and institutions) also cause the short-run aggregate supply curve to shift. But, in addition, the short-run aggregate supply curve can shift on its own. Typically, these shifts are due to changes that directly affect firms' costs of production and form their incentives for supply.

The primary cause of shifts in short-run aggregate supply is changes in input or resource prices. Aggregate supply is the total supply of GDP by firms in the economy, as it relates to the overall price level. When firms' production costs fall, firms produce more output at any given price level, which means that short-run aggregate supply increases, or shifts to the right. The short-run aggregate supply curve exists because input prices and other prices are sticky and do not always adjust immediately when aggregate demand shifts. So when these prices do change, the short-run aggregate supply curve shifts. For example, if input prices rise, short-run aggregate supply declines (the curve shifts to the left).

Input prices can change for many reasons. For example, unions often engage in collective bargaining that leads to wage agreements between large groups of workers and their employers. Perhaps workers underestimated inflation in the past and renegotiate to higher wages for the future. Let's say workers sign wage contracts under the assumption that the inflation rate will be about 2% in the next year. If the inflation rate turns out to be 5% at the end of the year, these workers will likely renegotiate with their employers. When workers renegotiate their wages upward, the short-run aggregate supply curve shifts to the left as input prices climb.

Along these lines, if you are going to sign a long-term wage contract, you'll want to form some expectation about future prices. After all, the real value of your future income depends on prices in the future. All else being equal, when workers and firms expect higher prices in the future, they negotiate higher wages. The result is higher labor costs, which reduce firms' profitability and make them less willing to produce at any price level. Therefore, higher expected future prices lead to a lower quantity of aggregate supply.

Freezing temperatures shock not only the orange crop but also the price in grocery stores.

Supply shocks are surprise events that change a firm's production costs.

The process works in reverse if workers and firms expect a lower price level. Subsequent negotiations produce a labor agreement with lower wages, which reduces labor costs. When labor costs fall, additional production is more profitable at any price level, and the short-run aggregate supply curve shifts to the right.

Sometimes, surprise events occur that affect input prices. For example, in December 2010, frigid temperatures across most of Florida caused orange crops to freeze. The freeze reduced total orange output in the state by 450 million pounds for the season. As a result, the price of oranges in grocery stores rose by more than 10%. Surprise events that change a firm's production costs are called **supply shocks**. When supply shocks are temporary, they shift only the short-run aggregate supply curve. Supply shocks can be negative or positive. Negative supply shocks lead to higher input prices and higher production costs; positive supply shocks reduce input prices and production costs.

A price change in an important factor of production is another supply shock. For example, from July 2007 to July 2008, oil prices in the United States doubled from $70 a barrel to over $140 a barrel. You may recall this period because gas prices rose from about $2 per gallon to more than $4 per gallon in the summer of 2008. Figure 26.10 plots the price of oil from 2004 to 2015. Oil is an important input to many production processes, so when its price doubles, a macroeconomic supply shock occurs. More recently, the price of oil has fallen below $50 per barrel. This is a positive supply shock for the macroeconomy.

Figure 26.11 shows how changes in input prices shift the short-run aggregate supply curve. Short-run aggregate supply increases (the curve shifts to the right to SRAS$_2$) when resource prices fall. This could occur when negotiation leads to lower worker wages or when there is a positive supply shock. Short-run aggregate supply decreases (the curve shifts to the left to SRAS$_3$) when resource prices rise. This happens when workers negotiate higher wages or when negative supply shocks increase resource prices.

FIGURE 26.10

Price of Crude Oil

The increase in crude oil prices is an example of a negative supply shock because production costs for firms throughout the economy rise drastically.

Source: U.S. Energy Information Administration.

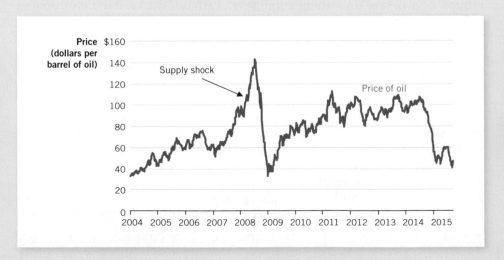

PRACTICE WHAT YOU KNOW

Long-Run Aggregate Supply and Short-Run Aggregate Supply: Which Curve Shifts?

In the real world, change is typical. In our aggregate demand–aggregate supply model, change means that the curves shift. Careful application of the model requires that you be able to determine which curve shifts, and in which direction, when real-world events occur.

Question: In each of the scenarios listed below, is there a shift in the long-run aggregate supply curve, the short-run aggregate supply curve, both, or neither? Explain your answer each time.

This oil rig sits atop the Bakken shale formation in North Dakota, where vast new shale gas resources have been discovered.

1. New shale gas deposits are found in North Dakota.
2. Hot weather leads to lower crop yields in the Midwest.
3. The Organization of Petroleum Exporting Countries (OPEC) meets and agrees to increase world oil output, leading to lower oil prices for six months.
4. U.S. consumers expect greater income in 2017.

Answers:

1. This scenario leads to an increase in both long-run aggregate supply and short-run aggregate supply. The shale gas discovery represents new resources, which shifts the long-run aggregate supply curve to the right. In addition, every shift in the long-run aggregate supply curve affects the short-run aggregate supply curve.
2. The lower crop yields are not permanent, so only the short-run aggregate supply curve shifts to the left. After the bad weather passes, the short-run aggregate supply curve shifts back to the right.
3. This scenario causes only the short-run aggregate supply curve to shift to the right because it doesn't represent a permanent change in oil quantities.
4. Neither the short-run aggregate supply curve nor the long-run aggregate supply curve shifts. A change in expected income shifts the aggregate demand curve, in this case to the right because consumers expect greater income.

How Does the Aggregate Demand–Aggregate Supply Model Help Us Understand the Economy?

In a market economy, output is determined by exchanges between buyers and sellers. As we will see, the economy tends to move to the point at which aggregate demand is equal to aggregate supply. In this section, we bring

FIGURE 26.11

How Changes in Input Prices Shift the Short-Run Aggregate Supply Curve

The short-run aggregate supply curve shifts to the right (from SRAS₁ to SRAS₂) when resource prices fall. This could occur when negotiations lead to lower wages or when there is a positive supply shock. The curve shifts to the left (from SRAS₁ to SRAS₃) when resource prices rise. This happens when workers negotiate higher wages or when negative supply shocks increase resource prices.

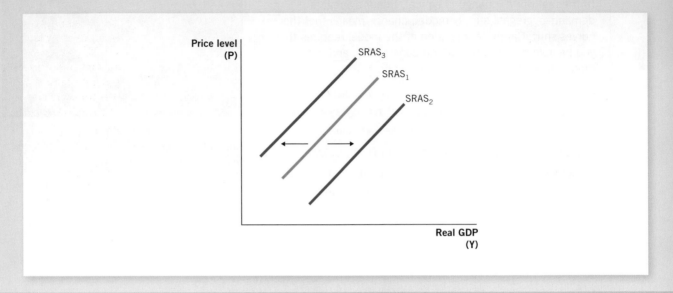

aggregate demand and aggregate supply together and then consider how changes in the economy affect real GDP, unemployment, and the price level.

Equilibrium in the Aggregate Demand–Aggregate Supply Model

Figure 26.12 plots the aggregate demand and the aggregate supply curves in the same graph. The point where they intersect, A, is the equilibrium point at which the opposing forces of supply and demand are balanced. At point A, the price level is P* and the output level is Y*. Prices naturally adjust to move the economy toward this equilibrium point.

To understand why the economy tends toward equilibrium at price level P*, consider other possible price levels. For example, if the price level is P_H, which is higher than P*, aggregate supply will be greater than aggregate demand. In this case, producers are producing more than consumers desire at current prices. Therefore, prices naturally begin to fall to eliminate a potential surplus of goods and services. As prices fall, the quantity of aggregate demand increases and the economy moves toward a new equilibrium at P*.

In contrast, if the price level is P_L, which is lower than P*, aggregate demand will exceed aggregate supply. At those prices, buyers desire more than produc-

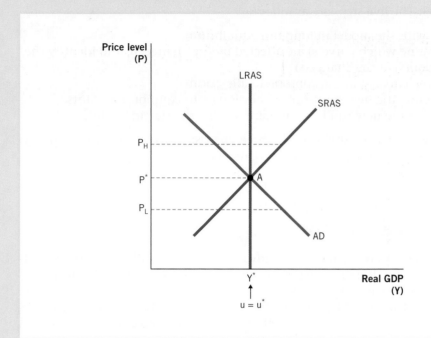

FIGURE 26.12

Equilibrium in the Aggregate Demand–Aggregate Supply Model

Forces in the economy naturally move it toward equilibrium at point A, where aggregate supply is equal to aggregate demand, $P = P^*$, $Y = Y^*$, and $u = u^*$. At P_H, aggregate supply exceeds aggregate demand, which puts downward pressure on prices and moves the economy toward equilibrium at P^*. At P_L, where aggregate demand exceeds aggregate supply, upward pressure on prices moves the economy toward equilibrium at P^*.

ers are willing to supply. Because aggregate demand exceeds aggregate supply, prices rise and the price level moves toward P^*. The only price level at which the plans of suppliers and demanders match is P^*. Market forces automatically push the economy to the price level at which aggregate demand is equal to aggregate supply.

We can also describe this equilibrium in equation form. In equilibrium, both long-run and short-run aggregate supply are equal to aggregate demand:

$$LRAS = SRAS = AD$$

(Equation 26.2)

Aggregate supply is the real GDP produced, which we indicate as Y. Aggregate demand derives from four components: C, I, G, and NX. Therefore, we can rewrite equation 26.2 as:

$$Y = C + I + G + NX$$

(Equation 26.3)

Now we know what equilibrium looks like in our model. Equation 26.3 is our reference point for thinking about the economy at a particular point in time.

In the real world, things are always changing: everything from technology to weather to wealth and expectations can change. Now that we've built our model of the macroeconomy, we can use it to examine how changes in the real world affect the economy.

In what follows, both in this chapter and for the remainder of the book, we consider many real-world factors that lead to changes in the macroeconomy. When we consider a change, we follow a particular sequence of steps that lead to the new equilibrium. Once we determine the new equilibrium, we can assess the impact of the change on real GDP, unemployment, and the price level. The five steps are as follows:

1. Begin with the model in long-run equilibrium.
2. Determine which curve(s) are affected by the change(s), and identify the direction(s) of the change(s).
3. Shift the curve(s) in the appropriate direction(s).
4. Determine the new short-run and/or long-run equilibrium points.
5. Compare the new equilibrium point(s) with the starting point.

Next we consider shifts in all three curves: long-run aggregate supply, short-run aggregate supply, and aggregate demand.

Adjustments to Shifts in Long-Run Aggregate Supply

We have seen that technological advances increase full-employment output and shift the long-run aggregate supply curve to the right. For example, the Internet is a relatively new and important technology that was made available to the general public in the 1990s. The Internet makes millions of workers more productive. The effect on the macroeconomy is illustrated in Figure 26.13. We begin at long-run equilibrium point A, with the full-employment output (Y^*) and the price level 100. But the introduction of new technology means that the long-run aggregate supply curve shifts from

FIGURE 26.13

How Long-Run Aggregate Supply Shifts Affect the Economy

Beginning at long-run equilibrium point A, the price level is at 100 and output is at the full-employment rate (Y^*). New technology shifts long-run aggregate supply positively from $LRAS_1$ to $LRAS_2$ because the economy can now produce more at any price level. The new long-run equilibrium is at point B, and there is now a new, higher full-employment rate of output (Y^{**}). Note that the unemployment rate (u) is equal to the natural rate (u^*) both before and after the shift.

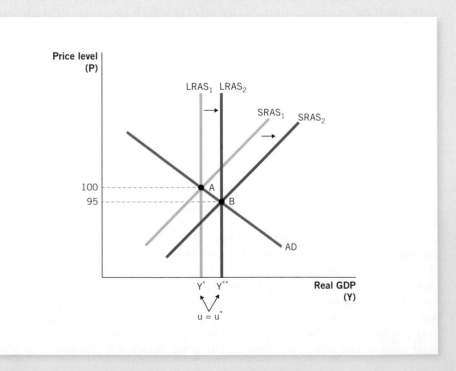

$LRAS_1$ to $LRAS_2$. Recall that changes in long-run aggregate supply also affect the short run, so the short-run aggregate supply shifts from $SRAS_1$ to $SRAS_2$. Assuming that this technological change is the only change in the economy, we move to long-run equilibrium at point B. Notice that at point B the economy has a new full-employment output level at Y^{**}.

All else being equal, technological progress leads to more output and a lower price level, which drops from 100 to 95. Before the Internet, the unemployment rate was at the natural rate (u^*). After the new technology becomes available, employment remains at the same level; but because we have better tools, workers are more productive. This analysis also applies to anything that shifts the long-run aggregate supply curve to the right, such as the discovery of new resources or the introduction of new institutions that are favorable for growth.

Adjustments to Shifts in Short-Run Aggregate Supply

Now let's examine the effects of a change in short-run aggregate supply. Consider what happens when there is a short-run supply disruption caused by an oil pipeline break. This is an example of a negative supply shock. Because oil is an input that is used in many production processes, the disruption temporarily raises production costs. We show this supply shock in Figure 26.14 by shifting the short-run aggregate supply curve to the left, from $SRAS_1$ to $SRAS_2$. The new equilibrium is at point b, with a higher price level (105) and a lower level of output (Y_1). Because this is a short-run equilibrium, we

FIGURE 26.14

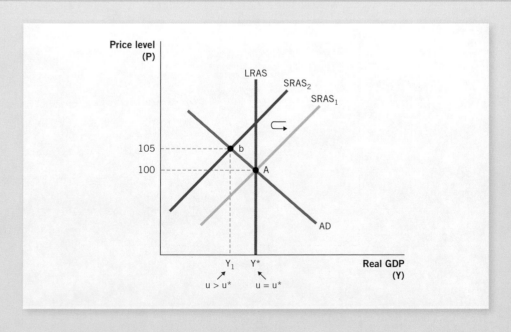

How Short-Run Aggregate Supply Shifts Affect the Economy

A temporary negative supply shock shifts short-run aggregate supply from $SRAS_1$ to $SRAS_2$. In the short run, the economy moves to equilibrium at point b (denoted with a lowercase letter to distinguish from long-run equilibrium). This equilibrium entails higher prices, lower real GDP, and higher unemployment. In the long run, the economy returns to equilibrium at point A.

use the lowercase b. The lower output means increased unemployment in the short run (u > u*). Notice that nothing happens to long-run aggregate supply—in the long run, the pipeline will be fixed and oil can be produced at full-employment output level Y* again.

Because the disruption is temporary, eventually the short-run aggregate supply curve will shift back to the right until it reaches $SRAS_1$ again. Short-run disruptions in aggregate supply do not alter the long-run equilibrium in the economy; eventually, the price level, output, and the unemployment rate return to their long-run equilibrium levels at point A. But in the short run, an economic downturn brings higher unemployment and lower real GDP.

ECONOMICS IN THE REAL WORLD

The Drought of 2012 Sends Prices Higher

According to an Associated Press article in August 2012, the summer of 2012 was the hottest on record for the United States. High temperatures led to extremely low yields in both corn and soybean crops. In fact, in 2012, each acre of corn planted in the U.S. yielded just 123 bushels, down from 147 bushels the year before and much lower than the 158 bushels in 2013.

According to the AP article, economist Rick Whitacre projected higher prices for many different consumer goods, such as cereal, soda, cake mixes, candy bars, and even makeup. Since corn is an important feed source for cattle, Whitacre projected a 4% to 6% rise in beef and pork prices.

The record temperatures are a classic example of a supply shock, and the result is exactly what the aggregate demand–aggregate supply model predicts: the short-run aggregate supply curve shifts to the left, leading to higher prices throughout the economy. ✷

These Iowa fields were supposed to be much greener in July 2012.

Adjustments to Shifts in Aggregate Demand

Aggregate demand shifts for many reasons. Some shifts occur because of expectations rather than actual events, yet they still affect the macroeconomy. For example, let's say that consumer confidence rises unexpectedly: consumers wake up one morning with expectations of higher future income. This change causes increased aggregate demand because consumers start spending more. Can this kind of change have real effects on the economy? That is, will a change in consumer confidence affect unemployment and real GDP? Let's look at the model.

Figure 26.15 illustrates the changes in the economy from the increased consumer confidence. We start with long-run equilibrium at point A, where the price level is 100, real GDP is at full-employment output Y^*, and unemployment is equal to the natural rate ($u = u^*$). Then aggregate demand shifts from AD_1 to AD_2, which moves the economy to short-run equilibrium at point b. The short-run equilibrium is associated with higher prices ($P = 105$) and higher real GDP (Y_1). In addition, the unemployment rate drops to u_1, which is less than u^*. Thus, changes in aggregate demand do affect the real economy, at least in the short run.

Our example presents a positive result—after all, unemployment falls and real GDP rises in the short run. Now let's complete this example by following

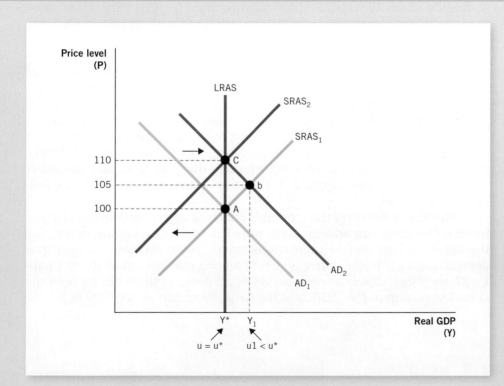

FIGURE 26.15

How Aggregate Demand Shifts Affect the Economy

An increase in aggregate demand moves the economy from the initial equilibrium at point A to a new short-run equilibrium at point b. The positive aggregate shift increases real GDP and decreases unemployment in the short run ($u_1 < u^*$). In the short run, prices adjust—but only partially, because some prices are sticky. In the long run, when all prices adjust, the short-run aggregate supply curve shifts to $SRAS_2$, and the economy moves to long-run equilibrium at point C, where $Y = Y^*$ and $u = u^*$.

TABLE 26.1

Summary of Results from Aggregate Demand Shifts

	Increase in aggregate demand		Decrease in aggregate demand	
	Short run	Long run	Short run	Long run
Real GDP	Y rises	Y returns to original level	Y falls	Y returns to original level
Unemployment	u falls	u returns to original level	u rises	u returns to original level
Price level	P rises	P rises even further	P falls	P falls even further

through to long-run equilibrium. Recall the difference between the long run and the short run: in the long run, all prices adjust. As all prices adjust, the short-run aggregate supply curve shifts to the left from SRAS₁ to SRAS₂. The economy moves to long-run equilibrium at point C. Notice that at C we are back to the original output level (Y*) and unemployment level (u*), but prices are higher (P = 110). The model is telling us that demand changes have no real effects in the long run because only the price level, a nominal variable, is affected.

What are the consequences of this move to long-run equilibrium, and how does it compare with the short-run equilibrium? At point b, real GDP is up and unemployment is down. But not everyone is happy. For example, workers with sticky wages are now paying more for their final goods and services, but their wages did not adjust upward in the short run. In fact, any sellers with sticky prices are hurt in the short run when other prices rise.

Because everyone can adjust their prices eventually, the economy moves to point C in the long run. Thinking about your coffee shop, in the long run you can renegotiate wages and all other long-term contracts. Thus, if there is a 10% increase in prices throughout the economy, both input and output prices rise by 10%. The price of a $4 latte rises to $4.40, and the barista wage of $10 per hour rises to $11 per hour. When input prices rise to match output price changes, the short-run aggregate supply curve shifts to SRAS₂. In the long run, after all prices have adjusted, the price level does not affect the quantity of output supplied. This is why output returns to Y*, the full-employment level.

Table 26.1 summarizes the economic effects of aggregate demand changes in both the short run and the long run. The last two columns summarize the effects of decreases in aggregate demand. These decreases in aggregate demand are a particular source of debate among macroeconomists. In Chapter 27, we'll look closely at negative aggregate demand shifts during both the Great Depression of the 1930s and the Great Recession of 2007–2009.

PRACTICE WHAT YOU KNOW

Using the Aggregate Demand–Aggregate Supply Model: The Japanese Earthquake and Tsunami of 2011

In 2011, a record-breaking earthquake hit Japan and was followed immediately by a tsunami. This natural disaster destroyed significant capital in Japan, including roads, buildings, and even nuclear power plants.

Question: How would you use the aggregate demand–aggregate supply model to illustrate the effect of this disaster on the Japanese economy?

Answer: People often think that natural disasters affect only short-run aggregate supply, because the effects are temporary. But if a disaster is so severe that it destroys resources, the long-run aggregate supply will also decline.

These devastating tsunami waves permanently destroyed many capital goods along part of Japan's seacoast.

Notice that the unemployment rate (u) is equal to the natural rate (u^*) both before and after the shift. Jobs remain because there is plenty of work to do in the aftermath of a natural disaster. However, in the long run Japan has fewer resources after the earthquake than it had before, and this outcome limits the nation's economic growth.

Question: How will the Japanese earthquake and tsunami affect the U.S. economy?

Answer: Real income falls in Japan, which leads to a decline in aggregate demand for U.S. goods and services.

Conclusion

We began this chapter with the misconception that recessions are normal occurrences that happen every few years. In fact, they are anything but normal. They occur with unpredictable frequency and are caused by many different factors. Recessions in business cycles are often caused by changes in aggregate demand, but the same symptoms can also reflect short-run aggregate supply shifts.

This chapter introduced the aggregate demand–aggregate supply model of the economy, which helps us understand how changes in the real world affect the macroeconomy. In the next chapter, we use the model to evaluate the two biggest macroeconomic disturbances of the past century: the Great Depression of the 1930s and the Great Recession of 2007–2009.

ANSWERING THE BIG QUESTIONS

What is the aggregate demand–aggregate supply model?

* The aggregate demand–aggregate supply model is a model that economists use to study business cycles (short-run fluctuations in the economy).

What is aggregate demand?

* Aggregate demand represents the spending side of the economy. It is the total demand for final goods and services in an economy. It includes consumption, investment, government spending, and net exports.
* The slope of the aggregate demand curve is negative due to the wealth effect, the interest rate effect, and the international trade effect.
* The aggregate demand curve shifts when there are changes in consumption factors (real wealth, expected future income, taxes), investment factors (investor confidence, interest rates, the quantity of money), government spending (at the federal, state, and local levels), or net export factors (foreign income and the value of the U.S. dollar).

What is aggregate supply?

* Aggregate supply represents the producing side of the economy. It is the total supply of final goods and services in an economy.
* The long-run aggregate supply curve is relevant when all prices are flexible. This curve is vertical at full-employment output and is not influenced by the price level.

✳ In the short run, when some prices are sticky, the short-run aggregate supply curve is relevant. This curve indicates a positive relationship between the price level and real output supplied.

How does the aggregate demand–aggregate supply model help us understand the economy?

✳ We can use the aggregate demand–aggregate supply model to see how changes in either aggregate demand or aggregate supply (or both) affect real GDP, unemployment, and the price level.

CONCEPTS YOU SHOULD KNOW

aggregate demand (p. 826)
aggregate supply (p. 826)
interest rate effect (p. 829)

international trade effect (p. 830)
long run (p. 837)
short run (p. 837)

supply shocks (p. 844)
wealth (p. 829)
wealth effect (p. 829)

QUESTIONS FOR REVIEW

1. What are three reasons the aggregate demand curve slopes downward? Name at least three factors that shift the aggregate demand curve.

2. What are three reasons the short-run aggregate supply curve slopes upward? Name at least three factors that shift the short-run aggregate supply curve.

3. How are the factors that shift the long-run aggregate supply curve different from those that shift the short-run aggregate supply curve?

4. Why is the long-run aggregate supply curve vertical?

5. How does strong economic growth in China affect aggregate demand in the United States?

6. Suppose the economy is in a recession caused by lower aggregate demand. If no policy action is taken, what will happen to the price level, output, and employment in the long run?

7. Consider two economies, both in recession. In the first economy, all workers have long-term contracts that guarantee high nominal wages for the next five years. In the second economy, all workers have annual contracts that are indexed to changes in the price level. Which economy will return to the natural rate of output first? Explain your response.

8. The interest rate effect can be viewed as a chain of reactions in the economy.

   a. Below is the chain of reactions with some of the steps filled in. Fill in the missing steps in the chain and be sure to indicate the direction of change (using an up or down arrow).

   b. What component (or piece) of aggregate demand is primarily affected by the wealth effect?

STUDY PROBLEMS (*solved at the end of the section)

1. Describe whether the following changes cause the short-run aggregate supply to increase, decrease, or neither.
   a. The price level increases.
   b. Input prices decrease.
   c. Firms and workers expect the price level to fall.
   d. The price level decreases.
   e. New policies increase the cost of meeting government regulations.
   f. The number of workers in the labor force increases.

2. Describe whether the following changes cause the long-run aggregate supply to increase, decrease, or neither.
   a. The price level increases.
   b. The stock of capital in the economy increases.
   c. Natural resources increase.
   d. The price level decreases.
   e. Firms and workers expect the price level to rise.
   f. The number of workers in the labor force increases.

3. On the following graph, illustrate the short-run and long-run effects of an increase in aggregate demand. Describe what happens to the price level, output, and employment.

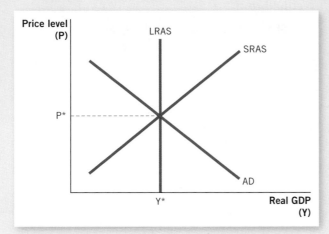

4. How does a lower price level in the United States affect the purchases of imported goods? Explain, using aggregate demand.

*5. Describe whether the following changes cause aggregate demand to increase, decrease, or neither.
   a. The price level increases.
   b. Investment decreases.
   c. Imports decrease and exports increase.
   d. The price level decreases.
   e. Consumption increases.
   f. Government purchases decrease.

*6. Suppose that a sudden increase in aggregate demand moves the economy from its long-run equilibrium.
   a. Illustrate this change using the aggregate demand–aggregate supply model.
   b. What are the effects of this change in the short run and the long run?

7. In the summer of 2008, global oil prices spiked to extremely high levels before coming down again at the end of that year. This temporary event had global effects because oil is an important resource in the production of many goods and services. Focusing only on the U.S. economy, determine how this kind of event affects the price level, unemployment rate, and real GDP in both the short run and the long run. Assume the economy was in long-run equilibrium before this change, and consider only this stated change.

*8. You work for Dr. Zhang, the autocratic dictator of Zhouland. After taking an economics course, you decide that devaluing your currency (Zhoullars) is the way to increase GDP. Following your advice, Dr. Zhang orders massive increases in the supply of Zhoullars, which reduces the value of Zhoullars in world markets. Use the AD-AS model to determine the effects on real GDP, unemployment, and the price level in Zhouland in both the short run and the long run. Assume the economy was in long-run equilibrium before this change, and consider only this stated change.

*9. Recently, the value of the U.S. dollar has been rising in world markets.
   a. Determine how the rising value of the dollar affects the U.S. price level, real GDP, and the unemployment rate in both the short run and the long run. For this part, assume that these changes are unexpected by market participants.

   You can use graphs to derive your answers, but place your answers in the boxes below (using an up arrow, a down arrow, or a dash if the level is consistent). Assume that the economy starts in long-run equilibrium, assume no other changes, and make all comparisons to the initial long-run equilibrium.

Short run			Long run		
P	Y	u	P	Y	u

   b. Under certain circumstances, it takes longer for the economy to adjust to long-run equilibrium following unanticipated changes. Do those circumstances apply here? Explain why or why not.
   c. If instead these changes in the value of the dollar are completely anticipated in advance, how will the results differ in the short run?

10. Let's say that in 2019 the United States experiences abnormally good weather. This weather is particularly beneficial for agricultural crop production. Determine how the run of good weather affects the U.S. real GDP, price level, and unemployment rate in both the short run and the long run.

You can use graphs to derive your answers, but place your answers in the boxes below. Assume that the economy starts in long-run equilibrium, assume no other changes, and make all comparisons to the initial long-run equilibrium.

Short run			Long run		
P	Y	u	P	Y	u

SOLVED PROBLEMS

5.a. Neither. A change in the price level (P) leads to a movement along the AD curve. When the price level rises, the quantity of aggregate demand declines along the curve.

b. Investment (I) is one component of aggregate demand, so a decrease in investment decreases aggregate demand.

c. Net exports (NX) is a component of aggregate demand. An increase in exports and a decrease in imports imply that net exports rise, so aggregate demand increases.

d. Aggregate demand neither increases nor decreases with a change in the price level (P). A change in the price level leads to movement along the AD curve. When the price level decreases, the quantity of aggregate demand increases along the curve.

e. Consumption (C) is a component of aggregate demand, so an increase in consumption means an increase in aggregate demand.

f. Government purchases (G) are a component of aggregate demand, so a decrease in government purchases causes a decrease in aggregate demand.

6.a. Aggregate demand increases from AD_1 to AD_2. In the short run, equilibrium will be at point b. In the long run, equilibrium will move to point C.

b. In the short run, real GDP rises, the unemployment rate falls, and the price level rises. In the long run, real GDP goes back to the full-employment level, the unemployment rate returns to the natural rate, and the price level rises further.

8. The reduction in the value of the Zhoullar means an increase or rightward shift in the aggregate demand curve. This change creates the same scenario pictured in the solution to problem 6; refer again to that figure.

In the short run, there is greater real GDP, lower unemployment, and a higher price level. This short-run equilibrium is pictured as point b in the figure.

In the long run, the only change is an increase in the price level (P), as indicated by the new long-run equilibrium at point C in the figure. Note that this explanation is consistent with the discussion of inflation in Chapter 22.

That is, the cause of inflation is monetary expansion. When Dr. Zhang commanded that the number of Zhoullars should increase, he guaranteed that inflation would eventually arrive.

9.a. When the value of the U.S. dollar rises relative to other currencies, it means that U.S. exports are relatively more expensive and imports from other nations are relatively less expensive. Therefore, net export demand falls and AD declines. The fall in AD leads to a new short-run equilibrium with a lower price level, lower real GDP, and higher unemployment. In the long run, the price level falls further, but real GDP and the unemployment rate return to their initial levels.

Short run			Long run		
P	Y	u	P	Y	u
↓	↓	↑	↓	—	—

b. It takes longer for the economy to adjust when prices are falling (rather than rising). That situation does apply here because prices need to fall to restore the economy back to long-run equilibrium.

c. If the results are completely anticipated, then the economy goes immediately to the long-run equilibrium. That is, even in the short run, prices fall, but real GDP and the unemployment rate remain at their long-run equilibrium levels.

The Great Recession, the Great Depression, and Great Macroeconomic Debates

The Great Recession was comparable to the Great Depression.
The Great Recession, which began at the end of 2007, was a very difficult period for both the U.S. economy and the global economy.

By almost any measure, it was the worst recession since the Great Depression of the 1930s. But many people have the false impression that this recession was nearly as difficult as the Great Depression. It wasn't even close. The effects on real GDP and unemployment were significantly smaller in the more recent contraction. Furthermore, living standards in the twenty-first century are much higher than they were during the Great Depression era. The Great Depression helped to birth the field of macroeconomics, and many of the lessons learned during the Depression era affect current policy responses to economic downturns.

In this chapter, we take a closer look at both of these infamous economic contractions. We first consider them in the context of the aggregate demand–aggregate supply model. We then give an overview of the major debates of macroeconomics and how they relate to the two contractions, again in the context of aggregate demand and aggregate supply.

On Inauguration Day in 2009, the U.S. economy was mired in the Great Recession.

BIG QUESTIONS

* Exactly what happened during the Great Recession and the Great Depression?
* What are the big disagreements in macroeconomics?

Exactly What Happened During the Great Recession and the Great Depression?

The Great Recession and the Great Depression are the two most significant economic downturns of the past 100 years in the United States. In this section, we examine both downturns with two goals in mind. First, we briefly put each one in historical perspective, in terms of both depth and duration. Second, we examine each one in the context of the aggregate demand–aggregate supply model (see Chapter 26). Analyzing these two crucial real-world events demonstrates the power of the aggregate demand–aggregate supply framework. We begin with the Great Recession.

The Great Recession

In December 2007, the U.S. economy entered the recession we now call the Great Recession, a name primarily adopted because the downturn was longer and deeper than typical recessions and because early on there were significant problems in the financial markets (as there was at the start of the Great Depression). Finally, the title stuck when the effects of the recession refused to subside for several years after the recession was officially over. Before discussing the causes of the Great Recession, let's look more closely at just how serious the contraction was.

The Depth and Duration of the Great Recession

The official duration of the Great Recession was 18 months (December 2007 to June 2009), making it the longest of all recessions since World War II. But even this length understates the full amount of time during which the economic downturn affected the U.S. economy. For several years after the recession was officially over, unemployment remained high and real GDP grew slowly.

One way to grasp the depth and duration of the Great Recession is to compare it with the other recessions that have occurred since World War II. Figure 27.1 shows comparative data on real GDP and the unemploy-

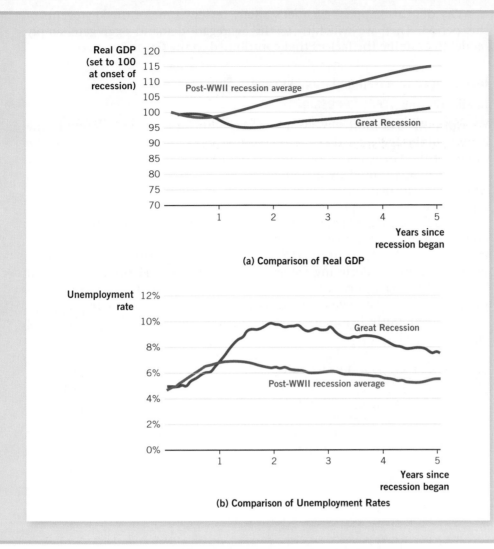

FIGURE 27.1

Real GDP and Unemployment Rate, Great Recession versus All Other Post-WWII Recessions

(a) During the Great Recession, real GDP fell further and rebounded more slowly than it otherwise did during a normal postwar recession.

(b) Also, the unemployment rate rose to levels far higher than have occurred in typical postwar recessions, and it remained high long after the rate typically falls.

Sources: (a): U.S. Bureau of Economic Analysis; panel (b): U.S. Bureau of Labor Statistics.

ment rate. Panel (a) compares the pattern of real GDP during the Great Recession and an average pattern of the other recessions since World War II. To illustrate the two paths of GDP, we set them to 100 at the onset of the contraction. Notice that during a typical recession, real GDP falls slightly and then comes back to its original level after about a year and a half. In contrast, during the Great Recession, output fell significantly and then recovered more slowly. In fact, it took nearly four years for real GDP to reach its prerecession level in the third quarter of 2011.

Panel (b) shows the monthly unemployment rate for the Great Recession compared with an average unemployment rate across the other post–World War II recessions. For a typical recession, the unemployment rate climbed to around 7% and then declined after about 12 to 15 months. But for the Great Recession, the unemployment rate climbed to 10% in October 2009 (22 months after the recession began) and remained at or near 8% even five years after the recession began. Taken together, panels (a) and (b) indicate that the Great Recession was more severe than a typical recession.

Why did this happen? First let's briefly review some of the key events of this period. Then we will turn to the aggregate demand–aggregate supply model to examine the factors that contributed to the Great Recession.

Using Aggregate Demand and Aggregate Supply to Analyze the Great Recession

We can now look more closely at this very difficult economic period in the context of the aggregate demand–aggregate supply model. In considering the causes of the Great Recession, most economists and policymakers initially assumed it was caused by a significant decline in aggregate demand. And while aggregate demand did indeed fall, it is clear in hindsight that aggregate supply also fell. We begin with the changes in aggregate supply.

The decline in aggregate supply was caused by problems with a key economic institution: the loanable funds market. In 2007, it became clear that there was trouble brewing in U.S. financial markets. Much of the trouble stemmed from the declining values of U.S. real estate. Figure 27.2 plots an index of U.S. house purchase prices from 2001 to 2012, with the Great Recession period shaded as a vertical blue bar. You can see that home prices began to fall in the months before the Great Recession, with the decline accelerating rapidly through 2008.

Many economists feel that the troubles of the Great Recession began in housing markets as a direct result of government policy with regard to the money supply. The view is that there was too much monetary expansion at the beginning of the twenty-first century As you can see from Figure 27.2, housing prices rose significantly until 2007. In Chapter 21, we talked about the problem of price confusion: when firms cannot tell whether price increases are due to real increases in demand or due to inflation. And this was the problem that builders faced in the lead-up to the Great Recession. Housing prices were rising rapidly, but many economists now believe that this was a result

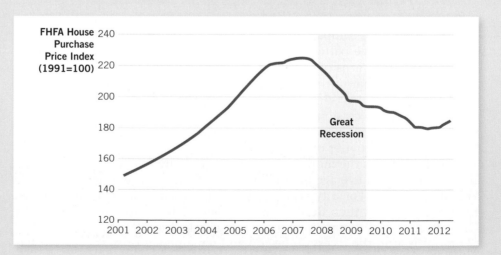

FIGURE 27.2

U.S. House Purchase Price Index, 2001–2012

U.S. house prices began falling in mid-2007 and then fell consistently through the Great Recession.

Source: Federal Housing Finance Agency.

of monetary expansion. The monetary expansion then led to a "bubble" in housing prices that burst in 2008.

During this time, very large investors, including financial institutions like Lehman Brothers, Bank of America, and Goldman Sachs, became very involved in the housing mortgage market, in particular the securitization of home mortgages. You might recall from Chapter 23 that at this time home mortgages had become securitized into mortgage-backed securities and that significant quantities of these securities were held by most of the largest financial institutions in the United States. Thus, when real estate values fell, that event led to a systemic problem in U.S. financial markets. Because of the financial firms' interdependence, the problem quickly spread throughout the United States and then to the rest of the world. A financial crisis signals a breakdown in the loanable funds market. When the loanable funds market does not function properly, firms cannot get funding to produce output, and aggregate supply falls.

A crucial issue as we analyze the Great Recession is identifying whether the decline in aggregate supply was temporary or permanent. Recall that in the aggregate demand–aggregate supply model, there are very different effects from changes in short-run and long-run aggregate supply. If the effect of the financial crisis was temporary, then we would view it as a short-run supply shock, illustrated in the aggregate demand–aggregate supply model with a leftward shift in the short-run aggregate supply curve. In this scenario, after the financial turmoil ends, the economy returns to its natural rate of output. (See Figure 26.14 for a refresher.)

But, in fact, the crisis in the loanable funds market had long-term effects. Why? First, there was a misallocation of resources during the lead-up to the great recession. Houses were built that were not needed, using workers and other resources. When this later became clear, the adjustment manifested as a decline in long-run aggregate supply (LRAS).

Second, the enactment of new financial regulations also affected the economy for the long-term. The **Dodd-Frank Act**, signed in July 2010, is the primary regulatory response to the financial turmoil that contributed to the Great Recession. This act established several new oversight bodies and regulations on financial institutions with the stated aim of reducing risk in financial markets. These regulations represent a permanent change in how financial institutions operate and shifted the long-run aggregate supply curve to the left.

The **Dodd-Frank Act** is the primary regulatory response to the financial turmoil that contributed to the Great Recession.

Consider the following analogy. Financial markets are like a bridge between savers and borrowers in an economy. If the economy is to grow, firms must be able to borrow, and so the bridge must be safe and efficient. But during the Great Recession, there were several accidents on the bridge, disrupting the flow of traffic and temporarily slowing the economy. The new financial regulations are like a stricter speed limit imposed on the bridge to make it safer. There will be fewer accidents in the future (we hope), but traffic will move more slowly across the bridge from now on. Therefore, we illustrate the permanent effects of the financial crisis and changes in institutions as a decline in long-run aggregate supply.

But aggregate demand was negatively affected as well. At least two factors contributed to a large decline in aggregate demand. The first was a fall in wealth: people's homes are often the largest piece of their overall wealth, so when real estate values fell, people's wealth dropped. (See again Figure 27.2.) In addition, U.S. stocks lost one-third of their value during 2008. For millions of people, this meant seeing their retirement savings drop by a full one-third. Both of these situations contributed to large declines in wealth, so aggregate demand declined significantly.

Aggregate demand also fell because of a decline in expected future income. Beginning in 2007, consumers realized that the economy was undergoing a downturn. Figure 27.3 shows the related Consumer Sentiment Index, which is a measure of consumers' confidence about their own financial situation and the future direction of the economy. The Consumer Sentiment Index began falling ahead of the recession and then fell significantly during 2008. Together, these two factors—a decline in wealth and a decline in expected future income—led to a decline in aggregate demand.

Let's now consider the aggregate demand–aggregate supply model to see the implications of these shifts for the macroeconomy. Figure 27.4 shows a decline in both aggregate demand and aggregate supply from 2007 to 2008. Aggregate demand shifted from AD_{2007} to AD_{2008}, and long-run aggregate supply shifted from $LRAS_{2007}$ to $LRAS_{2008}$. In 2007, the economy was in equilibrium at point A; at that time, the unemployment rate (not pictured in Figure 27.4) was below 5%, and real GDP was growing at a 3.6% rate in the second quarter of 2007. Then housing prices fell, leading to financial market turmoil, lower real wealth, and then lower consumer confidence. The declines in aggregate demand and long-run aggregate supply moved the economy to a new equilibrium at point B. During this time, the unemployment rate climbed to 10%, and by the last quarter of 2008, real GDP had shrunk by 8.9% (on an annual basis).

The unemployment rate rose significantly beginning in 2008 and then continued for several years. This was due in part to an increase in cyclical unemployment, but it was also due to an increase in structural unemployment

FIGURE 27.3

Consumer Sentiment Index, 2001–2012

The Consumer Sentiment Index is a measure of consumers' confidence about their own financial situation and the future direction of the economy. This index began falling in 2007 and then fell significantly during the Great Recession.

Source: St. Louis Federal Reserve FRED database. The Consumer Sentiment Index was developed at the University of Michigan.

FIGURE 27.4

The Decline in Both Long-Run Aggregate Supply and Aggregate Demand, 2007–2008

Financial market turmoil and lower consumer confidence led to decreases in both long-run aggregate supply and aggregate demand. The result was a new, lower level of real GDP and a higher rate of unemployment.

as the economy adjusted to new types of output in the wake of a decline in long-run aggregate supply.

One reason this recession has been called "Great" is that the decline in real GDP and the increase in the unemployment rate were large by historical standards. But another reason is that symptoms of the recession dragged on for several years after the recession was officially over. In 2012, real GDP was still expanding at less than 2%, and the unemployment rate remained at 8%. In response, the government employed many different tools to try to move

PRACTICE WHAT YOU KNOW

The Great Recession: What Made It "Great"?

Question: What are three reasons why the 2007–2009 recession came to be known as the Great Recession?

Answer:

1. Initially, the name appeared because the recession was clearly worse than a typical recession. For example, real GDP fell by an annual rate of 8.9% in the fourth quarter of 2008.

2. There was noticeable stress in financial markets, making the downturn similar to that aspect of the Great Depression.

3. The effects of the Great Recession, in terms of both high unemployment rates and slow real GDP growth, persisted long after the recession was officially over.

the economy back to normal growth and lower levels of unemployment. We will discuss these tools over the next four chapters. But the tools focused primarily on aggregate demand.

World financial institutions remained in poor health for quite a while, thus impacting aggregate supply—and this outcome kept many economies from quickly returning to previous output levels. Figure 27.5 shows U.S. real GDP from 1993 to 2015. In addition, we plot a dashed trend line that indicates the general path of real GDP prior to the Great Recession. This figure indicates that something permanent happened to the U.S. economy during the Great Recession. Long-run aggregate supply declined. The economy began growing again, but from a lower baseline level after the Great Recession.

The Great Depression

We have seen that the Great Recession was much worse than typical U.S. recessions. However, even though it has been termed "Great," we should not make the mistake of equating it with the Great Depression. In this section, we first examine economic indicators during the Great Depression era, and then we consider the severe contraction in terms of the aggregate demand–aggregate supply model.

The Magnitude of the Great Depression

To convey a sense of the historic magnitude of the Great Depression, we have plotted long-run U.S. real GDP data in Figure 27.6. The data go all the way back to 1870, but it is easy to identify the Great Depression—the significant drop in real GDP beginning in the 1930s. There have been several contractions in the U.S. economy since 1870, but none as severe as the Great Depression. During that period, real GDP fell from $1,057 billion in 1929 to

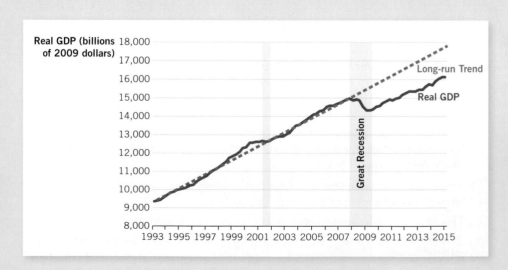

FIGURE 27.5

Real GDP versus the Previous Trend

There was a significant decline in real GDP during the Great Recession. In addition, there seems to be no tendency for the economy to return to its former trend line, indicating that there has been a permanent decline in long-run aggregate supply. In essence, the Great Recession led to a permanent loss of real GDP that the U.S. economy may never recover.

FIGURE 27.6

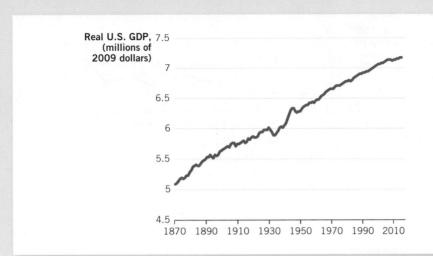

Real U.S. GDP,
(millions of
2009 dollars)

**Real U.S. GDP,
1870–2015**

When we look at U.S. real GDP growth over the long run, the Great Depression is easy to spot: it is the severe decline that occurred during the 1930s. To normalize across percentage changes, the plotted data appear as the logarithm of real GDP.

Source: U.S. Bureau of Economic Analysis.

$778 billion in 1933 (both equated to 2009 dollars). Imagine an economic contraction so severe that after four years the economy is producing almost 30% less than it was when the contraction started!

Furthermore, even though their names are similar, the Great Recession pales in comparison to the Great Depression. Figure 27.7 shows real GDP growth rates and unemployment rates beginning with the start of the two contractions. Panel (a) plots real GDP over the two contractions. Even though we earlier observed that the Great Recession was severe compared with typical U.S. recessions, when we compare it with the Great Depression, it looks like a harmless temporary decline. Real GDP fell by nearly 30% over the four years from 1929 to 1933, and it took seven years for real GDP to return to its prerecession level.

Panel (b) plots the unemployment rates. In 1929, the unemployment rate was just 2.2%, but just three years later it had climbed to over 25%! In other words, by 1933, one out of four workers were without a job. Particularly alarming was the length of the contraction: the unemployment rate remained above 15% for almost the entire decade of the 1930s.

During the Great Depression, shantytowns dubbed "Hoovervilles," after President Hoover, sprang up outside major U.S. cities.

Using Aggregate Demand and Aggregate Supply to Explain the Great Depression

The Great Depression was unusual because it was so deep and lasted so long. In fact, it was actually two separate recessions (August 1929 to March 1933 and May 1937 to June 1938). There is no technical definition of a depression—it is

FIGURE 27.7

Unemployment Rate and Real GDP for the Great Recession and the Great Depression

(a) During the Great Depression, real GDP fell by almost a third, and it took seven years to return to its prerecession level. In comparison, the decline in real GDP during the Great Recession seems meager. (b) During the Great Depression, the unemployment rate climbed to over 25% and remained over 15% for most of the entire decade of the 1930s. These levels far exceed the unemployment rates experienced during the Great Recession of 2007–2009.

Source: Panel (a): U.S. Bureau of Economic Analysis; panel (b): U.S. Bureau of Labor Statistics.

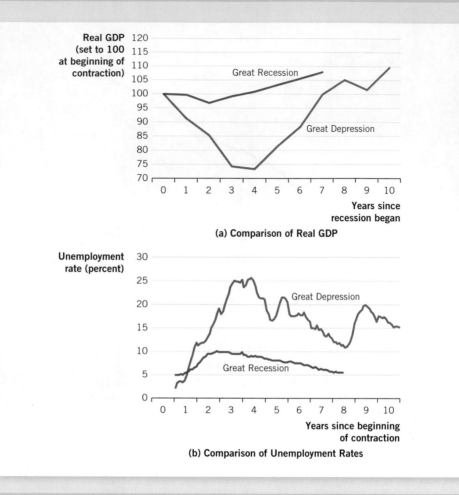

(a) Comparison of Real GDP

(b) Comparison of Unemployment Rates

really just a severe recession. But the Great Depression was also characterized by another striking condition: prices across the economy declined throughout the course of the decade. In fact, at the end of the 1930s, the general price level, as measured by the GDP deflator, was still 20% lower than it had been in 1929. The decline in prices indicates that the primary cause of the Great Depression was a decline in aggregate demand.

Figure 27.8 illustrates how a significant decline in aggregate demand affects the macroeconomy. In 1929, the economy was in equilibrium at point A, with aggregate demand designated as AD_{1929}. Then a significant decline in aggregate demand occurred for several years, as indicated by a shift to AD_{1930+}. As we have seen in our study of macroeconomics, lower aggregate demand leads to lower real GDP (shown in the figure as Y_1), higher unemployment rates (25%), and a lower price level (shown here as a decline from 100 to 80). These outcomes match the symptoms of the Great Depression.

What caused the decline in aggregate demand? Unfortunately, it turns out that much of the decline was caused by faulty macroeconomic policy.

FIGURE 27.8

The Decline in Aggregate Demand during the Great Depression

A significant decline in aggregate demand after 1929 can help to explain all three symptoms of the Great Depression: a decline in real GDP (from Y^* to Y_1), an increase in the unemployment rate (from 3% to 25%), and a decrease in the price level (from 100 to 80).

Macroeconomic policy encompasses government acts that influence the direction of the overall economy. Economists distinguish two different types of macroeconomic policy: fiscal policy and monetary policy. **Fiscal policy** comprises the use of government's budget tools, government spending, and taxes to influence the macroeconomy. **Monetary policy** involves adjusting the money supply to influence the economy. We are not yet ready to talk in detail about macroeconomic policies (those are the topics of the next section of this textbook), but we can outline the major determinants of the Great Depression based on aggregate demand and aggregate supply.

First, the stock market crashed on October 29, 1929. This day has come to be known as Black Thursday. But the economy did not crash just because the stock market experienced a severe downturn. A significant reaction to this event was a change in people's expectations for the future. In particular, expected future income declined—and we know that this factor decreases aggregate demand. Between 1929 and 1932, stock prices (as measured by the Dow Jones Industrial Average) fell by almost 90%.

The federal government had purposefully reduced the quantity of money in the economy in 1928 and 1929 in hopes of controlling stock prices, which policymakers thought were too high. As we will see in Chapter 31, tighter money (that is, a reduced money supply) leads to lower aggregate demand. In this context, the biggest policy error involved the banks. As financial panic spread across the country, people began withdrawing their deposits from banks. As a result, between 1930 and 1933, more than 9,000 banks failed in the United States. And while the government had the ability to lend to these ailing banks, it failed to do so. This policy led to even larger declines in the money supply. In fact, between 1929 and 1933, the quantity of money in

Macroeconomic policy encompasses government acts that influence the macroeconomy.

Fiscal policy comprises the use of government's budget tools, government spending, and taxes to influence the macroeconomy.

Monetary policy involves adjusting the money supply to influence the macroeconomy.

Was the stock market crash the only cause of the Great Depression?

Great Recession vs. Great Depression

The U.S. recession from December 2007 to June 2009 has been named the Great Recession. This name seems appropriate because it was the longest and most severe recession since the 1930s. But the name also ties it to the Great Depression era of the 1930s, and this comparison is misleading. While these two infamous contractions have similarities, they were drastically different in their economic impact. In terms of both real GDP and unemployment rates, the negative effects of the Great Depression dwarfed those of the Great Recession.

Real GDP

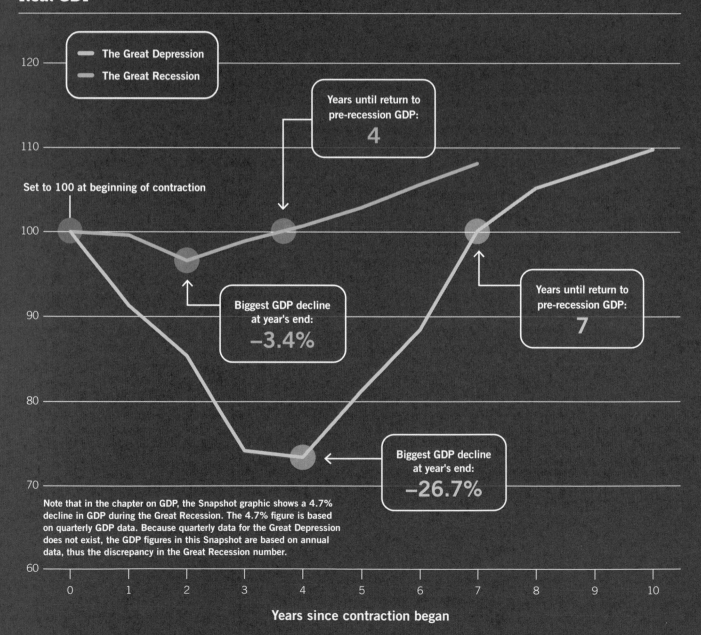

The Great Depression
The Great Recession

Years until return to pre-recession GDP:
4

Set to 100 at beginning of contraction

Biggest GDP decline at year's end:
−3.4%

Years until return to pre-recession GDP:
7

Biggest GDP decline at year's end:
−26.7%

Note that in the chapter on GDP, the Snapshot graphic shows a 4.7% decline in GDP during the Great Recession. The 4.7% figure is based on quarterly GDP data. Because quarterly data for the Great Depression does not exist, the GDP figures in this Snapshot are based on annual data, thus the discrepancy in the Great Recession number.

Years since contraction began

- If we assume a natural rate of unemployment equal to 5%, how much cyclical unemployment existed during the worst parts of the Great Recession and the Great Depression?

- Name two actions—or inactions—by the government that economists agree contributed to the depth and duration of the Great Depression.

Unemployment

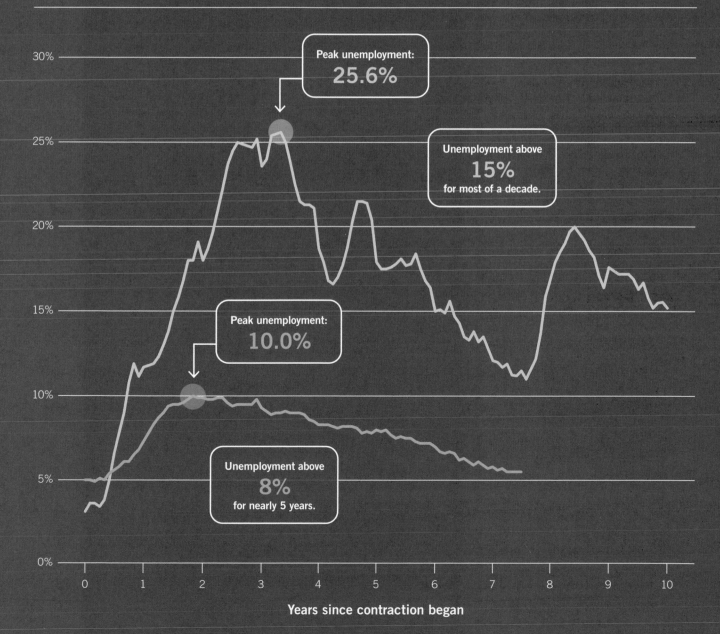

Peak unemployment:
25.6%

Unemployment above
15%
for most of a decade.

Peak unemployment:
10.0%

Unemployment above
8%
for nearly 5 years.

Years since contraction began

the U.S. economy declined by one-third. Economists today agree that these policy failures and the resulting decline in the money supply led to a significant decline in aggregate demand and were thus the primary contributors to the beginning of the Great Depression.

There were additional reasons why the economy dragged through the Great Depression for so long. In the early 1930s, Presidents Hoover and Roosevelt raised taxes in an attempt to balance the federal budget. And as we'll see in Chapter 29, higher taxes also reduce aggregate demand. Another policy blunder affected aggregate supply: in 1930, Congress passed the Smoot-Hawley Tariff Act. This legislation imposed tariffs (taxes) on thousands of imported goods and set off a global trade war as other nations reacted by imposing tariffs on U.S. exports.

In the end, most analysts agree that the economic contraction was primarily characterized by a significant decline in aggregate demand. In this context, the Great Depression was an event that reshaped the way both economists and noneconomists think about the economy. In the next section, we consider how the Great Depression changed economic thought.

What Are the Major Debates in Macroeconomics?

Here we consider the major debates in macroeconomics by building on the previous discussion of the Great Depression. Most economists agree with the basic implications of the aggregate demand–aggregate supply model. However, economists disagree about the role of government in the economy and whether the economy can correct itself. In this section, we try to clarify some of the issues around these debates.

One of the most contentious issues among economists involves the economy's adjustment to long-run equilibrium. Some economists believe that adjustment can and should occur naturally. This group, the **classical economists**, stresses the importance of aggregate supply. Others see the return to long-run equilibrium as an adjustment that occurs unpredictably and often with much delay; this group, the **Keynesian economists**, stresses the importance of aggregate demand and calls for the government to speed the process back to full employment. While not every economist fits completely in either camp, these distinctions help to clarify the debate.

Classical economists stress the importance of aggregate supply and generally believe that the economy can adjust back to full-employment equilibrium on its own.

Keynesian economists stress the importance of aggregate demand and generally believe that the economy needs help in moving back to full-employment equilibrium.

Classical Economics

At the beginning of the twentieth century, economics essentially focused on microeconomic issues. Economists had a good sense of the merits of supply and demand analysis for individual markets. As you know, when we consider basic supply and demand, the price of the good adjusts to draw the market toward equilibrium. To the extent that these economists considered macroeconomic issues, they extended their ideas from microeconomic analysis. In particular, they believed that since prices for individual goods are flexible, then prices across the economy are also flexible.

The classical economists dominated this era. One tenet of classical economics is the assumption that prices are flexible throughout the economy. If prices are completely flexible, then the economy is essentially self-correcting: no matter what factors change in the economy, no matter what curves shift, the economy automatically comes back to full employment. Figure 27.9 illustrates the classical view. Initially, the economy is in long-run equilibrium at point A. If aggregate demand increases from AD_1 to AD_2, price flexibility means that the economy moves to a new equilibrium at point B. At point B, real GDP is at full-employment output (Y^*), and the unemployment rate is at the natural rate ($u = u^*$). In short, the shift in aggregate demand is barely noticeable in the economy because prices adjust.

The results are not much different when aggregate demand declines. If aggregate demand falls from AD_1 to AD_3, price flexibility implies that the economy moves to long-run equilibrium at point C. (This outcome is very different from the actual experience we showed in Figure 27.8.) When prices are completely flexible, the economy comes back to full-employment output and the natural rate of unemployment relatively quickly. Classical economists probably slept well at night, without worries about long-term economic contractions.

Because they believed that the economy is self-correcting, classical economists were essentially laissez-faire in their policy recommendations. Because they had faith that market adjustments would take place quickly, they saw no significant role for a government macroeconomic policy focusing on short-run fixes when the economy is underperforming or overperforming.

Today, some economists are still in the classical camp. They don't worry much about aggregate demand shifts. These economists focus on economic policies designed to promote long-run growth; their main focus is on shifting

FIGURE 27.9

The Classical View of the Macroeconomy

In the classical view, prices adjust quickly in both directions. Therefore, shifts in aggregate demand do not lead to changes in output or employment because the output level stays at full employment. When prices are completely flexible, aggregate demand becomes less relevant, and changes in long-run aggregate supply are considered the primary source of economic prosperity.

long-run aggregate supply. Given this perspective, they see savings as a crucial positive factor in the economy: savings is translated into investment, which increases capital and shifts the long-run aggregate supply curve to the right.

Keynesian Economics

Although the classical economists dominated economics during the first part of the twentieth century, the Great Depression challenged the predominant view. In fact, the Great Depression set the stage for a new approach to macroeconomics. John Maynard Keynes, a British economist, formulated this new approach. In 1936, Keynes published *The General Theory of Employment, Interest, and Money*. This book vaulted him into the forefront of macroeconomic debates because it offered a theory about why cyclical unemployment might persist. Indeed, the title of the book—*The General Theory*—implies that Keynes believed that an economy out of long-run equilibrium is not unusual.

Keynesian economists emphasize that wages do not adjust downward quickly enough during recessions—in other words, are "sticky downward"—perhaps because of the presence of long-term contracts and money illusion (see Chapter 21). As a result, high real wages prevent the labor market from reaching equilibrium and restoring full employment. This outcome leads to prolonged recessions. Keynes believed that short-run economic circumstances could be improved through government intervention. He argued that the government should try to shift the aggregate demand curve back to its initial level. According to Keynes, it is foolish to wait for long-run adjustments. As he famously put it, "In the long run we are all dead."

Keynesian economists assume that prices are sticky downward, so they focus on the demand side of the economy as the source of instability. Look back at Figure 27.8, which shows the decline in aggregate demand between 1929 and 1930+. This large decline was due to a fall in consumer confidence and also the policy blunders of the 1930s. Notice that aggregate demand shifts from AD_{1929} to AD_{1930+}. According to Keynesian theory, individuals and firms both stopped spending as the stock market dropped in 1929, and firms became wary of future returns from capital—with the result that consumption and investment both fell significantly.

But if wages are sticky, there is no underlying tendency for the economy to return to full-employment equilibrium. In essence, the equilibrium at B is a long-run equilibrium in the Keynesian model. What is the source of the extreme price stickiness? Keynesian economists have posited that resource prices such as wages are very sticky downward, especially when negotiated through collective bargaining agreements by unions. Certainly, a larger percentage of the labor force was unionized in the 1930s, and this fact could have added to the wage rigidity. But money illusion may also have played a role. Consider yourself an employee in the midst of the Great Depression: times are tough, and now your employer is asking you to take a wage decrease. This would be a tough pill to swallow even if it were not a *real* wage decrease, so some might refuse a wage decrease. Employees that refused a pay cut would be laid off. This begins a troubling cycle. Workers without jobs drastically cut their spending, and this leads to a reduction in economic activity. Recall the circular flow diagram we discussed in Chapter 1. The welfare of businesses and workers are intertwined.

TABLE 27.1

Classical versus Keynesian Economics

	Classical economics	Keynesian economics
Key time period	Long run	Short run
Price flexibility	Prices are flexible	Prices are sticky
Savings	Crucial to growth	A drain on demand
Key side of market	Supply	Demand
Market tendency	Stability, full employment	Instability, cyclical unemployment
Government intervention	Not necessary	Essential

Keynes recommended that the British and U.S. governments take action to increase aggregate demand. Keynes felt that governments could play a role in stopping the decline with additional government spending, such as investing in social programs and additional infrastructure (we discuss this further in Chapter 29). During the Great Depression, a host of programs put into place as part of Franklin Delano Roosevelt's New Deal were designed to create immediate jobs and spending in the economy. If aggregate demand is too low because individuals and firms are reluctant to spend, Keynes argued, the government might fill the void by increasing the government-spending piece of aggregate demand. We cover this topic in more detail in Chapter 29.

The Keynesian view of the economy offered an explanation for the Great Depression (see the appendix to this chapter for more details on this view). In fact, after the nation emerged from the Great Depression, Keynesian theory became dominant in the field of economics.

Table 27.1 summarizes the major differences between classical and Keynesian economists.

Conclusion

We began this chapter with the misconception that the Great Recession is comparable to the Great Depression. But we have seen that other than having similar names, the two economic contractions were not much alike. The Great Depression lasted much longer and had a much greater impact on unemployment and real GDP. The two contractions are the two largest in the U.S. economy over the past 100 years, but the Great Depression was significantly more severe.

Going forward, we can use the aggregate demand–aggregate supply model as a tool for analyzing government policy. Most economists believe that the macroeconomy needs at least a little help from government. This help comes in the form of monetary policy, which adjusts the money supply, and fiscal policy, which adjusts taxes and spending. Over the next four chapters, we evaluate these policy alternatives and use the aggregate demand–aggregate supply model to understand how government policy affects the economy.

PRACTICE WHAT YOU KNOW

The Big Debates: Guess Which View

Which type of economist would recommend this shopping trip?

Question: Consider the four statements below. Which type of economist, Keynesian or classical, would likely make each statement? Explain your choice each time.

a. "If you want to help the economy, you should increase your spending."

b. "If you want to help the economy, you should increase your savings."

c. "Government policy should focus on counteracting short-run fluctuations in the economy."

d. "Government policy should not intervene in the business cycle because the economy can correct itself."

Answer:

a. *Keynesian.* The Keynesian approach focuses on spending, or aggregate demand, as the fundamental factor in the economy.

b. *Classical.* The classical approach focuses on long-run aggregate supply as the primary source of economic prosperity. In this view, increases in savings are necessary for increased investment, which shifts long-run aggregate supply to the right.

c. *Keynesian.* The Keynesian approach emphasizes inherent instability in the macroeconomy and the resulting need for government action to counteract the business cycle.

d. *Classical.* The classical approach emphasizes price flexibility, which means that the economy can correct itself and naturally move back to full-employment output levels.

ANSWERING THE BIG QUESTIONS

Exactly what happened during the Great Recession and the Great Depression?

* The Great Recession was characterized by shifts in both long-run aggregate supply and aggregate demand.
* The Great Recession was deeper and longer than typical U.S. recessions.
* The Great Depression was significantly worse than the Great Recession.
* Many factors contributed to the Great Depression, but most significant was a large and persistent decline in aggregate demand.

What are the big disagreements in macroeconomics?

＊ The big debates in macroeconomics focus on the flexibility of prices and the emphasis on aggregate supply or aggregate demand. The two key schools of thought are classical economics and Keynesian economics.

＊ If prices are assumed to be flexible, the implication is a generally stable macroeconomy without significant need for government help.

＊ If prices are assumed to be sticky, the implication is an inherently unstable economy in need of government assistance.

The Big Disagreements in Macroeconomics

ECONOMICS IN THE MEDIA

"Fear the Boom and the Bust"

This highly original rap video imagines what two giants of economics, F. A. Hayek and John Maynard Keynes, would have to say to defend their ideas. F. A. Hayek represents the classical economists. Here is one of the best lines:

> We've been going back and forth for a century
> **[KEYNES]** I want to steer markets,
> **[HAYEK]** I want them set free
> There's a boom and bust cycle and good reason to fear it.

F. A. Hayek was the twentieth century's most significant defender of free markets. In 1943, he wrote *The Road to Serfdom*, a book that cautions against central planning. Hayek characterizes markets as having the ability to organize spontaneously, to the benefit of an economy. *The Road to Serfdom* appeared in print just a few years after John Maynard Keynes published his *General Theory* in 1936. How could these two giants of economics see the world so differently?

Hayek, who received the 1974 Nobel Prize in Economics, lived long enough to observe that economics had come full circle. His Nobel acceptance speech was titled "The Pretense of Knowledge." In the talk, he criticized the economics profession for being too quick to adopt Keynesian ideas. Keynes had argued that the economy moves slowly to long-run equilibrium. Hayek countered that efforts to stimulate demand presume that economists know what they are doing; he argued that just because we

It's Keynes versus Hayek!

can build elaborate macroeconomic models does not mean that the models can anticipate every change in the economy. Hayek pointed to the high inflation rates and high unemployment rates of the 1970s as evidence that the Keynesian model was incomplete. Accordingly, he concluded, it would be best to put our faith in the one thing all economists generally agree on: that eventually the economy will naturally return to full-employment output levels.

"Fear the Boom and the Bust" presents the views of Hayek and Keynes to make you think. While there are many references in the rap that you might not "get" just yet, watch it anyway (and tell your friends to watch it). The subject it treats is an important, ongoing debate, and one of the goals of your study of economics is to acquire the information you need to decide for yourself what approach is best for the economy.

Understanding the Great Depression in Today's Context

You lived through the Great Recession. Perhaps it affected you personally. Certainly, many people experienced hardships as a result of the economic downturn. However, very few of us were forced to move into shanties on the street as a result of the downturn.

But the Great Depression was different. Living through it literally scarred an entire generation of Americans. Perhaps your great-grandparents were part of this generation. Now might be a good time to talk to them and ask how their life changed during the 1930s.

Many American families lost their homes and jobs during the Depression. The best alternative for many in some parts of the country was sharecropping, or living on a farm and harvesting the crops on behalf of the owners. For some other families, the best available living arrangement was in shantytowns outside of major cities. These shantytowns became known as Hoovervilles, named after President Hoover (who was in office from 1929 to 1933). Although homelessness and unemployment are still issues in the United States, the extent of the problems is far smaller today—and was far smaller during the Great Recession—than it was during the Great Depression.

We can use a familiar consumer item to illustrate the difference between the two contractions. During the Great Recession years of 2007–2009, the number of Starbucks locations in the United States grew from 10,684 to 11,128.* Thus, a chain of coffee shops that sell basic drinks for about $4 each actually expanded during the Great Recession. Yes, the coffee is very good, but that could never have happened during the Great Depression.

Now think again about how the Great Recession affected you or someone you know. How much more extreme might those effects have been during the Great Depression?

---

* "Starbucks Company Statistics," Statistic Brain, published September 2012. statisticbrain.com

Unemployed workers gather together in New York City, December 1937. They have a Christmas tree near their shanty.

Stores like this one would not have survived the Great Depression.

CONCEPTS YOU SHOULD KNOW

classical economists (p. 874) fiscal policy (p. 871) macroeconomic policy (p. 871)
Dodd-Frank Act (p. 865) Keynesian economists (p. 874) monetary policy (p. 871)

QUESTIONS FOR REVIEW

1. What were the cause(s) of the long-run aggregate supply shift during the Great Recession? What were the cause(s) of the aggregate demand shift during the Great Recession?

2. What specific numerical evidence would you give to explain why the Great Depression was so much worse than the Great Recession?

3. What is the key side (supply or demand) of the economy for Keynesian economists? What assumption about prices leads them to this emphasis? What is the key side of the economy (supply or demand) for classical economists? What assumption about prices leads them to this emphasis?

4. In Chapter 26, we covered three factors that shift long-run aggregate supply. What are those factors? Which of those factors changed during the period of the Great Recession, and how did they change?

5. In Chapter 26, we covered a list of factors that shift aggregate demand. Which of those fac-

tors changed during the Great Depression, and how did they change?

6. Consider the following statements about the macroeconomy. For each, indicate whether the statement best distinguishes the strict Keynesian view, strict classical view, or neither of these views.

   a. All prices are completely flexible.
   b. The primary focus is on aggregate supply.
   c. Spending is the key determinant of output.
   d. Capital is the key source of economic growth.
   e. Saving can be detrimental to the economy.
   f. The macroeconomy generally takes care of itself.
   g. Every dollar borrowed requires a dollar saved.
   h. The macroeconomy is inherently unstable.
   i. Full employment is at the natural rate of unemployment.
   j. Some prices don't adjust downward.

STUDY PROBLEMS (✶ solved at the end of the section)

✶ 1. Explain whether each of the following statements is more likely to come from a classical economist or a Keynesian economist:
   a. "The recent decline in consumer confidence will likely spell disaster for the economy."
   b. "Business managers making investment decisions play a crucial role in the short-run economy."
   c. "Consumer spending is down, but that is good news because it means that savings is up."
   d. "In the long run we are all dead."
   e. "There is no reason to believe that most prices will take more than several months to adjust in either direction."

2. For this problem, we want to practice working with the aggregate demand–aggregate supply model.
   a. Set up an aggregate demand–aggregate supply model in long-run equilibrium, with both short-run and long-run aggregate supply curves and an aggregate demand curve. Label the equilibrium price level as P* and the equilibrium level of real GDP as Y*. Draw this model twice.
   b. Using the first set of curves you drew in part (a), now assume that aggregate demand and aggregate supply (both short-run and long-run) decline. If all curves shift by the same amount, what is the resulting change in real

GDP and the price level? What is the implied change in the unemployment rate?

c. Now, using the second set of curves from part (a), let aggregate demand decline by a large amount while the aggregate supply curves decline by a relatively small amount. What are the resulting short-run changes in real GDP and the price level? What is the

implied short-run change in the unemployment rate?

d. Parts (b) and (c) describe the two different conditions of the Great Recession and the Great Depression. Which part refers to the Great Recession? Which part refers to the Great Depression?

SOLVED PROBLEM

1. a. *Keynesian.* The key here is that Keynesian economists emphasize the role of aggregate demand, which depends on consumer confidence.

b. *Keynesian.* The key here is the emphasis on the short run. Investment is a component of aggregate demand and can have an impact on spending in the short run.

c. *Classical.* The key here is the classical emphasis on savings, which can lead to greater

levels of lending in the loanable funds market—an outcome that increases capital in the long run.

d. *Keynesian.* In fact, this is a direct quote from John Maynard Keynes himself. The key here is that the quote de-emphasizes the long run in favor of the short run.

e. *Classical.* The key here is the emphasis on price flexibility.

The Aggregate Expenditures Model

27A

We have used the aggregate demand–aggregate supply (AD-AS) model to explain different reasons why the economy expands and contracts. In addition, we used the AD-AS model to explain the differences between classical economists and Keynesian economists. We observed that Keynesian economists focus on aggregate demand and sticky prices. In this appendix, we develop another model of the economy, the **aggregate expenditures (AE) model**, which extends the Keynesian perspective.

The AE model holds that prices are completely sticky and that aggregate demand therefore determines the economy's level of output and income. In fact, *aggregate expenditures* is another name for aggregate demand.

You may be wondering why some economists are willing to make the assumption that prices do not change. After all, we have seen that all prices adjust in the long run. We can therefore view the AE model strictly as a short-run model of the economy, where prices are inflexible. This model is particularly helpful in understanding economic downturns because, as we have seen, prices can be particularly inflexible in the downward direction.

The **aggregate expenditures (AE) model** is a short-run model of economic fluctuations. It holds that prices are completely sticky (inflexible) and that aggregate demand (aggregate expenditures) determines the economy's level of output and income.

The Components of Aggregate Expenditures

The four components of aggregate demand are consumption (C), investment (I), government spending (G), and net exports (NX). Aggregate expenditures is another way of describing aggregate demand. Let's consider each component.

Consumption

Recall that consumption expenditures constitute about 71% of all GDP spending. Because this component of aggregate expenditures is so large, it is the key to understanding the AE model. We start with a microeconomic example.

Let's say that your friend Kaitlyn has a job that pays her $3,000 a month after taxes. This $3,000 is Kaitlyn's monthly **disposable income** (Y_d), or income after taxes ($Y - T$). Kaitlyn is disciplined about saving a part of her income, using 80%, or $2,400 per month, for consumption. She saves the remaining 20%, or $600, of her disposable income. Last year was a productive year for Kaitlyn, and she is excited because her boss rewarded her with a raise that works out to $200 more disposable income every month. After the raise,

Disposable income is income after taxes ($Y - T$).

The **marginal propensity to consume (MPC)** is the portion of additional income that is spent on consumption.

The **marginal propensity to save (MPS)** is the portion of additional income that is saved.

Kaitlyn decides to continue saving 20% of her new disposable income, which leaves 80% for consumption.

We are talking about Kaitlyn's propensity to spend her income on consumption as opposed to saving. The **marginal propensity to consume (MPC)** is the portion of additional income that is spent on consumption. Kaitlyn's MPC is 80%, or 0.8. The **marginal propensity to save (MPS)** is the portion of additional income that is saved. Kaitlyn's MPS is 20%, or 0.2. MPC and MPS sum to 1 because income is either spent or saved:

(Equation 27A.1)

$$MPC + MPS = 1$$

This equation applies to individuals like Kaitlyn but also to entire economies. The MPC for a national economy is the average portion of additional income that people in the economy spend on consumption.

We can look at data from the United States over time to see how consumption spending rises with disposable income. Figure 27A.1 shows data on consumption and disposable income for the United States for the years 1964–2015. You can see the positive relationship in the slope: as disposable income rises, so does consumption.

The **aggregate consumption function** is an equation that specifies the relationship between national income and national consumption.

It is helpful to specify the relationship between national consumption spending and disposable income in equation form. This equation is called the **aggregate consumption function**:

(Equation 27A.2)

$$C = A + MPC*(Y - T)$$

Autonomous consumption spending is spending on consumption that is independent of the level of income.

This equation says that consumption rises with disposable income $(Y - T)$. Whenever disposable income increases by $1, consumption rises by MPC, the marginal propensity to consume. The letter A in the equation represents **autonomous consumption spending**, which is spending on consumption

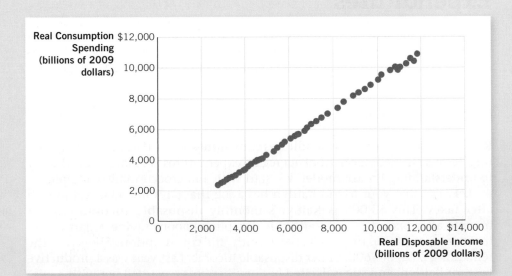

FIGURE 27A.1

U.S. Real Consumption and Disposable Income, 1965–2014

As real disposable income rises, consumption also increases. This is one way of viewing the consumption function for an entire economy.

Source: Bureau of Economic Analysis.

that is independent of the level of income. (The word "autonomous" means "independent.") Viewed this way, Equation 27A.2 implies that even when income is zero, some consumption must take place (A), and for every dollar that disposable income rises, consumption rises by MPC.

For the remainder of this appendix, we make a simplifying assumption with regard to disposable income. We assume that taxes do not change, so that all changes in income (Y) are the same changes in disposable income (Y − T). This assumption does not affect the major implications of the analysis, but it does make the model much simpler. With this assumption, the aggregate consumption function becomes

$$C = A + MPC*Y$$ (Equation 27A.3)

Consider the consumption function presented in Table 27A.1 (all dollar values are in billions of dollars). In this example, autonomous consumption is equal to $2,800 billion, and the marginal propensity to consume is 0.6. The first column shows real GDP, or real income levels, ranging from $10,000 billion to $14,000 billion. Column 2 is autonomous consumption spending, which does not change with income level (by definition). Column 3 shows the MPC of 0.6 times the value of Y from column 1. Column 4 is the sum of columns 2 and 3: total consumption (C) = A + MPC*Y.

Figure 27A.2 plots this hypothetical consumption function with real income (Y) on the horizontal axis and consumption spending (C) on the vertical axis (both measured in trillions of dollars). The consumption function starts at $2,800 billion, or $2.8 trillion, which is the level of autonomous consumption spending (A) in the economy. Then, for every dollar of additional income, consumption rises by $0.60, so that the slope of the consumption function is 0.6. This slope is the marginal propensity to consume.

Investment

Recall that investment is private spending by firms on tools, plant, equipment, and inventory to produce future output. Inventories play a critical role in the AE model. Inventory investment is not perfectly predictable because

TABLE 27A.1

An Aggregate Consumption Function (all dollars in billions; MPC = 0.6)

(1) Y Real GDP	(2) A Autonomous consumption	(3) MPC*Y	(4) C A + MPC*Y
$10,000	$2,800	$6,000	$8,800
11,000	2,800	6,600	9,400
12,000	2,800	7,200	10,000
13,000	2,800	7,800	10,600
14,000	2,800	8,400	11,200

FIGURE 27A.2

Aggregate Consumption Function

The aggregate consumption function shows how consumption is affected by changes in real GDP, which is real income. The equation for this function is C = $2.8 + 0.6*Y, which implies that autonomous consumption is $2.8 trillion and that the marginal propensity to consume (MPC) is 0.6.

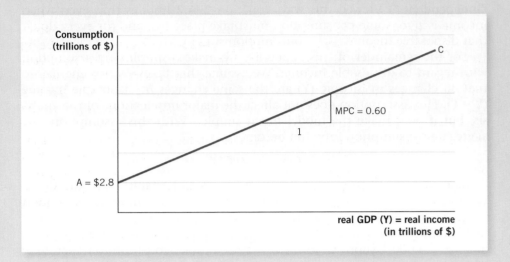

firms typically don't know the exact number of goods and services they will sell in a given period.

For example, consider a book publisher that is trying to plan for sales of a popular book in 2018. Imagine that the publisher begins the year with an inventory of 1,000 books on hand and anticipates selling 20,000 books in 2018. The publisher would like to have the same level of inventory (1,000 copies) at the end of 2018. Based on these expectations and the current inventory, the publisher prints 20,000 books in 2018.

Now consider the three scenarios displayed in Table 27A.2. In scenario 1, actual sales are 19,000, which is less than the firm anticipated. In scenario 2, actual sales are 21,000, which is more than the firm anticipated. In scenario 3, actual sales are 20,000, exactly equal to anticipated sales.

TABLE 27A.2

Planned and Unplanned Inventory

	Scenario 1 Sales = 19,000 books	Scenario 2 Sales = 21,000 books	Scenario 3 Sales = 20,000 books
Inventory at end of 2017	1,000	1,000	1,000
Production	20,000	20,000	20,000
Actual sales in 2018	19,000	21,000	20,000
Inventory at end of 2018	2,000	0	1,000
Unplanned investment	1,000	−1,000	0
Output adjustment for 2019	Decrease output	Increase output	No change

Consider scenario 1. Here, sales are less than anticipated, and so inventory at the end of 2018 is more than the firm expected. This unplanned inventory is positive **unplanned investment**, which occurs when a firm sells less than expected, causing inventory to rise beyond what was planned. All else being equal, this unplanned investment means that the firm enters the next year (2019) with more books on hand than it planned for, and it will react by producing fewer books in the next year. The last row in the table spells out this important result: positive unplanned investment leads to less output in the future, all else being equal.

(Positive) **unplanned investment** occurs when expected sales exceed actual sales, leading to an increase in inventory.

Now consider scenario 2, in which actual sales exceed anticipated sales. In this case, inventory at the end of the year is 1,000 books fewer than anticipated. This is an unanticipated decrease in investment, or **negative unplanned investment**. In this case, when people buy more books than the publisher expects, inventories decrease. All else being equal, the publisher will increase production of books in the next year.

Negative unplanned investment occurs when actual sales exceed anticipated sales, leading to a decrease in inventory.

The only scenario that does not require future adjustments is scenario 3. In this case, actual sales equal expected sales, and there are no unexpected changes in inventory: actual investment equals planned investment.

This example explains why firms across the economy adjust production each year, even when prices are fixed. When spending on output is greater than anticipated, inventories fall, which leads to output increases in subsequent periods. In contrast, if spending is less than anticipated, inventories pile up and then firms produce less in the future. Equilibrium occurs when spending plans match production plans.

An Economy without Government Spending or Net Exports

Before we consider the other components of AE, it is helpful to consider an economy without government spending or net exports. In this case, AE is equal to consumption (C) plus planned investment (PI):

$$AE = C + PI$$

(Equation 27A.4)

Let's return to our numerical example. Table 27A.3 is a continuation of the example presented in Table 27A.1 but adds planned investment expenditures. Column 4 indicates $2,000 billion in planned investment expenditures. Note that planned investment expenditures are autonomous with respect to income levels—that is, they don't change with the level of real GDP (Y). In Chapter 26, we identified three factors that do affect the level of investment demand: investor confidence, interest rates, and the quantity of money in the economy. This list does not include real income, and so we assume that planned investment expenditures are autonomous with respect to real income (Y). We add consumption (column 3) and autonomous planned investment (column 4) to derive aggregate expenditures in column 5.

Figure 27A.3 graphs the AE line. The lower line, labeled C, is the consumption function, which begins at a level of A. Recall that A is the level of autonomous consumption spending, or the amount that consumers spend in

TABLE 27A.3

Aggregate Expenditures with No Government Spending or Net Exports
(all dollars in billions, MPC = 0.6)

(1) Y Real GDP	(2) A Autonomous consumption	(3) C A + MPC*Y	(4) PI Autonomous planned investment	(5) AE C + PI
$10,000	$2,800	$8,800	$2,000	$10,800
11,000	2,800	9,400	2,000	11,400
12,000	2,800	10,000	2,000	12,000
13,000	2,800	10,600	2,000	12,600
14,000	2,800	11,200	2,000	13,200

a hypothetical case where income (Y) is zero. Consumption increases with Y, and the slope is equal to the marginal propensity to consume (MPC).

To get aggregate expenditures (AE), we add planned investment (PI) and consumption. Because planned investment spending is autonomous, adding PI to C simply shifts up AE by the same amount at all levels.

FIGURE 27A.3

Summing Consumption and Planned Investment to Get Aggregate Expenditures

Aggregate expenditures (AE) is the sum of all planned spending: consumption (C) and planned investment (PI). The lower line is consumption expenditures, which depend on the level of income (Y) in the economy. Consumption rises with income at a rate equal to the marginal propensity to consume (MPC). To get AE, we add planned investment (PI), which is assumed to be autonomous (unrelated) to income. As a result, the AE line is parallel to the C line. The distance between the two lines is planned investment expenditures.

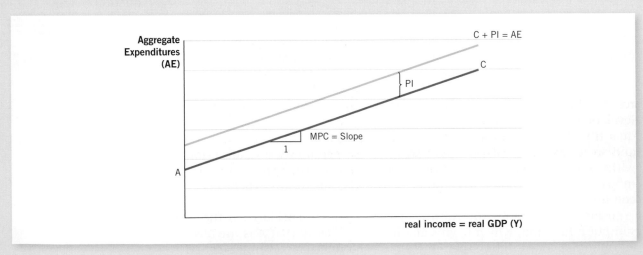

Equilibrium without Government Spending or Net Exports

Before we examine equilibrium in a general sense, let's consider a numerical example. Table 27A.4 continues our running example but adds column 6 to help us determine equilibrium.

In the AE model, equilibrium occurs when there is no reason for firms to adjust output decisions in the future. As we explained earlier, this point occurs when actual sales equal anticipated sales, so that unplanned inventory investment equals zero. In the language of the AE model, equilibrium occurs when actual spending (Y) is equal to anticipated spending (AE), or when AE = Y.

In our example, equilibrium occurs where real GDP equals $12,000 billion, where there is no difference between AE and Y (indicated in column 6 of Table 27A.4). At real GDP levels below $12,000, aggregate expenditures are greater than actual output (Y). As a result, inventories decrease, and so firms increase output toward $12,000 billion in future periods. On the other hand, at real GDP levels above $12,000 billion, real output exceeds aggregate expenditures. In this case, inventories increase unexpectedly, and firms react in future periods by reducing output toward $12,000 billion. In our example, the only equilibrium point occurs at $12,000 billion.

This is an important result: the equilibrium level of output in the economy is determined by the level of aggregate expenditures. For example, if aggregate expenditures are equal to $11,000 billion, output in the economy will adjust until equilibrium is reached at $11,000 billion. In fact, any point where AE = Y is a possible equilibrium. Panel (a) of Figure 27A.4 plots three possible equilibrium points for a macroeconomy. These always occur where actual real GDP is equal to aggregate expenditures. Panel (b) of Figure 27A.4 presents a line that includes all possible equilibrium points. Notice that this line splits the quadrant into two equal halves and so is at a 45-degree angle. This 45-degree line is a critical piece of the AE model because it shows us all possible equilibrium outcomes.

TABLE 27A.4

Equilibrium with No Government Spending or Net Exports (all dollars in billions; MPC = 0.6)

(1) Y	(2) A	(3) C	(4) PI	(5) AE	(6) AE − Y
Real GDP	Autonomous consumption	A + MPC*Y	Autonomous planned investment	C + PI	
$10,000	$2,800	$8,800	$2,000	$10,800	$800
11,000	2,800	9,400	2,000	11,400	400
12,000	2,800	10,000	2,000	12,000	0
13,000	2,800	10,600	2,000	12,600	−400
14,000	2,800	11,200	2,000	13,200	−800

FIGURE 27A.4

Equilibrium Points in the AE Model

Panel (a) shows three points that are possible equilibrium points in the AE model. For example, when AE is $12 trillion and Y is $12 trillion, then actual spending equals planned spending. In this case, there is no unplanned inventory change and the economy is in equilibrium. Panel (b) plots a line through all possible equilibrium points—that is, all points where AE = Y. This line is called the 45-degree line because it emanates from the origin at 45 degrees.

Let's put the 45-degree line together with aggregate expenditures (AE = C + PI) to determine which equilibrium will result. Figure 27A.5 plots the two lines we need for the AE model. The orange line is the 45-degree line that plots potential equilibrium points for the economy. The blue line is the actual level of AE for the economy, composed of expenditures on consumption and planned investment. Equilibrium occurs where planned AE is equal to actual (real) GDP. In this case, given the total level of AE, equilibrium occurs at $12 trillion. To see why this is the case, let's consider the adjustments that occur when actual (real) GDP is not equal to planned AE.

At a GDP of $11 trillion, planned spending (AE) is above actual output because the AE line (blue) is above the 45-degree equilibrium line (orange). In this case, spending is high relative to actual output, which leads to unplanned decreases in inventories. Thus, in the future, firms increase output to adjust to the higher level of planned spending, pushing output toward equilibrium at $12 trillion. This analysis applies to all points where the AE line is above the 45-degree line. That is, at all levels of output less than $12 trillion, firms increase future output and move toward $12 trillion of GDP.

What happens if, instead, firms produce real GDP of $13 trillion? In this case, AE (the blue line) is below actual output (the orange line). This means that spending is low relative to output, which leads to unplanned increases

FIGURE 27A.5

Equilibrium with No Government Spending or Net Exports

Equilibrium occurs at $12 trillion because that is the only point at which aggregate expenditures (AE) in the economy are exactly equal to what is produced (Y). At output levels below $12 trillion, such as $11 trillion, AE (planned spending, the blue line) is above Y (the orange line), which means that spending is above production, which leads to unplanned decreases in inventory. Firms will react by increasing output toward $12 trillion in future periods. At output levels above $12 trillion, such as $13 trillion, AE is below Y, which means that spending is above production, and this leads to unplanned increases in inventory. In this case, firms react by decreasing output toward $12 trillion in future periods.

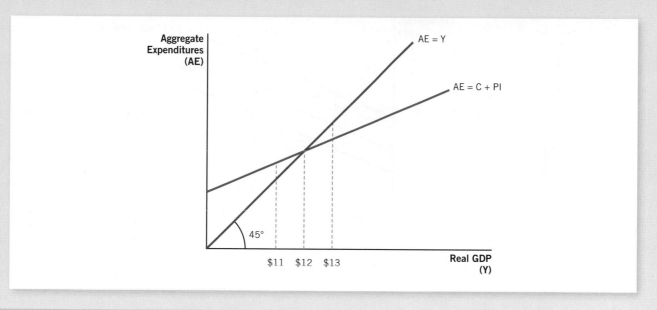

in inventories. Firms adjust in the future by reducing real output (Y) down toward equilibrium at $12 trillion.

In this example, output settles to equilibrium at $12 trillion. This is the only output level where firms' plans match the spending patterns of consumers and investors.

Aggregate Expenditures with Government Spending and Net Exports

More realistically, aggregate expenditures also includes government expenditures and net exports:

$$AE = C + PI + G + NX$$

(Equation 27A.5)

We can now add both government spending (G) and net exports (NX) to see how they affect the macroeconomic equilibrium. Figure 27A.6 shows the aggregate expenditures curve when we include consumption, planned investment, government, and net exports.

FIGURE 27A.6

Aggregate Expenditures with All Four Components

Aggregate expenditures (AE) are the total amount of spending in the economy from all four sources: consumption (C), planned investment (PI), government (G), and net exports (NX). Consumption spending depends on the level of income in the economy (Y) and increases at the rate of the marginal propensity to consume (MPC). The other components are assumed to be independent of the level of income, so the AE line shifts up in a parallel fashion when they are added.

TABLE 27A.5

Equilibrium with All Components of Aggregate Expenditures (all dollars in billions; MPC = 0.6)

(1) Y Real GDP	(2) A Autonomous consumption	(3) C A + MPC*Y	(4) PI Planned investment	(5) G Government spending	(6) NX Net exports	(7) AE C + PI + G + NX	(8) AE − Y
$16,000	$2,800	$12,400	$2,000	$2,000	$400	$16,800	$800
17,000	2,800	13,000	2,000	2,000	400	17,400	400
18,000	2,800	13,600	2,000	2,000	400	18,000	0
19,000	2,800	14,200	2,000	2,000	400	18,600	−400
20,000	2,800	14,800	2,000	2,000	400	19,200	−800

PRACTICE WHAT YOU KNOW

Spending and Equilibrium in a Small Economy

Consider a small economy with autonomous consumption of $700 billion, an MPC of 0.5, planned investment of $150 billion, government spending of $100 billion, and net exports of $50 billion.

Question: Determine AE in this economy when real GDP (Y) is equal to $1,500 billion, $2,000 billion, and $2,500 billion.

Answer: We can answer this question by filling in the values in the table below and then summing to get AE in the last column. Note that all dollars are in billions.

(1) Y Real GDP	(2) A Autonomous consumption	(3) C A + MPC*Y	(4) PI Planned investment	(5) G Government spending	(6) NX Net exports	(7) AE C + PI + G + NX
$1,500	$700	$1,450	$150	$100	$50	$1,750
2,000	700	1,700	150	100	50	2,000
2,500	700	1,950	150	100	50	2,250

Question: What is the equilibrium level of real GDP in this economy?

Answer: The equilibrium level of real GDP is $2,000 billion because this is the only output level for which AE (the value in the last column) is equal to Y (the value in the first column).

Consider the economy presented in Table 27A.5. Looking at the components of aggregate expenditures, we see that autonomous consumption expenditures are $2,800 billion and that the MPC is 0.6. Therefore, when income in the economy (Y) is equal to $17,000 billion, total consumption is $2,800 billion + 0.6 ($17,000) billion = $13,000 billion. This number appears in column 3. To get total AE, we also add planned investment ($2,000 billion), government spending ($2,000 billion), and net exports ($400 billion). These four components of aggregate expenditures sum to $17,400 billion. But $17,400 billion is greater than actual GDP, which is $17,000 billion. Inventories decrease by $400 billion, and so in future periods, firms increase output. The only output level that leads to equilibrium is $18,000 billion.

What Are the Implications of the AE Model?

In this section, we examine what the AE model implies about economic outcomes and potential government policy responses to those outcomes.

1. Spending Determines Equilibrium Output and Income in the Economy

One key implication of the AE model is that planned aggregate spending dictates the equilibrium level of GDP in an economy. That is, spending determines income completely. Consider the three different levels of aggregate expenditures plotted in Figure 27A.7. When spending is equal to AE_0, the equilibrium level of income in the economy is Y_0. If planned spending increases to AE_1, equilibrium income rises to Y_1. In the AE model, spending increases always lead to increases in real GDP. These increases can result from any of the four sources: consumption, planned investment, government spending, or net exports. No matter which component increases, the result is the same.

Consider the numerical example that we presented earlier in Table 27A.5. In that example, equilibrium output in the economy occurs at real GDP equal to $18 trillion, which comes from consumption spending of $13.6 trillion, planned investment spending of $2 trillion, government spending of $2 trillion, and net exports of $0.4 trillion. Now consider what happens if spending on one of these components increases.

Let's say planned investment rises by $0.4 trillion. Perhaps investor confidence rises and business decision-makers decide to invest in new factories for future production. Table 27A.6 shows the effect on equilibrium output in the economy. When planned investment rises from $2 trillion to $2.4 trillion, equilibrium real GDP in the economy rises from $18 trillion to $19 trillion.

FIGURE 27A.7

Equilibrium Points in the AE Model

The total level of spending in the economy (AE) determines equilibrium output (Y) in the AE model. When AE = AE_0, the level of output is Y_0. If AE shifts up to AE_1, real GDP rises to Y_1. If, instead, AE shifts down to AE_2, real GDP falls to Y_2.

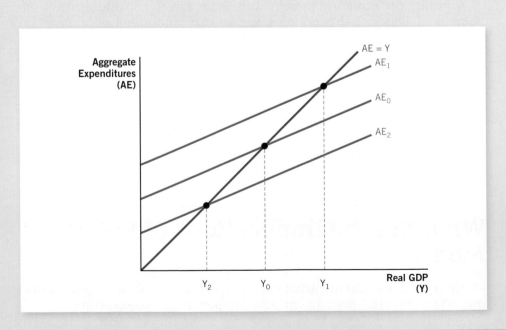

TABLE 27A.6

New Equilibrium with Higher Planned Investment Spending (all dollars in billions; MPC = 0.6)

(1) Y Real GDP	(2) A Autonomous consumption	(3) C A + MPC*Y	(4) PI Planned investment	(5) G Government spending	(6) NX Net exports	(7) AE C + PI + G + NX	(8) AE − Y
$16,000	$2,800	$12,400	$2,400	$2,000	$400	$17,200	$1,200
17,000	2,800	13,000	2,400	2,000	400	17,800	800
18,000	2,800	13,600	2,400	2,000	400	18,400	400
19,000	2,800	14,200	2,400	2,000	400	19,000	0
20,000	2,800	14,800	2,400	2,000	400	19,600	−400

The shift from AE_0 to AE_1 in Figure 27A.7 illustrates how an increase in spending leads to a higher level of real GDP in the economy. Anything that shifts AE upward—whether an increase in C, PI, G, NX, or a combination of these—will lead to an increase in real GDP. In short, spending determines real GDP.

Now consider the opposite scenario. Spending can also decline, and when it does, equilibrium GDP decreases. For example, suppose that investors become pessimistic about the future direction of the economy and decide to decrease investment spending by $0.4 trillion to $1.6 trillion. Table 27A.7 shows the new equilibrium. In this case, the equilibrium level of real GDP falls to $17 trillion.

This result holds no matter what the source of the decreased spending: C, PI, G, NX, or a combination of these components. This is why Keynesians favor government spending in an economic downturn: when G increases, real GDP rises.

TABLE 27A.7

New Equilibrium with Lower Planned Investment Spending (all dollars in billions; MPC = 0.6)

(1) Y Real GDP	(2) A Autonomous consumption	(3) C A + MPC*Y	(4) PI Planned investment	(5) G Government spending	(6) NX Net exports	(7) AE C + PI + G + NX	(8) AE − Y
$16,000	$2,800	$12,400	$1,600	$2,000	$400	$16,400	$400
17,000	2,800	13,000	1,600	2,000	400	17,000	0
18,000	2,800	13,600	1,600	2,000	400	17,600	−400
19,000	2,800	14,200	1,600	2,000	400	18,200	−800
20,000	2,800	14,800	1,600	2,000	400	18,800	−1,200

2. Equilibrium Can Occur Away from Full Employment

A second important implication of the AE model is that equilibrium output can occur when the economy is not producing full-employment output. In fact, the primary benefit of the AE model is how clearly it can explain the idea of an extended recession when spending is low in an economy. In the AD–AS model that we discussed in Chapter 26 and this appendix, there is an inherent tendency for the economy to adjust toward full-employment output, where the unemployment rate is equal to the natural rate of unemployment. But in the AE model, the equilibrium is completely determined by spending, regardless of whether or not the economy is at full employment.

This result implies that the economy can get stuck in a recession, with high unemployment and low real GDP, if spending drops. Notice that the tables and graphs in this appendix have not specified where full-employment output occurs. Equilibrium is determined by the level of spending in the economy, and this equilibrium may occur at less than full-employment output. For example, in Table 27A.5, equilibrium occurs at $18 trillion. But if full-employment output is $19 trillion, the unemployment rate might be 8% when output is at $18 trillion. This means that the economy is in a recession and there is no natural tendency for the economy to move up to $19 trillion.

3. The Spending Multiplier

In the example that accompanies Table 27A.6, we looked at the effects of an increase in planned investment spending from $2 trillion to $2.4 trillion. Let's think about how this spending increase leads to more income in the economy.

First, firms decide to increase planned investment by $0.4 trillion, or $400 billion. This means that firms spend $0.4 trillion more on factories, tools, inventory, and other equipment, which they buy from other firms. As a result, the income of these other firms and their employees rises by $400 billion. But that is just the first step, because this new income also generates additional spending in the economy.

If the MPC is 0.6, then $400 billion in new income leads to $240 billion more in consumption spending (0.6 × $400 billion = $240 billion). So the initial spending increase of $400 billion can generate spending of $640 billion ($400 billion + $240 billion). But the process doesn't stop there. Now there is another $240 billion of income to others in the economy, and they spend 60% of this income, which is $144 billion. And the process continues.

Table 27A.8 follows this spending example out for several rounds. In the end, if we add up all the new spending, we find a total increase in spending of $1,000 billion, or $1 trillion. Thus, any initial change in spending leads to a multiplied effect on real GDP.

To determine the total effect of a spending change on the economy, we use a formula for the **spending multiplier** (m^s), a number that tells us the total impact in spending from an initial change of a given amount. The formula for the spending multiplier is

The **spending multiplier** is a number that tells us the total impact on spending from an initial change of a given amount. The total impact on spending is the spending multiplier times the change in spending.

(Equation 27A.6)

$$m^s = \frac{1}{1 - \text{MPC}}$$

TABLE 27A.8

Spending Increase Multiplying through the Economy (all dollars in billions; MPC = 0.6)

Round	Spending increase*
1	$400
2	240
3	144
4	86.4
.	.
.	.
.	.
Total	$1,000

*This table assumes an initial increase in spending of $400 billion.

In our example, the MPC is 0.6. We can use this number to solve for the spending multiplier:

$$m^s = \frac{1}{1 - MPC} = \frac{1}{1 - 0.6} = \frac{1}{0.4} = 2.5$$

Thus, an MPC of 0.6 implies that any $1 change in AE eventually leads to a $2.50 change in real GDP. Spending changes are very powerful. But be careful: this statement is true of both increases and decreases. Decreases in AE can lead to large decreases in real GDP. The AE model makes it easier to understand the Keynesian view of the macroeconomy. Spending (aggregate demand or aggregate expenditures) is the key. Therefore, Keynesians often advocate for an increase in government spending. According to the AE model, the new spending in G increases income immediately and then also through the multiplier effect.

Conclusion

The AE model matches the way many people believe the economy works: spending drives the key economic results. Increases in spending lead to more income and lower unemployment. Decreases in spending lead to less income and higher unemployment. It doesn't matter why spending fluctuates—those spending changes have real effects on the macroeconomy.

The AE model implies that the economy is very unstable, driven by consumer and investor expectations and behavior. The results can be good, but they can also be very bad.

Even though the AE model is helpful in clarifying the Keynesian viewpoint, the same results can be demonstrated with the basic AD-AS model. As such, going forward in this text, we will rely on the AD–AS model to study the macroeconomy.

CONCEPTS YOU SHOULD KNOW

aggregate consumption function (p. 884)

aggregate expenditures (AE) model (p. 883)

autonomous consumption spending (p. 884)

disposable income (p. 883)

marginal propensity to consume (MPC) (p. 884)

marginal propensity to save (MPS) (p. 884)

negative unplanned investment (p. 887)

spending multiplier (p. 896)

unplanned investment (p. 887)

QUESTIONS FOR REVIEW

1. The slope of both the consumption function and the aggregate expenditures (AE) line is equal to the marginal propensity to consume (MPC).

   a. Explain why the slope of the consumption function is equal to the MPC.

   b. Explain why the slope of the AE line is equal to the MPC.

2. The AE model implies that a $1 change in government spending eventually leads to more than a $1 change in equilibrium real GDP. Explain how this multiplier process works.

3. Why is it that, in the AE model, all adjustments to equilibrium occur as changes in output? In other words, why does real GDP always change to move the economy to equilibrium?

STUDY PROBLEM (*solved at the end of the section)

*1. Assume that the following values apply to the Spanish economy:

   • Autonomous consumption (A) is $200 billion.
   • The marginal propensity to consume (MPC) is 0.8.

   • Planned investment expenditure is $50 billion across all income levels.
   • Government spending is $100 billion across all income levels.
   • Net exports are $50 billion across all income levels.

   a. Fill in the missing values in the following table. (All dollars are in billions.)

Y Real GDP (billions)	A Autonomous consumption	C A + MPC*Y	PI Planned investment	G Government spending	NX Net exports	AE C + PI + G + NX	AE − Y
$1,000							
1,500							
2,000							
2,500							
3,000							

b. What is the equilibrium GDP level for Spain as implied by the AE model in this example? How is this equilibrium determined?

c. At the current equilibrium GDP level, the unemployment rate in Spain is relatively high. Therefore, the government of Spain proposes to double the level of government spending (increase G to $200 billion). What is the new equilibrium level of real GDP?

d. What spending multiplier is implied by the MPC of 0.8?

SOLVED PROBLEM

1.a. All dollars are in billions.

Y Real GDP	A Autonomous consumption	C A + MPC*Y	PI Planned investment	G Government spending	NX Net exports	AE C + PI + G + NX	AE − Y
$1,000	$200	$1,000	$50	$100	$50	$1,200	$200
1,500	200	1,400	50	100	50	1,600	100
2,000	200	1,800	50	100	50	2,000	0
2,500	200	2,200	50	100	50	2,400	−100
3,000	200	2,600	50	100	50	2,800	−200

b. The equilibrium output level will be at $2,000 billion because this is the only level of real GDP where AE = Y.

c. If G doubles to $200 billion, the new equilibrium output level is $2,500 billion because this is where the new AE = Y.

d. The spending multiplier is

$$m^s = \frac{1}{1 - MPC} = \frac{1}{1 - 0.8} = \frac{1}{0.2} = 5$$

PART

8

Fiscal
POLICY

Federal Budgets
The Tools of Fiscal Policy

Governments never balance their budgets.

You don't have to look far to read about government budget problems. Does *any* government have enough money to pay its bills? Debt prob-

MIS CONCEPTION

lems seem to be mounting all over the globe, including in various U.S. states and localities. Nationally, the U.S. budget has seen record deficits in recent years, with spending vastly surpassing revenue. Given the current budget environment, one might assume that governments never balance their budgets. But, in fact, the United States had a balanced budget as recently as 2001.

So deficits are not inevitable. But then why are they so rampant? In this chapter, we examine the causes of budget imbalances and consider whether they can be avoided in the future. The primary goal of the chapter is to equip you with the knowledge you need to critically examine fiscal policy options. We frame the recent government budget struggles in their proper context to give you a better sense of the magnitude of these problems both historically and globally.

Of all the chapters in this text, this and the following chapter on government policy responses to the business cycle are among the most important for your postcollege life. Though you are not likely to actually work on government budgets, if you vote or otherwise participate in the political process, you'll need to decide what tax and spending plans endorsed by the various candidates make the most sense to you.

In this chapter, we first consider the spending side of the government budget. We then move to the revenue side, where we look closely at taxes. Finally, we bring these two sides together to examine budget deficits and government debt.

Budgets for the U.S. government are the result of negotiations between Congress and the president.

BIG QUESTIONS

* How does the government spend?
* How does the government tax?
* What are budget deficits?

How Does the Government Spend?

We live in interesting and historic macroeconomic times. Since the onset of the global financial crisis in 2007, federal budget crises have arisen in nations around the globe, including the United States, Japan, Greece, Italy, Peru, and Argentina. Government budgets have moved into the spotlight mainly because so many governments are deeply in debt. Here in the United States, the federal government's debt is a constant topic of political and economic debate.

A government budget is a plan for both spending and raising funds for the government. In this way, it is similar to a budget you may create for your own personal finances. There are two sides to a budget: the sources of funds (income, or revenue) and the uses of funds (spending, or outlays). We start with the spending side. If we were looking at your personal budget, the spending categories might include tuition, books, food, and housing.

Government Outlays

The U.S. government now spends over $3.5 trillion each year—more than $10,000 for every citizen. Figure 28.1 shows real U.S. government outlays from 1965 to 2014. Notice how steep the line gets around the year 2000 and then steeper yet in 2007. Between 2001 and 2010, real outlays grew by more than 37%. There are many reasons for this rapid growth in government spending. Much of the increase was due to spending during and after the Great Recession of 2007–2009 in an effort to keep the economy from sinking further. But there have also been significant spending increases in government programs such as Social Security and Medicare.

When you think of U.S. government spending, your mind probably jumps to goods and services like roads, bridges, military equipment, and government employees. These are part of the government spending component (G) in gross domestic product. But as we examine the total government budget, we must also include **transfer payments**, which are payments made to groups or individuals when no good or service is received in return. When making transfer payments, the government transfers funds from one group in the country to another. Transfer payments include income assistance (welfare) and Social Security payments to retired or disabled persons. As we'll see

Transfer payments are payments made to groups or individuals when no good or service is received in return.

FIGURE 28.1

U.S. Government Outlays, 1965–2014 (in billions of 2012 dollars)

Total outlays represent the spending side of the government budget. This graph shows real outlays (in billions of 2012 dollars) since 1965. In the decade between 2001 and 2010, real outlays grew by 37%. Total (nominal) outlays are now over $3.5 trillion per year, or $10,000 per U.S. citizen.

Source: U.S. Office of Management and Budget. Figures are converted to 2012 dollars using GDP deflator for government expenditures from the Bureau of Economic Analysis.

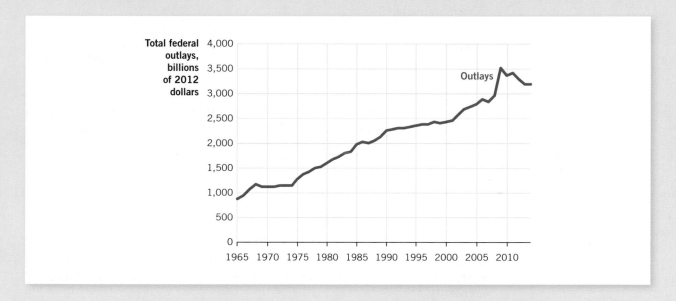

later in this chapter, transfer payments constitute a large and growing share of U.S. federal outlays.

When looking at government budgets, we include both spending and transfer payments in the broader category called **government outlays**. Table 28.1 shows the major divisions in U.S. government outlays in 2014. We divide the outlays into three groups: mandatory outlays, discretionary spending, and interest payments. By far the largest portion of the federal budget is dedicated to **mandatory outlays**, which constitute government spending that is determined by ongoing government programs like Social Security and Medicare. These programs are mandatory because existing laws mandate government funding for them. Mandatory outlays are not generally altered during the budget process; they require changes to existing laws. Sometimes, mandatory outlays are known as *entitlement programs* because citizens who meet certain requirements are entitled to benefits under current laws. We talk more about these mandatory programs in the next section.

Discretionary outlays comprise government spending that can be altered when the government is setting its annual budget. Examples of discretionary spending include monies for bridges and roads, payments to government workers, and defense spending. When you think of examples of government spending, you may think of these discretionary items. But total discretionary

Government outlays are the part of the government budget that includes both spending and transfer payments.

Mandatory outlays, sometimes called *entitlement programs*, comprise government spending that is determined by ongoing government programs like Social Security and Medicare.

Discretionary outlays comprise spending that can be altered when the government is setting its annual budget.

TABLE 28.1		
2012 U.S. Government Outlays		
Category	2014 outlays (billions of dollars)	Percentage of total
Social Security	$845	24%
Medicare	600	17%
Income assistance	613	17%
Other plus receipts	39	1%
Defense	595	17%
Nondefense discretionary	583	17%
Interest	229	7%
Total	**$3,504**	

Mandatory 59%

Discretionary 34%

Interest 7%

Source: Congressional Budget Office.

spending accounts for less than 35% of the U.S. government budget (see again Table 28.1).

The final category in Table 28.1 is interest payments. These are payments made to current owners of U.S. Treasury bonds. Such payments are not easy to alter, given a certain level of debt, so they are also essentially mandatory payments.

To better understand these three categories, consider how the spending side of your monthly budget might look after you graduate from college. You'll need to plan for groceries, gasoline, car payments, housing payments, utility bills, and perhaps student loan payments. Some of these categories will be discretionary—that is, you'll be able to alter them from month to month. These discretionary categories include groceries, gas, and utilities. Some categories will be mandatory, with a level that is predetermined each month. Mandatory categories include your monthly housing and car payments. Finally, your student loan payments are like obligatory government interest payments.

We clarify the distinction between mandatory and discretionary spending because it's important to note that certain categories are mandated by law and not negotiable from year to year. The distinctions also help us understand the recent growth of government spending in many nations. It turns out that much of the growth has been in mandatory spending. Returning to Table 28.1, we see that mandatory spending constituted 59% of the U.S. budget in 2014. In fact, if we include interest payments as obligatory, that leaves just 34% of the U.S. budget as discretionary. You might remember this the next time you read or hear about budgetary negotiations. While much of the debate focuses on discretionary spending items, like bridges or educational subsidies or defense

Discretionary government spending includes purchases of military equipment.

items, the majority of the budget goes to mandatory spending categories.

It wasn't always this way. Figure 28.2 plots U.S. federal budget categories as portions of total outlays for the years 1965–2014. The orange-shaded categories represent mandatory spending. Fifty years ago, mandatory spending was less than one-third of the U.S. federal budget. The cause of the growth in mandatory spending over the last 50 years is largely political: more programs have been added to the government outlay budget. Miscellaneous mandatory spending programs include unemployment compensation, income assistance (welfare), and food stamps. Medicare was added in 1966 and then expanded in 2006. In 2014, Social Security and Medicare together accounted for more than one-third of the U.S. federal budget, up from only 13% in 1965. Part of this increase was due to expanded benefits, such as Medicare coverage of prescription drug costs and increasing Social Security payments to retirees. In addition, as we shall see, the changing demographics of the U.S. population have contributed to the growth in mandatory spending.

Dining out on steak might be important to you, but it is not a mandatory category in your budget.

Social Security and Medicare

Because of the growing size of the Social Security and Medicare programs, it is important to understand what they are and why so many resources are devoted to these programs in the United States.

In 1935, as part of the New Deal and in the midst of the Great Depression, the U.S. Congress and President Franklin Roosevelt created the Social Security

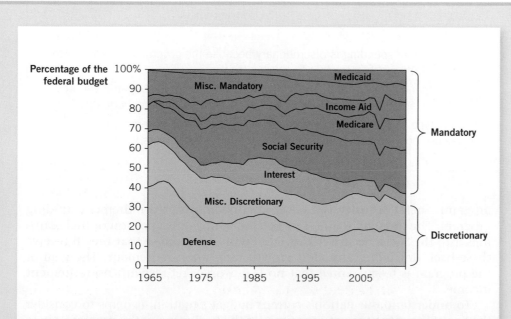

FIGURE 28.2

Historical Federal Outlay Shares, 1965–2014

The percentage of the budget allocated to mandatory spending programs has almost doubled since 1965. In contrast, discretionary spending is a shrinking part of the federal budget.

Source: Congressional Budget Office.

PRACTICE WHAT YOU KNOW

Is your mobile phone bill mandatory or discretionary?

Mandatory versus Discretionary Spending

Question: Of the following types of private spending, which are discretionary and which are mandatory components of a consumer's budget? Explain your response for each.

a. groceries

b. car payment

c. cell phone monthly fee

Answer:

a. This type of spending is discretionary. Even though groceries are a necessity, consumers can increase or decrease their spending on this budget component.

b. A car payment is typically mandatory because the consumer has signed a long-term loan agreement that entails monthly payments.

c. This type of payment is mandatory if the consumer has a long-term contract but discretionary if the phone plan is pay-as-you-go.

Question: Of the following types of government spending, which are discretionary and which are mandatory components of a government budget? Explain your response for each.

a. a new interstate highway

b. Medicare

c. international aid

Answer:

a. This type of spending is discretionary because the government can choose not to fund a new interstate highway.

b. This spending is mandatory because the government is obligated via previously enacted laws to pay Medicare expenses when recipients qualify.

c. This type of spending is discretionary. Each year, the government can choose how much to spend on aid to foreign governments.

Social Security is a U.S. government-administered retirement funding program.

program. **Social Security** is a government-administered retirement funding program. The program requires workers to contribute a portion of their earnings into the Social Security Trust Fund with the promise that they'll receive these back (including a modest growth rate) upon retirement. The goal of the program is to guarantee that no U.S. worker retires with no retirement income.

To understand our nation's current budget situation, it helps to consider the Social Security program over time. At the beginning of the program, there were just a few retirees receiving Social Security and many workers contributing to Social Security. As a result, payments into the Trust Fund began to pile up, even though at that time Social Security taxes were only 2% of wages. However, as time went on, more and more workers retired and became eligible for benefits. Thus, as workers retire and draw benefits from the program, the balance of the Trust Fund declines. To keep the Trust Fund from running out of funds, Social Security tax rates have increased. The tax rate is now up to 12.4%.

Medicare is a mandated federal program that funds health care for people age 65 and older. This program was established in 1965 with the goal of providing medical insurance for all retired workers. Like Social Security, the law requires current workers to pay Medicare taxes with the promise of receiving insurance upon retirement. In 2003, Medicare was extended into reimbursements for prescription drugs for retirees as well.

Franklin Delano Roosevelt signed the Social Security Act in 1935.

Both Medicare and Social Security are concentrated on the elderly population and so are greatly affected as population demographics shift. Given that these programs now account for more than 40% of all federal outlays, we need to consider the nation's demographic changes before we can completely understand the ongoing dynamics of the federal budget.

Medicare is a mandated U.S. federal program that funds health care for people age 65 and older.

Demographics

Entitlement programs have come to dominate the federal budget, with Social Security and Medicare taking up ever-expanding shares. There are three underlying natural demographic reasons. First, people are living longer today than ever before, which means that they draw postretirement benefits for a longer period of time. In 1930, life expectancy after age 60 was less than 13.7 years. The length of time that retirees would collect Social Security benefits was therefore limited. Today, Americans live an average of 22.6 years after age 60. This is a big change from the assumptions on which the system was founded.

Second, those who paid into the programs for many years are now retired and drawing benefits. To be eligible for Social Security and Medicare payments, workers have to pay taxes out of their earnings while they work. Thus, in the early years of Social Security and Medicare, very few workers were eligible for payouts, but millions of workers were paying in. So both programs naturally generated substantial tax revenue with very few outlays for many years. But the honeymoon is over.

Third, in addition to a normal flow of retirees, the baby boomers (people born between 1946 and 1964) are now retiring. Thus, over the next 15 to 20 years, workers will retire in record numbers. This demographic shift will require record spending on the mandatory programs.

Panel (a) of Figure 28.3 shows the U.S. population age 65 and over by decade since 1900. Notice how in each decade a larger portion of the population is older than 65—and therefore eligible for mandatory benefits from Social Security and Medicare. This portion will grow even larger over the next two decades. Panel (b) of Figure 28.3 shows the change in the number

FIGURE 28.3

The Effects of an Aging Population on Social Security, 1900–2010

Panel (a) shows how the U.S. population is aging, with an increasing percentage being age 65 and older. With the baby boomers now reaching age 65, the percentage will increase even further in coming years. More retirees also means that there will be fewer and fewer workers per Social Security beneficiary, as panel (b) illustrates.

Sources: U.S. Census Bureau and Social Security Administration.

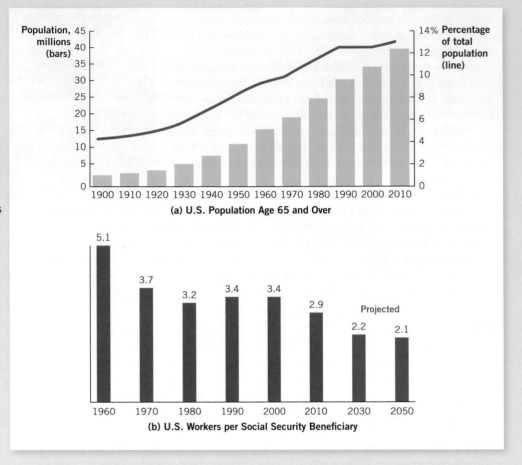

(a) U.S. Population Age 65 and Over

(b) U.S. Workers per Social Security Beneficiary

of U.S. workers per Social Security beneficiary, beginning in 1960. As you can see, in 1960 there were more than five workers per beneficiary in the Social Security system. With that number, it wasn't very difficult to accumulate a large trust fund. But now there are fewer than three workers per beneficiary, and as the baby boomers retire, this number is set to fall to just above two, as indicated by the projections for the years 2030 and 2050.

Any discussion about the national debt and deficits must necessarily focus on these programs. If we are serious about reducing the national debt, we cannot ignore them.

ECONOMICS IN THE REAL WORLD

Are There Simple Fixes to the Social Security and Medicare Funding Problems?

If the Social Security and Medicare programs are not revamped, the U.S. government budget will be strained by obligations to these programs in the future. Fortunately, many economists feel that a few relatively minor tweaks can solve the problems. The proposed solutions include the following:

1. *Increasing the retirement age from 67 to 70.* In general, people are living longer and healthier lives than when these retirement programs were implemented. If people were to work three years longer, they would have three more years of saving for retirement and three fewer years of drawing benefits.

2. *Adjusting the benefits computation to the consumer price index.* Benefit payments to retirees are adjusted for inflation on the basis of average wage levels when they retire. This policy is in place to ensure that workers' benefits keep up with standard-of-living changes during their working years. Currently, these benefits payments are adjusted on the basis of an average wage index, which has historically increased faster than the CPI. If, instead, the CPI were used to adjust benefits payments, the payments would not grow as fast and would still account for inflation.

3. *Means-testing for Medicare and Social Security benefits.* As it stands now, retirees receive benefits from Medicare and Social Security regardless of whether they are able to pay on their own. Thus, one suggestion is to decrease the benefits paid to wealthier recipients who can afford to pay for their own retirement and medical care.

While these three proposed solutions may help to shore up the federal budget, each one would involve a change in existing law. Moving the retirement age to 70 years would alter the labor force going forward, but it would mean billions of dollars in savings for these federal programs. In contrast, changing the benefits indexation from the average wage index to the CPI would yield mixed effects; the CPI has actually increased more rapidly than average wages in recent years. Finally, if means-testing were implemented, it would completely change incentives going forward. Means-testing would punish retirees who have saved on their own and can therefore afford more in retirement. In addition, Medicare and Social Security are mandatory programs that all workers must pay into (through taxes) during their time in the labor force. Means-testing implies that some workers wouldn't receive the benefits from a program they were required to pay into.

Incentives

These three simple solutions might reduce the benefits paid out in the short run and, in so doing, reduce pressure on the federal budget. But means-testing would likely lead to greater problems in the long run because of the incentive problem. ✳

Spending and Current Fiscal Issues

Before turning our attention to the revenue side of the budget, we should take a look at the recent history of U.S government outlays. Figure 28.4 shows real federal government outlays from 1990 to 2014. In the figure, you can clearly see that federal government spending began growing quickly around 2001. While there are many reasons for the increased spending, we can identify three major factors:

1. *Increased spending on Social Security and Medicare.* As we have seen, spending on these programs has grown significantly in recent years.

2. *Defense spending after the terrorist attacks of September 11, 2001.* Prior to 2001, defense spending had consistently declined as a portion of the federal budget since the fall of the Soviet Union in 1991, to just 16.5%

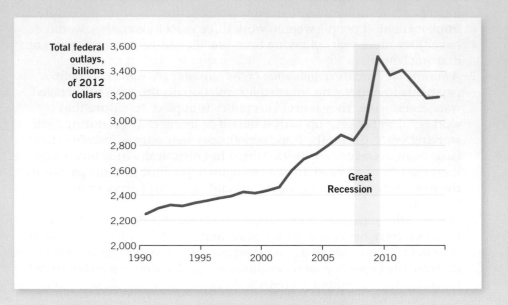

FIGURE 28.4

U.S. Government Outlays, 1990–2014 (in billions of 2012 dollars)

The rate of growth of U.S. government outlays has increased significantly in recent years. This graph shows a clear increase in spending after the terrorist attacks on September 11, 2001, as well as large spending increases during and after the Great Recession.

Source: U.S. Office of Management and Budget.

by 2001. But by 2010, defense spending had increased to 19.1% of the federal budget as a result of major conflicts, including the Iraq war.

3. *Government responses to the Great Recession, beginning with fiscal policy in 2008.* We'll cover these policy responses (including their rationale) more fully in Chapter 29, but it's important to note that real outlays increased by 25% from 2007 to 2009.

How Does the Government Tax?

Governments have several ways to raise revenues. Fees assessed for government services—for example, admission fees to national parks—contribute small amounts of revenue. However, virtually all government revenue is raised through taxes.

No one enjoys paying taxes, but government activity must be funded. If we want the government to provide Social Security, Medicare, national defense, highways, and public education, then we have to pay taxes. In this section, we detail the principal means by which the federal government raises tax revenue.

Sources of Tax Revenue

Figure 28.5 shows the sources of tax revenue for the U.S. government in 2014. The two largest sources are the individual income tax and the social insurance (Social Security and Medicare) tax. Together, these two categories accounted for 80% of all federal tax revenue in the United States in 2014. Both of these taxes are deducted from workers' paychecks, so they are referred to as *payroll taxes*.

The other major types of taxes together produced just 20% of the federal revenue. The largest of these is taxes on the income of corporations, which yielded $320.7 billion in 2014, or a little less than 10% of the total revenue. Estate and gift taxes are levied when property is gifted to others, particularly as an inheritance. Excise taxes are taxes on a particular good or commodity, such as cigarettes or gasoline. The federal excise tax on cigarettes is $1.01 per pack, and the federal tax on gasoline is 18.4 cents per gallon. Altogether, excise taxes yielded $93.4 billion in tax revenue in 2014. Customs taxes are taxes on imports, and these yielded just $33.9 billion in 2014. Because of the relative importance of payroll taxes to the financing of the U.S. government, we discuss them in greater detail in the next section.

Payroll Taxes

When you graduate from college and get a full-time job, you'll probably receive bigger paychecks than you have previously received. But those paychecks will probably be smaller than you expect. Remember, the government pays for activities with tax revenue predominantly raised from income. Let's look more closely at the two types of payroll taxes: the social insurance tax and the individual income tax.

Social Insurance Tax

Earlier in this chapter, we discussed Social Security and Medicare. You will recall that more than 40% of the U.S. federal government's outlays are for

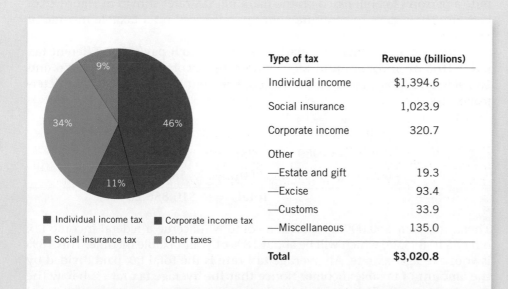

Type of tax	Revenue (billions)
Individual income	$1,394.6
Social insurance	1,023.9
Corporate income	320.7
Other	
—Estate and gift	19.3
—Excise	93.4
—Customs	33.9
—Miscellaneous	135.0
Total	**$3,020.8**

Pie chart legend:
- ■ Individual income tax
- ■ Corporate income tax
- ■ Social insurance tax
- ■ Other taxes

FIGURE 28.5

U.S. Federal Tax Revenue Sources, 2014

The major sources of tax revenue for the U.S. government are the two payroll taxes: the individual income tax and the social insurance (Social Security and Medicare) tax. Together, these two categories accounted for 80% of all tax revenue in 2014. Total tax revenue in 2014 was about $3 trillion.

Source: Congressional Budget Office, Historical Budget Data.

these two programs. And these programs are paid for with taxes on employees' pay; the benefits received by a retiree depend on the taxes paid in during his or her time in the labor force. Currently, the tax for these two programs amounts to 15.3% of a worker's pay. This amount is typically split in half, with 7.65% paid by the employee and 7.65% paid by the employer. People who are self-employed pay the full 15.3% (the Social Security portion of this tax is applicable to the first $118,500 an individual earns). These dollars go into the Social Security and Medicare trust funds that provide income and health care assistance to retirees.

Income Tax

In a **progressive income tax system**, people with higher incomes pay a larger portion of their income in taxes than people with lower incomes do.

The **marginal tax rate** is the tax rate paid on an individual's next dollar of income.

U.S. federal income taxes are set according to a scale that increases with income levels. In a **progressive income tax system**, people with higher incomes pay a larger percentage of their income in taxes than people with lower incomes do. Figure 28.6 shows 2014 U.S. federal tax rates for single individuals. Notice that the tax rate climbs with income level, indicating the progressiveness of the U.S. income tax system.

The tax rates specified in Figure 28.6 are marginal tax rates. A **marginal tax rate** is the tax rate paid on an individual's next dollar of income. Let's say your first full-time job after college offers you a salary of $66,200. For simplicity, we'll assume you take the standard tax deduction of $6,200 so that your taxable income is exactly $60,000. In terms of the tax rates presented in Figure 28.6, this income level puts you in the 25% tax bracket. This doesn't mean that you'll pay 25% of all your income in taxes; it only means that you'll pay 25% on every dollar of income *above $36,900*. You'll pay 10% on income up to $9,075 and 15% on the income between $9,076 and $36,900.

Marginal thinking

When we consider fiscal policy in Chapter 29, it will be critical to understand the way income tax rates affect an individual's total tax bill. For this reason, we will now go through a more extended example in which we compute a person's tax bill based on the marginal tax rates shown in Figure 28.6. Let's use these rates to compute your tax bill based on a taxable income of $60,000.

Before we go through the math, note that you'll pay three different tax rates: 10% on income up to $9,075; 15% on income between $9,076 and $36,900; and 25% on income above $36,900. Your total tax bill will be determined as

$$0.10 \times \$9,075 = \$907.50$$
$$+\ 0.15 \times (\$36,900 - \$9,075) = \$4,173.75$$
$$+\ 0.25 \times (60,000 - \$36,900) = \$5,775.00$$
$$\text{Total} = \$10,856.25$$

The **average tax rate** is the total tax paid divided by the amount of taxable income.

Therefore, your $60,000 in taxable income will accrue a federal income tax bill of $10,856.25, which will be about 18% of your taxable income. This 18% is your average tax rate. An **average tax rate** is the total tax paid divided by the amount of taxable income. Notice that the average tax rate is below the marginal tax rate. This is generally the case in a progressive tax system, and it is due to the fact that the marginal tax rate applies to the last few dollars taxed, not to all income.

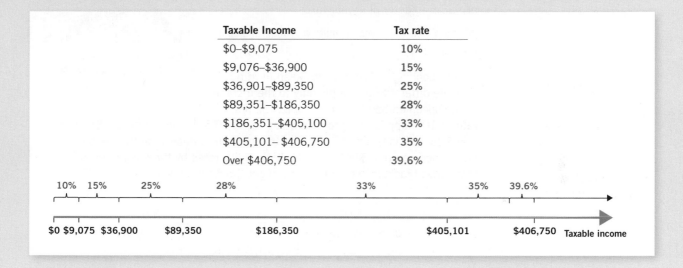

FIGURE 28.6

2014 U.S. Federal Tax Rates

These tax rates are marginal tax rates, which means that they apply only to dollars within the specified income ranges. For example, all income earned between $36,901 and $89,350 is taxed at 25%; but if someone earns $89,351, that last dollar is taxed at the 28% rate.

Source: Internal Revenue Service.

Taxable Income	Tax rate
$0–$9,075	10%
$9,076–$36,900	15%
$36,901–$89,350	25%
$89,351–$186,350	28%
$186,351–$405,100	33%
$405,101– $406,750	35%
Over $406,750	39.6%

Historical Income Tax Rates

Though taxes may seem like a fact of life now, the U.S. income tax is only about 100 years old. Prior to 1913, there was no income tax in the United States; most tax revenues were generated by taxes on imports. But import taxes were set to decline, so the government looked to income taxes as another source of revenue. The original income tax in the United States was similar to the current tax system in that the rates were progressive. However, the highest marginal tax rate in 1913 was just 6%, and that rate applied only to income greater than $500,000—over $11 million in today's dollars. Very few people were making this kind of income in 1913.

Once the income tax was instituted, marginal tax rates rose quickly. In fact, by 1918, the top marginal rate rose to 77%. This rate applied only to income over $2 million, but it meant that every dollar earned beyond $2 million yielded only 23 cents to the income earner. Figure 28.7 plots the top marginal income tax rates in the United States from 1913 to 2015. Note that while this figure shows only the top rate, it is a good indicator of the general level of rates over time.

There are several important dates in the evolution of income tax rates. During the 1930s, in the throes of the Great Depression, income tax revenues naturally fell. Presidents Hoover and Roosevelt, in attempts to balance the federal budget, pressed Congress to increase top marginal rates to 80%. Later, in 1963, with top marginal rates over 90%, President Kennedy pushed

PRACTICE WHAT YOU KNOW

Government Revenue: Federal Taxes

Assume that your taxable income is $100,000. Use the 2014 marginal tax rates from Figure 28.6 to determine your taxes.

Question: How would you compute your federal income tax?

Answer: Looking at Figure 28.6, keep in mind that the different rates apply only to the income in the specified bands. For example, the first tax rate of 10% applies only to income up to $9,075. Income between $9,076 and $36,900 is taxed at 15%. Use this pattern to determine the tax paid on all income up to $100,000. Multiply these rates by the income in the respective brackets, and sum these to get the total income tax:

Figuring out your income tax bill involves some basic math.

$0.10 \times \$9,075$	=	$907.50
$+ \, 0.15 \times (\$36,900 - \$9,075)$	=	$4,173.75
$+ \, 0.25 \times (\$89,350 - \$36,900)$	=	$13,112.50
$+ \, 0.28 \times (\$100,000 - \$89,350)$	=	$2,982.00
Total	=	**$21,175.75**

for rate reductions that decreased the top rate to 70%. Then, in the 1980s, President Reagan led the push to lower marginal tax rates even further. By the end of that decade, the top marginal rate was just 28%. In 1993, President Clinton proposed higher rates, and the top rate rose to 39.6%. President George W. Bush pushed through a temporary decrease in this top rate in 2003, and the lower rate of 35% persisted for 10 years, before the rate returned to 39.6% in 2013. Over the course of a century, there was a great deal of fluctuation in marginal tax rates. Going forward, it is not likely that rates will ever return to the levels witnessed prior to 1980.

How Are Taxes Distributed?

In a progressive tax system, the wealthy citizens pay more taxes than poor citizens with the very wealthy paying the highest share. In the United States, the wealthiest 20% of all households paid 69% of all federal taxes in 2010 (the latest year for which such data are available). Note that this amount includes both income and social insurance taxes. The poorest 40% paid just 4% of federal taxes in 2010. Figure 28.8 plots the shares of income tax liability by U.S. household income levels from 1980 to 2010. Notice that the top 1% of all households alone paid 24% of all federal taxes in 2010.

FIGURE 28.7

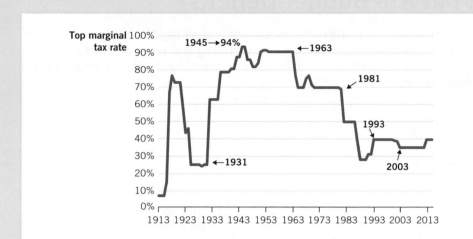

FIGURE 28.7

Historical Top U.S. Marginal Tax Rates, 1913–2015

Marginal rates are a good indicator of overall tax rates since 1913. There are several key historical dates. For example, after 1931, marginal tax rates increased significantly. Major downward revisions occurred in 1963 and in the 1980s.

Source: Internal Revenue Service.

FIGURE 28.8

Percentage of Total Federal Income and Social Insurance Taxes Paid by Various Income Groups, 1980–2010

In 2010, the middle-income group in the United States (labeled as Middle 20%) paid less than 10% of all income and social insurance taxes paid. The wealthiest 20% (the top line) of income earners paid almost 70% of all income and social insurance taxes in 2010. Digging deeper into this top 20%, we can see that the top 1% of all income earners paid nearly 25% of all income and social insurance taxes collected in 2010.

Source: Tax Policy Center.

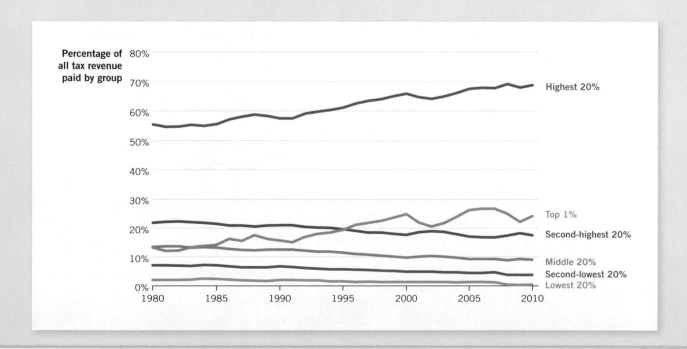

What Are Budget Deficits?

We are now ready to bring both sides of the budget together. Doing so enables us to examine the differences between spending and revenue. In this section, we define budget deficits and debt and also consider these in a long-run historical context.

Deficits

A **budget deficit** occurs when government outlays exceed revenue.

A **budget deficit** occurs when government outlays exceed revenue. Panel (a) of Figure 28.9 plots U.S. budget outlays and revenues from 1965 to 2014, in millions of 2009 dollars. Outlays, displayed in orange, have grown rapidly, especially since 2001. Over the long run, revenue has grown, but it fell from 2007 to 2010. You can see that outlays have generally exceeded revenue for much of the recent past. For example, in 2010, total outlays were almost $3.4

FIGURE 28.9

U.S. Federal Budget Data, 1965–2014 (in billions of 2009 dollars)

(a) Real outlays are shown in orange, and revenue in blue, for the U.S. federal government budget since 1965. When the outlays exceed revenue, the budget has a deficit for that year.

(b) In the plot of the real budget balance, negative values indicate a deficit. The Great Recession of 2007–2009 and the government's response to it helped to create the 2009 deficit of $1.4 trillion, the largest in U.S. history.

Source: U.S. Office of Management and Budget.

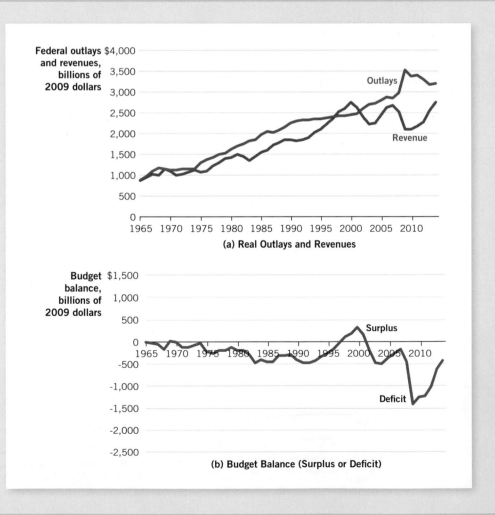

trillion, while revenue was about $2.1 trillion. The difference, $1.3 trillion, is the budget deficit for that year.

It is also possible for the government to have a **budget surplus**, which occurs when revenue exceeds outlays. The most recent federal budget surpluses came in the four years from 1998 to 2001. Panel (b) of Figure 28.9 graphs the budget balance from 1965 to 2014. When the budget is in deficit, the balance is negative; when the budget is in surplus, the balance is positive.

A **budget surplus** occurs when government revenue exceeds outlays.

The Great Recession and government responses during the recession helped to create the 2009 deficit of $1.4 trillion, the largest in U.S. history. This deficit is larger than the deficits generated during World War II in the 1940s. But dollar values for government budget figures are misleading over the long run, because the population and the size of the economy change. To control for both population and economic growth, economists look at the deficit as a portion of GDP. When we divide budget data by GDP, we essentially scale it to the size of the economy. Figure 28.10 shows the U.S. federal outlays and revenue, both as a fraction of GDP, from 1965 to 2014. Over the entire period, outlays averaged 19.7% of GDP and revenues averaged 17% of GDP. These averages are shown as dashed lines in the figure. The long-run averages can be viewed as a target benchmark for future budgets.

The blue vertical bars in Figure 28.10 indicate economic recessions. Since the onset of the Great Recession at the end of 2007, outlays, revenues, and

FIGURE 28.10

U.S. Federal Outlays and Revenue as a Percentage of GDP, 1965–2014

The deficit-to-GDP ratio is an informative gauge of the magnitude of deficits over time because it accounts for changes in population and economic growth. Here we illustrate outlays (orange) and revenue (blue) as a percentage of GDP. The deficit is the vertical distance between the lines. Dashed lines indicate long-run averages. These show us that recent spending has been above the long-run average and recent revenue has been below the long-run average. The blue bars indicate recessionary periods. As you can see, deficits grow during recessions.

Source: U.S. Office of Management and Budget.

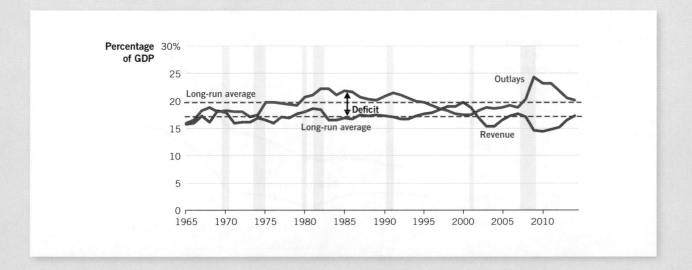

deficits have all reached historic magnitudes. Both outlays and revenues currently lie well outside their long-run averages. When a recession hits, tax revenue, which is largely tied to income, declines. In addition, for reasons we cover in the next chapter, government outlays often increase during recessions. Together these two results cause deficits to increase during recessions.

When the budget is in deficit, the government must borrow funds to pay for the difference between outlays and revenue. In Chapter 23, we introduced U.S. Treasury bonds as important financial assets in the loanable funds market. Now we can understand how those bonds originate: when tax revenues fall short of outlays, the government sells Treasury bonds to cover the difference.

Deficits versus Debt

In your personal budget, it might happen that your spending (outlays) in a given month exceeds your income. In other words, you find that you have a deficit. You might rely on funds from parents or grandparents to make up the difference, but this money counts either as income (if it's a gift) or as a loan (if you have to repay it). Often, you will have to borrow, perhaps by using a credit card. A loan, whether it is from a friend, relative, or credit card company, is a debt that must be paid.

FIGURE 28.11

U.S. National Debt, 1990–2013 (in billions of 2009 dollars)

The total amount of U.S. federal government debt (shown in blue) has grown to over $16 trillion in recent years, even exceeding annual GDP in the United States. But much of this debt is owned by agencies of the government itself (the government owes money to itself), so many economists focus instead on the debt that is held publicly (by anyone besides the federal government). This amount (shown in orange) is less than $10 trillion and constitutes about 60% of U.S. GDP. If you are curious about the current size of the U.S. national debt, you can visit the web site www.usdebtclock.org.

Source: U.S. Treasury, *Treasury Bulletin*.

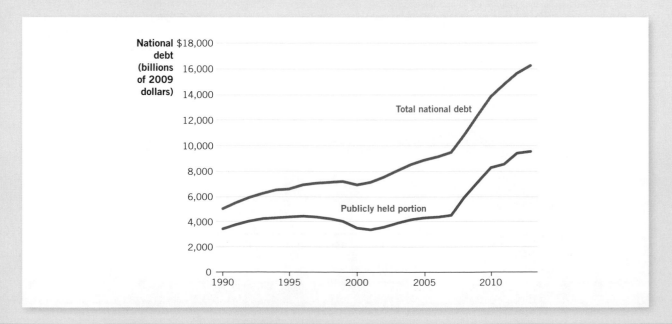

It's easy to confuse the terms "deficit" and "debt." A deficit is a shortfall in revenue for a particular year's budget. A **debt** is the total of all accumulated and unpaid budget deficits. Consider your tuition bill over the course of your time in college. If you borrow $5,000 to help pay for your first year of college, that is your first-year deficit. If you borrow another $5,000 for your second year, you have a $5,000 deficit for each year, and your debt grows to $10,000.

Figure 28.11 shows the U.S. national debt (in real terms) from 1990 to 2013. Notice that we distinguish between total national debt and debt held by the public. The difference between these is debt owned internally by one of the many branches of the U.S. government. Sometimes, a given federal agency will purchase Treasury bonds. For example, as part of its mandate to control the money supply, the Federal Reserve typically holds billions of dollars' worth of Treasury securities. Thus, it can be helpful to distinguish total government debt that is not also owned by the government itself, and this is the portion that is publicly held. Figure 28.11 indicates that both measures have risen in recent years, a result of the large budget deficits.

While the U.S. national debt is historically large, relative to the size of the economy it is still smaller than that of many other nations, including many wealthy ones. Figure 28.12 shows publicly held debt-to-GDP ratios for several nations in 2013. The United States came in at 100%, but Japan's ratio was nearly 220%.

A **debt** is the total of all accumulated and unpaid budget deficits.

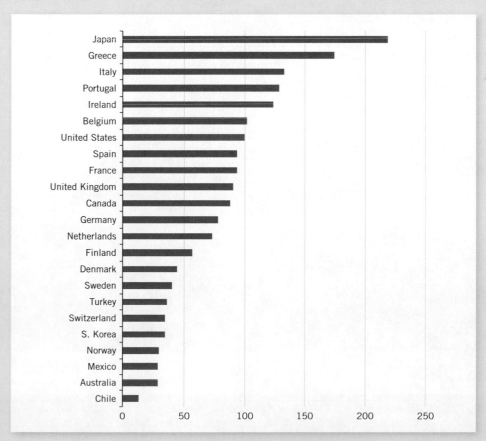

FIGURE 28.12

International Debt-to-GDP Ratios, 2013

While the U.S. debt-to-GDP ratio has grown to 100% in recent years, this amount is still smaller than that of some other developed nations.

Source: Eurostat and Trading Economics.

The Federal Budget Deficit

The U.S. federal government has run a budget deficit for almost the entire past half-century. The graph below plots federal revenue against outlays as a percentage of GDP, a measurement that stays consistent as the size of the economy changes. Note that the deficit is particularly likely to increase during recessions, as tax revenue declines and spending often jumps.

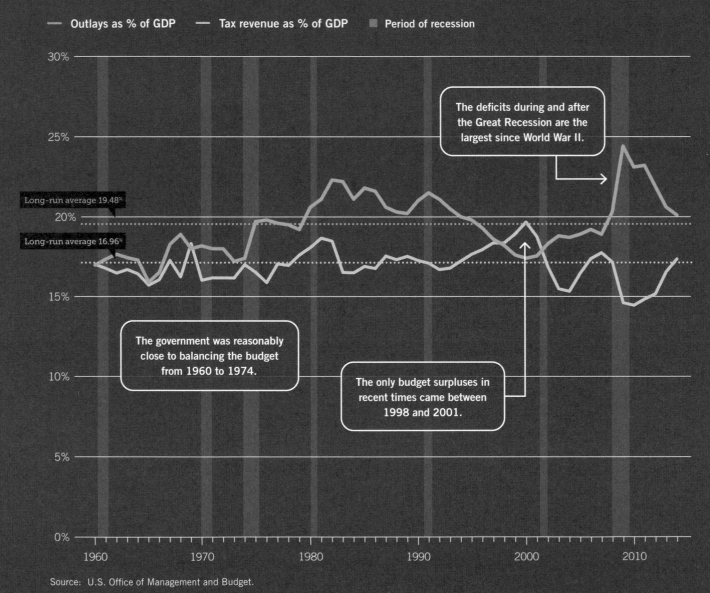

— Outlays as % of GDP   — Tax revenue as % of GDP   ■ Period of recession

Long-run average 19.48%

Long-run average 16.96%

The deficits during and after the Great Recession are the largest since World War II.

The government was reasonably close to balancing the budget from 1960 to 1974.

The only budget surpluses in recent times came between 1998 and 2001.

Source: U.S. Office of Management and Budget.

- The single worst deficit since 1960 occurred in 2009. When was the worst deficit since 1960 and prior to 2009?

- How do deficits seem to change at the beginning and end of recessions? How do they change in few years after a recession ends?

ECONOMICS IN THE REAL WORLD

Several European Nations Are Grappling with Government Debt Problems

In the summer of 2011, Greece erupted in a series of demonstrations, some marked by violent encounters between citizens and the national police. The issue at the heart of these protests was the Greek national debt, which climbed to almost 150% of its GDP in 2010. To avert a Greek debt default, other members of the European Union and the International Monetary Fund forged together aid packages of $146 billion in 2010 and $165 billion in 2011.

But the aid from Europe was granted only with strict austerity requirements. In this context, **austerity** involves strict budget regulations aimed at debt reduction. These austerity measures are what drove the Greek citizens to protest, because the measures included wage cuts and pension freezes for public and private workers, as well as an increase in the sales tax to 23%. The Greek government had agreed to these requirements in order to secure international aid and avert a default, but the Greek citizens rose up against their government after the agreements were signed.

Economic conditions worsened, with the unemployment rate climbing above 25% in mid-2012 and staying there for several years. In addition, real GDP fell by 26% between 2008 and 2014. These conditions are on a par with those of the Great Depression in the United States. Given the state of their economy, the Greek people rewarded the far left political party (Syriza) with the largest number of seats in their elected parliament. Their leader, Alexis Tsipras, became prime minister and promised no more austerity. This promise led to a standoff with Eurozone nations on the terms of Greece's debt repayment. But because Greek banks own significant portions of the country's national debt, a default would also harm the Greek economy. In the summer of 2015, the Greek government agreed to continue austerity measures and narrowly averted default. Most economists agree that this saga is far from over. ✳

Austerity involves strict budget regulations aimed at debt reduction.

Spanish police attempt to control demonstrators who oppose austerity measures in 2012.

Foreign Ownership of U.S. Federal Debt

As we saw in Chapter 23, many people are concerned about foreign ownership of U.S. debt. The concern stems from a fear that foreigners who own U.S. debt will control the country politically as well as economically. However, according to the U.S. Treasury, as of 2013, about 67% of U.S. national debt was held domestically, and just 33% internationally. China, Japan, and the United Kingdom are the major foreign holders of U.S. debt.

Figure 28.13 shows foreign and domestic ownership of total U.S. debt from 1990 to 2013. Total national debt grew from about $5 trillion to over $16 trillion. However, domestic investors and U.S. government agencies were the purchasers of most of the new debt. Still, the portion of U.S. government debt that is foreign owned more than doubled from 14% to 33% over that 24-year period.

While this foreign ownership of U.S. government debt is troubling for many Americans, it is important to realize the importance of the foreign funds to the U.S. loanable funds market. As we discussed in Chapter 23, foreign lending increases the supply of loanable funds in the United States, which helps keep interest rates low. Lower interest rates mean that firms and governments in the United States can borrow at lower cost. Furthermore, the increase in foreign ownership is a natural by-product of emerging foreign economies—as they get wealthier, they buy more U.S. Treasury bonds.

FIGURE 28.13

Foreign and Domestic Ownership of U.S. Government Debt, 1990–2013 (in billions of 2009 dollars)

Most U.S. government debt is owned by Americans or by the U.S. government itself. This graph shows total national debt and internationally owned debt. The percentage owned internationally has grown in recent years but is still only about one-third of the total.

Source: U.S. Treasury, *Treasury Bulletin.*

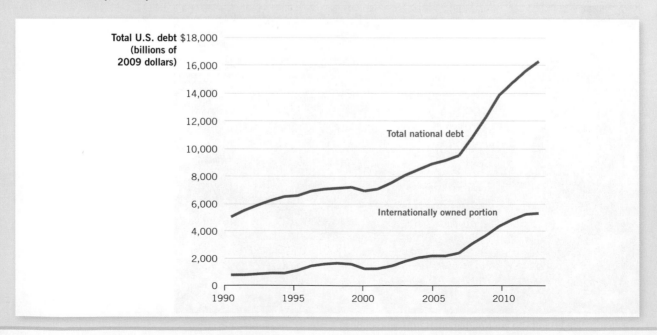

PRACTICE WHAT YOU KNOW

Federal Budgets: The U.S. Debt Crisis

The U.S. national debt grew substantially in the first decade of this century. The table below shows the data on the national debt from both 2001 and 2010.

Year	Total U.S. debt (billions of $)	Nominal GDP (billions of $)
2001	$5,807	$10,286
2010	$13,561	$14,499

Question: Using the data, compute the U.S. debt-to-GDP ratio in both 2001 and 2010.

Answer: For the year 2001, we compute the debt-to-GDP ratio as

$$\$5,807 \div \$10,286 = 0.56$$

For the year 2010, we compute the debt-to-GDP ratio as

$$\$13,561 \div \$14,499 = 0.94$$

Question: What are the major reasons why the national debt increased so much between 2001 and 2010?

Answer: First, on the outlay side, U.S. government spending increased due to higher costs for Social Security and Medicare, additional defense spending primarily funding conflicts in Iraq and Afghanistan, and government responses to the Great Recession beginning with fiscal policy in 2008.

Second, on the revenue side, tax receipts declined sharply during and after the Great Recession.

This running national debt clock is posted near Times Square in New York City.

Budgeting for Your Take-Home Pay

Most college students have not yet held full-time jobs. So you are probably still planning for that day when you graduate and get your first big paycheck. We certainly don't want to discourage you, but we will offer a few words of caution for when you are budgeting your major expenses.

Let's say you graduate and obtain a good job in the city of your choice. You agree to a salary of $60,000 per year. This is a good starting salary (probably due to the economics courses you took!), so you start thinking about your budget for the future. Consider a few of the biggest questions: How much can you afford for your monthly housing payment? How large a car payment can you afford? How much can you spend on groceries or dining out? How much should you save each month?

It's a smart move to think about these questions ahead of time. But when you plan, be sure to recognize that your take-home pay will be far less than $60,000. It is tempting to make a monthly budget based on the $5,000 per month that your basic salary promises. In the table shown here, we estimate the actual size of your paycheck.

First, we subtract federal income tax. Based on the 2015 tax rates and assuming a standard deduction of $6,200, we determine that your annual payment will be $9,240. Next we subtract 7.65% for Social Security and Medicare. After that, we subtract 5% each for state income taxes (this is about average), benefits (like health insurance, dental, and optical), and retirement contributions.

After these deductions, you are left with less than $3,000 per month! Your take-home pay is about 40% less than your salary.

Therefore, when you are making major spending decisions about things such as housing and car payments, be sure to budget based on this much smaller figure. If you budget based on your salary alone, you won't be able to save, and you may even become dependent on credit cards.

	Monthly	Yearly
Salary	$5,000.00	$60,000
Federal income tax	$770.00	$9,240
Social Security/Medicare tax	$382.50	$4,590
State income tax	$250.00	$3,000
Benefits	$400.00	$4,800
Retirement	$250.00	$3,000
Take-home pay	$2,947.50	$35,370

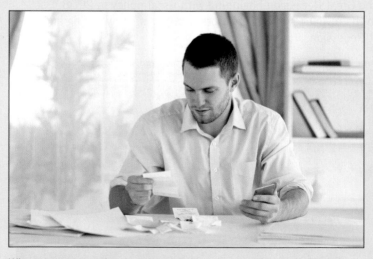

When you put together your budget, be sure to account for all the deductions from your paycheck.

Conclusion

We started this chapter with the misconception that governments never balance their budgets. Certainly, given the current size of U.S. budget deficits and the sovereign debt problems around the world, it would be natural to assume that national budgets are never balanced. But, in fact, as we have seen, the United States had a balanced federal budget as recently as 2001.

This chapter lays the groundwork for us to examine fiscal policy in Chapter 29. Much of the debt and deficits we've observed are a direct result of government budgetary maneuvers to affect the macroeconomy. Going forward, we now understand the institutions of fiscal policy. In Chapter 29, we'll learn about the economic theories that support fiscal policy.

ANSWERING THE BIG QUESTIONS

How does the government spend?

* Government spending has grown sharply since 2000, and it is now about $3.5 trillion per year.

* Mandatory spending programs now constitute almost 60% of government spending at the U.S. national level. These mandatory programs include Social Security, Medicare, and welfare programs.

* Interest on the national debt is about 7% of federal spending. Defense spending is 17% of federal spending. The remaining 17% of the discretionary budget goes to discretionary government spending like highways, bridges, and the salaries of many government employees.

How does the government tax?

* The U.S. government raises about 80% of its revenues through payroll taxes: the income tax and the tax for Social Security and Medicare. The income tax yields about $1.4 trillion in revenue per year. It is a progressive tax, so wealthier Americans pay more in taxes than the poor do.

What are budget deficits?

* If total government outlays exceed revenue in a given year, the budget is in deficit.

* Deficits add to the national debt, which is the accumulated deficit over time.

CONCEPTS YOU SHOULD KNOW

austerity (p. 923)
average tax rate (p. 914)
budget deficit (p. 918)
budget surplus (p. 919)
debt (p. 921)

discretionary outlays (p. 905)
government outlays (p. 905)
mandatory outlays (p. 905)
marginal tax rate (p. 914)
Medicare (p. 909)

progressive income tax system
  (p. 914)
Social Security (p. 908)
transfer payments (p. 904)

QUESTIONS FOR REVIEW

1. Since the 1960s, Social Security and Medicare have grown as portions of U.S. government spending.

    a. What major categories of government spending have shrunk during the same period?

    b. Has the U.S. budget become more or less flexible as a result of the growth in the mandatory programs? Explain your response.

2. Explain the difference between a budget deficit and the national debt.

3. Going back to 1965, there have been a few years in which the U.S. government budget was in surplus. What years were these? Why do you think those surpluses disappeared when they did? Figure 28.10 might be helpful in answering this question.

4. This question refers to Figure 28.10, which shows the U.S. outlays and revenue as portions of GDP.

    a. List three periods when the U.S. budget deficit was relatively large.

    b. What historical events were taking place in the United States during these three periods that may have led to these large deficits? Be specific.

5. Explain why mandatory outlays are predicted to grow (as a portion of the total budget) over the next two decades.

6. Explain the difference between average tax rates and marginal tax rates. Is it possible for a person's average tax rate to equal his or her marginal tax rate? If so, how?

STUDY PROBLEMS (*solved at the end of the section*)

1. Use the marginal income tax rates in Figure 28.6 to compute the following:
    a. tax due on taxable income of $100,000, $200,000, and $500,000
    b. average tax rate on taxable income of $100,000, $200,000, and $500,000

2. Greece, Ireland, Portugal, and Spain all went through national budget difficulties in recent years. Use the following data to answer questions regarding the sovereign debts of these nations. (All data come from the OECD and are in billions of current U.S. dollars.)

	2000		2010	
	Debt	**GDP**	**Debt**	**GDP**
Greece	$138	$127	$455	$308
Ireland	$34	$98	$124	$206
Portugal	$62	$118	$203	$231
Spain	$292	$586	$734	$1,420

    a. Compute the debt-to-GDP ratio for all four nations in both 2000 and 2010.
    b. Compute the average yearly budget deficit for each of the nations over this period.

c. In your judgment, which of the four nations was in the worst fiscal shape in 2010? Use your earlier computations to justify your answer.

3. There are three different ways to report budget deficit data: nominal deficits, real deficits, and deficit-to-GDP ratios. Which of the three is most informative? Why?

∗ 4. Greece has been through significant national budget turmoil. In 2010, it was discovered that the government had been concealing the true size of the national debt for several years. The data in the following table reveal just how much the nation's officially reported national debt grew between 2000 and 2010. The data are in billions of U.S. dollars. Use the data to answer the questions that follow.

2000		2010	
Debt	**GDP**	**Debt**	**GDP**
$138	$127	$455	$308

a. What was the average annual increase in the Greek debt over the 10-year span?
b. What was the average annual budget deficit for Greece over this period?

∗ 5. Use the table in problem 4 to compute the debt-to-GDP ratio for Greece in both 2000 and 2010.

SOLVED PROBLEMS

4.a. The debt grew from $138 billion to $455 billion over 10 years, which was an increase of $317 billion, or an average of $31.7 billion per year.

b. Given that the debt increased by $31.7 billion per year, this number was also the figure for the average annual deficit over this period.

5. For 2000: $138 \div 127 = 1.09$
For 2010: $455 \div 308 = 1.48$

Changing government spending is a simple and predictable tool for fighting recessions.

Many people believe that the government can quickly and predictably offset economic downturns, either through spending increases

or decreases in taxes to safely evade recessions. But if past experience has taught us anything, it is that government actions have uneven and unpredictable effects on the economy. While it's true that the government may be able to influence the macroeconomy, it is also easy to see that many government spending initiatives have not worked as planned. While we have lots of ideas, few economists feel we have found simple solutions.

In this chapter, we examine the case for fiscal policy, which includes both government spending and taxes. We begin by framing fiscal policy in the aggregate demand–aggregate supply model. We examine both expansionary and contractionary fiscal policies. We then consider potential shortcomings of fiscal policy and conclude with a view from the supply-side perspective.

The American Recovery and Reinvestment Act, which entailed almost $1 trillion in government spending, was passed to help the economy recover from the Great Recession.

BIG QUESTIONS

* What is fiscal policy?
* What are the shortcomings of fiscal policy?
* What is supply-side fiscal policy?

What Is Fiscal Policy?

Fiscal policy involves the use of government's budget tools, government spending, and taxes to influence the macroeconomy.

When the economy falters, people often look to the government to help push the economy forward again. In fact, the government uses many different tools to try to affect the economy. Economists classify these tools into two types of policy: *monetary policy* and *fiscal policy*. Monetary policy is the use of the money supply to influence the economy. We will study monetary policy in Chapter 31. **Fiscal policy**, the subject of this chapter, involves the use of government budget tools, spending, and taxes to influence the macroeconomy. In the United States, tax and spending changes are legislated and approved by both Congress and the president.

In this section, we first describe how the government can use fiscal policy to try to stimulate the economy; then we discuss how fiscal policy might be used to slow down rapid growth. Along the way, we consider how fiscal policy affects government budget deficits and debt. Finally, we examine the multiplier process, which describes the ways in which the effects of fiscal policy ripple through the economy.

Expansionary Fiscal Policy

Expansionary fiscal policy occurs when the government increases spending or decreases taxes to stimulate the economy toward expansion.

In the fall of 2007, the U.S. economy was slipping into recession. When this happens, most citizens expect the government should do something to keep the recession at bay, and 2007 was no exception. In particular, many expected the government to step in with tax reductions or spending programs to help stimulate the economy. **Expansionary fiscal policy** occurs when the government increases spending or decreases taxes to stimulate the economy toward expansion. In this section, we use the aggregate demand–aggregate supply model to examine the effects of expansionary fiscal policy.

In Chapter 26, we introduced the aggregate demand–aggregate supply model. In that model, we showed that recession can occur as a result of a drop in aggregate demand. In theory, the economy can move itself back to full employment in the long run when all prices adjust. Consider the example presented in Figure 29.1. Initially, the economy is in long-run equilibrium at point A, with $P = 100$, $Y = Y^*$ (full employment), and $u = u^*$ (the natural unemployment rate). If aggregate demand declines from AD_1 to AD_2, the economy moves to short-run equilibrium at point b, with output at Y_1, which is less than full-employment output, and an unemployment rate greater than the natural rate.

At equilibrium point b, government officials can wait for the economy to adjust back to full-employment equilibrium at point C. This adjustment occurs when all prices adjust downward and short-run aggregate supply (SRAS) shifts downward to $SRAS_2$. But prices can take a while to adjust. In addition, recessions are difficult times for many people, and they expect the government to take action to ease their plight. Thus, government officials often choose to use fiscal policy to try to shift aggregate demand back to its original level. If their policy works, the economy returns to full-employment equilibrium at point A.

Fiscal policy can make use of government spending, taxes, or a combination of the two. Government spending (G) is one component of aggregate demand. Therefore, increases in G directly increase aggregate demand. When private spending (consumption, investment, and net exports) is low,

FIGURE 29.1

Expansionary Fiscal Policy

A decrease in aggregate demand from AD_1 to AD_2 moves the economy from point A to equilibrium at point b, with less than full-employment output (Y_1) and unemployment (u) greater than the natural rate (u^*). In the long run, all prices adjust (short-run aggregate supply adjusts to $SRAS_2$), moving the economy back to full-employment equilibrium at point C. The goal of expansionary fiscal policy is to shift aggregate demand back to AD_1 so that the economy returns to full employment without waiting for long-run adjustments.

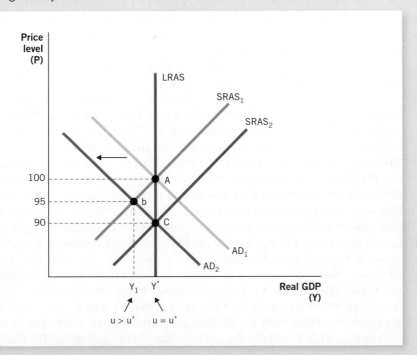

the government can increase demand directly by increasing G. Fiscal policy can also focus on consumption (C) by decreasing taxes. Decreases in taxes can increase aggregate demand because people have more of their income left to spend after paying their taxes. If people keep more of their paycheck, they can afford more consumption.

Recent history in the United States offers two prominent examples of expansionary fiscal policy. In the next section, we review these examples to clarify how fiscal policy uses both government spending and taxes.

Fiscal Policy during the Great Recession

In the fall of 2007, the U.S. unemployment rate climbed from 4.6% to 5%. As it became clearer that economic conditions were worsening in the United States, the government took action. Political leaders decided that fiscal policy could help. Figure 29.2 shows real GDP growth and the unemployment rate in the United States over the period of the Great Recession and beyond. The official period of the recession is shaded blue. The top panel shows quarterly real GDP growth over the period, which fell to −1.8% at the beginning of 2008. The bottom panel shows the monthly unemployment rate, which began climbing in late 2007 and remained at high levels through 2011, well after the recession officially ended.

Surrounded by congressional leaders, President Bush signed the Economic Stimulus Act of 2008 . . .

In this context, the government enacted two significant fiscal policy initiatives. The first, signed in February 2008 by President George W. Bush, was the Economic Stimulus Act of 2008. The cornerstone of this act was a tax rebate for Americans. They had already paid their taxes for 2007, and the stimulus act included a partial rebate of those previously paid taxes. The government actually mailed rebate checks to taxpayers. And these refunds were not insignificant: a typical four-person family received a rebate check for $1,800 ($600 per adult and $300 per child). The overall cost of this action to government was $168 billion; it refunded about 1 of every 7 dollars paid in individual income taxes for 2007. The expectation was that American taxpayers would spend rather than save most of this $168 billion, thereby increasing aggregate demand and stimulating the economy.

However, after the first fiscal stimulus was passed, economic conditions worsened. In Figure 29.2, notice that real GDP growth plummeted and the unemployment rate rose significantly in 2008 after the first fiscal stimulus legislation. National elections at the end of 2008 brought Barack Obama to the White House and changed the balance of power in Washington. In February 2009, less than one month after taking office, the new president signed the American Recovery and Reinvestment Act (ARRA) of 2009. The focus of this second act shifted to government spending. Seventy percent of the ARRA cost was due to new government spending; the remaining 30% focused on tax credits. In addition, the size of this second fiscal stimulus—$787 billion— was much larger than the first.

. . . and one year later, President Obama signed the much larger American Recovery and Reinvestment Act of 2009.

These two major pieces of legislation illustrate the tools of fiscal policy: taxes and spending. The first focused on taxes, the second on government spending. The two acts may seem very different, but both sought to increase aggregate demand; they are based on the analysis we presented in Figure 29.1.

Fiscal policy generally focuses on aggregate demand. At the end of this chapter, we consider an alternative approach—one that uses government spending and taxes to affect aggregate supply in the long run.

Major Fiscal Policy Initiatives during the Great Recession

The Great Recession began in December 2007. In February 2008, President Bush signed the Economic Stimulus Act of 2008, which introduced tax cuts to stimulate the economy and avoid recession. But during 2008, the economy sunk deeper into recession. In February 2009, President Obama signed the American Recovery and Reinvestment Act of 2009, which focused on government spending programs.

Source: GDP data are from the U.S. Bureau of Economic Analysis; unemployment rate data are from the U.S. Bureau of Labor Statistics.

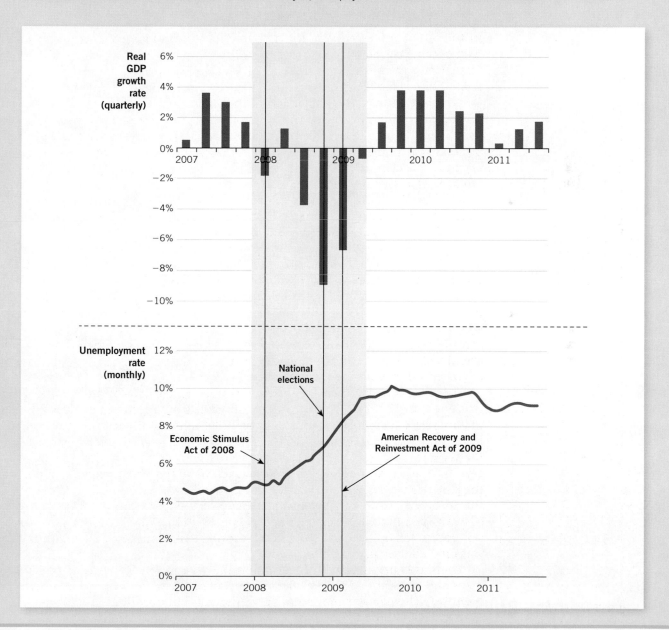

Recession, Stimulus, Reinvestment

The U.S. government reacted to the Great Recession with two of the most important fiscal policy initiatives in history. The Economic Stimulus Act of 2008, signed by President Bush that February, sought to stimulate aggregate demand by issuing rebate checks to taxpayers. A year later, conditions had worsened, and newly elected President Obama signed the much larger American Recovery and Reinvestment Act of 2009. This act also was an effort to increase aggregate demand, but mainly through boosting government spending instead of personal consumption.

— Unemployment rate — Real GDP growth ▮ Period of recession

1 National Stimulus Act
February 2008

This $168 billion stimulus act focused on tax reductions, including a rebate on 2007 taxes. The rebate was meant to spur consumer spending.

2 National Elections
November 2008

Barack Obama was elected.

3 American Recovery and Reinvestment Act
February 2009

the Obama administration enacted an aggressive $789 billion stimulus plan that focused on government spending in "shovel-ready" infrastructure projects.

Source: Real GDP growth data (quarterly) from U.S. Bureau of Economic Analysis; unemployment data (monthly) from the U.S. Bureau of Labor Statistics.

REVIEW QUESTIONS

- The GDP growth numbers from 2010 onward are similar to the GDP numbers from 2002 to 2008. What is different?

- What other factors beyond GDP growth might account for the high unemployment numbers since late 2008?

Fiscal Policy and Budget Deficits

We have seen that the typical prescription for an ailing economy is to increase government spending, decrease taxes, or both. You may be wondering how the government pays for all the spending or copes with the shortfall in tax revenue. The answer is through borrowing.

Let's start with a simplified example. Assume that the government is currently balancing the national budget so that outlays equal tax revenue. Then the economy slips into recession, and the government decides to increase government spending by $100 billion. The government must pay for this spending by borrowing; it must sell $100 billion worth of Treasury bonds. As a result, the federal budget is in deficit by $100 billion.

But that's only part of the story. In reality, the deficit will rise by more than $100 billion because tax revenue will fall. Recall from Chapter 28 that 80% of U.S. tax revenue derives from payroll taxes. In a recession, with income down and unemployment up, the amount of revenue that the government takes in from taxes falls, even if the tax rate stays the same.

It is easy to verify both of these phenomena by looking at recent U.S. recessions. Figure 29.3 shows U.S. federal outlays and tax revenue from 1985 to 2012, with recessionary periods indicated by vertical blue bars. First, look at the period of the Great Recession of 2007–2009. Note how spending (outlays) increased sharply in 2009, the year of the $787 billion fiscal stimulus. But falling income also led to less income tax revenue. Looking at the three recessions shown in this graph, we see that spending increased but that tax revenue fell during each one.

The bottom line is clear: expansionary fiscal policy inevitably leads to increases in budget deficits and the national debt during economic downturns. This policy prescription may seem odd to you. After all, if you personally fell on rough economic times, you might (reasonably) react differently. For example, if your employer were to cut you back to part-time employment, would it seem like a good idea to go on a spending binge? You might feel better while you were shopping, but it wouldn't help your financial situation

FIGURE 29.3

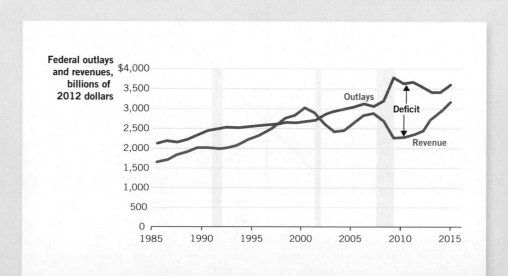

Real U.S. Outlays and Revenue, 1985–2015

The use of expansionary fiscal policy to counteract economic downturns leads to greater budget deficits. During recessionary periods, outlays increase and tax revenue falls. In 2001, these strategies erased the budget surplus; in 1990 and 2008, these strategies expanded the size of the deficit.

Source: Office of Management and Budget.

much. From a macroeconomic perspective, however, expansionary fiscal policy might work for the overall economy because spending by one person becomes income to another, which can snowball into income increases throughout the economy. We discuss this aspect of expansionary fiscal policy later in the chapter in the section on multipliers.

Contractionary Fiscal Policy

Contractionary fiscal policy occurs when the government decreases spending or increases taxes to slow economic expansion.

We have seen that expansionary fiscal policy is often used to try to increase aggregate demand during economic downturns. But there are also times when contractionary fiscal policy is used to reduce aggregate demand. **Contractionary fiscal policy** occurs when the government decreases spending or increases taxes to slow economic expansion.

There are two reasons why a government might want to reduce aggregate demand. First, as we discussed earlier, expansionary fiscal policy creates deficits during recessions. An increase in taxes or a decrease in spending during an economic expansion can work to reduce the budget deficit and pay off some government debt. For example, the U.S. government ran budget surpluses from 1998 to 2001, at the end of an extended period of economic expansion. These surpluses were not large enough to pay off the national debt entirely, but they did shrink it somewhat.

Second, the government might want to reduce aggregate demand if it believes that the economy is expanding beyond its long-run capabilities. Full-employment output (Y*) is considered the highest level of output sustainable in the long run. But if the unemployment rate falls below the natural rate (u*), output may be above Y*. Some economists then worry that the economy may "overheat" from too much spending, which can lead to inflation.

FIGURE 29.4

Contractionary Fiscal Policy

When policymakers believe that the economy is producing beyond its long-run capacity ($Y_1 > Y^*$), fiscal policy can be used to reduce aggregate demand. Contractionary fiscal policy moves the economy from short-run equilibrium at point a to equilibrium at point B, thus avoiding the inflationary outcome at point C.

Figure 29.4 illustrates this possibility, beginning at short-run equilibrium point a, with aggregate demand equal to AD_1. Notice that this level of aggregate demand leads to short-run equilibrium where real GDP is higher than its full-employment level ($Y_1 > Y^*$). In addition, at point a, the unemployment rate is below the natural rate ($u < u^*$), which is not sustainable in the long run.

When aggregate demand is high enough to drive unemployment below the natural rate, there is upward pressure on the price level, which is at 105 at short-run equilibrium point a. Further, without a reduction in aggregate demand, the economy naturally moves toward equilibrium at point C in the long run as prices fully adjust. But this equilibrium implies even more inflation. Thus, to avoid inflation, the government can use fiscal policy to try to reduce aggregate demand from AD_1 to AD_2. This strategy moves the economy back to long-run equilibrium with price stability at point B.

Together, contractionary and expansionary fiscal policy can serve to counteract the ups and downs of business cycles. We examine this combination more closely in the next section.

Countercyclical Fiscal Policy

All else being equal, people generally prefer smoothness and predictability in their financial affairs. In Chapter 22, we talked about this characteristic in reference to consumption smoothing; in Chapter 23, we considered how people are risk averse. Along these lines, an economy that grows at a consistent rate is preferable to an economy that grows in an erratic fashion. For these and other reasons, politicians generally employ fiscal policy to counteract the business cycle.

Fiscal policy that seeks to counteract business cycle fluctuations is known as **countercyclical fiscal policy**. It consists of using expansionary policy during economic downturns and contractionary policy during economic expansions. Figure 29.5 illustrates the goals of countercyclical fiscal policy. The

Countercyclical fiscal policy is fiscal policy that seeks to counteract business cycle fluctuations.

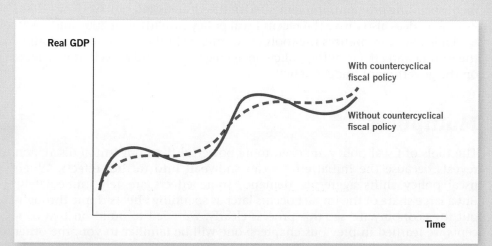

FIGURE 29.5

Countercyclical Fiscal Policy and the Business Cycle

The goal of countercyclical fiscal policy is to smooth out the fluctuations in the business cycle.

TABLE 29.1

Countercyclical Fiscal Policy Tools

Fiscal policy action	Timing	Objective: How it affects aggregate demand (AD)	By-product: How it affects the budget deficit
Expansionary			
↑ Government spending (G)	When the economy is contracting	G is one component of AD, so increases in G directly increase AD.	Increases budget deficit
↓ Taxes (T)		Decreasing T leaves more funds in the hands of consumers, who then spend more on consumption (C). When C rises, AD rises.	
Contractionary			
↓ Government spending (G)	When the economy is expanding	Decreases in G directly decrease AD.	Decreases budget deficit
↑ Taxes (T)		Increasing T leaves fewer funds in the hands of consumers, who then spend less on consumption (C). When C falls, AD falls.	

natural path of the economy (without countercyclical fiscal policy) includes business cycles during which income and employment fluctuate. The goal is that countercyclical fiscal policy can reduce the fluctuations inherent in a business cycle.

You might recall from Chapter 27 that Keynesian economists focus on aggregate demand (total spending) in the economy. Keynesian economics provides the theoretical foundation for countercyclical fiscal policy. In fact, Keynes's ideas provided a theoretical foundation for the New Deal government spending programs implemented in the United States in 1933 and 1935. But these ideas also drove the recent fiscal policy initiatives of 2008 and 2009.

Table 29.1 summarizes the tools of countercyclical fiscal policy, including the timing and effects of the policy on aggregate demand as well as its effects on the government budget deficit.

Multipliers

The tools of fiscal policy are even more powerful than our initial discussion reveals because the initial effects can snowball into further effects. When fiscal policy shifts aggregate demand, some effects are felt immediately. But a large share of the impact occurs later as spending effects ripple throughout the economy. To see this process clearly, we need to build on two concepts we learned in previous chapters; one will be familiar to you, the other is new.

First, the familiar concept: recall from Chapter 19 that what one person spends becomes income to others. This is true not only for private spending but also for government spending. For example, if the government uses fiscal policy to increase spending on new roads, the dollars spent on those roads become income to the suppliers of all the resources that go into the production of the roads.

Now the new concept: increases in income generally lead to increases in consumption. When a person's income rises, he or she might save some of this new income but might be just as likely to spend part of it, too. The **marginal propensity to consume (MPC)** is the portion of additional income that is spent on consumption:

The **marginal propensity to consume (MPC)** is the portion of additional income that is spent on consumption.

$$\text{MPC} = \frac{\text{change in consumption}}{\text{change in income}}$$

(Equation 29.1)

For example, say you earn $400 in new income, and you decide to spend $300 and save $100. Your marginal propensity to consume is then $300 ÷ $400 = 0.75. In other words, you spend 75% of your new income. The MPC isn't constant across all people, but it is a fraction between 0 and 1:

$$0 \leq \text{MPC} \leq 1$$

Let's consider a simple example of how spending changes affect the economy. For this example, let's say that the government decides to increase spending by $100 billion and spends all of the funds on salaries for government workers. This government spending becomes new income for the government workers. Now let's assume that these workers spend about 75 cents of each dollar of their new income, or that their MPC is 0.75. In total, the government workers spend $75 billion and save $25 billion of their new income. The government workers' spending becomes $75 billion worth of income to others in the economy. (Thus, in sum, we now have $175 billion in new income.) If the recipients of that $75 billion income also spend 75% of it, they create another $56.25 billion in new income for others in the economy, for a total of $231.25 billion.

It's clear that the initial $100 billion in government spending can create more than $100 billion in income; this effect occurs through the "multiplying" we just described. The effect continues on, round after round, as new income earners spend a portion of their new income.

The multiplier effect is significant when we focus on aggregate demand in the economy. Each time people earn new income, they spend part of it. After all the dust settles, the total impact is a multiple of the original spending created by the fiscal policy. Figure 29.6 illustrates this multiplier process for our current example. The table in the figure shows how spending becomes income and then how part of the new income is spent. The first round represents the government's initial spending of $100 billion. The following rounds represent the new income generated by consumption spending. Because the MPC is 0.75 in this example, each round generates 75% of the income produced in the preceding round.

Spend or save? What is your marginal propensity to consume?

FIGURE 29.6

The Spending Multiplier Process

Assume that MPC = 0.75 and the government increases spending by $100 billion. In the table, you can see how the spending multiplies throughout the economy; each round is 75% of the prior round. In the end, the total spending increase is four times the initial change in government spending. The graph illustrates the shifting aggregate demand curve as the spending multiplies throughout the economy.

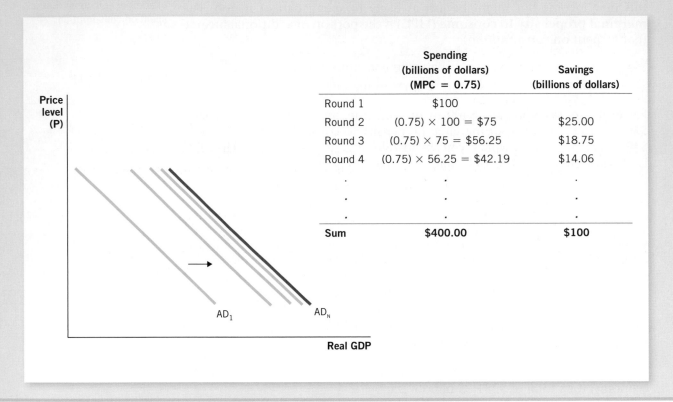

	Spending (billions of dollars) (MPC = 0.75)	Savings (billions of dollars)
Round 1	$100	
Round 2	(0.75) × 100 = $75	$25.00
Round 3	(0.75) × 75 = $56.25	$18.75
Round 4	(0.75) × 56.25 = $42.19	$14.06
.	.	.
.	.	.
.	.	.
Sum	**$400.00**	**$100**

In the graph, we show aggregate demand. Each time spending increases, aggregate demand increases (shifts rightward). The initial aggregate demand is labeled AD_1. Each round of spending shifts aggregate demand to the right. Finally, aggregate demand settles at AD_N, where N represents the completion of the multiplier process.

To determine the total effect on spending from any initial government expenditures, we use a formula known as the spending multiplier. The **spending multiplier (m^s)** tells us the total impact on spending from an initial change of a given amount. The multiplier depends on the marginal propensity to consume: the greater the marginal propensity to consume, the greater the spending multiplier. The formula for the spending multiplier is

The **spending multiplier** is a formula to determine the equation's effect on spending from an initial change of a given amount.

(Equation 29.2)

$$m^s = \frac{1}{(1 - \text{MPC})}$$

Spending Multiplier

Pay It Forward

In this movie, a drama from 2000, a young boy named Trevor (played by Haley Joel Osment) comes up with an idea that he thinks can change the world. Instead of paying people back for good deeds, Trevor suggests a new approach called "pay it forward." The idea is for him to help three people in some way. According to Trevor, "it has to be really big, something they can't do by themselves."

Then each of those three people helps three more. You can see how this idea leads to a multiplication of people helping other people.

Trevor's scheme is both similar to and different from the spending multiplier at the center of Keynesian fiscal policy. It is similar in that one person's "spending" leads to "spending" by others.

But we have seen that the spending multiplier is driven by the marginal propensity to consume, which is a fraction between 0 and 1, because people

Trevor explains his good-deed pyramid scheme.

generally save part of any new income they earn. So the spending multiplication process slows down and eventually dies out.

However, the multiplier in *Pay it Forward* exceeds 1 because each person helps three people. In fact, Trevor's multiplier will be infinity because each good deed leads to three more. So the good deeds can continue to expand to more and more good deeds.

Because the MPC is a fraction between 0 and 1, the multiplier is generally larger than 1. For example, if the marginal propensity to consume is 0.75, the multiplier is determined as:

$$m^s = \frac{1}{(1 - \text{MPC})} = \frac{1}{1 - 0.75} = \frac{1}{0.25} = 4$$

Sometimes, the spending multiplier is called the *Keynesian multiplier* or *fiscal multiplier*.

Note that the multiplier concept applies to all spending, no matter whether that spending is public or private. In addition, there is a multiplier associated with tax changes. A reduction in the tax rate leaves more income for consumers to spend. This spending multiplies throughout the economy in much the same way as government spending multiplies.

The multiplier process also works in reverse. If the government reduces spending or increases taxes, people have less income to spend, shifting the aggregate demand curve to the left. In terms of the aggregate demand curve in Figure 29.6, the initial decline in government spending leads to subsequent declines as the effects reverberate through the economy.

The spending multiplier implies that the tools of fiscal policy are very powerful. Not only can the government change its spending and taxing, but multiples of this spending then ripple throughout the economy over several periods.

The multiplier effects of fiscal policy on an economy are similar to the rippling effects of a stone thrown into the water.

Some government spending projects are more shovel-ready than others.

Expansionary Fiscal Policy: Shovel-Ready Projects

In early 2009, with the U.S. economy in deep recession, newly elected President Obama vowed to use fiscal stimulus spending on what was then termed "shovel-ready" projects, because they had already been approved by Congress and were just waiting for funding. Obama expected that his stimulus plan would create new jobs with minimal delays. To see the effect, let's first examine a simplified version of how economists might try to determine the effect of government spending projects (like the Obama proposal) on the macroeconomy.

Question: Assume that the economy is in short-run equilibrium with less than full-employment output. Also assume that the marginal propensity to consume (MPC) is equal to 0.5. What is the value of the government spending multiplier in this case?

Answer: Equation 29.2 gives us the formula for the spending multiplier:

$$m^s = \frac{1}{(1 - MPC)} = \frac{1}{(1 - 0.5)} = \frac{1}{0.5} = 2$$

Question: Given the size of the multiplier, what would be the implied change in income (GDP) from stimulus spending of $800 billion?

Answer: The total implied impact would be: $2 \times \$800$ billion $= \$1.6$ trillion.

What Are the Shortcomings of Fiscal Policy?

How would you like it if your medications worked with an 18-month lag?

At this point, you may wonder why fiscal policy doesn't always work perfectly in the real world. If fiscal policy is as simple as tweaking G and T and letting the multiplier go to work, why do recessions still happen? The first answer is that the real world isn't so simple. Millions of people make individual decisions that collectively affect the entire economy. While many economists try to forecast variables and outcomes (how much will people spend? how will people save?), they can never be certain of the answers to these questions ahead of time. Even the most informed and educated guesses are still guesses and not guarantees.

But there are also more specific shortcomings of fiscal policy. In this section, we consider three issues that arise in the application of fiscal policy: time lags, crowding-out, and savings shifts.

Time Lags

Both fiscal policy and monetary policy are intended to smooth out the economic variations that accompany a business cycle.

So timing is important. But there are three time lags that accompany policy decisions: recognition lag, implementation lag, and impact lag.

1. *Recognition lag.* In the real world, it is difficult to determine when the economy is turning up or down. GDP data are released quarterly, and the final estimate for each quarter is not known until three months after the period in question. Unemployment rate data tend to lag even further behind. In addition, growth is not constant: one bad quarter does not always signal a recession, and one good quarter is not always the beginning of an expansion. All these factors make it very difficult to recognize when expansion or contraction starts.

2. *Implementation lag.* It takes time to implement fiscal policy. In most nations, one or more governing bodies must approve tax and spending legislation. In the United States, such legislation must pass both houses of Congress and receive presidential approval before becoming law. For this reason, fiscal policy takes much longer to implement than monetary policy does. For example, as we discussed earlier in this chapter, the Economic Stimulus Act of 2008 entailed sending tax rebate checks to U.S. taxpayers. The act passed in early February, yet most checks did not go out until about six months later, even though the recipients were known ahead of time.

3. *Impact lag.* Finally, it takes time for the complete effects of fiscal or monetary policy to materialize. The multiplier makes fiscal policy powerful, but it takes time to ripple through the economy.

If lags cause the effects of fiscal policy to be delayed for a year or 18 months, there is a risk that the policy can actually magnify the business cycle. That is, if the effects of expansionary fiscal policy hit when the economy is already expanding, the result may be excessive aggregate demand and inflation. And if contractionary fiscal policy is implemented and followed by time lags, the effects could lead to even deeper recessions.

ECONOMICS IN THE REAL WORLD

Recognizing Lags

Hindsight is 20-20. But in reality, it is very difficult to determine how the economy is performing at any particular point in time. Looking back now, we know that the U.S. economy entered a recession in December 2007. But this development was far from clear at the time. In fact, as Edmund Andrews pointed out in a *New York Times* article in February 2008, the Bush administration was not convinced that the economy was in a recession. Reporting on February 12, Andrews wrote:

> The White House predicted on Monday that the economy would escape a recession and that unemployment would remain low this year, though it acknowledged that growth had already slowed. "I don't think we are in a recession right now, and we are not forecasting a recession," said Edward P. Lazear, chairman of the White House Council of Economic Advisers . . . . The administration's forecast calls for the economy to expand 2.7 percent this year and for unemployment to remain at 4.9 percent.

It's not inconceivable that this forecast was biased by political considerations, but according to Andrews, even independent economists were predicting a 1.7% growth rate for 2008. In reality, real GDP fell by 3.5% and the unemployment rate rose to 7.3% by the end of 2008. As this example demonstrates, it is very difficult to accurately recognize current economic conditions. ✳

Automatic Stabilizers

One possibility for alleviating lag problems are programs that automatically adjust government spending and taxes when economic conditions change. **Automatic stabilizers** are government programs that automatically implement countercyclical fiscal policy in response to economic conditions. Given that the prescription is to increase spending and decrease taxes during downturns and to decrease spending and increase taxes during expansions, there are several government programs that accomplish these goals automatically:

Automatic stabilizers are government programs that automatically implement countercyclical fiscal policy in response to economic conditions.

- *Progressive income tax rates* guarantee that individual tax bills fall when incomes fall (during recessions) and rise when incomes rise (during expansions).
- *Taxes on corporate profits* lower total tax bills when profits are lower (during contractions) and raise tax bills when profits are higher (typically during expansions).
- *Unemployment compensation* increases government spending automatically when the number of unemployed people rises and decreases government spending when fewer people are unemployed.
- *Welfare programs* also increase government spending during downturns and decrease government spending when the economy is doing better.

In short, automatic stabilizers can eliminate recognition lags and implementation lags and thereby alleviate some concerns about the destabilizing effects of fiscal policy.

Crowding-Out

A second challenge in implementing fiscal policy concerns the actual impact of government spending and the multiplier effects, in particular the idea that government spending may be a substitute for private spending. When government spending substitutes for private spending, the impact on aggregate demand is smaller. Economists call this effect crowding-out. **Crowding-out** occurs when private spending falls in response to increases in government spending.

Crowding-out occurs when private spending falls in response to increases in government spending.

For example, say the government starts a new program in which it buys a new laptop computer for every college student in America. (Don't get too excited; this example is just hypothetical.) But if the government is buying computers for students, then students won't buy as many computers for themselves. Students may continue to spend on other items, but they might save, too, which decreases aggregate demand as private spending is "crowded out" by government spending. When crowding-out occurs, then aggregate demand does not increase as anticipated and the fiscal policy becomes less effective.

Let's look more closely at how crowding-out can work. First, let's assume a nation that has a balanced government budget and a closed economy. Suppose the government increases spending by $100 billion but does not raise taxes. This means that it has to borrow the $100 billion in the loanable funds market. But as we know, every dollar borrowed requires a dollar saved. So when the government borrows $100 billion, the money has to come from $100 billion in savings.

Figure 29.7 illustrates what happens when this government enters the loanable funds market to borrow $100 billion. The graph shows that initially the market is in equilibrium at point A with demand for loans (that is, investment) designated as D_1. The initial interest rate is 5%, and at this rate there is $250 billion worth of savings. This amount of savings funds $250 billion in private borrowing. The table in Figure 29.7 summarizes these initial values in the column labeled "Before stimulus."

Now when the government borrows, the demand for loans increases by $100 billion at all points. This effect is indicated on the graph as a shift from D_1 to D_2. But the new demand for loans completely changes the equilibrium in the market. The increased demand drives the interest rate up from

If the government bought you a new laptop, would you spend your income on another one, too?

FIGURE 29.7

Crowding-Out in the Loanable Funds Market

Initially, at point A, private savings of $250 billion all becomes private investment of $250 billion. But government borrowing shifts the demand for loans from D_1 to D_2. The new demand for loans leads to equilibrium at point B, with a higher interest rate. At the new equilibrium there is $300 billion in private savings (S_B in the table), but $100 billion goes to the government (G_B) and $200 billion is left for private investment (I_B).

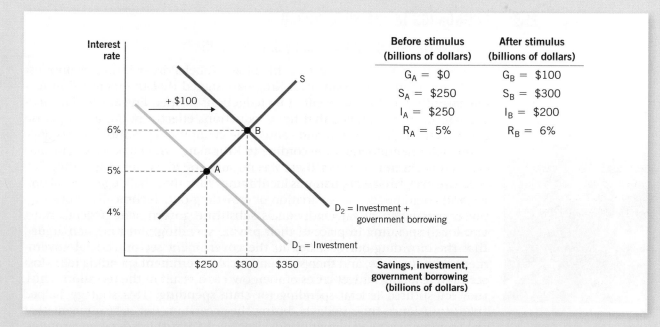

Before stimulus (billions of dollars)	After stimulus (billions of dollars)
$G_A = \$0$	$G_B = \$100$
$S_A = \$250$	$S_B = \$300$
$I_A = \$250$	$I_B = \$200$
$R_A = 5\%$	$R_B = 6\%$

5% to 6%, and the new equilibrium quantity of loanable funds increases to $300 billion, shown as point B on the graph. The interest rate rises because of the increase in demand for loans caused by government borrowing.

To demonstrate the overall effects of this new government borrowing, we compare the values of private savings and investment at the two equilibrium points. These are displayed in the table in Figure 29.7. The new equilibrium quantity of loans is $300 billion, but the government has borrowed $100 billion ($G_B$). This means that borrowing for private investment spending declines from $250 billion ($I_A$) to $200 billion ($I_B$). Essentially, the higher interest rate discourages some private investment; the government purchases crowd out private investment.

Finally, note that private savings increases from $250 billion ($S_A$) to $300 billion ($S_B$)—that is, by $50 billion—because the higher interest rate (R_B) has caused more individuals to devote more of their income to savings. But if savings rises by $50 billion, then consumption must fall by $50 billion. This is a direct relationship. The end result is that an increase of $100 billion in deficit-financed government spending leads to $100 billion less of private spending—$50 billion from lower private investment and $50 billion from higher savings.

In this example, we have complete crowding-out: every dollar of government spending crowds out a dollar of private spending. In reality, crowding-out may be less than complete, if new funds arrive from overseas or if consumers are encouraged to spend more as a result of the government spending. But this example does illustrate an important consideration of economists regarding the effects of fiscal policy.

ECONOMICS IN THE REAL WORLD

Did Government Spending Really Surge in 2009?

Why should states build new highways when the federal government offers to do it for them?

In a February 14, 2011, post on his blog, Nobel Prize–winning economist (and prominent Keynesian) Paul Krugman argued that the increases in federal spending in 2009 were offset by reductions in spending at the state government level. He argued that these reductions effectively put a damper on any potential GDP growth and caused the economy to continue to struggle with high unemployment. According to Krugman, "Once you take state and local cutbacks into account, there was no surge of government spending."

In a sense, what Krugman was identifying is another challenge of fiscal policy and could be seen as a variation of crowding-out. Technically, crowding-out occurs when private individuals substitute government (federal, state, and local) spending in place of their private spending. But Krugman argued that the crowding-out occurred in the government sector. Federal government spending rose, and then state and local government spending fell. Most states were facing budget crises of their own as a result of the recession. Thus, they substituted federal spending for state spending. This strategy helped them to balance their budgets during the recession. But it also meant that total government spending did not rise as much as the federal government intended. And this crowding-out may help explain why the 2009 fiscal stimulus failed to push the U.S. economy back to full employment. ✳

PRACTICE WHAT YOU KNOW

Crowding-Out: Does Fiscal Policy Lead to More Aggregate Demand?

Imagine that a small country is in recession and the government decides to increase spending. It commissions a very large statue for $50 million. To pay for the statue, the government borrows all of the $50 million. After the government borrows the $50 million, the interest rate rises from 3% to 4% and the equilibrium quantity of loanable funds increases from $500 million to $530 million.

Question: How would you sketch a graph of the loanable funds market representing this scenario? Be sure to indicate on this graph all the changes that take place after the borrowing.

Answer: Originally, the market is in equilibrium at point A, with an interest rate of 3% and savings and investment being equal at $500 million. Then the demand for loans increases by $50 million at all points when the government borrows $50 million. This change moves the market to a new equilibrium at point B.

Without crowding-out, a newly commissioned statue of economist Adam Smith could stimulate the economy.

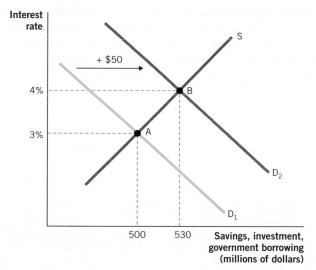

Question: Using the above information and assuming complete crowding-out, what would you predict will happen to C, I, G, and total aggregate demand (AD) in response to the government's action?

Answer: Government spending (G) will increase by $50 million. Total savings will increase from $500 million to $530 million, which means that total savings will increase by $30 million and consumption (C) will fall by $30 million. But because the government is borrowing $50 million of the savings, private investment (I) will fall to $480 million, a decrease of $20 million. All of this means a net change of zero in aggregate demand (AD). These changes are summarized below.

Component	C	I	G	AD
Change (millions of dollars)	$ −30	$ −20	$ +50	—

If your new income is temporary, are you more inclined to save it?

The **new classical critique** of fiscal policy asserts that increases in government spending and decreases in taxes are largely offset by increases in savings.

Savings Shifts

Imagine that you get a $1,000 check in the mail from the business office at your college. You would probably wonder why you got the check and whether you would have to return it. But you might also get excited and begin thinking about all the goods and services you could buy. How much would you spend, and how much would you save?

Let's consider two different scenarios regarding the source of these funds. First, imagine that you are awarded a $1,000 scholarship after your tuition bill is already paid. Thus, the money is yours to keep. In this case, you might spend much or all of the $1,000. If, instead, the funds were sent to you in error, then you would have to repay them. In this second scenario, you probably wouldn't spend any of the $1,000 you got from the college.

In some ways, government spending in the economy is similar to the second scenario. New spending today has to be paid for someday, which means that taxes must rise sooner or later. The **new classical critique** of fiscal policy, a model developed in the 1970s by a group of economists including Nobel Prize–winners Robert Barro, Robert Lucas, and Thomas Sargent asserts that increases in government spending and decreases in taxes are largely offset by increases in savings, because people know they'll have to pay higher taxes eventually. But if savings increases, then consumption falls, and this outcome mitigates the positive effects of the government spending.

Table 29.2 summarizes the three shortcomings that can diminish the effects of fiscal policy.

What Is Supply-Side Fiscal Policy?

We have considered typical fiscal policy, which focuses squarely on aggregate demand. It is also possible to implement fiscal policy with the intent of affecting the supply side of the economy. In this section, we begin by describing the supply-side perspective and certain popular supply-side policy proposals. We then look more closely at marginal tax rates and consider how changes in tax rates can affect the economy.

TABLE 29.2

Summary of Fiscal Policy Shortcomings

Shortcoming	Summary	Result
Time lags	The effects of fiscal policy may be delayed by lags in recognition, implementation, and impact.	If lags are significant, fiscal policy can be destabilizing and magnify business cycles.
Crowding-out	Government spending can serve as a substitute for private spending.	Even partial crowding-out reduces the impact of fiscal stimulus.
Savings shifts	In response to increases in government spending or lower taxes, people may increase their current savings to help pay for inevitably higher future taxes.	If current savings increases by the entire amount of the federal stimulus, the effects of the stimulus are negated.

The Supply-Side Perspective

We can illustrate the supply-side perspective in the aggregate demand–aggregate supply model. For most of this chapter, we have focused on using fiscal policy to shift the aggregate demand curve. Now we will explore how taxes and government spending can affect long-run aggregate supply. **Supply-side fiscal policy** involves the use of government spending and taxes to affect the supply, or production, side of the economy. Figure 29.8 indicates a shift from LRAS$_1$ to LRAS$_2$. When long-run aggregate supply shifts, the result is a shift to a new level of full-employment output, shown in the figure as a move from Y* to Y**.

Recall from Chapter 26 that shifts in long-run aggregate supply are caused by changes in resources, technology, and institutions. For example, we know that technological advances increase long-run aggregate supply: a technological advancement allows production of a greater quantity of output using the same or fewer resources. In the long run, much economic growth derives from technological advances. The government can implement fiscal policy and use the tax code to encourage technological advancement. Since 1981, for example, U.S. businesses have received tax credits for expenses related to research and development: firms that spend on research and development of new technology pay lower taxes than firms that don't. This incentive is designed to encourage innovation and with the goal of ultimately generating a greater supply of output. Thus, the goal of this fiscal policy is to shift long-run aggregate supply.

Many other fiscal policy initiatives are designed to focus on the supply side of the economy. These include:

1. *Research and development (R&D) tax credits.* Tax breaks are given to firms that spend resources to develop new technology. For example, if an alternative energy

Supply-side fiscal policy involves the use of government spending and taxes to affect the production (supply) side of the economy.

Subsidies for college education are a type of supply-side fiscal policy.

FIGURE 29.8

Supply-Side Fiscal Policy

Typical (demand-side) fiscal policy involves the use of government spending and taxes to shift aggregate demand. In contrast, supply-side fiscal policy involves the use of government spending and taxes to shift long-run aggregate supply (from LRAS$_1$ to LRAS$_2$), which moves the economy from one full-employment output level (Y*) to a new full-employment output level (Y**).

firm spends resources on a new lab to develop alternative energy sources, this spending reduces its overall tax bill.

2. *Policies that focus on education.* Subsidies or tax breaks for education expenses are given to help create incentives to invest in education. One example is the Pell Grant, which helps to pay for college expenses. Students receive these grants from the federal government to help them pay for college education. Eventually, education and training increase effective labor resources and thus increase aggregate supply.

3. *Lower corporate profit tax rates.* Lower taxes increase the incentives for corporations to undertake activities that generate more profit.

4. *Lower marginal income tax rates.* Lower income tax rates create incentives for individuals to work harder and produce more, because they get to keep a larger share of their income. We discuss marginal tax rates in the next section.

Incentives

All of these initiatives share two characteristics. First, they increase the incentives for productive activities. Second, each initiative takes time to affect aggregate supply. For example, education subsidies may encourage people to go to college and learn skills that will help them succeed in the workplace. But the full impact of that education won't be felt until after the education is completed. For this reason, supply-side proposals are generally emphasized as long-run solutions to growth problems.

Marginal Income Tax Rates

Marginal thinking

We have noted that lowering marginal income tax rates is one way that fiscal policy can affect the supply side of the economy. However the relationship between tax rates and tax revenue is one of the most highly controversial topics in politics, though by and large economists are not as divided over the

PRACTICE WHAT YOU KNOW

With congressional leaders at his side, President Bush signed a law that reduced top income tax rates from 39.6% to 35%.

Supply Side versus Demand Side: The Bush Tax Cuts

In mid-2001, the Bush administration won congressional approval for lower income tax rates. One stipulation of this rate cut was that the rates also be applied retroactively to taxes from the year 2000.

Question: Would you consider this fiscal policy to be demand-side focused, supply-side focused, or both? Explain your response.

Answer: Both! Tax rate cuts are generally supply-side initiatives, because they frame incentives for production going forward. So the rate cuts applying to income taxes for 2001 and beyond were focused on the supply side.

But the Bush tax cuts also applied to taxes already paid. This meant that refund checks were mailed to taxpayers, refunding part of the taxes they had paid for the year 2000. This provision was clearly demand focused, as the government hoped that taxpayers would use the funds to increase spending—that is, increase aggregate demand.

issue as the public at large is. In this section, we look more closely at how tax rates affect incentives for production.

Tax Rates and Tax Revenue

Raising income tax rates can increase tax revenue. But it turns out that if you raise them too high, tax revenue declines because the high rates provide negative incentives for production. This means that when tax rates are particularly high, a reduction in tax rates could actually lead to an increase in tax revenue. Tax rate cuts can be creative; that is, they can stimulate work effort, employment, and income and thereby generate *more* income tax revenue for the government.

Consider the following quote:

> The worst deficit comes from a recession. And if we can take the proper action in the proper time, this can be the most important step we can take to prevent another recession. That is the right time to make tax cuts, both for your family budget, and the national budget, resulting from a permanent basic reform and reduction in our rate structure. A creative tax cut, creating more jobs and income and, eventually, more revenue.

> —*35th president of the United States*

You may be surprised to learn that the president quoted is John F. Kennedy. He made this statement in 1962, when marginal tax rates were as high as 91%. Consider what a 91% marginal tax rate means: you would get to keep only 9 cents from an additional dollar's worth of income. Such an astronomical tax rate certainly diminishes incentives for work effort and production! And that was the state of the world when JFK gave his speech. Most economists agree that 91% marginal tax rates stifle economic growth. So although it may seem counterintuitive, it is possible to lower tax rates and increase overall tax revenue.

In contrast, at low initial tax rates, an increase in the tax rate leads to an increase in tax revenue. For example, there was no income tax in the United States in 1912. As we saw in Chapter 28, the United States instituted the income tax in 1913 with a top marginal rate of just 6%. Of course, income tax revenue rose between 1912, when there was no income tax, and 1913, when a modest tax was introduced. At low tax rates, increases in tax rates lead to revenue increases.

The Laffer Curve

In 1974, University of Chicago professor and economist Arthur Laffer famously tried to illustrate the relationship between tax rates and tax revenue, sketching a drawing on the back of a napkin at dinner. This relationship became known as the Laffer curve. Soon after, it became a centerpiece of Ronald Reagan's presidency in the 1980s and a central component of supply-side economists. Almost since its inception, this curve has been debated.

To understand this curve, let's first clarify the relationship between tax rates and tax revenue. Total income tax revenue depends on the level of income and the tax rate:

$$\uparrow \text{income tax revenue} = \uparrow \text{tax rate} \times \text{income}$$

JFK: Early supply-sider?

The **Laffer curve** is an illustration of the relationship between tax rates and tax revenue.

Incentives

This equation is straightforward. But because human beings react to incentives, it is not always easy to predict how tax revenue will change when tax rates change. The **Laffer curve**, shown in Figure 29.9, tries to illustrate the relationship between tax rates and tax revenue. Notice that we have labeled two regions of the Laffer curve. Region I, the blue portion of the curve, illustrates that increasing tax rates leads to increasing tax revenues:

$$\uparrow\text{income tax revenue} = \uparrow\text{tax rate} \times \text{income}$$

But at some point, tax rates become so high that they provide significant disincentives for earning income. This is the case in region II, illustrated by the orange portion of the curve, where decreases in the tax rate lead to more tax revenue. The United States was in region II in 1962, when some marginal tax rates were above 90% and President Kennedy gave his speech. At this point, an increase in the tax rate reduces income enough (illustrated by the double downward-pointing arrows) that net tax revenue falls:

$$\downarrow\text{income tax revenue} = \uparrow\text{tax rate} \times \downarrow\downarrow\text{income}$$

In region II of the Laffer curve, decreases in the tax rate lead to increases in tax revenue. At the lower rate, people have greater incentives to work and earn more income. Thus, the lower tax rates stimulate the economy and lead to more tax revenue overall.

At some specific tax rate, tax revenue is maximized. In Figure 29.9, this rate is labeled t*, though economists don't know exactly what this amount is. But there is evidence from the United States that t* is below 70%. The evidence comes from the 1980s. In 1980, the marginal tax rate on the wealthiest Americans was 70%, but then, marginal rates fell across all income brackets across the rest of the decade. Considering all U.S. taxpayers, average tax revenue (adjusted for both inflation and the number of tax returns filed) went from $6,954 to $6,202 between 1980 and 1991. Many analysts point to these figures and see them as proof that the Laffer curve doesn't exist or even that supply-side economics lacks merit.

FIGURE 29.9

The Laffer Curve

In region I of the Laffer curve, where tax rates are relatively low, increases in tax rates lead to increases in tax revenue. In region II, where tax rates are relatively high, increases in tax rates decrease tax revenue. Economists disagree over the size of t*, the tax rate that separates the regions.

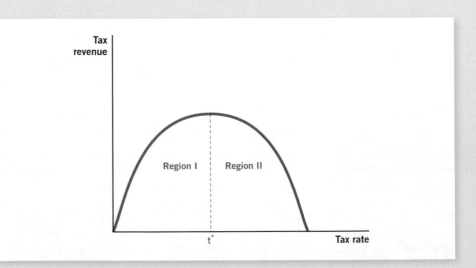

Planning for Your Future Taxes

The U.S. national debt is currently over $16 trillion, or more than $50,000 per person. In 2007, the national debt per person was only $30,000. Thus, we can infer that the increase is directly attributable to the Great Recession and the fiscal policy undertaken during that period.

What does this mean for you? It means that your taxes are going to be higher in the future. All Americans will need to contribute to pay down this large national debt. So taxes in the future will surely be higher, and you should plan accordingly.

In addition, economic growth will likely be lower until the debt is paid down. We know that higher income taxes reduce incentives for production, so it is safe to say that economic growth will be lower until this debt is paid off and taxes can come down again.

However, you can take actions to lower your future tax bills or make them more manageable. First, you probably ought to budget for higher taxes. This may mean saving more now than you would have saved otherwise. Second, in terms of personal investments, you might consider buying securities that

Government spending on highway projects was part of fiscal policy legislated during the Great Recession.

provide tax-free income. For example, the interest on municipal bonds (bonds issued by state and local governments) is not federally taxed. These simple steps might turn out to have significant benefits when your future tax bills arrive.

Others, however, look at the data and believes it shows that the rate reductions led to less tax revenue both overall and for those who were paying relatively low taxes in 1980. But for the wealthiest Americans, a rate reduction led to an increase in revenue. Table 29.3 shows data for U.S. taxpayers for both 1980 and 1991. Rate reductions led to greater tax revenue only from the top taxpayers. Overall, revenues declined when we adjust for both inflation and population.

The point to be taken from Table 29.3 is that data from the 1980s confirm that there really are two regions on the Laffer curve. Generally, conservative public figures tend to stress region II, where tax rate reductions lead to increased revenue. Liberals emphasize region I, where tax rate increases lead to more revenue. Both regions are important for economic policy.

TABLE 29.3

U.S. Income Tax Revenue for Different Income Levels, 1980 and 1991

	Income tax revenue per return (2009 dollars)		
	All taxpayers	**Bottom 50%**	**Top 1%**
1980	$6,954	$1,005	$131,307
1991	$6,202	$692	$153,675

Conclusion

We began the chapter with the misconception that government spending is a simple and predictable tool for fighting recessions—in other words, that government policy can quickly and predictably counteract business cycle fluctuations. It is certainly true that reductions in private demand accompany economic downturns. It is also true that government can use fiscal policy to increase expenditures or stimulate private spending through tax reductions. But the complete effects are difficult to predict. Recent experiences confirm this difficulty.

Looking ahead, we turn our attention next to monetary policy. In Chapter 30, we cover money and the Federal Reserve; in Chapter 31, we discuss how monetary policy affects the economy.

ANSWERING THE BIG QUESTIONS

What is fiscal policy?

* Fiscal policy involves the use of government's budget tools, government spending, and taxes to influence the macroeconomy, often through aggregate demand.

* Countercyclical fiscal policy is designed to counteract business cycle fluctuations by increasing aggregate demand during downturns and decreasing aggregate demand during expansionary periods.

What are the shortcomings of fiscal policy?

* Fiscal policy is subject to three significant lags: a recognition lag, an implementation lag, and an impact lag.

* In addition, crowding-out can diminish the effects of fiscal policy.

* Finally, according to the new classical critique, savings adjustments by private individuals can further diminish the stimulating effects of fiscal policy.

What is supply-side fiscal policy?

* Supply-side fiscal policy involves the use of government spending and taxes to affect the production (supply) side of the economy. This is a long-run view that concentrates on institutional changes.

* A key proposal of supply-side fiscal policy is that lower marginal income tax rates can actually lead to greater tax revenue when tax rates are high.

CONCEPTS YOU SHOULD KNOW

automatic stabilizers (p. 946)
contractionary fiscal policy
   (p. 938)
countercyclical fiscal policy
   (p. 939)

crowding-out (p. 946)
expansionary fiscal policy
   (p. 932)
fiscal policy (p. 932)
Laffer curve (p. 954)

marginal propensity to consume
   (MPC) (p. 941)
new classical critique (p. 950)
spending multiplier (p. 942)
supply-side fiscal policy (p. 951)

QUESTIONS FOR REVIEW

1. How are government budget balances affected by countercyclical fiscal policy? Be sure to describe the effects of both expansionary and contractionary fiscal policy.

2. Using the aggregate demand–aggregate supply model, one might argue that the economy will adjust on its own when aggregate demand drops. How does this adjustment work? Why might this adjustment take some time? (If necessary, review Chapter 27.)

3. Explain why the government budget deficit increases during a recession even without countercyclical fiscal policy.

4. Explain the three types of fiscal policy lags. What are automatic stabilizers? Which lags do automatic stabilizers affect?

5. In what circumstances would contractionary fiscal policy be recommended? How might you implement this type of policy? Why would you implement this policy—that is, what are the reasons why it might make sense to use fiscal policy to slow the economy?

6. Many people emphasize just one portion of the Laffer curve and forget that there are actually two sides. First, explain the math behind the positively sloped region of the Laffer curve. That is, explain why an increase in the tax rate sometimes leads to an *increase* in tax revenue. Second, explain the math behind the negatively sloped region of the Laffer curve. That is, explain why an increase in the tax rate sometimes leads to a *decrease* in tax revenue.

7. Assuming that complete crowding-out always holds, what happens to consumption, investment, and interest rates if the government *decreases* borrowing, all else being equal?

STUDY PROBLEMS (*solved at the end of the section*)

1. Explain the difference between typical demand-side fiscal policy and supply-side fiscal policy. For each of the following fiscal policy proposals, determine whether the primary focus is on aggregate demand or aggregate supply:
   a. a $1,000-per-person tax reduction
   b. a 5% reduction in all tax rates
   c. Pell Grants, which are government subsidies for college education
   d. government-sponsored prizes for new scientific discoveries
   e. an increase in unemployment compensation

2. To explore crowding-out, let's set up a simple loanable funds market in initial equilibrium.
   a. Draw a graph showing initial equilibrium in the loanable funds market at $800 million and an interest rate of 4%. Label your initial supply and demand curves as S_1 and D_1.
   b. Now assume that the government increases spending by $100 million that is entirely deficit financed. Show the new equilibrium in the loanable funds market. (*Note:* There is a range of possible numerical answers for this question. You should choose one number and then be sure the rest of your answer is consistent with this number.)

c. Write the new equilibrium interest rate and quantity of loanable funds in the blanks below:
New interest rate: _____
New quantity of loanable funds: _____

d. If we assume there was no government debt prior to the fiscal stimulus, determine the following new quantities and write them in the blanks below:
Savings: _____
Investment: _____
Government spending: _____

e. How much did private consumption change as a result of the change in the quantity of savings?

3. The new classical critique of activist fiscal policy is theoretically different from the crowding-out critique. Explain the difference by using a graph of the loanable funds market.

✳ 4. Fill in the blanks in the table below. Assume that the MPC is constant over everyone in the economy.

MPC	Spending multiplier	Change in government spending	Change in income
_____	5	$100	_____
_____	2.5	_____	−$250
0.5	_____	$200	_____
0.2	_____	_____	$1,000

✳ 5. Assume that the equilibrium in the loanable funds market is at an interest rate (R) of 3% and the total quantity of loans is $500 billion. In addition, in this initial situation, the government is borrowing $50 billion per year to fund the budget deficit.

a. What is private investment in this initial equilibrium? (It will help to draw a graph of the loanable funds market in this initial equilibrium.)

Now the government increases spending by $200 billion per year and finances this spending completely with additional borrowing.

b. At R = 3%, what would be the quantity demanded of loanable funds?

c. In which direction does the interest rate change to bring the market to equilibrium?
Assume that the new equilibrium is at $575 billion and assume complete crowding-out.

d. Determine the exact amount that each component of GDP changes, assuming no change in net exports.

e. What is the total change in AD from this action?

SOLVED PROBLEMS

4.

MPC	Spending multiplier	Change in government spending	Change in income
0.8	5	$100	*$500*
0.6	2.5	*−$100*	−$250
0.5	*2*	$200	*$400*
0.2	*1.25*	*$800*	$1,000

5.

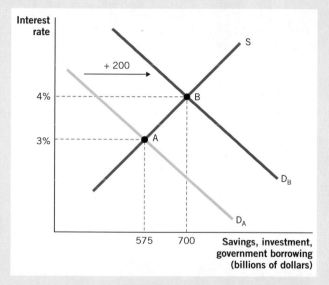

a. The initial equilibrium has an interest rate of 3% and total loans of $500 billion. This equilibrium is pictured as point A in the graph above. Because there is a total of $500 billion in loans but the government is borrowing just $50 billion of this amount, that leaves $450 billion for private investment.

b. The new demand curve is exactly $200 billion to the right of the old demand curve because the government increases the demand for loans by $200 billion at all interest rates. Therefore, at 3%, the new quantity demanded is $700 billion.

c. The interest rate rises to new equilibrium at point B. This increase is normal because at the old interest rate, the quantity demanded exceeds the quantity supplied.

d. Given the new equilibrium at $575 billion, we know that total savings is $575 billion because every dollar borrowed requires a dollar saved. The government is now borrowing $250 billion, which represents an increase in G of +$200 billion. But that leaves just $325 billion for private investment ($575 billion − $250 billion). As a result, I declines by $125 billion from the initial level of $450 billion (see part a). Finally, because total savings was initially $500 billion but is now $575 billion, C (consumption) falls by $75 billion.

e. The change in AD is the sum of the changes in C, I, G, and NX. We assumed no change in NX, but the changes in the others sum to zero (−$75 billion + −$125 billion + $200 billion).

PART

9

Monetary
POLICY

Money and the Federal Reserve

It's easy to control the amount of money in an economy.

Most people believe that controlling the amount of money in the economy is a simple task. After all, there is a fixed number of "green

pieces of paper" floating around the economy, and only the government has the authority to print more. But the job is actually very difficult. In fact, banks and private individuals influence the money supply with their daily private decisions. That's right: even *you* can make the money supply rise or fall.

We begin this chapter by looking closely at the definition of money. It turns out that money is more than just paper bills and coins. Because banks play an integral role in the money supply process, we will discuss how they operate and how their decisions affect the amount of money in the economy. Finally, we look at the role of the Federal Reserve System and examine how it oversees the amount of money in the economy. This background provides essential preparation for the discussion of monetary policy in Chapter 31.

Money is more than just green paper!

BIG QUESTIONS

* **What is money?**
* **How do banks create money?**
* **How does the Federal Reserve control the money supply?**

What Is Money?

It may seem strange to ask, what is money? After all, we use money all the time. Even children know we use money to buy goods and services. But what is included in the broad category of *money*? Certainly, the green pieces of paper we call currency are included. **Currency** is the paper bills and coins that are used to buy goods and services. But people also make many purchases without using currency. In this section, we define the functions of money and then explain how the quantity of money is measured.

Currency is the paper bills and coins that are used to buy goods and services.

Three Functions of Money

Money has three functions: as a medium of exchange, as a unit of account, and as a store of value. Let's look at each function.

A Medium of Exchange

If you want to buy groceries, you offer money in exchange for them; if you work, you accept money as payment for your labor. Money is a common **medium of exchange**—that is, it is what people trade for goods and services.

Modern economies generally have a government-provided medium of exchange. In the United States, the government provides our dollar currency. But even in economies without government provision, a preferred medium of exchange usually emerges. For example, in colonial Virginia, before there was any government mandate regarding money, tobacco became the accepted medium of exchange. Economist Milton Friedman wrote this about tobacco: "It was the money that the colonists used to buy food, clothing, to pay taxes—even to pay for a bride."

Invariably, some medium of exchange evolves in any economy; the primary reason is the inefficiency of barter, which is money's alternative. **Barter** occurs when there is no commonly accepted medium of exchange. It involves individuals trading some good or service they already have for something else that they want. If you want food in a barter economy, you must find a grocer who also happens to want whatever you have to trade. Maybe you can offer only your labor services, but the grocer wants a new cash register for their store. In that case, you have to try to find someone who has a cash register

A medium of exchange is what people trade for goods and services.

Barter involves the trade of a good or service in the absence of a commonly accepted medium of exchange.

and also wants to trade it for your labor. This takes more than a coincidence; it takes a double coincidence. Barter requires a **double coincidence of wants**, in which each party in an exchange transaction happens to have what the other party desires. A double coincidence is pretty unusual, which is why a medium of exchange naturally evolves in any exchange environment.

Historically, the first medium of exchange in an economy has been a commodity that is actually traded for goods and services. **Commodity money** involves the use of an actual good for money. In this situation, the good itself has value apart from its function as money. Examples include gold, silver, and the tobacco of colonial Virginia. But commodities are often difficult to carry around. Due to these transportation costs, money evolved into certificates that represented a fixed quantity of the commodity. These certificates became the medium of exchange but were still tied to the commodity, because they could be traded for the actual commodity if the holder demanded it.

Commodity-backed money is money that can be exchanged for a commodity at a fixed rate. For example, until 1971, U.S. dollars were fixed in value to specific quantities of silver and gold. A $1 U.S. silver certificate looks much like dollar bills in circulation today, but the print along the bottom of the note reads, "one dollar in silver payable to the bearer on demand." Until 1964, we also had commodity coins in the United States. U.S. quarters from 1964 look like the same quarters we use today, but unlike today's they are made of real silver.

While commodity money and commodity-backed money evolve privately in all economies, the type of money used in most modern economies depends on government. In particular, most modern economies make use of fiat money for their medium of exchange. **Fiat money** is money that has no value except as the medium of exchange; there is no inherent or intrinsic value to the currency. In the United States, our currency is physically just pieces of green paper, otherwise known as Federal Reserve Notes. This paper has value because the government has mandated that we can use the currency to pay our debts. On U.S. dollar bills, you can read the statement "This note is legal tender for all debts, public and private."

There are advantages and disadvantages to fiat and commodity monies. On the one hand, commodity-backed money ties the value of the holder's money to something real. If the government is obligated to trade silver for every dollar in circulation, a limit is imposed on the number of dollars it

Without money, what would you trade for this coffee and bagel?

A **double coincidence of wants** occurs when each party in an exchange transaction happens to have what the other party desires.

Commodity money involves the use of an actual good for money.

Commodity-backed money is money that can be exchanged for a commodity at a fixed rate.

Fiat money is money that has no value except as the medium of exchange; there is no inherent or intrinsic value to the currency.

The money pictured here looks much like our modern money, but the dollar bill is a commodity-backed silver certificate from 1957. At that time, it could be traded for a dollar's worth of actual silver. The quarter from 1964 is made of real silver.

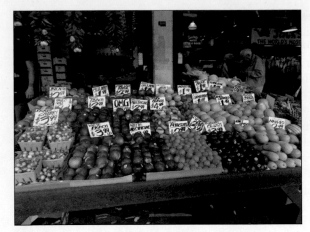

Thank goodness each of these fruits is priced in a common unit of account.

can print, which probably limits inflation levels. Fiat money offers no such constraint on the expansion of the money supply. Rapid monetary expansion and then inflation can occur without a commodity standard that ties the value of money to something real. We have and do see this especially in developing and less stable nations; as recently as 2016 Venezuela experienced inflation rates of over 150%.

On the other hand, tying the value of a nation's currency to a commodity is dangerous when the market value of that commodity fluctuates. Imagine how a new discovery of gold affects prices in a nation with gold-backed currency. An increased supply of gold reduces gold prices, and therefore more gold is required in exchange for all other goods and services. This situation constitutes inflation: the price of everything in terms of the money (gold) rises. This situation occurred in the mid-fifteenth and the mid-seventeenth centuries in Europe as Spanish conquistadors brought back tons of gold from Central and South America. Because a change in the value of a medium of exchange affects the prices of all goods and services in the macroeconomy, it can be risky to tie a currency to a commodity.

A Unit of Account

A unit of account is the measure in which prices are quoted.

A store of value is a means for holding wealth.

Money also serves as a unit of account. A **unit of account** is the measure in which prices are quoted. Money enables you and someone you don't know to speak a common language. For example, when the cashier says that the mangos you want to buy cost 99 cents each, the cashier is communicating the value of mangos in a way you understand. Consider a world without an accepted unit of account. In that world, goods would be priced in multiple ways. Theoretically, you might go shopping and find goods priced in terms of any possible currency or even other goods. Imagine how difficult it would be to shop! Using money as a unit of account is so helpful that a standard unit of account generally evolves, even in small economies.

Expressing the value of something in terms of dollars and cents also enables people to make accurate comparisons between items. Thus, money also serves as a measuring stick and recording device. Think of your checkbook for a moment. You don't write down in the ledger that you bought a bagel and coffee; instead, you write down that you spent $4. You use dollar amounts to keep track of your account and to record transactions in a consistent manner.

A Store of Value

If you keep your money in your sock drawer, you incur an opportunity cost of forgone interest from a bank account.

Money's third function is as a store of value. A **store of value** is a means for holding wealth. Money has long served as an important store of value. Think of bags of gold coins from the Middle Ages. In both fiction and nonfiction stories, pirates' treasures are generally represented by gold; this precious metal was the vehicle for storing great values. But in modern economies, this function is much less important. Today, we have other options for holding our wealth, many of which offer greater returns than keeping dollar bills in a sock drawer or stuffed under a mattress. We can easily put our dollars into bank accounts or investment accounts that earn interest. These options have caused money's role as a store of value to decline.

ECONOMICS IN THE REAL WORLD

The Evolution of Prison Money

In the past, cigarettes were often the preferred unit of account and medium of exchange in prisons. This commodity money was useful as currency in addition to its usefulness for smoking. But in 2004 the U.S. government outlawed smoking in federal prisons, and this decision led to the development of a new medium of exchange.

The evolution of prison money.

In an October 2008 *Wall Street Journal* article, Justin Scheck reported on one federal facility where cans of mackerel had taken over as the accepted money. According to one prisoner, "It's the coin of the realm." This "bartering" is not legal in federal prisons. Prisoners can lose privileges if they are caught exchanging goods or services for mackerel. Nonetheless, mackerel remains the medium of exchange and the unit of account. For example, haircuts cost about two "macks." The cans of fish also serve as a reliable store of value. Some prisoners even rent lockers from others so they can store their mackerel money.

But while mackerel is popular, it is not the only commodity used as money in federal prisons. In some prisons, protein bars or cans of tuna serve as money. One reason why mackerel is preferred to other alternatives is that each can costs about one dollar—so it's a simple substitute for U.S. currency, which inmates are not allowed to carry. ✳

Measuring the Quantity of Money

Now that we have defined the three functions of money, we need to consider how the total amount of money in the economy is measured. As we saw in Chapter 21, the quantity of money in an economy affects the overall price level. In particular, a nation's inflation rate is dependent on the rate of growth of its quantity of money. In addition, in Chapter 31 we'll see that the quantity of money can influence real GDP and unemployment rates. Because money has such profound macroeconomic influences, it is important to measure it accurately. But doing so is not quite as simple as just adding up all the currency in an economy.

To get a sense of the difficulties of measuring the money supply, think about all the different ways you make purchases. You might hold some currency for emergencies, to make a vending machine purchase, or to do laundry. On top of this, you might write checks to pay your rent, tuition, or utilities bills. Moreover, you probably carry a debit card that enables you to withdraw from your savings or checking account. To measure the quantity of money in an economy, we must somehow find the total value of all these alternatives that people use to buy goods and services. Clearly, currency alone is not enough—people buy things all the time without using currency. Currency is money, but it constitutes only a small part of the total money supply.

M1 and M2

Checkable deposits are deposits in bank accounts from which depositors may make withdrawals by writing checks.

As we broaden our definition of money beyond currency, we first acknowledge bank deposits on which checks can be written. **Checkable deposits** are deposits in bank accounts from which depositors may make withdrawals by writing checks. These deposits represent purchasing power that is very similar to currency, because personal checks are accepted at many places. Adding checkable deposits to currency gives us a money supply measure known as **M1**, the money supply measure that is composed of currency and checkable deposits. M1 also includes traveler's checks, but these account for a very small portion of M1.

M1 is the money supply measure that is composed of currency, checkable deposits, and traveler's checks.

A broader measure of the money supply, **M2**, includes everything in M1 plus savings deposits. M2 also includes two other types of deposits: money market mutual funds and small-denomination time deposits (certificates of deposit, or CDs). The key point to remember is that the money supply in an economy includes both currency and bank deposits:

M2 is the money supply measure that includes everything in M1 plus savings deposits, money market mutual funds, and small-denomination time deposits (CDs).

(Equation 30.1)

$$\text{money supply (M)} = \text{currency} + \text{deposits}$$

Equation 30.1 is an approximation of the general money supply. Actual data for both M1 and M2 are regularly published by the Federal Reserve. Figure 30.1 shows the components of M1 and M2 as of February 2015. Notice

---

FIGURE 30.1

Measures of the U.S. Money Supply, February 2015

M1 and M2 are the most common measures of the money supply. M1 includes currency, checking deposits, and traveler's checks. M2 includes everything in M1 plus savings deposits, small-denomination time deposits (CDs), and money market mutual funds.

Source: Federal Reserve, Money Stock Measures.

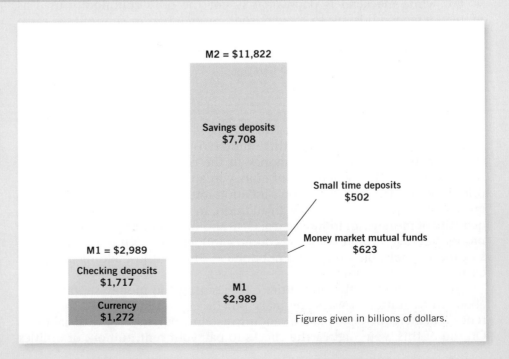

that currency in the United States is about $1.3 trillion. Adding checkable deposits of another $1.7 trillion yields M1 of about $3 trillion. But M2 was almost $12 trillion in 2015, almost $8 trillion of which was held in savings accounts. It will be important to remember that the money supply includes both currency and bank deposits when we discuss monetary policy in the next chapter.

Note that credit cards are not part of the money supply. Purchases made with credit cards involve a loan extended right at the cash register. When the loan is made, a third party is paying for the purchase until the loan is repaid. Because credit card purchases involve the use of borrowed funds, credit cards are not included as part of the money supply.

Until the 1970s, M1 was the most closely monitored money supply measure because it was a reliable estimate of the medium of exchange. But the introduction of automated teller machines rendered M1 obsolete as a reliable money supply measure. Prior to the arrival of the ATM, holding balances in checking accounts was very different from holding funds in savings accounts. Funds held in checking accounts could be accessed easily by writing checks. However, funds in savings accounts required the holder to visit the bank during business hours, wait in line, and fill out a withdrawal slip. Today, because of ATMs, depositors can make withdrawals at any time and at many locations. Because both checking and savings accounts are now readily available for purchasing goods and services, M2—which includes both types of deposits—is now a better measure of our economy's medium of exchange.

The invention of the ATM marked the beginning of the end for M1 as a reliable money supply measure.

PRACTICE WHAT YOU KNOW

The Definition of Money

People sometimes use the word "money" in ways that are inconsistent with the definition given in this chapter.

Question: Is each of the following statements consistent with our definition of money? Explain your answer each time.

a. "He had a lot of money in his wallet."

b. "She made a lot of money last year."

c. "I use my Visa card when I'm low on money."

d. "She has most of her money in the bank."

Is this M1 or M2? Yes.

Answers:

a. This statement is *consistent* with our definition, because currency is part of the medium of exchange.

(CONTINUED)

(CONTINUED)

b. This statement is *inconsistent* with the definition. It refers to income, not to money.

c. This statement is *inconsistent*. Payment with a credit card requires a loan, so using a credit card is technically not counted in the money supply.

d. This statement is *consistent*. Bank deposits count as money because they represent part of our medium of exchange.

How Do Banks Create Money?

We now have a working definition of money: money includes both currency and deposits at banks. And while private individuals and firms are not permitted to print currency, private actions do influence the total supply of money in the economy, because individuals and banks affect deposits. In this section, we explain how banks create money simply as a by-product of their daily business activity. Note that when we refer to "banks," we are talking about commercial banks, which take in deposits and extend loans. We distinguish commercial banks from investment banks, which serve a different role.

We begin by looking closely at the daily activities at typical banks. After that, we consider how banks influence the money supply.

The Business of Banking

Banks serve two very important roles in the macroeconomy. First, they are critical participants in the market for loanable funds. As we saw in Chapter 23, they provide a way for savers to supply their funds to borrowers without purchasing a financial security. In addition, they play a role in determining the money supply.

To understand how banks create money, let's look at the functions of a bank, illustrated in Figure 30.2. Banks are go-betweens in the market for loans. They are financial intermediaries; that is, they take in deposits and extend loans. Deposits are the primary source of funds, and loans are the

FIGURE 30.2

The Business of Banking: Financial Intermediation

The primary function of commercial banks is financial intermediation: they accept deposits and extend loans.

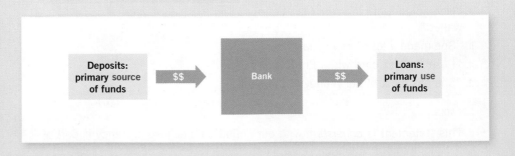

primary use of these funds. Banks can be profitable if the interest rate they charge on loans is higher than the interest rate they pay out on deposits.

Figure 30.3 illustrates the gap between interest rates on bank deposits and bank loans for U.S. banks for the period 1985–2013. The two rates go up and down together, but the interest rate on deposits is consistently lower than the interest rate on loans. The difference between the two interest rates pays a bank's operating costs and produces profits.

The Bank's Balance Sheet

Information about a bank's financial operations is available in the bank's balance sheet. A **balance sheet** is an accounting statement that summarizes a firm's key financial information. Figure 30.4 shows a hypothetical balance sheet for University Bank. The left side of the balance sheet details the bank's **assets**, which are the items the firm owns. Assets indicate how the banking firm uses the funds it has raised from various sources. The right side of the balance sheet details the bank's liabilities and owner's equity. **Liabilities** are the financial obligations the firm owes to others. **Owner's equity** is the difference between the firm's assets and its liabilities. When a firm has more assets than liabilities, it has positive owner's equity. Overall, the right side of the balance sheet identifies the bank's sources of funds.

As you can see, University Bank has extended $400 million in loans. Many of these loans went to firms to fund investment, but some also went to households to purchase homes, cars, and other consumer items. A second important asset held by banks is reserves. **Reserves** are the portion of bank deposits that are set aside and not loaned out. Reserves include both currency in the bank's vault and funds that the bank holds in deposit at its own bank, the Federal Reserve. Banks also hold U.S. Treasury securities and other

A **balance sheet** is an accounting statement that summarizes a firm's key financial information.

Assets are the items that a firm owns.

Liabilities are the financial obligations a firm owes to others.

Owner's equity is the difference between a firm's assets and its liabilities.

Reserves are the portion of bank deposits that are set aside and not loaned out.

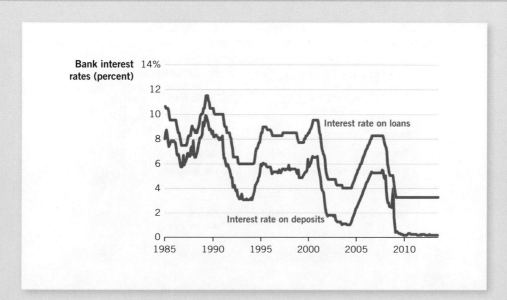

FIGURE 30.3

Interest Rates on Bank Deposits versus Loans, 1985–2013

Banks charge more interest for loans than they pay for deposits. The difference pays the banks' expenses and produces profits.

Source: FRED data, Federal Reserve Bank of St. Louis. The loan interest rate is the average prime interest rate across the United States; the deposit interest rate is the interest rate on one-month certificates of deposit.

government securities as substantial assets in their portfolio. These securities earn interest and carry very low risk. Finally, banks hold other assets, such as physical buildings and furniture.

Banks fund their activities primarily by taking in deposits. In fact, the deposits of typical households are the lifeblood of banks. But banks also borrow from other commercial banks and from the Federal Reserve. The third item on the right side of the balance sheet in Figure 30.4 is net worth, or the owner's equity in the bank. Because the University Bank owns $800 million in total assets but owes only $700 million in liabilities ($500 million in deposits plus $200 million in borrowings), the owners of the bank have $100 million in equity.

In the next section, we look more closely at bank reserves, which play an important role in money creation.

Bank Reserves

Fractional reserve banking occurs when banks hold only a fraction of deposits on reserve.

Our modern system of banking is called fractional reserve banking. **Fractional reserve banking** occurs when banks hold only a fraction of deposits on reserve. The alternative is 100% reserve banking. Banks in a 100% reserve system don't loan out deposits; these banks are essentially just safes, keeping deposits on hand until depositors decide to make a withdrawal.

Figure 30.5 illustrates the process of fractional reserve banking. Deposits come into the banks, and the banks send out a portion of these funds in loans. In recent years, U.S. banks have typically loaned out almost 90% of their deposits, keeping barely over 10% on reserve. Banks loan out most of their deposits because reserves earn very little interest; every dollar kept on reserve costs the bank potential income. In 2015, bank reserves paid just 0.25% interest.

Let's say a local business approaches a bank for a loan to expand its factory. Assume that the bank has reserves available to loan and that the current

FIGURE 30.4

Balance Sheet for University Bank

A bank's balance sheet summarizes its key financial information. The bank's assets are recorded on the left side; this side shows how the bank chooses to use its funds. The sources of the firm's funds are recorded on the right side; this side shows liabilities and owner's equity. The two sides of the balance sheet must match for the financial statement to be balanced.

Assets: Uses of funds (in millions)		Liabilities and owner's equity: Sources of funds (in millions)	
Loans	$400	Deposits	$500
Reserves	$60	Borrowings	$200
U.S. Treasury securities	$140	Owner's equity	$100
Other assets	$200		
Total assets	$800	Total liabilities and net worth	$800

interest rate on these commercial loans is 5%, which the firm is willing to pay. The alternative is to keep the funds on reserve, earning just 0.25% interest. If the bank rejects the firm's loan application and decides to keep the funds in its vault as reserves, the cost of this decision to the bank is the difference between these two interest rates: 5% − 0.25% = 4.75%.

Banks hold reserves for two reasons. First, they must accommodate withdrawals by their depositors. You'd be pretty unhappy if you tried to make a withdrawal from your bank and it didn't have enough on reserve to honor your request. If word spread that a bank might have difficulty meeting its depositors' withdrawal requests, that news would probably lead to a bank run. A **bank run** occurs when many depositors attempt to withdraw their funds from a bank at the same time.

Second, banks are legally bound to hold a fraction of their deposits on reserve. The **required reserve ratio** (rr) is the portion of deposits that banks are required to keep on reserve. For a given bank, the dollar amount of reserves that it is required to hold is determined by multiplying the required reserve ratio by the bank's total amount of deposits:

$$\text{required reserves} = \text{rr} \times \text{deposits}$$

Currently, the required reserve ratio is 10% for almost all deposits (rr = 0.10). This means that your bank can legally lend out up to 90 cents of every dollar you deposit.

Consider University Bank, whose balance sheet was presented in Figure 30.4. The bank currently has $500 million in deposits. University Bank pays some interest on the deposits and offers services, such as checking, to its depositors. University Bank can't afford to keep the $500 million sitting in the vault—the opportunity cost is too high. If the bank is going to stay in business, it will need to loan out at least part of the $500 million. With a reserve requirement of 10% of deposits, required reserves in this case are $50 million, so University Bank can loan out up to $450 million.

Banks rarely keep their level of reserves exactly at the required level. Any reserves above the required level are called **excess reserves**:

$$\text{excess reserves} = \text{total reserves} - \text{required reserves}$$

A **bank run** occurs when many depositors attempt to withdraw their funds from a bank at the same time.

The **required reserve ratio** is the portion of deposits that banks are required to keep on reserve.

(Equation 30.2)

Opportunity cost

Excess reserves are any bank reserves held in excess of those required.

(Equation 30.3)

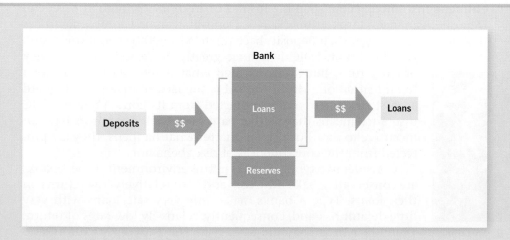

FIGURE 30.5

Fractional Reserve Banking

In a fractional reserve banking system, banks lend out only a fraction of the deposits they take in. The remainder is set aside as reserves.

The balance sheet of University Bank, presented in Figure 30.4, indicates that the bank currently holds total reserves of $60 million. Therefore, it has $10 million in excess reserves. Given the opportunity cost of holding these excess reserves, University Bank will probably seek to loan out most of this balance in the future.

The FDIC and Moral Hazard

Because a bank keeps only a fraction of its deposits on reserve, if all depositors try to withdraw their deposits at the same time, the bank will not be able to meet its obligations. But in a typical day, only a small number of deposits are withdrawn. However, if word spreads that a bank is unstable and may not be able to meet the demands of depositors—whether this rumor is true or not—depositors will rush to withdraw their funds, which will lead to a bank run. No bank can survive a bank run.

During the Great Depression, bank failures became common. From 1929 to 1933, over 9,000 banks failed in the United States alone—more than in any other period in U.S. history. It is clear that many banks were extending loans beyond their ability to collect and pay depositors in a timely manner. As a result, many depositors lost confidence in the banking system. If you became worried about your bank and were not certain that you could withdraw your deposits at some later point, wouldn't you run to the bank to get your money out?

This is precisely what happened to many banks during the Great Depression. The Hollywood film classic *It's a Wonderful Life* (1946) captures this situation perfectly. In the movie, the character George Bailey is set to leave on his honeymoon when the financial intermediary he runs is subject to a run. When a depositor asks for his money back, George tells him, "The money's not here. Well, your money's in Joe's house, that's right next to yours. And in the Kennedy house, and Mrs. Macklin's house, and, and a hundred others." This quote summarizes both the beauty and the danger wrapped up in a fractional reserve banking system. Fractional reserve banking allows access to funds by many individuals and firms in an economy, but it can also lead to instability when many depositors demand their funds simultaneously.

Moral hazard is the lack of incentive to guard against risk where one is protected from its consequences.

After the massive rate of bank failures from 1929 to 1933, the U.S. government instituted federal deposit insurance in 1933 through the Federal Deposit Insurance Corporation (FDIC). Deposit insurance now guarantees that depositors will get their deposits back (up to $250,000) even if their bank goes bankrupt. FDIC insurance greatly decreased the frequency of bank runs, but it also created what is referred to as a moral hazard situation. **Moral hazard** is the lack of incentive to guard against risk where one is protected from its consequences. FDIC insurance means that neither banks nor their depositors have an incentive to monitor risk; no matter what happens, they are protected from the consequences of risky behavior.

Consider two types of banks in this environment. Type A banks are conservative, take little risk, and earn relatively low returns on their loans. Type A banks make only very safe loans with very little default risk and, consequently, relatively low rates of return. Type A banks rarely fail, but they make relatively low profit and pay relatively low interest rates to their depositors. In contrast,

To end the bank run, George Bailey offers depositors money from his own wallet.

Type B banks take huge risks, hoping to make extremely large returns on their loans. Type B loans carry greater default risk but also pay higher returns. Type B banks often fail, but the lucky ones—the ones that survive—earn very handsome profits and pay high interest rates on their customers' deposits.

Moral hazard draws individual depositors and bankers to type B banking. There is a tremendous upside and no significant downside, because depositors are protected against losses by FDIC insurance. This is the environment in which our modern banks operate, which is why many analysts argue that reserve requirements and other regulations are necessary to help ensure stability in the financial industry—especially given that recessions often start in the financial industry.

ECONOMICS IN THE REAL WORLD

Twenty-First-Century Bank Run

For a modern example of a bank run, consider England's Northern Rock Bank, which experienced a bank run in 2007—the first British bank run in over a century. Northern Rock (which is now owned by Virgin Money) had earned revenue valued over $10 billion per year. But extensive losses stemming from investments in mortgage markets led it to near collapse in 2007.

In September of that year, depositors began queuing outside Northern Rock locations because they feared they would not get their deposits back. Eventually, the British government offered deposit insurance of 100% to Northern Rock depositors—but not before much damage had been done. In February 2008, Northern Rock was taken over by the British government because the bank was unable to repay its debts or find a buyer. To make matters worse, there is some evidence that Northern Rock was solvent at the time of the bank run, meaning that stronger deposit insurance could have saved the bank.

In the United States, over 300 banks failed between 2008 and 2011 without experiencing a bank run. (So these banks failed, but it did not lead to a bank run.) The individual depositors who funded the risky loans got their money back. So why the bank run in England? The difference is a reflection of the level of deposit insurance offered in the two nations. In England, depositors are insured for 100% of their deposits up to a value of $4,000, then for only 90% of their next $70,000. So British depositors get back a fraction of their deposits up to about $74,000. In contrast, FDIC insurance in the United States offers 100% insurance on the first $250,000. ✳

Depositors queue outside a Northern Rock Bank location in September 2007.

How Banks Create Money

We have seen that banks function as financial intermediaries. But as a by-product of their everyday activity, they also create new money. Modern U.S. banks don't mint currency, but they do create new deposits, and deposits are a part of the money supply.

Money deposited in the banking system leads to more money. To see how, let's start with a hypothetical example that involves the Federal Reserve, which supplies the currency in the United States. Let's say that the Federal Reserve decides to increase the money supply in the United States. It prints a single $1,000 bill and drops it out of a helicopter. Perhaps you are the lucky person who finds this brand-new $1,000 bill. If you keep the $1,000 in your wallet, then the money supply increases by only $1,000. But if you deposit the new money in a bank, then the bank can use it to create even more money.

Let's see how this process works. Consider what happens if you deposit the $1,000 into a savings or checking account at University Bank. When you deposit the $1,000, it is still part of the money supply, because both currency and bank deposits are counted in the money supply. You don't have the currency anymore, but in your wallet you have a debit card that enables you to access the $1,000 to make purchases. Therefore, the deposit still represents $1,000 worth of the medium of exchange.

But University Bank doesn't keep your $1,000 in reserve; it uses part of your deposit to extend a new loan that earns interest income for the bank. You still have the $1,000 in your account (as a deposit), but someone else receives money from the bank in the form of a loan. Thus, University Bank creates new money by loaning out part of your deposit. You helped the bank in the money creation process because you put your funds into the bank in the first place.

This is just the first step in the money creation process. We'll now explore this process in more detail, utilizing the bank's balance sheet. For this example, we need to make two assumptions to help understand the general picture:

Assumption 1: All currency is deposited in a bank.

Assumption 2: Banks hold no excess reserves.

Neither of these assumptions is completely realistic. But let's work through the example under these conditions, and later we can consider the effect of each assumption.

Consider first how your deposit changes the assets and liabilities of University Bank. The following t-account (an abbreviated version of a firm's balance sheet) summarizes all initial changes to the balance sheet of University Bank when you deposit your new $1,000 (assumption 1):

University Bank

Assets		Liabilities and net worth	
Reserves	+$1,000	Deposits	+$1,000

With a required reserve ratio of 10% (rr = 0.10), University Bank loans out $900 of your deposit (assumption 2 implies that only 10% of deposits are held on reserve). Perhaps the bank loans this amount to a student named Kaitlyn so she can pay her tuition bill. When University Bank extends the loan to Kaitlyn, the money supply increases by $900. That is, you still have your $1,000 deposit, and Kaitlyn now has $900.

Including your initial deposit and this $900 loan, the balance sheet changes at University Bank are summarized in this t-account:

University Bank

Assets		Liabilities and net worth	
Reserves	+$100	Deposits	+$1,000
Loans	+$900		

Kaitlyn gives her college the $900, and the college then deposits this amount into its own bank, named Township Bank. But the money multiplication process does not end here. Township Bank also keeps no excess reserves, so it loans out 90% of the $900, which is $810. This loan creates $810 more in money supply, so that total new money is now $1,000 + $900 + $810 = $1,710. Here are the balance sheet changes at Township Bank:

Township Bank

Assets		Liabilities and net worth	
Reserves	+$90	Deposits	+$900
Loans	+$810		

You can now see that whenever a bank makes a loan, it creates new money. As long as dollars find their way back into the banking system, banks multiply them into more deposits—which means more money. Table 30.1 summarizes this process of money creation. The initial $1,000 deposit ultimately leads to $10,000 worth of money. When monetary funds are deposited into banks, banks can multiply these deposits; and when they do, they create money.

TABLE 30.1

Money Creation

		Round	Deposit	
Assumption 1: All currency is deposited in banks.				
Assumption 2: Banks hold no excess reserves.		1	$1,000	← Initial deposit
Required reserve ratio (rr) = 10%		2	$900	
Initial new money supply = $1,000		3	$810	
		4	$729	
		.	.	
		.	.	
		.	.	
		Sum	$10,000	← Total money

The **simple money multiplier** is the rate at which banks multiply money when all currency is deposited into banks and they hold no excess reserves.

(Equation 30.4)

In the end, the impact on the money supply is a large multiple of the initial increase in money. The exact multiple depends on the required reserve ratio (rr). The rate at which banks multiply money when all currency is deposited into banks and they hold no excess reserves is called the **simple money multiplier** (m^m). The formula for the money multiplier is

$$m^m = \frac{1}{rr}$$

In our example, rr = 0.10, so the multiplier is 1/0.10, which is 10. When the money multiplier is 10, a new $1,000 bill produced by the Federal Reserve can eventually lead to $10,000 in new money.

Of course, in the real world our two assumptions don't always hold. There is a more realistic money multiplier that relaxes the two assumptions. Consider how a real-world money multiplier would compare with the simple money multiplier. First, if people hold on to some currency (relaxing assumption 1), banks cannot multiply that currency, so the more realistic multiplier is smaller than the simple money multiplier. Second, if banks hold excess reserves (relaxing assumption 2), these dollars are not multiplied, and again the real multiplier is smaller than the simple version. So, in reality, money doesn't multiply at quite the rate represented by the simple money multiplier. The simple money multiplier represents the *maximum* size of the money multiplier.

Note that the money multiplier process also works in reverse. When funds are withdrawn from the banking system, these are funds that banks cannot multiply. In effect, the money supply contracts. The maximum contraction is the withdrawal times the simple money multiplier.

How Does the Federal Reserve Control the Money Supply?

There's a good chance you've heard of the U.S. Federal Reserve (Fed), even outside economics class. Janet Yellen, the chair of the Fed's Board of Governors, is perhaps the most recognized economist in the world. And while we've referred to the Fed periodically throughout this text, now it's time to examine it closely.

The Many Jobs of the Federal Reserve

The Fed was established in 1913 as the central bank of the United States. The Fed's primary responsibilities are threefold:

1. *Monetary policy*: The Fed controls the U.S. money supply and is charged with regulating it to offset macroeconomic fluctuations.
2. *Central banking*: The Fed serves as a bank for banks, holding their deposits and extending loans to them.
3. *Bank regulation*: The Fed is one of the primary entities charged with ensuring the financial stability of banks, including the determination of reserve requirements.

Janet Yellen was appointed chair of the Fed's Board of Governors in 2014.

PRACTICE WHAT YOU KNOW

Fractional Reserve Banking: The B-Money Bank

Use this balance sheet of the B-Money Bank to answer the questions below. Assume that the required reserve ratio is 10%.

When banks extend loans, the money supply increases.

B-Money Bank

Assets		Liabilities and net worth	
Reserves	$50,000	Deposits	$200,000
Loans	$120,000	Net worth	$20,000
Treasury securities	$50,000		

Question: What are the required reserves of B-Money Bank?

Answer: B-Money is required to hold 10% of deposits, which is $20,000.

Question: What is the maximum new loan that B-Money can extend?

Answer: B-Money has $30,000 in excess reserves, so it can extend that total amount in new loans.

Question: How would you rewrite B-Money's balance sheet, assuming that this loan is made?

Answer: The only items that would change are reserves, which would decline by $30,000, and loans, which would increase by $30,000.

B-Money Bank

Assets		Liabilities and net worth	
Reserves	$20,000	Deposits	$200,000
Loans	$150,000		
Treasury securities	$50,000	Net worth	$20,000

Question: If the Federal Reserve now bought all of B-Money's Treasury securities, how large a loan could B-Money now extend?

Answer: B-Money would now have $50,000 in excess reserves, so it could make a loan in this amount.

Question: What would be the maximum impact on the money supply from this Fed action?

Answer: Using the simple money multiplier, we can see that the money supply could grow by as much as $500,000 from this action alone:

$$\$50,000 \times m^m = \$50,000 \times \frac{1}{rr} = \$50,000 \times 10 = \$500,000$$

In this section, we talk about the Fed's role as central bank and bank regulator. We then look at monetary policy in the remainder of the chapter and into the next chapter.

The Fed is a "central bank"—that is, it acts as a "bank for banks." In its role as central bank, it offers support and stability to the nation's entire banking system. The first component of this role involves the deposits that banks hold at the Fed. **Federal funds** are deposits that private banks hold on reserve at the Fed. The word "federal" seems to denote that these are government funds, but in fact they are private funds held on deposit at a *federal* agency—the Fed. These deposits are part of the reserves that banks set aside, along with the physical currency in their vaults.

Banks keep reserves at the Fed in part because the Fed clears loans between banks. When banks loan reserves to other banks, these are *federal funds loans*. The federal funds loans are typically very short-term (often overnight), and they enable banks to make quick adjustments to their balance sheets. For example, if our theoretical University Bank somehow dips below its required reserve level, it can approach Township Bank for a short-term loan. If Township Bank happens to have excess reserves, making a short-term loan enables it to earn interest. The interest rate banks charge each other on interbank loans is known as the **federal funds rate**.

Figure 30.6 illustrates how the relationship between the Federal Reserve and commercial banks is analogous to the relationship between commercial banks and households and firms. First, households and firms hold deposits at banks, and banks hold deposits at the Fed—these are the federal funds. Second, households and firms take out loans from banks, and banks take out loans from the Fed. The loans from the Fed to the private banks are known as **discount loans**.

Discount loans are the vehicle by which the Fed performs its role as "lender of last resort." Given the macroeconomic danger of bank failure, the Fed serves an important role as a backup lender to private banks that find difficulty borrowing elsewhere. The **discount rate** is the interest rate on the discount loans made from the Fed to private banks. The Fed sets this interest

Federal funds are deposits that private banks hold on reserve at the Federal Reserve.

The **federal funds rate** is the interest rate on loans between private banks.

Discount loans are loans from the Federal Reserve to private banks.

The **discount rate** is the interest rate on the discount loans made by the Federal Reserve to private banks.

FIGURE 30.6

The Federal Reserve as a Central Bank

The Federal Reserve operates as a central bank for commercial banks. Commercial banks make deposits at the Federal Reserve; these deposits are called federal funds. The Federal Reserve also extends loans to commercial banks; these loans are called discount loans.

Moral Hazard

Wall Street: Money Never Sleeps

This 2010 film is a sequel to the 1987 movie *Wall Street*. This film focuses on the historical events leading up to and during the financial crisis that began in 2007. One recurring theme in the movie is that some financial firms are "too big to fail." How can a firm be too big to fail?

If one bank fails, it is unable to repay its depositors and other creditors. This situation puts all the bank's creditors into similar financial difficulty. If the failing bank is large enough, its failure can set off a domino effect in which bank after bank fails and the entire financial system collapses. If regulators deem a bank too big to fail, they will use government aid to keep the bank afloat.

However, this situation introduces a particularly strong case of moral hazard. After all, banks have incentives to take on risk so that they can earn high profits. If we eliminate the possibility of failure by providing government aid, there is almost no downside risk.

Gordon Gecko understands moral hazard.

In this movie, Gordon Gecko, played by Michael Douglas, defines moral hazard during a public lecture. His definition is this: "when they take your money and then are not responsible for what they do with it."

Gecko is right: when a financial institution is not required to bear the costs of making poor decisions, it is not legally responsible for mishandling its depositors' funds.

rate because it is a loan directly from a branch of the U.S. government to private financial institutions.

Discount loans don't often figure prominently in macroeconomics, but in extremely turbulent times, they reassure financial market participants. For example, when banks were struggling in 2008, financial market participants were assured that troubled banks could rely on the Federal Reserve to fortify failing banks with discount loans. In fact, for the first time in history, other financial firms were allowed to borrow from the Fed. The Fed even extended an $85 billion loan to the insurance company American International Group because it had written insurance policies for financial securities based on failing home mortgages.

The Fed also serves as a regulator of individual banks. In this role, its responsibilities include the setting and monitoring of reserve requirements. The Fed monitors the balance sheets of banks with an eye toward limiting the riskiness of the assets the banks hold. One might ask why banks are subject to this kind of regulation. After all, the government doesn't monitor the riskiness of assets owned by other private firms. However, as we have seen, the interdependent nature of banking firms means that banking problems often spread throughout the entire industry very quickly. In addition, there is the moral hazard problem we discussed earlier: because of deposit insurance, banks and their customers have reduced incentives to monitor the risk of bank assets on their own.

Incentives

AIG: the first (and last?) insurance company to get a discount loan from the Fed.

PRACTICE WHAT YOU KNOW

Federal Reserve Terminology

Let's say the reserves at B-Money Bank fall below the required level, so it approaches University Bank for a loan. University Bank agrees to a short-term loan with B-Money Bank.

Loans from the Federal Reserve are not called federal funds. They are called discount loans.

Question: What is the name of the funds that private banks like University Bank loan to other private banks (like B-Money Bank)? What is the interest rate on these loans called?

Answer: The funds are called federal funds. The word "federal" makes it sound as if the funds are a loan from the federal government, but they are not. This wording has been adopted because the loan typically takes place through changes in the two banks' accounts at their bank, the Federal Reserve. The interest rate is the federal funds rate.

Now assume that B-Money Bank has made some particularly troublesome loans (perhaps a lot of high-risk mortgage loans) and that all private parties refuse to lend to B-Money, which then approaches the Fed for a loan to keep its reserves at the required level.

Question: What is the name of this type of loan? What is the name of the interest rate charged for this loan?

Answer: This is a discount loan, and the interest rate is the discount rate.

Monetary Policy Tools

When the Fed wants to alter the supply of money in the economy, it has several tools at its disposal. In this section we discuss these policy tools, but our emphasis is on the single tool the Fed uses every day: open market operations.

Open Market Operations

If the Fed decided to increase the money supply, it could do so in a number of direct ways. Here we list three possible means by which the Fed might directly increase the amount of money in the economy. See if you can guess which of the three is correct:

1. Drop money out of a helicopter.
2. Distribute $50,000 in new $100 bills to every private bank.
3. Use new money to buy something in the economy.

Open market operations involve the purchase or sale of bonds by a central bank.

If you chose option 3, you are correct. **Open market operations** involve the purchase or sale of bonds by a central bank. When the Fed wants to increase the money supply, it buys securities; in contrast, when it wishes to decrease the money supply, it sells securities. In Chapter 23, we introduced the U.S. Treasury security as a special bond asset. These are the securities (bonds) that the Fed typically buys and sells when implementing monetary policy.

Essentially, the Fed could realize its desired effects through buying any goods and services—real estate, fine art, or, for that matter, tons and tons of coffee and bagels. It would be as if the Fed created a batch of new currency and then goes shopping. When it is done shopping, it leaves behind all the new currency in the economy. Whatever it buys on its shopping spree becomes an asset on the Fed's balance sheet.

The Fed buys and sells Treasury securities for two reasons. First, the Fed's goal is to get the funds directly into the market for loanable funds. In this way, financial institutions begin lending the new money, and it quickly moves into the economy. Second, a typical day's worth of open market operations might entail as much as $20 billion worth of purchases from the Fed. If the Fed bought coffee and bagels, it would cause problems in that market. Imagine being the manager of a bagel shop in Washington, D.C., and having Janet Yellen walk in with a request for $20 billion worth of bagels. That would be an impossible request! But the market for U.S. Treasuries is big enough to accommodate this level of purchases seamlessly. The daily volume in the U.S. Treasury market is over $500 billion, so the Fed can buy and sell without difficulty.

Figure 30.7 summarizes how open market operations work. In panel (a), we see that when the Fed purchases bonds, it creates new money and trades this money with financial institutions for their Treasury bonds. The result is more money in the economy. On the other side, we see in panel (b) that when the Fed sells bonds to financial institutions, it exchanges bonds for existing money, taking the money out of the economy. The result is less money in the economy.

The Fed undertakes open market operations every business day. Typically, it intends to keep market conditions exactly as they were the day before. But

FIGURE 30.7

Open Market Operations

In open market purchases, the Fed buys bonds from financial institutions. This action injects new money directly into financial markets. In open market sales, the Fed sells bonds back to financial institutions. This action takes money out of financial markets.

(a) Open market purchase (expansionary): Fed buys bonds with new dollars.

$$

Fed → Financial Institutions

Bonds

RESULT: More money in the economy.

(b) Open market sale (contractionary): Fed exchanges bonds for existing dollars.

Bonds

Fed → Financial Institutions

$$

RESULT: Less money in the economy.

open market operations are also the primary tool that the Fed uses to expand or contract the money supply in order to affect the macroeconomy.

Quantitative Easing

Quantitative easing is the targeted use of open market operations in which the central bank buys securities specifically targeting certain markets.

The end of 2008 marked the single worst quarter for the U.S. economy in over half a century. Real GDP had declined by 8.9%, and the unemployment rate was ratcheting upward. In November 2008, hoping that more money would stimulate the economy, the Federal Reserve determined that it should take additional measures to increase the money supply. The method it chose is a new variety of open market operations known as quantitative easing. **Quantitative easing** is the targeted use of open market operations in which the central bank buys securities specifically targeting certain markets. Open market operations typically involve buying and selling short-term Treasury securities—that is, bonds that mature in less than one year. But with its quantitative easing in late 2008, the Fed expanded its purchases to include $300 billion in long-term Treasury securities. It also purchased $1.25 trillion in mortgage-backed securities, specifically targeting the housing market. Together with an additional $175 billion in purchases of securities from government-sponsored enterprises, the Fed's purchases amounted to almost $2 trillion in new funds injected into the economy.

This move was bold and unprecedented in both size and scope. It amounted to the Fed creating trillions of new dollars and injecting them into targeted sectors of the economy. The first round of quantitative easing started in November 2008 and continued into the first quarter of 2010. At that point, the Fed was convinced that economic recovery was well under way. But conditions deteriorated over the second half of 2010 as the unemployment rate stayed around 9% and real GDP growth stalled. Because of the lackluster U.S. economic performance in November 2010, the Fed decided to engage in a second round of quantitative easing, dubbed QE 2. This round involved purchasing an additional $600 billion in long-term Treasury securities. The Fed implemented these two rounds of quantitative easing when it was clear that traditional open market operations would not return the economy to stable growth rates. Then, in September 2011, as the economy continued to struggle toward consistent growth, then-Chairman of the Fed Ben Bernanke announced yet another variation of quantitative easing. In particular, the Fed would buy $400 billion in long-term Treasury securities and simultaneously sell $400 billion in short-term Treasury securities. This action became known as a "twist," because it was not really adding money to the economy but attempting to reduce long-term interest rates and thereby encourage business investment. However, the twist operation did not seem to have a significant effect on the economy, and lackluster growth continued through 2012. Thus, in September 2012, the Fed announced an ongoing program to buy $40 billion worth of securities per month (this amount was later increased to $85 billion). This program, which became known as QE 3, lasted until October 2014. Figure 30.8 illustrates the timeline for these quantitative easing programs along with the quarterly growth rates of real GDP.

In summary, quantitative easing was a new variation of open market operations that was introduced during the slow recovery from the Great Recession. Because the Fed had already bought so many securities on the open market, the lower interest rates caused by these huge purchases had already

FIGURE 30.8

Quantitative Easing, November 2008–October 2014

Beginning in 2008, the Federal Reserve began the unprecedented practice of quantitative easing (QE) to inject money into the economy. The QE initiatives were each implemented when traditional monetary policy seemed to be failing to push the economy back to consistent growth. QE 3 lasted until October 2014.

Source: GDP data are from the U.S. Bureau of Economic Analysis. QE data are from the Federal Reserve.

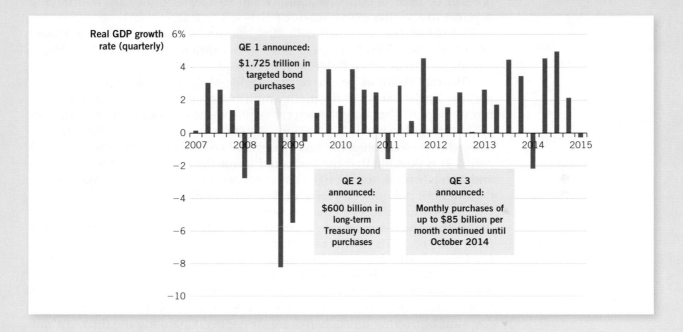

pushed short-term interest rates down to zero. Thus, traditional open market operations had reached a boundary and the Fed searched for other actions. Like most moves by the Fed, these actions are hotly debated, as critics of these programs note that quantitative easing did not quickly return the economy to strong growth. In the next chapter, we will look more closely at the Federal Reserve's influence on interest rates.

Reserve Requirements and Discount Rates

In the past, the Fed made use of two other tools in its administration of monetary policy: reserve requirements and the discount rate. Neither of these has been used recently for monetary policy, but they are available and historically important.

Recall our two earlier observations regarding reserve requirements:

1. The Fed sets the ratio of deposits that banks must hold on reserve. This ratio is the required reserve ratio.
2. The simple money multiplier (m^m) depends on the required reserve ratio (rr), because $m^m = \dfrac{1}{rr}$.

Taken together, these observations imply that the Fed can change the money multiplier by changing the required reserve ratio. If the Fed lowers the required reserve ratio, the money multiplier increases. If it raises the required reserve ratio, the money multiplier falls.

For example, consider what would happen if the Fed lowered rr to 5% from its current level of 10%. The new simple money multiplier would be $1 \div 0.05 = 20$. This action alone would double the simple money multiplier. Lowering the required reserve would mean that banks could loan out a larger portion of their deposits, enabling them to create money by multiplying deposits to a greater extent than before.

If, instead, the Fed raised rr to 20%, the simple money multiplier would fall to just $1 \div 0.20 = 5$. Table 30.2 shows different values of the simple money multiplier given different reserve requirements.

This tool is not as precise or predictable as open market operations are. Because small changes in the money multiplier can lead to large swings in the money supply, changing the reserve requirement can cause the money supply to change too much. In addition, changing reserve requirements can have unpredictable outcomes because the overall effects depend on the actions of banks. It is possible that the Fed could lower the reserve requirement to 5% and banks would not change their reserves. For these reasons, the reserve requirement has not been used for monetary policy since 1992.

The Fed has also used the discount rate to administer monetary policy. Recall that the discount rate is the interest rate charged on loans to banks from the Fed in its role as lender of last resort. In the past, the Fed would (1) increase the discount rate to discourage borrowing by banks and to decrease the money supply or (2) decrease the discount rate to encourage borrowing by banks and to increase the money supply. The Fed used this tool actively until the Great Depression era. Currently, the Fed discourages discount borrowing unless banks are struggling. Changing the discount rate to affect bank borrowing is no longer viewed as a helpful tool for changing the money supply.

TABLE 30.2

Required Reserves and the Simple Money Multiplier

$$m^m = \frac{1}{rr}$$

rr	m^m	
0.05	20	Increase in rr ⟶ Decrease in m^m
0.10	10	
0.125	8	
0.20	5	Decrease in rr ⟶ Increase in m^m
0.25	4	

ECONOMICS IN THE REAL WORLD

Excess Reserves Climb in the Wake of the Great Recession

The simple money multiplier assumes that individuals and banks do not hoard cash: individuals deposit their funds into the banking system, and banks hold no excess reserves. However, these assumptions are not always realistic.

Figure 30.9 shows the excess reserves held by banking institutions in the United States between 1990 and 2013. Until the autumn of 2008, banks held virtually no excess reserves. But then excess reserves climbed to unprecedented levels, reaching over $1,800 billion by 2013.

The cause of this increase was twofold. First, in the wake of the financial turmoil of the Great Recession, banks were probably more risk averse than before. Holding more reserves gave them a buffer against additional failures. But more important, the Federal Reserve began paying interest on reserves beginning in October 2008. This historic change in policy means that banks now have less incentive to loan out each dollar above the required reserve threshold. The Fed put this policy in place to reduce the opportunity cost of excess reserves.

Incentives

The increase in excess reserves means that the money multiplier is much smaller than our earlier analysis implied. When banks hold more dollars on reserve, fewer are loaned out and multiplied throughout the economy. ✳

FIGURE 30.9

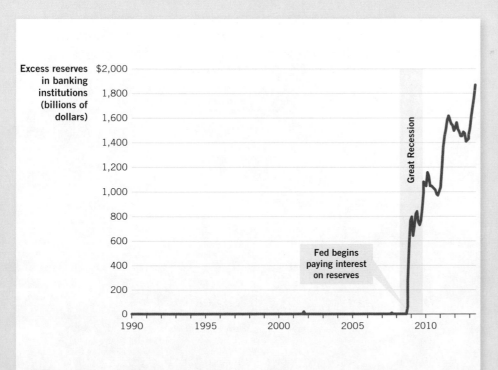

Excess Reserves, 1990–2013

Banks began holding significant excess reserves in 2008. Part of the explanation lies in the risky nature of loans during the Great Recession, but it is no coincidence that the excess reserves climbed immediately after the Fed began paying interest on reserves.

Source: Federal Reserve Bank of St. Louis, FRED database.

Show Me the Money!

In a modern economy, the trade of a good or service between a buyer and a seller is achieved by using money, which is the medium of exchange. Over the centuries, money has evolved from coins made of precious metals, to pieces of paper redeemable in a precious metal, to numbers on a computer screen that are redeemable in nothing and have value only because consumers have confidence in the entity issuing the money. In the United States, the government controls money through its central bank, the Federal Reserve Bank.

Measures of U.S. Money Supply (2015)

There are two main categories of money in the United States, M1 and M2. M1 is cold hard cash—that is, actual currency, plus funds in checking deposits at local banks. M2 includes M1 plus savings, traveler's checks and money-market funds.

M2 ($12,201.6 billion)

M1 ($3,035.8 billion)

M1 Breakdown	AMOUNT
CURRENCY	$1,326.6
CHECKING DEPOSITS	$1,706.6
TRAVELER'S CHECKS	$2.6

in billions of dollars

Credit cards don't count in the money supply.

M2 Breakdown	AMOUNT
M1	$3,035.8
SAVINGS DEPOSITS	$8,118.4
SMALL TIME DEPOSITS	$429.4
MONEY MARKET MUTUAL FUNDS	$618.0

in billions of dollars

A Timeline of Currency

Cattle	Seashells	Coins	Commodity-backed paper money	Wampum	Modern U.S. fiat currency
Widespread	Asia, Africa, North America	Asia Minor	China	North America	United States
9000 BCE	1200 BCE	640 BCE	800	1500 or earlier	1971

The Tools of the Fed

The Federal Reserve uses a small number of powerful tools when conducting monetary policy.

 ## Open Market Operations

This is the Fed's main tool for monetary policy. The Fed buys short-term U.S. Treasury securities to increase the money supply, or sells short-term U.S. Treasury securities to decrease the money supply.

 ## Quantitative Easing

This is a new tool that has been used since 2008. Quantitative easing is a type of open market operation that focuses on targeted securities purchases in both troubled markets (such as mortgage-backed securities) and long-term Treasury securities.

 ## Reserve Requirements

Changing the reserve requirement alters the money multiplier. An increase in the reserve requirement reduces the money multiplier and therefore the money supply; a decrease in the reserve requirement does the opposite. The Fed has not used this tool to actively manage monetary policy since 1992, but it remains a popular tool in other parts of the world.

 ## Discount Rate

This is the interest rate that banks pay on loans from the Fed. This was once the primary tool that the Fed used to control the money supply, before open market operations were employed. Nowadays the Fed does not use the discount rate for monetary policy.

REVIEW QUESTIONS

- What percentage of M1 does currency make up? Of M2?

- Which measure of money, M1 or M2, is the preferred measure of the nation's money supply in the twenty-first century?

Conclusion

We started this chapter with a common misconception about the supply of money in an economy. Many people believe that it is pretty simple to regulate the quantity of money in an economy. But while currency in modern economies is issued exclusively by government, money also includes bank deposits. Banks expand the money supply when they extend loans, and they contract the money supply when they increase their level of reserves. Even individuals have a significant influence: people like you and me cause the money supply to rise and fall when we change how much currency we hold outside the banking system. Taken together, these facts mean that the Fed's job of monitoring the quantity of money is very difficult. The Fed attempts to expand or contract the money supply, but its efforts may be offset by the actions of banks and individuals.

The material in this chapter sets the stage for a theoretical discussion of monetary policy and the way it affects the economy, which we undertake in the next chapter.

ANSWERING THE BIG QUESTIONS

What is money?

* Money is primarily the medium of exchange in an economy; it's what people trade for goods and services. Money also functions as a unit of account and a store of value.

* Money includes more than just physical currency; it also includes bank deposits, because people often make purchases with checks or cards that withdraw from their bank accounts. M1 and M2 are two measures of the money supply. M2 is the more commonly used measure today.

How do banks create money?

* Banks create money whenever they extend a loan. A new loan represents new purchasing power, while the deposit that backs the loan is also considered money.

How does the Federal Reserve control the money supply?

* The primary tool of monetary policy is open market operations, which the Fed conducts through the buying and selling of bonds. Quantitative easing is a special form of open market operations that was introduced in 2008. To increase the money supply, the Fed buys bonds. To decrease the money supply, the Fed sells bonds.

* The Fed has several other tools to control the money supply, including reserve requirements and the discount rate, but these tools have not been used in quite a while.

CONCEPTS YOU SHOULD KNOW

assets (p. 971)
balance sheet (p. 971)
bank run (p. 973)
barter (p. 964)
checkable deposits (p. 968)
commodity money (p. 965)
commodity-backed money
  (p. 965)
currency (p. 964)
discount loans (p. 980)
discount rate (p. 980)

double coincidence of wants
  (p. 965)
excess reserves (p. 973)
federal funds (p. 980)
federal funds rate (p. 980)
fiat money (p. 965)
fractional reserve banking
  (p. 972)
liabilities (p. 971)
M1 (p. 968)
M2 (p. 968)

medium of exchange (p. 964)
moral hazard (p. 974)
open market operations (p. 982)
owner's equity (p. 971)
quantitative easing (p. 984)
required reserve ratio (p. 973)
reserves (p. 971)
simple money multiplier
  (p. 978)
store of value (p. 966)
unit of account (p. 966)

QUESTIONS FOR REVIEW

1. What is the difference between commodity money and fiat money?

2. What are the three functions of money? Which function is the defining characteristic?

3. What are the components of M1 and M2? List them.

4. Suppose you withdraw $100 from your checking account. What impact would this action alone have on the following?

   a. the money supply
   b. your bank's required reserves
   c. your bank's excess reserves

5. Why is the actual money multiplier usually less than the simple money multiplier?

6. Why can't a bank lend out all of its reserves?

7. How does the Fed increase and decrease the money supply through open market operations?

8. How is the discount rate different from the federal funds rate?

9. What is the current required reserve ratio? What would happen to the money supply if the Fed decreased the ratio?

10. Define quantitative easing. How is it different from standard open market operations?

STUDY PROBLEMS (✴ *solved at the end of the section*)

1. Suppose that you take $150 in currency out of your pocket and deposit it in your checking account. Assuming a required reserve ratio of 10%, what is the largest amount by which the money supply can increase as a result of your action?

2. Consider the balance sheet for the Wahoo Bank as presented below.

Wahoo Bank Balance Sheet

Assets		Liabilities and net worth	
Government			
securities	$1,600	Liabilities:	
Required reserves	$400	Checking deposits	$4,000
Excess reserves	$0		
Loans	$3,000	Net worth	$1,000
Total assests	$5,000	Total Liablities	
		and Net worth	$5,000

Using a required reserve ratio of 10% and assuming that the bank keeps no excess reserves, write the changes to the balance sheet for each of the following scenarios:

a. Bennett withdraws $200 from his checking account.

b. Roland deposits $500 into his checking account.

c. The Fed buys $1,000 in government securities from the bank.

d. The Fed sells $1,500 in government securities to the bank.

3. Using a required reserve ratio of 10% and assuming that banks keep no excess reserves, which of the following scenarios produces a larger increase in the money supply? Explain why.

a. Someone takes $1,000 from under his or her mattress and deposits it into a checking account.

b. The Fed purchases $1,000 in government securities from a commercial bank.

4. Using a required reserve ratio of 10% and assuming that banks keep no excess reserves, what is the value of government securities the Fed must purchase if it wants to increase the money supply by $2 million?

5. Using a required reserve ratio of 10% and assuming that banks keep no excess reserves, imagine that $300 is deposited into a checking account. By how much more does the money supply increase if the Fed lowers the required reserve ratio to 7%?

6. Determine if the following changes affect M1 and/or M2:

a. an increase in savings deposits

b. a decrease in credit card balances

c. a decrease in the amount of currency in circulation

d. the conversion of a savings account to a checking account

7. Determine whether each of the following is considered standard open market operations or quantitative easing:

a. The Fed buys $100 billion in student-loan-backed securities.

b. The Fed sells $400 billion in short-term Treasury securities.

c. The Fed buys $500 billion in 30-year (long-term) Treasury securities.

✳ 8. What is the simple money multiplier if the required reserve ratio is 15%? If it is 12.5%?

✳ 9. Suppose the Fed buys $1 million in Treasury securities from a commercial bank. What effect will this action have on the bank's reserves and the money supply? Use a required reserve ratio of 10%, and assume that banks hold no excess reserves and that all currency is deposited into the banking system.

SOLVED PROBLEMS

8. When the required reserve ratio is 15%:

$$m^m = \frac{1}{rr} = \frac{1}{0.15} = 6.67$$

When the required reserve ratio is 12.5%:

$$m^m = \frac{1}{rr} = \frac{1}{0.125} = 8$$

9. The immediate result will be that the commercial bank will have $1 million in excess reserves, because its deposits did not change. The commercial bank will loan out these excess reserves, and the money multiplier process begins. Under the assumptions of this question, the simple money multiplier applies. Therefore, in the end, $10 million in additional deposits will be created.

Central banks can control the business cycle.

From 1982 to 2008—for 26 years—the U.S. economy hummed along with unprecedented success. There were two recessions during this

MIS CONCEPTION

period, but neither was severe or lengthy. Many economists and other observers actually believed that the business cycle had been tamed once and for all. Much of the credit for this "great moderation" was given to Alan Greenspan, the chairman of the Board of Governors of the Federal Reserve Board during much of this period. Analysts thought that his savvy handling of interest rates and money supply had been the key to the sustained economic growth and that enlightened supervision of central banks was the path to future economic growth throughout the world.

Unfortunately, the upturn did not last. The Great Recession, which started in late 2007, plunged the United States into the worst economic downturn since the Great Depression. Moreover, the slow recovery after 2009 seemed to punctuate the limits of monetary policy during significant downturns.

In this chapter, we consider how changes in the money supply and interest rates work their way through the economy. We build on earlier material, drawing heavily on the discussions of monetary policy, the loanable funds market, and the aggregate demand–aggregate supply model. We begin by looking at the short run, when monetary policy is most effective. We then consider why monetary policy can't always turn an economy around. We conclude the chapter by examining the relationship between inflation and unemployment.

The Federal Reserve plays a powerful role in the world economy, but not as powerful as some people think.

BIG QUESTIONS

* What is the effect of monetary policy in the short run?
* Why doesn't monetary policy always work?
* What is the Phillips curve?

What Is the Effect of Monetary Policy in the Short Run?

Across the globe, when economic growth stagnates and unemployment rises, we often look to the central bank to help the economy. Central banks in most countries use monetary policy to reduce interest rates and make it easier for people and businesses to borrow; this action generates new economic activity to get the economy moving again. In the last chapter, we saw that the U.S. Federal Reserve generally uses open market operations to implement monetary policy (increasing or decreasing the money supply). In this chapter, we look closely at how the effects of open market operations ripple throughout the economy.

We begin by considering the immediate, or short-run, effects. Recall the difference between the short run and the long run in macroeconomics. The *long run* is a period of time long enough for all prices to adjust. But in the *short run*, some prices—often the prices of resources such as wages for workers and interest rates for loans—are inflexible.

An Overview of Monetary Policy in the Short Run

To gain some intuition about the macroeconomic results of money supply changes, let's return to an example we talked about in an earlier chapter: your hypothetical college apparel business. Suppose you already have one retail location where you sell apparel, and you are now considering opening a second. Before you can open a new store, you need to invest in several resources: a physical location, additional inventory, and some labor. You expect the new store to earn the revenue needed to pay for these resources eventually. But you need a loan to expand the business now, so you go to the bank. The bank is willing to grant you a loan, but the interest rate is higher than your expected return on the investment. So you regretfully decide not to open a new location.

But then the central bank decides to expand the money supply. It buys Treasury securities from banks, which increases the level of reserves in the banking system. As a result, interest rates fall at your local bank. You then take out a loan, open the second apparel shop, and hire a few employees.

In this example, monetary policy affects your actions, and your actions affect the macroeconomy. First, investment increases because you spend on equipment, inventory, and a physical location. Second, aggregate demand increases because your investment demand is part of overall aggregate demand. Finally, as a result of the increase in aggregate demand, real GDP increases and unemployment falls as your output rises and you hire workers. This is what increasing the money supply can do in the short run: it expands the amount of credit (loanable funds) available and paves the way for economic expansion.

Now let's trace the impact of this kind of monetary policy on the entire macroeconomy. In doing so, we draw heavily on what we have presented in preceding chapters. Here is a short list of concepts from previous chapters that we will use in the discussion that follows. The chapters are identified so that you can review as necessary.

1. The Fed uses open market operations to implement monetary policy. Open market operations involve the purchase or sale of bonds; normally, these are short-term Treasury securities (Chapter 30).
2. Treasury securities are one important part of the loanable funds market, in which lenders buy securities and borrowers sell securities (Chapter 23).
3. The price in the loanable funds market is the interest rate. Lower interest rates increase the quantity of investment demand, just as lower prices increase the quantity demanded in any product market (Chapter 22).
4. Investment is one component of aggregate demand, so changes in investment demand indicate corresponding changes in aggregate demand (Chapter 26).
5. In the short run, increases in aggregate demand increase output and lower the unemployment rate (Chapter 26).

We have studied each of these concepts separately. Now it is time to put them together for a complete picture of how monetary policy works.

Expansionary Monetary Policy

There are two types of monetary policy: expansionary and contractionary. **Expansionary monetary policy** occurs when a central bank acts to increase the money supply in an effort to stimulate the economy, and it typically expands the money supply through open market purchases: it buys bonds.

When the Fed buys bonds from financial institutions, new money moves directly into the loanable funds market as an increase in the supply of loanable funds. As we saw earlier with the college apparel store example, this action increases the funds that banks can use for new loans. Figure 31.1 illustrates the short-run effects of expansionary monetary policy in the loanable funds market and also on aggregate demand. First, notice that with open market operations, the new funds directly enter the loanable funds market, as pictured in panel (a). The supply of funds increases from S_1 to S_2. This new supply reduces the interest rate from 5% to 3%. At the lower interest rate, firms take more loans for investment, and the quantity demanded of loanable funds increases from $200 billion to $210 billion.

Expansionary monetary policy occurs when a central bank acts to increase the money supply in an effort to stimulate the economy.

Because investment is a component of aggregate demand, an increase in the quantity of investment demand also increases aggregate demand, as pictured in panel (b) of Figure 31.1. Remember from Chapter 26 that aggregate demand derives from four sources: C, I, G, and NX. When investment (I) increases, aggregate demand increases from AD_1 to AD_2.

In the short run, increases in aggregate demand lead to increases in real GDP. In panel (b) of Figure 31.1, the economy moves from an initial long-run equilibrium at point A to a short-run equilibrium at point b. Real GDP increases from $18 trillion to $18.5 trillion. The increase in GDP leads to more jobs through the increase in aggregate demand; therefore, it also leads to lower unemployment. Finally, the general price level rises from 100 to 105. This price level increase is only partial; in the short run, output prices are more flexible than input prices, which are sticky and do not adjust.

In summary, in the short run, expansionary monetary policy reduces unemployment (u) and increases real GDP (Y). In addition, the overall price level (P) rises somewhat as flexible prices increase in the short run. These results are summarized in the table at the bottom of Figure 31.1.

FIGURE 31.1

Expansionary Monetary Policy in the Short Run

(a) When the central bank buys bonds, it injects new funds directly into the loanable funds market. This action increases the supply of loanable funds (S_1 shifts to S_2) and decreases the interest rate from 5% to 3%. The lower interest rate leads to an increase in the quantity of investment demand (D) from $200 billion to $210 billion, which increases aggregate demand (AD).

(b) The increase in aggregate demand causes real GDP (Y) to rise from $18 trillion to $18.5 trillion and reduces unemployment (u) in the short run. The general price level also rises to 105 but does not fully adjust in the short run.

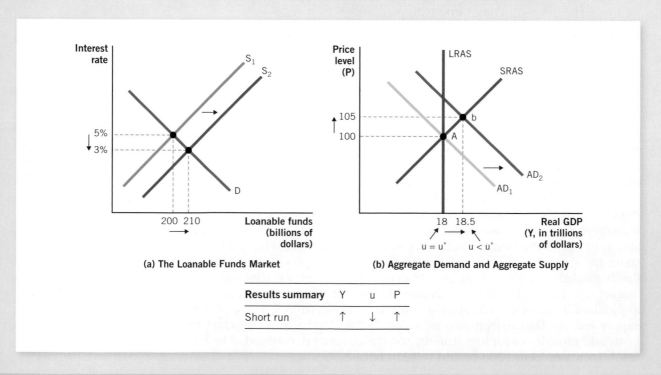

(a) The Loanable Funds Market

(b) Aggregate Demand and Aggregate Supply

Results summary	Y	u	P
Short run	↑	↓	↑

Before moving on, let's step back and consider the results of the expansion. They seem positive, right? After all, unemployment goes down, and real GDP goes up. This macroeconomic result is consistent with the way monetary policy affected your hypothetical college apparel firm. Real employment and real output expand as a result of increasing the quantity of money in the economy. However, later in the chapter, we will see that these benefits do not help everyone in the economy. Others see negative impacts, making these decisions decidedly more complex.

ECONOMICS IN THE REAL WORLD

Monetary Policy Responses to the Great Recession

In the fall of 2007, it was clear that the U.S. economy was slowing. The unemployment rate rose from 4.4% to 5% between May and June 2007, and real GDP grew by just 1.7% in the fourth quarter. The U.S. economy entered a recession in December 2007. We now know that the nation's economy was entering several years of low growth and high unemployment. Many economists believe that a decline in aggregate demand was one cause of the recession. The Federal Reserve's response was an attempt to increase aggregate demand.

We have seen that open market purchases drive down interest rates. This is exactly how the Federal Reserve responded, beginning in 2007. Figure 31.2 shows the *federal funds rate*, which is the interest rate on short-term loans between banks. Traditional open market operations involve buying short-term Treasury securities, which decreases the short-term interest rate, or selling short-term Treasury securities, which increases the short-term interest rate. As you can see, the Fed actively worked to keep the federal funds rate at nearly 0% for several years. This decision reflects a direct application of the monetary policy prescriptions that we have talked about in this section—expansionary monetary policy aimed at lower interest rates so as to increase real GDP and reduce unemployment. ✳

FIGURE 31.2

Monetary Policy during the Great Recession

When the Great Recession began, the Fed responded with expansionary monetary policy that led to lower short-term interest rates. The Fed continued to keep interest rates low even through 2015.

How would you like it if new money entered the economy through backpacks full of currency given to all college students?

Real versus Nominal Effects

We have seen that changes in the quantity of money lead to real changes in the economy. You may be wondering if the process is really that simple. That is, if a central bank can create jobs and real GDP by simply increasing the money supply, why would it ever stop? After all, fiat money is just paper! Well, while there is a short-run incentive to increase the money supply, these effects wear off in the long run as prices adjust and then drive down the value of money.

Think of it this way: Let's say the Fed's preferred method of increasing the money supply is to hand all college students backpacks full of newly printed bills. Not a bad idea, right? But let's focus on the macroeconomic effects. Eventually, the new money will devalue the entire money supply because prices will rise. But because you get the money first, you get it before any prices have adjusted. So these new funds represent an increase in real purchasing power for you. This is why monetary policy can have immediate real short-run effects: initially, no prices have adjusted. But as prices adjust in the long run, the effects of the new money wear off.

Injecting new money into the economy eventually causes inflation, but inflation doesn't happen right away and prices do not rise uniformly. During the time that prices are increasing, the value of money is constantly moving downward. Figure 31.3 illustrates the real purchasing power of money as time

FIGURE 31.3

The Real Value of Money as Prices Adjust

(a) If the central bank increases the money supply at time t_0, the price level begins rising in the short run. In the long run, all prices adjust and the price level reaches its new higher level. (b) As the price level increases, the real value of money declines throughout the short run. In the long run, at t_{LR}, the real value of money reaches a new lower level.

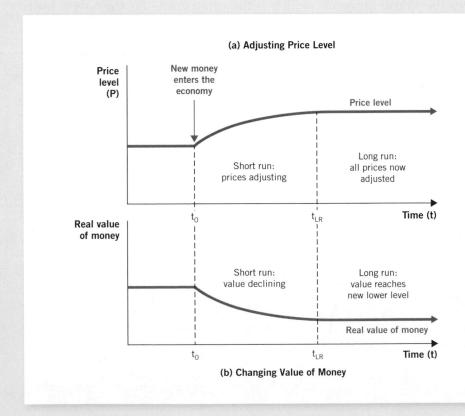

(a) Adjusting Price Level

Price level (P)

New money enters the economy

Price level

Short run: prices adjusting

Long run: all prices now adjusted

t_0 t_{LR} Time (t)

Real value of money

Short run: value declining

Long run: value reaches new lower level

Real value of money

t_0 t_{LR} Time (t)

(b) Changing Value of Money

goes by. Panel (a) shows adjustments to the price level. When new money enters the economy (at time t_0), the price level begins to rise in the short run and then reaches its new level in the long run (at time t_{LR}). Panel (b) shows the value of money relative to these price-level adjustments. When the new money enters the economy, it has its highest value because prices have not yet adjusted. In the short run, as prices rise, the real purchasing power of all money in the economy falls. In the long run, all prices adjust, and then the real value of money reaches its lower level. At this point, the real impacts of the monetary policy dissipate completely.

Unexpected Inflation Hurts Some People

Let's now consider how expansionary monetary policy affects different people across the economy. The basic macroeconomic results, summarized in Figure 31.1, seem very positive: real GDP goes up, the unemployment rate falls, and there is some inflation. Consider that you are living in an economy where these conditions exist. Everywhere you look, the news seems positive, as the media, politicians, and firms focus on the expanding economy. But this action does not help everybody.

For example, consider workers who signed a two-year contract just before the inflation hit the economy. These workers now pay more for goods and services such as groceries, gasoline, education, and health care—yet their wages were set before the inflation occurred. In real terms, these workers have taken a pay cut. Monetary policy derives its potency from sticky prices, but if your price (or wage) is stuck, inflation hurts you.

In general, inflation harms input suppliers that have sticky prices. In addition to workers, lenders (the suppliers of funds used for expansion) are another prominent group that is harmed when inflation is greater than anticipated. Imagine that you are a banker who extends a loan with an interest rate of 3%, but then the inflation rate turns out to be 5%. The Fisher equation, discussed in Chapter 22, implies that the loan's real interest rate is actually −2%. A negative interest rate will definitely harm your bank!

Later in this chapter, we talk about the incentives for these resource suppliers to correctly anticipate inflation. For now, we just note that unexpected inflation, while potentially helpful to the overall economy, is harmful to those whose prices take time to adjust.

Contractionary Monetary Policy

We have seen how the central bank uses expansionary monetary policy to stimulate the economy. However, sometimes policymakers want to slow down the economy. **Contractionary monetary policy** occurs when a central bank takes action that reduces the money supply in the economy. A central bank often undertakes contractionary monetary policy when the economy is expanding rapidly and the bank fears inflation.

To trace the effects of contractionary policy, we again begin in the loanable funds market. The central bank reduces the money supply via open market operations: it sells bonds in the loanable funds market. Selling the bonds takes funds out of the loanable funds market because the banks buy the bonds from the central bank with money they might otherwise loan out.

Contractionary monetary policy occurs when a central bank acts to decrease the money supply.

FIGURE 31.4

Contractionary Monetary Policy in the Short Run

(a) The central bank sells bonds, which pulls funds out of the loanable funds market. This action decreases the supply of loanable funds (S_1 shifts to S_2) and increases the interest rate from 5% to 6%. The higher interest rate leads to a decrease in the quantity of investment demand (D) from $200 billion to $190 billion, and this outcome decreases aggregate demand (AD).

(b) The decrease in aggregate demand (from AD_1 to AD_2) causes real GDP to decline from $18 trillion to $17.5 trillion and induces unemployment in the short run. The general price level also falls to 95 but does not fully adjust in the short run.

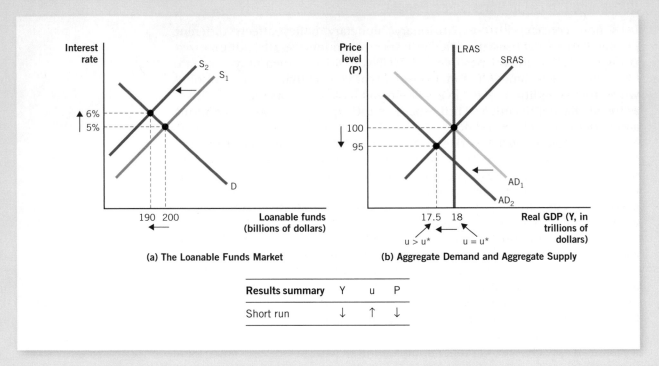

(a) The Loanable Funds Market

(b) Aggregate Demand and Aggregate Supply

Results summary	Y	u	P
Short run	↓	↑	↓

Financial institutions are not forced to buy the bonds, but the central bank enters the market and sells bonds alongside other sellers. The loanable funds market pictured in panel (a) of Figure 31.4 shows this reduction in supply from S_1 to S_2. The interest rate rises, and equilibrium investment falls from $200 billion to $190 billion.

When investment falls, aggregate demand falls. Panel (b) of Figure 31.4 illustrates a fall in aggregate demand from AD_1 to AD_2. In the short run, real GDP decreases from $18 trillion to $17.5 trillion, the unemployment rate increases, and the price level decreases.

These short-run results are again the result of fixed resource prices for the firm. A lower money supply leads to downward pressure on prices (P), but sticky resource prices mean that firms cannot adjust their workers' wages or the terms of their loans in the short run. Therefore, firms reduce output and lay off some workers. This is why we see real GDP (Y) falling and the unemployment rate (u) rising. These results are summarized in the table at the bottom of the figure.

ECONOMICS IN THE REAL WORLD

Monetary Policy's Contribution to the Great Depression

As if monetary policy is not hard enough, consider that the money supply is not completely controlled by a central bank. In Chapter 30, we explained how the actions of private individuals and banks can increase or decrease the money supply via the money multiplier. Banks increase the money supply when they loan out reserves, and they decrease the money supply when they hold more reserves. In addition, individuals like you and me increase the money supply when we deposit funds into bank accounts, and the banks multiply that money by making loans. When we withdraw our funds and hold on to more currency, we decrease the money supply because banks cannot multiply those funds.

What happens when all these people want to withdraw their funds?

Now imagine a scenario with massive bank failures and very little deposit insurance. As more and more banks fail, people withdraw their funds all over the country. While it makes sense that individuals would want to withdraw their money, as people all over the country continue to remove money from banks, the money supply declines significantly. The reduction in the money supply leads to an economic contraction, similar to the scenario we saw in Figure 31.4.

This type of monetary contraction is exactly what happened at the beginning of the Great Depression. From 1929 to 1933, prior to the establishment of federal deposit insurance, over 9,000 banks failed in the United States. Because of these bank failures, people began holding their money outside the banking system. This action contributed to a significant contraction in the money supply. Figure 31.5 shows the money supply prior to and during the Great Depression. After peaking at $676 billion in 1931, the M2 money supply fell to just $564 billion in 1933. This drastic decline was one

FIGURE 31.5

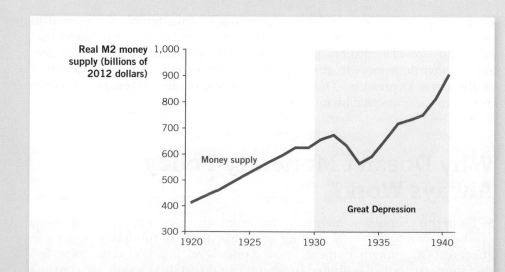

U.S. Money Supply before and during the Great Depression

The M2 money supply grew to $676 billion in 1931, but then plummeted to $564 billion by 1933. The huge decline in the money supply was a major contributor to the Great Depression. (Values for real money supply are expressed in 2012 dollars.)

Source: Historical Statistics of the United States, Colonial Times to 1970.

PRACTICE WHAT YOU KNOW

Expansionary versus Contractionary Monetary Policy: Monetary Policy in the Short Run

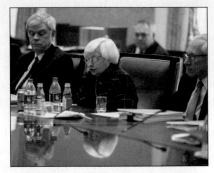

The Federal Open Market Committee is the group that determines monetary policy.

Question: In the short run, how does expansionary monetary policy affect real GDP, unemployment, and the price level in the economy?

Answer: Real GDP increases, the unemployment rate falls, and the price level rises as all flexible prices adjust.

Question: In the short run, how does contractionary monetary policy affect real GDP, unemployment, and the price level in the economy?

Answer: Real GDP decreases, the unemployment rate rises, and the price level falls as all flexible prices adjust.

Question: What real-world circumstance might lead to contractionary monetary policy?

Answer: If members of the Federal Open Market Committee at the Federal Reserve thought that inflation was an imminent danger, they might implement contractionary monetary policy.

of the major causes of the Great Depression. In Chapter 27, we referred to policy errors as one of the causes of the decline in aggregate demand that led to the Great Depression. Economists today agree that the Federal Reserve should have done more to offset the decline in the money supply at the onset of the Great Depression. This was perhaps one of the biggest policy errors in U.S. macroeconomic history. ✳

Why Doesn't Monetary Policy Always Work?

So far in this chapter, we have seen that monetary policy can have real effects on the macroeconomy. By shifting aggregate demand, monetary policy can affect real GDP, unemployment, and the price level. But most economists feel that monetary policy is limited in what it can do. In this section, we consider three of these limitations. First, we look at the diminished effects of monetary policy in the long run. Next, we consider how expectations can dampen the effects of monetary policy. Finally, we examine the limitations of monetary policy when economic downturns are caused by shifts in aggregate supply rather than aggregate demand.

Long-Run Adjustments

We have noted that some prices take longer to adjust than others and that the long run is a period long enough for *all* prices to adjust. Output prices can adjust relatively quickly. Think about the output prices at a coffee shop, which are often displayed in chalk behind the cash register; they are easy to change in the short run. In contrast, input prices, such as workers' wages, are often the slowest prices to adjust. After all, wages are at times set by contracts; moreover, money illusion (see Chapter 21) can make input suppliers reluctant to lower their prices. But the long run is a period sufficient for all prices to change, even wage contracts, which eventually expire.

Both types of prices affect the decisions made at firms across the economy, and therefore both affect output and unemployment. For example, consider your hypothetical small business producing and selling college apparel. Earlier in this chapter, you secured a loan to open a new retail location because the Fed increased the money supply, which expanded the supply of loanable funds. When you initially received your loan, costs for resources such as workers, equipment, inventory, and a physical plant were relatively low because prices for these resources are sticky and had not yet adjusted. But in the long run, these resource prices adjust. If everything works out well for you, the monetary expansion will lead to new demand for your product and you'll be able to keep your new store open. But it is also possible that when the prices of resources rise—in the long run—you may not be doing well enough to afford them. At that point, with your costs rising, you may have to reduce your output, lay off some workers, or perhaps even close your new retail location. In the long run, as prices adjust throughout the macroeconomy, the stimulating effects of expansionary monetary policy wear off.

Let's see how this process works for the entire economy. Figure 31.6 illustrates long-run macroeconomic adjustments to expansionary monetary policy. As you can see in the graph, expansionary monetary policy shifts aggregate demand from AD_1 to AD_2. This action moves the economy from long-run equilibrium at point A to short-run equilibrium at point b (with a temporary change in real GDP and unemployment). In the long run, as resource prices rise, short-run aggregate supply shifts to the left from $SRAS_1$ to $SRAS_2$, and the economy moves to a new long-run equilibrium at point C. When we compare the new long-run equilibrium to the situation prior to the application of monetary policy, we see that there is no change in real GDP (Y) or unemployment (u), but there is an increase in the price level from 100 to 110.

One important implication of these long-run results is the lack of real economic effects from monetary policy; in the long run, all prices adjust. Therefore, in the long run, monetary policy does not affect real GDP or unemployment. The only predictable result of more money in the economy over the long run is inflation. As we discussed in Chapter 21, the cause of inflation is monetary growth. You now can understand why in the context of the aggregate demand–aggregate supply model.

FIGURE 31.6

Expansionary Monetary Policy in the Long Run

Beginning in equilibrium at point A, an increase in the money supply shifts aggregate demand from AD_1 to AD_2; this action moves the economy to a new short-run equilibrium at point b. Equilibrium at point b is relevant only in the short run, because all prices have not yet adjusted. In the long run, resource prices adjust. This outcome shifts short-run aggregate supply from $SRAS_1$ to $SRAS_2$, and the economy moves to a new long-run equilibrium at point C.

Results summary	Y	u	P
Long run	No change*	No change*	↑

*Compared to original long-run equilibrium.

Monetary neutrality is the idea that the money supply does not affect real economic variables.

From one perspective, our long-run results may seem strange: central banks can't do much in the long run to affect the real economy. However, this statement might also seem logical, since it's possible to increase the money supply by just printing more paper money. But printing more paper money doesn't affect the economy's long-run productivity or its ability to produce; these outcomes are determined by resources, technology, and institutions. The idea that the money supply does not affect real economic variables is known as **monetary neutrality**.

Given that money is neutral in the long run, why do the Federal Reserve and other central banks employ short-run monetary policy? In fact, many of the substantive debates in macroeconomics focus on the relative importance of the short run versus the long run. Some economists believe it is best to focus on short-run effects, which are very real. After all, during recessions people often lose their jobs, which can be a very painful experience. When the money supply is expanded, firms can get loans more cheaply and then hire more workers. From this perspective, central banks ought to take a very active role in the macroeconomy by increasing the money supply during economic downturns and contracting the money supply during economic expansions. This policy can then potentially smooth out the business cycle.

Other economists discount the short-run expansionary effects of monetary policy and instead focus on the problems of inflation. In Chapter 21, we explored the negative effects of inflation. These include price confusion, wealth redistribution, and uncertainty about future price levels. These by-products of inflation can stifle economic growth.

In the next section, we consider the potency of monetary policy when market participants expect inflation ahead of time.

Adjustments in Expectations

Unexpected inflation harms workers and other resource suppliers who have fixed prices in the short run; therefore, workers normally expect a certain level of inflation and expect to see it reflected by annual pay adjustments or in contracted cost-of-living adjustments sometimes tied to inflation rates. The key incentive for anticipating the correct rate of inflation is straightforward: people are harmed when inflation is a surprise. But when it is expected, the real effects on the economy are limited.

Incentives

Let's look at inflation expectations in the context of the aggregate demand–aggregate supply model. Figure 31.7 shows how monetary expansion affects aggregate demand and aggregate supply when it is expected. Expansionary monetary policy shifts aggregate demand from AD_1 to AD_2. But if this effect is expected, short-run aggregate supply shifts to the left from $SRAS_1$ to $SRAS_2$.

In Chapter 26, we discussed how short-run aggregate supply shifts back when workers and resource suppliers expect higher future prices, because they do not want their real prices to fall. If short-run aggregate supply shifts along with the shift in aggregate demand, the economy goes immediately to equilibrium at point C. Therefore, monetary policy has no real effect on the economy—real GDP and unemployment do not change. The only lasting change is nominal, because the price level rises from 100 to 110. Monetary policy has real effects only when some prices are sticky. But if inflation is expected, prices are not sticky; they adjust because people plan on the inflation. To the extent that all prices rise, the effect of monetary policy will be limited, even in the short run.

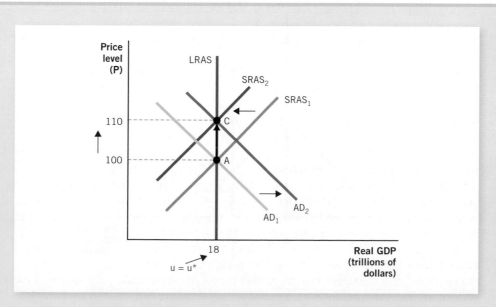

FIGURE 31.7

Completely Expected Monetary Policy

If expansionary monetary policy is expected, short-run aggregate supply shifts along with the shift in aggregate demand, and the economy moves directly from equilibrium at point A to point C. In this case, there are no real effects from the monetary policy, even in the short run. The only lasting change is nominal because the price level rises from 100 to 110.

Aggregate Supply Shifts and the Great Recession

We have seen that monetary policy affects the economy by shifting aggregate demand. Thus, if a recession occurs as a result of deficient aggregate demand, then monetary policy has a chance to stabilize the economy and return it to higher levels of real GDP and lower unemployment. But not all downturns are a result of aggregate demand shifts. Declines in aggregate supply can also lead to recession. And when supply shifts cause the downturn, monetary policy is much less likely to restore the economy to its prerecession conditions.

The Great Recession that began in 2007 seems to have included both shifts of aggregate supply and shifts of aggregate demand. In Chapter 27, we argued that the widespread problems in financial markets at that time negatively affected key institutions in the macroeconomy. Further, the financial regulations that were put in place restricted banks' ability to lend at levels equal to those in effect prior to 2008. The result was a shift backward in long-run aggregate supply. In addition, as people's real wealth and expected future income levels declined, aggregate demand shifted to the left.

Figure 31.8 shows how the decline in both aggregate demand and aggregate supply might affect the economy. Initially, the economy is in equilibrium at point A, with the aggregate supply and aggregate demand curves from 2007. Then aggregate demand and aggregate supply shift to the left, to the 2008 levels. When this happens, real GDP declines from $18 trillion to $16 trillion, and the unemployment rate rises from 5% to 8%—levels similar

FIGURE 31.8

Aggregate Supply–Induced Recession

Initially, in 2007, the economy is in equilibrium at point A. Then the long-run and short-run aggregate supply curves shift to the left, to $LRAS_{2008}$ and $SRAS_{2008}$. In addition, aggregate demand shifts to the left to AD_{2008}. This combination of shifts takes the economy to a new equilibrium at point B. At point B, monetary policy is limited in its ability to move the economy back to its original level of real GDP because monetary policy affects the economy through aggregate demand.

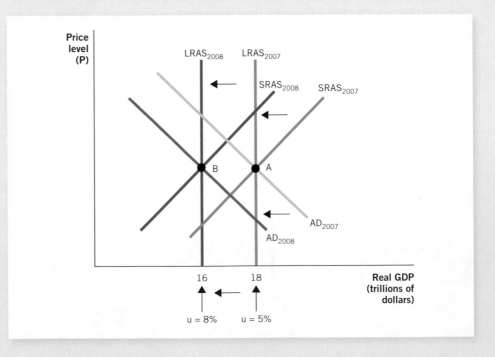

PRACTICE WHAT YOU KNOW

Monetary Policy Isn't Always Effective: Why Couldn't Monetary Policy Pull Us out of the Great Recession?

The Great Recession officially lasted from December 2007 to June 2009. But the effects lingered on for several years thereafter, with slow growth of real GDP and high unemployment rates. These effects all occurred despite several doses of expansionary monetary policy. Not only did the Fed push short-term interest rates to nearly 0%, but it also engaged in several rounds of quantitative easing, purchasing hundreds of billions of dollars' worth of long-term bonds.

Question: What are three possible reasons why monetary policy was not able to restore expansionary growth during and after the Great Recession?

Answer:

1. *Monetary policy is ineffective in the long run.* While we don't know the exact length of the short run, all prices certainly had time to adjust by 2010 or 2011, yet the economy was still sluggish. Thus, one possibility is that all prices adjusted, so the effects of monetary policy wore off. This answer alone is probably inadequate, given that the effects of monetary policy were not evident even in the short run.

2. *Monetary policy was expected.* It seems unlikely that monetary policy is much of a surprise nowadays. The Federal Reserve releases official statements after each monetary policy meeting and generally announces the direction it will follow for several months in advance.

3. *The downturn was at least partially due to an aggregate supply shift.* Because monetary policy works through aggregate demand, the effects of monetary policy can be limited if shifts in aggregate supply cause a recession.

to the actual experience during this period. Further, this rise in the unemployment rate was at least partially due to new structural unemployment that raised the natural rate of unemployment.

The dilemma is that at point B, monetary policy is limited in its ability to permanently move output back to its prior level. Even if monetary policy shifts aggregate demand back to AD_{2007}, this shift is not enough to eliminate the recession. Furthermore, as we have stressed throughout this chapter, the effects of monetary policy wear off in the long run.

Thus, in the wake of the Great Recession, the U.S. economy continued to struggle with slow growth and high unemployment, even after significant monetary policy interventions. The bottom line is that monetary policy does not enable us to avoid or fix every economic downturn.

What Is the Phillips Curve?

We have seen that monetary policy can stimulate the economy in the short run. Increasing the money supply increases aggregate demand, which can lead to higher real GDP, lower unemployment, and a higher price level (inflation). The relationship between inflation and unemployment is of particular interest to economists and noneconomists alike; it is at the heart of the debate regarding the power of monetary policy to affect the economy. In this section, we examine this relationship by looking at the Phillips curve.

The Traditional Short-Run Phillips Curve

The **Phillips curve** indicates a short-run negative relationship between inflation and unemployment rates.

In 1958, British economist A. W. Phillips noted a negative relationship between wage inflation and unemployment rates in the United Kingdom. Soon thereafter, U.S economists Paul Samuelson and Robert Solow extended the analysis to inflation and unemployment rates in the United States. This short-run negative relationship between inflation and unemployment rates became known as the **Phillips curve**. Before looking at Phillips curve data,

FIGURE 31.9

Aggregate Demand, Aggregate Supply, and the Phillips Curve

(a) This graph shows the effect of unexpected monetary expansion in the short run. Initially, the economy is in equilibrium at point A, with a price level of 100, real GDP of $18 trillion, and an unemployment rate of 5%. Aggregate demand shifts from AD_1 to AD_2, which moves the economy to short-run equilibrium at point b. The move to point b is accompanied by an increase in the inflation rate to 5% (the price level rises from 100 to 105) but a lower unemployment rate of just 3%.

(b) Here we see the two equilibrium points in a new graph that plots the negative relationship between inflation and unemployment rates. This graph, known as a Phillips curve, clarifies that higher inflation can lead to lower levels of unemployment in the short run.

(a) Aggregate Demand and Aggregate Supply

(b) Phillips Curve

let's consider the theory behind the Phillips curve in the context of the aggregate demand–aggregate supply model.

Panel (a) of Figure 31.9 shows how unexpected monetary expansion affects the economy in the short run. Initially, with aggregate demand at AD_1 and the price level at 100, the economy is in long-run equilibrium at point A with real GDP (Y) at $18 trillion and the unemployment rate equal to 5%. For this example, we assume that the natural rate of unemployment is exactly 5%.

Then expansionary monetary policy shifts aggregate demand to AD_2, which leads to a new short-run equilibrium at point b. Let's focus on the changes to prices and the unemployment rate. The monetary expansion leads to a 5% inflation rate as the price level rises to 105 (indicated in panel b). The unemployment rate drops to 3% as real GDP (Y) expands from $18 trillion to $18.5 trillion. The end result includes both inflation and lower unemployment.

This is the theory behind the Phillips curve relationship: monetary expansion stimulates the economy, and this outcome reduces the unemployment rate. Similarly, lower inflation is associated with higher unemployment rates. This negative relationship between inflation and unemployment is captured in panel (b) of Figure 31.9, which graphs a Phillips curve. Initially, at point A, the inflation rate is 0% and the unemployment rate is 5%. But when the inflation rate rises to 5%, the unemployment rate drops to 3%.

This negative relationship between inflation and unemployment rates is consistent with Phillips's observations and also with what Samuelson and Solow saw when they plotted historical data. Figure 31.10 plots U.S. inflation

FIGURE 31.10

U.S. Inflation and Unemployment Rates, 1948–1969

Data from 1948 to 1969 was very consistent with standard Phillips curve predictions: lower unemployment rates were consistently correlated with higher inflation rates. (Each number in the graph represents a particular year plotted for inflation and unemployment for that year. For example, 51 represents the year 1951, when the inflation rate was about 7% and the unemployment rate was about 3%.)

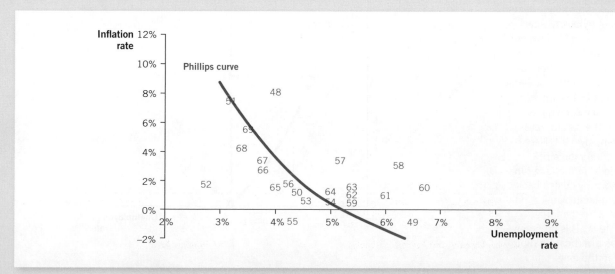

and unemployment rates from 1948 to 1969, which includes the period just before and just after the work of Samuelson and Solow. The numerical values plotted within the graph represent the years: for example, point 48 represents the year 1948. It is not hard to visualize a Phillips curve relationship in the data: most years with high inflation rates had low unemployment rates, while most years with low inflation rates had high unemployment rates.

The Phillips curve implies a powerful role for monetary policy. It implies that a central bank can choose higher or lower unemployment rates simply by adjusting the rate of inflation in an economy. If this is a realistic observation, then a central bank can always steer an economy out of recession, simply by creating inflation.

But we have already seen that monetary policy does not always have real effects on the economy. Next we consider the long run, when the real effects of monetary policy wear off. After that, we look at how expectations also mitigate the effects of monetary policy.

The Long-Run Phillips Curve

When all prices adjust, there are no real effects from monetary policy. That is, there are no effects on real GDP or unemployment. Therefore, the long-run Phillips curve looks different from the standard, short-run Phillips curve. Figure 31.11 shows both short-run and long-run Phillips curves. Initially, at

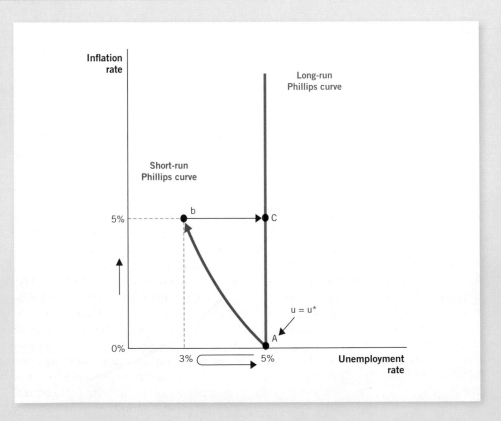

FIGURE 31.11

Short-Run and Long-Run Phillips Curves

In the short run, inflation can lead to lower unemployment, moving the economy from equilibrium at point A to point b. But in the long run, the effects of monetary policy wear off and the unemployment rate returns to equilibrium at point C. Under normal economic conditions, without inflationary surprises, the economy gravitates back to the natural rate of unemployment. Here the natural rate is 5%. Therefore, in the long run, the economy comes back to 5% unemployment, no matter what the inflation rate is. This outcome implies a vertical Phillips curve in the long run.

point A, there is no inflation in the economy and the unemployment rate is 5%. Then monetary expansion increases the inflation rate to 5%, and the unemployment rate falls to 3% in the short run. This short-run equilibrium is indicated as point b. But when prices adjust in the long run, the unemployment rate returns to 5% and the economy moves to a new equilibrium at point C. Inflation is the only result of monetary expansion in the long run.

In Figure 31.11, the unemployment rate is equal to the natural rate (5%) before inflation, and in the long run it returns to the natural rate. Thus, under normal economic conditions, including the situation in which there is no surprise inflation, we expect the unemployment rate to equal the natural rate $(u = u^*)$. Monetary policy can push the unemployment rate down, but only in the short run.

We have also learned that the effects of inflation are dampened or eliminated when inflation is fully expected. We saw this outcome earlier in the context of the aggregate demand–aggregate supply model. Now we look more closely at inflation expectations and how they affect the Phillips curve relationship.

Expectations and the Phillips Curve

We have seen that expected inflation has no real effects on the macroeconomy, even in the short run, because when inflation is expected, all prices adjust. To think about this topic further, we consider alternative theories of how people form expectations. This topic may seem like one for microeconomics or perhaps even psychology, but it is particularly relevant to monetary policy because the effects of expected inflation are completely different from the effects of unexpected inflation. When inflation is expected, long-term contracts can reflect inflation and mitigate its effects. But when inflation is unexpected, wages and other prices don't adjust immediately, and the result is economic expansion.

Adaptive Expectations Theory

In the late 1960s, economists Milton Friedman and Edmund Phelps hypothesized that people would adapt their expectations about inflation to something consistent with their prior experience. For example, if the actual inflation rate is consistently 2% year after year, people won't expect 0% inflation; they'll expect 2% inflation. The contributions of Friedman and Phelps came to be known as adaptive expectations. **Adaptive expectations theory** holds that people's expectations of future inflation are based on their most recent experience. If the inflation rate is 5% in 2017, then adaptive expectations theory implies that people will also expect a 5% inflation rate in 2018.

Consider the hypothetical inflation pattern presented in Table 31.1. The second column shows actual inflation over the course of six years. The inflation rate starts at 0% but then goes up to 2% for two years, then increases to 4% for two years, and then falls to 2% in the last year. If expectations are adaptive, actual inflation in the current period becomes expected inflation for the future. When actual inflation is expected inflation, there is no error, as indicated in the last column. For example, a 2% actual inflation rate in 2014 means that people will expect 2% inflation in the future. So when the actual inflation rate is 2% in 2015, people are not surprised. Adaptive expectations theory predicts that people do not always underestimate inflation.

Adaptive expectations theory holds that people's expectations of future inflation are based on their most recent experience.

TABLE 31.1

Adaptive Expectations

Year	Actual inflation rate	Expected inflation rate	Error
2013	0%	---	0%
2014	2%	0%	-2%
2015	2%	2%	0%
2016	4%	2%	-2%
2017	4%	4%	0%
2018	2%	4%	+2%

Incentives

Stagflation is the combination of high unemployment rates and high inflation.

Rational expectations theory holds that people form expectations on the basis of all available information.

When the inflation rate *accelerates*, however, people do underestimate inflation. For example, if people experience a 2% inflation rate in 2015, they will expect this level for 2016. But in our example, the rate increases to 4% in 2016, which leads to an error of −2%. Note that it is also possible under adaptive expectations theory to overestimate inflation. Overestimation happens when inflation rates fall. For example, in 2018, people might anticipate a 4% inflation rate because they experienced that level in 2017. If the rate is actually 2%, they will have overestimated inflation by 2%.

The idea behind adaptive expectations theory is not overly complex, but it revolutionized the way economists think about monetary policy. If expectations adapt, then monetary policy may not have real effects, even in the short run. Expansionary monetary policy can stimulate the economy and reduce unemployment—but only if it is unexpected.

This was the insight of Friedman and Phelps. Their basic reasoning was that people are not quite as simpleminded as the basic Phillips curve implies. Given that surprise inflation harms people, they have an incentive to anticipate inflation and, at the very least, learn from past experience. And yet, the data from the 1960s, shown in Figure 31.10, were certainly consistent with the traditional Phillips curve interpretation. But Friedman and Phelps challenged the accepted wisdom in 1968 and predicted that the Phillips curve relationship would not last. In particular, they predicted that high inflation would not always deliver low unemployment—a prediction that was proved correct.

Figure 31.12 shows U.S. unemployment and inflation rates for the period 1948 to 1979, with data for the 1970s presented in orange. (As in Figure 31.10, the numerical value represents the year.) Clearly, the 1970s were a difficult decade for the macroeconomy. The prior Phillips curve relationship fell apart—compare Figure 31.12 with Figure 31.10. In the 1970s, inflation was high, and so was unemployment. These macroeconomic conditions have come to be known as **stagflation**, which is the combination of high unemployment rates and high inflation. The stagflation of the 1970s baffled many economists who had come to believe in the validity of the Phillips curve.

Rational Expectations Theory

Expectations theory evolved yet again in the 1970s and 1980s, in part because of disenchantment with certain implications of adaptive expectations. For example, according to adaptive expectations theory, market participants consistently underestimate inflation when it is accelerating and overestimate inflation when it is decelerating. Expectations are seemingly always a step behind reality. And these errors are predictable.

Rational expectations theory holds that people form expectations on the basis of all available information. If people form expectations rationally, they use more than just today's current level of inflation to predict next year's. Rational expectations are different from adaptive expectations in that they are forward-looking, while adaptive expectations consider only past experience.

For example, imagine that inflation is trending upward. Perhaps the actual inflation rate for three periods is 0%, then 2%, and then 4%. Expectations formed rationally recognize the trend and, looking to the future, predict 6%. This outcome is different from what would occur under adaptive expectations, which would instead imply an expectation of 4% in the fourth period, since that number is consistent with the most recent experience.

Rational expectations theory does not imply that people always predict inflation correctly. No one knows exactly what the level of inflation will be next year. Prediction errors are inevitable. But people are unlikely to underpredict consistently, even when inflation is accelerating. Rational expectations theory identifies prediction errors as random, like the flip of a coin—sometimes positive and sometimes negative.

. . . tick, tock, tick, tock, tick, _____ . . . What comes next?

A Modern View of the Phillips Curve

The short-run Phillips curve is built on the assumption that inflation expectations never adjust. But economists today recognize that because inflation harms some people in the economy, there is an incentive to predict inflation in the future. Therefore, not all inflation is surprise inflation. And when inflation is not a surprise, it does not affect the unemployment rate. So we need to reconsider how different expectations affect the Phillips curve relationship.

Consider a hypothetical economy in which policymakers have never used inflation to try to stimulate the economy. Let's say that the inflation rate is

Incentives

FIGURE 31.12

U.S. Inflation and Unemployment Rates, 1948–1979

The 1970s (data points in orange) showed that it is possible to have both high inflation and high unemployment. This decade proved that policymakers could not rely on a permanent, exploitable downward-sloping Phillips curve.

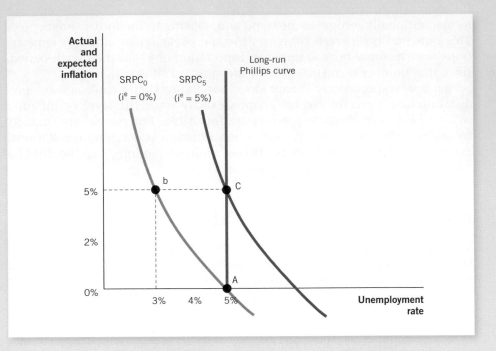

FIGURE 31.13

The Phillips Curve with Adjusting Expectations

Initially, at point A, inflation is 0% and people expect 0% inflation going forward. This expectation means that any positive inflation will reduce the unemployment rate. If the inflation rate is 5%, the unemployment rate falls to 3%, as indicated by movement to equilibrium at point b. But if actual inflation is 5% and expected inflation is also 5%, the unemployment rate moves to the natural rate at point C. There is a different short-run Phillips curve (SRPC) for each level of expectations about inflation.

0% and market participants expect 0% inflation going forward. Figure 31.13 shows this initial situation as point A. Now, if the central bank undertakes policy that raises the inflation rate to 5%, the unemployment rate drops to 3% in the short run. This increase in inflation moves the economy up along the short-run Phillips curve that is labeled $SRPC_0$ (to indicate that expected inflation is 0%: $i^e = 0\%$). The 5% inflation moves the economy to short-run equilibrium at point b on $SRPC_0$.

Now consider what happens if people come to expect a 5% inflation rate. If workers and employers expect 5% inflation, they embed this rate into all long-term contracts. Therefore, when the 5% inflation arrives, it does not stimulate the economy or reduce unemployment. The economy moves to a new equilibrium at point C, which is on $SRPC_5$ (to indicate that expected inflation is now 5%: $i^e = 5\%$). When actual and expected inflation are both 5%, inflation does not reduce the unemployment rate. In summary, there may be a downward-sloping Phillips curve relationship between inflation and unemployment, but this relationship holds only in the short run. In the long run, when expectations adjust, additional inflation cannot reduce the unemployment rate.

Figure 31.14 shows unemployment and inflation data from 1948 through 2015. In looking at this complete data set, we can see clearly that there is no long-run stable relationship between inflation and unemployment. In fact, the data appear to be randomly distributed around the average rate of 5.8%. Economists today believe that there are many factors that influence the unemployment rate in the economy, and the inflation rate is just one factor.

FIGURE 31.14

U.S. Inflation and Unemployment Rates, 1948–2015

Data over the long run present a picture of inflation and unemployment rates that looks random. Clearly, the unemployment rate is not always correlated with the inflation rate in the long run.

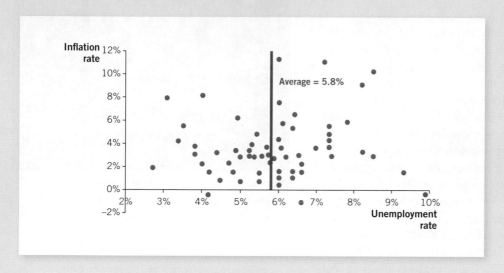

Implications for Monetary Policy

We can now use what we've learned about expectations theory and the Phillips curve to evaluate monetary policy recommendations. **Active monetary policy** involves the strategic use of monetary policy to counteract macroeconomic expansions and contractions. In the 1960s, before the development of expectations theory, monetary policy prescriptions were strictly activist: stimulate inflation during economic downturns, and reduce inflation when the economy is booming. This policy assumed that the Phillips curve relationship between inflation and unemployment would hold up in the long run.

Modern expectations theory prescribes greater caution. If people anticipate the strategies of the central bank, the power of the monetary policy erodes. If expectations adjust, the optimal monetary policy is to maintain transparency and stability. This conclusion holds if expectations are formed either adaptively or rationally. Let's consider each of these scenarios in turn.

Consider a scenario in which policymakers expand the money supply to decrease the unemployment rate. Say the unemployment rate is clearly above the natural rate, and real GDP is not growing. If expectations are adaptive, then inflation will reduce the unemployment rate in the short run. Eventually, expectations will adjust, and then the central bank will have to increase inflation again just to stay ahead of the adjusting expectations. For monetary policy to succeed in keeping the unemployment rate low, inflation has to accelerate and stay a step ahead of expectations. Essentially, the result will be

Active monetary policy
involves the strategic use of monetary policy to counteract macroeconomic expansions and contractions.

Expectations

The Invention of Lying

Imagine a world where no one lies. Ever. In the 2009 movie *The Invention of Lying*, this is the world that Ricky Gervais lives in. Then one day, Gervais accidentally lies. He misstates his bank account balance. After the bank adjusts his balance (upward!), Gervais realizes that no one expects him to lie, so they believe everything he says, no matter how outlandish. No matter how many lies Gervais tells, and no matter how unbelievable his statements, no one ever changes their expectations regarding the truth of his statements—they always believe him. Eventually, he claims to be God. People are stunned. But they completely believe him.

The insanity and irrationality of people's behavior in this movie illustrate exactly how silly it is to continually believe lies that come from the same source. The movie succeeds at being funny because no one in the real world would ever be as gullible or stupid as the people in this movie. In the real world, people would come to expect lies from Gervais. In economics lingo: expectations adjust.

What would you say if people were guaranteed to believe it?

Similarly, in the real world, people come to anticipate inflation when they experience it period after period. It makes no sense to expect 0% inflation if actual inflation has not been 0% for quite some time. In the real world, expectations adjust.

more and more inflation. Worse yet, if the central bank tries to reduce inflation levels, expected inflation will exceed actual inflation, which will lead to an increased unemployment rate in the short run. Thus, if expectations are adaptive, activist monetary policy will lead only to temporary short-run gains in employment. In the long run, it will lead to high inflation or unemployment or both, as it did in the 1970s.

If, instead, expectations are formed rationally, then activist monetary policy may yield no gains whatsoever. Because market participants use all available information when forming inflation expectations, the central bank is unlikely to get any positive results from activist monetary policy, even in the short run.

Many economists feel that monetary policy surprises should be minimized. **Passive monetary policy** occurs when central banks purposefully choose only to stabilize the money supply and price levels through monetary policy. In particular, passive policy does not seek to use inflation to affect real variables, including unemployment and real GDP. In the United States, the Federal Reserve has moved markedly in this direction since the early 1980s. Ben Bernanke, Janet Yellen, and other chairs of the Federal Reserve Board have consistently taken actions that lead to fewer surprises in monetary policy.

Passive monetary policy occurs when central banks purposefully choose only to stabilize money and price levels through monetary policy.

ECONOMICS IN THE REAL WORLD

Federal Reserve Press Conferences

On April 27, 2011, Ben Bernanke held the first press conference by a Fed chairman specifically to talk about the actions of the Fed's policymaking committee. This was an unprecedented leap toward transparency. In the past, the Fed always released carefully worded official statements that often used cryptic language to describe the Fed's outlook for the future.

In the spring of 2011, the economy was struggling to truly emerge from the 2008 recession; unemployment was still over 9%. Yet, in the midst of these economic troubles, the Fed still decided to lay all of its cards on the table. Many observers saw this move as risky. Jacob Goldstein, writing for NPR's *Planet Money* the day before the press conference, explained why it mattered:

> Because everything the head of the Federal Reserve says is a big deal. One off-hand comment can send global markets soaring or plunging. And because Fed chairmen, as a general rule, don't give press conferences. They release official statements that are very, very carefully worded. And they appear before Congress. Since the financial crisis, though, the Fed has come under increased scrutiny. The carefully worded statements and congressional appearances weren't carrying the day. So the leaders of the Fed have decided to send the chairman out for press conferences every few months ("to further enhance the clarity and timeliness of the Federal Reserve's monetary policy communication," in Fedspeak).

Bernanke's moves toward greater Fed openness reflected his belief that central bankers ought to be transparent. The move toward transparency reflects the modern view that expectations matter in macroeconomics— whether they are adaptive or rational. ✳

Chairman Bernanke's willingness to hold a news conference reflected his belief that central bankers should be more transparent.

Monetary Policy

It is very difficult for the government to exert any control over the forces of supply and demand. In fact, it's impossible. However, there is one component of the economy over which the government does exert great control—money. The Fed is the government entity that controls the money supply and sets monetary policy. It has a dual mandate—to control inflation and maximize employment. Traditionally, the Fed has used three tools in monetary policy: open market operations, the reserve requirement ratio, and the discount rate. During and after the Great Recession the Fed resorted three times to a new tool called quantitative easing.

Quantitative Easing

— Real GDP growth   — Unemployment rate   **QE** Quantitative easing   ▉ Periods of recession

QE **Quantitative Easing**

Quantitative easing refers to a type of open market operations. The Fed purchases securities in certain target markets—during the Great Recession, in mortgage-backed securities, long-term Treasury securities, and securities from government-backed enterprises. As you can tell from the still-high unemployment rate, quantitative easing has had only limited success.

- Knowing that in the long run inflation is the only result of expansionary monetary policy, why would the government act to increase inflation?

- How is quantitative easing similar to traditional open market operations?

Inflation and Unemployment: Is There a Phillips Curve?

If inflation is unexpected, it can reduce unemployment in the short run. But when inflation is expected, it does not reduce unemployment. In the long run, it is difficult to discern any relationship between inflation and unemployment rates. This suggests that the benefits of activist monetary policy may be severely constrained.

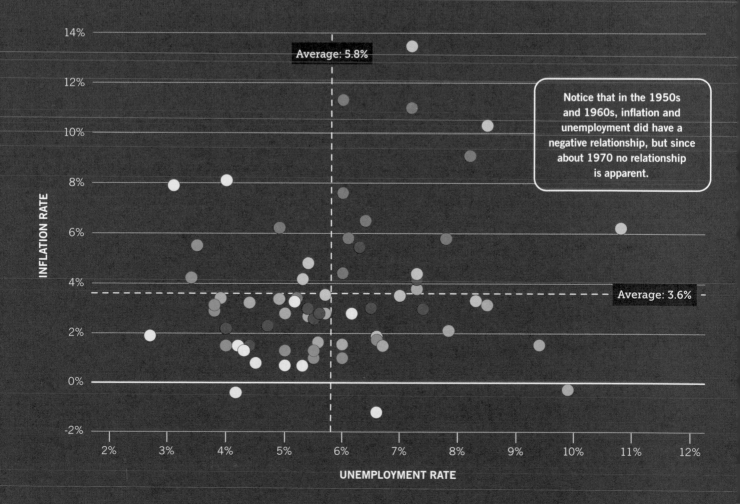

● 1948–1960　　● 1960–1969　　● 1970–1979　　● 1980–1989　　● 1990–1999　　● 2000–2014

Average: 5.8%

Average: 3.6%

Notice that in the 1950s and 1960s, inflation and unemployment did have a negative relationship, but since about 1970 no relationship is apparent.

INFLATION RATE

UNEMPLOYMENT RATE

PRACTICE WHAT YOU KNOW

The European Central Bank (ECB) undertakes monetary policy on behalf of the 19 nations that use the euro as their currency.

Monetary Policy: Expectations

Recently, unemployment rates in Europe have been relatively high and inflation has been low. Consider the European economy, in which all market participants expect a 2% inflation rate and the unemployment rate is 9%. Now assume that the European Central Bank (ECB) begins increasing the money supply enough to lead to a 4% inflation rate for a few years.

Question: If expectations are for 0% inflation, what happens to the unemployment rate in the short run?

Answer: The unemployment rate falls below 9% because the new inflation is a surprise and it can therefore stimulate the economy.

Question: If expectations are formed adaptively, what happens to the unemployment rate in both the short run and the long run?

Answer: The unemployment rate falls below 9% in the short run, because the new inflation is different from past experience. In the long run, expectations adapt to the 4% inflation, and all else being equal, the unemployment rate returns to 9%.

Question: If expectations are formed rationally, what happens to the unemployment rate in the short run?

Answer: If expectations are formed rationally, people understand the incentives of the central bank and therefore may anticipate the expansionary monetary policy. In this case, the unemployment rate does not fall.

Conclusion

We started this chapter with the misconception that central banks can always steer economies away from problems. If this were true, the U.S. economy certainly would not have experienced the sustained downturn that began at the end of 2007. So what can a central bank do? In the short run, if monetary policy is a surprise, a central bank can stimulate the economy and perhaps lessen the effects of a recession. But these results are mitigated when people come to anticipate monetary policy actions.

In the next two chapters, we turn to the international facets of macroeconomics. International trade, exchange rates, and international finance are becoming more important as the world economy becomes ever more integrated.

How to Protect Yourself from Inflation

In this chapter, we talked about how inflation harms some people. We also talked about how inflation doesn't harm people if they know it is coming—if it is expected.

If you are worried about inflation harming you, you can protect yourself from its effects. In recent history, U.S. inflation has been low and steady. In this case, inflation doesn't really harm anyone because it is easy to predict. But if you live in a country such as Argentina, where inflation has often been a problem because it has been high and unpredictable, or if you are worried about future inflation in the United States, these tips are for you.

The two types of people most often harmed by inflation are workers with fixed wages and lenders with fixed interest rates. Let's look at how to avoid inflation trouble in both instances.

Let's say you are a worker who is worried about inflation. One way to protect yourself is to avoid committing to long-term wage deals. If you must sign a contract, keep it short in duration. Better yet, include a clause in your contract that stipulates cost-of-living adjustments (COLAs) that are tied to a price index like the CPI. This way, your wages are hedged against future inflation.

But perhaps you are more worried about inflation's effect on your savings or retirement funds. In this case, you are a lender and thus susceptible to fixed interest rates. One way to avoid negative returns is to purchase securities or assets that tend to rise in value along with inflation. Stock prices generally go up with inflation, so you may want to invest more of your retirement funds in stocks rather than bonds. Gold is another asset that tends to appreciate in inflationary times because its value is tied to something real.

However, stocks can be risky, and the long-term returns on gold are historically very low. Thus, you might consider buying Treasury Inflation Protected Securities (TIPS). These are low-risk U.S. Treasury bonds that are indexed to inflation rates, so if inflation goes up, you get a higher rate of return. These bonds guarantee a particular real rate of return, no matter what the rate of inflation.

Gold is not a great long-term investment unless you really fear inflation.

ANSWERING THE BIG QUESTIONS

What is the effect of monetary policy in the short run?

 * In the short run, monetary policy can both speed up and slow down the economy.
 * Some prices are sticky in the short run. When some prices fail to adjust, changes in the money supply are essentially a change in real financial resources.
 * In the short run, expansionary monetary policy can stimulate the economy, increasing real GDP and reducing the unemployment rate.
 * In the short run, contractionary monetary policy can slow the economy, which may help to reduce inflation.

Why doesn't monetary policy always work?

 * Monetary policy fails to produce real effects under three different circumstances. First, monetary policy has no real effect in the long run because all prices can adjust. Second, if monetary policy is fully anticipated, prices adjust. Finally, if the economy is experiencing shifts in aggregate supply, monetary policy may be unable to restore normal growth, because monetary policy works primarily through aggregate demand.

What is the Phillips curve?

 * The Phillips curve is a theoretical negative relationship between inflation and unemployment rates. The modern consensus is that the Phillips curve is a short-run phenomenon that does not hold in the long run.
 * The power of inflation to reduce unemployment is directly related to how people's inflation expectations adjust throughout the economy. Modern expectations theory allows for adjusting expectations, which is why most economists now believe that the Phillips curve relationship does not hold in the long run.

CONCEPTS YOU SHOULD KNOW

active monetary policy (p. 1017)
adaptive expectations theory
   (p. 1013)
contractionary monetary policy
   (p. 1001)

expansionary monetary policy
   (p. 997)
monetary neutrality (p. 1006)
passive monetary policy
   (p. 1018)

Phillips curve (p. 1010)
rational expectations theory
   (p. 1014)
stagflation (p. 1014)

QUESTIONS FOR REVIEW

1. Why is it possible to change real economic factors in the short run simply by increasing the money supply?

2. Many people focus on the effect of monetary policy on interest rates in the economy.

   a. Use the loanable funds market to explain how unexpected contractionary monetary policy affects interest rates in the short run.

   b. Now explain how these changes affect aggregate demand and aggregate supply in both the short run and the long run. Also explain the changes in real GDP, the unemployment rate, and the price level.

3. During the economic slowdown that began at the end of 2007, the Federal Reserve used monetary policy to reduce interest rates in the economy. Use what you have learned in this chapter to give a possible explanation as to why the monetary policy failed to restore the economy to long-run equilibrium.

4. Explain why a stable 5% inflation rate can be preferable to one that averages 4% but varies between 1% and 7% regularly.

5. Who is harmed when inflation is less than anticipated? In what ways are they harmed? Who is harmed when inflation is greater than anticipated? In what ways are they harmed?

6. Explain the difference between active and passive monetary policy.

STUDY PROBLEMS (*solved at the end of the section)

1. Use the aggregate demand–aggregate supply model to illustrate the downward-sloping relationship between inflation and unemployment rates in the short-run Phillips curve.

2. Suppose the economy is in long-run equilibrium, with real GDP at $19 trillion and the unemployment rate at 5%. Now assume that the central bank unexpectedly *decreases* the money supply by 6%.

   a. Illustrate the short-run effects on the macroeconomy by using the aggregate demand–aggregate supply model. Be sure to indicate the direction of change in real GDP, the price level, and the unemployment rate.

   b. Illustrate the long-run effects on the macroeconomy by using the aggregate demand–aggregate supply model. Again, be sure to indicate the direction of change in real GDP, the price level, and the unemployment rate.

   c. Now assume that this monetary contraction was completely expected. Illustrate both short-run and long-run effects on the macroeconomy by using the aggregate demand–aggregate supply model. Be sure to indicate the direction of change in real GDP, the price level, and the unemployment rate.

3. Suppose the economy is in long-run equilibrium, with real GDP at $19 trillion and the unemployment rate at 5%. Now assume that the central bank *increases* the money supply by 6%.

   a. Illustrate the short-run effects on the macroeconomy by using the aggregate demand–aggregate supply model. Be sure to indicate the direction of change in real GDP, the price level, and the unemployment rate.

b. Illustrate the long-run effects on the macroeconomy by using the aggregate demand–aggregate supply model. Again, be sure to indicate the direction of change in real GDP, the price level, and the unemployment rate.

c. Now assume that this monetary expansion was completely expected. Illustrate both short-run and long-run effects on the macroeconomy by using the aggregate demand–aggregate supply model. Be sure to indicate the direction of change in real GDP, the price level, and the unemployment rate.

✱ 4. In the past, some people believed that the Federal Reserve routinely expanded the money supply during presidential election years to stimulate the economy and help the incumbent president. For this question, assume that the Fed increases inflation by 3% in every election year.

a. Describe the effect on the economy during election years if market participants expect 0% inflation.

b. Describe the effect on the economy during election years if expectations are formed adaptively.

c. Describe the effect on the economy during election years if expectations are formed rationally.

✱ 5. In each of the following scenarios, estimate the unemployment rate in comparison with the natural rate (u*).

a. Inflation is steady at 2% for two years but then increases to 5% for a year.

b. Inflation is steady at 10% for two years but then decreases to 5% for a year.

c. Inflation is steady at 8% for several years.

d. Inflation is steady at 2% for three years, and then the Fed announces that inflation will be 3% one year later.

6. The following table presents actual inflation rates for a hypothetical nation for 10 years.

Column 1	Column 2
Year	Actual inflation rate (i)
Year 1	4%
Year 2	4
Year 3	4
Year 4	6
Year 5	6
Year 6	7
Year 7	6
Year 8	4
Year 9	2
Year 10	1

a. Replicate the table on a separate sheet of paper and leave space for five more columns. Label column 3 "Expected inflation if expectations are adaptive." Fill in this column beginning with year 2.

b. Label column 4 "Unemployment rate if expectations are adaptive." In this column, compare the resulting unemployment rate with the natural rate of unemployment (u*) using the rule that u < u* when expected inflation is less than actual inflation, u > u* when expected inflation is more than actual inflation, and u = u* when expected inflation is equal to actual inflation.

c. Label column 5 "Random error." To fill in this column, you will need to flip a coin once for each year, beginning in year 2 (nine total coin flips). If the result of your first coin flip is heads, enter a "+1" for year 2, and if the result is tails, enter "−1." Repeat this process for years 3 through 10.

d. Label column 6 "Expected inflation if expectations are rational." For this column, sum together columns 2 and 5. The result is consistent with rational expectations in a world where errors in expectations are common but random.

e. Finally, label column 7 "Unemployment rate if expectations are rational." In this column, compare the resulting unemployment rate with the natural rate of unemployment (u*) using the rule that u < u* when expected inflation is less than actual inflation, u > u* when expected inflation is more than actual inflation, and u = u* when expected inflation is equal to actual inflation.

SOLVED PROBLEMS

4.a. If people expect 0% inflation, any positive inflation will stimulate the economy and lower the unemployment rate.

b. If people form their inflation expectations adaptively, they will not anticipate inflation in an election year because it would be a break from their recent experience. Therefore, inflation in election years will consistently lower the rate of unemployment.

c. If expectations are formed rationally, then people will consider the incentives of policy-makers during election years. Therefore, they will anticipate higher inflation in those years, and the inflation rate will have no effect on the unemployment rate.

5.a. The increase in inflation is likely a surprise, which means that it stimulates the economy and reduces the unemployment rate to a level below the natural rate.

b. The decrease in inflation is likely a surprise, which means that it slows the economy and increases the unemployment rate to a level above the natural rate.

c. Here there are no inflationary surprises, so the inflation rate does not influence the unemployment rate. Therefore, all else being equal, we should expect the unemployment rate to be near the natural rate.

d. Even though the inflation rate increases, it is not a surprise, so all prices have time to adjust. Therefore, all else being equal, we should expect the unemployment rate to be near the natural rate.

2/25		11:21	

11618.53	安	11562.10	
1部 1624.57	2部	15.96	
11600		+190	
11630	安	11550	
11600		+195	
979.26		+15.78	
981.80	安	976.21	
1611.68		42	
1612.68	安	1606.60	
1604.68		18	
124.05-15		-0.98	
96.66-72		-0.83	
14000.57		+119.95	
3161.82		+30.33	
22806.34		+28.90	

6728/T アルバック	6764/T ミツミ	カ
909	554	
+9	+9	
6752/T パナソニック	6770/T アルプス	695 ファ
687	608	
+16	+3	
6753/T シャープ	6773/T パイオニア	696 ロ
291	195	
-19	+5	
6754/T アンリツ	6796/T クラリオン	696 ホト
1349	125	
47	+4	
6756/T 日立国際	6841/T 横河電	697 京
801	987	
+10	+15	
6758/T ソニー	6857/T アドバンテ	69 太陽
1329	1296	

International
ECONOMICS

International Trade

A nation should never trade for goods and services that it can produce itself.

It is generally assumed that nations should try to produce their own goods and services. In particular, it seems intuitive that if the United States *can* produce a particular good more efficiently than any other nation can, then the United States *should* produce that good. But economics helps us understand that we may be better off letting another nation produce the good and then trading for it later. Trading enables us to specialize in production for another good that we can produce better. In addition, an increase in international trade is probably beneficial to nations.

Over the past few decades, the level of trade among the world's nations has risen dramatically. To help illustrate the extent of international trade, we begin this chapter with a look at global trade data. We then consider how international trade affects an economy. Finally, we examine trade barriers and the reasons for their existence.

Imports come into the United States from all over the globe. But does importing goods from other countries harm our economy?

BIG QUESTIONS

* Is globalization for real?
* How does international trade help the economy?
* What are the effects of tariffs and quotas?

Is Globalization for Real?

Over the past 75 years, nations all over the world have increased both imports and exports. What this means for you and me is that we now can buy fresh Peruvian strawberries (in February!), roses from Kenya, cars made in Mexico, and electronics produced in South Korea. But the United States also exports more now than in any earlier era. Imports and exports are both up, and this activity indicates that economies around the globe are becoming ever more interdependent. This increased interdependence is what we mean by *globalization*, and it is changing not only what you purchase but also your future job prospects.

Consider a single popular item: the iPhone. Inside the iPhone are parts made in Germany, Japan, Korea, and the United States. The phone is famously "designed by Apple in California," but it is assembled in China. This single item requires thousands of miles of global shipping before anyone ever receives a call on it.

The modern trade explosion has occurred for many reasons. Among these are lower shipping and communication costs, reduced trade barriers, and

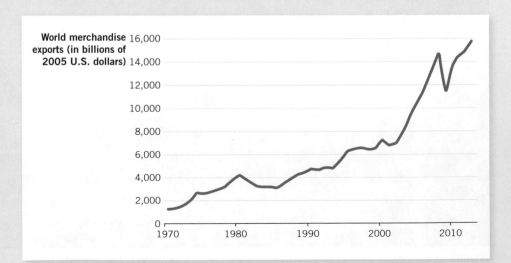

FIGURE 32.1

Real Value of World Merchandise Trade, 1970–2013

Over 40 years, world merchandise trade increased tenfold in real terms, from $1.3 trillion in 1970 to over $15 trillion in 2013. Between 2003 and 2013, world merchandise trade doubled.

Source: World Trade Organization.

How many borders does an iPhone cross before it is sold?

increased specialization in world economies. Total world exports of goods and services are now about one-fourth the size of world GDP. In this section, we look first at the growth in total world trade and then at trends in U.S. trade.

Growth in World Trade

"Globalization" is a buzzword that has gained traction in the past few decades as people have sensed a deeper interdependence between world economies. In this section, we look at the trade data that confirm this general sentiment. We start with a look at total world exports over time. Figure 32.1 shows total world trade in merchandise (goods) from 1970 to 2013. These data, which are adjusted for inflation, indicate that world trade in goods grew from $1.3 trillion to over $15 trillion. That's a tenfold increase in a little over 40 years. Furthermore, since 2003, world goods trade has doubled.

World trade has grown, but not just in market value. It has also grown as a percentage of total world output. That is, not only are nations trading more, but they are also trading a greater portion of their GDP. Figure 32.2 shows merchandise trade as a percentage of world GDP. This, too, has expanded dramatically, more than doubling over 40 years, from about 11% in 1970 to almost 25% in 2013. The data in Figures 32.1 and 32.2 tell us that international trade is now a significant portion of the world economy.

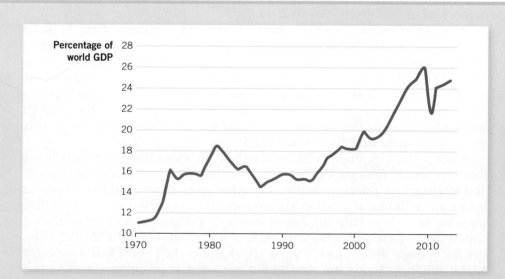

FIGURE 32.2

World Trade as a Percentage of World GDP, 1970–2013

Even as a percentage of world GDP, trade has grown significantly. It more than doubled from 11% in 1970 to almost 25% in 2013.

Sources: World Trade Organization; World Bank.

ECONOMICS IN THE REAL WORLD

Nicaragua Is Focused on Trade

Nicaragua, the second-poorest nation in the Western Hemisphere, is trying to escape poverty through international trade. Between 2003 and 2013, its real exports grew from $1.2 trillion to $4.2 trillion.

The Levi-Strauss company produces many of its blue jeans in Nicaragua.

Trade with Nicaragua is growing in part because the country has established "free zones," where companies can produce goods for export and avoid standard corporate tax rates. Typical Nicaraguan companies pay a myriad of sales taxes, value-added taxes, corporate profit taxes, and dividend taxes. But these do not apply to output that a company exports to other nations. U.S. companies that have taken advantage of production in these free zones include Levi's, Under Armour, and Nike.

All else equal, market-driven international trade certainly helps nations to prosper. Yet while the free zones are increasing exports, the effect on domestic consumers in Nicaragua may not be entirely positive. Because the goods have to be exported for the manufacturers to take advantage of the tax breaks, there is very little incentive to produce goods for domestic purchase and consumption. ✳

Trends in U.S. Trade

The United States is the world's biggest economy. A huge amount of trade takes place between the individual states *inside* the country. For example, residents of Michigan buy oranges from Florida, and Floridians buy cars from Michigan. Still, even with the ability to produce and trade so much within U.S. borders, the nation's participation in international trade has risen dramatically in recent years. Figure 32.3 shows U.S. imports and exports as a percentage of GDP from 1960 to 2014.

As you look at the data in Figure 32.3, note three features. First, in panel (a), you can see that both imports and exports increased significantly over the 50 years from 1965 to 2014. U.S. exports grew from less than 5% to over 13% of GDP. During the same period, imports rose from 4% to over 16% of GDP. Note also that these changes occurred even as real GDP grew by over 3% each year. These numbers provide another clear glimpse at the modern trend toward globalization: the world's largest economy is becoming ever more intertwined with those of other nations.

Since 1975, U.S. imports have exceeded U.S. exports. **Net exports** is the total exports of final goods and services minus total imports of final goods and services. The difference between a nation's total exports and total imports is its **trade balance**. If a nation exports more than it imports, it has a positive trade balance, or a **trade surplus**. However, if a nation imports more than it exports, it has a negative trade balance, or a **trade deficit**. The United States has had a trade deficit since 1975. In 2014 alone, the United States exported $2.34 trillion in goods and services but imported $2.85 trillion, leading to a trade deficit of $500 billion—no small sum.

Net exports is the total exports of final goods and services minus total imports of final goods and services.

A nation's **trade balance** is the difference between its total exports and total imports.

A **trade surplus** occurs when exports exceed imports, indicating a positive trade balance.

A **trade deficit** occurs when imports exceed exports, indicating a negative trade balance.

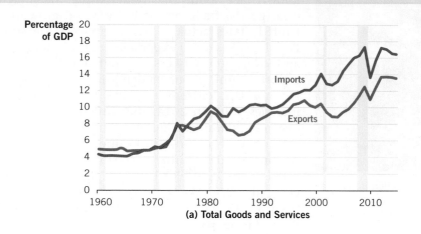

(a) Total Goods and Services

(b) Goods Only

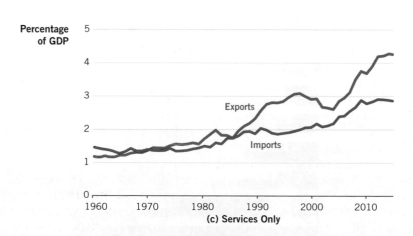

(c) Services Only

FIGURE 32.3

U.S. Exports and Imports, 1960–2014 (as a percentage of GDP)

(a) Both imports and exports are rising in the United States. In addition, the trade balance is becoming more negative over time, as imports are exceeding exports by an increasingly wider margin. This trade deficit grows larger during periods of economic growth and shrinks during recessions (shaded bars).

(b) The trade deficit is driven by a merchandise (goods) deficit, because (c) the United States enjoys a trade surplus in services.

Source: U.S. Bureau of Economic Analysis, *U.S. International Transactions*.

Foreign students who purchase their education in the United States are one type of U.S. service export.

Panels (b) and (c) of Figure 32.3 reveal a little-known fact about U.S. trade: while the merchandise (goods) trade deficit is large and growing, the United States actually has a service trade surplus. Popular U.S. service exports include financial, travel, and education services. To put a face on service exports, think about students in your classes who are not U.S. citizens (perhaps this category even includes you). In 2014, the United States exported over $21 billion worth of education services.

Finally, notice how the business cycle affects international trade. During recessionary periods (indicated by the light blue bars in Figure 32.3a), imports generally drop. As the economy recovers, imports begin to rise again. In addition, while exports often drop during recessions, the trade deficit tends to shrink during downturns. Part of this fluctuation reflects the way imports and exports are calculated. In short, note the strong relationship between trade and economic activity: trade expands during economic expansions and contracts during recessions.

Major Trading Partners of the United States

In 2014, the United States imported goods and services from 238 nations. However, 60% of goods imports came from just 10 nations. Figure 32.4 shows the value of imports from and exports to these top 10 trading partners of the United States.

FIGURE 32.4

Major Goods Trading Partners of the United States, 2014 (in billions of dollars)

Fully 60% of all U.S. goods imports come from the 10 nations shown here. We export more to Canada and Mexico than to other nations, but we import more from China. The U.S. trade deficit with China is almost $350 billion.

Source: U.S. Bureau of Economic Analysis.

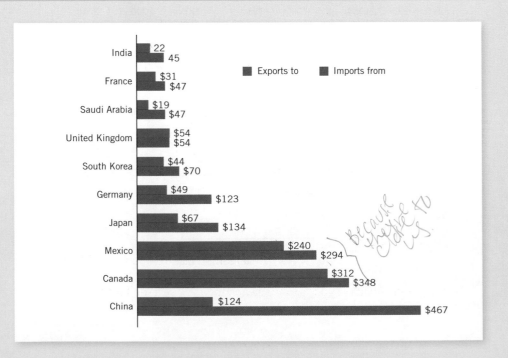

PRACTICE WHAT YOU KNOW

Trade in Goods and Services: Deficit or Surplus?

The United States imports many goods from Japan, including automobiles, electronics, and medical instruments. But we also export many services to Japan, such as financial and travel services. The table below reflects trade between the United States and Japan in 2014. (All figures are in billions of U.S. dollars.)

	Exports to Japan	Imports from Japan
Goods	$20	$103
Services	47	31

Sony PlayStations are a popular U.S. import from Japan.

Question: Using the data shown above, how would you compute the U.S. goods trade balance with Japan? Is the balance a surplus or a deficit?

Answer: The U.S. goods trade balance equals

goods exports − goods imports
$$= \$20 \text{ billion} - \$103 \text{ billion} = -\$83 \text{ billion}$$

This is a trade deficit. Imports exceed exports, and the trade balance is negative.

Question: Now how would you compute the U.S. service trade balance with Japan? Is the balance a surplus or a deficit?

Answer: The U.S. services trade balance equals

service exports − service imports
$$= \$47 \text{ billion} - \$31 \text{ billion} = \$16 \text{ billion}$$

This is a trade surplus. Exports exceed imports, and the trade balance is positive.

Question: Finally, how would you compute the overall U.S. trade balance with Japan, which includes both goods and services? Is this overall trade balance a surplus or a deficit?

Answer: The overall U.S. trade balance equals

Goods and service exports − goods and service imports
$$= \$67 \text{ billion} - \$134 \text{ billion} = -\$67 \text{ billion}$$

This is a trade deficit. Imports exceed exports, and the trade balance is negative.

Data source: Office of the United States Trade Representative.

Is there anything in this picture *not* produced in China?

In the past, our closest neighbors—Canada and Mexico—were our chief trading partners. From Canada we get motor vehicles, oil, natural gas, and many other goods and services. From Mexico we get coffee, computers, household appliances, and gold. Recently, transportation costs have decreased and we are trading more in volume with other countries as well. For example, total imports from China alone are now roughly $467 billion, up from $105 billion (adjusted for inflation) a little more than a decade ago. Popular Chinese imports include electronics, toys, and clothing.

Canada and Mexico buy the most U.S. exports. To Canada we export cars, car parts, computers, and agricultural products. To Mexico we export cars, car parts, computers, and meat, among many other items. Financial and travel services are major U.S. exports to all our major trading partners.

How Does International Trade Help the Economy?

Trade creates value

In this section, we explain how comparative advantage and specialization make it possible to achieve gains from trade between nations. To keep the analysis simple, we assume that two trading partners—the United States and Mexico—produce only two items, clothes and food. This example will enable us to demonstrate that trade creates value in the absence of any restrictions.

Comparative Advantage

Comparative advantage refers to the situation where an individual, business, or country can produce at a lower opportunity cost than a competitor can.

In Chapter 2, we saw that trade creates value and that **comparative advantage** makes the creation of value possible. Gains arise when a nation specializes in production and exchanges its output with a trading partner. In other words, each nation should produce the good it is best at making and trade with other nations for the goods they are best at making. Trade leads to lower costs of production and maximizes the combined output of all nations involved. (Comparative advantage is very important to the discussion that follows. If you don't remember the details of comparative advantage, be sure to review Chapter 2 before proceeding.)

Suppose the United States and Mexico both produce clothing and food. Also assume that the production of one unit of food requires a greater quantity of capital per unit of labor than the production of one unit of clothing (in economics, we say that food is *capital intensive* and clothing is *labor intensive*). Because the United States is generally viewed as abundant in skilled labor but not so much in unskilled labor, while at the same time abundant in capital, it makes sense that it will specialize and produce food. Mexico, which is generally viewed as abundant in unskilled labor, will specialize in clothing.

In Figure 32.5, we see the production possibilities frontier (PPF) for each country when it does *not* specialize and trade. In panel (a), Mexico can produce at any point along its PPF. It can produce 900 million units, or articles, of clothing if it does not make any food, and it can produce 300 million tons

FIGURE 32.5

The Production Possibilities Frontier for Mexico and the United States without Specialization and Trade

(a) Mexico chooses to operate along its production possibilities curve at 450 million articles of clothing and 150 million tons of food. Each ton of food incurs an opportunity cost of three articles of clothing—a food-clothing ratio of 1:3.

(b) The United States chooses to operate along its production possibilities curve at 300 million articles of clothing and 200 million tons of food. Each ton of food incurs an opportunity cost of one-half an article of clothing—a food-clothing ratio of 2:1.

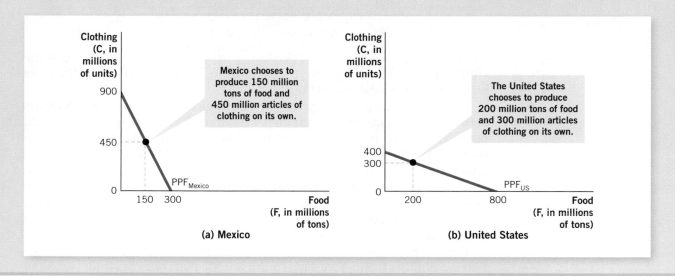

of food if it does not make any clothing. Neither extreme is especially desirable because it would mean that Mexico would have to do without either clothing or food. As a result, Mexico will prefer to operate somewhere in between the two extremes. We show Mexico operating along its production possibilities frontier at 450 million articles of clothing and 150 million tons of food. Panel (b) shows that the United States can produce 400 million articles of clothing if it does not make any food, and it can produce 800 million tons of food if it does not make any clothing. Like Mexico, the United States will prefer to operate somewhere in between—for example, at 300 million articles of clothing and 200 million tons of food.

To see whether gains from trade are able to make both countries better off, we must first examine the opportunity cost that each country faces when making these two goods. In Mexico, producing 150 million tons of food means giving up the production of 450 million articles of clothing (900 − 450 = 450). Thus, each ton of food incurs an opportunity cost of three articles of clothing, yielding a ratio of 150:450, or 1:3, or 1 ton of food per three articles of clothing. In the United States, producing 200 million tons of food means giving up production of 100 million articles of clothing (400 − 300 = 100). The ratio here is therefore 200:100, or 2:1. (Notice that both ratios are in the format food:clothing). In the United States, then, a ton of food incurs an opportunity cost of one-half an article of clothing. Table 32.1 shows the initial production choices and the opportunity costs for both nations. Because the United States

TABLE 32.1

Output and Opportunity Costs for Mexico and the United States

	Chosen output level		Opportunity cost	
	Food (millions of tons)	Clothing (millions of units)	Food (F)	Clothing (C)
Mexico	150	450	3 C	⅓ F
United States	200	300	½ C	2 F

Opportunity cost

has a lower opportunity cost of producing food than Mexico, we say that the United States has a comparative advantage in producing food and therefore will specialize in food production.

As long as the opportunity cost of the production of the two goods differs between the two countries, as it does here, trade has the potential to benefit both. The key to making trade mutually beneficial in this case is to find a trading ratio between 1:3 and 2:1. For instance, if Mexico and the United States establish a 1:1 trading ratio, Mexico would be able to acquire food at a lower cost from the United States than it would cost to produce food domestically. At the same time, the United States would be able to acquire clothing from Mexico at a lower cost than it would cost to produce clothing domestically.

Figure 32.6 shows the effects of a 1:1 trade agreement on the joint production possibilities frontier for each country. If the two countries trade, each can specialize in the good in which it has a comparative advantage. The United States will produce food and Mexico will produce clothing.

Suppose that 400 million units of clothing are traded for 400 million tons of food. Let's begin with Mexico, as shown in panel (a). Mexico specializes in the production of clothing, producing 900 million units. It then exports 400 million units of clothing to the United States and imports 400 million tons of food from the United States in return—this is the 1:1 trade ratio we identified previously. Therefore, Mexico ends up at point M_2 with 500 million units of clothing and 400 million tons of food. Notice that Mexico's production without trade (at point M_1) was 450 million units of clothing and 150 tons of food. Therefore, specialization and trade have made Mexico better off by enabling it to consume 50 million more units of clothing and 250 more million tons of food.

Now let's look at the United States in panel (b). The United States specializes in the production of food, producing 800 million tons. It exports 400 million tons of food to Mexico and imports 400 million units of clothing from Mexico in return. Therefore, the United States ends up at point US_2 with 400 million units of clothing and 400 million tons of food. Notice that U.S. production without trade (at point US_1) was 300 million units of clothing and 200 tons of food. Therefore, specialization and trade have made the United States better off by allowing it to consume 100 million more units of clothing and 200 million more tons of food.

The combined benefits that Mexico and the United States enjoy are even more significant. As we saw in Figure 32.5, when Mexico did not specialize

FIGURE 32.6

The Joint Production Possibilities Frontier for Mexico and the United States with Specialization and Trade

(a) After Mexico specializes in clothing and trades with the United States, it is better off by 50 million units of clothing and 250 million tons of food (compare points M_1 and M_2).

(b) After the United States specializes in food and trades with Mexico, it is better off by 100 million units of clothing and 200 million tons of food (compare points US_1 and US_2).

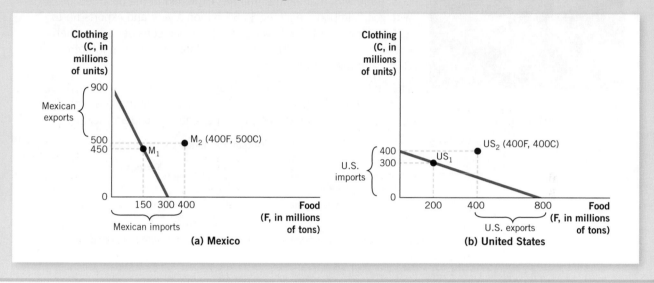

(a) Mexico

(b) United States

and trade, it chose to make 450 million units of clothing and 150 million tons of food. Without specialization and trade, the United States chose to produce 300 million units of clothing and 200 million tons of food. The combined output without specialization was 750 million units of clothing and 350 million tons of food. However, as we see in Figure 32.6, the joint output with specialization is 900 million units of clothing and 800 million tons of food. In economics, we call this a *positive-sum game* because both players, in this case both countries, win by trading with each other.

Other Advantages of Trade

Opportunity cost

Although comparative advantage is the biggest reason that many nations trade with other nations, there are other good reasons for nations to engage in trade. In this section, we consider how international trade encourages both economies of scale and increased competition and how these factors can help an economy to grow.

Economies of Scale

When a nation specializes its production, it can take advantage of the lower production costs that can accompany large-scale production processes. Economies of scale are especially important for smaller nations that do

PRACTICE WHAT YOU KNOW

Does China enjoy a comparative advantage in textile production?

Opportunity Cost and Comparative Advantage: Determining Comparative Advantage

U.S. trade with mainland China has exploded in the past decade, with goods imports reaching $467 billion a year and exports up to $124 billion. For the following questions, we consider a hypothetical production possibilities frontier for food and textiles in both China and the United States.

The table below presents daily production possibilities for a typical worker in both China and the United States, assuming that only two kinds of goods are produced in both countries: food and textiles.

	Output per worker per day (units)	
	Food	Textiles
China	1	2
United States	9	3

Question: What are the opportunity costs of food production for both China and the United States?

Answer: The opportunity cost of food production in China is the amount of textile production that is forgone for a single unit of food output. Because a Chinese worker can produce 2 textile units in a day or 1 unit of food, the opportunity cost of 1 unit of food is 2 textile units.

In the United States, a worker can produce 3 textile units in one day or 9 units of food. Thus, the opportunity cost of 1 unit of food is just ⅓ textile unit.

Question: What are the opportunity costs of textile production for both China and the United States?

Answer: The opportunity cost of textile production in China is the amount of food production that is forgone for a single textile produced. Because a Chinese worker can produce 1 unit of food in a day or 2 textile units, the opportunity cost of 1 textile unit is ½ unit of food.

In the United States, a worker can produce 9 units of food in one day or 3 textile units. Thus, the opportunity cost of 1 textile unit is 3 units of food.

Question: Which nation has a comparative advantage in food production? Which nation has a comparative advantage in textile production?

Answer: The United States has a lower opportunity cost of food production (⅓ versus 2 textile units), so it has a comparative advantage in food production. China has a lower opportunity cost of textile production (½ versus 3 units of food), so it has a comparative advantage in textile production.

not have a population big enough to support the domestic production of large-scale items such as automobiles, television sets, steel, and aluminum. However, once a smaller nation has free access to larger markets, it can effectively specialize in what it does best and generate low per-unit costs through exports.

In Figures 32.5 and 32.6, the production possibilities frontier is shown as a straight line, which makes the computation of the ratios fairly simple and holds the opportunity cost constant. However, in the real world, access to new markets allows countries to take advantage of economies of scale and therefore lower per-unit costs as production expands. Increased production gives companies the opportunity to economize on distribution costs and marketing and to utilize assembly lines and other forms of automation.

Consider how a small textile company based in Mexico fares under this arrangement. With international trade, the company can expand its sales into the United States—a much larger market. This move creates additional demand, which translates into added sales. A larger volume of sales enables the textile firm's production, marketing, and sales to become more efficient. The firm can purchase fabrics in bulk, expand its distribution network, and use volume advertising.

Increased Competition

Another largely unseen benefit from trade is increased competition. In fact, increased competition from foreign suppliers forces domestic firms to become more innovative and to compete in terms of both price and quality. Competition also gives consumers more options to choose from, which enables consumers to purchase a broader array of products that better match their needs. For example, many cars are produced in the United States, but foreign automobiles offer U.S. consumers greater variety and help to keep the prices of domestically made cars lower than they would be otherwise.

Trade Agreements

Although international trade can be beneficial, countries often restrict trade, particularly imports. To create opportunities for freer trade, nations often reach trade agreements that specify the conditions of free trade. For example, the North American Free Trade Agreement (NAFTA), which was signed in 1992, eliminated nearly all trade restrictions between Canada, Mexico, and the United States. Currently, the United States has trade agreements with 20 nations.

Even though trade agreements often stipulate protections for particular industries (most notably, agriculture), they still increase trade between nations. For example, as a result of NAFTA, real U.S. imports and exports of goods with Canada and Mexico have doubled. In 1993. the United States exported $183 billion worth of goods to Canada, but by 2014, this amount had risen to $312 billion. Over the same period, exports to Mexico grew from $80 billion to $240 billion. Imports from both nations also expanded: imports from Canada grew from $180 billion to $348 billion, and imports from Mexico grew from $76 billion to $294 billion. The reduction in trade barriers has enabled all three nations to move toward the production of goods and services in which they enjoy a comparative advantage.

NAFTA created a broad, geographically connected network of lower trade barriers, fostering growth across much of North America.

The World Trade Organization (WTO) is an international organization that facilitates trade agreements between nations. Created in 1995 by the 123 countries that were then signatories of the General Agreement on Tariffs and Trade, the WTO regulates the trade of various goods and services, including textiles, investment, intellectual property, even agriculture. Moreover, the WTO works to resolve trade disputes. For example, in 2012 the WTO helped to end a 20-year disagreement between Latin American banana exporters and the European Union over a tax on imported bananas.

What Are the Effects of Tariffs and Quotas?

Despite the benefits of free trade, significant trade barriers, such as import taxes, often exist. For example, almost every shoe purchased in the United States is made overseas; but with few exceptions, the U.S. government taxes each pair of shoes that comes across its borders to be sold. For example, a new pair of Nike tennis shoes imported from Vietnam is subject to a 20% import tax. If these shoes are valued at $100, the foreign producer has to pay a $20 tax on them.

Import taxes like those on footwear are not unusual. In this section, we explore two of the most common types of trade barriers: *tariffs* and *quotas*. We then look more closely at common economic and political justifications for **protectionism**, which is a blanket term for government actions and policies that restrict or restrain international trade, often with the intent of protecting local businesses and jobs from foreign competition. We close by examining whether or not protectionism is effective.

Protectionism is a blanket term for government actions and policies that restrict or restrain international trade, often with the intent of protecting local businesses and jobs from foreign competition.

Tariffs are taxes levied on imported goods and services.

Tariffs

Tariffs are taxes levied on imported goods and services. A tariff is paid by the producer of the good when the good arrives in a foreign country. A tariff can be a percentage of the value of the good (called an *ad valorem tax*), a per-unit tax (called a *specific tax*), or a mix of the two. Figure 32.7 illustrates the impact of a per-unit tariff on foreign shoes. To assess how a tariff affects the market price of shoes in the United States, we observe the relationship between domestic demand and domestic supply.

We begin by noting that domestic supply ($S_{domestic\ only}$) and domestic demand ($D_{domestic}$) would be in equilibrium at $140 per pair of shoes. However, this is not the market price if free trade prevails. If trade is unrestricted, imports are free to enter the domestic market, so that supply increases to $S_{free\ trade}$. Now, because trade is unrestricted, domestic producers who might wish to charge a price that is higher than that charged by foreign producers would find that they could not sell their shoes at that price. As a result, the domestic price (P_D) decreases to the world price (P_W), which is $100. At $100, the total quantity demanded is Q_W. Part of this quantity is produced domestically (Q_{D1}), and part is imported from foreign sources ($Q_W - Q_{D1}$).

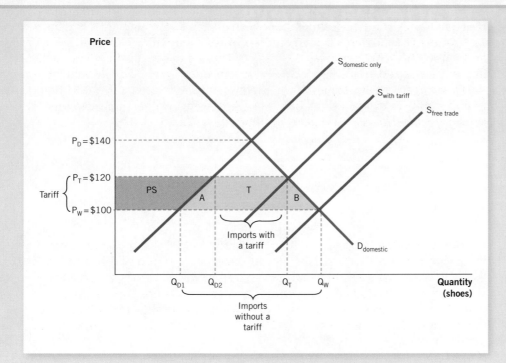

FIGURE 32.7

The Impact of a Tariff
Without a tariff, the domestic market is dominated by imports. However, when a tariff is imposed, the price rises and domestic production expands from Q_{D1} to Q_{D2}. At the same time, imports fall to $Q_T - Q_{D2}$. Tariffs also create deadweight loss (shaded areas A and B), revenue for the government (area T), and increased producer surplus for domestic firms (area PS).

Now let's see what happens when a tariff of $20 per pair of shoes is levied. When the country imposes the tariff per pair of shoes, the cost that foreign producers must bear when they export shoes rises by $20 per pair, the amount of the tariff. Supply decreases to $S_{\text{with tariff}}$. The tariff pushes the domestic price up from $100 to $120 (represented as P_T, reflecting the price with tariff). Foreign producers must pay the tariff, but domestic producers do not have to pay it. One consequence of this situation is that the amount imported drops to $Q_T - Q_{D2}$. At the same time, the amount supplied by domestic producers rises along the domestic-only supply curve from Q_{D1} to Q_{D2}. Because domestic suppliers are now able to charge $120 and also sell more, they are better off.

We can see this outcome visually by noting that domestic suppliers gain producer surplus equal to the shaded area marked PS. The government also benefits from the tariff revenue, shown as shaded area T. The tariff is a pure transfer from foreign suppliers to the government. In this case, the tariff is $20 per pair of shoes, so total tax revenue is $20 times the number of imported pairs of shoes. In addition, there are two areas of deadweight loss, A and B. Consumers are harmed because the price is higher and some people are forced to switch from foreign brands to domestic shoes. In addition, inefficient domestic producers now get to enter the market. Areas A and B represent the efficiency loss associated with the tariff—or the unrealized gains from trade. The economy as a whole loses from the tariff because the loss in consumer surplus is greater than the gains obtained by producers and the government.

Consider for a moment just how damaging a tariff is. Foreign producers are the lowest-cost producer of shoes, but they are limited in how much they

Major U.S. Trade Partners

Though the United States imports goods from over 230 nations in the world, just 7 of those countries account for over 60% of these imports. These same 7 countries also buy more U.S. goods exports than any other country. Clearly, our major trade partners produce numerous items that Americans demand, and the United States produces numerous items that these countries desire.

— **U.S. goods exports to trade partner (2014)** — **U.S. goods imports from trade partner (2014)**

Japan

Top Imports from
- Passenger cars
- Auto parts
- Industrial machines

Top Exports to
- Civilian aircraft
- Pharmaceuticals
- Medical equipment

$67B

$134B

South Korea

Top Imports from
- Passenger cars
- Auto parts
- Household goods

Top Exports to
- Semiconductors
- Industrial machines
- Civilian aircraft

$44B

$70B

China

Top Imports from
- Computers
- Household goods
- Apparel

Top Exports to
- Soybeans
- Civilian aircraft
- Passenger cars

$124B

$467B

The United States

Source: U.S. Bureau of Economic Analysis

- What U.S. industry generates the most universal demand from our trading partners?

- Based on the list of U.S. imports, how would you finish this sentence? "Americans sure love their _____!"

$312B

$348B

Canada

Top Imports from	Top Exports to
• Crude oil	• Auto parts
• Passenger cars	• Trucks/buses
• Petroleum products	• Passenger cars

$54B

$54B

United Kingdom

Top Imports from	Top Exports to
• Pharmaceuticals	• Nonmonetary gold
• Petroleum products	• Civilian aircraft
• Passenger cars	• Pharmaceuticals

$49B

$123B

Germany

Top Imports from	Top Exports to
• Passenger cars	• Passenger cars
• Pharmaceuticals	• Civilian aircraft
• Auto parts	• Pharmaceuticals

$240B

$294B

Mexico

Top Imports from	Top Exports to
• Crude oil	• Petroleum products
• Passenger cars	• Auto parts
• Auto parts	• Computer accessories

of America

can sell. This situation makes little sense from an import/export standpoint. If foreign shoe manufacturers cannot sell as many shoes in the United States, they will acquire fewer dollars to use in purchasing U.S. exports. So not only does the tariff mean higher shoe prices for U.S. consumers, but it also means fewer sales for U.S. exporters.

Quotas

Import quotas are limits on the quantity of products that can be imported into a country.

Sometimes, instead of taxing imports, governments use *import quotas* to restrict trade. **Import quotas** are limits on the quantity of products that can be imported into a country. Quotas function like tariffs with one crucial exception: the government does not receive any tax revenue. In the United States today, there are quotas on many products, including milk, tuna, olives, peanuts, cotton, and sugar.

One famous example of quotas comes from the automobile industry in the 1980s and 1990s. During that period, Japan agreed to a "voluntary" quota on the number of vehicles it would export to the United States. Why would any group of firms agree to supply less than it could? The answer involves politics and economics. By voluntarily limiting the quantity they supply, foreign producers avoid having a tariff applied to their goods. Also, because the quantity supplied is somewhat smaller than it would otherwise be, foreign suppliers can charge higher prices. The net result is that a "voluntary" quota makes financial sense if it helps a producing nation to avoid a tariff.

Figure 32.8 shows how a quota placed on foreign-made shoes would work. The figure looks quite similar to Figure 32.7, which is not an accident. If we set the quota amount on foreign shoes equal to the imports after the tariff illustrated in Figure 32.7, the result is exactly the same with one notable exception: the green tariff rectangle, T, in Figure 32.7 has been replaced with a green rectangle, F, which is called the tariff-equivalent quota.

The quota is a strict limit on the number of shoes that may be imported into the United States. This limit pushes up the domestic price of shoes from $100 to $120 (represented as P_Q, reflecting the price under a quota). Because foreign producers must abide by the quota, one consequence is that the amount imported drops to $Q_Q - Q_{D2}$ (where Q_Q represents the total quantity supplied after the imposition of the quota). The smaller amount of imports causes the quantity supplied by domestic producers to rise along the domestic-only supply curve from Q_{D1} to Q_{D2}. Because domestic suppliers are now able to charge $20 more and also sell more, they are better off. We can see this result visually by noting that domestic suppliers gain producer surplus equal to shaded area PS (as we observed in Figure 32.7). As a result, domestic suppliers are indifferent between a tariff and a quota that has the same results. So, like before, there are two areas of deadweight loss, A and B, in which consumers lose because the price is higher and some people are forced to switch from foreign brands to domestic ones.

As you can see by the deadweight loss in shaded areas A and B, a quota results in the same efficiency loss as a tariff. Even though domestic suppliers are indifferent between a tariff and a quota system, foreign producers are not. Under a quota, they are able to keep the revenue generated in the blue rectangle, F. Under a tariff, the equivalent rectangle, T, shown in Figure 32.7, is the tax revenue generated by the tariff.

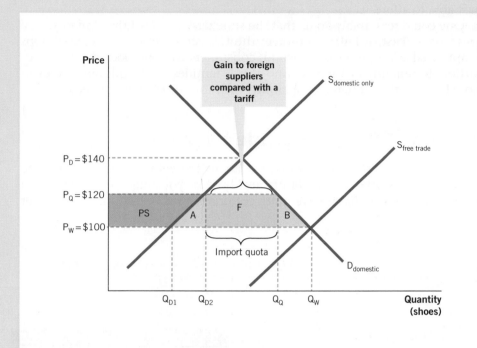

FIGURE 32.8

The Impact of a Quota
Without a quota, the domestic market is dominated by imports. However, when a quota is imposed, the price rises and domestic production expands from Q_{D1} to Q_{D2}. At the same time, imports fall to $Q_Q - Q_{D2}$. Quotas create deadweight loss (shaded areas A and B), a gain for foreign suppliers (area F), and increased producer surplus for domestic firms (area PS).

ECONOMICS IN THE REAL WORLD

Inexpensive Shoes Face the Highest Tariffs

Overall, U.S. tariffs average less than 2%, but inexpensive shoes face tariffs that are often 10 times or more than that amount. What makes inexpensive imported shoes so "dangerous"? To help answer this question, a history lesson is in order.

Just 40 years ago, shoe manufacturers in the United States employed 250,000 workers. Today, the number of shoe workers is less than 3,000—and none of those workers assemble cheap shoes. Most of the shoe jobs have moved to low-labor-cost countries. But the shoe tariff, which was enacted to save domestic jobs, remains the same. Not a single sneaker costing less than $3 a pair is made in the United States, so the protection isn't saving any jobs. In contrast, goods such as cashmere sweaters, snakeskin purses, and silk shirts face low or no import tariffs. Other examples range from the 2.5% tariff on cars, tariffs of 4% and 5% for TV sets, and duty (tax)-free treatment for cell phones.

Shoppers who buy their shoes at Walmart and Payless shoe stores face the impact of shoe tariffs that approach 50% for the cheapest shoes, about 20% for a pair of name-brand running shoes, and about 9% for designer shoes from Gucci or Prada. This situation has the

Why do cheap imported shoes face such a high tariff?

unintended consequence of passing along the tax burden to those who are least able to afford it.

One could reasonably argue that the shoe tariff is one of the United States' worst taxes. First, it failed to protect the U.S. shoe industry—the shoe jobs disappeared a long time ago. Second, consumers who are poor pay a disproportionate amount of the tax. And third, families with children pay even more because the more feet in a family, the more shoes that are needed. ✳

Reasons Given for Trade Barriers

Considering all that we have discussed about the gains from trade and the inefficiencies associated with tariffs and quotas, you might be surprised to learn that trade restrictions are quite common. In this section, we consider

ECONOMICS IN THE MEDIA

Free Trade

Star Wars Episode I: The Phantom Menace

The Phantom Menace (1999) is an allegory about peace, prosperity, taxation, and protectionism. As the movie opens, we see the Republic slowly falling apart. Planetary trade has been at the heart of the galactic economy. The central conflict in the movie is the Trade Federation's attempt to enforce its franchise by trying to intimidate a small planet, Naboo, which believes in free trade and peace.

The leader of the Naboo, Queen Amidala, refuses to pursue any path that might start a war. Her country is subjected to an excessive tariff and blockade, so she decides to appeal to the central government for help in ending the trade restrictions. However, she discovers that the Republic's Galactic Senate is ineffectual, so she returns home and prepares to defend her country.

Meanwhile, two Jedi who work for the Republic are sent to broker a deal between Naboo and the Trade Federation, but they get stranded on Tatooine, a desert planet located in the Outer Rim. In the Outer Rim, three necessary ingredients for widespread trade—the rule of law, sound money, and honesty—are missing. As a consequence, when the Jedi try to purchase some new parts for their ship,

Disruptive, barriers to trade are!

they find out that no one accepts the credit-based money of the Republic. The Jedi are forced to barter, a process that requires that each trader have exactly what the other wants. This situation results in a complicated negotiation between one of the Jedi and a local parts dealer. The scenes on Tatooine show why institutions, economies of scale, and competition matter so much for trade to succeed.

We encourage you to watch *The Phantom Menace* again with a fresh pair of eyes trained on the economics behind the special effects!

some of the reasons for the persistence of trade barriers. These include national security, protection of infant industries, retaliation for *dumping*, and favors to special interests.

National Security

Many people believe that certain industries, such as weapons, energy, and transportation, are vital to our nation's defense. They argue that without the ability to produce its own missiles, firearms, aircraft, and other strategically significant assets, a nation could find itself relying on its enemies. Thus, people often argue that certain industries should be protected in the interest of national security.

Although it is certainly important for any trade arrangement to consider national security, this argument has been used to justify trade restrictions on goods and services from friendly nations with whom we have active, open trade relations. For example, in 2002, the United States imposed tariffs on steel imports. Some policymakers argued that the steel tariffs were necessary because steel is an essential resource for national security. But, in fact, most imported steel comes from Canada and Brazil, which are traditional allies of the United States.

Infant Industries

Another argument in support of steel tariffs in the United States was that the U.S. steel industry needed some time to implement new technologies that would enable it to compete with steel producers in other nations. This **infant industry argument** states that domestic industries need trade protection until they are established and able to compete internationally. According to this point of view, once the fledgling industry gains traction and can support itself, the trade restrictions can be removed.

However, reality doesn't work this way. Firms that lobby for protection are often operating in an established industry. For example, the steel industry in the United States is over 100 years old. Establishing trade barriers is often politically popular, but finding ways to remove them is politically difficult. There was a time when helping to establish the steel, sugar, cotton, or peanut industries might have made sense based on the argument for helping new industries. But the tariffs that protect those industries have remained, in one form or another, for over 100 years.

> The **infant industry argument** states that domestic industries need trade protection until they are established and able to compete internationally.

Retaliation for Dumping

In 2009, the U.S. government imposed tariffs on radial car tires imported from China. These tariffs began at 35% and then gradually decreased to 25% before being phased out after three years. The argument in support of this tariff was that Chinese tire makers were *dumping* their tires in U.S. markets. **Dumping** occurs when a foreign supplier sells a good below the price it charges in its home country. As the name implies, dumping is often a deliberate effort to gain a foothold in a foreign market. It can also be the result of subsidies within foreign countries.

In cases of dumping, the WTO allows for special *countervailing duties* to offset the subsidies. Thus, the United States placed a tariff on the imported tires

> **Dumping** occurs when a foreign supplier sells a good below the price it charges in its home country.

PRACTICE WHAT YOU KNOW

Tariffs and Quotas: The Winners and Losers from Trade Barriers

In 2009, the United States imposed a tariff of 35% on radial car tire imports from China. The result of this tariff was a drop in imports of these tires from 13 million tires to just 5.6 million tires in one quarter. In addition, within a year, average radial car tire prices rose by about $8 per tire in the United States: the average price of Chinese tires rose from $30.79 to $37.98, while the average price of tires from all other nations rose from $53.94 to $62.05.

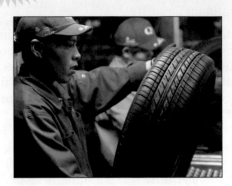

Why would we penalize Chinese tire imports?

Question: Who were the winners and losers from this tire tariff?

Answer: The primary winners were the producers of tires from everywhere except China. Because this tariff was targeted at a single nation, it did not affect tire producers in other nations. Non-Chinese tire producers realized an average of $8 more per tire. In addition, given that the tire tariff is a tax, it also produced some tax revenue.

The primary losers were U.S. tire consumers, who saw prices rise by about $8 per tire, or $32 for a set of four tires.

Data Source: Gary Clyde Hufbauer and Sean Lowry, "U.S. Tire Tariffs: Saving Few Jobs at High Cost," Policy Brief (Washington, D.C.: Peterson Institute for International Economics, April 9, 2012).

---

to restore a level playing field. In essence, anytime a foreign entity decides to charge a lower price to penetrate a market, the country that is dumped on is likely to respond by imposing a tariff or quota to protect its domestic industries from foreign takeover.

Favors to Special Interests

The imposition of trade barriers is often referred to as "protection." This term raises the questions *Who is being protected?* and *What are they being protected from?* We have seen that trade barriers drive up domestic prices and lead to a lower quantity of goods or services in the market where the barriers are imposed. This situation does not protect consumers. In fact, tariffs and quotas protect domestic producers from international competition. Steel tariffs were put in place to help domestic steel producers, and tire tariffs were put in place to help domestic tire producers.

When we see trade barriers, the publicly stated reason is generally one of the three reasons we have already discussed: national security, infant industry protection, or retaliation for dumping. But we must also recognize that these barriers may be put in place as a favor to special interest groups that have much to gain at the expense of domestic consumers. For example, as a result of sugar import regulations, U.S. consumers pay twice as much for sugar as the rest of the world does. Thus, while sugar tariffs and quotas protect U.S. sugar producers from international competition, they cost U.S. consumers more than $3 billion in 2014 alone. This outcome represents a special interest gain at the expense of U.S. consumers. If it were a tax that was transferred from consumers to producers, it would likely not persist. However, this kind of favor doesn't appear in the federal budget.

Conclusion

We began this chapter with the misconception that nations should not trade for goods and services that they can produce for themselves. The concept of comparative advantage contradicts this misconception by showing that nations can gain by (1) specializing in the production of goods and services for which they have the lowest opportunity cost and then (2) trading for the other goods and services that they wish to consume.

International trade is expanding all over the world. The United States now imports and exports more than at any time in its history. Increased trade is generally positive for all nations involved. However, trade barriers still exist around the globe for various reasons, including national security, the protection of infant industries, retaliation for dumping and subsidies, and favors to special interests.

ANSWERING THE BIG QUESTIONS

Is globalization for real?

* Since 1970, world exports have grown from 11% to about 25% of world GDP. In the United States, imports and exports have both grown rapidly over the past five decades. Between 1965 and 2014, U.S. exports grew from less than 5% of GDP to 13% of GDP. Over the same period, U.S. imports grew from 4% of GDP to over 16% of GDP. There's no doubt that the world economy is becoming more integrated.

How does international trade help the economy?

⁎ Gains from trade occur when a nation specializes in production and exchanges its output with a trading partner. For this arrangement to work, each nation must produce goods for which it is a low-opportunity-cost producer and then trade them for goods for which it is a high-opportunity-cost producer.

⁎ In addition, trade benefits nations' economies through economies of scale and increased international competition.

What are the effects of tariffs and quotas?

⁎ Protectionism in the form of trade restrictions such as tariffs and quotas is common. A tariff is a tax on imports; a quota is a quantity restriction on imports.

⁎ Proponents of trade restrictions often cite the need to protect defense-related industries and fledgling firms and to fend off dumping. But protectionist policies can also serve as political favors to special interest groups.

CONCEPTS YOU SHOULD KNOW

comparative advantage
  (p. 1038)
dumping (p. 1051)
import quotas (p. 1048)

infant industry argument
  (p. 1051)
net exports (p. 1034)
protectionism (p. 1044)

tariffs (p. 1044)
trade balance (p. 1034)
trade deficit (p. 1034)
trade surplus (p. 1034)

QUESTIONS FOR REVIEW

1. What are three problems with trade restrictions? What are three reasons often given in support of trade restrictions?

2. What would happen to the standard of living in the United States if all foreign trade were eliminated?

3. How might a nation's endowment of natural resources, labor, and climate shape the nature of its comparative advantage?

4. Why might foreign producers voluntarily agree to a quota rather than face an imposed tariff?

5. Tariffs reduce the volume of imports. Do tariffs also reduce the volume of exports? Explain your response.

STUDY PROBLEMS (✳ *solved at the end of the section*)

1. Consider the following table for the neighboring nations of Quahog and Pawnee. Assume that the opportunity cost of producing each good is constant.

Product	Quahog	Pawnee
Meatballs (per hour)	4,000	2,000
Clams (per hour)	8,000	1,000

a. What is the opportunity cost of producing meatballs in Quahog? What is the opportunity cost of harvesting clams in Quahog?
b. What is the opportunity cost of producing meatballs in Pawnee? What is the opportunity cost of producing clams in Pawnee?
c. Based on your answers in parts (a) and (b), which nation has a comparative advantage in producing meatballs? Which nation has a comparative advantage in producing clams?

2. Suppose that the comparative-cost ratios of two products—mangoes and sardines—are as follows in the hypothetical nations of Mangolia and Sardinia:

Mangolia: 1 mango = 2 cans of sardines
Sardinia: 1 mango = 4 cans of sardines

In what product should each nation specialize? Explain why the terms of trade of 1 mango = 3 cans of sardines would be acceptable to both nations.

3. What are the two trade restriction policies we discussed in this chapter? Who benefits and who loses from each of these policies? What is the new outcome for society?

✳ 4. Germany and Japan both produce cars and beer. The table below shows production possibilities per worker in each country. For example, one worker in Germany produces 8 cars or 10 cases of beer per week. (For a review of absolute versus comparative advantage, see Chapter 2.)

	Labor force	Cars (C)	Beer (B)
Germany	200	8	10
Japan	100	20	14

a. Which nation has an absolute advantage in car production? Which one has an absolute advantage in beer production? Explain your answers.

b. Which nation has a comparative advantage in car production? Which one has a comparative advantage in beer production? Explain your answers.

✳ 5. Continuing with the example given in the previous problem, assume that Germany and Japan produce their own cars and beer and allocate half their labor force to the production of each.

a. What quantities of cars and beer does Germany produce? What quantities does Japan produce?

Now suppose that Germany and Japan produce only the good for which they enjoy a comparative advantage in production. They also agree to trade half of their output for half of what the other country produces.

b. What quantities of cars and beer does Germany produce now? What quantities does Japan produce?

c. What quantities of cars and beer does Germany consume now? What quantities does Japan consume?

d. People often act as if international trade is a zero-sum game, meaning that when one party wins, the other party must lose an equal amount. State this book's foundational principle that contradicts this idea.

✳ 6. Determine whether each statement is true or false.
Developing countries stand to gain from international trade because

a. trade enables them to specialize in producing where they have a comparative advantage.

b. trade gives them access to the greater variety of goods produced abroad.

c. trade subjects their local producers to greater competition.

d. trade allows them to produce larger amounts than they could consume themselves, allowing them to take advantage of increasing returns to scale.

7. Is it possible for a producer to have both an absolute advantage and a comparative advantage?

SOLVED PROBLEMS

4. **a.** Japan has an absolute advantage in both because 20 > 8 and 14 > 10.
   b. Japan has a comparative advantage in car production because its opportunity cost is less than Germany's (0.7 < 1.25). Germany has a comparative advantage in beer production because its opportunity cost is less than Japan's (0.8 < 1.43).

5. **a.** Germany: (C, B) = (800, 1,000); Japan: (C, B) = (1,000, 700)
   b. Germany: (C, B) = (0, 2,000); Japan: (C, B) = (2,000, 0)
   c. Germany: (C, B) = (1,000, 1,000); Japan: (C, B) = (1,000, 1,000)
   d. Trade creates value for all involved because each party must benefit from the terms of trade or they would not agree to trade.

6. All four statements are true: (a) Trade is built on the concept of specialization and the application of comparative advantage in that process. (b) Trade allows countries to obtain a greater variety of goods and services from abroad than they could produce on their own. (c) Because trade effectively increases the number of potential competitors in the market, local producers are subject to more competition than would exist without trade. (d) When countries export goods, they benefit from being able to access a larger marketplace, which gives them the opportunity to produce at a larger scale than they would without trade.

International Finance

Trade deficits are harmful to an economy.

Since 1975, the United States has had a trade deficit with the rest of the world—we import more than we export. Many people believe that

MIS CONCEPTION

trade deficits are bad for an economy. After all, it seems unfair that we are buying goods from other nations but they are not buying goods from us. And the news media often perpetuates these beliefs by reporting trade deficit data in alarmist tones. After all, the word "deficit" never sounds good. Most economists are not bothered by trade deficits. A trade deficit does not indicate economic weakness. In fact, a trade deficit usually accompanies a strong and growing economy. A relatively wealthy economy can afford to buy goods and services from all over the world. But are trade deficits really something to worry about?

In this chapter, we explore the two most important topics in international finance: exchange rates and trade balances. We begin by explaining the determinants of exchange rates in both the short run and the long run, and then we come back to the topic of international trade balances.

These books that fill an Amazon warehouse are produced all over the world. Is the U.S. economy worse off if most of these books come into the United States and contribute to our trade deficit?

BIG QUESTIONS

✳ **Why do exchange rates rise and fall?**

✳ **What is purchasing power parity?**

✳ **What causes trade deficits?**

Why Do Exchange Rates Rise and Fall?

Have you ever tried to exchange one currency for another? Perhaps you've seen exchange rates displayed on a sign at a bank or in an airport. If so, you've seen national flags and a lot of confusing numbers. Each of these numbers represents an exchange rate. An **exchange rate** is the price of foreign currency. This price tells how much a unit of foreign currency costs in terms of another currency. For example, the price of a single Mexican peso in terms of U.S. dollars is about $0.08, or 8 cents. This is the exchange rate between the peso and the dollar.

A key message from Chapter 32 is that the world economy is becoming ever more integrated: globalization is real and increasing. As more goods and services flow across borders, exchange rates become more important. One goal of this chapter is to explain the reasons why exchange rates rise and fall.

Exchange rates matter because they affect the relative prices of goods and services. Any good that crosses a border has to pass through a foreign exchange market on its way to sale. For example, the price you pay in the United States for a Samsung television built in South Korea depends on the exchange rate between the U.S. dollar and the won, the currency of South Korea.

Zooming out to the macro view, exchange rates affect the prices of all imports and exports—and therefore GDP. The more integrated the world economy becomes, the more closely economists watch exchange rates because they affect both what nations produce and what nations consume.

Our approach to exchange rates is straightforward: *exchange rates are prices*. For example, the exchange rate between the U.S. dollar and the won is the dollar price of one won, or the number of dollars required to buy one won. It is just like the price of other goods that we buy. Exchange rates are prices that are determined in world currency markets. Just as there are global markets where people buy and sell commodities such as sugar, wheat, and roses, there are also world markets where people buy and sell currencies. These markets, often called *foreign exchange markets*, are places where people buy and sell international currencies.

Exchange rates are determined by the demand for and supply of currency in foreign exchange markets. Thus, if we

An **exchange rate** is the price of foreign currency, indicating how much a unit of foreign currency costs in terms of another currency.

Are you planning a trip abroad? If so, you'd better figure out how to use signs like this to exchange currency.

want to explore the factors that make exchange rates rise and fall, we must consider the factors that affect the demand for and the supply of foreign currency. In this section, we look at some characteristics of foreign exchange markets and then consider the demand for and supply of foreign currency. When we have finished, we will be able to consider why exchange rates rise and fall.

Characteristics of Foreign Exchange Markets

In a foreign exchange market, the good in question is a foreign currency. Very likely, you've held foreign currency at some point in your life—perhaps because a friend or relative saved some as a souvenir from a trip abroad or perhaps because you were fortunate to vacation or study in a foreign country. People purchase a foreign currency in order to buy goods or services produced in the foreign country that uses that specific currency. Don't lose sight of this simple truth, because it is at the core of our entire conversation about exchange rate determination.

The demand for foreign currency is a derived demand. **Derived demand** is demand for a good or service that derives from the demand for another good or service. For example, if you travel to Belgium, you will probably want to buy some Belgian chocolates. But first you must buy euros, because the euro is the currency of Belgium. The euro is an unusual currency because it is used by 19 separate European nations, including Belgium, Germany, France, Spain, and Portugal. The demand for euros in world markets is derived from the demand for Belgian chocolates and many other goods, services, and financial assets produced in those 19 nations.

Derived demand is demand for a good or service that derives from the demand for another good or service.

Today, it is easier to buy goods in foreign countries because you can often just use your credit or debit card to make foreign purchases; you don't have to physically buy foreign currency. This approach works because your bank or card company is willing to buy the foreign currency for you. To you, it feels like you are paying in U.S. dollars, since you use the same card all over the world and you see deductions from your bank account in dollars. But your bank literally takes dollars from your account and then exchanges them for foreign currency so that it can pay foreign companies in their own currency. Your bank charges a fee for this service, but it certainly makes the transaction simpler for you.

Exchange Rates Are the Price of Foreign Currency

In this section, we look more closely at exchange rates. First, we clarify how exchange rates are quoted; then we consider how appreciation and depreciation—two new terms—affect exchange rates.

Table 33.1 shows some actual exchange rates from August 2015. Exchange rates can be viewed from either side of the exchange. For example, the exchange rate between the U.S. dollar and the Japanese yen can be viewed as either of the following:

1. the number of yen required to buy one U.S. dollar (¥ per $)
2. the number of U.S. dollars required to buy one yen ($ per ¥)

While these two rates communicate the same information, they are not usually the same number, because they are reciprocals of each other. For

TABLE 33.1		
Exchange Rates between the U.S. Dollar and Other Currencies, August 2015		
	Units of foreign currency you can buy with one U.S. dollar	**Number of U.S. dollars required to buy one unit of foreign currency**
British pound	0.644	1.551
Chinese yuan	6.21	0.161
Euro	0.915	1.092
Indian rupee	62.5	0.016
Japanese yen	125	0.008
Mexican peso	16.4	0.061
Turkish lira	2.788	0.360

Source: Google Public Data.

consistency, we exclusively use the second option—the number of U.S. dollars required to buy one unit of foreign currency. This number is represented in the last column in Table 33.1. We choose this option because it is the way we quote all other prices. If you walk into Starbucks and look at the prices posted on the wall, they indicate the number of dollars it takes to buy different coffee drinks. So when we refer to exchange rates in this textbook, we're always talking about the number of dollars required to buy one unit of foreign currency.

Currency appreciation occurs when a currency becomes more valuable relative to other currencies.

If a currency becomes more valuable in world markets, its price rises, and this increase is called an appreciation. **Currency appreciation** occurs when a currency increases in value relative to other currencies. In contrast,

---

FIGURE 33.1

Exchange Rates and Currency Appreciation and Depreciation

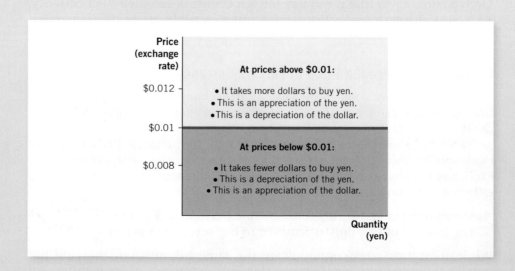

currency depreciation occurs when a currency decreases in value relative to other currencies. If the dollar depreciates, it is less valuable in world markets.

Figure 33.1 illustrates appreciation and depreciation with the exchange rate between the U.S. dollar and the yen. The exchange rate starts at $0.01. If the exchange rate rises above $0.01, it will take more dollars to buy a yen, which signals an appreciation of the yen and a depreciation of the dollar. If, instead, the price falls below $0.01, it will take fewer dollars to buy a yen, which signals a depreciation of the yen and an appreciation of the dollar.

> **Currency depreciation** occurs when a currency becomes less valuable relative to other currencies.

Some Historical Perspective

When exchange rates rise, foreign currencies become more expensive relative to the dollar. This means that imports become more expensive. But it also means that U.S. exports become less expensive, so foreigners around the globe can afford to buy more goods and services from the United States. These are the reasons why exchange rates are important macroeconomic indicators to watch.

The recent past offers a mixed picture of the world value of the dollar. Figure 33.2 plots exchange rates for the currencies of two different trading partners of the United States: one that uses the euro and one that uses the yen (Japan). The vertical axis in each panel measures the dollar price of one unit of the relevant foreign currency. Panel (a) shows the exchange rate with

FIGURE 33.2

Two Foreign Exchange Rates, 2005–2015

These exchange rates are reported as the number of U.S. dollars required to purchase a unit of foreign currency. (a) In looking at the euro exchange rate from 2005 to 2015, we see that the price of the euro rose from $1.30 to almost $1.60 but then fell below $1.10 more recently. (b) The Japanese yen grew very expensive from 2007 to 2013 but then fell dramatically.

Source: FRED Economic Data, Federal Reserve Bank of St. Louis.

(a) Exchange Rate for Euro

(b) Exchange Rate for Yen

the euro. The euro exchange rate fluctuated wildly over the 10 years pictured, rising from $1.30 to almost $1.60 during the recession year of 2008 but then falling to under $1.10 by 2015. Between 2013 and 2015, the value of the dollar grew significantly.

Panel (b) shows a similar story for the yen over the 10-year period. As the price of yen climbed, dollars were depreciating. But by 2015, the dollar value had grown, which means a lower price for yen.

The Demand for Foreign Currency

In this section, we discuss the factors that affect the demand side of the market for foreign currency. We distinguish three primary factors: the price of the currency (the exchange rate), the demand for foreign goods and services, and the demand for foreign financial assets.

Price of Foreign Currency (the Exchange Rate)

The law of demand holds in foreign currency markets. When the price of the yen falls, goods and services produced in Japan (such as Sony televisions or Toyota SUVs) are less expensive relative to goods and services produced in the United States. Therefore, if the price of the yen falls, the quantity of Japanese goods demanded increases. If, instead, the price of the yen rises, it becomes more expensive to purchase Japanese goods, and the quantity demanded falls.

Demand for Foreign Goods and Services

As we emphasized earlier, you purchase foreign currency so that you can buy goods or services produced in foreign countries. Perhaps you are thinking, "But wait, I buy goods from other countries quite often without purchasing foreign currency." This is true: you can buy imported TVs, cars, fruits, and clothing without ever touching a coin or bill of foreign currency. But in fact, those goods were originally purchased with the foreign currency of the nation where they were produced.

For example, a Sony television is produced in Japan, but you buy it in a retail store here in the United States. The workers and factory owners in Japan are paid in yen. This means that the U.S. company that imports the Sony TV from Japan has to buy yen so it can pay for the product. In short, someone has to buy the foreign currency to pay for the TV, even if it is not you. For this reason, the demand for a nation's currency depends on the demand for its exports.

When the demand for a nation's exports rises, the demand for its currency rises as well. For example, if the U.S. demand for Japanese TVs increases, the demand for yen will increase at all prices. Figure 33.3 illustrates changes in demand for yen. An increase in demand for Sony TVs shifts the demand for yen from D_1 to D_2. If the U.S. demand for Sony TVs decreases, then there is less reason to buy yen, so the demand declines. This decline is illustrated as a shift in the opposite direction, from D_1 to D_3.

If you want to snorkel in Mexico, you'd better buy some pesos.

Demand for Foreign Financial Assets

Another reason to purchase foreign currency is to buy financial assets in a foreign nation. To buy stocks or bonds in a foreign country, you have to convert to the local currency. Even to establish a foreign bank account, you must first buy the currency of that country. Likewise, if people from other nations want to buy U.S. stocks or bonds, they exchange their currency for U.S. dollars first.

A primary reason why foreigners demand U.S. dollars is to buy U.S. stocks, bonds, and real estate. Relative to the rest of the world, the United States is often seen as a stable, low-risk economy. Although U.S. stability weakened during the financial turmoil associated with the Great Recession of 2007–2009, the long-term productivity of U.S. firms still attracts foreign funds. For this reason, there is still a stable demand for U.S. dollars.

Along these lines, one key factor in foreign exchange markets is interest rates across nations. If interest rates rise in one country (relative to rates in the rest of the world), the demand for its currency will increase, since there is a greater demand for the assets with higher returns. For example, if interest rates in Japan rise relative to those in the rest of the world, it means that Japanese bonds provide a higher return than previously, and demand for these bonds will rise right along with the interest rate. In Figure 33.3, this move is indicated as a shift from D_1 to D_2. When interest rates fall, there is reduced demand for the nation's currency. We see this outcome in Figure 33.3 as a shift from D_1 to D_3.

The Supply of Foreign Currency

In Chapter 30, we talked about modern money, which is fiat currency. This kind of currency is printed and supplied by governments. From a market standpoint, it is fixed in quantity at any one time. Governments increase and

Shifts in the Demand for Foreign Currency

Increases in the demand for foreign currency (D_2) derive from an increased demand for foreign goods and services and/or foreign financial assets. Decreases in the demand for foreign currency (D_3) derive from a decreased demand for foreign goods and services and/or foreign financial assets. Here we illustrate these relationships with the U.S. dollar and the Japanese yen.

decrease the supply of fiat currency very often, and when they do, the supply curve shifts, as Figure 33.4 shows. For example, consider the possible actions of the Bank of Japan (BOJ), which is the central bank of Japan, the agency that determines monetary policy for the country. Initially, the supply of yen is vertical at S_1. If the BOJ increases the supply of yen relative to the supply of dollars, the supply curve shifts outward to S_2. If, instead, the BOJ reduces the supply of yen relative to the supply of dollars, the supply curve shifts in the opposite direction to S_3.

Applying Our Model of Exchange Rates

In this section, we consider some applications of our model of exchange rates. In reality, exchange rates fluctuate daily, and these prices affect the prices of all imports and exports. These fluctuations are the result of shifts in demand, supply, or both. We start with changes in demand.

Changes in Demand

In most of the world, car shoppers can choose from many cars; these include Toyotas produced in Japan and Jeeps produced in the United States. In microeconomics, you might study the impact on the auto manufacturers from a shift in consumer preferences away from Jeeps and toward Toyotas. But these kinds of demand changes, which occur quite frequently, also affect the market for foreign currency. For example, if consumer preferences in the United States shift away from Jeeps and toward Toyotas, the demand for the yen rises.

Figure 33.5 shows the results of a shift toward Toyotas. Initially, the market (for yen) is in equilibrium with supply S and demand D_1. The initial equilibrium exchange rate is $0.010. Then, after U.S. consumers demand more Toyotas, the demand for yen shifts outward to D_2. This shift causes the exchange rate to rise to $0.012.

How are exchange rates affected when consumers choose Toyotas over Jeeps?

FIGURE 33.4

Shifts in the Supply of Foreign Currency

The supply of any foreign nation's currency is determined by that nation's government. If the Bank of Japan increases the supply of yen relative to the supply of dollars, the supply curve shifts from S_1 to S_2. If the supply of yen decreases relative to the supply of dollars, the curve shifts in the opposite direction to S_3.

If the cause of the shift were an increase in the demand for Japanese financial assets, the result would be the same. Thus, if interest rates in Japan rise, this sends a signal to investors around the globe to buy financial assets in Japan. The increase in the demand for yen leads to an increase in the exchange rate. The higher exchange rate implies an appreciation of the yen and, by comparison, a depreciation of the dollar. People want more yen, so its value rises in relation to the dollar.

If, instead, global demand for goods, services, and financial assets moves away from Japan and toward the United States, the demand for yen will fall (shifting to D_3) as people move toward dollars. In this case, the exchange rate falls and the yen depreciates, but the dollar appreciates.

These shifts in demand occur naturally in a global economy in which consumers across different nations choose among products produced in a wide variety of countries. Even just focusing on cars, we can choose to buy from the United States, Germany, Japan, South Korea, the United Kingdom, Canada, and Italy, to name just a few car-producing countries. But as international demanders' product preferences change, exchange rates are affected. Table 33.2 summarizes how shifts in demand affect foreign exchange rates.

However, there are also "unnatural" changes in exchange rates, caused by intentional actions of government monetary authorities all over the globe. To understand these, we look at shifts in currency supply.

Changes in Supply

The supply side of currency markets is determined by government changes to the supply of currency. Figure 33.6 illustrates a scenario in which the Bank of Japan increases the supply of yen. This move shifts supply from S_1 to S_2 and causes the exchange rate to fall from $0.010 to $0.008. The drop in the exchange rate means that the yen depreciates relative to the dollar—a direct

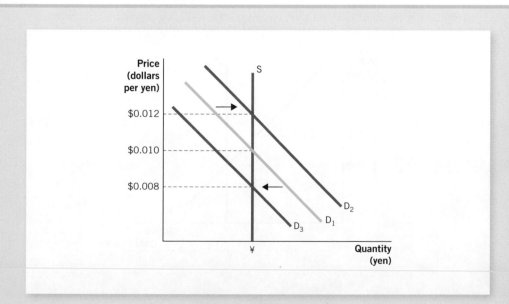

FIGURE 33.5

How Demand Shifts Affect the Exchange Rate

An increase in the demand for foreign currency leads to an increase in the exchange rate from $0.010 to $0.012. This signals a depreciation of the U.S. dollar relative to the yen. A decrease in the demand for foreign currency leads to a decrease in the exchange rate from $0.010 to $0.008. This signals an appreciation of the U.S. dollar relative to the yen.

TABLE 33.2

Shifts in Demand for Foreign Currency

Cause	Demand for foreign currency	Exchange rate change
Increase in demand for foreign goods and services or financial assets	Demand increases.	Exchange rate rises.
Decrease in demand for foreign goods and services or financial assets	Demand decreases.	Exchange rate falls.

Exchange rate manipulation occurs when a national government intentionally adjusts its money supply to affect the exchange rate of its currency.

result of the increase in yen. The BOJ action means that there are now more yen per dollar, so yen are worth less in relative terms.

The scenario pictured in Figure 33.6 is actually quite common. Government monetary authorities often intervene in markets to drive down their exchange rates. **Exchange rate manipulation** occurs when a national government intentionally adjusts its money supply to affect the exchange rate of its currency.

It may seem odd that a government would take action to purposefully depreciate the value of its own currency. After all, don't we typically want the value of our assets to *appreciate*? If you learned that the value of your car depreciated drastically in the last year, would you take that as good news? What if the value of your parents' home depreciates; is that good news? No, these are both bad news. However, nations depreciate their own currency in order to make their exports more affordable to buyers worldwide. If the yen

FIGURE 33.6

How Supply Shifts Affect the Exchange Rate

All else being equal, an increase in the quantity of yen shifts the supply of yen to the right, to ¥$_2$. This shift causes the exchange rate to decrease from $0.010 to $0.008. Thus, the yen depreciates and the dollar appreciates.

falls in value, then each dollar buys more yen. And a devalued yen makes Japanese products more affordable. All else being equal, the demand for Japanese products will rise in the United States.

Currency devaluation, by increasing the quantity of currency, can certainly have a short-run impact on aggregate demand. But to see how the currency devaluation affects the Japanese economy, we need to consider it in the context of the aggregate demand–aggregate supply model. In Chapter 23, we included the value of domestic currency among the factors that shift aggregate demand. We noted that a decrease in the value of domestic currency (depreciation) causes an increase in aggregate demand.

Let's now consider this observation in the context of our present discussion. If the Bank of Japan acts to depreciate the yen, then aggregate demand for Japanese goods and services increases, as shown in Figure 33.7 as a shift from AD_1 to AD_2. In the short run, this shift leads to greater real GDP (Y_1) and lower unemployment in Japan. This happens because some prices are inflexible in the short run. But when all prices adjust, output returns to its earlier level, leaving only inflation as the result of the increased quantity of yen—the price level rises from 100 to 110. In the end, yen are less expensive; but because of inflation, it takes more yen to buy Japanese goods. In the long run, there are no real effects from the action: the LRAS curve remains at Y^*.

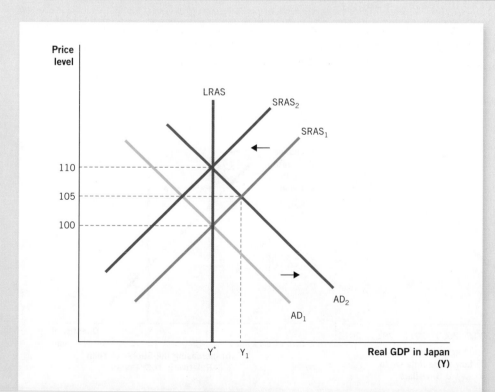

FIGURE 33.7

Increase in Aggregate Demand in Japan Arising from Yen Depreciation

A depreciation of the yen increases aggregate demand for Japanese goods and services. In the short run, real GDP increases and unemployment (not pictured here) decreases due to some sticky prices. In the long run, when prices adjust fully, there are no real effects, just inflation, because the price level rises from 100 to 110.

Pegging Exchange Rates

Panel (a) of Figure 33.8 plots the U.S. dollar exchange rate with the Chinese yuan. Notice the flat period between 2008 and 2010, then the gradual mostly evenly paced increases after that. This pattern is not due to natural market forces; it is because the Chinese government has chosen to maintain a pegged exchange rate with the dollar. **Pegged (fixed) exchange rates** are exchange rates that are fixed at a certain level through the actions of a government. The alternative to pegged exchange rates is flexible exchange rates. **Flexible (floating) exchange rates** are exchange rates that are determined by the market forces of supply of and demand for currency. Previously in this chapter, our discussions have assumed flexible exchange rates.

Many exchange rates today, such as those we have already considered, are flexible. However, China pegs its currency, the yuan, to the U.S. dollar. The yuan has been consistently pegged at a value below that which would prevail if the exchange rate were allowed to be flexible; the market-determined rate would be well above $0.160. For instance, the yuan was pegged at $0.147 between 2008 and 2010, as you can see in the flat part of the graph in panel (a) of Figure 33.8. But countries cannot pass a law that pegs the exchange rate, because world markets are not subject to the laws of other nations. Instead,

Pegged (fixed) exchange rates are exchange rates that are fixed at a certain level through the actions of a government.

Flexible (floating) exchange rates are exchange rates that are determined by the supply of and demand for currency.

FIGURE 33.8

How China Pegs the Yuan and Increases Its Supply

The Chinese government controls the exchange rate for its currency, pegging the yuan to a particular value relative to the U.S. dollar. Panel (a) shows that from mid-2008 until mid-2010, the pegged rate was set at $0.147; after this, it was allowed to rise but was still kept below the value that world markets would dictate. Panel (b) shows how the Chinese government keeps the exchange rate below the market rate. The government uses yuan to buy U.S. dollars and other U.S. assets in world markets. This strategy increases the supply of yuan, which shifts the supply curve to the right.

Source: FRED Economic Data, Federal Reserve Bank of St. Louis.

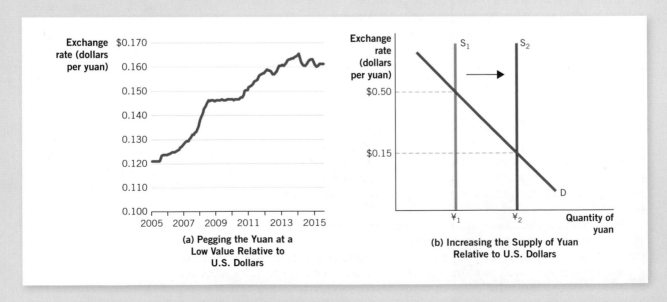

(a) Pegging the Yuan at a Low Value Relative to U.S. Dollars

(b) Increasing the Supply of Yuan Relative to U.S. Dollars

the Chinese government maintains the peg by adjusting its supply of yuan in world markets.

To decrease the price of the yuan, the Chinese government increases the supply of yuan relative to the supply of dollars. Panel (b) in Figure 33.8 illustrates how an increase in supply drives down the price of the yuan. In practice, the Chinese government buys U.S. dollars and U.S. Treasury securities in world markets. Notice the word "buy" in the last sentence. That's right: the Chinese government has to buy these, and when it buys them with newly minted yuan, the supply of yuan shifts to the right, to S_2. This action causes the Chinese currency to depreciate. Essentially, the Chinese government is conducting open market operations by purchasing U.S. Treasury securities. Ironically, this is exactly how the U.S. Federal Reserve enacts expansionary monetary policy for the United States.

The Chinese government devalues the yuan so that Chinese goods and services become less expensive on world markets. The government wants Chinese exports to be very affordable because it is trying to build the nation's economy through exports. The Chinese view this as a long-term strategy that will help their economy develop into an industrial economy. Since 2010, the Chinese government has been letting the yuan slowly rise in value, but as the Economics in the Real World feature explains, the Chinese government seems to be having second thoughts.

ECONOMICS IN THE REAL WORLD

Chinese Export Growth Slows

In August 2015, the Chinese government took action to devalue the yuan, letting the exchange value fall 3% in just two days. The goal of the Chinese government was to cheapen the yuan to make Chinese exports cheaper for Americans and others to buy. The devaluation of the yuan took place while the Chinese economy was struggling to maintain the phenomenal growth of the prior two decades. But many economists question whether continued currency devaluations can lead to sustainable economic growth.

In one sense, it is clear that the Chinese economy has been growing at historically high rates over the past two decades. This fact seems to indicate that the devaluation strategy is helping the Chinese economy overall, not just the export sector. Perhaps this is true, but let's be careful. After all, many other changes have taken place in China over the past two decades. Recall from Chapters 24 and 25 that institutional changes (especially the introduction of private property rights) have significantly altered production incentives in China. Therefore, it is inaccurate to pin China's success on currency devaluation alone.

Will the Chinese government continue to keep the value of the yuan down so that Americans can buy these toys at reduced prices?

In addition, the devaluation of the Chinese currency has other side effects. In particular, devaluation harms Chinese workers, who are paid in yuan. When the government devalues the currency, this move effectively gives the workers a real pay cut. Part of the reason why Chinese exports are so inexpensive is that the nation's labor costs are very low. But this is not a positive outcome for the wage earners. ✳

PRACTICE WHAT YOU KNOW

The Bahamian Dollar Is Pegged to the U.S. Dollar

While the Chinese government keeps the dollar–yuan exchange rate artificially low to encourage exports, other nations peg their currency to the dollar to guarantee stability. In fact, as of 2015, there were still dozens

This might not look like three U.S. dollars, but that's what it basically is.

of nations that pegged their currency to the U.S. dollar. Not all the exchange rates are held artificially low with their dollar peg.

Question: Assume that the Bahamian government wants to peg its currency to the U.S. dollar at a 1:1 ratio (one U.S. dollar = one Bahamian dollar). But the current exchange rate is at 90 cents (10 cents below the official peg). What must the Bahamian central bank do to return to the $1 exchange rate?

Answer: In this case, as illustrated in the graph below, the initial supply and demand curves intersect at $0.90 before the government intervenes to enforce the peg. Thus, the Bahamian central bank should reduce the supply of Bahamian dollars from S_1 to S_2 to increase the exchange rate to $1.00.

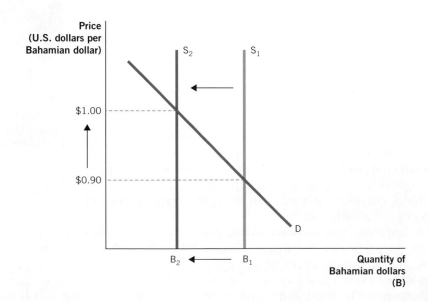

What Is Purchasing Power Parity?

As we have noted, the world economy is becoming ever more integrated. This closer integration affects both suppliers and demanders of goods and services. Suppliers can often choose where they wish to sell their output, and demanders can often choose where they want to buy their goods and services—even if doing so requires a little extra shipping.

In this section, we discuss the theory of how exchange rates are determined in the long run. We begin by examining how market exchanges determine the price of a particular good at different locations. Next we extend this discussion to the prices of all goods and services in different nations. Finally, we come back and consider limitations to the theory. We begin with the *law of one price*.

The Law of One Price

Let's consider a simplified example of trade within the borders of one country: Florida oranges are consumed in Michigan and many other states. What happens if the price of Florida oranges is different in Michigan and Florida? Figure 33.9 illustrates two different markets for Florida oranges—one in Florida and one in Michigan. Initially, as we see in panel (a), the price of a pound of oranges in Florida is $1.80; as we see in panel (b), the price of a pound of

FIGURE 33.9

The Law of One Price
(a) Initially, the price of a pound of oranges in Florida is $1.80, while (b) the same oranges sell for $2.20 per pound in Michigan. Thus, orange suppliers reduce supply in Florida and increase supply in Michigan. If transportation costs are zero, these supply changes will take place until the price is the same in both locations.

(a) The Market for Oranges in Florida

(b) The Market for Oranges in Michigan

the same oranges in Michigan is $2.20. Assume for now that there are no transportation costs and no trade barriers. In this case, sellers in Florida have an incentive to sell their oranges in Michigan, where the price is 40 cents higher. Thus, the supply in Florida will decline and the supply in Michigan will increase. These supply shifts will lead to an increased price in Florida and a decreased price in Michigan. The adjustment will continue until the prices are the same in both locations.

This adjustment process is the logic behind the **law of one price**, which says that after accounting for transportation costs and trade barriers, identical goods sold in different locations must sell for the same price. We can state the law of one price in equation form, where p_A is the price of a good in location A and p_B is the price of the same good in location B:

> The **law of one price** says that after accounting for transportation costs and trade barriers, identical goods sold in different locations must sell for the same price.

(Equation 33.1)

$$p_A = p_B$$

The law of one price also holds across international borders. For example, if Florida oranges are sold in Japan, the price should be the same once we account for the costs of shipping and trade barriers. But when oranges ship across international borders, a new issue arises because different nations generally use different currencies. We take up this issue in the next section.

Purchasing Power Parity and Exchange Rates

In Japan, the medium of exchange is the yen. The exchange rate between the U.S. dollar and the yen is about $0.01. Therefore, since each yen is worth about a penny, the law of one price implies that it should take about 100 times as many yen to buy oranges in Japan as it does dollars to buy the same oranges in the United States. Thus, if the price of a pound of oranges in the United States is $2, the price in Japan should be ¥200. This extension of the law of one price is the idea behind purchasing power parity (PPP).

Purchasing power parity (PPP) is the idea that a unit of currency should be able to buy the same quantity of goods and services in any country. For example, once you exchange $2 for ¥200, you should be able to buy a pound of oranges.

> **Purchasing power parity (PPP)** is the idea that a unit of currency should be able to buy the same quantity of goods and services in any country.

PPP is an extension of the law of one price. If, after converting currencies, the price of oranges is higher in Japan than it is in Florida, then supply to Japan increases and supply in Florida decreases until the prices are equal. We can also represent this in equation form:

(Equation 33.2)

$$p_A = \text{exchange rate} \times p_B$$

In the short run, PPP may not hold perfectly, and we explain the reasons for this in the next section. But in the long run, after all the adjustments have taken place, PPP holds.

So far, we have considered a single good—oranges. But we can extend purchasing power parity to all final goods and services in order to derive an important implication regarding exchange rates. If Equation 33.2 holds for all final goods and services, then the price levels (P) in different nations should be related as follows:

(Equation 33.3)

$$P_A = \text{exchange rate} \times P_B$$

Impossible Exchange Rates

Eurotrip

In this movie from 2004, four American high school graduates travel to Europe and end up in Bratislava, the capital of Slovakia. They are particularly concerned when they pool their remaining money and find they have just $1.83. But Slovakia is an impoverished country, and it turns out that the U.S. dollar is extremely valuable there. Using this small amount of money, the four friends are able to have an amazing night on the town. At one point, they tip a busboy just 5 cents, but this tip is so valuable that the man promptly retires from his job to enjoy his wealth.

An appreciating and strong U.S. dollar is good news to people who are paid in U.S. dollars. The stronger your home currency, the more you can buy around the globe.

But purchasing power parity means that the kind of wild overvaluation of the dollar that we see in *Eurotrip* is not possible in the real world. If the dollar were really this strong in some nation, tourists would

These friends don't have to look far to find a bargain when their dollars are strong relative to the local currency.

flood in with dollars and then drive the prices up to a more reasonable level. The movie's story makes for entertaining theater, but the law of one price and purchasing power parity mean that these kinds of bargains can't last long in the real world.

In Equation 33.3, P_A is the price level in nation A and P_B is the price level in nation B. We can rewrite Equation 33.3 to derive a key implication of PPP:

$$\text{exchange rate} = P_A \div P_B \qquad \text{(Equation 33.4)}$$

This equation is a direct extension of the law of one price to international trade in all goods and services. We can use Equation 33.4 to learn what causes big swings in exchange rates over time. For example, we have noted that the exchange rate between the U.S. dollar and the Japanese yen has consistently risen in recent years (see Figure 33.2b), which means that the dollar has depreciated relative to the yen. In 2007, each yen cost approximately $0.008, but the rate had risen to $0.013 by 2012. This long-run change reflects shifts in relative price levels over the period 2007–2012. While inflation in the United States averaged just 2.7% from 2007 to 2011, the price level in Japan actually declined over the same period, falling by 2.1%. These changing price levels led to an increase in the exchange rate, because $P_{US} \div P_{Japan}$ increased between 2007 and 2011. Thus, in the long run, exchange rate fluctuations are driven by relative changes in price levels.

ECONOMICS IN THE REAL WORLD

The Big Mac Index

We have said that purchasing power parity is a condition that should hold in the long run. The British magazine *The Economist* has devised a creative way to test PPP at any given point in time. It compares the price of a McDonald's Big Mac sandwich across many nations. The Big Mac is a good choice because it is roughly the same good all over the world. For example, in July 2015, the price of a Big Mac in the United States was $4.79. Given that the exchange rate between the U.S. dollar and the euro was about $1.10 in July 2015, we can use Equation 33.2 to find the implied price of the Big Mac in the Euro area:

$$4.79 = 1.1 \times P_{Europe}$$

Solving for the price in Europe, we find that 4.79 ÷ 1.1 = 4.35 euros. In fact, the actual price was 4.07 euros, so the PPP formula worked fairly well in this case.

But PPP doesn't always hold perfectly in the short run. Table 33.3 shows the Big Mac price across seven different nations, along with the price implied by PPP. The first column of numbers gives the actual price of the Big Mac in terms of the domestic currency for each nation. The last column shows the actual price of the Big Mac converted to U.S. dollars using the exchange rate. If PPP held perfectly, the prices in the last column would all be $4.79, the price of a Big Mac in the United States.

In the next section, we examine why PPP might not hold exactly in the short run. One of the key reasons is that the food must be identical across nations. ✳

Is the price of this McDonald's sandwich the same all over the world?

Why PPP Does Not Hold Perfectly

When we look at the Big Mac index, we see that PPP does not always hold perfectly. There are five reasons why PPP may not hold in the short run.

First, for the law of one price and PPP to hold, the goods or services sold in different locations must be identical. As Table 33.3 notes, the Indian version of the Big Mac is not even a hamburger; it is a chicken sandwich. Thus, we should not expect the prices to be the same.

Second, some goods and services are not tradable. One example is a haircut. Haircuts in China typically cost less than $5 (and often include a massage), whereas haircuts in the United States almost always cost more than $20. But we cannot import a "haircut produced in China"; you'd have to travel to China to buy that service. Therefore, the supply of foreign haircuts cannot adjust to force PPP to hold. This is the case for all nontradable goods and services.

Third, trade barriers inhibit the trade of goods across some international borders. If goods cannot be traded or if tariffs and quotas add to the costs of trade, then prices will not equalize and PPP will not hold. The higher the trade barriers, the higher the price of the good in the foreign country. For example, tariffs and quotas on Florida oranges imported to Japan would lead to higher prices in Japan than in Florida.

TABLE 33.3

The Big Mac Index, July 2015

	Actual price in domestic currency	Exchange rate	Price in U.S. dollars
U.S. dollar	4.79	1.000	$4.79
Chinese yuan	17.00	0.161	$2.74
Euro	3.70	1.100	$4.07
Indian rupee*	116.25	0.016	$1.86
Japanese yen	370.00	0.008	$2.96
Mexican peso	49.00	0.064	$3.14
U.K. pound	2.89	1.561	$4.51

Source: *The Economist.*

*In India, the Big Mac is not sold; the closest comparison is with the Maharaja Mac, which substitutes chicken for beef.

Fourth, shipping costs keep prices from completely equalizing. In fact, higher shipping costs will lead to higher prices of the same good in a foreign nation. The greater the shipping costs, the bigger the difference in prices that can persist.

Finally, we have emphasized consistently throughout this book that some prices take longer to adjust than others. PPP is a theory about long-run price adjustments across nations, with prices reacting to changes in demand and supply. The theory is by definition a long-run theory, which only holds after all prices have completely adjusted. Therefore, it will not typically hold perfectly in the short run.

In sum, PPP is a theory that teaches us a lot about the level of exchange rates in the long run—why exchange rates rise and fall over long periods of time. But in the real world, given these limitations, PPP typically does not hold perfectly at any point in time.

What Causes Trade Deficits?

At the beginning of this chapter, we noted that many people think that trade deficits are harmful. In this section, we consider why this is a misconception. We also look at the specific causes of trade deficits.

A trade deficit means that more goods and services are coming in than are going out. On a micro level, individuals can have trade deficits with other individuals or business firms. Think about your favorite place to eat lunch. Perhaps you go there once a week. You have a trade deficit with that restaurant; unless you also happen to work there, you buy more from it than it buys from you. Does this deficit make you worse off or indicate weakness on your part? No. In fact, the wealthier you are, the more you may eat at your favorite restaurant and the more your trade deficit with the restaurant may increase. If voluntary trade creates a trade deficit for you, it doesn't mean that you are worse off. Remember: trade creates value.

PRACTICE WHAT YOU KNOW

The Law of One Price: What Should the Price Be?

The Ikea furniture company sells Swedish bookshelves all over the world. One popular model is called the BILLY bookcase. According to the Bloomberg news agency, the 2011 price of the BILLY bookcase in the United States was $59.99, while the price in the United Kingdom was £29.90.

BILLY bookcases from Ikea can be shipped all over the world.

Question: In 2011, the exchange rate between the U.S. dollar and the British pound sterling was about $1.60. Using this figure, how would you determine the 2011 price implied by PPP for the BILLY bookcase in the United Kingdom? To be clear, we are asking for the price in British pounds sterling that is equal to the $59.99 price in the United States.

Answer: From Equation 33.2,

price in the United States = exchange rate × price in the United Kingdom

Therefore, substituting in the price in the United States and the exchange rate, we have

$59.99 = $1.60 × price in the United Kingdom

Solving this equation, we get

$$\frac{59.99}{1.60} = £37.49$$

Question: The 2011 price implied by PPP was £37.49, but the actual price in the United Kingdom at that time was £29.90. What are possible reasons why the price was relatively low in the United Kingdom?

Answer: Two reasons seem particularly likely. First, shipping costs to the United Kingdom may have been lower than shipping costs to the United States. In addition, there were likely lower trade barriers across Europe than between Europe and the United States.

Data source: Kristian Siedenburg, "Ikea Billy Bookshelf Index," Bloomberg.com, Sept. 15, 2010.

When we extend this concept to the entire economy, the result is the same: we are not worse off when more goods and services flow in. In fact, historical data reveal that the U.S. trade deficit often increases during periods of economic growth. Figure 33.10 shows the U.S. trade balance (imports/exports) with recessionary periods shaded as vertical blue bars. The solid blue horizontal line is drawn where exports exactly equal imports. As the orange graph line becomes increasingly negative, it indicates a bigger trade deficit. Notice that the trade deficit widens during periods of expansion and then shrinks during recessions. The data show us that trade deficits are often a by-product of positive economic periods.

Before we can explore the various causes of trade deficits, we need to discuss more about the accounting of international trade and financial flows. For this we turn to the balance of payments.

Your trade deficit with a local lunch spot does not make you worse off.

Balance of Payments

In this section, we introduce the terminology of international transactions accounts—the accounts used to track transactions that take place across borders. For a while, it may seem like we have left economics to study accounting. But we need to clarify how international transactions are recorded before we can fully explain the causes of trade deficits and surpluses.

A nation's **balance of payments (BOP)** is a record of all payments between that country and the rest of the world. Anytime a payment is made across borders, the payment is tracked in the BOP. For example, if you buy a car

The **balance of payments (BOP)** is a record of all payments between one nation and the rest of the world.

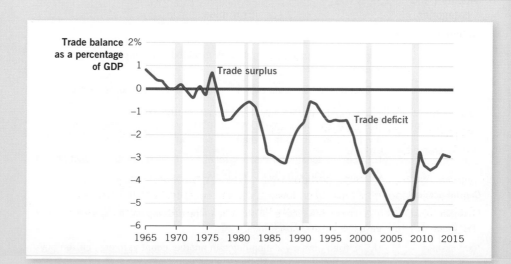

FIGURE 33.10

U.S. Trade Balance and Recessions, 1965–2015

Since 1975, the U.S. trade balance has been a deficit, with the deficit reaching its peak in 2006. The trade deficit typically grows during economic expansions and shrinks during recessions, which are indicated here with vertical blue bars.

Source: U.S. Bureau of Economic Analysis, *U.S. International Transactions.*

Trade balance as a percentage of GDP

Trade surplus

Trade deficit

made in Japan, the dollar amount of that transaction is recorded in the balance of payments. If someone from Canada buys shares of stock in a U.S. corporation, that payment is also tracked in the U.S. balance of payments, as well as in Canada's.

The **current account** is the BOP (balance of payments) account that tracks all payments for goods and services, current income from investments, and gifts.

The balance of payments is divided into two major accounts: the current account and the capital account. Different types of transactions are entered into each account. The **current account** tracks payments for goods and services, gifts, and current income from investments. When we import TVs from Japan or strawberries from Peru (goods) or when we utilize technical advice from a call center in Mumbai, India (a service), or when we supply international aid to refugees in the Middle East (a gift), these transactions are recorded in the current account.

The **capital account** tracks payments for real and financial assets between nations and extensions of international loans.

The **capital account** tracks payments for real and financial assets between nations. When residents of one nation buy financial securities such as stocks and bonds from another nation, these payments are recorded in the capital account. When the Chinese government buys U.S. Treasury securities, this transaction is recorded in the capital account. If someone from the United States deposits funds into a Swiss bank account, this transaction is recorded in the capital account. Even if you trade for the currency of another nation, your transaction is recorded in the capital account.

Purchases of real assets also enter in the capital account. If you buy a vacation home in Cozumel, Mexico, it counts as an outgoing payment in the capital account. When the Abu Dhabi Investment Council purchased the Chrysler Building in New York City, the transaction was recorded in the capital account as an incoming payment.

Because much of the activity in the capital account is in financial securities, it is sometimes called the *financial account*. Table 33.4 shows the major

TABLE 33.4		
Current Account Transactions versus Capital Account Transactions		
Account and categories	**Examples**	
Current account		
Goods	Domestically produced computer is exported; foreign-produced shoes are imported.	
Services	U.S. airline transports foreign passengers; foreign call center offers technical advice.	
Income receipt or payment	U.S. citizen earns income from a job in a foreign nation; foreign citizen earns dividends on ownership of shares of stock in a U.S. company.	
Gifts	U.S. citizen donates for disaster relief in a foreign country; foreign citizen donates to charity in the United States.	
Capital account		
Financial assets	U.S. citizen buys shares of stock in a foreign company; foreign government buys U.S. Treasury securities.	
Real assets	U.S. citizen buys a vacation home in another country; foreign citizen buys an office building in the United States.	

Did it hurt the U.S. economy when the Abu Dhabi Investment Council bought the Chrysler Building in New York City?

TABLE 33.5

U.S. Balance of Payments, 2014

Current account (millions of dollars)		Capital account (millions of dollars)	
Goods and services		Real and financial assets	
Exports	$2,343,205	U.S.-owned assets abroad	−$792,145
Imports	−$2,851,529	Foreign-owned assets in United States	$977,421
Income			
Receipts	$963,369	Net financial derivatives	−$54,372
Payments	−$844,571		
Gifts	−$45	Statistical discrepancy	$258,667
Balance	−$389,571		$389,571

Source: United States Bureau of Economic Analysis.

categories of the current account and the capital account, along with some examples of the types of transactions entered in each.

Table 33.5 shows actual values for the U.S. current and capital accounts in 2014. Goods and services are by far the largest entry in the current account, representing about 80% of total current account activity. For this reason, we focus primarily on goods and services when we discuss the current account.

The dollar amounts in this table represent changes in the various accounts during 2014. For example, on the current account side, the figures indicate that the United States exported about $2.3 trillion worth of goods and services but imported about $2.9 trillion worth. This trade deficit accounts for most of the current account deficit. On the capital account side, U.S. individuals (and government) purchased almost $800 billion worth of assets from abroad, but foreigners bought about $1 trillion in U.S. assets in 2014. In the short run, statistical discrepancies are common. We know that in the long run the two accounts sum to zero by definition.

When we evaluate the trade balance, we are really focusing on the current account. In fact, when you read about a "trade deficit," you are likely reading about a current account deficit. An **account deficit** exists when more payments are flowing out of an account than into the account. Generally, this means that we are importing more goods and services than we are exporting. Table 33.5 shows that the U.S. current account deficit in 2014 was $389,571 ($2,851,529 − $2,343,205) million.

An **account surplus** exists when more payments are flowing into an account than out of the account. Because goods and services constitute most of the current account, a surplus of the current account

An **account deficit** exists when more payments are flowing out of an account than into the account.

An **account surplus** exists when more payments are flowing into an account than out of the account.

Banana imports are recorded with other goods and services in the current account.

would be driven by a trade surplus. Table 33.5 shows a capital account surplus of $389,571 for the United States in 2014. You will notice that this surplus is exactly the same size as the current account deficit. This is no coincidence, and we explain the relationship in the next section.

The Key Identity of Balance of Payments

To talk about the major causes of trade deficits, we need to clarify the link between the current and capital accounts. Basically, when one of the accounts increases, the other decreases. We begin with an example before we state an important identity.

Let's say you are shopping for a new car, and you decide on a Toyota that is manufactured in Japan. Let's assume the following:

- Before you buy a Japanese car, the U.S. trade is completely balanced: imports = exports.
- Before you buy the car, the U.S. capital account is also balanced: U.S. ownership of foreign assets = foreign ownership of U.S. assets.
- The car costs $40,000.

Now when you buy the car, there are two sides to the exchange: from your perspective, you are trading dollars for an imported good; from the perspective of Toyota, the company is trading its car for a U.S. financial asset (dollars). Thus, the exchange is recorded twice in the U.S. balance of payments. First, it is recorded as an import in the current account, and it leads to a current account deficit of $40,000. Second, it is recorded as the purchase of U.S. currency, a U.S. financial asset, in the capital account, and this transaction implies a surplus in the capital account of $40,000. These are entries of equal but offsetting magnitude, which is the principle behind the *balance* of payments.

Now we arrive at an important principle with regard to the balance of payments, which we call the *key identity of the balance of payments*: while either account can be in deficit or surplus, together they sum to zero. A positive balance in the current account means there must be a negative balance in the capital account, and vice versa. We can also write this principle in equation form:

(Equation 33.5)   current account balance + capital account balance = 0

Thus, if the current account is in deficit, the capital account is in surplus by the same amount. If the current account is in surplus, the capital account is in deficit by the same amount.

Before moving on, let's consider two other scenarios stemming from our Japanese car example. First, what happens if the new foreign owners of the $40,000 in U.S. currency decide to use it to buy Microsoft software manufactured in the United States? This transaction involves $40,000 worth of U.S. exports, so the current account deficit disappears, as does the capital account surplus.

Finally, what happens if, instead, the Japanese owners of $40,000 in U.S. currency use it to purchase shares of Microsoft stock? In this case, the U.S. current account deficit stays at $40,000 and the capital account surplus stays at $40,000, because the Japanese have simply shifted to a different U.S. financial asset. These three scenarios are summarized in Table 33.6. In all cases, the current account changes are offset by opposite capital account changes.

TABLE 33.6

An Example of Balance of Payments

Example: A U.S. citizen buys a Japanese car for $40,000.

Scenario I: The Japanese company holds on to the $40,000.

U.S. current account: −$40,000

U.S. capital account: +$40,000

Total 0

Scenario II: The Japanese company buys $40,000 worth of U.S.-produced Microsoft software.

U.S. current account: −$40,000 + $40,000 = 0

U.S. capital account: +$40,000 − $40,000 = 0

Total 0

Scenario III: The Japanese company buys $40,000 worth of Microsoft Corporation stock.

U.S. current account: − $40,000

U.S. capital account: + $40,000

Total 0

We can see this identity when we examine actual balance of payments data for a nation. Figure 33.11 illustrates the identity with real historical data from the United States. The orange line is the U.S. current account balance—clearly in deficit since 1991. Figure 33.11 also plots the balance of the capital account, which is clearly in surplus since 1991. Notice that when the capital account surplus grows, it accompanies a larger current account deficit. As the

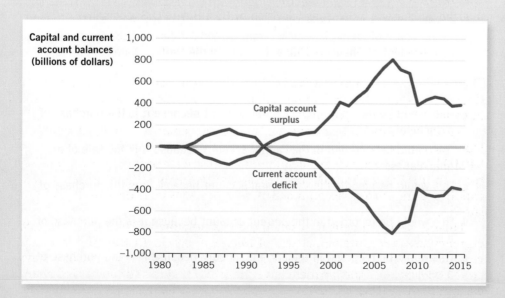

FIGURE 33.11

U.S. Current and Capital Account Balances since 1980

The current account and the capital account are essentially mirror images of each other. If we say that the United States has a current account deficit, we are also saying that it has a capital account surplus.

Source: United States Bureau of Economic Analysis.

current account deficit exceeded $750 billion in 2006, the capital account surplus also exceeded $750 billion. The two lines are very close to mirror images, which they should be, based on Equation 33.5.

This identity is important for practical purposes because it shows us that anything that affects the capital account also affects the current account. Thus, if we are interested in the major causes of trade deficits, we need to examine not only what causes a current account deficit to increase but also what causes a capital account surplus to increase, because the two are essentially mirror images.

PRACTICE WHAT YOU KNOW

Current Account versus Capital Account Entries

Question: Would the following international transactions be recorded in the U.S. current account or the capital account?

a. the purchase of a Canadian government bond by a resident of Pennsylvania

b. the sale of a U.S. Treasury bond to a resident of Ontario, Canada

c. the purchase of a condominium in Cancun, Mexico, by a U.S. resident

If a foreign student buys a ticket on a U.S. airline, how does this transaction affect the balance of payments?

d. the purchase of a Samsung television by Best Buy (a U.S. company)

e. the purchase of an airplane ticket from United Airlines (a U.S. company) by a resident of Chengdu, China, to come to the United States to attend college

Answers:

a. This would be recorded in the capital account because it is the purchase of a financial asset.

b. This would be recorded in the capital account because it is the sale of a financial asset.

c. This would be recorded in the capital account because it is the purchase of a real asset.

d. This would be recorded in the current account because it is the purchase of a good.

e. This would be recorded in the current account because it is the purchase of a service.

The Causes of Trade Deficits

People who are concerned about trade deficits often think about trade in terms of fairness. After all, if our economy is buying goods from nations around the globe, shouldn't these nations be buying goods from us? The way we calculate GDP seems to reinforce this point of view. Recall that GDP is the sum of four components—consumption (C), investment (I), government expenditures (G), and net exports (NX):

$$GDP = Y = C + I + G + NX$$

The fourth piece is net exports. All else being equal, the net exports component falls when a nation imports more goods. In this sense, the greater current account deficit implies lower GDP. While that implication might make you think that nations are better off with fewer imports or more exports, you shouldn't jump to this conclusion.

There are several causes of deficits in the current account. Although the United States has consistently had a current account deficit since 1975, the cause has varied over time. We consider three primary causes of current account deficits: strong economic growth, lower personal savings rates, and fiscal policy.

Strong Economic Growth

One cause of current account deficits is strong domestic growth. A nation that is growing and increasing in wealth relative to the rest of the world is also a nation that can afford to import significant quantities of goods and services.

Think of this first in terms of individuals. Imagine that you open a coffee shop and your business does very well. You earn significant profits, and your personal wealth grows. This new wealth enables you to purchase many goods and services that you would not be able to afford if you were less well off. With your new wealth, you'll likely develop trade deficits with many stores and restaurants in your town. You might even establish trade deficits with ski resorts, golf courses, and car dealerships. Bill Gates has personal trade deficits all over the world simply because he buys large quantities of goods and services.

Bill Gates seems to enjoy his trade deficits.

This scenario also applies to nations. During periods of rapid economic expansion in the United States, our current account deficit has grown. The prime example of this is the late 1990s. Look again at Figure 33.11. In the long growth period during the late 1990s, the economy was growing and the current account deficit was growing as well. U.S. wealth was increasing, which enabled us to afford more imports from around the globe. The reverse occurs during economic downturns. When U.S. wealth falls, we are less able to afford imports, and the current account deficit shrinks.

Certain distinct effects cause the trade deficit to grow during economic expansion. The first is in the current account: wealthy domestic consumers can afford to import more goods and services. The second is in the capital account: growing economies offer higher investment returns, so funds from around the globe flow in to take advantage of high rates of return. Table 33.7 summarizes these two complementary effects.

TABLE 33.7		
Why Strong Growth Leads to a Balance of Payments (BOP) Deficit		
Primary account	**Explanation**	**Result**
Current account	The growing economy leads to wealthier consumers who import more goods and services from around the world.	Net exports fall, which leads to a greater BOP deficit.
Capital account	The growing economy offers greater returns, which attracts international funds for investment.	The capital account surplus increases, which reinforces the greater BOP deficit.

When an economy is growing rapidly relative to the rest of the world, the firms in that economy are willing to pay more for investment funds. This demand for loanable funds shifts to the right and interest rates increase. Subsequently, international funds flow in to take advantage of these higher interest rates.

To clarify, let's return to the example where your coffee shop business is doing very well. One way to expand your business is to offer shares of stock in the business. People buy this stock, hoping to get in on the financial success of your great new business. The stock purchases represent a capital inflow for your business. It works in exactly the same way for nations that are growing relatively quickly: funds from around the globe flow in to take advantage of the high returns.

For a macro example, consider the case of China. In recent years, China has periodically experienced a current account deficit, largely owing to its rapid economic growth. This result seems almost counterintuitive, as the rapid Chinese growth has largely been in the area of manufacturing exports. Yet the income surge has also enabled Chinese citizens to import goods and services from all over the globe. In addition, greater returns have brought an influx of global investment funds. These effects were so strong that by late 2010, China was recording current account deficits.

Lower Personal Savings Rates

A second major cause of current account deficits is low domestic savings rates. When households are not saving much, funds can flow in from overseas to supplement domestic investment.

Let's return to the example of your coffee shop. Your business is doing well, and you are considering expansion. You decide you want to open another location for your coffee shop. If you have been frugal and saved a portion of your income, you can use your own savings to expand the business. However, if you have spent your income, you'll need to rely on the savings of others to pay for your expansion. You'll have to borrow from a bank or issue some bonds or perhaps sell shares of stock in your coffee shop business. The purchase of financial assets in your firm is analogous to capital account purchases in the balance of payments.

We can extend the analysis to a macroeconomy. If individuals and governments save a significant portion of their income, the savings can be used to fund investment. In contrast, if savings falls, investment must be funded with outside sources. In the United States, personal savings rates have dropped significantly since the early 1990s (see Figure 22.8). So while the U.S economy was growing throughout the 1990s and into the first decade of this century, the necessary financing was coming from savers around the globe. This activity increased the capital account surplus. Of course, any increase in the capital account surplus implies an increase in the current account deficit.

As we discussed in Chapter 22, the influx of funds from around the globe was instrumental in keeping interest rates low in the United States and enabling firms to fund expansion. These funds were critical as U.S. savings rates fell, but they did contribute to the widening current account deficit.

Fiscal Policy

Large budget deficits also contribute to current account deficits. This is part of the reason for large U.S. current account deficits in the 1980s and then again after 2000. Large government budget deficits devour both domestic and foreign funds. Recall this important principle from Chapter 22: *Every dollar borrowed requires a dollar saved.* So when the U.S. government borrows trillions each year, this is similar to a further reduction in personal savings: the government is using funds that could have been used for private investment.

Domestic savings are not enough to fund the budget deficit. International funds also flow in to fund the budget deficit. The influx of international funds increases the capital account surplus and thus increases the trade deficit.

Table 33.8 summarizes these different causes of trade deficits. The bottom line is that many factors cause trade deficits, some that don't even seem related to goods and services. The past few decades of U.S. experience offer examples of all three. The 1980s was a time of large budget deficits, and the trade deficit widened. Beginning around 1990, personal savings rates fell and the economy grew rapidly; the trade deficit widened, even as the federal government balanced its budget. Finally, in recent years historically large budget deficits have added to the pressure for capital inflows, reducing any prospects for elimination of the trade deficit in the near future.

TABLE 33.8

Causes of Current Account Deficits

Cause	Explanation
Rapid domestic growth	Domestic buyers are able to afford imports given the increase in wealth, which widens the current account deficit. At the same time, foreign funds are attracted to higher rates of return in the growing economy, which increases the capital account surplus.
Declining domestic savings	Falling domestic savings leaves a finance gap for investment. The gap is filled with foreign funds, which increases the capital account surplus.
Government budget deficits	Increased government borrowing means greater competition for investment funds. All else being equal, more foreign funds are needed to lend to government, and this activity widens the capital account surplus.

To Peg or Not to Peg?

Most of the United States' major trading partners allow their currency to "float," which means the market forces of supply and demand are allowed to determine the currency's exchange rate versus another. However, the United States' second-largest trading partner and the second-largest economy in the world—China—does not allow its currency to float. Rather, it "pegs" it to a specific value of the U.S. dollar. This activity has been very controversial—let's see why.

$0.14   **$0.17**

Step 1

In recent years, the yuan has had an exchange rate of between $0.14 and $0.17. If the Chinese government were not pegging the yuan, the exchange rate would be much higher.

Step 2

When the Chinese government observes the value of the yuan rising against the dollar, they print more yuan.

Step 3

The newly minted yuan are then used to purchase U.S. dollars and Treasury securities on world markets. These actions reduce the value of the yuan relative to the dollar, since the supply of yuan on the currency market increases while the supply of dollars decreases. Note that China has not declared a new exchange rate for the yuan—which is impossible for it to do— but rather has adjusted the supply of currency so that the market creates the desired outcome.

- Create a simple supply and demand graph showing how the Chinese purchase of U.S. dollars on currency markets reduces the value of the yuan.

- How do U.S. citizens benefit from the fact that China pegs its currency?

Lower prices for Chinese exports

The lower value of the yuan means a higher value of the dollar, and so Americans can afford to buy more Chinese goods and services. This stimulates the quantity of Chinese exports demanded.

Lower real wages for Chinese citizens

The main drawback for China is that the real wages of Chinese citizens decline, since the devalued yuan can purchase fewer goods worldwide.

For Rent

Higher prices for U.S. exports

China's actions reduce the quantity of U.S. exports demanded, which hurts domestic industries. This effect is what makes the Chinese monetary policy politically controversial in the United States.

Conclusion

We began this chapter with the misconception that trade deficits are harmful to an economy. But we have seen that there are many factors that affect a trade balance, and typically a trade deficit means that the domestic economy is actually doing well. Goods and service flows are interrelated with real and financial asset flows. Given this relationship, changes in personal savings rates and government budget deficits can affect trade balances.

We also studied exchange rates in this chapter and considered them as market prices that depend on the supply of and demand for foreign currency. But exchange rates are also subject to manipulation by governments. Depreciating a nation's currency makes its exports less expensive but doesn't always help all the residents of a nation.

ANSWERING THE BIG QUESTIONS

Why do exchange rates rise and fall?

* An increase in the exchange rate indicates a depreciation of the domestic currency. The exchange rate increases when there is an increase in demand for foreign goods, services, and financial assets relative to the demand for domestic goods, services, and financial assets.

* The exchange rate also increases when there is a decline in the supply of foreign currency relative to the domestic currency.

* A decrease in the exchange rate indicates an appreciation of the domestic currency. The exchange rate decreases when there is a decrease in demand for foreign goods, services, and financial assets relative to domestic goods, services, and financial assets.

* The exchange rate also falls when there is an increase in the supply of foreign currency relative to the supply of domestic currency.

What is purchasing power parity?

* Purchasing power parity (PPP) is a theory about the determinants of long-run exchange rates. PPP implies that the exchange rate between two nations is determined by a ratio of relative price levels in the two nations. If a nation experiences more inflation than its trading partners do, its exchange rate will rise, indicating a depreciation of its currency.

* PPP is based on the law of one price.

What causes trade deficits?

* Trade deficits are essentially synonymous with current account deficits. As such, they increase when the current account deficit or the capital account surplus increases.

✳ Economic growth increases the current account deficit as wealthier residents demand more imports. It also works through the capital account as higher rates of return attract foreign funds.

✳ A second cause of trade deficits is lower personal savings rates.

✳ A third cause of trade deficits is larger government budget deficits.

CONCEPTS YOU SHOULD KNOW

account deficit (p. 1081)
account surplus (p. 1081)
balance of payments (BOP)
   (p. 1079)
capital account (p. 1080)
currency appreciation (p. 1062)
currency depreciation (p. 1063)

current account (p. 1080)
derived demand (p. 1061)
exchange rate (p. 1060)
exchange rate manipulation
   (p. 1068)
flexible (floating) exchange
   rates (p. 1070)

law of one price (p. 1074)
pegged (fixed) exchange rates
   (p. 1070)
purchasing power parity (PPP)
   (p. 1074)

QUESTIONS FOR REVIEW

1. The United States imports Molson beer from Canada. Assume that Canada and the United States share the same currency and that a bottle of Molson beer costs $2 in Toronto, Canada, but just $1 in Chicago.

   a. What market adjustments will ensue in this case, assuming no shipping costs or trade barriers?
   b. If Canadians like Molson beer more than the residents of the United States do, can a price differential persist? Why or why not?

2. The United States currently has a current account deficit. How would each of the following events affect this deficit, assuming no other changes?

   a. U.S. economic growth slows relative to the rest of the world.
   b. U.S. personal savings rates increase.
   c. U.S. federal budget deficits decline.
   d. Foreign rates of return (in financial assets) rise relative to rates of return in the United States.

3. Why are current account balances generally mirror images of capital account balances?

4. Sometimes, official government reserves are singled out in the balance of payments accounts. For example, when China buys U.S. financial assets (currency and Treasury securities), this purchase is classified as "Official Government Reserves." On which side of the balance of payments should such purchases be reflected—the current account or the capital account? Explain your logic.

5. What are three factors that might make a capital account surplus grow?

6. Is a trade deficit a sign of economic weakness? Why or why not?

7. The rate of inflation in India from 2007 to 2011 was 8%. Over the same period, the inflation rate in the United States was 2.7%.

   a. What is the implication of these inflation rates for the exchange rate between the dollar and the rupee? In particular, does the PPP condition imply a rise or a fall in the exchange rate? Explain your answer.
   b. Is the change in the exchange rate an appreciation or a depreciation of the dollar? Is it an appreciation or a depreciation of the rupee?

STUDY PROBLEMS (*solved at the end of the section*)

1. If interest rates in India rise relative to interest rates around the world, how is the world value of the rupee affected? Illustrate these effects in the market for rupees.

2. From Chapter 21, we know that the primary cause of inflation is expansion of the money supply. In this chapter, we find an additional side effect of monetary expansion. What is this effect? Use demand and supply of foreign currency to illustrate your answer.

3. Explain the numerical effect on both the U.S. current account and the U.S. capital account from each of these examples.

   a. In the United States, the Best Buy company purchases $1 million worth of TVs from the Samsung corporation, a Korean firm, using U.S. dollars. In addition, Samsung keeps the U.S. dollars.
   b. Best Buy purchases $1 million worth of TVs from the Samsung corporation, using U.S. dollars. Samsung then trades its dollars to a third party for won, the Korean currency.
   c. Best Buy trades $1 million for Korean won and then uses the won to buy TVs from Samsung.

4. The price of a dozen roses in the United States is about $30. Use this information, along with the exchange rates given in Table 33.1, to answer the following questions.

   a. Assuming that PPP holds perfectly, what is the price of a dozen roses in Turkey? Express your answer in units of Turkish lira.
   b. If the actual price in Turkey costs more lira than the answer you found in part (b), how might you account for the discrepancy?

* 5. Explain why the supply curve for foreign currency is vertical. Let's say you return from a trip to Mexico with 1,000 pesos. If you decide to exchange these pesos for dollars, does your action shift the supply of pesos?

* 6. For each of the following transactions, determine whether it will be recorded in the U.S. current account or capital account and whether the entry will be positive or negative.

   a. A resident of the United States buys an airplane ticket to England on Virgin Atlantic Airways, a British company.
   b. The government of England buys U.S. Treasury securities.
   c. A U.S. citizen buys shares of stock in a Chinese corporation.

SOLVED PROBLEMS

5. The supply curve is vertical because the supply is completely controlled by the government and does not vary with changes in price. Your exchange does not shift the supply of pesos; only the government can do that. Instead, it signals a reduction in demand for pesos.

6. a. This is a purchase of a service, so it enters the current account. It enters negatively because it is an import; thus, funds are flowing out of the U.S. current account.
   b. This is a purchase of financial assets in the United States, so it is entered in the U.S. capital account. The entry is positive because funds are flowing into the capital account.
   c. This is a purchase of financial assets abroad, so it enters the U.S. capital account. It enters negatively because funds are flowing out.

GLOSSARY

absolute advantage: the ability of one producer to make more than another producer with the same quantity of resources

account deficit: condition existing when more payments are flowing out of an account than into the account

account surplus: condition existing when more payments are flowing into an account than out of the account

accounting profit: profit calculated by subtracting a firm's explicit costs from total revenue

active monetary policy: the strategic use of monetary policy to counteract macroeconomic expansions and contractions

adaptive expectations theory: the theory that people's expectations of future inflation are based on their most recent experience

adverse selection: phenomenon existing when one party has information about some aspect of product quality that the other party does not have

aggregate consumption function: an equation that specifies the relationship between national income and national consumption

aggregate demand: the total demand for final goods and services in an economy

aggregate expenditures (AE) model: a short-run model of economic fluctuations that holds that prices are completely sticky (inflexible) and that aggregate demand (aggregate expenditures) determines the economy's level of output and income

aggregate production function: the relationship between all the inputs used in the macroeconomy and the total output (GDP) of that economy

aggregate supply: the total supply of final goods and services in an economy

antitrust laws: laws that attempt to prevent collusion (that is, prevent oligopolies from behaving like monopolies)

assets: the items that a firm owns

asymmetric information: an imbalance in information that occurs when one party knows more than the other

austerity: policy involving strict budget regulations aimed at debt reduction

automatic consumption spending: spending on consumption that is independent of the level of income

automatic stabilizers: government programs that automatically implement countercyclical fiscal policy in response to economic conditions

average fixed cost (AFC): an amount determined by dividing a firm's total fixed costs by the output

average tax rate: the total tax paid divided by the amount of taxable income

average total cost (ATC): the sum of average variable cost and average fixed cost

average variable cost (AVC): an amount determined by dividing a firm's total variable costs by the output

backward-bending labor supply curve: supply curve occurring when workers value additional leisure more than additional income

backward induction: in game theory, the process of deducing backward from the end of a scenario to infer a sequence of optimal actions

balance of payments (BOP): a record of all payments between one nation and the rest of the world

balance sheet: an accounting statement that summarizes a firm's key financial information

bank run: event occurring when many depositors attempt to withdraw their funds from a bank at the same time

barriers to entry: restrictions that make it difficult for new firms to enter a market

barter: the trade of a good or service without a commonly accepted medium of exchange

behavioral economics: the field of economics that draws on insights from experimental psychology to explore how people make economic decisions

black markets: illegal markets that arise when price controls are in place

bond: a security that represents a debt to be paid; an IOU that joins two parties in a contract that specifies the conditions for repayment of a loan, where typically a firm or government the borrower and typically an individual is the lender

bounded rationality: the concept that although decision-makers want a good outcome, either they are not capable of performing the problem solving that traditional theory assumes or they are not inclined to do so; also called limited reasoning

budget constraint: the set of consumption bundles that represent the maximum amount the consumer can afford

budget deficit: condition occurring when government outlays exceed revenue

budget surplus: condition occurring when government revenue exceeds outlays

business cycle: a short-run fluctuation in economic activity

cap and trade: an approach used to curb pollution by creating a system of emissions permits that are traded in an open market

capital account: the balance of payments account that tracks payments for real and financial assets between nations and extensions of international loans

capital gains taxes: taxes on the gains realized by selling an asset for more than its purchase price

capital goods: goods that help produce other valuable goods and services in the future

cartel: a group of two or more firms that act in unison

causality: condition existing when one variable influences another

ceteris paribus: meaning "other things being equal," the concept under which economists examine a change in one variable while holding everything else constant

chained CPI: a measure of the consumer price index in which the typical consumer's "basket" of goods and services considered is updated monthly

checkable deposits: deposits in bank accounts from which depositors may make withdrawals by writing checks

classical economists: economists who stress the importance of aggregate supply and generally believe that the economy can adjust back to full-employment equilibrium on its own

Clayton Act: law of 1914 targeting corporate behaviors that reduce competition

club good: a good with two characteristics: it is nonrival in consumption and excludable

Coase theorem: theorem stating that if there are no barriers to negotiations, and if property rights are fully specified, interested parties will bargain to correct externalities

coinsurance payments: a percentage of costs that the insured must pay after exceeding the insurance policy's deductible up to the policy's contribution limit

collusion: an agreement among rival firms that specifies the price each firm charges and the quantity it produces

commodity-backed money: money that can be exchanged for a commodity at a fixed rate

commodity money: the use of an actual good in place of money

common-resource good: a good with two characteristics: it is rival in consumption and nonexcludable

comparative advantage: the situation where an individual, business, or country can produce at a lower opportunity cost than a competitor can

compensating differential: the difference in wages offered to offset the desirability or undesirability of a job

competitive market: a market in which there are so many buyers and sellers that each has only a small (negligible) impact on the market price and output

complements: two goods that are used together; when the price of a complementary good rises, the demand for the related good goes down

compounding: (1) in the context of borrowing money, the situation in which interest is added to an account balance so that the borrower ends up paying interest on an increasingly higher balance; (2) in the context of saving, the situation in which interest is added to the total savings so that you get paid interest on your savings plus any prior interest earned

constant returns to scale: condition occurring when long-run average costs remain constant as output expands

consumer goods: goods produced for present consumption

consumer optimum: the combination of goods and services that maximizes the consumer's utility for a given income or budget

consumer price index (CPI): a measure of the price level based on the consumption patterns of a typical consumer

consumer surplus: the difference between the willingness to pay for a good (or service) and the price that is paid to get it

consumption: the purchase of final goods and services by households, excluding new housing

consumption smoothing: behavior occurring when people borrow and save to smooth consumption

contractionary fiscal policy: a decrease in government spending or increase in taxes to slow economic expansion

convergence: the idea that per capita GDP levels across nations will equalize as nations approach the steady state

copayments: fixed amounts that the insured must pay when receiving a medical service or filling a prescription

cost-benefit analysis: a process that economists use to determine whether the benefits of providing a public good outweigh the costs

countercyclical fiscal policy: fiscal policy that seeks to counteract business cycle fluctuations

CPI: see *consumer price index*

creative destruction: the introduction of new products and technologies that leads to the end of other industries and jobs

credit history: a record of an individual's loan and payment history

credit report: a financial report card that reports your credit history (your ability to repay your loans)

cross-price elasticity of demand: measurement of the responsiveness of the quantity demanded of one good to a change in the price of a related good

crowding-out: phenomenon occurring when private spending falls in response to increases in government spending

currency: the paper bills and coins that are used to buy goods and services

currency appreciation: a currency's increase in value relative to other currencies

currency depreciation: a currency's decrease in value relative to other currencies

current account: the balance of payments account that tracks all payments for goods and services, current income from investments, and gifts

cyclical unemployment: unemployment caused by economic downturns

deadweight loss: the decrease in economic activity caused by market distortions

debt: the sum total of all accumulated and unpaid budget deficits

decision tree: diagram that illustrates all of the possible outcomes in a sequential game

deductibles: fixed amounts that the insured must pay before most of the policy's benefits can be applied

default risk: the risk that a borrower will not pay the face value of a bond on the maturity date

deflation: condition occurring when overall prices fall

demand curve: a graph of the relationship between the prices in the demand schedule and the quantity demanded at those prices

demand schedule: a table that shows the relationship between the price of a good and the quantity demanded

depreciation: a fall in the value of an asset over time

derived demand: the demand for an input used in the production process

diamond-water paradox: concept explaining why water, which is essential to life, is inexpensive, while diamonds, which do not sustain life, are expensive

diminishing marginal product: condition occurring when successive increases in inputs are associated with a slower rise in output

diminishing marginal utility: condition occurring when marginal utility declines as consumption increases

direct finance: activity in the loanable funds market when borrowers go directly to savers for funds

discount loans: loans from the Federal Reserve to private banks

discount rate: the interest rate on the discount loans made by the Federal Reserve to private banks

discouraged workers: those who are not working, have looked for a job in the past 12 months and are willing to work, but have not sought employment in the past 4 weeks

discretionary outlays: government spending that can be altered when the government is setting its annual budget

diseconomies of scale: condition occurring when long-run average costs rise as output expands

disposable income: income after taxes

dissaving: withdrawing funds from previously accumulated savings

dividend: a cash payment to stockholders for each share of stock owned

Dodd-Frank Act: the primary regulatory response to the financial turmoil that contributed to the Great Recession, enacted in 2010

dominant strategy: in game theory, a strategy that a player will always prefer, regardless of what his opponent chooses

double coincidence of wants: condition occurring when each party in an exchange transaction happens to have what the other party desires

dumping: behavior occurring when a foreign supplier sells a good below the price it charges in its home country

economic contraction: a phase of the business cycle during which economic activity is decreasing

economic expansion: a phase of the business cycle during which economic activity is increasing

economic growth: the percentage change in real per capita GDP

economic profit: profit calculated by subtracting both the explicit and the implicit costs of business from a firm's total revenue

economic rent: the difference between what a factor of production earns and what it could earn in the next-best alternative

economics: the study of how individuals and society allocate their limited resources to satisfy their unlimited wants

economic thinking: a purposeful evaluation of the available opportunities to make the best decision possible

economies of scale: condition occurring when long-run average costs decline as output expands

efficiency wages: wages higher than equilibrium wages, offered to increase worker productivity

efficient: describing an outcome when allocation of resources maximizes total surplus

efficient scale: the output level that minimizes average total cost in the long run

elasticity: a measure of the responsiveness of buyers and sellers to changes in price or income

endogenous factors: the variables that can be controlled for in a model

endogenous growth: growth driven by factors inside the economy

equation of exchange: an equation that specifies the long-run relationship between the money supply, the price level, real GDP, and the velocity of money

equilibrium: condition occurring at the point where the demand curve and the supply curve intersect

equilibrium price: the price at which the quantity supplied is equal to the quantity demanded; also known as the *market-clearing price*

equilibrium quantity: the amount at which the quantity supplied is equal to the quantity demanded

equity: (1) the fairness of the distribution of benefits among the members of a society; (2) the part of an asset that you own; in the case of a house, the part of the selling price you get to keep after paying off the balance on your mortgage

excess capacity: phenomenon occurring when a firm produces at an output level that is smaller than the output level needed to minimize average total costs

excess reserves: any reserves held by a bank in excess of those required

exchange rate: the price of foreign currency, indicating how much a unit of foreign currency costs in terms of another currency

exchange rate manipulation: a national government's intentional adjustment of its money supply to affect the exchange rate of its currency

excise taxes: taxes levied on a particular good or service

excludable good: a good that the consumer must purchase before having access to it

exogenous factors: the variables that cannot be controlled for in a model

exogenous growth: growth that is independent of any factors in the economy

expansionary fiscal policy: an increase in government spending or decrease in taxes to stimulate the economy toward expansion

expansionary monetary policy: a central bank's action to increase the money supply in an effort to stimulate the economy

explicit costs: tangible out-of-pocket expenses

external costs: the costs of a market activity imposed on people who are not participants in that market

externalities: the costs or benefits of a market activity that affect a third party

face value: the value of a bond at maturity—the amount due at repayment; also called *par value*

factors of production: the inputs (labor, land, and capital) used in producing goods and services

federal funds: deposits that private banks hold on reserve at the Federal Reserve

federal funds rate: the interest rate on loans between private banks

fiat money: money that has no value except as the medium of exchange; there is no inherent or intrinsic value

final goods: goods sold to final users

financial intermediaries: firms that help to channel funds from savers to borrowers

fiscal policy: the use of government's budget tools, government spending, and taxes to influence the macroeconomy

Fisher equation: equation stating that the real interest rate equals the nominal interest rate minus the inflation rate

fixed costs: costs that do not vary with a firm's output in the short run; also known as overhead

fixed exchange rates: see *pegged (fixed) exchange rates*

fixed interest rate: an interest rate that remains in effect for the full term of a loan

flexible (floating) exchange rates: exchange rates that are determined by the supply of and demand for currency; also called floating exchange rates

floating exchange rates: see *flexible (floating) exchange rates*

fractional reserve banking: a system in which banks hold only a fraction of deposits on reserve

framing effect: a phenomenon seen when people change their answer depending on how the question is asked (or change their decision depending on how alternatives are presented)

free-rider problem: phenomenon occurring when someone receives a benefit without having to pay for it

frictional unemployment: unemployment caused by delays in matching available jobs and workers

full-employment output: the output level produced in an economy when the unemployment rate is equal to the natural rate

gambler's fallacy: the belief that recent outcomes are unlikely to be repeated and that outcomes that have not occurred recently are due to happen soon

game theory: a branch of mathematics that economists use to analyze the strategic behavior of decision-makers

GDP: see *gross domestic product (GDP)*

GDP deflator: a measure of the price level that is used to calculate real GDP

Gini index: a measurement of the income distribution of a nation's residents

GNP: see *gross national product(GNP)*

government outlays: the part of the government budget that includes both spending and transfer payments

government spending: spending by all levels of government on final goods and services

Great Recession: the U.S. recession lasting from December 2007 to June 2009

gross domestic product (GDP): the market value of all final goods and services produced within a country during a specific period

gross national product (GNP): the output produced by workers and resources owned by residents of the nation

growth stock: a stock in a company that is expected to grow and become profitable

hot hand fallacy: the belief that random sequences exhibit a positive correlation

human capital: the set of skills that workers acquire on the job and through education

immediate run: a period of time when there is no time for consumers to adjust their behavior

imperfect market: a market in which either the buyer or the seller has an influence on the market price

implicit costs: the costs of resources already owned, for which no out-of-pocket payment is made

import quotas: limits on the quantity of products that can be imported into a country

incentives: factors that motivate a person to exert effort

incidence: the burden of taxation on the party who pays the tax through higher prices, regardless of whom the tax is actually levied on

income effect: phenomenon occurring when laborers work fewer hours at higher wages, using their additional income to demand more leisure

income elasticity of demand: measurement of how a change in income affects spending

income inequality ratio: ratio calculated by dividing the top quintile's income percentage by the bottom quintile's income percentage

income mobility: the ability of workers to move up or down the economic ladder over time

income stock: a stock that pays a predictable dividend over a relatively long period

indifference curve: a graph representing the various combinations of two goods that yield the same level of personal satisfaction, or utility

indirect finance: activity in the loanable funds market when savers deposit funds into banks, which then loan these funds to borrowers

individual retirement account (IRA): a retirement savings account that provides tax incentives to promote saving

infant industry argument: the idea that domestic industries need trade protection until they are established and able to compete internationally

inferior good: a good purchased out of necessity rather than choice

inflation: the growth in the overall level of prices in an economy

in-kind transfers: transfers (mostly to the poor) in the form of goods or services instead of cash

inputs: the resources (labor, land, and capital) used in the production process

institution: a significant practice, relationship, or organization in a society

interest rate: a price of loanable funds, quoted as a percentage of the original loan amount; the price a borrower pays to a lender to use the lender's money

interest rate effect: effect occurring when a change in the price level leads to a change in interest rates and therefore in the quantity of aggregate demand

intermediate goods: goods that firms repackage or bundle with other goods for sale at a later stage

internal costs: the costs of a market activity paid only by an individual participant

internalize: relating to a firm's handling of externalities, to take into account the external costs (or benefits) to society that occur as a result of the firm's actions

international trade effect: effect occurring when a change in the price level leads to a change in the quantity of net exports demanded

intertemporal decision-making: planning to do something over a period of time, which requires valuing the present and the future consistently

investment: the process of using resources to create or buy new capital

investment-grade bonds: bonds that pay lower interest rates but are issued by companies that are very likely to repay their creditors

investor confidence: a measure of what firms expect for future economic activity

invisible hand: a phrase coined by Adam Smith to refer to the unobservable market forces that guide resources to their highest-valued use

junk bonds: bonds that pay higher interest rates but are considered speculative

Keynesian economists: economists who stress the importance of aggregate demand and generally believe that the economy needs help in moving back to full-employment equilibrium

kinked demand curve: the theory that oligopolists have a greater tendency to respond aggressively to the price cuts of rivals but will largely ignore price increases

labor force: those who are already employed or actively seeking work and are part of the work-eligible population

labor force participation rate: the percentage of the work-eligible population that is in the labor force

Laffer curve: an illustration of the relationship between tax rates and tax revenue

law of demand: the law that, all other things being equal, quantity demanded falls when the price rises, and rises when the price falls

law of increasing opportunity cost: law stating that the opportunity cost of producing a good rises as a society produces more of it

law of one price: law stating that after accounting for transportation costs and trade barriers, identical goods sold in different locations must sell for the same price

law of supply: the law that, all other things being equal, the quantity supplied of a good rises when the price of the good rises, and falls when the price of the good falls

law of supply and demand: the law that the market price of any good will adjust to bring the quantity supplied and the quantity demanded into balance

liabilities: the financial obligations a firm owes to others

life-cycle wage pattern: the predictable effect that age has on earnings over the course of a person's working life

line of credit: the maximum amount that a lender is willing to lend to a borrower

loanable funds market: the market where savers supply funds for loans to borrowers

long run: (1) in microeconomics, the period of time when consumers make decisions that reflect their long-term wants, needs, or limitations and have time to fully adjust to market conditions; (2) in macroeconomics, a period of time sufficient for all prices to adjust

loss: the result when total revenue is less than total cost

M1: the money supply measure that is essentially composed of currency, checkable deposits, and traveler's checks

M2: the money supply measure that includes everything in M1 plus savings deposits, money market mutual funds, and small-denomination time deposits (CDs)

macroeconomic policy: government acts to influence the macroeconomy

macroeconomics: the study of the overall aspects and workings of an economy

mandatory outlays: government spending that is determined by ongoing programs like Social Security and Medicare; sometimes called entitlement programs

marginal cost (MC): the increase in cost that occurs from producing one additional unit of output

marginal product: the change in output associated with one additional unit of an input

marginal product of labor: the change in output associated with adding one additional worker

marginal propensity to consume (MPC): the portion of additional income that is spent on consumption

marginal propensity to save (MPS): the portion of additional income that is saved

marginal rate of substitution (MRS): the rate at which a consumer is willing to trade one good for another along an indifference curve

marginal tax rate: the tax rate paid on an individual's next dollar of income

marginal revenue: the change in total revenue a firm receives when it produces one additional unit of output

marginal thinking: the evaluation of whether the benefit of one more unit of something is greater than its cost

marginal utility: the additional satisfaction derived from consuming one more unit of a good or service

market-clearing price: see *equilibrium price*

market demand: the sum of all the individual quantities demanded by each buyer in the market at each price

market economy: an economy in which resources are allocated among households and firms with little or no government interference

market failure: condition occurring when there is an inefficient allocation of resources in a market

market power: a firm's ability to influence the price of a good or service by exercising control over its demand, supply, or both

markets: systems that bring buyers and sellers together to exchange goods and services

market supply: the sum of the quantities supplied by each seller in the market at each price

markup: the difference between the price the firm charges and the marginal cost of production

maturity date: on a bond, the date in the future when the loan repayment is due

maximization point: the point at which a certain combination of two goods yields the most utility

Medicare: a mandated U.S. federal program that funds health care people age 65 and older

medium of exchange: what people trade for goods and services

menu costs: the costs of changing prices

microeconomics: the study of the individual units that make up the economy

minimum payment: the smallest amount that a lender requires a borrower to pay each month so as not to damage the borrower's credit score

minimum wage: the lowest hourly wage rate that firms may legally pay their workers

monetary neutrality: the idea that the money supply does not affect real economic variables

monetary policy: the government's adjustment of the money supply to influence the macroeconomy

money illusion: the interpretation of nominal changes in wages or prices as real changes

monopolistic competition: a type of market structure characterized by free entry, many different firms, and product differentiation

monopoly: condition existing when a single company supplies the entire market for a particular good or service

monopoly power: measure of a monopolist's ability to set the price of a good

monopsony: a situation in which there is only one buyer

moral hazard: the lack of incentive to guard against risk where one is protected from its consequences

mutual interdependence: a market situation where the actions of one firm have an impact on the price and output of its competitors

mutual fund: an investment program that trades in diversified holdings and is professionally managed

Nash equilibrium: a phenomenon occurring when all economic decision-makers opt to keep the status quo

natural monopoly: the situation that occurs when a single large firm has lower costs than any potential smaller competitor

natural rate of unemployment: the typical rate of unemployment that occurs when the economy is growing normally

negative correlation: condition occurring when two variables move in opposite directions

negative unplanned investment: the situation when actual sales exceed anticipated sales, leading to a decrease in inventory

net exports: total exports of final goods and services minus total imports of final goods and services

net investment: investment minus depreciation

network externality: condition occurring when the number of customers who purchase or use a good influences the quantity demanded

new classical critique: the assertion that increases in government spending and decreases in taxes are largely offset by increases in savings

nominal GDP: GDP measured in current prices and not adjusted for inflation

nominal interest rate: the interest rate before it is corrected for inflation

nominal wage: a worker's wage expressed in current dollars

normal good: a good consumers buy more of as income rises, holding other things constant

normative statement: an opinion that cannot be tested or validated; it describes "what ought to be"

occupational crowding: the phenomenon of relegating a group of workers to a narrow range of jobs in the economy

oligopoly: a form of market structure that exists when a small number of firms sell a differentiated product in a market with high barriers to entry

open market operations: operations involving the purchase or sale of bonds by a central bank

opportunity cost: the highest-valued alternative that must be sacrificed to get something else

output: the product that the firm creates

output effect: how a change in price affects the number of customers in a market

outsourcing of labor: a firm's shifting of jobs to an outside company, usually overseas, where the cost of labor is lower

owner's equity: the difference between a firm's assets and its liabilities

par value: the value of a bond at maturity—the amount due at repayment; also called *face value*

passive monetary policy: a central bank's use of monetary policy only to stabilize money and price levels

payday loan: a short-term loan in which the borrower writes the lender a check against an upcoming paycheck and the lender waits until the borrower's payday to cash the check

pegged (fixed) exchange rates: exchange rates that are fixed at a certain level through the actions of a government

pension: an employer-funded retirement plan

per capita GDP: GDP per person

perfect complements: two goods the consumer is interested in consuming in fixed proportions, resulting in a right-angle indifference curve

perfect price discrimination: the practice of selling the same good or service at a unique price to every customer

perfect substitutes: goods that the consumer is completely indifferent between, resulting in a straight-line indifference curve with a constant marginal rate of substitution

Phillips curve: curve indicating a short-run negative relationship between inflation and unemployment rates

positive correlation: condition occurring when two variables move in the same direction

positive statement: an assertion that can be tested and validated; it describes "what is"

poverty rate: the percentage of the population whose income is below the poverty threshold

poverty threshold: the income level below which a person or family is considered impoverished

PPP: see *purchasing power parity*

predatory pricing: the practice of a firm deliberately setting its prices below average variable costs with the intent of driving rivals out of the market

preference reversal: phenomenon arising when risk tolerance is not consistent

price ceiling: a legally established maximum price for a good or service

price controls: an attempt to set prices through government involvement in the market

price discrimination: the practice of selling the same good or service at different prices to different groups

price effect: how a change in price affects the firm's revenue

price elasticity of demand: a measure of the responsiveness of quantity demanded to a change in price

price elasticity of supply: a measure of the responsiveness of the quantity supplied to a change in price; sometimes called elasticity of supply or supply elasticity

price floor: a legally established minimum price for a good or service

price gouging laws: temporary ceilings on the prices that sellers can charge during times of emergency

price leadership: phenomenon occurring when a dominant firm in an industry sets the price that maximizes profits and the smaller firms in the industry follow by setting their prices to match the price leader

price level: an index of the average prices of goods and services throughout the economy

price maker: a firm with some control over the price it charges

price taker: a firm with no control over the price set by the market

priming effect: phenomenon seen when the order of the questions influences the answers

principal-agent problem: a situation in which a principal entrusts an agent to complete a task and the agent does not do so in a satisfactory way

principal amount: the total amount of money borrowed

prisoner's dilemma: a situation in which decision-makers face incentives that make it difficult to achieve mutually beneficial outcomes

private good: a good with two characteristics: it is both excludable and rival in consumption

private property: provision of an exclusive right of ownership that allows for the use, and especially the exchange, of property

private property rights: the rights of individuals to own property, to use it in production, and to own the resulting output

producer surplus: the difference between the price that the seller receives and the price at which the seller is willing to sell a good or service

product differentiation: the process that firms use to make a product more attractive to potential customers

production function: the relationship between the inputs a firm uses and the output it creates

production possibilities frontier: a model that illustrates the combinations of outputs that a society can produce if all of its resources are being used efficiently

productivity: the effectiveness of effort as measured in terms of the rate of output per unit of input

profit: the total result when revenue is higher than total cost

profit-maximizing rule: the rule stating that profit maximization occurs when a firm chooses the quantity of output that causes marginal revenue to be equal to marginal cost, or MR = MC

progressive income tax system: income tax system in which people with higher incomes pay a larger portion of their income in taxes than people with lower incomes do

property rights: an owner's ability to exercise control over a resource

prospect theory: a theory suggesting that individuals weigh the utilities and risks of gains and losses differently

protectionism: a blanket term for government actions and policies that restrict or restrain international trade, often with the intent of protecting local businesses and jobs from foreign competition

public good: a good that can be jointly consumed by more than one person, and from which nonpayers are difficult to exclude

purchasing power: the value of your income expressed in terms of how much you can afford

purchasing power parity (PPP): the idea that a unit of currency should be able to buy the same quantity of goods and services in any country

quantitative easing: the targeted use of open market operations in which the central bank buys securities specifically targeting certain markets

quantity demanded: the amount of a good or service that buyers are willing and able to purchase at the current price

quantity supplied: the amount of a good or service that producers are willing and able to sell at the current price

rational expectations theory: the theory that people form expectations on the basis of all available information

real GDP: GDP adjusted for changes in prices

real-income effect: a change in purchasing power as a result of a change in the price of a good

real interest rate: the interest rate that is corrected for inflation

real wage: the nominal wage adjusted for changes in the price level

recession: a short-term economic downturn

rent control: a price ceiling that applies to the market for apartment rentals

rent seeking: Using resources to secure monopoly rights through the political process

required reserve ratio: the portion of deposits that banks are required to keep on reserve

reserves: the portion of bank deposits that are set aside and not loaned out

resources: the inputs used to produce goods and services; also called *factors of production*

reverse causation: condition occurring when causation is incorrectly assigned among associated events

risk-averse people: those who prefer a sure thing over a gamble with a higher expected value

risk-neutral people: those who choose the highest expected value regardless of the risk

risk-takers: those who prefer gambles with lower expected values, and potentially higher winnings, over a sure thing

rival good: a good that cannot be enjoyed by more than one person at a time

Roth IRA: an individual retirement account in which gains are not taxed at the time of withdrawal

rule of 70: rule stating that if the annual growth rate of a variable is x%, the size of that variable doubles approximately every $70 \div x$ years

samaritan's dilemma: a situation in which charity creates disincentives for recipients to take care of themselves

savings rate: personal saving as a portion of disposable (after-tax) income

scale: the size of the production process

scarcity: the limited nature of society's resources, given society's unlimited wants and needs

scatterplot: a graph that shows individual (x,y) points

secondary markets: markets in which securities are traded after their first sale

securitization: the creation of a new security by combining otherwise separate loan agreements

securitized loan: a loan in which a borrower's asset serves as collateral

security: a tradable contract that entitles its owner to certain rights

services: outputs that provide benefits without producing a tangible product

Sherman Antitrust Act: the first federal law (1890) limiting cartels and monopolies

shoe-leather costs: the resources that are wasted when people change their behavior to avoid holding money

shortage: market condition when the quantity supplied of a good is less than the quantity demanded; also called *excess demand*

short run: (1) in microeconomics, the period of time when consumers can make decisions that reflect their short-term wants, needs, or limitations and can partially adjust their behavior; (2) in macroeconomics, the period of time in which some prices have not yet adjusted

signals: information conveyed by profits and losses about the profitability of various markets

simple money multiplier: the rate at which banks multiply money when all currency is deposited into banks and they hold no excess reserves

single-payer system: government coverage of most healthcare costs, with citizens paying their share through taxes

slope: the change in the rise along the y axis (vertical) divided by the change in the run along the x axis (horizontal)

social costs: the sum of the internal costs and external costs of a market activity

social optimum: the price and quantity combination that would exist if there were no externalities

Social Security: a U.S. government-administered retirement funding program

social welfare: see *total surplus*

specialization: limiting one's work to a particular area

spending multiplier: a number that tells us the total impact on spending from an initial change of a given amount

stagflation: the combination of high unemployment rates and high inflation

status quo bias: condition existing when decision-makers want to maintain their current choices

steady state: the condition of a macroeconomy when there is no new net investment

strike: a work stoppage designed to aid a union's bargaining position

stocks: ownership shares in a firm

store of value: a means for holding wealth

structural unemployment: unemployment caused by changes in the industrial makeup (structure) of the economy

subsidy: a payment made by the government to encourage the consumption or production of a good or service

substitutes: goods that are used in place of each other; when the price of a substitute good rises, the quantity demanded of that good falls and the demand for the related good goes up

substitution effect: (1) the decision by laborers to work more hours at higher wages, substituting labor for leisure; (2) a consumer's substitution of a product that has become relatively less expensive as the result of a price change

sunk costs: unrecoverable costs that have been incurred as a result of past decisions

supply curve: a graph of the relationship between the prices in the supply schedule and the quantity supplied at those prices

supply schedule: a table that shows the relationship between the price of a good and the quantity supplied

supply shocks: surprise events that change a firm's production costs

supply-side fiscal policy: policy that involves the use of government spending and taxes to affect the production (supply) side of the economy

surplus: market condition when the quantity supplied of a good is greater than the quantity demanded; also called *excess supply*

switching costs: the costs incurred when a consumer changes from one supplier to another

tariffs: taxes levied on imported goods and services

technological advancement: the introduction of new techniques or methods so that firms can produce more valuable outputs per unit of input

technology: the knowledge that is available for use in production

third-party problem: a situation in which those not directly involved in a market activity experience negative or positive externalities

time preferences: the fact that people prefer to receive goods and services sooner rather than later

tit-for-tat: a long-run strategy that promotes cooperation among participants by mimicking the opponent's most recent decision with repayment in kind

total cost: the amount a firm spends to produce and/or sell goods and services

total revenue: the amount a firm receives from the sale of goods and services

total surplus: the sum of consumer surplus and producer surplus; a measure of the well-being of all participants in a market, absent any government intervention; also known as *social welfare*

trade: the voluntary exchange of goods and services between two or more parties

trade balance: the difference between a nation's total exports and total imports

trade deficit: condition occurring when imports exceed exports, indicating a negative trade balance

trade surplus: condition occurring when exports exceed imports, indicating a positive trade balance

tragedy of the commons: the depletion of a good that is rival in consumption but nonexcludable

transfer payments: payments made to groups or individuals when no good or service is received in return

Treasury securities: the bonds sold by the U.S. government to pay for the national debt

ultimatum game: an economic experiment in which two players decide how to divide a sum of money

underemployed workers: those who have part-time jobs but who would prefer to work full-time

underground economies: markets in which goods or services are traded illegally

unemployment: condition occurring when a worker who is not currently employed is searching for a job without success

unemployment insurance: a government program that reduces the hardship of joblessness by guaranteeing that unemployed workers receive a percentage of their former income while unemployed; also known as federal jobless benefits

unemployment rate: the percentage of the labor force that is unemployed

union: a group of workers who bargain collectively for better wages and benefits

unit of account: the measure in which prices are

unplanned investment: positive unplanned investment; the situation when expected sales exceed actual sales, leading to an increase in inventory

util: a personal unit of satisfaction used to measure the enjoyment from consumption of a good or service

utility: a measure of the level of satisfaction that a consumer enjoys from the consumption of goods and services

value of the marginal product (VMP): the marginal product of an input multiplied by the price of the output it produces

variable: a quantity that can take on more than one value

variable costs: costs that change with the rate of output

variable interest rate: an interest rate that can change based on market conditions or the borrower's creditworthiness

velocity of money: the number of times a unit of money exchanges hands in a given year

wage discrimination: unequal payment of workers because of their race, ethnic origin, sex, age, religion, or some other group characteristic

wealth: the net value of one's accumulated assets

wealth effect: the change in the quantity of aggregate demand that results from wealth changes due to price-level changes

welfare economics: the branch of economics that studies how the allocation of resources affects economic well-being

willingness to pay: the maximum price a consumer will pay for a good; also called the reservation price

willingness to sell: the minimum price a seller will accept to sell a good or service

winner-take-all: phenomenon occurring when extremely small differences in ability lead to sizable differences in compensation

CREDITS

Shutterstock.com; Pg. 234 (top): Stockbyte/Getty Images; Pg. 234 (bottom): Karl Dolenc/iStockphoto; Pg. 235: NASA/Goddard Space Flight Center; Pg. 236 (top): Stephanie Keith/Polaris/Newscom; Pg. 236 (bottom): kali9/iStockphoto; Pg. 237: June M Sobrito|Dreamstime.com;

CHAPTER 8

Pg. 242: Geoffrey Kidd/Alamy; Pg. 245: Marc F. Henning/Alamy; Pg. 246: Photoshot/ Newscom; Pg. 247: ZITS 2002 ZITS PARTNERSHIP, KING FEATURES SYNDICATE; Pg. 250: YinYang/ iStockphoto.com; Pg. 251: Justin Sullivan/Getty Images; Pg. 255: San Antonio Express-News/ZUMA Press/Newscom; Pg. 260: FOXTROT (2005) Bill Amend. Reprinted with permission of UNIVERSAL UCLICK. All rights reserved; Pg. 261: Mitch Haaseth/NBC-TV/The Kobal Collection; Pg. 262: John Verner/iStockphoto. com; Pg. 263 (top): Sandra Nicol/iStockphoto.com; Pg. 263 (bottom): JillKyle/iStockphoto.com; Pg. 264: Sandra Nicol/iStockphoto.com; JillKyle/iStockphoto. com; John Verner/iStockphoto.com; Pg. 266: Monty Brinton/CBS via Getty Images; Pg. 267: Antonio Jodice|Dreamstime.com; Pg. 269: Columbia/courtesy Everett Collection.

CHAPTER 9

Pg. 275: Graça Victoria|Dreamstime.com; Pg. 277 (top): Neilson Barnard/iStockphoto.com; Pg. 277 (2nd down): Manon Ringuette|Dreamstime.com; Pg. 277 (3rd down): Raine Vara/Alamy; Pg. 277 (bottom): Russell Shively/iStockphoto.com; Pg. 278: Michel Porro/ Getty Images; Pg. 279: Henry M. Trotter/Wikimedia Commons; Pg. 281: Michael Shake|Dreamstime.com; Pg. 282: 20th Century Fox. All rights reserved/courtesy Everett Collection; Pg. 284: Courtesy of Dirk Mateer; Pg. 289 (top): TRIPPLAAR KRISTOFFER/SIPA/Newscom; Pg. 289 (bottom): Laura Farr/Time Life Pictures/Getty Images; Pg. 290: Alexandr Mitiuc|Dreamstime.com; Pg. 294 (top): Judy Ledbetter/iStockphoto.com; Pg. 294 (bottom): adrian beesley/iStockphoto.com; Pg. 297: hywit dimyadi/iStockphoto.com; Pg. 299: CBS-TV /The Kobal Collection/Art Resource, NY; Pg. 300: Chrisyates|Dreamstime.com; Pg. 302: DNY59/ iStockphoto.com.

CHAPTER 10

Pg. 309: kali9/iStockphoto.com; Pg. 312: ROBYN BECK/AFP/Getty Images; Pg. 313: Michelle Del Guercio/Photo Researchers/Getty Images; Pg. 314: Howard Harrison/Alamy; Pg. 315: PARAMOUNT

PICTURES/Album/Newscom; Pg. 321: Tom Strickland/Bloomberg via Getty Images; Pg. 322: Colonel/Getty Images; Pg. 325 (top left): AP Photo/ Ric Feld; Pg. 325 (top right): AP Photo/Jessica Hill; Pg. 325 (bottom): Paul Souders/Getty Images; Pg. 326 (left): Debbi Smirnoff/iStockphoto.com; Pg. 326 (right): jfmdesign/iStockphoto; Pg. 327: rabbit75/ iStockphoto.com; Pg. 328: ONE MAN BAND, 2005. Buena Vista Pictures/courtesy Everett Collection; Pg. 330: AFP/Getty Images/Newscom; Pg. 334: John Mutrux/MCT/Newscom.

CHAPTER 11

Pg. 339: Arne9001|Dreamstime.com; Pg. 343 (top): Nacivet/Photographer's Choice/Getty Images; Pg. 343 (bottom): FOXTROT (2006) Bill Amend. Reprinted with permission of UNIVERSAL UCLICK. All rights reserved.; Pg. 345: Weldon Schloneger/Shutterstock. com; Pg. 347: M.G.M/TRACY BENNETT/Album/ Newscom; Pg. 348: Cynthia Farmer|Dreamstime.com; Pg. 349: vau902/iStockphoto.com; Pg. 351: Kyoungil Jeon/iStockphoto.com; Pg. 352: Photo by Dirk Mateer; Pg. 353: Benkrut|Dreamstime.com; Pg. 355: Jason DeCrow/Invision for SUBWAY Restaurants/AP Images; Pg. 356: TLC/Courtesy of Everett Collection/ Everett Collection; Pg. 358: AP Photo/Charles Agel.

CHAPTER 12

Pg. 363: ZUMA Press/Newscom; Pg. 366 (top left): swalls/i-Stock.com; Pg. 366 (top right): Marcnorman|Dreamstime.com; Pg. 366 (bottom): TravelCollection/Alamy Stock Photo; Pg. 372: ShutterWorx/iStockphoto.com; Pg. 374 (top): Monkey Business Images|Dreamstime.com; Pg. 374 (bottom): Serafino Mozzo/iStockphoto; Pg. 375: Courtesy of Anheuser-Busch; Pg. 377 (top): wsfurlan/istockphoto.com; Pg. 377 (2nd row): Anthony Seebaran/iStockphoto; Pg. 377 (3rd row): Stanley Marquardt/Alamy; Pg. 377 (4th row): AP Photo/Tom Gannam; Pg. 377 (5th row): Lynn Watson|Dreamstime.com; Pg. 377 (6th row): Carlos Gawronski/iStockphoto; Pg. 377 (bottom): David Paul Morris/Bloomberg via Getty Images; Pg. 379 (top): Universal/The Kobal Collection/Art Resource, NY; Pg. 379 (bottom): PEANUTS 1966 Peanuts Worldwide LLC. Dist. By UNIVERSAL UCLICK. Reprinted with permission. All rights reserved.; Pg. 383 (top left): Atm2003| Dreamstime.com; Pg. 383 (top right): Pedro Antonio Salaverr|Calahorra|Dreamstime.com; Pg. 383 (bottom): BOB FILA AND JAMES F. QUINN KRT/Newscom;

Pg. 385: RW3 WENN Photos/Newscom; Pg. 386: Kathy Kmonicek/Invision for Papa John's/AP Images.

CHAPTER 13

Pg. 391: STANCA SANDA/Alamy Stock Photo; Pg. 393: iStockphoto; Pg. 397: Jack Sullivan/Alamy; Pg. 398: Mary Evans/UNIVERSAL PICTURES/DREAMWORKS/IMAGINE ENTERTAINMENT/Ronald Grant/Everett Collection; Pg. 399: Icholakov|Dreamstime.com; Pg. 403: MURDER BY NUMBERS, Ryan Gosling, 2002, Warner Brothers/courtesy Everett Collection; Pg. 406: AP Photo/Sergey Ponomarev; Pg. 407: HAGAR 2006 KING FEATURES SYNDICATE; Pg. 408: THE DARK KNIGHT, Heath Ledger as The Joker, 2008. Warner Bros./Courtesy Everett Collection; Pg. 410: Nickilford/iStockphoto; Pg. 411: TheCrimsonMonkey/iStockphoto; Pg. 415 (bottom): (c) YvanDube/istockphoto.com; Pg. 415 (top): Richard Levine/Alamy; Pg. 416: Tim Boyle/Bloomberg/Getty Images; Pg. 417: Brandon Alms|Dreamstime.com; Pg. 418: (c) Anna Hoychuk/Shutterstock.com.

CHAPTER 14

Pg. 428: Picture Alliance/ZUMApress/Newscom; Pg. 431: Vivan Mehra/The India Today Group/Getty Images; Pg. 432: Ernesto Diaz/iStockphoto.com; Pg. 433 (top): Candybox Images|Dreamstime.com; Pg. 433 (bottom): Daniel Laflor/iStockphoto.com; Pg. 437 (top): AP Photo/The Daily Dispatch, Ashley Steven Ayscue; Pg. 437 (bottom): South West Images Scotland/Alamy; Pg. 438: Pzaxe|Dreamstime.com; Pg. 442: The Everett Collection, Inc; Pg. 443: Kts|Dreamstime.com; Pg. 445: Eric Hood/iStockphoto.com; Pg. 448 (top): AP Photo/Ajit Solanki; Pg. 448 (bottom): The Protected Art Archive / Alamy; Pg. 449: GRAND AVENUE 2003 Steve Breen and Mike Thompson. Reprinted by permission of Universal Uclick for UFS. All rights reserved; Pg. 451: jonathansloane/iStockphoto.com; Pg. 453: EPA/Newscom; Pg. 454: Columbia Pictures/courtesy Everett Co/Everett Collection; Pg. 456: MCT/Newscom; Pg. 459: Jasper Juinen/Bloomberg via Getty Images; Pg. 460: jez gunnell /iStockphoto.com; Pg. 462: iStockPhoto.

CHAPTER 15

Pg. 467: Redbaron|Dreamstime.com; Pg. 468: pete collins/iStockphoto.com; Pg. 470: Ljupco/iStockphoto.com; Pg. 471 (top): pete collins /iStockphoto.com; Pg. 471 (bottom): Matthew Simmons/Stringer/WireImage/Getty Images; Pg. 472: Getty Images; Pg. 473 (top, 1st row): pete collins/iStockphoto.com; Pg. 473 (top, 2nd row): Stockbyte/Getty Images; Pg. 473 (top, 3rd row): pete collins/iStockphoto.com; Pg. 473 (top, 4th row): Matthew Simmons/Stringer/WireImage/Getty Images; Pg. 473 (top, 5th row): Getty Images; Pg. 473 (bottom): (c) Eros Hoagland/Redux; Pg. 474: Nyul|Dreamstime.com; Pg. 475 (left): DFree/Shutterstock.com; Pg. 475 (center): Elizabeth Goodenough/Everett Collection/Newscom; Pg. 475 (right): Featureflash/Shutterstock.com; Pg. 478: DREAMWORKS SKG/FRANK MASI/Album/Newscom; Pg. 479: Photo Works/Shutterstock.com; Pg. 481: 5th Pillar (a citizens coalition against corruption), www.5thpillar.org; Pg. 486: nilgun bostanci/iStockphoto.com; Pg. 487: THE BORN LOSER 2005 Art and Chip Sansom. Reprinted by permission of Universal Uclick for UFS. All rights reserved.; Pg. 489: Design Pics/Carson Ganci/Getty Images/Perspectives; Pg. 490: Magali Delporte/eyevine/Redux; Pg. 491: Ken Backer|Dreamstime.com; Pg. 494: Murray Close/Lionsgate/Courtesy Everett Collection; Pg. 496 (top): Roberto Serra/Iguana Press/Getty Images; Pg. 496 (bottom): zhang bo/iStockphoto.com; Pg. 497: Daniel Loiselle/iStockphoto.com.

CHAPTER 16

Pg. 502: Tom Grill/Photographer's Choice RF/Getty Images; Pg. 505: Cristian Baitg/iStockphoto.com; Pg. 506 (top): Stephen Walls/iStockphoto.com; Pg. 506 (bottom): john shepherd/iStockphoto.com; Pg. 507: Rawpixel.com/Shutterstock.com; Pg. 509 (top): Mathias Wilson/iStockphoto.com; Pg. 509 (bottom): Michael Yarish/CBS via Getty Images; Pg. 510 (top): Christian Degroote|Dreamstime.com; Pg. 510 (2nd row): Robert Billstone/iStockphoto.com; Pg. 510 (3rd row): Juanmonino/iStockphoto.com; Pg. 510 (4th row): iStockPhoto; Pg. 510 (5th row): Joe Potato Photo/iStockphoto.com; Pg. 510 (bottom): Cal Vornberger/Alamy; Pg. 514: Vividpixels|Dreamstime.com; Pg. 516: Erin Cadigan/istockphoto.com; Pg. 519: SUPER SIZE ME, Morgan Spurlock, 2004, Samuel Goldwyn/courtesy Everett Collection; Pg. 522: Catonphoto|Dreamstime.com; Pg. 526: AiVectors/Shutterstock.com.

CHAPTER 17

Pg. 541: THE KOBAL COLLECTION/PARAMOUNT/BAD ROBOT; Pg. 542: iofoto/istockphoto.com; Pg. 543: Jennifer Pitiquen|Dreamstime.com; Pg. 544: NBC/NBCU Photo Bank/Getty Images; Pg. 545: Corbis RF; Pg. 546: Ryan Balderas/iStockphoto.com; Pg. 547: Laszlo Sovany/iStockphoto.com; Pg. 548 (top): Filmfoto|Dreamstime.com; Pg. 548 (bottom):

CHAPTER 27

Pg. 861: AP Photo/Tannen Maury, Pool; Pg. 869: Universal History Archive/Getty Images; Pg. 871: Underwood Archives/Getty Images; Pg. 878: Photographerlondon|Dreamstime.com; Pg. 879: Courtesy of John Papola/Emergent Order; Pg. 880 (left): Russell Lee/Getty Images; Pg. 880 (right): Britta Kasholm-Tengve/iStockphoto.com.

CHAPTER 28

Pg. 900: Liam Bailey/Getty Images; Pg. 903: Stephen Crowley/The New York Times/Redux; Pg. 906: U.S. Navy photo by Andy Wolfe courtesy of Lockheed Martin; Pg. 907: Luckydoor|Dreamstime. com; Pg. 908: svariophoto.iStockphoto.com; Pg. 909: AP Photo; Pg. 916: lucky336/iStockphoto. com; Pg. 923: JAVIER SORIANO/AFP/Getty Images; Pg. 925: Elizabeth Wake/Alamy Stock Photo; Pg. 926: Wavebreakmedia Ltd/Dreamstime.

CHPATER 29

Pg. 931: AP Photo/Amy Sancetta; Pg. 934 (top): Gerald Martineau/The Washington Post/Getty Images; Pg. 934 (bottom): AP Photo/Darin McGregor, Pool; Pg. 941: eurobanks/Shutterstock.com; Pg. 943 (bottom): Raja Rc|Dreamstime.com; Pg. 943 (top): PAY IT FORWARD, Haley Joel Osment, 2000/Everett Collection; Pg. 944 (top): BRIAN KERSEY/UPI/ Newscom; Pg. 944(bottom): Louis-Paul St-Onge/ iStockphoto.com; Pg. 947: Stephen Krow/iStockphoto. com; Pg. 948: Bohuslav Mayer|Dreamstime.com; Pg. 949: Ronnie McMillan/Alamy; Pg. 950: Edyta Pawlowska|Dreamstime.com; Pg. 951: iStockphoto; Pg. 952: KEVIN LAMARQUE/REUTERS/Newscom; Pg. 953: NASA; Pg. 955: AP Photo/Ed Reinke.

CHAPTER 30

Pg. 960: Andrew Harrer/Bloomberg via Getty Images; Pg. 963: Yekaterina Rashap/iStockphoto.com; Pg. 965 (top): Charles Islander/iStockphoto.com; Pg. 965 (bottom left): Dpenguinman/Wikimedia; Pg. 965 (bottom right): Scottnodine|Dreamstime.com; Pg. 966 (top): DeborahMaxemow/iStockphoto.com; Pg. 966 (bottom): Ken Tannenbaum/iStockphoto.com; Pg. 967 (left): Versluis Photography/iSockphoto.com; Pg. 967 (right): Maurice Crooks/Alamy; Pg. 969 (top): Baris Simsek/iStockphoto.com; Pg. 969 (bottom):

tomas del amo/Alamy; Pg. 974: RKO/Album/ Newscom; Pg. 975: ANDY RAIN/EPA/Newscom; Pg. 978: Drew Angerer/Bloomberg via Getty; Pg. 979: Ted Foxx/Alamy; Pg. 981 (top): TM Copyright 20th Centry Fox Film Corp. All rights reserved.; Pg. 981 (bottom): FRANCES M. ROBERTS/ Newscom; Pg. 982: Uschools University Images/ iStockhoto.com.

CHAPTER 31

Pg. 995: AP Photo/Manuel Balce Ceneta; Pg. 1000: Dani Simmonds/Alamy; Pg. 1003: Bettmann/Getty; Pg. 1004: Courtesy of Federal Open Market Committee (FMOC); Pg. 1015: Almir1968|Dreamstime.com; Pg. 1018: Warner Bros/Courtesy Everett Collection; Pg. 1019: Lin Yu/ZUMAPRESS/Newscom; Pg. 1022: Jackryan89|Dreamstime.com; Pg. 1023: Oleksiy Mark|Dreamstime.com.

CHAPTER 32

Pg. 1028: Natsuki Sakai/ALFO/Newscom; Pg. 1031: Rafael Ramirez Lee/iStockphoto.com; Pg. 1033 (left): Phil Crean A/Alamy Stock Photo; Pg. 1033 (right): Phil Crean A/Alamy Stock Photo; Pg. 1034: Aleksandra Yakovleva/iStockphoto.com; Pg. 1036: R. Gino Santa Maria|Dreamstime.com; Pg. 1037: Chris Ratcliffe/Bloomberg via Getty Images; Pg. 1038: Sanjay Pindiyath|Dreamstime.com; Pg. 1042: Andrew Rowat/Getty Images; Pg. 1044: TinaFields/iStockphoto .com; Pg. 1049: AP Photo/Damian Dovarganes; Pg. 1050: Mary Evans/LUCASFILMS/Ronald Grant/ Everett Collection.

CHAPTER 33

Pg. 1059: KIERAN DOHERTY/REUTERS/Newscom; Pg. 1060: david franklin/iStockphoto.com; Pg. 1064: Patryk Kosmider/iStockphoto.com; Pg. 1066: Anthony Dunn/Alamy; Pg. 1071: Feng Li/Getty Images; Pg. 1072: B.A.E. Inc./Alamy; Pg. 1075: 2004, (c) DreamWorks/courtesy Everett Collection; Pg. 1076: Niknikopol|Dreamstime.com; Pg. 1078: Alex Segre/Alamy; Pg. 1079: Courtesy of Lee Coppock; Pg. 1080: btrenkel/iStockphoto.com; Pg. 1081: AP Photo/ Peter Dejong; Pg. 1084: Chmiel/iStockphot.com; Pg. 1085: Sean Gallup/Getty Images; Pg. 1052: LARRY LEUNG/FEATURECHINA/Newscom.

INDEX